CONGRESS INVESTIGATES:

A Critical and Documentary History

REVISED EDITION

VOLUME II

CONGRESS INVESTIGATES:

A Critical and Documentary History

REVISED EDITION

VOLUME II

Edited by Roger A. Bruns, David L. Hostetter,
and Raymond W. Smock

A Congressional Research Project of the
Robert C. Byrd Center for Legislative Studies
Shepherd University
Shepherdstown, West Virginia

CONGRESS INVESTIGATES: A CRITICAL AND DOCUMENTARY HISTORY, REVISED EDITION

Facts On File, Inc.
An imprint of Infobase Learning
132 West 31st Street
New York NY 10001

Library of Congress Cataloging-in-Publication Data
Congress investigates : a critical and documentary history / edited by Roger A. Bruns, David L. Hostetter, Raymond W. Smock ; Robert C. Byrd Center for Legislative Studies. — Rev. ed.
p. cm.
Includes bibliographical references and index.
ISBN 978-0-8160-7679-6
1. Governmental investigations—United States. I. Bruns, Roger. II. Hostetter, David. III. Smock, Raymond. IV. Robert C. Byrd Center for Legislative Studies.
JK1123.A2B78 2010
328.73'07452—dc22 2010020268

You can find Facts On File on the World Wide Web at http://www.infobaselearning.com

Text design by Lina Farinella
Composition by Hermitage Publishing Services
Cover printed by Yurchak Printing, Landisville, Pa.
Book printed and bound by Yurchak Printing, Landisville, Pa.
Date printed: June 2011
Printed in the United States of America

10 9 8 7 6 5 4 3 2 1

This book is printed on acid-free paper.

CONTENTS

VOLUME I

VOLUME II

LIST OF DOCUMENTS

VOLUME I

VOLUME II

The Army-McCarthy Hearings, 1954

The Labor Racketeering Investigation, 1957–61

The Watergate Committee, 1973–74

The Church Committee on Intelligence Activities Investigation, 1975–76

The Iran-Contra Hearings, 1987

The Hurricane Katrina Inquiry, 2005–06

The Dies Committee and Un-American Activities, 1938–43

By Michael Wreszin

From the passage of the Alien and Sedition laws in 1798 to the mid-twentieth century attempt to outlaw the Communist Party, House and Senate committees have sporadically turned their attention to the activities of individuals and organizations charged with subversion. In 1919, during what is popularly known as the "Red Scare," a Senate committee was created to investigate the alleged propaganda activities of the brewery industry. Known as the Overman committee, it quickly turned the main focus of its attention from German to Bolshevik propaganda. This shift from concern with the danger from the Right to that from the Left previewed the circumstances surrounding the creation of the Dies committee, which was presumably fathered to expose Nazi and anti-Semitic propaganda but quickly turned its attention to Communist and leftist activities. The Overman committee was the first congressional committee to investigate alleged Communist activity, for even at that time it was customary for many Americans to link Bolshevism with "pro-Germanism" and to see both as alien, authoritarian ideologies.

Official concern with the Bolshevik menace died quickly in the 1920s and was replaced by a virulent racist xenophobia. Catholics, Jews, and blacks were lumped together with immigrants as a growing threat to the nation's Anglo-Saxon heritage. Demand for immigration restriction and the continued deportation of alien radicals occupied the minds of congressional defenders of Americanism. With the beginning of the Depression these racist and nativist anxieties were stimulated by a search for a scapegoat to explain the failures of the American system.

In May 1930 the House of Representatives was suddenly alarmed by New York police commissioner Grover Whalen's charge that the Russian Amtorg Trading Corporation was engaged in Communist propaganda. New York's aristocratic Republican representative, Hamilton Fish, was quickly appointed to chair the Special Committee to Investigate Communism in the United States. Fish, with an impeccable genealogy, was an appropriate choice to defend America against imported ideologies, but his direction of the committee revealed his

New York police commissioner Grover A. Whalen. (Library of Congress)

OVERVIEW

Background

With the rise of Adolf Hitler and the Nazi Party in Germany in the 1930s, concern in Congress over infiltration in the United States by subversive German agents led to the creation of the Special Committee on Un-American Activities in the House of Representatives, chaired by Representatives John W. McCormack (D-Mass.) and Samuel Dickstein (D-N.Y.). Although the committee held few hearings and was quietly disbanded in 1937, it was reconstituted by the House in 1938 as the Special House Committee on Un-American Activities, and in 1945 it became a standing (permanent) committee. Throughout its stormy history, the committee would be widely known as HUAC.

Congress Investigates

Chaired by Representative Martin Dies (D-Tex.), the committee at first primarily investigated German-American involvement in Nazi activities, pro-Fascist groups, and even the Ku Klux Klan. Most committee members, however, including Dies, did not see the Klan as "un-American" in the same manner as foreign subversives and the Klan therefore was never a focus of serious investigation. Under Dies's guidance, the committee quickly shifted to probe the activities of the American Communist Party and whether its agents had infiltrated the Works Progress Administration, especially the Federal Theatre Project, a popular New Deal program that had been created under the Roosevelt administration in 1935. The Federal Theatre Project put more than 30,000 people to work, almost half of whom were professional actors, directors, and writers. It conducted thousands of performances of new and often controversial subjects across the United States, but in the growing climate of Communist fear, a handful of plays struck the Dies committee as being Communist propaganda. The director of the Federal Theatre Project, Hallie Flanagan, a staunch opponent of censorship of artists, testified before the Dies committee in December 1938, when the entire federal program came under attack.

Impact

The Dies committee's greatest impact was that it significantly fostered anti-communist hysteria in the 1930s and paved the way for the atmosphere of fear and hatred of the Soviet Union that became a hallmark of the cold war after 1945. The investigation of the Federal Theatre Project resulted in the demise of the program, which Congress overwhelming rejected for further funding in 1939. Although Dies said in August 1938 that "this Committee will not permit any 'character assassination' or any 'smearing' of innocent people," he and his colleagues employed tactics of intimidation and guilt by association that later became the preferred method of investigation in the 1950s, when Senator Joseph McCarthy (R-Wis.) led the hunt for Communists in the federal government.

The extreme tactics of the Dies committee and HUAC and later those of Senator McCarthy ironically hindered efforts to expose real spies, double agents, and actual subversives who did exist in government service. In 1941 Dies issued a list of 1,000 people in the federal government who should be investigated for subversion. Only two were dismissed from government service.

scant knowledge of the subject. Although astonished by the very existence of avowed Communists in America, he treated the witnesses with the courtesy expected of a gentleman with his credentials. Congressman Carl Bachmann of West Virginia, on the other hand, played a role that became standard on such committees. Described by the hostile literary critic, Edmund Wilson, as the perfect caricature of the "lower type of Congressman . . . pot gutted . . . greasy looking . . . pig eyes," Bachmann's questions were designed to prove that communism was a weird belief held primarily by immigrants and other outcasts with no capacity to grasp the virtues of Americanism. His solution was to deport alien radicals and increase restrictions on immigration.

The findings of the Fish committee were a potpourri of conflicting assertions and drastic recommendations. While it discovered that there were only 12,000 registered Communist Party members in the United States, the committee estimated that there were also between 500,000 and 600,000 Communists and Communist sympathizers here. The American Civil Liberties Union was declared a bulwark of Communism, passing itself off as a defender of the Bill of Rights. American labor unions, it charged, were Communist-infiltrated, and in New York alone Communist youth camps were said to turn out 15,000 party members each year.

What should be done? The committee recommended outlawing the Communist Party, registering all aliens determined to be radicals, and censoring the mail service to thwart publication of Communist propaganda. It also requested that the State Department obtain permission for Treasury agents to go to Russia to investigate their use of forced labor—a peculiarly quixotic proposal given America's continued resistance to recognition of the Soviet government.

The report and its recommendations were ridiculed by even the relatively conservative *Outlook* as both "stupid and dangerous." One critic charged that the "proposals of the Fish Committee may be far more dangerous to liberty and freedom than the pitiful handful of Communists in the United States have ever been." Fish warned about Communist promotion of class hatred and race mixing, and issued a proclamation asserting that America, with the fairest, most honorable government in the world, must stand ever vigilant against this alien menace.

This was the national atmosphere when Martin Dies came to Congress from Orange County, Texas, in 1931. He was to make it his mission each year to present bills labeled "Aliens, for the deportation of certain," or "Immigration, to further restrict." He soon gained a seat on the Committee on Immigration and Naturalization, a hotbed of nativist and anti-radical sentiment. In May 1932 Dies's bill, HR 12044, for the expulsion and exclusion of alien Communists, passed in the House over the vigorous opposition of Congressman Fiorello LaGuardia. It was, however, tabled in the Senate under the leadership of Robert La Follette Jr.

In these initial years Dies was not taken seriously. He was known for his leadership of the House "Demagogues Club," which was made up of younger members like himself who sarcastically pledged to vote for any appropriation bill and against any tax measure. Making a great display at roll call, they would dash into the chamber and register their votes to the accompaniment of loud guffaws and clowning antics. This "good ole boy" contingent of aspiring Dixie Demagogues was tolerated with general good humor. Dies appeared to be a simple country lawyer from Texas who was glad to be on the federal payroll and was quick to admit that it was "better than working." Marquis Childs, an astute observer of the congressional beat, recalled that he had never encountered a more cynical man who, despite his display of good humor, seemed to have nothing but "utter scorn for the whole institution of Congress."

How Dies became obsessively devoted to the issue of subversive activities is open to speculation. Childs suggests it may simply have been the developing political climate of the 1930s, the "frustration of obscurity and neglect," or some "gnawing force beneath the outer surface of cynicism" that awakened a latent zealotry that fed on itself and was encouraged by others. Allan Michie and Frank Ryhlick, in their study *Dixie Demagogues,* attribute it to a self-serving ambition aimed at pleasing Texas oil and utility interests opposed to all New Deal regulatory measures.

As a member of the Committee on Immigration and Naturalization, Dies soon encountered Samuel Dickstein, who represented a largely Jewish immigrant constituency on New York's Lower East Side. Dickstein was devoted to the fight against anti-Semitism in extremist organizations that were encouraged by the rise of Hitler. If Martin Dies was to become an authority on Trojan horses designed to deceive God-fearing Americans, he found the right man for his purpose in this rabbi's son. He used Dickstein's concern with right-wing propaganda groups as a cover to launch an assault on the entire spectrum of the Left in America and to smear the New Deal with a red brush. It was a shrewd political manipulation, which was aided by the increasingly conservative congressional leadership.

In January 1934 Dickstein offered a resolution calling for an investigation of Nazi activities in the United States. After a rousing debate, during which opponents of the bill charged Dickstein with tarnishing the image of decent German Americans, the bill passed. Congressman John McCormack of Massachusetts was appointed chairman and Dickstein vice chairman of the investigating committee.

In light of subsequent investigations of subversive activity, the work of the McCormack-Dickstein committee was relatively sane and judicious. It concentrated on such organizations as the German American Bund and the Friends of New Germany, but it also reviewed the evidence on communism gathered by the Fish committee. It heard testimony from Earl Browder and James Ford, two high officials of the American Communist Party, and concluded that both Fascist organizations and the Communist Party served the interests of foreign governments. Neither, however, presented an immediate threat, but both were potential dangers to the country.

The committee's procedures were unique in that all witnesses were interviewed first in executive sessions before undergoing public hearings, thereby eliminating

CHRONOLOGY

1918–1919

- *September 1918–June 1919:* In the wake of World War I and the Russian Revolution of 1917, the U.S. Senate establishes subcommittee of the Committee on the Judiciary to investigate German and Bolshevik political activity and propaganda in the United States. Chaired by Senator Lee Slater Overman (D-N.C.) and called the Overman Committee, the committee contributes to a heightened fear of Bolshevik radicals infiltrating the United States.

1919

- The Communist Party of the United States of America is formed, attracting many liberal thinkers and artists.

1919–1921

- Unknown subversives, presumed to be socialists or Bolsheviks, set off bombs simultaneously in eight American cities on June 2, 1919, prompting U.S. Attorney General A. Mitchell Palmer to launch a major crackdown on radical elements, arresting, interrogating, and deporting thousands of people with "foreign" ideologies. J. Edgar Hoover leads the so-called Palmer Raids as head of the General Intelligence Division of the Justice Department.

1930

- The Fish committee, chaired by Representative Hamilton Fish III (R-N.Y.), investigates the American Civil Liberties Union and the Communist presidential candidate, William Z. Foster. Fish works to deport Communists and keep them from entering the country.

1934–1937

- The House of Representatives creates and operates the Special Committee on Un-American Activities. Chaired by Representatives John W. McCormack (D-Mass.) and Samuel Dickstein (D-N.Y.), the committee compiles information on how foreign subversive elements entered the United States and on the organizations that were spreading un-American propaganda. The committee disbands in 1937.

1935

- President Franklin D. Roosevelt establishes the Works Projects Administration (WPA) as part of the New Deal's attempt to combat the Great Depression.

wild charges and acrimonious debate. The committee retained the services of Thomas Hardwick, who had previously defended Communists during the Gastonia strike litigation as its counsel. Later committees would have hardly found such a man acceptable.

The most significant legislation to emerge from the committee's recommendations were the McCormack Foreign Agents Registration Act of 1938 and a bill that permitted congressional committees investigating subversive activity to subpoena witnesses when conducting hearings outside of the District of Columbia. But before this legislation had been passed, McCormack, whose committee had been charged with having produced no legislation, presented a forceful argument that became the predominant justification for many subsequent investigating committees. McCormack asserted that legislation should not be the cardinal criterion for measuring the accomplishments of such committees. Their major purpose was to alert the public to an important problem and aid in the formation of public opinion. Dies was later to argue that "simple exposure was the most effective weapon" against subversive activities. "When the light of day is brought to bear we can trust public sentiment to do the rest." This was indeed a prophetic analysis.

Historically, there were three purposes for congressional investigating committees: to obtain information that would assist Congress in designing wise legislation; to supervise the executive branch to see that the laws were faithfully executed; and, finally, to serve as a national forum—that is, to inform as well as shape public opinion. While the Supreme Court had only affirmed the first of these three purposes, it had generally agreed that the second and third were legitimate functions. The third, over the years, had broadened to mean the influencing of public opinion by the circulation of certain

CHRONOLOGY

Among the WPA's programs is the Federal Theatre Project (FTP), an attempt to offer work to theatrical professionals. During its four years of existence, the FTP would launch or establish the careers of such artists as Orson Welles, John Houseman, and Arthur Miller. In 1938 the WPA and the FTP would come under investigation by the Dies committee.

1938

- *May:* House Committee on Un-American Activities is established under the chairmanship of Martin Dies Jr. (D-Tex.). The committee is popularly known as the Dies committee.
- *August 12:* Dies makes opening statement before the committee.
- *October 25:* Roosevelt criticizes Dies committee for unfair attacks on Michigan governor Frank Murphy.
- *December:* Dies committee interrogates Hallie Flanagan, author, educator, and head of the Federal Theatre Project.

1940

- *January 11:* The journalist Walter Lippmann attacks Dies committee as a group of "official vigilantes."
- *May 17:* Dies delivers his "Trojan Horse" speech on House floor, warning of the infiltration of the United States by traitors and spies.
- *December:* Dies committee and U.S. Department of Justice agree to work together to combat subversive elements.

1941

- *Spring:* Dies committee releases more than 1,000 names of federal employees who should be investigated for sedition.

1942

- *September:* Attorney General Francis Biddle reports that a Justice Department investigation of the names gathered by the Dies committee resulted in only two cases that merited dismissal from the federal workforce.

1945–1975

- House Committee on Un-American Activities functions as a standing (permanent) committee of the House.

facts and ideas. This often became the sole defense of a committee's *raison d'être*.

In a defense of congressional investigations Woodrow Wilson pointed to the dire need for "instruction and guidance in political affairs," which the people might receive from a body that kept "all national concerns suffused in a broad light of discussion." He insisted that the "informing function of Congress should be preferred to its legislative function." The potential to abuse this "informing function" was quickly realized by astute politicians, sundry demagogues, and their victims.

During the twenties and thirties liberal reformers supported a host of congressional investigating committees that served to mobilize support for progressive social and economic legislation. In 1924 when Congress was investigating the moneyed interests and the Harding scandals, Felix Frankfurter, a champion of civil liberties, insisted that "the power of the investigative process should be left untrammeled." When conservatives attacked the committees as star chamber proceedings, liberals insisted on the "people's right to know."

It is not without significance, however, that the first hearings of the Dies committee began in August 1938, just one day after what appeared to be the final hearings of the La Follette committee, which concentrated on the violation of civil liberties by union-busting corporations. New Dealers were soon to discover that their effective weapon of securing favorable public opinion could also be used by a belligerent Congress to attack the New Deal administration. Telford Taylor observes, in his fine history of investigating committees, that during the late thirties the "chickens came home to roost."

Throughout the depression there had been a preoccupation with what Alistair Cooke called the "universal hobby of looking for a scapegoat." Conspiracy theories have not been the exclusive domain of paranoid rural populists, as some recent historians have suggested. The liberal supporters of the New Deal, in their search for a simple explanation for the breakdown of the economy, had been delighted with the exposure of the "money changers," the "merchants of death" in the munitions industry, and the "economic royalists" of the corporate hierarchy. But despite the exposure of these villains, the depression continued and soon the sophisticated "brain trusters" and social engineers of the New Deal bureaucracy found themselves in the rogue's gallery of scapegoats that marked the decade.

Southern Democrats, in league with vengeful Republicans, began to publicly voice their contempt for the wild schemes of the "lunatic professors." Others suggested a Machiavellian power play under the guise of fraudulent humanitarian rhetoric. From there it was only a short step to the old conservative charge that the New Deal program was a simple masquerade covering an alien and un-American conspiracy.

The Communist Party line in the late thirties lent weight to this argument. During the earlier hard-line period, the party had reviled Roosevelt as a "social fascist" and the New Deal as a sugarcoated pill of reaction. This had guaranteed the party's isolation from the main thrust of American reform. But with the rise of powerful Fascist forces in Italy and Germany, the party had somersaulted and embraced democratic reform in its enthusiasm for a popular front against fascism. Now Communism was defined by party spokesmen as nothing but twentieth-century Americanism, and Communists as the "sons and daughters of the American Revolution." Many American reformers had been fascinated by the "Soviet experiment" and saw in Russia a unity of purpose and collective social consciousness lacking in the United States. It was not difficult to accept the Soviet Union or even American Communists as crusaders against Hitler and fascism abroad and bigotry and reaction at home. This apparent agreement between New Deal reformers and Communists on a program of social and economic reforms gave sustenance to the growing anti–New Deal coalition bent upon exposing the New Deal as the vehicle for an alien radical ideology.

Representative Martin Dies of Texas, ca. 1938. Once a supporter of President Franklin Roosevelt's New Deal, Dies by the late 1930s became a forceful spokesman against organized labor and a champion of vigilance against foes of Americanism, especially Communist subversion. Under his direction, the House Committee on Un-American Activities became a strong political force. (Library of Congress)

By 1937 Martin Dies was on his way to becoming a leader in the anti–New Deal coalition. He had opposed the wages and hours legislation and had repeatedly called for an investigation of the "Communist instigated" sit-down strikes. Vice President Garner, who was beginning to make a sharp distinction between traditional Democrats and New Dealers, encouraged the young congressman. Big, boyish—an American to the core—Dies would make a perfect standard-bearer in defense of purity. He had all the qualifications—a fine-honed contempt for big-city sophistication, a hatred for big-labor lawlessness, and a suspicion of foreigners of any kind. In frequent speeches he recalled the example of his congressman father, who had bolted the party during the fight against the League of Nations because Wilson had been corrupted by "foreign advisors." Dies announced that he would always place the country before the party in a battle for true Americanism.

By the spring of 1938 the fortunes of the Roosevelt administration were approaching their lowest point. The abortive attempt at court reform had seriously strained liberal loyalties, and the sit-down strikes which accompanied a downturn in the economy had undercut the president's authority in Congress. Democratic ranks were bitterly divided, and Roosevelt had let it be known that he planned a purge of backsliding party members in the upcoming congressional election campaign. "Nothing," wrote the historian William Leuchtenburg, "divulged the sourish spirit of 1938 more than the creation of the House Committee on Un-American Activities."

Dies's bill (HR 282) had been in the works for nearly a year when it came up for debate again on May 26, 1938. It contained almost the same wording and provisions as the previous Dickstein resolutions for the investigation of subversive activities, which had failed to pass. But Dies, according to Robert Strippling, had, unlike Dickstein, the tacit support of the House leadership and had been requested by the vice president to gather support for an Un-American Activities Committee that would have "substance and specific duties."

Contrary to the assumption of Walter Goodman, who labeled the Dies committee "Dickstein's Monster," there is little irony in the bill initially proposed by Dickstein that resulted in the Dies committee. That appears to have been the plan from the start, and partisans on both sides were aware of it. The son of a Russian rabbi would hardly be a fit leader for champions of American nativism. Nor is it likely that the administration spokesmen in Congress had been caught napping, as another analyst suggests. In the past, Roosevelt had been able to inspire friendly congressional committees and thwart hostile probes, but those days were gone. The administration had lost much of its control of congressional leadership, and this had encouraged the ambitions of Martin Dies. New Dealers may have underestimated the subsequent power and popularity of the committee, but the debate of May 26 must have warned them of the ultimate designs held by the bill's supporters. Dickstein's initial anti-Nazi preoccupations had only served as a shallow cover for a committee with much broader political ambitions.

Necessary support had been mustered well in advance, so Dies was able to assume a moderate and diplomatic role during the debate. To the charge that such a committee might endanger individual civil liberties, Dies eloquently voiced his own fears. He warned that any "legislative attempt to prevent un-American activities . . . might jeopardize fundamental rights far more important than the objectives we seek." But that danger could be avoided simply by the way such a committee was chaired. Publicity-seeking politicians or sensation-mongers must, of course, be barred from serving on such a committee. This was a reference to Samuel Dickstein, who had been labeled as such by opponents of his anti-Nazi assaults.

In an indirect way, the public debate made several things clear to the politicians. Dies was assuring his colleagues that Dickstein would have no place on his committee. The exchange between Dies and John Cochran over appropriations for the committee revealed that Cochran understood that Dies was to be the chairman of the committee. And, as both John Rankin and J. Parnell Thomas had made it clear that no committee with Dickstein on it would receive their support, Dies was more than conciliatory on that point. He assured skeptical critics that the committee could achieve its modest goals during the remainder of the year and that it would not need a lavish appropriation. Evidence of Dies's calculated dissembling clearly supports Marquis Childs's opinion that the case history of Martin Dies is a story of "ambition, by Shakespeare, out of True Story Magazine."

If Dies took on the mantle of judicious statesmanship, a far cry from the earlier demagogue jeering at House protocol, the more flamboyant rhetoric demanded in such rituals was supplied by the traditional New Deal haters. Congressman Taylor of Tennessee was allotted an inordinate amount of time to defend the resolution, most of which he used to wrap himself in the flag, embrace red-blooded Americanism, and denounce the defilers of virtue who had only recently painted Plymouth Rock an unholy red. Scoundrels of this stripe, he shouted, should be "hunted down like rattlesnakes and kicked out of the country." Continuing on, he attacked Secretary Frances Perkins and the Department of Labor for their coddling of immigrants who "cared nothing about America."

J. Parnell Thomas pointed out that the Communist Party was a greater threat than Nazi organizations since, according to his research, Communists outnumbered Nazis by more than five to one. Worse than both were the Communist-influenced agencies of the federal government; these were the real sources of un-Americanism, and *they* must indeed be investigated.

It was left to F. Maury Maverick (D.–Tex.), Gerald Boileau (D.–Wis.), and John Main Coffee (D.–Wash.) to defend civil liberties and the integrity of the New Deal. They ridiculed the "pompous patriotism" of the bill's supporters and the potential spectacle of congressmen "swaggering around the country like inquisitors." The proposed committee was not designed to deal with fundamental problems facing the nation, but was a plot to dismantle the New Deal and harass liberal organizations. What constituted un-Americanism was a question that remained vague and ill defined. Dies argued that un-Americanism was simply the understanding that Americans derived their fundamental and inherent rights not from society or government but "from Almighty God." Maverick retorted that if one were for the wage and hours laws, for free speech, and for a living wage, he was apparently un-American, since these rights came from the determination of the courts and not from God. "Un-American is simply something that somebody else doesn't agree to," he concluded. Representative Harold Knutson (R.–Minn.) won the prize for brevity. He repeatedly answered the question "What is un-American?" with the single word, "Goosestepping." What his colleagues thought about that is not recorded, but he did know the purpose of the committee. It was just another machination improvised to provide hard-pressed congressmen with "room and board during the summer months."

For all the "ballyhoo and bunk," the tally was an overwhelming 191 to 41 in favor of the resolution. Representative Cochran explained the lopsided vote for an anti–New Deal measure in a House dominated by Democrats. Newspapers, he observed, would make it clear, if the resolution failed to pass, that the House had declined to investigate subversion. "I do not want to be accused of refusing to vote for legislation to investigate un-American activities." Eugene Lyons's later assertion that the Dies committee grew out of a tiny congressional faction is simply erroneous. It was not a victory for the "Dies-Dickstein strategy" as Walter Goodman observed. On the contrary, Dies had used Dickstein as his own Trojan horse upon which to ride the plains of anti–New Deal discontent. Dickstein, the reputed father of the committee, was not even permitted three minutes to address his colleagues at the end of the debate and was denied membership on the committee.

On June 6 Dies was predictably appointed chairman; the committee members, to no one's surprise, were five to two and often six to one against the Roosevelt administration. Conservative Democrats Dies, Joe Starnes of Alabama, and Harold G. Mosier of Ohio were allied with the two Republicans, J. Parnell Thomas of New Jersey, and Noah Mason of Illinois. Only John J. Dempsey of New Mexico could be described as a New Deal Democrat, albeit a wavering one. The seventh member, Arthur Healey of Massachusetts, was a will o' the wisp Democrat who voted one way and then another but was usually absent at crucial junctures. Jerry Voorhis, the most dependable of New Deal liberals and a constant critic of the committee's conduct, was appointed to replace Mosier when he was defeated in the 1938 elections. Dies would later point to Voorhis's membership on the committee to counter charges of political partisanship.

While some observers persisted in believing the committee's main target was Nazi propaganda, ideologues on the Right and the Left were aware of the reality. Father Coughlin's *Social Justice* assured its readers that the anticommunist bloc had backed the committee. The *New Republic* cited Dies's record against the New Deal and concluded that "if the principal energies of Mr. Dies are not given over to hounding Communists, it would be a miracle." But Dies was a knowledgeable performer and, as Walter Goodman has observed, he called upon anti-Nazi testimony intermittently during the investigations "like the comic who pops out between . . . skits with a broom and sets diligently to sweeping the stage until he is kicked off so the show may proceed."

During the months between the creation of the committee and its initial hearings in August 1938, Dies continued in his role with statesmanlike decorum. The committee, he informed the press, would conduct no "three-ring circus." As chairman he would not permit "any individual or organization to use the Committee as a sounding board to obtain publicity." Dies's opening statement on August 12, 1938, was perhaps his most magnificent performance; it was as though it had been composed by the American Civil Liberties Union. The committee would conduct all hearings on a "dignified plane" and maintain a "judicial attitude." To the merriment of cynics, he insisted that the committee members held no preconceived views and that their single goal was to discover the truth. All witnesses would be treated with courtesy, fairness, and impartiality. There would be no "character assassination" nor "smearing of innocent people." Reckless charges would not be condoned, as the gathering of facts, not opinions, was the prime objective. "Charges unsupported by facts" were of no value. "It is easy," he warned, "to smear someone's name or reputation and very difficult to repair the damage that has been done." In the investigation of un-American activities it must be kept in mind that "because we do not agree with opinions or philosophies of others does not necessarily make such opinions or philosophies un-American." Too often partisans branded their opponents with a pejorative label rather than engaging in argument with "facts and logic." Conservatives were inclined to call all liberals Communists and "so-called liberals" stigmatized all conservative ideas as fascistic. The committee would take the utmost care to distinguish between what was "un-American and what was no more or less than an honest difference of opinion" on economic, political, or social questions.

Walter Goodman, after a study of subsequent hearings, wondered if "the lady of breeding" who had made such "a dignified entrance into town" had not in fact established "a bawdy house." But the charade was maintained by the first witness, John C. Metcalf, a German-American who had infiltrated the Bund and had gathered a file on their bizarre activities. The stage seemingly set for a thorough investigation of Nazi propaganda, Dies dropped the curtain the following day and introduced John P. Frey, president of the metal trades department of the American Federation of Labor (AFL), who immediately launched a sustained attack, charging Communist domination of the rival Congress of Industrial Organizations (CIO). Here was the committee's response to the Senate's La Follette Committee, which had just ended its hearings on anti-union activities.

In three days, Frey provided 186 pages of testimony and accompanying documentation to support the AFL. allegations. Frey was encouraged to make charges, and few CIO unions of any consequence escaped his condemnation. He named 210 union officials as "Communistic," but supplied little documentation to prove his allegations. He received no challenge from the committee, however. He also charged that the La Follette Committee investigators had close contacts with members of the Communist Party; that charge proved to have some substance.

Frey's testimony received much attention in the press. *Communists Rule the CIO, La Follette Committee Linked to Communism* read the bold, black headlines. With roughly 85 percent of the press in opposition to the New Deal in 1938, Dies had little trouble monopolizing the front pages. Kenneth Crawford, a seasoned journalist, later declared that it was the "amazing success of the Frey testimony as an experiment in publicity that awakened Dies and his associates to a full realization of the . . . political gold mine they had struck. From Frey on it was catch as catch can with no holds barred."

Here James J. Metcalf explains to the Dies committee investigating un-American activities the difference between the salutes of the German Bunds in America and the German-American Bund. In the salute of the former, the left arm is held rigid against the side instead of at the belt buckle, as in German-American Bund. (©Bettmann/CORBIS)

The committee did not simply depend upon the hearings to produce publicity. It became standard practice for members and the staff to make statements outside of the public hearings; unfortunately, these often appeared in the press as part of the committee's findings. While Frey was testifying on August 14, Edward Sullivan, a committee investigator with a long history of labor spying and anti-Semitic associations, charged Harry Bridges, the longshoreman leader, with responsibility for 60 percent of the labor strife on the West Coast. In spite of his Communistic connections and inclination, Sullivan continued, Bridges was being protected by an "outstanding official" in the Department of Labor.

Dies did not vouch for the authenticity of the charge. However, he soon joined with those calling for the impeachment of Frances Perkins, who refused to deport Bridges as an alien Communist organizer because the Bridges case was already being litigated in the courts and the Department of Labor had no legal grounds upon which to initiate deportation proceedings. Bridges was

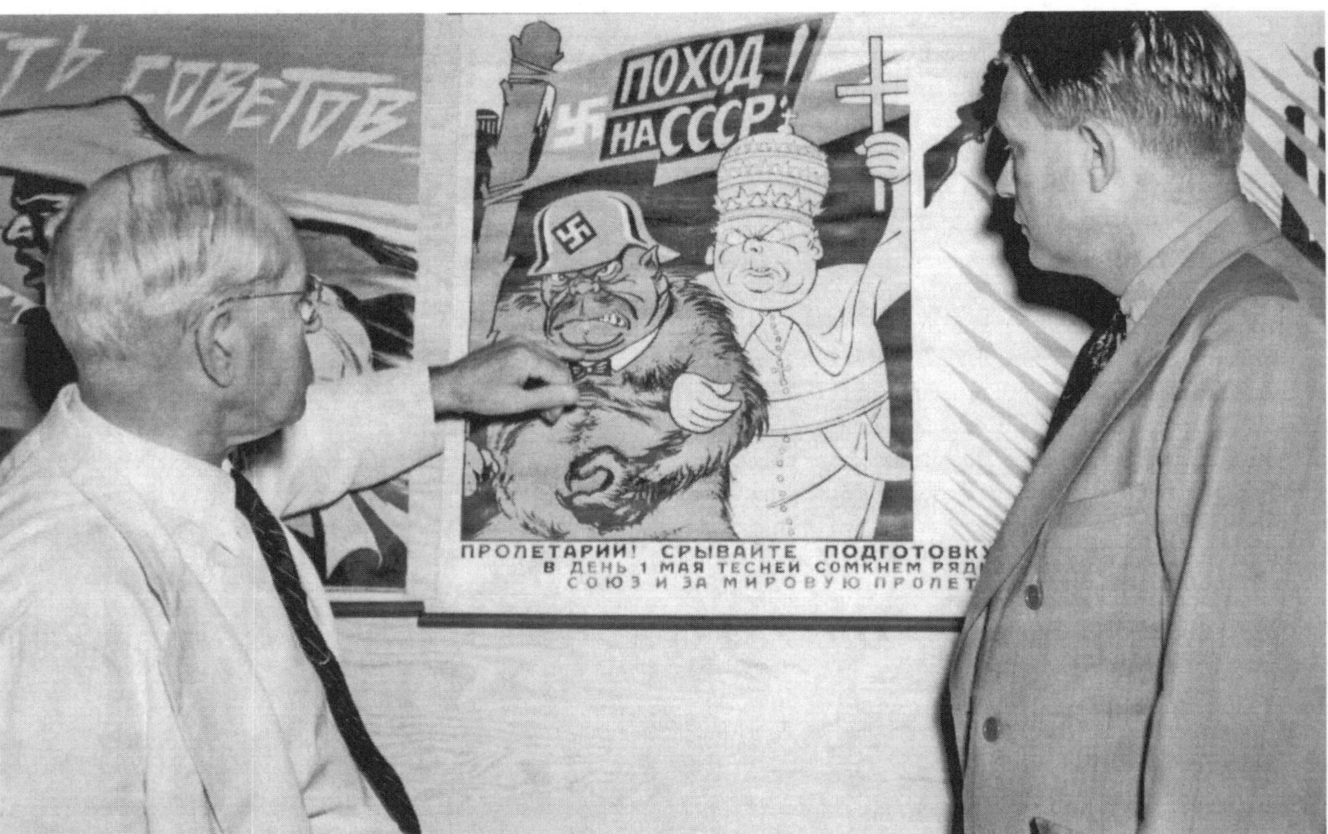

John Frey of the American Federation of Labor points to one of the posters used as exhibits at the hearings on un-American activities headed by Representative Martin Dies, right, August 13, 1938. (Associated Press)

hounded by the Dies committee and later by the whole House, which eventually passed a bill for his deportation on the grounds that it was "in the best interests of the United States." In 1945 Justice Murphy closed the case in Bridges's favor, with the observation that "seldom . . . in the history of the Nation has there been such a concentrated and relentless crusade to deport an individual because he dared exercise the freedom that belongs to him as a human being and that is guaranteed him by the Constitution."

Following Frey the committee offered a platform, in direct contradiction to Dies's opening day statement, to Walter S. Steele, a professional patriot and professional witness who made a career of testifying before subversive activities committees. Steele, claiming to represent 114 patriotic organizations and some 20 million Americans, named 640 organizations as Communistic and claimed that 6.5 million Americans were engaged in some form of foreign propagandistic activity. Even the Boy Scouts and Campfire Girls were suspect for their pacifist inclinations and their faith in internationalism.

Dies anticipated the response of critics to such absurd testimony and occasionally interrupted to suggest that the testimony would not be admissible in a court, and thus the committee should be wary of causing injury to innocent persons. Dies's duty done, the witness would then be allowed to continue the harangue, urged on by friendly and leading questions from the committee members.

Day after day it went on. A Legionnaire attacked the League for Peace and Freedom as Communist-dominated, and committee member Noah Mason, picking up the cue, named eight government officials as members of the organization. J. Parnell Thomas initiated his crusade against the Works Progress Administration (WPA) with an assault on the Federal Theatre Project. The committee exposed its racist underpinnings by boldly pursuing the lurid story of a black project worker who had the temerity to ask a woman fellow worker for a date. Sally Saunders, the witness, disclosed that Communist workers "hob-nobbed indiscriminately" with blacks and "threw parties with them left and right." In answer to a question from Joe Starnes, she agreed that "social equality and race merging" were part of the Communist program.

The Frey and Steele testimonies established the general conduct and atmosphere of the hearings for the committee's first year. After the first month Dies violated nearly every code of conduct that he had initially announced. The committee was used as a platform by partisan witnesses, who, with few exceptions, were given free rein to make damaging accusations unsupported by corroborative evidence. If they were friendly witnesses, there was virtually no cross-examination. Committee members would put words into their mouths and urge them on with provocative and leading questions. Testimony that attacked organizations and reputations and offered no effective opportunity for rebuttal was constantly released to the press. Individuals were named and condemned on the basis of simple associations with organizations described as "Communistic." Paul Douglas, John Dewey, Reinhold Niebuhr, even H. L. Mencken, were referred to derogatorily, as the reporters scribbled on. If the hearings themselves failed to produce immediate headlines on any given day, members were free to take to the public podium to make further charges and to capture attention.

The witnesses were either "experts" who filed long, unexamined briefs, or rabid partisans. Particularly acceptable to the committee were disgruntled bureaucrats who had failed to find a home in some New Deal agency and sought an outlet for their animosity. D. A. Saunders of the *Public Opinion Quarterly* concluded in April 1939 that the witnesses had hardly inspired confidence in the investigation. A large number seemed "to have been professed patriots, vigilantes, political stool-pigeons, labor spies, anti-Semites, Nazi sympathizers and even criminals." One grieving member of the press covering the hearing complained that "the mixture of plausible testimony with fantasy, the practice of Committee members putting words in the witnesses' mouths, their almost universal failure to seek development of proof of startling accusations or to develop the backgrounds of possible animus of the accusers, makes covering the inquiry a headache of major proportions." Unfortunately, his conscientious concern was hardly typical.

If ignorance of the field of investigation and vagueness of direction characterized the initial hearings, they were saved, so to speak, by the evangelical proselytizer, J. B. Matthews. Shortly after a lengthy testimony on Communist-front organizations, Matthews was made an investigator for the committee, a job he held through the Hiss-Chambers hearings in 1949. He later served briefly as a staff director on the McCarthy committee. Matthews was the classic American "seeker." He had traveled from evangelical fundamentalism to the humanitarianism of the Social Gospel, on down the road to the progressivism of the elder La Follette, through the pacifism of the Fellowship of Reconciliation, to the left wing of the Socialist party, into the Popular Front and militant consumerism, and, finally, back to the fundamentalism practiced by anticommunist converts. There is some humor in the fact that Matthews's conversion to anticommunism occurred when, as an executive of Consumers' Research, he was outraged by a strike of its employees, charging that it was a Communist plot to take over the organization. Benjamin Gitlow saw him as a lightweight on Marxist social and economic theory, but Matthews could chart every twist and turn in the tortured history of fellow traveling.

This was the man for Dies. He lent respectability to the committee and was deferentially referred to as "Doctor" by some of its members. Whether he analyzed any situation as a witness or as an interrogator, his testimony was filled with the most minute details of popular front organizational structure, lists, names, dates, and places. He was a master archivist and his exhaustive knowledge made him invaluable to the committee because he could make connections between liberals, fellow travelers, and the hidden Communist conspiracy. Dies was out to slander the New Deal, and Matthews served his purpose well.

Matthews first appeared as a witness on August 22, 1938. He listed at least twenty Communist fronts with which he had been affiliated and recalled the most inconsequential episodes down to the last detail. Like so many anticommunist witnesses, he inflated the Communist attributions of power and influence to organizations that were more accurately described by Murray Kempton as "structures of enormous pretension and pathetic foundation." But it was the meat and gristle of his life, and he did not believe that he had been on a feckless journey. He had heard the roar of the crowd in Madison Square Garden, as well as the mumblings in storefront temples.

It was Matthews who made the gaffe that the committee never lived down. In explaining how innocent, well-meaning people could be used by Communists, he noted that several movie stars such as Clark Gable, James Cagney, and Shirley Temple had been persuaded to send congratulations to a French Communist newspaper on its first anniversary. Matthews made a point of not saying they were Communists or Communist sympathizers but rather that their reputations had been exploited in the interest of Communist propaganda. But it was too late. Every critic of the committee leaped to the advantage. Harold Ickes conjured up visions of burly congressmen leading posses of investigators into Shirley Temple's nursery to gather evidence of Communist conspiracy. Frances Perkins thanked God that Shirley was a citizen and could not be deported.

Titled "Our Changing Tastes . . . in 1938," this drawing published on May 15, 1938, shows caricatures of Benny Goodman, Ginger Rogers, Fred Astaire, Orson Welles, Robert Taylor, Lily Pons, Salvador Dalí, Alfred Lunt, Lynn Fontaine, Walt Disney, Dorothy Thompson, and Shirley Temple. (Library of Congress)

By October 1938 the congressional election campaign was under way, and the political potential of the committee was apparent both to its chairman and to the administration. Heated election struggles were already going on in the crucial swing states of Minnesota, Michigan, and California. On October 17, after protesting that the committee was only interested in Communism and not political disputes, Dies produced Steve Gadler of St. Paul, who testified that the Democratic candidate for governor of Minnesota, Elmer A. Benson, had been endorsed by Browder, and the candidate had not repudiated the endorsement. Gadler went on to charge that the Farmer Labor Party had been captured by the Communists, and six other nondescript witnesses testified to the same general information.

From Minnesota on to Michigan—the committee went to work on a Roosevelt favorite, Governor Frank Murphy, who was running for reelection. Returning to the sit-down strikes of two previous years, the committee recruited Paul V. Gadola, a Republican judge, to testify that the timid negotiating policy of Governor Murphy had contributed to the breakdown of law and order in that state. Murphy, Gadola charged, had become nothing more than a pawn in the hands of a crew of Communist lawyers and had refused to support the judge's injunction against lawless seizures of private property. After further damaging testimony from American Legionnaires and some local police officers, the committee heard from John M. Barringer, a former city manager and director of public safety in Flint, Michigan. Dies played on Barringer's testimony as though it were a musical instrument, leading the questions all the way. "Would you say that [the sit-down strikes] would not have occurred if it had not been for the investigation and active leadership of the Communists?" Barringer obligingly replied, "No, it would not have occurred. And I can further answer that question—it would not have developed . . . if it had not been for the attitude of the members of the La Follette Committee, and Governor Murphy's treasonable action in not giving us help when we should have had it." Dies had hit a bull's-eye, gaining him headline dividends that surpassed even his wildest hopes.

Ignored during the questioning was the great potential for violence inherent in the organizing drive for industrial unionism. Murphy, under terrible pressure, had chosen the tactics of delay and negotiation over armed force, and the strike ended with no loss of life. From Murphy's perspective the situation had come close to civil war, with the American Legion at the head of assorted vigilante groups confronting a tough core of determined union militants.

Roosevelt, smarting under the steady attack on members of his administration and angered by the blatant political partisanship of the committee's conduct, issued a public condemnation. The president described the witnesses as a "coterie of disgruntled Republican office holders," led by a "disgruntled Republican judge," a "discharged city manager," and a group of "officious" policemen who had been recruited to make lurid" and unjustified charges that could not be verified. He eloquently defended Murphy as a "profoundly religious, able and law-abiding Governor" whose handling of the strike was such that "all peace loving Americans should praise him." The president indicted the committee for allowing itself to be used in a "flagrantly unfair and un-American attempt to influence an election." He hoped that the committee would abandon the practice of providing a forum for those who sought headlines.

Undaunted, Dies immediately reaffirmed all of the charges, insisting that despite the president's anger and opposition, he would continue to do his duty "undeterred and unafraid." Next to appear were two Californians who accused the Democratic candidate for governor, Culbert Olsen, of owing his nomination to Communist support. It was later asserted that these witnesses represented the interests of the Associated Farmers, a West

Coast antiunion organization of fruit growers and packers that supported Republican candidates.

The administration blamed the Dies committee for the defeat of Murphy in Michigan, and Dies was delighted to accept the credit. Arthur Krock in the *New York Times* acknowledged the influence of the committee when he asserted that the election returns had emphatically rebuked the sit-down strikes and the Democratic-CIO alliance.

Dies and his committee were the beneficiaries of a growing disenchantment with the New Deal program and a fearful anxiety over what lay ahead. He had no intention of losing momentum, so he and his colleagues kept up a running assault on officials in the executive bureaucracy. In an Armistice Day speech Dies accused Secretaries Ickes and Perkins of being purveyors of class hatred. Almost no agency or department head was immune from criticism as a collaborator or dupe of Communist design.

Harold Ickes was the only one to return the fire with any enthusiasm. In a press release he said that "anyone who wanted to get anything out of his system against any New Dealer" should apply to the accommodating Dies committee. Dies, Ickes quipped, was the "outstanding zany of American political history." The following day Dies called for the resignation of Ickes and Perkins because no American could feel secure with an administration staffed by Communists, Socialists, and the "ordinary garden variety of crackpots."

While this extracurricular activity went on, the committee conducted its final hearings in December 1938. They were designed to expose the criminal mismanagement of the Works Progress Administration, and particularly the writer and theater projects. With unerring instinct Dies and J. Parnell Thomas recognized that these projects constituted "the soft underbelly" of the WPA. Many Americans were indifferent or unsympathetic to a federal program providing employment for writers and actors whom they felt were, at best, loafers and, at worst, troublemakers. It was true, as Thomas repeatedly charged, that many Communists and fellow travelers of varying radical persuasions had found a home in the projects. This was notoriously true of the New York projects, which were frequently in a state of upheaval resulting from factional political struggles. In the eyes of middle-class

The Dies committee congressional investigation ends a series of hearings on December 18, 1938. Here, Chairman Martin Dies brings down his gavel signifying adjournment. Pictured as the final hearing closed are, left to right, seated: Representative Harold G. Mosier of Ohio, Chairman Martin Dies of Texas, and Representative J. Parnell Thomas of New Jersey. Standing, left to right: Representative John J. Dempsey of New Mexico; Robert E. Stripling, committee staffer; and John C. Metcalfe, chief investigator. (Library of Congress)

respectability, the projects were composed of a motley crew of wild-eyed and frequently drunken poets, writers, and assorted bohemians whose lifestyle was an affront to all that was pure and decent. Imagine what the suffering, self-reliant taxpayer thought of a mystical raconteur like the legendary Joe Gould who, when not writing his mythical "Oral History of the World," rambled around his Greenwich Village turf flapping his arms like a seagull and disrobing at parties. Nor is it likely that the general populace could appreciate the genius of the Village bohemian-turned-Communist Maxwell Bodenheim, who actually rose to the position of a supervisor in the writer's project until his penchant for spirits made it impossible for him to show up for work—even once a week.

This "gallery of grotesques," combined with the sectarian warfare between Stalinists and Trotskyites in the New York projects, gave the entire program a bad reputation and was a constant embarrassment to the administration. As the hearings proceeded it was obvious that no major administration official would exert much effort to protect this experiment in federal sponsorship of the arts, despite its many fine achievements.

The thrust of the attack on the projects rested on the testimony of disgruntled former employees. They charged that Communists controlled the employees' union and the Workers' Alliance and used their power to intimidate and harass non-Communists. The editorial staff, they accused, was dominated by Communists who insidiously introduced propaganda into literary and theatrical productions. Critics complained that the famous state guidebooks invariably employed Communist phraseology, stressed the struggle between capital and labor, referred to blacks as the downtrodden, and championed the virtues and nobility of the "underprivileged." It was noted that the Massachusetts guide devoted more pages to the Sacco-Vanzetti case than it did to the Boston Tea Party.

Committee members followed their all too familiar practice of putting words into the mouths of witnesses.

CONGRESSMAN MASON: Would you say that the federal Writers Project is being used by a group of radicals to propagandize the states through the use of these guides?

WITNESS: I do; and that is just the beginning.

CHAIRMAN DIES: Do you think Mr. Alsberg (director of Writers Project) is bringing into the department as many radicals as he can?

WITNESS: I don't know whether he is doing it under orders or voluntarily.

DIES: But he is doing it?

WITNESS: It has seemed to us for a long while that he has been bringing in such persons.

Ellen S. Woodward. (Library of Congress)

Friendly witnesses were seldom cross-examined. However, when Ellen Woodward, the assistant administrator, testified in defense of the project, her testimony was challenged at every point, proof demanded of any generalizations, and her fitness as a witness discussed at length.

After a score of accusatory witnesses were heard, Hallie Flanagan was finally permitted to defend the theater projects. She was a spirited witness not intimidated by the committee. When asked what her duties were, she remarked that she worked to combat un-American activities by providing jobs for professional men and women. Dies refused to allow her to testify to anything she had not personally witnessed, and no hearsay evidence was permitted. This was an astonishing switch from the usual procedure, which had encouraged reams of unsupported hearsay evidence.

During her testimony, an old article by Flanagan was dug up in which she referred to the "Marlowesque madness" of workers' theaters taking root in America. Congressman Starnes wanted to know who this Marlowe was. "Is he a Communist?" he asked. Flanagan respectfully replied that she had been referring to Christopher Marlowe, but Starnes, unsatisfied, pressed on. "Tell us who Marlowe is. . . ." To this Flanagan responded with delight: "Put in the record that he was the greatest dramatist in the period of Shakespeare, immediately preceding Shakespeare." A shout of laughter echoed through the chamber and out across the nation, and every opponent of the committee was comforted by the knowledge that the red-necked Starnes knew as little about drama as he did about Communism.

The theater and writers projects had produced an amazing variety of material, some first-rate and much of it little more than crude and inept political propaganda. But to the committee it was not so much Communist literary banality as it was the abominable association of the government with these disreputable figures. It is a toss-up as to who should be credited for ultimately killing these projects. The New Deal administration found the experiment a political liability and gave it little support once under attack. The Dies committee exploited every sensational facet of political and social nonconformity, thus damaging the reputation of the entire experiment, and the Communists' continuous, disruptive bickering and crude attempts at politicization made them vulnerable to ridicule.

The WPA hearings were a rehearsal for the first debate over the renewal of the committee. Dies had good reason to be optimistic, for despite the fact that a poll of journalists, solicited by Roosevelt, had declared the committee's conduct unfair and the administration had hired Paul Anderson, a journalist, to attack it on a national network, a Gallup poll showed that it had wide popular support.

Harold Ickes insisted that the only way to deal with Dies was to confront him directly. He planned a nationwide speech entitled "Playing with Loaded Dies," which would inform the public of the outrageous conduct of the hearings. But the president, increasingly wary of Dies's political influence, especially after the decisive defeat in the congressional elections, was persuaded to cancel Ickes's speech. He continued to entertain the hope that congressional leadership could either curb the committee's longevity or the size of its appropriation through careful political maneuvering. He was advised that an Ickes attack would simply rally anti–New Deal support for Dies.

Ickes replied that Dies was making gains because the president and his administration had refused to take the offensive. A number of cabinet sessions were turned over to a discussion of Ickes's strategy. He urged the administration to encourage an additional appropriation for the La Follette committee to counterbalance Dies's investigation, or to pack the Dies committee with loyal New Dealers.

The president vacillated between these two proposals but refused to allow administrative officials to lobby on the Hill. The degree to which Roosevelt feared Dies may be seen in his request that Frank Murphy, whom he had only recently appointed attorney general, begin an investigation of the organizations that the committee daily attacked as subversive. This, however, gave substance and respectability to the charges of the committee.

Ickes was disconsolate when the committee was renewed in February and received a sizable increase in its appropriation, while the La Follette committee's appropriation was cut in half in the Senate. He recorded in his diary that it was another example of "a complete falling down of Democratic leadership." They had "abjectly surrendered" to the demagogues. Sam Rayburn remarked: "Martin Dies could beat me right now in my own district."

When Congress convened in January 1939, Dies submitted the 125-page committee report. A considerable portion of the report was allotted to a defense of the investigation and an assault on the lack of cooperation from Roosevelt's administration. Reflecting the opinion of its chairman, the committee report emphasized the notion that Americanism was the recognition that a citizen's fundamental rights came from God. The preaching of class conflict was un-American. The real danger of Communism was not overt conspiracy, but the infiltration of organizations and the government itself.

Frank Murphy, new attorney general, arriving at the White House to call on President Roosevelt, January 1939. (Library of Congress)

In its survey of the hearings, what evidence the committee chose to include was highly selective. It carefully detailed the testimony covering Communist influence in the WPA, but the hostile testimony of Hallie Flanagan was entirely omitted. Frey's charges of Communist domination of the National Labor Relations Board and the CIO were reasserted, as was the testimony attributing treasonous action to Governor Murphy during the sit-down strikes. Walter Steele's rambling testimony was constantly quoted to support charges against alleged Communist-front organizations. The American League for Peace and Freedom was cited as a prime example of a Communist front, and it obviously was. The Workers' Alliance, the American Student Union, and the National Negro Congress were all castigated as suspect organizations willingly serving the ends of Communist propaganda.

The general reception of the report in Congress and in the press was favorable. All agreed that the menace of un-American activities was a real threat to national security and that the committee's purpose had been justified. The problem was that the frequently shoddy conduct of the committee violated the American sense of fair play. Here was the beginning of that haunting refrain, "I believe in the objectives but I deplore the methods," which later became the basis of anticommunist apologia during the next two decades.

The position of the *New York Times* was a classic of the genre. The committee, the newspaper asserted, had performed a useful service. It had exposed the deceit and hypocrisy of the so-called front organizations and the insidious nature of Communist tactics and had correctly linked Communism with Nazism and Fascism as another form of undemocratic authoritarianism. It was important that the public be alerted to propagandistic and subversive activities. On the other hand, the Dies committee was not the perfect instrument to achieve these ends, the *Times* said. It had entertained "hysterical tosh," arrived at conclusions in advance of evidence, and was guilty of "red-baiting." Despite these failings, the newspaper endorsed the committee, felt it should be continued, and hoped for some reform of its personnel.

The *New Republic,* a strong supporter of the popular front, condemned the committee and its works. But the depth of its civil libertarian principles seemed to depend on certain conditions. It urged support for the La Follette committee on the grounds that "nothing holds the forces of darkness in check like a Senatorial searchlight always in readiness to be turned upon their activities." Supporters of the Dies committee held the same view with respect to a congressional searchlight on alleged subversive activities. One might agree that the power of union-busting corporations presented a greater threat to genuine democracy than that of the Communist Left during these years and that the conduct, research, and documentation of the La Follette investigation far surpassed the unfair and slipshod methods of the Dies Committee, but this double vision, which accepted the political motivation of one committee while rejecting the other, set an example for the wavering integrity of some liberals who grew to accept the work of the un-American activities committees as a necessary evil in the fight against international communism.

While partisans of both sides discussed the needs, failings, and implications of the committee, *Collier's* magazine captured the popular attitude. In spite of some obvious theatrical flaws, phony witnesses, and fantastic stories, the public wished the show to go on, hoped for some improvement in the proceedings, and advocated a larger appropriation.

Dies was confident. In the congressional debate over renewal of the committee, the war horses of the opposition retreated. They no longer repudiated the committee's existence but simply demanded reform of committee conduct. Only one representative, Adolph Sabath, still angered over their neglect of anti-Semitic and Fascist groups, voted against renewal in the Rules Committee. After an hour of debate on the floor, Dies won an overwhelming vote of confidence, 344 to 35. Republicans supported the committee to a man; Democrats, reading public sentiment and noting the feeble opposition of the administration, went along. The committee was awarded $100,000 and another year's tenure.

Dies was jubilant. "We've proved the job should be done." To conciliate critics and prove nonpartisanship,

California representative H. Jerry Voorhis. (Library of Congress)

the liberal Californian, Jerry Voorhis, replaced Mosier, who had been defeated in the last election. For the next four years Voorhis played the role of the committee's conscience, invariably condemning its conduct while defending its continued existence.

In the spring of 1939 as the European horizon darkened, there was a lull in the headline accounts of the committee's activities. In the House, Dies continued to push for legislation to exclude and expel alien Communists, require registration of suspect, "Communist" organizations, and bar federal employment of known Fascists and Communists. The latter became law in August 1939, and it was not long before Dies would follow his triumph by prodding the House to attach riders to many appropriations bills demanding the dismissal of bureaucrats investigated by the committee.

The committee's first headlines of 1939 occurred on May 18. Committee investigators, a shadowy and elusive crew, had uncovered a Fascist, anti-Semitic plot allegedly threatening the entire nation. The plot involved the most bizarre of the right-wing fringe and a group of unknown red Jews. The story was shrouded in mystery, with secret sessions of the committee and unknown witnesses hidden from one another and the press. As details were leaked, it was learned that the anti-Semite, Dudley Pierrepont Gilbert, had discovered, through a waiter in a restaurant frequented by wealthy Jews, that there was a conspiracy afoot to take over the country. Gilbert had passed the information on to right-wing patriots who, in turn, planned a counterplot to rid the country of the Jewish menace.

As the story unfolded in the press, the emphasis shifted from an exposure of anti-Semitism to an account of the Communist-Jewish plot. Anti-Semitic right-wing leaders, testifying before the committee, expounded upon the nature of the worldwide Communist-Jewish conspiracy. The effect was the revival of the flagging careers of those fringe groups that insisted that their main purpose was to protect the country from Communism, a disease invariably carried by Jews. General George Van Horn Moseley, a retired army officer and leader of anti-Semitic groups, and George E. Deatherage, the national commander of the anti-Semitic, nativist Knights of the White Camelia, gave lengthy dissertations on the attempts his group had made to mobilize a counterforce against this conspiracy. Moseley's "astute" scholarship was summed up in his observation that "over two thousand years of recorded history shows very clearly that those traits which have made the Jew unwelcome every place he has domiciled cannot be bred out."

One is tempted to equate the fears of the Communist and Fascist menace as equally bizarre manifestations in American life during a period of hysteria. But if respectable institutions did not support the likes of Moseley and Deatherage, their tolerance of anti-Semitism was overt. Only a year later the genteel aristocrat Albert Jay Nock was commissioned to write an essay for the *Atlantic* on the "Jewish problem." In it he refined Moseley's message to assert that the Jew and the Gentile could never live amiably side by side and that some form of apartheid was necessary if the country was to survive. Neither could the press be excused for twisting this story and others so as to hang its headlines on the spectacle of an ancient Jewish conspiracy while playing down the anti-Semitic aspects of the affair. More than one historian of the committee has wondered why, with so much evidence of anti-Semitism, it failed to utilize its information to develop a full-scaled investigation of the native Fascist movement.

As was his practice, Dies delayed formal public hearings on this matter until the late summer and fall when Congress had adjourned. In August the approach of war in Europe brought the real menace of Hitler home to the American people. Dies obligingly investigated the German-American Bund and its national leader, Fritz Kuhn. The historian of nativist Fascist movements, Sandor Diamond, notes that in a "strange but understandable way" Kuhn owed much to Martin Dies. Because "Dies was more concerned with the Communist threat to America than with the Nazi menace," Kuhn's only hope of reviving his waning movement was by "converting it into a militant anti-Communist and isolationist group." The Dies hearings on the Bund provided his platform but could not help but mobilize anti-Fascist feelings. It was not the Dies Committee, however, that was responsible for Kuhn's subsequent conviction on a tax evasion charge; it was the liberal congressman Fiorello La Guardia of New York.

The diverse and rambling hearings of the summer of 1939 simply could not sustain attention. The Nazi-Stalin Pact of August 24, 1939, was a lifesaver to the committee and its chairman, for they now had the documentation for their long-held contention that there was no difference between Fascism and Communism. Both were Godless forms of totalitarianism which would stop at no form of deceit. The subsequent invasions of Poland and Finland only confirmed the charge, which was immeasurably strengthened by the slavish servility of American Communists and fellow travelers who went to absurd lengths to defend these events. The apologetics of the Communist Party, which involved the abandonment of their call for resistance to Fascism and an espousal of pacifism and isolationism, proved to the committee and to most Americans that the party was nothing more than a vehicle of Soviet foreign policy. The stupidity of party spokesmen was more than many fellow travelers and former sympathizers could take. Granville Hicks, a literary critic who had eloquently defended the nobility of the popular front, submitted his farewell to the party to the *New Masses,* which refused to publish it; but the *New Republic,* still reeling from the shock of the Pact, did. Hicks lamented that the party had abandoned all pretense of independence from the Kremlin with its shameful claim that the Pact was a contribution to peace and democracy. He was chagrined that the party had not even bothered to defend the agreement as an act of political expediency necessary to gain time to prepare a defense against future Nazi aggression (which did become the rationale of many). He charged that since they were ill-equipped "to defend the Soviet Union intelligently, they would defend it stupidly."

For the less ideological and more romantic supporters of Communist goals, the Pact dealt a devastating blow to their idealistic commitments and principles. Irwin Edman's reaction is perhaps the most representative of many of the left-wing partisans who had marched with the Communists in worthy causes. There could be no rational reason for the Pact. The fact that there were such rationalizations, Edman wrote, "had eaten like a canker into the bloom of every value we enjoy and every ideal we cherish." It had made "a mockery of all their former hopes and knowledge." Even the "private joys" of former comradeship were made "shamefaced and precarious." Edman lamented that men in the nineteenth century had been saddened because they could no longer believe in God. But he and his friends were "more deeply saddened because they could no longer believe in man."

Such a lament tells more about the Communist menace than anything ever alleged by an un-American activities committee. The betrayal of political decency by the party struck a blow against the foundations of liberal optimism and soured a generation of well-meaning men and women on all forms of social commitment, encouraging many to retreat into private visions or a resigned acceptance of the irrational. Others enthusiastically embraced the status quo as the best of all possible worlds. Adopting a sophisticated Niebuhrian pessimism, they proclaimed a cynicism tantamount to political maturity. *This* was the most devastating legacy of the American flirtation with Communism in the 1930s. It may also help to account for the conduct of jaded liberals during the cold war and in the 1960s when they, too, resorted to duplicity to justify actions beyond the understanding of reasonable men.

The undermining of liberal confidence and commitment was one of the goals of the Dies committee, and its chairman did not let the advantage offered by the Pact slip by. It provided an opportunity for the committee to exploit the more ludicrous dimensions of Communist logic. Earl Browder shamelessly declared that world peace would be the consequence of the agreement of Germany and Russia to refrain from mutual attack. William Z. Foster continued to insist that the American Communist party was independent of the Soviet Union. There were, he claimed, "tens of thousands" of times when the party had taken a stand independent of the Comintern. When pressed, however, he could think of no particular instance. He admitted that after a party member had been educated to a particular position but continued to oppose it, he would be expelled. None of this was startling information, but the committee presented it in such a way as to provide sardonic anticommunists with unsurpassed examples of Communist sophistry.

At one point during Browder's hearing the Communist official broadened the definition of "transmission belt," a term used in Communist jargon to mean independent organizations used by the party to transmit their words to the masses, to include the American Federation of Labor. J. Parnell Thomas, right on cue, read off a list of liberal organizations to which high officials in the New Deal, including the president and his wife, had given addresses and asked if they were not also part of the transmission belt. When Browder conceded, Thomas commented with smug satisfaction that it seemed that the New Deal was working "hand in glove with the Communist Party."

During this period of daily revelations by Communist functionaries, Dies was shaping the strategy that would become his principal method of maligning the Roosevelt administration. As early as 1938 Harold Ickes had confided in his diary that Dies had sent to the Department of State a long list of organizations that he insisted were "agents of a foreign government." Ickes had concluded then that Dies's strategy was "to put it up to the executive departments to take action." If they failed to respond, then Dies could go to the country urging the need for greater support and appropriations for his committee as the only defense against alien subversion.

In October 1939 the committee heard the testimony of the Reverend Harry Ward, one of the Social Gospelers who had found twentieth-century Christianity in left-wing causes and was currently president of the American League for Peace and Democracy (ALPD). During the Ward hearings, committee investigators broke into the files of the Washington, D.C., chapter of the league. After some bickering with committee members Dempsey and Voorhis, the committee released to the press what was either a mailing or membership list.

Representative Martin Dies thunders against Communism at a convention of the Grocery Manufacturers Association in New York, October 30, 1939. (Library of Congress)

Major newspapers across the country gave their readers 563 names of citizens who were allegedly members of the league and at the same time government employees. Since the committee had already informed the public of the Communist-front nature of the organization, it concluded that these were defiant Communists or fellow travelers who had no business in the United States government. When errors were corrected and names of people included who had no connection with the league or any knowledge of its activities, the committee blandly replied that the error was not theirs, but the league's. When others objected that many people named had long since left the league, committee members pointed out that they had had a full year to see that their names had been expunged from the list.

Through mass exposure, the Dies committee investigations illustrated the power of publicity in punishing American citizens who were guilty of no crime but that of holding opinions contrary to those of the committee. The committee did not have to assert that the people listed were Communists, only that the league was a Communist-front organization. With publicity, the committee applied effective "moral suasion" forcing their resignations. It became clear that Dies was not interested in the Communist menace or the Fascist menace so much as he was in what he frankly described as the "left-wingers and radicals who do not believe in our system of private enterprise." This was a sweeping category encompassing all dissenters, from the mildest liberal critics of laissez-faire orthodoxy to genuine revolutionaries. It obliterated all distinctions in opinion and victimized citizens guilty of nothing more than an association with unpopular causes.

Committee member Dempsey denounced the release of information as a damnable un-American act. Voorhis presented an eloquent but ambivalent appraisal of the situation: He denounced the committee for publishing the names but defended the sincere, if mistaken, motives of his colleagues. He argued that there were two real dangers to American democracy—"honest to goodness" subversive activities that had to be exposed at both extremes of the political spectrum, and the kind of political demagoguery of the moderate Right and Left, who branded their opponents with Fascist and Communist labels. He supported continued publicity concerning true subversives and defended the committee on the whole as having conducted itself "in a proper and fair way."

The president described the committee's action as a "sordid procedure," and Dies responded by denouncing the "sordid" policy of an administration that continued to hire and harbor Communist sympathizers. It was almost like a dress rehearsal for the McCarthy era, replete with lists, names, and an increasingly vulnerable administration.

Four days following the publication of the league's list of names, the *St. Louis Post Dispatch* and the *Washington Sunday Star* printed an article based on an interview with Dies in which he boasted about the accomplishments of his committee thus far. Among a long list of achievements were the following: The committee had succeeded in "paralyzing the left-wing influence in the Administration," discredited the CIO, defeated Murphy for governor of Michigan, brought about an investigation of the National Labor Relations Board, encouraged the congressional abandonment of the federal writers and theater projects, and stimulated the movement to cut the appropriation of the La Follette Committee. Dies never repudiated this article and later repeated most of the claims.

The last controversial event of the committee's activities in 1939 was the publication of J. B. Matthews's report on the Communist domination of the consumer movement. Matthews had been an executive official of Consumers' Research until its staff went on strike in 1935, when he abruptly lost his taste for Socialist militancy. Bent on personal revenge against his former associates, he founded the rival Consumers Union. Matthews, now working with business interests, warned the country that many consumer organizations were determined to undermine the noble services of American advertising and manufacturing in order to support the Communist critique of decadent capitalism. Apart from fulfilling Matthews's vendetta against his former associates, the report served to further Dies's growing political ambitions by encouraging the support of businessmen delighted with any attack on the consumer movement.

The Matthews report, released under the imprint of the committee, had never been discussed by its members. There had been no hearings, no witnesses called, and no vote taken. Matthews had simply aired his antagonism, courtesy of the official facilities of the committee.

It is astonishing that after a detailed account of such scurrilous violations of judicial procedure, a historian of the committee, August R. Ogden, could still find praise for the "uniformly high plane" of the committee's performance during its second year. The conduct of the hearings had improved and now compared "favorably with the average run of investigations and exhibit[ed] only the faults common to this method of legislative procedure."

This tolerance reflected the apologetics of the time. With the exception of the leftist critique, no act of the committee seemed so nefarious as to suggest that the committee should be abolished. Walter Lippmann's appraisal of January 11, 1940, is a masterpiece of rhetorical ambivalence. The committee, he observed, was not "really a legislative committee at all." It was, on the contrary, a "committee of public safety" designed to repress activities condemned by the majority of the people, but which "are in themselves either not unlawful, or even if they were . . . could not be dealt with by the ordinary procedure of the law." In short, the Dies committee, Lippmann conceded, was nothing more than a form of "official" vigilantism. Since its members operated in the absence of much needed legislation, they were, by necessity, often "lawless in spirit and disorderly in their methods."

But Lippmann was quick to insist that "only the very innocent and self-deluding have any doubt that the Dies Committee have been attacking a formidable evil in modern society. The menace is real. It is not imaginary," he warned. This posed the "ancient moral question of whether the end justifies the means." It was clear that Lippmann felt the seriousness of the problem simply had to be met and, while he went on almost routinely to indict the methods of the committee for their flagrant violations of "American morality," he conceded that the end, "which is to protect the American system," was being maintained by means which, "if used for some other end would be deplored by everyone . . . except . . . the revolutionists Mr. Dies is stalking."

According to Lippmann, the committee could not be abolished because the end did justify the means; it needed only to be reformed. He suggested the idea of adding "one or two learned lawyers" to the committee who "would make it their business to reform the procedure." He advocated a larger appropriation to ensure the hiring of competent investigators so that the committee would cease to rely upon "dubious informers and crackpots who always gather about an inquiry of this sort."

This argument was repeated in one way or another by liberal and conservative politicians and commentators, and it has remained the basis for many subsequent evaluations of the committee. It goes a long way toward explaining how a committee whose means were its ends became an integral part of the American political process for the next three decades. It remains one of the curiosities of historical analysis that Lippmann's article was cited years later as "the soundest criticism . . . voiced at the time."

By late November 1939, Dies was preparing for the renewal debate coming up in January. A Gallup poll published in mid-December indicated strong popular support, but within the committee there was a deepening factional struggle. Voorhis, Dempsey, and Joseph E. Casey, a New Deal Democrat from Massachusetts who replaced Healey, were still furious over the publication of the ALPD list and the discovery that Dies and Matthews had already drafted the second annual report without consulting them. Stunned by the belligerent flamboyance of the report, largely the work of Matthews, they threatened to destroy the bipartisan image of the committee by issuing a minority report. Dies, ill and apparently fearful that a break in the ranks of House support was a possibility, agreed to support a new report prepared by Voorhis and unanimously signed by the other members.

The second annual report of the committee was published on January 3, 1940. It was described by the *New York Times* as an "astonishingly able and balanced document . . . a model of sound democratic reasoning." Even some of the committee's most persistent critics found it a judicious statement on the problem of subversive activities and the achievements of the committee in combating these forces. Others on the left, while conceding the change in tone, suspected that it was designed to weaken the resolve of the opposition.

The report was a classic liberal defense of the need for the committee. It began with the observation that the preservation of constitutional liberties and an adjustment of the nation's economic life were the two major problems facing America. It then offered a more precise definition of un-American activities, describing them as the work of organizations or groups "subsidized, directed or controlled by a foreign government" for the purpose of changing the American form of government in accordance with the "wishes of a foreign government." While it still left plenty of latitude for a broad interpretation, it was an improvement on the vague religiosity of earlier definitions.

The report outlined a solid case against the Communist Party, U.S.A., proving that it was simply a branch of the Comintern, and associated with eleven front organizations serving Soviet propaganda interests. Noticeably lacking was a mention of the American Civil Liberties Union, which Dies and Matthews had repeatedly charged with Communist infiltration.

In a section devoted to Communist influence in the union movement, the report asserted that an overwhelming majority of CIO members and officers were neither Communists nor sympathizers and that at most the leadership of ten or twelve unions out of forty-eight were "more than tinged with Communism." But there was also encouraging evidence that the "leadership" of the CIO was making every effort to purge all Communist influence.

In marked contrast to the hysterical tone of its previous reports, the committee now argued that neither Communist nor Fascist organizations constituted much in the way of a direct threat to American institutions. The real danger was the possibility that totalitarian groups through deception might persuade a substantial number of citizens that their only defense lay in some form of violence against their opponents.

In its conclusion the committee listed the conviction of Earl Browder for traveling on a forged passport and the conviction of Fritz Kuhn for the mishandling of Bund funds among its achievements. However, in both cases, federal and state law enforcement agencies had begun investigations before the committee had held hearings, and it is doubtful that the committee played any substantial role in their arrests and convictions. Defenders of congressional committees invariably make these kinds of claims, but Telford Taylor has observed that few congressional investigations have ever turned up evidence contributing to criminal prosecution that was not well known and acted upon by state and federal agencies.

Equal space in the report was given to summaries of Communist and Fascist propaganda, suggesting that a broad American consensus believed it was faced with a threat equal from the Left as from the Right. This illusion of balance, used to refute the charge that the committee's primary purpose was to harass the Left, distorted the real political struggle of the 1930s, however. That conflict was not so much a confrontation between political extremists and the center as it was between the forces of reform and the defenders of the status quo. And it was not a struggle between equals. It is difficult to equate the power and influence of reform and leftist movements, even during this so called "red decade," with that of the conservative institutional forces opposed to fundamental changes in the American system. Surely the CIO, supported by the militant activism of many Communists and encouraged by members of the New Deal administration, never had the strength of America's corporate hierarchy. It is unlikely that the liberal and leftist press had anything comparable to the power, influence, and circulation of the nation's conservative newspapers. The allegedly dangerous and subversive front organizations like the League for Peace and Freedom or the American Student Union, both weakened, had nowhere near the influence of the patriotic organizations—the veterans' associations, the Chambers of Commerce, the National Association of Manufacturers, or even the

American Medical Association. Too often commentators, embroiled in what Telford Taylor calls the "Cold Civil War," have attributed far too much influence to the power of militant reform in this decade. Thus, even Voorhis's widely praised report hardly informed the people of the real issues at hand.

Once again, their report formed the basis for the defense of the committee's renewal during the debate in January 1940. That debate received a charge when Congressman Frank E. Hook, an ardent New Dealer from Michigan, fell victim to a clever hoax perpetrated by conservative supporters of the committee. Hook rose dramatically to offer documented evidence linking Dies with William Dudley Pelley of the anti-Semitic "Silver Shirts." The evidence consisted of an exchange of correspondence between Pelley and David Mayne, another official of the Silver Shirts, and confirmed charges made repeatedly by the radical press. However, within a week the letters proved to be forgeries sold to Gardiner Jackson, an agent of liberal opponents of the committee. The letters had then been turned over to Congressman Hook, who had been, in the words of Mayne, "played for a sucker." Hook was forced to make a humiliating apology to the entire House, which exonerated Dies from any connection with the extreme Right. However, the leftist press, which had taken the bait, continued to make the charge, claiming that the hoax failed to repudiate other solid evidence of Dies's warm associations with right-wing extremist organizations.

With the exception of this bizarre incident, in itself revealing of the atmosphere surrounding the committee's activities, the debate over renewal had become little more than a formality. Defenders championed the committee as the lone bulwark against all threats to the American way of life. Opponents damned it as an un-American violation of unpopular opinion. Representatives of labor remained silent, hoping that the committee would leave them alone. Liberal congressmen feared for their careers if they participated in an attack on Dies or the committee, but of course, Voorhis and Coffee played their standard roles; they continued to rebuke the committee for its conduct in certain particulars while eloquently insisting

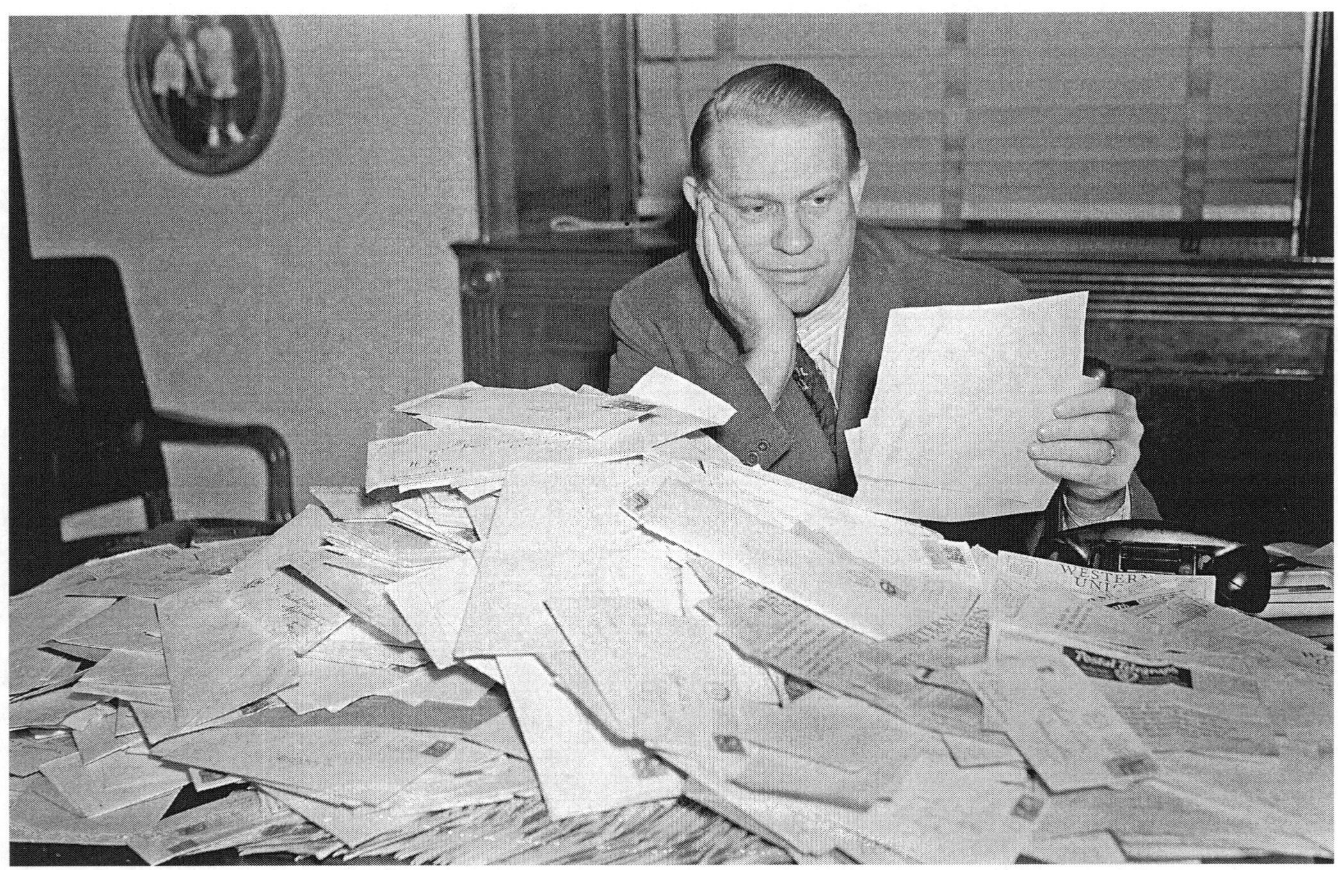

Chairman Martin Dies of the House committee investigation takes the time to read the hundreds of letters and telegrams that have accumulated on his desk, November 2, 1939. According to Dies, almost all of this correspondence endorsed the work of the committee and urged its extension, which Dies later requested. (Associated Press)

on the necessity for its continued existence. There was the usual talk of reform of committee procedure, but it was nothing more than talk. The committee had its own procedure.

The vote, 344 to 23, was another triumph for Dies. Voorhis's reasoned and moderate report had weakened what at one point looked like a faintly promising attack on the committee. Crawford, in the *Nation,* described the vote as Dies 344, Decency 23. Opponents of the committee feared that a vote against the committee would be widely interpreted as a vote for Communism.

Dies started off the new year by announcing that there were 7 million aliens in American industry who deserved serious investigation and exposure; Communist subversion in Hollywood was rampant; and there was a far-flung Soviet secret police operation in the United States. It soon became apparent that his real attention this year was directed to middle-rung Communist party functionaries who, he announced, would be subpoenaed and requested to supply names, under threat of congressional contempt citations.

In March and April 1940 committee investigators, with the aid of local law officers, raided several party headquarters in various cities and absconded with party records. A federal judge in Pennsylvania, George A. Welsh, ordered the arrest of the raiders and enjoined Dies not to make use of the stolen documents, and in May the judge ruled the raid an illegal violation of the Fourteenth Amendment. Communists were an unpopular minority, but their rights had been violated, rights, the judge declared, that are sacred to all Americans regardless of their political persuasions. Dies, in response, fumed over the state of a society that would extend fundamental rights to "agents of a foreign dictator."

Apparently the documents proved worthless because the committee, when it did subpoena a number of Communists to demand membership lists and the names of friends and associates, for the first time was defied by the Communists, who refused to answer questions. The committee, they charged, was establishing an illegal black list, their questions were prompted by the unlawful seizure of private property, and, more to the point, the committee was invading personal privacy by seeking information irrelevant to its stated investigative purpose.

Sol Cohn, the attorney for one of the witnesses, cited *Sinclair v. United States* (1929) as a defense of his client's right to refuse to answer questions regarding the Communist affiliations of members of his family. The limits of congressional inquiry had been raised in *McGrain v. Daugherty* as early as 1927, when the Court upheld the right of congressional investigations to demand information for the purpose of legislating, but also asserted that a witness "rightfully may refuse to answer questions . . . not relevant to the matter under inquiry." The *Sinclair* case was an elaboration on the *McGrain* case. The Court issued a ringing defense of civil liberties when it asserted in the majority decision that it had always been recognized that fewer rights were of greater importance than exemption from unauthorized, arbitrary, or unreasonable disclosures, in respect of "the citizens' personal and private affairs."

The committee's counsel insisted, however, that the only established grounds for refusal to respond to questions was "self-incrimination" under the Fifth Amendment. The committee preferred that plea because of the automatic inference of guilt it carried with it, the inference obviously serving the committee's purposes.

Dies did manage to have a number of witnesses cited for contempt, but only a few were ever convicted, and they received suspended sentences. The process involved court litigation and did not serve the publicity aims of the committee. Silent witnesses seldom produced headlines.

The first half of 1940 was chaotic, with the committee's seizure of worthless Communist records, hostile and unresponsive witnesses, and a rebuke by the courts for high-handed and illegal activities. In addition, the world's attention had become rooted on the German *blitzkrieg* of the Low Countries in May. The latter event gave strength to Dies's warnings against the threat of a fifth column, and his case was further aided when the Smith Alien Registration Act was passed in July, making it a crime to "teach and advocate the overthrow of the United States Government by force and violence." There were only four votes against that measure, further evidence of the solid ground upon which Dies was now working.

Dies naturally understood these events as support for the committee's work and requested additional funds, which he received in September ($35,000). Dies was riding high; the committee had become synonymous with his name. It became the rule to conduct one-man hearings out of which information was released to the press. He, or one of his colleagues, seemed to be everywhere, holding closed meetings and releasing sensational disclosures concerning sabotage and fifth column conspiracies.

Dies had promised not to conduct hearings during the presidential election campaign in 1940, but on the eve of the election his first book, *The Trojan Horse in America,* was published. It proved to be little more than a lengthy polemic indicting the administration: Public officials had deliberately harbored Communists; the president, Ickes, Wallace, Perkins, and countless lesser figures had served the evil designs of the "Trojan horse." Stalin, he charged, had "baited his hook with a 'progressive worm,'" and the New Deal suckers had "swallowed the bait—hook, line, and sinker." First Lady Eleanor Roosevelt had proved to be "one of the most valuable assets of the Trojan horse" because she had addressed countless subversive organizations, giving them prestige and respectability.

With President Franklin Roosevelt's reelection in November 1940, Dies believed it was essential to transform the committee from a congressional investigative unit into a law enforcement body coequal with the Department of Justice and the Federal Bureau of Investigation. Such a grandiose ambition was sure to promote a direct confrontation with both, and it was not long in coming.

Dies charged that the FBI's methods of fighting sabotage were not sufficient to cope with the present menacing situation. In October he claimed to have a list of over 300,000 active fifth columnists employed by the government, or by defense industries under contract to the government. He threatened to publish the list if the administration did not initiate a more aggressive policy of screening suspected subversives.

On November 20, 1940, Dies's challenge to the executive, the Department of Justice, and the FBI came to a head. The committee released a special report, the "White Paper," on alleged Nazi espionage and sabotage activities. Advertised weeks in advance, it proved to be an anticlimax; the information was widely known. The *Times* remarked that the report seemed to expose the "little schemes of little men" whose techniques hardly justified the extravagant claims made by the committee's chairman.

Two days after the publication of the "White Paper," Attorney General Robert H. Jackson publicly accused Dies and his committee of interfering with the work of the FBI. Jackson lectured the committee on the distinction between the responsibilities of an investigative committee and those of a law enforcement agency, a distinction that Dies was bent on ignoring. He charged that the publicity of the Dies committee had jeopardized the department's attempt at apprehension and prosecution in several cases.

Jackson's criticism of the committee was a shrewd ploy not only because it pitted Dies against J. Edgar Hoover, but in choosing to fight over Nazis rather than Communists, the administration also shifted the battlefield away from Dies's familiar stamping grounds. In late November the committee balanced its "White Paper" with the "Red Book" on Communist plans for sabotaging American industry. This was followed by a report from Hoover refuting Dies's claims to having exposed an extensive sabotage network in America. Hoover, while conceding the good work of the committee, insisted that it should not set itself up in competition with the FBI, thereby endangering the bureau's ongoing work.

Dies was aware that there was no political advantage in a dispute with Hoover. He requested a meeting with the president to work out a means of cooperation between his committee and the executive departments. Roosevelt agreed, but pointed out that the administration of justice was an executive responsibility and that "hasty seizure of evidence" and "premature disclosure of facts" were injurious to the administration's pursuit of real subversives.

Dies met with the president on November 29. His account of the meeting suggests that Roosevelt lightheartedly belittled Dies's crusade. He reported later that the president had jocularly boasted that some of his "best friends were Communists." However, if Roosevelt treated Dies lightheartedly before the public, it is clear that he continued to view the chairman and his committee as a powerful threat that must be handled with kid gloves. Roosevelt supported a firm agreement among the committee, the Department of Justice, and the FBI. The committee agreed to cease publication of information until it had been cleared by the Department of Justice, which checked to see that it did not interfere with secret investigations that might lead to prosecution. The Department of Justice agreed to furnish the committee with all of its information on cases that it felt could not be successfully prosecuted in a court of law.

The effect of this conciliation was to enhance the committee's reputation as an integral branch of the law enforcement apparatus. In addition it amounted to an official recognition and a sanction of the committee's tactic of punishing people by proscriptive publicity, even if their actions were not unlawful. Roosevelt belittled Dies publicly, but the administration accepted the committee and its methods as an established part of the system.

The committee's third annual report to Congress, published on January 3, 1942, defended the committee's existence by claiming to have been the "decisive force" in shaping the attitudes of the American people toward fifth column activity. The committee's work, it boasted, had been in the form of "public education," the importance of which could not be exaggerated. It noted that not a single country overrun by Hitler had had the protection of a similar committee preceding its downfall.

For the first time the annual report offered recommendations for legislation. The list was a veritable grab bag of restrictive prohibitions necessary to protect the nation. The committee called for the deportation of alien spies and saboteurs and all aliens who advocated "any basic change in the form of our government." (This supported Dies's assertion that attacks on capitalism were inherently un-American.) It insisted that the

This 1938 Herblock cartoon titled "Wait till the Dies Committee hears about this!" shows a six-panel strip distorting commonly understood information about Santa Claus to portray him as a Communist. (A Herblock Cartoon, copyright by The Herb Block Foundation)

government withdraw all financial aid to educational institutions that permitted advocates of Communism to remain on the faculty. It called for legislation barring immigration from countries refusing to accept the return of deported nationals. It called for new postal restrictions against "totalitarian propaganda," and asked for an extension of the statutory period during which citizenship might be revoked.

As a parting shot the committee closed its report with a hint as to its next major challenge to the administration. It recommended that it become official policy to deny employment in the government or in national defense to any "person who has been and is now active in any political organizations found to be under the control and guidance of a foreign government." Since the committee would make that determination, it was clear that Dies intended to mount a legislative assault on the executive by dictating his selection of executive personnel. It was also, indirectly, an attack on the judiciary because the committee would be free to determine guilt outside of due process of law, and, by mobilizing public opinion, they could punish the accused. This technique of exposure would become one of the most effective strategies of the committee in later years. Jerry Voorhis signed this report, objecting only to the proposed withdrawal of federal funds to educational institutions charged with harboring Communist faculty members. He felt such legislation would be impossible to administer fairly, but Voorhis's complaint was hardly a ringing defense of civil liberties.

The subsequent debate over renewal was a simple matter for the committee. Even Representative Coffee abandoned the opposition. Indeed, he had run for reelection in 1940 proudly endorsing the Dies committee. Congressman Sabath, usually a critic, lavishly praised the committee's work when he reported the resolution for extension out of the Rules Committee. Only the hapless Samuel Dickstein and the eternally belligerent Vito Marcantonio vigorously fought against renewal. When Dickstein charged that Fascists had a key to the back door of the committee, the House, spurred on by Mississippi's John Rankin, ordered Dickstein's remark expunged from the record. Rankin made it clear that Dickstein did not speak for "the old line Americans." The vote was 354 to 6, and the committee was awarded its highest appropriation—$150,000.

The activities of the committee after 1941 are difficult to trace because it had become a one-man investigation that seldom held public hearings; Dies had transformed the committee into a one-man "denunciatory agency." From the summer of 1940 to the end of his tenure as chairman in 1944, Dies never appeared at a public hearing. His activities and those of most of the committee's members were reduced to speeches, articles, and the constant barrage of press releases informing the people of the committee's constant vigilance against subversion.

The German invasion of the Soviet Union on June 22, 1941, hardly served the interests of Chairman Dies, however. Once again the Communists' policy reversed itself, and they presented themselves as comrades-in-arms against the Fascist menace. Although Dies never gave up the battle, he was driven to despair at the sight of Communists and their sympathizers masquerading as ardent patriots supporting the war effort. But, as the administration mobilized for war, the executive bureaucracy expanded, and it hired men and women whose names were found in Dr. Matthews's encyclopedic files as members or supporters of suspicious organizations operating in the thirties.

Periodically, Dies released lists of names and renewed his demand that the administration dismiss all persons remotely associated with alleged front organizations. Leon Henderson, head of the Office of Price Administration, was charged with membership in the Friends of Spanish Democracy. Robert Brady, Henderson's head consultant, had written a book critical of capitalism and was accused of being a Socialist and a destroyer of the church. Goodwin Watson, a broadcast analyst for the Federal Communications Commission (FCC), had been associated with a number of front organizations indicted by the committee and had supported Vito Marcantonio, a brazen and defiant fellow traveler who never lost an opportunity to denounce and ridicule Dies and his committee. Invariably, these charges were made without committee hearings or consultations. In fact, Voorhis and other members learned of these official findings in their daily papers.

In March 1942 Dies accused Vice President Henry Wallace of shoddy administration of the Board of Economic Warfare. Dies charged that thirty-five officials on the board had front affiliations, and, despite Wallace's outrage, he promised to see that the FBI checked all of the names on the list.

As ridiculous as Dies's activities appear, he was having a genuine impact on administrative policy. In the spring of 1941 Congress appropriated $100,000 to enable a willing Department of Justice to investigate federal employees accused by Dies. Attorney General Francis Biddle received a list of 1,121 names of suspects to investigate and indict if the sedition charges proved true. Biddle was under pressure from the president to follow through quickly in order to placate Dies's adherents. In September 1942 Biddle announced the results of his investigation. Only two persons were discharged as a result of information gathered by the Dies committee, but Biddle took the occasion to censure the reckless methods of the committee. A large proportion of the complaints, he charged, were unfounded and never should have been submitted in the first place. He denounced the inquisitorial behavior of the committee for having sapped the time and energy of FBI investigators. Dies responded by accusing Biddle of hamstringing the FBI and insisting that the committee should see the reports, not the department heads.

In January 1943 when the committee published its fourth annual report, Voorhis refused to sign it, submitting a minority report critical of the unilateral action of the chairman. Dies's report was the product of no hearings and had been presented to committee members for signature on a "take it or leave it basis." Voorhis's complaint was of the chairman's autocratic conduct. He continued to insist that the committee, with proper leadership, could serve a useful purpose by stiffening American resistance to Nazi propaganda. When Voorhis finally resigned from the committee in 1943, he admitted that his efforts to reform the committee had been "one hundred per cent unsuccessful" and arrived at the "novel" notion that the committee had become "more and more a political instrument of definite conservative bias" and less and less a "dignified, important and effective congressional committee." Many observers might have wondered when it had ever served in a dignified manner.

Dies cared little about this dissent, for he had discovered the old congressional weapon, the power of the purse. The attachment of riders to appropriation bills, insisting that suspected employees found guilty by verdict of the committee, i.e., Martin Dies, be dismissed or the department be denied its appropriation became a potent tool. This was perhaps the boldest attack on the executive branch during the entire history of the committee.

On February 1, 1943, Dies rose in the House to defend himself against repeated charges that he was aiding the Axis powers by his unrelenting attacks on the administration. The wartime alliance with the Soviet Union had made him and his committee vulnerable to criticism for hindering the war effort. In the course of his defense he came up with another list of names; this time it was thirty-nine government employees who were, according to Dies, irresponsible, unrepresentative, radical, and crackpots. He threatened the administration: "If you do not get rid of these people, we will refuse to appropriate money for their salaries." It was no idle threat. The House, in the Goodwin Watson affair, had excluded his salary from an FCC appropriation, but the Senate had killed the bill.

The House, intent on pursuing the Dies strategy, created on February 9 a special subcommittee of the Committee on Appropriations to review the charges. It was an extraordinary situation. Dies would be the prosecuting agent, the new House committee would serve as a jury, and the whole House would constitute "the Lord's High Executioners." The obvious encroachments on the prerogatives of the executive branch were ignored. Although the subcommittee dismissed the charges against most of the thirty-nine suspects, it did vote, after a heated debate, to demand that three be denied salaries before their respective departments received appropriations. The three victims were Goodwin Watson, William E. Dodd Jr., also of the FCC, and Robert Morss Lovett, formerly an eminent professor of English at the University of Chicago, a veteran of popular front causes, and presently the government secretary to the Virgin Islands. A House vote of 317 to 62 was unanimously rejected by the Senate, but during ensuing weeks Senate opposition weakened as the departments became pressed to meet their financial obligations.

The administration and even conservative supporters of the Dies committee denounced the act as a modern bill of attainder. The administration kept the accused at work, but they were deprived of their salaries. Finally, the Supreme Court, in *Lovett v. United States*, rebuked the House for its illegal action. Justice Hugo Black, speaking for the majority, reminded the Congress that "when the Bill of Rights were written, our ancestors had ample reason to know that legislative trials and punishments were too dangerous to liberty to exist in the nation of free men they envisioned. And so they proscribed bills of attainder."

The last significant public hearings of the Dies committee came in June and July 1943 and, fittingly, were related to one of the most shoddy episodes in American history. In 1942 the Roosevelt administration, bending before the hysteria following the attack on Pearl Harbor, inaugurated the evacuation of all persons of Japanese ancestry, citizens and aliens alike, from the West Coast. More than 100,000 Japanese Americans were transported to "relocation centers" under "protective custody." The reason for this flagrant violation of justice—military necessity.

There were other forces at work. For nearly 50 years prejudice against the Japanese had been prevalent on the coast. Nativist and racist sentiment was supported by hard economic interests. The efficient and hard-working Japanese farmers posed a constant threat of competition to Western growers and producers. Such organizations as the Sons of the Golden West and the Legionnaires allied with the Chambers of Commerce and growers associations to pressure West Coast politicians to support evacuation. Among those supporting this movement was the attorney general of California, Earl Warren.

The camps were directed by the War Relocation Authority (WRA) and staffed by men of goodwill who attempted to make the best of a bad situation. By 1943 they had mapped out a plan for the release of those evacuees whose "loyalty tests" showed they were of no danger to the nation. Those groups that had most enthusiastically championed evacuation, however, had never contemplated the return of the Japanese before the end of the war. Many had seen the program as the first step toward ultimate deportation. They immediately launched an attack on the WRA for faulty security, coddling of internees, failure to separate the loyal from the disloyal, and an ineffective Americanization program.

At this juncture the Dies committee was called in to serve a purely political purpose. Dies had claimed shortly after Pearl Harbor that the administration had thwarted a committee investigation of Japanese subversion by preventing the release of information that could have averted the sneak attack. The committee now leaped at the opportunity to further slander the administration. For tactical reasons it was decided to create a subcommittee chaired by a native Californian, John Costello. Congressman Costello was a member in good standing of the nativist Sons of the Golden West, with close

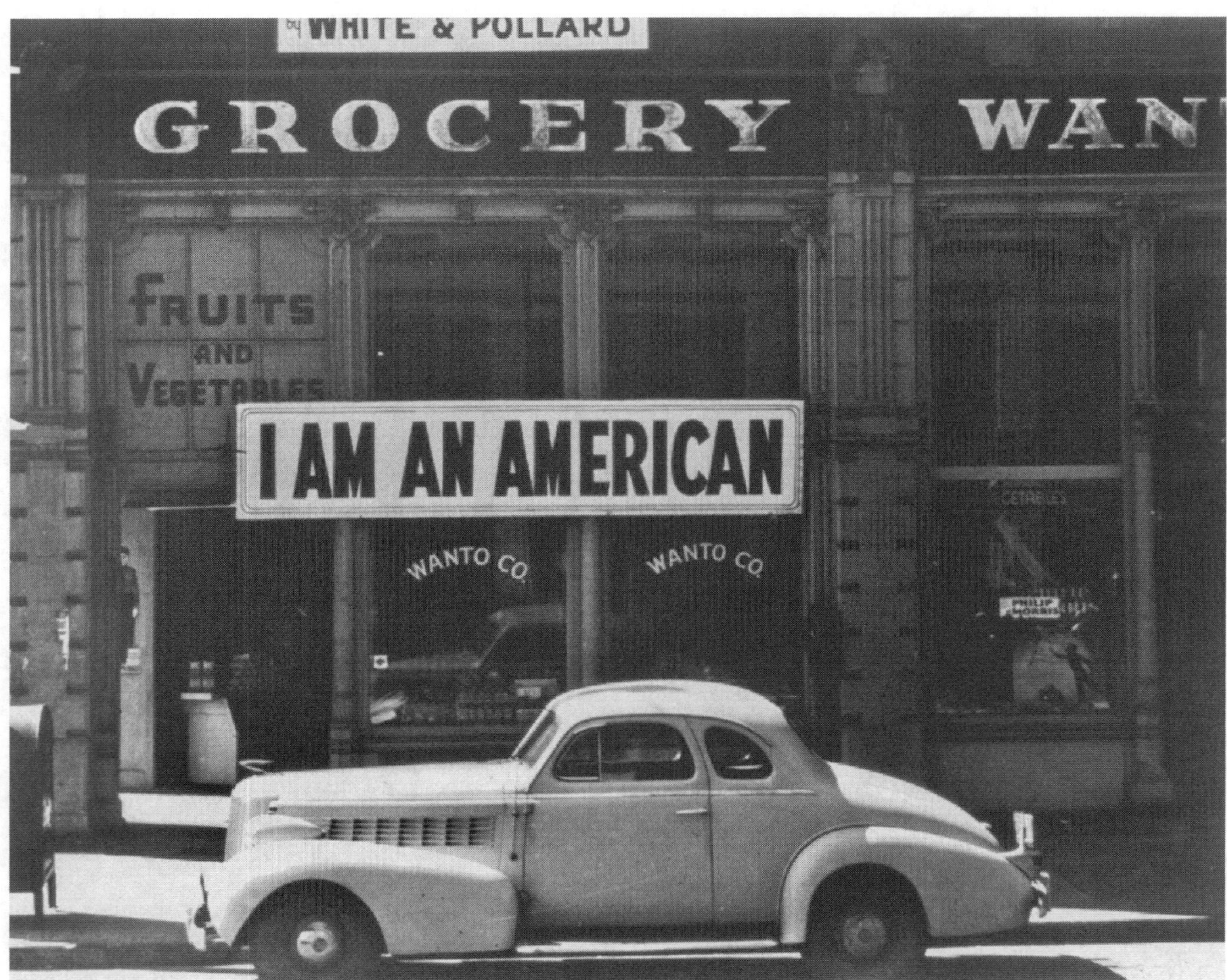

A large sign reading "I am an American" was placed in the window of a store at 13th and Franklin streets, in San Francisco, California, the day after the attack on Pearl Harbor in December 1941. The store was closed following orders to evacuate persons of Japanese descent from certain West Coast areas. The owner, a University of California graduate, was housed with hundreds of evacuees in a War Relocation Authority center for the duration of World War II. (Library of Congress)

ties to the Los Angeles Chamber of Commerce. The old tactic of advance publicity was again employed to promote the hearings, and J. Parnell Thomas went to Los Angeles in May, a full month before the hearings were to begin. He bombarded the local press with inflammatory press releases, which accommodating local editors turned into sensational headlines: *Rep. Thomas Reveals Jap Army in L.A.; Dies Prober Charges Relocation Plan Is a Farce.* Thomas lamented the deplorable spectacle of "fat-waisted Japs" being released while "American boys" on Guadalcanal "were barely receiving enough food to keep alive"; but Thomas had yet to go near a relocation center. Robert E. Stripling, the chief investigator for the committee, authorized a statement from Washington asserting that the WRA was releasing "spies and saboteurs."

When the hearings began in early June, Costello had recruited a motley crew of nativists, Legionnaires, and a disgruntled former employee of the WRA to smear the program and its administrators. They raised the old saw, "Once a Jap always a Jap," and ridiculed the notion that Asians could ever be assimilated into a Caucasian society. These racist ruminations went unchallenged by the committee. Only Representative Herman P. Eberharter attempted to keep the hearings within the minimal bounds of judicious behavior. As was standard practice, the committee entertained accusatory witnesses before it would permit supporters of the program to rebut the charges, thus allowing the press to spread abroad the damaging testimony. Later rebuttals seldom attracted headlines.

Carey McWilliams observed that the committee conducted an inquisition rather than a hearing. It had deliberately encouraged scare stories about "dynamite caches" in the desert to inflame the local populace and to serve the racist, nativist, and economic interests determined to prevent the Japanese citizens from returning to their homes in California. It was an inexcusable performance, playing upon every tactic the committee had used throughout its career to exploit the worst instincts in the body politic and to serve the most reactionary political interests, while at the same time impugning the competence and loyalty of the administration.

Despite the fanfare, the committee's final report was a relatively mild document calling for a more effective means of segregating the loyal from the disloyal prisoners, a more rapid Americanization program that did not bow to the ethnic eccentricities of the Japanese, and a review board that would investigate each evacuee who applied for release. Eberharter, in a minority statement, concluded that the report was marked by prejudice and that its charges against the WRA were unsubstantiated.

It is no mitigation of the deplorable conduct of the committee to recall that many of its liberal critics supported the evacuation program. Few challenged the right of the government to imprison American citizens guilty of no crime. Thus, it is difficult to conclude that this latest travesty of the committee was the sole work of extremists. On the contrary, the conduct of the committee was simply the last episode in an act of injustice initiated and condoned by the established liberal community.

Despite the contemptuous performance of the committee, the House in January 1944 again renewed its contract and appropriated another $75,000 to facilitate its work, bringing the total appropriation to $625,000. Nevertheless, its activities and its dignity had been severely tarnished. Dies, who had abandoned public appearances before the committee, continued to use its files to launch attacks on the administration, the labor movement, and organizations and individuals he deemed subversive. In the spring he engaged in a degrading public debate with Walter Winchell, a former ally. Winchell accused Dies, the committee, and other congressmen of hurting the war effort. So, even breast-beating patriots of Winchell's caliber came to the belated conclusion that the committee and its supporters no longer served the best interests of the nation. Dies, of course, demanded equal network time to call Winchell a liar.

By that time Martin Dies's days as chairman were numbered. He had lost a bid for a Senate seat in 1941 and faced stiff opposition for reelection in the fall of 1944. Militant labor groups in the Texas oil refineries had denounced him as a demagogue and were organizing to campaign against his reelection. Dies was tired and ill. He announced on May 12 that he would not seek reelection because he had "always had a dread of becoming a professional politician dependent upon the public" for his livelihood. One can fault his sincerity and integrity, but not his sense of humor.

Only a few weeks before the 1944 elections, the committee published a report denouncing the political action committee of the CIO and Dies promised to reveal more sensational documentation indicting the New Deal for disloyal collaboration with Communist forces. Dies ended his career as he had begun it, by using the committee's facilities for political purposes during an election campaign. The beneficial work of the Dies committee was quickly recognized when Congressman Rankin, by careful political maneuvering, persuaded the House to make the Un-American Activities Committee a permanent standing committee. Even without Dies the committee would go on to bigger battles in the days ahead, until it was finally eliminated by the Ninety-Fourth Congress in January 1975.

August Ogden, author of the committee's most detailed history, leaves the reader with an ambivalent judgment about its performance. He laments that the committee failed to take advantage "of a wonderful opportunity to render real service to the country." He concludes that while the committee's work was not a total failure, it "stands in the history of the House of Representatives as an example of what an investigating committee should not be." Ogden's conclusion proceeds upon the assumption that the committee was created to render responsible service to the American people, and the evidence fails to support that notion.

If the Dies committee and its successors were designed to serve such lofty ends, surely the House would not have appointed the likes of Fish, Dies, Thomas, Rankin, Velde, or Pool to chair such investigations. It is more reasonable to believe that the committees were designed to pander to popular fears during times of anxiety and to serve partisan political ends. Decent and responsible men were seldom persuaded to serve on these committees because they understood that the committee's conduct was rooted in the purpose for which it was created.

Too often commentators have presented the distorted notion that the liberal community constituted a united front against the committee. Evidence does not support such a self-serving interpretation. Liberals condemned the committee's questionable conduct but bowed before its political clout, justifying its continued existence. On occasion they tried to restrain the impact of the committee by supporting slightly weaker measures against the threat of subversion, as happened during the Truman administration. At other times they tried to prove they were tougher on communism by increasing the penalties advocated by the committee, hoping to counteract the "soft on communism" charge made by their political opponents.

During the cold war the established liberal community seldom challenged the existence of the committee in any effective way. While tolerating its excesses, they shifted the blame for its existence on to rural reactionary elements in American life. When that was insufficient, they apologized for the committee's undemocratic methods by stressing the disreputable character of its victims. At times some suggested that the results of the committee's activities were not so horrendous since the targets of its wrath were kooks, Stalinist hacks, and people of no account. By denouncing the character of the victim, one could mitigate the iniquity of the committee's criminal conduct.

The basic argument that justified the committee's existence proceeded upon assumptions that, from the advantage of hindsight, seem dubious at best. It was widely accepted that the Communist menace constituted a genuine internal threat to the republic. This notion came to be held as sacred orthodoxy—to be challenged only at the price of self-incrimination. It was asserted that Communist influence and power pervaded the intellectual community, infiltrated the government, and controlled unions and the communications industry, thereby constituting a force equal to the country's established conservative institutions. This assumption appears more and more to have been a form of self-delusion. By such rationalizations the liberal community helped to inhibit sincere dissent and genuine reform, which is the lifeblood of a democratic society.

But self-delusion lived on. In 1953, after Dies had returned to the House, a Senate subcommittee investigating possible ways of reforming the conduct of congressional inquiries called on Dies for his expertise. He advised the senators: "Primarily, if you get a good chairman and a good committee you will have a good investigation. Outside of that all you need is a few general rules to see that the witness and the public get a fair break."

DOCUMENTS

Opening Debate over House Resolution to Establish Un-American Activities Committee, May 26, 1938

In 1934, amid concerns that German agents were spreading Nazi propaganda throughout the United States, the U.S. House of Representatives at the behest of Representative Samuel Dickstein (D-N.Y.), formed the Special Committee on Un-American Activities. After holding a few hearings, the committee disbanded with little to show for its efforts. By 1938, with the tentacles of war in Europe threatening to reach the United States, new concerns beset segments of the American population. Some worried about Nazi infiltration; others about the possible spread of Communism. In May 1938, the House of Representatives formed a new Committee on Un-American Activities. This time, with disloyalty seemingly lurking around every corner, the committee would have greater power to investigate suspicious elements of American society.

OPENING DEBATE OVER HOUSE RESOLUTION TO ESTABLISH UN-AMERICAN ACTIVITIES COMMITTEE MAY 26, 1938

The Clerk read the resolution, as follows:

House Resolution 282

Resolved, That the Speaker of the House of Representatives be, and he is hereby, authorized to appoint a special committee to be composed of seven members for the purpose of conducting an investigation of (1) the extent, character, and objects of un-American propaganda activities in the United States, (2) the diffusion within the United States of subversive and un-American propaganda that is instigated from foreign countries or of a domestic origin and attacks the principle of the form of government as guaranteed by our Constitution, and (3) all other questions in relation thereto that would aid Congress in any necessary remedial legislation.

That said special committee, or any subcommittee thereof, is hereby authorized to sit and act during the present Congress at such times and places within the United States, whether or not the House is sitting, has recessed, or has adjourned, to hold such hearings, to require the attendance of such witnesses and the production of such books, papers, and documents, by subpena or otherwise, and to take such testimony as it deems necessary. Subpenas shall be issued under the signature of the chairman and shall be served by any person designated by him. The chairman of the committee or any member thereof may administer oaths to witnesses. Every person who, having been summoned as a witness by authority of said committee, or any subcommittee thereof, willfully makes default, or who, having appeared, refuses to answer any question pertinent to the investigation heretofore authorized, shall be held to the penalties provided by section 102 of the Revised Statutes of the United States (U.S.C., title 2, sec. 192).

MR. DIES. . . . Mr. Speaker, this resolution, as it shows on its face, is for the purpose of investigating un-American activities.

I desire to make it plain in the beginning of my remarks, Mr. Speaker, that this investigation is not directed at any race, and that the impression which has been created in some quarters that this investigation is directed at the German-American people is unfounded. I would not have anything to do with any investigation that sought to cast an aspersion upon the German-Americans of this country. I know of no more loyal citizens than the majority of German-Americans in this Nation. My own mother is of German descent. I desire to refute some of the unfounded charges that have been made to the effect that this investigation is aimed in that direction. This investigation is not directed at any race, for we all live in America, peoples of all races and of all creeds. While we may have our differences with regard to economic questions or methods that men use to achieve certain objectives, it seems to me that certainly all Americans of every political faith can agree upon those inherent and fundamental rights that distinguish this country from all foreign nations. I have often believed that the distinction between the American form of government and the forms of government which prevail in many European countries is the conception we have in America that we derive fundamental and inherent rights not from society, not from governments, but from Almighty God, and having derived those fundamental rights from God, no man or no majority of men can deprive us of the inherent right to worship God according to the dictates of our conscience or to speak our opinions and our convictions as we feel them. I can assure the House here and now that if I have anything to do with this investigation it will in no sense be an effort to abridge the undisputed right of every citizen in the United States to express his honest convictions and enjoy freedom of speech.

MR. WARREN. Mr. Speaker, will the gentleman yield?

MR. DIES. I yield to the gentleman from North Carolina.

MR. WARREN. The wording of this resolution is most unusual. I do not recall a similar case. This resolution seeks to set up an investigating committee, but nowhere in the resolution do you provide for a report to Congress. This means that the lid is off. It would mean that you could come back here next January and ask for permission to file a report or to extend the inquiry over a period of years, if you cared to do so. I believe 7 months is long enough to investigate any subject on earth. The gentleman controls the previous question, and I am wondering if he would accept an amendment for a new section providing that the committee shall file its report to the House on January 3, 1939, or may file its report earlier, in case the House is not in session, with the Speaker of the House for printing as a public document. I may say this has nothing to do with whether or not I support the resolution. All I am asking is, Will the gentleman permit the filing of the report?

MR. DIES. I may say to the gentleman it was my understanding and belief that any committee created by this Congress would terminate at the expiration of the Congress. I see no objection to the amendment, as far as I am concerned.

MR. WARREN. I hope the gentleman will accept the amendment. If not, we will just have to vote down the previous question so we can amend the resolution.

Mr. Dies. I see no objection to the acceptance of the amendment. It is perfectly all right with me, because I believe the committee ought to conclude its hearings by that date.

Mr. Maverick. Mr. Speaker, will the gentleman yield?

Mr. Dies. I yield.

Mr. Maverick. We do not want to be barred from offering other amendments, and if the resolution is to be open for one amendment, it ought to be opened for all amendments; and if the gentleman agrees that it may be opened for one amendment, would the gentleman agree to open it for all other amendments?

Mr. Dies. That is not a matter for me to agree to. That is a matter for the action of the House.

Mr. O'Connell of Montana. Mr. Speaker, will the gentleman yield?

Mr. Dies. I yield.

Mr. O'Connell of Montana. I have an amendment with respect to the Jersey City situation which I think ought to go in the resolution. [Laughter.]

Mr. Dies. As I was saying, Mr. Speaker, when I was interrupted, I have absolutely no patience with any effort in this country to abridge the rights of speech. I opposed a movement in my country which spread from one section to the other, and which was aimed at religious freedom and directed at certain races, and any effort in this country to create prejudice toward certain people on account of the fact that they happen to belong to certain racial groups is unworthy of the fundamental ideals of Americanism, as I understand them.

Now, I know the argument will be used, What is the value of an investigation? I have a mass of information that has been supplied to me that is shocking, information which shows the extent of the Nazi and Communist movements in the United States. I am not one of those who are inclined to be alarmists. I am not inclined to look under every bed for a Communist, but I can say to this House that there is in my possession a mass of information showing the establishment and operation of some 32 Nazi camps in the United States, that all of these camps have been paid for, that they claim a total membership of 480,000, that they assemble in these camps, and I have seen photographs that have been furnished from various sources showing the fact that in these camps men are marching and saluting the swastika, if that is the proper word for it. Not only is this true, but I have information in my possession that certain individuals and groups in America have contributed funds for the purpose of encouraging the Fascist or Nazi movement in this country, and may I say in that connection that so far as I am concerned I regard communism and nazi-ism and fascism as having one underlying principle—dictatorship—the theory that government should have the right to control the lives, the fortunes, the happiness, the beliefs, and every detail of the life of the human being, and that man is a pawn of the government, rather than the American conception that government is created for the benefit of mankind.

Mr. Johnson of Minnesota. Mr. Speaker, will the gentleman yield?

Mr. Dies. I yield.

Mr. Johnson of Minnesota. If the gentleman says he has positive information that there are 31 bund camps now organized in the United States, why does he not, as a member of the Rules Committee, see that the bill (H.R. 10003), the Voorhis bill, to forbid private military companies and organizations is passed by the House, rather than go on a fishing expedition all over the country when you have the information now?

Mr. Dies. I will say to the gentleman that I never knew there was such a bill until this morning, when it was shown to me, I believe, by the gentleman from Texas [Mr. Maverick].

Mr. Johnson of Minnesota. Will not the gentleman admit that when he knows the condition that exists in respect to Nazi activities in the United States, that the thing to do is not to waste 7 months on that committee, but to pass an act immediately?

Mr. Dies. That is easy to talk about, but the most difficult matter in the world is to deal with this subject. In the first place neither the gentleman, nor I, nor any Member of this Congress would sanction any legislation that might have as its effect the abridgment of the right of free speech in America. I care not what the gentleman's views are, I care not what his economic or religious or political views are, and I respect every man in this House who believes in his views, but I do believe that every man's right to express those views should be safeguarded.

Mr. Harlan. Mr. Speaker, will the gentleman yield?

Mr. Dies. Yes.

Mr. Harlan. Is it not true also that there is a matter involved here that is a great deal more comprehensive than mere military drilling, in that it is to the interest of the people of the United States to find where these funds are coming from?

Mr. Dies. That is right.

Mr. Harlan. And what other activities they are engaged in, and who is the leader, and the general program of undermining our institutions. They would not be covered by a merely military organization.

Mr. Dies. The gentleman is absolutely correct.

The Speaker. The gentleman from Texas has used 10 minutes.

MR. DIES. Mr. Speaker, I yield myself 5 minutes more. In connection with some of the information that has come to my attention. I have seen affidavits signed by supposedly reputable people, charging that in one of the principal Nazi camps only recently a speech was made by one member of this bund advocating the assassination of the President of the United States. In addition to that, on the other hand, I hold here a letter which was written to my colleague, the distinguished chairman of the Committee on Rules, the gentleman from New York [Mr. O'Connor]. I cannot read the name of the man who signed the letter, because I have been asked not to do that, but the charge is made in the letter that in the city of New York the Communists are preparing to picket the home of the gentleman from New York [Mr. O'Connor]—and I do not deny the right of men to picket industries where there is a labor dispute—and to harass and humiliate and to use every effort and purpose to bring about the political destruction of this Member of Congress.

MR. CRAWFORD. Mr. Speaker, will the gentleman yield?

MR. DIES. Yes.

MR. CRAWFORD. The gentleman made such a clear-cut statement, with which I agree, a moment ago with reference to communistic activities, that I ask him whether he heard Browder's radio address last night, beginning at 10:30 and ending at 10:40 on this subject, and I suggest if the gentleman did not hear it, that he move heaven and earth to get a copy of it, because it was a hair-raiser.

MR. DIES. I thank the gentleman.

MR. KELLER. Mr. Speaker, will the gentleman yield?

MR. DIES. Yes.

MR. KELLER. How many committees or commissions have already been appointed by this House for a similar purpose?

MR. DIES. There was one committee appointed some years ago headed by our distinguished colleague the gentleman from Massachusetts [Mr. McCormack] that performed a very useful function. Let me say to the gentleman that I believe all depends upon the way the committee is handled. I can conceive that a committee constituted or composed of men whose object it is to gain publicity, or whose object it is to arouse hatred against some race or creed, or to do things of that sort, might do more harm than good. On the other hand, investigations have a useful purpose. The other body creates committees constantly to investigate. I am not in a position to say whether we can legislate effectively in reference to this matter, but I do know that exposure in a democracy of subversive activities is the most effective weapon that we have in our possession. Always we must keep in mind that in any legislative attempt to prevent un-American activities, we might jeopardize fundamental rights far more important than the objective we seek, but when these activities are exposed, when the light of day is brought to bear upon them, we can trust public sentiment in this country to do the rest.

MR. KELLER. Was there not another committee headed by the gentleman from New York [Mr. Fish]?

MR. DIES. I do not know about Mr. Fish's committee.

MR. KELLER. And did they not get about all the publicity possible before this country?

MR. DIES. I know the gentleman from Illinois is a liberal-minded gentleman, but let me say to the gentleman that some of these groups, especially the Communists, are very strong in their advocacy of freedom of speech, and people throughout that great area are mere pawns in the hands of unscrupulous bureaucrats.

MR. KELLER. What was the recommendation of the McCormack committee and what have we done about it?

MR. DIES. Oh, I have only a few minutes, and the gentleman must not ask me to go into that.

MR. COCHRAN. Mr. Speaker, will the gentleman yield?

MR. DIES. Yes.

MR. COCHRAN. If this resolution passes, naturally the gentleman, or whoever is made chairman, will be appealing for an appropriation. Can the gentleman give us any idea as to the cost of this investigation?

MR. DIES. Let me say to the gentleman that so far as I am concerned, I am opposed to lavish expenditure of money on these investigations. I shall oppose any effort to create an army of useless agents running around over the country, and I shall be opposed to any effort to pad any rolls, or to put any political friends on the pay roll, and so far as I am concerned, if the House votes this investigation I shall insist upon an economical investigation with sufficient funds to do the work.

As to the amount involved, I do not know; that is a matter that the Committee on Accounts will go into. I am sure it will be handled properly.

MR. COCHRAN. As a member of the committee which will be required to vote this money—and, of course, the committee will consider it mandatory to vote the money if this resolution passes—I feel that the House should know now what sort of request is going to be made, how much money is going to be asked to carry out this resolution.

[Here the gavel fell.]

MR. DIES. Mr. Speaker, I yield myself 5 additional minutes. As I said a moment ago, the gentleman's committee will consider the matter, and that committee has shown a disposition in the past to be very careful about appropriating large sums.

MR. COCHRAN. There is no limitation whatsoever in the resolution pending. There is nothing in the world to prevent the gentleman from Texas or anyone else offering an amendment to a resolution appropriating a certain amount to double, triple, or even quadruple the amount recommended by the committee.

MR. DIES. I assure my distinguished friend from Missouri that that will not be done.

MR. COCHRAN. I think the House should have some information as to whether it will cost $5,000, $10,000, $20,000, or $25,000.

MR. DIES. I do not know. What does the gentleman think about it?

MR. COCHRAN. I do not think we should spend more than $20,000 on the investigation. I would like an expression from the gentleman on that.

MR. DIES. As I said, it is rather difficult for me to give an expression, because I do not know.

MR. COCHRAN. The gentleman will have an idea just the minute this resolution passes.

MR. STEFAN. Mr. Speaker, will the gentleman yield?

MR. DIES. I yield.

MR. STEFAN. I may say to the gentleman from Texas that while in his opening remarks he expressed deep sympathy to the patriotic German-Americans and that he is opposed to anything which would inflame Americans toward one particular race, I call the gentleman's attention to the fact that this country has been flooded with publicity regarding subversive activities. The gentleman's committee's investigation is going to be followed with a tremendous amount of publicity which I fear may inflame the American people against innocent but honest and good patriotic German-Americans. I caution the gentleman to use every effort in his power, if he is going to be chairman of this committee, to oppose anything that might be done in his committee to put publicity out into our country which will inflame one race against another.

MR. DIES. I am in entire sympathy with the gentleman's statement. As I said a moment ago, there is no one who detests more sincerely or more deeply than I any attempt to inflame the American people against any group within our boundaries.

MR. STEFAN. I hope the gentleman will carry that attitude throughout the investigation.

MR. DIES. . . . . This resolution has been endorsed by the American Legion. I ask unanimous consent to incorporate the resolution of endorsement at this point in the Record.

THE SPEAKER. Without objection, it is so ordered.

There was no objection.

Source: Congressional Record, 75th Congress, 3rd Session, 7568–70.

Opening Statement of Chairman Martin Dies, August 12, 1938

A Texas lawyer who was elected as a Democratic member of the U.S. House of Representatives from the congressional district once held by his father, Martin Dies was an early supporter of President Franklin D. Roosevelt. He championed many of Roosevelt's New Deal reform measures that stimulated the depression-ridden economy. By the late 1930s, however, Dies began displaying a radical change of heart. He soon spoke out against the corruption of organized labor, minimum-wage legislation, and regulation of the coal industry. But he soon decided his mission was to alert the American public to insidious foes of Americanism, especially Communist subversion, that threatened to control not only elements of the government but also other areas of American life. Under his direction, the House Committee on Un-American Activities would gain a strong foothold in American politics.

OPENING STATEMENT OF MARTIN DIES AUGUST 12, 1938

THE CHAIRMAN. The committee will come to order.

I understand that it is customary for the chairman to make a preliminary statement before the committee begins to take evidence. The Chair will make his statement very brief.

This special committee was created by a resolution of the House of Representatives, House Resolution 282, for the purpose of conducting an investigation of the extent, character, and objects of un-American propaganda activities in the United States; the diffusion within the United States of subversive and un-American propaganda that is instigated from foreign countries or of domestic origin and attacks the principle of the form of government as guaranteed by our Constitution; and, all other questions in relation thereto that would aid Congress in any necessary remedial legislation. . . .

The Chair wishes to reiterate what he has stated many times—namely, that this committee is determined to conduct its investigation upon a dignified plane and to adopt and maintain throughout the course of the hearings a judicial attitude. The committee has no preconceived views of what the truth is respecting the subject matter of this inquiry. Its sole purpose is to discover the truth and report it as it is, with such recommendations, if any, as to legislation on these subjects as the situation may require and as the duty of Congress to the American people may demand.

We shall be fair and impartial at all times and treat every witness with fairness and courtesy. We shall expect every witness to treat us in the same way. This committee will not permit any "character assassination" or any "smearing" of innocent people. We wish to caution witnesses that reckless charges must not be made against any individual or organization.

The Chair wishes to make it plain that this committee is not "after anyone." All that we are concerned with is the ascertainment of the truth, whatever it is.

It is the hope of the committee that we can admit the public to the hearings. However, in the interest of a dignified and judicial hearing we cannot tolerate any demonstration, disorder, or interruption on the part of those who are the guests of the committee. If any such demonstration, disorder, or interruption occurs, the person or persons responsible for it will be immediately ejected by the police and denied further admittance.

The Chair wishes to emphasize that the committee is more concerned with facts than with opinions, and with specific proof than with generalities. Opinions, conclusions, and generalities have no probative force in any court of justice and they cannot be made the basis of any findings on the part of this committee. It is the Chair's opinion that the usefulness or value of any investigation is measured by the fairness and impartiality of the committee conducting the investigation. Neither the public nor Congress will have any confidence in the findings of a committee which adopts a partisan or preconceived attitude. Statements and charges unsupported by facts have no evidentiary value and only tend to confuse the issue. It is easy to "smear" someone's name or reputation by unsupported charges or an unjustified attack, but it is difficult to repair the damage that has been done. As I previously stated, this committee is determined to be fair and just to everyone, and when any individual or organization is involved in any charge or attack made in the course of the hearings, that individual or organization will be accorded an opportunity to refute such charge or attack.

In investigating un-American activities it must be borne in mind that because we do not agree with opinions or philosophies of others does not necessarily make such opinions or philosophies un-American. The most common practice engaged in by some people is to brand their opponents with names when they are unable to refute their arguments with facts and logic. Therefore, we find a few people of conservative thought who are inclined to brand every liberal viewpoint as communistic. Likewise, we find some so-called liberals who stigmatize every conservative idea fascistic. The utmost care, therefore, must be observed to distinguish clearly between what is obviously un-American and what is no more or less than an honest difference of opinion with respect to some economic, political, or social question.

Source: U.S. House of Representatives, 75th Congress, 3rd Session, Hearings before a Special Committee on Un-American Activities, Vol. 1, 1–3.

Testimony of Sallie Saunders, August 20, 1938

Although Representative Martin Dies (D-Tex.), chairman of the House Committee on Un-American Activities, in his opening statement had promised a fair and unprejudiced examination of so-called un-American activities and had also promised that the proceedings would be held on a "dignified plane," it did not take long for a circus-like atmosphere to dominate. On August 20, 1938, just eight days into the hearings, the discussion had turned from possible Nazi activities in the United States to the testimony of a young actress named Sallie Saunders who had been employed by the Federal Theatre Project, one of the programs of the Roosevelt administration's Works Progress Administration, the largest of the New Deal agencies. In approaching the witness, Dies went straight to the point. The young white actress had been called on the phone for a date by a black artist, whom she did not know personally. Since Communist propaganda was, in Dies's view, part of the movement toward racial equality, could this incident in the life of an actress in the Federal Theatre Project be damaging evidence of subversion?

TESTIMONY OF SALLIE SAUNDERS AUGUST 20, 1938

THE CHAIRMAN. Before you testify, Miss Saunders, let me say we are not interested, as a committee, in the racial question, except only insofar as it forms a vital part of communistic teachings, practices, and doctrines. Later on it will be developed that Communists are working among the Negroes in certain sections of the country, and that their appeal is racial equality.

MISS SAUNDERS. That is right.

THE CHAIRMAN. Only as we link that in with Communist practices, doctrines, and methods—only to that extent, we are concerned with your testimony.

MISS SAUNDERS. And only to that extent can I testify.

THE CHAIRMAN. In your testimony I will ask certain questions, because we do not want to do anything that will stir up or increase any hatreds.

MISS SAUNDERS. It has much to do with racial hatred, if it is explained clearly.

THE CHAIRMAN. That is true. I will ask some questions, and you will limit yourself to answering the questions. This is a delicate matter, and I would like for you to answer the questions rather than make voluntary statements or get into a discussion of the fifteenth amendment, or something else than we have before us. I will ask certain pertinent questions, and I know you will cooperate in giving the material facts we want to develop by your testimony.

MISS SAUNDERS. I will be glad to, Congressman Dies, but I feel very strongly about the fifteenth amendment.

THE CHAIRMAN. But this is not the place nor the time to discuss the fifteenth amendment.

MISS SAUNDERS. That is exactly the point the Communists are making.

THE CHAIRMAN. We will reach that. Where were you from originally?

MISS SAUNDERS. Originally from Vienna, Austria.

THE CHAIRMAN. Are you a citizen of the United States?

MISS SAUNDERS. Yes, sir; since 1920. I believe my father took out citizenship papers then.

THE CHAIRMAN. How long have you been in New York?

MISS SAUNDERS. Since 1930.

THE CHAIRMAN. You have been employed by the Federal Theatre Project; is that true?

MISS SAUNDERS. Yes, sir.

THE CHAIRMAN. When were you first employed?

MISS SAUNDERS. March 3, 1936.

THE CHAIRMAN. How long did you remain with the project?

MISS SAUNDERS. Until October 8, 1937, when I took 90 days' leave of absence for private industry. I returned to the project January 7, 1938.

THE CHAIRMAN. You are on the project now?

MISS SAUNDERS. Yes, sir.

THE CHAIRMAN. What is the work that you are doing now?

MISS SAUNDERS. As an actress.

THE CHAIRMAN. Have you seen with your eyes evidence of communistic or subversive activities on this particular project?

MISS SAUNDERS. I can only say that literature has been sent around to me personally.

THE CHAIRMAN. Do you know that Communist literature has been distributed on the premises?

MISS SAUNDERS. Surely.

THE CHAIRMAN. On one occasion you were called on the telephone. Will you go into the details of that without going too much into it?

MISS SAUNDERS. Yes, sir. On Decoration Day I received a phone call from Mr. Van Cleave.

THE CHAIRMAN. This year?

MISS SAUNDERS. Yes, sir; and he asked me for a date. I lived at the Fraternity Club, and there are a great many men there. I thought it was someone I met at the Fraternity Club. I said, "Mr. Van Cleave, I do not remember you; when did I meet you?" He said, "I was the gentleman who sketched you in Sing for Your Supper." I said, "There were 289 people down there, and I do not know more than 25 of them." He said, "I am the fellow who was sketching you." The day before I had noticed a Negro making a sketch of me as I was dancing. He shoved the sketch in my face. I did not know his name, and did not know anything about him. All I knew was that a Negro had sketched me. I signed out and left the building. At first I thought it was someone trying to play a joke on me, and I became very angry about it and asked how he got my telephone number. He said that he took it from a petition blank or a petition to President Roosevelt, which we all signed regarding the $1,000 pay cut. He took my name and address from that petition.

MR. MOSIER. How did he know that was your address?

MISS SAUNDERS. He was one of the committee passing it around.

THE CHAIRMAN. After that time when he asked permission to make a date with you, did you report it to the supervisor?

MISS SAUNDERS. I reported it to Mr. Hecht.

THE CHAIRMAN. What did Mr. Hecht say to you?

MISS SAUNDERS. He said, "Sallie, I am surprised at you. He has just as much right to life, liberty, and pursuit of happiness as you have." He said, "It is in the Constitution." I said, "Mr. Hecht, that happens to be in the preamble to the Constitution."

THE CHAIRMAN. Let us not go into that. We know there is feeling in the matter, and we have to be very cautious about race feeling. You reported it to him, and he advised you, in effect, that he was in favor of social equality?

MISS SAUNDERS. According to the Constitution, and there was some press clipping about equal social rights.

THE CHAIRMAN. Did you report it to anyone else?

MISS SAUNDERS. I talked it over with Miss Coonan, and she was appalled. I requested for an immediate transfer, which was granted. I then reported the matter through a personal friend to Senator Pat Harrison.

THE CHAIRMAN. Who was Mr. Hecht?

MISS SAUNDERS. Mr. Hecht is in Sing for Your Supper.

THE CHAIRMAN. An employee of the Federal project?

MISS SAUNDERS. Yes, sir.

THE CHAIRMAN. I think that is far enough. Is he connected with the Workers Alliance?

MISS SAUNDERS. Mr. Hecht is of split nationality. He has a card in every organization which has the most power at the moment.

MR. MOSIER. What is his full name?

MISS SAUNDERS. Harold Hecht.

THE CHAIRMAN. Did you report it to Trudy Goodrich?

MISS SAUNDERS. She is a secretary of a Workers Alliance division, and she came to me to her own accord. She said she felt very sorry that I felt that way about it, because she personally encouraged Negro attention on all occasions and went out with them or with any Negro who asked her to.

MR. STARNES. Did she say that it was the policy of the Workers Alliance to do that?

MISS SAUNDERS. She did not say that; but she is a representative of that party, and they hobnob indiscriminantly with them, throwing parties with them right and left.

MR. STARNES. Is that a part of the Communist program?

MISS SAUNDERS. Yes, sir; social equality and race merging.

THE CHAIRMAN. I think that is all. I thank you for your testimony.

Source: U.S. House of Representatives, 75th Congress, 3rd Session, Hearings before a Special Committee on Un-American Activities, Vol. 1, 857–60.

Testimony of Hallie Flanagan, December 6, 1938

The Dies committee paraded before its hearings a number of witnesses who, like Sallie Saunders, expressed suspicions about the Federal Theatre Project. Finally, in early December 1938, the director of the project, Hallie Flanagan, testified. An internationally respected experimental theater director with a résumé that included a teaching stint at Harvard University, a Guggenheim Fellowship for work in Europe, and the creation of the Vassar Experimental Theatre, Flanagan accepted the directorship of the Federal Theatre Project in 1935. Although widely praised for bringing theater productions to many Americans who had never before attended the theater, including children, she also became the target of right-wing, anticommunist critics. They charged that the program was replete with productions tinged by socialistic and communist messages. Representative Martin Dies (D-Tex.) pressed Flanagan for answers. Beset by continuing criticism, the program would later be dropped from the New Deal agenda, and Flanagan would return to Vassar.

TESTIMONY OF HALLIE FLANAGAN DECEMBER 6, 1938

MRS. FLANAGAN. One of the great problems is that, while in the other art projects it is possible to establish them in every State in the Union, which we would also like to do here, it is not possible with us, because, while an artist can paint or a musician play or a writer write if there is no audience or only one or two people involved, we cannot set up theaters except in States where there are 25 or more people of satisfactory type on the relief rolls.

So that one of our problems is this centralization of the theater industry. Our big centers are New York, Los Angeles, and Chicago; and we, as much as possible, want to tour people out from those regions and want to set up small projects in the country.

However, it is very difficult to tour, because, as you know, it is very expensive business. We are touring a great deal out of the regional centers, covering the rural areas in Michigan and Illinois and so on. But we have not gone as extensively into touring as we would like to do.

May I go on for just a minute?

THE CHAIRMAN. Where have your audiences been? What localities have you played mostly?

MRS. FLANAGAN. We have played to, I think I am safe in saying, the widest variety of American audiences that any theater has ever played before.

THE CHAIRMAN. In what localities, Mrs. Flanagan?

MRS. FLANAGAN. The chief localities are, first, New York City, and next Los Angeles and Chicago, because that is where the greatest unemployment exists. They are the three largest centers. But if you are speaking now of the audiences themselves—I want to pick up that point, if you don't mind—

THE CHAIRMAN. It is quite all right, but I merely want to know the places where you have played. But if you want to discuss audiences, it is all right.

MRS. FLANAGAN. I do want to discuss them.

THE CHAIRMAN. That is all right.

MRS. FLANAGAN. Because that allegation was made here by one of your witnesses, which I would not like to remain in the minds of any of you around this table, because my impression is that you are trying to get at all the facts.

THE CHAIRMAN. That is correct. And if this statement is untrue, we want you to refute it.

MRS. FLANAGAN. I want to quote from her allegation. Miss Huffman says:

> "They couldn't get any audiences for anything except communistic plays."
>
> Now, gentlemen, I absolutely deny that allegation, and I have here the proof that that is an absolutely false statement.
>
> We have, as sponsoring bodies for the Federal Theater, lists of organizations covering 20 pages of this brief, which I intend to write into the record; and I will summarize them for you, if you like.
>
> Two hundred and sixty-three social clubs and organizations, 264 welfare and civic organizations, 271 educational organizations, 95 religious organizations, 91 organizations from business industries, 16 mass organizations, 66 trade-unions, 62 professional unions, 17 consumers unions, 25 fraternal unions, and 15 political organizations.
>
> Note, gentlemen, that every religious shade is covered and every political affiliation and every type of educational and civic body in the support of our theater. It is the widest and most American base that any theater has ever built upon; and I do request you not only to write that into the record, but to read the list of public schools and universities and churches and the civic and social groups that are supporting this Federal Theater.

MR. STARNES. I want to quote finally from your article, "A Theater Is Born," on page 915 of the Theater Arts Monthly, edition of November 1931.

MRS. FLANAGAN. Is this the same article, Mr. Starnes?

MR. STARNES. Yes. I want to quote this. This will be the final quotation. It is after you discuss the type of plays that are being used in this country at that particular time.

MRS. FLANAGAN. By workers' unions.

MR. STARNES. For instance they deal with unemployment and labor laws and those sort of things. This is your language that I am quoting.

> The power of these theaters springing up everywhere throughout the country lies in the fact that they know what they want. Their purpose—restricted, some will call it, though it is open to question whether any theater which attempts to create a class culture can be called restricted—is clear. This is important because there are only two theaters in the country today that are clear as to aim: one is the commercial theatre which wants to make money; the other is the workers' theater which wants to make a new social order.
>
> The workers' theaters are neither infirm nor divided in purpose. Unlike any art form existing in America today, the workers' theaters intend to shape the life of this country, socially, politically, and industrially. They intend to remake a social structure without the help of money—and this ambition alone invests their undertaking with a certain Marlowesque madness.

MR. STARNES. You are quoting from this Marlowe. Is he a Communist?

MRS. FLANAGAN. I am very sorry. I was quoting from Christopher Marlowe.

MR. STARNES. Tell us who Marlowe is, so we can get the proper reference, because that is all that we want to do.

MRS. FLANAGAN. Put in the record that he was the greatest dramatist in the period of Shakespeare, immediately preceding Shakespeare.

MR. STARNES. Put that in the record, because the charge has been made that this article of yours is entirely communistic, and we want to help you.

MRS. FLANAGAN. Thank you. That statement will go in the record.

MR. STARNES. Of course, we had what some people call Communists back in the days of the Greek theater.

MRS. FLANAGAN. Quite true.

MR. STARNES. And I believe Mr. Euripides was guilty of teaching class consciousness also, wasn't he?

MRS. FLANAGAN. I believe that was alleged against all of the Greek dramatists.

MR. STARNES. So we cannot say when it began.

MRS. FLANAGAN. Wasn't it alleged also of Gibson and against practically every great dramatist?

MR. STARNES. I think so. All right.

Now, I am quoting again:

> When we see, as we probably shall during the next year, their street plays and pageants, their performances on trucks and on street corners, we shall doubtless find them crude, violent, childish, and repetitious. Yet we must admit that here is a theater which can afford to be supremely unconcerned with what we think of it. It does not ask our advice, our interest, our advertising, or our money. We need not deplore the lack of art in the workers' theater for we shall not be invited to witness its performances. It is only in the event of the success of its herculean aim—the reorganization of our social order—that we shall become involuntary audience.

MRS. FLANAGAN. Well, you understand, Mr. Starnes, that that did not take place, did it? The great hope of the workers' theater professionals landed right in the lap of the United States Government; and I can again say that I am concerned today, and have been for 3 years, with the rehabilitation of those people.

MR. STARNES. Of course you are, but this is what you said in this article.

If there are no communistic activities on your projects, we want to know it. If there are, we think that that fact should be made public. And if the facts are made public, we feel that surely you, as the directing head, will take the necessary remedial action to rid the projects of such un-American activities.

MRS. FLANAGAN. You are quite right. . . .

THE CHAIRMAN. You have established the precedent of exhibiting a play championing the cause of ownership of public utilities. You said that was proper and you yourself thought you had a right to do that?

MRS. FLANAGAN. I think so.

THE CHAIRMAN. Now, what I am asking you is what would keep you or the policy board from continuing that same type of plays so as to cover other ranges of public ownership?

MRS. FLANAGAN. Let me answer it this way: If someone came up with a very good play proving that the private ownership of railroads was the best possible thing, and the play was a good play, we would do it.

THE CHAIRMAN. Then you would show it?

MRS. FLANAGAN. Yes.

THE CHAIRMAN. Then, on the other hand if the same play proved that the public ownership of railroads was a good thing you would do it too, would you not?

MRS. FLANAGAN. Absolutely, and the test is is it a good play and within the general range and the variety we have established.

THE CHAIRMAN. And if someone came with a play showing the public ownership of all the property in the United States, and it was a good play, you would also exhibit that, would you not?

MRS. FLANAGAN. Well, that is a very clever move on your part to maneuver me into a certain position.

THE CHAIRMAN. I do not pretend to any cleverness. I would not undertake to match my cleverness with you on this subject because you are thoroughly acquainted with it.

MRS. FLANAGAN. No; I would not. We would stop with that, because that would be recommending the overthrow of the United States Government, and I do not want that, gentlemen, whatever some of the witnesses may have intimated.

THE CHAIRMAN. In other words, you would favor doing it by degrees, but not all at once, isn't that right?

MRS. FLANAGAN. Well, we probably would not agree—

THE CHAIRMAN. Well, but you have said under oath the exhibition of a play championing the ownership of public utilities or railroads, if it were an entertaining play, that you would show it. You have said that yourself. Now, that is just the degree is it not?

MRS. FLANAGAN. Well, it is a degree that the Congress of the United States has passed upon, isn't it?

THE CHAIRMAN. Not yet; the question of public ownership of utilities, it has not passed on that.

MRS. FLANAGAN. You did it one time.

THE CHAIRMAN. Not that I know of.

MRS. FLANAGAN. During the war.

THE CHAIRMAN. Oh, well, you are going back now to emergency legislation.

MRS. FLANAGAN. Of course, we have gone back into history and covered so much geographic range that perhaps I—

THE CHAIRMAN. So, as I understand from your testimony, when a play is presented to you championing the public ownership of power, of railroads, if it is a good play you said you would exhibit it. Now, what I want to ask you and I want you to state is would you stop with those two forms of ownership, or would you go further and exhibit a play that would champion the cause of public ownership of other forms of private property?

MRS. FLANAGAN. I can't go into these hypothetical questions. I came up here under the distinct understanding that I was to refute testimony given by witnesses before your committee. You are proposing a long series of hypothetical questions. . . .

THE CHAIRMAN. You would not undertake to disprove that six of your supervisors on one project were Communists; would you?

MRS. FLANAGAN. I would like to know what the names are. You mean the ones mentioned in the brief?

THE CHAIRMAN. The ones in the testimony.

MRS. FLANAGAN. We have every one of those cases listed here with accompanying affidavits.

THE CHAIRMAN. That they are not Communists?

MRS. FLANAGAN. No; on the charges.

THE CHAIRMAN. Did you ever secure from any of the supervisors affidavits as to whether they were not Communists?

MRS. FLANAGAN. No.

THE CHAIRMAN. So you are not able to produce any evidence on the question as to whether they are not Communists?

MRS. FLANAGAN. No.

THE CHAIRMAN. So that it comes down to this, as a correct statement, does it not, that with reference to the plays themselves you can say unequivocally that none of them were communistic?

MRS. FLANAGAN. Right.

THE CHAIRMAN. That you have personal knowledge of?

MRS. FLANAGAN. I do have personal knowledge of.

THE CHAIRMAN. Because you have read each one of the plays, you supervised it, and so forth?

MRS. FLANAGAN. Yes.

THE CHAIRMAN. But outside of that you are not in a position to refute any of the testimony by any of the witnesses?

MRS. FLANAGAN. Oh, yes; I am.

THE CHAIRMAN. Dealing with the communistic activities charged on the project?

MRS. FLANAGAN. Yes. For example, I quoted this morning Miss Huffman as saying we could not get any audiences except for communistic plays.

THE CHAIRMAN. But that is not communistic activities on the project.

MRS. FLANAGAN. Let us narrow it down specifically to the solicitation of funds, and the posting of notices on bulletin boards, and so forth.

THE CHAIRMAN. In other words, we heard considerable testimony which forms an important part of this, that numerous people working on the project were Communists. We got that from one or two who are members of the Communist Party themselves. We got it from their own signatures, and statements that they were Communists, and received testimony that Communist literature was disseminated through the premises during project time, that they were printed on the bulletin board until this investigation began and it stopped, that meetings of the Communists units were held on project time in the premises, and other testimony.

I am just citing you some of the high lights. Now, that is the material fact involved here, as to whether that was done.

MRS. FLANAGAN. May I ask is that all in the record which I have studied, or are you referring to other records?

THE CHAIRMAN. I do not know what record you have studied, but that is in the record of the hearing, in all of the records.

MRS. FLANAGAN. I think you must be confusing some of our testimony, because I have read it very carefully, because I have not found a single witness brought up before us that said he was a Communist.

THE CHAIRMAN. Before us?

MRS. FLANAGAN. Before you.

THE CHAIRMAN. Well, Mr. DeSolo said he was a Communist.

MRS. FLANAGAN. But he is not on the Federal Theatre Project.

THE CHAIRMAN. He is on the Writers Project.

MRS. FLANAGAN. Yes; but not our project.

THE CHAIRMAN. You are dealing with the Federal Theatre Project.

MRS. FLANAGAN. Because that is what I have jurisdiction over.

THE CHAIRMAN. You do remember the statements with reference to dissemination of communistic literature on the premises?

MRS. FLANAGAN. I would like to say something about that. I spent about half of my time the first year in the New York project, it is half of our project, and I have never seen these activities carried on. I have never seen subversive literature or communistic literature on the project bulletin boards, nor to my knowledge, have I ever known of a Communist meeting being held on project property. So that, what I have to go on, is that your principal witnesses alleged that such things took place. I say I want this immediately traced and I want to find out about this. I have done that in every case.

THE CHAIRMAN. What have you done?

MRS. FLANAGAN. I have gone to the supervisor of the project, the administrative officer, Mr. Paul Edwards, and Mr. George Carnduff, head of the Theatre Project, and asked them to trace every one of those allegations.

THE CHAIRMAN. Have they done it for you?

MRS. FLANAGAN. They have done it, and the affidavits are in the brief of the whole testimony that I had hoped to be allowed to read, but which, in any case, I wish to write into the record.

THE CHAIRMAN. Now, they have all denied that communistic activities took place on the project as charged?

MRS. FLANAGAN. Yes.

THE CHAIRMAN. They did not cite a single instance where any of these things took place, did they?

MRS. FLANAGAN. No.

THE CHAIRMAN. So that, it was a complete denial on the part of all of the supervisors and everyone that reported to you that a single communistic activity had taken place on the premises?

MRS. FLANAGAN. Yes, but this sounds, as you say it, as though 3,000 people testified. Ten people testified about some fifty other people. This is a project of 4,000 people.

THE CHAIRMAN. What I am asking you is simply this, that all the reports you have—

MRS. FLANAGAN (INTERPOSING). Have denied the allegation of communistic activities.

THE CHAIRMAN. Denied them all?

MRS. FLANAGAN. Yes.

Source: U.S. House of Representatives, 75th Congress, 3rd Session, Hearings before a Special Committee on Un-American Activities, Vol. 4, 2856–85.

Critique of Committee by Walter Lippmann, January 11, 1940

After watching the Dies committee in action for well over a year, Walter Lippmann, perhaps America's most influential journalist, saw fit to draw some early conclusions about both its mission and its tactics. From his early days at Harvard University and his muckraking years as the editor of The New Republic, *Lippmann's views of the world had mellowed with his age. Like no other journalist of his time, Lippmann had an audience not only of millions of book and newspaper readers across the world but also of U.S. politicians. His opinion mattered. As for the mission of the Dies committee—to ferret out those anti-American individuals and influences that threatened the country's stability—the investigation and the hearings were necessary. Nevertheless, as he considered the moral issues surrounding the committee's work, Lippmann was troubled. The work needed to be done, but was this the best course?*

CRITIQUE OF COMMITTEE BY WALTER LIPPMANN JANUARY 11, 1940

The Dies committee are not really a legislative committee. They are a kind of committee of public safety set up by Congress to suppress activities which, though detested by the great majority of the people, are in themselves either not unlawful, or, even if they were outlawed, could not be dealt with by the ordinary procedure of the law. The Dies committee are official vigilantes operating in an area, that of the political underworld, where there is as yet no effective law and there is, therefore, no order. The committeemen, like their vigilante predecessors on the American frontier, are therefore themselves often lawless in spirit and disorderly in their methods.

This accounts for the somewhat shamefaced approval which thoughtful men have given to the work of the committee. The public is confronted with the ancient moral question of whether the end justifies the means. Thus, only the very innocent and self-deluding have any doubt that the Dies committee have been attacking a formidable evil in modern society. The menace is real. It is not imaginary. And it must be met. Yet there is no doubt also that the procedure of the Dies committee is itself a violation of American morality; it is a pillory in which reputations are ruined, often without proof and always without the legal safeguards that protect the ordinary criminal; it is a tribunal before which men are arraigned and charged with acts that are, as a matter of fact, lawful.

End Is Attained by Deplorable Means

Therefore the end, which is to protect the American system, is attained by means which, if used for some other end, would be deplored by everyone, by everyone, except, of course, the revolutionists whom Mr. Dies is stalking.

It is plain that the Dies committee cannot be abolished and must be continued since it offers a center of resistance to evils which could not otherwise be brought to light and checked. It is equally plain that the committee needs to be reformed, so that its methods will in spirit, at least, be lawful, and, therefore, capable of commanding the respect of law-abiding citizens.

I do not know how this can be done except by subjecting the procedure of the committee to public criticism, and by adding to the membership one or two learned and respected lawyers who will make it their business to reform the procedure, and by giving the committee enough money to hire competent investigators so that they may cease to rely upon dubious informers and the crackpots who always gather about an inquiry of this sort.

Source: New York Post, January 11, 1940; reprinted in *Congressional Record,* 76th Congress, 3rd Session, January 23, 1940, 597.

Sol Cohn's Defense of a Witness's Refusal to Testify, April 3, 1940

Although the Dies committee remained a formidable political force into the 1940s because of the widely held assumption that its activities were a genuine guard against subversive infiltration, its abuses were manifest even to the most casual observer. From witness intimidation to guilt by association to self-incrimination, its hearings damaged the reputations of legions of honest men and women who came under its whip. In its heyday, it was the target of few direct assaults against its tactics and legal maneuvers. In April 1940, Sol Cohn, an attorney for one of the witnesses at the hearings, challenged chairman Martin Dies (D-Tex.) and the committee's insistence that the witness testify. Citing the Supreme Court decision in Sinclair v. United States *(1929), Cohn asserted that his witness had the right in a congressional investigation to refuse to respond to questions that would lead to unreasonable and arbitrary personal disclosures threatening his personal and private affairs.*

SOL COHN'S DEFENSE OF A WITNESS'S REFUSAL TO TESTIFY APRIL 3, 1940

MR. MATTHEWS. Who is the secretary of the Harvard Young Communist League?

MR. O'DEA. I refuse to answer that question because I believe that by answering that question I will expose this person to economic persecution. He will be unable to get a job, and getting a job is the only way he will be able to live, and I think under the fourteenth amendment, that is due process, his only property will be his scholarship and his job, and he will lose that.

THE CHAIRMAN. Then you decline to answer?

MR. LYNCH. I think that that should be stricken from the record, all of the witness's statement except the statement that he refuses to answer, on the ground that it is entirely immaterial. The only right that he has to refuse to answer is one, that his answer might tend to incriminate him; and if he objects on that ground why, of course, that is all right, but otherwise he has absolutely no right to refuse.

MR. COHN. I think that is an incorrect statement of the law handed down by the United States Supreme Court in the case of Sinclair against the United States and other cases. I think that the objection of the witness is well taken.

MR. CASEY. What is the *Sinclair case?*

MR. COHN. In that case the Supreme Court said that the witness had other rights to object in addition to the one, the privilege against self-incrimination. It said that, for example, the committee had no right to delve into matters that were personal or private matters affecting the witness, and other cases held that the committee may only ask questions, and the witness has the right to refuse to answer questions which are not material to the investigation, questions that are not relevant to the investigation, questions that are not within the scope of the investigation.

The committee is limited by those decisions of the United States Supreme Court in addition to the constitutional provision against self-incrimination.

May I further say that it is my belief that the witness has a full right to explain his refusal to answer.

MR. LYNCH. I submit that none of the reasons advanced by Mr. Cohn are applicable to this witness. In other words, this witness does not say that they are not material, this witness does not say that they are personal to him, but he says that they are personal to someone else, and, of course, he has no right to attempt to protect somebody else.

MR. COHN. We are going to bring to the United States Supreme Court the question of whether a witness has a right to decline to answer questions, in view of what the chairman has already stated in the record, that he proposes to use any names of Communist members for a blacklist to see to it that those—

THE CHAIRMAN (INTERPOSING). That is stricken from the record; that is incorrect and will be stricken.

MR. COHN. That was the testimony when Mr. Cooes was examined. If my recollection is correct, the chairman then said that that was his purpose, and I said under those circumstances that the witness has a right to decline to answer.

THE CHAIRMAN. That is stricken from the record; you are incorrect.

MR. COHN. I respectfully object.

THE CHAIRMAN. The Chair will take under advisement the question of whether a witness can state the reasons for his declining to answer. The Chair is not familiar with the decisions with respect to that, but for the time being we will take that under advisement. The Chair now directs you to answer the question that was asked you. Do you decline to do so?

MR. O'DEA. I do, for the reasons stated.

THE CHAIRMAN. You have already said that. You decline to answer the question?

MR. O'DEA. I do, for the reasons stated.

Source: U.S. House of Representatives, 76th Congress, 2nd Session, Hearings before a Special Committee on Un-American Activities, 7561–62.

Martin Dies, "Trojan Horse" Speech, May 17, 1940

In May 1940, with the fall of a number of countries in World War II providing examples to him about the dangers of subversive infiltration by Nazis and Communists, committee chairman Martin Dies (D-Tex.) struck a theme in a speech to Congress that he would continue to press as the war grew closer to home. It was the ancient example of the Trojan horse, Dies said, against which Americans must remain ardently vigilant. But the attention of Dies was focused mainly on the Communist menace. At a time when pro-Nazi organizations were staging rallies in American cities, Dies warned of the danger of Soviet leader Joseph Stalin leading divisions of uniformed troops into the United States. Later in 1940, Dies turned the Trojan horse idea into a book titled The Trojan Horse in America.

MARTIN DIES, "TROJAN HORSE" SPEECH MAY 17, 1940

Mr. Chairman, democracy and the principles for which it stands are seriously challenged throughout the world today. Both as a form of government and as the spirit of free peoples, democracy is still young in the world. Democracy is everywhere threatened more seriously than it has been during the century and a half since our fathers drafted and proclaimed the Declaration of Independence. No man knows what new crisis for democracy each succeeding week holds. The paramount duty and the principal concern of every American must be the preservation of liberty and constitutional democracy.

We in America are not now in danger of any invasion of foreign enemies. Fundamentally no power or combination of powers could ever successfully invade our country even if they dare to try, so long as we are adequately prepared and stand united in allegiance to the God of our fathers and the Constitution upon which our economic and political institutions are founded. This confidence that we are invulnerable to attack rests only in part upon the strength of our armed forces, which we must maintain at maximum efficiency according to our defensive needs.

This confidence—if it is to be an enduring trust in our capacity for self-protection—must rest even more upon that strength of unity which we derive from the sacred commitment of all of our people to the principles of Americanism. It is this unity of our commitment to Americanism which the "fifth column," through Trojan-horse tactics, is now seeking to undermine. It is this unity of our commitment to Americanism whose strength we have not properly valued as a measure of national defense.

The safety of a modern republic lies, first of all, in ideological and spiritual defense erected throughout the length and breadth of its territory, in the hearts and minds of its people. It is this fundamental national defense which we have been far less diligent in building than we have been in preparing to stop armies and navies at our borders and coasts.

The experience of this generation, more than that of any other, has demonstrated that the enemies within a country constitute its greatest menace. Treason from within rather than invasion from without has been the cause of the speed with which modern governments have collapsed in the face of totalitarian assaults. Stalin and Hitler have pushed their Trojan-horse tactics to the point of perfection.

This Trojan-horse policy was adopted at the Seventh Congress of the Communist International held in Moscow. It was described by George Dimitrov in an address to the congress on August 20, 1935, in the following language:

> Comrades, you remember the ancient tale of the capture of Troy. Troy was inaccessible to the armies attacking her, thanks to her impregnable walls; and the attacking army, after suffering many sacrifices, was unable to achieve victory until with the aid of the famous Trojan horse it managed to penetrate to the very heart of the enemies' camp. We revolutionary workers, it appears to me, should not be shy about using the same tactics.

Years ago Adolf Hitler described in detail this new and diabolical method of destroying the governments and liberties of other countries. I ask you to ponder his words:

> When I wage war, troops will suddenly appear. . . . They will march through the streets in broad daylight. . . . No one will stop them. Everything has been thought out to the last detail. They will march to the headquarters of the general staff. . . . The confusion will be beyond belief. But I shall long have had relations with the men who will form a new government—a government to suit me. We will find such men; we shall find them in every country; we shall not need to bribe them. They will come of their own accord. Ambition and delusion, party squabbles and self-seeking arrogance will drive them. . . . Our strategy is to destroy the enemy from within, to conquer him through himself.

The Trojan-horse minorities within Austria, Czechoslovakia, Poland, Finland, and Holland made it impossible for these countries to offer any serious resistance to foreign invasion. The subversive work of Nazi and Communist sympathizers in the countries overrun by Hitler and Stalin has everywhere constituted a major factor in the spectacular success of the German war machine. In Czechoslovakia the Government permitted the formation of a Nazi organization of 1,500,000 citizens and noncitizens residing in Czechoslovakia. The fuehrer of this organization was Comrade Henline, a traitor to his own country and an agent of Adolf Hitler.

During the early stages of this Nazi movement in Czechoslovakia a few wise and patriotic statesmen of that Republic warned the Government that this movement was disloyal to the Republic and that Henline was contemplating the betrayal of his country.

The world has not yet appreciated the important role played by this Nazi organization in the easy conquest of Czechoslovakia by the Nazi legions. It is a fact, however, that this treasonable organization delivered the Republic into the hands of Hitler.

The next victim of the "fifth column" was Poland, with a population of 35,000,000 people and a standing army in excess of 1,000,000 soldiers. Polish officers now in exile have testified to the fact that there were so many Nazi and Communist agents and sympathizers in Poland, and their aid to Hitler and Stalin was so valuable and important, that the Polish Army, with thousands of traitors in its rear and with the ruthless war machine of Hitler in its front, virtually collapsed.

After the easy conquest of Poland, Hitler admitted in a public statement that he knew the military plans of the Polish high command 6 weeks before he gave the order to invade Poland.

In Finland we see another example of the success of Trojan-horse tactics. The Communist Party in Finland, which had been tolerated under the free institutions of that heroic country, set up a puppet government and furnished the pretext for the Communist invasion. Their treasonable cooperation with Stalin seriously handicapped the brave people of Finland in their immortal defense.

American correspondents who witnessed the working of this new combination of internal revolution and foreign invasion in Norway have reported its shocking details for our American newspapers. Editors all over the country have commented upon its despicable character. It has not been generally reported, however, that the Communist Party of Norway fully supported the invasion by Hitler's troops, and that the Communists of Norway, like the Nazi sympathizers in the country, welcomed the setting up of the Nazi totalitarian regime in Oslo. The Daily Worker, official Communist Party newspaper in the United States, even points with pride to this treasonable role of the Norwegian Communists. The Daily Worker of April 17 publishes in full a manifesto of the Norwegian Communist Party. In this manifesto there is not one line of criticism of Hitler's invasion. On the contrary, the entire blame for the present fate of Norway is laid at the door of England, which the Norwegian Communists accuse of violating the country's neutrality. The Communist Party of the United States has itself taken exactly the same line as that taken by the Norwegian Communist Party, and both act as Trojan-horse traitors for Stalin.

The most recent example of the fifth-column strategy is the case of Holland. It is not generally known, but it is a fact, that a Nazi organization composed largely of Dutch citizens and to some extent augmented by non-citizens of Holland, with a membership of 60,000, cooperated with the German soldiers in the conquest of that great country.

In the year 1935 the strategy of the Nazis, the Communists, and the Fascists underwent certain fundamental changes designed to perfect the Trojan-horse tactics. It is sometimes overlooked that nazi-ism, fascism, and communism were promulgated as world theories. In "Mein Kampf" Adolf Hitler advances his cult of nazi-ism as a world theory to be embraced and spread throughout the world with the zeal which characterized the early disciples of Christianity. The same thing is true with reference to fascism. In his book What is Fascism? Mussolini describes it as a world theory which cannot, and should not, be compressed within the narrow boundaries of any one country. In the many speeches and writing of Lenin, Karl Marx, and the other founders of communism it is stressed repeatedly that communism is a world theory, not to be confined to any one country, but to embrace the proletariat of every country. This being true, Italy, Germany, and Russia established organizations throughout the world which masked themselves as political parties in some instances, and in other instances as social, patriotic, or fraternal societies.

In France, Moscow played an important part in the formation of the Popular Front. The Communists were the most militant and aggressive group which comprised the Popular Front; and as a result of this militancy they exercised a preponderant influence in the front. They elected many members of the party to the Parliament, and they became so powerful that they were able to prevent France from adopting adequate measures of national defense. In the face of German aggression, the Communists and their allies threatened a general strike. And it was only by resort to oppressive and democratic methods that France was finally able, though too late, to prepare herself to resist the war machine of Adolf Hitler.

I stress the experience of France in order to illustrate the danger and effectiveness of a program which is able to go into a country and enlist the support and sympathy of some of its citizens in order to destroy the liberties and freedom of that country. I also desire to emphasize another truth that is sometimes overlooked. For 2 years I have been stressing the fact that communism, nazi-ism, and fascism are fundamentally alike. When Mussolini approved the definition of fascism—"Everything for the state, nothing against the state, nothing outside the state"—he was expressing in different language the philosophy of Adolf Hitler, who declared that the highest duty of the individual is to subordinate himself to the state. This declaration was not original with Mussolini and Hitler; it was merely an expression of Marxian theory predicated upon the erroneous premise that the individual should be nothing and the state should be everything; that the individual should lose his dignity and identity as a human being and become a cog in a collectivistic system.

Now, what I propose to do—and I wish I had more time to go into it—what I first propose to do is to show you that the Communist, Nazi, and Fascist organizations in this country are not political parties as some of them pretend to be; that they are not social or fraternal societies as others pretend to be, but that, as a matter of fact they are foreign conspiracies under the control of foreign dictators.

Lenin, who is the undisputed authority on which the Communist Party bases its teachings and tactics, describes the Communist Party as—

> A small kernel consisting of reliable, experienced, and steeled workers with responsible agents in the chief districts and connected by all the rules of strict conspiracy.

In that same book on organization Lenin mentions the word "conspiracy" 20 times. Not only does he emphasize the fact that the Communist Party is a conspiratorial organization, but in the program of the Communist Internationale, under which the American Communist Party operates, it states bluntly that legal methods must unfailingly be combined with illegal methods. That accounts for the fact that leaders of the American Communist Party, such as Browder, Wiener, Dozenburg, and others, have recently been indicted and convicted for violation of our laws as a result of one investigation. That accounts for the fact that the Communist Party in the United States openly violated the laws of this country when it enlisted and sent to Spain some 5,000 recruits.

In the city of Detroit indictments were returned against 17 of them for a violation of the passport laws, but, as a matter of fact, the committee received evidence from other sections of the country showing that the Communist Party as an organization, and in obedience to orders from Moscow, recruited American boys and sent them to Spain, often under phony passports, and paid their expenses to Spain in many instances.

Lenin said, "Revolutionaries who are unable to combine illegal forms of struggle with every form of legal struggle are very poor revolutionaries."

Earl Browder, the present head of the Communist Party in the United States, has himself estimated that there are nearly 2,000,000 Americans who go with the Communist Party all the way to its full program. Let me analyze the growth of the Communist Party, the German-American Bund, and the various Fascist organizations in the United States.

The Communist Party, according to Earl Browder, has 5,000 branches in the United States, members in 42 States, district organizations in 36 districts. In 1929 the party claimed 7,000 members; in 1935, 25,000; and from 1935 to 1939, the membership, according to Browder, grew from 25,000 to 100,000 members. The party claims 28,000 members in New York City, 7,000 in Chicago, 6,000 in California, and 4,000 in Washington and Oregon. But let me caution you not to accept—at face value—the statement of Communist leaders with reference to their full membership. When the committee obtained certain documents and files in Chicago it found membership books with membership numbers in excess of 100,000. In the spring of the revolution in Russia the Communist Party claimed to have had 60,000 paid members, and yet they were able to seize the Government of Russia.

In China the party claimed to have 416,000 members and yet they were able to control one-fifth of China.

In Germany the Communists were claiming 220,000 members in the fall before the Hitler election and at election they polled nearly 6,000,000 votes in Germany.

In Spain, according to their own documents, the Communists claimed, in 1933, 800 paid members in the party, and yet that fall they polled 400,000 votes.

I mention these facts to illustrate that it is the policy on the part of the Communist organizations, as well as the Fascists and Nazis, to underestimate their strength, in order to lull the people into a sense of false security. . . .

Let me make myself clear. The committee has said, and properly so, that the great majority of working people in both unions are loyal, patriotic American citizens, but the committee has unanimously designated 10 national unions as being under the control of Communist leadership, or, rather, that Communist leadership was intrenched in those unions.

Not only did the Communist Party by their policy seek to gain a foothold in the trade-union movement in the United States, but likewise it established a number of so-called front organizations. What do we mean by "front organizations"?

We can take the International Workers Order as an illustration, although there are numerous other organizations that this committee has unanimously found to be under the control of Communists. What evidence do we have to support such statements? I merely want to illustrate the type of evidence in order to convince you that the question is not even open to serious debate.

Here is the International Workers Order that now has 165,000 members in the United States, 1,900 branches or lodges scattered throughout this country. It maintains a school for the training of youth. This organization grew from 5,000 members in about 1930 to 165,000 members today. Who is the president of it? William Weiner, the financial secretary or treasurer of the Communist Party of the United States.

Who is secretary of the International Workers Order? Max Bedacht, who is a high functionary in the Communist Party, head of the International Publishers Association, which prints and distributes Communist literature and books in the United States. Here is one of the pamphlets issued by the International Workers Order. It was issued by the campaign committee of the International Workers Order in 1932. In this pamphlet they openly advocate the election of Communist candidates for office. I cannot take the time to read excerpts from this, but it is a document prepared by the International Workers Order openly sponsoring Communist candidates.

We charged the American League for Peace and Democracy with being one of the organizations under the control of the Communist Party. There was a great hue and cry throughout the United States. We based that charge upon documentary evidence, upon printed and verbal admissions, and upon what I conceive to be absolutely indisputable evidence. The American League, in obedience to the Trojan horse policy dictated by Dimitrov in 1935, succeeded in obtaining recruits or members throughout the United States and at one time during the height of its power in this country it claimed 4,000,000 members, directly and indirectly affiliated with it. Of course, no one is intimating that those 4,000,000 members were all Communists. The great majority of them were not Communists.

I wish to illustrate for the benefit of the House the cleverness, the subtlety, the intrigue, and the strategy of the Communists in setting up so-called liberal organizations in the country for the purpose of deceiving many gullible people who otherwise would not associate with the Communist movement.

As I said a moment ago, according to the report of our committee, Communist leadership is entrenched in 10 of the labor unions affiliated with the C. I. O. Do you know that a trade union of technical men led by the Communist Party has a unit in every navy yard in the United States and that the total membership of this union of technicians is 7,000?

In the confidential minutes of the Communist Party of New York is the following statement:

> At the present time, while all are not functioning perfectly, we have, nevertheless, some 300 factions in the trade-unions, and in about 150 trade-unions there are party comrades who are either fully or partially in the leadership of these unions.

Fred Howe, secretary of Local No. 2 of the American Communications Association, recently testified that there were 150 radio operators in our merchant marine in the Communist

Party, and that it was an easy task for these operators to transmit messages to Moscow or Berlin. . . .

It may be interesting to the Members of this House to know that as a result of the audit of the bank accounts of the Communist Party and their controlled organizations—I am speaking now of organizations where they are in control through secretaryships and presidencies of the organization or through the executive committees which they control—the audit that our committee made of their books shows that their receipts in the United States total about $10,000,000 a year. You are dealing with an organization that is able to collect $10,000,000 and to distribute some 600 publications throughout the United States. Let us take certain typical examples of it. Here was William Browder, brother of Earl Browder, who was secretary of the Communist Party of the State of New York.

The audit of his bank account showed that he ran an account in one New York bank of $1,300,000 for 1 year and 11 months. He testified before the committee that the funds belonged to the Communist Party. But, as a matter of fact, there was nothing in the record of the bank deposit to indicate that the funds belonged to the party. I asked him the question: "Did you render an income-tax return, did you pay an income tax on this?" And he said he had not. I then called this fact to the attention of the Internal Revenue Department. Now, let us inquire somewhat further into their financial transactions in the United States, because I want to convince you that you are not dealing with a small and poorly financed movement. According to Earl Browder in his testimony before our committee much of their revenue comes from thousands of contributors and the contributions range from $10 to $3,000. Some of the men who are the backbone of this movement in the United States, are men like A. A. Heller, who is a wealthy man in New York and who has financed the International Publishing Co. since the day of its inception by subsidizing it.

These contributors are not people who are in dire financial straits; they are people who are able to make contributions from $10 to $3,000, according to the testimony of the head of the Communist Party; and, according to Earl Browder's statement, something like 50,000 members of the party are now members of labor organizations in the United States. He said further that two-thirds of that number are in the C. I. O. and one-third in the A. F. of L., as I recall his testimony. Let us consider the financial transaction in the case of Sam Carp, who, according to his own admission, went to Moscow to see his brother-in-law, Molotov (Premier of Russia), and there received a commission to spend $100,000,000 in the United States for supplies, largely military equipment. He is a citizen of this country through naturalization, and he returned to the United States from Russia with $100,000 in $1,000 bills, according to his testimony. But when we checked his bank account we found that he had made other cash deposits totaling about $400,000. We traced $52,000 of it and found that this amount had been spent to buy political influence. We have not yet traced the remainder of the cash brought from Russia, although I have information where that money went, and I hope before long we shall be able to show the country where at least some of it went.

I think I have shown you that the Communist Party is not a political organization, that its members, according to the testimony of Earl Browder, William Weiner, and the other leaders, must obey the decisions of the party leadership upon penalty of expulsion. Communist leaders have also admitted in their testimony before the committee that the Communist Party of the United States must obey the decisions and follow the policies of the Communist International if it is to continue its affiliation with the International. The Communist International is controlled by the Presidium, a small group that governs when the Congress is not in session. This Presidium is completely controlled by Joseph Stalin. For a period of 7 years the Congress of the International did not meet and during that interval the dictator of Russia, Joseph Stalin, was not only in absolute control of the Communist Party in the United States but of every other country.

We asked a Communist leader, James Dolsen, who, by the way, was lecturing on a W. P. A. project in Pittsburgh, whether it would be the duty of a Communist to give information to his party leadership, and, in answer to the question, he frankly said that it would be the duty of a Communist to give such information. This means, in effect, that we have an espionage system in the United States which Russia does not have to pay for. This new method has many new advantages over the orthodox system employed by other countries. In the first place, Stalin and Hitler are able to enlist the services of many sincere and fanatical followers who can be depended upon to be loyal, faithful, and zealous. In the second place, the system can be operated at a profit to Stalin and Hitler. Through it they have been able to obtain financial aid. In addition to these advantages, the espionage agency is able to carry on its activities and propaganda under the cloak of legality. While the primary function of this espionage system is to gather important industrial and military information to transmit to Russia, the ultimate objective is to promote class hatred and overthrow the free institutions of America by force and violence and, in the interim, to undermine the unity of this country as the Communists and Nazis were able to do in France and Poland, and as they have been able to do in every other country in order to prevent adequate preparedness.

The Communists have formed many "front" organizations in the United States. For 2 years our committee has repeatedly warned everyone with reference to the identity and aims of these "front" organizations. When we expose one organization like the American League for Peace and Democracy and it dissolves, immediately another organization is established. . . .

In the case of the Communist Party of California, its report shows that one half of the membership was born abroad and the other half in the United States. In the case of the German-American Bund, I venture to say that 95 percent of the 100,000 members of that organization are Germans who came to the United States after the World War and have become citizens of the United States through naturalization. Many of them served in the German Army during the World War.

Let us take up that organization. What is its constitution?

> To be and remain worthy of our Germanic blood, our German motherland, our German brothers and sisters, and to cultivate our German language, customs, and ideals, and to be outstandingly proud of these principles.

This organization has in the United States 100 units, and a unit must have not less than 20 members, according to the testimony of the head of that organization. It has 47 districts in the United States. It has a membership composed of regular members who have voting privileges and sympathizing members who do not have voting privileges but who pay dues without any record being kept of their affiliation with the organization.

New York City has 5 bund units and New York State has 15 bund units; New Jersey has 4 bund units; New England has 7 units; California 9 units; Philadelphia 1 unit; Pittsburgh 1 unit; Wheeling, W. Va., 1 unit. There are units in Chicago, Detroit, and Flint. The application blank, written in German, calls for a person who will vouch for the applicant in Germany. In other words, the applicant has to furnish a German witness, living in Germany, for reference. Initiation fee is $1, and monthly dues amount to 75 cents per month per member. One-third of the fees that the members pay their local units goes to the headquarters. Voluntary contributions from members and outsiders for the last half of 1938 and the first half of 1939 amounted to $18,000. The German-American Business League is a separate organization but closely affiliated with the bund. It is composed of German-American merchants who pay $3 a year to be registered in a special book which the Business League puts out. The league has a membership of 800 in New York. There are similar German-American business leagues located in 11 other States. The Prospective Citizens' League is affiliated with the bund. To be eligible for membership the applicant must have first papers and establish a residence of at least 2 years in this country. The bund cooperates with the Christian Front, Christian Mobilizers, and the Christian Crusaders. The head of the bund states that its purpose was to establish a separate political party. The bund maintains summer camps, and the youth movement where boys and girls are trained.

In the Weckruf, dated May 12, 1937, page 3, is an article which includes a reprint of literature which was sent in by George Deatherage, president of the American Nationalist Confederation. In the issue of June 23, 1938, is a report from the Los Angeles chapter of the bund, stating that Roy Zachary, field marshal of the Silver Shirts, declared in an address to the bund that the Silver Shirts were similar to the bund. The Weckruf published James True's material. In the Weckruf, dated May 26, 1938, is an article by Edmondson. And it was also admitted by bund leaders that the Italian Fascist groups cooperated with the bund. Seven different Italian groups and organizations met with the bund upon different occasions. On June 18, 1937, at Camp Nordland, a large group of Italian black shirts were present and participated in a demonstration. The Weckruf for May 26, 1938, contains an item from the Los Angeles bund paper concerning a meeting of 100 Italian Fascists, attended by a man by the name of Ferri, who spoke to the organizations of the bund, and at the close of the meeting there were three cheers for Hitler and three for Mussolini.

The Committee received evidence with reference to an organization in Chicago composed entirely of German citizens with a total membership of approximately 1,000. We discovered that most of them were working in the important industries in and about Chicago. As a matter of fact, the 100,000 members of the German-American Bund in the United States are, for the most part, working in basic industries, and many of the members of the bund are skilled workmen, such as chemists and technicians.

In the 1937 yearbook of the German-American Bund is a statement from Adolf Hitler to the bund members of the United States in which he uses the expression, as translated:

> Your fatherland is Germany; love it more than anything in words and in accomplishments.

The German-American Bund sent a delegation of its members to Berlin. This delegation carried $3,000 in cash, which was donated to the winter relief campaign in Germany. These delegates were American citizens. They saluted and marched under the swastika. They were addressed by Goebbels and upon their return they published the special message to them of Adolf Hitler. Let me make it clear that the great majority of the people of German descent in America, are loyal and patriotic Americans, let us make no mistake about that. We are dealing with minority groups with respect to nationalities and labor unions. But the people who compose these minority groups are so imbued with zeal and enthusiasm for Nazi Germany or Communist Russia or Fascist Italy that they cannot conceal it.

I do not mean to imply that all the members of the Communist Party and the German-American Bund are traitors to this country, but fifth-column technique is to use innocent and sympathetic people for the purpose of obtaining valuable military and industrial information, and to support the foreign policies of the dictatorships and to undermine national unity.

Fascist Italy has used the same tactics in this country. The committee received evidence that there are Fascist organizations in this country; that these organizations are seeking to train and indoctrinate American boys and girls in Fascist ideology; that they have raised funds to aid the Fascist regime in Rome; and that they have cooperated with the German-American Bund. For instance, the committee received in evidence a letter written by Consul Decicco, of New Haven, Conn., addressed to all Italian-American fraternal societies. In this letter the consul says:

> There are a big number of Italian-American societies in the State of Connecticut. It is necessary that this office be in possession of the names and addresses of all those who belong to such societies. Therefore, I would appreciate it very much if you would send me the names and the addresses of those who belong to your society.

The committee also received evidence that there is a branch of the Italian Government secret service known as the O. V. R. A., which corresponds to the G. P. U. of Nazi Germany. There are letters from other members of the Italian consular service, which may be found in volume 2 of the committee's hearings.

I have examined some of the textbooks used in the Italian schools which glorify the Fascist regime in Italy. American children of Italian descent have been sent to Italy as guests of the Italian Government. These children were given Fascist uniforms and taken to training camps. They have participated in services, meetings, and parades on the streets of Rome, Genoa, and other cities.

It is clear from the evidence that there are in the United States certain Italian organizations which are Fascist in principle and belief.

Now, what are we going to do about these organizations? There has been a demand that we suggest legislation, and the committee is undertaking to do so. The gentleman from California [Mr. Voorhis], a very sincere and tireless worker on the committee, as is indeed true of every member of our committee, has conferred with the State Department and the Justice Department with reference to the preparation of a bill requiring the registration of these organizations, but I would not be honest and truthful with you if I led you to believe that the solution of this problem is through new legislation. The first thing you have to do is to enforce existing law. [Applause.]

Now, we might as well be frank about this. I wrote letters to the State and Justice Departments about a year ago naming organizations in this country that are the agents of foreign governments, and recommending that these organizations be prosecuted for failure to register in accordance with the provisions of existing laws.

If the Government of the United States and the States in which the Trojan-horse agencies are incorporated will enforce existing laws without fear or favor, we can go a long way toward solving this problem. In the enforcement of these laws, however, the Federal Government and the States must be prepared for the opposition which they will encounter from certain influences in the C. I. O. Before we had any hearings of the committee, we invited Mr. John L. Lewis to appear before the committee and give us the benefit of any information which he had. Mr. Lewis did not see fit to accept this invitation. At a later date, when the testimony of certain witnesses who appeared before our committee was challenged by Labor's Non-Partisan League, I invited the representatives of that organization to appear before the committee and deny under oath this testimony. They declined to do so. The committee unanimously found that on the basis of the evidence submitted Communist leadership is entrenched in the following organizations: National Maritime Union; United Cannery, Packing, and Allied Workers; Federation of Architects, Engineers, Chemists, and Technicians; Fur Workers' International Union; International Longshoremen's and Warehousemen's Union; Transport Workers' Union; United Office and Professional Workers' Union; American Communications Association; United Electrical, Radio, and Mechanical Workers of America; and the United Furniture Workers of America.

These unions exist in and largely control vital and basic industries in America that affect our whole national defense. I hope that the Members of this House can read the testimony of witnesses dealing with these unions, and especially the testimony of the heads of these unions, such as Joe Curran, Michael Quill, and Merwyn Rathbourne. It cannot be stressed too often that the enforcement of existing laws is absolutely essential if we are to check these undemocratic minorities in our midst. We must enforce our laws dealing with immigration, deportation, income-tax evasion, registration of foreign agents, passport requirements, and so forth.

I recognize the fact that many people in this country have been deceived by the insidious wiles of foreign influence. There were some sincere liberals in the United States who were deceived by the pretensions of the Communist Party that it was a democratic organization. On the other hand, there were some so-called patriots who, on account of racial and religious prejudice, joined organizations that were used by foreign governments for their own purpose and benefit in the United States. There is no longer any excuse for these misguided people to continue their affiliation with organizations which our committee has exposed as agents of foreign countries.

It is true that we can supplement existing laws by making more stringent our deportation and immigration requirements and by requiring registration and full publicity of Fascist, Communist, and Nazi organizations in this country. I hope and believe that our committee can offer legislation along these lines at an early date. However, I am now pleading for positive and vigorous action on the part of the Federal Government of the United States in the enforcement of existing laws. I do this not in the spirit of rancor but because the national welfare requires it without further delay. The strengthening of our national defense is necessary and urgent, but it will be wholly inadequate if we fail to check the progress of the enemy within our country and the "Trojan horse" organizations under which he masks his treasonable designs and activities.

This committee has been fair to John L. Lewis. It has found in its report that a great majority of the members of his organization are patriotic Americans. It has specifically exonerated Mr. Lewis of being a Communist. But I say to Mr. Lewis that it is his patriotic duty to expel men like Quill, Joe Curran, and Harry Bridges, and certain other leaders in these vital unions and thereby make known to the American people that there is no place for such men in the American trade-union movement. If Mr. Lewis will accept this challenge, the C. I. O. can clean its own house, and when it does this committee will give it a clean bill of health. We are dealing here with a vital question—a question as to whether or not we shall permit agents of foreign governments and their dupes, who are masquerading under high-sounding titles and objectives, to do in the United States what they did in Poland and what they did in Czechoslovakia and other European countries, or whether through democratic processes and in accordance with the Constitution of the United States we will here and now reckon with them and say to them: "At least it is not a violation of the Bill of Rights to enforce the laws of this country."

This Government should have deported Harry Bridges. [Applause.] There was sufficient evidence before our committee to justify his deportation, and in justice to the American people it should have been ordered.

There are some mistaken ideas and misunderstandings in official Washington but I plead with those in control, first of all let us enforce the laws of this country. This committee will submit supplemental legislation, but you must remember that in dealing with this question in peacetime it is not an easy matter. There is always the charge that if we undertake in the slightest manner to expose these subversive organizations we are violating the Bill of Rights. We subpena them to bring their records, and they arrogantly defy the committee. We have sat there for 2 years and endured the insulting remarks, arrogance, defiance, evasions, and perjury of these groups not because we wanted to, but in order that we might make a record of who these people are and what they are doing, so that in the event of a great national emergency we will at least have some means to check them and to deal with them.

Our great mistake was to sit idly by during the period in which they increased from a few thousand to the several million that now comprise, either wittingly or unwittingly, the Fascist, Nazi, and Communist movements in the United States.

There was a time when these organizations operated so openly and boldly that it would have been easy for the Department of Justice to obtain the names of all of their officers and make a permanent record. I am sorry to say that was not done. Five months ago when a representative of the Department of Justice came to my office and when I tendered him our fullest cooperation—he was a friend of mine, a former Member of this House—he frankly admitted to me that they knew very little about the subject, and had no valuable or dependable information.

I say that, although I run the danger of having someone charge that I am attacking the Department of Justice. I am not. This is a new problem that has baffled the peoples of every country. It has deceived England, it has deceived France, and it has deceived all the countries. All I am asking as a Member of this House, in a spirit of good will and harmony, is that the Government of the United States here and now cooperate with this committee to the fullest extent possible. We are now in such a critical condition throughout the world that there is no justification for the slightest feeling between any agencies of government. We need the help of this Government. We have never had more than seven or eight investigators.

In dealing with the most difficult problem that the Government can deal with we have been handicapped in every conceivable manner. I say to this House and to our Government that we need your help. We need the help of the F. B. I. We need trained men in order that we may do a full and complete job, and for that help I now plead.

I appreciate very much the opportunity I have had to bring some of these facts to the attention of the House. I want to make myself perfectly clear, that there is no indictment or intended indictment of a great majority of the American people. But minority movements, highly organized, constitute the greatest threat to modern democratic governments. We have seen the ability of a small group, tightly organized as a kernel, holding strategic and vital jobs in utilities, in shipping, in transportation, and in communications, to deliver a whole country over to an invading host.

We have seen their ability to promote strife and hatred in a country in order to divide it into hostile camps either along racial, religious, or class lines. We have seen the disastrous results that have come to other republics and other democracies by such a course.

If we are to be preserved as a democracy we must match the brains, the ingenuity, the patriotism of men who believe in democracy against this new and sinister influence. We must revitalize democracy and offer it as a challenge to the fanatical followers of Hitler, Stalin, and Mussolini. I believe that democracy can develop a tremendous enthusiasm for the principles of freedom and constitutional government. I believe that through voluntary and cooperative union on the part of all classes in America, labor and capital, all races and all creeds, that we can meet the challenge that has been flung at every democracy on the face of the earth; and, as one people under one God, regardless of our differences of race, religion, or class, we can unite in the defense of the greatest democracy the world has ever seen. . . .

Source: Congressional Record, 76th Congress, 3rd Session, 6295–6304.

Summary of Third Annual Report, January 3, 1941

As Representative Martin Dies (D-Tex.) and his fellow Un-American Activities Committee members continued their crusading work against groups and individuals who, they believed, would infest the country with alien and evil philosophies and who threatened American lives and values, the committee produced an extraordinary document in early 1941. In the summary of its third annual report, the committee's self-congratulatory posture reached an epic level. The committee boldly declared that it had foiled plots and stymied enemies from both the Left and the Right. In its language and claims of conquest, the report's stance seemed nearly messianic, as if its work had in itself saved America from a wretched future. Dies and his group even boasted about the huge files they had accumulated on Americans from all walks of life and on groups that posed grave threats. A decade later, Senator Joseph R. McCarthy (R-Wis.) would take up Dies's mantle with the same rallying cries.

SUMMARY OF THIRD ANNUAL REPORT JANUARY 3, 1941

One accomplishment will, by universal consent, be credited to the committee: We have educated and awakened the American people to a far better understanding of the sinister character and wide extent of subversive activities. We may justly claim to have been the decisive force in shaping the present attitudes of the American people toward the activities of the "fifth columns" which aim at our destruction. Our work has been a type of public education whose importance cannot be exaggerated. Not a single one of the countries of Europe which have been overrun by Stalin and Hitler had the protection of a committee like ours during the years that preceded its supreme crisis.

When we began our work, the German-American Bund had a hundred thousand followers who were pledged to its fuehrer, Fritz Kuhn. The very first exposure which our committee undertook in the summer of 1938 was that of the German-American Bund. The first volume of our hearings opens with a hundred pages of detailed testimony on the un-American and subversive character of the bund.

During the past week the committee published a translation of the official, confidential Manual of the Storm Troopers of the German-American Bund. That document proves conclusively that the German-American Bund is an organization which is highly militarized, and which requires absolute loyalty on the part of its members.

Today Fritz Kuhn is in Sing Sing prison and the German-American Bund has been thoroughly discredited. James Wheeler-Hill, former secretary-treasurer of the bund, is also in prison. Our exposures have provided thousands of innocent people with adequate protection against the false claims of the bund. Its drastically reduced membership and following may now be held to consist only of those whose loyalty is to Hitler.

When we began our work, the bund and a score of Nazi-minded American groups were laying plans for an impressive united front federation—a federation which would be able to launch a first-rate Nazi movement in the United States. By our exposure of these plans, we smashed that Nazi movement even before it was able to get under way.

In like manner, the committee had a large part in breaking up the People's Front. This was more difficult than the breaking up of the Nazi Front. The People's Front was composed of several million adherents and scores of organizations, which bore high-sounding names. The People's Front exercised real political influence. But one by one we took its component organizations and showed by incontrovertible evidence that each was a tool of Stalin's revolutionary conspiracy. It is true that Stalin helped greatly by his alliance with Hitler to bring the People's Front into general disrepute; but, even in that, Stalin was only confirming the committee's indictment of his movement. Long before the Nazi-Soviet pact, we had exposed the hypocrisy of the People's Front in its pretended espousal of democracy.

The largest unit of the People's Front movement was the American League for Peace and Democracy. When we began our work, the American League boasted of 7,000,000 adherents. We kept the spotlight of publicity turned upon this organization until it finally gave up in despair and went out of existence. It was killed by exposure. It would have been a great thing for the protection of our country if our disclosures about the league could have been made in 1933 instead of in 1938 and 1939. Our exposure of the league was not premature; it was long overdue.

Other organizations which formed units in the People's Front movement have been greatly crippled in their effectiveness as a result of our exposures. The American Youth Congress once enjoyed a very considerable prestige and an impressive following among the youth of our country. Today many of its distinguished former sponsors refuse to be found in its company. Best of all, it has been deserted by American youth. We kept the spotlight of publicity focused upon the American Youth Congress, and today it is clear to all that, in spite of a degree of participation in its activities by many fine young people, it was never at its core anything less than a tool of Moscow.

Another of the important People's Front units was the Workers Alliance. At one time in its history, the alliance had an actual dues-paying membership of 600,000. It had an influential lobby in Washington, and claimed to be the only Government-recognized bargaining agency for the unemployed. The alliance became so bold that it took physical possession of the State capitols in New Jersey and Wisconsin. Our committee kept the spotlight of publicity turned upon the Workers Alliance. Finally, its influence was destroyed when it became apparent to all that its control was in the hands of the agents of Moscow. Its non-Communist element withdrew under the leadership of David Lasser in June of this year, and today the Workers Alliance is a mere shadow of its former self—without influence anywhere and completely discredited.

In 1938 William Dudley Pelley was spreading a million pieces of literature over the country. The religious bigots organized in Pelley's Silver Shirts have now lost their leader. Immediately after Pelley was placed on the stand before our committee, he ordered the dissolution of his silver-shirted band. We had exposed it out of existence. One of Pelley's agents who tried to secure a job with our committee by falsely representing himself before us while under oath was tried and convicted for perjury.

Deatherage and his Knights of the White Camellia, who tried to make themselves the nucleus of an American Nazi group, under the name of the American Nationalist Confederation, have likewise gone the way of those who could not bear up under the full exposure of their true purposes. Our committee heard all that Deatherage could say for himself under questioning, and that was enough to put an end to his propaganda of religious bigotry.

The same thing happened to Gilbert and Campbell when we obtained their records under the authority of our congressional subpena, and exposed the falsity of their propaganda of religious hatred.

The country did not know that Earl Browder had traveled on false passports until our committee placed him on the stand and obtained the damaging admission from his own lips. After that exposure, Browder was successfully prosecuted and now awaits a prison term.

The case of Nicholas Dozenberg was fully aired before our committee. The whole country was apprised of the fact that this former leader of the American Communist Party had entered the espionage branch of Stalin's machine. Three months later, Dozenberg was apprehended by the Secret Service of the Treasury Department. He was then tried, convicted, and sentenced. The American public learned through our exposure of Dozenberg's case that members of the Communist Party are subject to draft into Stalin's espionage ring.

For 2 years our committee piled proof upon proof that the Communist Party was nothing more or less than a foreign conspiracy masked as a political party. In our annual report at the beginning of the present year, we showed in detail how the Communist Party was tied to Moscow. One of our members introduced legislation which will require such foreign-controlled agencies as the Communist Party and the German-American Bund to make a public record of all pertinent facts concerning themselves. His bill was passed unanimously by both Houses of Congress. In its effort to evade the provisions of the Voorhis Act, the Communist Party has now made the gesture of severing its connections with Moscow. Our relentless exposure of the party has it on the run.

Recently, our committee gave to the country the clearest picture it has yet received of the technique and aims of Hitler's subsidized propaganda in the United States. Because the German diplomatic and consular agents were involved in this un-American propaganda campaign, our committee took every possible precaution not to embarrass the State Department in its conduct of our foreign relations.

During the recent election campaign our committee obtained the names of more than 200,000 persons who had signed the election petitions of the Communist Party. We made an extensive investigation and exposed the fact that these election petitions were tainted with wholesale fraud, perjury, and misrepresentation. On the basis of our exposures, local law-enforcement authorities have obtained more than a hundred indictments and from 50 to 60 convictions. Without a single exception throughout the United States, we have found State and local authorities prepared to cooperate to the fullest with our committee.

In addition to all these things, the committee has built up very complete files on "fifth column" organizations. These files contain the names and records of several hundred thousand individuals. They contain many thousands of pieces of literature and practically all of the publications which "fifth column" organizations have put out during the past 20 years. They also contain thousands of signed letters which have passed between "fifth columnists." These files cannot be duplicated anywhere else in the world today.

Finally, the committee has shown that there is a way to combat the "fifth column" without creating a Gestapo. It is the way of exposure—a way which conforms to the letter and the spirit of a democracy, and is at the same time more effective than a Gestapo. In both Russia and Germany, half the population spies on the other half. That is the logical end of a system which depends exclusively on methods of counterespionage.

Source: U.S. House of Representatives, 77th Congress, 1st Session, House Report No. 1, Investigation of Un-American Propaganda Activities in the United States, 1–25.

Bibliography

Bentley, Eric, and Frank Rich. *Thirty Years of Treason: Excerpts from Hearings Before the House Committee on Un-American Activities, 1938–1968.* New York: Nation Books, 2002.

Buckley, William. *The Committee and Its Critics: A Calm Review of the House Committee on Un-American Activities.* New York: Putnam Books, 1962.

Dies, Martin. *The Trojan Horse in America.* Reprint. Manchester, N.H.: Ayer, 1977.

Gladchuk, John Joseph. *Hollywood and Anticommunism: HUAC and the Evolution of the Red Menace, 1935–1950.* New York: Routledge, 2006.

Goldstein, Robert. *American Blacklist: The Attorney General's List of Subversive Organizations.* Lawrence: University Press of Kansas, 2008.

Goodman, Walter. *The Committee: The Extraordinary Career of the House Committee on Un-American Activities.* New York: Farrar, Straus & Giroux, 1968.

Heineman, Kenneth. "Media Bias in Coverage of the Dies Committee on Un-American Activities, 1938–1940." *Historian* (Autumn 1992).

Kutulas, Judy. *The American Civil Liberties Union and the Making of Modern Liberalism, 1930–1960.* Chapel Hill: University of North Carolina Press, 2006.

Latham, Earl. *The Communist Controversy in Washington.* Cambridge, Mass.: Harvard University Press, 1966.

Leuchtenburg, William. *Franklin D. Roosevelt and the New Deal.* New York: Harper Perennial, 1963.

Mangione, Jerry. *The Dream and the Deal: The Federal Writers Project.* Reprint. New York: Avon Books, 1972.

Ogden, August. *The Dies Committee: A Study of the Special House Committee for the Investigation of Un-American Activities, 1938–1944.* Washington, D.C.: Catholic University of America Press, 1945.

O'Reilly, Kenneth. *Hoover and the Unamericans: The FBI, HUAC, and the Red Menace.* Philadelphia: Temple University Press, 1983.

Seldes, George. *Witch Hunt: The Technique and Profits of Redbaiting.* New York: Modern Age Books, 1940.

The Truman Committee on War Mobilization, 1941–44

By Theodore Wilson

The Senate Special Committee to Investigate the National Defense Program (popularly known as the Truman committee) is often characterized as the most successful congressional investigative effort in United States history. Whether or not this is correct, this committee certainly played an important role in the ebb and flow of executive-legislative relations that shaped the mobilization effort of the United States during World War II. The Truman committee, created to satisfy a junior senator's pique regarding the allocation of defense contracts, evolved into the dominant congressional body scrutinizing the defense program. As such, it became enmeshed in numerous critical questions—constitutional, political, economic, and ethical—regarding the organization and administration of America's wartime mobilization efforts. Although the committee and its chairman did not resolve certain of these questions (and, indeed, refused to confront certain of them), its record of responsible, restrained investigation established an admirable standard.

In times of national crisis, especially in time of war, the constitutional demarcations of authority between the legislative and executive branches of government have wavered and shifted dramatically. During the nineteenth century and into the twentieth, Congress and the president struggled periodically for supreme control over the process of war-making and its attendant responsibilities. This struggle was a result of the ambiguous language of the Constitution regarding executive and legislative responsibilities for declaring, prosecuting, and concluding wars. Each branch possessed strong claims to primacy. Certainly, the Constitution's grant of authority was great: "The executive power shall be vested in a President of the United States of America"; he shall recommend "such measures to Congress as he shall judge necessary and expedient"; and, most important, "the President shall be Commander-in-Chief of the Army and Navy." On the other hand, the Constitution empowered Congress "to provide for the common defense and general welfare of the United States, . . . to declare war, . . . to raise and support armies," and "to provide and maintain a navy." Further, Congress was given authority "to make all laws which shall be necessary and proper for carrying into execution the foregoing powers, and all other powers vested by this Constitution in the government of the United States, or in any department or officer thereof." These phrases, ambiguous in content, would appear to make possible a titanic struggle for domination should the two branches find themselves disagreeing about the necessity for military action or the manner of conducting a war.

On the basis of explicit constitutional authority, Congress would appear to have the upper hand in any such conflict. It possessed power over both the purse and the sword, it guarded the sole authority to declare war, and the executive's war power was but rhetoric unless Congress bestowed its approval via appropriations and other legislation. That the president, by virtue of his role as supreme military commander and other powers that have accrued to him, has come to dominate almost all phases of the nation's activities in time of war was the result of executive aggrandizement and, equally, of legislative ineptitude and abdication. It is, nevertheless, the central fact in any analysis of executive-legislative relations during wartime.

Before the Civil War, Congress held the upper hand in both constitutional theory and practice. The "Commander in Chief" clause, upon which expansion of executive authority was later based, was viewed only as stating the obvious fact that the president was "top

OVERVIEW

Background

In 1940, the Roosevelt administration and Congress, preparing for possible U.S. involvement in World War II, appropriated large funds for defense contracts. By early 1941, however, stories surfaced regarding contractor mismanagement. Alarmed by the information, Senator Harry S. Truman (D-Mo.) began a 10,000-mile tour of military bases and other defense installations to gather information. Many of the stories and rumors, he discovered, turned out to have substance. He found inefficient work in some of the plants; he also found that a handful of companies in the eastern United States were receiving a huge share of the contracts. Convinced that corruption and waste in defense contracting must be examined more closely, Truman pushed for a congressional investigation.

Congress Investigates

On March 1, 1941, the Senate, by unanimous consent, created the special Senate Committee to Investigate the National Defense Program. Chaired by Truman, it became known as the Truman committee. Although senior military officials in the Roosevelt administration opposed the creation of the Truman committee, warning that it could interfere with executive authority and could be used by Roosevelt's political opponents as a weapon, Truman was determined that its work would benefit the nation's military structure.

Impact

During the three years of Truman's chairmanship, the committee earned nearly universal respect for its determined efforts to stop corruption and cost overruns. Through hundreds of hearings and extensive travel to contractors across the country, committee members not only saved the nation's taxpayers billions of dollars but also encouraged the government to hold manufacturers of defense equipment and munitions to higher standards. The Truman committee stands as one of the most successful and sustained efforts to provide much-needed oversight in government military contracting during wartime. In addition to saving money and exposing corrupt practices, the work of the committee saved countless American servicemen and women whose lives were at risk due to faulty aircraft engines, poorly manufactured munitions, and other equipment and materiel. The committee also raised Truman's stature and influence, leading to his selection as the Democratic Party's vice-presidential candidate in 1944.

general and top admiral" of the armed forces. As Chief Justice Roger Taney observed of the president in 1850:

> His duty and his power are purely military. As commander-in-chief, he is authorized to direct the movements of the naval and military forces placed by law at his command, and to employ them in the manner he may deem most effectual to harass and conquer and subdue the enemy. . . . But his conquests do not enlarge the boundaries of this Union, nor extend the operation of our institutions and laws beyond the limits before assigned to them by the legislative power.

President Abraham Lincoln interpreted his role as commander in chief as authorizing executive intervention in areas previously reserved to Congress. On his own, during the period after Fort Sumter, Lincoln created an enormous army, paid it out of Treasury funds without authorization or appropriation, proclaimed a blockade of Southern ports, suspended the writ of habeas corpus, and undertook various other actions without statutory authorization. He justified these measures by claiming that his position as commander in chief, combined with the president's duty "to take care that the laws be faithfully executed," produced a war power sufficient to carry out all necessary steps. Taken together, these acts amounted to an assertion that the president has, as Edward S. Corwin wrote, "for the first time in our history, an initiative of indefinite scope and legislative in effect in meeting the domestic aspects of a war emergency." President Lincoln "had laid hold upon vast emergency powers not describable in the usual terms of military command, the results of which, nevertheless, Congress had accepted, willy-nilly; and in these regards

CHRONOLOGY

1941

- *February 10:* Senator Harry S. Truman proposes that the Senate create a special committee to investigate defense contracts.
- *March 1:* By unanimous consent, the Senate creates the special Senate Committee to Investigate the National Defense Program.
- *March 8:* Truman is appointed chairman of the committee, which soon becomes known as the Truman committee.
- *April 15:* Truman committee opens hearings by calling Secretary of War Henry Stimson as its first witness.
- *August:* Because of its early successes in revealing problems and challenges in defense contracting, the Truman committee is extended and its budget increased.
- *December 7:* Japan attacks the U.S. Naval Base in Pearl Harbor, Hawaii, leading the United States to declare war the following day and enter World War II.

1942

- *January 13:* Based on the recommendations of the Truman committee, President Franklin D. Roosevelt replaces the Office of Production Management with the more powerful War Production Board.
- *January 15:* The Truman committee presents its first annual report to the Senate, five weeks after the Japanese attack on Pearl Harbor.
- *February 8:* Published reports estimate that savings attributable to the work of the Truman committee since its inception were approximately $11 billion.
- *May:* With pressure from the Truman committee to centralize war production authority, Roosevelt creates the Office of War Mobilization and appoints James Byrnes as its director.
- *July:* The Truman committee's investigation of aerospace giant Curtiss-Wright finds that the company had delivered defective motors to the Army Air Corps and had covered up the wrongdoing. The committee's work eventually leads to the prosecution of one U.S. general and executives of Curtiss-Wright.

1944

- *August 3:* After his selection to run for vice president with Roosevelt in the 1944 election, Truman resigns chairmanship of the committee.

1944–1948

- Committee continues its defense watchdog role until its abolition in April 1948.

the Civil War was the prototype of both the First World War and the Second." But Congress did not accede to the president's actions without a struggle.

Indeed, the Joint Committee on the Conduct of the War, an intensely partisan investigatory committee that harassed the president throughout the war, did assert a powerful check on presidential authority. The committee was established on December 9, 1861, following the Union defeats at Bull Run and Balls Bluff, to "inquire into the conduct of the present war." Dominated by Radical Republicans and chaired by a leading radical senator, Benjamin F. Wade, the Joint Committee claimed the right not only to investigate executive acts and advise the president, but attempted to take over direction of the war effort. Hearings were convened in late December 1861 and continued until early 1865. At these sessions, the committee discussed past and future battles and strategic plans, disloyal employees, and war supplies and contracts. In this effort the committee was partly successful, for the Confederate leader Robert E. Lee commented that "the Committee was worth about two divisions of Confederate troops." The committee repeatedly questioned the strategy and tactics of the Union, establishing a standard for meddling to which later congressional investigations might aspire, though the more responsible ones, such as the Truman committee, consciously rejected the presumptions and behavior of the Joint Committee on the Conduct of the War. Senator Truman and his colleagues would have agreed with one later writer who shuddered at the War Committee's "undocumented insinuations, loud publicity against the reputations of men who were not permitted to defend themselves, its suppression of testimony which did not support the official thesis about the war, its star chamber atmosphere, and its general disregard of the rules of fair procedure." The Joint Committee played a powerful role in the conduct of the Civil War, but its power derived from political, not constitutional, sources. Thus, its influence was of brief duration and, by any estimate, the presidency emerged the victor.

The experience of World War I further strengthened the hand of the president, though Congress also acquired enormous, hitherto unimagined, authority over personal and property rights. Edward S. Corwin has written: "First and foremost of the constitutional problems that confronted the President and Congress in 1917 . . . was that of adapting legislative power to the needs of 'total war.' Congress was suddenly called on to extend its power to a vast new range of complex subject matter that had hitherto existed outside the national orbit, and at the same time to give its legislation a form capable of keeping it easily responsive to the ever changing requirements of a fluid war situation. The problem was solved by the delegation to the president of the broadest discretion." The President received and, in some cases, merely took authority over a wide range of activities. While Congress might have originally bestowed these powers, the active role of the president in implementing them, and the pattern of delegating powers to persons and agencies acting solely in his name, tended to exclude Congress from any meaningful part in directing the war effort.

To meet the challenge of rearmament during World War II, as early as 1938 President Franklin D. Roosevelt began to establish executive offices responsible for the nation's defense. Shortly after the bombing of Pearl Harbor, a White House organization chart listed forty-two executive agencies, of which thirty-five had been created by executive order rather than by statute. The agencies that were given congressional authorization, such as Selective Service and the Office of Lend-Lease Administration, were staffed and operated with little regard for the sensibilities of Congress.

Despite the broad latitude permitted the president, the nation's defense mobilization moved forward slowly because of inadequate planning. The War and Navy Departments assumed that, prior to a declaration of war, "it was unlikely that an appreciable mobilization, either in manpower or materials, could be expected." There was no provision for gradual mobilization, and the Industrial Mobilization Plan, a sketchy document drafted without consultation of civilian leaders, would go into effect only when war was imminent. Because of congressional indifference, as late as March 1940, the House Appropriations Committee reduced a War Department request for replacement airplanes from 496 to 57, denied funds for an air base in Alaska, and discouraged any rapid expansion of the armed services.

The German blitzkrieg in the Low Countries and France during May 1940 reversed congressional opposition to rearmament and opened the floodgates for extensive defense expenditures. On May 16, 1940, the president requested an urgent appropriation of $1.2 billion for the armed services; two weeks later he requested another billion. Congress quickly authorized these sums. On July 10 Roosevelt proposed further authorizations and appropriations totaling almost $5 billion, which were approved in less than two months. Altogether, between June 1 and December 1, almost $10.5 billion in defense-related contracts was awarded.

At this point, however, the lack of careful preparation and the peculiar administrative philosophy of President Roosevelt became critically important. The president could request billions for defense and Congress could appropriate funds, but production of weapons and munitions remained largely beyond their control in a country that was officially at peace. Factory production capacity, still at depression levels, could be quickly increased, but the nation's resources were not unlimited, and priorities had to be established.

The Roosevelt administration's penchant for overlapping organization, the growth of competing bureaucracies, and the president's inability to delegate authority realistically produced conflicts between existing defense agencies and the president's newly created organizations. No organization had complete control of any defense program; instead, each agency had partial control of many operations. On May 26 FDR created a National Defense Advisory Commission (NDAC), with members drawn from business, labor, and government. Though the NDAC acquired a staff and assorted responsibilities (including approval of defense contracts), it never overcame its administrative deficiencies. Individual members acquired considerable power (in 1940 Donald Nelson became administrator of priorities; William S. Knudsen, industrial production; and Sidney Hillman, manpower), but coordination proved impossible. In December 1940 FDR responded to the clamor for unified direction of the defense program by establishing another new agency, the Office of Production Management (OPM). Although OPM had only two chairmen, Knudsen and Hillman, their ability to coordinate the war effort was impaired, as they were not given the authority to establish priorities, place orders, or allocate resources.

Despite the administration's failure to achieve internal cohesion, once the United States entered the war, the president and his subordinates accepted responsibility for the conduct of the war. Indeed, President Roosevelt, in an address to Congress on September 7, 1942, asserted his right to ignore an act of Congress if necessary to win the war.

By 1941, Congress had accepted (and by its acceptance given tacit approval to) the executive's claim to major authority in conducting the war effort. Given the political situation of 1941–1945—an inordinately skilled politician occupying the White House and his party dominating both houses of Congress—it appeared that the wartime role of Congress would be passive. Executive predominance was based on claims of superior knowledge; since this knowledge was derived from the executive's accessibility to vital elements of information and organization that were denied to Congress, Congress could only acquiesce, thus excluding itself from meaningful participation in directing the war effort.

Executive control of America's participation in World War II was not questioned until March 1941, when the Senate Special Committee to Investigate the National Defense Program was created. Indeed, the investigatory power of Congress, hallowed by a great tradition of legislative practice in English and American history, appeared to offer Congress an effective means of challenging claims of executive preeminence: "We are called the Grand Inquest of the Nation, and as such it is our duty to inquire into every step of publick management, either Abroad or at Home, in order to see that nothing has been done amiss," William Pitt had informed the House of Commons in 1742. No one seriously questioned the right of Congress to conduct investigations for, as Donald H. Riddle has noted, "the purpose of informing itself, controlling the executive branch, or informing the public."

Senator Truman and his colleagues could not match the president's domination of the mechanisms of government, especially his control over information vital to a public challenge to his authority. Also, Truman did not intend to duplicate the shoddy work of the Civil War investigation. Therefore, much of the potential for legislative-executive conflict, embodied in the Truman committee's charge to make a full and complete study of the national defense program, was siphoned off at the outset.

The creation of the Senate Special Committee to Investigate the National Defense Program is an undramatic story, perhaps befitting the sober mien of its chief sponsor and first chairman. In early 1941, Harry S. Truman, newly reelected junior senator from Missouri, was returning to work after an exhausting campaign. As a strong supporter of the Roosevelt administration, Senator Truman was naturally interested in the measures then under way to achieve the president's "arsenal of democracy" program. Truman, a member of the Military Affairs Committee and the Military Subcommittee of the Appropriations Committee, possessed a lifelong interest in military issues. He had visited a number of army installations and had become alarmed about the waste, favoritism, and lack of direction that he found in the defense program. Letters from constituents made him aware of the enormous economic benefits to be gained from the assignment of defense plants and military installations, and he was determined that Missouri communities should receive a fair share of this lucrative defense business.

Harry S. Truman, Democratic senator from Missouri. In 1941 newly reelected senator Truman announced his intention to file a resolution to establish a committee to investigate the national defense system, its procedures for awarding contracts, and the progress being made by those contractors involved in war mobilization. The Special Committee on War Mobilization, commonly known as the Truman committee, would be one the most successful congressional probes in the history of congressional investigations. (Library of Congress)

On August 15, 1940, Senator Truman wrote confidently to his friend, Lou E. Holland, president of the

Mid-Central War Resources Board in Kansas City, that Missouri possessed a great opportunity to obtain defense plants and defense-related contracts. "I have been interviewing the people here who are at the source of the fountain, and I believe that with proper organization Missouri can get its proper place in the set-up," Truman told his friend. He went on to describe the mobilization program, as army and administration officials had explained it to him: The key was decentralization. "The program, as outlined, contemplates the location of Government plants and key industries in five different sections between the Appalachians and the Rocky Mountains. . . . We are in Area C, which consists of southern Indiana and southern Illinois, Missouri and Kansas. The plan is to make each area a complete unit, with every sort of set-up needed in the National Defense program. Powder plants, loading plants, small arms factories, and so forth will be in each one of these areas. They are urging factories to decentralize all over the whole area. . . . This is our opportunity, if we ever had it." Within a few months, however, Truman recognized the favoritism given to Eastern states. "I think they are working with a little private clique of their own and not giving the local people a chance to do the work," he charged the War Department. Although Missouri had received 55 percent of all defense expenditures between the Mississippi River and Rocky Mountains by mid-1941, Truman decided that he had to defend the interests of the Midwest and the little businessman.

On February 10, 1941, after weeks of preparation, Truman rose in the Senate to address the problems he had identified in the defense program. This speech, a rare event for Truman, was given before a small but increasingly interested audience of colleagues, journalists, and professional gallery-sitters. Truman had previously stated that his purpose was "heading off scandals before they started." This speech dealt mainly with possibilities for corruption and the geographical and economic injustices that the present system of letting war contracts perpetrated. "There seems to be a policy in the national-defense set-up to concentrate all contracts and nearly all manufacturing that has to do with the national defense in a very small area," he observed indignantly. "I am reliably informed that from 70 to 90 percent of the contracts let have been concentrated in an area smaller than England." Such concentration was militarily unwise and also unfair to those regions that were being denied an opportunity to participate in the defense program, a result of the federal bureaucracy's preference for dealing with large corporations located in a few heavily industrialized areas. "The little manufacturer, the little contractor, and the little machine shop have been left entirely out in the cold. The policy seems to be to make the big man bigger and to put the little man completely out of business."

Personal favoritism, the sort of palm-greasing, "do a favor for a friend" attitude that had produced so much waste and graft during World War I, was widespread. For example, a Detroit company had won an ammunition plant contract from equally qualified construction firms in Missouri. Was it accidental that a partner in the Detroit firm was a good friend of a member of the War Department's Construction Advisory Board? Similarly, nonlocal companies had obtained contracts for the St. Louis Ordnance Plant and Ft. Leonard Wood and, in the latter case, the firm awarded this huge contract possessed no construction experience. This was simply not fair, Truman concluded, especially since the War Department was blatantly ignoring suggestions from members of Congress. "It is considered a sin for a United States Senator from a State to make a recommendation for contractors, although he may be more familiar with the efficiency and ability of our contractors than is anybody in the War Department," he said.

One means of correcting this deplorable situation, Senator Truman proposed, was to establish a committee to investigate the manner in which defense contracts were being awarded. Since tax money was being spent, the Senate should make use of "every safeguard possible to prevent their being misused and mishandled." Such a committee, empowered to ascertain the facts, would perform an important service in maintaining public confidence in the defense program. To that end, Truman announced his intention to introduce a resolution calling for such an investigation: "I am merely stating what I believe to be conditions that deserve investigation. If nothing is wrong, there will be no harm done. If something is wrong, it ought to be brought to light." He introduced Senate Resolution 71 three days later and had it referred immediately to the Committee on Military Affairs. On February 22, the committee unanimously reported the resolution to the Senate. At this point, however, Truman's proposal was frozen, being referred back to another committee, the Senate Committee to Audit and Control the Contingent Expenses of the Senate, chaired by James F. Byrnes, a confidant of President Roosevelt.

The administration naturally was concerned about any proposal for a congressional investigation of the defense program. Congressional snooping into such sensitive matters as contracts and the progress of the mobilization effort might produce unwelcome publicity, thus upsetting the president's carefully orchestrated campaign to swing public opinion in favor of America's support of Great Britain. A call for such a committee in May 1940 by Republican senator Arthur H. Vandenberg had been immediately scotched, but by early 1941 pressures for a congressional inquiry were mounting. In January two such resolutions had been introduced in the House of Representatives. One, by Representative Eugene Cox, a conservative Georgian hostile to organized labor, called for a joint committee "to investigate and keep itself currently informed on all activities of the Federal Government in connection with the national defense." As well, a young Republican congressman, Henry Cabot Lodge Jr., had introduced a resolution that proposed a congressional committee with authority "to formulate and develop a consistent and complete defense policy for the United States." Lodge's proposal "amounted to a committee to conduct the war." No one in the administration wanted either of these probes, and the only other alternative appeared to be the comparatively mild investigation proposed by Senator Truman. When the Cox resolution was discussed at a White House meeting, Byrnes informed the president: "I can fix that by putting the investigation into friendly hands." Truman later implied that he had given such assurances to the White House: "I couldn't get Jimmy Byrnes to act. Everybody thought I wanted to set up a headline business like the Dies Committee. . . . After much haggling and delay he recommended that I be given the magnificent sum of $15,000 with which I started the activities of that committee." Byrnes permitted Senate Resolution 71 to be reported on March 1, 1941. It was unanimously adopted the same day, with two alterations: an increase in the size of the committee from five to seven members, and, as noted above, a reduction of Truman's funds from $25,000 to $15,000.

Senator Truman, sponsor of the resolution, became committee chairman. His proposal had been authorized by the Senate (and tacitly, at least, by the administration); he had $15,000 to spend and, if he and the committee proved themselves worthy of the Senate's trust, the prospect of additional funds and a renewed authorization at some point in the near future.

Although initially it proved difficult to persuade senatorial colleagues to serve on the committee, within a week all seven had been selected. On March 8, the committee's membership was officially appointed: Truman as chairman; Joseph H. Ball (R.-Minn.); Owen Brewster (R.-Me.); Tom Connally (D.-Tex.); Carl Hayden (D.-Ariz.); James M. Mead (D.-N.Y.); and Monrad C. Wallgren (D.-Wash.). Carl A. Hatch (D.-N.M.) soon replaced Hayden, who resigned on April 15, 1941, and perhaps should be considered an original member. The committee was comprised of five Democrats and two Republicans, probably a reflection of the administration's anxiety that it not spawn a political vendetta. The membership reflected impressive geographical balance and considerable diversity of background and political outlook. Notably, however, all save Connally, Hatch, and Truman were serving their first terms in the Senate.

At the time he became chairman of the Special Committee, Harry S. Truman was fifty-seven years old. The junior senator from Missouri had been in the Senate since 1934, but was virtually unknown outside his home state and the Senate chambers. A quiet, hardworking, physically unprepossessing man, Truman had served a long political apprenticeship. When he first came to Washington, he was identified with the political organization of Kansas City boss Thomas Pendergast; he gradually made a name for himself by supporting the New Deal. In 1941, Truman was just coming into his own, having won a tight battle for reelection with almost no assistance from the administration. Intelligent, pragmatic, and deeply conscious of the historical dimension of the committee's work, Truman was determined to make a success of this assignment, the most important he had been given during his tenure. Nevertheless, no one would have predicted that he would demonstrate great ability, and that his dedicated and crusty leadership of the investigation would make his name a household word within a few months.

Ball had been appointed to the Senate in 1940 and won reelection in 1942. An ardent internationalist, Ball strongly supported FDR's program in foreign affairs and accepted the administration's conduct of the war. The committee's senior Republican, Brewster, had also entered the Senate in 1940. Connally was the ranking Democrat on the committee. Connally had enjoyed a long career in Texas and national politics and by 1941 was one of the most powerful men in the Senate. Hatch did not attend committee sessions regularly, but he had served in the Senate since 1933 and could be counted an administration loyalist. One of the most active members of the committee, Mead had served nineteen years in the House, was then appointed to the Senate in 1938, and was elected in his own right in 1940. Mead was an administration regular and perhaps the most liberal among the committee members. Elected in 1940, Wallgren was a little-known Democrat interested primarily in problems affecting his home state, such as lumber, light metals, and aircraft.

The membership of the committee was remarkably stable, and these seven members served throughout Truman's chairmanship. The group was enlarged to ten members in November 1941, when Styles Bridges (R.-N.H.), Harley M. Kilgore (D.-W.Va.), and Clyde

L. Herring (D.-Iowa) were appointed. Bridges resigned from the committee, pleading other responsibilities, in March 1942. He was replaced by Harold H. Burton (R.-Ohio), who took an active part in the committee's inquiries until he was appointed to the Supreme Court in 1945. Because Herring was defeated in the 1942 elections, Homer Ferguson (R.-Mich.) was appointed and became an aggressive critic of the military, particularly interested in the administration of the defense program.

Senator Truman once said of his colleagues on the committee: "I have . . . been extremely lucky in having associates who are sound thinkers and honest men." From small towns and middle class in background, the committee members appeared to share Truman's pragmatic approach to their job, viewing it as a vehicle for exposure and correction of abuses (especially where big business was concerned) rather than a platform for ideological disputation. Although every member had at least six committee assignments (Truman served on seven committees), the seven freshman senators were less heavily burdened than their elders and, undoubtedly, considered the Truman committee a superb opportunity to gain quick recognition. As a whole, the committee established a standard of participation and knowledgeability considerably above the norm.

The committee's second urgent chore was to obtain a qualified staff. On the recommendation of Attorney General Robert Jackson, Truman appointed Hugh Fulton, a young lawyer who had served as a U.S. attorney, as chief counsel. After a second appropriation in August 1941, Truman and Fulton then recruited the remainder of the staff, consisting of an associate counsel, an assistant counsel, a chief investigator, twelve to eighteen investigators, and various clerical persons. Matthew Connelly, who later became President Truman's appointment secretary, was the first chief investigator, and he recommended many of the other investigators, mostly young lawyers or accountants. For a time the committee, following a tradition of some years, co-opted employees from various executive agencies (such as the Justice Department, Labor, the U.S. Housing Authority, the Federal Power Commission, and the Office of Price Administration [OPA]) as investigators.

In all, between 1941 and 1948, the Truman Committee held 432 public hearings at which 1,798 witnesses appeared (giving 27,568 pages of testimony), and another 300 executive sessions that produced 25,000 additional pages of transcript. Fifty-one reports totaling 1,946 pages were published; and, as a result of the committee's careful attention to relations with the media, thousands of press releases were issued. All this was the end product of uncounted hours of research, hundreds of field trips, and thousands of interviews. Throughout its existence, the committee was almost never embarrassed by sloppy or inaccurate staff work. Indeed, the Truman committee's thoroughness soon became so highly regarded that other congressional committees which became involved with defense issues often borrowed the committee's documentation, tacking on their own conclusions.

Together, Truman and Fulton decided upon guidelines for staff investigations and committee sessions. The Truman committee asked only for the right to subpoena witnesses, as they normally dealt with readily available information and cooperative witnesses. The committee received thousands of letters during its existence, many describing alleged graft or waste; but it usually made independent decisions to launch investigations. Hearings were but a small part of the committee's activities; Truman and the staff often arranged numerous private meetings before deciding whether to schedule a hearing on a particular topic.

These public hearings (and the executive sessions that were convened if issues directly affecting the national security or the individuals' reputations were involved) were conducted by explicit though unwritten rules. Although Truman was not always able to control the conduct of his colleagues, he insisted upon a modicum of fairness and objectivity. The committee decided not to act as a court of law, and witnesses were accorded an impressive range of legal protections. They were permitted to submit prepared statements, to be attended by counsel, to place in the record documents supporting their views, and to review the pertinent hearing transcripts. The committee stated that it recognized, without prejudice, recourse to the Fifth Amendment, though a careful search of the record suggests that no witness ever invoked this provision. In sum, the Truman committee followed a code of procedures that was rational, fair, and efficient; perhaps as objective as such an agency—which, after all, was created and conducted by politicians for political purposes—can be.

Overlapping jurisdiction greatly worried Truman, for the committee faced potential friction from standing committees and other investigatory groups. Fortunately, the Truman committee encountered little hostility from the Senate establishment. Neither Naval Affairs nor Military Affairs evinced any interest in procurement and contract procedures; the Small Business Committee did have certain interests in common, but Truman and its chairman worked out a compromise. Truman kept his colleagues informed of the committee's work; senators were welcome at committee hearings and were invited to take part in examination of witnesses. Further, the members of the Truman committee, via service on other committees, strengthened the committee's position.

Two House committees, Naval Affairs and Military Affairs, occasionally grumbled about the Truman committee's intrusions into their spheres. Their dissatisfaction may have been caused by the favorable headlines earned by Truman and his colleagues. An army officer stated as much in September 1941: "Confidentially I sat in on a meeting . . . where the House Naval Affairs Committee were bemoaning the fact that the Truman Committee has grabbed all the glory, has received the maximum of publicity, and has dampened the efforts of the other investigatory committees." Fortunately, relations with the House Select Committee to Investigate Defense Migration, which under the leadership of Representative John Tolan looked at a variety of defense-related problems, were quite friendly. The Tolan committee might be termed the House equivalent of Truman's inquiry, though it never received the public recognition accorded its Senate counterpart.

The resolution that created the committee bestowed it with a remarkably broad grant of authority. Empowered to investigate all phases of the national defense program, the committee was specifically requested to study the following:

1. the types and terms of contracts awarded by the government;
2. methods by which such contracts are awarded and grantees selected;
3. use of small business facilities, through subcontracts or otherwise;
4. geographic distribution of contracts and location of plants and facilities;
5. effects of the defense program on labor and the migration of labor;
6. the performance of contracts and the accountings required of contractors;
7. benefits accruing to contractors;
8. practices of management or labor, and prices, fees, and charges that interfere with the defense program or unduly increase its cost;
9. such other matters as the committee deems appropriate.

Again and again, Truman and other members stated that their aim was to serve as a watchdog, a "benevolent policeman," to dig out the facts and present them to the American people. Originally, the Truman committee was concerned with possible corruption and waste stemming from the rapid and enormous expansion of the defense

Senator Harry Truman, center, at a meeting of the Senate Committee to Investigate the National Defense Program, April 26, 1943. From left to right are Senator James Meade, Charles Patrick Clark, Senator Truman, Senator Ralph Brewster, Senator Joseph Ball, and Senator Gerald Nye. (©CORBIS)

production program. "I have had considerable experience in letting public contracts," Truman observed in an early speech, "and I have never yet found a contractor who, if not watched, would not leave the Government holding the bag. We are not doing him a favor if we do not watch him." The deplorable experiences of the aftermath of World War I, during which numerous investigations uncovered widespread corruption and waste in the government's war production activities, was a powerful argument for careful scrutiny while contracts were being awarded and weapons manufactured.

The Truman committee fulfilled this assignment with admirable efficiency and fairness. During the most active period of its existence—from summer 1941 to spring 1944—the committee investigated an incredible list of problems alleged to be retarding progress of the nation's domestic war effort and hundreds of cases of supposed graft and corruption. They maintained close scrutiny over the government's policies with regard to the award of contracts, labor-management relations, the geographical distribution of war plants, and the treatment of small business (Truman's pet concern). The committee held hearings and issued reports on such diverse problems as the aluminum shortage, camp and cantonment construction, light metals, aircraft, rubber, the conversion program of the War Production Board, Senator Albert B. Chandler's swimming pool, manpower, gasoline rationing, barges, farm machinery and equipment, renegotiation of war contracts, fake inspections of steel plate by Carnegie-Illinois Steel Corporation, shipbuilding and shipping, the comparative merits of rayon and cotton tire cord, magnesium, Ream General Hospital, conditions at Curtiss-Wright Corporation, and transactions between Senator Theodore G. Bilbo and various contractors. Its watchfulness certainly resulted in diminished graft, since potential wheeler-dealers were deterred from engaging in shady activities. One estimate of the actual monetary savings for which the Truman committee was responsible is $15 billion. More important, perhaps, thousands of lives were saved as a result of the committee's success in ferreting out cases of production of defective weapons, aircraft, and other war supplies.

Nevertheless, the work of the Truman committee, judged in historical perspective, was to prove not entirely successful. Increasingly, as mobilization picked up speed, it became apparent that the greatest threat to full production and to efficient and equitable use of the nation's resources was the chaotic administrative situation in Washington. The Truman committee, as with previous investigatory committees in similar circumstances, found itself in a quandary regarding the issue of governmental waste and inefficiency. Should the committee have wished to do so, it might have found a justification in its grant of authority (especially its charge to investigate "such other matters as the Committee deems appropriate") to undertake a full inquiry into the Roosevelt administration's conduct of the war. Such a step was repugnant to Truman, the other Democrats on the committee, and even to their Republican colleagues, for they sincerely desired to "help the President to win the war." They feared that public exposure of the full dimensions of bureaucratic confusion and conflict in Washington—and of its effects on the defense effort—would weaken, and perhaps destroy, public confidence in the administration. That, in turn, might have caused the United States to lose the war.

Senator Truman clearly was aware of this conflict and of the dangers it posed. During a Senate debate in August 1941, he was pressed by Senator Vandenberg to admit that the president was culpable.

VANDENBERG: In other words, the Senator is now saying that the chief bottleneck which the defense program confronts is the lack of adequate organization and coordination in the administration of defense. . . . Who is responsible for that situation?

TRUMAN: There is only one place where the responsibility can be put.

VANDENBERG: Where is that—the White House?

TRUMAN: Yes, sir.

VANDENBERG: I thank the Senator.

To face this problem squarely, however, would be to open a Pandora's box. Truman and his Democratic colleagues certainly wished to avoid doing political injury to the president. At the same time, no one on the committee wanted to risk charges of whitewash because they ducked legitimate questions. Even if the committee had raised the issue of presidential responsibility directly, Truman must have doubted whether his committee—or even Congress as a whole—possessed sufficient clout to force the sort of changes that were necessary. Above all, Truman wished to avoid the kind of disgusting spectacle evoked by the internecine warfare carried on between 1861 and 1865 by the Joint Committee on the Conduct of the War. The Truman committee stated repeatedly that it would not concern itself with matters of strategy and tactics. Whenever Truman was informed that a committee inquiry threatened to enter this realm (as defined by the executive branch), he abandoned that line of investigation. This, of course, proved a source of continuing frustration, for strategy and even tactics were even more intimately connected with matters of production and the allocation of resources during World War II than they had been during the Civil War.

At almost every turn, the Truman committee, pursuing legitimate and seemingly innocuous inquiries, found itself in potential conflict with executive prerogatives and policies. It may be that the value of tracing the committee's route is not so much in measuring their boldness under fire, not even in discovering how far they traveled; rather, any benefit may derive from recognition of the dangers they faced and being better prepared to avoid or defuse them if ever the nation again undertakes such a journey.

At its first meeting on March 12, 1941, the Truman committee decided that it should not undertake the investigation of any controversial subjects until it had established its legitimacy before the Senate and the American people. For the time being, Truman eschewed study of such sensitive topics as the location of defense facilities and racial discrimination in hiring at these plants. Public relations, the members correctly recognized, was of foremost importance for any congressional investigatory committee; without popular acceptance, its efforts would be worthless. Thus, the committee agreed that "its first duty would be to give to Congress and the public a clear picture of the present state of the program." On April 15, the committee convened hearings on this subject and sat back to hear Secretary of War Henry L. Stimson, Undersecretary of War Robert P. Patterson (soon to be a familiar visitor), Secretary of the Navy Frank Knox, and OPM's Hillman and Knudsen discourse on how smoothly the program was proceeding. The session gained favorable publicity for the committee and introduced it to certain of the complex issues to be dealt with in the next few years.

The committee's next target in this preliminary phase was the camp and cantonment construction program, a matter of great interest to the public. Some 229 projects had been started at an estimated cost of slightly over $500 million; thus, the likelihood of waste and chicanery was large. Investigators of the Truman committee failed to uncover corruption, but they did raise further questions about the concentration of contracts, and they discovered that the construction program was far in excess of its original estimated cost. Ultimately, the cost was $828,424,000, over $300 million above the original estimates. General Brehon Somervell, the arrogant chief of the army's Services of Supply, complained bitterly about the Truman committee's meddling, a forewarning of other clashes. Somervell admitted increased expenditures of over $100 million but justified them on grounds of the urgency of the situation. This, too, would become a familiar refrain. The committee gave the army a fair opportunity to rebut its findings, sending Somervell a copy of its draft report and expressing willingness to reevaluate its conclusions. The report, released on August 14, 1941, placed blame for the enormous cost of the construction program on the cost-plus contract scheme (whereby a contractor received all costs incurred in fulfilling a contract, plus a percentage profit) and the inability of the Quartermaster Corps (which was responsible for all construction) to administer efficiently such projects. The committee did not recommend outright abolition of cost-plus contracts. It did, however, suggest that responsibility for construction be shifted to the Engineers Corps. Some months later the War Department accepted this recommendation, a decision that greatly enhanced the Truman committee's reputation.

Two other investigations in the committee's first months of operation—a one-day session on labor problems in the coal industry and a careful look at aluminum shortages—were typical of the watchdog dimension of its activities. In April the committee decided reluctantly that it should take a hand in the bitter dispute between the United Mine Workers and the coal operators. Concerned about the effects of the coal strike on steel production, Truman convened a one-day hearing, which accomplished little aside from giving United Mine Workers chief John L. Lewis a forum for some flamboyant oratory. However, a settlement was reached a few hours after the committee adjourned.

A study of the critical shortages of aluminum that had come to light during the spring was much more serious. The Aluminum Company of America, which possessed a virtual monopoly over production of aluminum, had repeatedly given assurances that it could supply the needs of both the defense program and the private sector. However, in recent months demand had outstripped Alcoa's production by more than 100 percent. The Truman committee held hearings during May–June 1941, responding with impressive speed once the bottleneck was brought to its attention. In the June 26 report the committee criticized Alcoa for acting selfishly to protect its monopoly and blasted the Office of Production Management's handling of the situation. Faulting OPM for underestimating aluminum requirements and for indecision once the problem had been discovered, the Truman committee pressed for better coordination of the defense program. Truman commented: "We rapped some knuckles to be sure, but we tried to do it in a constructive way. We didn't take the easy course and blame the President. We want aluminum, not excuses." Unfortunately, the only way to obtain more aluminum immediately was to let Alcoa off the hook. This would not be the last time the Truman committee would encounter this sort of genteel blackmail: the necessity to ignore principle in order to obtain immediate production.

The Truman committee, particularly its inexperienced chairman and staff, performed with the skill of veterans. Truman was greatly encouraged, believing that "we have justified the existence of the Committee." He wrote a friend: "I don't believe there will be any serious difficulty for us to get the necessary funds from now on to carry out our work." His confidence was justified, for in August 1941 the Senate increased the committee's budget and authorized use of facilities and personnel drawn from the executive branch. Thereafter, the Truman committee's position never was seriously challenged, and its mandate was routinely renewed each year.

Senator Truman, as committee chairman, was receiving favorable recognition as well, as he was eager to dig into what he believed to be glaring inequities regarding the location of defense plants and the treatment of small business. In part, this resulted from an emotional distrust of "bigness" in any form. Writing in a populist vein to a Missouri friend, Truman stated:

> I am trying my best to carry on my investigation of the . . . contract racket as fairly as I possibly can. It is a most difficult job to perform but I believe we are getting some results. . . . It has been the policy of the Army and Navy to let contracts to big contractors and to big business because it is the easiest way out. A half a dozen big construction companies and manufacturers have more than seventy-five per cent of all the contracts. They obtained all the priorities on basic metal, and the little manufacturers like Chapman Brothers there in Independence are simply being put out of business.

Bringing every sort of pressure at the committee's command to bear on this problem, Truman and his colleagues obtained a measure of improvement. However, the War Department, concerned with getting as much production as quickly as possible, persisted in dealing mainly with large firms. All through the war, unhappy constituents deluged Congress with complaints. Truman himself admitted: "If you should see my correspondence, you would think that every little businessman in the country is going out of business." Frustrated by its inability to correct the problem, the Truman committee gradually realized that the government's method of awarding contracts was not solely responsible, but that the total approach to defense production, including such problems as cost-plus contracts, allocation of scarce materials, reliance on dollar-a-year men, and the stubborn impassivity of the War Department, was also involved. Exerting pressure on OPM to correct these inequities was futile, since OPM was helpless to bring into line the agencies it supposedly managed.

This realization caused the Truman committee to confront the most important issues it would deal with during the war. Fearful for the defense program if the current state of administrative chaos in Washington was permitted to continue, the committee faced awkward alternatives: it could blow the whistle and subject OPM and the entire administration—including, if necessary, the president—to indictment and trial in the forum of public opinion; or the committee could work behind the scenes, hoping to force the administrative *apparat* to pull together for the common good. Neither strategy was very appealing, and either course entailed considerable risk for the committee's members and for the nation. Not surprisingly, the committee adopted a compromise strategy, borrowing from both of the above alternatives as the situation warranted. None of its members wanted to run the war, a possible outcome if a publicity barrage attacking the administration had been totally effective. "The Committee," its first annual report affirmed, "has not and does not intend to substitute or attempt to substitute its judgment . . . for the judgment of the executive agencies involved." Its proper role, Senator Truman stressed again and again, was "auditor of the national defense program," not dictator. But, at the very least, OPM must be replaced by a new agency with real power over the assorted satrapies that had sprung up. If that was done, the committee could provide powerful support for the administration, using its publicity leverage against recalcitrant bureaucrats instead of the president.

Senator Truman unveiled the committee's plan in his presentation of the first annual report to the Senate on January 15, 1942, just five weeks after Pearl Harbor had propelled the United States into war. There was little drama in Truman's awkward summary of the committee's findings; but the conclusions he diffidently offered had a dramatic effect on his audience. The report was, clearly, a devastating indictment of the Office of Production Management. "Its record has not been impressive," the report began. "Its mistakes of commission have been legion; and its mistakes of omission have been even greater. It has all too often done nothing when it should have realized that problems cannot be avoided by refusing to admit that they exist." The report criticized the practice of using dollar-a-year men and lambasted OPM for ignoring the tremendous contribution that small companies could make. "Fundamentally," Truman observed, "the disappointing record of the Office of Production Management is not so much due to its lack of power as to its failure to perform the functions for which it was created." Cynically, one might view this as an attempt to absolve the president of blame by placing that blame on ineffective subordinates. Nonetheless, Truman sincerely believed in this explanation. The report also blasted selfish interests, especially organized labor, concerned solely with their own aggrandizement; but it returned repeatedly to OPM as the chief bottleneck in the defense program. The report recommended that a single person be appointed to direct the production and supply program, and that OPM be abolished and a new agency be created.

The Truman committee's major proposal already had been implemented when Truman spoke. Two days before, on January 13, President Roosevelt had announced the creation of a new superagency, the War Production Board (WPB), which would "exercise general direction over the war procurement and production program." He appointed as its head Donald M. Nelson, the experienced and highly regarded former Sears Roebuck executive. While the president was being pressed from all quarters to straighten out the administration of the domestic war effort, Truman's submission, some days before its formal release, of the committee report to Roosevelt may well have prodded him into a decision. Certainly, the press credited the Truman committee with a major role in this reorganization of defense programs.

It appeared that the committee's efforts to obtain central direction of the war production program had been amply rewarded. Nelson, who had been permitted to draft the executive order that set up the War Production Board, had inscribed therein sweeping powers for himself. The chairman's authority over other agencies was explicitly stated: "Federal departments, establishments, and agencies shall comply with the policies, plans, methods, and procedures in respect to war production and procurement as determined by the Chairman." However, Nelson's authority was seriously circumscribed, for it depended, as did all such administrative arrangements under the New Deal, on his personal relationship with Roosevelt and the coterie of presidential intimates surrounding the president. Nelson did not possess the complete confidence of the White House. Lacking this, officials of agencies theoretically subordinate to Nelson's authority could (and did) go over his head, taking their objections to Roosevelt or one of his advisers. Further, Nelson was no "production czar" but rather a super-coordinator. His decisions had to be enforced on those agencies that negotiated procurement contracts and supervised the production of war supplies. As the Truman committee was soon to learn, Nelson simply was not aggressive enough to protect and extend his authority. Preferring persuasion to coercion, Nelson avoided confrontations with imperious representatives of other government departments. This defect was obvious in his relations with General Somervell, chief of the Army Services Forces. Somervell's procurement activities clearly placed him under Nelson's authority, but he operated the agency with almost total private freedom. "Nelson was not aggressive about his jurisdiction and his powers," the historian of WPB admitted. "He allowed [the Army-Navy Munitions Board] to elude his group, although it was subordinate to him, and he permitted the War Department's Services of Supply, over which he said he had control, to become something decidedly other than what he thought it ought to be." In Nelson's favor were his flexibility, openness, and enthusiasm.

These latter qualities favorably impressed the Truman committee. Nelson quickly gained good relations with committee members and, in particular, with Truman. The WPB was careful to keep the committee fully informed and normally dealt with Congress through Truman. In response, the committee adopted a proprietary attitude toward the WPB. At Nelson's first appearance before the committee in late January, Truman stated: "Mr. Nelson, this Committee has been working for seven months to get the responsibility for the war effort centered in one man, with the power to act. . . . We have fought to get you this job. We are going to fight to support you now in carrying it out." Nelson had come to discuss the dollar-a-year-men issue, and the committee objected vehemently to his statements in support of the practice. However, Senator Truman's comments revealed the situation in

Sears Roebuck executive Donald M. Nelson was appointed head of the War Production Board. (Library of Congress)

which the committee found itself following Nelson's appointment. Truman first remarked:

> We want you to understand . . . that we want the war won as quickly as possible. If you have to have dollar-a-year men to win the war, this Committee is not going to interfere with that procedure on your part, because we want the war won, but we still have some ideas on dollar-a-year men and the ethics and things that are brought to bear on that subject. But this committee does not want to hamper you in carrying out your job. That comes first. . . . Here is the situation. Whether you are right or wrong under the present circumstances, this Committee feels . . . that your idea ought to prevail, because we have to win the war.

Arranging Truman's emotional statement in a roughly logical sequence demonstrates the committee's helplessness. Although the committee believed that reliance on dollar-a-year men, favoritism of big business, *et al.* were ethically wrong and boded ill for the future, they had to be accepted if they contributed to the war effort. The committee accepted the sole competence of the executive branch to judge whether something did or did not contribute to winning the war. The Truman committee certainly never gave automatic approval of WPB decisions. During the next twelve months, the committee objected strenuously to a number of WPB policies and decisions, and relations between Nelson and Truman were at times decidedly strained. The possibility of a total break was minimal, for Nelson recognized that the Truman committee was his strongest ally, and the committee believed WPB was its best hope for centralized control and, thus, protection of civilian interests.

The fatal defect in this strategy was that the Truman committee could not force Nelson to use the powers he had been given. It could only offer encouragement, as Truman stressed during Nelson's first appearance before the committee: "If you meet any obstacles . . . where this committee can turn the light of publicity on the subject or call attention to legislation that should be enacted to give you the necessary means to carry the job out, we want to be informed, and we are at your service." But what if Nelson refused to fight, what if the process of bureaucratic imperialism continued unabated, what if the president permitted these quarrels to persist? Truman and his colleagues were obligated by their own definition of the proper role of an investigatory committee in wartime not to mutiny. Notably, the Truman committee first opposed proposals that were introduced to Congress in mid-1942 for the creation of a top-level liaison committee between Congress and the executive branch. Many congressmen were unhappy about their lack of knowledge of the defense program. "All is not well with us. . . . We do not always have the information which we should have," lamented one senator in October 1942. Roosevelt rejected the liaison proposal, and the Truman committee at this time also opposed it, largely because its members believed the committee served this function.

Of course, Harry Truman was psychologically incapable of restraining his irritation and repressing frustration with WPB's failures. Throughout 1942 and into early 1943, the Truman committee held hearings on critical areas where production bottlenecks had developed. The rubber program (which proved a source of great embarrassment for Nelson), defense housing, steel shortages, and gasoline rationing were some of the topics it examined. The committee criticized the greedy actions of both large corporations and the unions, and gained enormous support for this position. Truman's outspoken statements regarding those who used the war as an opportunity for private profit made him one of the most popular figures in America.

Increasingly, however, Truman and the committee zeroed in on the War Department as the greatest source of difficulties in the war effort. This resulted from the committee's bitterness about the army and navy procurement agencies' role in destroying the effectiveness of Nelson and the War Production Board. It certainly was possible to date the downfall of the WPB to March 12, 1942, when an agreement setting forth the relationship between the WPB and War Department purchasing agencies was signed by Nelson and Undersecretary of War Robert Patterson. In effect, the WPB abdicated to the armed services full responsibility for military procurement and, given shortages, tight production schedules, and conflicting priorities regarding military and civilian needs, that inevitably produced further conflict.

The Truman committee remained steadfastly loyal to Nelson, but it could not tolerate the erosion of his authority. Other agencies asserted their independence, leading eventually to a reorganization of the WPB in September. Further rebellions during the fall culminated in February 1943 in a decision by Roosevelt to replace Nelson with the World War I "czar," Bernard Baruch. The Truman committee regretfully abandoned Nelson and began to speak in favor of a legislative solution to the need for centralized authority. A bill to establish a Department of Supply, long advocated by Senator Kilgore, a committee member, was introduced and received Truman's support. In April the committee scheduled hearings on "conflicting war programs" and

Senator Harry Truman, accompanied by members of the special committee on war mobilization (Truman committee), visit the Ford Motor Company, April 13, 1942. During World War II, Ford mass-produced the B-24 Liberator. (Library of Congress)

its report on this subject, released on May 6, stated forcefully: "Today discussion of the overall legal authority of the War Production Board is mere pedantry. Although the authority may exist it has not been exercised." Four days later, the Senate enthusiastically approved a bill to establish an independent, civilian-dominated supply agency. White House alarm at this threatened congressional revolt led to Roosevelt's appointment of his "assistant president," James Byrnes, to the post of director of an Office of War Mobilization. Byrnes was given essentially the powers to coordinate the procurement and production programs that the WPB had possessed.

This decision ended the struggle for primacy over war production. The Truman committee applauded Byrnes's appointment and justifiably claimed that the congressional and popular pressure it had mobilized was a major cause of Roosevelt's decision. Certainly, the committee had played an important role throughout the struggle, although the objectives for which it originally had entered the fray—eliminating favoritism toward big business, wasteful procedures regarding contracts, overemphasis on military needs, and so forth—had not been achieved. Nor would they receive significant attention in the future, for Byrnes, a conservative Southerner who was sympathetic to the military's viewpoint, had no need to look for support to the Truman committee.

The committee's involvement in overall control of the domestic war effort did, however, continue, though its emphasis shifted. As the battle for domination of the domestic war effort progressed, Truman and several other members began referring to the critical issue not as centralized administration but in terms of a struggle for civilian control of the war effort. This concern emerged quite early, though it was largely obscured by other problems until the WPB's disintegration. On November 26, 1942, for example, Truman took part in a "March of Time" interview. Responding to a question about the problem of civil-military relations, Truman bluntly stated:

> That is the most important question of the day. The function of generals and admirals is to fight battles, and to tell us what they need to fight battles with. They have no experience in business and industry, and the job of producing what they ask for should be left to business men under the direction of experienced civilians. I am firmly convinced that any attempt on the part of these ambitious generals and admirals to take complete control over the nation's economy would not only place vital functions in inexperienced hands, but would present a definite threat to our postwar political and economic structure.

He was referring specifically to the conflict then raging over utilization of manpower but the threat, as perceived by Truman and others, involved every phase of American economic and social life. The generals and admirals in no way pursued a calculated plan to take over the country, though they might have succeeded had they made a serious effort. They were interested solely in obtaining everything necessary to win the war, and they approached the wartime economy from this narrow perspective. Military bureaucrats such as General Somervell, who once described the Truman committee as "formed in iniquity for political purposes," had no patience with arguments that the people at home required a fair share of rubber, aluminum, gasoline, and other scarce materials. Civilians had to make do; military requirements—which often reflected an assessment of actual needs and all possible contingencies—came first.

The Truman committee cooperated with other groups to resist the War Department's efforts to impose its priorities on the nation. Where the military's challenge of civilian control was blatant—the manpower issue, stockpiling of truck tires, or the conflict between the army program and legitimate domestic requirements—resistance was remarkably effective. The principle of civilian authority was maintained, though the pervasiveness of the military in domestic matters continued to increase until the end of the war.

As noted previously, the Truman committee repeatedly renounced any desire to meddle in strategy or tactics. But that did not resolve the problem of civil-military relations, for what was a legitimate military program and what represented an illegitimate military effort to overturn civilian rule? There were no clear guidelines, and the committee did not possess sufficient information—or the power to compel the military to make such information available—to devise effective rules. Access to information was crucial: with junior officers, the committee believed that it possessed the power to force military representatives to testify. Writing to Patterson in March 1943, Truman strongly objected to a War Department claim that executive privilege excused Colonel John H. Amen from responding to the committee's questions. "Since the Committee obtained from other officers of the Army the information which it expected to obtain from Colonel Amen," Truman informed Patterson, "it will not take the necessary steps to cite him for contempt. But the Committee desires to make it clear that in so doing it does not in any sense acquiesce in your contention that any officer in the Army has the right to refuse to divulge to the Committee within the scope of its powers of investigation." However, when principal officers of the War Department refused information on the ground of military necessity, the committee willingly complied. Undoubtedly the most significant case of this sort arose when committee investigators ran across enormous and unexplained expenditures for something identified only as the Manhattan Project. Truman telephoned Secretary of War Henry L. Stimson, who told him: "Now that's a matter which I know all about personally, and I am only one of the group of two or three men in the whole world who know about it."

TRUMAN: I see.
STIMSON: It's part of a very important secret development.
TRUMAN: Well, all right then &
STIMSON: And I—
TRUMAN: I herewith see the situation, Mr. Secretary, and you won't have to say another word to me. Whenever you say that to me that's all I want to hear.

Truman was not to learn the Manhattan Project's purpose until the day he became president.

More typical of the information imbroglio was the ill-starred Canol Project, a scheme to supply high-octane gasoline, using locally produced and refined petroleum, for the Alcan Highway and U.S. airfields in the region. The project was clearly impractical and required enormous expenditures of manpower and scarce goods. Nevertheless, the War Department, and specifically General Somervell, forged ahead, ignoring the question of cost-effectiveness and practicality. "Military necessity requires that the Canol Project be completed as rapidly as possible," was Somervell's stock answer when objections were raised by civilian agencies.

The Truman committee launched an investigation of the Canol Project in summer 1943 and in September a subcommittee looked at the site and convened hearings. Gathering a huge amount of evidence, the committee soon decided that the scheme was indefensible, and should be closed down. The WPB, the Department of Interior, and various other civilian agencies supported this recommendation. Although $100 million already had been spent, an immediate shutdown would save $30 million already authorized but not expended. The War Department flatly ignored the committee's judgment, stating without elaboration that Canol was "necessary to the war effort." Since no executive agency was able to overrule the army, the Truman committee's only recourse was to place the facts in the record. This was done via public hearings in late 1943 and a report by Truman to the Senate. Despite continued pressure from members of the committee, the army obtained a further appropriation from Congress and completed all phases of the project in October 1944. The fifth annual report of the Truman committee, released in September 1946, reported that Canol had cost $134 million and had produced about as much fuel as could have been transported by one medium tanker in a period of three months. The Canol Project, though certainly not typical of wartime development programs, showed the limits of the Truman committee's influence.

The committee performed splendidly in its principal role as production watchdog. Perhaps the greatest of the committee's accomplishments was the high level of public confidence in the Roosevelt administration's conduct of the war. The committee served as an important source of information on what the government was doing to win the war, and most Americans accepted its assurances that the domestic war effort, despite administrative tangles and bureaucratic incompetence, was going well. Notably, the public seemed little concerned about the committee's reluctance to investigate charges of congressional graft and influence-peddling. Only three such inquiries took place (only one, involving Senator "Happy" Chandler's swimming pool, during Truman's tenure) in almost seven years.

In April 1942 Truman wrote his friend, Lou Holland: "We have the political campaign coming on, and with the Republican Committee endorsing the war program the campaign will be made of course on the efficiency of the conduct of that program. So unless the Democrats whole-heartedly endorse what my Committee is trying to do I fear very much I will become a political issue, and then the fat will be in the fire sure enough." Truman's anxieties proved unwarranted, for the committee attained such recognition and public acceptance that it became virtually invulnerable to political attack. Ironically, the committee's unique status largely stemmed from Truman's request that the committee's deliberations be conducted as impartially and reasonably as possible.

It may be said that Truman's resignation on August 4, 1944, to accept the Democratic Party's vice-presidential nomination was a watershed in the history of the committee. Although it was to continue in existence until April 1948, after Truman's departure there occurred a large turnover in the committee's membership, erosion of its prestige, and growth of partisan bickering. The committee, headed by James M. Mead, Harley Kilgore, and then Owen Brewster, conducted some forty-five public hearings. It issued reports on such important topics as reconversion, disposal of surplus property, the proposed loan to Great Britain, and the renegotiations of war contracts. However, if "congressional investigations are essentially exercises in the creation of public opinion," the heyday of the Senate Special Committee to Investigate the National Defense Program ended with Truman's resignation. Indeed, recognition of the feisty Missourian's centrality to all that the committee accomplished—and failed to do—perhaps is the most useful insight to be gained from study of its activities.

DOCUMENTS

Speech of Senator Harry S. Truman to the Senate, February 10, 1941

Fresh from his reelection as a U.S. senator, Harry S. Truman (D-Mo.), in early February 1941, announced his intention to file a resolution to establish a committee to investigate the national defense system, its procedures for awarding contracts, and the progress being made by those contractors involved in war mobilization. From his early days as a businessman running a clothing store to his years as a judge of the Jackson County Court, Truman had gained a reputation as a man of both honesty and efficiency. As a first-term senator, he had taken major roles in securing passage of the Civil Aeronautics Act of 1938 and the Transportation Act of 1940. As World War II intensified in Europe in 1940, Congress had appropriated more than $10 billion in defense contracts. Truman, a member of the Committee on Military Affairs, learned of evidence of contractor mismanagement, wasteful spending, and possible fraud. After visiting military bases and defense production sites, he became increasingly concerned about these

problems and proposed a congressional investigation to ensure that war profiteering did not fill corporate coffers to the detriment of small businessmen and laborers.

SPEECH OF SENATOR TRUMAN TO THE SENATE FEBRUARY 10, 1941

Mr. President, I expect to submit a resolution asking for an investigation of the national-defense program and the handling of contracts.

I feel that it is my duty at this time to place before the Senate certain information which I have, and which I am sure is of vital importance to the success of the national-defense program.

There seems to be a policy in the national-defense setup to concentrate all contracts and nearly all the manufacturing that has to do with the national defense in a very small area. This area is entirely outside the location which the Army survey, itself, has shown to be safe. The little manufacturer, the little contractor, and the little machine shop have been left entirely out in the cold. The policy seems to be to make the big man bigger and to put the little man completely out of business. There is no reason for this that will stand up, because plans have been presented to the National Defense Committee which would solve the condition of the little manufacturer and the little machine-shop owner.

A perfectly practical and concrete plan was presented by the Mid-Central War Resources Board. A survey of the region within 100 miles of Kansas City was made by this Board, and 160 small machine shops and manufacturing plants were located. It was proposed to combine the facilities of these little machine shops and allow them to take a contract, or contracts, which they could, working as a unit, carry out successfully.

Under this program there would be no housing problem. The shops are in the small towns. The people already have their houses. They are the best workmen and the most loyal citizens in the whole country.

The same sort of a survey was made in St. Louis and the immediate surrounding territory, and the same conditions exist there. I have no doubt that these conditions exist in Iowa, Illinois, and Indiana.

When this matter was put up to the Defense Committee, an effort was made to find out where the machines in these small shops were located so that the big fellows could go and buy them and move them. They are buying these machines wherever they can find them, shipping them to Detroit, Philadelphia, Norfolk, and industrial cities in Massachusetts and Connecticut. They are hiring our young men and moving them to the Atlantic and Pacific seaboards and to Detroit, leaving us denuded of manpower as well as machines. This makes a double housing problem. It leaves our cities with vacant property which is rapidly depreciating in value, and creates a condition at Norfolk, Philadelphia, Detroit, Hartford, Conn., and Los Angeles, Calif., where housing problems have to be met. It just does not make sense. The policy seems to be to make the big men bigger and let the little men go out of business or starve to death, and they do not seem to care what becomes of these little fellows. . . .

Now I wish to read a few extracts from a confidential letter which I received just the other day. This letter is from a man who knows what he is talking about.

> I think I can say that enough evidence is accumulating here in Washington of the "dog in the manger" attitude of the big fellows to provide the tinder for a rather serious blow-up a little later on. In the last analysis, of course, the Government itself is to blame. Unless the matter can be policed at the time and place where contracts are given out, i.e., unless the Government intervenes to exercise some supervision over new plant installation, it is almost certain to result in the prime contractor "tooling up" to handle the bulk of the business himself. As I see it, here is more or less the attitude the Government should take when it gives out a contract (for example) to Westinghouse Electric & Manufacturing Co. for the construction of two big ordnance plants—one at Louisville, Ky., the other at Canton, Ohio. "We are ready to give you a contract. That contract provides for the amortization of indispensable new plant equipment and buildings over a 5-year term, in 60 monthly installments, in accordance with the law. Now, let us see just what new capital investment your corporation proposes to amortize." At this point Westinghouse presumably submits a list of what it will provide in the way of new plant facilities. Somewhere along the line of scrutiny, the Government should say, "Sorry, but you cannot include in your price for the finished articles any amortization charge for this and this and this item of equipment. Our surveys indicate beyond the possibility of a doubt that the facilities already exist in the following plants, which we are satisfied will be in a position to collaborate with your concern as subcontractors on a farming-out basis." My guess is that if it were feasible to look into the situation in any large contract that has been given out recently, it would be disclosed that the Government's agreement to amortize new plant facilities covered machine-shop and metal-working facilities already available in other plants.
>
> Now, it is essential to the functioning of this idea, however, that when the Government in Washington says, "We know the facilities are available," it should be in position to cite chapter and verse. This is where our regional pooling associations (Mid-Central War Resources Board, etc.) come into the picture. Or, to put it another way: When the Government is in negotiation with Westinghouse for the construction of the two new ordnance plants, it should start with the proposition: "Where do you propose to locate these plants?" In the discussion as to location, the Government should raise its voice in terms of the

availability of facilities in different regions that could supplement the new ordnance plants to the best advantage. Really, the office for production management should take the lead in determining where new Government-owned plants are to be located. It should start out by asserting that a certain plant is to be located in a certain place, because, among other reasons, there are facilities in smaller shops in the area tributary to that location which could effectively supplement the new plant. This is really national-defense planning. Of course, nothing like this point of view exists anywhere in official Washington, and I don't see any signs of such an attitude developing anywhere in the new set-up.

To illustrate a little further: One of the reasons why North American's new assembly plant is to be located in Kansas City is that in the region tributary to your metropolis there are so many plants that can effectively supplement the facilities of North American as "subcontractors."

So long as the present "let the big fellows do it" attitude governs in the national-defense set-up, you can be sure that they will tool up in order to do everything possible under their own roofs—why not, there's more money in it that way. There is no risk for the prime contractor. He knows this national-defense show is going on for several years; it probably signifies the entry of our Nation on a totally different path of destiny than it has ever trod before. In any case, the prime contractor is protected. At the end of 5 years he has gotten back all of his capital expenditure. If, for any reason, he wants the plant, he has an option to buy it. If he doesn't want it, well, let the taxpayers have it as scrap iron. The same thing happened in 1919 in the liquidation of war plants.

The position we are in, as I see it, is this: The forces of the times run more and more strongly in the direction of bigger and bigger business. Unless the Government intervenes to reverse this trend, there will be no stopping the concentration of business in fewer and fewer hands. Under separate cover we send you our bulletin 3, a list of 650 corporations classified as to State and locality, that have something like $6,000,000,000 of war contracts. But something like 114 of them have the bulk of the business. This simply will not do.

Similarly, with regard to the new shipyards. Something like 50 new ways are to be constructed in about 10 years. Assuming 2 ships per way per year, the 200 ships would be turned out by December 31, 1942. Query: Is the Maritime Commission permitting the ships constructors to duplicate facilities which already exist in other plants inland? Incidentally, these 200 new ships are to be 100 percent welded. You might inquire of the boys in K.C. Structural what effect this decision has on the availability of the inland fabricating shops for collaboration in this program. . . .

Mr. President, under the War Department there are three types of contracts—the lump-sum contract, the purchase-and-hire contract, and the fixed-fee contract. Under the lump-sum contract the contractor is awarded the contract for the work, either on a low-bid basis or on a negotiated lump-sum basis. The purchase-and-hire form of contract is, as it would imply, a straight cost-plus contract. With the cost-plus-a-fixed-fee contract, under which most of the present construction work is being performed, the contractor is selected and a fee for his work fixed. The fixed fee amounts to approximately 3.2 percent. All costs allied with the construction work, including all overhead, blue prints, telephone calls, stenographers, clerks, field inspectors, labor, and material, are paid for by the Government. The fee can be interpreted as a profit to the contractor for the use of his services and his organization.

I do not pretend to be entirely familiar with the workings of any of these departments. However, the fixed-fee branch is now in the process of being reorganized. General Hartman has been retired, due to overwork. Colonel Somervell, former P. W. A. chieftain of New York City, is now at the head of the fixed-fee branch. Mr. Loving was formerly the construction chief. Colonel Groves is now very important in the construction branch.

Fixed-fee contracts are also being awarded to large industrialists, such as Chrysler, Du Pont, Remington, Atlas, and Hercules. These industrialists are given a fixed fee for the use of their engineering facilities. After the building has been erected and the plant completed by Government money, these industrialists lease the plant and supply the Government with the product of the plant at a fixed cost per unit.

On August 15, the Chrysler Corporation was awarded a contract in the amount of $53,000,000. The fee for construction which is paid by the Government to Chrysler is in the amount of $1. This looks exceedingly patriotic. Nevertheless, during the 1-year period of the Chrysler Corporation's lease of the factory facilities they will produce 1,000 tanks at a cost to the United States Government in the amount of $33,000,000. I doubt if anyone could give the method by which the cost of $33,000 per tank was fixed. Chrysler has full jurisdiction over the spending of all money and the inspection of all work at the job. I am sure the constructing quartermaster at the job is sincere in his effort to guard every penny of the United States Government's money; but with Chrysler having full control, it is almost impossible to do anything else but what Chrysler wants. I do not say that the Chrysler Corporation is performing anything other than its patriotic duty, but I do feel that even the large corporation should be subject to a full accounting for every nickel spent and the profit accrued on every task.

The same procedure followed in the award of the contract to the Chrysler Corporation has been pursued in awarding all contracts to the large corporations. The Remington Co. get $600,000 for acting as advisers to the Government. No one knows what this advice is or what it is worth. In addition to the $600,000, they will receive a profit of no one knows how much for each 30-caliber and 50-caliber shell they produce in a factory which has been financed by the United States Government. After the operating company—the large industrialist—has been selected, an architect, an engineer, and a construction contractor are selected.

Every contractor in the country, with but few exceptions, and every architect and engineer have registered with the Quartermaster General and with the Navy. Each firm presents a portfolio including a statement of Government fixed-fee contracts.

The information which the contractor, the architect, and the engineer furnish the Quartermaster General is turned over to the Construction Advisory Board.

The Construction Advisory Board consists of three men: Messrs. F. Blossom, F. Harvey, and F. Dresser. Mr. Blossom is a member of the firm of Sanderson & Porter, engineers and contractors of New York City. Mr. Dresser is a former civil-service employee who was employed by the U. S. H. A., has been in business for himself in the Middle West, and has had considerable interest in the Association of General Contractors.

After the information is submitted to the Quartermaster General, it is reviewed by the Board, which interviews the prospective contractor or engineer. The contractor is then given a rating which is filed for future use. The Board could really be considered an indexing committee of contractors and architects throughout the country.

The contractor is supposed to be financially sound. He should have an organization equipped to do the work. He should have done work of a similar character, or at least of similar size. Because he is a local contractor, he is considered conversant with local labor conditions and material markets; and, being in the vicinity of the project, he can serve better than one who is removed from the project because of geographical location. Were these requirements religiously carried out, no one could find fault with them; but the rules do not fit with the facts.

If there is a job in St. Louis after the operating company has been selected, the Board is requested to submit the names of those who, in its judgment, are the most competent contractor and architect for the job. The Board usually selects three.

In selecting the contractor for the job in question, the Board is supposed to bear in mind the geographical location of the contractor with reference to the job.

The name of the contractor selected by the Board is then submitted to Mr. Loving. Mr. Loving, after perusing the files of the contractor, requests that the contractor come to Washington for negotiations. Contractor No. 1 selected by the Board is then called into conference with Mr. Loving, Mr. O'Brien, and Captain Kirkpatrick and one of the section chiefs. Negotiations then take place, and generally at that meeting the contractor is informed, confidentially, that he has the job.

After negotiations a proceed order, in the form of a letter, is sent to the contractor. Final contracts are drawn up and submitted to the office of the Under Secretary of War for final signature.

One of the first jobs awarded was an $18,115,000 project at Fayetteville, N.C. This contract, strange as it may seem, was awarded to T. A. Loving & Co., at Charlotte, N.C. Mr. Loving, former construction branch chief, bears the same name and is from the same town. It is said that no relationship whatsoever exists between the two Mr. Lovings. Another instance occurred where a contractor and an architect had been selected because they have special merit for a reasonably small project. The Philadelphia quartermaster depot was awarded to the Ballinger Co. and Wark & Co. in the amount of $700,000. Within a month's time this same group received an additional contract in the amount of $9,911,000 as an extra. There were no negotiations. The same thing occurred at Camp Blanding, Fla., Camp Edwards, Mass., and at Camp Meade, Md.

Many of the contracts which have been awarded have been traced to a connection between a member of the contractor's firm and Mr. Dresser, namely, they have been personal friends in the past. This, however, should not effect any criticism. Friends may have been made because of their quality performance. Friendship should not be a handicap to anyone seeking work in the War Department. When a friendship, however, dominates the selection of an inferior contractor, then that selection is wrong. Colonel Wahlbridg of Wahlbridg and Aldinger was a personal friend of Mr. Dresser, so I am told. Wahlbridg & Aldinger of Detroit, and Foley Bros. of St. Paul, Minn., were awarded the $8,000,000 Remington small arms ammunition plant at Lake City, Mo. The two firms were neither geographically located in regard to the job, nor were they in any way better equipped than local contractors of Kansas and Missouri.

The same policy was followed in letting the contract at Camp Leonard Wood at Rolla, Mo. I am told that the gentlemen who got this contract were dirt movers and had never had a construction job in their lives. They are having much trouble getting organized and are having a great deal of difficulty with local labor conditions.

Smith, Hitchman & Grylls, architects and engineers, of Detroit, were awarded the architectural work at Lake City. Smith, Hitchman & Grylls are personal friends of Mr. Harrison, who is in the Housing Section of the National Defense Council. Mr. Harrison, I believe, and from what I am told, was the booster of Smith, Hitchman & Grylls. Smith, Hitchman & Grylls, after having had the contract since September 23, were unable to produce a suitable plot plan for a reasonably simple project until December 31, and it was not until the section chief handling the particular project forced construction, whether right or wrong, and against the wishes of both Remington and Smith, Hitchman & Grylls. Smith, Hitchman & Grylls were considered for the second Remington Arms plant in Denver.

On the Western Cartridge small-arms ammunition plant, to be known as the St. Louis ordnance plant, negotiations were held with two firms who were combined by the Dresser committee. Albert P. Greensfelder, of the Fruco Construction Co., formerly known as the Fruin-Colon Contracting Co., is a personal friend, so I am told, of Mr. Dresser. The Fruco Co. was combined with the Massman Construction Co. Massman is a river contractor. The particular project on which he was selected to be the contractor is within the city limits of St. Louis, and all the barges which Massman may own would serve no useful purpose for this project. The Fruco Co. had, a month prior to the negotiations, so I am told, a B rating. The second choice for the St. Louis job was Winston, or Winston & Turner, of New York. For some reason Winston has been pushed into practically every job in the Middle West by the Advisory Committee. A short time ago they were awarded, as co-contractors with

Sollit Construction Co., the bag-loading plant, at Charlestown, Ind. The operators of this plant were intent on using a contractor close to the job, the H. K. Fergeson Co., of Cleveland. Winston, however, seems to have gotten the job.

At Camp Blanding, Fla., Starrett Bros. & Eakin, Inc., general contractors, of New York City, were awarded a $9,000,000 project, and 8 days later, awarded an additional $8,000,000 project—a total of $17,463,777 in construction. This particular job was supposed to be completed January 15, 1941, but as of December 27, 1940, was but 48 percent completed. There has been much discussion on this particular project. Fischbach & Moore, electrical contractors, of New York City, received the contract for the electrical work. So, too, did a New York contracting firm, J. L. Murphy, for all the plumbing work on the project. No one knows why Starrett Bros. & Eakin, of New York City, should have received the contract for this particular project.

One of the first projects that was awarded was the Ellwood ordnance plant at Wilmington, Ill. This project was in the amount of $11,564,000, and was awarded to Mr. Blossom's firm, Sanderson & Porter. Mr. Blossom is on the committee.

I have been informed—and this also needs verification—that John Griffiths & Son Construction Co., of Chicago, were bankrupt 5 years ago, but through a Colonel Paddock, chief Washington representative of the firm, they were awarded a $6,268,669 contract for the construction of Camp Grant in Illinois. At Falmouth, Mass., the Walsh Construction Co., of Boston, a tunnel contractor, received the contract for the construction of Camp Edwards in the amount of $7,000,000 first and $12,000,000 second, a total of $19,697,948 for construction. Fischback-Moore, electrical contractor of New York, is in on this job. The estimated date of completion was February 1 and December 20. To date they are about 70 percent complete. On this particular job, I have been told on good authority that there was a local union consisting of about 100 members who so organized the labor on this job that the 5,000 men employed would have to pay $50 apiece to the local union before they set foot on the job. Labor conditions similar to this have existed on many of the camp jobs, including Fort Dix, Fort Meade, Lake City, St. Louis and Rolla, Mo.

Maureen, Russell, Crowell & Mullgardt were awarded, as associated with Giffels & Vallet, the contract for the design of the $30,000,000 St. Louis Ammunition Plant. Russell, again, is a personal friend of Mr. Dresser, so I have been informed. Russell's firm has never done this type of work before. It is said that this firm received approximately $76,000,000 worth of national-defense construction. There has been good reason for criticism of the Fixed Fee Branch of the War Department.

It is also said that Albert Kahn, Associated Architects & Engineers, Inc., have received between three hundred and five hundred millions of dollars in engineering and architectural contracts. Giffels & Vallet are, I am told, an offshoot of Albert Kahn. The Senate will remember what a tremendous fuss was raised when it was discovered that Chip Robert and his engineering firm in Atlanta, Ga., had received engineering and architectural contracts to the sum of $76,000,000. It looks as if Chip has been a piker and was not in at the right time.

I do not believe that any contracts should be let on the basis of friendship or political affiliation. We are facing a national emergency. Patriotism would require that these contracts be let to the man best fitted to carry out the contracts. I believe the Senate ought to go to the bottom of the whole procedure.

It is my opinion, from things I have heard, that the violations of ethics and common-sense procedure are just as flagrant in the lettering of contracts for the Navy.

They say the selection of a contractor and architect is based on their financial stability and their past experience. If the contractor and the architect were selected on the basis of their familiarity with labor and local material markets, and if the contractors were provided with a suitable method of reimbursement, and if the red tape connected with the payments were removed, smaller contracting firms would be judged on the same basis as the larger firms are now judged. Past performance is really no guide for judging a contractor today. In the past 11 years there has been little, if any, industrial expansion. The building industry throughout the United States, as we all know, has suffered for the want of work. The only work that contractors have been performing has been P.W.A. and W.P.A. projects. The firms who were good prior to 1929 are not necessarily the firms who are good today.

I am calling the attention of the Senate to these things because I believe most sincerely that they need looking into. I consider public funds to be sacred funds, and I think they ought to have every safeguard possible to prevent their being misused and mishandled. . . .

I think the Senate ought to create a special committee with authority to examine every contract that has been let, with authority to find out if the rumors rife in this city have any foundation in fact. This will be a protection to the men who are responsible for letting these contracts, and will also insure a more efficient carrying out of the contract itself.

I have had considerable experience in letting public contracts; and I have never yet found a contractor who, if not watched, would not leave the Government holding the bag. We are not doing him a favor if we do not watch him.

When safeguards are removed from a man who is entrusted with funds it does him a disservice, for the simple reason that it is much better to place the necessary guards around public funds and keep men from embezzling them than it is to prosecute men after embezzlement has taken place. When a bank teller is permitted to run loose without bond and without the necessary supervision, in the long run he gets his money mixed up with the money of the bank. The same thing happens in letting Government contracts. I do not like a cost-plus contract. I think it is an abomination; but, under the present conditions, I do not see how else this situation could have been met, although in the time that has been wasted as this matter has been handled, plans and specifications could have been drawn and contracts could have been let to the lowest and best bidder, which is the only proper way to let contracts.

I am particularly alarmed at the concentration of national-defense industrial plants. I am reliably informed that from 70 to 90 percent of the contracts let have been concentrated in an area smaller than England. It undoubtedly is the plan to make the big manufacturers bigger, and let the little men shift for themselves.

I think the "educational order" program ought to be gone into thoroughly. If it is necessary to give Henry Ford and Chrysler and General Motors millions of dollars for educational purposes for mass production, then we are certainly out on a limb. I understand that they have been given $11,000,000 apiece for educational purposes. The educational-order program was instituted along in the 1920's and 1930's by the War Department and the Navy Department to educate certain manufacturers in what the Army and the Navy might need in case an emergency should arise. Those educational orders are things of the past, and ought now to be abandoned. They are merely a gift. That phase of our national-defense program should be thoroughly gone into.

I am merely stating what I believe to be conditions that deserve investigation. If nothing is wrong, there will be no harm done. If something is wrong, it ought to be brought to light. The location of these national-defense plants and the profits that are supposed to be made on tanks, planes, and small arms should be a matter of public record, unless we are to have the same old profiteering situation that we had in the last war.

Everyone connected with the national-defense program should have a patriotic interest in seeing that it is properly carried out; and the Senate ought to know whether such persons have this interest, whether they be manufacturers or laboring men.

Source: Congressional Record, 77th Congress, 1st Session, 830–38.

Senate Resolution Establishing Special Committee on War Mobilization, March 1, 1941

Three days after addressing the Senate in February 1941 on his proposed investigation of war mobilization, Senator Harry S. Truman (D-Mo.) introduced a formal resolution to create a Special Senate Committee to Investigate the National Defense Program. It was not until March 1, 1941, after considerable assurances to the Roosevelt administration that Truman was not planning the kind of media circus that the Dies Committee had become, that the Senate approved the resolution, allotting the committee, as Truman said sarcastically, "the magnificent sum of $15,000" to begin its work. A week later, the committee's membership was set—five Democrats and two Republicans. It would soon be known as the Truman committee, and no member of Congress has ever gained greater political benefits from chairing a congressional investigating committee than Truman.

SENATE RESOLUTION MARCH 1, 1941

Resolved. That a special committee of seven Senators, to be appointed by the President of the Senate, is authorized and directed to make a full and complete study and investigation of the operation of the program for the procurement and construction of supplies, materials, munitions, vehicles, aircraft, vessels, plants, camps, and other articles and facilities in connection with the national defense, including (1) the types and terms of contracts awarded on behalf of the United States; (2) the methods by which such contracts are awarded and contractors selected; (3) the utilization of the facilities of small business concerns, through subcontracts or otherwise; (4) the geographic distribution of contracts and location of plants and facilities; (5) the effect of such program with respect to labor and the migration of labor; (6) the performance of contracts and the accountings required of contractors; (7) benefits accruing to contractors with respect to amortization for the purposes of taxation or otherwise; (8) practices of management or labor, and prices, fees, and charges, which interfere with such program or unduly increase its cost; and (9) such other matters as the committee deems appropriate. The committee shall report to the Senate, as soon as practicable, the results of its study and investigation, together with its recommendations.

For the purpose of this resolution the committee, or any duly authorized subcommittee thereof, is authorized to hold such hearings, to sit and act at such times and places during the sessions, recesses, and adjourned periods of the Seventy-seventh and succeeding Congresses, to employ such clerical and other assistance, to require by subpena, or otherwise, the attendance of such witnesses and the production of such correspondence, books, papers, and documents, to make such investigations, to administer such oaths, to take such testimony, and to incur such expenditures as it deems advisable. The cost of stenographic services to report such hearings shall not be in excess of 25 cents per hundred words. The expenses of the committee, which shall not exceed $15,000, shall be paid from the contingent fund of the Senate upon vouchers approved by the chairman of the committee.

Source: Congressional Record, 77th Congress, 1st Session, 1615.

Truman Committee News Release, April 18, 1941

In mid-April 1941, the Truman committee issued one of thousands of news releases that would keep the public informed of the committee's progress. The members had heard from the first witnesses to come before the committee, several heads of agencies involved with war mobilization. In the years to come, from 1941 to 1948, the committee would hold 432 public hearings at which 1,798 witnesses would appear. It would also hold 300 executive sessions.

Under Senator Harry S. Truman's leadership, the committee was scrupulous in its research, was careful with its dealings with both the Roosevelt administration and the news media, and established a code of procedures that was fair and efficient. Throughout the life of the committee, there would be no parade of witnesses invoking the Fifth Amendment.

TRUMAN COMMITTEE NEWS RELEASE APRIL 18, 1941

The Senate Special Committee investigating the National Defense Program had just finished its first week's sessions. The Committee heard the Secretary of War, Mr. Stimson, the Under Secretary of War, Mr. Patterson, the Secretary of the Navy, Mr. Knox, and William S. Knudsen, Office of Production Management.

Each witness reviewed the difficulties and handicaps encountered in their several departments at the beginning of the National Defense program, due to the government's lack of facilities to execute it, and to provide equipment. Contrast was made between the conditions prevailing in 1917 and those at the time our defense program began. Then, England and France were intact and we purchased most of our heavy weapons from them; now every weapon must be built in this country.

In overcoming the obstacles it was pointed out that the government was obliged to develop and expand many private plants at great cost. The Selective Draft Act, Secretary Stimson said, necessitates planning a program of training which may last for five years. He discussed cantonment construction and explained the methods and operation of contracts and told of the present status of the projects. The percentage of those behind schedule was small and steadily diminishing while others were being completed ahead of the time expected.

He emphasized the fact that the Army places orders but that business must fill them. In doing so the principal contractors had entered into many subcontracts which scattered the work widely in different parts of the country.

The Lease-Lend bill, he said had superimposed a vast new program to cover the needs of other nations, over our own requirements. It is proceeding with even greater speed and efficiency than marked the programs which were instituted last summer.

Testimony of Mr. Patterson

Mr. Patterson took up the subject of procurement with which he is charged. Of the $6,623,000,000 made available, ninety-five per cent has been obligated. Under a decentralized system purchases in a large measure had been made in the field. Pursuing further the subject of contracts touched upon by Mr. Stimson, the Under Secretary told of contracts awarded "with and without advertising," and under the "cost-plus-fixed-fee" method. These negotiated contracts were made to expedite the program. From July 1, 1940 to March 1, 1941, the Department had entered into approximately 739,000 such contracts at an aggregate cost of $6,062,000,000. He denied that any political or personal favoritism had been exercised in making the awards. The industrial mobilization plan he said had worked well in emergency and months of valuable time had been saved. Fixed fees on construction at military posts never exceeded six per cent and in practice ranged down to two per cent. Architect-engineer fees averaged 3/4 per cent. By the end of November, 1940, the Quartermaster Corps had made contracts aggregating $900,000,000. He deplored intermediaries in obtaining contracts, a pernicious practice, but the Department was using its efforts to prevent the abuse.

Summarizing, Mr. Patterson said the shelter, clothing and rations provided for troops are the best the army has ever provided. Barracks are comfortable and built to last for years. The armament is of advanced design and thoroughly efficient; tanks are superior to those of any other army. Combat planes, bombers and pursuit are of advanced designs and incorporate meritorious features developed from the European war.

The program is huge and mistakes have been made; errors have been discovered and corrected and the work prosecuted with skill and vigor.

Testimony of Secretary Knox

Secretary Knox told of the navy's expansion following a steady decline in the shipbuilding and munitions industry from 1920 to 1936. No battleships were laid down after the World War until 1937. The Navy now has 2,226,950 tons of combat ships under construction and 282,507 tons of auxiliaries. Nearly all yards are working on three shifts. Future difficulties which may cause a hold up lie in the production of structural steel, aluminum, steel forgings and armor.

Of aircraft, 840 planes were contracted for in 1940 and 6,038 in 1941. The program of expansion calls for 15,000 planes. The work is proceeding with rapidity and training capacity for pilots has increased to thousands a year. Formerly all major purchases were made on a competitive basis, but the practice was not adapted to speed nor a rational plan to utilize industrial resources. It became necessary to expand capacity and the government had given aid to manufacturers who in turn gave subcontracts to many hundreds of smaller manufacturers for parts.

In supplying material to Great Britain, Mr. Knox said allocations had been received from the President for $128,963,000 and $272,422,000 have been requested. It is on its way but shipping orders are not publicly known. Mr. Knox said of the OPM "it works" and he would not change its character to "a one-man outfit."

Of price fixing he said he wanted "to hold up a bit" but thought some price control must be exercised. He did not think it would seriously affect the cooperative attitude of industry. He considered the designation of Harry Hopkins as a clearing house under Lease-Lend procurement, a very desirable setup. Mr. Knox expressed much concern over a possible shortage of aluminum. Ultimately we may have to come to commandeering aluminum of every character in private hands. The cartel control of magnesium he considered an indefensible monopoly.

Testimony of William S. Knudsen

Mr. Knudsen said planes were his first consideration when he took up his present work. There were then 7,000 on order; the number was pushed up to 33,000 in July, of which 19,000 were for our own needs, and 14,000 for the British. Next came the machine tool problem. The industry's production had been quadrupled.

Seven plants are now making tanks, medium and light. They will be in full production by October 1st, and bomber plants by the latter part of this year. Last month 1,400 planes were delivered, three times the number produced last June.

Describing the procedure under the Lease-Lend bill Mr. Knudsen said the specifications came from the Army and Navy and were handled as if they were for these services. He does not deal directly with Mr. Hopkins.

"When we get going" Mr. Knudsen declared, "we will have more production capacity than any two European countries" and he was "not afraid." Around 2,800,000 men have been placed in defense work since last June and the number may go to four million more before the close of the year. He did not think anything more would be heard of unemployment.

Mr. Knudsen said that his committee had gone over the action taken by Mr. Henderson in the matter of price fixing. He did not think it would cut down production. There had been some howls; but he added "A howl never hurts anybody."

He felt better about the labor situation than he did a year ago.

None of the witnesses dwelt upon strike conditions but insisted that capital and labor would work together to accomplish the job undertaken.

Source: Papers of Harry S. Truman, Senatorial and Vice-Presidential Files, Harry S. Truman Library, Independence, Missouri.

Truman Committee Statement of Policy, December 10, 1941

The original Senate resolution that established the Truman committee in March 1941 had empowered it with broad authority to examine war mobilization contracts and the methods used to make them, the geographic distribution of the plants and facilities receiving government contracts, and the performance, benefits, and possible graft that might be involved. As Senator Harry S. Truman later said, "The minute we started spending all that defense money, the sky was the limit and no questions asked . . . just the fact that there was such a committee, that there was an investigation going on, caused a lot of people to be more honest that they'd had in mind being." But Truman was careful to distinguish the boundaries of the committee's role.

On December 10, 1941—two days after the United States entered World War II—the committee issued a statement of policy. The committee was a watchdog over the nonmilitary aspects of the defense program, the statement declared, not a forum to debate military strategy or tactics. Unlike the Committee on the Conduct of the War that hounded President Abraham Lincoln and his generals during the Civil War, Truman and his colleagues were careful not to attempt to inject themselves into areas of military policy pursued by the Roosevelt administration.

TRUMAN COMMITTEE STATEMENT OF POLICY DECEMBER 10, 1941

MR. TRUMAN. Mr. President, I ask unanimous consent to make a brief report from the Special Committee to Investigate the national-defense program. The committee held an executive session this morning for the purpose of determining how the committee could best contribute to the defense of the Nation.

> The committee never has investigated, and it still believes that it should not investigate, military and naval strategy or tactics. Such matters should be handled strictly by the Military and Naval Affairs Committees of the Congress.
>
> From its inception the special committee has concerned itself with the nonmilitary aspects of the defense program—that is to say, with seeing to it that the defense articles which the Army and Navy have determined that they need are produced in a minimum of time at a minimum of cost and with as little disruption of the civilian economy as possible.
>
> During the 8 months in which the special committee has operated, it has noted and called attention to many things which have adversely affected production, particularly the failure to increase the production of strategic materials soon enough and fast enough, and the failure to utilize in the defense program the existing facilities of the intermediate and small manufacturing establishments. By its action, the special committee believes that it has forced a greater attention to these problems; it believes that the various defense agencies are giving now more adequate attention to them; but it believes also that it is necessary to continue a constant watch for the purpose of assuring that such problems are met head-on and solved.
>
> The special committee has no doubt of the ability of the United States to win this war. It is simply a question of when and at what cost the war will be won, but that is a most important question. The committee is determined the war should not continue

weeks or months longer because of the failure to get the production which we need as soon as possible. An unnceessary prolongation of war, caused by failure to produce as fast, efficiently, and economically as possible, would cause an unnecessary loss of life and property.

There were present at the meeting of the committee this morning 9 of the 10 members, ant it was the unanimous opinion that what I have outlined should be the continuing policy of the committee.

The special committee has no doubt of the ability of the United

Source: Congressional Record, 77th Congress, 1st Session, 9600–01.

Radio Address by Senator Truman, Shenandoah, Iowa, October 4, 1943

By the fall of 1943, the Truman committee, in its watchdog role over wartime production, had taken to task such large business interests as the United States Steel Corporation and the Curtiss-Wright Corporation. If the companies had produced subgrade materials or had violated contractual agreements with the government, the committee was there to make those problems public, whatever the size of the business. In some cases, those companies fought back fiercely, charging the committee with overzealous and inaccurate charges. Some business-friendly reporters attacked the committee for governmental interference with American capitalist enterprise. With each attack, however, Senator Harry S. Truman, the feisty chairman of the committee, gave a speech or issued his own news release setting the record straight.

RADIO ADDRESS BY SENATOR TRUMAN, SHENANDOAH, IOWA OCTOBER 4, 1943

Today we are engaged in total war. Victory or defeat depends upon our armed forces, but they, in turn, are dependent upon what we give them with which to fight. They are risking their lives. They are entitled to the best that we can give them.

Their needs are determined by the procurement officers of the Army and Navy. The Army and Navy specify what war materials they want, and ask business to produce them in accordance with the Army and Navy specifications.

Business contracts to supply materials that conform to these specifications. Common honesty requires that business should not foist off upon the Government materials that do not conform to contract. But more than honesty is involved here. Our soldiers and sailors are dependent upon those materials for their lives, and our Nation is dependent upon them for its liberty, and even for its continued existence.

For these reasons, the committee of the Senate, of which I have the honor to be the chairman, has considered itself obligated to check charges that come to it from Government inspectors that certain corporations are delivering war material that does not meet specifications. These Government inspectors are patriotic men. They are honest and conscientious. They make no profit from the sale of the war materials. They gain nothing by making unfounded charges, and by complaining at all, they risk their jobs.

The committee has investigated a number of such charges. Unfortunately, it has found several outstanding examples in which they were true. In all such cases, the committee has insisted that the corporation involved should correct the situation, and that it should either produce material according to specifications, or obtain the approval of the armed service using the material for the delivery of substandard items to be paid for as substandard material and used only where it can safely be used.

The committee will continue this policy. It will not accept excuses from management, except where it is convinced that management is acting promptly, and in good faith, to remedy the situation and to discharge those responsible for the fraud upon the Government. By the latter, the committee does not mean the little fellows at the plant who pass the materials, but the plant superintendents who, through carelessness and incapacity, are responsible for the existence of the situation.

Such a policy seemed to the committee to be so clearly right and necessary that it expected that the press and radio would join it in requiring management to conform to Government specifications, and in telling defense workers that they would receive support in their efforts to make good war material.

This is not asking too much. Practically all of industry is producing good, high-grade material. The great mass of companies are giving our Government what it pays for. Only a very few of our large corporations have strayed from the path. And honest business and industry have been unanimous in condemning such practices. I want it perfectly clear that I have no criticism of industry or business in general. The few whom I have had to criticize are the exceptions and not the rule.

By and large the committee's efforts have received such support. The press and radio deserve a great deal of credit for this, because the companies which have had to be corrected include several of the largest corporations in the United States. They spend millions of dollars for advertising, which the press and radio risk if they publicize their mistakes.

These corporations also employ staffs of publicity men, who occupy themselves in attempts to confuse the issues and obtain public comment favorable to the companies based on a misunderstanding by the press or radio of the underlying facts.

A few of our better known newspapers and one popular radio news columnist have misunderstood the situation and by their reports to the public have unwittingly assisted in creating a false impression.

For example, the committee found that the Carnegie-Illinois Steel Corporation, the principal subsidiary of the United States Steel Corporation, was producing steel plate for the Navy and the Maritime Commission and Lend-Lease in its Irvin Works, and that the physical tests to which the finished steel plates were subjected to determine their tensile strength were faked and falsified. The company men in charge of the operation of the testing machines testified that about 5 percent or more of the tests were deliberately faked for the purpose of falsely reporting that the steel plate was in accordance with specifications. To do this they instructed the testers under them to cheat.

The case required particular emphasis because of the improper and obstructive attitude which was taken as to it by the Carnegie-Illinois Corporation when the matter was first brought to its attention. Instead of cooperating in an investigation of a serious situation, which had arisen by reason of the carelessness and negligence of the management, it attempted to delay and obstruct the investigation by refusing access to records and an opportunity to examine witnesses. When it became impossible to continue such tactics, it resorted to attempts to minimize the importance of the dishonesty which it was forced to admit had been practiced by its employees. The presentation of its case before the committee was marked by a lack of frankness and candor.

The situation was so bad that Mr. Fairless, the president of the United States Steel Corporation, stated to the committee: "We are just as shocked to get these facts as you and we are just as desirous of correcting them as you are," and "I consider it was very, very poor management."

Mr. Charles E. Wilson, executive vice chairman of the War Production Board, informed the United States Steel Corporation that:

> Although the evidence adduced to date does not prove that the culpability for the falsification goes higher than the chief metallurgist, Mr. McGarrity, it does nevertheless indicate, in our opinion, poor management on the part of the officials of the Carnegie-Illinois Steel Corporation.
>
> Needless to say, this entire situation has deeply disturbed us at the War Production Board, and we are determined, as we feel certain you are, too, that immediate steps shall be taken to put an end to all falsifications, to take appropriate disciplinary action with regard to those responsible for such practices, no matter how high in the organization they may be, and finally so to readjust your organization that, in the future, we can look forward with the fullest confidence to effective, efficient, and straightforward operation of your corporation and its subsidiaries.

Mr. Wilson could not have used plainer language, and he acted only after consulting with the Navy Department and the Maritime Commission and being assured that they concurred in his opinion.

This was not the first time that Carnegie-Illinois Steel Corporation had been guilty of faking tests on steel supplied to the Navy. Forty-nine years ago, in 1894, the House Naval Affairs Committee investigated charges against the Carnegie Steel Co. and found the following charges to have been proven:

> False reports of the treatment of the plates were systematically made to the Government inspectors.
>
> Specimens taken from the plates both before and after treatment to ascertain the tensile strength of each plate were stretched without the knowledge of the Government inspectors, so as to increase their apparent tensile strength when actually tested.
>
> False specimens taken from other plates were substituted for the specimens selected by the Government inspectors.
>
> The testing machine was repeatedly manipulated by order of the superintendent of the armor-plate mill so as to increase the apparent tensile strength of the specimens.

The similarity between the frauds practiced today and the frauds practiced 50 years ago is so striking that a single report might well have served to summarize both investigations.

The committee believed that it was time that such practices should stop and was extremely surprised when a leading Pittsburgh paper ran a scare headline all the way across the front of its paper as follows: "Steel slump blamed on Truman—Committee's bungling slows war output."

The story referred to an exhaustive independent inquiry just completed by that newspaper. In all this exhaustive inquiry the newspaper had not once contacted the committee for any information. The article proceeded to say that although official production figures for April were not available:

> Preliminary and informal reports to the W. P. B. on production trends show that instead of April being the month in which all records for steel-plate production would have been broken, this month's production may fall seriously below previous months—possibly fall off as much as 35 percent.

As I understand the newspaper article, it was a charge that because the Senate had dared to require the United States Steel Corporation to be honest we were going to lose up to 35 percent of our steel-plate production, and that that loss should be attributed to the committee's bungling.

This article with its prediction of a 35-percent slump for April was published on April 16, after half the month had expired.

The fact is that after the month had ended and the figures were in, the War Production Board announced that April was a record-breaking month, and that the steel industry produced more steel plate than it had ever before produced in a similar month.

I wonder, and I think you will wonder, who told that newspaper that there was going to be a steel slump and why was such a ridiculous rumor circulated.

Shortly afterward the committee found that the Wright Aeronautical Corporation, a subsidiary of the Curtiss-Wright Corporation, was guilty of selling for installation in Army and Navy planes airplane engines that were not in accordance with specifications.

The engines in question were made at Lockland, Ohio, near Cincinnati, in a plant designed by Curtiss-Wright, but built by the Government at a cost of more than $140,000,000.

I want to tell you just how this investigation started and was conducted. In order to make sure that the engines being produced could properly be used in our military aircraft, both Curtiss-Wright and the Government employed many inspectors, at a total cost of several million dollars a year. The committee received letters from a number of these inspectors, particularly the Government inspectors, complaining that they were being forced to pass parts and engines which were not in accordance with the specifications. Now, these specifications were prepared by Curtiss-Wright itself, and approved by the War Department. Curtiss-Wright has never claimed that the specifications were needlessly made too strict.

A committee investigator was sent to Cincinnati. He found that the majority of the Government inspectors looked to the Senate to correct a situation which they had lost hope of having corrected by Curtiss-Wright. In fact, one of the inspectors broke down and cried as he told his story, saying that he had two nephews in the Air Forces. Before our investigator had finished, not only a majority of the Government inspectors, but also a number of the Curtiss-Wright inspectors made the same charge, namely, that the inspectors were not being permitted to reject parts and engines that failed to conform to specifications.

These men had come to the committee only as a last resort. They had tried to tell their story to Curtiss-Wright. They had tried to tell their story to their own superiors in the United States Army. The only reward of those who attempted to do this was that they were transferred under a cloud, or otherwise penalized. Morale was almost completely destroyed.

Their complaints were unanimous. There were no discrepancies. They had been forced to accept bad materials. In many cases, where they attempted to reject material which was clearly bad, Curtiss-Wright succeeded in having them overruled by appealing, over their heads, to their superiors.

They did not charge their superiors with dishonesty—they simply pointed out that, again and again, material which was clearly and dangerously bad, had been accepted. They were able to show our investigator defective parts which had been accepted. They were able to point out engines which had been accepted with defects.

The committee did not make any public announcement of the conditions which its investigator had found, because it wanted to be absolutely sure that it was fair to Curtiss-Wright and to the Army. What the committee did do was to call in both Curtiss-Wright and the Army, and give them each a week or two within which to make their own investigation of the inspection procedures at the Lockland plant. Both later reported to the committee that they had found nothing. Some of the Curtiss-Wright personnel, who claimed to have made an investigation, have since been discharged or removed from their jobs, and the Army has instituted court-martial proceedings against some of the officers upon whom it relied for an investigation.

A subcommittee of the Truman committee then went to Cincinnati to inspect the plant and to hold hearings. Before it finished, it had heard scores of witnesses. One witness would suggest several others. A group of inspectors would go out, voluntarily, and dig up a number of other inspectors who had the same story to tell. The subcommittee took 1,200 pages of testimony, and found a situation which was appalling.

At the subcommittee's invitation, an Army officer accompanied it, and was at its hearings. At his request, the testimony taken by the subcommittee was made available to the Army, which also made a further investigation of its own. The Army and the committee are in substantial agreement that the situation at the Lockland plant was extremely bad, and required drastic corrective action.

General Arnold, commander of the Army Air Force, recently complimented me on the accomplishments of the committee at Lockland and informed me that the committee's action has been of great value and assistance to the Army Air Force.

Maj. Gen. Charles Branshaw, commanding general, matériel command, at Wright Field, recently informed Senator Wallgren, the chairman of the Subcommittee on Aircraft, that in his opinion the situation was three times worse than the committee had said it was.

The committee leaned over backward in this case to be certain that it was fair to Curtiss-Wright. It even submitted its report to Curtiss-Wright, as well as to the Army, in advance, so that both would have an opportunity to present any evidence they desired, and to suggest any changes which they thought might merit the approval of the committee. I do not know how we could have been more fair.

Very significantly, Curtiss-Wright confined itself to a few generalities. It could not discuss the detailed facts themselves because they did not admit of argument.

The committee issued a report to the Senate to force Curtiss-Wright and the Army to take further additional corrective action, and to take it promptly.

In its report, the committee specifically called attention to the fact that Curtiss-Wright, through the Wright Aeronautical Corporation, was producing and causing the Government to accept defective and sub-standard material and that this was accomplished in the following ways:

1. By the falsification of tests.
2. By destruction of records.
3. By improperly recording results of tests.
4. By forging inspection reports.
5. By failing to segregate substandard and defective material.
6. By failing to promptly destroy or mutilate such defective and substandard material.
7. By orally changing tolerances allowed on parts.

8. By circumventing the salvage committee set up to pass on the usability of parts outside of tolerances.
9. By allowing production to override the inspection force, thereby destroying morale of both company and Army inspectors.
10. By skipping inspection operations.

The committee found no evidence that Curtiss-Wright was deliberately disregarding the specifications for the purpose of sabotage. We understood that the reason why some of its officials wanted lax inspection was that they were not able to produce engines in quantity that conformed to the specifications. For these reasons, the committee expected that the rate of production of engines would fall off when the plant was required to produce engines which conformed to Curtiss-Wright's own specifications. In other words, to get the quality which both the company and the War Department thought was necessary for engines going into military aircraft, it would be necessary to sacrifice quantity until Curtiss-Wright could improve the management and the procedures at the Lockland plant. Of course, this was distasteful to the plant managers whose negligence and incapacity were being demonstrated, and to Curtiss-Wright which would suffer a financial loss because less engines would be accepted and paid for by the Government.

Most newspapers and radio commentators thoroughly understood this situation, but a few of them allowed themselves to be confused by Curtiss-Wright officials who wanted to make it appear that it was the Senate, and not themselves, who should be censured for their inability or unwillingness to produce airplane parts and engines in accordance with their own specifications.

These newspaper articles and radio talks insinuated and, in some cases, stated: First, that the loss of production at the Lockland plant was due to bungling by the Truman committee which had caused inspectors to reject parts that should have been passed; second, that the committee's report was unnecessary and issued only for sensational purposes because Curtiss-Wright had already corrected the situation; third, that in any event, all the defective parts had been found before the engines were finally accepted for use in airplanes; fourth, that the quality of the engines was demonstrated by the job they were supposed to have done in the Tokyo raid; and fifth, that airplane production was going to suffer for lack of these engines.

You may be interested to know that the same man who predicted for the Pittsburgh paper the steel slump that never materialized somehow got himself substituted for a well-known radio commentator. For several days he attacked the Truman committee over the radio for daring to call Curtiss-Wright to account.

If these reporters were not duped, I suggest that they were, themselves, the sensation mongers. It is very significant that no official of Curtiss-Wright has ever publicly to you, or privately to the Senate committee, made any such statements as these.

Let us look at what Mr. Guy Vaughan, president of Curtiss-Wright, had to say as to the charge that production was lowered because the inspection procedures were too rigid:

QUESTION. The stoppages you refer to are your own stoppages which you have had to instigate to correct a situation that was not right?

MR. VAUGHAN. That is right. . . .

QUESTION. Does the company, through you now, publicly take the position that the reason for your reduction in production is the fact that the Army inspection service is blocking production by its inspection procedure?

MR. VAUGHAN. No; it could not. . . .

QUESTION. And any articles to that effect you would repudiate as not being in accordance with the facts?

MR. VAUGHAN. Publicly, internationally, any other way.

Mr. Vaughan could not take any other position because Major LaVista, resident representative of the Army for the Lockland plant had just testified that he had contacted three of the principal officials of the Lockland plant and that they had been unable to point out any cases where their production had been held up by being forced to comply with inspection procedures.

The suggestion that Curtiss-Wright had taken full corrective action before the committee's report was equally unfounded.

QUESTION. You do not disagree with General Echols in his conclusion that the management of the company at present is not satisfactory.

MR. VAUGHAN. I will agree to the fact that we have had a number of things that are not called good management, but I won't agree that the people who have been building up this thing have done a bad job. I think it can be made better as time goes on. It has got to be made better.

Major General Echols, in charge of matériel for the Army Air Force, officially testified on behalf of the War Department that:

GENERAL ECHOLS. In my opinion, the management which has been there for the past several months has not shown itself qualified to accomplish the job as laid out by that plant.

General Echols further testified that:

GENERAL ECHOLS. The Government has had discussions with the top management of the Wright Aeronautical Corporation with regard to getting men to strengthen the management in this plant.

QUESTION. You mean by that, I take it, General, that in addition to the question of the top man in the plant you are dissatisfied with what you might term the management group in the highest brackets in the plant and have desired that they be strengthened by the addition of other qualified men.

GENERAL ECHOLS. This is my opinion. They should be.

QUESTION. Why has not the Wright Aeronautical Corporation, of its own volition, provided that kind of management?

GENERAL ECHOLS. I don't know.

QUESTION. What reasons have they given you for their failure to do it?

GENERAL ECHOLS. The reasons they have given me were that they believed that the present management could work the problem out.

Thus, 6 weeks after the committee had issued its aircraft report, Curtiss-Wright had still failed to provide good management at the Lockland plant, and the situation was still so bad as to require both the Army and the Truman committee to give the company the ultimatum "produce or get out."

As to the suggestion that the engines produced were not defective, Major LaVista testified:

> Three engines which were on the shipping dock, finally inspected and sealed, ready to ship to the destination, were brought back, disassembled, and reinspected 100 percent. Everyone of the three engines were found to be in such a condition that they could not have been installed in an airplane. In fact, the conditions found were bad enough that the company immediately ordered 89 engines, which were ready to ship, returned to the assembly department to be completely disassembled and reinspected 100 percent.

Major LaVista also testified that over 400 engines were turned down on final run due to high oil flow because no effort had been made to maintain a close tolerance on the connecting-rod bearings. When 33 engines out of these 400 were reassembled with a proper fitting, all 33 went through the penalty run without trouble. Major LaVista also testified that parts which had been rejected and which had not been found suitable for salvage were discovered in the so-called green assembly line ready to be assembled into engines.

Major LaVista concluded, and I quote:

> It can be readily seen from the above facts that production could be completely bottled up until such time as these engines and parts are out of the way.

Since the Cincinnati hearing the Army has torn down and reexamined 64 of the 89 engines referred to by Major LaVista. It has also called in 100 engines as a sample selection of the engines produced from January to April prior to the committee's report. So far 10 of these have been torn down and reexamined. The results were obtained from the Army by the committee, in confidence, and I would like to set them forth here for your information as a direct, final, and conclusive answer to the contention that the engines produced were not defective and were fit for use in airplanes.

However, Under Secretary of War Patterson has specifically requested that this information not be made public. Without his consent, I will not make it public.

Since this speech was announced, further conferences have been had with officials of the Army, including Under Secretary of War Patterson. The Under Secretary stated to the committee on Saturday, "Investigations made by the Army confirm the findings made by the Truman committee as to the construction and inspection of engines." I am happy to say that the Army officials have reiterated their views that the Truman committee has performed the most worthwhile service in connection with the Curtiss-Wright plant at Lockland.

Under Secretary of War Patterson and other officials of the War Department agree with us that the results of the investigation made by the Truman committee, the matters about which we complained and which we pointed out, were matters of serious import and concern. We also agree that, happily, through vigorous efforts of the Army and the Truman committee, these conditions recently have been largely corrected. Since the committee's report the Curtiss-Wright Co. has installed much better management and procedures of every kind. Rigid inspection is now required, not only by the War Department but also by the company itself. Fathers and mothers of American boys who are pilots, and the boys themselves, can be assured that the Truman committee, the Army, and all branches of the armed forces will continue the most careful scrutiny of every plant in order that the lives and safety of our boys may be protected as far as it is humanly possible.

As to the contention that the Lockland plant must be good because its engines powered the Tokyo raiders, the fact is that Mr. Vaughan, president of Curtiss-Wright, has written the committee apologizing for that assertion. When he checked up—and it is to his credit that he checked up—he found that none of the planes raiding Tokyo had an engine manufactured at Lockland.

The suggestion that the requirement that these engines be made properly in conformance to Curtiss-Wright's own specifications is holding up airplane production is likewise unfounded. The War Production Board informs the committee that these engines are used in eight types of planes, and that deliveries of completed aircraft have been affected in only one instance, a Navy flying boat.

Let me repeat, I am very glad to be able to tell you that since our report Curtiss-Wright has taken drastic action and recently has made real progress. It has obtained some experienced personnel from other industries. Curtiss-Wright has hired a new senior vice president, who is giving all of his attention to correcting the situation. It has obtained a new manager for the Lockland plant and has relegated the former manager to other work. It has fired some of the principal assistants. It has sought and obtained outside advice as to how to better its inspection and production procedures. The improvements have borne fruit. Production is better and is expected to become much better.

These steps are all to the good, and the committee will support fully every effort of Curtiss-Wright to produce good planes and engines. It will unhesitatingly call attention to any failures where it believes that Curtiss-Wright or any other company is failing to produce good material and is slow or unwilling to take action to correct its failure.

A constructive and timely investigation of failure to conform to Government specifications may be painful to the businessmen involved, but it may also be very useful even to them. Some weeks ago there was a most unfortunate accident to a glider, which resulted in the loss of a number of lives, including that of the mayor of St. Louis and the president of the company manufacturing the glider. I checked on the cause of this glider crash and was informed that it was due to a strut fitting which had been improperly machined down to a point far below Government specifications. As a result it broke under stress and caused the glider to crash. Had we checked earlier and criticized the company for installing these defective parts the president of the glider company might, like United States Steel and Curtiss-Wright officials, have resented it. But he would have been alive today.

The committee will disregard newspaper articles and radio programs which confuse the issues and seek to absolve corporations for their failures. The next time you read such an article or hear such a program, I would appreciate it if you would write me. I will send you a copy of the report of the public hearings in question. After you have read them, if you disagree with the committee, I would appreciate your writing and telling me so. If you disagree with the newspaper or radio commentator, I would appreciate your writing him and telling him so.

Source: Congressional Record, 78th Congress, 1st Session, A4145–48.

Memorandum of Hugh Fulton, Chief Counsel, Truman Committee, May 26, 1944

On January 17, 1943, the tanker S.S. Schenectady *snapped in half and sank off the coast of Portland, Oregon. An investigation by the American Bureau of Shipping indicated that the sinking was caused by a brittle steel plate on the ship that was "more like cast iron than steel." Truman and his colleagues on the committee swept into action, calling witnesses from the Carnegie-Illinois Corporation and its parent company, the giant U.S. Steel Corporation. The testimony revealed that Carnegie-Illinois had delivered faulty material to the Navy, the Lend Lease Administration, and the Maritime Commission, which had contracted for the S.S.* Schenectady. *Officials had later falsified the steel test records to cover their tracks. The faking of tests had covered at least 28,000 tons of low-grade plate. Some workers who had complained to their superiors about the faking of the tests were reprimanded. U.S. Steel officials called the investigation unnecessary, blaming a few "lax" employees for the failure. Nevertheless, the Truman committee's investigation led to a federal grand-jury indictment in Pittsburgh against the Carnegie-Illinois Corporation itself, not a few employees. On May 23, 1944, the corporation was acquitted of the charges, and U.S. Steel trumpeted the results in a news release. But the Truman committee fired back. Hugh Fulton, chief counsel of the committee and a shrewd investigative attorney, explained that the acquittal was largely a technicality. The findings of the committee had been vindicated, he said, because Carnegie-Illinois had admitted at the trial "that records had been falsified and substandard steel furnished."*

MEMORANDUM OF HUGH FULTON, CHIEF COUNSEL, TRUMAN COMMITTEE MAY 26, 1944

To All the Members of the Truman Committee:

The Committee has obtained a copy of a press release, prepared by the United States Steel Corporation, with respect to the acquittal of the Corporation in the criminal proceedings brought in Pittsburgh. A copy of the release is attached.

After discussion with several members of the Committee, Senator Truman requested that I inform the members of the Committee as to the facts in case any of them should have occasion at any time to discuss the Carnegie-Illinois case with persons who might not understand the true situation. Senator Truman suggested that in the next annual report of the Committee the situation could be reviewed. He was of the opinion, however, that no release in answer to the United States Steel Corporation was necessary.

The Corporation was the only defendant. A verdict was directed as to the charge that records had been destroyed, because the Judge was of the opinion that the Corporation could not be held criminally responsible unless it was established that the destruction of the records had been made by a company policy-making official. He was of the opinion that the chief metallurgist of the Plant was not a company policy-making official.

With respect to the second charge concerning the faking of inspections of steel plate and the testing of steel beneath the standard of the Government in the purchase contracts, the Corporation made no attempt to deny those facts, but instead assured that there was no criminal intent on the part of the Corporation, and that the steel, although substandard, was not defective because there was no proof that it had failed to stand up under the uses to which it was put. The Department of Justice states that it was given no cooperation whatever by the Navy Department and Maritime Commission on this point. In addition, some of the witnesses who testified before the Committee as to the faking and forging of tests, did not testify at the trial because they claimed their constitutional privilege against self-incrimination.

Under these circumstances, the Corporation of course is entirely inaccurate in inferring that it was cleared of "unfair and unsubstantiated accusations made by the Truman Committee" because it admitted at the trial that the accusations the Truman Committee made were that records had been falsified and substandard steel furnished.

In addition, a verdict of acquittal in a criminal proceeding is not an exoneration of anyone, and merely means that the Judge was not convinced beyond a reasonable doubt that the Government had proved every point in its case.

—*Hugh Fulton*

NEWS RELEASE OF U.S. STEEL CORPORATION MAY 23, 1944

"We are happy to have the public know that the unfair and unsubstantiated accusations made by the Truman Committee of the delivery by Carnegie-Illinois of defective plates have been completely refuted," J. L. Perry, President of Carnegie-Illinois Steel Corporation, a U.S. Steel subsidiary, said in commenting upon today's acquittal of Carnegie-Illinois in the criminal suit prosecuted by the Government against it in the Federal Court at Pittsburgh.

"No witness," Mr. Perry continued, "testified either before the Truman Committee or before the Federal Court at Pittsburgh that any defective steel plates were ever supplied by Carnegie-Illinois Steel Corporation from Irvin Works or elsewhere."

Mr. Perry added:

"About a year ago, when indictments were found against Carnegie-Illinois Steel Corporation, relative to alleged false reports of tests of steel plates at Irvin Works, I stated that Carnegie-Illinois was confident that when it was afforded the opportunity to present in court the full facts, the outcome would be complete exoneration. Such statement reflected my firm conviction that none of the plates supplied by Irvin Works were either defective or inferior, and that any irregularities in test reports which might have occurred concerned relatively unimportant variations from the specifications. My statement has since been proved to have been entirely accurate.

"After an exhaustive three week's trial, just concluded before Judge Robert M. Gibson in the United States District Court at Pittsburgh, such complete exoneration has been obtained. Today the jury in that case acquitted Carnegie-Illinois of the charges contained in 47 counts of an indictment, that it had falsely certified tests on certain plates furnished to or for various government agencies. During the trial, Carnegie-Illinois introduced evidence to establish the actual heat numbers of the steel involved in each of these 47 counts, as well as evidence to prove that all of the steel in question had, in fact, been properly tested and had met the chemical and physical requirements of the contract specifications.

"Federal Judge Gibson directed a verdict of acquittal on another indictment, charging Carnegie-Illinois with the destruction of pertinent records. The Government was unable to present any evidence connecting Carnegie-Illinois with destruction of records.

"Carnegie-Illinois is justly proud of its outstanding productive record in support of our country's great war effort, including the delivery of more than 10 million tons of steel plates of all kinds since Pearl Harbor. About one-sixth of these very considerable plate deliveries came from Irvin Works."

Source: Papers of Harry S. Truman, Senatorial and Vice-Presidential Files, Harry S. Truman Library, Independence, Missouri.

Truman Committee News Release, June 15, 1944

By June 1944, war production in some industries had outperformed the needs of the military. Private industry would begin to turn from a war to a civilian economy. In a news release, Senator Harry S. Truman spoke about imminent cutbacks and a need for an orderly transition within large industries. As always, his advice was: "The best way is the American way of encouraging individual initiative." For Truman, his work with the committee that bore his name was almost over. The committee itself would live on for a few years after World War II. But Truman was destined for a larger place in American politics. Because of his superb work with the committee, his experience in working with business, labor, agriculture, and executive-branch agencies, and his reputation for honesty and efficiency in government, President Franklin D. Roosevelt asked Truman to be his running mate as vice president in the November election. He accepted.

TRUMAN COMMITTEE NEWS RELEASE JUNE 15, 1944

Senator Harry S. Truman, Chairman of the Special Senate Committee Investigating the National Defense Program, announced today:

In its Third Annual Report issued in March, the Truman Committee emphasized the necessity of declaring materials free for the manufacture of civilian articles as soon as it became clear that there was a surplus of such materials over and above the quantity necessary for the production of war materials. The Committee foresaw that there soon would be sufficient supplies of many articles of war, and that it would be necessary to cut back or cease production in many lines. In November 1943 the Committee had recommended that the Armed Services analyze their needs and give notice of expected termination as far in advance as possible.

There has been much discussion recently of creating adequate machinery to distribute contracts for whatever war material is still needed among manufacturers whose contracts have been cut back. That work is important but, at best, it is only a stop-gap. Obviously, as the cutbacks begin to involve more and larger contracts, it will become impossible for any agency, however efficient it might be, to parcel out new contracts to the companies affected. If the Government should attempt to provide contracts for those affected, the Government would be assuming a control of civilian business that would be a major step towards regimentation of industry.

American business is so complicated that I do not believe that there is or can be any substitute for the individual initiative and experience of American manufacturers. They should be told when and to what extent their contracts are expected to be cut back; the materials which are in surplus should be made free and available for any use to which they want to put them except in areas of manpower shortages; and they not only should be allowed but should be encouraged to place orders now for the acquisition of plants, machine tools and dies necessary to resume production of any articles that they can make out of the materials that are free, in any design and quantity that they see fit.

It is particularly important that progress along these lines be made now because cutbacks and cancellations of major proportions already are contemplated, and it is reasonably certain that the necessity for still others will be ascertained within the near future.

Mr. Donald Nelson, Chairman of the War Production Board, has assured the Committee that he is prepared to end general restrictions on materials that are in surplus, as recommended by the Committee, and to substitute specific restrictions which will apply only to the materials or semi-finished articles as to which there is still a scarcity. I am convinced that that is the most effective action that can be taken, and that it should be taken right away. The only way to begin any job is to start doing it.

Mr. Nelson will explain his views in further detail at a public hearing in Room 318 in the Senate Office Building at 10:00 o'clock A.M. on Monday, June 19.

For a number of months there has been a surplus of aluminum and magnesium. It has even been necessary to shut down a number of production units. Yet, the general limitation orders have been continued. These, undoubtedly, will be among the first to be eliminated.

It is now up to the aluminum industry to take the initiative and to show what uses it can make of aluminum and magnesium and, if possible, of the facilities for the production of aluminum and magnesium built by the Government at a cost of more than a billion dollars.

At the public hearing on Monday the Committee will ask the Aluminum Company of America and the Reynolds Metals Company, the two principal manufacturers of aluminum and principal fabricators and users of magnesium and aluminum products, to inform the Committee as to what they think can be done with respect to those metals.

I believe that all other manufacturers should be thinking along these lines and making preparations that will enable them to provide employment for their workers when their war contracts are cut back or terminated.

There are some industrialists who want to control their competitors and who think in terms of industry planning, whereby those who run out of war contracts will be restricted as to what they can make. Such plans are dangerous because of the self interest involved and because no one is intelligent enough to make worthwhile plans for the future of entire industries. The best way is the American way of encouraging individual initiative.

Source: Papers of Harry S. Truman, Senatorial and Vice-Presidential Files, Harry S. Truman Library, Independence, Missouri.

Bibliography

Dallek, Robert. *Harry S. Truman: The 33rd President, 1945–1953* (The American Presidents Series). New York: Times Books, 2008.

Donovan, Robert. *Conflict and Crisis: The Presidency of Harry S. Truman, 1945–1948.* Columbia: University of Missouri Press, 1996.

Ferrell, Robert. *Harry S. Truman: A Life.* Columbia: University of Missouri Press, 1996.

Flynn, George. *The Mess in Washington: Manpower Mobilization in World War II.* Westport, Conn.: Greenwood Press, 1979.

Huzar, Elias. *The Purse and the Sword.* Reprint. Westport, Conn.: Greenwood Press, 1971.

Janeway, Eliot. *The Struggle for Survival: A Chronicle of Economic Mobilization in World War II.* New Haven, Conn.: Yale University Press, 1951.

Koistinen, Paul. *Arsenal of World War II: The Political Economy of American Warfare, 1940–1945.* Lawrence: University Press of Kansas, 2004.

McCulloch, David. *Truman.* New York: Simon & Schuster, 1993.

Lever, Harry, and Joseph Young. *Wartime Racketeers.* New York: G. P. Putnam, 1945.

Riddle, Donald H. "The Truman Committee: A Study in Congressional Responsibility." *Journal of American History* (September 1964).

———. *The Truman Committee.* New Brunswick, N.J.: Rutgers University Press, 1964.

Toulmin, Harry. *Diary of Democracy: The Senate War Investigating Committee.* New York: R. R. Smith, 1947.

Willson, Roger. "The Truman Committee." PhD. diss., Harvard University, 1966.

The Pearl Harbor Committee, 1945–46

By Wayne Thompson

General Douglas MacArthur's plane landed at an airfield near Tokyo on the afternoon of August 30, 1945. He relished the occasion not least because subordinates had expressed concern that Japanese soldiers, defeated but still armed, might try to kill him. As he expected, the arrival of America's conquering general passed without incident. When Americans awoke a few hours later at the dawn of their August 30, the news that MacArthur was in Japan confirmed the victory which nearly four years of combat and two atom bombs had brought. But the morning papers also carried other news. In their hour of victory, Americans were called to reconsider the defeat at Pearl Harbor, the event that had brought the war to them.

General Douglas MacArthur is seated at a desk during the formal surrender ceremonies in Tokyo Bay as soldiers look on, August 31, 1945. (Library of Congress)

While MacArthur was preparing to oversee the American occupation of Japan, President Harry Truman, after four months in the White House, began to deal with an unpleasant matter left unsettled when Franklin Roosevelt died. Truman made public two reports on the Pearl Harbor disaster, reports that had been submitted in 1944 by an army board and a navy court of inquiry. Attempting to explain the ineffectiveness of American resistance to the Japanese air attack on the Pacific Fleet at Pearl Harbor, Hawaii, December 7, 1941, the army board criticized General George Marshall, army chief of staff, for whom Truman had the highest regard. The board charged that Marshall not only had been officially responsible for army preparedness in Hawaii, but also that he personally had missed opportunities to keep the local commander well informed. Truman was not particularly receptive to the board's charges, because he considered Marshall the best general of his time.

During the war Marshall had received far less publicity than MacArthur and General Dwight Eisenhower. At Roosevelt's request, Marshall had remained in Washington and permitted Eisenhower to have the more glamorous job directing the liberation of France. Marshall was identified, nonetheless, with the policy of achieving victory in Europe before embarking upon an all-out campaign in the Pacific. For critics of the Europe-first policy, Marshall was the man who had helped Roosevelt keep MacArthur and the navy from winning a quick victory against Japan. Though Marshall never voted and always tried to maintain a nonpartisan political reputation, he had become the Democrats' favorite general, as MacArthur was the favorite of Republicans, particularly conservatives. Eisenhower, who had served under both MacArthur and Marshall, was less controversial, and an interesting presidential prospect who enjoyed

OVERVIEW

Background

On Sunday, December 7, 1941, naval and air forces of Japan attacked the U.S. Pacific Fleet and other army installations in and around Pearl Harbor, Hawaii. The attack killed more than 2,400 people. The United States lost 18 warships and more than 180 aircraft. On December 8 the United States declared war on Japan, entering World War II. How had this catastrophe occurred? How could the U.S. forces have suffered such a defeat? The lack of preparedness of U.S. forces seemed extraordinary, and the press, politicians, and the general public demanded an accounting. Who was to blame?

Within days of the attack, Navy Secretary Frank Knox flew to Hawaii to undertake an assessment of the damage and the causes of the disastrous humiliation. Following Knox's investigation, no less than seven separate boards of inquiry and military inquiries probed the background and factors that led to the Japanese attack. Early inquiries focused primarily on the actions of Admiral Husband E. Kimmel, commander of the Pacific Fleet, and General Walter C. Short, commander of the Hawaiian Department. Both Kimmel and Short were demoted and relieved of command, and both men retired from the military within months. Later inquiries spread the fault more evenly between the commanders and members of the Roosevelt administration. At the same time that the various hearings rebuked Kimmel, Short, and leading figures in Washington, rumors surfaced of a conspiracy reaching all the way to the White House that the nation's leaders had sought to bring on a Japanese attack in order to pave the way for American entry into World War II. Shortly after the war ended, Congress passed a joint resolution on September 6, 1945, calling for its own investigation, under the chairmanship of Senator Alben W. Barkley (D-Ky.).

Congress Investigates

On November 15, 1945, the Joint Committee on the Investigation of the Pearl Harbor Attack held its first session. This investigation had the advantage of access to classified documentation released to the committee by the Truman administration. In addition, all of the major figures were still alive and, with the exception of Secretary of War Henry Stimson, who was ill, they all agreed to testify. The joint committee heard from many witnesses, but key testimony came from top military officials, including General of the Armies George C. Marshall, Admiral Harold Stark, and Kimmel.

Impact

The committee's investigation did not lay to rest rumors that high government officials, including President Franklin D. Roosevelt, knew of the attack in advance, but it was the most complete investigation of the Pearl Harbor attack, having benefited from earlier wartime inquiries. The committee's report provided some relief to Kimmel and Short, the two military officials in charge of Pearl Harbor, who resigned shortly after the incident, concluding that they had made "errors of Judgment [but] not derelictions of duty." The 40-volume report also concluded that "high authorities in Washington" failed adequately to inform Kimmel and Short of the immediacy of war and the possibility of a Japanese strike at Pearl Harbor. The public and Congress were fascinated to learn that U.S. intelligence had managed to decipher the Japanese code with the decryption machine dubbed MAGIC. But despite breaking the code, very little intelligence about the impending Pearl Harbor attack materialized, and neither Kimmel nor Short was privy to messages decoded by MAGIC. By July 1946, when the committee issued its report, most Americans, weary of war and its aftermath, and the many investigations of Pearl Harbor, were ready to move on to other issues. The committee's report remains a gold mine of information for historians, but its impact on the politics of postwar United States was minimal.

much favorable publicity. President Truman, however, vigorously endorsed Secretary of War Henry Stimson's exoneration of Marshall in Stimson's statement accompanying the army board report. The president drew the attention of reporters to that statement: "The conclusion of the Secretary of War," Truman emphasized, "is that General Marshall acted throughout this matter with his usual 'great skill, energy and efficiency.' I associate myself

CHRONOLOGY

1941

- *December 7:* Japanese naval aircraft attack U.S. Pacific Fleet and Army in the Pearl Harbor base in Hawaii and destroy many American ships and aircraft. In a little over two hours, 18 U.S. warships and more than 180 aircraft are totally destroyed or knocked out of action with the loss of 2,400 lives.
- *December 8:* United States declares war on Japan, entering World War II.
- *December 9:* Navy Secretary Frank Knox flies to Hawaii to investigate the damage. He concludes that neither the army nor the navy had been adequately prepared. He also credits the disaster to superior Japanese planning.
- *December 18–23:* The Roberts Commission, established by presidential executive order and chaired by Supreme Court Justice Owen Roberts, pins principal blame for the disaster on area commanders Admiral Husband E. Kimmel and General Walter C. Short.

1944

- *February 15–June 15:* Admiral Thomas Hart, former commander of the Asiatic Fleet, conducts a one-man inquiry on the orders of the Navy Department.
- *July–October 20:* In response to an act of Congress, the army's adjutant general convenes hearings. The Army Pearl Harbor Board takes testimony from 151 witnesses. The board censures Generals George C. Marshall and Leonard Gerow for not fully advising Short of the situation.
- *July–October:* A Naval Court of Inquiry exonerates Kimmel and blames Admiral Harold R. Stark, chief of naval operations at the time of the attack, for failing to adequately advise Kimmel of the critical situation prior to the attack.

1945

- *September 2:* Japan surrenders, ending World War II.
- *September 6:* Congress agrees by concurrent resolution to establish the Joint Committee on the Investigation of the Pearl Harbor Attack.
- *November 15:* Joint congressional hearings begin under the chairmanship of Senator Alben W. Barkley (D-Ky.).
- *December 6–13:* Marshall, general of the armies, testifies before committee.

1945–46

- *December 31, 1945–January 3, 1946:* Admiral Harold Stark testifies before committee.

1946

- *January 15–21:* Kimmel testifies before committee.
- *July 20:* Committee issues final report.

whole-heartedly with this expression by the Secretary of War."

In his eagerness to clear Marshall, Truman neglected to give similar consideration to other men criticized by the reports. His failure to defend former secretary of state Cordell Hull against army board charges (Hull's diplomacy was said to have triggered the war before the army could prepare itself properly) caused a brief stir among Hull's many friends until Truman hastily called another press conference to announce his support for the popular old man. The president remained silent about others named in the reports, however. Nor did the helping hand for Hull and Marshall extend to Admiral Harold Stark, who had been chief of naval operations in 1941. Truman's silence on Stark's case seemed to affirm Secretary of the Navy James Forrestal's decision that the navy's Pearl Harbor report justified removing Stark from command of the Atlantic Fleet. Forrestal had declared that Stark was unfit to hold a position of responsibility. While Stark, Hull, and Marshall were the highest-ranking officials criticized by the army and navy reports, many others in the government hierarchy were also charged with similar imperfections. Though Truman bowed to Secretary Forrestal's views on Stark, political advantage as well as natural loyalties dictated that Truman and his fellow Democrats would try to push the responsibility for the Pearl Harbor disaster down the hierarchy where it could be safely diffused, while Republicans would try

to push that responsibility upward through Marshall and Hull to Stimson and Roosevelt.

Ever since that Sunday morning late in 1941 when 343 Japanese planes rained destruction on Pearl Harbor, many senators and congressmen (especially, but not exclusively, Republicans) had demanded a thorough investigation. How, they asked, after Congress had appropriated a fortune to make Pearl Harbor impregnable, did the Japanese, at a cost of only 29 planes, sink or damage all 8 battleships in the American fleet, destroy 188 American planes, and kill more than 2,400 Americans? The Roosevelt administration's initial response to congressional curiosity was a commission headed by Supreme Court Justice Owen Roberts. In February 1942 the Roberts Commission reported that the blame for America's unreadiness at Pearl Harbor rested solely with the local commanders, Admiral Husband E. Kimmel and General Walter Short. Despite cries of whitewash, Kimmel and Short were not court-martialed and had no opportunity to make public their side of the story. The administration explained that courts-martial would interfere with the war effort by requiring generals and admirals to appear as judges and witnesses. From time to time, nevertheless, the matter was raised in Congress, especially after December 1943, when the statute of limitations should have run out on misdeeds preceding the Pearl Harbor attack.

Though Kimmel and Short waived the statute, Congress sought to ensure their liability (and the liability of anyone else who might be found responsible) by passing periodic extensions of the statute of limitations with regard to Pearl Harbor. In June 1944 Congress directed the army and the navy to undertake investigations of Pearl Harbor in preparation for courts-martial. The reports completed in the fall of 1944 were those Truman released to the press in August 1945. In 1944 the press was told only that Kimmel and Short probably would not be court-martialed, but not that the administration's new attitude toward them derived from the claim that the blame for Pearl Harbor ought to be shared by Washington officials.

When Truman released the army and navy reports, there was already talk that after the summer recess Congress would demand an investigation of Pearl Harbor. Truman wisely took the initiative, but his error in praising Marshall, while overlooking the army board's charges against Hull, was compounded by his awkward attempt to rectify it. During Truman's press conference on August 30, he explained that he had not read the reports before releasing them, and that of course he wished to associate himself with Stimson's defense of Hull also. That explanation considerably reduced the value of his earlier defense of Marshall. Truman's theory of guilt for Pearl Harbor did not do much to help himself or his friends. Recalling the administration of his predecessor, Truman declared that "whenever the President made a statement about the necessity of preparedness, he was vilified for doing it. I think the country is as much to blame as any individual in the final situation that developed in Pearl Harbor." Republicans would remind Truman frequently that he had blamed the whole country for Pearl Harbor.

The Pearl Harbor affair seemed to offer Republicans considerable political leverage, but the party leadership was also worried about several drawbacks. For the moment, the leader of the party's moderates, Governor Thomas E. Dewey of New York, the 1944 presidential candidate, kept silent. The party's conservative leader, Senator Robert Taft of Ohio, moved warily on the issue. Before Pearl Harbor, Taft had been a leading isolationist, an opponent of America's entry into World War II—a stand that he had never recanted, but which had become so unpopular that he did not wish to resume debate. No doubt he would have liked to prove that Roosevelt and his administration had bungled into an unnecessary war or, worse, conspired to enter the war after promising to remain at peace. Yet, if the country could not be persuaded of Roosevelt's malevolence, those who sought to spoil his martyrdom could be in an uncomfortably exposed position. Taft preferred to concentrate his fire on New Deal domestic policies where Truman appeared most vulnerable.

Taft's ally, Arthur Vandenberg, the senior senator from Michigan, was even more sensitive about having been an isolationist. In January 1945 he had made a widely hailed speech announcing his conversion to a more flexible and popular international outlook. Vandenberg had striven to associate himself prominently with the war effort; now he wanted to be identified with the United Nations and participation in world affairs. There was, however, another Republican senator from Michigan who was relatively immune to charges of isolation, since he had not come to Washington until 1943. Homer Ferguson, the junior senator from Michigan, would lead the Republican investigation of Pearl Harbor.

While much of the country was debating the proper relationship of the United States to the wars in Europe and China, Homer Ferguson had been liberating Detroit from crime and corruption. Judge Ferguson had been chosen by his fellow judges in Wayne County as a one-man grand jury to probe allegations of wrongdoings in the police department. The trail led all the way to the mayor's office, and Ferguson had followed it

Michigan senator Homer L. Ferguson. (Library of Congress)

relentlessly. In three years, he personally interrogated 6,000 people; even the county prosecutor went to jail. With Ferguson's consequent reputation, he had no trouble wresting Michigan's 1942 Republican senatorial nomination from Gerald L. K. Smith. Ferguson's Democratic opponent, Senator Prentiss Brown, proved a more formidable obstacle, but when Brown suggested that Ferguson would be lost in the Democratic woods, Ferguson responded that as a bird hunter, he knew his way around the woods, where he intended to use the Constitution as a compass. The voters sent him into the Washington woods, and he arrived in January 1943 ready to investigate.

Republican leaders promptly found a place for the veteran interrogator on the Senate committee investigating the National Defense Program, chaired by Senator Harry Truman of Missouri. At a time when Republican opposition was muted to avoid the stigma of being unpatriotic obstructors of the war effort, the Truman Committee offered a rare, if limited, outlet for criticism of the Roosevelt administration. Truman did not permit, however, any probing of strategy or tactics—he was determined to prevent a repetition of the harassment suffered by Abraham Lincoln and his generals eighty years earlier at the hands of the Joint Committee on the Conduct of the War. Anything connected with supply was fair game, unless General Marshall said no. Within those limits, Homer Ferguson set to work, peering at witnesses through thick glasses and asking pointed questions. His affability, advertised by a crop of disheveled gray hair, could not hide a persistence that often gave the impression that Homer Ferguson did not believe the witness.

Senator Ferguson played a prominent role in wartime floor debates over extending the statute of limitations on the Pearl Harbor affair. When interest began to fade after the 1944 elections, he tried to keep the issue alive by introducing a resolution calling for a Senate investigation of the Pearl Harbor attack. When Truman finally released the army and navy reports in 1945, Ferguson's resolution was revived. He redrafted it to provide for a joint investigating committee, but before he could introduce his new resolution, the Democrats came forward with their own.

The administration's most reliable Senate troubleshooter, the majority leader, Alben Barkley of Kentucky, on September 7, 1945, proposed the creation of a joint committee to investigate the Pearl Harbor attack. After the resolution was passed by both houses, Barkley became chairman of a joint committee that would absorb an enormous amount of his time for the next year. Ever since becoming majority leader in 1937 as a supporter of Roosevelt's attempt to pack the Supreme Court, Barkley had gone down the line for the administration. Some said that his one moment of rebellion over Roosevelt's veto of a 1944 tax bill had cost Barkley that year's vice presidential nomination, which went to Truman, but if Barkley felt any bitterness toward Roosevelt or Truman, he did not show it.

Republicans were suspicious of the administration's sudden willingness to probe the Pearl Harbor disaster. Senator Taft wanted to know whether Barkley's resolution was "broad enough to go back to the beginning of the war, that is, I mean to the general policy, the application of the Neutrality Act, the shipment of scrap and so forth?"—a polite way of asking whether Democrats would let Republicans have enough rope to hang Roosevelt. Barkley replied that the resolution was "broad enough to go back to the Japanese invasion of Manchuria or to any other period in past history that can in any way be connected with or related to the attack on Pearl Harbor"—a polite way of saying that the Republicans could have all the rope they needed to hang themselves. Barkley intended to let Republicans ask all the questions they wanted, though he probably would have been surprised to learn that his new joint committee, which was supposed to report in January, would not report until July.

The new committee was composed of six Democrats and four Republicans. The two Democratic senators chosen to join Barkley on the committee were Senator Walter George of Georgia and Senator Scott Lucas of Illinois. Both were influential members of the Foreign Relations Committee who had displayed no unusual interest in the Pearl Harbor attack and had consistently stood behind the administration's foreign policy, if not the New Deal. Senator George was the powerful chairman of the Finance Committee. Though Roosevelt once had tried to prevent his reelection, they did agree about America's role in the world. Senator Lucas, the majority whip, was tall, handsome, athletic, a natty dresser. Except for his special interest in farm legislation, he showed few traces of the fact that he, like Barkley and George, started life on a tenant farm. Of the three Democratic senators, only Lucas would have much to say during the investigation. A former American Legion state commander and a colonel in the reserves, Lucas had an interest in military affairs. He was ever ready to point out that several hours after General MacArthur, stationed in the Philippines, learned about the Pearl Harbor attack, his planes were destroyed on the ground by another Japanese air attack—a matter that never had been investigated. Senator Barkley was slightly sensitive on this point, since his daughter was married to General MacArthur's nephew and namesake.

House Democrats chose a less potent trio to represent them on the committee, for once again reliability was the watchword. Congressmen such as Montana's Mike Mansfield, who had called for an investigation of the attack, were passed over. The co-chairmanship of the committee went to Jere Cooper of Tennessee, who eventually inherited the chairmanship of the Ways and Means Committee. He was a reclusive widower, almost wholly given to the study of taxation. He had some interest in military affairs, having served in France during World War I, and like Senator Lucas, he had been a state commander of the American Legion. The other two House members were almost unknown outside their districts; J. Bayard Clark of North Carolina was near the end of a long, quiet career in the House, and second-term Pennsylvania representative John W. Murphy quit to become a federal judge toward the end of the hearings.

The principal function of the six Democrats on the Pearl Harbor Committee would be to restrain the four Republicans whenever necessary. The Democrats had more power, and the Republicans had more questions. To ask their questions the Republicans did not choose their most powerful Senate leaders, like Taft or Vandenberg, who either did not want to spend the time or else thought it best to stand back a little distance in case the investigation backfired. Instead, the assignments went to others who were already probing the military as members of the Truman Committee—Senator Homer Ferguson and a somewhat quieter, more experienced senator from Maine, Ralph Owen Brewster. Brewster had been in Washington for more than a decade. In the 1920s he had served two terms as governor of Maine. His acquaintance with Robert Taft commenced about 1910, when he and President Taft's son were attending Harvard Law School. Like Ferguson, however, Brewster could not easily be labeled an isolationist. In March 1941 he had voted for the lend-lease program to aid Britain, and though he had voted against arming merchant vessels in the fall of 1941, at that time he had made a speech carefully differentiating himself from isolationists. He considered himself an advocate of preparedness, of a strong navy (he served on the Naval Affairs Committee), and of air power (he was an amateur pilot). In addition, he had volunteered for army service during World War I, he belonged to the American Legion, and had an ancestor who had arrived on the *Mayflower.* Not only were his patriotic credentials impeccable, but he had pressed for a Pearl Harbor investigation from the beginning. Soon after the attack, he and Senator Taft had urged Senator Truman to conduct an investigation, but Truman kept them at bay for over three years.

Unlike the well-coordinated team of Ferguson and Brewster, the House Republicans on the committee were never quite comfortable with each other. The more vocal isolationists who had pushed for an investigation, men like Hamilton Fish of New York and Dewey Short of Missouri, were passed over in favor of an obscure congressman from Wisconsin who had kept fairly quiet about his isolationist votes—Frank Keefe, a banker from Oshkosh who proved to be one of the committee's more thoughtful members. The committee's other House Republican, Bertrand Gearhart of California, was more energetic and less thoughtful. Gearhart had been a pilot in France during World War I and like Senator Lucas and Congressman Cooper, he became an American Legion state commander. An active member of the Native Sons of the Golden West, before the Pearl Harbor attack he had spoken in favor of a tough policy toward Japan, including war if necessary. Here was a man who would not be charged with being soft on Japan—but before long that charge was made.

The United States naval base at Pearl Harbor, December 7, 1941, in flames after aerial assault by Japanese planes. (Library of Congress)

The ten men who composed the special joint committee to investigate the Pearl Harbor attack had all graduated from law school, and all, except Murphy, were over fifty years of age—traits they shared with many others in Congress. Aside from the three former American Legion state commanders, the committee was not notable for its military expertise. Only Senator Brewster was a member of one of the four standing committees on military and naval affairs. The administration had attempted to steer the Pearl Harbor issue clear of those standing committees, partly because two of the chairmen were critical of the administration's handling of that issue. Besides, Truman wanted the committees on military and naval affairs to pursue an objective upon which he placed a high priority: the unification of the army, the navy, and the emergent air force into a single Department of Defense.

Truman favored an army proposal calling for only one chief of staff for all three services. Secretary of the Navy Forrestal and the admirals waged a desperate fight against the army proposal, arguing that it would mean the end of the navy as such, for the navy would be absorbed by the army. A central intelligence agency would be a sufficient cure for whatever ailed the services. In the end, the navy had to accept the Department of Defense, but Forrestal managed to kill the proposal for a single chief of staff. Throughout the Pearl Harbor attack hearings, this army-navy struggle was being discussed before the military and naval affairs committees. In fact, many navy and army representatives testifying before the Pearl Harbor Committee took the opportunity to put in a plug for their side of the debate.

From the outset the administration exploited apparent connections between the lack of preparedness at

Pearl Harbor and the need for a unified defense organization. The *New York Times* expressed the administration point of view in an editorial of August 31, 1945. The *Times* claimed that "Pearl Harbor was not so much the fault of men as the fault of a system that was not geared to cope with such an eventuality. . . . The first step in the direction of great preparedness would seem clearly to be the creation of a single Department of Defense with a straight line of both command and responsibility from the very top to the very bottom." While evidence obtained by the Pearl Harbor Committee tended to promote the need for defense unification, the Democrats' emphasis on weaknesses within the system tended to diffuse responsibility for any errors that may have been made before Pearl Harbor. The army was completely comfortable blaming the system; the navy was not, since it wanted to prove that the system worked well enough and that therefore individuals were usually to blame for errors (if any). The Republicans on the Pearl Harbor Committee inclined toward the navy point of view. However, they handled admirals as roughly as generals in seeking out the guilty individuals.

Long hearings and frayed tempers lay ahead of the committee, but in September 1945 all members were cordial, promising no politics would enter into the proceedings; it would be a thorough investigation. The Democrats tried to find a counsel agreeable to the whole committee. They found such a man in William D. Mitchell, a New York Democrat who had been President Hoover's attorney general. At 71, he was a bland, methodical, legal authority, whose memories reached back into the nineteenth century when his father had been a prominent Minnesota judge and when the outbreak of the Spanish-American War had inspired him to become a volunteer army officer. By the end of World War I he had risen to the rank of colonel in the reserves. The Pearl Harbor Committee approved him unanimously, and Senator Ferguson told the press that Mitchell's party affiliation made no difference. "We are determined," Ferguson proclaimed, "not to have any politics in the investigation."

Counsel having been chosen, Chairman Barkley hoped that hearings could begin in a week or two, but Mitchell soon disabused Barkley of that notion. Even with the help of three assistants, counsel required more than a month to prepare. There had been seven earlier investigations of the Pearl Harbor attack, excluding an initial report by Frank Knox, then secretary of the navy. In addition to the Roberts Commission, the Army Pearl Harbor Board, and a navy court of inquiry, all of which had published reports, the navy had ordered other investigations, as had Secretary of War Stimson and General Marshall. Thousands of pages of testimony had already accumulated, and Mitchell wished to study them. When it became apparent that the hearings would not begin until the middle of November, the Democrats canceled plans to visit Pearl Harbor. Senator Brewster, the only committee member who had visited Hawaii, pressed hard for the junket, but Barkley would tolerate no further delay in beginning the hearings. It had become apparent that the Republican members would not mind if the hearings extended far past their January reporting deadline toward the elections in November 1946.

An important dispute between the committee's Republicans and Democrats erupted before the hearings began. At Truman's news conference the day after he released the army board report, he fielded a question about a fifty-two-page deletion. When would the deletion be made public? Never, he replied—there were sources of information that had to be protected. Despite Truman's caution, the secret found its way into print. *Life* magazine revealed that in 1944 General Marshall had asked Governor Dewey, the Republican presidential candidate, not to reveal that American cryptanalysts had cracked Japanese codes before the attack on Pearl Harbor. When the *Life* article appeared in September 1945, Dewey had no comment, but his associates confirmed the story. As a result, the question around which the hearings were to revolve now took shape: If the Roosevelt administration had access to secret Japanese messages, how could it have been surprised by the Pearl Harbor attack? The Republicans on the committee were determined to answer that question and to confirm their belief that the Truman administration was trying to prevent them from obtaining necessary information.

Republican committee members were particularly angry about Truman's directive of August 28 (the day before he released the army board report), which forbade anyone in the government from releasing information about cryptanalysis without Truman's express approval. On October 23 Counsel Mitchell obtained a new presidential directive authorizing government agencies to turn over pertinent information on cryptanalysis to the committee and permitting government employees to testify about cryptanalytic activities. Senators Ferguson and Brewster were not satisfied. They wanted the right as individuals to investigate government files because they did not trust counsel to find and produce all relevant information. Thus began their rift with Mitchell. They publicly reminded Democrats that the Truman Committee had permitted individual members to investigate government records on their own initiative, but to no avail.

The desire of Senators Ferguson and Brewster to explore the records of cryptanalytic offices applied with equal force to the papers of President Roosevelt. The Truman administration, however, was not about to let the dead president's enemies rummage through his papers. Not even counsel would be permitted to search there. Grace Tully, President Roosevelt's private secretary, was directed to give the committee any records she thought relevant. The process of moving Roosevelt's disorganized papers from Washington to Hyde Park was far from complete, and even had Tully the knowledge and the inclination to supply the committee's needs, she would have had extreme difficulty. Whatever the committee might learn about Roosevelt would have to come from other sources.

Though committee Republicans grumbled through the hearings that they were not receiving all pertinent evidence, they could not deny that they were given an immense amount. This, too, became a source of complaint. Before the hearings began, counsel sent them a number of exhibits, including two printed volumes and several hundred pages of Photostats. It was the first trickle of a deluge. Ferguson and Brewster protested that many of the Photostats were unreadable and that the hearings ought to be postponed to allow proper study of the documents. The Democrats voted down the request for delay, and the hearings opened in the Senate caucus room on November 15, 1945.

The exhibits introduced by counsel on the first day seemed to indicate that the whole Pearl Harbor story would now be told. Sensational news leaks about American cryptanalysis of Japanese codes and ciphers were confirmed. Exhibit number one was a printed volume of radio messages between the Japanese government and its embassies, particularly Washington, from July 1 to December 8, 1941. Those messages had been intercepted and decrypted by the army and navy. Exhibit number two was a similar volume of intercepted messages between the Japanese government and its agents near various American naval and military installations, including those in Hawaii, the Philippines, and Panama. The first two exhibits also provided a selection of MAGIC, the code name applied by American intelligence to decrypted Japanese messages. Counsel assured the committee that though the volumes did not include all the intercepts of the designated period, he believed that all pertinent intercepts were included.

Mitchell said the intercepts would become the subject of testimony by numerous witnesses. He had a neat schedule that would permit the committee to complete hearings before Christmas. The first few witnesses would give the committee a quick overview of the attack and explain why the Pacific Fleet was based at Pearl Harbor. Then several witnesses from army and navy intelligence would explain the process of acquiring and distributing MAGIC. Next, top officials from Washington in late 1941 would be questioned: Admiral Stark, General Marshall, Secretary of State Hull, and Secretary of War Stimson. Finally, personnel in Hawaii at the time of the attack would testify, culminating with General Short and Admiral Kimmel. As it turned out, the committee called the more famous witnesses early, questioned them until well beyond Christmas, and reserved close examination of the intelligence process until last. Mitchell's orderly presentation of evidence dissolved, along with his tight schedule. According to the committee's procedures, counsel was free to question witnesses without interruption. Then each member of the committee in turn had the same privilege. The Democrats had few questions, but the Republicans, especially Senator Ferguson, had a multitude; frequently a single witness was grilled for several days. Since Mitchell asked all the questions he thought pertinent, the Republican performance seemed to him foolishly repetitive or irrelevant. Though there was no minority counsel, Ferguson had the help of Percy L. Greaves Jr., a research consultant who sat beside the senator throughout the hearings.

The feud between counsel and the Republicans was already going strong on the first day of hearings. To provide an introductory description of the attack on Pearl Harbor, Mitchell asked the current chief of naval intelligence, Admiral T. B. Inglis, and Colonel Bernard Thielen of the army general staff to give a joint briefing, replete with charts and maps. The briefing was to cover all noncontroversial data about the attack, hoping to save the committee the tedium of securing elementary information from eyewitnesses. But Admiral Inglis and Colonel Thielen had not been in Hawaii or Washington at the time of the attack. The Republicans declared that this was nothing more than an official, hearsay version of the Pearl Harbor attack. Senator Ferguson cross-examined the witnesses at length. What had been planned as a crisp military briefing stretched into an interrogation lasting four days.

At last Admiral Inglis and Colonel Thielen were allowed to leave. The Republicans were much happier with the next witness, Admiral James Otto Richardson. In 1940 Admiral Richardson had commanded the U.S. Fleet, which until that spring had been based primarily in southern California, with detachments at Pearl Harbor and on the Atlantic. Admiral Richardson never agreed with the decision to base the fleet at Pearl Harbor to gain leverage with the Japanese. He thought the fleet was unprepared for war, would therefore not intimidate the Japanese, and ought to be returned to California where it could be supplied, manned, and trained prop-

Admiral James O. Richardson, one of the most popular U.S. Navy chiefs, stands on board one of the U.S. Navy's ships on June 5, 1941. At 62, Richardson was chief of America's Pacific Fleet. (Associated Press)

erly. According to Richardson, he urged his views on President Roosevelt during a luncheon at the White House on October 8, 1940. Roosevelt replied that the fleet was a restraining influence on the Japanese, and that he did not wish to give the impression of retreat by returning the fleet to California. When Richardson asked Roosevelt if the United States would go to war, Roosevelt answered that it would not if Japan attacked Thailand, the Kra Peninsula, the Dutch East Indies, or perhaps even the Philippines, but that "sooner or later" the Japanese "would make a mistake and we would enter the war." This was tantalizing testimony. Roosevelt was portrayed as ready to write off the Philippines, while still expecting to be at war with Japan; these were purported to be his thoughts while he was campaigning on the promise that the United States would remain at peace. What kind of Japanese "mistake" he was expecting is unknown, but Admiral Richardson was relieved of the Pearl Harbor command only three months after his interview with Roosevelt. Admiral William D. Leahy, the next witness, cast doubt upon Richardson's testimony. Though present at Roosevelt's luncheon with Richardson, Leahy could not remember anything but Richardson's complaints about the poor condition of the fleet. Leahy recalled being shocked and telling Richardson that he had better do something about the fleet's deficiencies quickly. Republicans distrusted Leahy, however, because he had become Roosevelt's chief of staff during the war and was still serving in that capacity in Truman's administration.

After a short Thanksgiving recess, the hearings focused on diplomacy rather than intelligence, as Mitchell had originally planned. From the day Truman released the army board report, the board's charges against former secretary of state Hull had generated controversy. The principal allegation was that on November 26, 1941, ignoring military and naval pleas against a war for which they were unready, Hull had given the Japanese an ultimatum that triggered their attack on Pearl Harbor. A major question before the committee was whether Hull's ten-point proposal of that date was in fact an ultimatum. In return for a relaxation of American trade embargoes that had especially threatened Japan's supply of oil, Japan was to withdraw all its armed forces from China and Indochina. If they could show that in the minds of both Hull and the Japanese the ten-point proposal spelled an end to negotiations, then the charge that Hull had triggered the war might hold.

An attempt to discredit Cordell Hull would have been fraught with difficulties no matter what the evidence. At 74, he had attained political sanctity. Not only had he been secretary of state longer than anyone else, but previous to that he had spent more than two decades in Congress, where he had championed the income tax and tariff laws. He was a veritable monument who had become less and less controversial with the passing years. Even after more than a decade in Roosevelt's cabinet, no one identified Hull with the New Deal.

As for Hull's 1941 negotiations with the Japanese ambassador, the one incident with which almost everyone was familiar had occurred just after the Pearl Harbor attack when Hull vented his anger and that of the nation. Indeed, only two days before the Pearl Harbor hearings opened, Hull had received a Nobel Peace Prize for fathering the United Nations. On the troublesome matter of the ten-point proposal, the navy came to Hull's aid. A Japanese cruiser sunk in Manila Bay was found to contain war plans dated November 5, 1941, outlining the Pearl Harbor attack, along with orders of November 7, 1941, directing the attack. Secretary of the Navy Forrestal made this discovery public at the end of October, and it was hailed by Secretary of State James Byrnes as proof that Hull's proposal of November 26 could not have triggered the war. Though the orders of the Japanese Pearl Harbor task force were subject to change, the edge of the army board's criticism of Hull had been dulled irreparably.

To their misfortune, committee Republicans did not immediately recognize the political risk in criticizing Hull. After the second day of hearings, when Admiral Inglis presented data accumulated by the navy about Japanese planning for the attack, the Republicans held a press conference during which they leveled reckless charges at the navy and at Hull. Ferguson called Inglis's testimony an "investigation of the Navy by the Navy." Brewster commented that the navy was "obviously taking a partisan attitude" in order to save Hull. But it was Congressman Gearhart who went off the deep end, saying: "The Japanese, in fact, were doing everything in their power to get an acceptable agreement and got slapped in the face on November 26th. That precipitated the war." Gearhart then darkly observed that the events preceding Pearl Harbor were "strangely significant." His companions obviously thought he had gone too far, for the press conference came to a hasty conclusion. Ferguson said that he did not want to "prejudge the case." Gearhart, who was known to his California constituents as one who had always taken a tough stance toward the Japanese, was not permitted to forget that day's remarks; he did not repeat them.

Gearhart had come as close as any of his Republican colleagues on the committee would ever come to expressing the theory that many Democrats insisted was behind Republican questions. That theory held that Roosevelt and his subordinates had wanted the Japanese to attack Pearl Harbor so that Americans united in a common cause would go to war against Japan and Germany. Could that be the purport of Gearhart's allusions? Numerous Democrats charged that it was. On November 20 Senator James Tunnell, Democrat of Delaware, attacked Republicans on the Pearl Harbor Committee for slandering Roosevelt: "In their desperation, his opponents have, in effect, put on Japanese kimonos and hissed, 'excuse Japan, please. Honorable Roosevelt and Honorable Hull teased us into honorable surprise attack.'" Tunnell noted that General MacArthur had forwarded data from Japan supporting the navy's evidence that Japan had planned the Pearl Harbor attack months in advance. "All through the war," Tunnell gibed, "General MacArthur's work has been complicated by the efforts of the Roosevelt-haters to put him into a position of rivalry with the late President. . . . May we now expect the 'kimono' boys to smear MacArthur?" Attacks like Tunnell's infuriated committee Republicans but also sobered them. In 1945 one had to avoid any suggestions of being soft on Japan and by the time Hull came before them, they had developed a new caution.

On the morning after Thanksgiving, Cordell Hull, tall, white-haired, and frail, appeared in the Senate caucus room with a lengthy written statement. After a few minutes he left, and the associate counsel, Gerhard Gesell (who eventually became a prominent Washington judge), read Hull's statement. Hull returned in the afternoon for the hour of questioning that his health permitted, and he came back for another hour on each of three more days. Every time he left the hearing room, the audience gave him an ovation. The climax of his testimony came when he answered a question from Senator Lucas, who wondered how Hull felt about the Army Pearl Harbor Board report. "If I could express myself as I would like," Hull rasped, "I would want all of you religious-minded people to retire." His language was, nonetheless, blunt with regard to the Japanese. He referred to the government led by General Hideki Tojo as "that bunch of savages and outlaws" who were on a "world rampage" in company with Adolf Hitler. "They were off on this final attack," Hull concluded, "and no

This cartoon shows an outraged Uncle Sam holding his hip and glaring at a small boy (labeled "Lyttleton") who holds a gun. The boy protests, "I didn't know it was loaded." A police officer (labeled "Hull") approaches, brandishing his nightstick. In June 1944, British minister of production Oliver Lyttleton provoked a diplomatic flurry when he said in a speech that U.S. policy had "provoked" Japan into attacking Pearl Harbor. Secretary of State Cordell Hull angrily responded that American actions had been taken in self-defense. The next day, Lyttleton retracted his statement saying it was "poorly phrased." (Library of Congress)

one was going to stop them unless we yielded and laid down like cowards, and we would have been cowards to have lain down."

Between Hull's daily visits, the committee questioned two of his former subordinates. The first, Sumner Welles, was deemed by Hull the more insubordinate, though of course Hull did not refer to their discordant relationship. As undersecretary of state in 1941, Welles had been closer than Hull to Roosevelt, who often bypassed Hull. Like Roosevelt, Welles had gone to Groton and Harvard. The committee was far more interested in what he had to say about Roosevelt than in what he had to say about Hull, and Welles obliged by saying as little as possible about him.

The committee was eager to learn about the Atlantic Conference of August 1941, when Roosevelt met with British prime minister Winston Churchill on an American cruiser off the coast of Newfoundland. The conference was famous for its master stroke of propaganda, the Atlantic Charter. Welles wished to associate himself with the composition of that famous statement of Anglo-American ideals; he said that he had worked on almost nothing else at the conference. The committee asked about the truth of allegations that Roosevelt had made a secret deal with Churchill to go to war against Japan if Japan attacked Malaya or the Dutch East Indies. Welles answered "no" when Associate Counsel Gesell asked, "Did you at that time participate in any discussion between President Roosevelt and Prime Minister Churchill concerning Japan or developments in the Far East?" Welles did say that at the end of the conference Roosevelt instructed him to draft a warning to Japan against further expansion, that the warning had been suggested by Churchill, that he, Welles, had muffled Churchill's warning slightly, and that it was further watered down in the State Department before Roosevelt gave it to the Japanese ambassador.

Senator Ferguson repeatedly asked Welles if he were telling all he knew about the Roosevelt-Churchill discussions of Japan. Not satisfied with Welles's answers, Ferguson pressed counsel to look for additional State Department records on the Atlantic Conference. Three weeks later, counsel obtained memoranda about the conference written by Welles, memoranda that were at variance with his testimony. He had kept an extensive record of the conference, and by his own account had participated in the Roosevelt-Churchill meeting at which it was decided that the British and American governments would present parallel warnings to Japan. Welles's lapse of memory about so significant a discussion was odd, especially since his return to Washington with a draft of the warning had provoked Hull's wrath. Hull had been responsible for diluting the warning, which had seemed to him the irresponsible handiwork of Welles and Roosevelt. In testimony before the committee, both Welles and Hull kept silent about their disagreement. After obtaining Welles's memoranda, committee Republicans did not press the matter further, perhaps because the memoranda indicated that Roosevelt had declined Churchill's request for a formal commitment to stop Japanese expansion in Southeast Asia by going to war if necessary. Still, there were grounds for thinking that the nature of the Atlantic Conference had been misrepresented to the American people.

In August 1941 British and American leaders at the Atlantic Conference had been especially concerned with Japanese expansion because the United States recently had taken steps that were apt to provoke further Japanese expansion. These steps in effect prevented Japan from receiving further shipments of American oil, and it seemed likely that Japan would be forced to seize the Dutch East Indies to obtain a dependable source of oil. The American oil embargo had been an act of retaliation against the Japanese occupation of southern French Indochina. The American government, however, did not offer to eliminate the oil embargo in exchange for Japanese withdrawal from southern French Indochina, including the northern portion that Japan had held for a year. Finally, in Hull's ten-point proposal of November, the Japanese were asked to withdraw from both Indochina and China in exchange for oil. Hence the oil embargo of July 1941 was perhaps the most important American move on the long road to Pearl Harbor.

Yet the oil embargo received relatively little attention during the congressional Pearl Harbor hearings. First, committee members had not yet begun to master the tangled story of American-Japanese diplomacy when they tried to question State Department personnel. The committee floundered, and the witnesses did not volunteer to enlighten them. Committee Republicans were sidetracked along lines of questioning that gave promise of disclosing conspiracy, but a mysterious mist seemed to hang over the Atlantic Conference.

The oil embargo was broached during testimony by another Groton and Harvard alumnus, Joseph Grew, who had been ambassador to Japan in 1941 and throughout the preceding decade. The Army Pearl Harbor Board had quoted him indirectly as saying that Hull's ten-point proposal had "touched the button that started the war." Grew, however, easily demonstrated that he had said merely that the Japanese military had pushed the button for war perhaps "about the time of the receipt of Mr. Hull's memorandum." He could not be coaxed into criticism of American diplomacy even with regard to Roosevelt's refusal to meet with Prince Konoye, the Japanese premier, in the fall of 1941—a meeting Grew had sponsored. He did agree that Konoye's failure to obtain a meeting with Roosevelt had contributed to the fall of the Konoye government, which was replaced by the more militant government of General Tojo. As to the oil embargo, that, said Grew, was merely a part of the policy of firmness he had recommended in 1940. Republicans on the committee suggested that Grew's hindsight was less valuable than his diary. "My diary," Grew objected, ". . . contains the records of many talks with foreign diplomatic colleagues, sometimes of a nature the confidential character of which I am in honor bound to respect." From the standpoint of disappointed committee Republicans, Joseph Grew, who had opposed the diplomacy of Roosevelt and Hull, now joined in their coverup.

The committee's perplexed wanderings through diplomatic ambivalence were interrupted by General Patrick Hurley, who, having grown bitter about his own diplomatic adventures, resigned on November 25, 1945, as American ambassador to China. Hurley's clumsy attempt to reconcile Nationalists and Communists had been trampled in the race to occupy territory evacuated by the Japanese. Blaming his difficulties on career diplomats whom he charged with supporting the Communists, Hurley stormed back to Washington. President Truman immediately appointed General Marshall special envoy to China. The Republicans on the Pearl Harbor Committee were startled to find that their star witness might leave the country at any moment. The focus of the hearings moved abruptly to Marshall.

General Marshall had become the subject of acclaim since the release of the Army Pearl Harbor Board report criticizing him. When Secretary of War Stimson retired in September, his farewell address was devoted principally to a recitation of Marshall's virtues. Marshall was, according to Stimson, a "great and modest man" who had tried to prepare the country for its "inevitable involvement" in the world war. "The destiny of America at the most critical time of its national existence," Stimson concluded, "has been in the hands of a great and good citizen. Let no man forget it." When Marshall stepped down as army chief of staff in November, President Truman, while decorating Marshall with an oak leaf cluster for his Distinguished Service Medal, read a citation that was at once unusually lavish and sincere. "To him, as much as to any individual, the United States owes its future. He takes his place at the head of the great commanders of history."

General Marshall could not have managed the war effort effectively without making enemies. For every officer like Eisenhower who was rapidly promoted by Marshall, there were numerous others who believed themselves slighted. The president of the Army Pearl Harbor Board, General George Grunert, was an officer with an excellent reputation who had not received such prestigious assignments; that might explain some of his willingness to criticize the chief of staff. Yet, the board's criticisms were not directed at Marshall's competence or the handling of his overall duties; rather, he was charged with behaving imperfectly on three specific occasions. The warning message sent in Marshall's name to General Short in Hawaii, on November 27, 1941, was thought by the board to have been confusing and insufficiently strong in view of the fact that negotiations with Japan probably had terminated. When Short reported that he had alerted his command for sabotage, Marshall did not order him to alert his command for attack. When, during the twenty-four hours before the attack, military intelligence obtained information indicating the strong possibility of imminent Japanese attack somewhere, a warning to that effect did not reach General Short until after the attack; Marshall was charged with responsibility for the delay. These specific allegations stimulated Senator Ferguson, whose lengthy questioning of previous witnesses paled beside the nearly four days he spent interrogating Marshall.

Counsel Mitchell and committee members asked about Marshall's activities on December 6 and 7, 1941, but Marshall could not remember where he had been on Saturday evening, December 6; he guessed he had been at home as usual. On Sunday morning he had gone horseback riding as he did every Sunday morning. After his ride, at about 10:30, he learned that Colonel Rufus Bratton of army intelligence had something important for him. Marshall reached his office about 11:20, and Bratton brought him some decrypted messages sent from Tokyo to the Japanese ambassador. Oblivious to the requests of subordinates that he read the short message immediately, Marshall first read the longest one, transmitted in fourteen parts, announcing that all negotiations with the American government were at an end. Finally, Marshall turned to the short message instructing the Japanese ambassador to present the memorandum to the American government, preferably the secretary of state, at 1 P.M.—an extraordinary procedure, directing delivery at a specific time on a Sunday. After a brief conference with subordinates, Marshall sent a warning message through army radio communications to Pacific commands, with priority to the Philippines.

The 1 P.M. deadline chosen for delivery of the Japanese memorandum turned out to be highly significant, though the Japanese embassy was unable to deliver the memorandum until after 2. One P.M. in Washington is about 7:30 A.M. in Hawaii; the Japanese attacked at 7:55 A.M. The interception and decrypting of the fourteen-part message and the short message constituted the most dramatic achievement of American intelligence before the Pearl Harbor attack. American intelligence was decrypting almost all messages from Tokyo to Washington, and yet no better hint of an attack on Pearl Harbor was received. Japan's ambassador in Washington knew nothing about the attack until he heard the news reports.

The Pearl Harbor Committee was fascinated by this achievement of American intelligence. Before Marshall's testimony, General Sherman Miles, former chief of military intelligence, had been brought before the committee to explain MAGIC, the decrypted Japanese messages. The more committee members learned about MAGIC, the more intrigued they became. MAGIC was read by only a few officials. Colonel Bratton and navy Lt. Commander Alwyn Kramer, both translators, carried MAGIC in locked briefcases to these select few. Ordinarily the readers did not retain copies; although copies were kept by military and naval intelligence, no one was assigned to analyze the accumulated intercepts as a whole and correlate them with other intelligence. General Short and Admiral Kimmel in Hawaii were not among the readers of MAGIC. Outside Washington only the navy in Manila and the British had the machines necessary to decrypt the most difficult Japanese diplomatic cipher, PURPLE. The few who read MAGIC were hesitant to communicate even its substance to the Pacific commanders for fear the Japanese would learn that some of their codes and ciphers had been broken and would change them. General Marshall did not permit any of the MAGIC information to be sent to General Short. Admiral Kimmel learned more, but by no means everything.

The secrecy of MAGIC limited its use, but it produced relatively little important intelligence before Pearl Harbor that could not be derived from other sources. Aside from the messages of December 6 and 7, 1941, its major contribution was the revelation in late November and early December that several Japanese embassies, including that in Washington, had been ordered to destroy code and cipher machines. In addition, it was learned early in November that Japanese negotiators were working under a November 25 deadline. Washington officials, however, did not need MAGIC to tell them that negotiations were going badly, or that on November 25 a Japanese convoy was moving south from Shanghai, or that on December 6 three Japanese convoys were off the southern coast of French Indochina. Far from disclosing Japanese plans to attack Pearl Harbor, MAGIC gave officials confidence that nothing really surprising would occur. The Japanese would attack Thailand or Malaya, and then the British would want American assistance, or, possibly, the Japanese would attack the Philippines.

If little more, MAGIC supplied the one o'clock message, an indication that the Japanese might make a move soon. It was in the hands of Colonel Bratton at 9 a.m. on Sunday, December 7, 1941. Four years later Senator Ferguson wondered aloud why General Marshall had not been able to warn General Short in time. After making as much as possible of Marshall's horseback ride, Ferguson focused on Marshall's failure to use the telephone to alert the Pacific commands after he had read the one o'clock message that morning.

Marshall's responses to this question were a little odd. No one would have been surprised had he said that he did not want to betray MAGIC by using a means of communication so insecure as a telephone, even with a scrambler. But he gave other reasons as well. He said that he did not want to try to get hold of people at that hour, since they would still be in bed; it would have been about midnight in the Philippines, the American post which seemed to him most threatened—about dawn in Hawaii. Under Senator Ferguson's dogged questioning, Marshall recalled another more important reason. The Japanese might have claimed that such a warning was an "overt act" justifying retaliation. Ferguson was incredulous, but Marshall insisted: "I think, Senator, that the Japanese would have grasped at most any straw to bring to such portions of our public that doubted our integrity of action that we were committing an act that forced action on their part." Marshall added that he could not recall clearly his decision to use encrypted radio messages rather than the telephone. Not only had he ruled out the telephone, Marshall also rejected Admiral Stark's offer of the navy's superior communications network. Army communications would do the job, he had assured Stark. As it turned out, army communications lost radio contact with Hawaii. Consequently, Marshall's warning message was sent via Western Union to Short, whom it reached after the attack. The delayed message did not warn of an attack on Pearl Harbor, but that the Japanese might do something somewhere at about 1 p.m. Washington time.

Committee Republicans pursued details about Marshall's activities during the last hours before the attack, both because those hours were dramatic and because Marshall's responsibility to act seemed personal, not just official. He was responsible officially, of course, for almost everything anyone on the general staff did or did not do. Since most communications that bore

The battleship USS Arizona *sinks into the harbor during a Japanese surprise attack on Pearl Harbor, Hawaii, December 7, 1941. The ship sank with more than 80 percent of its 1,500-person crew. The attack, which left 2,343 Americans dead and 916 missing, broke the backbone of the U.S. Pacific Fleet and forced America out of a policy of isolationism. President Franklin D. Roosevelt announced that it was "a date which will live in infamy," and Congress declared war on Japan the morning after. This was the first foreign attack on American territory since 1812.* (Associated Press)

his name were not written by him, but were products of his bureaucracy, his personal role was usually obscure. The warning message sent to General Short in Hawaii on November 27, for instance, was the work of many hands. Just before Marshall's appearance at the Pearl Harbor hearings in December 1945, General Leonard Gerow, who had been chief of the general staff's War Plans Division in 1941, took responsibility for drafting the November 27 warning to Short. That warning was the result of the combined efforts of Gerow, Gerow's subordinates, Marshall, and Secretary of War Stimson. On November 26, with the knowledge that negotiations with Japan probably were coming to an end, Marshall had decided to send warnings to the commanders in the Pacific, particularly to General MacArthur in the Philippines. Marshall then left Washington to watch army maneuvers in North Carolina. While he was away on November 27, General Gerow and Secretary of War Stimson conferred about the wording of warnings to MacArthur and Short; the warnings were sent that day in Marshall's absence. Marshall read copies of the messages on November 28 and saw nothing wrong with them.

The November 27 message sent to MacArthur was shorter and less confusing than the one sent to Short. Both messages cautioned that while preparations for hostilities should go forward, the United States wanted Japan to "commit the first overt act." The message to Short, however, contained two additional notes of caution: whatever measures Short took were to be "carried out so as not, repeat not, to alarm civil population or disclose intent"; dissemination of the warning must be limited to "minimum essential officers." Short deduced that he was not expected to order a full alert, an action that would have been obvious to the civil population. He informed the War Department that Hawaii was alerted for sabotage.

No one in Washington raised any question about the adequacy of Short's alert. From the vantage of December 1945, Marshall's failure to notice that inadequacy was the softest spot in his armor. Congressman Keefe, the quietest Republican on the Pearl Harbor Committee, displayed rare aggressiveness in poking at this apparent flaw in Marshall's performance. Marshall had not initialed Short's message, but admitted the probability of his having seen it, because in the files it was clipped behind a MacArthur message that Marshall had initialed. "Now, in all fairness, General Marshall," Keefe pressed, "in the exercise of ordinary care as Chief of Staff, ought you not to have proceeded to investigate further and give further orders to General Short when it appeared that he was only alerted against sabotage?" Marshall agreed that he had missed an opportunity to intervene. Was it not a responsibility rather than an opportunity Keefe suggested? Marshall retorted that he was responsible, of course, for all actions, large and small, of the general staff, but that he was "not a bookkeeping machine."

Most of the time General Marshall maintained his characteristic unruffled dignity. He gave the committee a clear picture of how he had viewed Hawaii and the Philippines in the fall of 1941—why he was concerned about a possible attack on the Philippines but not on Hawaii. Hawaii was an apparently impregnable bulwark, better supplied than any other American outpost. The Philippines were a tenuous foothold just south of Japanese Formosa and just north of the Dutch East Indies with their oil. From Formosa the Japanese could bomb Manila with ease. An invasion of the Philippines would pose no severe supply problem for the Japanese, but Hawaii would be nearly impossible for them to occupy. The only threat to Hawaii he perceived was sabotage. Since many Japanese lived there, the army worried about internal rather than external security.

The Philippines were also on the flank of Japan's southward movement through Indochina. For the Pearl Harbor Committee, Marshall described his desperate last-minute efforts to supply the Philippines with more bombers. A squadron of bombers on their way from California to the Philippines landed unarmed in Hawaii on December 7, 1941, during the attack. On the day of the attack and on preceding days, warning messages from Washington went to MacArthur before they went to Short. MacArthur responded to the November 27 warning by moving some of his bombers to the southern island of Mindanao, less accessible to a Japanese air raid. Yet, nine hours after he had learned about the Pearl Harbor attack, most of MacArthur's planes were destroyed on the ground.

In view of MacArthur's losses in the initial Japanese air attack on the Philippines, Republicans on the Pearl Harbor Committee were not disposed to explore the Marshall-MacArthur feud, though its well-known existence pervaded the atmosphere. Marshall had been General John Pershing's aide after World War I, when Pershing was army chief of staff. Pershing (then in his sixties) was said to have taken an interest in a woman MacArthur soon married. Later, MacArthur's stint as superintendent at West Point was cut short by Pershing, who sent MacArthur to the Philippines, and when MacArthur was army chief of staff, he was said to have been an obstacle to Marshall's advancement. During the congressional Pearl Harbor hearings, Marshall's references to Pershing conveyed respect for the old general then ending his days in a nearby hospital. At the same time, however, Marshall asserted that he had done everything he could in 1941 to help MacArthur hold the Philippines.

Like MacArthur and Pershing, Marshall had served as a young officer in the Philippines. Secretary of War Stimson had been governor general of the Philippines, and a high percentage of senior officers in the army and navy had served in the Philippines, including Admiral Leahy, Admiral Stark, Admiral Kimmel, and General Short. These men could remember the Philippine war scares four decades earlier when a Japanese invasion of the islands seemed possible. These men were accustomed to following Theodore Roosevelt in thinking of the Philippines as America's Achilles' heel. But FDR was ready to defend them in 1941; so much attention was paid to the Philippines then that Pearl Harbor was taken for granted.

If during Marshall's testimony Douglas MacArthur seemed to loom silently over one shoulder, committee Republicans strained to see Franklin Roosevelt over the other. They were disappointed. Marshall had kept his distance from Roosevelt so that the president could not manipulate him. Besides, in 1941 Marshall had not yet acquired all the power he wielded during the war. In the days preceding Pearl Harbor Marshall had relatively little contact with Roosevelt. As vehicles for reaching the president, Marshall and Hull were poor choices. They were men whose backgrounds and temperaments did not adjust easily to Roosevelt's flippancy.

Marshall was able to testify that Roosevelt had not known about the 1944 letters in which Marshall asked Governor Dewey not to raise the Pearl Harbor issue in the presidential campaign. Marshall, worried by congressional debates about Pearl Harbor, feared that a public investigation would force the government to disclose that it was deciphering Japanese messages. His top-secret letter to Dewey of September 25, 1944, explained the risks to national security inherent in such a disclosure. A colonel carried the letter to Dewey's campaign train in Oklahoma, but Dewey refused to read it. Two days later Marshall sent a similar letter to Albany, where Dewey read the letter and kept quiet about Pearl Harbor for the rest of the campaign. At Roosevelt's funeral in April 1945, Marshall saw Dewey and asked him to come to the War Department, where he was shown examples of MAGIC. Counsel Mitchell elicited the information on Dewey early in Marshall's testimony, but it was not a matter Republicans wished to pursue. MAGIC had not given explicit advance warning of an attack on Pearl Harbor and had provided a legitimate national security justification for covering up the Pearl Harbor affair.

Marshall's testimony was the climax of the hearings; thereafter public interest waned. Senator Ferguson's exhaustive interrogation of Marshall dismayed the general's admirers, who thought it particularly rude because he was waiting to begin his important China mission. On December 14, the morning after Marshall was permitted to leave the witness table, General Counsel Mitchell and his three assistants resigned. In a prepared statement Mitchell left no doubt that he was upset about the way "extensive examination" of witnesses by Republicans had destroyed his plans to present evidence efficiently, thus the hearings were not finished before Christmas. After a month of daily hearings only ten witnesses had been introduced out of the sixty scheduled.

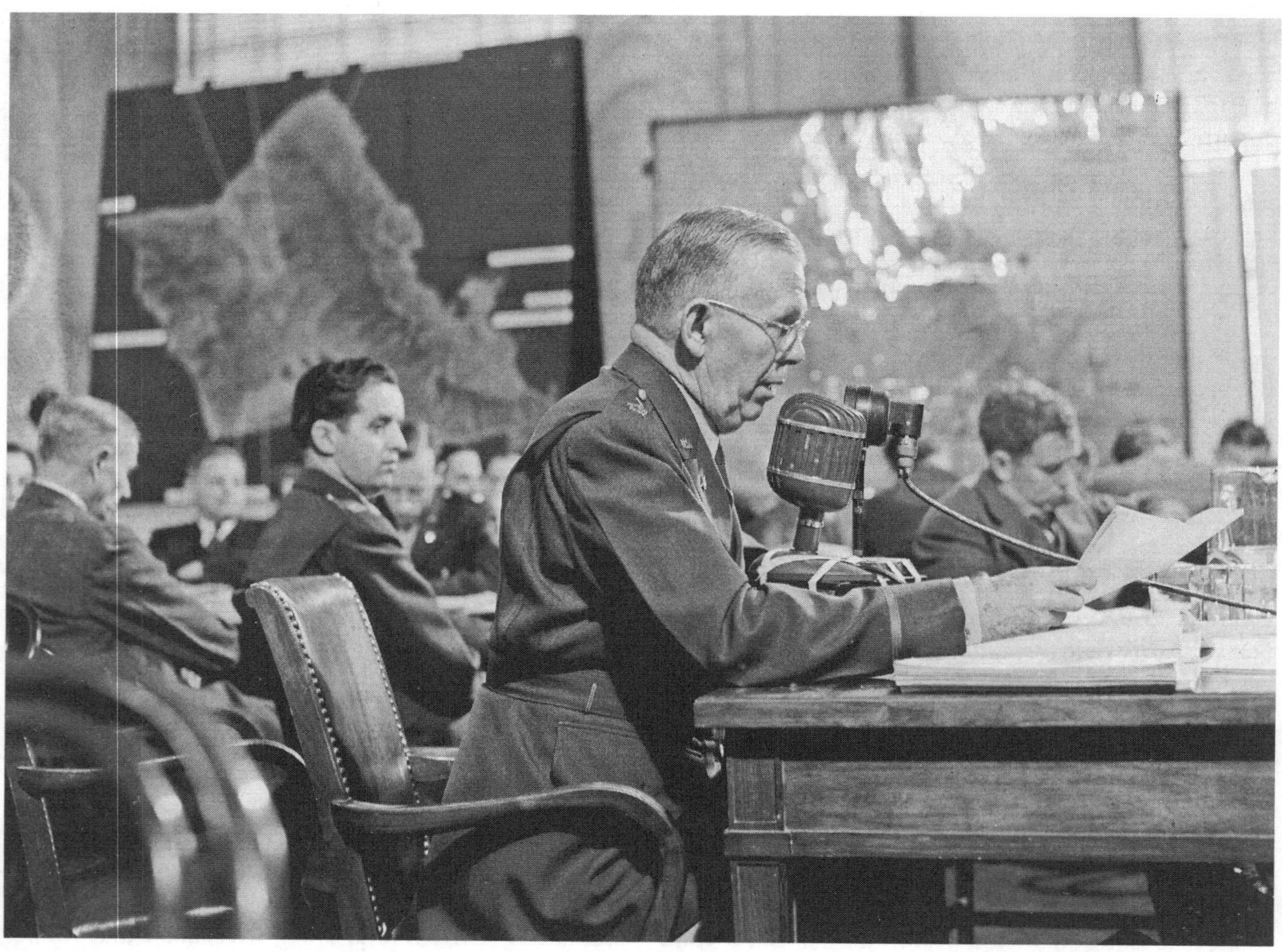

General George C. Marshall, former U.S. Army chief of staff, testifies before the Pearl Harbor Committee, December 8, 1945. (Associated Press)

"Since the start of the hearing," Mitchell declared, "it has become increasingly apparent that some members of the committee have a different view than that entertained by counsel, either as to the scope of the inquiry or as to what is pertinent evidence." Chairman Barkley soberly intoned his admiration for Mitchell. "The chairman feels like saying to Mr. Mitchell, and to his entire staff, that in his experience as a legislator covering 33 years, and a longer experience in public life and in the practice of law, he does not recall a more diligent, earnest, painstaking, unselfish effort made by a lawyer or a group of lawyers to perform their service as a public duty." Barkley said he had no idea where the committee would find a new legal staff or how long the hearings would last. He was having difficulty keeping up with his duties as majority leader and might have to resign from the committee as well. Senator George's remarks suggested that he was also considering resigning. Nothing more was heard about resignation, however, and the committee resumed its task. Mitchell agreed to stay until early January while new counsel was selected.

Mitchell performed his last service for the committee by questioning Admiral Harold Stark, who had been chief of naval operations in 1941. Beginning with Stark, the committee heard from three men (Stark, Kimmel, and Short) whose careers had been most damaged by the American reaction to the Pearl Harbor attack. After commanding the Atlantic Fleet during the war, Stark had been banned by Secretary of the Navy Forrestal from holding any position of responsibility. Yet Stark usually had given Admiral Kimmel better information before the attack than Marshall had given Short. While Marshall's workload had dried up his personal correspondence with Short by the fall of 1941, Stark continued to send Kimmel personal letters describing the outlook in Washington. Stark was more willing than Marshall to have Kimmel know the substance of MAGIC; indeed Stark was under the impression that Kimmel had the machine necessary to decrypt PURPLE-enciphered Japanese messages intercepted in Hawaii. On December 3, 1941, when MAGIC had betrayed code destruction at several Japanese embassies, including Washington and London, Kimmel was informed. Even Stark's warning message to Kimmel of November 27 had a more urgent tone than the parallel War Department message to Short. Stark's message began unequivocally: "This despatch is to be considered a war warning." Their effect on Kimmel, however, was cushioned by two qualifications: the message specified that the Japanese probably would move against Thailand or the Philippines; it instructed Kimmel to prepare to carry out war plan 46, which was an offensive war plan having nothing to do with the defense of Hawaii. Like everyone else in Washington, Stark had not expected an attack on Pearl Harbor.

The one instance when Stark's conduct appeared markedly inferior to Marshall's with regard to Pearl Harbor occurred on the morning of December 7. Stark read the Japanese one o'clock delivery message at about 10:40 A.M. Unlike Marshall, Stark did not conclude immediately that there was any special significance in specifying a particular time on a Sunday. When Marshall telephoned him an hour later about having the army's warning message sent to navy commanders also, Stark initially said no. A few minutes later Stark changed his mind, but his hour of indecision badly scarred a career that bore few other blemishes.

In 1941 Stark had been closer than Marshall to Roosevelt. Stark was an easier man with whom to talk than Marshall, less reserved. Roosevelt called Stark "Betty," his naval academy nickname, and they had known each other for nearly three decades. They met in 1914 when Roosevelt was assistant secretary of the navy. Stark was Roosevelt's personal choice for chief of naval operations. The Roosevelt-Stark relationship offered Republicans on the Pearl Harbor Committee another chance to search for Roosevelt's connection with the events that led to the attack, but committee Republicans had grown more reticent about this line of questioning due to a barrage of unfavorable criticism. Senator Lucas, whose turn to ask questions came before the Republicans', suggested as others had that the Republicans were trying to prove an outrageous theory about the late President. "Do you know of any man or group of men high in the Executive branch of the Government," Lucas asked Stark, "that trapped the Japs or lied to the Japanese to get them to attack us in Pearl Harbor in order to make it easier to get Congressional action to declare war against Japan?" To no one's surprise, Stark said he did not. He went on to say that as recently as the summer of 1944 Roosevelt had assured him that he had been surprised by the attack on Pearl Harbor. With unusual force, Stark added that "the Japs were the real cause for the attack on Pearl Harbor, sir."

Though Senator Lucas may have been the committee's most adept needler of Republicans, he proved instrumental in obtaining a new counsel satisfactory to them. Lucas occasionally played golf with one of Washington's most successful corporation lawyers, Seth Richardson, who knew the committee's first chief counsel, William Mitchell, from the Hoover administration, when Richardson was assistant attorney general and Mitchell was attorney general. Unlike Mitchell, Richardson was a staunch Republican who had never made any secret of his antipathy for Franklin Roosevelt, and he used his intimate knowledge of the Justice Department to protect corporate clients from the trust-busting and regulatory proclivities of the New Deal.

As the Pearl Harbor Committee's new chief counsel, Richardson announced his preference for tough, exhaustive questioning of witnesses. Committee Republicans would have been delighted to have had Richardson's approach applied to the well-known witnesses who had already testified, but they would not be quite their former selves in questioning those who remained. As the investigation of witnesses moved down from the highest level of the government, the Democrats became more critical, the Republicans less so. The Democrats were so pleased with Richardson's subsequent performance that President Truman made him chairman of the Loyalty Review Board a year later.

The new counsel's first two witnesses had been waiting impatiently ever since the attack to give their testimonies. The congressional hearings gave Admiral Kimmel and General Short their first opportunity to defend themselves publicly. From the beginning of the hearings, they were seen in the Senate caucus room every day. Short heard Marshall testify that on December 7, 1941, Short had been given sufficient warning and sufficient equipment to put up a much better fight than he had. Kimmel heard Stark agree to the same premise in Kimmel's case, though Stark was reluctant to blame anyone. Kimmel and Short, forced to retire from active service in 1942, had gone to work for companies thriving on government defense contracts. Kimmel had helped to design a floating drydock used in the war, but he and Short must have felt cheated each time they considered what their roles could have been had the disaster at Pearl Harbor not occurred.

Admiral Kimmel began his testimony on January 15, 1946. He was justifiably proud of his long career. He had gone around the world with Theodore Roosevelt's Great White Fleet in 1908, when fears that the Japanese would attack it had evaporated with the warm greeting they received in Tokyo. Kimmel had early impressed the naval hierarchy with his expertise in gunnery and his talent for strategy. He wanted to assure the committee that the favor of Franklin Roosevelt had not been responsible for his jump over senior officers to the command of the Pacific Fleet in 1941. Though he had been special aide to the assistant secretary of the navy briefly in 1915, he had not communicated with Roosevelt from 1918 to 1941. Kimmel had reached the top of his profession, thanks to his abilities. How then did he explain the devastating success of the Japanese attack?

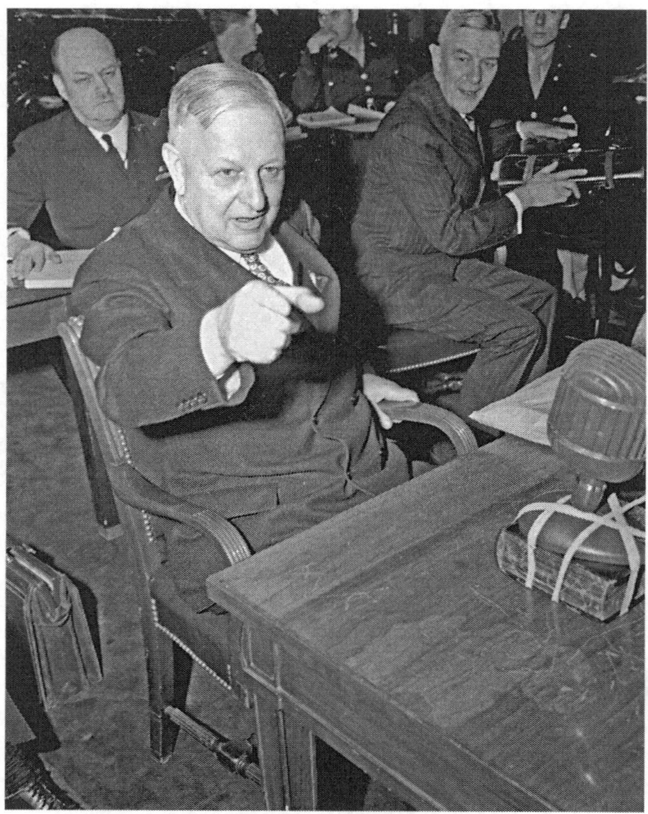

On January 15, 1946, Rear Admiral Husband E. Kimmel appeared before the Pearl Harbor Committee. (©Bettmann/CORBIS)

At that time Kimmel judged a Japanese attack on Pearl Harbor to be highly unlikely. In his opinion there was no possibility that a Japanese air attack could do much harm, because planes would need torpedoes, not just bombs, to damage battleships. So far as he knew, torpedoes dropped from planes would not run in the shallow waters of the harbor. (The Japanese had added special fins to their torpedoes, and practiced dropping them into shallow water until they ran straight to their targets. Then, too, of course, a freak bomb went down one of the *Arizona*'s stacks and eliminated that battleship.) In any event, the main reason he was surprised by the attack, Kimmel asserted, was Washington's failure to keep him informed; it was the failure of Stark, Knox, and Roosevelt to tell him what they knew. Naval intelligence in Washington had decrypted a September 1941 message from Tokyo to an agent in Hawaii; the agent was directed to send information on the exact location of warships in the harbor; Kimmel was not told about this message. Stark's war-warning message of November 27, 1941, Kimmel deemed misleading. It directed him to prepare for offensive warfare in case the Japanese attacked Thailand or the Philippines; it said nothing about an attack on Pearl Harbor. When asked if it was not Kimmel's responsibility to react to an unprecedented war warning by preparing for any eventuality, Kimmel said that he could not prepare to defend Pearl Harbor and prepare to engage in offensive action at the same time. He had been preoccupied with bolstering the outposts on Wake and Midway islands, more likely targets than Pearl Harbor; his two aircraft carriers had been away ferrying planes to those islands on December 7, 1941. Although he had never seen the term "war warning" used in a message before November 27, he did not consider it an extraordinary term—the United States and Japan had been on the verge of war for months.

Richardson was disturbed by the casual way Kimmel seemed to have tossed aside clues of impending attack that *did* come to his attention. A few days before the attack, Kimmel had learned from Washington that Japanese embassies there and in London were destroying codes; Kimmel did not react to that news, nor did he inform General Short. The day before the attack, one of Kimmel's intelligence officers informed him that after the recent change in call signs used by radio operators on Japanese ships, naval intelligence had lost track of many Japanese naval vessels, including six aircraft carriers. Kimmel had asked jokingly whether he was expected to believe that the carriers were coming around Diamond Head. Not only did Richardson seem to doubt that Kimmel would have been any more perceptive about clues that Washington officials failed to send him, but the new counsel also had doubts about the importance of the most dramatic of such clues, the one o'clock delivery message of December 7. Had Stark or Marshall notified either Kimmel or Short, would two or three hours warning have made any difference? Kimmel was sure that such a warning would have helped Short, but his own case was another question. He had already testified that his ships were arranged in the harbor to facilitate anti-aircraft fire; all guns, he said, had opened fire within seven minutes of the beginning of the attack, so only minutes would have been saved by having them all manned beforehand. Kimmel admitted that the most he could have done with a few hours' warning was get some of the ships out of the harbor. What is more, he said that he probably would not have bothered to send out the battleships. In addition to his skepticism about their vulnerability to air attack in the harbor, he believed they would be relatively useless on such an occasion. "As a matter of fact," Kimmel explained, "one of my problems all the time there, against a fast raiding force, if any should come, was the fact that my battleships would have been of very little use to me. They couldn't go fast enough, and the only ones that were of use were the ones that could get out and do something to the enemy.

Without criticizing Short, Kimmel repeatedly declared that the defense of Pearl Harbor was the army's responsibility. While the navy got ready to do battle at sea, the army was expected to provide protection for them. To clarify the army's role and his own, General Short succeeded Kimmel at the witness table. Short's defense closely resembled Kimmel's, but the general was less shrill, less apt to protest too much, less inclined to a conspiratorial view of events. Short did insist that, if he had known everything known in Washington, he would have gone on full alert, rather than on partial alert for sabotage. Short had a quality of quiet substance, not unlike Marshall; coincidentally, they had been two of the army's most effective teachers. Both instructors at Fort Leavenworth, Kansas, and Fort Benning, Georgia, they counted themselves among the small group of army officers who had risen to high positions without being alumni of West Point. Marshall was less extraordinary than Short in this regard, because Marshall had graduated from the Virginia Military Institute. Short, on the other hand, was a Phi Beta Kappa liberal arts graduate of the University of Illinois. By the end of World War I, Short had become an expert on the use of machine guns; he had even written a book on the subject.

When General Marshall sent General Short to command the Hawaiian department in February 1941, the chief of staff emphasized the importance of establishing a good relationship with Admiral Kimmel. The Pearl Harbor Committee was especially interested to know how well Short and Kimmel had gotten along. They had played golf together (they even had a golf date for the morning of December 7), but the warmth of their social relationship did not produce adequate official communication. Their most important misunderstandings concerned reconnaissance.

The navy bore the principal responsibility for long-range sea and air patrols, and Short assumed that the patrols operated constantly. Short also knew that naval intelligence was keeping track of Japanese ships through their radio call signals. The army had a new radar system, and Kimmel assumed that it was functioning around the clock. Short did not know, however, that Kimmel was saving his planes (which were not numerous enough for full reconnaissance) for offensive operations; air patrols were irregular training missions rather than regular reconnaissance missions. Nor did Short know that naval intelligence had recently lost track of six Japanese aircraft carriers. Kimmel did not know that the army did not yet have sufficient spare parts and trained personnel to operate their radar screens more than a few hours a day. On the morning of December 7, 1941, there was no long-distance naval air patrol operating north of

Hawaii; the army radar system was turned on at 4 A.M. and off at 7 A.M. One radar station, however, was kept running an additional half hour by two privates who were working hard at learning their new jobs. The privates informed a lieutenant that numerous planes were approaching from the north; the lieutenant told them to forget it. None of them ever did. Nor did General Short.

Noting the misunderstandings about reconnaissance and Kimmel's mistaken belief that Short had put his command on full alert, Democrats on the Pearl Harbor Committee pressed Short for his opinion of command unity. "If you had one man in command," Senator Lucas asked, "where you could place all of the responsibility over the Hawaiian Islands and the fleet, would that eliminate what I am talking about here, eliminate the possibility of any confusion or conflicting interests in the future which might be responsible for a similar disaster?" Short agreed that command unity would be "decidedly helpful." Lucas then extended his argument to include unity of intelligence in Washington so that "there can't be any buck-passing when a serious thing happens." Short concurred. Neither Lucas nor Short, however, attempted to expound the extreme army reorganization position, which proposed a single chief of staff in Washington for all services.

Despite the admirable accomplishments of American intelligence in 1941, it became the object of increasing criticism from all members of the committee as the hearings drew to a close. This concern did not rest solely on their awareness of the need for a central intelligence agency. The committee was subject to the romantic attraction of things secret, such as cryptanalysis. This natural tendency was exacerbated by Republican interest in a radio intelligence adventure of dubious relevance and remarkable fascination, the pursuit of something called the "winds code execute."

On November 19, 1941, the Japanese government informed its Washington embassy that, in case international communications were cut, a coded message disguised as a weather forecast in a shortwave news broadcast would indicate when codes should be destroyed and the country with which Japan was breaking relations. If diplomatic relations were endangered while normal channels were still open, a similar coded warning would be included in a regular intelligence broadcast. American intelligence thought this code arrangement important enough to send MAGIC recipients a card inscribed with the basic code: "east wind rain" meant a rupture in Japanese-American relations; "north wind cloudy" meant a rupture in Japanese-Russian relations; "west wind clear" meant a rupture in Japanese-British relations. If American intelligence intercepted a broadcast that seemed to employ the winds code, that is, a winds code "execute," an intelligence officer could telephone the code phrase immediately to MAGIC recipients since they had the explanatory cards. The search for a winds code execute sharply increased the workload on American intelligence; all normal news broadcasts had to be examined with care. A winds code execute was intercepted on December 8 after the Pearl Harbor attack. Whether an execute was intercepted before Pearl Harbor was the question that absorbed the congressional committee. By December 4, however, the quest for a winds code execute had lost importance because American intelligence had intercepted other Japanese messages ordering code destruction at embassies in London, Washington, and elsewhere. Thenceforth the winds code was a distraction rather than a critical source of intelligence.

One intelligence officer, nevertheless, was convinced that a winds code execute had been received on December 4, 1941, and that all traces of its receipt had been removed as part of an attempt to frame Admiral Kimmel by destroying war signs that were received and not communicated to him. This testimony would have seemed insane had it not been for the importance of the witness and several suspicious changes in the testimony of a fellow officer. Captain Laurence F. Safford was a significant figure in the development of American cryptanalysis. He had established the navy's radio intelligence unit in 1924, and he was still running it in 1941. At the time of the Pearl Harbor attack, he was a commander.

According to his testimony before the congressional committee, on the morning of December 4, Safford received the Japanese text of a winds code execute on a scrap of teletype handed him by the principal translator, Lt. Commander Alwyn D. Kramer, who said, "This is it." Safford could not read Japanese, though he was familiar with the Japanese words used in the winds code; Kramer or someone else had already scribbled a translation on the teletype sheet; war with England and the United States, peace with Russia. Safford took the execute immediately to Admiral Leigh Noyes, chief of naval communications, who was supposed to telephone recipients of MAGIC. According to Safford, copies of the execute were filed by navy and army intelligence. Those copies could no longer be found, and Safford assumed they had been destroyed by unidentified officers involved in a conspiracy to clear Stark and frame Kimmel. Though Safford was nervous in the face of Chief Counsel Richardson's aggressive interrogation, the cryptanalyst stood his ground as he had throughout the various investigations of Pearl Harbor. His steadfastness required undeniable courage; his career could not profit and might suffer. As Richardson suggested, however, he had been overworked in the days before the attack. Perhaps fatigue could explain his story, but how did one explain the changing testimony of Alwyn Kramer?

Kramer, who had risen to the rank of captain by 1946, ought to have known better than anyone whether or not a winds code execute had been received. He was the navy's leading Japanese translator, in charge of translating and distributing MAGIC for the navy. During the various Pearl Harbor investigations, Kramer had proceeded from agreement with Safford about the validity of a pre-attack winds code execute to agreement with Admiral Noyes that it had been a false claim. Just before the congressional hearings opened in November 1945, Congressmen Gearhart and Keefe had studied Kramer's previous testimony. Their suspicions about his change in testimony mushroomed when they discovered that he was currently in Bethesda Naval Hospital. After visiting him there, the two Republican congressmen declared that he was undergoing psychiatric treatment necessitated by pressures exerted upon him to change his testimony. Kramer and the hospital issued denials; that he had changed his testimony was, however, clear.

When Kramer finally came before the congressional committee in February 1946, he attempted to reconcile his various testimonies. On December 3, 4, or 5, he had been shown teletype that the watch officer believed might contain a winds code execute. Kramer did not check to see whether it had appeared in a news broadcast as required; he assumed that the watch officer had. At the time he believed the intercept was a winds code execute indicating ruptured relations with Britain. But when he was asked about the intercept by a navy court of inquiry, he became confused and testified incorrectly that the execute had specified the United States. Now he believed that the supposed execute was a false alarm, because word had come from General MacArthur's headquarters in Japan that Japanese officials denied sending a winds execute before Pearl Harbor. Senator Ferguson, who had been somewhat less active in the hearings since General Marshall's testimony, rose to the occasion. He observed that the testimony of those Japanese officials was worthless because they also denied any knowledge of the winds code arrangement. The senator, quoting contradictory passages in Kramer's testimony during previous investigations, wondered why Kramer's recollection should have improved, contrary to the normal tendency to forget.

As the winds code execute remained lurking in the shadows gaining an undeserved importance, yet another more intriguing figure held sway over the committee. Try as they might, committee Republicans learned few particulars about Roosevelt's connection with Pearl Harbor except that the deceased president was generally responsible for all decisions made. A rare glimpse of Roosevelt was provided by Commander L. R. Schulz. On the evening of December 6, Schulz had been an assistant naval aide at the White House. Sometime after 9 P.M., Lt. Commander Kramer came to the White House with a locked briefcase, which Schulz took to the president's study, where he found Roosevelt and his adviser, Harry Hopkins. After reading the first thirteen parts of the intercepted Japanese fourteen-part message that announced the end of negotiations (the last part was not available until the next morning), Roosevelt said in substance, "This means war." Hopkins remarked that it was too bad the United States could not strike the first blow, to which Roosevelt replied, "No, we can't do that. We are a democracy and a peaceful people." Then, raising his voice, he added, "But we have a good record." When Schulz testified on February 15, 1946, he was the only surviving witness to the conversation, Hopkins having died two weeks earlier.

The only source who promised to provide the committee with more information about Roosevelt was former secretary of war Henry Stimson. The Army Pearl Harbor Board report had revealed that Stimson's testimony, which included quotations from his diary, had been the basis for their criticism of Secretary of State Hull. After retirement Stimson's health deteriorated rapidly, making it impossible for him to testify. The ill-informed were invariably startled to learn that Stimson had first served as secretary of war in 1911. As Hoover's secretary of state he had spoken out against Japan's conquest of Manchuria and had closed down the State Department's cryptanalytic unit with the epitaph that "gentlemen do not read each other's mail." He had forfeited the esteem of many fellow Republicans in 1940 by joining the Roosevelt administration, where his duties included presiding over a new and flourishing cryptanalytic operation, and where he was a leading advocate of intervention in Europe and Asia. On his own account and on account of what he knew about Roosevelt, Hull, and Marshall, committee Republicans wanted to question Stimson and read his diary. In March 1946 he agreed only to give the committee a written statement, a few excerpts from his diary, and answers to some of the questions composed by Senator Ferguson.

Though Stimson already had quoted most of the diary excerpts in testimony before the Army Pearl Harbor Board, they were the most valuable part of his contribution to the congressional committee. They revealed that Stimson argued with a sometimes reluctant Roosevelt for a tough policy in the Pacific. Roosevelt had been concerned about the willingness of Americans to assist Britain if Japanese expansion in Southeast Asia continued southward toward Malaya. On November 25,

1941, Roosevelt told his top advisers that the Japanese were notorious for making surprise attacks, and might make one as early as December 1. He was concerned about an attack on the Kra Isthmus in Thailand, just north of Malaya, and he wondered what should be done in the meantime. As Stimson recalled the discussion, the "question was how we should maneuver them into the position of firing the first shot without allowing too much danger to ourselves." Roosevelt and Stimson mulled this problem over for three days while reports came to them about Japanese convoys moving southward. Roosevelt decided to warn Japan against further expansion through a personal message to the emperor and a presidential speech before Congress. The message to the emperor had just been sent, and the message to Congress was still being drafted when the Japanese attacked Pearl Harbor. Extracts from Stimson's diary indicated that Roosevelt had been ready to take the country into an Asian war if Japan moved against the British in Malaya or Thailand.

It was Roosevelt's desire to help the British that most disturbed Republicans on the Pearl Harbor Committee. Their interest in the Atlantic Conference of August 1941 was driven by their suspicions that Roosevelt had a secret arrangement with Churchill. Late in the hearings, a navy captain testified that, as a naval attaché in Singapore just before the attack on Pearl Harbor, he had been informed by a British officer that the United States had made a firm commitment to give the British armed support in case of a Japanese attack on Thailand, the Dutch East Indies, or Malaya. Republicans on the committee wanted to learn more about Roosevelt's relationship with Churchill, and at one point Senator Ferguson even proposed that Churchill be called as a witness. The former prime minister, whose Conservative party had been voted out of power by the end of the war, was visiting the United States at the time. The Democrats dismissed Ferguson's proposal as a publicity stunt. Churchill had no comment.

During his visit to the United States, Churchill did comment memorably on a subject far removed from the Pearl Harbor attack. Early in March 1946 at Westminster College in Missouri, Churchill declared that a Communist "iron curtain" had descended across Europe. The menace of Japan and Germany was gone, but new menaces were on the march. As the weeks passed, anti-Japanese rhetoric in the press was replaced by expressions of concern about Russia, China, and, more importantly, about striking workers in the United States.

Long before its demise, the joint committee on the Pearl Harbor attack was out of date. It had lost most of its audience. By the time the main round of hearings ended in February, the few citizens who came to listen were usually officers sympathetic to Kimmel and Short. The hearings were reopened for a few days in April and May while the committee tried to pin down the exact whereabouts of General Marshall and Admiral Stark on the evening of December 6. More testimony was taken from Marshall, who was in Washington to report on his China mission, the early promise of bringing the Communists and Nationalists together already beginning to sour. At last on May 31, 1946, the Pearl Harbor Committee closed its records and turned its attention to writing reports.

Chairman Barkley wanted to avoid a straight party split on majority and minority reports, an action that would give credence to charges that the investigation was a Democratic whitewash. The Democrats' tactic of blaming the poor American performance at Pearl Harbor on the national defense system served them well. They could agree to a critical report so long as it did not attribute blame to specific individuals, at least not to individuals who had been high in the government hierarchy. The Democrats were willing to reduce the charges against Admiral Kimmel and General Short from dereliction of duty to mere "errors of judgment." The two Republican congressmen on the committee were interested in going along with the majority. Congressman Gearhart had harvested nothing from his criticisms of Hull's negotiations with the Japanese. They had been thrown back at him again and again, and he could ill afford a reputation for being pro-Japanese in Fresno, California, with the fall elections only a few months away. Gearhart decided that the majority report on Pearl Harbor was accurate enough for him to sign.

Congressman Keefe of Wisconsin also decided to go along with the Democrats, but he was not entirely comfortable with the majority conclusion that "the President, the Secretary of State, and high Government officials made every possible effort, without sacrificing our national honor and endangering our security, to avert war with Japan." At the same time, he had not gone along with Ferguson and Brewster, who had been unwilling to participate in committee deliberations about a report and had begun immediately to prepare a minority report. Keefe gained the most independent voice on the committee by signing the majority report and supplying appending reservations. He was disturbed by a gap evidenced between Roosevelt's diplomacy in 1941 and the American people's desire to remain at peace. "In the future," he wrote toward the end of his reservations, "the people and their Congress must know how close American diplomacy is moving to war so that they may check its advance if imprudent and support its position if sound."

Obtaining the signatures of Gearhart and Keefe for the majority report of July 20, 1946, Chairman Barkley won the political battle of Pearl Harbor. In the summer of 1946, however, that battle no longer had much importance. The Republicans won the fall elections on other issues, chiefly economic. No one on the committee lost his seat in Congress that fall, except Murphy, who resigned to become a judge. Apart from its strictly political role, the committee gathered an enormous quantity of data useful to historians, and it contributed to the climate of opinion in which the Department of Defense and the Central Intelligence Agency were born. No one could know whether adjustments within the system would compensate for a failure of imagination and deduction as massive as the one that blinded American officials before the Pearl Harbor attack. Partly because the Democrats were eager to prove that the Roosevelt administration had not provoked a Japanese attack as a means of uniting Americans behind a declaration of war, the majority report stressed the most astonishing revelation about Pearl Harbor: In a government expecting war with Japan at any moment, no one worried about a surprise attack on the Pacific Fleet. America's excellent intelligence-gathering apparatus provided few clues, and those few were buried in a mountain of less relevant information. "Reading other people's mail" had encouraged its readers to think they knew everything of importance about what other people were going to do. That smugness, that want of imagination, proved disastrous.

Much credit for the length and thoroughness of the congressional investigation must go to Senators Ferguson and Brewster, Republicans who did not let the Democrats finish the investigation by January and kept them at it until July, but even then minority standards of thoroughness were not satisfied. The Roosevelt papers, the Stimson and Grew diaries, and perhaps other important documents had not been perused; and the minority refused to draw any conclusions about diplomatic questions for want of evidence. What distinguished the minority report from the majority report was the minority's list of individuals who had failed to perform their duties. Minority criticism encompassed Kimmel and Short, but their names were at the bottom of a list that ascended through Stark and Marshall to Stimson and Roosevelt. Apart from the political motivation for the list, there was a theoretical justification worthy of consideration. "In our opinion," Ferguson and Brewster concluded, "the evidence before this Committee indicates that the tragedy at Pearl Harbor was primarily a failure of men and not of laws or powers to do the necessary things, and carry out the vested responsibilities."

Senator Ferguson assumed primary responsibility for preparing the minority report, while Senator Brewster traveled as a representative of the United States at the Philippines independence celebration, July 4, 1946. Brewster visited China on the way home, but he was not yet ready to publicly criticize General Marshall's conduct there. Later, in 1949 when Marshall had left China, had served as secretary of state, and at last apparently had retired, he did so. By then Nationalist rule was crumbling throughout China. On the floor of the Senate, Brewster and Ferguson asked each other leading questions. Was it not true that General Marshall's Chinese armistice of 1946 had enabled the Communists to take Manchuria? Had not the United States fought a war against Japan to maintain the open door policy in China? Did not the senator think that the Communists were much more dangerous than the Japanese? Senator William Knowland, Republican of California, interrupted to note that on November 26, 1941, Secretary of State Cordell Hull had handed the Japanese ambassador a proposal that called upon Japan to leave China in the hands of the Nationalist government, a proposal that had been answered by the attack on Pearl Harbor. "I think that is a very pertinent contribution," Brewster replied. The situation in China now was comparable with that before Pearl Harbor, Brewster agreed: "I point out, however, that the implication that therefore we would immediately go to war to assist China, is a step I have not yet been prepared to agree is wise, although, as the Senator from Michigan points out, it would be exactly as logical today as it was when Secretary Hull presented his note in November 1941." But, added Ferguson, there was much that might be done short of sending soldiers. In China, Brewster and Ferguson found a political issue more explosive than anything dredged out of Pearl Harbor.

DOCUMENTS

Senate Debate over Resolution to Establish Pearl Harbor Committee, September 6, 1945

Nearly four years after the United States' greatest military debacle, the December 7, 1941, attack on Pearl Harbor, Congress was now ready to try to unravel what various commissions and boards of inquiry had failed to explain satisfactorily following the attack: How could the military have been so unprepared? With World War II now over, Alben W. Barkley, the Democratic Senate majority leader from Kentucky, offered a resolution in September

1945 to establish a joint congressional committee to investigate the Pearl Harbor military disaster. From the various inquiries already undertaken and other information made available to them since December 1941, a number of Republican members of Congress were eager to begin an investigation that would pin much of the blame on the administration in Washington rather than on the commanders in the field. In moving to create the committee, Barkley was attempting to position the administration and its allies out front in the inquiry and to show that Democrats as well as Republicans sought the truth about Pearl Harbor. In November 1945, the hearings opened. They would be shot through with politics.

SENATE DEBATE OVER RESOLUTION TO ESTABLISH COMMITTEE SEPTEMBER 6, 1945

MR. BARKLEY. Mr. President, the Japanese attack upon Pearl Harbor occurred on December 7, 1941.

On December 18, President Roosevelt appointed by Executive order a board or commission to ascertain and report the facts relating to the attack made by Japanese armed forces upon the Territory of Hawaii on December 7, 1941.

This commission was composed of Justice Owen J. Roberts, as chairman, Admiral William H. Standley, Admiral J. M. Reeves, Gen. Frank H. McCoy, and Gen. Joseph T. McNarney.

The commission made its report to the President on January 29, 1942, and this report was immediately made public.

In June 1944, by joint resolution approved June 13, Congress in effect directed the Secretary of War and the Secretary of the Navy to designate appropriate boards or courts of inquiry "to ascertain and report the facts relating to the attack made by Japanese armed forces upon the Territory of Hawaii on December 7, 1941, and to make such recommendations as it may deem proper."

The board appointed on behalf of the War Department was composed of Lt. Gen. George Grunert, as president, Maj. Gen. Henry D. Russell, and Maj. Gen. Walter H. Frank.

This board made its report to the Secretary of War on October 20, 1944, and the report was released to the public on Wednesday, August 29, 1945. The report consists of more than 300 pages of typewritten matter detailing the circumstances of the Pearl Harbor attack, indulges in criticisms of certain military and other officials, and makes no recommendations to the Secretary of War.

The board appointed on behalf of the Navy consisted of Admiral Orin G. Murfin, as president, Admiral Edward C. Kalbfus, and Vice Admiral Adolphus Andrews.

This board finished its inquiry on October 19, 1944, then adjourned to await the action of the conning authority.

The report of the Navy board went into some detail concerning the circumstances of the Pearl Harbor attack, and recommended that no further proceedings be had in the matter.

This report was also made public by the President on August 29, 1945.

Since these reports were made public, I have spent a large portion of my time studying them, and also, in connection with them, I have reread the report of the Roberts commission.

The official report of the board appointed by the Secretary of War, I have here, and, as I have said, it consists of 304 pages of typewritten matter on what we call legal size paper, not letter size. The report of the board appointed by the Secretary of the Navy contains various divisions, all of which add up to something like 100 pages of typewritten matter.

Reading these reports and studying them, insofar as I could in the limited time at my disposal, required my attention not only during the daytime since the reports were made public on last Wednesday, but required practically all of two nights, in order that I might read not only the reports, but the statement or summary made by the Secretary of War based upon the report of the Army board and the statement made by the Secretary of the Navy based upon the report of the naval board of inquiry, as well as other documents pertaining thereto. I have not been away from the city of Washington during the entire adjournment since the first day of August, when the Senate adjourned.

Mr. President, I shall not at this time attempt to discuss these various reports in detail, but after studying them to the extent possible in the time at my disposal, I am convinced that a further searching inquiry should be made under the authority and by the direction of the Congress of the United States.

In forming this opinion, Mr. President, I cast no reflection upon the ability, the patriotism, the good faith, or the sincerity of the boards which have thus far investigated and reported upon the Pearl Harbor disaster, nor of any member of these various boards. They are all outstanding American citizens and officials, who have rendered signal service to their country over a long period of time in various capacities. That includes the members of the Roberts commission, the War Department board, and the Navy Department board, as well as all those officials who have commented upon these reports or are in any way involved in them.

But these reports, Mr. President, are confusing and conflicting when compared with one another, and to some extent contain contradictions and inconsistencies within themselves.

Under these circumstances, it is not strange that widespread confusion and suspicion prevail among the American people and among the Members of Congress.

In these several reports men in the armed services and in civilian positions of executive responsibility and authority are subjected to criticism, and the defenses are themselves inconsistent and contradictory. It would be easy now, if time allowed and if it were necessary, to point out these inconsistencies between the report made by the naval board and the report made by the Army board, and both of them as compared to the Roberts report. I do not deem it necessary to go into that at this time.

It is my belief, therefore, Mr. President, arrived at immediately upon the conclusion of my study of these reports, that under all the circumstances Congress itself should make its own thorough, impartial, and fearless inquiry into the facts and circumstances and conditions prevailing prior to and at the time of the Pearl Harbor attack, no matter how far back it may be necessary to go in order to appraise the situation which existed prior to and at the time of the attack.

This inquiry, Mr. President, should be of such dignity and authenticity as to convince the Congress and the country and the world that no effort has been made to shield any person who may have been directly or indirectly responsible for this disaster, or to condemn unfairly or unjustly any person who was in authority, military, naval, or civilian, at the time or prior thereto.

Ever since the day of Pearl Harbor there have been discussions of courts-martial in the Army and in the Navy. We have here extended from time to time the Statute of Limitations pertaining to courts-martial. The report of neither the naval nor the military board of inquiry recommends any further proceedings in these matters. It is my understanding that the law is that in the Army no man has a legal right to demand that he be court-martialed. Charges must be filed against an Army officer or an enlisted man setting out the offense which he is alleged to have committed. He has no right, as I understand the law, to go into the War Department and demand that he be court-martialed upon any accusation or any charge of misconduct on his part.

I understand that in the Navy any officer or man who is charged with an offense that would constitute a violation of the Articles of War or Navy Regulations has the right to demand or request—I am not certain that he has the right to demand, but has the right to request, and it may be to demand—that he be given a court-martial.

So that as it applies to any Army officer who may have been responsible prior to or at the time of this attack, as I understand, he has no right to demand that he be given a trial in order that he may be vindicated or that the facts may be brought out. Whether in the Navy formal request has been made by any naval officer for a court-martial I am not in position to say, though the newspapers have carried stories that such a request has been made.

But if it were possible or appropriate, Mr. President, to subject high-ranking military or naval officers to courts-martial, the trials might be conducted in secret, and would relate themselves principally, if not entirely, to the guilt or innocence of the person against whom the specific charges were leveled. I do not here feel called upon or competent to determine whether court-martial should be inaugurated in any case involving any officer of the Army or Navy or any person in the armed forces.

But I am convinced that the Congress and the country desire an open, public investigation which will produce the facts, and all the facts, so far as it is humanly possible to produce them.

Such an investigation should be conducted as a public duty and a public service.

It should be conducted without partisanship or favoritism toward any responsible official, military, naval, or civilian, high or low, living or dead.

It should be conducted in an atmosphere of judicial responsibility, and it ought to be so complete and so fair that no person could doubt the good faith of the report and the findings made in it, or those who make it.

It ought not to be conducted or undertaken for the purpose or with the sole view of vindicating or aspersing any man now in office, or who has been in office during the period involved.

It ought not to be undertaken or conducted for the purpose of enhancing or retarding the welfare of any political party, or any person now in office, or any person who desires or aspires to hold public office.

It should not be conducted for the purpose of attempting to bedaub the escutcheon of any innocent man, high or low, living or dead, with the infamy of imputed wrong.

It should not be conducted with the purpose of gratifying the misanthropic hatreds of any person toward any present or past public servant, high or low, living or dead.

It should not be conducted for the purpose of casting aspersions upon the names and records of men who have rendered outstanding service to their country and to the world; nor should it be conducted for the purpose of whitewashing any person who may have been guilty of wrongdoing in connection with the whole affair.

Such an investigation should look solely to the ascertainment of the cold, unvarnished, indisputable facts so far as they are obtainable, not only for the purpose of fixing responsibility, whether that responsibility be upon an individual or a group of individuals, or upon a system under which they operated or cooperated, or failed to do either. It should be conducted with a view of ascertaining whether, in view of what happened at Pearl Harbor and prior thereto, or even subsequent thereto, it might be useful to us in legislating in regard to the operations of our military and naval forces and the executive departments having control of them, or which are supposed to work with them.

In my opinion this investigation should be a joint effort of the two Houses of Congress. If the two Houses should undertake separately to investigate, going their separate ways, the result might be divergent reports made by the two Houses, which would contribute to further confusion in the minds of the public, as well as in the minds of Members of Congress. Whatever the findings may be, they will carry more weight and bear greater authority if both Houses of Congress jointly and concurrently conduct the investigation.

For these reasons, Mr. President, acting in my capacity as a Member of the Senate and in my capacity as majority leader of this body, I am submitting a concurrent resolution directing such an investigation by a joint committee of the two Houses, consisting of five Members from each House, no more than three of whom shall be members of the majority party, to be appointed by the respective Presiding Officers of the two Houses, with all the authority they will need; and, in order that there may be no unnecessary delay in making the investigation and the report to Congress, directing that such report be made not later than January 3, 1946.

It is now nearly 4 years since the disaster occurred at Pearl Harbor. During the war, for certain military reasons, it was deemed inexpedient to do what I am now proposing. I believe that the decision on the part of the Congress and the Government as a whole was a wise decision. But the war is now over, and there is no military reason of which I am cognizant which would make it advisable any longer to delay a complete revelation of all the facts and circumstances leading up to this disaster, and the events which occurred while it was in progress.

Mr. President, I am submitting this resolution with the full knowledge and approval of the President of the United States. After I had studied the reports and made up my own mind as to what my duty was, I called upon the President and discussed the matter with him, because obviously I would not want to take such a step without discussing it with him, or at least letting him know what I had in mind and what I thought about it. He not only approved, but urged that I be not dissuaded for any reason from my purpose to submit the resolution calling for this investigation.

Also, since the preparation of the resolution, I have discussed the matter with the Speaker of the House of Representatives, and I have his assurance that if and when the Senate acts upon the concurrent resolution, it will receive prompt consideration by the House.

Mr. President, I express the earnest hope, which the President shares, that the two Houses may promptly agree to the resolution; that the investigation may proceed forthwith, without further delay; and that the Congress and the country may expect a full and impartial report, without regard to the consequences, within the time limit designated in the resolution. I send the resolution to the desk and ask that it be read and appropriately referred.

MR. FERGUSON. Mr. President, will the Senator yield?

MR. BARKLEY. I yield.

MR. FERGUSON. I think it would be appropriate to ask that the concurrent resolution be immediately considered and agreed to.

MR. BARKLEY. That is what I had in mind. I should like to ask that that be done. Under the rule, a resolution providing for an investigation and calling for the expenditure of funds is supposed to be referred to a standing committee, reported back, and then referred to the Committee to Audit and Control the Contingent Expenses of the Senate. Personally I should like to obviate those necessities, and I suppose it could be done by unanimous consent. I make the parliamentary inquiry now as to whether, notwithstanding the rule, the Senate could, by unanimous consent, proceed to consider and agree to the concurrent resolution.

THE PRESIDENT PRO TEMPORE [KENNETH MCKELLAR]. It could be done by unanimous consent. . . .

MR. FERGUSON. Mr. President, I had prepared to offer a concurrent resolution nearly identical in terms to the concurrent resolution which is now before the Senate. I merely had in mind that probably seven Members from each House would be better because of the question of attendance, but I should like in the time of the Senator from Kentucky to say a few things now in relation to why I believe a resolution such as the one which has just been read should immediately be adopted.

MR. BARKLEY. Mr. President, if the Senator will permit me to do so, I should like to make a remark in regard to his attitude and situation. I appreciate his attitude and his cooperation. I did not know that he contemplated the introduction of a resolution until I saw mention of it in the newspapers last night. But in the meantime I had already prepared mine and, as I have said, I had conferred with the President and with others about it. So it was not prepared and offered in any way for the purpose of interfering with the introduction of any other resolution. But I felt that probably it should be offered and considered and, if possible, adopted immediately. So that the country will understand that the Senate, and, I am sure, the House of Representatives, feel that they owe a public duty to go into this whole matter; and I wish the Senator from Michigan and all other Senators to know that I deeply appreciate the cooperation which seems evident in regard to the matter.

MR. FERGUSON. Mr. President, I appreciate and I understand the situation. It is not a question as to who introduces or offers the resolution, but it is a matter of having the job done. I should like to make a few remarks at this time regarding why I believe such a resolution should be adopted.

At the very outset I want to make clear precisely what I think should be investigated. The question is why our Army and Navy were not able either to avoid or to cope with the initial attack launched by the Japanese at Pearl Harbor. Everybody—those who opposed the war and those who favored it—was shocked at the swift liquidation of our

Pacific naval strength; I am sure that everybody—men of every point of view—will agree that we ought to have the whole truth about this unfortunate event.

Source: Congressional Record, 79th Congress, 1st Session, 8338–45.

Excerpt from Testimony of Fleet Admiral William D. Leahy, November 21, 1945

William D. Leahy was a Navy man all his life. A graduate of the U.S. Naval Academy in 1887, he served in the Spanish-American War, the Boxer Rebellion in China, and World War I. By 1937 he had risen to chief of naval operations, serving for more than two years during a period marked by increasing tensions in the Far East and Europe. Following his retirement in August 1939, Leahy was appointed governor of Puerto Rico, and in late 1940 he became the U.S. ambassador to France. A little over a year before the attack on Pearl Harbor, Leahy was in Washington, where he lunched with President Franklin D. Roosevelt and Admiral James Richardson. At the time Richardson was commander in chief of the U.S. Pacific Fleet and had held that position when the fleet had been redeployed from its traditional base in San Pedro, California, to Pearl Harbor, Hawaii. Richardson had opposed that deployment, arguing that the burden of defending such a large perimeter was problematic. At the lunch with the president and Leahy, Richardson expressed deep concern that the fleet in Hawaii was not prepared for war. Leahy was shocked. After all, he told William Mitchell, counsel of the Pearl Harbor committee, "I had been telling the Congress and the people of this country for some time that the Navy was ready for war and I was distressed to find that it was not."

EXCERPT FROM TESTIMONY OF FLEET ADMIRAL WILLIAM D. LEAHY NOVEMBER 21, 1945

Mr. Mitchell. Were you present at the White House at a luncheon on or about October 8 of that year at which Admiral Richardson was present?

Admiral Leahy. I did have luncheon with the President on October 8, 1940, and Admiral Richardson was also present at the luncheon.

Mr. Mitchell. Will you state in your own way just what occurred at that luncheon?

Admiral Leahy. I was at that time in Washington on duty connected with the Government of Puerto Rico and the President asked me to have luncheon with him on October 8. I found after I arrived that Admiral Richardson was also to be at lunch.

Many matters were discussed at the luncheon, some in connection with my affairs in Puerto Rico and some with Admiral Richardson in regard to the condition of the fleet.

Perhaps it would be best for this inquiry for me to state as well as I can remember the discussion that took place between Admiral Richardson and the President in regard to the condition of the fleet. My memory in that matter is good, principally because I was exceedingly surprised to learn that the commander in chief of the fleet did not consider the fleet prepared for war and at that time I was apprehensive in regard to an early war situation in the Pacific, although I was very far from sources of information and I had no late information in regard to that matter.

I do not remember how the subject was brought up but Admiral Richardson told the President that the fleet in Honolulu was not ready for war for numerous reasons.

He said the ships did not have their war complements; that the facilities in Pearl Harbor were not sufficient to keep the ships in a top condition at all times; that he had not a sufficient number of fuel ships to make it possible for him to operate the fleet at any distance from the Hawaiian Islands; that the personnel of the fleet, the officers and the crews, did not know why they were in the Hawaiian Islands; that apparently nobody expected to be called upon for war duty; that the families of the men and officers were in the continental United States and they wanted to get home and see their families; that the recreation facilities and the means for taking care of his men when they were on shore in Honolulu were almost nonexistent, at least they were entirely insufficient and that he felt that if there was a prospect of calling upon the fleet for war service it could be done much more advantageously in a port on the Pacific Coast of the United States where he could clear his ships for action, get the additional things that would be needed and reinforce his peacetime crews.

I think that covers very well all of the conversation that went on between the President and Admiral Richardson at this luncheon which I attended with them in the President's office.

Mr. Mitchell. Did the President himself say anything about basing the fleet there that you heard?

Admiral Leahy. I do not remember that the President made any comment whatever as to why the fleet was in Pearl

Harbor or as to whether or not it might be required to remain there. He may have made a remark of that kind but I have no recollection of it.

MR. MITCHELL. Did you leave the White House with Admiral Richardson?

ADMIRAL LEAHY. We left the White House together and we rode to where we were going, he to the Navy Department and I to the Interior Department, either in a car which I had or in his car.

During this short ride I expressed to Admiral Richardson my surprise to find that the fleet was in the condition which he had stated to the President and I said that I hoped he would manage to correct as many of the deficiencies as possible without any delay because I had been telling the Congress and the people of this country for some time that the Navy was ready for war and I was distressed to find that it was not.

Source: U.S. Congress, Pearl Harbor Attack, Hearings Before the Joint Committee on the Investigation of the Pearl Harbor Attack, 79th Congress, 1st Session, Part 1, 342–43.

Excerpt from Testimony of General of the Armies George C. Marshall, December 6–13, 1945

For a week in mid-December 1945, the Pearl Harbor committee questioned General of the Armies George C. Marshall. It was Marshall's role in Washington at the time of the Pearl Harbor attack that Republicans were especially anxious to clarify. How much did Marshall know about a possible attack, and what measures did he take or refuse to take to combat it? Marshall began his testimony on December 6, 1945, one day shy of four years since the Pearl Harbor disaster. Committee counsel William Mitchell began the rounds of questioning that would last for several days, just before the planned departure of Marshall for China. From the relatively friendly exchanges between Marshall and Mitchell to the more pointed questioning by Republican senators, Marshall often gave elusive responses or had difficulty remembering certain facts or events. When asked when he first saw Japanese decoded messages indicating that an attack was imminent, Marshall was not quite sure. Mitchell then led the general through the events of December 6–7, 1941, trying to ascertain whether the base at Pearl Harbor could have been alerted to an imminent attack.

EXCERPT FROM TESTIMONY OF GENERAL OF THE ARMIES GEORGE C. MARSHALL DECEMBER 6–13, 1945

MR. MITCHELL. You attended the Atlantic Conference at Argentia [Newfoundland], did you not?

GENERAL MARSHALL. Yes, sir; I did.

MR. MITCHELL. What part did you take in that?

GENERAL MARSHALL. I was concerned with what amounted to a first getting-together, coming to know the British Chiefs of Staff. We had no agenda for our meeting.

We met and discussed general matters, largely regarding the matériel desired by the British, and then we broke up into groups, myself and Field Marshal Sir John Dill, the head man of the ground forces of the British Army.

There was no question of matériel between us because we had given them all of the matériel we could afford to dispense at that time.

I believe on the Navy side, and I am quite certain on the Air side, there was considerable discussion on matériel.

With Field Marshall Sir John Dill and myself, our conversations were almost entirely devoted to a general résumé of the war situation, what the hazards were, what the anticipations were, particularly as to the Middle East and the Mediterranean, and Singapore.

MR. MITCHELL. Did you at that meeting know of any commitment that the United States made at that meeting to engage the Nation in war if we were not attacked?

GENERAL MARSHALL. No, sir; I did not. I was not involved in the political discussions.

MR. MITCHELL. Did you learn anything at that meeting about this proposal to make the parallel protests to the Japanese by England and the United States?

GENERAL MARSHALL. My recollection as to that is that I knew nothing of that until a meeting of the liaison group of the State, War, and Navy Departments in Mr. Sumner Welles' office after my return from Argentia.

MR. MITCHELL. And what did you learn then about that, do you remember?

GENERAL MARSHALL. I was given either the information, general information with regard to, or heard read—I do not recall which—a message the President had sent.

MR. MITCHELL. After he had sent it?

GENERAL MARSHALL. After he had sent it. . . .

MR. MITCHELL. Now, General Marshall, with all these documents before us showing your contacts with Hawaii and your knowledge about the situation there and the question of defense against air attack, will you cast your mind back, if you can, to the latter part of November 1941 and give us the estimate you then had as to the capacity of the forces at Hawaii to resist an air attack, an air raid? I am not asking you now whether you expected one but what your estimate then was of the situation and the capacity with the matériel they had to resist such an attack successfully.

General Marshall. The Hawaiian garrison on the Army side was short of four-engined bombers, only having 12; it was short a few three-inch antiaircraft guns and it was short more seriously in lesser calibers of antiaircraft guns. It had been built up to a considerable extent in fighter aircraft.

It had a moderate radar set-up of the portable type then functioning. It had what I thought were ample troops to defend the beaches successfully against a landing attack.

The military forces on Hawaii were in numbers and in equipment more nearly up to the desired standards than any other installation in the Army. My own impression was that the garrison was sufficiently established and equipped and organized to prevent a landing and to successfully resist an air attack and to defend the naval base.

I was always of the opinion, as indicated particularly by my letter to General Short of February 7, I believe, that the principal problem there was to be prepared against an emergency of a surprise attack which might come at any time, presumably with the least possible advance notice. In that letter I stated, if you recall:

> My impression of the Hawaiian problem has been that if no serious harm is done us during the first six hours of known hostilities, thereafter the existing defenses would discourage an enemy against the hazard of an attack. The risk of sabotage and the risk involved in a surprise raid by Air and by submarine, constitute the real perils of the situation. Frankly, I do not see any landing threat in the Hawaiian Islands so long as we have air superiority.

Would you repeat your question again to me, please, to see if I got it straight?

Mr. Mitchell. Well, I was trying to draw out your judgment as of the latter part of November 1941 and the early part of December as to the capacity of the forces at Hawaii, assuming they used all they had to the best advantage to—

General Marshall. I think they had a sufficient amount of matériel at their disposal there to successfully resist an enemy effort in the form of either a raid or a more serious attack.

Mr. Mitchell. Well, these reports of Admiral Bloch and the Martin-Bellinger reports and all these other documents we have in evidence dealt very heavily with the question of reconnaissance. The general tenor of them was the conclusion that if you wanted a complete, sure defense against a carrier-borne air attack you should have a reconnaissance the evening before and catch the carriers at dusk before they started their night run, and the alternative, if that was not done, was to try to get the planes out and break up the attack after the carrier planes left the carriers the next morning, which was not so certain.

Now, the studies that were presented there that we have been offering and considering this morning indicate that a pretty large number of patrol planes would be needed for the long reconnaissance and then a very large number of bombing planes would be needed to go out and smash the carriers after they were discovered and I notice that in the recommendation of General Martin made in his study of the air situation in Hawaii under date of August 20, 1941, exhibit 13, which we referred to this morning, he made this recommendation [reading from Exhibit No. 13]:

> It is recommended that the War Department give immediate consideration to the allotment of 180 B–17D type airplanes or other four-engine bombers with equal or better performance and operating range and 36 long-range torpedo-carrying medium bombers to the Hawaiian Air Force for the performance of search and attack missions in an area bounded by a circle whose radius is 833 nautical miles and center is Oahu, as follows:
>
> 72 for daily search missions.
>
> 36 for attack missions (these airplanes will be in readiness daily, fully armed and loaded with bombs for a mission).
>
> 72 for maintenance and reserve from which 36 may be used to augment the attack force.
>
> 180 total B–17D's.
>
> 36 torpedo-carrying medium bombers of the B-26 or other suitable type.

Now, his report shows that he was considering a 360° reconnaissance, all around the circle and which was the extreme requirement for a perfect defense against any attack from any direction.

Now, there are other figures in his report as to reconnaissance over limited arcs.

Now, compared with what Martin recommended on August 20 for a complete security there against air attack we had a very slim equipment, did we not?

General Marshall. Well, I stated, if you recall, we had a serious shortage in four engine bombers. We only had 12.

Mr. Mitchell. As an aid to Navy PBY air reconnaissance, that was practically nothing, wasn't it, or almost nothing?

General Marshall. Little more than that, sir. Not only a small supplement to the Navy reconnaissance, but it left no striking force.

Mr. Mitchell. That is it. After you located them, you had not any bombers to sink the carriers?

GENERAL MARSHALL. No, sir.

MR. MITCHELL. It seems to be the fact, according to these figures, and your judgment is, isn't it, that as far as security by long-distance reconnaissance and bombing the carriers the night before the proposed air attack is concerned, the equipment was quite inadequate.

GENERAL MARSHALL. Was deficient.

MR. MITCHELL. What would be the result of that—that they would have to confine their long-distance reconnaissance to the limited sector that you stated, or what could they do under those circumstances?

GENERAL MARSHALL. The provision of General Martin there is for complete and perfect reconnaissance. That is all right. That certainly is to be done, if you can provide the planes. I might, incidentally, say even at the top of our production, we were never able to give Hawaii, in 1943 and 1944, what the commander of Hawaii wanted, any more than we were able to give any commander all he wanted. That was an unavoidable situation always, in a war of the character we were involved in. However, there were ways to improve the situation by increased vigilance, by the operation of the attack planes, the interceptor planes, in every way we could in that fashion.

There was also this to be considered, which we always had in mind, and that is the great hazard the enemy undertook in sending his people so far from home. A surprise is either a triumph or a catastrophe. If it proved to be a catastrophe, the entire Japanese campaign was ruined, and advance into Malaysia, and advance into the East Indies would have been out of the question.

Singapore would not have been captured, the Burma Road would not be cut off, and the attack on New Guinea probably would not have occurred. So you have an enemy hazarding a great risk in this stroke. Therefore you measure somewhat your means of defense against the hazard he is accepting in doing it.

I agree with General Martin that if the planes were available that was a very appropriate assignment. It was on the side of conservatism which is certainly a good side to take in the defense of a fortress such as Hawaii, and the fleet more than the fortress against air attack. Does that explain my point of view?

MR. MITCHELL. Yes. Your answer deals with two problems: One is the question whether you expected an attack and the other one, what position you were in to defeat it.

GENERAL MARSHALL. Yes, sir.

MR. MITCHELL. I was intending to confine my first question to this proposition: Assuming the attack is made, to what extent, under the circumstances, and with the material they had available, would you conclude that they had adequate means for either breaking up the attack at sea, or on the carriers, or else destroying it, mitigating it the next morning?

GENERAL MARSHALL. I think they had at least the means to so have broken up that attack that it could do limited harm. . . .

MR. MITCHELL. By that, you mean if everybody had been on the alert and the radar operating and reporting planes at distances of 130 to 150 miles, and every pilot was in the seat, the motor going, everybody on the alert, and the antiaircraft men with ammunition, with that amount of warning that you could get from that sort of reconnaissance, you could have mitigated the attack.

GENERAL MARSHALL. Roughly, sir. I would not say every pilot in his seat, but in a condition of alert.

MR. MITCHELL. Your idea is with the forces available, they could have broken up the Jap planes in the air to an extent?

GENERAL MARSHALL. It would have greatly lessened the damage done. . . .

MR. MITCHELL. Well, now, we come up to this question of the modus vivendi. You and Admiral Stark had been working for more time. Were you aware that on November 20 the Japs had made a proposal to the United States that involved practically our termination of aid to China and our opening up of the freezing regulations and furnishing the Japs with oil?

GENERAL MARSHALL. I have no definite recollection, but I am quite certain there was.

MR. MITCHELL. Did you have access to those diplomatic intercepts during that period, that is, the decoded Japanese messages to and from Tokyo and Washington?

GENERAL MARSHALL. Yes, sir. The majority of them went over my desk, those that were supposed to be critical.

MR. MITCHELL. Do you remember seeing any of those in which the Japs instructed their Ambassadors here to get an affirmative agreement first by the 25th of November and later at least by the 29th?

GENERAL MARSHALL. I remember that very well, sir.

MR. MITCHELL. Do you remember those messages which said, if they did not get it signed, sealed, and delivered at that date something automatically would happen?

GENERAL MARSHALL. Yes, sir; I remember that.

MR. MITCHELL. Well, then, when the modus vivendi came up—what date was it, do you remember? Around the 25th or 26th?

GENERAL MARSHALL. I think it was earlier than that. About the 21st, was it not?

MR. MITCHELL. The 21st?

GENERAL MARSHALL. Yes.

MR. MITCHELL. What part did you have in that discussion?

GENERAL MARSHALL. I was absent on that particular day on an inspection trip, as I recall, and I learned of the matter on my return from General Gerow. I believe there was a memorandum from him to me. He had attended the meeting with Admiral Stark and he had expressed a view in regard to the outcome.

MR. MITCHELL. That is right.

GENERAL MARSHALL. And he submitted the memorandum to me describing the conditions and giving me the data.

MR. MITCHELL. Did you agree with General Gerow's position?

GENERAL MARSHALL. Yes, sir.

MR. MITCHELL. Which he reported in that memo?

GENERAL MARSHALL. Yes, sir; particularly that portion where he states that he informed Admiral Stark verbally that he regretted the reference to Army Forces in the Navy comments on proposition A–1. He felt that no restrictions should be placed on the Army's preparations to make the Philippines secure.

The point was we had almost nothing there, we had everything to put there, and if we did not do anything we were helpless, and we continued helpless if the thing broke.

MR. MITCHELL. You learned that that proposal had been dropped?

GENERAL MARSHALL. Yes, sir; I learned that.

MR. MITCHELL. Did you learn at that time of the fact that Mr. Churchill had wired him about it and that it was sent back for the Chinese, and did you know about Chiang Kai-shek's protest in which he said the Chinese Army would collapse if anything like that occurred?

GENERAL MARSHALL. I have no recollection of seeing Mr. Churchill's message, but I have a very clear recollection of Mr. Hull describing the Generalissimo's reaction. Whether or not I read his message I do not know, but I know I was clearly aware of his very energetic opposition to the proposal.

MR. MITCHELL. In the light of what you just said and what you knew, were you reconciled to the Secretary's decision not to attempt the modus vivendi proposal?

GENERAL MARSHALL. I think I was, sir. I recall this, that we were very much disappointed that we could not get this through, because it looked like a very slender hope of delaying matters to give us more time, and as I also recall, and the records will show, we had movements on the ocean at that time that were very critical, Marines coming out of Shanghai, and hazard to some movement, a more serious one was a group, I think, of four vessels of fair speed that were moving to the north of Guam straight into the Philippines and a large convoy of slow vessels that was moving south toward Torres Strait.

MR. MITCHELL. Now did you know, in advance of its submission to the Japanese, the contents of Mr. Hull's statement to them of November 26, 1941?

GENERAL MARSHALL. No, sir; I did not.

MR. MITCHELL. Were you consulted about that?

GENERAL MARSHALL. I do not think I was, sir. . . .

MR. MITCHELL. General Marshall, we have here a transcript of proceedings before the Army Pearl Harbor Board, volume 35, as of Tuesday, September 26, 1944, and on page 4050 there is testimony given by Mr. Stimson about a statutory war council meeting in the Department.

Secretary Stimson said:

> General Marshall read a long letter from General MacArthur in the Philippines, telling us of the progress of the reorganization of the Philippine Army and the construction of airports throughout the Islands.

Then again—I think Mr. Stimson was reading from his own diary here.

Well, I started too soon. I meant to start with November 25, 1941. He read:

> At 9:30 Knox and I met in Hull's office for our meeting of three. Hull showed us the proposal for a three-months' truce which he was going to lay before the Japanese today or tomorrow. It adequately safeguarded all of our interests, I thought, as we read it, but I don't think there is any chance of the Japanese accepting it because it was so drastic.
>
> Then we had a long talk over the general situation there which I remember.
>
> Then he quotes from his diary:
>
> We were an hour and a half with Hull, and then I went back to the Department, and I got hold of Marshall. At 12 o'clock I went to the White House where we were until nearly half past one. He says:
>
> That's an hour and a half.
>
> Then the diary proceeds as follows:
>
> At the meeting were Hull, Knox, Marshall, Stark, and myself. There the President brought up the relations with the Japanese. He brought up the event that we were likely to be attacked perhaps as soon as—perhaps next Monday for the Japs are notorious for making an attack without warning, and the question was what we should do.
>
> We conferred on the general problem.
>
> The diary continues:

When I got back to the Department I found news from G–2 that a Japanese War had started. Five divisions had come down from Shantung and Shansi to Shanghai, and there they had embarked on ships, 30, 40, or 50 ships and have been sighted south of Formosa. I at once called up Hull and told him about it and sent copies to him and to the President, of the message.

Do you remember that conference?

GENERAL MARSHALL. I have no detailed recollection of the conversations back and forth, but I have a very distinct recollection of the situation that was developing at that particular moment in the China Sea.

MR. MITCHELL. Have you any recollection of this beyond the statement of President Roosevelt, have you any memory of that?

GENERAL MARSHALL. I don't remember, sir.

MR. MITCHELL. That was on the 25th.

Now, I call your attention to this message that was sent to General Short over your signature on November 27. Were you in the city on the 27th?

GENERAL MARSHALL. I was not, sir.

MR. MITCHELL. Where were you?

GENERAL MARSHALL. I was in North Carolina.

MR. MITCHELL. What was going on there?

GENERAL MARSHALL. General McNair was having a very large maneuver, I imagine about 300,000 troops, or thereabouts. It was a vital day, and I flew down on the afternoon of the 26th to see the operations on the 27th, and flew back late that evening, so that I appeared in the office on the early morning of the 28th.

MR. MITCHELL. Before you left on the 26th, had this proposal to send a warning message out to the overseas posts been discussed with you?

GENERAL MARSHALL. Yes, sir. My recollection of it, which is rather confirmed by the memorandum of General Gerow under date of the 27th, I believe that we had a considerable discussion on the joint board on the morning of the 26th, at which it was decided that an alert should be drafted and dispatched immediately.

General Gerow had the task of drafting the alert. Whether or not he had a draft copy with him at the time or whether he was to prepare it after he returned to the War Plans Division I do not recall. I left in the afternoon following this meeting of the joint board in the morning. Present at the meeting was Admiral Stark, myself, the Deputy Chief of Staff of the Army, General Bryden, General Gerow, and I believe at that time the officers of the Air Corps, and their opposites were present from the Navy.

MR. MITCHELL. The message was sent over your name then while you were away?

GENERAL MARSHALL. Yes, sir.

MR. MITCHELL. When did you see the draft after you returned?

GENERAL MARSHALL. I saw it, the actual message, as it was sent, I think, the moment I reached my desk on the morning of the 28th.

MR. MITCHELL. This memorandum referred to by General Gerow of November 27 is the one in which he states, "The Secretary of War sent for me about 9:30 A.M. November 27, 1941." That is the one you refer to, is it?

GENERAL MARSHALL. Yes, sir.

MR. MITCHELL. When you saw the message of the 27th to General Short after you returned from maneuvers, what was your reaction as to its contents and sufficiency?

GENERAL MARSHALL. I concurred in the message and the manner in which it was drawn.

MR. MITCHELL. Did you see at the same time the identical message sent to the Commander on the West coast?

GENERAL MARSHALL. I saw the message—

MR. MITCHELL. To all the commanders?

GENERAL MARSHALL. Pacific commanders.

MR. MITCHELL. Did you see General Short's response and the responses of the other commanders to the warning message that had been sent to them?

GENERAL MARSHALL. I assume I did. I find in looking at the copy I did not initial it. I assume I must have seen it.

MR. MITCHELL. Have you seen this photostat?

GENERAL MARSHALL. Well, I saw the actual—

MR. MITCHELL. The original of it?

GENERAL MARSHALL. The original of it.

MR. MITCHELL. The photostat showing the report of General MacArthur of November 28 and the report of General Short on November 28.

GENERAL MARSHALL. Yes, sir.

MR. MITCHELL. It is our exhibit 46.

You are not relying on your present recollection but on the existence of this document?

GENERAL MARSHALL. In what respect?

MR. MITCHELL. To know whether you received it or not?

GENERAL MARSHALL. Well, I know I received this because there is my own reference of that to the Secretary of War and my initials on the copy, and the two were clipped together.

Mr. Mitchell. You remember that they were both clipped together?

General Marshall. No; I don't remember the clipping together. When I checked back to find out about the thing I found them clipped together and noticed I had not initialed the under copy but I assumed that I saw it.

Mr. Mitchell. How did you happen to route it to the Secretary of War?

General Marshall. Because I thought it was very important that he should see this particular message. It had been my custom always when there was anything up that was out of the ordinary that he might miss I always initialed it for him and had it taken directly to his room.

Mr. Mitchell. The fact that he participated in your absence in the drafting of the message to which these were responses, did that have anything to do with your sending it to him?

General Marshall. It might have; I don't recall, sir.

Mr. Mitchell. What do you remember now about your appraisement of or reaction to General Short's message of the 28th?

General Marshall. I have not a clear-cut recollection at all because shortly after the attack—I presume about an hour and a half—I was in conversation with Colonel Bundy in regard to the measures we were then taking to reestablish ourselves on the west coast, to get the convoys straightened out, and see what other measures we had to take throughout the United States for security, and he mentioned this message, which he apparently had reexamined, and referred to the sabotage factor in it, and also referred to the implication he had gotten, from the liaison with the Navy which is included in the message.

He did that while he was standing at my desk just before his departure from my room, when we concluded the other part of the conversation, which was the virtual redeployment of all our military sources to meet the situation as it developed.

Mr. Mitchell. What was the date of that talk with Colonel Bundy?

General Marshall. I would say that was an hour and a half or an hour, thereabouts, after the news of the attack on Pearl Harbor.

Mr. Mitchell. On December 7?

General Marshall. Yes, sir.

Mr. Mitchell. Well then, at that time Colonel Bundy brought up with you the question of Short's report of November 28?

General Marshall. My recollection of it is that when we finished this business I had him in there for, he being the officer in immediate charge of all details relating to the Pacific, that was his subsection of the War Plans Division, or the section of the War Plans Division, he would be in charge, and so I was doing business with him direct as to what we were to do to reestablish the situation, and when we finished that, as I recall the incident he was leaving the room and stopped about halfway out of the room and made a reference to the message, which he evidently had looked back on it to see what was going on, and referred to this sabotage clause, and I have forgotten just what his reference to it was. I recall his reference to liaison with the Navy. He referred to that. They had gone ahead with the procedure.

Now, my difficulty in answering your question was it is very hard for me to associate myself with the statement about what came next because from that instant on I was completely involved in the most active period during the war, the next 6 weeks.

Mr. Mitchell. Well, I was referring more especially to your appraisement of or reactions to this message of Short's on November 28 when it was shown to you, or you saw it on the 28th?

General Marshall. Yes, sir.

Mr. Mitchell. Did you notice the brevity of it or the difference in contents—

General Marshall. I have no recollection regarding it at all.

Mr. Mitchell. (Continuing)—by comparison with any of the other reports that you received?

General Marshall. I have no recollection regarding it at all, other than the fact that I find the two messages together and that I signed the upper one. . . .

Mr. Mitchell. Now, when we closed last evening I had just asked you a question. I will repeat it now:

> Do you remember this diplomatic message from Tokyo to their Ambassadors here, what we call for short the 14 part message and the 1 p.m. message?
>
> Your answer was, "Yes, sir."
>
> Will you state in your own way just when you first knew about that and under what circumstances?
>
> And you got as far as saying: "I first was aware of this message when I reached the"—and then we adjourned.
>
> Will you give us now the answer?

General Marshall. When I reached the office on the morning of Sunday, December 7th.

On that particular morning I presumably had my breakfast at about eight, and following the routine that I had carried out on previous Sundays, I went riding at some time thereafter.

I think in one of the previous statements I made in this investigation of Pearl Harbor incidents that I said I probably rode at 8:30. Discussions with the orderlies and also evidence that I had seen of other individuals leads me purely by induction and not by definite memory to think that I must have ridden later; just what time I do not know; but between 8 o'clock and the time I went to the War Department I ate my breakfast, I probably looked at the Sunday papers and I went for a ride.

Now, as to the probable duration of such a ride, I can only say that there were very limited places to which one might ride unless you crossed from the Arlington side of the river up over Memorial Bridge and the park system on the Washington side, which I did not do but once, I think, in the previous 6 years. My rides took me almost invariably down to the site of the present Pentagon Building, which is the Government experimental farm.

On a few occasions I crossed the approaches to the Memorial Bridge, not the bridge itself, and rode along the Potomac about two-thirds of the way down to where the present National Airport is, but no farther. The average length of my rides was about, the time period of my rides is about 50 minutes because I rode at a pretty lively gait, at a trot and a canter and at a full run down on the experimental farm where the Pentagon now is and returned to the house, so I would say that the high probability is that the ride was an hour or less, generally or certainly not longer.

My recollection beyond that is that while I was taking a shower, either as I went into the shower or while I was actually taking a shower, word came to me that Colonel Bratton had something important and wished to come out to Fort Myer. I sent word that I was coming to the War Department, so I finished my shower, dressed and left for the War Department.

My average time of taking a shower and dressing would be about 10 minutes, possibly less. As to what time I arrived at the War Department is a matter of conjecture; I have no recollection.

On my arrival there Colonel Bratton handed me these intercepts which included the 14 sections of the Japanese message, and I started reading them through. You recall it is a rather lengthy document and of such a nature that there were portions of it that I read twice.

When I reached the end of the document the next sheet was the 1 o'clock message of December 7.

Mr. Mitchell. That is the message that directed the Ambassadors to deliver this thing at 1:00 p.m. Sunday to the American Government?

General Marshall. Yes, sir, that message. That, of course, was indicative to me, and all the others who came into the room, of some very definite action at 1:00 o'clock, because that 1:00 o'clock was Sunday and was in Washington and involved the Secretary of State, all of which were rather unusual put together.

I think that I immediately called Admiral Stark on the phone, and found he had seen the message, and I proposed a message to our various commanders in the Pacific region, the Philippines, Hawaii, the Caribbean, that is the Panama Canal, and the west coast, which included Alaska. Admiral Stark felt that we might confuse them, because we had given them an alert and now we were adding something more to it.

I hung up the phone, which was the White House phone, and in longhand wrote out the message. My recollection was that he called me back. I am told now that the White House telephone records show that I called him back. I had no recollection of reading the message to him. I thought, on the contrary, he called me just as I finished the message, saving the last sentence.

However, one way or the other, there was a call or conversation between Stark and myself, the effect of which was he wished me to add to the message specifically "Show this to your Naval officers," which I did in longhand.

I then directed Colonel Bratton to take it immediately to the message center and start it. There was a proposal then that we have it typed. The decision was there was no time for typing, and Colonel Bratton left with the message.

On his return I questioned him as to the length of time involved and I could not make out whether or not he was talking about the time of encoding as well as the time of dispatching and the time of receipt, so I sent him back accompanied by Colonel Bundy, the officer in charge of the immediate details of all Pacific affairs.

They came back and gave me the estimates of the time of deliveries in these various parts of the world. My recollection is that I sent at least Colonel Bundy back again, and I thought Colonel Bratton with him. I believe others state that there was no third trip. There were certainly two—my own recollection is there were three. However that may be, that was the procedure on the dispatching of the message.

Do you wish me to go ahead?

Mr. Mitchell. Yes.

General Marshall. The next information I had was the notification of the actual attack on Pearl Harbor. Of my own recollection I do not recall whether I was at the War Department or at the house. I am told on one side by the Secretary of the General Staff at that time, the Acting Secretary at that time, General Dean, that I had returned to the house. I am told, on the other hand by my orderly that I was at the War Department. I do not know where I was.

Anyway, shortly thereafter, if not immediately then, I was at the War Department, because it was a very quick drive, and on Sunday there was no traffic. It was a matter of about 7 minutes from my house to the Munitions building.

The information then came in fuller detail, and telephone communication was established and I talked to General Short's Chief of Staff, Colonel Phillips. You could hear the explosions at the time. He was endeavoring to tell me what was actually happening.

My questioning, as I recall, was with relation to a report that had come from somewhere—and there were many reports of course at that time, rumors and authentic, confusion—that a Japanese landing was being attempted, as I recall, below Barber Point, and my recollection is my inquiry of Colonel Phillips was to the facts in regard to that.

I talked to Colonel Phillips because, as I recall, at that time General Short had gone to his command post and therefore was not able to talk to me directly.

The procedure on the dispatch of the messages did not come to my attention in detail until I was before the Roberts Board. The fact that the one message had been sent by the Western Union to San Francisco on a direct line, relayed by the RCA and presumably teletyped, which was not done in Hawaii, I did not know about that.

Admiral Stark tells me, and I am quite certain he is right—I do not recall it but he is undoubtedly right—that he asked me at the time of our second conversation that morning, or he said that they had rapid means of communication and if I wished to use it, and I told him no. That must be a fact—I do not recall—that must be a fact.

That, I think, covers the main details.

Mr. Mitchell. Now do you remember your movements on the evening of December 6, as to where you were?

General Marshall. I can only account for them by sort of circumstantial evidence. The only definite thing I have is that I had no dinner engagement. I found our engagement book, or Mrs. Marshall's engagement book, and between the 1st of November and 7th of December I had one dinner engagement, that was the 2d of December.

Also they checked on the post movie. It was about our only recourse for relaxation, and I had never seen the picture. So I was not there.

We were not calling. We were leading a rather monastic life. There was also in that record the affairs of the day for her, which involved, I think, an old-clothes sale, I think, all day long, to raise money for one of these industries they had down there, so the probability is she was tired and we were home.

Mr. Mitchell. You are sure you were not at the White House that evening?

General Marshall. No, sir; not at all.

Mr. Mitchell. There is a statement in the Army Board report that the warning message that you got out on the morning of the 7th you telephoned to the Philippines. Is that your recollection?

General Marshall. No, sir; I talked to Colonel Phillips, as I explained here, after the attack was going on, because we could hear the explosions at the time.

Mr. Mitchell. You did not telephone any such message yourself?

General Marshall. I did not telephone anywhere.

Mr. Mitchell. After you drafted this warning message to the outposts that you were prepared to send as the result of having seen this 1 p.m. message, is it your recollection that you called Admiral Stark first before he called you? Originally, I mean.

General Marshall. I am quite certain of that. I called him first.

Mr. Mitchell. What did you say to him?

General Marshall. As nearly as I can recall, I asked him if he had seen the message. He stated that he had, and I proposed that we send a message apropos of this to the various commanders concerned, and he replied as I have outlined, he feared that that would tend to confuse them, that we had given them an alert and now we were putting something else into the picture.

I then went ahead and wrote the message, and I don't think I said to him in concluding that first conversation whether or not I was going to do it, but I did write it out immediately in longhand.

Mr. Mitchell. Then your recollection is he called you?

General Marshall. My recollection is he called me, but the records of the White House telephone exchange show I called him.

Mr. Mitchell. And what was the subject of the second conversation?

General Marshall. I had thought that he called me to say he wanted this shown to the naval officer. It would seem from the record at the White House that I called him and maybe read the message. In any event he did ask me, and I am specific about that, he did ask me to put into the message that it be shown to the naval officer.

Mr. Mitchell. Have you exhibit 58 before you?

General Marshall. No.

Mr. Mitchell. I will have to show it to you, General.

This is a record of telephone calls on December 7 by outside parties through using the White House exchange.

It says, and I will show it to you—the record says "11:40 A" which means "A.M.," I suppose.

General Marshall cld Ad'm Stark—O. K.

11:30 A—Gen. Marshall cld Ad'm Stark—O. K.

In that particular instance, according to the White House records, these hours are reversed. The 11:40 A is ahead of 11:30, which does not seem to be the practice, and we are not sure just what it means.

Will you look at it and see if it means anything to you? That is exactly what the record shows there, that the time 11:40 precedes the entry of the 11:30 message.

General Marshall. I would not know what the significance of that is.

Mr. Mitchell. You would not know anything about it?

General Marshall. No, sir. It does this, though. It gives the time one way or another of the completion of the message following the reading of the 14-point thing and the preparation of this other message.

Mr. Mitchell. Then at least you did read the message and were in the act of preparing a warning by 11:30 or 11:40?

General Marshall. Yes, sir; 11:40 would be quite evidently the completion of it, because I had it all written except the last sentence.

Mr. Mitchell. I will offer now, as Exhibit 61, a photostat which reads as follows: "December 7, 1941." It is typed.

> Memorandum for the Adjutant General
> (Through Secretary, General Staff)
>
> Subject: Far East Situation
>
> The Secretary of War directs that the following first priority secret radiogram be sent to the Commanding General, U. S. Army Forces in the Far East; Commanding General, Caribbean Defense Command; Commanding General, Hawaiian Department; Commanding General, Fourth Army;
>
> And the message is this:
>
> Japanese are presenting at one p.m. Eastern Standard time today what amounts to an ultimatum also they are under orders to destroy their Code machine immediately stop Just what significance the hour set may have we do not know but be on alert accordingly stop Inform naval authorities of this communication.
>
> —*Marshall*

It has the signature of General Gerow on it. Has the committee a copy?

The Chairman. Yes.

Mr. Mitchell. And the committee will note that underneath it is a record:

> Radios as follows dispatched 11:52 a.m., 12-7-41 by Code Room WDMC.

General Marshall. War Department Message Center.

Mr. Mitchell. And another was dispatched 12:05 to Manila; another one to Hawaii at 12:17; the one to the Caribbean Command is blurred. It looks like 12:00 o'clock, and the one to the Fourth Army at San Francisco at 12:11.

The Vice Chairman. That is Exhibit 61?

Mr. Mitchell. Exhibit 61.

(The document referred to was marked "Exhibit No. 61.")

Mr. Mitchell. Did you give any instructions to the Communications Center as to the means of transmitting this message to Hawaii?

General Marshall. No, sir. Their business was to dispatch it in the most efficient and rapid manner possible. This photostat of this document of General Gerow's should be read in the light that it was written after the event. The message was sent from a longhand pencil copy on an ordinary ruled sheet of paper—which, incidentally, was before the Roberts board.

Mr. Mitchell. The original message was in your handwriting and you gave directions that it should not be typed?

General Marshall. Yes, sir. It was carried by hand by Colonel Bratton and checked on the second trip by Colonel Bratton and Colonel Bundy, and then I thought there also should be a third trip by Colonel Bundy, but there was a difference of opinion on that.

Mr. Mitchell. In the message center it was necessary to take your handwritten draft and encode it?

General Marshall. Yes, sir; encode it first.

Mr. Mitchell. And then put it on the way?

General Marshall. Yes, sir.

Mr. Mitchell. Was there any report made to you at that time that there was any difficulty in reaching Hawaii on the telephone?

General Marshall. No, sir.

Mr. Mitchell. I mean before the attack?

General Marshall. No, sir. I did not ask the question.

Mr. Mitchell. You didn't ask the question as to means of transportation?

General Marshall. I didn't ask the question about the telephone.

Mr. Mitchell. What did they estimate to you would be the required time for delivery to Fort Shafter of the Hawaiian message?

General Marshall. I don't recollect, sir. I have a faint recollection of being told that it would take 8 minutes to get it through, but I think you will have positive testimony on that.

Mr. Mitchell. You sent the message to all Commands without any special selection of Pearl Harbor?

General Marshall. Exactly. I sent each commander involved in the Pacific situation. The Western Defense Command, which is the Fourth Army, the Caribbean Command, the Philippine Command, and the Hawaiian Command.

MR. MITCHELL. Did you make any inquiry of the communications people or your subordinates as to the prospective time of delivery of that message to Hawaii?

GENERAL MARSHALL. That was the reason I sent Colonel Bratton back with Colonel Bundy, to give me a clear picture of what the time involved was, because when I first questioned Colonel Bundy I couldn't tell whether he was including the time necessary to encipher the message, and so I sent him back to determine that for me.

MR. MITCHELL. Well, what report did he make to you, do you remember, about that?

GENERAL MARSHALL. I do not recall the minutes. I think it is shown in one of the documents. I couldn't tell you offhand. I think they are prepared to give you that, sir.

MR. MITCHELL. Did anybody in your office, when you were reading the 14-part message and the 1 P.M. supplement, on the morning of the 7th, make any mention of the fact that 1 P.M. in Washington would be about 7:30 A.M. in Honolulu?

GENERAL MARSHALL. There was no mention of the 1 P.M. message until I came across it at the end of the pile. I am quite clear about that, because I was very much taken back by the time I had spent on the preceding lengthy message in trying to understand its significance, and then arriving at this, to me, very critical one of 1 P.M.

MR. MITCHELL. You thought you ought to have been shown the 1 p.m. part first?

GENERAL MARSHALL. I don't know about that. I am just talking about my own reaction.

MR. MITCHELL. Well, was any discussion had when you saw the 1 P.M. message? Any discussion about the corresponding time of day in Honolulu or the Philippines?

GENERAL MARSHALL. I don't recall that. I don't recall that at all. The whole thing was, it was a significant message, and what would we tell these commanders, and I went ahead and wrote it out myself. . . .

MR. MITCHELL. You stated in your testimony before the Army Board, I think you used this phrase. I think "we" did not expect the attack at Pearl Harbor. When you said "we," were you speaking generally of the high officers in the War Department?

GENERAL MARSHALL. That was a rather careless expression. I will make that "I."

MR. MITCHELL. And when you say the enemy would judge whether he would attack on whether he knew you were going to be ready, did you, in that conclusion take into account the fact that the Japs knew we weren't alert?

GENERAL MARSHALL. I didn't take that into consideration because I thought we were on the alert.

MR. MITCHELL. Your estimate that you didn't expect it was based on the theory that what you had was ready and if ready, the Japs probably knew it was ready?

GENERAL MARSHALL. It is a little bit like, in my mind, the present discussion as to the postwar organization of our Army. If we are ready, the other man will not involve us.

Source: U.S. Congress, Pearl Harbor Attack, Hearings Before the Joint Committee on the Investigation of the Pearl Harbor Attack, 79th Congress, 1st Session, Part 3, 1051–52, 1081–84, 1091–92, 1095–98, 1107–13, 1118–19, 1132–39, 1212–13, 1417–18, 1421–22, 1528–31.

Excerpt from Testimony of Admiral Harold R. Stark, December 31, 1945–January 3, 1946

A veteran naval officer who led antisubmarine and escort duties in the Mediterranean Sea during World War I, Harold Stark won three Distinguished Service Medals in his career. In 1939 President Franklin D. Roosevelt promoted Stark to admiral and named him chief of naval operations. With the threat of war looming, Stark successfully sought the funding necessary to strengthen the navy to help prepare strategy for facing both Germany and Japan. Yet, it would be Stark's actions immediately prior to the Pearl Harbor attack that would blemish his career. Like Marshall, Stark was privy to the decoded Japanese messages. Indeed, he had kept Admiral Husband E. Kimmel well informed about the content of the messages and the current thinking in Washington about a possible attack. But Stark's hesitation on December 7, 1941, in sending the message that suggested an attack in the near future made him one of the scapegoats for the navy's unpreparedness. Also, like General George C. Marshall and just about every administration official in Washington, Stark believed that the Japanese would attack the Philippines or Thailand, not Hawaii.

EXCERPT FROM TESTIMONY OF ADMIRAL HAROLD R. STARK, DECEMBER 31, 1945–JANUARY 3, 1946

MR. MITCHELL. I will . . . call your attention to what we have been calling here the 14-part and 1 P.M. message. It appears of record here that on December 6 there was intercepted and decoded here in Washington a pilot message sent from the

Jap Government to their ambassadors here stating there would come shortly a longer message containing their answer to the American Government's position, and then it appears on the evening and before midnight December 6–7, the first 13 parts of that message were translated, decoded, and made available to certain officials here, and on the next morning, the 14th part and 1 p.m. part, which directed the presentation of the message to our Secretary of State at 1 p.m. on the 7th, were translated and disseminated. When did any part of that message first come to your attention?

ADMIRAL STARK. It first came to my attention Sunday forenoon when I came to the office in the Navy Department. I had no information of it prior to that time.

MR. MITCHELL. Nobody endeavored to reach you, that you know of, Saturday evening, about the early 13 parts?

ADMIRAL STARK. Nobody reached me.

MR. MITCHELL. Where were you, if you know?

ADMIRAL STARK. I don't know, sir. I thought I was home but if they had tried to reach me I should have been there. Also if I were not there word would have been left where I was. Also the duty officer was generally informed of my whereabouts. Unfortunately, Mrs. Stark has destroyed her date calendar of that time. I have tried to run down two or three blinds. There was a party given in the Navy yard that night for Governor Edison, ex-Secretary of the Navy. I knew that I had been there on a party with him. I wrote the Commandant at that time. He said that he had completely forgotten they had given the party and his wife said she was sure I wasn't there, in any case. So that blind went by the board.

MR. MITCHELL. The record shows that Secretary Knox had it that night; your Chief of Naval Intelligence had it that night.

ADMIRAL STARK. That is right.

MR. MITCHELL. And Knox called up and made an appointment with Stimson and Hull the next morning. You didn't hear anything about that?

ADMIRAL STARK. No, sir, not a word.

MR. MITCHELL. In the afternoon of the Saturday before, during office hours, this pilot message came in, which was the preliminary message from the Japs to their ambassadors stating that they were going to send this message along.

Did you see that?

ADMIRAL STARK. I have no recollection of having seen or heard of the pilot message. The first information that I had on the subject was Sunday forenoon.

MR. MITCHELL. I noticed in your statement about this incident you make no mention of the hour you got in the office or the hour you first saw this 13- or 14-part message Sunday morning. Have you no recollection about the hour?

ADMIRAL STARK. I can only guess on that and I did guess last summer. I usually got down to the office Sunday mornings around 10:30 and I just assumed that I had gotten there somewhere around 10:30 or 11 o'clock. I was lazy on Sunday mornings unless there was some special reason for getting up early. I usually took a walk around the grounds and greenhouse at the Chief of Naval Operations' quarters and didn't hurry about getting down and my usual time, as I recall, was about 10:30 or 11. What time it was on this particular Sunday morning I couldn't go beyond that.

MR. MITCHELL. I believe there are some officials in your Department, who have not yet been called as witnesses, whose job it was to deliver and consider messages of that type, who think you got there at 9 o'clock and saw a part of this message as early as that and the balance of it, the fourteenth part, at least by 1:30.

Would that be contrary to the fact if they should so testify?

ADMIRAL STARK. They have told me the same thing and they are also estimating. You will have those people before you. And as regarding the 1 o'clock message I think you will have, probably, from one of the witnesses who kept some track of his time, the fact that he got to my office, and he can testify, about 10:40, with the 1 o'clock message, but I have no recollection.

MR. MITCHELL. The records show, the White House phone records show that General Marshall called you at 11:30 about it, he had written out a message to Pearl Harbor, to the Army commander there about this 1 p.m. business.

Do you recall that?

ADMIRAL STARK. That is the one thing on that morning which stands out very clearly in my memory, was General Marshall's call to me about that message. At that time I was talking over that message with Admiral Schuirmann, as to what it might mean. He pointed out, he said, we don't know what the significance of it is, but it might mean something, and he said he thought it would be a good thing to inform the people in the Pacific.

My first reaction was that we had sent so much out that—and as there was no deduction from the message, as to what it meant, at least we had made none at that time, that it would be just as well not to send it. A few days previous, when we had a discussion whether to send out anything more, the question came up, be careful not to send too much, it might create the story of "wolf."

That was my first conversation with General Marshall.

I put the phone up and, as I recall it, I put it up and stopped, and in a matter of seconds, or certainly only a few minutes, and thought, well, it can't do any harm, there may be something unusual about it. General Marshall states he doesn't know what the significance is, but there might be something, and I turned back and picked up the phone, he had not yet sent the message, and I said, perhaps you are right, I think you had better go ahead and I would like to have you make sure that it goes to the naval opposites where this message was going, which was throughout the commands in the broad Pacific.

I also asked General Marshall, knowing that the time was rather short, whether or not he would get it out quickly. I told him our own system under pressure was very fast. And he said, no, that he was sure he could get it out quickly also. And with that I did nothing more.

MR. MITCHELL. What was your system?

ADMIRAL STARK. Radio.

MR. MITCHELL. You had a powerful sending apparatus, did you?

ADMIRAL STARK. Yes, sir; very.

MR. MITCHELL. Well, if we are right in our assumptions as to the fact that you had this 1 p.m. message in your hands an hour before Marshall did, that is at least 10:30, you are not willing to concede that, are you?

ADMIRAL STARK. My remembrance, as I said, was 10:40. When you say "at least 10:30," I think you will find testimony to that effect by a witness, and if he states that, and I think he probably has good supporting data, I accept it, that it was delivered to my office and then after that was given, by whomever he gave it, to me.

MR. MITCHELL. Is it fair to say that if Marshall hadn't spotted that message and started to send word out to Pearl Harbor that you probably wouldn't have sent anything?

ADMIRAL STARK. I don't know that I would. I think that might be a fair deduction.

MR. MITCHELL. Now didn't you have somebody more than Schuirmann in there discussing this 1 P.M. business?

ADMIRAL STARK. Well, sir—

MR. MITCHELL. Didn't Commander Kramer—

MR. GESELL. I believe one witness says there were 15 officers in there.

MR. MURPHY. Admiral Schuirmann.

ADMIRAL STARK. Admiral Schuirmann. I said when Marshall called I was talking it over with Schuirmann.

MR. MITCHELL. After you got the 1 P.M. message wasn't there some discussion in your office then about it?

ADMIRAL STARK. There may have been. I don't recall it.

MR. MITCHELL. Commander Kramer—

ADMIRAL STARK. I can give you what I know by hearsay.

MR. MITCHELL. I don't want that. I just want whether any of these officers spoke to you about it.

ADMIRAL STARK. I don't recollect it that morning. I recollect it since.

MR. MITCHELL. There were some younger officers that spotted the 1 p.m. business and made some suggestion about it being daylight at Honolulu?

ADMIRAL STARK. I am certain nobody mentioned Honolulu with reference to a daylight attack. I am positive of that.

MR. MITCHELL. Well, this was what we lawyers call a last clear chance. These people were not ready at Pearl Harbor; the Jap Fleet was piling in; here was a chance to get a message to them that might have saved them; it reached your hands, we will say, at 10:40; the chance wasn't taken.

Does that sum up the situation as you see it?

ADMIRAL STARK. Well, I gather from your—

MR. MITCHELL. You might have intervened and done something.

ADMIRAL STARK. I gather from your question you are now pointing that dispatch directly at Pearl Harbor. It didn't mention Pearl Harbor. It gave no inference with regard to Pearl Harbor any more than it did the Philippines or the Netherlands East Indies.

MR. MITCHELL. Are you right about that? 1 P.M. here was dawn at Pearl Harbor and 1 P.M. here was in the middle of the night in the Philippines.

ADMIRAL STARK. I would say that dawn at Pearl Harbor was about an hour—that can be checked by the Naval Observatory—before the time specified in the message; and as regards midnight in the Philippines, as to whether that would mean anything, that could have been an attack at night. Taranto was an attack just a few minutes after midnight.

MR. MITCHELL. Why not send a message to all three of those places saying something is liable to happen at 1 P.M. Washington time?

ADMIRAL STARK. In the light of hindsight, if we had read into that message that it meant an attack at that hour, and had sent it out, of course, it would have been helpful. I wish such an inference could have been drawn.

MR. MITCHELL. The fixing of an exact hour to deliver the diplomatic message and rout out the Secretary of State on a Sunday at 1 p.m., wasn't it obvious that there was some special significance, having in mind the history of the Japs striking first and declaring war afterwards?

ADMIRAL STARK. If so, Mr. Mitchell, I would like to say that so far as I know the Secretary of War didn't read that inference into it, the Secretary of State didn't read that inference into it, the Secretary of the Navy didn't read that inference into it, General Marshall and his staff didn't read that inference into it, and nobody mentioned it to me.

MR. MITCHELL. Are you quite right about General Marshall? The first thing he did was to spot that message and he wouldn't even allow his answer to be typed, he put it into longhand and told them to encode it without typing it.

ADMIRAL STARK. I would like to read this:

> Just what significance the hour set may have been we do not know.

MR. MITCHELL. Of course, you didn't know.

ADMIRAL STARK. (reading):

> But be on the alert accordingly.

MR. MITCHELL. That means, to you, being alerted at 1 P.M. Washington time, doesn't it?

ADMIRAL STARK. Yes, sir; but I would like to invite attention also to the fact that we had thought that they were on the alert. I am not attempting to argue the fact, sir, that I don't think it would have been a good thing to have gotten this message out, drawn the inference and sent it. I wish we could have. We didn't.

MR. MITCHELL. You didn't know they weren't on the alert?

ADMIRAL STARK. No, sir. On the contrary, we felt they were.

MR. MITCHELL. You don't know what time Stimson and Hull got this 1 P.M. message, do you, or saw it?

ADMIRAL STARK. I think, if I may say so, Kramer can tell you that. And if Kramer says that message was delivered to my office at 10:40, I accept it.

MR. MITCHELL. It has been suggested to me that Kramer may have told you about the text of that message before delivery of the document. Do you recall that?

ADMIRAL STARK. No, sir. . . .

THE CHAIRMAN. In view of your message to Admiral Kimmel of the 24th and the 27th, and General Marshall's dispatch to General Short of the same date, that is, the 27th, which he instructed him to convey to Admiral Kimmel, what was the duty of the naval commander there during the days following the receipt of that message on the 27th?

ADMIRAL STARK. Well, my thought was, we assumed that there would be a conference between the senior Army and Navy commanders there, that a conference would occur, and that they would implement their plans against surprise, and in the protection of the Island of Oahu, particularly of the Fleet, Pearl Harbor, for what ships were kept there, and the alerting of ships at sea, with the fact that Japan was expected to attack and the officers in charge of the ships at sea, of course, would be very much on the alert against surprise anywhere.

THE CHAIRMAN. Did that alertness include day and night?

ADMIRAL STARK. Yes, sir.

THE CHAIRMAN. In view of these instructions contained in the Army and Navy dispatches to Pearl Harbor, was it or was it not in compliance with or in violation of them not to have any reconnaissance, say on the 6th day of December, the day before the attack. The evidence shows there was no reconnaissance of any kind on that day. I am speaking now of the 6th.

ADMIRAL STARK. Yes, sir. We had assumed when we sent out dispatch that reconnaissance would be started and kept up.

THE CHAIRMAN. That is from the 27th or the 24th?

ADMIRAL STARK. Well, I would say from the 27th in any case.

THE CHAIRMAN. 27th.

ADMIRAL STARK. Yes, sir.

THE CHAIRMAN. Do you know whether it was kept up from the 27th until the attack?

ADMIRAL STARK. I don't know just what they did at that time. Marshall's dispatch particularly directed reconnaissance. Ours directed the deployment. And just what action was taken there I don't know.

THE CHAIRMAN. Deployment means the arrangements of whatever forces there are, the grouping or separation or movement in such a way as to facilitate the greatest possible defense in the event of an attack?

ADMIRAL STARK. That is correct, yes, sir.

THE CHAIRMAN. Well, you didn't answer my question as to whether if there was no reconnaissance of any kind on the 6th that that would be considered as being in violation of the orders or in compliance.

ADMIRAL STARK. I would say it would be not carrying them out.

THE CHAIRMAN. That is a very diplomatic way to answer my question. It was not in compliance with the instructions.

ADMIRAL STARK. Yes, sir.

THE CHAIRMAN. It was not?

ADMIRAL STARK. It was not.

THE CHAIRMAN. In other words, they did not obey the instructions that were received?

ADMIRAL STARK. That is my understanding, yes, sir.

THE CHAIRMAN. That is, if they had no reconnaissance at all on that day, that was in disobedience?

ADMIRAL STARK. That is correct, yes, sir.

THE CHAIRMAN. Now, do you agree with—first, did you hear Admiral Turner's testimony in which he said that if they had been properly alerted, with the material and with the men they had, and the forces they had, if they had been alerted on the day of the attack, that the damage done to us might have been considerably lessened and the damage done to the Japanese might have been considerably increased and thereby lessening the success of the raid—what is your view on that?

ADMIRAL STARK. I agree with that. That is, of course, on the assumption they might have scouted for that Japanese attack and might have missed it. But there was a chance of their getting it. And if they had located it, if the radar station which did pick it up, if that had been reported, there was a chance of the Army fighters being in the air, and other measures which could have been taken with antiaircraft batteries which, I think, unquestionably would have considerably lessened the damage which the Japs inflicted.

THE CHAIRMAN. It is conceivable the planes might have gone up and missed the Japanese planes, but if they didn't go up they were sure to miss them.

ADMIRAL STARK. Yes, sir.

THE CHAIRMAN. It made it easy for the Japanese planes?

ADMIRAL STARK. That is correct. If they had used everything they had they still might have missed that flight; depending on where they made their estimate as to where the Japanese might come in.

THE CHAIRMAN. You mean if they had gone out it would have been possible to have gone out on a reconnaissance and not discovered the approaching Japanese airplanes?

ADMIRAL STARK. That is correct.

THE CHAIRMAN. Now, whose duty was it, whose obligation or responsibility was it to decide whether this Fleet should have been in Pearl Harbor at that particular time, or at any other particular time?

ADMIRAL STARK. That was the Commander in Chief Pacific.

THE CHAIRMAN. That was Admiral Richardson's responsibility when he was Commander of that Fleet and it became Admiral Kimmel's after he took charge?

ADMIRAL STARK. That is right.

THE CHAIRMAN. And the frequency of the visits of the fleet to Pearl Harbor and the length of its stay was altogether then within the control of the Commanding Officer out there?

ADMIRAL STARK. That is correct; yes, sir.

THE CHAIRMAN. And were there any general instructions from Washington about that, or was that left entirely to the Commanding Officer?

ADMIRAL STARK. That was left to the Senior Officer there. There may have been a general understanding of the fact on the so-called employment schedule that ships periodically have certain periods assigned for repairs, but generally speaking, which I believe you refer to, the fleet going in or out, except for vessels that might be sent to the navy yard, or might be repairing there on a periodic overhaul, that was up to the Commander in Chief there. . . .

SENATOR LUCAS. One other question: From your intimate knowledge of the naval, military and diplomatic conditions as they existed in the United States in the summer and fall of 1941 was there any one man or group of men who maneuvered the Japanese crisis so as to deliberately invite the Pearl Harbor attack?

ADMIRAL STARK. Not to my knowledge, or I had never thought such.

SENATOR LUCAS. Well, you were in on the conversations, practically all of the conversations with respect to Pearl Harbor previous to December 6, 1941?

ADMIRAL STARK. Yes, sir.

SENATOR LUCAS. As Chief of Naval Operations that was one of your duties, to know and understand what was going on?

ADMIRAL STARK. Yes, sir, and I may say that on the contrary we were trying to maintain peace in the Pacific.

SENATOR LUCAS. Do you know of any man or group of men high in the Executive branch of the Government that trapped the Japs or lied to the Japanese to get them to attack us in Pearl Harbor in order to make it easier to get Congressional action to declare war against Japan?

ADMIRAL STARK. I did not get the first part of that question.

SENATOR LUCAS. Do you know of any man or group of men high in the Executive branch of the government, including the naval, military and diplomatic group, who trapped the Japanese or who lied to the Japanese in order to get them to attack Pearl Harbor so as to make it easier for Congress to give a declaration of war?

ADMIRAL STARK. No, I do not.

SENATOR LUCAS. You had frequent conversations, you have told me, with the President of the United States from time to time. You also had frequent conversations with Col. Frank Knox, who was then Secretary of the Navy. I take it that he was familiar with all of these messages that were sent to Admiral Kimmel between November the 24th and December the 6th?

ADMIRAL STARK. He was. I had no secrets from the Secretary of the Navy.

SENATOR LUCAS. Well, now, from your intimate knowledge of the diplomatic and military activities and your conversations with the President and the Secretary of the Navy, did the President of the United States have every reason to believe that the naval command in Hawaii was properly alerted for any emergency when the Japs struck us on December the 7th, 1941?

ADMIRAL STARK. He knew of the dispatch that we had sent there, he knew how I felt about it and I felt that he agreed with me.

SENATOR LUCAS. Well, did he have every reason to believe from all that had been done by yourself and Marshall at that time with respect to alerting the commands that the Hawaii command at the time was properly alerted? That was your belief, wasn't it?

ADMIRAL STARK. Yes, sir; I think he felt that they were properly alerted. I may say, and I have hesitated to quote the President unless I am dead certain, but I specifically recall his statement to me that he was surprised at the attack on Pearl Harbor and he stated that to me as late as last summer and I told him that I had just previously a day or two before that testified to that effect myself before the Navy Court of Inquiry. It was some comfort to me to have him reiterate it.

SENATOR LUCAS. Well, I guess everybody was surprised except the Japs, were they not?

ADMIRAL STARK. The Japs were the real cause for the attack on Pearl Harbor, sir.

Source: U.S. Congress, Pearl Harbor Attack, Hearings Before the Joint Committee on the Investigation of the Pearl Harbor Attack, 79th Congress, 1st Session, Part 5, 2182–86, 2202–04, 2271–72.

Excerpt from Testimony of Rear Admiral Husband E. Kimmel, January 15–21, 1946

Admiral Husband E. Kimmel had begun his career in 1915 as an aide to the assistant secretary of the Navy, Franklin D. Roosevelt. After serving admirably on battleships in World War I and winning command of other ships between the wars, Kimmel attained the rank of rear admiral and commanded the cruiser forces at Pearl Harbor. In early 1941, he was promoted to commander of the Pacific Fleet, replacing Admiral James Richardson, whom Roosevelt relieved of duty when he objected to basing the fleet at Pearl Harbor. As it became clear that Japan was planning an attack on U.S. forces, Kimmel believed that a sneak attack at Wake Island or Midway Island was the most likely plan of the Japanese and that the chances of an attack on Pearl Harbor were very slight. Following the events of December 7, 1941, Roosevelt appointed Supreme Court justice Owen Roberts to investigate the circumstances of the tragic losses. The Roberts commission primarily blamed Kimmel and General Walter C. Short, commander of the Hawaiian Department. The conclusions of the committee led to the removal of the two men from their positions. When Roberts testified before the Pearl Harbor committee four years after the event, he was bitter about the treatment he had received from the administration. In 1955, Kimmel wrote an autobiography in which he made it clear that he believed Roosevelt had sacrificed him and Short to take suspicion of negligence away from the administration itself.

EXCERPT FROM TESTIMONY OF REAR ADMIRAL HUSBAND E. KIMMEL JANUARY 15–21, 1946

MR. RICHARDSON. You thought on December 7 that the danger of air attack on Hawaii was very slight?

ADMIRAL KIMMEL. That is right.

MR. RICHARDSON. In fact, Admiral, the danger was exceedingly great as the event proved to be?

ADMIRAL KIMMEL. Yes; I think that is fair.

MR. RICHARDSON. Then the disaster at Hawaii was the result of an error of judgment?

ADMIRAL KIMMEL. Well, not entirely. It was not entirely the result of an error of judgment. If we had had available in Oahu at this time all of the facilities which you have outlined and we had been able to take the precautions which you have outlined, that would have been one thing.

We had to make a choice. We felt that we had to make a choice. We had to provide for what we knew was coming in all probability against what we conceived at that time to be a very small chance of an attack on Oahu.

Now, you can never be absolutely secure, there is no such thing as absolute security and with a fleet that is particularly true and this estimate that we made—that I made—was made after mature consideration of balancing probabilities and when you balance probabilities you must take into account the means which you have to meet these various possibilities.

MR. RICHARDSON. In reaching such a judgment, Admiral, do you have to consider the possible result of a mistake?

ADMIRAL KIMMEL. You should; yes.

MR. RICHARDSON. And if the mistake on the one hand might result in the destruction of the fleet as against a delay in training what have you to say to that?

ADMIRAL KIMMEL. It was not a delay in training that was involved in this. The primary thing that we had in mind all the time was to be ready for offensive action.

MR. RICHARDSON. Well, then, let me restate my question. In reaching a judgment as to what you were to do, what weight would you give the fact that a mistake with respect to a possible air attack on Hawaii which might result in the destruction of your fleet as compared with the preparation of your fleet for future offensive action outside of Hawaii?

ADMIRAL KIMMEL. In the first place, I never believed that an air attack on Hawaii, on Pearl Harbor would result in the destruction of the fleet. I was firmly convinced at the time that torpedoes would not run in the waters of Pearl Harbor and if it had not been for the destruction accomplished by the torpedoes at that time the damage would have been comparatively negligible. . . .

MR. RICHARDSON. Now, Admiral, it is also a fact, isn't it, that on December 6 it was reported to you by one of your staff, under circumstances showing his nervous interest in the fact, that for 6 days the Japanese carriers had been lost?

ADMIRAL KIMMEL. I thought I covered that pretty completely.

MR. RICHARDSON. You did. Let me finish.

And in response to his anxiety about it you made the remark, "Do you expect me to believe that the carriers are coming around Diamond Head?"

Now do you recall the incident and will you give us your version of it?

ADMIRAL KIMMEL. You are talking about the twinkle in my eye, I suppose.

MR. RICHARDSON. Well, that is part of it.

ADMIRAL KIMMEL. I do not recall the exact words that I used to Captain Layton, but I was very much interested in the location of all Japanese ships, not only the carriers but the other types. I felt if I could locate the carriers I would be able to determine pretty closely where the main Japanese effort was going to be. I went over these traffic analyses reports with Captain Layton every morning. Captain Layton was a very excellent officer. He was very intense, and I have no doubt that I made such remark as that to him, not in any way to decry his efforts, or to treat the matter lightly. I did not treat the matter lightly, and he would be the last one to ever say that I treated the matter lightly.

MR. RICHARDSON. But you had a very different reaction to the suspected fact than he did?

ADMIRAL KIMMEL. No; I had no different reaction from what he had. If you have gotten that impression I think it is entirely erroneous.

MR. RICHARDSON. Did he come to you with a twinkle in his eye when he told you that he had not heard anything of the carriers for 6 days?

ADMIRAL KIMMEL. He came to me because I told him to come.

MR. RICHARDSON. Well, that is all right.

ADMIRAL KIMMEL. He came to me every morning. The first thing I did when I reached the office in the morning was to go over everything that had come in during the night.

MR. RICHARDSON. Did you get any idea from him when he came that he was not serious in this report about the loss of the 6 carriers?

ADMIRAL KIMMEL. Serious?

MR. RICHARDSON. Yes.

ADMIRAL KIMMEL. Of course he was serious. There was never any question of being serious. Not about the loss of the carriers. As far as we were concerned the carriers were never lost, and when people say the carriers were lost they might as well say the whole Japanese fleet was lost.

MR. RICHARDSON. Well, Admiral—

ADMIRAL KIMMEL. Just one second, sir.

MR. RICHARDSON. Yes.

ADMIRAL KIMMEL. We had during this period a wealth of traffic. There was a great deal of traffic. The only trouble was we were unable to identify it, and we were not only unable to identify the Japanese carriers, we were unable to identify pretty nearly all the Japanese fleet. It was not that we had lost six carriers, that was not the thing. We did not even know we had lost them. We could not identify them.

MR. RICHARDSON. Did not Layton use the word "lost" in reporting to you?

ADMIRAL KIMMEL. As far as I remember, no. All he said was he was unable to identify them. . . .

MR. RICHARDSON. Now, on that Sunday morning of the attack, you had your ships so arranged in the harbor as to facilitate the use of your antiaircraft batteries on the ships?

ADMIRAL KIMMEL. That is a fact.

MR. RICHARDSON. That was a matter of definite policy which you had worked out to guide your ships when in the harbor?

ADMIRAL KIMMEL. That is correct.

MR. RICHARDSON. So in event of an air attack they could concentrate their fire in the most scientific way?

ADMIRAL KIMMEL. Yes, sir; instantly.

MR. RICHARDSON. And you testified that your information is that your fleet guns, aircraft, antiaircraft guns were firing on this attack within 4 to 7 minutes after the attack started?

ADMIRAL KIMMEL. My understanding and my belief is that in from 4 to 7 minutes, variously estimated, all the guns of the fleet were firing, all the antiaircraft guns of the fleet, but that those that were manned before the attack opened fire at once.

MR. RICHARDSON. Is that in your opinion as great a state of readiness as could have been provided for for those ships under those circumstances that morning?

ADMIRAL KIMMEL. I think it was a very reasonable condition to maintain. When any gun, or group of guns, one-quarter to one-half of them, opened fire at once, and began to shoot at the first planes coming in, and when the rest of them chime in to the extent of the whole outfit within 4 to 7 minutes, I don't believe you will beat that much anywhere. . . .

MR. RICHARDSON. If you had sent your battleships to sea on the morning of the 7th, if you had had sufficient information so that it would have been possible to maneuver them and make a sortie with your battleships, wouldn't those battleships have been in greater danger from air attack in the open sea without any planes of yours that could protect them than they were in the harbor?

ADMIRAL KIMMEL. On the morning of December 7, it was a little late to send the battleships to sea, but on the night of December 6 I could have arranged a rendezvous with Halsey and gotten out pretty much in the same vicinity with him. I could have had the patrol planes out, and such planes as we had in the fleet at that time. I could have called back Newton with the *Lexington*, and he would have been in supporting distance of the fleet by daylight the next morning.

MR. RICHARDSON. How long would it take to sortie the battleships out of the harbor into the open sea?

ADMIRAL KIMMEL. Three hours, perhaps.

MR. RICHARDSON. If you had had every possible warning of the 1 o'clock message which was so delayed on Sunday, the most you could have done with your battleships in that time would have been to sortie them, wouldn't it?

ADMIRAL KIMMEL. Yes, but I think now, and again this is hindsight, I can't help but believe I wouldn't have sent the battleships to sea.

MR. RICHARDSON. That is just the point I was making.

ADMIRAL KIMMEL. I would have sent all the light forces to sea. I would have gotten the destroyers and cruisers out. As a matter of fact, one of my problems all the time there, against a fast raiding force, if any should come, was the fact that my battleships would have been of very little use to me.

They couldn't go fast enough, and the only ones that were of use were the ones that could get out and do something to the enemy.

Source: U.S. Congress, Pearl Harbor Attack, Hearings Before the Joint Committee on the Investigation of the Pearl Harbor Attack, 79th Congress, 1st Session, Part 6, pp. 2590–91, 2597–98, 2606, 2612–13, 2629–30.

Conclusions of the Majority Report of the Pearl Harbor Committee, July 20, 1946

The Pearl Harbor committee held hearings from November 15, 1945, to May 31, 1946. Although the Democratic majority managed to steer the hearings in such a manner as to deflect as much criticism as it could from President Franklin D. Roosevelt, Republican members, led by Senator Homer Ferguson of Michigan and Senator Ralph Brewster of Maine, pushed hard to fix blame on administration officials in Washington and not on the commanders in the field. In the summer of 1946, the committee issued its final report, along with evidence, exhibits, and testimony that came to more than 40 volumes. The Majority Report concluded that Japan's attack had been entirely unprovoked. There was no evidence, it declared, that the Roosevelt administration had maneuvered Japan into attacking U.S. forces in order to persuade Congress to declare war. The Pearl Harbor disaster, said the majority, was due to the failure of the local commanders to take adequate measures to detect a possible attack and maintain proper readiness. The majority did say that during the 48 hours prior to the attack, the War and Navy Departments should have notified Pearl Harbor about the impending diplomatic break that the Japanese had scheduled to take effect from 1 P.M. Washington time on December 7, 1941. A Minority Report, signed by Ferguson and Brewster, blamed Roosevelt for failing to enforce clear and timely communications between civilian and military officials about an imminent war with Japan.

CONCLUSIONS OF THE MAJORITY REPORT OF THE PEARL HARBOR COMMITTEE JULY 20, 1946

Conclusions with Respect to Responsibilities

1. The December 7, 1941, attack on Pearl Harbor was an unprovoked act of aggression by the Empire of Japan. The treacherous attack was planned and launched while Japanese ambassadors, instructed with characteristic duplicity, were carrying on the pretense of negotiations with the Government of the United States with a view to an amicable settlement of differences in the Pacific.
2. The ultimate responsibility for the attack and its results rests upon Japan, an attack that was well planned and skillfully executed. Contributing to the effectiveness of the attack was a powerful striking force, much more powerful than it had been thought the Japanese were able to employ in a single tactical venture at such distance and under such circumstances.
3. The diplomatic policies and actions of the United States provided no justifiable provocation whatever for the attack by Japan on this Nation. The Secretary of State fully informed both the War and Navy Departments of diplomatic developments and, in a timely and forceful manner, clearly pointed out to these Departments that relations between the United States and Japan had passed beyond the stage of diplomacy and were in the hands of the military.
4. The committee has found no evidence to support the charges, made before and during the hearings, that the President, the Secretary of State, the Secretary of War, or the Secretary of Navy tricked, provoked, incited, cajoled, or coerced Japan into attacking this Nation in order that a declaration of war might be more easily obtained from the Congress. On the contrary, all evidence conclusively points to the fact that they discharged their responsibilities with distinction, ability, and foresight and in keeping with the highest traditions of our fundamental foreign policy.
5. The President, the Secretary of State, and high Government officials made every possible effort, without sacrificing our national honor and endangering our security, to avert war with Japan.
6. The disaster of Pearl Harbor was the failure, with attendant increase in personnel and material losses, of the Army and the Navy to institute measures designed to detect an approaching hostile force, to effect a state of readiness commensurate with the realization that war was at hand, and to employ every facility at their command in repelling the Japanese.
7. Virtually everyone was surprised that Japan struck the Fleet at Pearl Harbor at the time that she did. Yet officers, both in Washington and Hawaii, were fully conscious of the danger from air attack; they realized this form of attack on Pearl Harbor by Japan was at least a possibility; and they were adequately informed of the imminence of war.
8. Specifically, the Hawaiian commands failed—

   (a) To discharge their responsibilities in the light of the warnings received from Washington, other information possessed by them, and the principle of command by mutual cooperation.
   (b) To integrate and coordinate their facilities for defense and to alert properly the Army and Navy establishments in Hawaii, particularly in the light of the warnings and intelligence available to them during the period of November 27 to December 7, 1941.
   (c) To effect liaison on a basis designed to acquaint each of them with the operations of the other, which was necessary to their joint security, and to exchange fully all significant intelligence.
   (d) To maintain a more effective reconnaissance within the limits of their equipment.
   (e) To effect a state of readiness throughout the Army and Navy establishments designed to meet all possible attacks.
   (f) To employ the facilities, matériel, and personnel at their command, which were adequate at least to have greatly minimized the effects of the attack, in repelling Japanese raiders.
   (g) To appreciate the significance of intelligence and other information available to them.
9. The errors made by the Hawaiian commands were errors of judgment and not derelictions of duty.
10. The War Plans Division of the War Department failed to discharge its direct responsibility to advise the commanding general he had not properly alerted the Hawaiian Department when the latter, pursuant to instructions, had reported action taken in a message that was not satisfactorily responsive to the original directive.
11. The Intelligence and War Plans Divisions of the War and Navy Departments failed:

   (a) To give careful and thoughtful consideration to the intercepted messages from Tokyo to Honolulu of September 24, November 15, and November 20 (the harbor berthing plan and related dispatches) and to raise a question as to their significance. Since they indicated a particular interest in the Pacific Fleet's base this intelligence should have been appreciated and supplied the Hawaiian commanders for their assistance, along with other information available to them, in making their estimate of the situation.
   (b) To be properly on the *qui vive* to receive the "one o'clock" intercept and to recognize in the message the fact that some Japanese military action would very possibly occur somewhere at 1 P.M., December 7. If properly appreciated, this intelligence should have suggested a dispatch to all Pacific outpost commanders supplying this information, as General Marshall attempted to do immediately upon seeing it.

12. Notwithstanding the fact that there were officers on twenty-four hour watch, the Committee believes that under all of the evidence the War and Navy Departments were not sufficiently alerted on December 6 and 7, 1941, in view of the imminence of war.

Source: U.S. Congress, Investigation of the Pearl Harbor Attack, Report of the Joint Committee on the Investigation of the Pearl Harbor Attack, 79th Congress, 2nd Session, Senate Document No. 244, 251–66; 266s–66w; 572–73.

Bibliography

Beard, Charles. *President Roosevelt and the Coming of the War, 1941*. Reprint. Edison, N.J.: Transaction Publishers, 2003.

Bland, Larry. *The Papers of George C. Marshall: "We Cannot Delay, July 1, 1939—December 6, 1941*. Baltimore: Johns Hopkins University Press, 1986.

Clausen, Henry, and Bruce Lee. *Pearl Harbor: Final Judgment*. New York: Crown Publishers, 1992.

Ferrell, Robert. "Pearl Harbor and the Revisionists." *The Historian* (Spring 1955).

Greaves, Percy L. Jr. "Senator Homer Ferguson and the Pearl Harbor Congressional Investigation." *Journal of Historical Review*. Available at: www.ihr.org/jhr/v04/v04p405_Greaves.html.

Hoehling, Adolph. *The Week Before Pearl Harbor*. New York: Hale, 1963.

Morton, Louis. "1937–1941." In *American-East Asian Relations: A Survey*, edited by Ernest May and James C. Thomson Jr. Cambridge, Mass.: Harvard University Press, 1972.

"Pearl Harbor: Documents: The Attack." *Foreign Affairs* (Winter 1991/92). Available at: www.foreignaffairs.org/19911201faessay6120/joint-congressional-committee/pearl-harbor-documents-the-attack.html.

Pogue, Forrest. *George Marshall: Ordeal and Hope, 1939–1942*. New York: Viking Press, 1966.

Prange, Gordon, Donald Goldstein, and Katherine Dillon. *Pearl Harbor: The Verdict of History*. New York: McGraw-Hill, 1986.

Smith, Stanley. *Investigations of the Attack on Pearl Harbor*. Westport, Conn.: Greenwood, 1990.

Stinnett, Robert. *Day of Deceit: The Truth About FDR and Pearl Harbor*. New York: Free Press, 2000.

U.S. Congress. Pearl Harbor Attack: Hearings Before the Joint Committee on the Investigation of the Pearl Harbor Attack. 79th Cong., 1st sess. Available at: www.ibiblio.org/pha/pha/invest.html.

Wohlstetter, Roberta. *Pearl Harbor: Warning and Decision*. Palo Alto, Calif.: Stanford University Press, 1962.

The Kefauver Committee on Organized Crime, 1950–51

by Theodore Wilson

The Senate Special Committee to Investigate Organized Crime in Interstate Commerce, popularly known as the Kefauver committee, is one of the most famous congressional investigations of recent times, despite its failure to prove conclusively its principal thesis or to obtain legislative approval for its major recommendations. One factor, television, was largely responsible for fixing the public consciousness upon this one investigation from among the dozens of important congressional inquiries in the decade after World War II. For the first time millions of Americans (some 20 million by one estimate) observed the periodic bouts of drama and boredom that comprised a congressional hearing as it unfolded. Americans gaped as the denizens of other worlds—bookies, pimps, and gangland enforcers, crime bosses and their slippery lawyers—marched across their television screens. They watched and were impressed by the schoolmasterish Estes Kefauver, the dignified Tennessean who was the committee's first chairman, as he condemned criminals and the system of ineffective law enforcement, graft, and popular apathy that permitted them to thrive. Most important, they turned away from this spectacle persuaded that Senator Kefauver and his colleagues had uncovered the "true" causes of crime in America and that the crime committee had the problem under control. Certainly, the credibility and public support extended to the Kefauver committee, a litmus test of the success of any congressional investigation, suggest that this inquiry deserved its impressive reputation.

Tennessee senator Estes Kefauver. (Library of Congress)

Nonetheless, one is nagged by the thought that something more than television (and the fact that the committee's endeavors made Estes Kefauver a presidential contender) explains the Kefauver committee's powerful impact. A partial explanation may be found, perhaps, by studying the Kefauver committee within the context of those frantic years, 1949–1952—a time of bitter partisanship and of deep divisions within American society. Looked at in this way, as an example of oracular utterances to a people desperately clamoring for reassurance, the Kefauver committee's popularity makes considerable sense. A cynic might assert that the Kefauver committee was the social counterpart of Senator Joseph McCarthy's pursuit of a domestic political conspiracy aimed at the destruction of the United

OVERVIEW

Background

Following World War II, the United States faced a wave of violence. Crime statistics reflected an increase in burglary, murder, illegal gambling, and prostitution. As citizen crime commissions, journalists, and law enforcement officials searched for answers, Congress turned its investigative authority to the illicit underworld of organized crime.

Congress Investigates

In May 1950, the Special Committee to Investigate Organized Crime in Interstate Commerce, under the chairmanship of Senator Estes Kefauver (D-Tenn.), began hearings in cities across the country. The first congressional investigation to attract a large television audience, the committee interrogated a parade of more than 600 gangsters, pimps, gamblers, lawyers, and politicians with apparent underworld connections. For 15 months in 14 cities, the committee questioned 800 witnesses.

Impact

After the New York hearings in March 1951, during which more than 50 witnesses provided extensive information regarding the crime syndicate led by Frank Costello, *Life* magazine said, "the week of March 12, 1951, will occupy a special place in history." Following the hearings, legalized gambling proposals were defeated in Arizona, California, Massachusetts, and Montana. More than 70 local crime commissions were established in cities across the country as public awareness of the danger of crime increased. The committee's work also led the Special Rackets Squad of the FBI to launch investigations. As a result of the hearings, one crime figure, Joe Adonis, was deported to Italy, while another underworld character, Willie Moretti, an associate of Costello's, was murdered to keep him from talking. Even though there were relatively few television sets in the United States in 1951, the hearings were watched with great intensity, especially in bars and public places as the nation became aware of the extensive nature of organized crime.

The hearings made Senator Kefauver a national figure, and he would later run for president in 1952 and 1956. As a result of the exposure from the hearings and the murder of Moretti, Costello would face charges that resulted in several jail sentences, weakening his underworld power.

States. According to reputable sources, McCarthy and Kefauver competed for the authority to mount a crusade against organized crime during the period when McCarthy was thrashing around in search of an issue to further his twisted ambition. Kefauver's inquiry and McCarthy's assorted "investigations" had almost nothing in common in terms of procedures, purposes, and achievements; but they did reflect the yearning of Congress—and the American people—in these parlous times for easy solutions, for scapegoats upon which to dump the frustration of accepting less than had been promised, and of having apparently simple problems reach levels of complexity beyond their understanding. Both reflected and exemplified a general feeling of dissatisfaction and insecurity that was only hazily expressed but was no less ominous because of its vagueness.

The nation's affairs had seemed to collapse into an unending downward spiral since the glorious days of mid-1948—when the Marshall Plan and tremendous prosperity confirmed the innate superiority of American institutions—and since Harry Truman's come-from-behind victory in the presidential sweepstakes of that year. Soon after Truman's reelection, serious national and international problems and difficulties within the Truman administration arose, challenging the optimism with which the president and most of his countrymen had looked to the future. Less than a year after Truman's triumphal inauguration, the country faced growing external problems, a serious economic recession, and debilitating political scandals. In particular, the humiliating flight of Chiang Kai-shek's Chinese Nationalist regime to Formosa, the revelation in September 1949 that Russia had exploded an atomic bomb, the sensational trial of Alger Hiss, and mushrooming suspicions that the federal government harbored numerous traitors eroded public confidence in Truman's leadership. In part, Truman's conduct of the presidency was also responsible. One of his closest advisers later confessed:

CHRONOLOGY

1949

- *May:* Department of Justice reports to President Harry S. Truman that a serious crime was committed at the rate of one every 18.7 seconds in the United States in 1948.
- *December:* American Municipal Association calls on the Justice Department to help embattled state and municipal agencies in their efforts to combat an escalating crime wave.

1950

- *January 5:* Senator Estes Kefauver (D-Tenn.) introduces a resolution calling for examination of organized crime in the United States.
- *May 2:* Senate approves resolution establishing the Special Committee to Investigate Organized Crime in Interstate Commerce.
- *May 26:* Special committee opens its hearings in Miami, Florida.
- *June:* Truman orders federal agencies to open their files to the committee.
- *November 15:* The Kefauver committee arrives in Las Vegas. Most of the high-profile casino operators had already left town.

1951

- *February 28:* The committee issues a preliminary report saying at least two major crime syndicates were operating in the United States.
- *March 13–15:* In New York City, the gangland boss Frank Costello makes his first appearance before the committee. Television cameras are allowed to focus only on his hands as part of a deal to protect his identity and gain testimony.
- *March 29:* Truman acknowledges the committee's efforts to publicize the need for all levels of government to work harder to eradicate crime.
- *April:* After an exhausting tour of major cities, Senator Kefauver decides to wrap up the investigation.
- *May 1:* The committee issues an interim report outlining the roots and activities of the Mafia, a new word for organized crime in the lexicon of many Americans who first heard it during the Kefauver hearings.
- *August 31:* Kefauver committee issues its final report.

> Something happened between Truman's first and second terms that is hard to pin down. There was a change of atmosphere around the White House. . . . During the first term, we were all playing it pretty much by ear—sensing what had to be done and getting on with it. There wasn't much pressure from the outside, from the lobbies and the special interest pleaders or the big politicians. . . . And then came the 1948 election, and—my God—how cocky he was after that. . . . Now he was all bustle and decisiveness and full of big plans, and to hell with the details. . . . But now the outside pressures began to close in on him and on us. . . . The people who wanted things now knew they had to deal with him or not deal at all. So now they began to scheme and to ponder and to sort of feel around to see what was the best way of getting to him. . . . There was nothing sinister about this you could put your finger on. But it was a new mood and a new climate, and in a way Mr. Truman was a captive of it.

The discovery of "Commies" in high places weakened President Truman's credibility, but he could not be held personally responsible. However, the disclosures of shady dealings by administration officials threatened to reach inside the doors of the White House itself.

In August 1949 a special Senate committee was investigating "influence-peddlers," lobbyists, and others who, for fat fees, arranged favors for businessmen eager to obtain lucrative government contracts. Investigators found evidence that General Harry Vaughan, Truman's military aide and an old and close friend from Missouri, had permitted his office to be used by lobbyists to exert pressure on various government officials. This had been going on for some years in fact. Vaughan, it appeared, was friendly with several "five-percenters," men who helped businessmen gain preferential treatment from government agencies for a 5 percent fee. It was learned that Vaughan had assisted one friend in obtaining an allocation of structural steel for the construction of a race track and had used his influence to open doors for various others. "Evidence before the Senate subcommittee showed," Cabell Phillips has noted, "that he poked his nose into the fields of public housing and surplus property disposal, into Federal trade regulations, and even into the Department of Agriculture, where the legitimate interests of the military aide to the President would seem to be minimal." Vaughan appears to have been more a victim of his desire to be a "good guy" than a man on the take. He apparently did not accept cash payoffs for these favors, and he believed that his actions, taken to assist the president and the Democratic Party, were entirely proper. The Senate investigation did dredge up evidence that Vaughan had received numerous large contributions for the party, and that he also had accepted a deep freeze, a scarce item because of lingering controls, from the client of one of his lobbyist buddies.

The practice of influence-peddling had a long and venerable history in Washington. People who "knew the ropes"—often ex-congressmen, retired military men, or civil servants—had been functioning as middle men since the Jackson administration and even before. The activities of this particular group of five-percenters were hardly in the same class as Teapot Dome and other instances of corruption; however, heightened public awareness, partly the result of Harry Truman's determined pursuit of "wheeler-dealers" as chairman of the wartime Special Committee to Investigate the National Defense Program, produced an enormous outcry against Vaughan and the "mess in Washington." Newspapers were still carrying cartoons that caricatured Vaughan and his deep freeze when a serious scandal involving the Reconstruction Finance Corporation broke in early 1950. Here again, one of Truman's principal assistants was charged with improper conduct.

The Reconstruction Finance Corporation (RFC), a depression agency created to assist businesses that could not obtain loans from commercial sources, had expanded into other fields during World War II and continued after the war's end as a bulwark against economic difficulties and a source of development capital. By the late 1940s the RFC was issuing loans for a variety of speculative enterprises and had gained a reputation as being one of the most "political" of federal agencies. Responding to charges of political deals, influence-peddling, and financial irregularities supposedly rife in this sprawling, semi-autonomous organization, the Senate Banking and Currency Committee launched an investigation of the RFC in February 1950. A subcommittee, headed by Senator J. William Fulbright (whom President Truman violently disliked), eventually reported that the RFC was suffering from mismanagement and found numerous instances of loans awarded in return for political favors. Truman's personnel director, fellow Missourian Donald Dawson, was singled out by the Fulbright subcommittee as "the man to see" where pressure on the RFC was concerned. The Democratic National Committee and its chairman, William M. Boyle, another Missourian, were accused of imposing political conditions on RFC loans and of extracting large contributions from applicants.

Before Truman left office, corrupt practices by Internal Revenue Service officials had been uncovered, and charges of a vast network of influence peddling in the nation's capital were under investigation by Congress. The president was forced to submit proposals for the reorganization of the RFC and the IRS. After much debate he also established a special White House commission to investigate the whole issue of governmental corruption. These decisions were made under strong public and congressional pressure and further intensified tension between the executive and legislative branches. The president's impassioned defense of his friends did not help his cause. Indeed, by insisting, "My people are honorable—all of them are," Truman subjected himself to ridicule and suspicion regarding his own possible involvement.

The significance of these unfortunate episodes—which by no means can be compared with Teapot Dome or Watergate—derives largely from their crippling effects on Truman's authority and public image. For a variety of reasons, Truman's second term degenerated into political bickering and ineptitude. One cause, certainly, was the "mess" in Washington. In addition, the bipartisan coalition that had sustained Truman's bold initiatives in foreign affairs fell apart under the strain of widespread dissatisfaction with the administration's China policy and parallel unhappiness about the demonstrable effects of economic and military assistance to Europe. Assorted explanations for the perilous position in which America found itself were offered. The most popular one, that Communist agents strategically located in the government bureaucracy were distorting and delaying the achievement of American foreign policy goals, produced a witch hunt that further crippled the authority of Truman and his administration. To a considerable degree Congress was the temporary beneficiary of this reversal in presidential fortunes. By early 1950 eager congressmen were charging off in all directions, using the investigatory power of Congress to dig into the

Truman administration's handling of various domestic and international problems. Investigations were undertaken of such previously sacrosanct issues as the giving of economic assistance to Socialist governments abroad, East-West trade, and United States policy toward Spain, Yugoslavia, and, of course, China. Other probes dealt with domestic subversion (within and outside the federal bureaucracy), housing, the motion picture industry, civil rights, shipping problems, and organized crime, to name but a few.

Of these, the crime investigation is among the most interesting—on its own merits and because it reflected so many aspects of the confused, unhappy public mood. There is little doubt that an investigation of "organized crime," which implicitly questioned existing federal law enforcement programs and which focused on criminal operations in cities almost exclusively dominated by Democratic political machines, would not have taken place in normal circumstances. Even so, despite the Truman administration's siege mentality and the widespread belief that America confronted a moral crisis of apocalyptic dimensions, the decision of a Democratic Senate to appoint a committee controlled by Democrats to investigate a problem involving and likely to embarrass powerful Democratic leaders was astounding. One may argue that the Kefauver crime investigation was intended to head off a dangerous, Republican-initiated study; but even if Kefauver's original purpose was to protect the administration—which is highly doubtful—the Senate Special Committee to Investigate Crime in Interstate Commerce soon was caught up in the fervent moral absolutism that swept the nation. Sidney Shalett began the introduction to *Crime in America,* Senator Kefauver's "personal account" of the crime investigation, by observing:

> In the spring of 1951 the American people were a little sick of politicians. Some of the contemporary exhibitions of what passed for political morality didn't sit well against the gnawing heartache of the Korean War and the awful feeling that here we go again. Rising taxes and the return of economic restrictions the people could take, though they didn't like it. But when they saw their children being drilled from kindergarten up to lie down on the dirt and cover their heads with their hands as protection against the atom bomb that the Russians were supposed to drop on us, the people were heartsore and angry—and, Americanlike, they started looking around for a whipping boy. Rightly or wrongly, the politicians filled the bill.

In such a climate, it was perhaps inevitable that the Kefauver committee's investigation of organized crime would also become an inquest into the state of America's moral health.

I

The involvement of Congress in efforts to combat criminal activities stretched back into the nineteenth century. Although the dominant tradition in the United States supported local rather than national law enforcement programs, the federal government had always been responsible for prevention of certain crimes (counterfeiting, smuggling, tax evasion, and so forth). State governments, of course, exercised most "police powers" either directly or by delegation to county or municipal law enforcement agencies. Until the progressive period, crimes against person and property remained the exclusive domain of state and local government, as did immoral activities such as gambling and prostitution. There existed, however, one exception to the general pattern of decentralized responsibility for law enforcement: federal authority over interstate commerce. By the late nineteenth century, certain problems arising from industrialization and the centralization of American business grew beyond the regulatory power of individual states. "Americans had seen nothing quite like the industrial sabotage, collusion, stock manipulation, use of private armies, and public corruption that accompanied the development of Big Business in the United States," William H. Moore has written. Responding to popular clamor for control of labor violence, financial manipulations, and corruption, the federal government attempted—by means of its taxing authority and powers over interstate commerce—to dampen the fires through regulation. In addition, Congress enacted legislation to eradicate certain illegal (or immoral) activities: interstate lotteries, and the "white slave trade," transportation of women across state lines. Congressional investigations were conducted on several of these problems.

The most notable action of Congress in the crusade against vice and the criminal operations it supposedly spawned was Prohibition, making it illegal to manufacture and distribute alcoholic beverages. The Eighteenth Amendment, which made liquor illegal, produced the Volstead Act, a federal effort to ensure its enforcement. Since little provision was made for implementation of the Prohibition concept, the Volstead Act and the Eighteenth Amendment itself soon became a mockery. Sociologists and historians are still debating whether Prohibition spawned the well-organized criminal gangs that typified the "roaring twenties," or whether the presence of Dutch Schultz, Al Capone, and their brethren prevented the "noble experiment" from achieving complete acceptance by the American people. Certainly, the era of Prohibition focused public attention for the first time on the problem of *organized* criminal elements and the threat they posed to public safety and the nation's morals. Gangland murders, gleefully reported in big city newspapers, appeared an almost everyday occurrence; and gangsters such as "Scarface" Al Capone, head of a Chicago mob that at times seemed to exert total control over the city's police and political leadership, were portrayed as glamorous if also frightening figures.

Partly as a result of the enormous publicity given criminal leaders and their murderous jousts for supremacy, the federal government moved more aggressively to control crimes that had some interstate dimension. The Justice Department received expanded authority and manpower, and the Federal Bureau of Investigation was reorganized under the control of a tough young lawyer, J. Edgar Hoover. The view of federal law enforcement agencies and of the numerous crime commissions (such as the Wickersham Commission created by President Herbert Hoover in 1929) was that crime was somehow inherent in certain groups and classes of Americans. Thus, it could be eradicated only by tough, swift, and determined enforcement of the law. Actually, the FBI and other police agencies paid little attention to organized crime, for they were forced by public opinion to concentrate their meager resources on dramatic but isolated criminal acts such as the Lindbergh kidnapping and bank robbers such as Pretty Boy Floyd, Bonnie and Clyde, and John Dillinger.

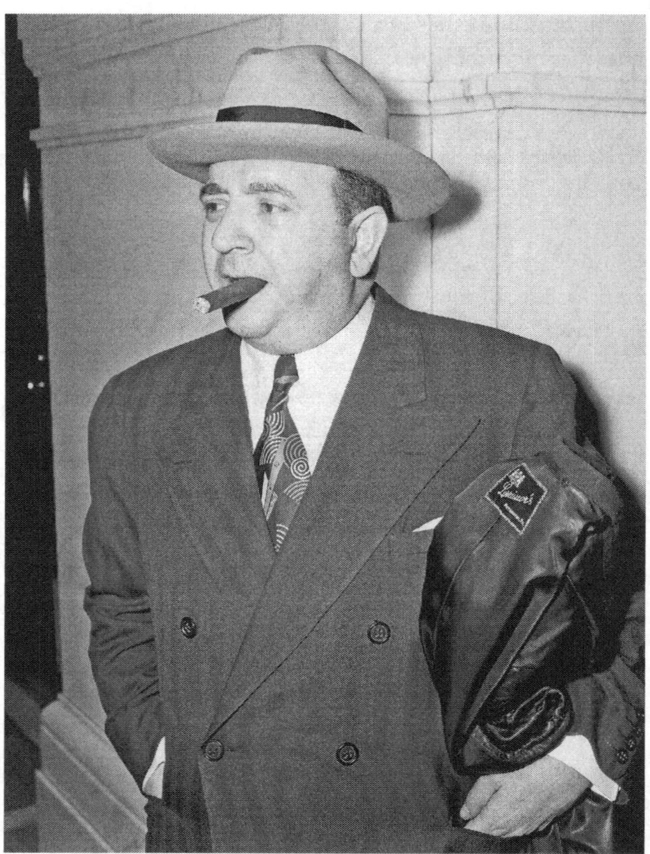

Joe DiCarlo, described by police as a rackets organizer, refused to answer questions when he appeared before Senator Estes Kefauver's crime investigation committee held in Cleveland, Ohio, on January 19, 1951. The Kefauver committee held the hearing as part of the U.S. Senate probe into interstate crime. (Associated Press)

A subcommittee of the Senate Commerce Committee held hearings on "racketeering" for two years beginning in 1933; however, its vague conclusions regarding the potential threats of organized, deeply entrenched criminal operations were ignored. The phenomenon of racketeering, which implied the existence of a nationwide criminal conspiracy, was "discovered in the early 1930s, though organized extortion, comprising a private tax on the exchange of goods and services" by extralegal agencies, had long been a familiar practice in urban life. Also during the 1930s ambitious efforts to control prostitution and gambling rackets were launched. Once again, however, federal and state law enforcement programs dealt largely with a few "big fish," leaving undisturbed the substructure of illegal activities and linkages between criminal bosses and political leaders. Concern about "crime syndicates" did increase, but mostly as a result of such inflammatory books as *Crime Incorporated* and its bestselling successor, *Murder, Inc.* Notably, the criminal geniuses portrayed in books and journalistic exposés increasingly were Italian-Americans, and the public came to accept the thesis, which the Kefauver committee later propounded vigorously, that, "behind the local mobs which make up the national crime syndicate is a shadowy, international criminal organization known as the Mafia, so fantastic that most Americans find it hard to believe it really exists." Regrettably, little was done by Congress or the executive branch to prove whether a "Mafia" did control crime in America—or to explore the causes and implications of this complicated issue.

World War II shifted government's and the public's attention to external threats, and few efforts, except for certain investigations of the Truman Committee, were given to expose organized criminal activities. This was doubly unfortunate, because the tremendous opportunities for vice, racketeering, and graft, and the equally tremendous powers assumed by the federal government during the war provided impressive means by which it might have carried through an effective crime control program. The years immediately after the war witnessed an even greater growth of crimes against people and property. Sociologists might argue with civil servants that the causes of this new "crime wave" were wartime pressures on family life leading to juvenile delinquency, the widespread violations of rationing, price control measures, and the draft system that made Americans tolerant of the "black market" and other devices to avoid government regulations, or simply the complexity of life, with its attendant frustration and alienation, in postwar America. Most people, however, blamed organized crime.

That a frightening increase in crime of all types had occurred was beyond question. A memorandum prepared in May 1949 for President Truman by the office of the attorney general observed: "It is shocking to realize that in the United States in 1948 a serious crime was committed at the rate of one every 18.7 seconds. Moreover, the increase in the number of crimes involving violence and brutality has been too great to pass unnoticed. In 1948, aggravated assaults and rape, to mention only a few, increased 68.7 per cent and 49.9 per cent, respectively, over prewar averages (1938–1941). The crimes of burglary, murder and robbery all are on the increase." The Justice Department, which for a time supported the position that juvenile delinquency was a major cause of the problem, did launch several efforts to stem the tide. It convened a National Conference on Prevention and Control of Juvenile Delinquency in November 1946, and some months later it supported increased FBI programs and created a "racket squad" to work with federal grand juries in various big cities. In mid-1949 Attorney General J. Howard McGrath, on the advice of the FBI and in response to vocal pressures from state and municipal leaders, proposed a National Conference on Crime and Law Enforcement. This group was supposed to "discover, study, and analyze the causes of this dangerous crime trend in the United States and . . . devise methods to improve and remedy the situation." At this point municipal officials and crime-fighting reporters, unhappy with Attorney General McGrath's "lackadaisical" approach to crime, especially national crime operations such as slot machines and the racing news wire service, decided to go directly to Congress with their tale of an organized criminal conspiracy bent on taking over America.

In September 1949 Mayor deLesseps Morrison of New Orleans, then president of the American Municipal Association (AMA), had requested that the federal government investigate the political influence of criminal elements (which he believed to be organized on a national scale) in numerous cities throughout the country. Three months later the AMA itself asked that the Justice Department give extraordinary assistance to embattled state and municipal agencies, asserting that "the matter is too big to be handled by local officials alone; the organized criminal element operates across state boundaries on a national scale." It appeared to activists that the Truman administration's sole response was to revive the idea of a national conference on crime, to meet in February 1950 in conjunction with the annual convention of U.S. attorneys. Assisted by powerful journalists such as Drew Pearson, Mayor Morrison and his colleagues pressed for congressional action. Among the congressmen most sympathetic to the anticrime forces was Estes Kefauver, freshman senator from Tennessee.

Kefauver later said that his interest in an investigation of organized crime derived from several factors, an important one being his participation some years before in a House Judiciary Committee inquiry into the activities of a Pennsylvania federal district judge. "In the process of gathering the evidence that subsequently resulted in the retirement of this man who disgraced his robes," Kefauver recalled, "the full import of what rottenness in public life can do to our country came home to me. From then on the subject never was far from my mind." After Kefauver moved to the Senate, having won a bitterly fought election from the Crump political machine in 1948, he became somewhat obsessed with "the phenomenon of politico-criminal corruption and what it was doing to the country." Also, of course, the Tennessee senator, who possessed a driving ambition, was anxious to find some means of obtaining national recognition. While he perceived risks in the "crime problem," involving as it did possible laxity of federal agencies, collusion between criminal forces and politicians in Democratic strongholds, and uncertain political alignments in Congress, Kefauver decided that the risks were acceptable and the potential benefits unlimited. Perhaps only in the confused atmosphere of 1949–1950 could a very junior senator have so boldly thrust aside the constraints of party loyalty, executive primacy, and the procedures of that exclusive club, the U.S. Senate.

Senator Kefauver was not alone in his desire to head a congressional investigation of organized crime, however. As noted previously, the aggressive and ambitious junior senator from Wisconsin, Joseph McCarthy, was wavering between crime and Communism as sure-fire reelection issues. Also, soon after the attorney general's conference on crime concluded (with a great deal of publicity but almost nothing in the way of positive recommendations), Representative Kingsland Macy, a New York Republican, stepped forward to propose a sweeping congressional investigation of organized crime, especially its evil influence over local, state, and federal governments. However,

Kefauver was first in the field, and, though he faced deep and continuing opposition from many in the Senate to his proposal, the Tennessean eventually emerged with authorization for an investigation and approval of himself as the investigatory committee's chairman.

It should be noted that Kefauver, despite his junior standing, possessed impressive credentials. First, he already owned a considerable reputation as a political comer on the strength of his surprising victory over the powerful political machine of "Boss" Crump in 1948. He had accomplished this with almost no support from the Democratic national organization, and thus was not tied in any way to the embarrassing situation that the Democratic Party faced in 1949–50. Although Kefauver's victory was not so remarkable as a sympathetic press claimed (Crump's power was already declining, and Kefauver won by a rather narrow margin in a three-man race), the public remembered him as the shyly articulate Southerner who wore a coonskin cap and who was, nonetheless, praised as one of the most promising and effective liberals to enter the Senate in decades. In addition, Kefauver had made himself knowledgeable about the crime issue. From close contacts with crime reporters and Justice Department investigators he received information about their fascination with the threat of organized crime. In particular, he was made aware of the findings of the California Crime Commission, which had dredged up an enormous store of evidence about criminal activities in that state and elsewhere. Kefauver was already at work on bills to deal with specific abuses, such as a curb on the racing news wire service and the slot machine distribution question, when the opportunity arose to conduct a full-scale investigation of crime and political corruption.

On January 5, 1959, Senator Kefauver introduced Senate Resolution 202 calling for "a full and complete study and investigation of interstate gambling and racketeering activities and of the manner in which the facilities of interstate commerce are made a vehicle of organized crime." He proposed that this investigation be conducted by the Judiciary Committee (of which he was a member) or by a subcommittee thereof. In justification of the resolution, Kefauver offered the following statement:

> Responsible and nationally known reporters and magazine writers have for the past several years been writing of a national crime syndicate which they allege is slowly but surely through corruption gaining control of, or improper influence in, many cities throughout the United States.
>
> On September 14, 1949, Mayor deLesseps S. Morrison as President of the American Municipal Association, and speaking for that association, asked the Federal government to investigate the encroachment by organized national racketeers on municipal governments throughout the United States with the intent to control their law enforcement agencies.
>
> The Chicago and California Crime Commissions in 1949 reported the insidious influence wielded by this crime syndicate through corruption of public officials and its political and financial control.
>
> Also, . . . the mayors of several large cities, such as Los Angeles, New Orleans, and Portland, and many others, have complained in the past year of attempts being made by national crime syndicates to control and corrupt the local political affairs of their respective cities, and that they do not have adequate means to cope with this well organized and powerful criminal organization, and have asked the Federal government for assistance in coping with this alleged criminal aggression.
>
> There appears to be no adequate Federal statute which can be invoked against the activities of this organized syndicate. The Resolution I am filing today would authorize and direct the Committee on the Judiciary of the Senate to make investigation to determine whether there is an organized syndicate operating in interstate commerce which is menacing the independence of free municipal governments, for the benefit of the criminal activities of the syndicate, and determine and report to the Senate their findings on whether the states and municipalities can, without Federal assistance, adequately cope with this organized crime movement. The Committee would also be directed to investigate the jurisdiction of the Federal government over the activities of any criminal syndicate, and make recommendations for any necessary legislation.

Senator Kefauver clearly was reflecting the contention of the AMA, the crime-fighting journalists, and others that a nationwide criminal conspiracy did exist and that it already possessed sufficient strength to threaten democratic control of American life in various places. Further, the statement implied that the "Federal government"—by which he meant the Truman administration—was negligent in meeting this threat and must be forced to take action. Kefauver's commitment to these preconceived views never wavered. Perhaps the most remarkable achievement of his investigation was that these assumptions were accepted as correct by the general public and by a majority of Congress.

The path of Senate Resolution 202 from its introduction to ultimate approval by the full Senate comprises an excellent case study in the complex issues affecting a congressional investigation. Tracing the course of Kefauver's proposal through the halls and committee rooms of Congress would demand far more space than is possible here; however, a brief description is essential, for the treatment accorded Senate Resolution 202 made obvious the problems and pressures that confronted any investigation—and especially one involving such a sensitive issue as "politico-criminal corruption"—during a difficult period.

It has been stated that numerous similarities exist between the Kefauver committee and the Truman committee, especially regarding the problems each encountered in obtaining support and funding from the Senate leadership; however, the traumatic early history of Kefauver's project makes Harry Truman's problems with his attempt to carry out a study of the defense program appear mild by comparison. There were three potential roadblocks: the attitude of President Truman and federal law enforcement agency heads, the issues of jurisdiction and propriety raised by the Senate leadership, and the vulnerability of any such inquiry to partisan political maneuvering. Kefauver was required, of course, to drag his proposal over all three of these obstacles simultaneously; but in order to comprehend the scope of the problems they posed, each will be analyzed separately.

In some ways, the danger of an attempt by the president or his advisers to squelch the proposed investiga-

Members of the Senate crime investigating committee, left to right, are Senator Charles Tobey of New Hampshire, Senator Herbert O'Conor of Maryland, chief counsel Rudolph Halley, Senator Estes Kefauver of Tennessee, and Senator Alexander Wiley of Wisconsin, as they arrived at the White House, June 1, 1950. (Library of Congress)

tion was least worrisome. By early 1950 the Truman administration simply did not have sufficient strength to oppose a congressional study of organized crime, for any such act would lead to charges that the administration had something to hide. Attorney General McGrath and, undoubtedly, President Truman were concerned about the baneful effects of Kefauver's investigation. They feared that the inquiry might get out of control, and they specifically worried about the embarrassment it might cause Democratic candidates in the 1950 elections. There was, however, little they could do to stop Kefauver, though a number of the president's supporters in the Senate were pressed to cool down the impudent Tennessean.

Kefauver seems to have been so little concerned about White House reaction that he neglected to consult either the president or the attorney general before filing his resolution. (He did send a copy of the proposal to McGrath on January 9 with the comment: "I tried to reach you before filing this resolution, but was unable to do so, and circumstances were such that it was necessary to go ahead with it, at the time I did.") There were certainly no conditions imposed by the executive comparable to those Truman had had to swallow ten years earlier. It appears that the administration sought only to restrain Kefauver from going overboard (as was happening with McCarthy's investigation of internal subversion) and to use delaying tactics whenever possible. Kefauver did meet with the attorney general in mid-January and as a concession to the administration agreed to take part in the upcoming crime conference and to postpone formal presentation of his resolution until the conference had ended. For his part, McGrath blocked an effort to have the crime conference issue a resolution of support for a congressional investigation, and the Justice Department and other executive agencies offered only formal assistance for some months after the committee launched its inquiries.

Possible countermoves by the administration undoubtedly worried supporters of the Kefauver project; but they had their hands full warding off friendly enemies and competitors in Congress. Kefauver had planned that the Judiciary Committee would oversee any investigation of organized crime. That idea was immediately caught up in a jurisdictional squabble between the Judiciary Committee and the Interstate and Foreign Commerce Committee, neither of which was especially enthusiastic about Kefauver's proposal. At the same time, Senator McCarthy made an abortive effort to have the Special Investigations Committee, which had examined the "five-percenters" scandal the previous year, and on which he served, assume principal responsibility for any crime investigation. Suggestions were also made that the investigation be converted into a joint House-Senate affair. Because the resolution focused on criminal operations which crossed state lines, the Commerce Committee, which had conducted similar inquiries in the past, appeared to have clear title to control an investigation that, in Kefauver's own words, would study "the manner in which the facilities of interstate commerce are made a vehicle of organized crime." Objections by Kefauver and his supporters were simple: Kefauver was not a member of the Commerce Committee and thus could not have taken part in any investigation sponsored by it. On the other hand, the Judiciary Committee, according to the Senate Democratic leadership, was hardly a wise choice. It was chaired by Senator Pat McCarran, an old-line conservative who despised the Truman Administration and, being from Nevada, was certainly not sympathetic to an investigation of organized crime. Further, the Judiciary Committee contained Republicans Homer Ferguson of Michigan and Forrest Donnell of Missouri, both of whom were eager to seize upon an investigation of crime and corruption in urban centers for partisan political advantage.

A wild melee of cloakroom discussions and parliamentary maneuvers, lasting for some four months, ensued. Kefauver later admitted: "As I look back on the struggle to set up the committee I sometimes wonder that we were ever able to bring it into existence." First, McCarran blocked progress of Senate Resolution 202 for two months by assigning it to a study group which he dominated, and then tacked on impossible amendments when the full committee did consider it. Eventually, the favorable publicity Kefauver's idea was receiving forced McCarran to release the resolution. However, at this point a further effort was made to assign the crime investigation to the Commerce Committee. Belligerent Republicans attempted to put over a *fait accompli* by having a commerce subcommittee undertake a study of the race wire service question and later to extend the scope of its activities. The only notable result of this short-lived probe was a statement by Attorney General McGrath that the Justice Department had no persuasive evidence that a "national crime syndicate" did exist.

The stalemate was broken in mid-April 1950 when the Democratic Policy Committee, composed of the Democratic leadership of Congress, recommended that a special investigatory committee, with members from both the Judiciary and Commerce Committees and with Estes Kefauver as its chairman, be created. It has been suggested that this compromise was the result of the discovery on April 6, 1950, of two murdered Kansas City gangsters and political figures, their crumpled bodies found in a Democratic club, sprawled under a huge photograph of President Truman. The publicity from this incident certainly had its effect, but the Democratic leadership probably acted because of the threat of a Republican takeover of the crime investigation. Certainly partisan politics played a large role in the final chapter of Senate Resolution 202's hegira. Republicans, outraged by the blatant move to avoid Commerce Committee (and thus, Republican) sponsorship of the investigation, worked furiously to defeat authorization by the full Senate. Amid shouts of "whitewash" and "cover-up" the Senate voted and found itself deadlocked. Vice President Alben Barkley, acting as a faithful Democrat, cast the tie-breaking vote, and the Senate Special Committee to Investigate Organized Crime in Interstate Commerce came into existence.

It is perhaps unnecessary to reiterate that the Kefauver committee was born amid political antagonisms and would be involved in partisan politics for its duration. Democrats assumed that the investigation would tread lightly past questionable relationships between gangsters and big-city Democratic organizations. Republicans were equally sure that the purpose behind the inquiry, which after all had been proposed and organized by Democrats, was to whitewash the iniquities perpetrated by Democratic political machines. Such assessments ignored the personality and outlook of Estes Kefauver. He had always gone his own way and kept his own counsel, refusing to give blind allegiance to a political party or its leaders. One writer was to comment later: "Kefauver's handling of the crime hearings was a very special feat. To a lesser man, such an assignment could have been political suicide." Kefauver was permitted to assume a comparatively independent position not because he was trusted, but because few people in either party believed that his investigation would receive much attention. Probably no one was more surprised than Kefauver when his dream of winning national recognition as a crime-fighting congressman came true.

II

Senate Resolution 202, as amended, was approved by the Senate on May 2, 1950. It established the Special Committee to Investigate Organized Crime in Interstate Commerce, with all the scope that its title suggested. It was given authority to conduct its study of crime until March 1, 1951 (later extended until September 1, 1951), a budget of $150,000, and the usual subpoena and other powers. The committee was charged with three tasks: "to determine whether organized crime utilizes the facilities of interstate commerce" to carry on illegal activities; to investigate the "manner and extent of such criminal operations," identifying the guilty parties; and to discover if the activities of organized crime "were developing corrupting influence in violation of the Federal law or the laws of any state." This was an impressively broad mandate.

Senator Kefauver, who naturally assumed he would be chairman of the committee, began immediately to press for office space and staff; but for a time he found himself without authority or even colleagues. Vice President Barkley deliberated for a week over the appointment of the committee's members, but finally announced his selections on May 10, 1950. He chose the ranking Republican members of the Commerce and Judiciary Committees—Charles W. Tobey of New Hampshire and Alexander Wiley of Wisconsin—as the minority representation. Then, from a large list the vice president appointed Kefauver, Lester C. Hunt of Wyoming, and Herbert R. O'Conor of Maryland as the Democratic members. At its first meeting the next day, May 11, the committee formally elected Kefauver as their chairman.

In his impressive biography of Kefauver, Joseph B. Gorman has observed: "All five [committee members] were known as relatively quiet, mild-mannered, and fair men, and the attention the committee was to attract stood in sharp contrast to the personalities of the senators serving on it." Despite his aggressive efforts in behalf of the investigation, Kefauver was determined that the probe proceed cautiously and with a minimum of sensationalism. "The temptation to become a publicity-grabber, a table-thumper, a modern Torquemada was great," one of Kefauver's associates has noted; but the scholarly Tennessean abjured McCarthy-style tactics. Such tactics were risky and, more important, flamboyance and inquisitorial pressures made Kefauver uncomfortable. His colleagues on the committee agreed with this view of the investigation, though on more than one occasion members were to violate the spirit if not the letter of the agreement.

In 1951 Estes Kefauver was forty-six years old. Born in Madisonville, Tennessee, in 1903 to a socially prominent and wealthy family, Kefauver attended the University of Tennessee and Yale Law School, obtaining great popularity for his athletic and academic exploits. He practiced law in Chattanooga for a decade, joining "everything in town," and then won a seat in the House of Representatives in 1939. For the next ten years he worked steadily at this job, earning a reputation as one of the brightest and most effective of the southern liberal bloc in Congress. He also became known as something of a political maverick, challenging the House

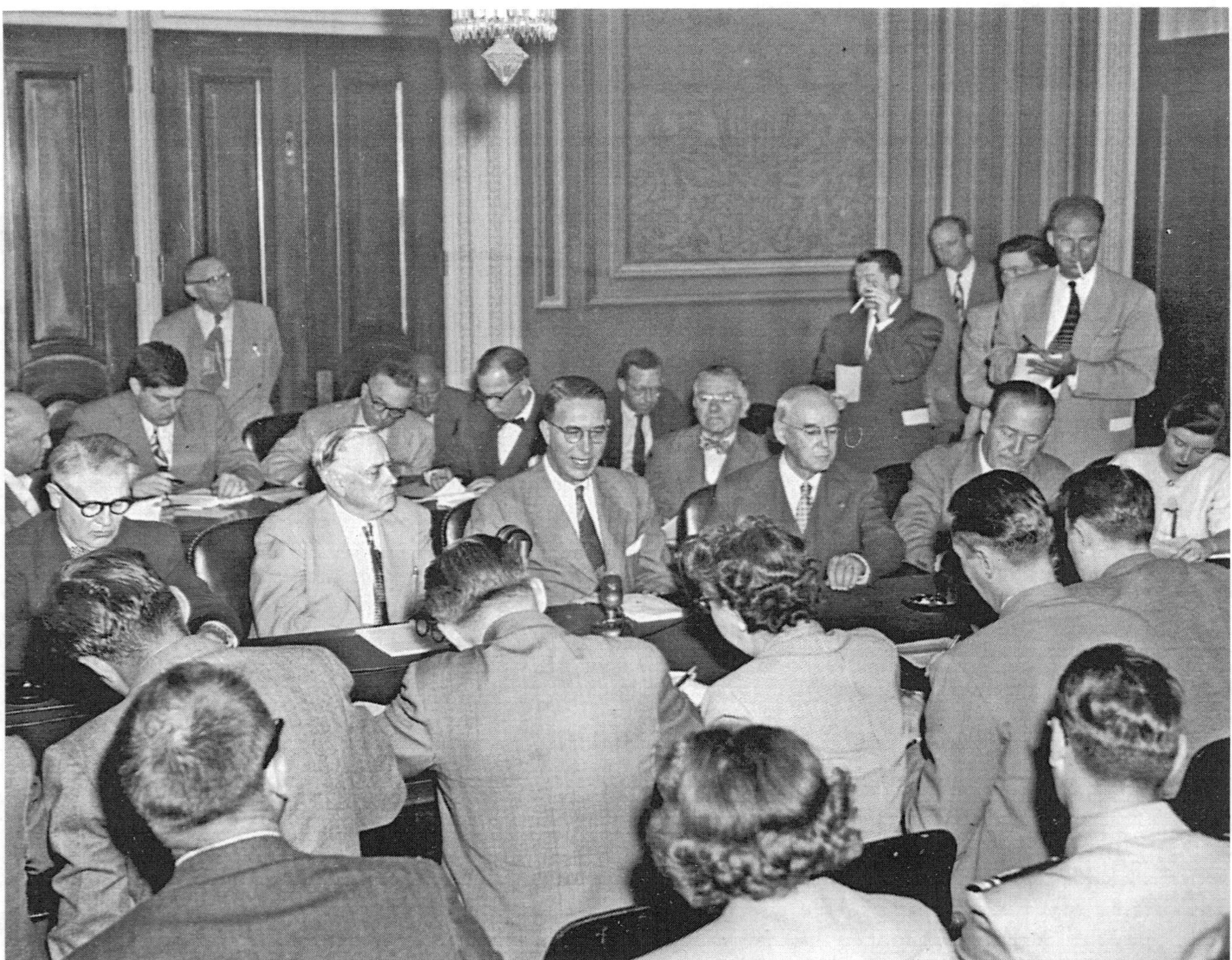

Members of the Senate crime investigating committee meet with reporters at a news conference. Left to right: Senators Lester Hunt, Alexander Wiley, Chairman Estes Kefauver, Charles Tobey, and Herbert O'Conor. (National Archives)

leadership on such issues as TVA and civil rights. By personal inclination and experience, Kefauver was a single-minded student of each issue that claimed his attention. He clearly was determined to put all else aside to conduct the crime investigation, though, of course, having just been elected to a six-year term, he could afford to ignore his constituents. Kefauver, like Harry S. Truman before him, was the moving force in the investigation he headed.

Kefauver's Democratic colleagues on the committee were both experienced politicians but relative newcomers to Washington. Lester C. Hunt had been elected to the Senate in 1948, after holding various state offices in Wyoming and serving as governor for three terms. Hunt, a former dentist, was considered an administration "regular" and had already obtained two prestigious committee assignments: Armed Services and Commerce. Although he had been initially reluctant to serve on the crime committee, Hunt soon recognized its potential, and he became a fairly active member. Herbert R. O'Conor, one of three lawyers on the committee, was a onetime reporter who had served as governor of Maryland during World War II. O'Conor came to the Senate in 1947, and had been a member of the Special Committee to Investigate the National Defense Program, then tottering toward dissolution, and of the Internal Security Subcommittee. He was close to Senator McCarran and was known as a conservative, opposed to much of Truman's domestic program. O'Conor was always doubtful about the wisdom of Kefauver's investigation of organized crime and took only an occasional interest in the committee's hearings.

Despite the fact that the two Republicans, Tobey and Wiley, were running for reelection in 1950 and that both faced serious challenges, they took an active part in the committee's deliberations. Clearly, both were eager to seize any political (or partisan) advantage that service on the crime committee might offer; but the two senators, especially Tobey, became deeply interested in the outcome of the investigation. Charles W. Tobey, a veteran of New Hampshire and national politics, had been in the Senate since 1939. Entering political life as a Bull Moose Republican, Tobey was counted among the liberal Republicans, though perhaps more for his eccentric personality than for substantive reasons. One writer has described his participation as follows: "Tobey used his appointment to the Kefauver Committee to his political advantage in New Hampshire and made it into a forum for his intense showmanship, but he also genuinely enjoyed the sleuthing, energetically pursuing leads from taxicab drivers and porters, and continually referring rumormongers to an indulgent Committee staff." Alexander Wiley, also a colorful, veteran campaigner, had entered the Senate in 1938. Though Wiley was a member of several powerful committees, including Foreign Relations, he had *sought* an appointment to the Kefauver crime probe. His participation was limited by the other demands on his time, but he did take part when topics with vote getting potential, such as the Chicago crime situation and Democratic corruption, were raised.

In sum, the membership of the special crime committee was typical of such inquiries but perhaps reflected better qualifications and greater involvement than most. The committee was less important in some ways than the staff that served it. Kefauver recognized this fact. He insisted that the committee hire the best-qualified staff to be found and that their selection be on a non-partisan basis. He later expressed his viewpoint on this crucial issue:

> Before choosing anyone for the staff, we had several committee meetings at which I stated my position to my fellow members. I told them I felt we had a great challenge to prove that we really were going to carry out our promise of a sincere, thorough, and non-partisan investigation. . . . My colleagues all agreed with me that the way to confound . . . critics was for us to forget that we were Democrats or Republicans, to select a non-partisan staff, and to investigate without regard as to whom we might benefit or hurt. I told my colleagues firmly that I never did believe in committees being divided into majority and minority factions; that if we were to do any good at all we had to work as a team. I told them that I had no favorite lawyers or investigators from my home state of Tennessee to place on the committee . . . and that I would like to see all personnel chosen without regard for patronage or politics. Competence rather than influence was to be the yardstick for choosing the staff. The committee, I believe, faithfully utilized that yardstick.

Given the difficult political climate in which the crime investigation was launched, Kefauver's desires were carried out with surprisingly few difficulties. A major factor was the appointment of Rudolph Halley as chief counsel to the committee. Halley had impressive experience with congressional investigations, having served on the staff of the Truman committee and later as chief counsel for its successor, the Mead committee. A brilliant and aggressive lawyer, Halley left a lucrative New York law practice to work for the crime committee. He quickly assumed responsibility for planning the committee's schedule and, recognizing the tremendous publicity to be gained from public hearings, pointed Kefauver toward the "grand finale" confrontation with the "big shots" of organized crime in New York.

Both Kefauver and Halley agreed that the crime committee should rely primarily on information dredged up by other inquiries, especially state crime commissions, and that this should be supplemented by interviews and testimony. Thus, the staff should be composed of persons with solid contacts with law enforcement agencies and study groups. The investigative component was headed by Harold Robinson, who had worked for the Truman committee and was then chief investigator on the California Crime Commission, and included several newspapermen, former FBI agents and race track investigators, police officers on leave from various urban police departments, and narcotics, gambling, and wiretapping experts. The legal staff in Washington possessed equally diverse and intensive backgrounds in law enforcement and related fields. In addition, investigators were hired or borrowed from cooperating agencies in each city through which Kefauver's "crime show" moved on its journey across the country. At times this caused confusion and tension within the committee staff and between the staff and disgruntled outsiders. But the staff did manage to schedule and complete preparatory work on over six hundred witnesses in less than one year.

The course to be followed by the Kefauver Committee was written during the weeks prior to its first hearings, held in Miami on May 26, 1950. As mentioned previously, Kefauver did not intend that the committee would undertake a comprehensive study of crime in America. His concern was whether a nationwide crime organization existed, where the sources of its power lay, and the

Senator Estes Kefauver, standing, chairman of the Senate crime investigating committee, opens a one-day hearing in Las Vegas into Las Vegas gambling enterprises. The first witness, William J. Moore, executive director of the Last Frontier Hotel, is at right foreground. (Harold P. Matosian/Associated Press)

degree to which criminal elements had purchased the cooperation and acquiescence of local governments in their activities. The principal means of uncovering information about these three issues was through a probe of gambling, "the life blood of organized crime"; that meant that Kefauver and his colleagues first focused on urban areas, the strongholds of both gangsters and Democrats. During the fifteen months of its existence, the crime committee convened hearings in fourteen major cities: Miami, Kansas City, St. Louis, Philadelphia, Chicago, Tampa, Cleveland, Detroit, New Orleans, Las Vegas, San Francisco, Los Angeles, New York, and Washington. Of course, investigators visited numerous other areas, but the committee itself confined its activities to these cities, with the exception of a brief foray into Saratoga County, New York, the location of a famed gambling spa and racetrack.

Kefauver's conception of the committee's task was that it should reveal and dramatize to the American people the extent to which organized crime had infiltrated the nation's economic and political life. Therefore, he was much more interested in confrontations with known bosses and corrupt politicians than in the tedious job of uncovering all others involved in criminal activities. Thus, the committee could rely heavily on information garnered from previous investigations at the local level. J. Edgar Hoover once asserted, in fact, that local authorities already knew enough about criminal operations that they could "clean up organized gambling in forty-eight hours if they wanted to." Kefauver readily admitted that the crime committee was turning up little that was new; but, he said, "the fact that certain information is known to some people and the assembly of that information in such a way that a legislative program can be based on it are two quite different things." The investigators did uncover fascinating and significant details about criminal activities. Further, the decision of President Truman in June 1950 to order appropriate agencies of the federal government to open their files to the committee produced some important breakthroughs. Information from income tax files controlled by the Treasury Department and the Internal Revenue Service was especially helpful, though this source was closed off as the investigation proceeded.

The critical procedural issue faced by the crime committee was not accessibility of records but availability of witnesses. Since the public impact of the investigation was based upon face-to-face interrogations of "real live criminals" (as well as assorted police chiefs, district attorneys, and federal officials), the ability of the committee to compel witnesses to appear and, then, to have them respond to direct questioning was basic. The committee made enormous use of the subpoena power, but it encountered considerable difficulty in enforcing its subpoenas because of the archaic procedures imposed upon it by the Senate's rules.

Kefauver recalled this problem: "As soon as we served subpoenas on certain hoodlums many of their partners in crime, whose testimony was vital, went into hiding—some even fleeing the country. We felt it was urgently necessary for us to be able to go directly to the full Senate and obtain immediate warrants of arrest for subpoena-dodgers. . . . We found ourselves saddled with a time-wasting procedure which required us to go through the formality of requesting the Senate sergeant-at-arms to search for the missing witnesses before the arrest warrants were issued. The estimable Senate sergeant-at-arms, of course, is a parliamentary officer rather than a policeman and simply has no facilities of his own for tracking down fugitive gangsters." This difficulty was never resolved.

Secondly, there arose the thorny problem of compelling witnesses to answer questions once they did appear before the committee. Kefauver and Halley decided at the beginning to follow rules regarding the rights of witnesses established by the Truman committee. Witnesses were permitted the aid of counsel and could submit prior statements to the committee. Kefauver insisted that persons accused in testimony be given an opportunity to refute charges against them and instituted other safeguards. The American Civil Liberties Union later commented: "The hearings were conducted, with one or two exceptions, in an atmosphere of fairness and sober fact-finding, without resort to the hysteria and wild accusations which have marked other Congressional probes." Nevertheless, there arose serious questions regarding the committee's procedures: with regard to the effect of television (a problem that will be discussed later), and the right of witnesses to plead the Fifth Amendment.

At the time the Kefauver Committee conducted hearings, the use of the Fifth Amendment safeguard was under attack from various quarters. Although Kefauver and chairmen of other investigatory committees admitted that congressional hearings were not judicial proceedings and that they were held to obtain information and not to ascertain guilt or innocence, the temptation to assume the position of a prosecutor was often irresistible. When witness after witness answered even the most innocuous questions with the bland phrase, "I refuse to answer on the ground that it may tend to incriminate or degrade me," Kefauver and his colleagues sought to force compliance by issuing contempt-of-Congress citations. The committee's view was that the Fifth Amendment did not excuse witnesses from answering "legitimate" (non-self-incriminating) questions or from answering questions relating to state or local offenses. Voting contempt citations in such circumstances clearly represented an attempt to punish hostile witnesses, and federal courts, recognizing that fact, overturned the first twenty-two contempt cases stemming from the crime committee hearings; after two years the courts had upheld only three such citations. In the court of public opinion, however, the committee won a smashing victory. Each time a Frank Costello, Joe Adonis, or some other sullen-faced gangster uttered the fateful words, he was found guilty by the public.

III

Many of the above questions had still to be faced when the crime committee convened its first hearings in Miami. The "Miami story" did not prove especially noteworthy or unique, but as the first of many visits to urban centers, it focused public attention on the committee and provided a powerful impetus for continuation of the crime committee's activities. Kefauver's purpose in going to Miami was to look into the gambling situation—and he found evidence of gambling everywhere. "Card games, dice games, numbers games, roulette and other gambling wheels operated in establishments varying from the well-appointed air-conditioned casinos set up for the purpose, to night clubs and restaurants and private rooms in various hotels. Bookmaking operated out of newsstands, cigar stands or elaborate horse rooms, in most hotels, and even from specially fitted cabanas on the beach." The most shocking information dramatized by the committee was an apparent connection between persons close to Florida's Democratic governor, Fuller Warren, and a bookmaking syndicate controlled by the Capone mob in Chicago. Until 1949, most bookmaking in Miami had been conducted by the "S. and G. Syndicate," a local organization that operated betting shops in some 200 hotels and had grossed $26.5 million in 1948 alone. Then, in January 1949, Governor Warren appointed W. O. Crosby as a special investigator to control gambling; Crosby was later found to have been involved with the Capone organization, but he did lead some gambling raids in Dade County, though only against S. and G. establishments. S. and G. suffered further difficulties when the Continental Press Service, a racing news organization also controlled by Capone people, cut off the flow of information about horse and dog races to S. and G. About this time a Capone associate, Harry Russell, was made a full partner in the S. and G. Syndicate. The Kefauver Committee later learned that Russell had paid $20,000 for half of a $26 million business. Shortly thereafter, raids on S. and C. bookies ceased and the racing news service was restored. The committee also learned that another Capone representative had given $100,000 to Governor Warren's campaign fund. Further, when it was disclosed that the sheriff of Dade County had become a wealthy man after five years in office and had tried to block a crime study by the Greater Miami Crime Commission, only to be upheld by Governor Warren, the Kefauver committee had uncovered a real case with which to dramatize gangsterism and political corruption.

Unfortunately, pursuit of the mess in Miami forced the committee to attack the state Democratic organization—from Governor Warren down. The committee limited its criticism to a summary statement in its report, but the damage was done. Governor Warren began a bitter vendetta against Kefauver and other committee members, but his attacks served only to hasten his own demise and to generate favorable publicity for the committee. However, the episode also produced some nervous foreboding in the headquarters of the Democratic National Committee—and anger in the White House. Soon thereafter, cooperation from the Truman administration noticeably cooled down.

The committee's next stop was Kansas City, the place from which Harry Truman had emerged to national prominence and in which the president still retained close ties with the local Democratic organization. The crime committee's findings regarding criminal activities in Kansas City were not particularly shocking, but they may be viewed as typical of the developing emphases of the investigation. As Kefauver observed in *Crime in America:* "Between Miami Beach and Kansas City, we had been assembling small pieces of the national crime mosaic which would fit later into the big picture. We had not been overwhelmed yet by the repetitious mass of evidence we were to accumulate all over the country, pointing to raw and brutal rule by criminals and utter prostitution of their oaths of office by some officials who were supposed to serve the public. Hence the Kansas City situation hit us with doubly powerful impact. . . . I shall never forget my first impression of the city as a place that was struggling out from under the rule of the law of the jungle." What the committee found (or believed it found) there "was a staggering example of a prosperous city . . . which, through indifference and civil inertia, had fallen under the influence of as vicious a bunch of criminals as existed anywhere." In particular, the committee considered Kansas City to be dominated by the Mafia.

The Kansas City example completely justified the crime committee's investigations, for it possessed all those ominous developments that the committee had dedicated itself to exposing. First, there was clear proof of a nationally organized criminal conspiracy operating within the city. Second, Kansas City offered abundant information and clues as to who led this conspiracy and their motives. Third, the committee's study also revealed the connection between these criminal leaders and state and local elected officials. Hearings were held in Washington and in Kansas City, and forty-eight witnesses, including Governor Forrest Smith, various law enforcement representatives, and "a number of the city's known gamblers and racketeers," were questioned.

Kefauver decided that information obtained in Kansas City provided indisputable proof that the racing wire services represented the principal vehicle by which organized crime was spreading its influence across state lines and throughout the nation. This conviction, a basic support of the committee's assertion that an organized criminal conspiracy did exist, received constant reiteration. Kefauver termed the racing news service (particularly the Continental Press, the nation's largest racing wire operation) "America's Public Enemy Number One." Continental Press, which leased 23,000 miles of telegraph circuits from Western Union for the purpose of distributing racing information, was supposedly an independent, lawfully operated business. In fact, the Kefauver committee concluded, it was "a powerful and indispensable ally of the underworld," and was totally controlled by the Capone organization. Kansas City was a vital distribution center for the Continental News Service (CNS) racing news operation.

Of note was the observation that the persons behind CNS and almost every other gambling-vice activity in Kansas City were Italian-American. The list of witnesses called before the Kefauver committee in Kansas City included Joseph Di Giovanni, James Balestere, Tony Gizzo, and Tano Lococo. The committee was convinced that this was not coincidental, that the domination of Kansas City crime as elsewhere by Italian-Americans was further proof that the Mafia, an international criminal conspiracy, controlled crime throughout the United States. "In past years," the committee's *Third Interim Report* proclaimed, "Kansas City was known as a center for the activities of the Mafia, or Unione Siciliano, which is said to be a secret organization operating throughout the country and internationally." Though witnesses claimed total ignorance of any such organization, the committee refused to credit their testimony. It listed sixteen unsolved murders as Mafia-arranged, and suggested that the killings of Charles Binaggio, a gambler and Kansas City Democratic leader, and his henchman, Charles Gargotta, in April 1950 were masterminded by the Mafia leadership after Binaggio failed to fulfill a promise to use his political influence to "open up Kansas City."

The Binaggio case led the committee into an ugly case of political corruption and influence-peddling that stretched from the headquarters of the First Ward Democratic Club possibly as far as the statehouse in Jefferson City. "The Committee heard considerable testimony," its *Report* cautiously admitted, "relating to attempts by Binaggio to exert political influence to open up for gambling and other illegal operations the State of Missouri, and particularly St. Louis and Kansas City." Rumors of enormous contributions by Binaggio to Governor Smith's campaign fund were discussed, but no solid evidence was presented. It was clear that Smith and Binaggio were friendly, and that the governor had appointed police commissioners "who were at least acceptable to Binaggio"; however, the committee refused to accuse Governor Smith of willful wrongdoing.

By its very presence, nonetheless, the Kefauver committee was calling attention to an awkward, politically embarrassing mess in President Truman's backyard. Kefauver could say, as he did in a concluding statement in Kansas City on September 30, "We haven't been out here with the intention of protecting anyone, of harming anyone, but of carrying out the mission that we were given by the United States Senate." Even so, Democrats were being harmed, some badly, by the committee's disclosures. The committee itself might struggle mightily not to take sides, but others inevitably drew politically motivated conclusions from the crime committee's reports. An example of this phenomenon was the Chicago hearings, hurriedly arranged by Kefauver after the killings of two men who were at work gathering evidence on ties between organized crime and the Cook County Democratic organization. Senator Scott Lucas, then fighting an uphill battle for reelection, had been assured that the crime committee would not come into Chicago until after the election. Having agreed reluctantly to support Kefauver's proposed investigation the previous spring, Lucas was furious when the committee convened hearings in Chicago in late October. On November 1 Police Captain Dan Gilbert admitted to permitting widespread violations of gambling laws and other irregularities. This testimony, given in closed session, found its way to Chicago newspapers and was published just days before the election. Senator Lucas and numerous other Democrats were defeated, an occurrence Lucas attributed completely to the Kefauver committee's inopportune appearance in Chicago.

As the crime committee traveled from city to city during the fall and early winter of 1950, it seemed that Kefauver had accomplished—though at what cost no one then knew—his aim of conducting a fair, nonpartisan inquiry in order to bring the staggering dimensions of organized crime before the American people. Joseph B. Gorman has effectively summed up this first phase of the committee's endeavors. "The pattern was the same everywhere the committee went. Local crime commissions, grand juries, crusading newspapers, and sympathetic law enforcement officers all made available everything that might be of interest to the committee, and the staff had all it could handle just organizing the information supplied to it. Even though almost all the local evidence had been made public before, there was nevertheless a shock on reviewing the accumulated evidence of years, and the Kefauver Committee made headlines wherever it went." Favorable publicity, combined with the stance of absolute impartiality assumed by the committee (despite internal conflict and external attacks), made the crime committee, for a time, almost invulnerable to attack. By the end of the year Senator Kefauver had been transformed into a modern Sir Galahad, crisscrossing the country in search of evildoers upon whom to wield the fatal sword of public exposure. Of course, Kefauver was protected not by some magic talisman but rather by the continuing decline of popular support for President Truman and the partisan bickering of Congress. In the unhappy days of early 1951, with the Korean "police action" grinding on and the country caught in a spiral of inflation and shortages, any hero, even such an unlikely one as Estes Kefauver, was welcomed.

Opposition to the crime committee was growing in Congress, however, and was led by the vengeful Scott Lucas, Pat McCarran (who had been outraged by Kefauver's report on organized crime's domination of Las Vegas), and others. Little could be done, though, while the committee enjoyed such enormous popularity. "Let's face it," a Democratic stalwart admitted, "the Kefauver committee hurts the party and the longer it keeps going, the more we'll be hurt. But we can't stop it, not while it possesses glamour. Any effort to block it would be a political blunder, maybe suicide." The Democratic leadership's helplessness was reflected in the Senate's quick approval of Kefauver's request that the committee's authorization be extended in order to conduct hearings already planned for New York City. Senators could grumble, but they dared not oppose the request. Not even a protest emerged from the White House, where an embattled president kept his own counsel. Possibly, leaders of both the legislative and executive branches hoped that the crime committee's claim on popular attention was about exhausted and that after the hearings in New York, it would fade away into oblivion. If so, they were soon disabused. The New York hearings, which introduced television audiences to numerous "Mr. Bigs" in the underworld, proved to be the high point of the entire investigation.

That the Kefauver committee in one day of televised hearings became a "national phenomenon" was totally unexpected, for the decision to permit a New York station to televise the proceedings was made only a day or so before the first session. It must be emphasized, however, that Kefauver and the committee staff had been pointing toward New York as a perfect final act for their traveling show since the beginning. The committee stated: "The New York hearings were vital . . . for a number of reasons. New York City, because of its size, location, dominance in the country, complexity of its population and governmental problems, is one of the major centers of organized crime." Rudolph Halley, the committee's ambitious chief counsel, was particularly determined that the New York hearings be a smashing success. In fact, Halley seems to have considered the other city investigations as something like out-of-town rehearsals. They certainly had that effect, for the New York hearings featured impressive performances by the committee, the staff, and their totally believable supporting cast of gangsters and their mouthpieces.

The Kefauver committee was the fifth congressional committee to allow television cameras into a hearing room. The most notable use of television previously had been at the House Committee on Un-American Activities interrogation of Alger Hiss. Of course, congressional investigations had authorized the presence of film crews for some two decades, and newsreels had given most Americans some familiarity with the setting and procedures of a congressional hearing. Thus, no one apparently considered television to be in a different category. The committee's hearings in New Orleans already had been televised live. The favorable response to that experiment persuaded Kefauver to allow television in New York, but neither he nor anyone else grasped clearly the essential difference between television and film: that viewers were observing events as they happened. The tremendous power of television derived from this fact, and its discovery made Kefauver a presidential contender and perhaps did even more for the fledgling television industry.

When the committee opened hearings in New York on March 12, 1951, only New York and a few other stations carried the broadcast, but stations in twenty cities blanketing the Eastern seaboard and much of the Midwest quickly picked up the hearings. *Time* agreed to sponsor New York coverage; the response astonished everyone. Kefauver's personal assessment was most revealing: "The hour-by-hour television coverage of the proceedings . . . reached an estimated audience of between 20,000,000 and 30,000,000, and the effect was unbelievable. In New York City itself . . . businesses were paralyzed; many movie houses became 'ghost' halls. . . ; and housewives did their ironing and mending in front of their TV sets. Throughout the country the Crime Committee became . . . a national crusade, a great debating forum, an arouser of public opinion on the state of the nation's morals."

A statistical-demographic analysis suggests certain obvious explanations for the popularity accorded the crime hearings. First, the percentage of homes with television sets in the New York metropolitan area had jumped from 29 to 51 percent during the previous year. At that time the typical daytime programming was so poor that only 1.5 percent of those sets were in use on an average morning. The incredible rise in viewing (seventeen times normal) and equally rapid growth in the viewing audience could be easily explained. At certain times 86.2 percent of those watching television in the New York area were tuned to the crime committee hearings.

Still, statistics cannot convey the incredible impact of the hearings upon their audience. For eight days Americans watched spellbound as some forty witnesses marched confidently forward to be sworn in (eight days of public hearings and five private sessions were held; the committee heard eighty-nine witnesses and conferred with approximately five hundred others), only to be reduced to an incoherence of belligerent silence by Halley's devastating questioning and the calm, confident behavior of Kefauver and his colleagues. "It was as if everything . . . had been designed to reinforce the simplistic concepts of American politics conveyed through thousands of high school government classes and textbooks," one scholar has written. "Good and evil, heroes and villains, black and white categorization made each specific encounter between committee and witness easy to follow. All five senators played their roles perfectly." The committee was eager to explore such topics as the links between crime and politics in New York, criminal operations on the waterfront, bookmaking and gambling activities, especially at Roosevelt Raceway, and the narcotics situation. However, the hearings pivoted upon the presentation of the argument that one criminal organization, a syndicate headed by gangsters Joe Adonis, Frank Costello, and Meyer Lansky, dominated New York crime. Both personal conviction and popular fascination with these underworld tycoons prompted the committee to zero in on the Costello-Adonis-Lansky operation and its influence over local government.

Frank Costello, alleged leader of the largest crime syndicate in America that engaged in bootlegging, slot machines, and gambling, testifies before the Kefauver committee, March 1951. (Library of Congress)

Frank Costello's appearance on March 13, and repeat performances later, proved the dramatic high point of the hearings. In part this was the result of both the man's reputation and the manipulative effects of television. Costello objected violently to the television cameras, and the committee decided that only his hands would be shown. Those hands twisted and clenched, revealing Costello's inner fears and confusion as Halley fired question after question at this "elder statesman" of crime. Increasingly frustrated by the committee's interrogation, Costello lapsed into incoherence and refused to answer many questions on grounds of self-incrimination. During the hearings on March 15 Costello abruptly claimed he was too ill to testify and walked out, pursued by Kefauver's ringing indictment. He returned the next day but proved so uncooperative that the committee cited him for contempt. This episode was significant because Frank Costello came to symbolize organized crime for millions of Americans, and they greeted his condemnation by the crime committee with unreserved approval, despite the committee's inability to substantiate many of its assertions about the New York situation.

Other interesting witnesses presented themselves before Kefauver, his colleagues, and the omniscient television camera before the hearings closed on March 21, 1951. Joe Adonis, his pomaded hair and tailored clothes a gangster caricature, bombastically described himself as a law-abiding citizen, but then had to resort to the Fifth Amendment when his involvement in gambling, extortion, and gang warfare was explored. Then came Virginia Hill, a stereotypical gangster moll, who told an incredible story of her relationships with Adonis, Costello, and Bugsy Siegel. Perhaps most disturbing of all was the painful exploration of former New York mayor William O'Dwyer's association with Costello and other gang leaders. O'Dwyer, who was currently serving as ambassador to Mexico, was asked to answer charges of influence-peddling and corrupt practices. His responses proved so unsatisfactory that the committee recommended perjury action be initiated and that his income

Joe Adonis turns his head as he sits in the witness chair before the Kefauver Senate crime investigating committee hearings on interstate crime, March 12, 1951, at the federal courthouse in New York. (Pool/INP/Associated Press)

Virginia Hill testified to the Kefauver committee in March 1951 about her relationships with mobsters. (Library of Congress)

tax returns be investigated. His testimony, however, did raise the matter of the committee's integrity for the first and only time (aside from Governor Warren's persistent but unsubstantiated sniping). O'Dwyer claimed he possessed evidence that Senator Tobey had received underworld money for political campaigns. Tobey made an emotional denial of the charge, and it turned out that O'Dwyer's "evidence" was worthless. The ambassador soon resigned his position, but the episode caused much embarrassment to the administration. As elsewhere, the New York hearings left the local Democratic organization in difficult circumstances.

The Kefauver committee returned to Washington, persuaded, as *Life* magazine proclaimed, that "the week of March 12, 1951 will occupy a special place in history." Scheduled hearings were conducted in Washington but then, though public interest in the investigation continued to be high, Kefauver decided that the committee had accomplished its principal goals and should be dissolved. "I do not think that the kind of investigative committee that we have had . . . is justified any longer, because we've found out what we were supposed to determine," he told US. *News and World Report* in April 1951. "Now that we have determined that, I think it's time to recommend legislation and see what we can get passed in the Congress." Kefauver's reasons for recommending an end to the inquiry were personal, pragmatic, and political. He had traveled over 50,000 miles on committee business and had conducted hearings on ninety-two days; thus, he was desperately eager to return home again. As well, Kefauver sincerely believed that the committee had proved its case and that its task now was to prepare a comprehensive legislative crime control program on the basis of the information it had acquired. Thirdly, Kefauver may have sensed that the committee could not continue on its independent course much longer without risking violent retaliation from the White House. Immediately after the conclusion of the New York hearings, the Truman administration began to formulate new initiatives on the "crime front" and to publicize the efforts of federal law enforcement agencies. At a press conference on March 29, for example, President Truman said: "We have been studying quietly but consistently the problems of adult crime, particularly organized crime which spills over state boundaries." Joseph McCarthy might have ignored these signals, given the comparative powerlessness of the Truman administration; but Kefauver was not prepared to risk an open break with the administration. In addition, he was advised to begin immediately the consolidation of the national reputation he had gained by a coordinated schedule of lectures, interviews, and writing.

Other members of the committee, more interested in the direct exposure from further hearings, demanded that an extension of the committee's mandate until at least September 1, 1951, be requested. Kefauver finally agreed to the extension but insisted on resigning as chairman. Senator O'Conor replaced him and the crime committee conducted a few desultory inquiries, largely following up leads uncovered earlier in the summer of 1951. Its effective end came, however, when Kefauver resigned as chairman and after the *Third Interim Report,* containing the crime committee's basic findings and recommendations, was released in May 1951.

IV

It must be said that the Kefauver committee left as many questions unanswered as had the most reticent of the hundreds of witnesses who appeared before it. Even today the real purposes of Senator Kefauver and the crime committee remain something of a mystery. Equally uncertain is any full assessment of the committee's accomplishments. One recent study of the committee, William Moore's impressively researched *The Kefauver Committee and the Politics of Crime, 1950–1952,* concludes that Kefauver launched the investigation almost entirely for political gain and, further, that the committee's basic thesis—that an organized, national crime conspiracy was at work—was erroneous. This is not the place to debate the existence of the Mafia, though it is clear that Kefauver and his colleagues, responding to public pressures, were determined from the beginning to find a scapegoat, some type of conspiratorial group with responsibility for much of America's crime.

Whether or not the Mafia or the syndicate or the mob was central, one must point to the almost total lack of success the committee experienced in getting crime control laws through Congress. Kefauver agreed with other law enforcement experts that crime control remained essentially a local responsibility. A federal police force or any of the other alarmist reactions to the crime committee's disclosures were, he believed, impractical and possibly dangerous. The committee's recommendations included the following:

Creation of a Federal Crime Commission "to coordinate and bring together and avoid duplication in the investigative services of the Federal Government."

Establishment of a "racket squad" in the Justice Department.

Establishment of a mechanism for maintaining "a list of known gangsters, racketeers, gamblers, and criminals whose income tax returns should receive special attention by a squad of trained experts."

Effective enforcement by the Internal Revenue Bureau of existing laws requiring adequate records of income and expenses by all taxpayers.

Strict controls over the records of gambling casinos.

"The law and the regulations of the Bureau of Internal Revenue should be amended so that no wagering losses, expenses, or disbursements of any kind . . . incurred in or as a result of illegal gambling shall be deductible for income-tax purposes."

Regulation of the transmission of gambling information across state lines by telegraph, telephone, television, radio, or other means "so as to outlaw any service devoted to a substantial extent to providing information used in illegal gambling."

Prohibition of the transmission of bets or wagers across state lines via the methods described above.

Prohibition of the transportation of slot machines in interstate commerce extended to include other gambling devices, such as punchboards, roulette wheels, and so forth.

Substantial increase in the penalties against illegal sale of narcotic drugs.

Amendment of the immigration laws to facilitate deportation of "criminal and other undesirable aliens." Other changes were also proposed.

Substantial expansion in the numbers of federal law enforcement personnel.

Clarification of the existing federal statute with respect to perjury.

The attorney general of the United States should be given authority to grant immunity from prosecution to witnesses whose testimony may be essential to an inquiry conducted by a grand jury, or in the course of a trial or of a congressional investigation.

Passage of legislation to compel the presence of evasive witnesses before a congressional investigation.

Legislation to prevent racketeers from entering the liquor industry and to eliminate any criminal elements presently involved in the production or distribution of liquor.

Recommendation that the Interstate Commerce Commission "be required by law to consider the moral fitness of applications" for certificates of necessity.

In one sense this list of recommendations comprised a comprehensive program for effective control of organized crime. Unfortunately, very few of the committee's proposals were enacted into law. Of some 221 legislative recommendations submitted to Congress as a result of the committee's activities, only a handful obtained a full hearing by standing committees of Congress. But the pressure generated by the crime committee and by an alarmed public did produce stronger enforcement of existing laws, and this must be considered a positive achievement.

In general, any assessment of the Kefauver Committee must deal with the tremendous effect it had on public awareness of the problem of organized crime. For better or for worse, the "publicity function" is basic to the work of any congressional investigation. There can be no doubt about the success of the crime committee in this field. As a result of the committee's dramatization of the problem, public concern about organized crime and instances of local corruption attained a level of awareness heretofore unimagined. More than seventy local commissions were created, and those already in existence received fresh support. There existed the danger of vigilantism and, even more worrisome, the possibility that local groups would conclude that the crime committee had shown that the problem was beyond their capabilities or that such groups could rely solely on the federal government for solutions to the threat of organized crime. Something like this did occur over the next decade, but Senator Kefauver and the crime committee did not intentionally foster vigilante sentiment or the belief that a "man on horseback" would appear to save America from organized crime. Yet the nature of the investigation and the manner in which the committee presented its case led inevitably to such judgments. The "times were out of joint," and it would have demanded men of extraordinary courage and vision to resist the yearning for simple, easy solutions to problems and concerns then sweeping the nation.

Indeed, placed against this backdrop of popular tensions and political turmoil, the procedures followed by the Kefauver committee were remarkably enlightened and objective. Kefauver and his colleagues were essentially fair-minded men, and their investigation, though limited by preconceptions regarding the problem of organized crime, did reflect concern for fair play. The committee faced certain difficult procedural questions: applicability of the Fifth Amendment, the punitive nature of contempt citations, and the provision of immunity from prosecution. It may be stated that the committee sincerely believed that its position was correct and that the rights of witnesses would be safeguarded. In any event, the courts would be compelled to clarify these questions because of the activities of other congressional investigations then being conducted.

This Charles George Werner cartoon, published March 14, 1952, shows Senator Estes Kefauver of Tennessee, wearing his trademark coonskin cap, holding up a fur coat (labeled "administration scandals") and a stack of "protest votes" next to a television showing a "TV Crime Buster Series." The series of television hearings on organized crime conducted by Kefauver implicated some Democratic supporters. The cartoon suggests that the senator used this publicity to launch his campaign for the Democratic nomination for president in 1952. (Library of Congress)

Only with regard to the status of television did the Kefauver committee introduce a new element into the structure of congressional investigations. The committee did not recognize any important difference between filming hearings for theater showings and the use of live television. However, it soon became clear that television posed serious issues. Lawyers feared that television would distort the legal process, giving the aura of truth to unsubstantiated testimony and influencing prospective jurors. The Federal Bar Association of New Jersey asserted that the "glaring melodrama" created by the presence of television apparatus would produce a warped atmosphere. Somewhat later the federal courts, in *United States v. Kleinman et al.,* adopted a similar position with regard to the atmosphere created by television. Others worried about the effects of commercial sponsorship of government hearings and the danger that investigators, conscious of the enormous audiences watching their every move, might "play to the galleries." Thurman Arnold warned of what might happen if Joe McCarthy or someone like him were given a television spot. "When the Senator does put on his show," Arnold commented soon after the Kefauver committee's hearings in New York, "I'll lay a substantial wager with my bookie . . . that McCarthy will make the efforts of the present committee look like the work of inept amateurs." However, the House of Representatives ruled out televised coverage of hearings in February 1952. The Senate Rules Committee recommended in January 1955 that witnesses have the right to request that television or other cameras not be directed at them during testimony. The precise effects of televising congressional hearings are still being disputed, though the advocates of the "Congress as classroom" viewpoint would seem to have the upper hand.

Had Estes Kefauver been successful in converting the popular approbation he received for his "crimebusting" exploits into a successful campaign for the presidency, as he attempted to do in 1952, historical evaluations of the crime committee might have been quite different. As president, Kefauver would have been in a position to throw the full weight of the federal government into the fight against organized crime, and there might have occurred a test of the thesis that chopping off the heads of the criminal hydra would destroy the beast itself. However, Kefauver discovered that the investigation which made him a presidential contender also served to deny him the prize.

Not an excited public but professional politicians selected the Democratic candidate for the presidency, and at the 1952 convention Kefauver, despite successes in the primaries, faced a hostile array of urban bosses, vengeful congressmen, and an outgoing president who violently opposed his candidacy. Kefauver had sought to reach the White House via the same route carved out by Harry Truman; but instead of following the markers of party loyalty and obeisance to the president's leadership, as had Truman, he set his own course. Perhaps an independent stance could not have been avoided in the difficult circumstances of 1950–51, but so long as the system endured, retribution was sure to be visited on violators of the political code, no matter how powerful or secure their positions might appear to be. Then, too, circumstances changed, and people soon forgot yesterday's heroes.

DOCUMENTS

Summary of Crime Conditions by FBI Director J. Edgar Hoover, May 11, 1949

During the years following World War II, the United States experienced a fiercely escalating crime rate. From murders to armed robberies to rape, the rise in violence exposed a society facing great difficulties transitioning from a wartime economy. In 1949, FBI director J. Edgar Hoover outlined the growth of crime in a memorandum directed to Attorney General Tom Clark. "It is shocking to realize," Clark later declared, "that in the United States in 1948, a serious crime was committed at the rate of one every 18.7 seconds." Reports from local and state officials as well as investigative reporters alarmed congressional leaders, who were now ready to call for a major investigation.

SUMMARY OF CRIME CONDITIONS
BY FBI DIRECTOR
J. EDGAR HOOVER
MAY 11, 1949

The Attorney General

Director, FBI

In response to your recent inquiry concerning the crime situation in the United States with particular reference to offenses involving violence and brutality and abuses of parole and probation, I thought you might be interested in the following summary of current crime conditions and also information on prior commissions and conferences organized for the purpose of studying such problems:

I. Present Crime Trends

(a) 1948 Compared to Prewar Averages

A study of crime trends on a long-term basis reflects some very sharp increases when the year 1948 is compared with the prewar averages (1938 to 1941). This study which is based on cities with a population in excess of 25,000 shows that aggravated assaults in 1948 were 68.7 per cent above the prewar average. Rape was 49.9 per cent above the average of the prewar years. Burglary was 16.7 per cent higher followed by murder, 14.1 per cent, and robbery, 8.9 per cent. These figures alone tend to show the aggravated conditions which exist today.

(b) Current Crime Statistics

During 1948 a serious crime was committed every 18.7 seconds and by the year's end the total reached an estimated 1,686,670 offenses. On the average, 36 persons were feloniously slain during each day of 1948, 255 persons were the victims of either aggravated assaults or rape and during the same day 150 robberies were committed. During an average 24-hour period 1,032 places were burglarized, 463 automobiles were stolen and, in addition, 2,672 miscellaneous larcenies were committed.

A further analysis of the crime figures for present-day America reflects that in the urban areas crime in 1948 remained practically the same as in 1947. It was, however, alarming to note that in the rural areas, crime rose over 4 per cent.

(c) Factors Causing Crime

There is nothing new about the crime problem. It is obvious that many factors contribute to crime causation but essentially the problem must resolve itself to the simple one of character and moral conduct which comes from proper home training and discipline exercised by the church, school and community.

As the figures noted above indicate, our present alarming crime picture can certainly in part be attributed to World War II particularly when we note the comparisons made between prewar and postwar figures. Wars have always brought about changes in the mores of the people. The last war was no exception. Strained emotions, a large segment of the male population in the Armed Services, with the consequent disruption of family life, migration of families, disrupting of community services and a strained economic condition all were contributing factors to the present situation. In 1944 and 1945 more youths 17 years old were arrested and fingerprinted than any other age group. During the war period many adults were too occupied with other pursuits to spend time with youngsters. At a time when strong family unity was needed to strengthen our home front, children were exposed to broken homes, neglectful parents, immorality, lack of discipline, lack of religious training and an over-all lack of adult guidance. A bumper crop of young people were introduced to the ways of crime.

It was, of course, hoped that when the war ended the crime rate particularly among young people would begin a downward spiral. Unfortunately, this has not been true. It now appears that youth of modern-day America are being brought up in the midst of new notions of happiness and a new sense of values. Too many young people have absorbed false attitudes and notions of law and order. Certainly the best way to force the crime rate down is to educate the parents of America as to their responsibility and to make them realize that they are the prime factor in our present-day crime picture. Secondly, the community must be awakened to its responsibility if we are to meet the challenge of crime.

II. Recidivism

(a) Repeaters (1945–1948)

As of possible further assistance in analyzing recent crime trends, an analysis was made of fingerprint arrest records received by the FBI Identification Division from 1945 to 1948. This analysis was made to determine the percentage of persons who already had fingerprint arrest records on file and are commonly known in law enforcement circles as repeaters.

In 1945, 2,201 individuals arrested and fingerprinted for the crime of *homicide* were repeaters. In 1948, 2,992 of those arrested for this offense were repeaters, which is an increase of 35.9 per cent.

In analyzing the crime of *rape,* it was found that the percentage of repeaters increased 39.4 per cent in 1948 over 1945.

The number of repeaters who were arrested for the crime of *assault* showed an increase of 47.5 per cent when comparing 1945 to 1948. In 1945, 21,507 repeaters, were arrested for *assault* and 31,719 in 1948.

The same formula applied to the crime of *robbery* showed that the percentage of repeaters rose 48.9 per cent between 1945 and 1948.

Repeaters arrested for the crime of *prostitution* in 1945 numbered 4,647. In 1948 the number of repeaters was 5,030, showing an increase of 8.2 per cent.

An analysis of the figures on repeaters who were arrested for *other sex offenses* showed that 43.3 per cent more were repeaters in 1948 than in 1945.

(b) Parole, Probation and Repeaters (Special One-week Survey)

In order to bring the crime problem to a current status, a special analysis was made of the fingerprint arrest records received during the period of April 26 to May 2, 1949. These figures include both state and federal arrests.

This sample survey included a study of 15,523 fingerprint arrest records received during the specified week and 9,205 or 59.3 per cent of these fingerprint records were of persons who already had fingerprint arrest records on file.

Of these 9,205 instances, 916 or 10 per cent had been pardoned or paroled one or more times prior to the current arrest and 1,892 or 20.6 per cent had received probationary sentences one or more times prior to the current arrest.

In addition, the study reflected that of the 9,205 fingerprint records considered representing persons with previous arrest records on file 4,605 or 50 per cent had previously been arrested on a charge similar to the one placed against them in connection with the current arrest. Further, 578 or 6.3 per cent were the fingerprints of persons whose current arrest occurred prior to the expiration of a previous sentence.

These figures are considered conservative inasmuch as there are probably many occasions when arrested persons whose fingerprints are on file may have received parole treatment and the like but such disposition may not be on record at the FBI.

In connection with the problem of probation and parole, it is interesting to note that as of April 30, 1949, there were 84,524 fugitives on whom wanted notices had been posted by America's law enforcement agencies. Included in this total are 10,406 parole violators and 1,253 probation violators.

To further clarify the present problems connected with parole and probation, a special survey was made of 127 FBI fugitives on whom Identification Orders were outstanding as of April 30, 1949. These are individuals against whom Federal process is outstanding and whose criminal activities are sufficiently grave to warrant the issuance of Identification Orders.

Of the 127, 28 of them have been the recipients of paroles. Fifteen of them had previously been placed on probation or given suspended sentences.

As a by-product of this survey it was found that 44 of the fugitives had previously escaped custody on one or more occasions. It was also found that 44 of the fugitives had committed the crimes for which they were being sought by the FBI prior to the expiration of a previous sentence.

A further analysis of the 127 fugitives reflects that they had received 258 previous convictions for various crimes.

(c) Crimes of Violence

An analysis of the fingerprint arrest records in the more brutal and shocking types of crime for the past four years reflects alarming trends. The number of persons arrested for the crime of murder has gradually climbed from 5,381 in 1945 to 6,703 in 1948. The same is true in regard to the crime of robbery. In 1945, 14,795 persons were arrested for this offense, while in 1947, 21,509 were fingerprinted and 20,583 in 1948.

Persons arrested for assault in 1948 totaled 58,364. This figure can be compared with the 43,006 arrested in 1945. In regard to the crime of rape, figures have shown a steady increase, climbing from approximately 6,700 in 1945 to over 9,500 in 1948. Persons arrested for prostitution over the four-year period have totaled 39,596 with the average being close to 10,000 a year. Individuals arrested for other sex offenses totaled 17,602 in 1948, compared to 13,923 in 1945.

III. Current Efforts

(a) Local Law Enforcement

Recent years have seen a tremendous change take place in the progress of law enforcement. Gradually local law enforcement agencies have been able through their own efforts to train their men and to assume a greater share in the responsibilities of their respective communities. The modern law enforcement officer is more aware today that he is not only an individual who must apprehend the criminal but that he is a crime prevention instrument in his own community. Work done by various Police Boys Clubs and related police boys organizations throughout the country has had a marked effect. There are many communities where young people have been led away from crime by the helping hand of the police department. This is a continuing and ever growing process.

Recent years have also seen a marked increase in the efficiency of law enforcement. For example, the FBI National Academy with its more than 1,900 graduates has imparted to all levels of law enforcement a higher degree of training and efficiency than has ever been attained. In addition, the FBI has cooperated with local law enforcement agencies on a national scale by cooperating in thousands of schools which have had a marked effect in improving their methods and techniques. In fact in the 1948 fiscal year the FBI participated in 1,237 local police training schools with an estimated attendance of 61,850 officers.

(b) Public Awakening

In recent years the better elements of the press, radio and motion pictures have awakened to the fact that the serious crime problem is also their responsibility. These media are now more than ever being used to educate the public to its responsibility and to make people aware of the dangers inherent in the present crime situation.

(c) The Attorney General's National Conference on Prevention and Control of Juvenile Delinquency

One of the more recent outstanding efforts was the Attorney General's National Conference on Prevention and Control of Juvenile Delinquency which met in Washington, D. C. in November of 1946.

Realizing that the crime problem was a youth problem, many prominent officials including law enforcement officers, religious leaders, educators and other civic minded individuals met to discuss means of coping with juvenile crime. As a result of the Conference there was created the Continuing Committee of the National Conference on Prevention and Control of Juvenile Delinquency which set up a pattern for organizing state and local conferences on the delinquency problem. The Committee urged the establishment in local communities of conferences which would take action rather than merely discuss the problem. The Committee has issued a handbook on the establishment of such conferences and also a series of eighteen booklets dealing with various phases of the Conference's work. These booklets which have been disseminated by the Government Printing Office cover such topics as mental health, recreation, housing, the role of the police, juvenile detention, juvenile court law, juvenile court administration, home responsibilities, schools and teachers, responsibility of the church, case work and many others helpful to those who desire to work out problems of crime and youth on a local level.

Source: Papers of Harry S. Truman, Official File, The Harry S. Truman Library, Independence, Missouri.

Senate Resolution to Establish Investigation of Gambling and Racketeering, January 5, 1950

Estes Kefauver, a little-known but ambitious Democratic senator from Tennessee, stepped into the eye of the national news media with his resolution in early 1950 to launch a congressional investigation into organized crime. Despite the doubts of FBI director J. Edgar Hoover that Mafia-type crime syndicates had muscled into American businesses, Kefauver believed that the investigative stories in the press and other reports from government officials had enough credence for the federal government to take an investigative role. Illegal gambling, drug trafficking, extortion, and prostitution—all of it, he suspected, was controlled by mobsters whose power had overwhelmed local law enforcement. Kefauver's resolution calling for an investigation by the Senate Committee on the Judiciary sparked much contentious debate.

SENATE RESOLUTION TO ESTABLISH INVESTIGATION OF GAMBLING AND RACKETEERING JANUARY 5, 1950

MR. KEFAUVER. Mr. President, I submit a resolution providing for an investigation of interstate gambling and racketeering activities, and I ask unanimous consent that a statement by me in explanation thereof be printed in the Record.

THE VICE PRESIDENT. The resolution will be received and appropriately referred, and, without objection, the statement will be printed in the Record. . . .

The explanatory statement presented by Mr. Kefauver is as follows:

Statement of Senator Estes Kefauver on Resolution to Investigate Interstate Gambling and Racketeering

MR. KEFAUVER. Mr. President, today I am filing a resolution to authorize and direct the Committee on the Judiciary to make a full investigation of interstate gambling and to make recommendations for such legislation as may be deemed necessary.

Responsible and nationally known reporters and magazine writers have for the past several years been writing of a national crime syndicate which they allege is slowly but surely through corruption gaining control of, or improper influence in, many cities throughout the United States.

On September 14, 1949, Mayor deLesseps S. Morrison, as president of the American Municipal Association, and speaking for that association, asked the

Federal Government to investigate the encroachment by organized national racketeers on municipal governments throughout the United States with the intent to control their law-enforcement agencies.

The Chicago and California crime commissions in 1949 reported the insidious influence wielded by this crime syndicate through corruption of public officials and its political and financial control.

Also, Mr. President, the mayors of several large cities, such as Los Angeles, New Orleans, and Portland, and many others, have complained in the past year of attempts being made by national crime syndicates to control and corrupt the local political affairs of their respective cities, and that they do not have adequate means to cope with this well-organized and powerful criminal organization, and have asked the Federal Government for assistance in coping with this alleged criminal aggression.

There appears to be no adequate Federal statutes which can be invoked against the activities of this organized syndicate. The resolution I am filing today would authorize and direct the Committee on the Judiciary of the Senate to make investigation to determine whether there is an organized syndicate operating in interstate commerce which is menacing the independence of free municipal governments, for the benefit of the criminal activities of the syndicate, and determine and report to the Senate their findings on whether the States and municipalities can, without Federal assistance, adequately cope with this organized crime movement. The committee would also be directed to investigate the jurisdiction of the Federal Government over the activities of any criminal syndicate, and make recommendations for any necessary legislation.

The resolution is as follows:

> *Resolved,* That the Committee on the Judiciary, or any duly authorized subcommittee thereof, is authorized and directed to make a full and complete study and investigation of interstate gambling and racketeering activities and of the manner in which the facilities of interstate commerce are made a vehicle of organized crime. The committee shall report its findings, together with its recommendations for such legislation as it may deem advisable, to the Senate at the earliest practicable date.
>
> Sec. 2. For the purposes of this resolution, the committee, or any duly authorized subcommittee thereof, is authorized to employ upon a temporary basis such technical, clerical, and other assistants as it deems advisable. The expenses of the committee under this resolution, which shall not exceed $100,000, shall be paid from the contingent fund of the Senate upon vouchers approved by the chairman of the committee.

Source: Congressional Record, 81st Congress, 2nd Session, 67–68.

Excerpt from Senate Debate over Establishment of Crime Committee, May 2–3, 1950

The Senate did not take action on the resolution introduced by Senator Estes Kefauver (D-Tenn.) in January 1950 to launch a crime investigation until early May. Political jockeying over the resolution was intense as several senators sought to place the investigation in their own committees. But in April 1950, the bodies of two Kansas City gambling kingpins, Charles Gargota and Charles Binaggio, were found in the First Ward Democratic Club slumped beneath a large portrait of President Harry S. Truman. The gangland-type slayings further intensified national concerns about the post–World War II growth of powerful crime syndicates in the nation's larger cities and spurred Congress finally to establish the Special Committee to Investigate Organized Crime in Interstate Commerce. Headed by Kefauver and composed of five members, the committee would hold hearings for 15 months across the United States in 14 cities. Its proceedings would reach the living rooms of Americans as, for the first time, a major Senate hearing would be covered on national television. According to Life *magazine, "people had suddenly gone indoors into living rooms, taverns, and clubrooms, auditoriums and back-offices. There, in eerie half-light, looking at millions of small frosty screens, people sat as if charmed. Never before had the attention of the nation been riveted so completely on a single matter." On the cover of the May 12, 1951, issue of* Time *magazine was a drawing of the face of a smiling Kefauver next to a masked octopus with its arms stretched around guns, liquor, horses, dice, prostitutes, and other elements of the crime wave that his committee was charged to investigate.*

EXCERPT FROM SENATE DEBATE OVER ESTABLISHMENT OF CRIME COMMITTEE MAY 2–3, 1950

There being no objection, the Senate proceeded to consider the resolution (S. Res. 202) to investigate interstate gambling and racketeering activities, which had been reported from the Committee on the Judiciary with amendments, and from the Committee on Rules and Administration, with additional amendments. . . .

MR. KEFAUVER. Mr. President, I send to the desk a proposed amendment which is in the nature of a substitute, which I shall offer at the proper time, and I ask that it be printed. . . .

MR. DONNELL. I was about to ask, Mr. President, whether we might have the amendment read with reasonable deliberation, if the clerk would be so kind.

THE VICE PRESIDENT. The Chair has so ordered.

THE LEGISLATIVE CLERK. It is proposed to strike out all after the resolving clause and insert in lieu thereof the following:

> That a special committee composed of five members to be appointed by the President of the Senate from the Committee on Interstate and Foreign Commerce of the Senate and the Committee on the Judiciary of the Senate is authorized and directed to make a full and complete study and investigation of whether organized crime utilizes the facilities of interstate commerce or otherwise operates in interstate commerce in furtherance of any transactions which are in violation of the law of the United States or of the State in which the transactions occur, and, if so, the manner and extent to which, and the identity of the persons, firms, or corporations by which such utilization is being made, what facilities are being used, and whether or not organized crime utilizes such interstate facilities or otherwise operates in interstate commerce for the development of corrupting influences in violation of law of the United States or of the laws of any State: *Provided, however,* That nothing contained herein shall (1) authorize the recommendation of any change in the laws of the several States relative to gambling, (2) effect any change in the laws of any State relative to gambling, or (3) effect any possible interference with the rights of the several States to prohibit, legalize, or in any way regulate gambling within their borders. For the purposes of this resolution, the term "State" includes the District of Columbia or any Territory or possession of the United States.
>
> Sec. 2. The committee shall select a chairman from among its members. Vacancies in the membership of the committee shall not affect the power of the remaining members to execute the functions of the committee and shall be filled in the same manner as the original selection. A majority of the members of the committee, or any subcommittee thereof, shall constitute a quorum for the transaction of business, except that a lesser number, to be fixed by the committee, shall constitute a quorum for the purpose of taking sworn testimony.
>
> Sec. 3. The committee, or any duly authorized subcommittee thereof, is authorized to sit and act at such places and times during the sessions, recesses, and adjourned periods of the Senate, to require by subpena or otherwise the attendance of such witnesses and the production of such books, papers, and documents, to administer such oaths, to take such testimony, to procure such printing and binding, and to make such expenditures as it deems advisable. The cost of stenographic services to report such hearings shall not be in excess of 25 cents per hundred words.
>
> Sec. 4. The committee shall have power to employ and fix the compensation of such officers, experts, and employees as it deems necessary in the performance of its duties, but the compensation so fixed shall not exceed the compensation prescribed under the Classification Act of 1949 for comparable duties. The committee is authorized to utilize the services, information, facilities, and personnel of the various departments and agencies of the Government to the extent that such services, information, facilities, and personnel, in the opinion of the heads of such departments and agencies, can be furnished without undue interference with the performance of the work and duties of such departments and agencies.
>
> Sec. 5. The expenses of the committee, which shall not exceed $150,000, shall be paid from the contingent fund of the Senate upon vouchers approved by the chairman of the committee.
>
> Sec. 6. The committee shall report to the Senate not later than February 28, 1951, the results of its study and investigation, together with such recommendations as to necessary legislation as it may deem advisable. All authority conferred by this resolution shall terminate on March 31, 1951. . . .

[MR. KEFAUVER.] Mr. President, referring to the interest of the junior Senator from Tennessee in the resolution, in the summer of 1945, at which time I had the pleasure of serving as a member of the Judiciary Committee of the House of Representatives, the chairman of that committee, Representative Sumners, a great statesman from the State of Texas and one of the finest men, I think, who ever served in Congress, appointed a subcommittee consisting of six members, three Democrats and three Republicans, of which I had the privilege of being chairman, to investigate alleged judicial corruption in the middle district of Pennsylvania, involving Judge Albert Johnson.

The committee, composed of six members, devoted most of the summer and fall of 1945 to this inquiry. There had been a great many complaints about corruption and mismanagement and barter of justice in the middle district of Pennsylvania. Many investigations had been made by local bar associations, grand juries, and other agencies. There was a great deal of smoke about it, most of the lawyers and bar associations felt that justice had reached a very low ebb, and that there was no respect for the judiciary and little respect for the enforcement of laws in the middle district of Pennsylvania. However, they had been unable to find out anything definite about Judge Johnson. The 6 members of the committee were Mr. Reed, of Illinois, Mr. Gwynne, of Iowa, Mr. Talbot, of Connecticut, Mr. Cravens, of Arkansas, Mr. Russell, of Texas, and myself as chairman. Mr. Russell was unable to attend many of the meetings.

After making some investigations in the middle district of Pennsylvania—and we had very fine cooperation from the Department of Justice and the Federal Bureau of Investigation and other governmental agencies—we found that Mr. Max Goldschein, who was in the Criminal Division of the Department of Justice—I did not know it at the time, but I found out later that he had originally come from Nashville, Tenn.—had been conducting a grand jury investigation in Scranton, Pa., for some short time in connection with this matter. We engaged him as counsel for the committee. After quite a lengthy inquiry we finally uncovered—and without the cooperation we received it would have been impossible—one of the most notorious and disgraceful judicial rackets which had ever been heard of in the history of the American judiciary. One judge was receiving money for the dispensation of justice, and he had sons located in strategic sections throughout the district. It involved referees in bankruptcy, auditors, and attorneys for referees. The whole judicial system was in a terrible state of corruption. Respect for the law was almost absent.

During that time we had an opportunity of seeing how this corruption fitted in with other kinds of rackets and betting in which these people were engaged. We had occasion also to see how some of the money which was criminally taken had been used in efforts to bribe local officials, both Democrats and Republicans, to keep out of the hands of the law. During this time members of the committee had an opportunity of meeting and talking with such young men as Boris Kostelanetz, who, at that time, was with the Department of Justice and was doing some special work there. He is now in the private practice of law. He had successfully prosecuted Bioff and Brown, some of the Capone group, and others, and was a very successful prosecutor and a certified public accountant. He had a great record with the Department of Justice. We also conferred with FBI agents concerning rackets and interstate crime in general.

From that time on I took a special interest in the reports of various crime commissions throughout the country. I think, Mr. President, a word of praise and tribute should be said about the voluntary associations which have been formed in various sections of the United States, whose expenses are paid by interested citizens who have no motive except that they want good law enforcement and to rid their communities of the influence of gamblers and racketeers. I have had an opportunity of reading reports of the Greater Miami Crime Commission, of which Colonel Springer is chairman and Daniel Sullivan is the operating director, and of talking with these men about conditions in that section of Florida. I have read the various reports of the California Crime Commission. There have been three of them. This commission has been operating under the direction of former Admiral William H. Standley. Their deputy director is Frank E. Crane, and they have with them an investigator by the name of Robinson, who used to be with the Federal Bureau of Investigation and is one of the top investigators of crime in the United States. Then there is the great Massachusetts Citizens Committee, of which Mr. Godfrey L. Cabot is honorary president and the Reverend Dana Greeley is president. Dwight S. Strong is the secretary.

Further, there is the Chicago Crime Commission, with Mr. Guy L. Reed as president and Virgil W. Peterson as operating director. He also was a former FBI agent and has done very excellent work in investigations which have been made and the reports which have been filed. All the investigations by these commissions have been made, Mr. President, without the power of subpena. The amount of information which they have set forth in their various reports is an eye opener for anyone who is interested in good law enforcement in the United States and the riddance from society of the influence of the criminal element. . . .

Mr. President, I think I need not go into the matter of the public interest and demand for an inquiry of this kind. The press of the Nation has served a very great purpose in calling to the attention of the public, through newspaper articles and editorials, the efforts and the activities of certain alleged criminals and law violators to try to corrupt local officials in some cases. The radio commentators have performed a great public service in explaining the extent of the operations of some of the persons who are alleged to operate illegally in interstate commerce. Many articles have appeared in most of the great magazines of the Nation.

It should also be pointed out that the Attorney General of the United States, the Intelligence Service of the Treasury Department, the enforcement division of the Treasury Department, and the Federal Bureau of Investigation all have taken steps in the effort to expose these alleged criminals and to protect the public from their operations. It should be pointed out, however, that most of their operations, according to newspaper reports, are not in violation of the present Federal laws, but they are operating in interstate commerce in violation of the laws of many States.

In November of last year I drafted a bill designed to prohibit the interstate shipment, of certain gambling devices, which are in violation of the law of the State to which the shipment is to be made. I also began the preparation, with the assistance of the legislative counsel, of a bill imposing penalties upon the users for illegal purposes of information coming over the wires in interstate commerce. After working on the bills and after talking with a number of experts who know a great deal about the operations in interstate commerce of gamblers and of criminals, I came to the conclusion, that, as stated by the experts, before any laws could be very intelligently considered by the Congress, or before the reaction of public opinion could be secured on them, there should be a development at least to the extent it was possible to get it of the over-all picture of interstate syndicates, if there are such, who operate them, how they operate, what the source of their power is, what communications they use, and what corrupting influence if any they may have or attempt to have on governing bodies and officials.

So, Mr. President, on January 5, I filed a resolution for the purpose of investigating generally the subjects I have stated, in order to develop if possible the over-all picture of interstate gambling and crime. . . .

It would be my purpose, if I had anything to do with the direction of the committee, in the first place to have it understood with the committee that the object was not to smear anybody or to whitewash anybody, that what we wanted to get were the facts, and if anybody got hurt with the facts, he would just get hurt; that on the other hand we did not want to harm the names of good, innocent people, and we would try to work with people, either in executive meetings of the committee or in private meetings, or through staff consultations, and go over the facts and circumstances, before they were actually brought out in the public hearings, so that we would be sure we had something to go on when charges were made in public hearings.

I think the practice of allowing charges to be made in committees which do damage to the names of good people is not reflecting too much credit on Congress. There are proper ways of conducting congressional committees. I have always had the feeling that the way the Truman committee went about its business was most commendable and that the Truman committee was the greatest congressional committee I have ever known anything about. I have talked with many persons about the methods of the Truman committee . . . in the first place finding out what we had in the way of facts, what sort of case we could make, and whether it would stand up. We would determine by staff investigation where we were going before we had a public hearing and any charges were made. I understand that there was a kind of a pretrial practice in the Truman committee of any case to see whether they did have facts and circumstances which could be made public.

Mr. President, another consideration is that this is going to be a committee's committee, at least I hope so. I trust the work can be done on the basis of nonpartisanship, that no one on the committee will feel that there is anyone to be prosecuted or smeared, and also that there is nobody to be protected, that we can go at our investigation on the basis of the facts, and develop them.

I know that some men think we are not getting after some people hard enough, and others may feel we are pushing some too hard.

MR. KERN. Mr. President, will the Senator yield for a question?

MR. KEFAUVER. Permit me to finish my statement. I know also that there will be some disappointment respecting the amount of work we may be able to perform in various local communities. I now have in my files requests from law-enforcement officers or officials of 19 important cities in the country setting forth that conditions involving interstate crime exist in their communities, which they would like to have investigated. But I think the public should understand in the first place that, as has been stated so often, the crimes committed in various communities are largely of local concern. While some local officials perhaps would like to transfer their burdens to the FBI to enforce their laws where they have been unable to do so yet, it is almost always primarily a matter for local enforcement if we are really to have law enforcement. The Federal Government is not interested in getting into everyone's back yard and trying to enforce laws which the local communities should themselves enforce. So I am quite sure we are not going to be able to go into as much detail in the investigation as we would like to. Many persons may be disappointed.

For instance, this afternoon I received copies of two stories from the Providence Journal-Bulletin, written by John Strohmeyer, one dated May 1, the other dated May 2. If half the allegations made in these two stories can be proved, it would take a senatorial committee 6 months, I am sure, to investigate all the matters involving Boston, Providence, and other cities in New England. So there may be some disappointment as to the number of cities and the number of towns in which we can make investigations and as to the time that can be granted. I think, however, that the committee can obtain a notion of what the picture is; that we can present cases and do our work with courage, so as to enable the Federal Government to consider whether legislation should be passed, and if so, what legislation.

MR. HUMPHREY. I have been very much interested in the remarks of the Senator from Tennessee, because I am particularly interested in the objective of his resolution and the purposes for which it is prepared and to which it is directed. I want to make a comment, if the Senator will permit.

MR. KEFAUVER. I am glad to yield.

MR. HUMPHREY. It is this: There seems to be some concern as to what the public might think regarding the purpose and objective of the resolution. I think one thing ought to be crystal clear, namely, that the resolution itself will not save America from sin or from crime.

MR. KEFAUVER. No. I should be glad if the Senator would expand on that idea. I think it needs enlargement.

MR. HUMPHREY. The purposes of the resolution are to aid the municipal, county, and State officials, and to extend the helping hand of the Federal Government insofar as the interstate commerce aspects of organized crime may be concerned. I surely want to commend the Senator particularly on the proposals which he has suggested as possibly being within the purview of the committee, legislative suggestions for proposals such as the banning of shipment of gambling devices between the States, and also the matter of sending communication materials or information. But I think it is important, as this resolution is discussed and as the body of the Record is developed about the nature of the resolution, to realize that law enforcement cannot take place out of the Congress, that what the Congress can do under the terms of the resolution is to redefine certain laws, to prepare some new laws. But, basically, law enforcement is a local governmental responsibility.

I desire to make a further observation, because I have had a little bit of experience along this line. All too often one of the real reasons for the lack of good law enforcement in a community is the failure of the citizen population to take any interest in their local governmental affairs. I hope that as this committee goes into the interstate aspects of crime and as it makes investigations of the respective municipalities or areas, questions will be asked as to how many people voted in the last municipal election. Another question: How much money do you appropriate for your police department? Another question: How many police officers do you have in your city per square mile? Another question: To what extent have you mechanized or modernized your police department? Do you have a crime laboratory? Do you have motor-vehicle equipment? Are you up-to-date in your police-training methods?

I may take a look at my own State. The Governor of my State is not a member of my political party, but there are no slot machines in my State. They are not there because the Governor of the State drove them out. Interstate crime or no interstate crime, there simply are no slot machines. I may say with equal candor there are none left in the city of Minneapolis. We have plenty of interstate crime. If we get Federal, State, and county officials who have the will and the intestinal fortitude to enforce the law, they will do a great deal of law enforcing, particularly if the people will support them.

One of the worst things that could happen would be to have the Federal Government take over the responsibility of local law enforcement. I know that the purpose of this resolution is to have the Federal Government only aid in it, and I think it is a wonderful and, let me say, a very important aspect, of a law-enforcement program.

I mention this, because I am of opinion that somehow or other some persons are going to get the idea that if we investigate crime, crime will, in a way, disappear, and that we shall have a nice moral utopia. That simply is not going to be the case, because, even though we pass a new Federal law, there will still be violators, and those violators will not all be apprehended by an FBI. They will have to be apprehended by local police officers as well as by Federal officers. . . .

MR. DONNELL. . . . I want to emphasize, Mr. President, two facts to which I have already made reference, but which I think will bear repetition and which should be emphasized. First, that the membership of the special committee, cannot, by virtue of the odd number, the number of five, be equal from each of the two standing committees. Therefore, a majority of the members of the special committee will come from either the Committee on Interstate and Foreign Commerce or the Committee on the Judiciary, and therefore the members from one or the other of the two said standing committees will be in the minority on the special committee.

Second, that if the Senate creates a special committee, not a single Member of the Senate, unless possessed of some information not known to the entire Senate, will, when the vote creating the special committee is announced, know which of the two committees, namely, the Committee on Interstate and Foreign Commerce or the Committee on the Judiciary, will be the one which shall furnish the majority of members of the special committee. It is entirely conceivable, Mr. President, that some Members of the Senate might desire to have such knowledge. They might feel that the subject matter is peculiarly one as to which the Committee on Interstate and Foreign Commerce, for illustration, should have the majority, or, conversely, that the subject matter is such that the Committee on the Judiciary should have the majority. But in voting upon the substitute amendment proposed by the Senator from Tennessee all of us are in the dark as to which of the two standing committees will furnish the majority of the members of the special committee.

I am opposed, Mr. President, to the creation of a special committee. The first of my reasons for being opposed to the creation of a special committee is that there is no need to bypass the standing committees of the Senate by authorizing the employment of a special committee.

Press reports indicate that it has been asserted that adoption of the Kefauver substitute is needed in order that there may not be a duplication resulting from the making of two separate investigations, one by the Senate Committee on Interstate and Foreign Commerce and the other by the Senate Committee on the Judiciary.

A few moments ago I read from the Washington Evening Star, in which the Senator from Illinois [Mr. Lucas] is stated to have announced that the setting up of a special five-man committee would avoid the duplication caused by having two separate inquiries, one by the Judiciary Committee and the other by the Committee on Interstate and Foreign Commerce. That newspaper account illustrates very clearly the reports which have appeared in the press in regard to the reason for the proposal to create a special committee.

Mr. President, the argument that adoption of the Kefauver substitute is needed in order that there may not be a duplication resulting from having two separate investigations made, one by the Committee on Interstate and Foreign Commerce and the other by the Committee on the Judiciary, is not well founded. The reason why it is not well founded is that Senate Resolution 249, the

Johnson resolution, which provides for an investigation by the Committee on Interstate and Foreign Commerce, has not been adopted by the Senate, and no hearings under that resolution have been authorized by the Senate. There is no compulsion upon the Senate to permit two separate investigations to occur, if the Kefauver substitute is not adopted. The Senate is not obligated to permit the Committee on Interstate and Foreign Commerce to make an investigation. The Senate has a right to authorize its Judiciary Committee to be the only committee to conduct the investigation. Likewise the Senate has a right to authorize its Committee on Interstate and Foreign Commerce to be the only committee to conduct the investigation. Certainly the ability of the members of either of those standing committees is such that either one of them could conduct the investigation and study. . . .

Mr. President, I am opposed to the special committee on the general proposition, first, that there is no need to bypass standing committees; that the standing committees, with their power of subpena, their investigatory power, their ability to exercise a high degree of watchfulness, and with all the facilities of a staff, members of which are chosen solely on the ground of merit, and without regard to political considerations, are amply able to conduct such an investigation as is proposed. The standing committees are able to do all that it is sought here to have the special committee do. Therefore, Mr. President, there is no need to bypass the standing committees.

In the second place, I oppose the Kefauver substitute because the special committee would violate the intent of the Legislative Reorganization Act. To substantiate that contention, I have produced before the Senate this afternoon witness after witness of undeniable ability and undeniable knowledge, headed up, I may say, by the distinguished senior Senator from Illinois [Mr. Lucas], as to his views respecting the intent of the Legislative Reorganization Act; in the case of the senior Senator from Illinois not only as to the intent of the Legislative Reorganization Act, but as to the sound reason which existed even before the Reorganization Act was passed.

Then, Mr. President, I have pointed out that a special committee would not be subject to the discipline to which a standing committee would be subject.

I have pointed out the lack of efficiency of a special committee.

I have pointed out the precedent which the appointment of such a special committee would constitute; and in that connection I have referred to the fact, as was so picturesquely stated by the Senator from Oregon, that it might very well result in a rash of other special investigating committees.

Mr. Taft. Mr. President, I send to the desk an amendment to the substitute and ask unanimous consent that it be read by the clerk. I understand that it is not in order to offer it at this time, but I wish to make a few remarks on it.

The Vice President. Without objection, the amendment to the amendment will be read for the information of the Senate.

The Chief Clerk. On page 2, at the end of line 17, of the so-called Kefauver substitute, it is proposed to insert the following:

> Two members of such special committee shall be appointed from among the minority members of the Committee on Interstate and Foreign Commerce and the Committee on the Judiciary on the nomination of the minority floor leader of the Senate.

Mr. Taft. Mr. President, in case the substitute should be adopted, I have submitted the amendment for two reasons. The first reason is that while two Republicans should be on a committee consisting of five members, perhaps not one Republican would be appointed. The appointment of Republican members of the committee is left entirely in the discretion of the Presiding Officer. In fact, so far as I can see, there is no requirement that he appoint any Republicans. Recently we had a proposal to appoint members of a Special Committee on Small Business. At that time the Presiding Officer determined that there should be eight Democrats and five Republicans on the committee. It seems to me that if the proposed committee is to be a committee of only five members, there should be at least two Republicans on it.

In the second place, my amendment proposes that the Republican members of the committee be appointed on the nomination of the minority leader.

I realize that there were certain special circumstances involved in the appointment of the members of the Special Committee on Small Business. I do not know about the majority members of the committee, but the fact is that so far as the minority members were concerned the Presiding Officer undertook to appoint them and did appoint them without any consultation whatsoever with the minority floor leader or the minority policy committee. The appointment of minority members of regular standing committees has always been upon the nomination of the minority floor leader. There has never been any question that the majority has always permitted the minority to choose its own members on committees. That was the practice ever since I have been a Member of the Senate until the appointment of the members of the Special Committee on Small Business, when that practice was ignored. I have said that I thought probably there were special circumstances which might have justified such procedure at that time. However, I think it would be exceedingly unfortunate to proceed to make it the permanent policy of the Senate. Therefore, I have submitted an amendment which would provide, first, that there shall be two minority members of the committee, consisting of five members, and, second, that the minority members shall be appointed upon the nomination of the minority floor leader.

Mr. Lucas. Mr. President, in reply to the distinguished Senator from Ohio, I think that an examination of Senate precedents will show that similar resolutions have been adopted which gave the presiding officer power to appoint members of a special committee.

I do not have any particular objection to one phase of the suggestion made by the Senator from Ohio, and that is with respect to the suggestion that two Republicans be appointed on the committee. However, I do object to the other part of the suggestion. In other words, it is the theory of the minority that the Vice President will not be fair in the appointment of a committee of five. There is no man in public life in the United States today who enjoys greater respect and who has a higher reputation for integrity and honor than the Vice President of the United States. A suggestion that the Vice President would not be fair and just in the appointment of a committee of this kind does not square with the background of the distinguished Vice President of the United States.

Mr. Taft. Mr. President, will the Senator yield?

Mr. Lucas. No; I do not have the time to yield.

Furthermore, Mr. President, it is a strange thing that it is the Senator from Missouri [Mr. Donnell] and the Senator from Michigan [Mr. Ferguson] who should seek to defeat the so-called Kefauver substitute. Why is that? The Senator from Michigan has been talking about the Committee on the Judiciary. The distinguished chairman of the Judiciary Committee [Mr. McCarran] has definitely agreed to the proposed arrangement. The Senator from Tennessee [Mr. Kefauver], the author of the resolution in the first instance, has agreed to the arrangement. Therefore the two members of the Committee on the Judiciary who are most interested in the resolution, along with the distinguished chairman of the Committee on Interstate and Foreign Commerce [Mr. Johnson of Colorado] and the Senator from Arizona [Mr. McFarland], the chairman of the subcommittee which has been handling matters of this kind for that committee, have agreed that this is the proper procedure to be followed.

Why is it, Mr. President, that certain Senators on the Republican side of the aisle are practically demanding to be appointed to this committee? I know the reason, and the Senate knows. It is the first time in my experience that Senators almost demand they be put on a committee charged with conducting an investigation. I do not know what the Vice President of the United States would do with respect to the appointment of the committee. However, whomever he appoints—and I know he will appoint two Republicans and three Democrats, because that is the way it should be—will be men who enjoy the respect of the people of the country and the people of their respective States, and who will do a thorough and convincing job so far as investigating crime syndicates is concerned.

Mr. President, other Senators are capable of conducting investigations, and certain Senators do not have a monopoly on ability to make investigations simply because they came to the Senate with reputations of having been successful investigators.

The Vice President may decide to appoint the Senator from Missouri [Mr. Donnell], the Senator from Michigan [Mr. Ferguson], the Senator from North Dakota [Mr. Langer], the Senator from Vermont [Mr. Tobey], or other Senators who are members of the two committees concerned. Whomever the Vice President appoints certainly will be satisfactory to the majority, and they should be satisfactory to the minority. However, Mr. President, the minority wants to place its special Senators on the committee. They want that power. In the Eightieth Congress, I remember whenever there was a time the minority wanted something, they got nothing. In the Eightieth Congress, so far as any suggestions were concerned as to what the majority should do, the minority received no consideration at all. The provision for the appointment of the committee as it now stands in the resolution is in line with precedents, it is in line with what was done in the case of the Pearl Harbor investigation, when the then Vice President appointed a special committee.

Mr. President, I hope that the amendment submitted by the Senator from Ohio will be voted down. I rely upon the Vice President of the United States to appoint to the committee Senators who will make the kind of investigation which the resolution demands. I want the Senate to understand that the Senator from Illinois is in favor of the Kefauver substitute. I want the committee to have the money that is necessary to make the proper kind of an investigation. I want it to have the kind of investigators who are necessary, and I want it to be surrounded by the kind of personnel who will do a job which will add dignity and prestige to the Senate of the United States.

Mr. President, I do not want a fishing expedition. I want an honest-to-God investigation, without any politics involved, and let the chips fall where they may—not the kind of an investigation we have seen around here in the Senate at different times in the past. . . .

The Vice President. The question is on the amendment of the Senator from Ohio to the amendment of the Senator from Tennessee in the nature of a substitute, as modified.

Mr. Taft. Mr. President, I ask for a division. . . .

So Mr. Taft's amendment to the Kefauver amendment in the nature of a substitute, as modified, was rejected.

The Vice President. The question now is on agreeing to the amendment in the nature of a substitute, as modified, offered by the Senator from Tennessee [Mr. Kefauver].

Mr. Wherry and other Senators asked for the yeas and nays, and they were ordered. . . .

The result was announced—yeas 35, nays 35. . . .

The Vice President. Under the Constitution, the Vice President, having the right to vote in case of a tie, casts his vote in the affirmative.

So Mr. Kefauver's amendment in the nature of a substitute, as modified, was agreed to.

The Vice President. The question recurs on agreeing to the resolution as amended.

Mr. Donnell. I ask for the yeas and nays.

The yeas and nays were ordered, and the legislative clerk called the roll. . . .

The result was announced—yeas 69, nays 1. . . .

So the resolution (S. 202), as amended, was agreed to.

Source: Congressional Record, 81st Congress, 2nd Session, 6148–6245.

Excerpt from Testimony of Frank Costello, March 13, 1951

For nine days in New York City, from March 12 through 20, 1951, more than 50 witnesses described the highest-ranking crime syndicate in America, allegedly led by Frank Costello. Bootlegging, slot machines, gambling—Costello's enterprises made huge amounts of money from a wide range of illegal operations. Costello gained the reputation, as no one before him, of building bridges between legitimate businesses and the mob. He had the contacts and clout. He could arrange fixes of judges or politicians. From March 13 to 15, 1951, Costello himself sat before the Kefauver committee. Averse to having his face shown on television, Costello testified as the cameras ranged over his hands while he spoke. His nervous hand gestures betrayed the pressure that the most notorious gangster in America felt while before the Kefauver committee.

EXCERPT FROM TESTIMONY OF FRANK COSTELLO MARCH 13, 1951

Senator O'Conor. Do you solemnly swear the testimony you will give this committee shall be the truth, the whole truth, and nothing but the truth, so help you God?

Mr. Costello. Yes, sir.

Senator O'Conor. Just for identification purposes, will you give your full name?

Mr. Wolf. May I understand whether or not this proceeding—

Senator O'Conor. Will you identify yourself?

Mr. Wolf. Senator, my name is George Wolf.

Senator O'Conor. You are a member of the bar?

Mr. Wolf. I am a member of the bar, and I am appearing as attorney for Mr. Costello. I would like to know whether you intend to televise this proceeding.

Senator O'Conor. The proceedings have been televised. May I ask whether you have any objection?

Mr. Wolf. Strenuously object.

Senator O'Conor. Upon what basis do you register objection?

Mr. Wolf. On the ground that Mr. Costello doesn't care to submit himself as a spectacle. And on the further ground that it will prevent proper conference with his attorney in receiving proper advice from his attorney during the course of the testimony.

Senator O'Conor. I gather, then, Mr. Wolf, that you feel that this proceeding, or proceedings, under those circumstances would adversely affect the interests of your client?

Mr. Wolf. Absolutely.

Senator O'Conor. Would it in any way have effect upon his giving a complete and full statement to the committee, and of answering questions freely?

Mr. Wolf. I think it would interfere with Mr. Costello testifying properly.

Senator O'Conor. I see. Well, under the circumstances, then, it is the view of the committee, counsel, that the defendant not be televised, or the individual who is here, the witness, not be televised at the time.

Mr. Wolf. And I presume that applies to radio broadcast, for this reason, Senator:

For the reason I assume that if it is broadcast by radio, every whisper between the witness and myself will be heard; so that there will be no privacy at all between counsel and client. I will not be able to advise him as to his rights; he will not be able to ask me as to his rights.

I think the witness will be absolutely helpless under those circumstances, Senator.

Senator O'Conor. Counsel, the committee cannot agree with you in that statement. It is our duty and obligation, of course, to afford the witness every proper safeguard, so that he be permitted to have the benefit of counsel to the fullest extent, and such a conference can be held without it being audible to anyone else; and we shall certainly see to that.

Mr. Wolf. With that provision, I concede, then.

Will you permit me, then, on occasions, if necessary, to have the privacy of conference with my client, if he so desires?

Senator O'Conor. We will not only permit it, but encourage it; because he is fully expected to have every possible benefit of counsel, and that should be his, not as a matter of gratuity from this committee, but as a matter of right.

MR. WOLF. Then we have no objection to it being broadcast by radio. In fact, the witness himself would prefer it.

SENATOR O'CONOR. Very good.

I, incidentally, improperly referred to him just before as a defendant. I didn't mean that at all, but just as a witness.

MR. WOLF. That is not unusual, Senator. He has been referred to as a defendant, even though he is only a witness.

SENATOR O'CONOR. That does not, of course, apply to the presiding officer.

MR. WOLF. That is a very common thing, Senator.

SENATOR O'CONOR. You have already given your full name. Just for purposes of identification, will you give your address.

MR. COSTELLO. 115 Central Park West.

SENATOR O'CONOR. It is understood by the television persons that the witness is not to be televised during the course of the proceedings.

MR. WOLF. Senator—

MR. HALLEY. May we have the witness' name first—Frank Costello?

MR. COSTELLO. Frank Costello, 115 Central Park West.

MR. HALLEY. Have you ever used any other names—

MR. WOLF. Before he answers any further questions, may the witness make a statement through me?

SENATOR O'CONOR. Yes.

MR. WOLF (reading):

> On January 2, 1951, chief counsel for this committee telephoned Mr. George Wolf, my attorney, and stated that the committee desired to examine me as a witness. On January 3, at a conference with chief counsel, Mr. Wolf stated that I was anxious to testify in order to deny under oath and forever silence the false stories and rumors that I was connected with any crime syndicate and that I was guilty of grave criminal offenses but that, judging from press reports of statements made by certain members of this committee, I could not expect fair treatment or consideration.
>
> However, my attorney was assured by chief counsel that the committee had not concluded its investigation about me, would treat me fairly as a witness, and would withhold judgment until after I had testified.
>
> Thereupon I agreed to accept service of subpena and, pursuant to arrangements, accepted service at my attorney's office on the following morning, January 4. This subpena was made returnable forthwith, but I agreed to appear at any future time upon notice to my attorney. Later my attorney was requested to have me appear on February 13, 10 A.M., in this room; and I did so. Before testifying I made the following statement:
>
> "I am here as a witness pursuant to forthwith subpena dated January 3, 1951, served upon me on January 4, 1951.
>
> "For years I have repeatedly been falsely charged with the most serious and vicious crimes and with being the leader of a national crime syndicate. Whenever possible I have sought to deny these charges and on many occasions have offered to testify before impartial investigating agencies. As recently as April 26 last I voluntarily appeared as a witness before the Senate Subcommittee on Interstate and Foreign Commerce, investigating interstate gambling. To the best of my ability I then testified fully and frankly, claiming and being granted by the committee privilege against self-incrimination on only one subject; namely, whether gambling was conducted in the Beverly Country Club of New Orleans.
>
> "In spite of my denials under oath, these accusations continue to be made. According to reports of the Congressional Record and the press throughout the country, some of the very members of this Senate committee have charged me with the commission of grave criminal offenses and with being a leader of organized vice and crime in this country and have also announced their intention to have me prosecuted for perjury if no other crimes can be proved against me.
>
> "I respectfully submit that I am a witness, not a defendant. I respectfully request that I be treated as impartially as any ordinary witness, that no attempt be made to single me out and make a field day of my examination, that my rights and privileges be respected, and that my interrogation be fairly conducted and kept within the bounds of the subject matter of your investigation."

That is the end of the quote of the statement that Mr. Costello made on February 13.

At the conclusion of the statement the chairman made the following remarks:

> "Thank you, Mr. Wolf. That is a very good statement, and I don't know as to some of the things you referred to, but it is the policy of this committee to try to treat every witness as fairly as we know how."
>
> Within a few moments after I started to testify, the committee again sought to reassure me that my examination was to enable me to establish the falsity of the malicious reports about me. The chief counsel said, and I am quoting from the record:
>
> "I might say, Mr. Costello, that the committee is well aware of your contention that you have been misrepresented. Mr. Wolf has made that very clear to me.
>
> "The purpose of a detailed examination privately is to give you every opportunity to establish your contentions."

For 2 hours on February 13 and for 6 hours on February 15 I testified. I did my level best to furnish the committee with every bit of information they asked for and to answer every single question directly and honestly.

When my examination was ended, I had every right to believe that I had completely disposed of the fantastically untrue stories built up around me and that I would now be recognized for what I actually am and have been, without defending gambling and bootlegging activities of which I am not particularly proud but for which I prefer not to be eternally punished.

I felt that I was fortunate for having accepted the assurances of the committee at face value. In fact, the concluding remarks of the chairman did much to strengthen my belief that my testimony had done much to destroy the mythical tales about me. I quote the following from the record:

"Mr. Halley. Do you think you have got your rights as you demanded them in your statement, Mr. Wolf?

"Mr. Wolf. . . . although the examination was quite vigorous and thorough, I think he was treated quite fairly. I also think that Mr. Costello as a witness was very frank and cooperative to the fullest extent. I think you will agree with me on that, Mr. Halley."

And I am pointing out, gentlemen, this is what took place at the close of the examination of 8 hours.

"Mr. Halley. He certainly cooperated.

"The Chairman. He answered most questions forthrightly. He was a little vague about things back in the prohibition days, and there were some of these matters that he seemed to have forgotten as to what he told Mr. Hogan, but that has been quite a number of years ago."

On March 1 the newspapers reported the submission of an interim report by this committee describing the criminal activities of an alleged major crime syndicate composed of two parts and naming me as one of the two heads of one part. While I then realized that the committee's pretenses of fairness were empty words, I was not prepared for the shocking discovery that the report was completed before I had even begun to testify and that nothing I could have said or done would have altered it one iota. I was informed that chief counsel not only admitted that the report had been prepared before I started to testify but that it was, to use the chief counsel's own language, "based upon inference upon inference" and without a single shred of direct evidence against me, after over a year of an extensive investigation, aided by virtually every local and Federal investigating agency in the United States.

Over my repeated denials and my testimony under oath, which you said was "forthright," without any direct evidence, and without permitting me to defend myself, you have branded me as an archcriminal. You have prejudged me without a bit of respectable proof to support your judgment.

Under our system of law a man is presumed to be innocent until his guilt is proved beyond a reasonable doubt. I do not ask to be measured by the same rules as should be applied to all of us. I am willing to assume the burden of proving my innocence to you and to the world.

Give me, I ask you, this last opportunity of proving that your charges against me are unjustified and that they should be retracted. Confront me with evidence if you have it; if your charges are based on inferences, let me know what those inferences are. Then give me the right to publicly reply to your evidence or construe your surmises.

I am not only asking that you respect fundamental rights and principles, I am begging you to treat me as a human being.

The Chairman. Mr. Chairman, I think there is one matter that should be straightened out before we start. Senator O'Conor is acting as chairman today.

That matter is the statement that the report was written before Mr. Costello testified. That is absolutely untrue. The report was not completed, it was not written, until 1 week before it was published; and Mr. Costello testified many, many weeks before that time.

I think also, Mr. Wolf, that you mistake forthrightness with proof of innocence or no wrongdoing.

It is quite correct, and we always try to state whether the witness is forthright or not, and at the conclusion of the hearing I stated for the record and to the press that most of the questions Mr. Costello had answered forthrightly, that he only refused to answer, or avoided answering, one question, and that was in connection with the Beverly Country Club; that as to matters in the prohibition era, and also as to what he had told Mr. Hogan, that his memory was dim, and that he did not answer those questions very fully, or his memory wasn't full about them.

However, it should not be construed that, because we said he answered forthrightly, he exonerated himself of any connection with crime or contacts with other people who may have been engaged in it.

That was what my statement was, and I stand by that statement today.

But your statement, sir, that the report was written before you testified is absolutely incorrect. It was to a considerable extent on his testimony in executive session that certain things were brought out in the report. . . .

Mr. Halley. The last time you appeared before the committee, the committee asked you for a complete financial statement of your assets, and I believe at that time you said you would produce it, but that since then Mr. Wolf has stated that in view of the committee's report he would not produce such a financial statement; is that correct?

MR. WOLF. I said so. I said that in view of the fact that I had believed the committee would await any determination until the witness testified, the release of this interim report in condemning him as it did would be a reason, one of the reasons why he would not furnish that financial statement, and I want to say further, Mr. Halley, and I think you will agree with me, that every bit of information that you requested as to data concerning his operations in the oil business, concerning his income for 1950, concerning all of his income tax returns between 1940 and date, were turned over to the committee and furnished to you. The only items that were left open was the request by Senator Tobey for a financial statement.

Mr. Costello, in spite of the fact that he might have raised a question, and object to the furnishing of that, felt that in justice to him he would forego any claim of immunity and give the committee this information.

That financial statement was to be given 2 weeks after, I think, February 15. We were busy preparing that statement. I attempted to get hold of Mr. Halley several days before the end of the 2-week period to tell him that we needed much more time, that this question of a financial statement was an important question to this witness, but when I heard that this interim report had come down I told Mr. Halley it could serve no useful purpose as far as this witness is concerned and that we would not comply with the request to furnish a financial statement.

MR. HALLEY. And I believe I pointed out to you at that time there was no way I could force you to produce such a statement, but that I would of course expect Mr. Costello to answer with full particularity all questions concerning his assets and liabilities.

MR. WOLF. You said that you believed it was your right to question him about that.
I said I have no concern with that.

MR. HALLEY. Now, Mr. Costello, have you brought with you a financial statement showing your net worth today?

MR. COSTELLO. No.

MR. HALLEY. What is your net worth today?

MR. COSTELLO. I refuse to answer that question.

MR. HALLEY. On what ground?

SENATOR O'CONOR. Why do you refuse to answer?

MR. COSTELLO. I am going to exercise my rights that it might incriminate me.

Source: U.S. Senate, Investigation of Organized Crime in Interstate Commerce, Hearings Before a Special Committee to Investigate Organized Crime in Interstate Commerce, 81st Congress, 2nd Session, Part 7, New York-New Jersey, 877–80; 905–09; 912–14.

Excerpt from Kefauver Committee Final Report, August 31, 1951

In the summer of 1951, Senator Estes Kefauver (D-Tenn.) and his colleagues on the committee wrapped up their investigation and issued a final report. Although the principal suggestion of the committee members—the creation of a National Crime Coordinating Council chaired by a nominee of the president—was not acted upon, the hearings did have significant results. The Kefauver committee's vast publicity and exposure spurred states and localities to create crime commissions to attempt to combat the criminal elements that had been exposed. In addition, the U.S. Senate established a Permanent Subcommittee on Investigations, or the "rackets committee." Chaired by Senator John McClellan (D-Ark.), the rackets committee would soon hold its own national hearings that would stir the national interest.

EXCERPT FROM KEFAUVER COMMITTEE FINAL REPORT, AUGUST 31, 1951

CONCLUSIONS

A. Constant Vigilance

As the result of the committee's activities there exists a great public awareness of the nature and extent of organized crime. The public now knows that the tentacles of organized crime reach into virtually every community throughout the country. It also knows that law enforcement is essentially a local matter calling for constant vigilance at the local level and a strengthening of public and private morality.

People everywhere are pleading for a means of keeping alert to crime conditions and avoiding a return to the state of public complacency and indifference under which gangsterism has thrived for so long. The demand for a permanent force that can, in some measure, replace this committee must be met.

With a view to answering this demand, the committee, in its Third Interim Report, proposed the establishment of a Federal Crime Commission, and a bill to accomplish this has been introduced. The Commission contemplated by this proposal is an independent Federal agency in the executive branch of the Government, organized and staffed independently of other Government agencies, and required to report to the Congress.

This bill is opposed by the Treasury Department and the Department of Justice, and Senator Wiley has expressed his dissent. Although the committee does not recede from the proposal, a realistic approach compels the committee to recognize that enactment of the bill cannot be accomplished in a short period of time.

In the meantime, it is highly desirable that some action be taken promptly to afford local communities a means of obtaining help in their attacks upon organized crime.

The answer seems to lie partly in the field of local, privately constituted crime commissions. Several of these have been in operation for a number of years and they have shown themselves to be highly effective. They are not investigative or policing agencies. Their function is to observe local crime conditions, to cooperate with civic, educational, and enforcement agencies where possible, and to report to the public any evidence of laxity or corruption.

A great step forward would be accomplished in the field of law enforcement if privately constituted crime commissions of this character could be established in every city in the United States where organized crime presents a serious problem, and if a central agency could be established which would foster the establishment of local commissions and serve as a clearing house and coordinating agency for their information and experience.

Experience has shown that the crime commission movement cannot progress unless it has a national parent body with sufficient prestige and funds to give it drive. It is believed that if Congress fosters the establishment of such an organization, funds from private foundations or philanthropists can be obtained to give it permanent life.

This report contains a recommendation for establishment of an organization of this character.

B. Narcotics

1. The illegal sale of narcotic drugs represents an evil of major proportions requiring for its eradication the combined efforts of law enforcement bodies, legislators, educators, and parents. It should be attacked at all levels of the Nation's social structure. If not successfully overcome in the near future, it may do lasting damage to the youth of the Nation.
2. The organized gangster syndicates will unquestionably turn to the sale of narcotic drugs when they are driven out of the presently lucrative field of gambling. As they did at the end of the prohibition era, when bootlegging no longer offered substantial profits, they will turn to another form of illegal activity. Under present conditions, narcotic drugs offer them the most profitable opening. Their protestations that they would not stoop so low are hollow in the light of the recent arrest of Waxey Gordon in New York City on a narcotics charge.
3. There has been a startling increase in the abuse of drugs by young people, many of whom are unaware of its frightful consequences. They fail to realize that they are dealing with what is, in effect, a contagious disease which brings degradation and slow death to the victim and tragedy to his family and friends.
4. There has been a tendency to shroud the subject of drug addiction in a veil of secrecy. The result is that young people learn about drugs from bad associates or from the drug peddlers in the back streets and alleys, rather than from qualified sources of information. It is for this reason that many young people have tried drugs, innocently unaware of the dangers they face.
5. Addiction is extremely difficult to cure. It is a chronic condition with a high rate of recurrence. If discovered in time, addiction may be prevented, but once it occurs the victim can overcome it only through a painful and bewildering perplexity of treatment entailing difficult physical and psychological readjustment.
6. Members of the public generally are not aware of the fact that voluntary, noncriminal patients may be treated at the United States Public Health Service Hospital at Lexington, Ky., and that patients who cannot afford to pay are treated without charge.
7. The United States Public Health Service Hospitals at Lexington, Ky., and at Forth Worth, Tex., do not have sufficient facilities for caring for all of the women patients in need of treatment. Furthermore, there is not sufficient segregation of young patients from older, hardened addicts. There is considerable danger that youngsters going to these institutions for the first time are retarded in their recovery by mingling with the older addicts.

   If the public should become fully aware of the availability of these hospitals for voluntary patients, it is entirely possible that the demands upon them will increase materially. In that event additional Federal facilities may be required.

   At the State level, the facilities for treatment appear to be wholly inadequate.
8. The illegal sale of narcotic drugs pays enormous profits to the lowest form of criminal, namely, the peddler who is willing to wreck young lives to satisfy his greed. No penalty is too severe for a criminal of such character. Until recently the courts have been far too lenient toward narcotic violators. Short sentences do not deter the potential peddler and suspended sentences are a waste of judicial effort.
9. The drug representing the greatest problem is heroin, the importation and possession of which are forbidden in the United States. All of the heroin now used in this country is smuggled in from abroad, for the most part by passengers and seamen carrying it off ships on their persons. Because of the ease of concealment, checking its flow through customs search is extremely difficult. Present practices and procedures for canceling the sailing papers of seamen convicted of narcotics violations are unsatisfactory.
10. The most effective means of combating the narcotics problem is through effective enforcement facilities. The Narcotics Bureau of the Treasury Department is efficient and effective as far as it is able to go, but it is pitifully undermanned considering the enormity of the task assigned to it. With sufficient personnel, the Narcotics Bureau could do more than any other force toward stamping out the illegal importation and sale of narcotic

drugs. Most addicts would like to see the traffic stamped out so that it will not be available to them.

At the local level, there are too few enforcement officers who have had experience in specialized fields, especially in the field of narcotics. Although the Narcotics Bureau of the Treasury Department works in close cooperation with State authorities, its manpower is not sufficient to permit it to furnish training to local agents.

11. Barbiturate drugs, such as luminal, seconol, amytol, and the other products popularly known as sleeping pills have not yet become an object of organized crime. However, in its study of narcotics the committee learned that their addiction properties when used in large quantities are as severe as those other narcotic drugs. Their sale should be the subject of strict regulation under both State and Federal law.
12. The Commission on Narcotics of the United Nations has made great strides in bringing about cooperation among the nations of the world regarding control of the production of opium and of the manufacture of drugs derived from opium. The countries in which the drugs are manufactured have been fairly successful in limiting the output to the actual medical needs of the world.

On the other hand, the countries where the opium poppy is grown have found it to be impossible, in spite of strenuous efforts, to regulate the quantities planted and cultivated by the farmers. These countries grow enough opium poppy plants to produce 40 times the amount of opium needed for legitimate medical purposes.

It is believed that, whereas in the growing countries the quantity cannot be regulated, complete prohibition against the planting of opium poppy plants could be enforced.

Except in the case of cocaine, which represents a minor problem, adequate synthetic substitutes have been developed for opiate drugs, especially for morphine, which is the principal pain-relieving product. Although the synthetics are easy to produce, it is believed that their manufacture could be regulated within reasonable limits. The medical profession would not be materially handicapped if opium poppy growing were prohibited throughout the world.

C. Crime and Corruption

1. The same pattern of organized crime found in large metropolitan areas exists in the medium-size cities with similar evidence of official sanction or protection. In some cases the protection is obtained by the payment of bribes to public officials, often on a regular basis pursuant to a carefully conceived system. In other cases, the racketeering elements make substantial contributions to political campaigns of officials who can be relied upon to tolerate their activities. Sometimes these contributions will support a whole slate of officers in more than one political party, giving the racketeers virtual control of the governing body. Democracy vanishes in a captive community because the ordinary citizen for practical purposes has nothing to say about his Government.

   In many cities, large and small, there is evidence of active and often controlling participation by former bootleggers, gangsters, and hoodlums in the political affairs of the community. In some cases this participation extends to other cities and even to the government of the State. Underworld characters do not engage in politics for the good of the community or the Nation. They do so for the purpose of increasing their power and wealth and gaining greater protection for their illegal activities.

   Organized crime has been able to flourish and grow largely because of the economic power wielded by gangsters. The ordinary, honest citizen cannot expect to be able to compete in either business or government with persons who obtain wealth and power through illegal means.
2. Wiretapping is a powerful tool in the hands of law-enforcement officers. Federal agents are seriously handicapped in their regular enforcement work by the legal restrictions which presently surround this valuable instrument of investigation. If properly safeguarded by the same restrictions that are imposed by law upon searches and seizures, wiretapping does not infringe upon the right of privacy of the honest citizen. Several States, notably New York, have laws which permit the use of wiretapping pursuant to court order and subject to reasonable safeguards. These laws work satisfactorily and without objection on the part of law-abiding citizens. A similar Federal law would represent an important contribution to law enforcement.

RECOMMENDATIONS AND SUGGESTIONS

A. Recommendations for Action at the Federal Level

1. Establishment of National Crime Coordinating Council

In order to keep the searchlight of public vigilance turned upon crime and corruption in a manner that leaves at the local level the basic responsibility for law enforcement and at the same time affords centralized guidance and coordination, the committee proposes the establishment of a privately constituted National Crime Coordinating Council.

The Council would be a body composed of representatives of privately established local crime commissions. Its first chairman would be designated on an interim basis by the President of the United States to serve until appointment of his successor. As soon as the organization was established it would nominate five persons from whom the President would select a chairman to succeed the interim chairman. The chairman so designated would serve for a term of not more than 2 years at which time the same procedure would be followed for selection of his successor.

Congress would appropriate the sum of $100,000 to be applied as a grant in aid to the Council for the purpose of permitting it to organize and begin its activities. It is not contemplated that the Congress would be called upon for any additional funds. Thereafter, the Council would be expected to obtain its funds from charitable foundations or other private sources.

Solely to provide the mechanics for establishing the Council at the initial stages, the Attorney General of the United States would have the responsibility of drafting its charter and bylaws, arranging for its organizational meetings, and otherwise sponsoring its creation. Local crime commissions now in existence would be invited to serve as its charter members and thereafter it would sponsor throughout the country other local crime commissions which would also become members or chapters of the national organization.

The functions of the Council would be as follows:

- *(a)* To foster the establishment of privately constituted local crime commissions wherever needed throughout the country.
- *(b)* To serve as a clearinghouse for information of interest to local crime commissions.
- *(c)* To inquire into and study such new patterns or innovations in organized crime as may develop and to make the results of its studies available to appropriate agencies and to legislative bodies so that immediate deterrents may be devised.
- *(d)* To sponsor meetings for the purpose of exchanging ideas and information regarding local crime conditions to which would be invited representatives of local social and civic organizations, religious groups, educational bodies, women's clubs, law enforcement agencies, and all other groups having an interest in crime conditions.

The committee believes that establishment of the proposed National Crime Coordinating Council would constitute a great contribution toward the cause of law enforcement because it would provide at the local level the civic vigilance without which the evil of complacency and indifference may soon return.

As previously pointed out, this plan differs substantially from the proposal for a Federal Crime Commission as described in the third interim report. The Federal Crime Commission would be an official agency in the executive branch of the Government; whereas the National Crime Coordinating Council would be a private agency serving the local, privately established crime commissions constituting its membership. If the bill now pending in the Senate for establishment of the Federal Crime Commission should be enacted, the official functions of the Commission would not be in conflict with the private activities of the Council, although a demarcation of responsibilities between them might be advisable to avoid duplication of effort.

2. Continuation of Crime Investigation

Section 7 of Senate Resolution 202 as added by Senate Resolution 129 provides that on or before September 1, 1951, this committee "shall transfer all of its files, papers, documents, and other pertinent data to the Senate Committee on Interstate and Foreign Commerce, which committee shall, under and by virtue of the authority of section 136 of the Legislative Reorganization Act of 1946, continue the study and surveillance of the subject matter of this resolution."

This committee hopes that the study of organized crime will continue and it is gratified that the Committee on Interstate and Foreign Commerce has already taken cognizance of the foregoing provision. It is suggested that serious consideration be given to the problem presented by the witnesses who have evaded the committee's process.

With regard to the District of Columbia, this committee has, on several occasions, received evidence that the city of Washington may be a pivotal point for gambling operations of considerable size. There is also evidence before this committee of widespread traffic in narcotic drugs within the District. The committee therefore strongly recommends that an appropriate committee of the Senate undertake a thorough investigation of crime conditions in the District of Columbia, including the relationship of such conditions to crime in adjoining areas.

3. Coordinate Information Regarding Narcotics

It is recommended that one of the activities of the proposed National Crime Coordinating Council be to serve as a clearinghouse for information regarding local action taken in connection with the illegal sale and use of narcotic drugs.

At the present time, aside from the information on enforcement supplied by the Bureau of Narcotics, there is no central agency to which civic, educational, religious, and enforcement agencies may turn for information regarding the subject of narcotics. Each community is approaching the matter in its own way without having the benefit of experience gained in others. Duplication and waste of effort would be reduced if coordination of activities could be brought about by use of a central clearing agency.

4. Narcotics Bureau Training Squad

A squad should be organized in the Narcotics Bureau of the Treasury Department having as its function the training of local enforcement officers in the specialized techniques required for narcotics law enforcement. The squad should consist of at least 10 experienced Federal narcotics agents who would furnish instruction to local enforcement agencies everywhere.

Such a program would increase greatly the number of trained narcotics agents serving throughout the country on both Federal and local levels.

5. Increase Staff of Narcotics Bureau

The Appropriations Committees and the Congress are to be commended for action in increasing the appropriation of the Narcotics Bureau to provide for 30 additional agents. The studies of this committee, however, indicate that the problem presented by the importation and sale of narcotic drugs has reached such magnitude that at least 40 more agents, in addition to the 30 provided for, are urgently needed. This would cover the enforcement needs as well as the local training program described in the previous recommendation.

Enforcement is the one point in the entire narcotics problem where results of a tangible nature will be evident immediately. Given the men, the Bureau, with the help of local agencies, can do much more to erase this evil than it is able to do under present conditions.

6. Promote Narcotics Education
A nation-wide educational program regarding the character and effects of narcotic drugs and the nature and results of addiction should be developed by the Federal Security Agency and made available to educational institutions, civic organizations, and enforcement authorities throughout the country. The objective of the program should be to lift the veil of secrecy from the subject and to bring it out into the open where it can be dealt with in an intelligent and effective manner. The present authority and funds of the Federal Security Agency are sufficient for this purpose.

7. Increase Drug Peddlers' Penalties
Federal laws increasing the penalties that the courts may impose upon convicted drug peddlers should be enacted without delay.

8. Increase Treatment Facilities
The facilities for treating drug addicts in Federal institutions should be increased to permit accommodation of more women patients and segregation of young addicts. Public awareness of the fact that the United States Public Health Service Hospital at Lexington, Ky., is open to voluntary patients and that its services are free to those who cannot pay, may result in a substantial increase in patients. In that event the facilities of that hospital should be increased to meet the needs then found to exist.

9. Require Notice to Seamen's and Longshoremen's Unions of Narcotics Convictions
The Narcotics Bureau should notify the appropriate national unions of all narcotics law convictions of seamen and longshoremen in order that the unions may more easily enforce their rules calling for expulsion of such cases.

10. Cancel Sailing Papers of Narcotics Violators
The Coast Guard should be empowered and required to cancel the sailing papers of any seaman convicted of a violation of the narcotics laws, irrespective of whether the violation occurred on land or at sea.

11. Prohibit Opium Production Throughout the World
The United States representatives at the United Nations should work toward the adoption of measures that will prohibit the growing of opium poppy plants in any country of the world.

12. Attorney General's Crime Conference
The Attorney General of the United States made a substantial contribution in the effort to combat organized crime in calling an Attorney General's Crime Conference which had its meeting in Washington in February 1950. The importance of the conference was shown by the fact that it was addressed by the President of the United States. It was attended by Federal and local enforcement officers, prosecuting attorneys and by representatives of municipal, county, State, and Federal officials.

The conference made notable achievements among which were the recommendation for enactment by the Congress of legislation preventing the use for gambling purposes of interstate communication facilities and prohibiting interstate shipment of gambling devices. The legislative committee of the conference in cooperation with the Attorney General prepared bills to effectuate these recommendations. The bill preventing interstate shipment of slot machines was passed by the Eighty-first Congress.

Extensive hearings were held by the Interstate and Foreign Commerce Committee of the Senate, and the wire-service bill was unanimously reported favorably, the report being made by Senator McFarland of Arizona, now majority leader.

The committee strongly recommends that the Attorney General call annual conferences of this kind and that the legislative and other committees of the conference have more frequent sessions to study and propose legislation at both Federal and local levels to combat organized crime. . . .

USE OF TELEVISION, NEWSREELS, AND RADIO IN CONGRESSIONAL HEARINGS

As the first congressional committee to encounter television on an extensive scale at its hearings, this committee feels that a report regarding its experience and attitude in that connection would be desirable.

There has been a great deal of public discussion regarding the advisability of permitting congressional hearings to be televised. It should be understood at the outset, however, that the issue does not relate to television as such. Television is essentially another improved method of public communication.

If hearings are to be conducted in public, obviously public access to the proceedings cannot be limited to those who are able to attend in person. No one can object to having reporters present who report everything they believe to be of public interest irrespective of whether the witness likes it or not. No serious objection has been raised to the use of flash-bulb photographs for newspaper publication and the use of radio to broadcast public hearings has been a common practice. Newsreel cameras present the most difficult problem because of their bulk and the brilliance of the lights required for their use.

All of these media of news collection and dissemination have been in use for many years. Adding television merely has the effect of increasing the number of people who can actually see the proceedings. Television cameras are quiet and unobtrusive and they require considerably less light than newsreel cameras.

If the subject matter being investigated by a congressional committee is of limited public interest the demand made upon it for access to the hearing by the various media of public news collection and dissemination will be similarly limited. If its subject matter is of great public interest, it will be besieged with requests from the press, the radio, the newsreel producers, and the television firms for the right to publish and broadcast the hearings. It is incumbent upon a committee faced with these requests not to discriminate unjustly among the various media.

The committee found, for example, that when its hearings involved large cities or notorious characters whose names were of great public interest, all of these media of communication sought access to the hearings, whereas hearings covering medium-size cities, where the subject matter was less spectacular, attracted the press only. Presumably, because of the expense of handling their equipment, newsreel and television firms attend only if the material has unusual publicity value.

Accordingly, it is the degree of public interest, not the desires of the committee, which governs the number of news representatives and the amount of equipment that the committee will be asked to allow in the hearing room.

The public has a right to be informed of the activities of its Government and it is entitled to have access to public hearings of congressional committees. The witnesses appearing before the committee also have rights that must be respected, but a witness does not have any inherent right to interfere with the rights of the public in this regard. There falls upon the shoulders of the committee conducting the hearing the responsibility of maintaining a fair and equitable balance between the rights of both the public and the witness.

The degree to which a witness is distracted by news devices depends on many factors, including the health and temperament of the witness. Giving testimony of any kind under any conditions may be nerve-wracking to some witnesses. Some can bear the strain more easily than others. Much depends upon the willingness of the witness to cooperate. A friendly and cooperative witness seldom objects to being photographed or televised and does not find these factors to be distracting. The reluctant witness, on the other hand, is necessarily under greater strain and is more easily distracted by outside forces. This gives rise to the question of whether the friendly witness should be given less favorable treatment than the recalcitrant one.

The committee must always be conscious of its responsibility to obtain from its witnesses the information required to fulfill its mission. If a witness refuses to testify unless all media of news dissemination are diverted from him, the committee either may recommend that he be cited for contempt of Congress or it may accede to his request for the purpose of obtaining the information the witness is able to supply. This requires a careful exercise of judgment as to which course will be in the best interests of the public.

Crime is nearly always a matter that attracts wide public attention and it is for this reason that at some of the more newsworthy hearings of the committee, the various media of news dissemination requested the right to bring in all of their facilities and equipment. Drawing the line was not easy.

In order to reduce the amount of equipment in the hearing room, the committee ordinarily required the television networks to form a pool so that only one set of cameras would be in the room. It also attempted to limit the number of newsreel cameras and in some instances it forbade the taking of still photographs with flash bulbs during the time when a witness was actually testifying. In other cases where the witness requested it, cameras, both newsreel and television, were required to be turned away from the witness during his testimony. In one case, where the testimony of the witness was deemed to be of considerable importance, all cameras, radio, and recording devices were silenced.

The policy adopted generally by the committee throughout was to attempt to recognize the public's right of access to the hearings, to avoid unfair discrimination between the various news media and at the same time to avoid subjecting the witness to an ordeal that would unduly interfere with the giving of his testimony. The committee exercised its judgment according to the individual circumstances of each case.

One of the important factors that affects the decision of a congressional committee in regard to the amount of facilities and equipment to be allowed in a hearing room is the size and character of the room itself. Congress does not have a hearing room adequately suited for a hearing that is of such widespread interest that newsreels and television networks will be attracted to it. Such rooms as it has are not equipped to accommodate modern photographing and televising equipment in an inconspicuous manner.

An example of the modern method of handling such equipment is found in the United Nations assembly room at Lake Success where the room itself is well lighted and newsreel and television cameras are installed behind a glass partition which blocks all operational noise. In such an arrangement the equipment is hardly noticed. If similar facilities were available for the hearings of congressional committees there would be few occasions when a witness could justifiably claim that his ability to testify was unduly hampered by the presence of news disseminating equipment.

Considerable confusion of thought has resulted from the error of placing congressional hearings in the same category as trials in court. While it is true that gangsters and hoodlums when called before this committee and asked to give information regarding organized crime, were in an uncomfortable position while being interrogated by counsel and Senators, they were not on trial.

A court trial is entirely different. It is a judicial proceeding involving the specific facts of an individual case. A jury is present and must be able to hear and weigh the evidence without distraction. The fate of an individual defendant is at stake and great weight must be given to his right to be tried in an atmosphere that is strictly calm and judicial. It is for these reasons that the Federal Rules of Criminal Procedure specifically forbid radio broadcasting of court proceedings.

The function of a congressional committee, on the other hand, is to obtain information for the purpose of enacting legislation. The legislative process includes the important step of enlightening the public regarding the matters under inquiry in order that intelligent public opinion will be developed. The more access the public has to the hearings the more thoughtful will its opinion be. This is a necessary part of the democratic process.

A final point that deserves comment is the question of commercial sponsorship of the broadcasting of committee hearings. Unlike most public-interest programs, a congressional hearing if fully broadcast, occupies long periods of time, often extending over several days. During this period, a radio or television station or network, in order to carry the hearings, is required to cancel all of its regular commercial programs. This involves not only loss of revenue but also, in some cases, the payment of cancellation penalties. Seldom can a station or network afford to bear this enormous financial burden.

Unless sponsorship is permitted, the public will be deprived of the privilege of witnessing many important events. At the same time, it is important to avoid a type of sponsorship which permits the broadcasting to be done in a manner that detracts from the dignity of the proceedings.

After extensive study by the committee and its staff, and discussion with representatives of the radio and television industry, the committee in an effort to reach an understanding with the industry adopted a proposed code of conditions covering the use of sponsored radio and television at its hearings. The plan adopted is as follows:

1. No television network or station shall use for the hearings a commercial sponsor not specifically approved in writing by the committee or its designated representative, and no sponsor shall be charged by a network or station more than such reasonable amount as may be consistent with the usual charges for other programs emanating from a public source.
2. No commercial announcement shall be broadcast from the hearing room.
3. Breaks for station identification during the hearings shall be limited to 10 seconds.
4. No network or station shall make any comment or commercial announcement during the testimony of a witness, or interrupt the broadcasting of the testimony of a witness for the purpose of making any such comment or announcement.
5. During each pause or intermission in the hearings, the network may make a commercial announcement lasting not more than 1 minute and, except in the case of a newspaper, magazine, or other publication of general circulation referring to reports of the hearings to appear in its columns, such commercial shall be institutional in character and shall make no reference to the hearings.
6. No local station shall interrupt any portion of the broadcasting of the hearings as received from a network for the purpose of making any spot or other commercial announcement.
7. A network or situation may, at any time, make a complete break from the broadcasting of the hearings for the purpose of broadcasting other programs.
8. At the beginning and end of the broadcasting of the hearings for any day, the network carrying the hearings shall make the following announcement or its equivalent:

> These hearings are brought to you as a public service by the X Company in cooperation with the Y Television Network.
>
> It is hoped that the committee's experience in this matter will be of some guide to other congressional committees faced with similar problems.

The committee, immediately after its creation in May 1950, adopted a code of procedure for its hearings. This code provided among other things that a witness before the committee should have the benefit of counsel when requested. Also the counsel could ask his client questions designed to bring out full information on a particular matter; questions or interrogatories could be submitted to the committee to be asked other witnesses who gave testimony concerning a particular witness. The code also provided that any persons or organizations whose names were mentioned in a hearing should be afforded an opportunity to give their side of the story by testifying or filing a statement or data in the record designed to clarify any point in controversy.

Later, when requests were made to permit televising of the hearings, the committee gave a great deal of consideration to this problem and ultimately adopted the set of conditions for sponsored broadcasts set forth heretofore. The committee had to act on all matters in its hearings without the benefit of precedent of other committees.

The committee feels that much time in the development of individual codes for congressional committees would be saved and hearings would be expedited if the Senate or the Congress would adopt an over-all code of procedure for all such committees. Witnesses appearing before the committees and their counsel would then know the rules of the game and much bickering, questioning and delay would be avoided.

The committee gives its wholehearted approval to the proposals which are now pending before the Senate Committee on Rules and Administration and other congressional committees for the adoption of such an overall code of procedure.

Source: U.S. Senate, Final Report of the Special Committee to Investigate Organized Crime in Interstate Commerce, 82nd Congress, 1st Session, Senate Report No. 725, 2–13; 99–103.

Bibliography

Campbell, Rodney. *The Luciano Project: The Secret Wartime Collaboration of the Mafia and the U.S. Navy.* New York: McGraw-Hill, 1977.

Cressey, Donald. *Theft of the Nation: The Structure and Operations of Organized Crime in America.* Reprint. Piscataway, N.J.: Transaction Publishers, 2008.

"Final Report of the Special Committee to Investigate Organized Crime in Interstate Commerce." Available at: http://www.nevadaobserver.com/Reading%20Room%20Documents/Kefauver%20Final%20Report.htm.

Gorman, Joseph. *Kefauver: A Political Biography.* New York: Oxford University Press, 1971.

Kefauver, Estes. *Crime in America.* Garden City, N.Y.: Doubleday, 1951.

"Kefauver Hearings." The American Mafia. Available at: http://www.onewal.com/maf-kef.html.

Kennedy, Robert F. *The Enemy Within: The McClellan Committee's Crusade Against Jimmy Hoffa and Corrupt Labor Unions.* New York: Harper, 1960.

Moore, William Howard. *The Kefauver Committee and the Politics of Crime.* Columbia: University of Missouri Press, 1974.

Reppetto, Thomas. *American Mafia: A History of Its Rise to Power.* New York: Macmillan, 2004.

Schlesinger, Arthur. *Robert Kennedy and His Times.* New York: Houghton Mifflin, 1978.

Stolberg, Mary M. *Fighting Organized Crime: Politics, Justice, and the Legacy of Thomas E. Dewey.* Boston: Northeastern University Press, 1995.

Swados, Harvey. *Standing Up for the People: The Life and Work of Estes Kefauver.* New York: E. P. Dutton, 1952.

The Committee on the Conduct and Firing of General Douglas MacArthur, 1951

by John Edward Wiltz

On the morning of Friday, August 17, 1951, the twenty-six members of the Senate's Armed Services and Foreign Relations Committees assembled in Room 212 of the Senate Office Building in Washington for their last meeting in connection with their "inquiry into the military situation in the Far East and the facts surrounding the relief of General of the Army Douglas MacArthur from his assignments in that area." The inquiry had been triggered by President Harry S. Truman's dismissal the previous April of MacArthur as commander in chief, United Nations Command; supreme commander for the Allied powers in Japan; commander in chief, Far East Command; and commander in chief, army forces in the Pacific. The main issue to be resolved that morning was whether the committees, which in their joint inquiry had taken 2 million words of testimony from thirteen witnesses during forty-two days of hearings in May and June 1951, should prepare a report. After more than an hour of discussion the senators resolved that there should be no report but that members of the two committees could file their views and conclusions with the chairman, who would see that they were printed in an appendix. A fortnight later, in accord with that resolution, eight Republican members—Owen Brewster (Maine), Styles Bridges (New Hampshire), Harry P. Cain (Washington), Ralph E. Flanders (Vermont), Bourke B. Hickenlooper (Iowa), William F. Knowland (California), H. Alexander Smith (New Jersey), and Alexander Wiley (Wisconsin)—submitted their "individual views."

Those views betray none of the euphoria about differences between Communist countries and the so-called free world which, in light of President Richard M. Nixon's pilgrimages to Beijing and Moscow in the 1970s and optimistic talk about détente and peaceful coexistence, later captivated large numbers of Americans. They reveal instead disillusion and frustration over the failure of America's military crusade of 1941–45 to make the world safe for the principles of liberty and justice—as Americans of the time perceived those principles.

Nearly all Americans in 1951, whether admirers of Douglas MacArthur or Harry Truman, shared the conviction that "international Communism," under the disciplined control of the Kremlin, had ruthlessly enslaved millions of people in the aftermath of World War II. In that grim catalogue of tragedies, the greatest catastrophe had been Communism's conquest of China, the most populous country on earth, one that the United States, so the senators asserted and most Americans seemed to believe, had befriended and protected and whose people felt special esteem for America. Not satisfied by the swallowing of China, the appetite of international Communism—and here was an article of faith even of people considered Socialists by the right-wing of American politics—proved to be nothing short of subjugation of the entire world.

If nearly all Americans in 1951 seemed to share this estimate of the evil character and global ambitions of communism, they differed in their views of why Communism in recent years had dramatically enlarged its influence and power. Some credited Communist successes to a combination of ruthlessness, postwar chaos, and the failure of non-Communist leaders (notably in China) to meet the problems of grinding poverty. Others, including the eight senators, contended that the key to Communism's triumphs had been the unwitting (or witless) and treasonable assistance it had received from Americans; that had been the case most notably and tragically in China. By pursuing policies of expediency and appeasement, they wrote, particularly at the Yalta

OVERVIEW

Background

On August 9, 1945, the same day that the United States dropped the second atomic bomb on Japan, the Soviet Union entered the war against Japan with an invasion of Manchuria and other Japanese-occupied territory, including the Korean Peninsula. The next day, two officers at the Pentagon, Dean Rusk (later secretary of state) and Colonel Charles Bonesteel, under the pressure of wartime circumstances and an advancing Soviet army, hastily drew up occupation zones for Korea. Using a National Geographic map, they divided the peninsula roughly in half at the 38th parallel. The Soviet army, by a prior agreement between President Harry Truman and Soviet leader Joseph Stalin, stopped its advance at the 38th parallel, and the U. S. Army eventually occupied the southern part of Korea. Two countries formed, one under Soviet influence and the other under the protection of U.S. military occupation, both claiming to be the legitimate government of all of Korea. In 1948, with the election of Syngman Rhee as president of South Korea, formally known as the People's Republic of Korea, U.S. occupation ended, but political tensions remained high in both North and South Korea on the question of unification.

On June 25, 1950, North Korea invaded South Korea, crossing below the 38th parallel. The United States came to the military aid of South Korea, partly to limit the spread of Communism in the region. Under the provisions of a United Nations Security Council resolution, Truman was authorized to pick the commander of U.N. forces mobilized to repel the invaders. Truman selected 70-year-old General Douglas MacArthur, one of the most decorated soldiers in American history and the commander of U.S. forces in occupied Japan. Congress did not declare war against North Korea, but it appropriated billions of dollars to fund U.S. and U.N. military personnel in what was technically called a United Nations "police action" rather than the full-scale war it was.

By September 1950, United Nations forces had turned back attempts by communist forces in North Korea to take over South Korea. MacArthur then made an aggressive attempt to sweep the Communists from North Korea. When vast numbers of Chinese troops joined those of North Korea to turn back U.N. forces, inflicting heavy casualties, MacArthur pressed for the authority to bomb Chinese targets and blockade Chinese coastal cities that were supplying Chinese troops in North Korea. MacArthur was willing to risk an all-out war with China, something that was far beyond the plans of Truman and his administration, which wanted to limit the war to Korea. MacArthur's actions, his threats to the Chinese, his attempts to influence congressional leaders behind the president's back, and his undermining of Truman's efforts to seek peace led Truman to relieve MacArthur of his command on April 11, 1951.

Congress Investigates

Truman's dismissal of MacArthur became not only an intensely personal conflict but also a major political bombshell. On April 25, 1951, two weeks after the dismissal, the Senate unanimously approved a resolution calling for its Committees on Foreign Relations and Armed Services to "conduct an inquiry into the military situation in the Far East and the facts surrounding the relief" of MacArthur. Chaired by Senator Richard B. Russell (D-Ga.), the hearings began in the Senate Office Building on May 3 and continued until June 25. The hearings comprised well over 2 million words of official transcript.

Impact

From the early days of the hearings, when MacArthur defended his aggressive posture in relation to the war, the highly partisan investigation constituted what historians have called "the Great Debate" on the wartime strategies of Communist containment followed by the Truman administration. Congress, which never seriously debated U.S. involvement in the Korean War, at least was able to debate the policy of containment of Communist aggression while the war was still under way. The hearings gave both sides—MacArthur and the Republicans and the Truman administration and the Democrats—opportunity to lay out their cases. Although MacArthur's freewheeling arguments remained convincing to some, his defiance of authority, the majority insisted, had given Truman no recourse but to act as he had done. MacArthur's immense personal popularity at the time of his firing led some to consider him a serious candidate for the presidency of the United States, but the congressional hearings on the reasons for his dismissal quickly dispelled any possibility of a political future for him.

CHRONOLOGY

1950

- *June:* Korean War begins. U.S. armed forces enter battle to resist Communist North Korea's invasion of South Korea.
- *September:* With victory at the battle at Inchon, South Korea, Communist forces are driven north of the 38th parallel.
- *December 5:* President Harry Truman issues an order primarily directed at General Douglas MacArthur, who was pressing to continue the fight into North Korea, that says that no civil or military official is to make any public statement on foreign or military policy without clearance from the Department of State or the Department of Defense.

1951

- *January:* After United Nations forces advance into North Korea, Chinese forces join battle and drive U.N. troops back in a humiliating retreat.
- *March 20:* Truman drafts a statement indicating that the United Nations should consider a cease-fire and peace negotiations.
- *March 24:* MacArthur, in defiance of Truman's order of December 5, 1950, makes an offer to personally negotiate with the North Koreans.
- *April 11:* Truman relieves MacArthur of his command and replaces him with Lieutenant General Matthew Ridgway.
- *April 19:* MacArthur addresses both houses of Congress and concludes with the words "Old soldiers never die; they just fade away."
- *April 25:* The Senate unanimously approves a resolution calling for its Committees on Foreign Relations and Armed Services to "conduct an inquiry into the military situation in the Far East and the facts surrounding the relief" of MacArthur.
- *May 3:* Hearings begin in Washington. MacArthur, the first witness, testifies for three days, from May 3 through May 5.
- *May 7:* Secretary of Defense George C. Marshall begins his testimony.
- *June 25:* MacArthur hearings conclude.
- *August 17:* Committees on MacArthur inquiry meet for the last time.

Conference in February 1945 and during General George C. Marshall's famous mission to China, December 1945 through January 1947, in failing to consult General MacArthur or follow the counsel of Lieutenant General Albert C. Wedemeyer regarding China, and in refusing to provide adequate support for the Nationalist regime of Generalissimo Chiang Kai-shek, "the victory won by our Armed Forces in the Pacific [in 1941–45] has been squandered by our diplomats." The eight senators, all identified with the Republican Party's "Old Guard" and in general agreement with Senator Joseph R. McCarthy's contention that the federal bureaucracy had been penetrated by Communists or Communist-sympathizers, also argued that what they termed vicious propaganda against Chiang Kai-shek and Communist subversion in the State Department had contributed to Communism's triumph in China.

Americans in 1951 likewise differed on how the presumed threat of international Communism should be met. Many favored a policy whereby the United States, working closely with allies, would try to contain Communism within its existing territory, thus guarding against Communist expansion in Europe. Others, including the eight senators, took a suspicious view of America's allies, particularly Great Britain, and thought the United States never should pull its punches for the sake of maintaining harmony with foreigners. Feeling a particular attachment to Chiang Kai-shek, Americans of the latter persuasion also contended that Communism in East Asia was as much a menace to America's security and interests as in Europe. In many respects, the world view of such individuals seemed a maze of vague and conflicting ideas. On the one hand, they looked with some contempt upon the outer world and exalted Americans and their institutions, sometimes betraying a yearning to retreat from world responsibilities to something approximating a "Fortress America." On the other hand, they often deplored the containment policy of the Truman administration and spoke of rolling back the Iron Curtain in Europe and Asia. While urging a

This Edwin Marcus cartoon shows General George C. Marshall surveying a broken vase (labeled "Our Chinese Policy"). Marcus drew this cartoon in December 1945, when President Truman sent Marshall as his envoy to China to see if he could bring an end to the civil war between the Chinese Nationalists and Communists. (By Permission of the Marcus Family)

reduction of American strength in Europe, which hardly squared with the rollback conception, some were willing to risk World War III to rescue China from the clutches of Communism.

What prompted the thinking of the eight senators and their political and intellectual companions? A simple answer might be that it resulted in part from misgivings over the government's departure, via the Truman Doctrine, Marshall Plan, and North Atlantic Treaty, from the historic peacetime policy of nonentanglement, relative aloofness, or national reserve (as it had been variously called)—or isolation (a popular if inadequate and misleading label). Such misgivings certainly seem to explain the flirtation of neo-isolationists (as the eight senators and other critics of Truman's foreign policies frequently were referred to) or nationalists (as they preferred to be called) with the Fortress America conception. In seeking an answer to this question, one might also note the vision of Communism held by neo-isolationists. While it was true that nearly all Americans of 1951 despised and feared Communism, the hatred and fear of the neo-isolationists exceeded that of many of their countrymen. Neo-isolationists accordingly rejected the idea of peaceful coexistence with the Communists and inclined to the view that America had two choices in foreign affairs: conceding most of the world to international Communism while building Fortress America as a bastion of liberty and democracy, or acting aggressively to bring about the collapse of Communism.

There was more to neo-isolationism, however, than concern over new departures in foreign policy and aggravated anticommunism. Most neo-isolationists, including the eight senators, were attached to the conservative wing of the Republican Party, and nearly all had been noninterventionists or isolationists in the period before America's entry in World War II. For such individuals the psychic burden of recent history had been almost unbearable. The ascendency of the principles of the Democratic welfare state brought about by President Franklin D. Roosevelt's New Deal in the 1930s, the universal repudiation of the central assumption of prewar isolationism, namely, that Axis aggression presented no threat to the United States, and five consecutive defeats in presidential elections had brought the conservative wing or Old Guard of the Republican Party to the depth of frustration. As the cold war unfolded and seemed to go from bad to worse, the Old Guard saw an opportunity to refurbish its reputation, recapture the White House, and turn back the clock of history to those revered days before Roosevelt and the welfare staters had taken the American republic on a radical binge. This opportunity appeared in the national disillusionment over the failure of World War II to bring forth the kind of world envisioned by the Atlantic Charter and the Charter of the United Nations, the great victories of Communism in Eastern Europe and China, and the alleged infiltration of legions of Communist traitors into the federal bureaucracy. Since Democratic welfare staters had been the managers of the republic's affairs during this time, it followed in accord with the iron law of American politics that blame for the great tragedy rested with them.

Encouraged by the stunning reelection victory of their acknowledged leader, Senator Robert A. Taft of Ohio in November 1950, and already deploying for a grand effort to put Taft in the White House in January 1953, Old Guard Republicans in late autumn 1950 touched off what news commentators were soon referring to as a Great Debate over American foreign policy. The debate reached the floor of Congress in early 1951 when the Old Guard made a strenuous effort to prevent President Truman from sending two army divisions to Europe to bolster America's commitment to the North Atlantic Treaty Organization (NATO). They succeeded in persuading the Senate to pass a resolution declaring that the president should not send additional troops to Europe without congressional consent. When Truman dismissed MacArthur, a Republican who shared the conservative political and social philosophy of the Old Guard and a renowned national hero who had clashed with their sworn enemy, "Give 'em Hell Harry" Truman, the Old Guard inevitably embraced MacArthur and made him a symbol of their views (although in truth MacArthur's ideas about world affairs in some ways varied with their own). MacArthur returned the embrace.

So began the MacArthur inquiry of 1951, for by the time the inquiry got under way nobody was questioning the president's authority to dismiss the general. The brainchild of Old Guardsmen (but not managed by them, inasmuch as Democrats were in control of Congress), the inquiry was a new and climactic chapter in the Great Debate over American foreign policy. By presenting MacArthur as the champion of their views and concentrating on the Far East, where Communism had registered its most staggering postwar triumphs (and hence American policy under the Democrats had suffered its most staggering defeat), the Old Guard hoped to demolish its opponents, force a dramatic revision of American foreign policy, and, most important of all, prepare the way for the capture of the White House a year and a half later by "Mr. Republican," Senator Taft.

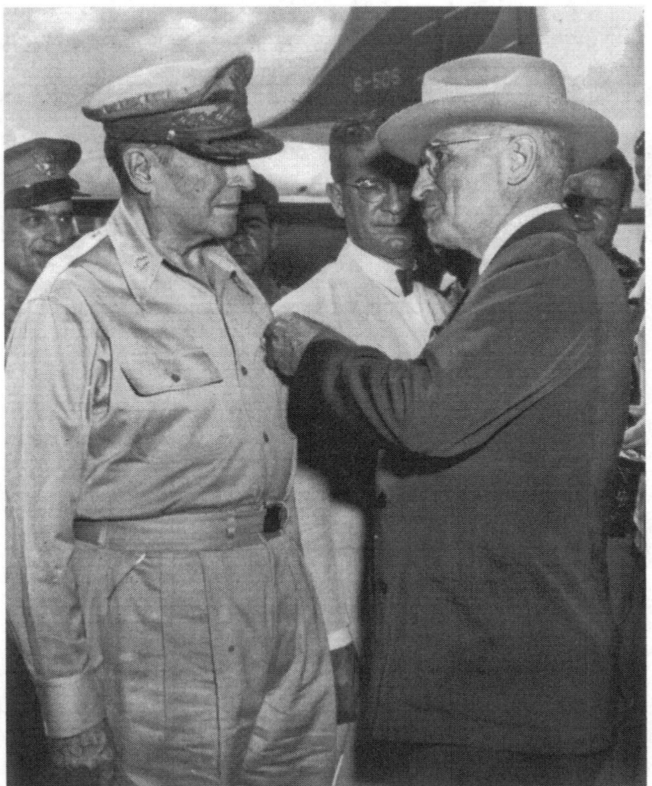

General Douglas MacArthur receives the Distinguished Service Medal from President Harry Truman on Wake Island, October 14, 1950. Within six months, President Truman would fire General MacArthur on grounds of insubordination. (Library of Congress)

I

Whatever their views about the origin of the cold war and how it should be prosecuted, most Americans had acquiesced in President Truman's decision at the end of June 1950 to throw American armed forces into the battle to resist Communist North Korea's invasion of South Korea. They agreed with the Truman logic that failure to stop this first overt act of aggression by "international Communism" since 1945 would only encourage further aggression and, ultimately, result in a new world war. They were pleased, even reassured, when the president placed the seventy-year-old General MacArthur in command of American forces in Korea and, when the United Nations assumed responsibility for resisting North Korea's attack, it asked the United States and MacArthur to assume command of U.N. operations in Korea.

After stopping the North Korean offensive along the Pusan perimeter at the southeastern corner of Korea, American forces, in one of MacArthur's most celebrated maneuvers, struck the North Korean flank and rear at Inchon, the Eighth Army broke out of the Pusan perimeter, and by the end of September 1950 South Korea (Korea below the thirty-eighth parallel) had been cleared of Communist forces. Then came a fateful decision, sanctioned by the U.N. but made in Washington, that directed U.N. troops to cross the thirty-eighth parallel and sweep Communism from the northern half of Korea. Leaders in the United States were anxious, however, lest the Chinese enter the war, particularly if U.N. troops advanced toward the Yalu River, the border between North Korea and China. During a dramatic meeting on Wake Island in mid-October, the president raised this possibility with MacArthur. The general either speculated or expressed reasonable certainty, depending on whose account of the discussion one accepts, that the Chinese would not intervene.

U.N. forces then pressed forward, and in an offhand remark, MacArthur expressed hope that American troops would be home by Christmas. Even as the commanding general uttered those words, however, Chinese soldiers were streaming across the Yalu into the rugged territory between MacArthur's separated contingents, and at the end of November they struck out savagely against the outnumbered U.N. infantrymen. When the U.N. retreat ended in January 1951, the Communists had recrossed the thirty-eighth parallel

A truck loaded with soldiers from the U.S. First Cavalry Division troopers are greeted by Koreans north of Seoul on the way to the 38th parallel. A South Korean flag flies in foreground. (Library of Congress)

and driven U.N. forces, then under the field command of Lieutenant General Matthew B. Ridgway, to a line fifty miles below Seoul, South Korea's battered capital city. For MacArthur, a proud and sometimes brilliant soldier, defeat came as a bitter pill, and to salvage the victory that had seemed within his grasp the previous November, he requested authority to send U.N. bombing planes against Communist supply depots, staging areas, and railroads in Manchuria, to impose a naval blockade against China's coastal cities, and introduce Chinese Nationalist troops from Formosa into the Korean combat. Determined to keep the war limited to Korea, Truman turned aside MacArthur's increasingly public appeals and finally, on April 11, 1951, dismissed the five-star general from his commands.

In retrospect, one is tempted to wonder why Truman put up with MacArthur as long as he did. The previous July, while U.N. troops were dug in along the Pusan perimeter, the general had flown to Formosa to check on the defenses of Chiang Kai-shek's island, and while there he expressed subtle disapproval of Washington's policy of preventing Nationalist attacks on China's Communist-ruled mainland. (When America intervened in the Korea conflict, Truman had ordered the Seventh Fleet to the Formosa Strait to protect Formosa and also to prevent Chiang from attempting an attack against his adversaries on the mainland.) In the last days of August 1950 MacArthur's public relations office in Tokyo handed reporters a copy of a statement by the general that was scheduled to be read in America on August 28 at the annual encampment of the Veterans of Foreign Wars. Although its theme was that Formosa should not be permitted to fall into hostile hands, the statement emphasized the importance of Formosa to the defense of

American interests in the Pacific and seemed inconsistent with Truman's statement of June 27 in which he stated his policy was to neutralize Formosa until such time as "restoration of security in the Pacific, a peace settlement with Japan, or consideration by the United Nations" was secured. Infuriated and concerned that the world might begin to wonder what America's policy regarding Formosa was, the president, as he later recorded in his *Memoirs,* considered relieving MacArthur of his command in Korea, but settled for an order directing him to withdraw the statement.

Truman's pique with MacArthur seemed to evaporate a few weeks later in the aftermath of the operation at Inchon and the subsequent rush of U.N. forces up the Korean peninsula. It appeared in those euphoric days of September–October 1950 that the American-inspired action of the U.N. in Korea was going to achieve its original objective and a good deal more besides; that is, it would succeed in repelling the North Korean invaders from South Korea and in addition bring a non-Communist reunification of the Korean nation, all without turning the so-called limited war of "police action" into a general war. But then came China's intervention and the heartbreaking U.N. retreat of November–January.

As exhausted U.N. units fell back across the thirty-eighth parallel in early December 1950, MacArthur advised the Joint Chiefs of Staff that China's entry into the war "calls for political decisions and strategic plans in implementation thereof adequate fully to meet the realities involved." Unable or unwilling to accept the logic of his superiors for keeping the war limited to Korea, he made a transparent appeal for authority to enlarge the war by carrying hostilities to the Chinese territory. Unfortunately, MacArthur was not content to keep his thoughts in military channels. In response to questions by *U.S. News and World Report* the first week in December, he maintained that orders preventing U.N. attacks beyond the Yalu were "an enormous handicap, without precedent in military history." More pointed were comments given about the same time in a statement to the president of the United Press. After explaining the advantage the "privileged sanctuary" in Manchuria gave the Communists, he scolded European proponents of limited war in Korea—and by implication American proponents, including the president—for failing to comprehend the importance of the conflict in East Asia: "If the fight is not waged with courage and invincible determination to meet the challenge here, it will indeed be fought, and possibly lost, on the battlefields of Europe." The general's broadsides irritated Truman, who wrote in his *Memoirs,* "I should have relieved General MacArthur then and there." But, Truman recalled, he did not want it to appear that the general was being made a scapegoat for the debacle in Korea. Instead, the president, on December 5, issued an order directing that no civil or military official (namely MacArthur) was to make any public statement on foreign or military policy without first getting a clearance from the Department of State or Department of Defense.

In the last days of December 1950 MacArthur composed a communication to the Joint Chiefs of Staff urging a dramatic expansion of the war in East Asia: a naval blockade of China, unrestricted air and naval attacks against Chinese industry, employment of Chiang Kai-shek's Nationalist troops in Korea, and removal of restrictions preventing the Nationalists on Formosa from attacking the Communists on China's mainland. On receiving a message from Washington turning aside his appeal, MacArthur, as he later recalled, "shot a query back" in which he advised the Joint Chiefs that his forces, weary and pinned down in Korea, no longer could guarantee the safety of Japan, the centerpiece of America's interests in the Far East; he requested substantial reinforcements or authority to evacuate Korea. In the words of Truman's secretary of state, Dean Acheson, recorded nearly two decades later in his memoirs, "here was a posterity paper if there ever was one, with the purpose not only of clearing MacArthur of blame if things went wrong but also of putting the maximum pressure on Washington to reverse itself and adopt his proposals for widening the war against China." Under heavy pressure from the U.N. and allies in Europe to keep the war in East Asia limited to Korea, which they were committed to do in any case, civil and military leaders in Washington were much annoyed. Finally, they dispatched a message to Tokyo that offered no reinforcements and directed MacArthur to stay in Korea "unless actually forced by military considerations." To provide any clarification that might be required, and also to discuss with MacArthur what might be done in the event matters got worse in Korea, two members of the Joint Chiefs of Staff, Generals J. Lawton Collins of the army and Hoyt S. Vandenberg of the air force, flew to Tokyo. A few days later Truman sent a long personal message to MacArthur explaining with uncharacteristic tact the global considerations underlying American policy.

Meanwhile the Communist offensive in Korea was running out of steam, and in late January 1951 U.N. troops under Ridgway, strung across the peninsula from a point fifty miles below Seoul, began to edge forward once more. In mid-March U.N. forces recaptured the remnants of the South Korean capital (the fourth time the city had changed hands in nine months), and within a few days were approaching the thirty-eighth parallel.

Thereupon MacArthur rekindled his campaign for widening the war. In a public statement on March 7 he observed that "as our battle lines shift north the supply position of the enemy will progressively improve, just as inversely the effectiveness of our air potential will progressively diminish, thus in turn causing his numerical ground superiority to become of increasing battlefield significance." He concluded: "Vital decisions have yet to be made—decisions far beyond the scope of the authority vested in me as the military commander, decisions which are neither solely political nor solely military, but which must provide on the highest international levels an answer to the obscurities which now becloud the unsolved problems raised by Red China's undeclared war in Korea." If couched in subtleties, the statement left little doubt about what MacArthur wanted to do. On March 15, in clear violation of Truman's order regarding public statements on high policy, the commanding general issued another communication to the president of the United Press. In it he expressed his opposition to stopping the U.N. advance at the thirty-eighth parallel or short of "accomplishment of our mission in the unification of Korea." As Acheson later recalled, "he had been told over and over again that this was not his mission."

From the U.N. and NATO allies, leaders in Washington were receiving different signals, namely, urgent appeals that they seek a cease-fire in Korea. The conditions for a battlefield truce certainly seemed opportune. The battle line was roughly where it had been when the war broke out, and neither side could advance without incurring devastating losses. A cease-fire along the present line, moreover, would not result in any substantial loss of face for either side, for if neither had achieved total victory in the war, the United States and U.N. could claim that they had saved South Korea from the Communist aggressors, and the Chinese could boast that they had prevented destruction of a Communist sister-state, North Korea. Weary of the war and unwilling to incur the expense in blood and treasure that further offensive action would require—and also concerned about reports that the Soviets were assembling troops in Siberia for possible commitment in Korea if the U.N. pushed ahead—the Truman administration needed no prodding. On March 20 the White House completed the draft of a statement to be issued by the president indicating that because the aggressors had been cleared from South Korea the U.N. would consider a cease-fire and peace negotiations. Copies of the draft statement went to fourteen other governments that had furnished troops for the U.N. effort, and General MacArthur was advised by radio that the president was about to make a peace overture. Leaders in Washington summarily dismissed MacArthur's response, an urgent request that "no further military restrictions be imposed upon the United Nations Command in Korea."

Then came a bombshell—labeled a routine communiqué a few years later by MacArthur in his reminiscences, but in Washington's eyes, an act of open defiance of the president's December 5 order. In a statement dated March 24, 1951, the commanding general made his own offer to negotiate with the enemy! MacArthur declared that despite inhibitions restricting its operations, his command had thwarted aggression in Korea and that the enemy "must be painfully aware that a decision of the United Nations to depart from its tolerant effort to contain the war to the area of Korea, through an expansion of our military operations to his coastal areas and interior bases would doom Red China to the risk of imminent military collapse." Seeing no reason the Communists should continue the struggle, MacArthur stood ready to confer with the enemy commander in chief.

Officials at the U.N. and in the capitals of America's allies were aghast, leaders in Washington furious. In addition to committing what his superiors considered an arrogant act of insubordination, MacArthur had cut the ground from under Truman's proposed peace overture. Clearly the general had to go. But Harry Truman, often impulsive in personal matters, was surprisingly cautious in matters of state. Before recalling MacArthur, he was determined to weigh the military and political consequences of such a dramatic move.

On April 5, 1951, the Republican leader in the House of Representatives, Joseph W. Martin Jr. of Massachusetts, stood in the House chamber and reported that several weeks before he had written MacArthur soliciting his views on the use of Chiang Kai-shek's Nationalist forces "in the opening of a second Asiatic front to relieve the pressure on our forces in Korea." He explained that he had asked the general to express himself either on or off the record, and since MacArthur's reply had not stipulated confidentiality, "I owe it to the American people to tell them the information I have from a great and reliable source." He then read MacArthur's letter. After supporting the idea of a Nationalist attack on the Chinese mainland MacArthur asserted: "It seems strangely difficult for some to realize that here in Asia is where the Communist conspirators have elected to make their play for global conquest, and that we have joined the issue thus raised on the battlefield; that here we fight Europe's war with arms while the diplomats there still fight it with words; that if we lost the war to Communism in Asia the fall of

In 1951 Massachusetts representative Joseph William Martin Jr. was House Minority Leader. He served two terms as Speaker from 1947–49 and 1953–55. (Library of Congress)

Europe is inevitable; win it and Europe most probably would avoid war and yet preserve freedom. . . . There is no substitute for victory." From London that same day came a news dispatch quoting MacArthur as having told a reporter that a web of artificial conditions was circumscribing U.N. forces in Korea, that the war had no definite objective, that it was not the soldier who had encroached on the realm of the politician. The general also allegedly said that the true object of a commander in war was to destroy the forces that opposed him, that such was not the case in Korea, and that the situation would be ludicrous if men's lives were not in the balance.

After consulting with diplomatic advisers and the Joint Chiefs, the president on April 10 signed the orders relieving MacArthur of all commands in the Far East. It was intended that the orders be cabled to Secretary of the Army Frank Pace, who was on an inspection mission in Korea, and that he would deliver them personally to MacArthur, before their release to the news media. At approximately seven o'clock in the evening, however, the presidential press secretary, Joseph Short, reported that the *Chicago Tribune* had learned of MacArthur's dismissal and would print the story the next morning. Hurrying to Blair House where Truman was having dinner (because the renovation of the White House living quarters was then in progress), General Omar N. Bradley, chairman of the Joint Chiefs, advised the president that if MacArthur learned of his dismissal via the *Tribune* story, he probably would try to resign. The President was purported to have snapped: "He's not going to be allowed to quit on me. He's going to be fired!" Unable to contact Pace to have him deliver the dismissal orders at once, Bradley, after another conference with Truman, dispatched the dismissal message directly to MacArthur's headquarters. It was a few minutes before midnight, Washington time; a few moments later Short summoned reporters to the White House and at 1:00 A.M. read the dismissal message. Before Bradley's communication got through to MacArthur, however, the embassy in Tokyo picked up a report of the dismissal in a commercial broadcast; an aide of the general at the embassy then telephoned MacArthur's residence, relayed the news to Jean Faircloth MacArthur, who in turn informed her husband. The general replied: "Jeannie, we're going home at last." It had been nearly fifteen years since the MacArthurs had last been in the United States.

What followed must seem, in retrospect, almost unreal to Americans whose memories do not reach back to 1951. Across the republic, expressions of outrage over the dismissal of the imperious MacArthur, the architect of victory in the southwest Pacific in World War II and the bearer of democracy to conquered Japan, drowned out the few voices raised on behalf of the president, whose reputation had recently been tarnished by disclosures that some of his subordinates had been peddling influence. When MacArthur, his wife, and young son arrived a few days later in San Francisco it seemed, so the general later recalled, "that every man, woman, and child . . . turned out to cheer us." On April 19 came perhaps the climax of MacArthur's long career—an address to both houses of Congress and the national television and radio audience. In his speech he restated his views on foreign policy and the Korean War and concluded by quoting the familiar refrain of an old barracks ballad—"Old Soldiers never die, they just fade away." From the capital MacArthur moved on to tumultuous receptions in New York, Chicago, and Milwaukee, the city of his childhood.

Old Guard Republicans, meanwhile, had been discussing the idea of a congressional investigation into MacArthur's dismissal and America's Far Eastern policy. Democrats, including Truman, also spoke out in favor of such an inquiry, and on April 25 the Senate unanimously approved a resolution offered by Richard B. Russell,

Democrat of Georgia, providing for a joint investigation by the Armed Services and Foreign Relations Committees. On the suggestion of Tom Connally of Texas, chairman of the Foreign Relations Committee, the honor of presiding over the joint inquiry went to Russell, chairman of the Armed Services Committee and a lanky and baldish bachelor of fifty-three. An eighteen-year veteran of the Senate, by 1951 he was one of the most respected (and powerful) men on Capitol Hill. The two committees agreed to commence hearings on May 3 by interrogating MacArthur himself, but before the interrogation could get under way Republicans and Democrats brawled over the question of whether the hearings should be open to the public or conducted behind closed doors. Counting on MacArthur's Olympian manner and polished phrases to strengthen support for their views, especially if the hearings were televised, Republicans demanded open hearings. Democrats countered that the inquiry would be dealing with secret documents and sensitive subjects, hence national security required closed hearings and censorship of transcripts of testimony before their release to the news media. Because Democrats had a majority of the votes, their view carried.

II

The MacArthurs had taken up residence in a $130-a-day suite in the Waldorf-Astoria in New York, and on the three days he testified before the Armed Services and Foreign Relations Committees the general commuted between New York and Washington by plane. On his arrival at the Senate Office Building the first day, May 3, 200 reporters and photographers scrambled about as he made his way through the corridors. Wearing his famous khaki campaign cap and accompanied by his long-time aide, Major General Courtney Whitney (who had quit the army in the aftermath of MacArthur's dismissal), he waved and half-smiled. When he entered the caucus room, site of the early hearings, the newsmen followed, and in the words of one reporter, "cameramen clambered on chairs to capture the firm jaw, the still-dark hair and serious mien, for the afternoon editions." While reporters and photographers milled about, MacArthur shook hands with the twenty-six members of the two committees and other senators who were also present. At length the journalists were ushered out of the room, the doors closed, and at 10:15 the interrogation began.

Hour after hour over the next three days the general, dressed in a ribbonless "Eisenhower jacket" and khaki necktie, slouched in a padded swivel-chair behind a table, puffing on a briar pipe as he answered questions, occasionally consulting Whitney, who was seated to his left. Democrats as well as Republicans treated him with elaborate courtesy, and only Senators Brien McMahon of Connecticut and J. W. Fulbright of Arkansas displayed enthusiasm for barbed or embarrassing questions. The general never seemed to tire or show any strain; he never appeared irritated. It was clear nonetheless that he was anxious to get on with other things, and to hasten the proceedings he persuaded the senators on the second and third days to lunch on sandwiches and coffee in the hearing room and continue the interrogation until seven o'clock each evening.

As was the case with all witnesses, the interrogation of MacArthur was confusing. Instead of moving logically from topic to topic, the questioning moved from senator to senator—from a member of the Armed Services Committee to a member of the Foreign Relations Committee, back and forth in accord with seniority—and when not asking questions, those senators in attendance often wandered in and out of the hearing room. The interrogation, as a result, touched on an incredible array of topics, some only remotely connected with the central purpose of the inquiry. The hearings were plagued by endless repetition of questions and answers (Secretary of State Acheson having to give an almost identical answer on six different occasions when queried about the use of the veto to keep China's Communist government out of the United Nations), and only with great effort could one ascertain the points being explored in the hearing room.

Among the points developed during the three days of MacArthur's appearance was that the general, in his judgment, had made no errors in his conduct of military operations in Korea.

It was inevitable that MacArthur's management of the Korean campaign would come under scrutiny, for the general received considerable criticism for having divided his forces as they advanced toward the Yalu in October–November 1950, thus leaving vacant a vast corridor through which the Chinese had entered and lashed out against the flanks of the Eighth Army and Tenth Corps. It was just as inevitable that MacArthur would give no quarter to his critics. The five-star general insisted that the first American troops dispatched to Korea from his command in Japan in July 1950, contrary to reports of nearly every observer, had been intensively trained and brought to a high state of professional efficiency. MacArthur explained that he had divided his forces because the northern extremity of Korea was so wide that he did not have the manpower to maintain a continuous line across the peninsula in that area. But was it not true that there had been virtually no liaison between the Eighth Army and the Tenth Corps? he was asked. "All that sort of stuff . . . is scuttlebutt written 10,000 miles away from the scene by these skillful propagandists who were trying to destroy the confidence of the American people in their own institutions." What about MacArthur's attack toward the Yalu in late November 1950 that was supposed to have ended the war by Christmas? It had not been an attack, the general maintained; it had been a reconnaissance in force to determine the strength of the Chinese in North Korea. As for the subsequent withdrawal from the Yalu by U.N. forces, "the concept that our forces withdrew in disorder or were badly defeated is one of the most violent prevarications of the truth that ever was made." The withdrawal, MacArthur contended, had been planned from the beginning, was orderly, and resulted in minimal losses. The entire action would have been obviated, of course—and victory assured—had he been permitted to destroy the Yalu bridges and attack supply bases and lines of communication in Manchuria as soon as it became apparent that the Chinese were entering Korea.

On the matter of his dismissal, MacArthur professed not to know why he had been relieved of his commands in the Far East. Never in his long career, he insisted, had he ever been insubordinate, nor would he do anything to undermine the principle of civilian control of the military: "Any idea that a military commander in any position would possess authority over the civil functions of this Government is a treasonable concept in my mind." Hence, he did not question the president's right to relieve him, explaining that Truman had acted "within his complete authority, and his responsibility, and I don't challenge either, in any way, shape, or manner." Reiterating a theme set out in his

U.S Marines halted by a Chinese roadblock during the push across the Yalu River on December 14, 1950. Harsh, subzero temperatures prevailed during this operation in northern Korea. (Associated Press)

address to Congress and widely trumpeted by his supporters, MacArthur intimated that his quarrel with the administration had resulted from the failure of officials in Washington to issue clear directives defining his mission in Korea. His own recommendations for expanding the war, he testified, had been intended to secure policy directives, for "I could not go on ordering men to their deaths by the thousands, in such a complete vacuum of policy decision." Had Truman been forthcoming with such policy directives, "I would, to the best of my ability, have carried them out completely and absolutely."

Regarding his statement of March 24 in which he offered to negotiate a truce with the enemy commander, MacArthur testified that "the notice I put out was merely that which every commander at any time can put out." The message from Washington of March 20 advising him that the president was about to make a peace announcement "hadn't the slightest bearing" on his own statement, and he could not imagine that his statement might have embarrassed the president or influenced what he and the U.N. were trying to do. As for his letter to Congressman Martin, he said he always had felt that any member of Congress was entitled, within the limits of security requirements, to any information he might ask for: "That is what I visualize is the proper courtesy and respect that is due to the legislative leaders of the country." Otherwise, the letter "was merely a routine communication such as I turn out by the hundreds" and "made so little impression upon me . . . that later on when somebody said a great deal of commotion had been raised by that letter, I had to consult my files to see what the letter was."

General MacArthur was nothing if not forthright, and in commenting on the larger aspects of American foreign policy he must have sent chills down the spines of such Old Guardsmen as former President Herbert Hoover, who had recently been championing a retreat to "Fortress America"; the general, it seemed, was an unreconstructed globalist. He portrayed himself as a more confirmed globalist than were those leaders of the Truman administration who had recently completed America's emancipation from the shackles of isolationism. According to the general, "You can't let one-half of the world slide into slavery and just confine yourself to defending the other. You have got to hold every place." As for Europe, its first line of defense was in Korea, and if the Communists succeeded in breaching that line, the fighting "will roll around to Europe as sure as the sun rolls around."

All this meant that MacArthur had no patience with the idea of waging a limited war in Korea for the limited goal of securing South Korea from Communism. The war in Korea, he insisted, had to be conducted without restriction until the Chinese, and with them Communism, were driven north of the Yalu and the entire Korean nation united under a non-Communist regime—this had been the U.N. objective, he maintained with dubious accuracy, from the onset of the Korean War. As he had said in his address to Congress on April 19: "War's very object is victory, not prolonged indecision. In war there is no substitute for victory." Restricting the use of one's forces in war, the general thought, was a form of appeasement, and "if you hit soft, if you practice appeasement in the use of force, you are doomed to disaster." Such a disaster, he reasoned, already was taking shape in Korea, where the opposing armies at dreadful expense had pushed one another up and down the Korean Peninsula in "an accordion war" and now seemed headed toward a bloody and inconclusive stalemate. MacArthur urged "that some plan be carried out that will bring this dreadful slaughter to a definite end." What he wanted, of course, was expansion of the war by lifting restrictions on bombing Chinese territory, imposing a naval blockade against the China coast, and putting the troops of Chiang Kai-shek in the battle against the "Red Chinese." Guessing that between 5 and 10 million Chinese died of starvation every year, he contended that the economic disruption resulting from the execution of his proposals would turn great segments of China's population to disorder and discontent, and "the internal strains would help to blow up her potential for war."

But might not expansion of the war in Korea provoke the Soviets and raise the risk of World War III? That, as Senator Wiley noted, was "the most serious question, and probably the most speculative one, and the one that most concerns our associates in the United Nations" regarding MacArthur's proposals.

The general's answer to the question was negative. In his view the Soviets had a timetable for world conquest and could be diverted from it only if it was transparently advantageous for them to do so. A small provocation in East Asia, in a word, was not apt to bring a Soviet response. MacArthur believed the Soviets would be more tempted to act if the war in Korea dragged on inconclusively; hence "I believe that the program I have suggested will tend to not precipitate a world war, but to prevent it." To reinforce his contention that the Soviets would not intervene if the U.N. expanded the war in Korea, the general minimized the Soviet Union's current involvement in the conflict: "It has been quite apparent to me . . . that the linking of the Soviets to this Korean War has paled out as the events have progressed." The interests and prestige of the Soviet Union, therefore, would not be imperiled by an expansion of the war, since the only objective of such an expansion would be to drive the Chinese from Korea. As a matter of fact, the Soviets might consider it to their advantage to have the U.N. administer a setback to "this new Frankenstein that is being gradually congealed and coalesced in China." Asked MacArthur: "Would the Soviet desire to have China become so powerful that it might even challenge the Soviet? Would it be the desire, would it be possible for the Soviet to retain a maximum degree of control if China became too powerful?"

Some senators remained unconvinced. McMahon observed that MacArthur's speculations on the probable course of events had been wrong in the past—notable was the case of China's entry in the Korean War. The general countered that in that instance the secretary of state and the CIA had made the same mistake. Senators Estes Kefauver of Tennessee and Wayne Morse of Oregon raised the question of whether the Sino-Soviet Pact of 1950 might require a Soviet response if the U.N. carried the war into Chinese territory. MacArthur dismissed the question as speculative. Morse wondered about the Soviet response to the bombing of the rail lines in Manchuria, which the Soviets jointly owned and operated with the Chinese and which served Soviet interests in Siberia. Replied MacArthur: "In my opinion, it is a minor point." Morse also wondered about the Soviet response to a naval blockade, inasmuch as the blockade proposed by the general would include the Soviet naval base in Manchuria, Port Arthur. MacArthur retorted: "I do not believe the small incident involved would materially affect in any way the great decisions that would be involved in bringing the Soviet into a global war."

Showing a figure labeled "China" chained to and pulling a rickshaw carrying a Stalin-like figure, this cartoon refers to the Sino-Soviet Pact, announced in September 1952, that allowed the Russians to retain control of Port Arthur. This agreement was interpreted in some Western circles as providing continued Soviet control of Manchuria and relegating China to the role of a Communist satellite. (Library of Congress)

Even if one accepted the contention that expansion of the war would not trigger a Soviet response, questions nonetheless remained. How much of a build-up of U.N., principally United States, forces would be required to execute MacArthur's proposals? The general could give no precise figures but was confident that expansion of the war would require the commitment of only a few more ground troops and several additional naval and air units to the East Asian conflict. Could not China match such an enlargement of U.N. forces? MacArthur did not think so: "I believe that practically the maximum effort that she is militarily capable of is being exerted in Korea at the present time." What about the so-called American sanctuaries in South Korea and Japan? If the United States carried the war into Chinese territory might not they retaliate by turning their air and naval forces loose against South Korea, America's bases in Japan, and the American navy off the Korean coast? "I don't believe that Red China has the potential to bomb any of those places," MacArthur told the senators. "I don't believe she has got the air or the navy to make any threat." Well, what about America's European allies? They seemed adamantly opposed to expansion of the war in Korea. "My hope would be of course that the United Nations would see the wisdom and utility of that course [expansion of the war], but if they did not, I still believe that the interest of the United States being the predominant one in Korea, would require our action." "Alone?" Senator Theodore Green of Rhode Island asked. MacArthur replied: "Alone, if necessary. If the other nations of the world haven't got enough sense to see where appeasement leads after the appeasement which led to the Second World War in Europe, if they can't see exactly the road that they are following in Asia, why then we had better protect ourselves and go it alone." But what if the MacArthur plan failed in its objective of driving the Chinese from North Korea? "I believe that the methods I have proposed will be completely effective. . . . I believe I wouldn't attempt to predict the exact time that that would be accomplished but, applied long enough, I believe its results would be a certainty." What if after being pushed out of Korea the Chinese remained in large formations in Manchuria along the Yalu? Might they present a continuing threat to Korea? "Such a contingency is a very hypothetical query," MacArthur countered. "I can't quite see the possibility of the enemy being driven back across the Yalu and still being in a posture for offensive action."

Whether to deploy Chiang Kai-shek's Nationalist forces against the Communists had been an aspect of MacArthur's controversy with his superiors in Washington, and during the general's appearance in the witness chair the question came up repeatedly. Less interested in the prospect of introducing Nationalist troops in Korea than he had been several months before, MacArthur now seemed consumed with the idea of helping Chiang return to China's mainland. A first step in executing such a return would be the removal of the Seventh Fleet from the Formosa Strait, a step he considered long overdue inasmuch as the mere threat of a Nationalist foray across the strait, he thought, would have taken pressure off U.N. forces in Korea after China's intervention across the Yalu and saved many thousands of U.N. lives. As for the danger of a Communist invasion of Formosa if the Seventh Fleet was withdrawn, MacArthur reverted to his contention that the Chinese Communists were already fully committed in Korea and thus did not have the capacity to make an amphibious assault across the Formosa Strait. What sort of operation by the Nationalists against the mainland did the general have in mind? Well, that would be up to the generalissimo but it probably would be "an infiltrative effort at various points" rather than a large-scale amphibious movement. Citing alleged reports that there were a million and a half anti-Communist guerrillas in China, MacArthur expected that Nationalist troops would coordinate their operations with those guerrillas. Because of their experience with the ways of the Communists, he also thought "most sincerely" that great numbers of ordinary Chinese would rally to the Nationalist banner when Chiang's troops returned to the mainland.

The senators inevitably raised more questions. In view of the widespread belief that Chiang Kai-shek was not well respected by other non-Communist Asians, would the United States risk losing its remaining friends in East Asia if it helped him return to the mainland? MacArthur replied that to the average Asian the generalissimo stood out as a great symbol of anticommunism and that those who favored Communism opposed him "completely and absolutely." Moreover, supporting Chiang, the general testified, did not mean that the United States was required to endorse everything he did or said. The overriding consideration was that Chiang's interests paralleled those of America. About the alleged corruption in Chiang's regime, MacArthur said: "In great international decisions, if they are to be based upon the details of corruption in government, Senator, there would be few countries that would pass unscathed." In any event, Chiang apparently had his administrative problems under control, for during his visit to Formosa the previous year MacArthur had found contentment and prosperity and evidence that Chiang was establishing a standard of government that compared favorably with many of the world's democracies.

The senators wondered about the quality of Nationalist forces and their capacity to get across the Formosa Strait and secure themselves on the mainland. MacArthur conceded that Chiang's soldiers were short of artillery and trucks and that his navy amounted to little. Of the Nationalist air force he said it had only a couple of hundred planes, but the pilots were capable "and for such a jerk-water group, they make a pretty brave showing." Accordingly, the Nationalists would require large-scale assistance by the United States. In the MacArthur scenario the American navy would transport the Nationalists to the mainland and with the American air force cover their operations. Perhaps 500 American technicians and military advisers would accompany the Nationalists, and the burden of supplying the operation would be assumed by the United States. Under no circumstances, however, would American combat units be introduced into the ensuing struggle. Said MacArthur: "No man in his proper senses would advocate throwing our troops in on the Chinese mainland." Well, what if the Nationalists went to the mainland and were wiped out? "I am unable to answer a hypothetical question," MacArthur replied, "in which you put up a suggestion that the forces of the Generalissimo would be destroyed. I do not believe that they are going to be destroyed; and, if we gave him the proper support, they would not be destroyed."

As he continued to respond to this question raised by Senator Henry Cabot Lodge of Massachusetts, MacArthur reiterated a point that he had been making over the past year and during the hearings: "I would insure that Formosa shall not fall into Red hands." The general's vision of the strategic importance of Formosa, in truth, seems incredible in retrospect—and seemed so to some Americans in 1951. Declaring that the "loss" of Formosa would make Japan and the Philippines indefensible, he said: "I believe that from our standpoint we practically lose the Pacific Ocean if we give up or lose Formosa. . . . If the enemy secured Formosa and secured thereby the Pacific Ocean, that would immeasurably increase the dangers of that ocean being used as an avenue of advance by any potential enemy. And Alaska is on that ocean; it would unquestionably increase the dangers to Alaska as well as it would be to the State of California, the State of Washington, and Oregon, Central and South America." When Senator Russell Long of Louisiana doubted that Formosa had so much strategic importance, the general repeated his contention with uncompromising vehemence.

The immediate effect of the MacArthur testimony, printed in its entirety by some newspapers, was hard to measure. If some of his ideas seemed outlandish and others not clearly formed, the general nonetheless remained a magnetic personality who in spite of his arrogance and vanity had touched many Americans, just as he had nine years before when, as he left the island of Corregidor, he uttered those memorable words: "I shall return."

MacArthur's simplistic declaration that there was no substitute for victory appealed to the large segment of the American populace that always had sought simplistic solutions to complicated problems and which presently felt demoralized by cold war setbacks and frustrated by the vagaries of the limited conflict in Korea. Then, there was a top-secret memorandum dated January 12, 1951, to which MacArthur had referred over and over during his three days in the witness chair and which seemed to strengthen his position. The general claimed the document proved that three months before his dismissal the Joint Chiefs of Staff had supported most of his proposals for expanding the war in East Asia. Because the memorandum was classified as top secret, it had remained unpublished, but if what the general said was true, it would appear that he had not been alone in calling for dramatic action against the enemy. If his interpretation of the memorandum was correct, moreover, the stature of the Joint Chiefs, who had concurred in his dismissal and whose alleged opposition to his ideas was central to the case against MacArthur, would be seriously diminished. It would appear that they had been persuaded by political leaders to support the dismissal of a distinguished fellow officer, even though they shared his view of what should be done in Korea.

As for the general's detractors, they must have found some reason for cautious encouragement in his testimony. MacArthur's case for expanding the war in East Asia was full of holes, his statements on the strategic importance of Formosa had been ludicrous, and most important, the senators on several occasions had forced him to admit that as a theater commander he had not had access to the requisite information for making high policy decisions and that his perspective on the East Asian war accordingly was limited.

III

Following MacArthur into the witness chair during the next month were spokesmen for the anti-MacArthur view, or the view of President Truman's administration: General of the Army George C. Marshall, the secretary of defense; General of the Army Omar N. Bradley, chairman of the Joint Chiefs of Staff; General J. Lawton Collins, chief of staff of the army; General Hoyt S. Vandenberg, chief of staff of the air force; Admiral Forrest P. Sherman, chief of naval operations; and Dean G. Acheson, the secretary of state.

Marshall, the seventy-year-old chieftain of the Department of Defense who conceded that he answered more readily to the title of general than to that of Mr. Secretary, proved a patient and effective witness, and by the time he completed his seven days of testimony it was evident that he had considerably weakened the convictions of those senators who espoused General MacArthur's cause. In his first minutes in the witness chair Marshall just about demolished MacArthur's argument that the Joint Chiefs of Staff's (JCS) memorandum of January 12, 1951, proved that military leaders in Washington had agreed with his prescription for expanding the Korean War. At the time the memorandum was prepared, Marshall explained, officials in Washington faced the possibility that U.N. forces might be compelled to evacuate Korea, and the proposals put forward by the JCS in the memorandum, which included preparations for a naval blockade of China and logistical support for operations by Chiang Kai-shek's Nationalists against China's Communists, were offered as tentative actions if an evacuation of Korea appeared imminent. But then, over the next week, came a dramatic improvement in the military situation in Korea. Clearly the Communists were not going to drive U.N. armies off the peninsula, so it was unnecessary to put into effect all of the actions outlined in the memorandum.

In his testimony Marshall observed that the American objective in Korea was to defeat aggression and restore peace, and to that end the United States had sought to confine the conflict to Korea and prevent it from escalating into World War III. "General MacArthur, on the other hand, would have us, on our own initiative, carry the conflict beyond Korea against the mainland of Communist China, both from the sea and from the air. He would have us . . . risk involvement not only in an extension of the war with Red China, but in an all-out war with the Soviet Union. He would have us do this even at the expense of losing our allies and wrecking the coalition of free peoples throughout the world. He would have us do this even though the effect of such action might expose Western Europe to attack by the millions of Soviet troops poised in Middle and Eastern Europe."

This editorial cartoon by Herblock captioned "We've been using more of a roundish one" shows Douglas MacArthur, seated on the left with a cubed globe that focuses only on the Far East, and George Marshall, seated on the right with a spherical globe and a more global view of foreign policy. (A Herblock Cartoon, copyright by The Herb Block Foundation)

He said that the differences in judgment between officials in Washington and MacArthur had arisen "from the inherent difference between the position of a field commander, whose mission is limited to a particular area and a particular antagonist, and the position of the Joint Chiefs of Staff, the Secretary of Defense, and the president, who are responsible for the total security of the United States, and who, to achieve and maintain this security, must weigh our interests and objectives in one part of the globe with those in other areas of the world so as to attain the best over-all balance." Conceding that it was both understandable and commendable for a field commander to become so wrapped up in his own operations and responsibilities that he would find some directives from higher authorities not to his liking, Marshall explained that "what is new, and what has brought about the necessity for General MacArthur's removal, is the wholly unprecedented situation of a local theater commander publicly expressing his displeasure at and his disagreement with the foreign and military policy of the United States." Marshall also implied, for he dared not attack MacArthur's soldierly integrity, that because MacArthur was so critical of established policies, there had been some doubt about his ability to execute those policies, if not in the letter at least in their spirit.

Old Guardsmen tried with little success to chip away at Marshall's case for MacArthur's dismissal. "Do you mean to say," Senator Alexander Wiley of Wisconsin asked, "that a man in General MacArthur's position, who was the Chief of Staff when you were a colonel, had no right to discuss or advise or recommend to you leaders in Washington?" Marshall said: "There was no limit whatever on his representations of his views to the officials in Washington. There is a great difference between that and the public announcements." What if Marshall, during World War II, when he was chief of staff of the army, had differed very strongly with the Roosevelt administration over military policy? "I would have done my best directed to the President to have it changed, and I might say I had some very difficult scenes with Mr. Roosevelt over certain phases of the matter . . . ; but I didn't make any public speeches," he replied. Still, was not a member of Congress, like Congressman Martin, entitled to a frank reply when writing to a military leader? "No, sir," Marshall said, "I don't think from the senior commander, when he knows he is advocating something to the leader of the opposition party to the administration that he as the commander is in total disagreement with his own people." As for the contention that in the weeks before his dismissal MacArthur had operated virtually without instructions from Washington on official policy and thus somehow was justified in setting out his own policy views, Marshall testified that "he was given full information [regarding policy] right along the line."

As expected, Marshall gave short shrift to MacArthur's proposals for expanding the war in East Asia. Execution of the general's proposals, he maintained, might have drastic consequences: a falling-out between America and its allies, a Soviet strike westward in Europe, or a nuclear confrontation between the Soviet Union and the United States. There was no way, he told the senators, that the gains that might be realized from an expanded war in Korea could justify such risks. But, MacArthur's supporters demanded to know, had the United States not risked a Soviet response when it organized the Berlin airlift in 1948 and set about arming the countries of Western Europe in accord with the North Atlantic Treaty of 1949? The situation in Europe in 1948–1949 had not been parallel with the present one in Korea, Marshall countered. Failure to act decisively in Europe in 1948–1949 would have left the way open for a Communist conquest of Western Europe. Failure to take the risks implicit in the MacArthur plan for Korea would leave exposed no American interest in East Asia.

In testimony deleted from the public transcript by the censor, Marshall went further in his critique of MacArthur's proposals. He told the senators that the United States plainly did not have the armed strength that would be required to conduct an expanded war in East Asia. More intriguing, he observed that just as the United States was keeping its air and naval forces in check in East Asia, so were the Communists. The advantage of mutual restraint, he said, rested with the United States and its allies. Bombing targets in Manchuria, for example, were widely scattered, while those of the U.N. forces in Korea were concentrated. Particularly vulnerable to a large-scale Communist attack was Pusan, the U.N. command's major port and logistical center. Marshall intimated that military leaders in Washington were concerned over the vulnerability of U.N. troops, communications, and installations if the Communists suddenly unleashed their air and naval forces known to be in the Far East. Marshall took a low view of MacArthur's proposal for employing Chiang Kai-shek's Nationalist troops either in Korea or in an assault on China's mainland. Putting the Nationalists in Korea or on the mainland would weaken the defenses of Formosa, might provoke an escalation of the war by the Communists, and was certain to cause friction between America and its allies. In addition, the Nationalists, he made clear in testimony later excised by the censor, were not nearly as strong as was commonly thought; they did not even have the capacity to hold Formosa without external help. "The record of the Chinese Nationalist troops for losing equipment furnished them," he also observed, "increases the reluctance of the Joint Chiefs of Staff to equip them and employ them in battle."

Since it was clear that Washington had no intention of ordering an expansion of the war or of trying to expel the Communists from North Korea by pushing the war much beyond the thirty-eighth parallel, pro-MacArthur senators demanded to know how Marshall and the Joint Chiefs of Staff proposed to terminate the conflict in East Asia. If the combat in Korea remained on its present course, they contended, the probable outcome would be a long and costly battlefield stalemate. Surely an expansion of the war in accord with MacArthur's ideas would be preferable to that. Marshall conceded that he and the Joint Chiefs looked with trepidation on the prospect of an extended stalemate in Korea. But in testimony deleted by the censor he expressed hope that the war might soon be brought to an end along the present battle line. The idea was to use the U.N.'s firepower superiority to extract such a toll of soldiers and equipment from the Communists that within a short time they would consent to an armistice. Marshall hoped that the Communists would keep up the offensive they had opened in recent weeks: "The best possibility that we see at the present time is immediately a continuation of the attack by the Communists, with the hope that we get fair weather, and inflict such tremendous losses on them in proportion to what has occurred in the past two weeks that we have broken the power of their trained armies."

In accord with their mandate, the senators grilled Marshall on the larger aspects of America's Far Eastern policies in recent years as well as on the dismissal of MacArthur. There was the matter of Marshall's "mission" to China in 1945–47 during which the general had pressed the Nationalists of Chiang Kai-shek and the Communists of Mao Zedong to terminate their civil war. Marshall insisted that his purpose had not been to urge the disputants to accept a coalition government; the Nationalists and Communists had agreed to a coalition government a short time before he left for China. His purpose had been to work out an armistice and a program for demobilization, although he eventually became involved in political affairs to the extent that he sought to help the opposing sides execute agreements they had made previously. Marshall pointed out that the operating document for the coalition gave Chiang a veto over government action and, more importantly, provided that China's army would comprise fifty Nationalist divisions and only ten Communist.

Another facet of this controversy was the celebrated report on China and Korea drafted by Lieutenant General Albert C. Wedemeyer following his own mission to East Asia in 1947. Marshall, as secretary of state, had prevented its publication or, in the parlance of the Old Guard, suppressed it. The senators wondered why. According to Marshall, Wedemeyer had proposed putting the China problem before the U.N. and placing Manchuria and Korea under a U.N. trusteeship, but that would have complicated discussions in Congress and at the U.N. concerning current affairs in Greece. "I know that they [people in the State Department] did go through it to see how we could delete, and it seemed to be so woven into the report, that part of the United Nations phase, that it would excite more speculation and more complications than would be desirable."

The chairman of the Joint Chiefs of Staff, Omar Bradley, followed Marshall to the witness chair, and in the early minutes of his interrogation Senator Wiley asked him to tell the committee what had been said in a meeting on April 6, 1951, involving Bradley, Marshall, Secretary Acheson, W. Averell Harriman, and President Truman. Bradley responded: "Senator, at that time I was in a position of a confidential adviser to the President. I do not feel at liberty to publicize what any of us said at that time." That response touched off a sometimes angry debate among the senators over the relationship of advisers to a president. The debate consumed nearly two days of the hearings and occupied more than a hundred pages in the printed transcript. At length, by a vote of 18–8, the two committees sustained Bradley's refusal to divulge presidential conversations.

Otherwise, Bradley reinforced the points made by Marshall, and in a prepared statement before his interrogation began made the most publicized utterance of the inquiry, saying that in the estimate of the Joint Chiefs the MacArthur strategy "would involve us in the wrong war, at the wrong place, at the wrong time, and with the wrong enemy." To execute the MacArthur program, he told the senators, the United States would have to strip its defenses in other areas of the world, and having done that he doubted that expansion of the war would bring victory in Korea. On the contrary, he suspected that expansion might result in a new world war—a war that the United States simply was not prepared to fight. If careful to avoid offending the proponents of air power, he expressed limited faith in MacArthur's view that bombing planes striking targets in Manchuria and elsewhere in China with non-nuclear bombs would cripple the Communist military effort in Korea. He observed that U.N. bombers presently had 200 miles of Communist supply lines in North Korea to patrol and were unable to stop the movement of men and matériel to the battlefront. As for an attempt to destroy the source of the enemy's military production by sending strategic bombing planes against China's cities, Bradley pointed out that the sources of production for the Communist war effort in Korea were in the Soviet Union, not China.

Of MacArthur's dismissal, Bradley explained that the Joint Chiefs had concurred in the decision to relieve MacArthur because he had violated Truman's directive of December 5, 1950, regarding public statements on high policy and undermined the president's proposed peace overture of March 1951, and because in their view "General MacArthur's actions were continuing to jeopardize the civilian control over military authorities." His only concession to MacArthur supporters was that the dismissal might have been executed more adroitly. About MacArthur's failure in November 1950 to act on a warning by the Joint Chiefs in Washington that the flank of the Tenth Corps in North Korea was exposed, Senator Fulbright asked if that action had influenced the Joint Chiefs in their decision to support MacArthur's dismissal. Bradley was not sure. It might have had some relevance, but they had not discussed it at the time they made the decision.

The three service chiefs, Generals Collins and Vandenberg and Admiral Sherman, were next to testify in the MacArthur inquiry. Each man spent two days in the witness chair in the last days of May 1951.

Although posing Collins the same questions about the expansion of the war in Korea and receiving answers similar to those offered by Marshall and Bradley, the senators seemed particularly interested in eliciting more comments on MacArthur's dismissal. Why, they asked, had the Joint Chiefs endorsed the decision? Because of an accumulation of incidents, Collins testified, "and a growing conviction that General MacArthur was not in sympathy with the basic policies under which he was operating; and that the President of the United States, as the Commander in Chief, was entitled to a field commander who was in consonance with the basic policies of his Government." Was it not a fair assumption, Senator Bourke Hickenlooper of Iowa asked, that the Joint Chiefs merely contrived to justify a decision already made at the White House? Reiterating that the Joint Chiefs had sought to give the president an honest opinion, Collins said: "You can ask me it in 10 different ways and I am going to give you the same answer." If the rea-

This Reg Manning cartoon, showing a military hat surrounded by the silk hats of "appeasing diplomats," suggests that President Truman caved in to timid diplomats when he relieved General MacArthur of command of the U.N. forces during the Korean War. (Library of Congress)

sons for the dismissal had been cumulative and existed before April 1951, why had the Joint Chiefs not recommended MacArthur's relief at an earlier date? Collins replied that it had not been known before April that the president was becoming, in Collins's words, "fed up" with MacArthur. That was a lame answer, and, indeed, senators who were critical of MacArthur's ideas and behavior, notably Morse and Fulbright, suspected that the Joint Chiefs were vulnerable to criticism for having kept silent in the face of those accumulating incidents.

If he was intimidated by MacArthur's reputation before April 1951, Collins was not reluctant to fault the general's behavior in testimony to the two committees. MacArthur's response to an attempt by Old Guard senators to justify his statement of March 24, 1951, by citing two appeals by MacArthur in autumn 1950 that the enemy in Korea stop fighting, was called into question. Collins explained that the autumn appeals had been made with the concurrence of leaders in Washington and on the basis of detailed instructions regarding surrender terms. MacArthur had received no similar sanction in March 1951 and was, in fact, operating at that time under a clear directive (Truman's December 5, 1950, proclamation) that he make no such statement without clearance from higher authorities. More significant was his response when asked by Senator Alexander Smith of New Jersey if MacArthur ever had violated a military directive by the Joint Chiefs of Staff—a question touching on MacArthur's military integrity, to which Smith obviously expected a negative answer. Collins replied that as a matter of fact MacArthur had violated a directive by the Joint Chiefs in November 1950, when he sent American troops to the banks of the Yalu. To reassure the Chinese that U.N. armies had no aggressive designs on Manchuria, Washington had wanted no American troops visible along the river and had given MacArthur notification to that effect, but he ignored the directive and dispatched GIs to the Yalu. Collins did not back down when Senator Harry Cain of Washington charged that, unintentionally perhaps, he had done "a first-rate hatchet job" on a man whose "splendid reputation . . . has been the pride of our Nation for many years." Far from backing down, Collins testified that the incident of late November had raised fears among the Joint Chiefs about MacArthur's obedience to orders; this ultimately contributed to the decision to dismiss him: "I think this was one indication among others . . . that General MacArthur was not in consonance with the basic policies that led us gradually to fear that just as he violated a policy in this case without consulting us, perhaps the thing might be done in some other instance of a more serious nature."

A man who radiated much confidence, General Vandenberg did not dwell on MacArthur's alleged violation of the directive of autumn 1950 but testified—several times for the benefit of senators who increasingly were absent from the hearing room when colleagues were interrogating witnesses—that it was difficult for a field commander to carry out the spirit and intent of orders that conflicted with his own views: "You had broad policies that you had to give to a commander, and in those broad policies, he had to have considerable latitude; in the use of that latitude, if he felt strongly in opposition to the policy that the Chiefs had felt necessary, there was a danger." It had seemed prudent, therefore, that someone else should be put in command in the Far East.

Vandenberg's testimony in response to questions relating to MacArthur's ideas about expanding the air war in the Far East was highly significant. Although MacArthur had bestowed lavish praise on the air force and the effectiveness of air power (which must have gladdened the hearts of all disciples of Billy Mitchell), Vandenberg stood unalterably opposed to MacArthur's proposals for carrying the air war to Chinese territory. In view of the fact that Vandenberg was an airman and MacArthur was not, his arguments were not easy to refute, especially since they did not rest primarily on the supposition that an expanded bombing campaign might trigger World War III, but on a realistic appraisal of the strength and global responsibilities of the U.S. Air Force (USAF). Execution of the MacArthur plan, Vandenberg told the senators, would require double the strategic power that the air force could muster, and in testimony deleted from the public transcript he said that if compelled to operate over the expanse of China, an air force four times the size of the existing USAF would be "a drop in the bucket." He observed that Communist bases in Manchuria were defended by anti-aircraft batteries controlled by radar and that in combat around the Yalu the air force had learned that such batteries could be very effective. Accordingly, he advised the senators that an expanded bombing campaign in the Far East would result in such serious losses of planes and pilots that the defenses of the United States and its allies would be imperiled: "In my opinion the shoestring United States Air Force that we are operating today, in view of our global commitments, must not be utilized until it is larger for anything except holding it intact as nearly as possible against a major threat, against a major power, because in my opinion again it is the sole deterrent to war up to this time; and if we emasculate it, that sole deterrent will be gone."

If the testimony of Vandenberg was devastating to MacArthur's plan to expand the air war in the Far

East, that of Admiral Sherman was equally destructive of MacArthur's proposal that the United States subject the Chinese ports to a naval blockade. Sherman viewed blockades as more effective than aerial bombardment in hostilities with countries such as China and told the senators that a blockade of China's ports in late 1950 would have compelled the Chinese to turn to the Soviet Union for many of the necessities of their existence. The Trans-Siberian Railroad, he thought, could not have handled the increased traffic. A blockade in 1950 would have opened the way for plagues and epidemics that would have sapped the strength of the Chinese people. Sherman also indicated that the American navy had the ships and personnel to manage a blockade of China without jeopardizing its ability to meet commitments elsewhere, and said that he would favor a blockade if it had the sanction and support of the United Nations. But, he explained, there was no possibility that the U.N. would approve a blockade, and unlike MacArthur, who was willing to "go it alone," Sherman wanted no part of a unilateral blockade. Such a blockade, according to Sherman, would not be effective unless applied to Hong Kong, and a blockade of Hong Kong would strain relations with the British. More serious, the blockade would also have to be applied to the Soviet leaseholds of Dairen and Port Arthur, thus inviting a war with the Soviet Union. The goal of the United States, for the time being, should be to achieve results similar to those that might be expected from a blockade by persuading U.N. members to honor a recent resolution calling for an economic boycott of China.

IV

With the testimony of Vandenberg and Sherman, the Old Guard senators lost much of their enthusiasm for MacArthur's proposals for expanding the war in Korea. That did not mean, however, that they were ready to urge an adjournment of the inquiry. On the contrary, they determined to press on, concentrating on America's policies in East Asia over the past six or seven years. Their object was transparent: establishment of their thesis that since about 1944 the Democratic administrations of Roosevelt and Truman had taken a "soft" stance on Communist expansions in East Asia, that resultant policies had virtually delivered China to the Communists and invited Communist aggression in Korea, and that if not checked by an aroused citizenry and vigilant Congress, the Democratic leadership was apt to continue the discredited policies of the past with equally disastrous consequences. To that end they subjected the last of the so-called administration witnesses, Secretary Acheson, to an intensive interrogation and then pursued the matter with several other prominent individuals who had been involved in East Asian affairs.

The atmosphere in the hearing room was charged on June 1, 1950, when Dean Acheson, dressed in a gray tropical suit, made his first appearance before the committees. Twenty-three of the twenty-six members were in their places. But interest in the tedious and repetitious questioning quickly faded, and during much of the interrogation of the secretary of state only a few senators were present. Inasmuch as such administration stalwarts as Connally, Fulbright, Green, Johnson, Kefauver, and McMahon were among the most frequent absentees, Acheson spent most of his time in the witness chair responding to the queries of Old Guardsmen: Brewster, Bridges, Cain, Hickenlooper, Knowland, Smith, and Wiley. Like Acheson, who had spent many hours going over testimony already given in the inquiry and preparing answers to probable questions, the Old Guardsmen had done their homework and entered the hearing room with brief cases bulging with notes and documents upon which they would base their interrogation.

With his patrician accent and Ivy League manners and dress, appearing suspiciously British in the minds of the Anglophobic Old Guardsmen, the secretary of state represented everything that they despised about the management of America's foreign relations. Old Guardsmen, in truth, already had made Acheson the scapegoat for frustrations that they and other Americans felt over the way international affairs had unfolded in the recent past, particularly those frustrations emanating from the Communist takeover in China. Acheson had been under continuous attack for many months. Demands that he resign or be fired were a daily occurrence, and by spring 1951 most observers in Washington doubted that he would last out the year in the State Department. Even Democrats who endorsed his views about international affairs, but considered him a political liability, had begun to express the hope that he would step aside.

For his part, Acheson clearly had the unwavering confidence and support of the combative man in the White House, had lost none of his own self-assurance (interpreted as arrogance by his critics), and gave no hint that he might quit. Still, it was manifest throughout his eight days in the witness chair—the longest stint of any witness—that the incessant attacks upon him and the policies of the Truman administration had not been without effect. Acheson, for example, betrayed none of the contempt for repetitious questions that sometimes had surfaced in previous testimonies, and instead displayed such tact and patience that Old Guardsmen treated him with a larger measure of courtesy and restraint than anyone expected. (Acheson himself must

This Reg Manning cartoon shows President Truman, Defense Secretary George C. Marshall, and Secretary of State Dean Acheson, talking to figures representing Congress and the general public, refusing to consider an expansion of the bombing during the Korean War on the grounds that "we might hit some of our friends." The drawing reflects general conservative frustrations at the refusal of the Truman administration to agree to General MacArthur's recommendations that the United States bomb Manchuria. In addition, it snipes at Acheson's support for a congressional resolution that would express the friendship of the American people for "all other peoples including those of the Soviet Union." (Library of Congress)

have felt confounded when near the end of his ordeal Senator Wiley, one of the most volatile of the Old Guardsmen, said: "You have had a long chore, sir, and you have done a grand job for yourself, I would say, with that mind of yours. Keeping everything in mind it is a remarkable accomplishment.") Much of the civility that prevailed during his interrogation may be attributable to the fact that Acheson seemed bent on establishing that he yielded to no Old Guardsmen in his determination to resist Communist expansion in East Asia and sustain Chiang Kai-shek on Formosa, a position not entirely consistent with that which he had taken a year and a half before.

Civility notwithstanding, the Old Guardsmen never lost sight of their goals for the inquiry; thus, they were constantly maneuvering and probing in an effort to find weak points in Acheson's defense of recent East Asian policy. Inevitably, they dwelled on the famous speech the secretary had delivered to the National Press Club in Washington on January 15, 1950, in which Acheson had sketched America's defensive perimeter in the Far Pacific, indicating that both South Korea and Formosa were outside it. Had not that speech been a veritable invitation to the Communists in North Korea, six months later, to make their lunge across the thirty-eighth parallel? In what must have sounded to his critics like a tortured explanation, and perhaps to some of his friends as well, Acheson explained that the United States in early 1950 had felt committed to defend only those areas in which American troops were on station, and at that time no GIs were in South Korea or Formosa. But whatever the location of the American defensive perimeter, the Communists were given no reason to believe that the United States had no interest in such areas as South Korea and Formosa and would not respond to Communist aggression against them, for, Acheson went on, the United Nations, of which the United States was a member, was obliged to respond to aggression, and the U.N. thus far had held its ground on that point.

During Acheson's appearance before the committees, many senators pressed a point that for many months had been a source of irritation to many Americans, namely, the behavior of America's allies with respect to the Korean War. Why had such allies as Britain and France made only token contributions to the U.N. military effort? Why had those allies, notably the British, continued to ship strategic materials to China at a time when the Chinese were killing U.N. soldiers in Korea? As had the Joint Chiefs of Staff before him, Acheson reminded the senators that the British were fighting Communists in Malaya, and the French were doing the same in Indochina—and indeed, the combined Anglo-French military effort in Southeast Asia was roughly equivalent to that of the United States in Korea. The United States, however, was continuing to urge U.N. members who had made no contribution at all in Korea to make some; Acheson, of course, was hopeful that some governments would respond. On the matter of the shipment of strategic materials to China, the secretary of state was decidedly upbeat. Despite some differences of opinion over what constituted strategic materials (for example, the British were not inclined to consider rubber a strategic item), governments allied with the United States had tightened controls over what they shipped to China, and as member states had responded to the U.N. resolution of May 18, 1951, urging an embargo on shipments of strategic commodities to China, there was hope that the supplies that the Chinese military mechanism in Korea was receiving from America's allies might soon be terminated.

As important as the prosecution of the Korean War, or so it seemed to the senators, was how the United States proposed to deal with the rival claimants to authority in China; in particular, the senators wanted to know whether the United States one day might extend diplomatic recognition to the Communist government in Beijing, tolerate the admission of "Red China" to the United Nations, and permit Formosa to pass to the control of the Communists. On the matter of diplomatic recognition of the Beijing regime, Acheson testified: "We are not recognizing the Communist authorities in China. We are not contemplating doing it. We are opposed to it." He denied that the United States ever had indicated conditions under which it might recognize Mao's government and emphasized that the United States recognized Chiang Kai-shek's regime in Taipei as the legitimate government of China. Regarding a U.N. seat for the Communist Chinese, Acheson reiterated (several times) the opposition of the Truman administration to that proposal. To date, he said, there had been seventy-seven attempts to seat representatives of the Beijing government in the U.N. or on one of the world organization's many special agencies or associated bodies. The United States, he said, had led the fight against seating the Communist Chinese on each occasion and had been successful in every instance save one. As for Formosa, Acheson believed that MacArthur had exaggerated its strategic importance. Still, the United States, he told the senators, had every intention of preventing the island from falling into hostile, Communist hands.

Old Guardsmen were only partially reassured. They called attention to a secret document of December 1949 in which the State Department had professed Formosa to be of no strategic importance and intimated that its takeover by the Communists would threaten no American interests in East Asia, a position that hardly squared with the current one. The secretary of state testified that there had been no change in the State Department's view of Formosa; the Old Guardsmen simply did not understand the circumstances that had prompted the so-called Formosa document. Even in December 1949, Acheson explained, leaders in Washington looked on Formosa as a territory of importance and hoped that it might be saved from the Communists. At that time, however, there seemed no way to prevent a Communist takeover of the island short of armed intervention by the United States; indeed it was generally assumed that the Communists would conquer Formosa sometime in 1950. In order to make the best out of a bad situation and to minimize the damage to American prestige when Formosa passed to the Communists, the State Department prepared the document of December 1949 for use by the Voice of America in its broadcasts. Six months later, of course, the Communist aggression in Korea afforded the United States the opportunity to put a naval force between Formosa and the Communists.

Then what about America's support of a U.N. resolution in January 1951 in which the world organization promised to consider the disposition of Formosa and the question of China's representation in the U.N. in exchange for an armistice in Korea? the senators asked. Had not that promise been a veritable offer of Formosa and a seat in the U.N. to the Communist Chinese if they would agree to a cease-fire? Not at all, Acheson told the senators. The resolution had provided that upon termination of hostilities in Korea, the future of Formosa and China's representation in the U.N. would be discussed. If the Communists had accepted the resolution—and American leaders had felt certain they would not—the United States would have continued to oppose both the transfer of Formosa to the Communists and a U.N. seat for the Beijing regime, and given America's influence within the world organization, leaders in Washington had been confident that their arguments would prevail. As it turned out, Acheson said, America's support of the cease-fire resolution, coupled with its rejection by the Chinese, had prepared the way for adoption by the U.N. a month later of a resolution branding the government in Beijing as an aggressor in Korea.

As expected, Old Guardsmen consumed many hours grilling Acheson about the China policy of the Democratic administrations of Roosevelt and Truman in the time before Chiang Kai-shek's expulsion from the mainland. But the interrogation brought few surprises, for the Old Guardsmen presented questions and Acheson recited answers that had been explored many times in recent years. Why had American leaders at the Yalta Conference of February 1945 supported concessions to the Soviets in Manchuria in return for a Soviet pledge to enter the war against Japan? To save American lives during the anticipated invasion of the Japanese home islands. Why had Chiang Kai-shek not been immediately informed of the Yalta concessions? Because his regime was notorious for leaking information to the Japanese, and the Yalta conferees did not want to risk a sudden strike by the Japanese against the Soviets in Siberia. Why had the United States in 1945–46 encouraged China's Nationalists to form a coalition government with the Communists? Because every Chinese expert in Washington considered a political arrangement the best solution to the problem of China—as did Chiang

Kai-shek, who had first proposed that solution in 1937. When had the State Department begun to view the Chinese Communists as agrarian reformers? The State Department never had viewed China's Communists as anything other than rigid Marxists. Why had the United States been so miserly in its support of Chiang Kai-shek in the years after World War II? On the contrary, the United States had provided more than $2 billion to Chiang from the end of the war to the time of his flight to Formosa.

More interesting were the recitations of Senators Sparkman and (during a couple of rare appearances in the hearing room) McMahon, who cited a range of documents showing that down to 1949 Republicans had not taken a particularly hard line against China's Communists or viewed the preservation of Chiang Kai-shek as an overbearing American interest. For example, Congressman Walter H. Judd of Minnesota, by 1951 one of the Old Guard's most vocal proponents of Chiang, had issued a statement at the end of 1945 in which he announced support for the idea of including Communists in China's government. Congressman George H. Bender of Ohio, the floor manager of Senator Taft's presidential bid at the Republican national convention of 1948, had delivered a speech to the House of Representatives in spring 1947 in which he referred to Chiang's regime as the "present Fascist Chinese Government." Congressman Howard H. Buffett of Nebraska in that same period had made a blistering attack on Chiang's government and deplored the prospect of any further American aid to it. In 1948 Senator Arthur J. Vandenberg of Michigan had declared that the United States could not underwrite the destiny of China, whereupon the Republican-controlled Eightieth Congress pared down President Truman's request for $570 million in aid to China and voted $400 million, instead.

The interrogation of Acheson finally droned to a conclusion late in the afternoon of June 9, 1951, a Saturday; the following Monday morning, promptly at 10:15 A.M., Lieutenant General Albert C. Wedemeyer was seated in the witness chair. Presently the commander of the Sixth Army in the western part of the United States, Wedemeyer in 1943–44 had served as deputy chief of staff of the Southeast Asia Command and in 1944–46 commanded American forces in China, where he was chief of staff to Generalissimo Chiang Kai-shek. A year after his departure from China, in summer 1947, he was again in the Far East, this time appraising the political, economic, and military situation in China and Korea as the personal representative of President Truman. After less than eight weeks of moving about the principal cities and countrysides of China and Korea, he had returned to Washington and submitted the so-called Wedemeyer Report, which the State Department declined to publish. Later, in the aftermath of Chiang Kai-shek's defeat on the mainland of China, "suppression" of the Wedemeyer Report had become a rallying point in the national controversy over East Asian policy. According to critics of Democratic management of affairs in the Far East, nonpublication of the report was the result of the fact that Wedemeyer's views and recommendations ran counter to the prevailing notion in the State Department that Chiang's days of power in China were numbered and that new outlays of aid to his Nationalist regime could not prevent a Communist takeover of the country. Inasmuch as Wedemeyer had been out of step with official policy in 1947, it was taken for granted in 1951 that he still was out of step—and anybody who was out of step with official policy in the Far East was assumed to be an advocate of the ideas of General MacArthur. Wedemeyer, in truth, owed his summons to testify at the inquiry to the insistence of Old Guardsmen who expected that he would counter the testimony of "administration" witnesses like Marshall, the Joint Chiefs, and Acheson.

The expectations of Old Guardsmen were only partially fulfilled. During his three-day interrogation Wedemeyer spoke out in favor of MacArthur's proposal for bombing Manchuria, even at the risk of provoking the Soviets, and announced his support of a unilateral naval blockade of the China coast. If America's European allies refused to go along with expansion of the war in Korea, the United States, as MacArthur had urged, should "go it alone," or as Wedemeyer expressed it, "their alternative is enslavement of mind and body; and we ought to make it crystal clear to them that our way is a selfless, Christian approach to international problems; and if they don't follow us, they have the alternative of enslavement." He told the senators that a field commander ought to be allowed to conduct a military campaign without restriction, and he endorsed MacArthur's plan for "taking the wraps" off Chiang Kai-shek's Nationalist forces. But Wedemeyer disagreed with MacArthur's contention that Formosa was a territory of critical importance, and in one astonishing statement declared that China "is not a critical, decisive, strategic area insofar as I am concerned." Regarding MacArthur's controversial peace overture of March 24, 1951, Wedemeyer felt that a field commander never should take such action without clearance from higher authority, and when Senator Sparkman asked to whom the people and Congress should look for guidance in the event of a disagreement between a field commander and the Joint Chiefs, Wedemeyer answered: "The Joint Chiefs of Staff, without question, sir."

Wedemeyer was an exasperating witness. He often obscured his points in rambling, almost incoherent discourses. At other times he strayed far off the points of questions put to him by senators, and on occasion appeared to take positions different from those expressed in earlier testimony. In addition, there was his proposal, so preposterous that even Old Guardsmen blinked, that South Korea be abandoned to the Communists. Although U.N. forces in Korea were at or beyond the thirty-eighth parallel and seemed in no danger of being shoved back, he urged an immediate withdrawal of U.N. armies from the Korean peninsula. Since there was no likelihood of expanding the war to achieve total victory, he argued, the only alternative was a long and expensive stalemate in a peripheral area, namely Korea, which in his judgment had no strategic importance. Moreover, Wedemeyer, who had a veritable obsession with psychological warfare, thought the United States was suffering from a psychic defeat in Korea because of its inability to liquidate the armies of a third-rate power. In his words, America's first team had been unable to defeat Communism's third team. The best course, therefore, was for America to cut its losses, both military and psychological, and leave the South Koreans to the mercies of the Communists.

If sometimes casting an image of confused innocence, Wedemeyer nonetheless seemed a man of candor and integrity. At the start of his interrogation he pointed out that as soon as it had become apparent that he might be called to testify he determined to have no conversations with MacArthur or anyone else connected with the inquiry. He wanted to be able to offer unvarnished opinions. When discussing Chiang Kai-shek and the reasons for the generalissimo's defeat in China's civil war, he made no concessions to the fantasies of Old Guardsmen. He emphasized that corruption had been pervasive in Chiang's government, and he categorically refuted the Old Guard contention that Chiang had lost the mainland for want of greater support by the United States. The Nationalists had gone down to defeat, he told the senators, because the Communists effectively employed the tactics of psychological warfare. Communist propagandists had exploited the corruption and maladministration in Chiang's regime, capitalized on the national war weariness, and persuaded Nationalist soldiers and civilians that life might be better under a Communist regime. Dean Acheson and men in the State Department, of course, had been saying the same thing for at least two years.

Wedemeyer's successor on the stand was Louis A. Johnson, the secretary of defense in the Truman administration from January 1949 until September 1950, when he resigned as a result of pressure by the White House. Because of the circumstances of his resignation, it was widely thought that Johnson might speak out against the administration's position in the MacArthur controversy and thus buttress the contentions of Old Guardsmen. That did not prove to be the case. If resentful of the criticism that his economy-minded management of the Defense Department had been responsible for the weakened state of the military establishment at the outbreak of the Korean War, Johnson claimed no bitterness over his dismissal. In his two days of testimony he betrayed no inclination to even any scores with the president and his top advisers. On the contrary, he told the senators that Truman was a man who did not seek to hurt people unnecessarily, and he said that if the president had lost confidence in MacArthur, he certainly should have dismissed him. As for MacArthur's proposals for prosecuting the war in East Asia, he favored a blockade of the China coast provided it did not include the Soviet leaseholds of Dairen and Port Arthur, but opposed the bombing of Manchuria, felt no enthusiasm for using Chiang Kai-shek's Nationalists in Korea or putting them on the mainland, and testified that for the time being the present policy, not MacArthur's, was the best one for Korea. About the only satisfaction he gave Old Guardsmen was expression of the view that during his time in the Truman cabinet the State Department had shown little enthusiasm for Chiang Kai-shek and his regime.

By the time of Johnson's appearance, the MacArthur inquiry no longer was commanding the front page of newspapers, and even Old Guard senators were finding it increasingly convenient to absent themselves from the hearing room. The sentiment among members of the Armed Services and Foreign Relations Committees was unanimous that it was about time to bring the hearings to an end. The two committees, therefore, drastically pruned their list of possible witnesses (which at one time had numbered more than a hundred) and set about concluding the hearings. The last witnesses would be Vice Admiral Oscar C. Badger (one day of testimony), Major General Patrick J. Hurley (two days), Major General David C. Barr (one day), and Major General Emmett O'Donnell Jr. (one day).

The navy's current Eastern Sea Frontier commander, Admiral Badger had been in charge of America's demobilization in the Pacific after World War II, and in that capacity had made frequent visits to China to arrange shipment of surplus war matériel from islands in the western Pacific to Chiang Kai-shek. In the witness chair he expressed little support for expansion of

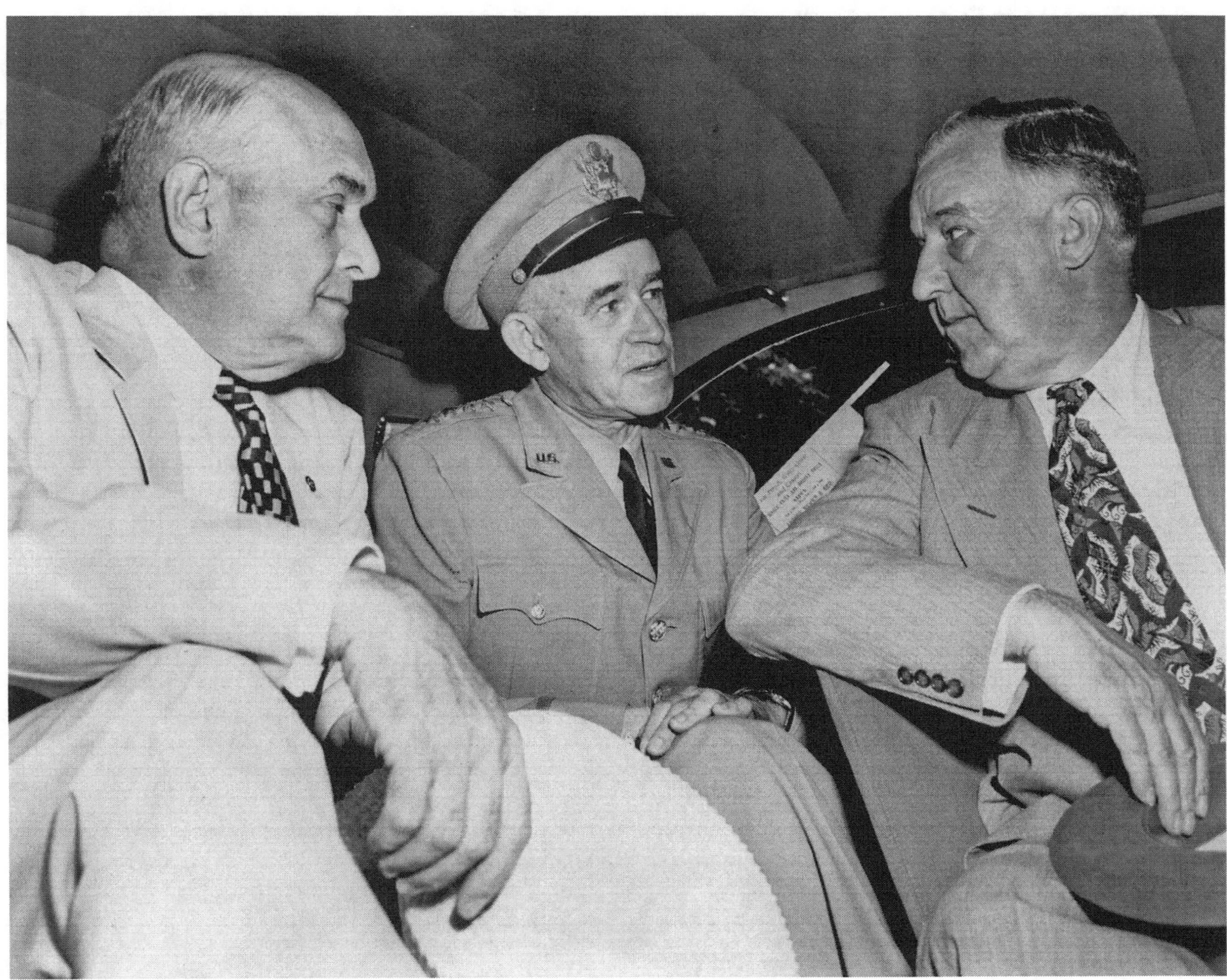

President Truman's military chiefs leave the White House after conferring with him on the Korea situation. Left to right are Defense Secretary Louis Johnson; Gen. Omar Bradley, chairman of the Joint Chiefs of Staff; and Undersecretary of Defense Stephen Early. (Library of Congress)

the war in Korea, and on the matter of the conflict of views between the Joint Chiefs and the theater commander, he testified: "There is no question in my mind but that the Joint Chiefs of Staff are the senior of the two, and are fully informed as to world conditions and circumstances which a theater commander may not be familiar with." Noting that the island's harbors were too small and its facilities too restricted, he dismissed MacArthur's notions about the strategic importance of Formosa. Formosa's principal value, he thought, was psychological, inasmuch as economic and political progress on the island provided material for propaganda aimed against the Chinese mainland. Other remarks by Badger afforded more comfort to Old Guardsmen, however. The admiral said that the people of South China were sick of Communism, and by dispatching bands of Nationalist soldiers to stir up guerrillas, it might be possible to wrest China south of the Yangtze from Communist control. He conceded, nonetheless, that he was "a little inclined to accept China as being gone," and thus believed the United States ought to concentrate on saving Southeast Asia from Communism. As for American aid to the Nationalists during the struggle for control of the mainland, Badger told the senators that considerable amounts of American equipment from the South Pacific had gone to the Nationalists without spare parts or technicians to supervise their use. More interesting, he said that if American aid intended for General Fu Tso-yi in summer 1948 had arrived in time, the entire civil war in China might have been turned around. At that time, he explained, Fu was in command of armies fighting against the Communists along the Great Wall.

Following Badger into the witness chair was General Hurley, a volatile Republican from Oklahoma who had served as secretary of war in President Hoover's cabinet and been ambassador to China from November 1944 until November 1945. Hurley had become a churlish critic of the China policies of the Democratic leadership, and was summoned to testify at the behest of the Old Guardsmen. It is doubtful that he did much to advance the interests of the Old Guard, however. His oratorical broadsides against Secretary Acheson, the State Department, and the Yalta agreements appeared unreasonable, and his unstinting praise of President Roosevelt, who he insisted had been a sick man in early 1945 and thus was without blame for the alleged disasters at Yalta, must have caused Old Guardsmen to cringe. Otherwise Hurley's principal concern appeared to be to defend his record as ambassador and counter the Democratic contention that he had been a good deal less than a stalwart anti-Maoist in 1944–45 and, indeed, had favored a coalition government in China. Countering the Democratic contention proved difficult, especially when Senator McMahon read into the record a string of documents quoting Hurley in 1944–45 as asserting that there were no essential differences between China's Communists and the Nationalists, that the Chinese Communists favored government by and for the people, and that the Soviets did not consider the Maoists bona fide Communists and thus were not supporting them.

A more articulate witness was General Barr, chief of the American military advisory group in China in the period of January 1948–January 1949 and commander of the Seventh Infantry Division in Korea from September 1950 to February 1951. He expressed his opposition to MacArthur's proposal for expanding the Korean War, saying that expansion could trigger a global clash with the Soviets. If one ignored political considerations, was there not a compelling military argument for expanding the war? he was asked. As a trained military man, Barr told the senators, he could make no clear distinction between political and military considerations. Did Barr favor the introduction of Chiang Kai-shek's Nationalist troops in Korea? He did not. "Knowing the Chinese as I do, they would be entirely dependent upon us" if dispatched to the Korean battlefront. Besides, the Nationalists were needed to defend Formosa. What did Barr think of the idea of putting the Nationalists back on the mainland? He thought poorly of it; so far as he knew—and the observation was deleted by the censor—there were no organized anticommunist resistance groups anywhere in China with whom the Nationalists could link up; hence a commitment of American troops would be a requisite if a Nationalist invasion of the mainland was to stand any chance of success.

If Barr's testimony on the Korean War offered little comfort to Old Guardsmen, that pertaining to the Nationalist defeat in China's civil war brought still less. Denying that the Yalta concessions to the Soviets had any important bearing on the disasters that eventually befell the Nationalists, Barr explained that at the end of World War II the Nationalists had been stronger than the Communists, but "the Communists were smart and the Nationalists were not." The Communists, for example, looked out for the welfare of their soldiers. In the Nationalist army the officers expropriated much of the pay of the enlisted men—if a soldier got breakfast, it was by his own initiative; dependents of soldiers were ignored. The outcome showed a great disparity in the fighting spirits of the combatants. Leadership in the Nationalist army, moreover, had been atrocious. While Communist commanders maneuvered their armies about the countryside, the Nationalists preferred to draw up behind the walls of cities where they were easily besieged. Barr denied that the Nationalists had suffered serious shortages of equipment and ammunition, although breakdowns in the supply system often prevented equipment and ammunition from reaching troops in the field. In addition to quantities of American ordnance, most of which he said ended up in Communist hands, the Nationalists had received more than half of the war matériel left behind in China by the departing Japanese. As for the renowned General Fu, who Admiral Badger thought might have saved the situation for Chiang along the Great Wall, Barr recalled telling Chiang that Fu could not hold the line in North China and thus should be ordered southward. When Chiang ignored the advice, Fu surrendered without a fight and joined up with the Communists.

The MacArthur hearings finally played themselves out on June 25, 1951, with the interrogation of O'Donnell. In command of the Fifteenth Air Force headquartered in California at the time of the investigation, O'Donnell, in the days after the outbreak of the Korean War, had organized the Far East Bomber Command and stayed on as its commander for six months. On June 25 he was in the witness chair for less than four hours, the shortest stint of any witness, and apart from testifying that Formosa was of no importance to the air force, he contributed little of substance to the discussion at hand. He told the senators that the United States had made a terrible mistake at the end of World War II when it failed to issue an ultimatum, presumably one packing a nuclear threat, directing the Soviets to give up their conquests and go home. Although he now opposed a bombing campaign against Manchuria (for like Vandenberg he feared that resultant losses of bombers and crews would weaken the Strategic Air Command as a deterrent to global war), he believed the bombers should have been loosed against Manchuria when the Chinese entered the Korean War in late 1950. Inasmuch as air defenses in Manchuria at that time were not menacing, the air force could have struck Manchurian targets without risking its ability to deliver a "Sunday punch" (O'Donnell's term) against the Soviets if they got out of line. Ignoring the fact that America's bombers in recent months had been unable to stop the flow of soldiers and supplies from Manchuria to the battlefront in Korea two hundred miles below the Yalu, he declared that bombing raids against Manchuria in late 1950 might have proved decisive. Exalting the destructive capacity of the bombing plane, he said: "I would say that the entire, almost the entire Korean Peninsula is just a terrible mess. Everything is destroyed. There is nothing standing worthy of the name." Why Communist soldiers and supplies were continuing to make their way down from the Yalu, nobody bothered to ask.

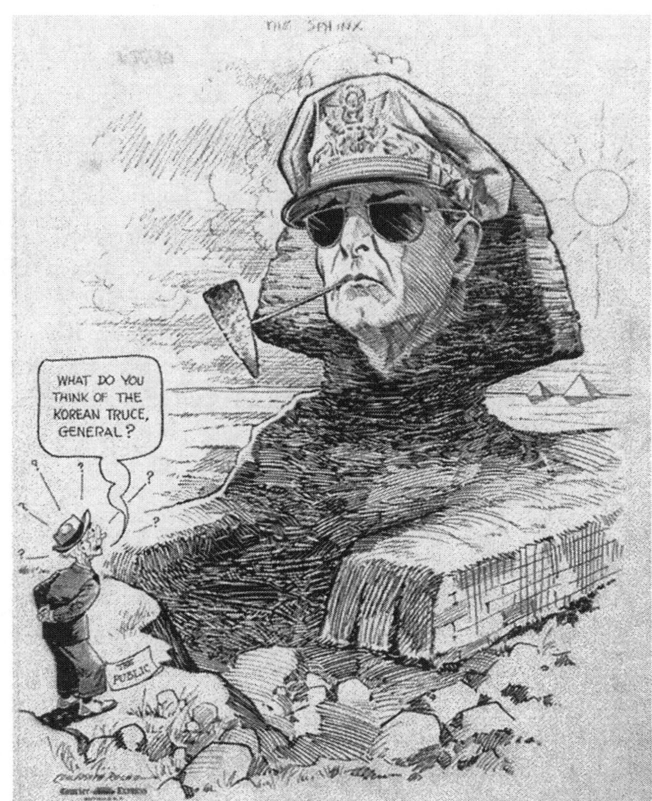

This Leo Joseph Roche cartoon shows a small man labeled "The Public" asking General Douglas MacArthur (pictured as the Sphinx), "What do you think of the Korean truce, General?" The drawing questions the General's reaction to the Korean Armistice signed in July 1953. MacArthur, who had advocated all-out war, had been removed from his position as Supreme Commander by President Truman in April 1951. (Library of Congress)

V

It is not an easy task to sort out impressions from conclusions after surveying the many sides and confusing events of the MacArthur inquiry, but one might begin by offering a few comments on the event's management. In truth, the inquiry was hardly managed at all. The attorneys for the Armed Services and Foreign Relations Committees played no discernible part in determining who should be called to testify or in the nature of the questions to be presented to witnesses. It was the senators who nominated prospective witnesses, who then were summoned after a majority vote by the combined committees, and it was the senators who fashioned the questions that were asked in the hearing room. Presiding over the entire affair, of course, was Senator Russell, an indefatigable committee chairman if there ever was one. After much pontificating that the MacArthur inquiry was one of the most important congressional exercises in the history of the republic, a majority of the members of the two committees, as already mentioned, found it convenient to absent themselves from the hearing room most of the time. Russell did not; he remained anchored in his chair throughout.

Russell merits further comment, for during the MacArthur inquiry he acted as an almost model chairman. In addition to maintaining an exemplary attendance record, introducing witnesses and interrupting the interrogation upon expiration of the time (eventually fifteen minutes) allotted to each senator during a round of questioning, he went to extreme lengths to appear fair and nonpartisan. He refused to discuss the MacArthur controversy with any representative of the White House. He was unfailingly courteous and evenhanded in his treatment of witnesses and senators—so much so that he won plaudits from Old Guardsmen and spokesmen of the Truman administration alike. He tolerated the endless rounds of interrogation of each witness, however repetitious or off the subject the questions might be, and when his own turn to query witnesses came around, his questions contained no barbs and were calculated to do nothing more than elicit pertinent information. (So nonpartisan was Russell's behavior, so noncontroversial were his questions, that newsmen were forced to speculate on where he actually stood on the issues raised by the MacArthur imbroglio.) Apart from an occasional lament about the absenteeism of his colleagues, he seldom betrayed any irritation, even when senators pressed witnesses with questions that had been asked and answered, often several times, while they were away from the hearing room.

It is transparent, of course, that the hearings would have proceeded more expeditiously and certainly been more enlightening if the chairman and counselors, with the approval of the full membership of the two committees, had prepared an agenda of topics to be explored with each witness and then adhered to the agenda in the hearing room; for example, if the interrogation had moved from topic to topic or from issue to issue instead of from senator to senator. But neither expedition nor enlightenment appeared to be Chairman Russell's principal purpose. His object seemed to be to use the inquiry as a vehicle for calming the passions that the MacArthur controversy had stirred across the republic, and he clearly understood that achievement of that goal required that he, as presiding officer, protect himself against charges of partisanship or unfairness and that he permit the senators, particularly the Old Guardsmen, to press on until they exhausted their arguments or were exhausted themselves.

If Chairman Russell was its most dedicated participant, General MacArthur in his three days in the witness chair established himself as the inquiry's central personality. Apart from his displays of humility, his flattery of senators, or his assertions that he had no idea that his statement of March 24, 1951, might upset Truman's peace initiative or why the president had relieved him of his Far Eastern commands, MacArthur's Olympian manner and finely turned phrases utterly dazzled most of the senators (a notable exception being Senator McMahon). Most awestruck, of course, were the Old Guardsmen, who seemed to be competing to see who could heap the most extravagant praise upon the general. Even Senator Morse, the maverick from Oregon who already was renowned as a hard-nosed independent, seemed star-struck in the presence of the imperious MacArthur, and when presenting him with provocative questions, he virtually apologized and explained that he merely was trying to get certain points in the record. The contrast in their behavior toward General Marshall, who followed MacArthur into the witness chair, but whose military reputation at least rivaled that of MacArthur, was striking. Perhaps the senators had seen so much of Marshall in recent years that, in the proverbial phrase, familiarity had bred a measure of contempt. Marshall's interrogation brought little flattery, a good deal of sharp questioning, and occasional flashes of animosity.

MacArthur's mesmerization of the senators prevented any serious scrutiny of the proposition that underpinned many of the arguments in behalf of his proposals, namely, that the general was America's premier expert on the military and political affairs of East Asia—including China. Accepted as an article of faith by Old Guardsmen, the proposition was expressed in the early minutes of the inquiry when Senator Wiley asked MacArthur: "Do you know of any man in America that has had the vast experience that you have had in the Orient, getting acquainted with various nations in the Orient? Do you know of any other man that has lived there so long, or known the various factors and various backgrounds of the peoples, and their philosophy, as yourself?" Flattered, and conceding that "it is something else again" as to whether he had profited in terms of knowledge and wisdom from his long tenure in the Far East, the general allowed that "the scope of my duties were complete and enveloping, as far as the Far East was concerned and, to some extent, involved the entire world." Numerous references testifying to MacArthur's expertise regarding the Far East, by Democrats as well as Republicans, found their way into the record during the general's three days in the witness chair. Later suggestions by General Marshall and Secretary Acheson that the general might not have been well informed about China, the country at the center of the controversy, seemed to make no impression.

On the basis of the hearings, it appeared beyond dispute that MacArthur's reputation as a Far Eastern expert was exaggerated and probably rested largely on myth. The general had been in the Far East, or more accurately, in the Far Pacific (Philippines, Australia, and Japan), for many years. As for the East Asian mainland, MacArthur acknowledged that he had not been in China since 1937, and it was apparent that before the Korean War he rarely had visited Korea. Then in the closing minutes of his interrogation Senator Fulbright casually asked a question that any expert on East Asia should have been able to answer in an instant: "We have been told that Mao Tse-tung was trained in Moscow and had close personal relations in Moscow. Is that not true?" Blurted MacArthur: "How would I know, Senator?" An observer of the inquiry might even have wondered about the extent of the general's knowledge of Japan—whether he had often strayed far from the Dai Ichi Building in Tokyo. There was no evidence that he knew anything about the Japanese language, no mention of contacts with ordinary Japanese, and he admitted that he never had visited Hiroshima, but had merely flown over it. MacArthur's reputation as a Far Eastern expert remained intact, nonetheless. By comparison, General Marshall, who had spent three years in China in the 1920s and the better part of a year during his postwar mission to China, was not conceded to have any special understanding of China or the Chinese. And when Senator Cain became nettled by General Barr's assessment of probable Communist strength in South China in 1951, he dismissed his testimony on the ground that Barr had not been in China for two years.

Yet, the interrogation of MacArthur and other witnesses did establish the point that, however expert he may have been on affairs of the Far East, the general had been a theater commander. As such he had not been privy to the spectrum of political and military intelligence that would enable him to speak with authority on global strategy or grasp the larger ramifications of recommendations he might make—for instance, the effect on the deterrent capacity of the Strategic Air Command (SAC) resulting from a bombing campaign against Manchuria. Thus a resounding "no" was given to one of the central questions raised by the MacArthur controversy: Was it conceivable that a theater commander, particularly one of such an illustrious reputation as MacArthur, might have a clearer vision of the requirements of world strategy than that of political leaders and the Joint Chiefs of Staff in Washington? If the MacArthur inquiry did nothing more than provide that answer, the arduous exercise probably was worthwhile. After a few feeble attempts at presenting himself as one who had sufficient global expertise to view the situation in the Far East in a larger perspective, even MacArthur was compelled to concede that officials in Washington alone had the requisite information and viewpoint to fashion world policy. Similarly, when Vandenberg demonstrated that MacArthur simply did not understand the military ramifications of his proposal for expanding the air war in the Far East, nothing substantial remained of the case for MacArthur in the controversy that had triggered his dismissal. Henceforth, the general's Old Guard defenders, when not pressing the argument that the Democrats had made possible a Communist victory in China, were more or less reduced to insisting that MacArthur had not been insubordinate and that Truman and his administration had treated him with unpardonable shabbiness in the manner of his dismissal.

If captivated by the myth that General MacArthur had unmatched expertise regarding the Far East, most participants in the MacArthur inquiry also seemed persuaded by the myth of the unlimited capacity of air power in modern war. In the words of General Wedemeyer: "We must have undisputed control of the air. It isn't on the ground that the future wars are going to be settled, sir, it is in the air." And nobody, it appeared, had more faith in the aerial weapon than did General MacArthur. Like O'Donnell, MacArthur believed that if he had been allowed to hurl the big bombers against Chinese bases and lines of communication in Manchuria in late 1950, the U.N. would have been spared the monstrous defeat it suffered when the Chinese entered the Korean War. Nobody pressed the point that since early 1951, in addition to the usual supply depots and staging areas, the air force had had two hundred miles of communications lines in North Korea to pulverize but had been unable to stop or even seriously impede the southward movement of Communist soldiers and supplies. In the climate of 1951, of course, it was perhaps understandable that such old soldiers as Wedemeyer and MacArthur and such senators as Russell and Knowland would be taken in by the proponents of air power. The sight of one of the new F-86 Sabrejets streaking across the sky or one of SAC's giant B-36 bombers approaching a landing field was awesome, and the self-assurance and bravado of the men who flew them was hard to resist. One wonders, however, if the air enthusiasts of 1951 might have exhibited greater humility about the capacity of the aerial weapon had they been able to look ahead to 1952, and see the failure of a concerted air force campaign that did little more than sever the rail lines reaching down from the Yalu to the thirty-eighth parallel, or if they could have

This Herblock cartoon shows General Douglas MacArthur walking with Chiang Kai-shek, who asks if he has much trouble with President Truman. While they walk, MacArthur is pulling a small cart upon which is a treadmill, and walking on the treadmill, headed in the opposite direction, is President Harry Truman holding a sign "U.S. Policy in Asia." (A Herblock Cartoon, copyright by The Herb Block Foundation)

peered a decade and a half into the future and witnessed the limits of incredibly more powerful and sophisticated aircraft in the war in Vietnam.

Another myth that remained throughout the MacArthur inquiry was that China had been a victim of Soviet conquest and presently functioned as a subservient appendage of the Kremlin's monolithic empire. In truth, the way in which witnesses and senators interpreted the relationship between the Soviet Union and "Red" China—so as to buttress their own arguments—was one of the more arresting aspects of the MacArthur inquiry.

Skirting the question of whether the Soviets via Chinese stooges had actually conquered China, MacArthur gave surprisingly little credence to the idea of the Soviet domination of the Communist government in Beijing. He testified: "I believe there is an interlocking of interests between Communist China and the Kremlin. The degree of control and influence that the Kremlin may have in China is quite problematical." At another point, in a statement that appears almost clairvoyant in retrospect, he said that "there is a point that might well be reached where the interests of Red China and the interests of the Red Soviet did not run parallel, that they started to traverse and become antagonistic." Adherence to the proposition that the connection between the Soviet Union and China was tenuous was almost imperative, if one was to accept MacArthur's contention that bombardment of Manchuria and a naval blockade of the China coast were not apt to provoke the Soviets and plunge America into World War III.

But Old Guard supporters blandly ignored the logic of his position. While they endorsed MacArthur's proposals for expanding the war in the Far East, they continued to insist that China was a docile satellite of the Soviet Union. They also clung to the notion that the Soviets, not Mao Zedong and his followers, had managed to defeat Chiang Kai-shek and his Nationalist regime in the civil war, and thus they could be legitimately styled as the conquerors of China. As with MacArthur's perception of the relationship between the governments in Moscow and Beijing, the view of the Old Guardsmen seemed self-serving. The proposition that Mao's regime was an arm of the Kremlin justified continued recognition of Chiang's government on Formosa as the legitimate government of China and hence the legitimate representative of China in the United Nations. The proposition that the Soviets had conquered China, in addition to strengthening the argument for continuing to recognize and support the Nationalists, reinforced the Old Guard contention that the Democrats had grossly misunderstood the civil war in China and this misunderstanding had provoked policy decisions that had opened the way for the Communist takeover of the country.

Equally self-serving seemed statements on the relationship between China and the Soviet Union by witnesses who spoke for President Truman's administration, particularly Secretaries Marshall and Acheson, although those statements were consistent with positions taken by Acheson in July 1949 in his letter of transmittal accompanying the celebrated White Paper on China. Whatever his purpose (and the purpose may have been to tell the truth as he saw it), Marshall told the senators: "I have gone on the assumption that she [China] was operating not only in conjunction with but literally under the direction of the Soviet Union." Acheson agreed with MacArthur on the possibility of an eventual fissure between China and the Soviet Union, but testified that he thought the connection between the two countries was greater than the general had indicated. (In the White Paper he had asserted that "the Communist leaders have foresworn their Chinese heritage and have publicly announced their subservience to a foreign power, Russia.") Such a view certainly reinforced the argument that expansion of the war in Korea in accord with the MacArthur conception was likely to provoke the Soviets and perhaps bring about a global confrontation. At the same time, the view also justified the current policy of nonrecognition of the government in Beijing and support of Chiang Kai-shek's regime on Taiwan. On the other hand, Marshall and Acheson conceded nothing to the Old Guard argument that in the civil war in China the principal weight in the balance had been Soviet power, nor did the two men, notably Acheson, retreat from the position taken in the White Paper that the Communist victory in China had resulted largely from Nationalist corruption and ineptitude, not from any lack of support by a confused United States.

Other myths intruded upon the MacArthur inquiry, especially that which blamed America's alleged misunderstanding of the realities of the civil war in China on those Communist subversives whom many Americans, thanks to the rantings of Senator Joseph R. McCarthy and others, thought were slithering about the State Department. To their discredit, the Old Guard senators made certain that the stench of McCarthyism never entirely subsided in the hearing room. They demanded to know the extent of the influence on America's Far Eastern policies of Professor Owen Lattimore of Johns Hopkins University, described by Senator McCarthy only a year before as the premier agent of the Soviet conspiracy in the United States. Acheson's statement that he never had met Lattimore and that the professor had never been an official of the State Department made no impression, and Lattimore's name continued to surface intermittently. The Old Guardsmen also wanted to know more about the activities of John

Stewart Service, John Carter Vincent, John Paton Davies, and Raymond Ludden, foreign service officers who had been in China in the 1940s and were subsequently tarred as pro-Communists. General Wedemeyer, under whom the four men had functioned while he was commander of American forces in China, vouched for their integrity and intelligence and observed that their criticisms of Chiang Kai-shek, a centerpiece of the charges made against them by the Red-hunters, had been no more severe than his own. It did not seem to matter; their names continued to be injected into the interrogation. Old Guard senators, meanwhile, asked when it was that the State Department had begun to view China's Communists as "agrarian reformers," wondered if Alger Hiss and others in Washington had been largely responsible for America's reverses in foreign affairs in recent years, and demanded the name of an obscure public information officer whom General Marshall had ordered home shortly after his arrival in China in late 1945, on the ground that the man's press releases had seemed unduly sympathetic with the Maoists.

Turning away from the omnipresent myths, one may ask: Did the MacArthur inquiry fall within the bounds of the investigative authority of the Armed Services and Foreign Relations Committees? It is questionable whether a sanction for the inquiry could be found in the Supreme Court's opinion of 1928 that said the legislative responsibilities of Congress justify congressional investigations. No legislation pertaining directly to the military and diplomatic affairs scrutinized by the two committees in May–June 1951 was pending, although the senators could have made a strong argument that matters taken up in the MacArthur inquiry doubtless would have a bearing on a range of legislative decisions that Congress would have to make in the near future. If, of course, one accepted the proposition set out by Woodrow Wilson in the 1880s that every affair of government is a legitimate subject of scrutiny by committees of Congress, in order that both Congress and the national populace receive maximum enlightenment, he could not easily dispute the legitimacy of the MacArthur investigation.

A more important question, however, is whether the MacArthur inquiry served any useful purpose. The answer is an unqualified yes. Reinforced by U.N. military successes in Korea and rumors that the Communists were about to consent to armistice negotiations, the inquiry defused the MacArthur controversy, if not the related controversy over why the so-called free world had "lost" China. After the testimony of General Marshall and the Joint Chiefs of Staff, particularly that of General Vandenberg, few Americans retained much enthusiasm for expanding the war in Korea. The MacArthur inquiry, indeed, was a veritable national seminar on foreign affairs. In their interrogations the senators ranged across the spectrum of issues that were troubling and dividing Americans in the area of foreign policy, and their endeavors received unprecedented media coverage. Accordingly, as Richard H. Rovere and Arthur M. Schlesinger Jr. wrote in their book *The General and the President*, published a few months after the inquiry: "One clear result of the MacArthur hearings was to improve popular understanding, not alone of the complexities of Far Eastern policy, but of the whole precise and delicate course to which the United States had committed itself." Most important, perhaps, Americans began to shed that obsession with total victory in diplomacy and war that had afflicted them at least since that memorable night in 1862 when the telegraph tapped out the news that U.S. Grant had insisted on unconditional surrender of the Confederate garrison at Fort Donelson. This notion had received further reinforcement by MacArthur's dramatic pronouncement that there was no substitute for victory. However belatedly and even reluctantly, Americans began to grasp the truth of the words set out more than a century before by the great Prussian military philosopher, Von Clausewitz: "As war is no act of blind passion, but is dominated by the political object, therefore the value of that object determines the measure of the sacrifices by which it is to be purchased."

The MacArthur inquiry must have reassured allies of the United States, not to mention many Americans who shuddered at the prospect of a nuclear confrontation with the Soviet Union, that America's leaders would not rashly risk global war. The leaders of the republic, on the contrary, appeared cautious and prudent and even courageous in their resisting of the firestorm touched off by the dismissal of MacArthur. Then, too, the inquiry generated renewed reflection on the principle of civilian control of the military, and established beyond dispute that political and military leaders in Washington alone, not theater commanders in Asia or Europe, even if the latter had such names as MacArthur and Eisenhower, had access to the necessary intelligence and had the requisite perspective from which to formulate global policy for the United States.

The MacArthur inquiry possibly had at least one unfortunate consequence: it may have contributed to the prolongation of the Korean War. So adamant were such witnesses as Marshall and Bradley against expansion of hostilities in East Asia that they announced a virtual commitment by the Truman administration to keep the war confined to the Korean peninsula so long as the Communists did likewise. (In testimony deleted from the public record by the censor, Bradley at one point indicated that after the military build-up

This Charles George Werner cartoon titled "A real fire-side chat!" shows General Douglas MacArthur addressing Congress against a backdrop of devastation and flames labeled "Communism in Asia." The title refers to the popular radio broadcasts to the nation made by President Franklin D. Roosevelt. The cartoon refers to the impassioned speech MacArthur made to Congress on April 19, 1951, after President Truman relieved him of his command for insubordination. (Library of Congress)

then under way had strengthened the armed forces, the United States might consider a MacArthur-style expansion of the war in East Asia should the present policy fail to bring satisfactory results. But there was no indication that such a possibility had been communicated to the Communists.) They also made it clear that U.N. forces in Korea would not press the war much beyond the thirty-eighth parallel. In so doing they conveyed an unmistakable signal to the Communists that they need be in no hurry to reach a cease-fire agreement. So long as they were willing to bear the cost of a stalemated conflict, the Communists could prolong the armistice negotiations with every expectation of wringing concessions from the war-weary Americans and their allies. The outcome was that truce talks dragged on intermittently at Kaesong and later Panmunjom for many months in 1951 and 1952. But then, in early 1953, Dwight D. Eisenhower took over the White House. Not wedded to the existing policy in Korea, the new president shortly threatened the Communists with expansion of the war and implied that he might order the use of nuclear weapons if the hostilities did not come to an early termination. Perhaps the Communists took him at his word; perhaps they assumed that as a professional military man he did not share his predecessor's inhibitions about expanding the war. A few months later, however, they agreed to a cease-fire. (One must acknowledge, of course, that other circumstances and events, for example, the uncertainties in the Communist world resulting from the death of Joseph Stalin in March 1953, may have had as much influence as Eisenhower's threats in persuading the Communists to accept a cease-fire in Korea.) Could the leaders in Washington in 1951–52 have threatened the Communists with equal effect? We shall never know; at the time of the MacArthur inquiry they virtually foreswore such threats as a possible tactic for ending the nightmare in Korea.

In retrospect, one is left with the suspicion that at the time of the MacArthur inquiry Marshall and other military men may have exaggerated the danger of World War III inherent in an expansion of the conflict in East Asia along the lines recommended by General MacArthur if the Communists rejected an ultimatum to make peace in Korea. Although testimony deleted from the public record indicated that the Soviets had the means of delivering enough nuclear warheads to the United States to render great damage to American cities, it was apparent that the Strategic Air Command, notwithstanding Vandenberg's lament that it was a shoestring instrument, was capable of inflicting far greater devastation on the Soviet Union. Thus it seems doubtful that leaders in the Kremlin might have risked a global confrontation with the United States following a limited expansion of the war involving a bombing campaign against Manchuria and a blockade of China's ports. Also, one wonders if America's allies, as Marshall and others intimated, might have seriously considered severing their connections with the United States had leaders in Washington acted upon MacArthur's proposals. In view of their dependence on the United States for defense and economic assistance, what alternative did the allies have than to acquiesce in whatever America elected to do in East Asia?

The foregoing observation is not intended as a criticism of President Truman and his advisers for turning aside MacArthur's appeal for an expansion of the East Asian war in the spring of 1951. In light of the military situation in Korea and the signals emanating from Communist capitals that the Chinese and North Koreans were ready to consider a battlefield armistice, expansion of the war at that time would have been totally irresponsible. What is intended as a criticism of the Truman administration is that they virtually threw away their trump card in the diplomatic game in East Asia; specifically, the threat that a Communist refusal to accept a reasonable cease-fire agreement at an early date might have very serious consequences was compromised.

This does not imply that a belated endorsement of General MacArthur is due, for the general never suggested that his object in urging an expansion of the war in East Asia was to force the Communists into early armistice negotiations and acceptance of a cease-fire line near the thirty-eighth parallel. A truce at the parallel, he insisted, would be appeasement of the Communists and would mean a defeat for America and its allies. Rather, his purpose was to expel the Communists from the entire Korean peninsula and implant the Stars and Stripes along the Yalu—where that banner had been implanted by soldiers under his command in November 1950. Incredible as it may seem in retrospect, nobody during the MacArthur inquiry demanded an answer to the question that logically derived from MacArthur's purpose: Would the conquest of North Korea for President Syngman Rhee of South Korea and the non-Communist world, the resultant enlargement of America's reputation as an inconquerable foe of Communism, and the corresponding decline in prestige of the government in Beijing justify the human and material sacrifices required to execute MacArthur's strategic ideas? The only answer that prudent individuals could make to that question in 1951 was an unqualified no, and nothing has transpired in the ensuing decades that might persuade the student of history to answer otherwise.

Other questions that begged for answers in the spring of 1951 went largely unanswered during the MacArthur inquiry. One question had to do with relations between MacArthur and his superiors in Washington in the months before his dismissal: Why had Truman, Marshall, and the Joint Chiefs not made a more concerted effort to harness the five-star general? The answer was obvious: they were awed by his reputation and intimidated by the strength of his personality. Still, it seemed that leaders in the capital had almost encouraged MacArthur to commit acts such as the issuance of the peace statement of March 24, 1951, and the posting of the letter to Congressman Martin—acts that they considered insubordinate and certainly injurious to what the United States was trying to accomplish in the Far East. When MacArthur dispatched his letter to the Veterans of Foreign Wars in August 1950, Truman gave him no dressing-down; he merely required him to withdraw the letter. When in the aftermath of the disaster along the Yalu in December 1950 the general made public his dissatisfaction with restrictions on his management of the war, the president again declined to reprimand MacArthur and instead confined himself to a general directive requiring *all* officials to refrain from public statements on high policy. Later, in February and early March 1951, when MacArthur made fresh comments indicating continued displeasure over Far Eastern policy, there was no response from Washington. One can only speculate as to the effect on the conduct of the war and the search for peace of an early and more forthright stance vis-à-vis the general.

Then there was the question of America's relations with China: Was it in the United States' best interest to align itself so uncompromisingly with Chiang Kai-shek and his regime in Taipei and virtually proclaim perpetual enmity toward the Maoists in Beijing? Granted, a calm and more searching discussion of America's interests in East Asia and the best policy to pursue in dealing with the Chinese was not possible in the spring of 1951, for passions in the United States were too inflamed in light of events in China and Korea in recent years not to mention news stories cascading out of the Far East at the time of the MacArthur inquiry that a massive and bloody purge of non-Communists was taking place on the Chinese mainland. Yet, a time or two during the MacArthur hearings, Senator Fulbright clearly was edging toward the proposition that the chief threat to American interests was the Soviet Union, not Communism, and that perhaps the United States should think in terms of separating such Communist states as the People's Republic of China from their bonds with the Kremlin—that is, it should abandon its crusade against "international communism" and actively encourage other Communist leaders outside the Soviet Union to emulate the example of President Tito of Yugoslavia.

* * *

In July 1961 Douglas MacArthur made a final return to the Philippines to participate in that republic's celebration of fifteen years of independence. MacArthur seemed increasingly a relic of a bygone era, the more so as the Korean War passed farther into history. He had not lost his old charisma and rhetorical skill—far from it. In 1962 the general, a tottering old man, traveled to West Point to accept the Sylvanus Thayer Award for distinguished service to the United States. In the peroration of his remarks to the corps of cadets, supposedly extemporaneous, he said:

The shadows are lengthening for me. The twilight is here. My days of old have vanished—tone and tint. They have gone glimmering through the dreams of things that were. Their memory is one of wondrous beauty, watered by tears and coaxed and caressed by the smiles of yesterday. I listen vainly, but with thirsty ear, for the witching melody of faint bugles blowing reveille, of far drums beating the long roll.

In my dreams I hear again the crash of guns, the rattle of musketry, the strange, mournful mutter of the battlefield. But in the evening of my memory always I come back to West Point. Always there echoes and re-echoes: Duty, honor, country.

Today marks my final roll call with you. But I want you to know that when I cross the river, my last conscious thoughts will be of the corps, and the corps, and the corps.

I bid you farewell.

A short time later the general had lunch at the White House and exchanged pleasantries with President John F. Kennedy, the first Democrat since his nemesis, Harry Truman, to command the Oval Office. The event seemed to demonstrate that the wounds wrought by the bitter controversy of spring 1951 had about healed. Still, as MacArthur had told the cadets at West Point, the shadows were lengthening. A few months after his eighty-fourth birthday, in spring 1962, he underwent surgery at Walter Reed Hospital in Washington for a malfunctioning gall bladder, and was visited by and photographed with (his last photograph) a man who was to become another Democratic president, Lyndon B. Johnson, who had interrogated him during the MacArthur inquiry of

General Douglas MacArthur delivering his farewell address to a joint session of Congress, April 19, 1951. Seated behind MacArthur are Vice President Alben Barkley and Speaker of the House Sam Rayburn. (Library of Congress)

1951. Then, on April 5, 1964, the old soldier died, and six days later, as a bugler sounded taps, his body was placed in a crypt in the MacArthur Memorial in Norfolk.

DOCUMENTS

Statement of General Douglas MacArthur, March 24, 1951

A former Army chief of staff, who had commanded the Southwest Pacific Theater in World War II, who had accepted Japan's surrender, and who oversaw that country's occupation in the postwar years, General Douglas MacArthur was placed in command of United Nations forces during the early years of the Korean War. He was now commander in chief, United Nations Command; supreme commander for the Allied forces in Japan; commander in chief, Far East Command; and commander in chief, army forces in the Pacific. Brilliant, exceedingly arrogant, and, unlike President Harry Truman, wildly popular with the American people, MacArthur did not agree with Truman's reluctance to expand the war into the People's Republic of China. At a meeting in Wake Island, Truman specifically ordered MacArthur to use tact and caution. But MacArthur had decided to violate his constitutional duty to serve his commander-in-chief. Increasingly, the general issued public pronouncements that clearly amounted to insubordination as he tried to push the United States into a broader war with China. On March 24, 1951, he issued another statement pointing out the weaknesses of China "even under inhibitions which now restrict activity of the United Nations forces and the corresponding military advantages which accrue to Red China." He ended the statement with a blatant offer to meet and negotiate with the military commander in chief of the enemy forces. MacArthur, in open defiance of the president, was now trying to make his own foreign policy.

STATEMENT OF GENERAL DOUGLAS MACARTHUR, MARCH 24, 1951

Operations continue according to schedule and plan. We have now substantially cleared South Korea of organized Communist forces. It is becoming increasingly evident that the heavy destruction along the enemy's lines of supply caused by our 'round-the-clock massive air and naval bombardment, has left his troops in the forward battle area deficient in requirements to sustain his operations.

This weakness is being brilliantly exploited by our ground forces. The enemy's human wave tactics definitely failed him as our own forces become seasoned to this form of warfare; his tactics of infiltration are but contributing to his piecemeal losses, and he is showing less stamina than our own troops under rigors of climate, terrain, and battle.

Of even greater significance than our tactical success has been the clear revelation that this new enemy, Red China, of such exaggerated and vaunted military power, lacks the industrial capacity to provide adequately many critical items essential to the conduct of modern war.

He lacks manufacturing bases and those raw materials needed to produce, maintain, and operate even moderate air and naval power, and he cannot provide the essentials for successful ground operations, such as tanks, heavy artillery, and other refinements science has introduced into the conduct of military campaigns.

Formerly his great numerical potential might well have filled this gap, but with the development of existing methods of mass destruction, numbers alone do not offset vulnerability inherent in such deficiencies. Control of the sea and air, which in turn means control over supplies, communications, and transportation, are no less essential and decisive now than in the past.

When this control exists, as in our case, and is coupled with the inferiority of ground firepower, as in the enemy's case, the resulting disparity is such that it cannot be overcome by bravery, however fanatical, or the most gross indifference to human loss.

These military weaknesses have been clearly and definitely revealed since Red China entered upon its undeclared war in Korea. Even under inhibitions which now restrict activity of the United Nations forces and the corresponding military advantages which accrue to Red China, it has been shown its complete inability to accomplish by force of arms the conquest of Korea.

The enemy therefore must by now be painfully aware that a decision of the United Nations to depart from its tolerant effort to contain the war to the area of Korea through expansion of our military operations to his coastal areas and interior bases would doom Red China to the risk of imminent military collapse.

These basic facts being established, there should be no insuperable difficulty arriving at decisions on the Korean problem if the issues are resolved on their own merits without being burdened by extraneous matters not directly related to Korea, such as Formosa and China's seat in the United Nations.

The Korean nation and people which have been so cruelly ravaged must not be sacrificed. That is the paramount concern. Apart from the military area of the problem where the issues are resolved in the course of combat, the fundamental questions continue to be political in nature and must find their answer in the diplomatic sphere.

Within the area of my authority as military commander, however, it should be needless to say I stand ready at any time to confer in the field with the commander in chief of the enemy forces in an earnest effort to find any military means whereby the realization of the political objectives of the United Nations in Korea, to which no nation may justly take exceptions, might be accomplished without further bloodshed.

Source: U.S. Senate, 82nd Congress, 1st Session, Military Situation in the Far East, Hearings Before the Committee on Armed Services and the Committee on Foreign Relations, Part 5, Appendix and Index, 3181.

Message Relieving General MacArthur of Command and Presidential Statement, April 11, 1951

Incensed by the rogue defiance of his chief military officer, President Truman realized that General Douglas MacArthur must be fired. Making sure of his support within the Joint Chiefs of Staff, who also saw in MacArthur's actions the kind of rank insubordination that demanded his dismissal, the president fired MacArthur on April 11, 1951. As MacArthur was welcomed home as a hero with massive parades across the country, outraged Republicans in Congress threatened impeachment proceedings against the president because of his action. Fortunately for Truman, his support within the Joint Chiefs gave the president political cover.

MESSAGE RELIEVING GENERAL MACARTHUR OF COMMAND AND PRESIDENTIAL STATEMENT, APRIL 11, 1951

Message Relieving General MacArthur of Command

I deeply regret that it becomes my duty as President and Commander in Chief of the United States military forces to replace you as Supreme Commander, Allied Powers; Commander in Chief, United Nations Command; Commander in Chief, Far East; and Commanding General, U.S. Army, Far East.

You will turn over your commands, effective at once, to Lt. Gen. Matthew B. Ridgway. You are authorized to have issued such orders as are necessary to complete desired travel to such place as you select.

My reasons for your replacement will be made public concurrently with the delivery to you of the foregoing order, and are contained in the next following message.

Statement of the President

With deep regret I have concluded that General of the Army Douglas MacArthur is unable to give his wholehearted support to the policies of the United States Government and of the United Nations in matters pertaining to his official duties. In view of the specific responsibilities imposed upon me by the Constitution of the United States and the added responsibility which has been entrusted to me by the United Nations, I have decided that I must make a change of command in the Far East. I have, therefore, relieved General MacArthur of his commands and have designated Lt. Gen. Matthew B. Ridgway as his successor.

Full and vigorous debate on matters of national policy is a vital element in the constitutional system of our free democracy. It is fundamental, however, that military commanders must be governed by the policies and directives issued to them in the manner provided by our laws and Constitution. In time of crisis, this consideration is particularly compelling.

General MacArthur's place in history as one of our greatest commanders is fully established. The nation owes him a debt of gratitude for the distinguished and exceptional service which he has rendered his country in posts of great responsibility. For that reason I repeat my regret at the necessity for the action I feel compelled to take in his case.

Source: U.S. Senate, 82nd Congress, 1st Session, Military Situation in the Far East, Hearings Before the Committee on Armed Services and the Committee on Foreign Relations, Part 5, Appendix and Index, 3546–47.

Address of General MacArthur to Joint Meeting of Congress, April 19, 1951

MacArthur came back to the United States from Korea not humbled by his firing but defiant, a martyr in his mind for attempting to lead his country the way it should have been run, not down the road taken by President Truman. It was not only the cheering crowds along the parade routes that convinced him that he was right about the war; it was also his supporters in Congress. In MacArthur, Republicans had a champion show horse, and now, in April 1951, they gave him a grand forum. Here, before Congress, here on this national stage, he would take on the "appeasers" and the "cowards." He would show them all the stuff of which a true leader is made.

ADDRESS OF GENERAL MACARTHUR TO JOINT MEETING OF CONGRESS APRIL 19, 1951

Mr. President, Mr. Speaker, distinguished Members of the Congress, I stand on this rostrum with a sense of deep humility and great pride; humility in the wake of those great American architects of our history who have stood here before me; pride in the reflection that this forum of legislative debate represents human liberty in the purest form yet devised. [Applause.]

Here are centered the hopes, and aspirations, and faith of the entire human race.

I do not stand here as advocate for any partisan cause, for the issues are fundamental and reach quite beyond the realm of partisan consideration. They must be resolved on the highest plane of national interest if our course is to prove sound and our future protected. I trust, therefore, that you will do me the justice of receiving that which I have to say as solely expressing the considered viewpoint of a fellow American. I address you with neither rancor nor bitterness in the fading twilight of life with but one purpose in mind, to serve my country. [Applause.]

The issues are global and so interlocked that to consider the problems of one sector oblivious to those of another is but to court disaster for the whole.

While Asia is commonly referred to as the gateway to Europe, it is no less true that Europe is the gateway to Asia, and the broad influence of the one cannot fail to have its impact upon the other.

There are those who claim our strength is inadequate to protect on both fronts, that we cannot divide our effort. I can think of no greater expression of defeatism. [Applause.] If a potential enemy can divide his strength on two fronts, it is for us to counter his effort.

The Communist threat is a global one. Its successful advance in one sector threatens the destruction of every other sector. You cannot appease or otherwise surrender to communism in Asia without simultaneously undermining our efforts to halt its advance in Europe. [Applause.]

Beyond pointing out these general truisms, I shall confine my discussion to the general areas of Asia. Before one may objectively assess the situation now existing there, he must comprehend something of Asia's past and the revolutionary changes which have marked her course up to the present. Long exploited by the so-called colonial powers, with little opportunity to achieve any degree of social justice, individual dignity, or a higher standard of life such as guided our own noble administration of the Philippines, the peoples of Asia found their opportunity in the war just past to throw off the shackles of colonialism and now see the dawn of new opportunity and heretofore unfelt dignity and the self-respect of political freedom.

Mustering half of the earth's population and 60 percent of its natural resources these peoples are rapidly consolidating a new force, both moral and material, with which to raise the living standard and erect adaptations of the design of modern progress to their own distinct cultural environments. Whether one adheres to the concept of colonization or not, this is the direction of Asian progress and it may not be stopped. It is a corollary to the shift of the world economic frontiers, as the whole epi-center of world affairs rotates back toward the area whence it started. In this situation it becomes vital that our own country orient its policies in consonance with this basic evolutionary condition rather than pursue a course blind to the reality that the colonial era is now past and the Asian peoples covet the right to shape their own free destiny. What they seek now is friendly guidance, understanding, and support, not imperious direction [applause]; the dignity of equality, not the shame of subjugation. Their prewar standards of life, pitifully low, is infinitely lower now in the devastation left in war's wake. World ideologies play little part in Asian thinking and are little understood. What the peoples strive for is the opportunity for a little more food in their stomachs, a little better clothing on their backs, a little firmer roof over their heads, and the realization of a normal nationalist urge for political freedom. These political-social conditions have but an indirect bearing upon our own national security, but do form a backdrop to contemporary planning which must be thoughtfully considered if we are to avoid the pitfalls of unrealism.

Of more direct and immediate bearing upon our national security are the changes wrought in the strategic potential of the Pacific Ocean in the course of the past war. Prior thereto, the western strategic frontier of the United States lay on the littoral line of the Americas with an exposed island salient extending out through Hawaii, Midway, and Guam to the Philippines. That salient proved not an outpost of strength but an avenue of weakness along which the enemy could and did attack. The Pacific was a potential area of advance for any predatory force intent upon striking at the bordering land areas.

All this was changed by our Pacific victory. Our strategic frontier then shifted to embrace the entire Pacific Ocean which became a vast moat to protect us as long as we held it. Indeed, it acts as a protective shield for all of the Americas and all free lands of the Pacific Ocean area. We control it to the shores of Asia by a chain of islands extending in an arc from the Aleutians to the Marianas held by us and our free allies.

From this island chain we can dominate with sea and air power every Asiatic port from Vladivostok to Singapore and prevent any hostile movement into the Pacific. Any predatory attack from Asia must be an amphibious effort. No amphibious force can be successful without control of the sea lanes and the air over those lanes in its avenue of advance. With naval and air supremacy and modest ground elements to defend bases, any major attack from continental Asia toward us or our friends of the Pacific would be doomed to failure. Under such conditions the Pacific no longer represents menacing avenues of approach for a prospective invader—it assumes instead the friendly aspect of a peaceful lake. Our line of defense is a natural one and can be maintained with a minimum of military effort and expense. It envisions no attack against anyone nor does it provide the bastions essential for offensive operations, but properly maintained would be an invincible defense against aggression.

The holding of this littoral defense line in the western Pacific is entirely dependent upon holding all segments thereof, for any major breach of that line by an unfriendly power would render vulnerable to determined attack every other major segment. This is a military estimate as to which I have yet to find a military leader who will take exception. [Applause.]

For that reason I have strongly recommended in the past as a matter of military urgency that under no circumstances must Formosa fall under Communist control. [Applause.]

Such an eventuality would at once threaten the freedom of the Philippines and the loss of Japan, and might well force our western frontier back to the coasts of California, Oregon, and Washington.

To understand the changes which now appear upon the Chinese mainland, one must understand the changes in Chinese character and culture over the past 50 years. China up to 50 years ago was completely nonhomogeneous, being compartmented into groups divided against each other. The war-making tendency was almost non-existent, as they still followed the tenets of the Confucian ideal of pacifist culture. At the turn of the century, under the regime of Chan So Lin, efforts toward greater homogeneity produced the start of a nationalist urge. This was further and more successfully developed under the leadership of Chiang Kai-shek, but has been brought to its greatest fruition under the present regime, to the point that it has now taken on the character of a united nationalism of increasingly dominant aggressive tendencies. Through these past 50 years, the Chinese people have thus become militarized in their concepts and in their ideals. They now constitute excellent soldiers with competent staffs and commanders. This has produced a new and dominant power in Asia which for its own purposes is allied with Soviet Russia, but which in its own concepts and methods has become aggressively imperialistic with a lust for expansion and increased power normal to this type of imperialism. There is little of the ideological concept either one way or another in the Chinese make-up. The standard of living is so low and the capital accumulation has been so thoroughly dissipated by war that the masses are desperate and avid to follow any leadership which seems to promise the alleviation of local stringencies. I have from the beginning believed that the Chinese Communists' support of the North Koreans was the dominant one. Their interests are at present parallel to those of the Soviet, but I believe that the aggressiveness recently displayed not only in Korea, but also in Indochina and Tibet and pointing potentially toward the south, reflects predominantly the same lust for the expansion of power which has animated every would-be conqueror since the beginning of time. [Applause.]

The Japanese people since the war have undergone the greatest reformation recorded in modern history. With a commendable will, eagerness to learn, and marked capacity to understand, they have, from the ashes left in war's wake, erected in Japan an edifice dedicated to the primacy of individual liberty and personal dignity, and in the ensuing process there has been created a truly representative government, committed to the advance of political morality, freedom of economic enterprise and social justice. [Applause.] Politically, economically, and socially Japan is now abreast of many free nations of the earth and will not again fail the universal trust. That it may be counted upon to wield a profoundly beneficial influence over the course of events in Asia is attested by the magnificent manner in which the Japanese people have met the recent challenge of war, unrest, and confusion surrounding them from the outside, and checked communism within their own frontiers without the slightest slackening in their forward progress. I sent all four of our occupation divisions to the Korean battle front without the slightest qualms as to the effect of the result in power vacuum upon Japan. The results fully justified my faith. [Applause.] I know of no nation more serene, orderly, and industrious—nor in which higher hopes can be entertained for future constructive service in the advance of the human race. [Applause.]

Of our former wards, the Philippines, we can look forward in confidence that the existing unrest will be corrected and a strong and healthy nation will grow in the longer aftermath of war's terrible destructiveness. We must be patient and understanding and never fail them, as in our hour of need they did not fail us. [Applause.] A Christian nation, the Philippines stand as a mighty bulwark of Christianity in the Far East, and its capacity for high moral leadership in Asia is unlimited.

On Formosa, the Government of the Republic of China has had the opportunity to refute by action much of the malicious gossip which so undermined the strength of its leadership on the Chinese mainland. [Applause.]

The Formosan people are receiving a just and enlightened administration with majority representation on the organs of government; and politically, economically, and socially appear to be advancing along sound and constructive lines.

With this brief insight into the surrounding areas I now turn to the Korean conflict. While I was not consulted prior to the President's decision to intervene in the support of the Republic of Korea, that decision from a military standpoint proved a sound one. [Applause.] As I say, a brief and sound one as we hurled back the invaders and decimated his forces. Our victory was complete and our objectives within reach when Red China intervened with numerically superior ground forces. This created a new war and an entirely new situation, a situation not contemplated when our forces were committed against the North Korean invaders, a situation which called for new decisions in the diplomatic sphere to permit the realistic adjustment of military strategy. Such decisions have not been forthcoming. [Applause.]

While no man in his right mind would advocate sending our ground forces into continental China—and such was never given a thought—the new situation did urgently demand a drastic revision of strategic planning if our political aim was to defeat this new enemy as we had defeated the old. [Applause.]

Apart from the military need as I saw it to neutralize sanctuary, protection given to the enemy north of the Yalu, I felt that military necessity in the conduct of the war made necessary:

First, the intensification of our economic blockade against China.

Second, the imposition of a naval blockade against the China coast.

Third, removal of restrictions on air reconnaissance of China's coastal areas and of Manchuria. [Applause.]

Fourth, removal of restrictions on the forces of the Republic of China on Formosa with logistical support to contribute to their effective operation against the Chinese mainland. [Applause.]

For entertaining these views all professionally designed to support our forces committed to Korea and bring hostilities to an end with the least possible delay and at a saving of countless American and Allied lives, I have been severely criticized in lay circles, principally abroad, despite my understanding that from a military standpoint the above views have been fully shared in the past by practically every military leader concerned with the Korean campaign, including our own Joint Chiefs of Staff. [Applause, the Members rising.]

I called for reinforcements, but was informed that reinforcements were not available. I made clear that if not permitted to utilize the friendly Chinese force of some 600,000 men on Formosa; if not permitted to blockade the China coast to prevent the Chinese Reds from getting succor from without; and if there were to be no hope of major reinforcements, the position of the command from the military standpoint forbade victory. We could hold in Korea by constant maneuver and at an approximate area where our supply advantages were in balance with the supply line disadvantages of the enemy, but we could hope at best for only an indecisive campaign, with its terrible and constant attrition upon our forces if the enemy utilized his full military potential. I have constantly called for the new political decisions essential to a solution. Efforts have been made to distort my position. It has been said in effect that I was a warmonger. Nothing could be further from the truth. I know war as few other men now living know it, and nothing to me is more revolting. I have long advocated its complete abolition as its very destructiveness on both friend and foe has rendered it useless as a means of settling international disputes. Indeed, on the 2d of September 1945, just following the surrender of the Japanese Nation on the battleship *Missouri*, I formally cautioned as follows:

"Men since the beginning of time have sought peace. Various methods through the ages have been attempted to devise an international process to prevent or settle disputes between nations. From the very start, workable methods were found insofar as individual citizens were concerned, but the mechanics of an instrumentality of larger international scope have never been successful. Military alliances, balances of power, leagues of nations, all in turn failed, leaving the only path to be by way of the crucible of war. The utter destructiveness of war now blots out this alternative. We have had our last chance. If we will not devise some greater and more equitable system, Armageddon will be at our door. The problem basically is theological and involves a spiritual recrudescence and improvement of human character that will synchronize with our almost matchless advances in science, art, literature, and all material and cultural developments of the past 2,000 years. It must be of the spirit if we are to save the flesh." [Applause.]

But once war is forced upon us, there is no other alternative than to apply every available means to bring it to a swift end. War's very object is victory—not prolonged indecision. [Applause.] In war, indeed, there can be no substitute for victory. [Applause.]

There are some who for varying reasons would appease Red China. They are blind to history's clear lesson. For history teaches with unmistakable emphasis that appeasement but begets new and bloodier war. It points to no single instance where the end has justified that means—where appeasement has led to more than a sham peace. Like blackmail, it lays the basis for new and successively greater demands, until, as in blackmail, violence becomes the only other alternative. Why, my soldiers asked of me, surrender military advantages to an enemy in the field? I could not answer. [Applause.] Some may say to avoid spread of the conflict into an all-out war with China; others, to avoid Soviet intervention. Neither explanation seems valid. For China is already engaging with the maximum power it can commit and the Soviet will not necessarily mesh its actions with our moves. Like a cobra, any new enemy will more likely strike whenever it feels that the relativity in military or other potential is in its favor on a world-wide basis.

The tragedy of Korea is further heightened by the fact that as military action is confined to its territorial limits, it condemns that nation, which it is our purpose to save, to suffer the devastating impact of full naval and air bombardment, while the enemy's sanctuaries are fully protected from such attack and devastation. Of the nations of the world, Korea alone, up to now, is the sole one which has risked its all against communism. The magnificence of the courage and fortitude of the Korean people defies description. [Applause.] They have chosen to risk death rather than slavery. Their last words to me were "Don't scuttle the Pacific." [Applause.]

I have just left your fighting sons in Korea. They have met all tests there and I can report to you without reservation they are splendid in every way. [Applause.] It was my constant effort to preserve them and end this savage conflict honorably and with the least loss of time and a minimum sacrifice of life. Its growing bloodshed has caused me the deepest anguish and anxiety. Those gallant men will remain often in my thoughts and in my prayers always. [Applause.]

I am closing my 52 years of military service. [Applause.] When I joined the Army even before the turn of the century, it was the fulfillment of all my boyish hopes and dreams. The world has turned over many times since I took the oath on the plain at West Point, and the hopes and dreams have long since vanished. But I still remember the refrain of one of the most popular barrack ballads of that day which proclaimed most proudly that—

"Old soldiers never die; they just fade away." And like the old soldier of that ballad, I now close my military career and just fade away—an old soldier who tried to do his duty as God gave him the light to see that duty.

Good-by.

Source: U.S. Senate, 82nd Congress, 1st Session, Military Situation in the Far East, Hearings Before the Committee on Armed Services and the Committee on Foreign Relations, Part 5, Appendix and Index, 3553–58.

Excerpt from Testimony of General MacArthur, May 3–5, 1951

In May and June 1951, the Senate Foreign Relations Committee and the Senate Armed Services Committee convened to look "into the military situation in the Far East and the facts surrounding the relief of General of the Army Douglas MacArthur from his assignments in that area." Thirteen witnesses took 2 million words of testimony during 42 days of hearings. The investigation was chaired by Senator Richard B. Russell (D-Ga.), chairman of the Armed Services Committee. On May 3, MacArthur was the lead-off witness. Dressed in his khaki army clothes, he made his way through the hundreds of reporters and photographers who pressed to get a word or a picture. Through three days of testimony that ranged over an array of issues surrounding war policy in the Far East, MacArthur let it be clear that in his mind he had made no errors whatsoever in his conduct in Korea.

EXCERPT FROM TESTIMONY OF GENERAL MacARTHUR MAY 3–5, 1951

The committees met, pursuant to adjournment, at 10:30 A.M. in the caucus room, Senate Office Building, Senator Richard B. Russell (chairman, Committee on Armed Services) presiding.

Present: Senators Russell, Connally (chairman, Committee on Foreign Relations), George, Green, McMahon, Fulbright, Sparkman, Gillette, Wiley, Smith (New Jersey), Hickenlooper, Lodge, Toby, Byrd, Johnson (Texas), Kefauver, Stennis, Long, Bridges, Saltonstall, Morse, Knowland, Cain, and Flanders.

Also present: Mark H. Galusha and Verne D. Mudge, of the staff of the Committee on Armed Services; Francis O. Wilcox, chief of staff; Thorsten V. Kalijarvi, staff associate, Committee on Foreign Relations; C. C. O'Day, clerk; and Pat M. Holt, associate clerk.

(Subheadings within the text have been inserted by committee staff in order to make hearings more readable and easier to follow.)

THE CHAIRMAN. Gentlemen of the Committee on Armed Services and the Committee on Foreign Relations, today we are opening hearings on momentous questions. These questions affect not only the lives of every citizen, but they are vital to the security of our country and the maintenance of our institutions of free Government.

We shall attempt to obtain the facts which are necessary to permit the Congress to discharge its proper functions and make correct decisions on the problem of war and peace in the Far East and indeed throughout the world.

General of the Army Douglas MacArthur has consented to be the first witness at these hearings. I am sure it is unnecessary for me to attempt to recount in detail the deeds and services which have endeared General MacArthur to the American people.

On the permanent pages of our history are inscribed his achievements as one of the great captains of history through three armed conflicts; but he is not only a great military leader, his broad understanding and knowledge of the science of politics has enabled him to restore and stabilize a conquered country and to win for himself and for his country the respect and affection of a people who were once our bitterest enemies.

The general is here today to counsel with our committees and to help us in the fulfillment of our legislative responsibilities. . . .

SENATOR WILEY. You have indicated in your public addresses that there has been a failure to take certain needed political decisions in the Korean matter. Can you tell us what you think those decisions might well have been?

GENERAL MACARTHUR. I can tell you what I would have done.

SENATOR WILEY. Yes.

GENERAL MACARTHUR. I would have served—as soon as it became apparent that Red China was throwing the full might of its military force against our troops in Korea, I would have served warning on her that if she did not within a reasonable time discuss a cease-fire order, that the entire force of the United Nations would be utilized to bring to an end the predatory attack of her forces on ours.

In other words, I would have supplied her with an ultimatum that she would either come and talk terms of a cease fire within a reasonable period of time or her actions in Korea would be regarded as a declaration of war against the nations engaged there and that those nations would take such steps as they felt necessary to bring the thing to a conclusion. That is what I would have done, and I would still do it, Senator.

SENATOR WILEY. Have you ever been embarrassed as commanding general in Korea by the actions or policies of any of your UN partners in Korea?

GENERAL MACARTHUR. None whatsoever. The United Nations, the various nations who have contributed there, the troops, the actual commands there, have been splendid in every respect.

SENATOR WILEY. General, when you were recalled when the message came through, were there any reasons assigned to your recall?

GENERAL MACARTHUR. The only reasons were contained in the order that I received and the reason that was given was that it was felt that I could not give my complete support to the policies of the United States and of the United Nations.

That reason seems to be to me—there was no necessity to give any reason.

Senator Wiley. I understand.

General MacArthur. But it seems to me to be completely invalid. I have not carried out every directive that I have ever received, but what I was trying to do was to find out what the directives were to be for the future.

I was operating in what I call a vacuum. I could hardly have been said to be in opposition to policies which I was not aware of even. I don't know what the policy is now. You have various potentials:

First is that you can go on and complete this war in the normal way and bring about just and honorable peace at the soonest time possible with the least loss of life by utilizing all of your potential.

The second is that you bring this thing to an end in Korea by yielding to the enemy's terms and on his terms.

The third is that you go on indecisively, fighting, with no mission for the troops except to resist and fight in this accordion fashion—up and down—which means that your cumulative losses are going to be staggering. It isn't just dust that is settling in Korea, Senator; it is American blood.

Now, my whole effort has been since Red China came in there to get some definition, military definition, of what I should do. There has been no change from the directions that I had—to clear North Korea.

As far as the United Nations are concerned, as far as the Joint Chiefs of Staff are concerned, my directives have been changed and I have been informed that my main objective, which takes precedence over everything else, was the security of my forces and the protection of Japan. And I have been operating on that.

Now, that is not a mission.

Now, when you say that I have enunciated my recommendations, they are plain and clear. The only reason that you can logically say that I would disagree was the concept that something else than what I recommended was going to be done.

Now, I don't know what is going to be done, but I can assure you had I stayed in command, whatever was ordered to be done I would have done it to the best of my ability.

Senator Wiley. General, when were you appointed to take over Japan, so to speak? What was the date you went to Japan?

General MacArthur. My appointment as the Supreme Commander for the Allied Powers in Japan, as I recall, was made either on August 14 or August 15.

Senator Wiley. How many years previously thereto had you lived in the Far East?

General MacArthur. My professional career has extended over a half-century, and more. I think that my foreign service, Senator, amounts to about 24 years on foreign service, nearly half.

Senator Wiley. Now, after you were appointed to the position in Japan, there began a systematic utilization of folks in America to try to formulate some kind of a Chinese policy.

Were you ever consulted?

General MacArthur. The Congress of the United States did me the very signal and high honor of asking my views; and while the pressure of my duties in Japan did not permit my coming here, I did make a report to the Congress in 1947, to the House Foreign Affairs Committee.

As far as any consultation on the future of China, by Washington authorities, outside of the legislative branch, the answer is in the negative.

My views have never been required.

Senator Wiley. Has the State Department ever consulted with you when they were sending General Marshall or General Hurley or sending the others over there?

General MacArthur. None whatsoever.

Senator Wiley. Did you ever receive any requests from anybody in Government, outside of the legislative branch, that were mentioned, for your views on, or as to how to handle the far eastern situation?

General MacArthur. No official request.

A great many personal friends of mine have written me and discussed it with me, but no official request, so far as I recall.

Senator Wiley. What I am getting at, there, is this:

Do you know of any man in America that has had the vast experience that you have had in the Orient, getting acquainted with various nations in the Orient? Do you know of any other man that has lived there so long, or known the various factors and various backgrounds of the peoples, and their philosophy, as yourself?

General MacArthur. That is a very flattering estimate you make, Senator.

I think that I have probably lived in the Far East as long as anybody that I know of, in an official position in the United States.

Whether I have profited by it, by the wisdom that you imply, is something else again.

Senator Wiley. Well, let me put it to you another way:

When you were in Japan, were you cognizant of the internal affairs that were going on in Russia, China—the fight between the Commies and the Nationalists?

General MacArthur. Naturally.

Senator Wiley. And, you were—

General MacArthur. For 5½ years, Senator, I have had to govern Japan. I was provided, by the nations concerned—I, as the sole executive authority for Japan; so naturally the scope of my duties were complete and enveloping, as far as the Far East was concerned and, to some extent, involved the entire world.

SENATOR WILEY. Did you have any idea at that time how the situation in China might have been solved, instead of running into the mess that we are in now?

GENERAL MACARTHUR. It is my own personal opinion that the greatest political mistake we made in a hundred years in the Pacific was in allowing the Communists to grow in power in China.

I think, at one stroke, we undid everything, starting from John Hay, through Taft, Leonard Wood, Woodrow Wilson, Henry Stimson, and all those great architects of our Pacific policy.

I believe it was fundamental, and I believe we will pay for it, for a century.

SENATOR WILEY. Well, let us ask the direct question:

What would you have done—what would you have advised, under the circumstances that existed back there in 1945—what would you have done?

GENERAL MACARTHUR. I would have given such assistance to the conservative Government of China as to have checked the growing tide of communism.

A very little help and assistance, in my belief, at that time, would have accomplished that purpose.

SENATOR WILEY. For a good many years you have been acquainted, I take it, with the Russians and with the Communist infiltration.

Would you have sought to have gotten those two forces together?

GENERAL MACARTHUR. I did not catch the question.

SENATOR WILEY. Would you have sought to have amalgamated the Commies and Nationalists—have gotten them together?

GENERAL MACARTHUR. Just about as much chance of getting them together as that oil and water will mix.

SENATOR WILEY. That was your idea at that time, too; was it not?

GENERAL MACARTHUR. It would have been then, and always. The whole history of the world shows that.

SENATOR WILEY. That is all, Mr. Chairman. . . .

SENATOR MCMAHON. . . . We have been proceeding on the assumption, as our mobilizer-in-chief said the other day, of no attack until 1953. By then, we will be so strong that they can't attack us, because by that time we will have the planes, we will have the bombs—amounts that we haven't got today—we will have the men in uniform, and we may be in shape to meet this attack, which we are not in shape to meet today.

GENERAL MACARTHUR. And in 2 years what will be your casualty rate of American boys in Korea?

SENATOR MCMAHON. And, General, I ask you what our casualty rate will be in Washington, D.C., if they put on an attack, an atomic attack—and I had better change it from Washington lest I be thinking about myself, to New York or the other cities of the United States, to say nothing of the American boys who are going to die in the air and sea in this logistical sort of support of the forces into China?

GENERAL MACARTHUR. All those risks, I repeat, were inherent in the decision of the United States to go into Korea.

SENATOR MCMAHON. General, I am not saying that they were not. What I am trying to say is that now is the time, it would seem to me, to stop, look, and listen and see where we are before we plunge into a course that may take us over the precipice before we are ready.

GENERAL MACARTHUR. What is your plan, then, to end Korea?

SENATOR MCMAHON. I would like to quote to you your language on going into Korea, which was very beautifully written, and I think it ought to be in the record:

> The decision of President Truman on June 27 lighted into flame a lamp of hope throughout Asia that was burning dimly toward extinction. It marked for the Far East the focal and turning point in this area struggling for freedom. It swept aside in one great monumental stroke all of the hypocrisy and the sophistry which has confused and deluded so many people distant from the actual scene.

General, do you regard the threat to us and to our national survival—

GENERAL MACARTHUR. The quotation that you read, Senator, is quite true. It did restore at one stroke the enormous prestige of the United States. It confirmed the people of the Far East that we were not going to let them slide into slavery, that we were determined we were going to meet aggression on every front that it showed itself, that we were not going to confine ourselves and say we will defend in this sector but all the other sectors globally we will let go.

It was the enunciation which was the very antithesis of defeatism, which has been so pronounced that we could not meet aggression except in one area of the world. It meant that we, if the enemy was going to encroach in two areas, we would meet him on two areas; in three areas, we would meet him on three areas; that he was just as divided as we were; that if we could not defend wherever he aggressed or started to attack, you admit before the conflict that you are going to be defeated.

This is global, as you said yourself this is a global proposition, and you can't let one-half of the world slide into slavery and just confine yourself to defending the other. You have got to hold every place.

Now, in the Far East there was a tremendous belief that we were not going to defend the Far East, and when we moved in to defend Korea, it gave an enormous uplift throughout that entire section of the world.

If there is anything that I have said that led you to believe that I was critical of the decision to defend Korea, I would correct it immediately.

SENATOR MCMAHON. No, General; I just thought that was such a fine statement.

GENERAL MACARTHUR. The only thing I am trying to do, Senator, is to settle the thing in Korea to bring it to a decisive end. I believe it can be brought to a decisive end without the calamity of a third world war. I believe if you let it go on indefinitely in Korea, you invite a third world war. I believe the chances of the terrible conflict that you so rightly dread—and all the rest of us dread with you—would be much more probable if we practice appeasement in one area even though we resist to our capacity all along the line.

That is all I am saying. I am saying it with the acute consciousness of the dreadful slaughter that is going on in Korea today. If it is possible to bring it to a successful and an honorable end, I believe we should take the chance of doing so. . . .

SENATOR FULBRIGHT. Certainly if we should accept your basic philosophy of war, and that is to proceed to victory without any dilly-dallying along, without any what you call appeasement, without anything short of a decisive victory, then there is no stopping point once we become committed. Then what happens to us? As to my own thinking, I am a little more worried about Russia not coming in than I am of her coming in in China, because if we become committed there, it seems to me she really is given a free hand in Europe and in the rest of the world. What really bothers us is the situation in the Middle East and Europe, if we really become committed to the point of having to supply very large forces of ground troops, and particularly air power in China.

I think that central question of whether or not this can be done in a relatively quick and definite decisive way is the key point to many other problems. That was why I was hoping you would develop it in a little fuller way, because this precedent of Japan's recent experience in that area makes it rather difficult to accept that it would be an easy sort of undertaking.

GENERAL MACARTHUR. The alternative, Senator, is to sacrifice thousands and thousands and thousands of American boys month after month after month.

Not only that, but you will have sacrificed, if you keep on indefinitely, the entire Korean Nation and people. The high moral reason for our intervention in Korea was to save Korea. If you do not continue and save her, you are going to destroy her.

She is pretty well destroyed now. This question of stopping halfway, of completely destroying the moral tone which caused us to intervene in Korea, completely ignoring the enormous bloodshed which goes on there month after month, that very concept shocks me, old soldier as I am. If these risks that you speak of were so real and so compelling, why did we intervene in Korea?

There is nothing that has happened that has changed those risks or increased those risks. The whole moral tone of the world resounded when in its nobility the United States and the United Nations following them intervened to save Korea.

At one stroke you would abandon that, at one stroke. You don't pay the slightest conception to that 30,000,000 of people in Korea, and that great nation and our own boys by the thousands and thousands.

I have been here 2 days now, and I have heard no proposition yet, outside of the ones that the Joint Chiefs made and myself, which would offer any hope for a successful conclusion of the Korean struggle.

I believe it would mean that if you don't attempt to bring this thing to a short and honorable conclusion, it means not only the indefinite sacrifice of life, but it means what is almost equally important, the complete degradation and sacrifice of our moral tone.

SENATOR FULBRIGHT. Well, General—

GENERAL MACARTHUR. I am not trying to sell my ideas to you, Senator, in any way, shape, or manner. I have expressed them with the greatest fullness, and I don't want you to get the idea that with a fellow Arkansas man, we are trying to jam anything down each other's throats.

SENATOR WILEY. Don't forget Wisconsin.

SENATOR FULBRIGHT. General, I realize that it takes a great deal of patience on your part to listen to a lot of people who are wholly unfamiliar with this type of thing. Certainly I am. I happen to be a member here of the Foreign Relations Committee and not of the Armed Services Committee, and some of these matters, which I am sure seem to you to be crystal clear, seem very, very difficult to understand on our part.

As I said, I hesitate to labor them. But that one point seemed extremely difficult to me. I think you said there had been no change in Korea. I had understood all along the intervention of China changed the situation, changed the risks, and that it came as a surprise to you and to all of us. If it had not changed—in other words, if the Chinese had not intervened, that particular undertaking in Korea might well have been long since wound up, as you so properly thought it would be, I think, at that time, last fall.

So that it has changed to some extent. Now, I think there is room for honest difference of opinion in matters of this kind. I think you could grant to all of us, certainly in the Foreign Relations Committee, even though we do not understand military matters, that our objective is to minimize the loss of American lives as well as the expenditure of treasure.

It seems to me that this loss of life which is going on today is so sad and terrible, that it is perfectly proper to consider that a mistake in the present circumstances might result in a 10 times greater loss within the near future.

That is what we are trying to balance off. I grant to you that if the choice is between the present loss and no loss—if there is any reasonable opportunity for that—we ought to take it.

The point at issue is whether there is a reasonable opportunity to stop our losses rather than to vastly increase them.

Now, there is a school of thought, as you have already seen exhibited here. I don't know that I say it is a school of thought but what we are really doing is examining these things to see if there is any validity in them.

I can't tell you at this minute whether I think it is right or wrong to proceed, but I am trying to develop the reasons which I hope may give us some guidance.

There are very definite cleavages of opinion about Russia and what she may do in Europe. It does seem to me that if we become bogged down in China, if by chance it proved to be a little more difficult than you think, that then the thing would come about that you mentioned earlier in your testimony. One of the major things that might induce Russia to attack all out would be a relative increase in her strength, which would come about if we expended very large resources in Asia, and if perchance at the same time our budget was cut $20 billion as suggested by the Senator from Ohio. All those things might happen.

A cautious attitude might be justified under your own suggestion that one of the things that might induce an attack would be a rather large increase in the power of Russia relative to our own. . . .

SENATOR MORSE. Do you think it would be a fair statement that the disagreement if any which arises between you and the administration is that apparently some in the administration feel that we cannot take a chance now that Russia will not become involved in the war until more time has elapsed for the strengthening of our defenses both in Asia and in Europe? Is it your understanding that that is the attitude of some in the administration?

GENERAL MACARTHUR. I really couldn't speak for the administration, Senator.

SENATOR MORSE. Let me put the question this way. Is it your understanding that one of the reasons why you did not get authorization to broaden the Korean War was because it was felt that such action at this time might bring Russia into the war?

GENERAL MACARTHUR. It is quite possible.

SENATOR MORSE. Have you heard it said, General, that that was one of the reasons for your recall?

GENERAL MACARTHUR. Senator, I do not know why I was recalled. The only statement that I have seen on it is the order for my recall.

SENATOR MORSE. Well, what I said is, Was it your understanding that that was one of the reasons?

GENERAL MACARTHUR. That statement was of a nature which expressed the President's belief that I could not give wholehearted support to the policies of the United States and of the United Nations in the Far East.

So far as I know, I have completely implemented, to the best of my ability, every directive, every policy that was given to me, but there is no possible charge that I have failed to carry out and implement or even to take exception to any announced policy that the United States or the United Nations has made.

I can only interpret that order that the administration, knowing the views I held, was going to act in a very contrary way, and believed it was advisable not to place any strain upon my loyalty, if you might put it that way, and relieved me of the command.

SENATOR MORSE. As I said the other day—

GENERAL MACARTHUR. It must have been based upon what they had in mind for the future. It could not possibly have been based upon anything in the past.

I had made certain recommendations, most of which—in fact, practically all, as far as I know—were in complete accord with the military recommendations of the Joint Chiefs of Staff, and all other commanders.

Now, I have no knowledge whatsoever, today, as to why I was relieved, except the orders of the President.

I have said before that the President is under no obligation to explain his actions. He acted within his complete authority, and his responsibility, and I don't challenge either, in any way, shape, or manner.

SENATOR MORSE. I think you have made an—

GENERAL MACARTHUR. But, as to the reasons of my recall, I am still completely uninformed, because the reasons contained in the order are not valid.

If the President had given a decision which was exactly contrary to the recommendations I had made, I would, to the best of my ability, have carried them out completely and absolutely.

My recommendations were seeking decisions, seeking policy directives. I felt that the position I was in, the military position, was untenable without having some directive, some mission which was more realistic than that which existed at the time; and I felt, in all conscience, I could not go on ordering men to their deaths by the thousands, in such a complete vacuum of policy decision.

There is nothing that I am aware of, of the slightest tinge of insubordination, or of dictation or anything that conflicted with any decision that has been made.

I merely first asked for decisions, and when they were not forthcoming, I gave my own recommendations.

Now, many of those, as I said, are completely in accord with the military and professional opinions that at that time were given by the Joint Chiefs of Staff.

Now, the opinion that the President expressed, as I read the order, and try to interpret it, is that something was in mind, that the administration had in mind, that was so violative of the concept that I had that it was thought best to relieve me, rather than charge me with their execution.

There has no charge ever been made to me, or publicly, that I know of, that I failed in any respect to try to carry out the directives I received; or any charge that I had disagreed with what had been decided upon.

Source: U.S. Senate, 82nd Congress, 1st Session, Military Situation in the Far East, Hearings Before the Committee on Armed Services and the Committee on Foreign Relations, Part 1, 1–287.

Excerpt from Testimony of Secretary of State Dean Acheson June 4–9, 1951

Educated at Yale University and Harvard Law School, a lawyer in a prestigious firm in Washington, undersecretary of the treasury and then assistant secretary in the Department of State in the Roosevelt administration, Dean Acheson brought his sterling credentials to the Truman administration in 1945 as undersecretary of state. Acheson played a pivotal role advising Truman on issues relating to the containment of Communism and European recovery after World War II. He believed the best way to halt the spread of Communism was by working with progressive forces in those countries threatened by revolution. After he became secretary of state in 1949, Acheson and Defense Secretary George Marshall came under increasing fire from Republicans on the right who considered both to be "soft on communism." In February 1950, Senator Joseph McCarthy (R-Wis.) slammed Acheson as "a pompous diplomat in striped pants." Acheson was fully on the side of Truman in his dispute with MacArthur. He took the stand in the hearings in June 1951 ready give his reasons.

EXCERPT FROM TESTIMONY OF SECRETARY OF STATE DEAN ACHESON JUNE 4–9

SENATOR WILEY. Mr. Secretary, a few days ago I had a little difference with my colleagues on the committee over a question asked General Bradley. I want to read into the record at this time a little statement from a wonderful article in the Yale Law Review under title of "Government Immunity From Discovery," written by two very prominent lawyers. I read as follows:

> Historically the claim of Executive immunity founders upon the ruling of Chief Justice Marshall in the Burr case; harks back to a royal prerogative which found scant favor on our soil and even in the field of sovereign immunity is regarded in increasing disfavor. In a state that rests upon the consent of the governed, the claim of the government to greater privileges than accorded citizens must rest not on administrative conveniences, not on archaic notions or prerogatives alien to our institutions, but on genuine necessity. Our Nation has again and again risen above partisan strife because of general confidence in the fairness of the Government. That confidence is indispensable to continuance of our domestic institutions. It can only be impaired by governmental claims of special privilege against the citizenry.

I repeat:

> It can only be impaired by governmental claims of special privilege against the citizenry.

On page 1458 is this statement:

> It was on this state of facts that Chief Justice Marshall ruled. He said, "That the President of the United States may be subpenaed as a witness and required to produce any paper in his possession is not controverted."

Now, in the Burr case, the President was not a party. To me, at least, investigating the reasons for the recall of General MacArthur, the President is in the position voluntarily of justifying his act, and thus, to all intents and purposes, he is a party.

He apparently voluntarily submits his Secretary of State, his Chief of Staff and other advisers to establish his position before the bar of public opinion; and at the present time he has given no reason for not permitting the Chiefs of Staff and others to tell what was said in the various meetings between the 5th and 11th of April.

With this preface, I shall pursue a few questions.

Mr. Secretary, your appearance is without subpena, and voluntary on your part, is it not?

SECRETARY ACHESON. I am appearing here at the request of the committee.

SENATOR WILEY. You have been subpenaed?

SECRETARY ACHESON. No, sir.

SENATOR WILEY. If I were to ask you what was said in the conversations that took place between you and the President and others in relation to the MacArthur matter, between the 5th and 11th of April, would you claim such conversations were privileged; would you say they were confidential; or make the claim of both privileged and confidential?

SECRETARY ACHESON. If you were to ask me what was said, I should have to say that I could not answer that question, because I am under direct instruction of the President of the United States not to repeat what was said at these meetings at his office.

If you wish me to say what matters were taken up, what the outcome of each particular meeting was, what conclusions were reached, what action was agreed upon and taken, I shall be very glad to go into that.

If you wish me to answer questions in regard to my own attitude on the relief of General MacArthur, I shall be glad to answer those questions, though I cannot say what I said at any one of these meetings.

SENATOR WILEY. I want to thank you, Mr. Secretary. I think that statement you just made clarifies everything. You say you are under instructions from the President. I presume, as a lawyer, you claim the President's privilege then or that they were confidential, and of such a nature that, within certain decisions, you are not privileged to repeat the conversations; is that right?

SECRETARY ACHESON. I think that is what I said; yes, sir.

SENATOR WILEY. Would you claim that what was said in those conversations would be against the public interest to disclose or against the President's interests to disclose?

SECRETARY ACHESON. I wouldn't say either. I would just say that the President has the right to instruct his subordinates as to what they should say or not say in regard to conversations in his presence of an official nature, and when he gives that instruction, so far as I am concerned, that instruction has to be obeyed.

SENATOR WILEY. Well, do you claim it is the privilege of the Government or the privilege of the President?

SECRETARY ACHESON. Well, I am not trying to analyze the matter, Senator.

SENATOR WILEY. No, no; I know you are not.

SECRETARY ACHESON. It seems to me that the whole structure of our Government means that in carrying out its highest functions the three coordinate branches cannot interfere with one another, and require the disclosure of confidential material.

I should think that it would be very clear, indeed, for instance, that neither the executive nor the legislative branch could require the members of the Supreme Court to disclose what was said by any of them in their conferences when they decide cases.

SENATOR WILEY. Do you claim it constitutes a state secret, these discussions, in relation to the planning and the execution of the recall of General MacArthur?

SECRETARY ACHESON. I think that it—I don't know whether you would call it a state secret—it is a confidential matter that took place with the President among his advisers.

SENATOR WILEY. I wonder if you see any similarity between these proceedings and any proceedings in court?

SECRETARY ACHESON. I have not thought about that, sir.

SENATOR WILEY. Do you think the same rule should apply in Senate investigations in relation to discovery as in a trial in court?

SECRETARY ACHESON. I should think the same rule would apply in court in regard to the conversation about which you are asking me, and if I were examined in court on this subject I should make the same reply.

SENATOR WILEY. Well, now, my question was more or less a legal question, whether or not the rules of discovery, the Federal rules, which have the effect of law, would apply in an investigation by the Senate the same as they apply in civil cases in Federal court. What is your judgment on them?

SECRETARY ACHESON. I should think they would not apply to this situation at all.

SENATOR WILEY. Is not one of the issues in this investigation, was the President justified by the fact even though he had the arbitrary power to recall MacArthur?

SECRETARY ACHESON. I don't think I am competent to say just exactly what the issues are in this investigation.

SENATOR WILEY. In your opinion should the Government or the President in a case like this, when he has exposed part of his hand with the facts, be obliged to expose all?

SECRETARY ACHESON. No, sir; I think the President is the sole judge of what he should disclose in regard to confidential private discussions with his own Cabinet.

SENATOR WILEY. . . . What reasons, diplomatic or otherwise, are there to believe that if MacArthur's suggestions in Korea had been carried out that Russia would strike? Have you got any intelligence source or anything to indicate that if MacArthur's suggestions had been carried out that Russia would intervene?

SECRETARY ACHESON. The grave danger, I think, which would be created by the suggestions which involve an attack on the territory of China, would be that that creates a situation which directly involves both Russian self-interest and may very well involve Russian treaty obligations.

I pointed out, I think, in my opening statement that if air and sea attacks were made on China, these would be attacks on the territory of the Soviet Union's principal satellite.

SENATOR WILEY. I remember that statement very well, Mr. Secretary. Have you any specific information from your intelligence sources or diplomatic sources that would be in addition to what you said in the beginning?

SECRETARY ACHESON. Well, I am not referring in this to any specific information which anyone has reported as to the intention of any particular person. I am talking about the danger of action and the possibility of action which the Russian Government might feel itself called upon to take.

SENATOR WILEY. Then I think your answer is that there is no additional information from any intelligence source or diplomatic source outside of what you see as a danger situation that would be created. You have no specific information on the subject?

SECRETARY ACHESON. Well, we have, as you know, a good deal of intelligence information, but what I am trying to say is that is not the sort of information which says that so-and-so stated that he would or would not do something.

SENATOR WILEY. If the Chinese Reds are pushed practically out but we do not destroy the feeder rail lines and the Chinese north thereof, do you think the Chinese Reds will remain quiet?

SECRETARY ACHESON. The problem of the future possibility of any Chinese attack has some, of course, important relation to where the fighting at any time might end, but fundamentally it is not I think influenced by that. It doesn't make any difference exactly where the fighting may end.

The point is, is a settlement going to be made or is it not going to be made where the Chinese will not have the will and the desire to come back in and fight again?

If the forces were pushed back to the Yalu River in accordance with your hypothesis here, if installations behind that were attacked, then their tack would be to recreate them or find some substitute for them. The important element in bringing this thing to a stable end would be to change the will to do this.

SENATOR WILEY. Well, let me substitute the name "Kremlin" for the "Chinese Reds" and say that if the Chinese Reds are pushed back of the Yalu but you do not destroy the feeder rail line and the nests north thereof, do you think the Kremlin will remain quiet and not intervene?

SECRETARY ACHESON. Well, I don't believe that the destruction of those facilities would have any bearing on whether they would remain—well, I shouldn't say that. Let me start over again.

I do not believe that destruction of those rail lines would operate to induce them to remain quiet. I think it would have the opposite effect.

SENATOR WILEY. Well, I guess that is one way of answering it, but the real question was if we do not destroy them, but we do push them back, do you think the Russians will remain quiet?

In other words, if we just get them back of the Yalu and leave them up there, have you any information or any judgment that we haven't got so far as to what the Russians will or will not do under those circumstances?

SECRETARY ACHESON. I think that we have given you the information which bears on this question.

SENATOR WILEY. Do you think that General MacArthur, 8,000 miles away, fighting a real war, due to the message of March 20, had less power to negotiate with an enemy commander than he had before?

SECRETARY ACHESON. I should think that the message of May 20 pointed out to him the situation as it existed before and should continue to exist.

SENATOR BREWSTER. May 20?

SECRETARY ACHESON. March 20. In other words, the negotiations carried on by a commander in the field with enemy forces is, in cases that I know about, conducted at the direction of his Government.

That was the case in the earlier statement which General MacArthur made along, I believe, in September or October of 1950. That statement was one prepared in Washington, sent to him, and was issued by him at the direction of this Government, and when he repeated it later, that was again done upon the direction of this Government.

SENATOR WILEY. What is the answer, "Yes" or "No"? Do you think General MacArthur had less power to negotiate with an enemy because of this message than he had before?

SECRETARY ACHESON. Well, I am pointing out that I think he had the same power that he had before. . . .

SENATOR WILEY. Now if we take the President's message . . . you will notice that the President says:

> . . . I have concluded that General of the Army Douglas MacArthur is unable to give his wholehearted support to the policies of the United States Government and of the United Nations in matters pertaining to his official duties.

I think you said you helped with others to get out that statement; am I correct? . . .

SECRETARY ACHESON. Yes. This statement by the President was one of the papers which had been prepared following the President's decision on Monday, April 9, I believe it was, and which was brought back to a meeting in the White House on the afternoon of Tuesday, the 10th of April.

I did see this paper and I did collaborate with General Marshall in the preparation of it.

SENATOR WILEY. In view of the fact that the President says he is unable to give his wholehearted support to the policies of the United States Government and of the United Nations in matters pertaining to his official duties, I am asking you: What evidence is there of his failure to carry out any policies in view of your previous statement that said he was not insubordinate, and he had not violated any military directive? We are talking about broad terms—policy.

SECRETARY ACHESON. What these words mean to me is very clear, Senator, that it is the President's statement that General MacArthur is unable to give his wholehearted support to the policies of the United States Government and the United Nations in matters pertaining to his official duties.

The policies, I believe, which are in particular reference here are those policies which have to do with limiting the hostilities to Korea and not taking steps which may extend them into Manchuria or China and possibly beyond that.

I think it was very clear indeed that General MacArthur was unable to give his wholehearted support to those policies, that he had stated so publicly, and that there was a situation there in which there was public disagreement between the President of the United States, with his responsibilities under the Constitution, and his responsibilities under the United Nations resolution, and General MacArthur, who was the instrument in the field for carrying out those policies.

SENATOR WILEY. Then if you refer to the second paragraph, where the President says it is fundamental, however, that military commanders must be governed by the policies and directives issued to them in the manner provided by our laws and Constitution—the same explanation goes for that, too?

SECRETARY ACHESON. The explanation of that is that I believe it is one of the most fundamental concepts of American constitutional thought, that a military commander must be governed by the policies and by the directives issued to him in accordance with law.

In other words, it is the doctrine of the civil supremacy.

SENATOR WILEY. Well, our difference, Mr. Secretary, is that you have already said, and others have said, he was not insubordinate, he violated no military directive, it was his privilege to make suggestions, and he made such suggestions; you have shown no place where he violated any of them.

He just differed in what he thought the policy should be. Now, if I am wrong in that, I would like to be corrected.

SECRETARY ACHESON. He differed and he differed publicly.

SENATOR WILEY. Yes.

SECRETARY ACHESON. He, in effect, challenged the policies as laid down by the President. . . .

SENATOR BYRD [HARRY FLOOD BYRD SR.]. . . . Do you regard the combat in Korea as a police action?

SECRETARY ACHESON. I regarded it as a military action to repulse the attack made against the Republic of Korea.

SENATOR BYRD. When does a military action or police action cease to be such and become a war?

SECRETARY ACHESON. Well, I think in the ordinary popular sense it is a war if you have fighting with military formations.

SENATOR BYRD. You recognize it as a war now?

SECRETARY ACHESON. Yes, sir; in the usual sense of the word there is a war.

SENATOR BYRD. There is a war.

Now, the Constitution provides, of course, as you know, that Congress is the only agency of the Government that can declare war.

SECRETARY ACHESON. Congress is the only agency that can declare war, yes, sir; but that does not mean that Congress is the only agency that can start fighting. A war is declared when somebody else attacks you, whatever happens; but what the Constitution is referring to is the declaration of war which has a whole lot of legal and other consequences.

SENATOR BYRD. Under what conditions—I would like you to name the conditions under which you think that a war should not be fought until it is first declared by Congress.

SECRETARY ACHESON. I don't think I am able to do that, Senator Byrd.

SENATOR BYRD. I think that is a pretty fundamental question. I don't understand why you can't do that, because the Constitution clearly says that all wars must be declared by Congress, and you say this is a war.

SECRETARY ACHESON. Well, I think if you consider it for a moment, you will see that it is an almost impossible question to answer.

The last war, where Congress had a declaration, was being fought quite vigorously before Congress got to do that.

SENATOR BYRD. Which war was that?

SECRETARY ACHESON. World War II. We were fighting at Pearl Harbor before Congress had any declaration of war.

SENATOR BYRD. That was a direct attack upon us.

SECRETARY ACHESON. Yes, sir; and I suppose if there is a direct attack upon us now, we would be fighting. . . .

SENATOR BYRD. Did you justify the order of June 26, directing that our forces go into combat at the thirty-eighth parallel, on the ground that it was a United Nations action?

SECRETARY ACHESON. No, sir; I don't think so.

SENATOR BYRD. How did you justify that, without the action of Congress?

SECRETARY ACHESON. I said that the orders of the 26th provided the Navy and Air Force be instructed to offer the fullest support to the South Korean forces, south of the thirty-eighth parallel.

The orders were issued to the Seventh Fleet to prevent an attack on Formosa, and so forth.

SENATOR BYRD. Now; the orders went beyond that, didn't they?

SECRETARY ACHESON. That was the 26th. Those orders were issued by the President in exercise of his authority as President and Commander in Chief.

They had primarily to do with getting our people out of the Seoul area and giving support to these South Korean forces.

SENATOR BYRD. Actually the June 26 instructions were furnished General MacArthur by the Joint Chiefs of Staff, and MacArthur then had not been made the commander by the United Nations, for the employment of the United States Naval and Air Forces against North Korean units south of the Thirty-eighth parallel. Was that taken under what authority—as the Commander in Chief? Was it taken in connection with our membership in the United Nations?

SECRETARY ACHESON. Sir, that was taken by the President under his authority as President and Commander in Chief. It was in part to get our own people out of that area. And in part it was in support of the resolution of the 25th which asked everybody to help in the purposes of that resolution.

SENATOR BYRD. That resolution of the 25th, as I understand it, was a cease-fire resolution.

SECRETARY ACHESON. The resolution called on the North Koreans to withdraw, asked no one to give any help to the other side. That determined that the action was a breach of the peace, called for the immediate cessation of hostilities, called upon the authorities of North Korea to withdraw forthwith their armed forces to the Thirty-eighth parallel, requests the Commission to do various things, and called upon all members to render every assistance to the United Nations in the execution of this resolution and to refrain from giving assistance to the North Korean authorities.

SENATOR BYRD. But you did not rely upon that resolution in the action taken by the President, which I understand you to say was done as Commander in Chief.

SECRETARY ACHESON. Well, I said all his actions here in relation to American forces are based upon his powers under the Constitution.

SENATOR BYRD. Well, you referred to the last war. It is true that the attack, that we attempted to resist the attack at Pearl Harbor when it was made, but the next day we declared war on Japan and Germany.

SECRETARY ACHESON. That is right.

SENATOR BYRD. There has been no war declared in this case.

SECRETARY ACHESON. That is right.

SENATOR BYRD. Where is the analogy here between the two?

SECRETARY ACHESON. I was not trying to draw an analogy.

SENATOR BYRD. What I want to know, and I think it is a pretty vital constitutional provision which says that Congress only can declare war. You say this is a war. The President calls it a police action. But you admit it is a war. In what different category is this particular war to other wars we have been engaged in when Congress has declared war? What is the difference?

SECRETARY ACHESON. What I was saying is from the point of view of constitutional law, I presume that the phrase "declare war" means declare a state of war with the various legal and other consequences which follow from that. Now Congress is the only body that can do that.

SENATOR BYRD. You are a great constitutional lawyer, but I think the provision in the Constitution was to protect the people of America by the fact that only Congress could declare war, the President or no one else could place us into war except by the action of the Congress.

Now I would like to know what the difference, what special category this particular war is in whereby it does not require a declaration of war, but that the President, as you say, can start the war and conduct the war.

SECRETARY ACHESON. We have filed a memorandum which shows that for over a hundred years, perhaps 150 years, the President has employed the Armed Forces for various situations where there was not a declaration of a state of war. I believe that his powers and precedents are ample to cover what he has done in this case.

SENATOR BYRD. To rely on the membership of the United Nations—in other words, the President can start a war any place in the world if he chooses to do it, without a declaration of war by Congress? If he had difficulty in Iran, for example, he can have a war there simply by having troops directed to go there into combat, that can be done—and the United Nations took such action on June 27.

Now, I assumed that the President had relied at least to some extent on the membership of the United Nations, until yesterday you responded to a question by Senator Gillette that the President—you said he relied on his authority as Commander in Chief alone, to send American troops. You may recall Senator Gillette asked, and I have the record here:

> Is it your contention that the President as Commander in Chief alone, Commander in Chief of the United States forces, without reference to the United Nations, would have authority to send American troops to the number of a quarter-million into such action as may be taking place in Korea without action by the Congress of the United States and declaration of war?

And you said you believed he had that power.

Now, it is your opinion as Secretary of State that you could advise the President that he has a right to begin a war as he sees fit any place in the world, acting as Commander in Chief? And if that is your opinion, I would like to ask you the question: Under what conditions do you believe the Congress should declare war?

SECRETARY ACHESON. Senator Byrd, I did not say that was my opinion and I never would have advised the President he can declare war.

SENATOR BYRD. You stated that yesterday, Mr. Secretary, in response to the question of Senator Gillette. I do not know whether you advise the President or not, but I assume you as Secretary of State would—but you did advise the President with respect to Korea, did you not?

SECRETARY ACHESON. What, sir?

SENATOR BYRD. Did you not advise the President with respect to Korea?

SECRETARY ACHESON. Oh, yes, sir.

SENATOR BYRD. And so then you could advise him again, as long as you are the Secretary of State. I would like now to know would you advise the President that he had the power in your judgment under the Constitution to start a war wherever he pleases without having a declaration of war from Congress?

SECRETARY ACHESON. No, sir; I would not advise the President he had power to start war whenever he wanted it.

SENATOR BYRD. Well, you did in this instance?

SECRETARY ACHESON. No, sir; I did not.

SENATOR BYRD. What did you do?

SECRETARY ACHESON. I advised the President that certain steps were necessary and desirable in Korea.

SENATOR BYRD. Did you advise him to issue the order of June 27?

SECRETARY ACHESON. I was at the meeting in which we discussed that order and joined in recommending its issue.

SENATOR BYRD. That was to send our troops into combat, was it—

SECRETARY ACHESON. Well, send our Air Force and Army into combat.

SENATOR BYRD. And that means war, and you admit that that means war, and now you are unwilling to state under what conditions, if there are conditions, where the Congress should declare war preliminary to hostilities. Do you think that Congress should have the right as stated in the Constitution to declare war?

SECRETARY ACHESON. Yes, sir; I think Congress is the only body that has the power to declare war.

SENATOR BYRD. But as I understand your position, then, it is that we are having a war without a declaration of war.

SECRETARY ACHESON. You may have fighting a great many times without the declaration of war, and throughout our 150 years of history it has happened a great many times, and they are all mentioned in these memoranda we filed with this committee and others.

SENATOR BYRD. Have we ever had a war in our history for this length of time without a declaration of war, where we have had casualties of 170,000?

SECRETARY ACHESON. I can't answer that, Senator Byrd; I don't know.

Source: U.S. Senate, 82nd Congress, 1st Session, Military Situation in the Far East, Hearings Before the Committee on Armed Services and the Committee on Foreign Relations, Part 3, 1748–2017.

Committee Invitation and MacArthur Reply, June 16 and 19, 1951

When the last of the witnesses had given testimony, the chairman of the committee, Senator Richard Russell (R-Ga.), invited MacArthur to return to the stand to rebut any inconsistencies and errors he felt had followed his own testimony the previous month. MacArthur politely declined but made it clear that much of what was on the record had, indeed, been incorrect or misleading, charging that officials in Washington did not have the direct experience with or knowledge about the events in question. "The full facts," said MacArthur, ". . . have not been elucidated due to the orders of the President silencing the pertinent witnesses as to his own part in the action." The debate over the firing of MacArthur did not end with the work of the committee. Historians would continue to argue the facts. And, in the immediate aftermath, the principals themselves would continue to fire personal salvos. In later writings, President Truman pointed to the fact that the decision to fire MacArthur had been unanimously endorsed by Secretary of Defense George Marshall, Secretary of State Dean Acheson, Presidential Adviser Averell Harriman, and General Omar Bradley and his entire Joint Chiefs of Staff. MacArthur replied by simply accusing each of these men with personal prejudice and animus against him. Acheson, for example, "had frequently exhibited petulance" because of MacArthur's interference with the State Department's "socialistic concepts" for Japan.

COMMITTEE INVITATION AND MACARTHUR REPLY JUNE 16 AND 19, 1951

June 16, 1951

General of the Army Douglas MacArthur
New York, N.Y.

Dear General MacArthur:

The Senate Committee on Armed Services and the Committee on Foreign Relations are endeavoring to terminate as soon as possible the series of hearings which began with your appearance before the committees on May 3.

As you were the first witness before the committees, the testimony presented by you during the first 3 days of the hearings was available to succeeding witnesses. You had no knowledge of the testimony of the succeeding witnesses at the time of your appearance before the committees. I am sure that the committees will feel that you should be afforded an opportunity to again appear before the committees to present any rebuttal testimony that you may think desirable.

If you wish to appear before the committees again, I shall appreciate your advising me of your decision as promptly as possible.

With assurances of esteem, I am,

Sincerely,
Richard B. Russell

New York, N.Y., June 19, 1951

Hon. Richard B. Russell,
United States Senate, Washington, D.C.

Dear Senator Russell:

I appreciate very much the opportunity offered by your letter of the 16th instant to appear again before the Senate committee, but in view of the voluminous record which has already been taken wherein is included my own personal views in most complete detail, I do not believe it in the public interest for me to do so.

I think it should be understood, however, that certain of the testimony which was given by some of the subsequent witnesses did not coincide with my own recollection and record of the events, and with many of their opinions and judgments I am in direct disagreement. I especially take sharp exception to interpretations of events of campaign given with little local knowledge thereof by those thousands of miles away from the scene of action. In some cases such witnesses had never even visited the area and none had direct knowledge of the events discussed. I suggest that the bimonthly official reports to the United Nations be incorporated into the committees' proceedings as they represent factually the views of the Commanders on the spot at the time of the actual occurrence of events, entirely uninfluenced by any extraneous issues or pressures.

Much opinion testimony was given of a nature which was never either by word or deed communicated to me and of which I had no slightest inkling. There has been, too, a lack of accuracy in the paraphrased documentation presented and some lifting from context—which could not fail to have been misleading.

Insofar as the investigation dealt with my relief from the Far East Command, I feel that the full facts have not been elucidated due to the orders of the President silencing the pertinent witnesses as to his own part in the action.

With renewed expressions of personal esteem.

Most sincerely,
Douglas MacArthur

Source: U.S. Senate, 82nd Congress, 1st Session, Military Situation in the Far East, Hearings Before the Committee on Armed Services and the Committee on Foreign Relations, Part 4, 2825–26.

Bibliography

Acheson, Dean. *Present at the Creation.* Reprint. New York: W. W. Norton, 1987.

Lowitt, Richard. *The Truman-MacArthur Controversy.* Chicago: Rand McNally, 1967.

MacArthur, Douglas. *Reminiscences.* New York: McGraw-Hill, 1964.

Manchester, William. *American Caesar: Douglas MacArthur 1880–1964.* Boston: Little, Brown, 1978.

Pearlman, Michael. *Truman and MacArthur: Policy, Politics, and the Hunger for Honor and Renown.* Bloomington: Indiana University Press, 2008.

Rees, David. *Korea: The Limited War.* New York: St. Martin's Press, 1964.

Rovere, Richard H., and Arthur Schlesinger. *The MacArthur Controversy and American Foreign Policy.* New York: Farrar, Straus & Giroux, 1965.

Smith, Robert. *MacArthur in Korea.* New York: Simon & Schuster, 1981.

Spanier, John. *The Truman-MacArthur Controversy and the Korean War.* Cambridge, Mass.: Belknap Press, 1959.

Truman, Harry. *Memoirs: Years of Trial and Hope.* Garden City, N.Y.: Doubleday, 1956.

U.S. Congress. Senate Committee on Armed Services. *Individual Views of Certain Members of the Joint Committee on Armed Services and Foreign Relations of the U.S. Senate Relating to Hearings Held on the Dismissal of General MacArthur and the Military Situation in the Far East, May 3–June 27, 1951.* Washington, D.C.: GPO, 1951.

Wainstock, Dennis. *Truman, MacArthur, and the Korean War.* Westport, Conn.: Greenwood Press, 1999.

Wiltz, John Edward. "The MacArthur Hearings of 1951: The Secret Testimony." *Military Affairs* (December 1975).

The Army-McCarthy Hearings, 1954

By Donald A. Ritchie

Political dictionaries define "McCarthyism" as the use of smears, exaggerations, and unsubstantiated charges that trample rights and reputations. The label derives from public perception of the tactics employed by Senator Joseph R. McCarthy, a Republican senator from Wisconsin, who chaired the Senate's Permanent Subcommittee on Investigations from 1953 to 1954. McCarthyism has been applied indiscriminately to anticommunist investigations that McCarthy himself had little or nothing to do with, ranging from the hearings on Hollywood conducted by the House Committee on Un-American Activities (HUAC) to the Red-hunting committees that operated in various state legislatures. McCarthy himself held widely publicized hearings into allegations of subversion and espionage in such federal agencies as the Department of State, U.S. Information Libraries, and the Government Printing Office. His investigation of the Army Signal Corps culminated in the nationally televised Army-McCarthy hearings, when the tables were turned and Chairman McCarthy and his chief counsel, Roy Cohn, became subjects of the inquiry. The confrontation not only undermined McCarthy's public standing but also diminished confidence in all congressional investigations for years to come.

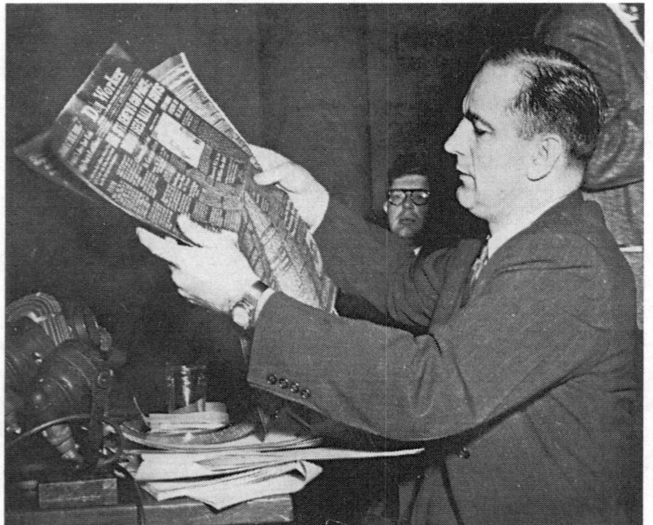

Joseph McCarthy, Republican senator from Wisconsin, whose anticommunist crusade profoundly shaped the American political landscape in the early 1950s. McCarthy is seen here reading from the Communist newspaper Daily Worker. (National Archives)

Prelude to the Investigations

McCarthy's career as a Senate investigator achieved a remarkable arc, soaring to the heights of power and popularity before crashing in censure and disgrace. He had spent a hardscrabble youth on a Wisconsin chicken farm before obtaining a delayed education—attending high school at 19 and completing it in a year, then going to college and earning a law degree. He won election as a circuit judge but resigned from the bench during World War II to enlist in the Marine Corps. While still in uniform in 1944, he lost the Republican nomination to run for the U.S. Senate. In the 1946 primary, however, McCarthy upset the incumbent, Senator Robert M. La Follette Jr., and he then won the Senate seat at the age of 38. Brash and unpredictable, he earned media notice as "The Senate's Remarkable Upstart." McCarthy often disregarded Senate traditions of decorum, and he lost one of his committee assignments because the chairman regarded him as a "troublemaker." Yet he could affably throw his arm around the shoulders of a colleague he had just attacked, and he would otherwise demon-

OVERVIEW

Background

Senator Joseph R. McCarthy (R-Wis.) gained immediate national attention in 1950 with his allegations that hundreds of Communists had infiltrated the State Department and other federal agencies. At a time of much anxiety about the spread of Communism and its threat to the country's national institutions, his charges sounded an alarm that not only rocketed him into a glaring political spotlight but also launched an era of partisan investigation rarely seen in American history.

Congress Investigates

As chairman of the Senate Permanent Subcommittee on Investigations, McCarthy shifted that body's focus from investigating fraud and waste in the executive branch to hunting for communists. He conducted scores of hearings, calling hundreds of witnesses in both public and closed sessions. Often without substantial evidence, he directed hearings on possible Communist infiltration of the State Department, the Voice of America, the U.S. Information Libraries, the Government Printing Office, and the Army Signal Corps. He also subpoenaed such prominent writers as Dashiell Hammett and Langston Hughes, and the newspaper editor James Wechsler to examine their politics—as if they had any control over how their books got into government libraries.

By early 1954, McCarthy's aggressive tactics had sparked derisive comment. On March 9, 1954, CBS television journalist Edward R. Murrow, on his *See It Now* program, blasted McCarthy and his methods. Nevertheless, shortly after Murrow's attack, McCarthy was again on the march. The Subcommittee on Investigations launched the so-called Army-McCarthy hearings, a televised spectacle that pitted the Wisconsin senator against the U.S. Army's clever lawyer from Boston, Joseph Welch. On June 9 McCarthy charged that one of Welch's young attorneys had ties to a Communist organization. As an enormous television audience looked on, Welch responded with the lines that ultimately ended McCarthy's career: "Until this moment, Senator, I think I never really gauged your cruelty or your recklessness." When McCarthy tried to continue his attack, Welch angrily interrupted, "Let us not assassinate this lad further, Senator. You have done enough. Have you no sense of decency, sir, at long last have you left no sense of decency?"

Impact

Six months after Welch's devastating assault on McCarthy, the Senate, on December 2, 1954, voted 67–22 to censure McCarthy for "conduct contrary to senatorial tradition." He died a few years later. Following the Army-McCarthy hearings, the Supreme Court considerably strengthened the rights of witnesses appearing before congressional committees. The Senate and the permanent subcommittee also revised the rules of inquiry to prevent a continuation of the abuses evident during McCarthy's tenure.

strate his congeniality. A boxer in his youth, McCarthy approached politics like a prizefighter who landed blows on his opponents without rancor or remorse.

Midway through his first term, McCarthy expressed concern over his chances of reelection and sought an issue that would attract some publicity. In February 1950, speaking at a Lincoln's Day dinner in Wheeling, West Virginia, he broke into national headlines by accusing the State Department of harboring known Communists. Newspapers quoted McCarthy as claiming to hold in his hand "a list of 205 who were known to the Secretary of State as being members of the Communist Party and who, nevertheless, are still working and shaping policy in the State Department." To investigate these allegations, the Senate Foreign Relations Committee appointed a special subcommittee, chaired by Millard Tydings (D-Md.). Actually having no list of names, McCarthy employed the aid of sympathetic journalists from the Hearst and McCormick newspaper chains, who compiled cases of security risks he could present as evidence. After some stormy confrontations, the Tydings committee denounced his charges as a "fraud and a hoax." Yet, rather than discredit McCarthy, publicity from the inquiry established him as the nation's most outspoken

CHRONOLOGY

1938

- The House of Representatives establishes the Dies committee, a special committee to investigate subversive, un-American elements infiltrating the United States. The Dies committee becomes the precursor to the House Committee on Un-American Activities (often known as HUAC), which the House establishes as a standing committee in 1945.

1948

- HUAC hears testimony from Whitaker Chambers, who says that Alger Hiss, a former State Department official, spied for the Soviets. Hiss denies the charges.

1950

- *January 25:* Hiss found guilty of perjury and sentenced to five years in prison.
- *February 9:* In Wheeling, West Virginia, Senator Joseph McCarthy (R-Wis.) gives his first speech against Communist subversion in the federal government.
- *September:* The McCarran Act, or Internal Security Act of 1950, is passed. President Harry S. Truman vetoes the legislation, but the Senate overrides him by a vote of 89 to 11.

1951

- *March 29:* Julius and Ethel Rosenberg are convicted of espionage. Both are sentenced to death and executed in 1953.

1953

- *January:* McCarthy becomes chairman of the Senate Permanent Subcommittee on Investigations.
- *Fall 1953–Spring 1954:* McCarthy's subcommittee conducts an investigation of the Army Signal Corps. During the hearings, McCarthy fails to uncover information regarding a supposed espionage ring. During the interrogations, however, he insults General Ralph Zwicker, declaring that he was not fit to wear his uniform.

1954

- *March 9:* On his *See It Now* program, CBS television journalist Edward R. Murrow attacks McCarthy and his methods.
- *March 11:* The Senate Permanent Subcommittee on Investigations votes to investigate the Army's charges against McCarthy, and his countercharges against the Army. It also votes to allow live television coverage of the inquiry. McCarthy relinquishes the committee chairmanship to Karl Mundt (R-S.D.) and becomes, with the committee's chief counsel, Roy Cohn, a contestant and witness in a live television drama.
- *April 22–June 17:* Hearings are broadcast for 188 hours to 22 million viewers. McCarthy's frequent interruptions of the proceedings with calls of "point of order" make him the object of ridicule, and his approval ratings in public-opinion polls decline sharply.
- *June 9:* After McCarthy charges that one of the Army's attorneys had ties to a Communist organization, Joseph Welch, an Army attorney, declares: "Until this moment, Senator, I think I never really gauged your cruelty or your recklessness. . . . Let us not assassinate this lad further, Senator. You have done enough. Have you no sense of decency?"
- *December 2:* The Senate votes 67–22 to censure McCarthy for "conduct contrary to senatorial tradition."

anticommunist and a political power as well, when Tydings unexpectedly lost his race for reelection that fall.

McCarthy's charges had struck a vein of American national insecurity over the threat of international Communism and the effectiveness of the nation's foreign policies. The United States and the Soviet Union had been allied against Nazi Germany until World War II ended in 1945, when relations dissolved into a tense cold war. The Soviet army occupied Eastern Europe, ruthlessly installing Communist governments, while Communist parties made political gains in Western Europe. In 1949, the Soviet Union exploded its first atomic bomb, sooner than the U.S. government had expected, and Communist forces seized control of China.

In 1950, Communist North Korea invaded South Korea, and the United States was drawn into the war. To make sense of these troubling events, McCarthy gave a simple answer: Communists had infiltrated and sabotaged the U.S. government. He blamed the Democratic administrations of Franklin D. Roosevelt and Harry Truman for laxity in allowing "twenty years of treason," impugning the loyalty of such leading architects of American foreign policy as Secretaries of State George C. Marshall and Dean Acheson.

American authorities knew about Soviet espionage within the U.S. government. During World War II, the Army's Signal Intelligence Service had intercepted messages between Moscow and Soviet agents in the United States, and by 1946 it had cracked the code. Named Project Venona, the intercepts revealed that an underground wing of the American Communist Party worked within key government agencies and provided information to the Soviets. Venona's evidence would remain secret for a half-century (and therefore unknown to McCarthy), but the defections of a Russian code clerk in Canada and a Communist courier in Washington produced headlines about Soviet spying right after the war. The Soviets responded by shutting down most of their American operations, recalling agents, and sending others into hiding. In 1947, President Truman instituted a government-wide loyalty program. Loyalty boards within government agencies screened the civil service for security risks. The attorney general compiled a list of subversive organizations, and federal employees suspected of Communist sympathies could be fired. By 1951, the loyalty boards had investigated 3 million federal employees and dismissed 212 for questionable loyalty. Security officers had suspicions about some additional individuals, but not enough hard evidence to warrant their dismissal.

As a member of the minority party in the Senate, McCarthy could make sensational charges without responsibility for acting on them, since he had no control over a committee that could conduct investigations. In 1952, the anticommunist issue helped elect a Republican president, Dwight D. Eisenhower, and Republican majorities in both houses of Congress. Seniority elevated McCarthy to the chairmanship of the Senate's Committee on Government Operations and its Permanent Subcommittee on Investigations. Under the Senate's rules, jurisdiction for investigations into subversive activities belonged to the Judiciary Committee's Subcommittee on Internal Security. Republican leaders hoped that McCarthy would accept his committee's established role of rooting out corruption in government, but he interpreted its authority broadly enough to investigate anything related to government wrongdoing, which included subversion and espionage. The other Republican members of the subcommittee—Karl Mundt (South Dakota), Everett McKinley Dirksen (Illinois), and Charles E. Potter (Michigan)—generally sympathized with his aims, while the Democrats—John L. McClellan (Arkansas), Henry M. Jackson (Washington), and Stuart Symington (Missouri)—gave McCarthy leeway to prove his charges, in case they were true.

Acting on the recommendation of the Hearst newspaper columnist and staunch anticommunist George Sokolsky, McCarthy hired for his chief counsel Roy M. Cohn, the 25-year-old son of a New York State appellate division judge. Cohn had graduated from Columbia University Law School and become an assistant U.S. attorney on the day he was admitted to the bar. He had taken part in the prosecution of Julius and Ethel Rosenberg for providing atomic secrets to the Soviet Union. In 1952, Cohn joined Truman's Justice Department, where he handled other cases of suspected subversion. A registered Democrat, Cohn had a reputation as a tough and relentless interrogator. The fact that he was Jewish also helped McCarthy counteract the charges of anti-Semitism that often were leveled against anticommunist investigations, since many of the witnesses were Jewish. McCarthy confided to Cohn that although Senate Republicans had been trying to persuade him to drop the Communist issue and play it safe, he had won reelection on the issue and did not intend to hand it off to anyone else.

Lacking previous legislative experience, Cohn ran the Subcommittee on Investigations' hearings in the style of a prosecutor before a grand jury, collecting evidence to seek an indictment rather than conduct a fair hearing. Congressional investigations traditionally work from the top down, requiring the top officials in an agency to explain policy, and then determining how they carried it out. McCarthy and Cohn reversed the order, beginning their investigations by calling suspect witnesses from the lowest levels of an agency and then working their way up the chain of command to determine who had protected them.

As chief counsel, Cohn promptly recruited his friend G. David Schine to be an unpaid consultant. Young, handsome, and an executive in his family's chain of hotels and theaters, Schine took no salary because he had no need for one and because he lacked the credentials to justify hiring him. Neither a lawyer nor an investigator, he accepted the assignment out of his interest in the subject, having written a pamphlet on the definition of Communism for distribution in his family's hotel rooms. Cohn and Schine exhibited conspicuous self-indulgence.

This Edwin Marcus cartoon shows Senator Joseph McCarthy, who has painted himself into a corner using a can of "Red Paint." The painted floor is labeled "Accusations." The cartoon was drawn in March 1950, soon after the Wisconsin senator began his round of sensational charges regarding Communist subversives in government, when it appeared that his smear campaign might fail. He was not discredited until 1954. (By Permission of the Marcus Family)

They chose not to work in the subcommittee's cramped offices in the Senate Office Building, instead renting a suite in a nearby office building stocked with plush furnishings. They signed McCarthy's name to a letter to the Senate Committee on Rules and Administration, in an abortive appeal for them to use the senators-only pool and steam bath. Whenever their hearings were televised, Schine would call friends on the West Coast to encourage them to watch, running up long-distance phone bills that the subcommittee could not pay since he was not on the payroll (the chief clerk dunned Cohn instead).

Cohn became the driving force behind McCarthy's investigations, and together the chairman and chief counsel conducted a rush of well-publicized hearings. Their hectic schedule stretched the subcommittee's staff and often resulted in their insufficient preparation. To gather evidence, McCarthy and Cohn relied chiefly on closed executive-session hearings, where they took testimony from hundreds of witnesses, winnowing out those to call back to testify in public. After each closed hearing, the chairman would step into the hall to provide waiting reporters with his own version of what had happened, ensuring that his side of the story appeared first in the newspapers, long before the witnesses could explain themselves publicly.

The marathon executive sessions revealed McCarthy's complex nature. Witnesses alternately encountered his solicitude and his contempt. He would advise them of their rights and then berate them for exercising those rights. He showed his "true believer" side by devoting long hours to grilling witnesses on the assumption that he could force them to confess their subversive ties or contradict their previous statements and perjure themselves. His cynical side came out when he gave reporters distorted versions of the testimony, selectively quoting them and overstating the case against them. A lack of evidence rarely deterred him, and he seemed to believe that any tactic was justifiable in combating an international conspiracy. His public hearings opened with headline-grabbing fanfares and then ended without resolution as the subcommittee shifted to another subject. Robert F. Kennedy, who served as a member of McCarthy's staff in 1953 before becoming the Democrats' minority counsel in 1954, commented that no real research was ever done: "Most of the investigations were instituted on the basis of some preconceived notion by the chief counsel or his staff members and not on the basis of any information that had been developed."

Interrogations

Chairman McCarthy started his investigations, in January 1953, by returning to the familiar territory of the State Department. He examined irregularities in the department's filing system that might have permitted Communists to avoid detection. When nothing startling turned up, he shifted abruptly to the United States Information Agency (USIA) to find out why it had books by known Communist writers on its library shelves. Rather than call the library administrators, McCarthy subpoenaed the authors of the questionable books, grilling left-leaning authors about their politics and encouraging them to renounce their past writings. During a congressional recess in the spring of 1953, Cohn and Schine traveled to Europe to tour USIA libraries. The European media mocked them as junketing "book burners." Eventually the subcommittee learned that the USIA had not bought any of the books—they had been donated by well-wishing citizens to American soldiers during World War II. The army had given them to the libraries after the war, and the USIA had chosen not to eliminate books by radical authors, on the premise that the collection should reflect the wide range of opinion that existed in a democracy. McCarthy's investigation reversed this policy, and the libraries hastened to remove anything controversial from their shelves.

Neither McCarthy nor Cohn paid much attention to administrative details, and Cohn's brusque personality antagonized others on the staff. Disorganization and personnel turnover persuaded the chairman to appoint J. B. Matthews as staff director in June 1953. A former "fellow traveler" (the term used to describe someone who adopted the Communist Party line without joining the party), Matthews had collected extensive files on suspected Communists as director of research for HUAC from 1938 to 1945. Soon after he took the job, Matthews's article on "Reds and Our Churches" appeared in the *American Mercury* magazine, accusing Protestant clergymen of being the largest single group supporting "the Communist apparatus in the United States." This caused a public uproar, and Democrats on the subcommittee demanded Matthews's dismissal. The Democratic minority had cooperated with McCarthy until then, but his hiring of staff without prior consultation had grown too arbitrary to tolerate. Senator Potter signaled that he intended to vote with the Democrats, which compelled McCarthy to announce Matthews's resignation. In July, he named Francis P. Carr, a former FBI agent, as the committee's executive director, while turning down the three Democratic senators' request to hire a minority counsel. The three senators resigned from the subcommittee in protest, so for the rest of that year, the chairman operated without minority-party senators to keep him in line. By holding hearings outside Washington, often at short notice, he was often the sole senator present.

McCarthy bent Senate rules that required committees to vote on issuing individual subpoenas by providing his staff with blank subpoenas that they issued "as regularly as traffic tickets," according to the army's chief counsel, John G. Adams. Witnesses complained of receiving notice to appear on the night before or the morning of the hearing, forcing them to rush to obtain legal representation. Even if lawyers accompanied witnesses, the chairman would not permit them to raise objections or to talk for the witnesses. Senate committees normally required a quorum of one-third of their members to take sworn testimony, although they also allowed a single senator to hold hearings if authorized by that committee. McCarthy's "one-man rule" gave witnesses the impression that they were facing "judge, jury, prosecutor, castigator, and press agent, all in one," according to Adams. On occasions when even McCarthy was absent, Cohn held "staff interrogatories" that resembled committee hearings. Schine would preside, with Cohn addressing him as "Mr. Chairman."

Behind closed doors, McCarthy and Cohn interrogated more than 500 witnesses, confronting them with the allegations against them in an attempt to force confessions. When witnesses exercised their right under the Fifth Amendment to the Constitution not to answer questions that might incriminate them, McCarthy interpreted this as tantamount to an admission of guilt and branded them as "Fifth Amendment Communists." During McCarthy's two years as chairman, 106 witnesses invoked the Fifth Amendment in their public testimony. Nine others cited the First Amendment to justify their refusal, two claimed marital privileges, and one who did not respond declined to invoke any constitutional grounds. Taking the Fifth Amendment generally cost the job of anyone who worked in the federal government, for a defense contractor, or as a public school teacher.

The Justice Department in 1948 had defined the Communist Party as advocating the overthrow of the U.S. government by force and violence, and the Supreme Court, in *Dennis v. U.S.* (1951), had upheld convictions obtained under that premise. Active Communists therefore took the Fifth Amendment; but if witnesses no longer belonged to the party, why were they still reluctant to talk about it? Former party members and fellow travelers might have admitted their own pasts, except that would have exposed them to a line of questioning that required them to "name names" of others with whom they had associated, including family and friends. They asserted their Fifth Amendment protection, but in *Rogers v. U.S.* (1951) the Supreme Court had ruled that a witness could not refuse to answer questions simply out of a "desire to protect others from punishment, much less to protect another from interrogation by a grand jury." The Justice Department assured McCarthy that he had authority as a congressional investigator to order witnesses to answer questions about the identities of any Communists who might be working for the government.

While court rulings backed McCarthy's assumptions, the Federal Bureau of Investigation provided him with little help. FBI Director J. Edgar Hoover maintained a friendship with the senator, but Hoover worried that McCarthy's charges made it look as if the FBI was not doing its job. The only reports the subcommittee obtained from the FBI came through back channels, via personal contacts by the former FBI agents serving on the subcommittee's staff. The subcommittee relied instead on information from "people outside of Government," particularly from patriotic organizations and former Communists, and from "certain people in Government" who leaked information about possible security risks. Cohn acknowledged that the success or failure of their investigations depended upon what they could get from within the executive branch. "If we don't get it," he said, "we are out of business." This made the subcommittee dependent upon the cooperation of

Roy M. Cohn, chief counsel to the Government Committee on Operations of the Senate, confers with Senator Joseph McCarthy during the Army-McCarthy hearings, 1954. (Library of Congress)

disgruntled security officers who questioned their agencies' official loyalty review process, such as allegations of security risks among civilian personnel of the Army.

The origins of McCarthy's investigation of the U.S. Army were disputed, but the inquiry quickly became intertwined with Schine's draft status. In July 1953, a nationally syndicated column by the well-known journalist Drew Pearson asked how Cohn and Schine had managed to evade the military draft. Cohn had joined the National Guard, but Schine, who looked healthy, had been classified 4-F (or physically unfit for military service). The glare of publicity caused Schine's draft board to reexamine his case and reclassify him 1-A. As soon as McCarthy saw Pearson's column, he called the army's chief congressional liaison, Major General Miles Reber, and asked that Schine be commissioned an officer. Schine said that he was willing to go right away to the Pentagon and "hold up my hand." Reber sent the request to three divisions of the army, as well as the navy and air force, but none found Schine qualified for a commission. Once Schine received notice that he would be drafted as a private, Cohn began making demands on army officials that he be released from basic training and temporarily detailed back to the subcommittee.

According to McCarthy and Cohn, the army investigation began months before Schine's draft notice arrived. In April 1953, President Eisenhower had issued Executive Order 10450 requiring all federal agencies to reinvestigate and "readjudicate" cases of staff with any information in their files regarding loyalty and security. In line with this order, the army's intelligence unit, known as G-2, reopened the files of the civilian engineers at the Army Signal Corps laboratories at Fort Monmouth, New Jersey, whom they had previously investigated and cleared. Although he could not recall the date when it occurred, McCarthy said that he received a phone call from "someone in the army" who was disturbed because the FBI had reported Communist infiltration of the top-secret laboratories at Fort Monmouth, and that "nothing was being done" about it. From an army intelligence officer, the subcommittee obtained a copy of a letter from FBI director Hoover regarding security risks at the labs. Cohn further claimed that during the spring "various members of the staff" had received information about Communist infiltration of army installments.

Yet, while the subcommittee communicated regularly with the army about other investigations during these months—on the level of the sale of gift cigarettes by army personnel in South Korea—it sounded no alarms about espionage. Not until the end of August 1953 did it hold any executive-session hearings on civilians working for the army. A week later, McCarthy and Cohn invited the secretary of the army, Robert Ten Broeck Stevens, to a breakfast at Schine's spacious apartment in the Waldorf Astoria Towers in New York City (they often used Schine's apartment and limousine while holding hearings in Manhattan) to discuss the subcommittee's investigation of the Army, and Schine's desire for a commission. Eager to avoid controversy, Stevens—until recently an executive in his family's textile mills—assured the chairman and his counsel of his willingness "to correct anything that may be wrong."

As a subcommittee of one, McCarthy held closed hearings on civilian employees in the Army at the federal courthouse in New York City. His lead witness, Doris Walters Powell, was a 31-year-old African American clerk-stenographer for the New York Quartermaster Corps who had been on maternity leave for the past year. McCarthy informed her that he had information about her Communist Party membership, and that if she lied about it they would prosecute her for perjury. When Cohn asked her if she had ever been a member of the Communist Party, she replied, "I don't feel as though I have been—not to my knowledge." Nervously, she recounted how during her earlier employment, from 1944 to 1948, as a secretary for the *People's Voice* newspaper in Harlem, there had been "a lot of disturbance" in the office that had made her suspicious. She testified that she had been given a card to attend some lectures on "Negro history," which she came to realize were organized by the Communist Party.

Despite its radical-sounding title, the *People's Voice* had been founded by a Baptist preacher, Adam Clayton Powell Jr., to promote his political career. Doris Walters Powell (no relation to Adam Clayton Powell Jr.) was his secretary. When Adam Clayton Powell was elected to Congress in 1944, she continued to work for his successor as editor, Doxey Wilkerson, who was also an official in the Communist Party (CP). She told McCarthy that in 1948 she raised questions about Communist activities at the *People's Voice* and "got together with a whole lot of the editorial staff trying to find out who was Communist. I got very unpopular when I found out it was a Communist organization. I wanted to get the paper for the benefit of the Negro people, and I had gotten together with this group who were found to be Communists."

Brushing aside her explanations, McCarthy told reporters waiting outside the hearing room that he had interviewed a "Miss Q" who posed a serious threat to military security. Although Doris Walters Powell's job in the army was clerical and involved no classified information, McCarthy extrapolated that her access to paperwork on food shipments enabled her to learn troop movements. When she returned to testify, her lawyer protested the lurid accounts that had appeared in the press. McCarthy dismissed his concerns: "If the papers called her a card-carrying Communist, there is no control that we have over that." Without hope of getting her job back, Powell this time took the Fifth Amendment when asked if she had ever been a member of the Communist Party.

To build his case, McCarthy called Marvel Jackson Cooke, a known Communist who had worked at the *People's Voice*. She refused to answer his questions about whether she or Doris Walters Powell had been Communists. McCarthy cautioned her in regard to Doris Walters Powell: "You understand, of course, that when you refuse to state whether Doris Walters was a Communist on the ground a truthful answer might tend to incriminate you . . . in effect, so far as the committee is concerned, you are saying she is a Communist, and I assume she is a friend of yours." To McCarthy, her silence confirmed his assumptions; but he was wrong. Years later, in an oral history, Cooke commented on the irony that Walters, a "Red-baiter," had lost her job with the army because she was a suspected Communist: "Anytime we would have a union meeting and a progressive motion came before the floor you would hear this sibilant whisper: 'CP! CP! CP!' I hated that woman! Her name was Doris Walters. . . . Not even a good trade unionist. . . . And certainly not a Communist."

Besides Doris Walters Powell ["Miss Q"], McCarthy interrogated a security guard, Francesco Palmiero, from the Army Signal Corps Photographic Center, who had once signed a Communist Party nominating petition. He denied being a Communist Party member but was suspended from his job after his battered former wife testified that he said he "liked Stalin." While Powell and Palmiero were decidedly small fish, Senator McCarthy demanded that the Army produce the names and personnel files of those individuals higher up who had shielded them, arguing that the members of the Army loyalty board who had cleared Miss Q had been either "incompetent beyond words, or in sympathy with Communism." Schine phoned the office of Army Secretary Stevens to set up an appointment on the matter. Troubled over the escalating inquiry, Stevens hired John G. Adams as the department's legal counselor, assigning him to handle problems with McCarthy.

Allegations of Espionage

On September 29, 1953, Senator McCarthy was married in a ceremony attended by Stevens and a host of other Washington dignitaries. During the chairman's honeymoon, Cohn and Schine looked into the complaints of security officers at the Army Signal Corps laboratories in Fort Monmouth, over their inability to dislodge suspected security risks. During World War II, the FBI and Army intelligence had investigated reports of Communists working at the Signal Corps laboratories, which were engaged in highly classified work on the development of radar. These inquiries led to the wartime dismissal of three electrical engineers, Julius Rosenberg, Joel Barr, and Alfred Sarant. Losing their government

Close-up photographs of Senator Joseph R. McCarthy taken while Army Secretary Robert T. Stevens was testifying at the Army-McCarthy hearings. (Library of Congress)

jobs for being security risks did not prevent them from getting work with private defense contractors that supplied the Signal Corps. In 1950, Rosenberg was arrested and charged with delivering information about the atom bomb to the Soviet Union. Barr and Sarant defected to Moscow. The FBI interrogated everyone at Fort Monmouth who had any connection to them. G-2 military intelligence officers looked into the possibility that espionage might still be going on at Fort Monmouth, but they found no substantial evidence.

Convicted of conspiracy to commit espionage, Julius Rosenberg and his wife, Ethel, were executed on June 19, 1953. Following the massive publicity that surrounded these executions, Cohn became convinced that he could expose remnants of a Rosenberg spy ring at Fort Monmouth, where the rest of the federal government had failed. The subcommittee had obtained a letter from FBI director Hoover to the head of Army G-2, identifying Aaron Coleman and several other scientists, engineers, and technicians at Fort Monmouth as possible security risks. Coleman's name "rang a bell" with Cohn, who recalled that it had been mentioned in the course of Julius Rosenberg's espionage trial. With this evidence, Cohn flew to West Palm Beach to meet with the vacationing McCarthy. "I brought some of the transcripts of the testimony with me," Cohn later recalled, "and I told him that there had been a few suspensions, but there were still a sizable number of people working in the secret radar laboratories at Fort Monmouth with records of Communist affiliation to a greater or lesser degree." At Cohn's urging, McCarthy cut short his honeymoon and dramatically returned to Washington to hold hearings.

What purported to be a Hoover letter was actually an excerpt from a longer letter that Hoover had sent to Army G-2 in 1951. The original letter made no specific allegations of espionage or subversion, but cataloged all of the unsubstantiated allegations collected during FBI field examinations regarding Julius Rosenberg. The subcommittee staff also learned of intelligence reports about an East German defector who had seen microfilmed copies of documents that had originated at Fort Monmouth. The army had concluded that the United States had turned over the microfilmed documents to the allied Soviet government under Lend-Lease agreements during World War II. Throughout the war, Soviet representatives had been stationed at Fort Monmouth and had access to classified material in the laboratories. During the war's last months, one security officer counted 286 Russian officers living on the post. The Hoover letter had prompted G-2 to conduct its own investigation, but the army had reprimanded some of these security officers for making unfounded accusations that fostered antagonism among personnel at the base. Despite the failure to uncover subversion, the camp's commanding officer, Major General Kirke B. Lawton, had complained about the potential security risks among the large number of engineers who had attended such "left-wing" schools as the City College of New York (CCNY).

The academically rigorous CCNY provided a tuition-free education for those who could not afford it, primarily to students from New York City's immigrant communities. During the depression, it had been a hotbed of radical politics, reflecting a feeling prevalent among students that the economic collapse called for noncapitalist solutions. Young socialists and communists debated and played table tennis against each other in the alcoves of the student center. After graduation, social prejudices denied Jewish graduates jobs in the city's more prestigious engineering firms, and many of them applied instead for work in the government. Julius Rosenberg had been one of the CCNY-trained engineers hired by the Army Signal Corps. With his arrest for espionage, all of his classmates working at Fort Monmouth fell under suspicion.

Major General Lawton, exercising his authority as base commander, suspended 42 Signal Corps employees. The first suspensions occurred on August 19, 1953, just prior to the subcommittee's hearings, and the rest were made by mid-October, while the hearings were in full swing. All of the suspended employees subpoenaed by the subcommittee had been previously interviewed by the FBI and Army G-2. In light of McCarthy's hearings, FBI agents reopened their Fort Monmouth investigations, but they concluded that there was no proof to support charges of a spy ring. An internal FBI report reasoned this would not stop the congressional proceedings, since "Cohn is smart enough to know that it is not necessary for him to produce factual evidence to establish an espionage connection."

The Jewish service organization B'nai B'rith provided the suspended engineers with legal counsel on the suspicion that they were victims of anti-Semitism. "Well, that is an outrageous assumption," Cohn responded. "I am a member and officer of B'nai B'rith." One of his witnesses suggested that Cohn "look at the statistics." Thirty-nine of the 42 suspended were Jewish. One of them, Louis Leo Kaplan, testified that he believed he had been confused with another Louis Kaplan who had written pro-Communist letters to the local newspaper. When Cohn later interviewed a Jacob Kaplan, who also had been suspended despite having had no contact with any Communists, it dawned on him that the army had suspended "everybody with the name of Kaplan." The

Louis Kaplan who had written the inflammatory letters to the editor had run a nearby agricultural cooperative.

Army Secretary Stevens met frequently with McCarthy and Cohn, alternately discussing Fort Monmouth and David Schine. Insisting that he would oppose Communist infiltration of the army to the best of his ability, Stevens tried to persuade them that Army G-2 could investigate Fort Monmouth and send the subcommittee progress reports. McCarthy rebuffed this offer with the assertion that "G-2 was badly infiltrated by Communists." Despite Stevens's efforts, McCarthy went public with allegations after an executive session on October 15, telling reporters that the recently executed Julius Rosenberg had formed a Communist spy ring at Fort Monmouth during World War II, and he believed it was still operating in the top-secret laboratories. Stevens considered these charges spurious and privately expressed his dismay over Lawton's suspension of so many engineers at Fort Monmouth. "When he suspends a fellow because he lives next door to a person who thought he was a Communist," Stevens told the head of Army intelligence, ". . . it is going to make us look foolish." The army removed Lawton from his command and retired him for reasons of health.

The day after he broke the news of a "Rosenberg spy ring," Senator McCarthy stepped out of a closed hearing to tell reporters that a witness had broken down and cried after "some rather vigorous cross-examination by Roy Cohn." The senator added, "I have just received word that the witness admits that he was lying the first time and now wants to tell the truth." Although McCarthy declined to name the witness, reporters had seen the ashen-faced man escorted from the closed hearing and identified him in their stories as Carl Greenblum. Once his name appeared in the papers, a hammer and a sickle were painted on his house. The truth, as it emerged, was far less incriminating than McCarthy intimated.

Greenblum's mother had died, and he was sitting shivah (a Jewish ritual mourning) when he was subpoenaed to testify. Another witness, Joseph Levitsky, who had taken the Fifth Amendment when asked if he had ever been a member of the Communist Party, testified that before World War II he had shared a car pool to the Signal Corps with Greenblum and Julius Rosenberg. Greenblum denied knowing whether Levitsky had been a Communist or having associated with Rosenberg. Cohn pressed him on the car pool, insisting that he must have lied about not having contact with Rosenberg since he rode with him every day for months in a car pool. One of them had committed perjury, McCarthy conjectured, "and we intend to have the man who was guilty of perjury prosecuted." Greenblum grew visibly distraught, and the subcommittee recessed for lunch to let him think over his testimony. When they resumed, Greenblum said that he wanted to clear the record. He confessed that he knew Levitsky had been a Communist at CCNY. In those days, Greenblum had been a member of the Trotskyite Young Socialists, who despised Stalinists. He insisted that he had no contact with Rosenberg after they left school. McCarthy kept pressing him: "It seems to me that knowing Rosenberg, he having been executed for espionage since then, it should ring a very definite bell in your mind if, as Levitsky has testified, you rode in this car pool over a period of about two months." It took another witness to unravel the mystery, explaining that Greenblum had replaced Rosenberg in a group apartment. They had not overlapped and had never ridden together in the same car pool.

McCarthy thought he had a stronger case against Greenblum's section chief, Aaron Coleman, since Rosenberg himself had admitted inviting Coleman to attend a Young Communist League meeting at CCNY, and had talked of contacts with him later in the Army Signal Corps. The Civilian Personnel Office at Fort Monmouth gave Coleman's personnel file to the subcommittee without removing information regarding his security investigations, contrary to the presidential directive. From the unexpurgated file, the subcommittee staff learned that he had been suspended for 10 days in 1946 after G-2 officers found classified material in his apartment. It was this combination of evidence that had encouraged McCarthy to tell reporters in 1953 that Rosenberg's spy ring might still be at work at Fort Monmouth. Coleman became the centerpiece of that investigation and was called repeatedly to testify in private and public.

As a witness, Coleman disappointed the chairman. Rather than confess or stonewall, he offered explanations for the evidence against him. In 1938, when he was a 19-year-old student, he had accompanied his classmate Rosenberg to a Young Communist League meeting because Rosenberg had urged him to keep an "open mind." He arrived late and left before the meeting ended, unimpressed by so much ranting. As a commuter from Brooklyn to the Manhattan campus, he had no time for any extracurricular activities, political or otherwise. He did not recall having seen Rosenberg in the Army Signal Corps laboratories, suggesting this was because travel related to their jobs kept both of them away from Fort Monmouth for long periods.

During World War II, Coleman took a leave of absence from the Signal Corps to serve as a radar officer in the Marine Corps. When he returned to Fort Monmouth in January 1946, he took work home with

Army counsel Joseph Welch, left, and Senator Joseph McCarthy, right, during the Army-McCarthy hearings in 1954. (Library of Congress)

him at night to catch up with developments in the program during his absence. In September 1946, a security guard questioned him about documents he was removing from the base. Coleman allowed G-2 officers to search his apartment, where they found 43 documents, a few of them classified. He explained that his superiors had authorized him to check out documents, some of which were his personal notes, but G-2 reprimanded him for storing the documents under his bed rather than in a safe. His suspension for "carelessness" was balanced by official praise for his "outstanding record of achievement" in radar research and development, and it did not prevent his later being promoted to division chief. Following Rosenberg's arrest, the FBI interviewed Coleman and other engineers—the subject of Hoover's letter to G-2. Still suspicious, in January 1952 the army lifted Coleman's security clearance and assigned him to a nonsecure building outside the post. It suspended him when the subcommittee called him to testify.

Having uncovered nothing new against Coleman, McCarthy and Cohn applied a sinister spin. When Coleman said he could "only guess" why he had removed those particular documents seven years earlier, McCarthy snapped, "You can only guess why you stole secrets from the radar laboratories?" Coleman responded, "I am sorry, sir, but I did not steal." McCarthy described the 1946 search of his apartment as a "raid," although Coleman had signed a waiver to permit the search without a warrant. Cohn referred to the "secret" meeting of the Young Communist League he had attended, but Coleman insisted that it had been an open meeting. Coleman objected to their conflating recent events with those that had happened before the cold war began, and reminded the committee that things had changed: "When we realized that Russia is our enemy, and everybody didn't realize that in 1946, and we didn't know, everybody didn't know that the Communists were infiltrating the Government at that time, that a guy sitting next to you might be a Communist. We were fighting a different kind of enemy, and he didn't use that type of word, and everybody here in this room knows that there is a difference between 1946 and 1953."

As a rebuttal witness, the subcommittee called Nathan Sussman. In an interview with the FBI, Sussman had named Coleman as a member of the Young Communist League. In his executive-session testimony, however, Sussman had no definite memory of Coleman at league meetings. He thought he "probably" had met Coleman there, but he explained that Coleman had been two years behind him at CCNY, that he never saw him again after graduation, and that he had no idea whether Coleman had joined the Communist Party. McCarthy therefore kept Sussman's public testimony brief, allowing no more than a flat assertion that Coleman had been a member of the Young Communist League.

In the end, McCarthy conceded to Coleman's lawyer that he could produce no witnesses who saw Coleman turn over any material to an enemy agent, but he insisted that the mere act of removing classified documents from the Signal Corps laboratories had been a violation of the Espionage Act. At a news conference, Senator McCarthy linked Coleman to the Signal Corps documents that had surfaced in East Germany—despite his lack of any evidence to support that charge—and announced that the subcommittee would refer the case to the Justice Department to seek Coleman's indictment. When Justice Department attorneys found insufficient grounds to prosecute, Coleman appealed to the courts to get his job back. In 1958, the army reinstated him, and he continued to work for the Signal Corps until his retirement in 1978.

For all the fireworks, McCarthy's investigation of Fort Monmouth brought out little that the Army did not already know. At the same time, the subcommittee's work managed to cast the Army in a poor light in the newspapers. As part of his campaign to appease McCarthy, army secretary Stevens accompanied him and Cohn on a personal tour of the Signal Corps laboratories on October 20. The gesture backfired, however, when guards stopped Cohn from entering the laboratories on the grounds that he lacked the necessary security clearances. Army officers who stood outside with Cohn described him as extremely upset. "They let Communists in and keep me out," he protested, embarrassed that reporters had seen him denied entry. "We will now really investigate the army." Cohn later admitted his anger but denied the vituperation. The next day, in a phone call to the army secretary, Schine learned that he could not avoid basic training. Cohn stepped up pressure on army officials for them to furlough Schine to the subcommittee. When Schine entered the military on November 3, the army granted him temporary duty in New York, where the closed-door hearings on Fort Monmouth were under way.

News of Private Schine's special treatment was leaked to Drew Pearson, who realized that the Pentagon's catering to Cohn's incessant demands could turn the incident into a "national rhubarb." The columnist collected evidence of Schine's being excused from KP duty and guard duty, fraternizing with officers, and receiving excessive leave. On December 22, Pearson ran his fifth column on Schine in six months. While this column failed to attract attention from the rest of the news media, it encouraged the army to launch an internal investigation. Not until March 1954, when stories surfaced that the army had been monitoring Cohn's telephone calls and had transcripts of his intercessions for Schine, did other news reporters pick up the story. The transcripts revealed Cohn's fixation with Schine, and McCarthy's lack of enthusiasm for him. "For God's sake, don't put Dave in service and assign him back to my committee," McCarthy implored Stevens in a call before Schine's induction. "If he could get off weekends—Roy—it is one of the few things I have seen him completely unreasonable about. He thinks Dave should be a general and work from the penthouse of the Waldorf."

Stevens invited McCarthy for lunch at the Pentagon on November 6. The army secretary protested the army's "constant hammering in the headlines" and said that the image of spying at Fort Monmouth "was not in accordance with the facts." McCarthy demanded more information about the members of the army's loyalty boards. He wanted to know who in the hierarchy had cleared these lower-level security risks. Recounting his earlier investigation of the Government Printing Office (GPO), where he had uncovered some printers with Communist leanings, he advised Stevens that those hearings had been shortened by the "complete, 100 percent, not lip-service, but actual cooperation" the subcommittee received from Raymond Battenberger, the head of the GPO. The analogy was faulty, however, since the GPO was a legislative-branch agency and Battenberger, the public printer, worked directly for Congress. The same did not hold true when the subcommittee examined the army, which took its orders from the commander in chief.

President Eisenhower despised McCarthy but refused to "get into the gutter" with him through an open confrontation. McCarthy thrived on publicity, he believed, and the best course would be to ignore him. Yet Eisenhower could not hide his irritation over McCarthy's investigation of the army, the institution in which he had spent most of his adult life prior to the presidency. He had no intention of permitting McCarthy access to the names and files of members of the loyalty boards in the Army or any other federal agency. Eisenhower perceived that McCarthy would cause more trouble if congressional committees could force loyalty boards to justify their decisions and defend their own loyalty. He therefore kept in force former president Truman's executive order: "No information shall be supplied as to any specific intermediary steps, proceedings, transcripts of hearings or actions taken in processing an individual under loyalty of security programs."

The Subcommittee's Hearings

The subcommittee's public hearings on the Army Signal Corps opened on November 24, 1953, and adjourned on March 11, 1954. The open hearings mixed current and former employees as witnesses, creating confusion over whether those who took the Fifth Amendment still had some connection with the laboratories. As the only senator present at most of the hearings, McCarthy held twice-a-day news conferences in which he promised to produce proof of ongoing espionage. By January 1954, the publicity had elevated him to his highest point of public esteem in the polls, with a majority of Americans indicating they believed his charges of Communist infiltration of the government. At the same time, the hearings laid the groundwork for his downfall. McCarthy summoned Gen. Andrew J. Reid, the G-2 chief at Fort Monmouth, but the general drew his ire by declining to violate the president's directive against providing information on government loyalty investigations, marking the beginning of a pattern that would provoke the chairman to throw tantrums.

As much as McCarthy relished not having to share the spotlight, when the second session of the 83rd Congress convened in January 1954, the Democrats' boycott jeopardized his subcommittee's appropriations. Members of the Senate Appropriations Committee threatened to cut off the subcommittee's funds, and other senators called on their colleagues to restrict the subcommittee's scope and prohibit it from overlapping other committees' jurisdictions. Senator McCarthy called this "a vote against the exposure of spies and saboteurs," but he backtracked at a subcommittee meeting, agreeing to let the Democrats hire a minority counsel and requiring confirmation of future staff appointments by a majority of the subcommittee. Senators McClellan, Jackson, and Symington rejoined the subcommittee and selected Robert F. Kennedy as their counsel, and the Senate approved the subcommittee's appropriation.

Then in February, McCarthy's mercurial temper exploded during the testimony of Brigadier General Ralph Zwicker, which dealt with the subcommittee's discovery of an army dentist, Irving Peress, who had been promoted despite having refused to deny his membership in the Communist Party. McCarthy regarded this as a "graphic example" of what was wrong with army security. While even Cohn realized that the system had promoted the dentist because he met the statutory criteria, McCarthy saw more devious forces at work. The

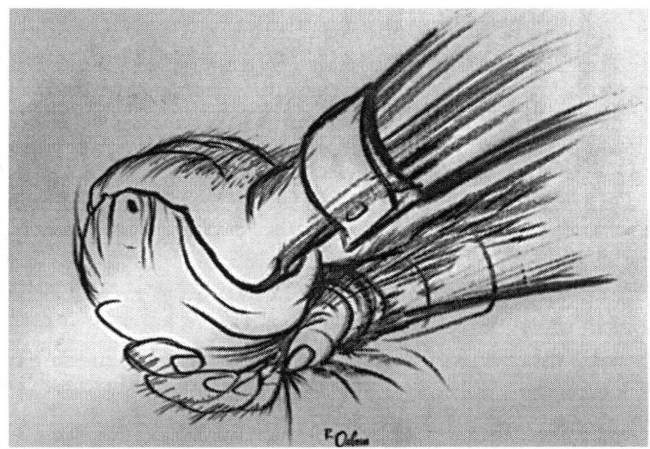

Titled "Silence Dissenters," this 1954 Robert Chesley Osborn drawing shows a man being gagged by the palm of one hand covering his mouth and face, and choked by another hand around his throat. (Library of Congress)

senator's charges boiled down to the headline phrase: "Who Promoted Peress?"

A dentist from Queens, New York, Peress had been commissioned under the Doctors Draft Act, which required him to certify that he was not a member of any organization "advocating a subversive policy." Once inside the Army Dental Corps, Peress declined to answer further questions about his political affiliations, which flagged his case in the Army G-2 files. Peress, who started on active duty on January 1, 1953, was first stationed on the West Coast and then transferred to Camp Kilmer, in New Jersey. While the paperwork from his investigation followed him back and forth, intelligence officers did not seek his immediate dismissal since he did not hold a sensitive position. In October, they briefed Zwicker, the base commander at Camp Kilmer, and he sent a message to the Pentagon recommending Peress's discharge. Two days later came word that Peress had been promoted from captain to major. Peress had applied for the promotion under an amendment to the Doctors Draft Act, which mandated a readjustment in rank for medical officers. Some 1,600 doctors and dentists were promoted under this provision, and his case went through with the rest despite the warnings in his file. As Peress later reflected, "Somebody was eating lunch or making a telephone call when my promotion passed across the desk." Chagrined over its error, the army scheduled Major Peress for release from service on March 31, 1954.

In the interim, someone in the army tipped off the subcommittee (years later, Cohn named Zwicker as the source of this leak). In January 1954, one of McCarthy's staff, George Anastos, called the base for information about an unnamed medical officer being investigated as a member of the Communist Party, and Zwicker volunteered Peress's name and the derogatory information that G-2 had collected against him. Adams, the Army's counsel, also learned that McCarthy's staff was asking about Peress, but he considered the matter settled because of the dentist's pending discharge. McCarthy acted first. On January 30, 1954, he called Peress to an executive session and then told reporters outside the hearing room about all the questions he had refused to answer. In the glare of the publicity that followed, Peress asked that his discharge take effect at once. Army investigators regarded the process for discharging someone for security reasons slow and cumbersome, and preferred the quicker method of a reduction in force, a route that gave Peress an honorable discharge. Having called for a court-martial, McCarthy was outraged. He insisted that the most important issue was not a Communist dentist, but who higher up had protected and promoted him.

In a closed hearing on February 18, Zwicker cited President Truman's executive order prohibiting the release of files relating to loyalty investigations, which the Eisenhower administration had kept in effect, as his reason for not providing information on who had promoted Peress. McCarthy responded with a torrent of abuse: "Any man who has been given the honor of being promoted to general and who says, 'I will protect another general who protected Communists,' is not fit to wear that uniform, General." The attack on Zwicker finally put some starch in army secretary Stevens. He realized that McCarthy was trying to "make somebody the goat," and he could not allow the senator to berate a general without undermining the confidence of the entire officer corps. Stevens issued an order forbidding Zwicker or other officers from giving further testimony, and he refused to provide the subcommittee with the names of those who had promoted and discharged Peress. McCarthy called on the army secretary to stop the "disgraceful coddling of Communists" at Camp Kilmer, and he told reporters that Zwicker had testified that he could do nothing to hold up Peress's discharge. Zwicker disputed this account and accused McCarthy of slanting his testimony. To resolve the dispute, the subcommittee voted to release the transcript of the closed hearing. The record of McCarthy insulting a decorated military officer shocked even his strongest supporters. An editorial in the *Chicago Tribune* advised him to learn to "distinguish the role of investigator from the role of avenging angel."

Had McCarthy been satisfied to cite the Peress case as an example of a flawed security system, the army and the Eisenhower administration would have been willing to concede the point and institute necessary corrections. Lax security, however, lacked the headline appeal of a Communist conspiracy. McCarthy's and Stevens's mutual intransigence threatened a constitutional showdown between the legislative and executive branches. To repair relations, Vice President Richard Nixon convened a group of administration officials and Republican senators. At their urging, Republicans on the subcommittee invited Stevens to a private fried-chicken luncheon at the Capitol on February 24. Assured that the gathering would be off the record, Stevens arrived to find reporters and photographers clustered outside the luncheon room. Inside, the senators persuaded Stevens to permit Zwicker to testify in public and give the committee the names of all who had promoted and honorably discharged Peress. But the memorandum of agreement they produced failed to include the secretary's insistence on proper treatment of military witnesses. Stevens left thinking he had won the encounter, but everyone else read the "chicken lunch" statement as a surrender to McCarthy. That afternoon, the *New York Times* reporter Bill Lawrence called Senator McCarthy to get his views on the luncheon. If Lawrence wanted to be a general, he could arrange it, McCarthy kidded: "I'm running the Army now."

Pentagon officials read wire service reports about the agreement and told Stevens that the senators had gotten the better of him. Badly shaken, Stevens announced that he would never accede to army personnel being abused and humiliated. President Eisenhower's press secretary confirmed that the administration endorsed Stevens's words. Senator Mundt, who had typed the memorandum, commented that the senators thought they had parted on the friendliest terms after the lunch, but by that night "the clouds opened up and the hailstones started running down." To Mundt, it appeared that the Pentagon had "decided to tear the memorandum into shreds and come out swinging."

Stevens had agreed to appear before McCarthy's subcommittee, but before that could take place, Senator McCarthy called a news conference and announced his plan to call a Pentagon employee who handled coded documents despite FBI evidence of her membership in the Communist Party. "This is primarily for Stevens's benefit," McCarthy told the reporters, claiming this would give the army secretary "the full picture" before he testified. His witness was Annie Lee Moss, an African American who had been suspended from her government job because of his inquiry. She would prove another public relations disaster for the chairman. Until then, McCarthy's expansive charges had gained extensive newspaper and television coverage. He had adroitly manipulated reporters, providing his own summaries of executive sessions that they could not attend and making his charges close to their deadlines so there would be no time for fact checking. Even skeptics reported what he said because they lacked the time and resources to disprove it. Most reporters felt constrained by the rules of objective journalism, which prevented them from expressing an opinion about his charges.

Subpoenaed to testify first in closed session, Moss fell ill with bronchitis, so it was not until she appeared before the television cameras at a public hearing that McCarthy had an opportunity to take her measure. Mary Stalcup Markward, a paid FBI informant who had served as membership director and treasurer for the Washington, D.C., branch of the Communist Party, testified that Moss's name and address appeared in the party's membership rolls from 1943 to 1945. "In my position, I knew almost all of the party members in Washington," Markward had previously avowed, but she testified that she had never met Moss and could not identify her personally. In 1943, Moss had joined the Washington Cafeteria Workers Union, a chapter of the United Federation of Workers of America (UFWA), as a condition of getting a job as a pastry cook at the Pentagon. The Congress of Industrial Organizations (CIO) later expelled the UFWA for having Communist leadership. During the two years she belonged to the union, her name and address appeared in the Communist Party's membership rolls. Her family received copies of the *Daily Worker,* but when someone came to collect the subscription fee, she refused to pay, saying she had never subscribed. Subsequently, Moss was interviewed by security officers at several federal agencies where she held low-level jobs, but she always denied having been a Communist, having paid dues, or having attended any party meetings. The FBI, the Army, and the House Committee on Un-American Activities had investigated her inconclusively.

This 1954 Herblock cartoon shows an angry man watching television while holding a newspaper with the headline "Army vs. McCarthy." A man on the television screen is seen pulling down a shade with the phrase "This program has been discontinued temporarily while the committee tries to find a way to discontinue it permanently." (A Herblock Cartoon, copyright by The Herb Block Foundation)

Senator McCarthy dismissed Moss as being "not of any great importance" personally, but he wanted to know "who in the military, knowing that this lady was a Communist, promoted her from a waitress to a code clerk?" He implied that she had access to secret intelligence, although the Army described Moss's position as a relay machine operator who received and transmitted "unintelligible code messages." When she testified at the televised hearing on March 11, 1954, Moss seemed an unlikely threat to the republic. Aware that her pitiful appearance put him at a disadvantage, McCarthy abruptly excused himself and left midway through her testimony. The TV cameras panned his empty seat for the rest of the hearing. Democratic senators, taking advantage of the chairman's discomfort, promised the unemployed woman help in finding another job. The army reinstated Moss, shifting her to a "nonsensitive" post.

McCarthy's handling of Annie Lee Moss contrasted with his treatment of Doris Walters Powell. Despite the senator's claim that he had proved that Powell was a Communist and had gotten her dismissed from her job, he never called her to testify in public. A meek witness would not have played well on television, and McCarthy could more easily claim victory through newspaper accounts, without exhibiting her. Had he interrogated Moss privately, he would not likely have called her back in public, no matter how strong a case he thought he had against her.

The drama of the Annie Lee Moss hearing appealed to McCarthy's leading critic in the media, CBS broadcaster Edward R. Murrow. A week before Moss testified, Murrow had devoted his entire half-hour nationally televised program *See It Now* to Senator McCarthy, saying, "Often operating as a one-man committee, he has traveled far, interviewed many, terrorized some, accused civilian and military leaders of the past administration of a great conspiracy to turn the country over to Communism, investigated and substantially demoralized the present State Department, made varying charges of espionage at Fort Monmouth. The Army says it has been unable to find anything relating to espionage there." Murrow made the Moss hearing the subject of his next program, which aired on March 16, 1954, and created a public furor that astonished the broadcaster. He attributed this reaction to his decision to forgo narration and simply show film clips from the hearing, allowing viewers to draw their own conclusions. Senator McCarthy demanded equal time and went on the program the following week to accuse Murrow of Communist sympathies.

Newspapers reported how Cohn had hectored the army for special treatment for Schine, and members of Congress turned to the Department of Defense for confirmation. The army provided them with the "chronological series of events" that Adams, the army's counsel, had prepared, documenting all the phone calls and meetings that dealt with Schine getting a commission, weekend passes, and other favors. The chronology left the impression that the subcommittee's investigation of the army might have had something to do with easing Schine's life as a soldier. Senator Potter questioned the staff's behavior, and since he held the swing vote on the subcommittee, he jeopardized McCarthy's working majority. Had the chairman been willing to compromise, Potter would have been satisfied with McCarthy's dropping Cohn as chief counsel and promising no further abuse of army brass. Whenever McCarthy felt cornered, however, he instinctively counterattacked. He charged the Army with trying to derail his investigation by holding Schine hostage. The subcommittee members met to consider the charges and countercharges, and determined that their investigation would require that McCarthy relinquish his chairmanship during the inquest. He reluctantly turned the gavel over to Mundt, and agreed that Senator Henry Dworshak, an Idaho Republican sympathetic to his anti-Communist crusade, could replace him on the subcommittee, to maintain the Republicans' one-vote majority.

The Case Against McCarthy

At 10:30 A.M. on April 22, 1954, before an overflowing audience in the Senate Office Building's vast Caucus Room, Senator Mundt gaveled open the first public session of what became known as the Army-McCarthy hearings. For the next nine weeks, the nationally televised hearings captured public attention and allowed citizens to see what McCarthy was all about. The Republican majority appointed Ray Jenkins of Knoxville, Tennessee, as special counsel, while Robert Kennedy served as minority counsel. Since John Adams had become a subject of the inquiry, the army hired a Boston attorney, Joseph N. Welch, to represent its interests. The Iowa-born Welch had graduated Phi Beta Kappa from Grinnell College and won a scholarship to Harvard Law School, before joining the prestigious firm of Hale & Dorr in 1923. A shrewd trial lawyer, his courtroom style blended humor, logic, theatrics, and moral outrage. The subcommittee set rules stipulating that McCarthy could not "participate in the deliberations of the subcommittee; in any of its votes; or in the writing of the report." This meant that, in principle, Senator McCarthy and Secretary Stevens had the same rights during the proceedings. The rules indeed created very different circumstances for McCarthy. He would no longer run the hearings, and opposing counsel could immediately challenge his charges.

"A point of order, Mr. Chairman," McCarthy interjected before anyone could testify. "May I raise a point of order?" Using points of order, he inserted himself into the proceedings in ways that subverted the subcommittee's rules of fairness, seizing the initiative and the spotlight. McCarthy would never have tolerated such grandstanding from another senator when he chaired the subcommittee, but Mundt proved incapable of silencing him, and endless repetition turned "point of order" into a national catchphrase.

As the first witness, the army's congressional liaison, Major General Reber, testified about all the calls he had received from McCarthy and Cohn regarding Schine. When it came McCarthy's turn to interrogate the witness, his key question had nothing to do with Schine. He asked instead: "Is Sam Reber your brother?" McCarthy demanded whether Reber knew that his brother had been forced to resign from the State Department as a "bad security risk" because of his investigation of the USIA libraries. Surprised, Reber replied that he had not known of any investigation of his brother, who had retired from the State Department. McCarthy insisted that his questions went to the issue of motive, but it was guilt by association. He was signaling from the start that he would strike back hard at his critics.

Spectators waited in long lines to view the hearings in the Senate Caucus Room, but far more Americans watched on television. The leading television networks—NBC, CBS, ABC, and DuMont—had planned to film gavel to gavel, but the subcommittee ruled that the television broadcasts could not be interrupted for commercials, and NBC and CBS decided to return to their lucrative daytime programs and run late-night syn-

This Herblock cartoon on the Army-McCarthy hearings shows Senator Joseph McCarthy holding a "doctored photo" and a "faked letter," which he claims are FBI documents. (A Herblock Cartoon, copyright by The Herb Block Foundation)

opses of the hearings instead (NBC later resumed live coverage). Since ABC and DuMont had few sponsored daytime programs, they broadcast the entire hearings live.

For years, McCarthy's critics had accused him of using spurious evidence and waving papers around without letting others examine them closely. The Army-McCarthy hearings were replete with questionable documentation that reinforced that image. Early in the hearings, McCarthy's staff produced a photograph showing Schine standing alone beside Secretary Stevens, to suggest their close relationship. Welch, the army's counsel, denounced it as a "doctored" photograph. McCarthy's staff had cropped a high-ranking military officer out of the picture to make it appear that Schine and Stevens had not been part of a group. Despite McCarthy's denials of any intended deception, the altered photograph became an icon of the hearings, reproduced widely in the media to highlight his ends-justify-the-means tactics.

McCarthy came under similar fire when he produced the letter from Hoover to the Army G-2 about Coleman. Welch pointed out that the copy had not come from the army's files: "And I have an absorbing curiosity to know how in the dickens you got hold of it." When McCarthy declined to name his informant, Welch likened his response to taking the Fifth Amendment. The Army called it a "phony" letter, since it was actually an extract from Hoover's longer letter, retyped to look unique. McCarthy insisted that none of this mattered—that someone had simply removed information not pertaining to Coleman—yet once again the senator left the impression that he had tampered with the evidence. The Hoover letter also made it clear that federal agencies had been investigating possible security risks at Fort Monmouth long before McCarthy and Cohn picked up the trail.

The hearings dragged on for months, and McCarthy grew increasingly testy, interrupting others and then expressing offense over being interrupted himself. When Senator Stuart Symington interjected that McCarthy had been making an argument rather than a point of order, McCarthy snapped, "Oh, be quiet." Watching the kinescopes of his own testimony, which TV rebroadcast each evening, Cohn saw that he had been "brash, smug, and smart-alecky," while McCarthy came across as a "dictatorial, brutal, obstructive, utterly humorless bully." Cohn recognized that McCarthy had grown addicted "to dramatic techniques in presenting information" and had become overly aggressive and dramatic: "He acted on impulse. He tended to sensationalize the evidence he had." McCarthy displayed this behavior daily to television audiences.

Stevens testified that between mid-July 1953 and early March 1954, Schine had been discussed between his department and the subcommittee in at least 65 telephone calls and 19 meetings, and he cited the special privileges the private had received. Under cross-examination, it became clear that Stevens had gone out of his way to appease McCarthy and Cohn whenever possible. While the charge of favoritism had triggered the hearings and consumed most of the testimony, McCarthy countered that the real issue was the attempt to stall his investigation of loyalty boards that had been "clearing Communists." Despite presidential directives by Truman and Eisenhower that barred members of loyalty boards from discussing their cases with congressional committees, McCarthy insisted that no Americans were immune from testifying under subpoena. The army rebutted that if the committee should call members of loyalty boards to testify, it would be only fair for the committee to review all evidence, including unproven allegations.

Rather than concentrate his fire on Stevens, McCarthy painted him as an unwitting pawn. The senator insisted that "somebody is trying to cover up his improper conduct over in the Pentagon, that they are using a fine, not overly experienced Secretary as their tool. These individuals, who they are I don't know, but they are somebody deathly afraid of being exposed." In order to prove that "men who themselves had long Communist records" were passing judgment on the loyalty of others in the army, he demanded the right to call other witnesses, but the Republicans on the subcommittee were not eager to broaden the investigation into the Republican administration. Jenkins, their counsel, dismissed McCarthy's request as "entirely improper," and he made it clear that Stevens and Adams were the only parties in the Pentagon against whom charges would be heard. Then, on May 12, Adams complicated matters by testifying that he had compiled his chronology regarding Schine at the suggestion of the White House chief of staff, Sherman Adams (no relation to John G. Adams), and other high-level administration officials. To prevent the subcommittee from calling them to testify, President Eisenhower sent a letter to Secretary of Defense Charles Wilson on May 17, making an absolute claim of executive privilege. Eisenhower asserted his right to withhold from Congress any information about conversations or communications within the executive branch. McCarthy called this an "iron curtain" designed to obscure the real instigators of the army's charges against him. He had a point, but members of Congress and the news media who would normally have protested such a sweeping executive edict accepted it as necessary to check the renegade senator.

Throughout the hearings, news photographs captured Cohn whispering in McCarthy's ear, giving the impression of a young Svengali manipulating his boss. Gossip circulated about a homosexual relationship between Cohn and Schine—and even about McCarthy, who had married for the first time at age 44 (the allegations ran contrary to his reputation as a womanizer). During an exchange over the disputed photograph of Schine and Stevens, Welch asked whether a witness thought it came from a pixie. McCarthy interrupted to make him define a pixie. "I should say, Mr. Senator," Welch parried, "that a pixie is a close relative of a fairy." Cohn's behavior suggested a personal obsession with Schine, leading to descriptions of the pair as "intimate friends" and "constant companions," but the committee also heard closed-door testimony from Schine's girlfriend, Iris Flores, for whom he had requested all those weekend passes. (Schine later married Miss Universe 1955, with whom he had six children.) The attacks on McCarthy were an ironic twist on his own homophobic denunciations of "those Communists and queers" who he claimed had undermined American foreign policy. He regularly laced his speeches with references to "powder puff diplomacy" and "softness" toward Communism, portraying himself in manly terms as willing to do "a bare-knuckle job" in defense of American freedom.

In June, McCarthy engaged in a verbal confrontation with Symington. To a burst of applause from the audience, Symington said: "I am not afraid of anything about you or anything you got to say, at any time, any place, anywhere." McCarthy responded: "I am glad we are on television. I think millions of people can see how low a man can sink." Soon after that exchange, Welch questioned Cohn on why he had not immediately given information about a spy ring at Fort Monmouth to the army and the FBI: "May I add my small voice, sir, and say whenever you know about a subversive or a Communist or a spy, please hurry." Welch needled Cohn until McCarthy could no longer control himself. He interrupted with an impromptu attack on the army counsel for including on his defense team Fred Fisher, who had once belonged to the National Lawyers Guild, labeled "subversive" by HUAC. By 1954, Fisher was a registered Republican, but Welch had dropped the young lawyer from the army's defense team to avoid giving McCarthy an opening for attack. In a preemptive move, Welch gave the story to the *New York Times*. It appeared buried inside the paper, along with Fisher's picture. The story made no splash since the rest of the news media left it alone. Reviewing it on television during the hearings would broadcast it nationwide. When Welch tried to stop him, McCarthy persisted, rifling through his files and promising to produce the clipping of the news story for the record. Welch then asked for a point of personal privilege. "Until this moment, Senator, I think I never really gauged your cruelty or your recklessness," he said. "Let us not assassinate this lad further, Senator. . . . Have you left no sense of decency?" As the committee then went into recess, McCarthy sat in his chair, shrugging.

The Aftermath

McCarthy's gratuitous attack on the absent lawyer's loyalty, and Welch's emotional condemnation of him for it, served as the climax of the hearings. The incident both deflated McCarthy and invigorated his opponents in the Senate. Welch and Cohn had earlier reached an understanding that if McCarthy said nothing about Fisher, Welch would not bring up the draft-dodging charges against Cohn. According to Cohn, McCarthy had approved the trade, but simply could not restrain himself. Welch may have anticipated this behavior and baited a trap, but McCarthy stepped into it voluntarily. Early in the hearings, McCarthy had advised Cohn that audiences would never remember what any of them said, and instead would retain general impressions. By then, he had forgotten his own advice.

At 6:32 P.M., on June 17, 1954, Senator Mundt adjourned the hearings after 36 days and 2,986 pages of transcripts. Mundt issued "subpoenas" for a party for all the participants on Saturday, but he canceled the affair when Senator Lester Hunt committed suicide in his Senate office that day. A popular Democrat from Wyoming, Hunt shot himself after some of McCarthy's allies in the Senate warned him not to run for reelection or they would expose a homosexual scandal in his family. The incident became a plot device in the reporter Allen Drury's 1959 best-selling novel, *Advise and Consent*, which revealed the dark side of Senate politics.

That summer, Schine resumed his regular army duties, while Cohn went to Biloxi, Mississippi, for two weeks of summer training with the National Guard as a first lieutenant. When Cohn returned to Washington, he learned that Senator Potter intended to vote with the Democrats to fire him. He resigned instead and never again held a government post. As a private attorney, his reputation for ruthlessness attracted some unsavory clients, and he frequently faced charges of unethical conduct. A panel of judges in New York eventually disbarred him. Robert Kennedy—who went on to become attorney general and a U.S. senator—spent the summer of 1954 at a beach house in Cape Cod, where, with the assistance of a former Harvard Law School dean, James M. Landis, he wrote the final report on the Army-McCarthy hearings. Their report was so thorough that the Republicans adopted it as the committee report, minus its conclusions.

The four Republicans on the subcommittee, Senators Mundt, Dirksen, Potter, and Dworshak, absolved McCarthy of exercising improper influence over the army, but they criticized him for not exercising greater discipline over his staff. They condemned Cohn for being "unduly aggressive and persistent" in his dealings with the army on behalf of Schine, but they concluded he had not used the investigation of Fort Monmouth as leverage against the army. They found no evidence of dishonesty or bad faith on the part of Stevens or Adams, but they criticized them for "not registering a vigorous protest with the committee" when the demands grew unreasonable, and accused Stevens of following a "course of placation, appeasement, and vacillation" in dealing with McCarthy and Cohn. The Republican majority recommended that there be no more unpaid consultants on the subcommittee, that staff of the subcommittee no longer have contacts with executive-branch policy makers, and that hearings held outside of Washington be authorized by a majority vote and attended by at least two senators.

The three Democratic senators, McClellan, Jackson, and Symington, drew their own conclusions. The minority considered it improper for McCarthy or Cohn to have made any requests of the army while investigating it. They noted that Schine had received passes for all or part of 34 of the 67 days he had spent in basic training, and there was no evidence he had done any work for the subcommittee during those leaves. They absolved the army of holding Schine hostage and instead criticized army officials for awarding him too many special privileges. They vouched for the loyalty and patriotism of Stevens and Adams and dismissed McCarthy's charges against them as "reckless irresponsibility." However, the Democrats added that "we know of no statute, or of any Executive order, that makes members of loyalty boards immune from subpoena."

On the day after the Army-McCarthy report was released, a select committee created by the Senate opened hearings on censure charges against Senator McCarthy. Heedlessly, the senator made plans to resume investigating the defense industry, which he said had been "completely immobilized" by the Army-McCarthy hearings. His intention of holding hearings in Boston went awry, however, when Senate Majority Leader William F. Knowland denied permission for any committee to meet outside of Washington for the remainder of the session. The subcommittee instead held sporadic executive sessions in Washington, looking into allegations of subversion among defense contractors in New York and Massachusetts, where the Communist-led United Electrical Workers represented some of the employees.

Of the 42 suspended engineers at Fort Monmouth, the Army Signal Corps offered jobs back to all but two. Eleven had been automatically reinstated after the army failed to bring charges against them. Twenty-three were reinstated after hearings or on appeal. A federal court order reinstated another six, including Aaron Coleman. The majority of them chose not to return to the Signal Corps. They had been among the best engineers on the base, and the *Bulletin of Atomic Scientists* lamented that the loss of so many scientists and engineers had "seriously hampered the research and development program."

President Eisenhower had been convinced that he could withstand McCarthy by ignoring him, but even the president acknowledged the powerful impact of the televised Army-McCarthy hearings. The president called Welch to the White House to thank him. Welch responded that he felt he had kept McCarthy in front of the television cameras long enough for the public to see "how disgracefully he acted." Although Eisenhower remained immensely popular, his party lost their majorities in the congressional elections of 1954. After that election, the Senate met in a lame-duck session in December and voted 67 to 22 to condemn McCarthy

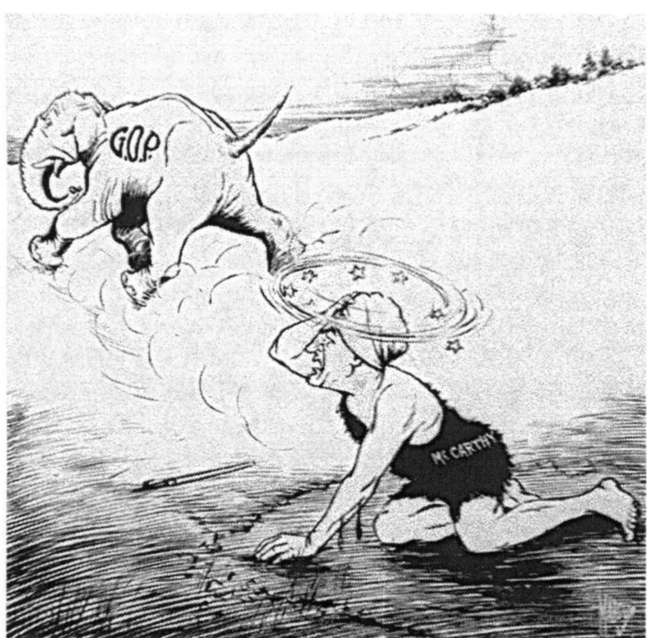

This Edwin Marcus cartoon shows Senator Joseph McCarthy as a battered elephant boy in a turban who has just been thrown off the back of an angry GOP elephant. McCarthy's red-baiting tactics had the reluctant support of most Republicans until he went too far in his televised investigations of the Army in the spring of 1954. In December, many Republicans joined Democrats in condemning his behavior. (By Permission of the Marcus Family)

for conduct "contrary to senatorial tradition." The loss of the majority deprived McCarthy of his chairmanship. Reporters began to ignore his news releases, and his name faded from the front pages. His health and spirit declined rapidly, and he died in 1957 at the age of 48.

As a senator, McCarthy passed no legislation to resolve the issues he raised, and his investigative record proved equally barren. McCarthy had regularly threatened witnesses with indictment for perjury and contempt of Congress, but not a single witness who appeared before him while he chaired the subcommittee went to jail for perjury, contempt, espionage, or subversion. A few witnesses were convicted of contempt, but the courts overturned every case on appeal. The Supreme Court also acted to broaden the rights of witnesses. On June 17, 1957, the high court handed down a set of sweeping decisions that rebuked the investigators' presumptions. In *Yates v. U.S.* the Supreme Court found that joining the Communist Party was not synonymous with advocating the overthrow of the government by force and violence. In *Watkins v. U.S.* the justices decreed that an investigating committee must demonstrate a legislative purpose to justify probing into private affairs, that public education was an insufficient reason to force witnesses to answer questions under the penalty of being held in contempt, and that the Bill of Rights applied in full to those subpoenaed by congressional committees.

The permanent subcommittee revised its rules to require a majority vote to authorize any investigation, issue subpoenas, or hold hearings outside of Washington, and stipulated that a majority of members be present to hear testimony. Despite these reforms, public skepticism of congressional investigations continued until the Watergate investigation in 1973. That committee was chaired by the folksy Democratic senator Sam Ervin of North Carolina, whose self-presentation as "just a country lawyer" resembled Joseph Welch more than Joseph McCarthy. It operated in a bipartisan manner and relied on a diligent and well-prepared staff. Its hearings sent a number of high-level administration officials to prison, led to President Richard Nixon's resignation, and helped pass legislation to rectify the abuses of power it had uncovered. The Watergate hearings demonstrated that a successful investigation requires committee members and staff to treat witnesses with some respect and humanity, to do the necessary homework to compile evidence to build its case, and to rise above any perception of partisanship.

Despite the Senate's rebuke, Joseph McCarthy's supporters later claimed that the Venona intercepts vindicated him. But Venona offered no confirmation of his allegations about a spy ring among the Signal Corps engineers. Fort Monmouth was a dead end for his historical reputation. While espionage had existed during the cold war, the weight of evidence indicates that McCarthy's investigations misled the public about its extent and perpetrators, and misjudged the federal government's determined response to threats against national security.

DOCUMENTS

Speech of Senator Joseph R. McCarthy, Wheeling, West Virginia, February 9, 1950

On February 9, 1950, a little-known, Republican junior senator from Wisconsin named Joseph R. McCarthy addressed a Republican club in Wheeling, West Virginia. Against a restive national fear of Communism in the United States, Senator McCarthy directly charged that the administration of President Harry Truman had allowed Communist sympathizers and traitors to occupy positions of trust and authority within the U.S. government.

Waving a piece of paper, he claimed to have information proving that more than 200 employees in the State Department alone were "card-carrying" members of the Communist Party. Delivered shortly after Alger Hiss, a State Department official, had been convicted of perjury in a case involving espionage, McCarthy's speech ignited an already combustible atmosphere of mistrust and growing fears of treason on the part of the government. McCarthy's great salvo that day in West Virginia gave him a national stage for his crusade against Communism and triggered his rise to the chairmanship of the Senate Permanent Subcommittee on Investigations. It was from that position of power that he would wage a relentless political attack that, in its hysteria and recklessness, would give name to "McCarthyism."

SPEECH OF SENATOR JOSEPH R. McCARTHY, WHEELING, WEST VIRGINIA FEBRUARY 9, 1950

Ladies and gentlemen, tonight as we celebrate the one hundred forty-first birthday of one of the greatest men in American history, I would like to be able to talk about what a glorious day today is in the history of the world. As we celebrate the birth of this man who with his whole heart and soul hated war, I would like to be able to speak of peace in our time—of war being outlawed—and of world-wide disarmament. These would be truly appropriate things to be able to mention as we celebrate the birthday of Abraham Lincoln.

Five years after a world war has been won, men's hearts should anticipate a long peace—and men's minds should be free from the heavy weight that comes with war. But this is not such a period—for this is not a period of peace. This is a time of "the cold war." This is a time when all the world is split into two vast, increasingly hostile, armed camps—a time of a great armament race.

Today we can almost physically hear the mutterings and rumblings of an invigorated god of war. You can see it, feel it, and hear it all the way from the Indochina hills, from the shores of Formosa, right over into the very heart of Europe itself.

The one encouraging thing is that the "mad moment" has not yet arrived for the firing of the gun or the exploding of the bomb which will set civilization about the final task of destroying itself. There is still a hope for peace if we finally decide that no longer can we safely blind our eyes and close our ears to those facts which are shaping up more and more clearly . . . and that is that we are now engaged in a showdown fight . . . not the usual war between nations for land areas or other material gains, but a war between two diametrically opposed ideologies.

The great difference between our western Christian world and the atheistic Communist world is not political, gentlemen, it is moral. For instance, the Marxian idea of confiscating the land and factories and running the entire economy as a single enterprise is momentous. Likewise, Lenin's invention of the one-party police state as a way to make Marx's idea work is hardly less momentous.

Stalin's resolute putting across of these two ideas, of course, did much to divide the world. With only these differences, however, the east and the west could most certainly still live in peace.

The real, basic difference, however, lies in the religion of immoralism . . . invented by Marx, preached feverishly by Lenin, and carried to unimaginable extremes by Stalin. This religion of immoralism, if the Red half of the world triumphs—and well it may, gentlemen—this religion of immoralism will more deeply wound and damage mankind than any conceivable economic or political system.

Karl Marx dismissed God as a hoax, and Lenin and Stalin have added in clear-cut, unmistakable language their resolve that no nation, no people who believe in a god, can exist side by side with their communistic state.

Karl Marx, for example, expelled people from his Communist Party for mentioning such things as love, justice, humanity or morality. He called this "soulful ravings" and "sloppy sentimentality."

While Lincoln was a relatively young man in his late thirties, Karl Marx boasted that the Communist specter was haunting Europe. Since that time, hundreds of millions of people and vast areas of the world have come under Communist domination. Today, less than 100 years after Lincoln's death, Stalin brags that this Communist specter is not only haunting the world, but is about to completely subjugate it.

Today we are engaged in a final, all-out battle between communistic atheism and Christianity. The modern champions of communism have selected this as the time, and ladies and gentlemen, the chips are down—they are truly down.

Lest there be any doubt that the time has been chosen, let us go directly to the leader of communism today—Joseph Stalin. Here is what he said—not back in 1928, not before the war, not during the war—but 2 years after the last war was ended: "To think that the Communist revolution can be carried out peacefully, within the framework of a Christian democracy, means one has either gone out of one's mind and lost all normal understanding, or has grossly and openly repudiated the Communist revolution."

This is what was said by Lenin in 1919—and quoted with approval by Stalin in 1947:

> "We are living," says Lenin, "not merely in a state, but in a system of states, and the existence of the Soviet Republic side by side with Christian states for a long time is unthinkable. . . . One or the other must triumph in the end. And before that end supervenes, a series of frightful collisions between the Soviet Republic and the bourgeois states will be inevitable.

Ladies and gentlemen, can there be anyone tonight who is so blind as to say that the war is not on? Can there be anyone who fails to realize that the Communist world has said the time is now? . . . that this is the time for the show-down between the democratic Christian world and the communistic atheistic world?

Unless we face this fact, we shall pay the price that must be paid by those who wait too long.

Six years ago, at the time of the first conference to map out the peace, there was within the Soviet orbit, 180,000,000 people. Lined up on the antitotalitarian side there were in the world at that time, roughly 1,625,000,000 people. Today, only 6 years later, there are 800,000,000 people under the absolute domination of Soviet Russia—an increase of over 400 percent. On our side, the figure has shrunk to around 500,000,000. In other words, in less than 6 years, the odds have changed from 9 to 1 in our favor to 8 to 1 against us.

This indicates the swiftness of the tempo of Communist victories and American defeats in the cold war. As one of our outstanding historical figures once said, "When a great democracy is destroyed, it will not be from enemies from without, but rather because of enemies from within."

The truth of this statement is becoming terrifyingly clear as we see this country each day losing on every front.

At war's end we were physically the strongest nation on earth . . . and at least potentially the most powerful intellectually and morally. Ours could have been the honor of being a beacon in the desert of destruction . . . shining proof that civilization was not yet ready to destroy itself. Unfortunately, we have failed miserably and tragically to arise to the opportunity.

The reason why we find ourselves in a position of impotency is not because our only powerful potential enemy has sent men to invade our shores . . . but rather because of the traitorous actions of those who have been treated so well by this Nation. It has not been the less fortunate, or members of minority groups who have been traitorous to this Nation . . . but rather those who have had all the benefits that the wealthiest Nation on earth has had to offer . . . the finest homes, the finest college education and the finest jobs in government we can give.

This is glaringly true in the State Department. There the bright young men who are born with silver spoons in their mouths are the ones who have been most traitorous.

Now I know it is very easy for anyone to condemn a particular bureau or department in general terms. Therefore, I would like to cite some specific cases.

When Chiang Kai-shek was fighting our war, the State Department had in China a young man named John Service. His task, obviously, was not to work for communization of China. However, strangely, he sent official reports back to the State Department urging that we torpedo our ally Chiang Kai-shek . . . and stating in unqualified terms (and I quote) that "communism was the only hope of China."

Later, this man—John Service—and please remember that name, ladies and gentlemen, was picked up by the Federal Bureau of Investigation for turning over to the Communists secret State Department information. Strangely, however, he was never prosecuted. However, John Grew, the Under Secretary of State, who insisted on his prosecution, was forced to resign. Two days after, his successor, Dean Acheson, took over as Under Secretary of State. This man, John Service, who had been picked up by the FBI and who had previously urged that communism was the only hope of China, was not only reinstated in the State Department, but promoted . . . and finally, under Acheson, placed in charge of all placements and promotions. Today, ladies and gentlemen, this man Service is on his way to represent the State Department and Acheson in Calcutta, by far and away the most important listening post in the Far East.

That's one case. Let's go to another—Gustavo Duran, who was labeled as (I quote) "a notorious international Communist," was made assistant to the Assistant Secretary of State in charge of Latin American affairs. He was taken into the State Department from his job as a lieutenant colonel in the Communist International Brigade. Finally, after intense congressional pressure and criticism, he resigned in 1946 from the State Department. And, ladies and gentlemen, where do you think he is now? He took over a high-salaried job, as Chief of Cultural Activities Section in the office of the Assistant Secretary General of the United Nations.

Then there was a Mrs. Mary Jane Kenney, from the Board of Economic Warfare in the State Department, who was named in a FBI report and in a House committee report as a courier for the Communist Party while working for the Government. And where do you think Mrs. Mary Jane is—she is now an editor in the United Nations Document Bureau.

Then there was Julian H. Wadleigh, economist in the Trade Agreements Section of the State Department for 11 years. And who was sent to Turkey and Italy and other countries as United States representative. After the statute of limitations had run so he could not be prosecuted for treason, he openly and brazenly not only admitted but proclaimed that he had been a member of the Communist Party . . . that while working for the State Department he stole a vast number of secret documents . . . and furnished these documents to the Russian spy ring of which he was a part.

And, ladies and gentlemen, while I cannot take the time to name all the men in the State Department who have been named as active members of the Communist Party and members of a spy ring, I have here in my hand a list of 205 . . . a list of names that were made known to the Secretary of State as being members of the Communist Party and who nevertheless are still working and shaping policy in the State Department.

One thing to remember in discussing the Communists in our Government is that we are not dealing with spies who get 30 pieces of silver to steal the blue-prints of a new weapon. We are dealing with a far more sinister type of activity because it permits the enemy to guide and shape our policy.

In that connection I would like to read to you very briefly from the testimony of Larry E. Kerley, a man who was with the Counterespionage Section of the FBI for 8 years. And keep in mind as I read this to you that at the time he is speaking there was in the State Department Alger Hiss (the convicted traitor), John Service (the man whom the FBI picked up for espionage), Julian Wadleigh (who brazenly admitted he was a spy and wrote newspaper articles in regard thereto).

Here is what the FBI man said: "In accordance with instructions of the State Department to the Federal Bureau of Investigation, the FBI was not even permitted to open an espionage case against any Russian suspect without State Department approval."

And some further questions:

MR. ARENS. "Did the State Department ever withhold from the Justice Department the right to intern suspects?"

KERLEY. "They withheld the right to get out process for them which, in effect, kept them from being arrested, as in the case of Schevchenko and others."

ARENS. "In how many instances did the State Department decline to permit process to be served on Soviet agents?"

KERLEY. "Do you mean how many Soviet agents were affected?"

ARENS. "Yes."

KERLEY. "That would be difficult to say because there were so many people connected in one espionage ring, whether or not they were directly conspiring with the ring."

ARENS. "Was that order applicable to all persons?"

KERLEY. "Yes, all persons in the Soviet espionage organization."

ARENS. "What did you say the order was as you understood it or as it came to you?"

KERLEY. "That no arrests of any suspects in the Russian espionage activities in the United States were to be made without the prior approval of the State Department."

Now the reason for the State Department's opposition to arresting any of this spy ring is made rather clear in the next question and answer.

SENATOR O'CONNOR. "Did you understand that that was to include also American participants?"

KERLEY. "Yes, because if they were arrested that would disclose the whole apparatus, you see."

In other words they could not afford to let the whole ring which extended to the State Department, be shown.

This brings us down to the case of one Alger Hiss who is important not an individual any more, but rather because he is so representative of a group in the State Department. It is unnecessary to go over the sordid events showing how he sold out the Nation which had given him so much. Those are rather fresh in all of our minds.

However, it should be remembered that the facts in regard to his connection with this international Communist spy ring were made known to the then Under Secretary of State Berle 3 days after Hitler and Stalin signed the Russo-German Alliance Pact. At that time one Whittaker Chambers—who was also part of the spy ring—apparently decided that with Russia on Hitler's side he could no longer betray our Nation. He gave Under Secretary of State Berle—and this is all a matter of record—practically all, if not more, of the facts upon which Hiss' conviction was based.

Under Secretary Berle promptly contacted Dean Acheson and received word in return that Acheson (and I quote) "could vouch for Hiss absolutely"—at which time the matter was dropped. And this, you understand, was at a time when Russia was an ally of Germany. This condition existed while Russia and Germany were invading and dismembering Poland, and while the Communist groups here were screaming "warmonger" at the United States for their support of the Allied nations.

Again in 1943 the FBI had occasion to investigate the facts surrounding Hiss. But even after that FBI report was submitted, nothing was done.

Then late in 1948—on August 5—when the Un-American Activities Committee called Alger Hiss to give an accounting, President Truman and the left-wing press commenced a systematic program of vilification of that committee. On the day that Truman labeled the Hiss investigation a "red herring," on that same day (and listen to this, ladies and gentlemen) President Truman also issued a Presidential directive ordering all government agencies to refuse to turn over any information whatsoever in regard to the Communist activities of any Government employee to a congressional committee.

Incidentally, even alter Hiss was convicted it is interesting to note that the President still labeled the exposé of Hiss as a "red herring."

If time permitted, it might be well to go into detail about the fact that Hiss was Roosevelt's chief advisor at Yalta when Roosevelt was admittedly in ill health and tired physically and mentally . . . and when, according to the Secretary of State, Hiss and Gromyko drafted the report on the conference.

According to the then Secretary of State, here are some of the things that Hiss helped to decide at Yalta. (1) The establishment of a European High Commission; (2) the treatment of Germany—this you will recall was the conference at which it was decided that we would occupy Berlin with Russia occupying an area completely circling the city, which, as you know, resulted in the Berlin air lift which cost 31 American lives; (3) the Polish question; (4) the relationship between UNRRA and the Soviet; (5) the rights of Americans on control commissions of Rumania, Bulgaria and Hungary; (6) Iran; (7) China—here's where we gave away Manchuria; (8) Turkish Straits question; (9) international trusteeship; (10) Korea.

Of the results of this conference, Arthur Bliss Lane of the State Department had this to say: "As I glanced over the document, I could not believe my eyes. To me, almost every line spoke of a surrender to Stalin."

As you hear this story of high treason, I know that you are saying to yourself—well, why doesn't the Congress do something about it. Actually, ladies and gentlemen, the reason for the graft, the corruption, the dishonesty, the disloyalty, the treason in high government positions—the reason this continues is because of a lack of moral uprising on the part of the 140,000,000 American people. In the light of history, however, this is not hard to explain.

It is the result of an emotional hang-over and a temporary moral lapse which follows every war. It is the apathy to evil which people who have been subjected to the tremendous evils of war feel. As the people of the world see mass murder, the destruction of defenseless and innocent people, and all of the crime and lack of morals which go with war, they become numb and apathetic. It has always been thus after war.

However, the morals of our people have not been destroyed. They still exist. This cloak of numbness and apathy has only needed a spark to rekindle them. Happily, this has finally been supplied.

As you know, very recently the Secretary of State proclaimed his loyalty to a man guilty of what has always been considered as the most abominable of all crimes—being a traitor to the people who gave him a position of trust—high treason. The Secretary of State in attempting to justify his continued devotion to the man who sold out the Christian world to the atheistic world, referred to Christ's Sermon on the Mount as a justification and reason therefor.

. . . And the reaction of the American people to this would have made the heart of Abraham Lincoln happy.

Thus this pompous diplomat in striped pants, . . . with a phony British accent, tells the American people that Christ on the Mount endorsed communism, high treason, and betrayal of a sacred trust, this blasphemy was just great enough to awaken the dormant, inherent decency indignation of the American people.

He has lighted the spark which is resulting in a moral uprising and will end only when the whole sorry mess of twisted, warped thinkers are swept from the national scene so that we may have a new birth of honesty and decency in government.

Source: U.S. Senate, 81st Congress, 2nd Session, State Department Loyalty Investigation Committee on Foreign Relations, 1759–63.

Senate Agreement to Investigate the Army-McCarthy Conflict, April 20, 1954

Senator Joseph R. McCarthy's (R-Wis.) trail to ferret out Communists from the U.S. government led him in 1953 to the Army Signal Corps at Fort Monmouth, New Jersey, where he raised the possibility of subversive activities among civilian workers. Antagonizing the military would ultimately lead to McCarthy's downfall, for the army not only fought back against his charges but leveled their own against him and his staff. In November 1953, G. David Schine, a consultant on McCarthy's staff, was drafted into the army. Even before Schine's formal induction, Roy M. Cohn, McCarthy's chief counsel, had begun a personal campaign to pressure military officials into giving Schine special privileges. On March 11, 1954, the army issued a detailed chronology documenting Cohn's improper intrusions into Schine's military career. The charges and countercharges between McCarthy and the Senate Permanent Subcommittee on Investigations on the one hand and the U.S. Army on the other led to a decision to postpone other investigative business of the subcommittee in order to resolve the dispute. Members of the subcommittee voted to hold hearings on the Army-McCarthy matter and to allow live television coverage of the inquiry. McCarthy relinquished the chairmanship to Senator Karl Mundt (R-S.D.) for the duration of the hearings.

SENATE AGREEMENT TO INVESTIGATE THE ARMY-McCARTHY CONFLICT APRIL 20, 1954

The committee met at 4:25 P.M., pursuant to notice, in the office of the Secretary of the Senate, Senator Karl E. Mundt presiding.

Present: Senator Karl E. Mundt, Republican, South Dakota; Senator Henry C. Dworshak, Republican, Idaho; Senator Everett McKinley Dirksen, Republican, Illinois; Senator Charles E. Potter, Republican, Michigan; Senator John L. McClellan, Democrat, Arkansas; Senator Henry M. Jackson, Democrat, Washington; Senator Stuart Symington, Democrat, Missouri.

Also present: Walter L. Reynolds, chief clerk, Government Operations Committee.

SENATOR MUNDT. The committee will come to order. Let me say first of all that as ranking Republican member of the Committee on Government Operations, and in conformity with the memorandum which is herewith submitted in this record, I have at the request of Senator Joseph McCarthy called this meeting today for the purpose of confirming his nomination to the subcommittee on investigations, to replace him during the current investigation, and to take action on the rules which have been recommended to the full committee by the unanimous vote of the subcommittee.

[The memorandum of Senator McCarthy is as follows:]

> I would appreciate it if you would call a meeting of the Committee on Government Operations and act as Chairman thereof for the purpose of presenting to that Committee the Subcommittee rules and the confirmation of another Republican to take such part as set forth in those rules during the current hearing. You are authorized to vote my proxy in favor of the rules which you read to me over the phone and also for the confirmation of Senator Henry C. Dworshak.

I respectfully request that the purpose of the meeting be limited solely to the purposes as set forth above and to rules and other matters that are taken up at that time.

I further request that the meeting be held either today or tomorrow so that this matter may be disposed of before the hearings begin. . . .

SENATOR DIRKSEN. Now, I think as a first order of business, Mr. Chairman, I move that the committee empower the subcommittee, known as the temporary subcommittee of which Senator Mundt of South Dakota is chairman, to proceed with the conduct of the hearings in response to the controversy which has developed.

I move that the committee authorize the special subcommittee to conduct the hearings with respect to the controversy in which we are presently engaged.

SENATOR MCCLELLAN. I second the motion.

SENATOR MUNDT. You have heard the motion made by Senator Dirksen, and seconded by Senator McClellan. Is there any discussion? All in favor say "aye"; contrary minded "no." It is a unanimous vote.

SENATOR MCCLELLAN. Now, I move that Senator Mundt, as the ranking Republican member on the subcommittee since Senator McCarthy has stepped down from the committee, for the purposes of these hearings, be the chairman of this subcommittee for the purposes of these hearings.

SENATOR DIRKSEN. Second the motion.

SENATOR MUNDT. You have heard the motion made by Senator McClellan and seconded by Senator Dirksen. Is there any discussion? Those in favor signify by saying "aye." Contrary? The chair votes present. It is unanimously carried except for the chairman's vote of "present."

SENATOR MCCLELLAN. I move that the actions taken by this subcommittee to date with respect to employing counsel and requiring bills of particular and specifications and charges and so forth be ratified by the full committee. I will add that the full committee authorizes the subcommittee to employ counsel and to ratify the actions taken by the counsel thus far, and to validate all actions taken and obligations incurred with respect to the committee staff.

SENATOR POTTER. That includes issuance of subpoenas?

SENATOR DIRKSEN. Yes.

I second that motion, Mr. Chairman.

SENATOR MUNDT. It is moved by Senator McClellan and seconded by Senator Dirksen and you have all heard it. Is there any discussion? Those in favor signify by saying "aye"; contrary "no." The motion is unanimously approved.

SENATOR DIRKSEN. Now, Mr. Chairman, I move that the rules which have been under consideration and perfected by the deliberations of the subcommittee which were unanimously presented and recommended to us by the subcommittee be approved and adopted.

SENATOR MUNDT. Is there a second?

SENATOR JACKSON. Seconded.

SENATOR MUNDT. Is there any discussion? Those in favor signify by saying "aye"; contrary "no." It is carried.

[The rules are as follows:]

1. For all purposes of these hearings, Senator McCarthy will not participate in any of the deliberations of the Subcommittee; in any of its votes; or in the writing of the report; and he will nominate some other Republican member of the Committee on Government Operations to replace him on the subcommittee during these hearings for such purposes. It is the understanding and the rule of this subcommittee that during these hearings Senator McCarthy or his counsel and counsel for Messrs. Stevens and Adams (or Messrs. Stevens and Adams themselves), or other principals involved in the controversy, shall have the same right to cross-examine as the members of the subcommittee. These same rights shall also prevail for the new Republican member of the subcommittee to be nominated by Senator McCarthy and confirmed by the Committee on Government Operations, and for Messrs. Cohn and Carr, or other principals, or any counsel selected by them.
2. During the course of these hearings, it is the rule of this Subcommittee that counsel for the Subcommittee will first complete his questioning of all witnesses without interruption or limitation as to time, then the Chairman will proceed with questions for a maximum of ten minutes without interruption, then alternating from Democratic to Republican sides of the table and from senior members down the line, each Senator shall proceed with questions without interruption for a maximum of ten minutes. At the conclusion of these questions, Senator McCarthy and Mr. Welch, or those associated with them, shall proceed with questions for a maximum of ten minutes to each side, after which, starting with counsel for the subcommittee, the same procedure will be repeated until all those having questions to ask shall have concluded their interrogatories.
3. All examinations in each case shall proceed without interruption except for objections as to materiality and relevancy.
4. If in the course of the proceedings any motion is presented or any objection is raised by anyone competent to make an objection, and it is submitted to the Committee for its determination and there is a tie vote as to whether the motion will be adopted or the objection sustained, such motion or objection will not prevail.
5. There shall be no votes by proxy except where the absent Senator files with the Chairman of the Committee a wire or letter stating his position upon the specific issue before the Committee and in which

he asks that his vote be recorded and directing the Chairman to record it accordingly.

6. Any matter or issue that may be presented during the course of these hearings not specifically covered by the Special Rules adopted for these hearings, or covered by the standing rules of the Subcommittee, shall immediately be submitted to the Subcommittee for its determination by a majority vote.
7. Any member of the Committee may at any time move that the Committee go into executive session for the purpose of discussing any issue.
8. Where these special rules of the Subcommittee do not apply, the standing rules of the Subcommittee, where applicable, shall control; provided, however, that, where these special rules may conflict with the regular standing rules of the Subcommittee these special rules shall prevail.
9. Because of the peculiar nature of the current controversy and the unusual problems created because of the positions of the individuals involved, these procedural rules are not in any way intended to establish a precedent.

SENATOR DIRKSEN. Now, Mr. Chairman, I move you that the vacancy temporarily occasioned by the action of Senator McCarthy in stepping down for the purposes of these hearings be filled by Senator Dworshak who is nominated by Chairman McCarthy to replace himself.

SENATOR MCCLELLAN. Seconded.

SENATOR MUNDT. It is seconded by Senator McClellan and moved by Senator Dirksen. Is there any discussion? Those in favor signify by saying "aye" contrary "no." Let the record show that the six members have voted "aye"; Senator Dworshak voted "no." If there is no further business, we can adjourn.

SENATOR DIRKSEN. I move the committee do now adjourn.

SENATOR SYMINGTON. Seconded.

SENATOR MUNDT. It is moved and seconded that the full committee now adjourn. Those in favor signify by saying "aye"; contrary "no."

We are adjourned.

[Whereupon, the committee adjourned at 4:40 P.M.]

Source: U.S. Congress, 83rd Congress, 2nd Session, Executive Sessions of the Senate Permanent Subcommittee on Investigations of the Committee on Government Operations, Vol. 5, 1954, 209–12.

Excerpt from Testimony of Secretary of the Army Robert T. Stevens, April 22, 1954

Led by Senator Joseph McCarthy (R-Wis.) and his chief counsel, Roy Cohn, the Senate Permanent Subcommittee on Investigations called hundreds of witnesses, including government officials, for both public and closed sessions. In the spring of 1954, McCarthy picked a fight with the U.S. Army, claiming that a top-secret Army Signal Corps facility at Fort Monmouth, New Jersey, had demonstrated lax security. As various army officers and staff faced down abusive queries from the committee, Secretary of the Army Robert T. Stevens began to suffer criticism from military leaders and the news media that he had been too timid in defending those who served under his command. On April 22, 1954, Stevens, former chairman of a major textile manufacturing company, took his turn before the committee in the witness chair of the Senate Caucus Room. Although Stevens fared rather poorly in his appearances, in the end it was the committee, and McCarthy in particular, that suffered during the month-long Army-McCarthy hearings. With television networks broadcasting gavel-to-gavel coverage, an estimated 22 million viewers watched as McCarthy's badgering of men such as Stevens began to take a toll on the Wisconsin senator's credibility.

EXCERPT FROM TESTIMONY OF SECRETARY OF THE ARMY ROBERT T. STEVENS APRIL 22, 1954

I now turn to the charges made by Senator McCarthy:

1. That I urged the Senator to go after the Navy and the Air Force; and
2. That I am guilty of blackmail.

I would like first to recall briefly at this point certain events arising out of the General Zwicker incident.

On Thursday evening, February 25, I made a public statement from the White House. In that statement I said that from assurances which I had received from members of this committee, I was confident that Army witnesses would not be abused in the future.

Shortly after my statement of February 25 became public, Senator McCarthy said that my statement was "completely false." This was widely quoted in such papers as the New York Times, the Baltimore Sun, and the Washington Evening Star.

In contrast to this, the Washington Post of February 26, the very next day, carried the following comment:

> Subcommittee Member Karl E. Mundt (Republican, South Dakota), however, said he "agreed entirely" with Stevens' statement. Mundt said he felt Stevens was justified in saying he received "assurances" from "members" of the subcommittee, meaning "individual members," about the treatment of witnesses.

A United Press dispatch, also dated February 26, reported as follows:

> Senator Charles E. Potter (Republican of Michigan) also told newsmen "Stevens was absolutely correct" in saying he had received assurances that Army witnesses "would not be browbeaten and humiliated."

Against this background of confirmation of my statement from two members of this committee, I submit for your determination the correctness of Senator McCarthy's charge of "complete falsehood." It is well to bear this incident in mind as we turn to the new attack which Senator McCarthy has made against me.

Now, as to the Senator's charges that I urged him to "go after" the Navy and the Air Force and that I was guilty of blackmail, I call your attention to the fact that these charges have nothing whatsoever to do with the issue raised by Senator Potter's letter as to whether undue influence was used by Senator McCarthy and his staff to obtain preferential treatment for Private Schine.

The first of these charges relates to my luncheon with Senator McCarthy, Cohn, Carr, and Mr. Adams in my office on November 6, which I mentioned earlier.

At this luncheon I commented on the lengths to which I had gone in working with the committee. I said I felt the inquiry by the committee at Fort Monmouth had served its purpose. I thought the Army should itself follow up the suggestions of the committee and take whatever further steps were necessary to eliminate any possible security risks.

I added that I would make progress reports to the committee. However, I did not welcome the damaging effect upon the Army of Senator McCarthy's statements to the press which gave the impression that there was much current espionage at Fort Monmouth, when such was not the case.

The Senator then brought up the plans the committee had to investigate subversion in certain industrial plants engaged in Army work. I told him that the question of security in industrial plants engaged in secret work was of real concern not only to the Army but to the entire Defense Establishment.

The memoranda released March 12 by Senator McCarthy state that I had at this luncheon suggested that the committee "go after" the Navy and the Air Force. At no time on that day, or at any other time, did I suggest that the committee "go after" the Navy and Air Force. The Senator said that the Army would furnish information about the other services. I never made any such statement. I never had any such information. I never supplied any such information.

Gen. Matthew B. Ridgway, Chief of Staff; Maj. Gen. G. C. Mudgett, Chief of Information; and Maj. Gen. A. G. Trudeau, Chief of Intelligence, were present during approximately half of the 3-hour meeting. General Trudeau is presently overseas, but General Ridgway and General Mudgett are available to answer any questions that may be asked of them regarding the discussion that took place while they were present.

The second episode in this connection began on November 16, when Cohn, accompanied by Mr. Adams, came to my office. Cohn referred to a statement by me at a press conference on November 13 to the effect that I was not then aware of any current espionage at Fort Monmouth. Cohn said that Senator McCarthy was considerably upset as he felt that my statement had "pulled the rug out from under him." I told him that had not been my intention. I said that I thought I had been more than fair to Senator McCarthy and his investigation of Fort Monmouth.

I flew to New York the next morning and again invited Senator McCarthy to lunch. He was plainly provoked at the comments I had made regarding the lack of any current espionage at Fort Monmouth. We finally agreed on a statement that I would make at a joint press conference which Senator McCarthy and I held following lunch. It boiled down to my saying that the Army had no evidence of current espionage, and, in making that statement, I made it clear that I was speaking only for the Army and not for the committee. This was no different in substance from my statement of November 13 to which Senator McCarthy had objected. I still have no evidence of current espionage at Fort Monmouth.

An unsigned memorandum of November 17, also made public March 12 by Senator McCarthy, states it was at this luncheon in New York that I again suggested the committee go after the Navy and Air Force. That is not true. Colonel Cleary and Mr. Adams were present throughout. They heard no such suggestion and are available to supply information regarding what was said at this luncheon.

My oath of office requires me to do everything in my power for the defense of the United States. That means the most forthright and honorable dealings with the Navy, the Air Force, and the Marines. That kind of cooperation I have both given and received. If confirmation is needed, I suggest you check with those services.

It is a singular thing to me that this serious charge—that I tried to persuade the chairman of this committee to investigate the Navy and the Air Force—was kept secret so long. Why should it have only come to light 4 months later on the day after the Army chronology of events became public?

Now as to Senator McCarthy's charge of blackmail.

This charge was included in the Senator's memorandum dated December 9 and also made public March 12. In this case, for more than 3 months, this most serious charge—that the chairman of this committee had been blackmailed by the Secretary of the Army—was kept secret not only from the public but from the other members of this committee, as I understand it.

I do not know what the Senator had in his mind when he made this charge.

SENATOR MCCARTHY. Mr. Chairman, a point of order.

The Secretary, and I assume by an honest mistake, or whoever wrote this, is constantly referring to my being blackmailed. There was a charge that there was an attempt to blackmail, a very, very unsuccessful attempt, and I think the record should be cleared on that at this time.

SENATOR MUNDT. The Senator will have a chance on cross-examination to bring that out when he interviews the Secretary of the Army.

SECRETARY STEVENS. I do not know what the Senator had in his mind when he made this charge. But during the 90 days when he kept it secret, he continued to make flattering remarks about me in public. On December 16 Senator McCarthy was quoted by the New York Times as follows:

> I may say, just so this will not be misinterpreted as an attack upon Secretary Stevens and those who are now in charge, they have been cooperating fully with us, and I think they are just as concerned as we are about the very, very unusual picture unfolding. More and more they are doing something about it.

On February 23, the Senator was quoted in the Washington Evening Star as follows:

> I don't think Bob Stevens wants Communists in the Army any more than this committee does.

On February 26, the Washington Daily News quoted the Senator as saying:

> I think on the overall he (referring to me) has done a very good job.

On March 11, the day before the blackmail charge was made public, Senator McCarthy was quoted in the Washington Times-Herald as follows:

> Bob Stevens is doing a good job. We have disagreed and will disagree in the future. It's impossible to do a job without having some disagreements.

The occasion of the blackmail outburst on March 12 was, of course, publication of the Army's chronological account of the Schine affair. Nevertheless, 6 days later—on March 18—Senator McCarthy was quoted in the New York Herald Tribune as saying that he had no "ill feelings" against me, that I was a "very fine fellow" and "honest."

Is that the description of a blackmailer?

The fact remains that this most serious charge is still on the record. I therefore state that it is absolutely false.

By way of summary may I say again that I am proud to have had this chance to speak for the Army today. The Army is of transcendent importance to this Nation and to the friends of freedom and justice and peace around the world. Its integrity and morale are priceless commodities in these times, and I count it a welcome duty to testify to their soundness here today.

The Schine case is only an example of the wrongful seeking of privilege, of the perversion of power. It has been a distraction that has kept many men from the performance of tasks far more important to the welfare of this country than the convenience of a single Army private.

In conclusion, I want to make it clear that the United States Army does not coddle Communists. This committee knows that. The American people know that. I share the view of Senator Leverett Saltonstall, chairman of the Senate Committee on Armed Services when he said on March 24 this year:

> . . . as one who has served and as a parent whose children have served, I share the disbelief and the resentment felt by millions that there were either significant numbers of Americans whose loyalty was not in our finest tradition, or that disloyalty was coddled by the very uniforms whose heroic sacrifices in Korea have spoken so eloquently. . . .

Source: U.S. Senate, Committee on Government Operations, Permanent Subcommittee on Investigations, Special Senate Investigation on Charges and Countercharges Involving: Secretary of the Army Robert T. Stevens, John G. Adams, H. Struve Hensel and Senator Joe McCarthy, Roy M. Cohn, and Francis P. Carr (Washington, D.C., 1954), 96–99.

Excerpt from Testimony of Iris Flores in Executive Session, April 24, 1954

Many witnesses in the Army-McCarthy investigation did not appear in public session before the cameras. One such witness was Iris Flores, a striking 29-year-old woman from California, who listed her occupation as "inventor." She told investigators that she had two patents on file for a new line of brassieres. Why did investigators have an interest in Flores? Army investigators had evidence that she was a girlfriend of David Schine and was on the receiving end of frequent calls from him while he was on government business. Did Schine misuse his government privileges and fritter away his time in pursuing his relationship with Flores? Following her testimony before the executive session, there was much discussion about whether she should be brought before the hearings in a formal setting. Would she hurt or help Senator Joseph R. McCarthy (R-Wis.) or the U.S. Army? Eventually Senator Karl Mundt (R-S.D.), chairman of the Senate Permanent Subcommittee on Investigations, decided that the testimony of the glamorous Iris Flores would not be pertinent but merely a sideshow for the press and television audiences across the country. She testified, but not in public session.

EXCERPT FROM TESTIMONY OF IRIS FLORES IN EXECUTIVE SESSION, APRIL 24, 1954

The subcommittee met at ten o'clock A.M., pursuant to call, in the office of Senator Mundt, Senator Mundt presiding.

Present: Senator Karl E. Mundt, Republican, South Dakota.

Also present: John Kimball, Jr., army counsel; Thomas R. Prewitt, assistant counsel; Sol Horowitz, assistant counsel.

SENATOR MUNDT. Do you solemnly swear that the testimony you are about to give will be the truth, the whole truth, and nothing but the truth, so help you God?

MISS FLORES. I do.

TESTIMONY OF IRIS FLORES

MR. PREWITT. Miss Flores, this is a private hearing, an executive hearing of the subcommittee. You were subpoenaed by counsel for the subcommittee. This is in the nature of an—I use the phrase pretrial hearing for investigative purposes. That is the reason why we subpoenaed you, with the idea in mind that we want to dispose of all extraneous matters, that is, matters that might not bear on the issues of this controversy in advance of any open hearing.

I understand that through your letter to us that you have taken the position that you do not want to testify in an open hearing which is televised; is that correct?

MISS FLORES. That is correct.

MR. PREWITT. And that matter can be disposed of at a later date.

MISS FLORES. I also said at a public hearing. Do you remember my letter?

MR. PREWITT. Those matters can be disposed of later because this is not a public hearing.

MISS FLORES. I understand.

MR. PREWITT. Now, you do not have counsel with you?

MISS FLORES. No, I do not.

MR. PREWITT. Now, will you state your name for the record?

MISS FLORES. Iris Flores.

MR. PREWITT. Your residence?

MISS FLORES. Twenty-third East 64th Street, New York City.

MR. PREWITT. And your occupation?

MISS FLORES. I am an inventor.

MR. PREWITT. Are you employed by any person or concern?

MISS FLORES. No. I sold an invention to I. Newman and Company and it has to do with brassieres and it is a gadget and DuPont working on it, a man from DuPont, and a brassiere designer for them. I have been working closely with them for working models. We hope to bring it out in a few months.

MR. PREWITT. What is your age?

MISS FLORES. Twenty-nine.

MR. PREWITT. Do you know one G. David Schine?

MISS FLORES. I do.

MR. PREWITT. For how long have you known him?

MISS FLORES. For about three and a half years. Approximately four years. 1951 I met G. David Schine.

MR. PREWITT. Has your association with him been on a casual basis or a closer basis?

MISS FLORES. I have had a great friendship for Mr. Schine and it certainly has been always proper.

MR. PREWITT. Miss Flores, are you familiar with the fact that Private Schine was inducted into the army last November?

MISS FLORES. Yes, I am.

MR. PREWITT. Did you know of that fact at the time?

MISS FLORES. Yes, I did.

MR. PREWITT. Did you know that he was assigned to Fort Dix, New Jersey?

MISS FLORES. Yes, I did.

MR. PREWITT. Can you recall, if you know, the approximate date when he was assigned to Fort Dix?

MISS FLORES. Everyone knows, the third of November.

MR. PREWITT. I will ask you if you received any telephone calls from Fort Dix from Private Schine?

MISS FLORES. Yes, I did.

MR. PREWITT. Subsequent to November 3 last?

MISS FLORES. Yes.

MR. PREWITT. Did you receive many, or few calls?

MISS FLORES. I don't remember how many calls. I don't remember how many.

MR. PREWITT. Did you receive calls daily?

MISS FLORES. Perhaps. I don't know. I don't remember more or less whether it was daily.

MR. PREWITT. Did you receive more on the average of one call a week?

MISS FLORES. Yes I did.

MR. PREWITT. Will you give us your best estimate of the number of calls which you received weekly?

MISS FLORES. I don't know. I am in and out of my house so much that I miss a great many calls. I am on these inventions and many things I do. I don't know if I could have been home when he called or if I had a message. You know, it is hard to say. I don't quite remember that far.

MR. PREWITT. Without going into the details of these various telephone calls from Private Schine to you while the latter was at Fort Dix, tell us what the purpose of the calls were, if they had any particular purpose?

MISS FLORES. No, just to say hello I suppose, and what he was doing. He was in the army, he was very happy the way things had turned out. I suppose he was busy. That is all. Just social. It was purely a social call.

MR. PREWITT. During the period when Private Schine was at Fort Dix, did you see him socially?

MISS FLORES. Yes, I did.

MR. PREWITT. On many or few occasions?

MISS FLORES. Well, they were sort of few, because I went away part of November. I was in Florida. I went to Palm Beach. I believe I saw Private Schine a few times. I don't know; we had a quick dinner; and very late at night because he was always busy with things to do, and Roy Cohn. I imagine he was sort of annoyed because he never made a special—

MR. PREWITT. Tell us if Private Schine called you on any occasion while he was at Fort Dix and made a prearrangement to see you?

MISS FLORES. What was that question again? I don't understand.

MR. PREWITT. Did he make any engagement with you over the telephone to see you while he was at Fort Dix?

MISS FLORES. I don't know. He may have. If he didn't, he would say, "I would love to see you if I am not tied up, if I am not busy, if I have a chance I will call."

MR. PREWITT. I am not trying to confuse you, Miss Flores.

MISS FLORES. No, but there was no definite, anything definite, I never had a definite commitment or definite date because he always seemed so terribly tied up with all kinds of things.

MR. PREWITT. Did Private Schine after calling you from Fort Dix ever have an engagement with you?

MISS FLORES. After calling me from Fort Dix?

MR. PREWITT. Yes, on the same day of the call, or shortly thereafter?

MISS FLORES. Possibly, but it might have been at the last minute, very late like I say. I dined with him once or twice, dinner quickly. You know, it was always hurried.

MR. PREWITT. Where did you dine with him?

MISS FLORES. I believe at Pen and Pencil one day, about an hour. That was all. And one evening at the Drake Hotel. I don't remember.

MR. PREWITT. That was while he was stationed at Fort Dix?

MISS FLORES. Yes.

MR. PREWITT. Did you ever go to Trenton, New Jersey and meet Private Schine?

MISS FLORES. No.

SENATOR MUNDT. Did you see Private Schine while you were in Florida?

MISS FLORES. No, I saw no one that knows Private Schine. This is a different group of people in Palm Beach.

MR. PREWITT. Miss Flores, we have information that Private Schine on December 8, 1953, telephoned you four different times. Now, is that true or not, or do you remember it?

MISS FLORES. December 8? Frankly, to tell you the truth, I do not remember it.

MR. PREWITT. Do you remember whether Private Schine on any one day called you as much as four times from Fort Dix?

MISS FLORES. To the best of my recollection, I don't remember. It might have been so. I don't remember.

MR. PREWITT. Did you see Private Schine while the latter was at Fort Dix at any time during any week from Monday to Friday, that is, any week day?

MISS FLORES. Yes, I did. Christmas Day, on the twenty-fifth, he had a gift for me and it was very late. He called me and told me he had just come in from Fort Dix. I spent a great deal of time in bed in December because I had laryngitis, I was sick, and I remember it. I saw him on the twenty-fifth, but it was very late in the day. He said he had things to do and he would call me when he was through. Then I saw him again on the thirty-first, at Mr. Cohn's house, on New Year's eve. He called me and said, he asked me if I would not mind going to Mr. Cohn's because he had several things he had to talk to Mr. Cohn about and I wouldn't want to spend New Year's there. I said no. I had been so sick. I had engagements during December. I went to some and others I couldn't get there. I was very sick. So I didn't have plans for New Year's. I made no definite plans.

Source: U.S. Congress, 83rd Congress, 2nd Session, Executive Sessions of the Senate Permanent Subcommittee on Investigations of the Committee on Government Operations, Vol. 5, 1954, Testimony of Iris Flores, pp. 223–241.

Excerpt from Joseph Welch–Joseph McCarthy Confrontation, June 9, 1954

Leading the defense of the U.S. Army against the onslaughts of Senator Joseph R. McCarthy (R-Wis.) and the committee attorney, Roy Cohn, was an avuncular Boston lawyer, Joseph N. Welch, of the law firm Hale & Dorr, hired by the military as a special counsel. With a calm manner that contrasted with the outbursts of the investigators, Welch fended off various attacks and insinuations against military personnel. In early June 1954, McCarthy made a tactical blunder. He targeted one of Welch's young legal aides named Fred Fisher, who had once worked for the National Lawyers Guild, an organization sus-

pected of Communist ties. When McCarthy began an assault on Fisher, who was not present in the hearing room, Welch dramatically cut him off. "Until this moment, Senator, I think I never really gauged your cruelty or your recklessness. . . . Have you no sense of decency, sir, at long last? Have you left no sense of decency?" A short hush in the room was suddenly punctuated by applause. A stunned McCarthy backed down. Welch had delivered a rhetorical dagger blow from which McCarthy never recovered.

EXCERPT FROM JOSEPH WELCH–JOSEPH McCARTHY CONFRONTATION JUNE 9, 1954

MR. WELCH. Mr. Cohn, tell me once more: Every time you learn of a Communist or a spy anywhere, is it your policy to get them out as fast as possible?

MR. COHN. Surely, we want them out as fast as possible, sir.

MR. WELCH. And whenever you learn of one from now on, Mr. Cohn, I beg of you, will you tell somebody about them quick?

MR. COHN. Mr. Welch, with great respect, I work for the committee here. They know how we go about handling situations of Communist infiltration and failure to act on FBI information about Communist infiltration. If they are displeased with the speed with which I and the group of men who work with me proceed, if they are displeased with the order in which we move, I am sure they will give me appropriate instructions along those lines, and I will follow any which they give me.

MR. WELCH. May I add my small voice, sir, and say whenever you know about a subversive or a Communist or a spy, please hurry. Will you remember those words?

SENATOR McCARTHY. Mr. Chairman.

MR. COHN. Mr. Welch, I can assure you, sir, as far as I am concerned, and certainly as far as the chairman of this committee and the members, and the members of the staff, are concerned, we are a small group, but we proceed as expeditiously as is humanly possible to get out Communists and traitors and to bring to light the mechanism by which they have been permitted to remain where they were for so long a period of time.

SENATOR McCARTHY. Mr. Chairman, in view of that question—

SENATOR MUNDT. Have you a point of order?

SENATOR McCARTHY. Not exactly, Mr. Chairman, but in view of Mr. Welch's request that the information be given once we know of anyone who might be performing any work for the Communist Party, I think we should tell him that he has in his law firm a young man named Fisher whom he recommended, incidentally, to do work on this committee, who has been for a number of years a member of an organization which was named, oh, years and years ago, as the legal bulwark of the Communist Party, an organization which always swings to the defense of anyone who dares to expose Communists. I certainly assume that Mr. Welch did not know of this young man at the time he recommended him as the assistant counsel for this committee, but he has such terror and such a great desire to know where anyone is located who may be serving the Communist cause, Mr. Welch, that I thought we should just call to your attention the fact that your Mr. Fisher, who is still in your law firm today, whom you asked to have down here looking over the secret and classified material, is a member of an organization, not named by me but named by various committees, named by the Attorney General, as I recall, and I think I quote this verbatim, as "the legal bulwark of the Communist Party." He belonged to that for a sizable number of years, according to his own admission, and he belonged to it long after it had been exposed as the legal arm of the Communist Party.

Knowing that, Mr. Welch, I just felt that I had a duty to respond to your urgent request that before sundown, when we know of anyone serving the Communist cause, we let the agency know. We are now letting you know that your man did belong to this organization for either 3 or 4 years, belonged to it long after he was out of law school.

I don't think you can find anyplace, anywhere, an organization which has done more to defend Communists—I am again quoting the report—to defend Communists, to defend espionage agents, and to aid the Communist cause, than the man whom you originally wanted down here at your right hand instead of Mr. St. Clair.

I have hesitated bringing that up, but I have been rather bored with your phony requests to Mr. Cohn here that he personally get every Communist out of government before sundown. Therefore, we will give you information about the young man in your own organization.

I am not asking you at this time to explain why you tried to foist him on this committee. Whether you knew he was a member of that Communist organization or not, I don't know. I assume you did not, Mr. Welch, because I get the impression that, while you are quite an actor, you play for a laugh, I don't think you have any conception of the danger of the Communist Party. I don't think you yourself would ever knowingly aid the Communist cause. I think you are unknowingly aiding it when you try to burlesque this hearing in which we are attempting to bring out the facts, however.

MR. WELCH. Mr. Chairman.

SENATOR MUNDT. Mr. Welch, the Chair should say he has no recognition or no memory of Mr. Welch's recommending either Mr. Fisher or anybody else as counsel for this committee.

I will recognize Mr. Welch.

SENATOR MCCARTHY. Mr. Chairman, I will give you the news story on that.

MR. WELCH. Mr. Chairman, under these circumstances I must have something approaching a personal privilege.

SENATOR MUNDT. You may have it, sir. It will not be taken out of your time.

MR. WELCH. Senator McCarthy, I did not know—Senator, sometimes you say "May I have your attention?"

SENATOR MCCARTHY. I am listening to you. I can listen with one ear.

MR. WELCH. This time I want you to listen with both.

SENATOR MCCARTHY. Yes.

MR. WELCH. Senator McCarthy, I think until this moment—

SENATOR MCCARTHY. Jim, will you get the news story to the effect that this man belonged to this Communist-front organization? Will you get the citations showing that this was the legal arm of the Communist Party, and the length of time that he belonged, and the fact that he was recommended by Mr. Welch? I think that should be in the record.

MR. WELCH. You won't need anything in the record when I have finished telling you this.

Until this moment, Senator, I think I never really gauged your cruelty or your recklessness. Fred Fisher is a young man who went to the Harvard Law School and came into my firm and is starting what looks to be a brilliant career with us.

When I decided to work for this committee I asked Jim St. Clair, who sits on my right, to be my first assistant. I said to Jim, "Pick somebody in the firm who works under you that you would like." He chose Fred Fisher and they came down on an afternoon plane. That night, when he had taken a little stab at trying to see what the case was about, Fred Fisher and Jim St. Clair and I went to dinner together. I then said to these two young men, "Boys, I don't know anything about you except I have always liked you, but if there is anything funny in the life of either one of you that would hurt anybody in this case you speak up quick."

Fred Fisher said, "Mr. Welch, when I was in law school and for a period of months after, I belonged to the Lawyers Guild," as you have suggested, Senator. He went on to say, "I am secretary of the Young Republicans League in Newton with the son of Massachusetts' Governor, and I have the respect and admiration of my community and I am sure I have the respect and admiration of the 25 lawyers or so in Hale & Dorr."

I said, "Fred, I just don't think I am going to ask you to work on the case. If I do, one of these days that will come out and go over national television and it will just hurt like the dickens."

So, Senator, I asked him to go back to Boston.

Little did I dream you could be so reckless and so cruel as to do an injury to that lad. It is true he is still with Hale & Dorr. It is true that he will continue to be with Hale & Dorr. It is, I regret to say, equally true that I fear he shall always bear a scar needlessly inflicted by you. If it were in my power to forgive you for your reckless cruelty, I will do so. I like to think I am a gentleman, but your forgiveness will have to come from someone other than me.

SENATOR MCCARTHY. Mr. Chairman.

SENATOR MUNDT. Senator McCarthy?

SENATOR MCCARTHY. May I say that Mr. Welch talks about this being cruel and reckless. He was just baiting; he has been baiting Mr. Cohn here for hours, requesting that Mr. Cohn, before sundown, get out of any department of Government anyone who is serving the Communist cause.

I just give this man's record, and I want to say, Mr. Welch, that it has been labeled long before he became a member, as early as 1944—

MR. WELCH. Senator, may we not drop this? We know he belonged to the Lawyers Guild, and Mr. Cohn nods his head at me. I did you, I think, no personal injury, Mr. Cohn.

MR. COHN. No, sir.

MR. WELCH. I meant to do you no personal injury, and if I did, I beg your pardon.

Let us not assassinate this lad further, Senator. You have done enough. Have you no sense of decency, sir, at long last? Have you left no sense of decency?

SENATOR MCCARTHY. I know this hurts you, Mr. Welch. But I may say, Mr. Chairman, on a point of personal privilege, and I would like to finish it—

MR. WELCH. Senator, I think it hurts you, too, sir.

SENATOR MCCARTHY. I would like to finish this.

Mr. Welch has been filibustering this hearing, he has been talking day after day about how he wants to get anyone tainted with communism out before sundown. I know Mr. Cohn would rather not have me go into this. I intend to, however, Mr. Welch talks about any sense of decency. If I say anything which is not the truth, then I would like to know about it.

> The foremost legal bulwark of the Communist Party, its front organizations, and controlled unions, and which, since its inception, has never failed to rally to the legal defense of the Communist Party, and individual members thereof, including known espionage agents.

Now, that is not the language of Senator McCarthy. That is the language of the Un-American Activities Committee. And I can go on with many more citations. It seems that Mr. Welch is pained so deeply he thinks it is improper for me to give the record, the Communist-front record, of the man whom he wanted to foist upon this committee. But it doesn't pain him at all—there is no pain in his chest about the unfounded charges against Mr. Frank Carr; there is no pain there about the attempt to destroy the reputation and take the jobs away from the young men who were working in my committee.

And, Mr. Welch, if I have said anything here which is untrue, then tell me. I have heard you and every one else talk so much about laying the truth upon the table that when I hear—and it is completely phony, Mr. Welch. I have listened to you for a long time—when you say "Now, before sundown, you must get these people out of Government," I want to have it very clear, very clear that you were not so serious about that when you tried to recommend this man for this committee.

And may I say, Mr. Welch, in fairness to you, I have reason to believe that you did not know about his Communist-front record at the time you recommended him. I don't think you would have recommended him to the committee if you knew that.

I think it is entirely possible you learned that after you recommended him.

SENATOR MUNDT. The Chair would like to say again that he does not believe that Mr. Welch recommended Mr. Fisher as counsel for this committee, because he has through his office all the recommendations that were made. He does not recall any that came from Mr. Welch, and that would include Mr. Fisher.

SENATOR MCCARTHY. Let me ask Mr. Welch. You brought him down, did you not, to act as your assistant?

MR. WELCH. Mr. McCarthy, I will not discuss this with you further. You have sat within 6 feet of me, and could have asked me about Fred Fisher. You have brought it out. If there is a God in heaven, it will do neither you nor your cause any good. I will not discuss it further. . . .

SENATOR MUNDT. Are there any questions?

MR. JENKINS. No further questions, Mr. Chairman.

SENATOR MUNDT. Senator McClellan?

SENATOR MCCLELLAN. I just want to ask 1 or 2 questions, Mr. Chairman.

SENATOR MUNDT. The Chair's attention has been called to the fact that it is a quarter to four. Shall we have our recess before that, Senator McClellan.

SENATOR MCCLELLAN. That will be all right.

SENATOR MUNDT. We will have a recess for 5 minutes.
(Brief recess.)

SENATOR MUNDT. The committee will resume activities.

Senator McClellan had the first 10 minutes which we interrupted for the customary afternoon recess.

Mr. Cohn, take the stand.

SENATOR MCCLELLAN. Mr. Chairman, I may say this. In view of the climax that occurred just before we recessed and in view of the fact that I could not possibly conclude any questioning of Mr. Cohn until I have had the opportunity to check the files of documents that Mr. Schine is supposed to have worked on, I cannot conclude my questioning of Mr. Cohn until then. So I withhold any questions for the moment until such time as I can get prepared to question about the other matters.

SENATOR MUNDT. The Chair would suggest, then, that Mr. Cohn step down temporarily and we call the next witness. We will recall Mr. Cohn when members will have had an opportunity to read the document.

Senator Symington?

SENATOR SYMINGTON. Mr. Chairman, I was not here. Unfortunately, I was in my office. Based on some of the calls that I have received, I would respectfully move that the Chair recess this hearing now until tomorrow morning.

SENATOR MUNDT. The Chair believes we have had enough delays without adding another delay of that kind now. We will agree to call Mr. Cohn back for any questions that you would like to have, or any other member, but I do think Senator McClellan's point is well taken. I have not had an opportunity either to read the documents, and I would like to read them. Mr. Cohn is not being dismissed. We will recall him tomorrow. He will still be in town tomorrow.

Mr. Jenkins, you may begin the direct examination of the next witness after he has been sworn.

Will you stand and be sworn. Do you solemnly swear the testimony you are about to give will be the truth, the whole truth, and nothing but the truth, so help you God?

SENATOR MCCARTHY. I do.

Source: U.S. Senate, Committee on Government Operations, Permanent Subcommittee on Investigations, Special Senate Investigation on Charges and Countercharges Involving: Secretary of the Army Robert T. Stevens, John G. Adams, H. Struve Hensel, and Senator Joe McCarthy, Roy M. Cohn, and Francis P. Carr (Washington, D.C., 1954), 2426–30.

Excerpt from Senate Permanent Subcommittee on Investigations on Personnel, July 15, 1954

For Senator Joseph R. McCarthy (R-Wis.) in the sweltering summer of 1954, no amount of air conditioning in the U.S. Capitol could help. The crusade was crumbling around him. Faced with accusations that members of the Permanent Subcommittee on Investigations had tampered with evidence and falsified information in their zeal to nail Communist sympathizers and fellow travelers within government,

Senator Charles Potter (R-Mich.), a moderate on the committee and often a severe critic of its actions, called for an investigation and possible change of staff members. Although McCarthy was keen to continue hearings, Senate Majority Leader William Knowland (R-Calif.) blocked additional public hearings for the rest of the congressional session. Soon, several members of the staff resigned, including counsel Roy Cohn. And, in a little over a month, Senator McCarthy himself would face censure charges that he had abused his power.

EXCERPT FROM SENATE SUBCOMMITTEE ON INVESTIGATIONS ON PERSONNEL JULY 15, 1954

The subcommittee met at 2:30 P.M., July 15, 1954, pursuant to notice, in room F–82, Capitol, Senator Joseph R. McCarthy presiding. Present: Joseph R. McCarthy, Republican, Wisconsin; Senator Karl E. Mundt, Republican, South Dakota; Senator Everett McKinley Dirksen, Republican, Illinois; Senator Charles E. Potter, Republican, Michigan; Senator Henry M. Jackson, Democrat, Washington; Senator Stuart Symington, Democrat, Missouri.

Also present: Roy M. Cohn, chief counsel; Francis P. Carr, executive director; Ruth Young Watt, chief clerk. . . .

SENATOR POTTER. Before you leave, Karl, I am going to make a motion. This is the motion.

SENATOR DIRKSEN. Charlie, let me ask, in fairness to you, do you want the staff present?

SENATOR POTTER. I don't care. This is nothing tricky.

Whereas, the Rules of the subcommittee as amended January 1954, provide for confirmation by a subcommittee majority of all staff appointments, and

Whereas, no such confirmation has been effected,

Therefore, I move that as of July 31, 1954, all present staff appointments shall automatically terminate except in those individual instances where a Subcommittee majority in formal session shall have voted such specific confirmation prior to that date.

THE CHAIRMAN. May I say two things: Most of the staff members have been confirmed. I think the minority counsel has not been confirmed. I got a call from Senator McClellan to put him on. I think you may find two or three other members who have not been confirmed. Could I suggest this——

SENATOR JACKSON. The rule provides that the present staff, as well as the future staff, had to be approved by a majority vote of the subcommittee.

THE CHAIRMAN. Could we do this? Why not do this; if there are some staff members that anyone has objection to, then I would say move that they be removed. It has the same effect. There is nothing to be gained by taking up the time of this committee to go over the list of secretaries on the committee, for example, or go over the investigators where there is no question.

Charlie, let me say this: As far as I am concerned, whenever any member of the committee wants to make a motion to remove a member of the staff, there will be a meeting for that. If you pass this motion, we may be in the position of not having a staff after the thirty-first. . . .

SENATOR POTTER. Joe, can I open on this, speak on it a moment?

Now, as I recall, when we had the meeting when the Democrats came back on the committee, that it was agreed that the committee could, by majority vote hire and fire members of the staff. Questions of certain members of the staff have been current in the press as the result of the past hearings, and, in all fairness to the staff and in fairness to the subcommittee, and in fairness to the public which we serve, I think the staff should have but affirmative vote. Now, rather than the suggestion that the chairman has made, I would like to take them up individually. There are members of the committee staff that I don't know. One man, whose name I have seen in the paper, I don't think I would know him if I saw him. I understand he has done a good job with the committee. I assume there are others that way. I assume there are other members of the committee in the same position as I. There is nothing tricky with this move . . .

SENATOR DIRKSEN. I make this brief representation. I find it very difficult to go along with Charlie's resolution. First, I don't want to hurt anybody who shouldn't be hurt. I think the committee amended its rules in January, six months ago, and there was never any question raised until now. After all, there is some implication we were satisfied and no questions were raised to the chairman, so I don't want to hurt him now in that respect.

Third, Henry raised this question about giving the staff members a hearing. I don't think that strange. All in all, they served on the committee and we are getting ready to terminate them and I think, in the good old American tradition, if we are going to terminate their services, we ought to let them know why and if they have got something to say, let them have an opportunity to say it before the action by the committee shall be conclusive. I think it is the essence of fair play. I never like to get put up on a stool I can't defend myself on good legal or moral grounds. This is an affirmative substitution. It will accomplish what everybody wants to accomplish. Henry raised the question that suppose there should be no meeting. If there is no meeting it is only because the members of the committee do not respond. This makes it mandatory on the chairman of the committee; it makes it mandatory to call a meeting before next Thursday.

THE CHAIRMAN. I can say there definitely will be.

SENATOR DIRKSEN. It gives us time to get briefs on the staff members.

SENATOR MUNDT. If Henry seriously thinks we will not call a meeting, we could put the date of the meeting.

SENATOR JACKSON. I think Charlie's motion is preferable as it ensures positive action prior to July 31st, number one. Number two, it does not single out any member of the staff. It means that the committee will have to go through the members of the staff and approve or disapprove affirmatively each member of the staff in accordance with the rules. I think it is the fairer of the two proposals, at least that is my——

SENATOR MUNDT. Henry, there is the same voting procedure under Dirksen's motion as Potter's. Take the staff members and either vote them up or vote them down. The preferential feature of Dirksen's motion quite apart from this other is the hearing, which I am not so much concerned with, but I think anybody is entitled to that. The preferential feature is not to slander anybody who ultimately will be accepted by the committee.

SENATOR JACKSON. I think there is one thing also for the record that should be corrected. It is my recollection after the rule with reference to majority approval of the committee was passed the latter part of January, Senator McClellan did speak to the chairman about the same situation at that time. He has so stated in public hearings and elsewhere. It is my understanding, if the facts bear me out, it wasn't very long after we came back to the committee that the now famous Army-McCarthy dispute came into being and made it impossible to implement this rule. I think everybody agrees we didn't have an opportunity, and it would have prejudiced people involved in the hearing.

THE CHAIRMAN. Number one, Scoop, you were in a peculiarly pleasant position because you had no monitored phone calls, number two, McClellan did not testify.

SENATOR JACKSON. I didn't say he testified. I said he stated.

THE CHAIRMAN. The testimony that he was visited six days before he came back on the committee by one of a group who took part in a conclave which resulted in the thirty-six days of hearings, so that there is no testimony by McClellan, as far as I know, and just in complete fairness to McClellan, I don't want to make this unqualified unless I would check, I don't think McClellan ever told me before he came back on the committee that he was going to try and get rid of staff members.

SENATOR JACKSON. I didn't say that. I said this. I want to make the record clear. I said this: When he came back and at the hearing or shortly after the meeting at which we came back, I recall his having stated to you that there were some staff matters which he wanted to speak to you about. I believe that statement you referred to now was made during what is now known as the Army-McCarthy hearings. I believe he did tell you there were some matters he had been informed about he wanted to speak to you about and bring to your attention in connection with the staff. If I am wrong, I stand corrected.

THE CHAIRMAN. I think you may be right. At this particular moment I don't remember. I don't think Senator McClellan would misstate the facts.

SENATOR SYMINGTON. I think Scoop is right on that. I know that is what Senator McClellan told me. I believe somewhere in the record, that is my recollection that he mentioned that in the hearings. Whether it was in an executive meeting, or public, I don't know.

SENATOR MUNDT. To me, as far as my sentiment, I would like to have a meeting next week for the purpose of confirming the staff; for the purpose of looking at the biographical data, finding out what their jobs are and deciding to continue or not continue them. To me, the Potter motion contains a blanket indictment of people I don't know and I don't want to embarrass them. Senator Dirksen's motion serves the same purpose—to have a subcommittee meeting next week and we have to confirm or disapprove them. That way we do it affirmatively and not hurt innocent people that we are subsequently going to keep on in our employment. We will get the same results. I think in all common decency we should retain the staff and not put them under suspicion for a couple of weeks and then say the subcommittee has reconsidered and accepted them.

SENATOR POTTER. Will the Senator yield at that point?

THE CHAIRMAN. I don't believe that——

SENATOR POTTER. Under the Dirksen motion you are putting the committee in the position of firing members of the staff. Now, I believe that the committee has every right and the staff has every right to expect the committee's approval of them as a staff member. Now, the only thing, I have been on other committees where you vote on staff members——

THE CHAIRMAN. May I say, here is the thing that bothers me. If you insist upon a vote on your motion, under the rules governing proxies, I would have to, with the greatest reluctance, rule out John McClellan's wire, which does not mention your position. I don't want to do that. I think John has an absolute right to vote on any matters that come up.

I think he should know what is coming up. I don't like to leave this room with a three and three vote, which means that the motion would lose, lose because we don't recognize the improper form of proxy.

SENATOR JACKSON. Is it agreed that he can submit his proxy in specific terms relating to this motion?

THE CHAIRMAN. No, his proxy does not cover this.

SENATOR JACKSON. I am not saying that. I thought it was understood that he could submit a proxy covering this.

THE CHAIRMAN. Yes, he certainly should be entitled to do that.

SENATOR JACKSON. We have never done this before, Mr. Chairman. We are invoking rules which have never been invoked before.

THE CHAIRMAN. Senator Dirksen has a motion accomplishing everything you want, a motion to hold a meeting next Thursday. There is certainly no delay about that.

SENATOR POTTER. As I understand, you will rule the proxy out of order.

THE CHAIRMAN. I think I would have to until John wired us or wrote us and told us what he wanted done. In doing that, I want to write McClellan myself. Senator Dirksen, Senator Mundt, Senator Jackson, I tried to get an opinion from the disbursing officer as to what effect this would have upon the retirement rights of these people. I don't have that opinion yet. I would want to write John McClellan exactly what effect that would have upon their retirement rights. We discussed that, Scoop, in great detail when John took over from Aiken and I just want to have McClellan know what he is voting on. It would be a matter of a couple of days. I will quite beating this horse, Senator Dirksen. Why doesn't Senator Dirksen's motion completely cover your situation. Every member would be up for you to vote for or against.

SENATOR POTTER. Because I think Senator Dirksen's motion is more of a reflection on the staff; however, if you are not going to recognize the proxy, I will accept Senator Dirksen's substitute.

SENATOR SYMINGTON. I think I know how Senator McClellan feels about this.

SENATOR JACKSON. Senator McClellan should certainly have the right to wire in his vote.

SENATOR SYMINGTON. I am certain he will approve Potter's motion. Senator McClellan should be given the opportunity to vote on this.

THE CHAIRMAN. Just one previous question: We have right now, we have some 130 people in defense plants who have Communist records. I think we should start holding hearings immediately. I would like to know in what way your motion would affect that. That has nothing to do with the army. I think it is pretty generally agreed among the senators that it would be improper to proceed with this investigation of any improper conduct on the part of army officials until the final report is submitted to the Senate, except I would like to know, Charlie, how you anticipate this would affect defense plant hearings. I would like to, and unless the committee votes me down on it, I will proceed to bring in Communists from defense plants, starting at the earliest convenience. I am going to ask the senators on the committee, Potter, Jackson, Dirksen, Mundt, McClellan and Symington, in view of the fantastic amount of work involved, in view of the fact it would be impossible for me to sit as chairman of all these committees, I think this is something we can all agree on; I don't think there will be any dispute by the Democrats or Republicans. I would like to ask all senators to take a spell chairing the committee. We have got 133, roughly. It means about five months of steady work.

May I say, and I don't want to take your time up, but the heads of defense plants have taken the position they can't fire these people unless and until they are called in and take the Fifth Amendment, Communists committing subversion, espionage, sabotage, what have you. I would just like to know if there is any indication, any inclination on the part of members to try to keep us from holding hearings, number one. Number two, under the rule, or proposed rule, while the Democrat members could prevent any new public hearings being started, it was agreed completely and fully that would not apply to any hearings in progress. In other words, the chairman, once he had authority to conduct a certain line of investigation, would not have to call the committee not together each day and say, "Can I hold hearings?" My proposal is not to start those hearings. They have nothing to do with the army loyalty setup, nothing to do with Stevens, nothing to do with Adams. There has been no claim by anyone that Carr, McCarthy, or Cohn, who were the principals on one side of this case, in any way improperly handled those defense plant hearings. I am just curious to know, Charlie, how your motion, in your opinion, would affect that?

SENATOR POTTER. Joe, my motion could be all cleared away by Tuesday of next week, if Frank got together the biographical sketches, and it would be completely out of the way.

THE CHAIRMAN. I want to hold hearings Saturday. Frankly, there are some pretty urgent matters.

SENATOR SYMINGTON. We have waited four weeks today or tomorrow, and I don't think we should have hearings before we get the staff situation clarified.

THE CHAIRMAN. Stu, let me tell you something. You and I had gotten along very well until we got into these hearings. There is no reason, as far as I know, Stu Symington, why you should keep us from exposing Communists in defense plants. If the Democrats want to keep me from exposing Communists in defense plants, I am inclined to think they can perhaps do it.

SENATOR JACKSON. We have been waiting four weeks to hear from you.

THE CHAIRMAN. I have been hearing it from the press every day——

SENATOR SYMINGTON. What did you hear from the press?

THE CHAIRMAN. I have been hearing that you have taken the position there can be no exposure of Communists until after the report is written, a report involving five million words, roughly. Make that two million. I read that in the papers.

SENATOR SYMINGTON. You never read that statement, not from me.

SENATOR JACKSON. Or from me.

THE CHAIRMAN. I have yet to hear one of my Democrat colleagues say, "We want to help expose some Communists." We have got in their files, Karl, we have got the most fantastic amount of work, months and months of it. It doesn't have anything to do with Stevens, McCarthy, or Adams hearing. There is no reason on earth why we shouldn't go ahead.

SENATOR JACKSON. We haven't been able to have a meeting of the committee for a month.

THE CHAIRMAN. Scoop, if you are going to hold it up until you can vote on each little girl on the committee, and each investigator, I just want to make—I just want to know it, number one, if that is your intention.

Number two, I just want to make that clear to the country because that is awfully important. That has nothing to do with Charlie Potter's motion.

SENATOR JACKSON. We haven't held up anything. We requested a meeting of the committee dated June 30th; then I will go ahead with the hearings.

THE CHAIRMAN. There has been a meeting today, July 15th.

SENATOR JACKSON. Not on any member of this committee.

THE CHAIRMAN. Then do I understand that there is no objection if I proceed to start holding hearings Saturday.

SENATOR JACKSON. Well, I think staff matters should be disposed of first.

SENATOR SYMINGTON. We have been waiting four weeks since the hearings closed to have a meeting. Taking Senator Potter's thought, he says that the staff problem can be cleared up by next Tuesday evening under his motion. As I understand it, I believe that is right. I would wait four more days, which includes Saturday and Sunday, until we clear up this staff situation before we go ahead with any hearings. That would be my recommendation and vote.

THE CHAIRMAN. Just so I can't be accused by members of the committee of deceiving you, unless the committee votes to deny me the right to do it, I intend to start exposing Communists in defense plants on Saturday. Now, I won't do all that work myself. I want every member of this committee to take a part in chairing those committees, and I think maybe some of us may have a better picture of this threat than we have now. I just want to say that. My position is that if there were a new hearing being held, I would have to get permission of the senators and the three Democrats could block it; it being a current hearing, they cannot, except by a motion on the part of a senator, if you want to make a motion to deny me the right, if that is carried, obviously I can't hold the hearings. I am bound by the majority rules of the committee. When I leave this room, I want the press outside to know who is going to hold up the hearings.

SENATOR JACKSON. I think the record should disclose that a whole month has elapsed since the conclusion of the Army-McCarthy hearings.

SENATOR MUNDT. I can't understand why we have a meeting which lasts a couple of hours about a problem which we say we all want to solve by having a meeting to vote on confirmation of the staff members. The vote is going to be the same way. This is just a question of approach shots. We have got Charlie's motion, which I take exception to on two scores mentioned, first the intermediate step, which in the hometown papers of every employee will cast a shadow of suspicion on them automatically, that they are suspended July 31st unless the committee votes them back in; and second, it denies them any possibility of a hearing. To me, that isn't the way of operation. In the first place, I don't believe in belittling people, and in the second place, we get the same results by Dirksen's resolution, plus giving them a hearing.

SENATOR DIRKSEN. You can't separate the humblest civil service worker under the federal laws without giving them a hearing. I don't want to bring myself into that position.

SENATOR JACKSON. Let's vote.

THE CHAIRMAN. Senator Potter says that he would like a ruling from the chair on the proxy of Senator McClellan.

The chair is prepared to rule on that. I will have to rule that under the rules of procedure, adopted by the Committee on Government Operations on January 14, 1953, which provides that the proxy must be in such details so that it clearly appears that the member voting the proxy knows what he is voting on relating to the specific subject. This proxy does not. I would have to rule the proxy out.

SENATOR JACKSON. Wherein does the proxy fail to comply?

THE CHAIRMAN. Let me rule first. I would say this: That is, if Senator Symington wanted to contact Senator McClellan or Senator Jackson wanted to contact him, and if they told me—I wouldn't have to talk to McClellan myself if I had the assurance from either one of you that you had given him the details of what this motion was—and he said, "My proxy still applied," I would perhaps be leaning away over backwards, but I would recognize the proxy unless the committee outvoted me.

I understand that Senator Potter's position is that he feels this matter is rather urgent and that if we rule out Senator McClellan's proxy, that Senator Dirksen's motion will perhaps accomplish the desired results. Therefore, I gather, Charlie, that you will go on and support that, not because you feel your motion is not better; you feel your motion is more desirable, but because of the time limit——

SENATOR JACKSON. Can we recess until tomorrow on that, so Senator McClellan can vote on these two specific resolutions?

SENATOR SYMINGTON. We have Senator McClellan's proxy on that vote. We have never denied a member of a committee——

THE CHAIRMAN. Let's be a little frank about this thing. You are Stu Symington—and let's make this completely clear—you are doing the most unfair job on the staff members that anyone could do. Let's get this clear, and this is on the record. You were not trying to take action which will remove any employee guilty of improper conduct from the committee; you are trying to stay action, Senator Symington, which is strictly 100 percent political, and you are entitled to do that. I don't accuse you of any dishonesty in this matter, but let's have it clear, I know what you are doing. You just go right ahead as far as I am concerned. I am going to call for a vote.

SENATOR SYMINGTON. Mr. Chairman, you have expressed your opinion. May I express mine? I did not know the details of Senator Potter's resolution. I believe that it is a wiser and kinder resolution to the staff than any other and we can have an honest difference of opinion on that. I believe that represents the thinking of Senator McClellan because of that. I want to assure you I have no political thinking of any kind whatever. The motion was made by one of your colleagues and supported by the Democrats. It is not a political action on my part of any kind whatever.

SENATOR MUNDT. I have another substitute motion if Senator Dirksen's motion loses, which I want to offer.

SENATOR JACKSON. We are granted the right to vote by proxy and I think it is most unfair to Senator McClellan. I don't object at all to an adjournment until tomorrow.

[Off-record discussion.]

SENATOR POTTER. Let me say one thing. I am offering my motion as an individual member of the committee. I hope it prevails, but if it doesn't carry, then I am going to vote for the next best motion offered to get action. I don't want to delay it. This thing has been hanging fire a long time, and in all fairness to the staff, the committee, and the public, it should be out of the way.

SENATOR DIRKSEN. Joe, let's not vote now. May I respectfully suggest, I think not only the chairman but the committee is inviting a good deal of hostility if a proxy is disqualified. I would prefer—I know it is your prerogative to rule it out, but I would prefer if you did consider the proxy valid for the purpose here. Let Senator Potter make his motion and I have one or two other motions I would offer which would come within the exception clause in Potter's motion.

THE CHAIRMAN. I will defer it to the judgment of my very able neighbor senator, if he insists. However, I think this, Senator Dirksen.

We had this question come up, the question of discharging all staff members and then rehiring them. That was up when John McClellan took over the chairmanship of the Government Operations Committee from Aiken, either that or vice versa. It is a very important question. I would like to get the opinion from the Disbursing officer, Senator Dirksen—I would like an opinion from the Disbursing officer as to how that would affect the pension rights of these employees. You see, they all have pensions. If there is a gap in employment, I understand their pension rights are affected. I would like to strongly urge, Charlie, if you would do this, just so we don't have to worry and it will accomplish the same results. Take the Dirksen resolution, and we could have a meeting earlier than the one called for on the 22nd.

Let me say this, Senator Dirksen. I don't like to accept a proxy unless I know that the man voting it knows how it will affect the young ladies on the committee. Take for example, Ruth Watt——

SENATOR DIRKSEN. Let me make an inquiry. In Charlie's motion he says, "except in those individual instances where a subcommittee majority in formal session all have voted such specific confirmation prior to that date." I offer a motion that all names of staff members shall be submitted to the subcommittee on or before the 22nd of July for specific confirmation in accordance with the exception in the Potter motion.

SENATOR POTTER. I see nothing wrong with that.

SENATOR DIRKSEN. That will take care of any possibility of endangering their retirement rights or pension rights or annuity rights.

SENATOR MUNDT. That still leaves in the objectionable language——

SENATOR JACKSON. I think that these various proposals ought to be put in writing and made available by Saturday morning. In the meantime, Senator Symington or myself can get in touch with Senator McClellan and we can reconvene on Tuesday. I think it is a dangerous precedent if you are going to turn down a proxy. I think it is a pretty fair statement of the subject matter before the committee, and I do believe that in fairness to any member, I don't care if he is a Republican or Democrat, that such member of the committee should have an opportunity to vote by proxy.

[Off-record discussion as to next meeting.]

THE CHAIRMAN. Can we do this? In the meantime, Stu, so we don't have a fight about this, can you get an opinion from the disbursing officer. I will get one also.

SENATOR SYMINGTON. You get it.

THE CHAIRMAN. Let John know what effect it has before he casts a ballot. I will ask for that jointly under my name and your name.

SENATOR SYMINGTON. May I make this observation? If you had the 31st, or any particular day, those would be off and back on all on the same day, so from the standpoint of the Disbursing Office, it would not be a problem.

THE CHAIRMAN. I will give you a copy of the letter I write to him.

SENATOR JACKSON. One point before we meet on Tuesday. I think the chairman should be requested to get all necessary biographical and background data on all members of the staff in the meantime.

THE CHAIRMAN. Senator Jackson, we will try and get that to you Monday, so you will have that twenty-four hours ahead of time. There is only one problem. Whenever I get a name check from the FBI it is marked personal and confidential to me personally. I think there has been some violation of that. I let the former chief of staff, Flanagan, look at those. It may be I won't be able to incorporate that, but I will call Hoover and ask him if I can incorporate that FBI name check in that thing.

Number two, we have got the press waiting, and I think, Stu, even though you and I exchange rather rough language, I think we substantially——

SENATOR SYMINGTON. In this case all the roughness was on your side, not mine.

THE CHAIRMAN. Let me say there that I can see no reason on earth—we have got Communists in defense plants, so why shouldn't we go ahead and hold hearings, unless somebody makes a motion to deny me the right.

SENATOR DIRKSEN. That has been authorized by the committee before.

SENATOR SYMINGTON. I want to say this for the record. I know, Senator McCarthy, this I am sure of, that there is going to be no further investigatory action on the part of the committee until the staff matters have been cleared up. I want to make that for the record with respect to how I feel on that point. Does that differ from the way you feel?

SENATOR DIRKSEN. Well, it runs in my mind that the only controversy is over the language in the record at one hearing that said there should be no regular function of the committee pursued until the investigation had been concluded. Well, the investigation has been concluded. I assume from that we could go ahead with the hearings and have it authorized. I see the point, of course, of any new investigations.

Source: U.S. Congress, 83rd Congress, 2nd Session, Executive Sessions of the Senate Permanent Subcommittee on Investigations of the Committee on Government Operations, Vol. 5, 1954, 295–315.

Senate Censure of Senator McCarthy, December 2, 1954

Near the close of the hearings, Senator Stuart Symington (D-Mo.) scolded Senator Joseph McCarthy (R-Wis.). "The American people has had a look at you for six weeks," Symington said. "You are not fooling anyone." Indeed, Senator McCarthy, under the glare of a national television audience, had through his excesses been reduced to a caricature of a bully. On July 30, 1954, almost two weeks after the hearings ended, Senator Ralph Flanders (R-Vt.) introduced a resolution (S. 301) calling for Senate censure of McCarthy for his behavior in the hearings. After three days of debate, the Senate voted 75–12 to refer the resolution to a six-member select committee chosen by Vice President Richard Nixon. On September 15 the committee released its report recommending censure on two counts: abuse of witnesses and contempt of a senatorial committee. On December 2, the abuse-of-witnesses count was dropped, and the Senate voted 67–22 in favor of the contempt censure.

SENATE CENSURE OF SENATOR McCARTHY DECEMBER 2, 1954

Resolved, That the Senator from Wisconsin, Mr. McCarthy, failed to cooperate with the Subcommittee on Privileges and Elections of the Senate Committee on Rules and Administration in clearing up matters referred to that subcommittee which concerned his conduct as a Senator and affected the honor of the Senate and, instead, repeatedly abused the subcommittee and its members who were trying to carry out assigned duties, thereby obstructing the constitutional processes of the Senate, and that this conduct of the Senator from Wisconsin, Mr. McCarthy, is contrary to senatorial traditions and is hereby condemned.

Sec. 2.

The Senator from Wisconsin, Mr. McCarthy, in writing to the chairman of the Select Committee To Study Censure Charges (Mr. Watkins) after the select committee had issued its report and before the report was presented to the Senate charging three members of the select committee with "deliberate deception" and "fraud" for failure to disqualify themselves; in stating to the press on November 4, 1954, that the special Senate session that was to begin November 8, 1954, was a "lynch party"; in repeatedly describing this special Senate session as a "lynch bee" in a nationwide television and radio show on November 7, 1954; in stating to the public press on November 13, 1954, that the chairman of the select committee (Mr. Watkins) was guilty of "the most unusual, most cowardly thing I've heard of" and stating further: "I expected he would be afraid to answer the questions, but didn't think he'd be stupid enough to make a public statement"; and in characterizing the said committee as the "unwitting handmaiden," "involuntary agent," and "attorneys in fact" of the Communist Party and in charging that the said committee in writing its report "imitated Communist methods—that it distorted, misrepresented, and omitted in its effort to manufacture a plausible rationalization" in support of its recommendations to the Senate, which characterizations and charges were contained in a statement released to the press and inserted in the Congressional Record of November 10, 1954, acted contrary to senatorial ethics and tended to bring the Senate into dishonor and disrepute, to obstruct the constitutional processes of the Senate, and to impair its dignity; and such conduct is hereby condemned.

Source: Congressional Record, 83rd Congress, 2nd Session, 16392.

Bibliography

Adams, John G. *Without Precedent: The Story of the Death of McCarthyism.* New York: W. W. Norton, 1983.

Anderson, Jack. *Confessions of a Muckraker: The Inside Story of Life in Washington During the Truman, Eisenhower, Kennedy and Johnson Years.* New York: Random House, 1979.

Bayley, Edwin R. *Joe McCarthy and the Press.* Madison: University of Wisconsin Press, 1981.

Cohn, Roy. *McCarthy.* New York: New American Library, 1968.

Doherty, Thomas. *Cold War, Cool Medium: Television, McCarthyism, and American Culture.* New York: Columbia University Press, 2003.

Evans, M. Stanton Jr. *Blacklisted by History: The Untold Story of Senator Joe McCarthy and His Fight Against America's Enemies.* New York: Crown Forum, 2007.

Ewald, William Bragg Jr. *Who Killed Joe McCarthy?* New York: Simon and Schuster, 1984.

Ewig, Rick. "McCarthy Era Politics: The Ordeal of Senator Lester Hunt," *Annals of Wyoming* 55 (Spring 1983), 9–21.

Griffith, Robert. *The Politics of Fear: Joseph R. McCarthy and the Senate.* Lexington: University Press of Kentucky, 1970.

Haynes, John Earl, and Harvey Klehr. *Venona: Decoding Soviet Espionage in America.* New Haven, Conn.: Yale University Press, 1999.

Herman, Arthur. *Joseph McCarthy: Reexamining the Life and Legacy of America's Most Hated Senator.* New York: Free Press, 2000.

Oshinsky, David M. *A Conspiracy So Immense: The World of Joe McCarthy.* New York: Free Press, 1983.

Potter, Charles E. *Days of Shame.* New York: Coward-McCann, 1965.

Reeves, Thomas C. *The Life and Times of Joe McCarthy: A Biography.* New York: Stein and Day, 1982.

Ritchie, Donald A. *Reporting from Washington: The History of the Washington Press Corps.* New York: Oxford University Press, 2005.

The Labor Racketeering Investigation, 1957–61

By Roger A. Bruns

The Confrontation

Robert F. Kennedy and James R. Hoffa exchanged steely glares. Kennedy, the young counsel of the Senate's Select Committee on Improper Activities in the Labor or Management Field, better known as the "Rackets Committee," prepared to stalk his prize prey, Hoffa, leader of the Teamsters union. Kennedy had first met Hoffa at a Washington dinner party, where they had begun a relationship of mutual contempt. And now, in a Senate hearing room in the summer of 1957, they would engage in a historic confrontation.

To Kennedy, Hoffa and those with whom he consorted represented the worst elements of the American economic system. On the backs of the workers whom he had been chosen to represent, Kennedy charged, Hoffa had powered his way to incredible influence and had injected unparalleled graft, corruption, violence, and intimidation into the labor movement. He was convinced that Hoffa had stolen millions of dollars from union accounts and entered into numerous sweetheart contracts with business leaders in return for payoffs. He saw him as an evil that had to be brought down.

The short, stocky union leader, who had fought and bullied his way from a near destitute childhood to a position of national power, looked at the Massachusetts, Ivy League lawyer and son of privilege and wealth as a silk-stocking, a spoiled brat, an unworthy opponent. He kept referring to him as a "boy."

Pierre Salinger, an investigative newspaper reporter and superb researcher hired by the committee, called the relationship between Hoffa and Kennedy a "blood feud." And now they eyed each other as their battle amid a major congressional investigation on national television was set to begin.

Kennedy and the Origins of the Investigation

Hoffa was right about Kennedy's lineage. Born in 1925, the seventh of nine children, he was the son of the Massachusetts businessman and political figure Joseph Kennedy and the younger brother of Senator John F. Kennedy (D-Mass.). After an elite prep school education, Kennedy followed his brothers to Harvard University. Shortly before his 18th birthday, he enlisted in the Naval Reserve, and in late 1945 he began serving as an apprentice seaman aboard the U.S.S. *Joseph P. Kennedy,* a destroyer named for his eldest brother, Joe, a Navy flier who had been killed in the war a year earlier.

Returning to Harvard, he played football, even though he weighed only about 160 pounds. Later, he graduated from the University of Virginia Law School and went to work for the Criminal Division of the U.S. Department of Justice. The following summer, in 1952, he managed John Kennedy's successful campaign for the Senate. Soon, he took a position working for Francis Flanagan, the general counsel for the Senate Permanent Subcommittee on Investigations, then chaired by Senator Joseph McCarthy (R-Wisc.). It was McCarthy who took the committee down its long road to ferret out Communists in the U.S. government.

For a short time, Kennedy left the committee. However, in February 1954, at the request of Senate Democrats, he returned as the panel's minority counsel. Following victories in the congressional elections of 1954, the Democrats regained control of Congress, so in January 1955, McCarthy relinquished the chairmanship of the committee. His successor was John L. McClellan (D-Ark.). Just 29 years old, Robert Kennedy was now chief counsel.

OVERVIEW

Background

In 1957, in the glare of a national television audience, two figures who would forge careers of towering national importance faced off as Congress probed the inner workings of certain labor unions and their ties to organized crime. Robert F. Kennedy, chief counsel of the Senate Select Committee on Improper Activities in the Labor or Management Field, probed the activities of James R. Hoffa, the new president of the International Brotherhood of Teamsters union, whose rise to power, Kennedy believed, was rife with bribes, payoffs, and close associations with mob figures. The link between organized crime and the Teamsters and other unions had been the subject of several investigative reports. In April 1956, when reporter Victor Riesel, who had written a series of articles alleging connections between organized crime and labor unions, was blinded with sulfuric acid in an attack on the streets of New York, the shock and outrage helped stir Congress to act.

Congress Investigates

Chaired by Senator John McClellan (D-Ark.), the committee for more than two years interrogated numerous organized-crime figures and union bosses.

Impact

The work of the committee highlighted the excesses of the Teamsters, and it vindicated the work of Walter Reuther, head of the United Auto Workers. The committee's findings brought down Teamsters head Dave Beck, Hoffa's predecessor, who was eventually imprisoned. It led to the passage of the Labor Management Reporting and Disclosures Act, known as the Landrum-Griffin Act, which placed certain curbs on union activity. It also led the way to a determined effort by the federal government under the presidency of John F. Kennedy in the early 1960s to expose and attack the illegal activities of organized crime.

In what directions would the new chairman take the committee? By 1955, the excesses of McCarthy's Communist hunt were all too glaring for many of the people who had seen much of it on television. McCarthy had used the committee much like a crazed general on a one-man crusade. McClellan, who had watched with disgust as the reputation of the committee diminished with each of its reckless investigative thrusts, was determined to bring civility, order, and responsibility back to the process.

The direction that the committee's work might take was given impetus on the night of April 5, 1956. A respected newspaper reporter named Victor Riesel, who was vigorously investigating corruption in organized labor, finished up his late-night radio show. On the show he attacked Local 138 of the International Union of Operating Engineers for racketeering. He also attacked Hoffa, who, he said, was maneuvering to take over the national leadership of the Teamsters.

As he left the radio studio, Riesel was approached by a man outside the famous Lindy's Restaurant in Manhattan's Times Square. The man rushed at Riesel and threw sulfuric acid in his face. The attack permanently blinded the reporter. No one was arrested but, as they began an investigation, police believed that organized crime was behind the attack.

The act was so despicable and horrifying that it elicited a heated comment from President Dwight D. Eisenhower. While attending the dedication of the new American Federation of Labor–Congress of Industrial Organizations (AFL-CIO) headquarters, Eisenhower said that his administration intended to take whatever steps were necessary to prevent the infiltration of labor unions by organized crime.

Soon federal authorities linked the crime to John Dioguardi, a man known in crime circles as Johnny Dio. The trail to Dio also led to his friend Sam Berger, head of Local 102 of the International Ladies' Garment Workers' Union, who had close ties to Hoffa and the Teamsters.

That summer, Clark Mollenhoff, an investigative reporter with the *Des Moines Register* and a friend of Kennedy's, gathered information on mob activities regarding corruption and abuses by the Teamsters, especially in a case in Portland, Oregon. In Kennedy's office, Mollenhoff urged the counsel to use his position and influence to direct the committee toward an investigation of the Teamsters.

CHRONOLOGY

1953

- *January:* Robert F. Kennedy becomes a counsel to the Senate Subcommittee on Investigations, chaired by Senator Joseph McCarthy (R-Wisc.).

1956

- *April 5:* A newspaper reporter, Victor Riesel, who was investigating corruption in organized labor, is blinded by an attacker who throws sulfuric acid in his face.
- *Fall:* Kennedy, as chief counsel of the Senate subcommittee, now headed by Senator Joseph McClellan (D-Ark.), begins to gather evidence on labor racketeering.

1957

- *January 30:* The Senate unanimously authorizes a Select Committee on Improper Activities in the Labor or Management Field to investigate labor racketeering.
- *March 26:* Dave Beck, president of the International Brotherhood of Teamsters, begins testifying before the committee about missing union money. During one session of his testimony, Beck takes the Fifth Amendment 140 times. Because of the information uncovered by the committee, Beck resigns his presidency and is later convicted and jailed.
- *August:* James R. Hoffa, Beck's successor, recently acquitted of a bribery charge, faces questioning before the committee.
- *December 6:* AFL-CIO members vote to expel the International Brotherhood of Teamsters because of alleged racketeering by its executives exposed by the Senate committee.

1959

- *August:* The Senate committee issues a special report attacking Hoffa's relationship to organized crime.
- *September:* Kennedy resigns from the committee in order to manage the presidential campaign of his brother, Senator John F. Kennedy (D-Mass.).
- *September 14:* Congress passes the Landrum-Griffin Act, restricting certain union activities.

1961

- The committee hearings end. Largely because of the work of the investigation, 141 Teamsters officials were accused of dishonest union dealings.

1964

- *July 26:* Hoffa and six others are convicted of fraud and conspiracy in the handling of a union pension fund.

By the mid-1950s, the research of Mollenhoff and a number of other investigative reporters had suggested that corrupt union officials had taken crooked paths to personal wealth and power at the expense of the hard-working membership of their organizations. They had looted union funds, negotiated sweetheart deals with companies in return for payoffs, and extorted money from businessmen with threats of pickets and labor unrest. Many of the racketeers stayed in power, evidence showed, through rigged elections within the unions themselves.

The events of the spring and summer convinced Kennedy. In August 1956, he gathered his staff and talked about the possibility of the committee's launching a major investigation of labor racketeering. For members of the Democratic Party, the idea seemed to carry much political risk. After all, big labor was a powerful constituent of Democrats nationwide, providing not only money but also manpower during election years. Although Kennedy was sensitive to the political risks, he was also convinced that exposing and cleaning out the corruption at the top of certain unions would make the organizations stronger, and the reform efforts would ultimately benefit the Democratic Congress.

Gathering Evidence of Racketeering

In November 1956, Kennedy traveled west using the alias of "Mr. Rogers." Accompanied by Carmine Bellino, a former FBI agent now working for the committee, he talked to several newspaper reporters about stories they

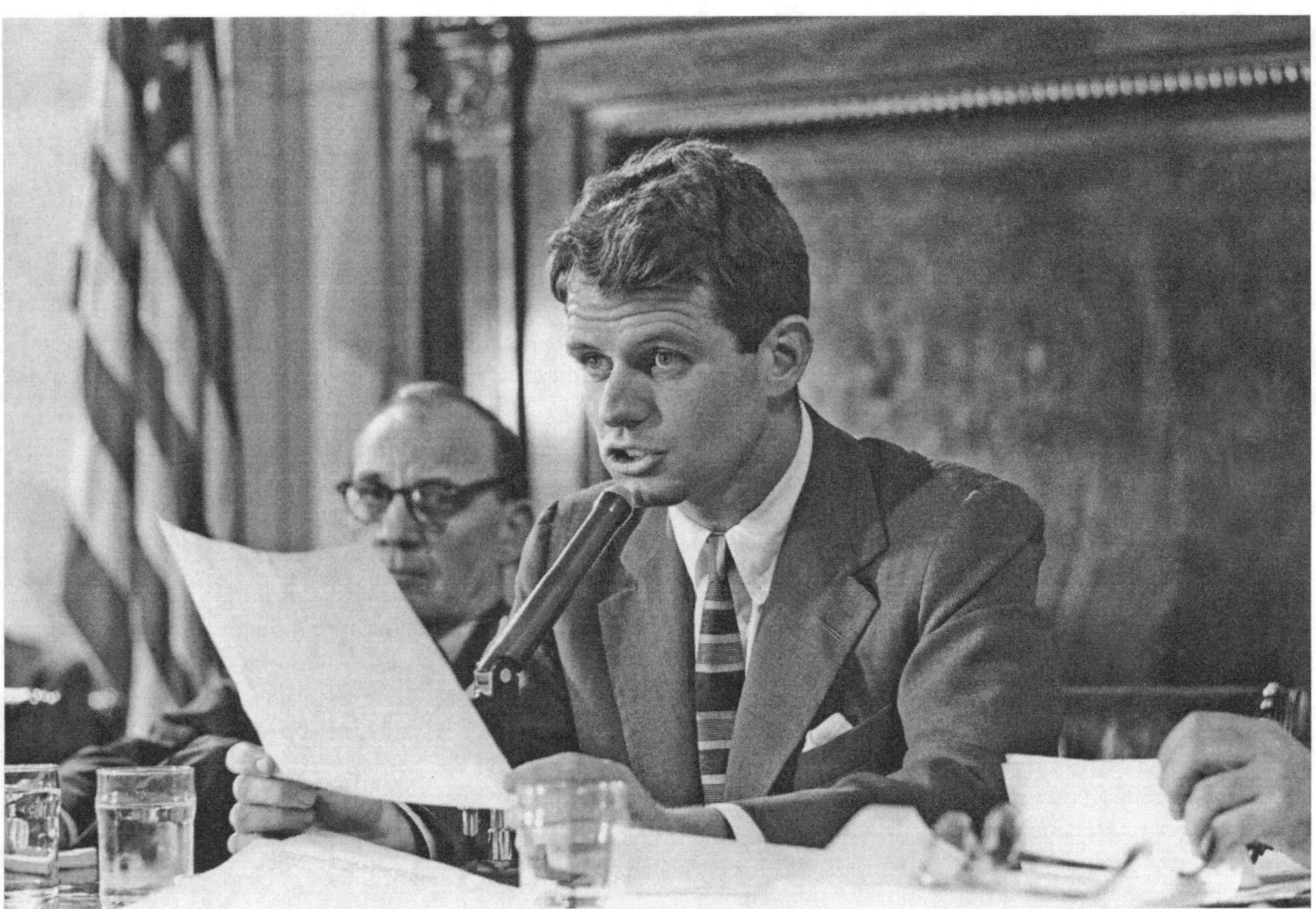

Robert Kennedy, chief counsel of the Senate Labor Rackets Committee, is shown at the hearing on March 19, 1957, in Washington. (Associated Press)

had written regarding union activities. They explored investigative avenues in Portland, Oregon, and Seattle, Washington, the home of Teamsters President Dave Beck.

Through his newspaper contacts, especially with Pierre Salinger, who had researched the Teamsters for *Collier's* magazine, Kennedy traced the nefarious activities of a so-called labor consultant named Nathan Shefferman of Chicago, who had personally helped Beck buy a few things "wholesale" in return for his sweetheart deals. Shefferman, as Kennedy would soon learn, was one of the major "fixers" working with business executives to offer bribes to union officials for favorable contracts. He also counseled businesses on the best methods to resist unionization efforts.

Kennedy and his assistant Bellino then traveled to Chicago with a subpoena to investigate Shefferman's records. At a room in Chicago's Palmer House hotel, Kennedy and Bellino spread around documents from Shefferman's files, following the trail of money from Teamsters accounts directly into the hands of Beck, much of it for his lavish home in Seattle. "In an hour," Kennedy later wrote, "we had come to the startling but inescapable conclusion that Dave Beck, the president of America's largest and most powerful labor union, the Teamsters, was a crook."

At Hyannisport, Massachusetts, the large Kennedy clan gathered for Christmas. With his wife, Ethel, and his five children at his side, Kennedy arrived to greet his relatives with some news. Tough and feisty, aching to please a father who always demanded the best, Kennedy announced that he was going to lead a congressional investigation into the corruption and the grip of organized crime on labor-management relations.

The relatives were stunned. His father was outraged. Such an investigation, argued Joseph Kennedy, would accomplish nothing, would antagonize organized labor, and would jeopardize the political path of John Kennedy to the presidency. For several days, the Kennedy patriarch railed against the idea. Hurt and disappointed, Robert Kennedy refused to back down. His sister Jean remembered the family confrontation as "the worst ever."

But Kennedy returned to Washington committed to the idea of a committee probe into union activities. He laid out his case for such an investigation to Chairman McClellan. The Arkansas senator agreed to go forward.

The Select Committee Takes Form

On January 30, 1957, the Senate passed a resolution, sponsored by Senators McClellan and Irving Ives (R-N.Y.), calling for the establishment of the Select Committee on Improper Activities in the Labor or Management Field.

The hearings would take place in the Caucus Room on the third floor of the Senate Office Building, a famous chamber with its vaulted ceiling and red carpeting. It was the same room where, in 1912, the Senate held hearings regarding the sinking of the *Titanic;* where J. Pierpont Morgan, titan of industry, faced charges of corruption; and where, only a few years earlier, Senator Joseph McCarthy conducted his politically charged televised hearings to expose Communists in the American government.

For the next two and a half years, the committee would hold periodic hearings. In that span, more than 1,500 witnesses would march to the witness table and take the oath. When the investigation was completed, the record of its testimony would fill nearly 50 volumes.

As in many congressional investigations, the committee divided sharply along ideological lines. Republican Senators Barry Goldwater of Arizona, Karl Mundt of South Dakota, and Carl Curtis of Nebraska took a consistent anti-union stance throughout the investigations, advocating strong legislation to control union activities. Chairman McClellan, along with Senator Sam Ervin (D-N.C.), was less hostile to union activities and took a middle ground between the Republicans and three prolabor members—John F. Kennedy, Patrick McNamara (D-Mich.), and Irving Ives.

Over the life of the committee, the Republicans were generally hostile to Robert Kennedy. They resented the wide latitude that McClellan gave the general counsel in deciding avenues of investigation and were convinced that he was steering the probe to benefit the Democratic Party.

Senator John Kennedy, a member of the select committee, gave a speech in which he laid out its aims. "I would say this investigation has two purposes," Kennedy declared. "The first follows the advice of Woodrow Wilson, who said: 'The best thing that you can do with anything that is crooked is to lift it up to where all the people can see that it is crooked—and then it will either straighten itself out or disappear.' Our second objective is to determine what Federal legislation or administrative action is necessary to remedy this evil."

The term *labor racketeering* was not yet firmly set in the mind of the public. The investigation would clearly lay out the practices in which labor leaders, mob gangsters, and business executives connived to skim money and power from the masses of hard-working Americans.

The committee would probe several areas of graft and corruption. First, certain labor racketeers, it was alleged, used their union positions as a front for criminal operations, directing union funds to finance gambling, prostitution, and other criminal activities. Others used their powerful positions as labor leaders to bribe, shake down, and extort money from employers by threatening strikes. Some union leaders embezzled union pensions and health funds for personal gain and channeled union business to certain contractors in return for kickbacks.

As the committee took form, its members also were determined to look into charges that some union bosses were engaging, along with mobsters, in the age-old tactics of strong-arm coercion and violence. In New York City, for example, a trucking union was formed to steer all garbage business to one company headed by a friend of the mobster Frank Costello.

The Chairman

The dour, stern chairman of the Senate Select Committee on Improper Activities in the Labor or Management Field had also many years ago been a prodigy. Born in 1896 in Sheridan, Arkansas, John McClellan was admitted to the state bar at the age of 17, four years before the minimum age requirement. It had taken a special act of the Arkansas legislature to accomplish this unusual career leap. McClellan became the youngest practicing attorney in the United States.

His career in the law soon took a path into politics. He was elected as a Democrat to the U.S. House of Representatives in 1934 and again in 1936. Strongly conservative, especially on the major social issue dear to the South, racial politics, he made a run for the Senate in 1938, suffering defeat. For a young man unused to losing anything, the blow to the ego and reputation was hard to bear. He blamed the more liberal elements of the party for thwarting his ambitions. Nevertheless, he ran again, and in 1943, he took a place in the U.S. Senate, where he would become a fixture.

In the early 1950s, McClellan became the ranking member of the Senate Government Operations Committee. It was here that he watched as the Republican chairman of the committee, Joseph McCarthy of Wisconsin, pressed on with his inquisition-like crusade to ferret out Communist infiltrators in the U.S. government. Although for a time McClellan did little to deflect the zeal of his colleague, he finally erupted during the

Army-McCarthy hearings in 1955, leading fellow Democrats on a dramatic walkout.

When the Democrats regained control of Congress and McClellan ascended to the chairmanship of the Government Operations Committee, one of the first things he ordered was a detailed code of procedures for the orderly and democratic processes of investigations. McClellan hoped that such a code would afford fair treatment to witnesses. Other Senate committees soon followed this lead and enacted their own codes of conduct. And now, in the spring of 1957, McClellan himself took up the gavel before television cameras in the most anticipated congressional hearing since the heated days of McCarthy.

Of Plots and Intrigue

Shortly after the committee investigation opened, Washington lawyer Eddie Cheyfitz, who worked in public relations for the Teamsters, suddenly appeared in Kennedy's office. Cheyfitz invited Kennedy to a dinner at his house, where he could get to know Cheyfitz's good friend Jimmy Hoffa. Suspicious but curious, Kennedy accepted the invitation. The dinner took place on February 19, 1957.

A week before the dinner, Kennedy's suspicions reached greater heights. He received a call from another lawyer, this one from New York. On the phone was a man named John "Cy" Cheasty. He announced to Kennedy that he had information that would make his hair curl.

The next day, the two sat together at lunch in Washington as Cheasty told Kennedy that he had been given $1,000 to get a job as an investigator with the Rackets Committee to act as a spy. His prospective employer in the plot, he said, was none other than Hoffa. Sensing an opportunity right out of a spy thriller, Kennedy offered Cheasty a job with the committee. He would act as a double agent.

Kennedy arrived at Eddie Cheyfitz's for dinner and his first meeting with Hoffa. Although Kennedy had seen many pictures of Hoffa, he was first surprised that the famous Teamster was short, about 5 feet 5, but stocky and muscled. After some small talk, Kennedy wasted little time quizzing Hoffa about union business. Such quizzing, it would turn out, would go on for years.

Kennedy asked Hoffa about Johnny Dio, the New York crime tough reputedly involved with the attack on Victor Riesel the previous year. Hoffa turned the questioning into a recitation of his own power and influence and the dangers of messing with him. He bragged about his brushes with the law and how he always came out on top.

As the tense evening wore on, Kennedy became aware that some of the information that Hoffa and Cheyfitz knew about the Rackets Committee had most likely come from John Cheasty. It was also clear that Hoffa, through Cheasty, was anxious to feed damning information about Dave Beck to the committee. Hoffa, after all, would ascend to the top job of the Teamsters if Beck took a fall.

Kennedy, of course, did not bring up Cheasty's name, fearful that he might tip off his new role as a double agent. As the evening drew to a close, the mutual personal contempt between Hoffa and Kennedy had been firmly seeded. Kennedy was already planning a scheme to trap the labor leader.

In early March 1957, Kennedy contacted his new double agent. Cheasty, Kennedy reasoned, could help him make quick work of Hoffa. With the help of the FBI, Kennedy orchestrated a plot to snare Hoffa while the Teamsters boss was giving money to Cheasty for his work in infiltrating the Senate committee.

On March 13, 1957, Hoffa walked into the Dupont Plaza Hotel in Washington, D.C. He soon walked out under arrest. As Hoffa handed an envelope containing $2,000 in $50 bills into Cheasty's hand, the FBI's cameras caught it all on tape.

At the courthouse, Kennedy, accompanied by his wife, Ethel, watched as Hoffa was arraigned. The Teamsters boss could not take his eyes off Kennedy, contempt written clearly on his face. The two men talked briefly, with the conversation degenerating into the subject of who could do more push-ups. A confident Kennedy told more than 50 reporters alerted to the scene that if Hoffa were acquitted he would jump off the Capitol building. Hoffa's trial and also his appearance before the Rackets Committee would be scheduled for later in the year.

Launching the Hearings

In early March 1957, the committee, setting the stage for the weeks and months ahead in exposing labor racketeering, spotlighted scandals in the Pacific Northwest. The story of mob penetration into the labor movement in Portland, Oregon, surfaced through the investigative reporting of Wally Turner and William Lambert of the Portland *Oregonian*. Their work on the story would land them a Pulitzer Prize.

The Portland case involved a central figure in the city's underworld. He was James B. Elkins, a man who had at one time manufactured whiskey during Prohibition and had been imprisoned for assault with intent to kill and for possession of narcotics.

Elkins was part of a syndicate that included mobsters, members of the Teamsters, and a district attorney. The operation controlled much of the gambling in Portland. When other members of the syndicate wanted to expand operations to include a prostitution ring, Elkins wanted no part of it. He thus became enmeshed in a quarrel that

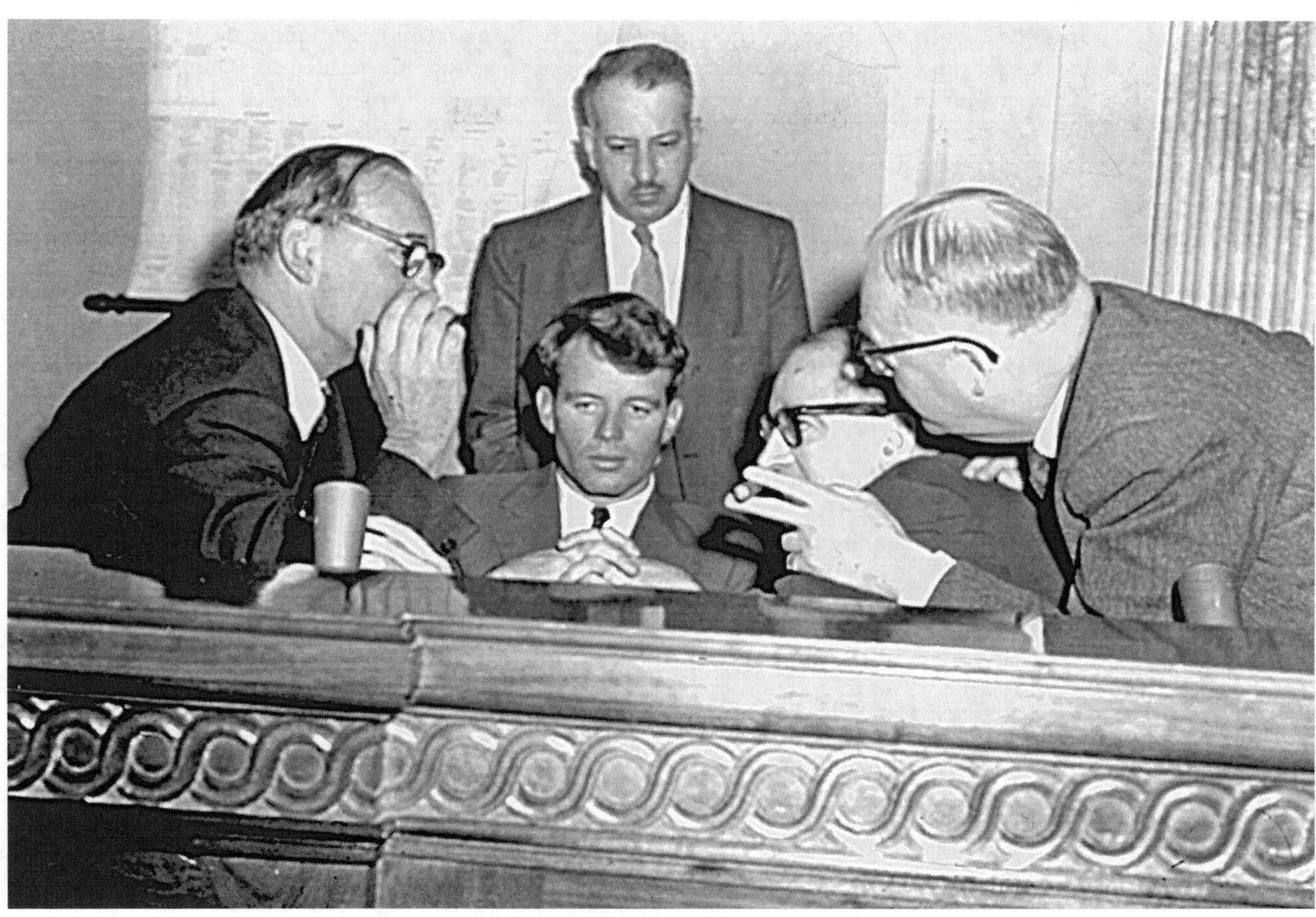

Members of the special Senate committee investigating alleged racketeering in labor and industry gather around the committee's counsel, Robert F. Kennedy, to decide whether to institute contempt proceedings against a witness who refuses to testify, March 7, 1957. (Associated Press)

threatened not only his power in the city but also his safety. At one point, Elkins said, one of the Teamsters men involved with the syndicate demanded that he go along with the plan or "you will find yourself wading across Lake Washington with a pair of concrete boots."

The threats and intimidation did not bring Elkins into line; instead, they brought the opposite reaction. He began to consider the possibility of telling his story to the press or the law. Because of his shady background, he knew that he would have to have corroborating evidence to back up his story. He began making tape recordings of his discussions with the fellow mobsters and their accomplices in the Teamsters and the Portland city government. He would eventually turn over the tapes to Wally Turner and William Lambert.

In his West Coast trip in late 1956, Kennedy had collected information on the charges made by Elkins that two Teamsters officials, Frank Brewster, a top lieutenant of Dave Beck, and Clyde Crosby, were involved in vice racketeering. The two *Oregonian* reporters made Elkins's tape recordings available to Kennedy and the McClellan committee. And now in March, armed with the recordings, Kennedy brought Elkins to the witness stand. His testimony on March 14, 1957, was explosive.

He told of threats to him and his wife by mobsters. He told of a confrontation in front of his house early one morning with two thugs. He said he made them go away.

SENATOR MCCLELLAN: You did what?

MR. ELKINS: I talked to them. Well, I pointed the shotgun at them and I talked to them, and they didn't come back any more.

MR. KENNEDY: Did you do anything else with them?

MR. ELKINS: Yes, I did. One of them, yes. I treated him a little rough.

MR. KENNEDY: What did you do with him?

MR. ELKINS: Well, I hit him on the head and knocked him around a little bit and put him back in the car and told his buddy that I was going to shoot the next person that came in my yard.

The gripping testimony of Elkins, bolstered by his tape recordings, delivered a stinging blow to the vice syndicate of Portland. As a result of the Senate hearings, two members of the district attorney's office in Portland faced indictments. The role of Teamsters officials in corruption and scandal now made national news. The Rackets Committee investigation had made a rousing bolt from the starting gate.

Its next target: Dave Beck, head of the Teamsters.

Dave Beck at the Witness Table

Born in 1894 in California, Dave Beck moved with his family to Seattle when he was four years old. Raised in a ramshackle house in the city's old Belltown district, the red-haired Beck helped make his own way from an early age, selling newspapers, catching and selling fish, selling Christmas trees, and even shooting wharf rats to sell to the city health department at $5 a head for those that showed signs of bubonic plague.

After serving in the military he took a job at Mutual Laundry, driving an old Ford truck. At his first union meeting after returning from World War I, dressed in his navy blues, he argued the laundry workers out of supporting a general strike in Seattle. "All I want for our members is a fair share of the profits; no more, no less," he said.

Soon, he became a full-time organizer for the Teamsters union. Although averse to personal confrontations, Beck assembled a formidable goon squad to protect his troops and intimidate his enemies. Under Beck's boys, the usual head-busting techniques were spiced with other weaponry. For example, one of the young Turks from his force recalled once paying a Northwest trapper $100 a quart for attar of skunk juice to be used in stink bombs.

But Beck's leadership acumen transcended the ordering of simple attacks of goon squads. He intellectually grasped the immense power of his rising union in the whole scheme of American capitalism and his own growing personal power. The members of the Teamsters rode the wheels of 10 million trucks, a massive force that moved the country's economy. As he began to consolidate the power of the union throughout the United States, he could feel the tug of power at his fingertips. Such power was exhilarating. He became president of the Teamsters in 1952.

Beck built a grand headquarters in Washington very close to the U.S. Capitol known informally as the "Marble Palace." With his gracious ways, Beck won access to the Eisenhower White House and attended many Washington social functions. Under Beck, the Teamsters increased their membership to nearly 1.5 million, making it the largest union in the country. The membership included not only drivers but also brewery and dairy workers, cannery employees, and potato-chip salesmen. He was an aggressive organizer and a well-liked leader but an ardent believer in capitalism. At a time when many other labor leaders defied business at every turn, Beck, who generally argued against strikes, wanted to work with business leaders.

Like corporate executives themselves, he did not look to the rank and file for guidance. He was there to make decisions. He once quizzically asked, "Why should truck drivers and bottle washers be allowed to make decisions affecting policy? No corporation would allow it." It is not surprising that he became a favorite outside the labor community, especially of such groups as the Chamber of Commerce.

He did not smoke, drink, play cards, bet on the horses, or become fodder for tabloid journalists looking for sexual indiscretions. He and his organization gave generously to civic and charitable enterprises, such as the City of Hope Medical Center near Los Angeles. A man who had never completed high school, he was appointed by the Washington state governor to the Board of Regents of the University of Washington. In 1950, he became its president.

He spent most of his time in his luxurious home in Seattle. On the underground level of the compound was a 45-seat theater with its 35mm CinemaScope movie projector. For the guests, the bar was stocked with both union-labor liquor and union-labor soft drinks. Next to the theater was a ballroom, complete with an electric organ, a piano, and an illuminated portrait of the president of the largest union in the United States—Dave Beck.

And now, on March 26, 1957, as he maneuvered his portly shape through crowds in the hearing room, Beck, attired in a tailor-made suit, flashed his three-diamond ring and sat down before his interrogators. He tried to present an air of nonchalance. When a reporter shouted out, "Are you nervous?" Beck grinned and shot back, "Nervous? Me? Haw!"

Kennedy, McClellan, and others on the committee had expected Beck to invoke the Fifth Amendment in answer to some of the questions. Nevertheless, they were eager to place in the formal record the results of the months of grinding, tedious investigation undertaken by the staff.

As McClellan read an opening statement, Beck, ensconced in the red-leather witness chair, began quietly but incessantly tapping one foot, perhaps betraying at least some concern at his predicament. The chairman declared that the committee had information indicating that "the president of the International Brotherhood of Teamsters, Chauffeurs, Warehousemen and Helpers of America, the largest and most powerful union in our country, may have misappropriated over $320,000 of union funds."

Beck's lawyer, Arthur Condon, had prepared a careful statement for his client to deflect any embarrassing questions—a standard recitation about constitutional articles and amendments and other constitutional protections involving self-incrimination. "I must decline to do so because this committee lacks jurisdiction or authority under Articles 1, 2, and 3 of the Constitution," he would mutter, "and, further, because my rights and privileges granted by the Constitution as supplemented by the Fourth and Fifth Amendments are violated."

For the most part, Beck stuck to the script, droning on time after time before the committee members, who gamely continued the questioning. On some occasions, however, a flummoxed and combative Beck, his face turning even more red than usual, took umbrage at certain characterizations and attacks and began to challenge his questioners. In those cases, Condon jabbed a knuckle into Beck's back to bring him back to the script. At the first sign of a temper outburst, Beck would get yet another knuckle in his spine.

On a number of occasions, Beck's labored reading of his prepared statement would draw more than a small amount of sarcasm:

MR. KENNEDY: Do you feel that if you gave a truthful answer to this Committee on your taking of $320,000 of union funds that might tend to incriminate you?
MR. BECK: It might.
MR. KENNEDY: Is that right?
MR. BECK: It might.
MR. KENNEDY: You feel that yourself?
MR. BECK: It might.
MR. KENNEDY: I feel the same way. . . .

Completing his first day before the committee, the Teamsters president and his retinue hastily marched out of the Capitol building and headed to the union's headquarters, a mere half a mile away. In his third-floor office, Beck sat down at his walnut desk, ordered a steak dinner, and prepared to watch the news of his appearance on television.

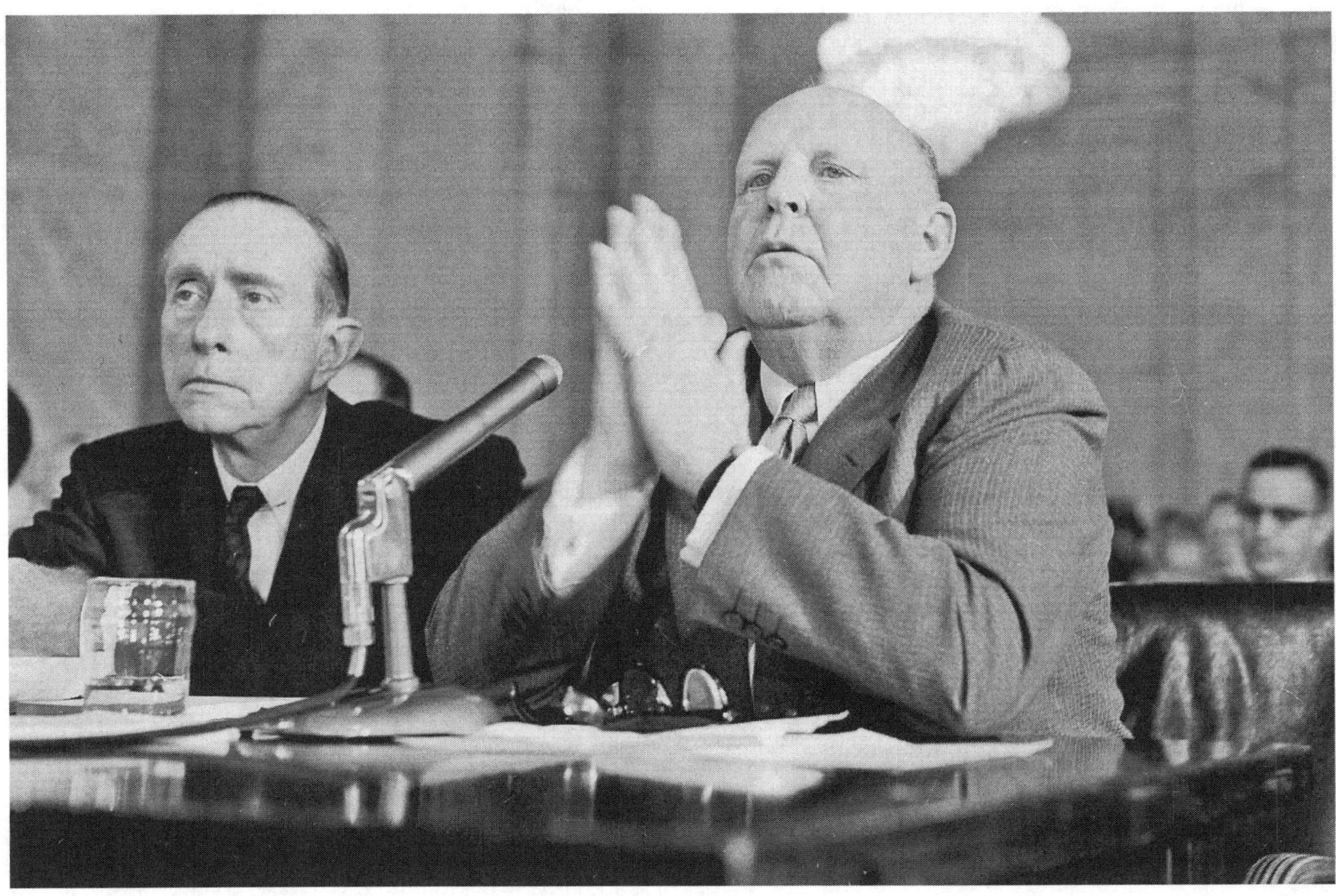

Dave Beck of the Teamsters Union strikes a prayerful attitude as he listens to a question during the interrogation by members of the Senate committee investigating labor racketeering. (Associated Press)

In the following days, things got worse. The committee's star witness against Beck was Nathan Shefferman, the "labor-relations consultant" from Chicago. Shefferman's business largely involved representing employers in their dealings with organized labor. A business wanting to avoid unionization altogether or wanting to ameliorate the possible actions that unions might take against the business, such as strikes and boycotts, might be willing to make an under-the-table deal with an unscrupulous labor leader willing to sell out his union members. Shefferman was there to make it happen, the one to negotiate the shakedown deal. He was a contact man, a go-between, the one who knew how much the graft market could bear, the one who could size up the amount of the payoff and swing the deal.

Kennedy and his investigators had struck gold when they discovered the ties between Shefferman and Beck. And now Kennedy pressed Shefferman at the hearing. He raised the question of why Shefferman had given Beck a gift of $24,500. Shefferman responded: "Mr. Beck, if you will permit me, is a terrific personality. . . . He is very attentive to his friends and very generous to his folks and people who surround him." Laughter broke out in the hearing room. Strangely, among those laughing the loudest was Dave Beck, sitting a short distance from Shefferman.

Kennedy began to list items that Shefferman, acting as a kind of personal gofer for Beck, had procured using Teamsters funds. There were silk shirts, golf clubs, football tickets, love seats, rugs, a refrigerator, two boats, a gun, six pairs of "knee drawers," a Bendix washing machine, sheets and pillowcases, and even a bow tie.

As the laughing grew louder, Shefferman paused: "Well, wait a minute, gentlemen. Please, the implication—I happen to know Mr. Beck is a moral man, and so it was perfectly all right."

Beck made his last appearance before the committee on May 16, 1957. By now, the evidence of his corruption had already essentially buried him. The boisterous, cocky man who had first walked into the committee room a few months earlier now looked like a nervous wreck, sometimes idly whistling to himself between questions.

Shortly before Beck escaped from his chair in the hearing room for the last time to head for the airport and his beloved Seattle, Senator McClellan seized the moment for a final parting short. Glowering at the witness, the chairman, with his usual astringent demeanor, declared, "Mr. Beck has shown flagrant disregard and disrespect for honest and reputable unionism and for the best interests and welfare of the laboring people of his country."

"They can make all the goddam fine headlines they want to out of Washington, D.C.," Beck retorted. "The way we are now organized we can launch a fight in every nook and corner of America. I've fought and struggled and worked to bring the Teamsters to that position. You can mark my words: Dave Beck and the Teamsters will come out on top, but if we're unfairly pushed, business and the community will suffer."

Dave Beck soon faced indictments for income-tax fraud and grand larceny involving Teamsters funds. He was found guilty and sentenced to five years in prison. He would begin his prison term on June 20, 1962. As reporters gathered in Tacoma, Washington, at the dock where the ferry would take the prisoner to his new residence, Beck likened himself to a general headed for temporary exile. "What was it General MacArthur said at Corregidor?" Beck shouted out. "'I'll be back.' Well, that goes for me, too."

But it would not be Dave Beck who would lead the Teamsters. In his place now was the fiery Teamsters organizer who had so lusted after the position that he had leaked unfavorable information on Beck to Senate committee investigators. James Hoffa would now ease his stocky, short body into the plushest seat in the "Marble Castle."

On the Trail of Hoffa

In April 1957, *Time* magazine ran a story about Robert Kennedy and his pursuit of labor corruption. It talked about his indefatigable energy—horseback rides at dawn before going to work, endless hours at the office sifting through a growing avalanche of anonymous tips. "Since they have a staff of servants at home," *Time* reported, "Mrs. Kennedy has sat in at almost all of the Teamsters hearings to watch her husband at work. In the hearing room, Kennedy took a terrier grip on recalcitrant witnesses, accusing, badgering and interrupting in his high-pitched, bean-and-cod-accented voice, drawing on a remarkable store of information."

And now that information and that energy would be directed toward Kennedy's chief target, James Hoffa. Born in Brazil, Indiana, on February 14, 1913, Hoffa was the son of a coal miner who died of black lung disease when the boy was seven years old. By 1924, the family was in an apartment house in a working-class neighborhood of Detroit. While in junior high, the youngster worked as a delivery boy, and he dropped out of school in the ninth grade.

Lying about his age, he soon took a job at the Kroger Company, working in the grocery warehouses a few blocks from his house, unloading railroad cars for about 30 cents an hour. As a teenager he got involved with the local union, displaying an unusual grit and determination to fight for the cause—not only with energy and passion but also with his fists. Later, he landed a job as an organizer for the International Brotherhood of Teamsters.

In his early days with the Teamsters, he roamed Detroit's loading docks for Local 299, trying to recruit truck drivers and warehouse men into the union. Constantly assaulted by police and strikebreaker thugs hired by business leaders, he refused to be intimidated. "I was hit so many times with nightsticks, clubs and brass knuckles that I can't even remember where the bruises were," he recalled. He saw the inside of jail cells time and again, he said, and "every time I showed up on the picket line, I got thrown in jail. Every time they released me, I went back to the picket line."

So dangerous was union organizing in the 1930s that many on the front lines learned to take special precautions. Joe Franco, one of Hoffa's fellow Teamster organizers, later described one safety technique that Hoffa taught him and others. "To this day," Franco said, "I still have the habit he drilled into me about getting into a car. I put my right leg in and my left leg stays out, and then I start my car. If the car is rigged and you start your car that way, you have a 50–50 chance of surviving because if it blows up, it will blow you out of the car."

"Our cars were bombed out," Hoffa remembered. "Cars would crowd us off the streets. Then it got worse. . . . Your life was in your hands every day. There was only one way to survive . . . fight back. And we used to slug it out on the streets. They found out we didn't scare." Hoffa's reputation as a resilient battler had spread so widely by the early 1950s that he was elected international vice president.

Unlike Beck, Hoffa did not lust after the high life and its trappings. Instead, he had lived in the same working-class Detroit neighborhood with his wife and family for two decades.

But his rise was not due entirely to his energy, organizing skills, and toughness. Kennedy and the committee sought to demonstrate that Hoffa courted members of organized crime to help him build his power base; that he used many of the corrupt and violent methods of the mob; that he robbed union pension funds to engage in questionable business practices; and that he sold out union interests in return for kickbacks.

In July 1957, shortly before his first committee appearance, Hoffa was tried in Washington, D.C., on the charge of attempting to bribe a committee member. The prosecutors had the testimony of the man Hoffa paid to infiltrate the committee; they also had photographs taken at the Dupont Circle Hotel in Washington that showed Hoffa paying the money and receiving documents relating to committee business.

Hoffa secured the services of two of the most high-priced, veteran lawyers in Washington, Edward Bennett Williams and George Fitzgerald. The defense attorneys used every trick to influence a jury. Their tour-de-force move was to bring in America's African American icon, the boxer Joe Louis, from Detroit to sit in the audience before an almost all-black jury and publicly embrace Hoffa.

The Teamsters leader walked, found not guilty on July 19, 1957. Williams, remembering Kennedy's mocking humor at the arraignment that he would jump off the Capitol if Hoffa were found innocent, joked with reporters that he would send Kennedy a parachute.

Hoffa explained simply, "It proves once again if you are honest and tell the truth you have nothing to fear."

Hoffa: The Elusive Prey

In August 1957, fresh from his acquittal in a D.C. courtroom, Hoffa first appeared before the committee. It was the first of several visits by the Teamsters boss to the hearing room. Unlike Beck earlier in the year, Hoffa did not resort to the Fifth Amendment and other constitutional protections. Instead, he displayed an unfailingly faulty memory. The man could not recall anything of interest to the committee. "To the best of my recollection I must recall on my memory I cannot remember," he would say. "I can say here to the Chair that I cannot recall in answer to your question other than to say I just don't recall my recollection."

So frustrated and infuriated did Chairman McClellan become that at one point he declared, "If these things do not refresh your memory it would take the power of God to do it. The instrumentalities of man obviously are not adequate."

At another point, after one of Hoffa's lack-of-memory answers, Kennedy mocked him with his own words. "'To the best of my recollection I must recall on my memory that I cannot remember,' is that your answer?" Kennedy retorted. As the caucus room erupted in cheers and jeers, the chairman gaveled for order. The same routine played out a number of times.

Hoffa was, to say the least, an elusive prey. In attempting to link the Teamsters boss with illegal payoffs and bribes, the committee trudged along a nearly invisible road. Hoffa dealt only in cash. He had no bank accounts in his name. He did not use a checkbook. Most of his business records had been trashed. When questioned about large amounts of cash that he always seemed to have on hand, he attributed them to racetrack winnings.

Sitting at the center table, right, James R. Hoffa, head of the Teamsters, faces off against the racketeering committee, August 20, 1957. (Library of Congress)

Ethel Kennedy was often in the hearing room, transfixed like everyone else by the confrontation. On a couple of occasions, some observers heard her exclaim, "Give it to him!"

In September 1957, the committee stated its case against Hoffa. Accusing the Teamsters boss of manipulating $2 million of union funds, the committee declared, "James R. Hoffa has taken the part of employers and convicted extortionists against members of his own union. James R. Hoffa has constantly defended and given aid and comfort to Teamster Union officials who were selling out the interests of Teamster Union members by setting themselves up in highly improper business activities and by entering into collusive agreements with employers."

Such damning charges might have seemed damaging to Hoffa's bid to retain control of the union. They proved to be no such thing. In October 1957 Hoffa was elected president of the Teamsters again by a margin of nearly 3 to 1.

Nevertheless, George Meany, the head of the AFL-CIO, and other labor leaders became especially concerned that the continuing drip-by-drip revelations from the Senate committee, especially about the Teamsters and their criminal associations, were doing major harm to the image of all unions in the United States. Meany clearly wanted the activities of the Teamsters to be publicly disassociated from those of other unions. Shortly after the Teamsters overwhelmingly stood behind the embattled Hoffa, Meany and others in the AFL-CIO leadership ousted the Teamsters from the larger labor organization.

Hoods in the Woods

On a chilly day in November 1957, in the small upstate New York town of Apalachin, dozens of men stood around a barbecue preparing to feast on fancy steaks, veal chops, and hams from Armour & Company in Binghamton. As the men chatted, renewing acquaintances, a car with two police officers and two U.S. Treasury agents rolled up the dirt road toward the open compound. The law-enforcement officials, responding to a tip-off, thought they were on the trail of men involved in bootlegging.

But the number of cars parked in the field piqued their curiosity. They soon realized that the cars were from a variety of states. This was more than a simple bootlegging operation. They called for backup police and a roadblock.

This was the home of Joseph Barbara. In organized crime circles he was known as "Joe the Barber." Now 52 years old, Barbara, a native Sicilian, had taken charge of an underworld syndicate controlling beer and soft-drink distribution. The mob boss had invited other crime figures to his estate to ease tensions that had been building among some of the crime families. Police officials, it turned out, had stumbled onto a gathering of many of the most notorious gangland figures in the United States. Fifty of the 58 men had arrest records involving everything from illegal use of firearms to murder.

As the police encircled the house, the men inside it panicked. With a cold drizzling rain falling, they ran out into the dark, into nearby woods. These were men used to high-level dangerous situations, tough guys, many in their fifties and sixties, who got to the top by terrorizing and outmaneuvering their rivals. Now, they scattered through the unfamiliar terrain of trees and brush, ripping their clothes and falling down, soaked and muddy.

One by one they were pulled out or wandered back onto a road where they were picked up, shivering, humiliated, and angry beyond measure. As police gathered up the bedraggled lot, names began to match the faces.

There was Vito Genovese from New Jersey, who liked to be called "Don Vito" and who aspired to be the head of all the Mafia families; Santo Trafficante, a Tampa, Florida, crime boss who presided over a gambling empire in Cuba; Joe Profaci, the "Olive Oil King," from New York; Carlo Gambino from New York, who was a Mafia member from his earliest days in Sicily and rose to head a mob family that profited from many things, including illegal alcohol; Joe Bonnano, known as Joe Bananas, a major crime family leader from New York active in gambling, racketeering, and other enterprises; and Joseph Civello from Texas, who was involved in narcotics trafficking.

As both public and government scrutiny would soon reveal, a number of these men were deep into racketeering. Some of them would be called before the Senate committee.

The United Auto Workers and Walter Reuther, 1958

For the Republican members of the committee, Kennedy's war with Hoffa, Beck, and the Teamsters, an organization not especially friendly to the Democratic Party, began to appear obsessively and suspiciously focused on that single union. What about the rest of organized labor? What about the man and his organization that had been a constant rock in the shoe of American capitalism—Walter Reuther and his United Auto Workers (UAW)?

Vito Genovese. (Library of Congress)

In July 1957, Kennedy, under constant pressure from Senator Barry Goldwater and other Republicans, recommended to McClellan that the committee investigate Reuther, the UAW, and its actions in a strike against Wisconsin's Kohler Company that had begun in April 1954.

Born in 1907, Reuther, like many prominent union organizers, grew up with a working-class background and joined a union at an early age. His father was a brewery-wagon driver and union leader in Wheeling, West Virginia. Walter and his two brothers, Roy and Victor, moved to the Detroit area to find jobs in the auto industry and, like their father, became actively involved in union affairs. At Detroit City College, Reuther helped organize a club that was affiliated with the League for Industrial Democracy, a socialist organization.

He was 29 years old in 1936 when he became president of Local 174 of the UAW. In a little over a decade, he reached the presidency of the national organization. Although Reuther was staunchly anticommunist, it was his ties to socialist organizations that fueled the mistrust and anger of Republican politicians and big business executives.

And now in 1957, Barry Goldwater, Karl Mundt, and others on the Rackets Committee trained their sights on Reuther, the UAW, and the Kohler Company strike. Founded in 1873, Kohler had a long history of antagonistic relations with organized labor. A manufacturer of bathroom and other plumbing fixtures, the Sheboygan, Wisconsin, company reached a negotiating impasse with union workers in April 1954 over pay, working conditions, and other matters.

After a strike and a two-month closure of the plant, the factory resumed production with scab labor, a move that touched off violence along the picket lines. Some picketers wore gas masks. Several clashes between union supporters and company police turned bloody. In one confrontation, more than 300 people were arrested.

The strike ground on into its third year. By early 1957 and the beginning of the McClellan investigations, a number of national business organizations such as the Chamber of Commerce sought to use the committee as a force to limit union power and especially to discredit Walter Reuther.

Of all the committee's hearings, those involving the UAW and the Kohler strike proved to be the most politically contentious among the committee members. The hearings began on February 26, 1958, and lasted slightly longer than a month.

Restless while he waited three days to testify, Reuther decided to tell his own story even before he was given a forum. He gathered reporters at a lunchtime news conference in the Senate caucus room during a break in the testimony. He charged Kohler with attempting to destroy the union. He talked about company officials establishing a private army and storing weapons at the plant to inflict violence on strikers. He charged that Kohler had simply refused to bargain and had rebuffed all attempts at arbitration. It was, he said, a calculated effort by Kohler to wipe out all union representation at their plant.

Conceding that the UAW was responsible for some of the violence, Reuther nevertheless quoted an October 1957 National Labor Relations Board report that stated that the company was out to "teach the union a lesson." Reuther said that the acts of violence "were the inevitable by-product of the company's acts of extreme provocation, the intense hatred generated by the company's continuous and vicious campaign of anti-union propaganda." Impassioned observers from both sides of the strike told of numerous acts of violence. The hearings concluded with the testimony of leaders of the organizations involved—Reuther and Herbert Kohler, president of the company.

On March 26, 1958, Kohler charged that the UAW had engaged in mass picketing that was illegal and included vandalism, threats, intimidation, and invasion of private property. The union, he said, was simply attempting to strangle the company and wreck its business in order to enforce its demands.

After Kohler's appearance, which lasted less than two hours, Reuther strode to the witness chair. Pugnacious as well as highly informed, he began by reading a statement that took nearly as long as Kohler's entire appearance before the committee. Reuther spoke of the history of the union and its role in forging better lives and working conditions for its members. He defied the committee to find any evidence of undemocratic voting or irregular or corrupt financial dealings. He rejected the notion that the union was affiliated in any way with mob bosses. Not surprisingly, Reuther blamed Kohler for the strike, arguing that the company refused to bargain in good faith and had brought in an arsenal of weapons to intimidate those on the picket lines.

Often, Reuther turned attempted attacks on the UAW into impassioned defenses. When Senator Goldwater showed a 16-year-old picture of a UAW official hitting an individual with a baseball bat during a strike at a Ford plant, Reuther became incensed. "We were fighting out there against the gangsters and getting no help from the police," Reuther shouted at Goldwater. "You drag out a photograph. . . . Sure this is wrong, but why did we get into this kind of thing? . . . Because the company was controlled by gangsters, because they beat us up in our homes, they beat us up in public places, and because the police department wouldn't protect us."

The committee heard reports on Reuther's personal finances on the last day of testimony. Carmine Bellino, the committee investigator, told the senators that he had never seen more meticulous books for any union or corporation than those kept by the UAW.

The investigation essentially exonerated the UAW. Even the Republicans were convinced of Reuther's honesty regarding his personal finances. After the hearings, Goldwater admitted to Kennedy, "You were right. We never should have gotten into this matter. This investigation was not one in which we should have been involved."

Nevertheless, the fact that Reuther and his fellow officers had been forced to testify before a congressional committee, even though there had been essentially no evidence of wrongdoing uncovered by committee staffers before the hearings began, worked to the detriment of the UAW and its leader.

The McCarthy hearings, which had preceded the formation of the McClellan committee, had left the public with a general impression of widespread conspiracy and corruption in labor unions. Unfortunately, merely appearing before a congressional investigating committee in the 1950s suggested some sort of wrongdoing to much of the public. For the UAW, its vindication before Congress did not make up for the general unfavorable taint of scrutiny that it and organized labor had undergone.

Despite the clean bill of health given to the UAW, the committee unearthed enough documentation that eventually led to criminal proceedings against not only the Teamsters Union but also top officials of the bakery workers, operating engineers, textile workers, meat cutters, and carpenters unions.

August 1958: The Second Hoffa-Kennedy Showdown

In August 1958, about a year since his first grilling before the committee, James Hoffa once again faced Robert Kennedy. Onlookers in the Senate caucus room were hushed as the two combatants readied for battle a second time. Kennedy sat at the edge of his chair, sometimes pushing his horn-rimmed glasses onto his forehead. Hoffa, giving off his usual air of confidence and bravura, grinned at Kennedy. At times the two exchanged long, mutual stares like prizefighters before the opening bell.

Kennedy soon launched into prepared remarks painting the Teamsters head as nothing less than a glorified crook, extorting money from his union, cavorting with notorious mobsters, and building a dangerous power base that threatened the fabric of labor-management relations.

Throughout the course of the investigation, Kennedy, McClellan, and other members of the committee had emphasized that all of the evidence accumulated had indicated that, overwhelmingly, the members of the Teamsters union were hard-working, honest individuals. As the investigation unfolded, it also became clear that many were unusually courageous. As committee investigators fanned out across the United States accumulating evidence against corrupt Teamsters and company officials and their mobster connections, a large number of the rank-and-file members were intimidated and, in a number of cases, physically assaulted when they spoke with committee investigators.

On September 9, 1958, Amos Reniker, a truck driver from Joplin, Missouri, defied warnings and appeared in the committee witness chair. He told of being attacked by four men after he had spoken to a committee investigator. He told of another driver who had been beaten with a hammer. To Kennedy and McClellan, these were a special breed of men, the kind who would wash clean

This Vaughn Shoemaker cartoon shows Uncle Sam (labeled "U.S. Patience") glaring from under the brim of his hat on which is perched triumphant labor leader Jimmy Hoffa (labeled "Hoffa's Arrogance"). Hoffa's footprints can be seen marching up Uncle Sam's arm and shoulder. Both Hoffa and his International Brotherhood of Teamsters had been accused of racketeering by the U.S. government. At its first unsupervised election in 1961, the union showed its scorn for the government by reelecting Hoffa president by acclamation and tripling his salary. (Library of Congress)

from their union the grafters and cheats who had taken over the leadership.

Kennedy's battle to take down Hoffa was nearly obsessive. One night, as Kennedy drove with Pierre Salinger from the Capitol past the Teamsters building, they spotted a light on in Hoffa's office. Not to be outworked, Kennedy suddenly turned the car around and returned to his office. "If he's still at work," Kennedy told Salinger, "we ought to be." It was after midnight.

On September 20, 1958, after yet another exhausting round of questions and rebuttals, accusations and denials, the chairman called a recess. Hoffa snickered to one of his aides that Kennedy was tired. He was right. The counsel later wrote in his journal, "I am mentally fatigued—more than during any other hearing. We have been going on for a long time without a break & I have about had it. I shall be happy when Hoffa is finished next week. McClellan also very tired. This year seems to have been tougher than last. Plodding grind. . . . I feel like we're in a major fight. We have to keep going, keep the pressure on or we'll go under."

Kennedy was fatigued but undeterred. As documents piled up on his desk and telephone calls flooded his office, he was determined to stay on top of the work, to keep moving forward.

Organized Crime on Display

In the highly publicized congressional investigation headed by Senator Estes Kefauver (D-Tenn.) in 1950, the committee had been unequivocal in declaring that a national crime syndicate existed in the United States, and its pervasive power was like that of a "second government." Although many continued to believe that the existence of a mafia was something of an exaggeration, the roundup of mobsters gathering in one location for a central meeting suggested otherwise. And, most important for the Rackets Committee, 22 of the men at Apalachin had union or labor-management ties.

Now Kennedy was ready to lay evidence before Congress and the powerful eyes of television, to expose the full extent of the gangster infiltration of union management. In a committee hearing, Kennedy portrayed Johnny Dio as the master racketeer of organized crime. In return for kickbacks to union officials, Kennedy said, Dio negotiated sweetheart deals with unions for his garment factories that allowed him to use non-union, immigrant labor and thus avoid the usual contractual obligations of labor agreements that burdened his competitors.

With Hoffa's blessing, Johnny Dio, along with his partner, Anthony "Tony Ducks" Corallo, set up six "paper locals" in New York, Kennedy charged. The locals were phantoms; they had no actual workers as members, just associates of the Mafia.

Hoffa's collaboration with Dio, Kennedy charged, proved lucrative to both: Hoffa got kickbacks, and Dio and the other hoods, now part of the Teamsters organization, got control of airport trucking in New York City.

The further the committee investigated the affairs of some labor leaders and their business confidants, the greater the number of notorious organized-crime figures that surfaced in the probe. By 1959, the witnesses included a veritable parade of underworld characters, many of whom had been picked up in the woods on that rainy day on November 14, 1957, in Apalachin, New York.

Ruth Young Watt, chief clerk of the Permanent Subcommittee on Investigations, later recalled the visit of Vito Genovese, known in hoodlum quarters as "king of the rackets." "Oh, he was the scariest one," Watt said. "He was the only one that really frightened me. . . . I would stand in back of where the senators were when he was testifying, and he had the coldest eyes. He would look right through you and just make chills. He was about the coldest individual I think I've ever seen."

During Genovese's appearance before the committee, Kennedy repeatedly asked the crime king about allegations of a wide range of schemes, including black-market intrigues and goon squads committing murder. In answer to each question, Genovese, glaring through amber-tinted glasses, took the Fifth Amendment.

And then there was Joey Gallo and his brother Larry. The brothers ran with local street gangs in Brooklyn, eventually hooking up with the Profaci family. By the time they walked into the Senate hearing room on February 17, 1959, Joey, 28 years old, had been arrested 17 times and Larry, age 30, was close behind at 13. Joey became known as "Crazy Joe," an accurate moniker for his unpredictable ruthlessness. The appellation also had some psychiatric accuracy: He had spent some time in the psychiatric unit at Kings County Hospital, in Brooklyn.

The committee was interested in the connection of the Gallo brothers with the coin-operated machine business in New York, Ohio, Pennsylvania, and West Virginia. The brothers not only were key men in Local 19 of the Federated Service Workers Union but also had connections with the Teamsters. Over the years, a number of jukebox owners and proprietors of various coin-operated businesses had been severely beaten by hoods working for crime families that were taking over many of the coin-operated businesses and collaborating with labor union bosses to keep their operating costs low.

Larry Gallo, short, his jet black hair combed straight back, wore a dark suit; Joey, his hair in a ducktail, sported a black suit, a black sport shirt buttoned at the collar, and sunglasses.

Chairman McClellan opened the questioning:

CHAIRMAN: You, on my left, give your name, your address, and your place of business or your business occupation, please sir.

MR. LAWRENCE GALLO: Lawrence Gallo, 2031 East 67th Street, Brooklyn, N.Y.

CHAIRMAN: What is your business or profession, or occupation?

MR. LAWRENCE GALLO: I respectfully decline to answer because I honestly believe my answer might tend to incriminate me.

And so it went. Although they refused to answer questions, the Gallo brothers did not bring with them the open hostility displayed by Vito Genovese. The Gallos tried to make small talk with Kennedy outside the hearing room.

Ruth Young Watt remembered Gallo at the witness table: "He was testifying one day and sitting at the hearing table and he flicked his glass and it went right into an ashtray on the floor where the photographers sat facing him. It broke into a million pieces. So I had to sit down and clean it up. He said, 'Oh, I wouldn't have done that if I'd known you had to clean it up.' So apparently he had done it on purpose, just to cause a diversion."

When Joe Profaci took the stand, no one could understand a word he said. The Brooklyn-based racketeer, whose front was an olive-oil import business, had been born in Italy. And now, as he replied to Kennedy's questions, his Italian accent suddenly became overwhelming. A frustrated Kennedy retorted, "We had a nice talk yesterday. Your English was very good. Your accent has gotten so bad today. You understand very well. What happened to you overnight?"

The parade of gangsters continued. Kennedy was satisfied that he had made his case that organized crime had become entrenched in the business affairs of some of the nation's unions.

In August 1959, in a special report to the Senate, the McClellan committee, in unequivocal terms, attacked Hoffa and his ties to organized crime. "In the history of this country," the report declared, "it would be hard to find a labor leader who has so shamelessly abused his members or his trust."

The report alleged 21 counts of "improper actions" by Hoffa and his lieutenants. Among the most incendiary indictments were that Hoffa, allied with gangsters Johnny Dio and Tony "Ducks" Corallo, made deals that resulted in low wages and poor working conditions for workers; that he and his associates manipulated votes at union elections; that Hoffa, through his lawyers, accepted bribes; and that he steered Teamsters Health and Welfare Fund money to mobsters such as Morris "Moe" Dalitz, one of the mob's builders of Las Vegas. Dalitz used the money from the Teamsters pension fund to build the Desert Inn and the Stardust Hotel.

The report warned: "If Hoffa remains unchecked he will successfully destroy the decent labor movement in the U.S." Asked to comment by *Time* magazine, Hoffa said simply, "To hell with them."

In September 1959, after 1,525 sworn witnesses, more than 500 separate hearings, and more than 46,000 pages of testimony, Robert Kennedy resigned as chief counsel of the Rackets Committee. He would now turn his attention to organizing the presidential campaign of his brother, John F. Kennedy.

Legacy

From the earliest congressional investigations in American history, committees have emphasized one important goal—possible new government legislation to correct systemic wrongs and inequities. Even before they concluded, the Rackets Committee hearings produced an important, if controversial, piece of legislation.

In September 1959, Congress passed the Labor-Management Reporting and Disclosure Act of 1959, known as the Landrum-Griffin Act, after its sponsors Democratic representative Phillip Landrum of Georgia and Republican representative Robert Griffin of Michigan. The act provided a worker's bill of rights, guaranteeing a union member's right to have a say in the running of the union and protection from intimidation. But essentially the law wounded the labor movement in concrete ways.

The legislation featured a formidable list of requirements and restrictions on union activity. Unions now faced a mountain of bureaucratic red tape in reporting to the government their financial affairs, contract negotiations, contracts signed, strikes conducted, procedures followed when calling strikes, bonding of officers, and much more.

A number of the restrictions limited what unions could do in strike situations. For example, the law prohibited "hot-cargo" arrangements—the organized refusal of unionized workers to carry cargo or work on goods produced by non-union companies or companies on strike. Added to the various provisions of the 1947 Taft-Hartley Act that had made it harder, as well as time-consuming, to call a strike, these provisions also made it illegal for strikes to spread beyond those who were first involved in the issue.

The Rackets Committee released its final report in March 1960. Chairman McClellan wrote, "There is much evidence of infiltration by criminal elements into the labor and management field. The committee found wholesale looting of union treasuries by unscrupulous and dishonest labor leaders and found instances where management conspired and connived with the dishonest leaders to gain favorable contracts to the detriment of the rank-and-file members. I am convinced that such activities of these unsavory elements in labor and management require careful and continuous scrutiny."

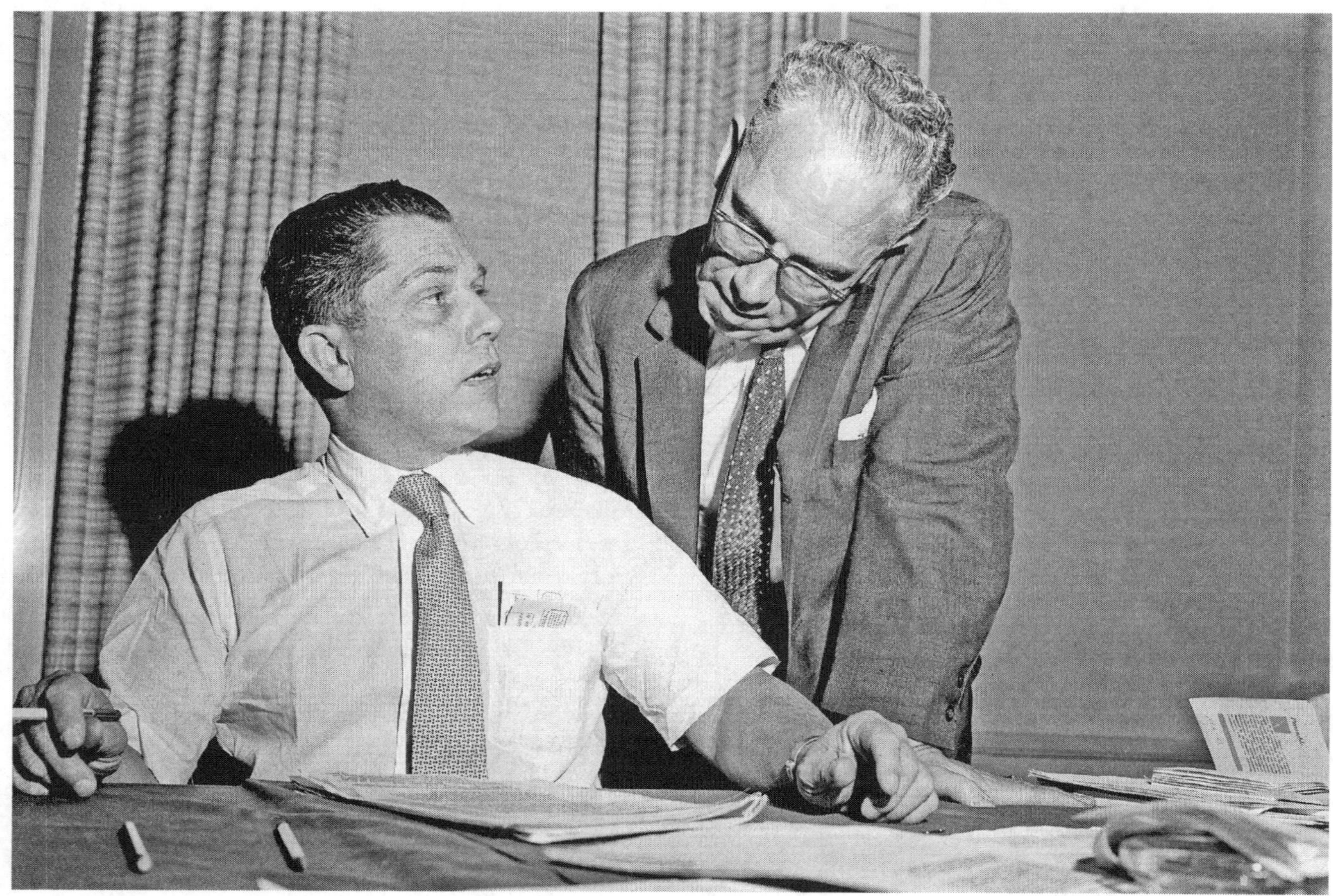

Teamsters Union leader Jimmy Hoffa works in his shirtsleeves as he confers with Milwaukee attorney David Previant during a break in a meeting of the union's Constitution Committee in San Francisco, California, August 1957. (Associated Press)

David Previant, a Teamsters lawyer, denounced the committee for abusing its power. "We had guilt by association," he charged, "guilt by marriage, guilt by eating in the same chop house, guilt by the general counsel's amazement, guilt by somebody else taking the Fifth Amendment, guilt by somebody else refusing to testify."

The historian Arthur Schlesinger, friend and later biographer of Robert Kennedy, vigorously disagreed. "It was not as if Kennedy had decided to go after the mob and the Teamsters out of abstract prejudice," he said. "The Rackets Committee had dug up a mass of concrete information of lawbreaking."

When John Kennedy became president of the United States in 1961 and Robert Kennedy took over as U.S. attorney general, the new administration forged a vigorous war on organized crime. Thus, the Rackets Committee investigation had made a significant impact, not only in spurring new legislation but also in influencing major government policy.

DOCUMENTS

Remarks of Senator John F. Kennedy, Washington, D.C., April 29, 1957

In late January 1957, the Senate authorized an investigation of labor racketeering. The Senate Select Committee on Improper Activities in the Labor or Management Field, chaired by Senator John McClellan of Arkansas, focused on allegations of corruption and abuse of power in labor unions. The chief counsel of the committee was Robert F. Kennedy. One of its members was his brother, Senator John F. Kennedy of Massachusetts. A rising star in the Democratic Party, John Kennedy realized that the hearings on labor racketeering would generate much national excitement. In late April, in a speech in Washington, Kennedy outlined the goals of the committee.

REMARKS OF SENATOR JOHN F. KENNEDY, WASHINGTON, D.C., APRIL 29, 1957

. . . I would like to discuss with you briefly tonight the Senate's investigation of labor racketeering through a Special Committee of which Senator McClellan is the Chairman and of which I am a member. Many have asked me: What is going to come of this investigation? What are your objectives? I would say this investigation has two purposes. The first follows the advice of Woodrow Wilson, who said: "The best thing that you can do with anything that is crooked is to lift it up to where all the people can see that it is crooked—and then it will either straighten itself out or disappear." Our second objective is to determine what Federal legislation or administrative action is necessary to remedy this evil. Permit me to discuss our progress with respect to each of these objectives.

I.

The first objective of the McClellan Committee is to obtain an exact understanding of what constitutes labor racketeering, and to separate these practices of a few dishonest, disreputable men, including hoodlums who invaded the labor movement from the outside and purchased or falsified union charters like so much merchandise, from the legitimate activities of the great mass of union leaders and members. As many of you who are lawyers know, laymen—particularly those already biased—are likely to describe as racketeering legitimate collective bargaining, legal boycotts, and union political activities. Whatever you may think of these activities, they should not be labeled racketeering. Based upon my experience as a member of the Special Senate Committee and 11 years on Congressional labor committees, I suggest that when you see headlines about labor racketeering you keep the following five types of activities in mind:

First—Labor racketeers are those who are using labor organizations, founded originally to protect the worker's welfare, as a front for criminal operations, as a means of organizing vice, gambling, prostitution and other rackets; using union funds to finance and extend these illegal or questionable activities, and to influence or corrupt public officials into permitting them. In Portland, Oregon, for example, vice king Jim Elkins and several of his associates and employees in a variety of rackets were all made Teamsters Union members in good standing, engaging in so-called union activities that would have made Samuel Gompers, founder of the American Federation of Labor, turn in his grave.

Secondly—Labor racketeers are those who are using their positions with a union to practice extortion, shakedowns and bribery; threatening strikes, physical violence or property damage to employers who fail to give them under-the-table payments, personal gifts or other contributions which the union members never see; or securing, to the detriment of their own membership, the waiver of certain labor and health standards set forth in the union's collective bargaining agreement, in return for a large fee going into the racketeer's own pocket. Our Committee's investigation of Mr. Nathan Shefferman, for example, intends to go into the matter of whether there is any connection between his services as a management representative and consultant on labor relations on the one hand, and, on the other hand, as a supplier of funds, services and discount purchases to Dave Beck whose union was involved with his management clients. In a more blatant case in Southern Illinois a short time ago, a contractor for the Atomic Energy Commission was asked for a private contribution of more than one million dollars by a labor racketeer who sabotaged the project for 18 months, and who boasted at his trial: "When I left Chicago I threw away my shovel for a blackjack, and I have been using it effectively ever since. I have carved out an empire."

Third—Labor racketeers are those who are abusing and manipulating for personal gain union pension, welfare and health funds; embezzling welfare funds, receiving kickbacks from employers or insurance brokers; or channeling a monopoly of a union's welfare fund business to personal friends or business associates, without regard to the cost, or to those willing to give them a commission on the side. Teamsters leader Frank Brewster, for example, channeled a multi-million dollar monopoly in his union's welfare plans to an insurance broker who also turned out to be Brewster's partner in a stable of race horses, a supposedly equal partnership that was unusually profitable for Mr. Brewster to the tune of $40,000, while his partner lost exactly that amount.

Fourth, and somewhat similarly, labor racketeers are those who are converting union treasuries for their own personal use and profit; financing their investments, hobbies, private affairs and even their homes with dues contributed by members to strengthen their union; and obtaining this money either through questionable loans, so-called gifts, or outright larceny. One Chicago union official, for example, spent $3,400 of his members' money on what he called a "good-will" tour of Europe. "To whom were you spreading goodwill?" he was asked. "Myself," came the reply.

Fifth and finally, labor racketeers are those who are conspiring with employers to use union power to wreck other businessmen and other unions; to prevent, by methods which include strong-arm coercion and violence, other employers from marketing their products or other unions from organizing even within their appropriate jurisdiction. In New York City, the local crime committee found that a trucking union was formed to steer all garbage business to one company headed by an old friend of Frank Costello's, intimidating all other companies and truckers out of the market.

All of these are practices I call labor racketeering. What about management, some have asked. Why isn't your committee investigating improper management practices? The fact is that our committee was primarily established to investigate labor-management or racketeering—improper management activities as such are subject for other investigations by other committees, except to the extent that they show collusion with labor rackets. Some of the small-time racketeers and others called in our Portland hearing were businessmen, not labor leaders. Mr. Shefferman is a businessman [?]—and so, some of the time, are Dave Beck, Frank Brewster, Jimmy Hoffa, Johnny Dio, Three Fingers Brown, Albert Anastasia, and others, all of whom own factories, trucking lines or other enterprises.

And it is a shocking fact that many employers have collaborated in labor racketeering practices, forcing their competitors out of business, obtaining monopolies for themselves, fighting legitimate union organizations and paying off racketeers in the process. Other employers are honest but timid—fearful of the labor trouble that may result if they refuse to yield to racketeers or if they testify before public authorities.

Thus, the problem of labor racketeering is not one for the Federal Government alone, or even primarily—the responsibility for cleaning up this foul situation is divided also among union members, employers, local government, and the general public.

Union members and honest union leaders should write their own regulations, and do their own policing. Conspiracy, violence, fraud and similar crimes are state and local offenses, not Federal.

But the Federal Government does have a responsibility in many ways. Involved are violations of the anti-trust laws, the Taft-Hartley Act, the Hobbs Anti-Racketeering Act, and the Internal Revenue Code.

II.

This leads me to the second objective sought by our Special Committee—the possible development of a need for new legislation. Such legislation must not be undertaken prematurely or in a spirit of vengeance or prejudice.

Nevertheless it now appears that additional legislation in some areas may be necessary.

As Chairman of the Labor Subcommittee of the Senate Committee on Labor and Public Welfare, I have a special interest in and responsibility for this aspect of the current investigations. Some matters must and should await the completion of the investigation—others, in my opinion, are presently ready for legislative hearings on the basis of information already uncovered by our Special Committee and past investigations.

There are five subjects into which we may inquire in these hearings:

1. The full disclosure of the financial operations of employee health and welfare funds, whether operated by unions, management or jointly.
2. The requirement of minimum standards or safeguards in union trust funds, including adequate reserves, independent audits and bans on collusion and discrimination.
3. The full disclosure of, and possible limitations on, conflicts of interest (transactions in which a union official has a personal or financial interest) in the handling of these trust funds and other union funds.
4. Safeguards to facilitate democratic control by union members of both types of funds (welfare and union treasuries) and their management, including safeguards for those workers arbitrarily excluded from membership, denied participation by the device of trusteeship or penalized for objecting to union policies.
5. Improvement in the apparently inadequate provisions of the Taft-Hartley Act for the reporting to the Government and the membership of all kinds of union funds and financial transactions; and the policing of those reports so that abuses of the type recently disclosed before our Select Committee might be more readily identified and corrected.

Many people have written or spoken to me about this labor racketeering investigation. They consider it to be exciting, and crusading adventure with crime. They are wrong. It is a discouraging, difficult task, taking the Committee into a seamy side of American life and American labor that would be more pleasant to ignore, and stirring hostilities and prejudices that are politically better left dormant. But this is our assignment, and we have accepted it—and with the understanding and assistance of well-informed members of the public like yourself, we shall continue our efforts to bring a little more light and a little more justice to this dark and troubled area on the American scene.

Source: John F. Kennedy Presidential Library and Museum, www.jfklibrary.org/Historical+Resources/Archives/Reference+Desk/Speeches/JFK/JFK+ Pre-Pres/1957/002PrePres12Speeches_57APR29.

Exerpt from Interview with Ruth Young Watt, Chief Clerk, Permanent Subcommittee on Investigations, 1948–79, October 5, 1979

Ruth Young Watt personally participated in congressional investigations for three decades. In 1947, Senator Owen Brewster of Maine hired Watt as clerk of the Special Committee to Investigate the National Defense Program, which President Harry Truman had chaired when he was a senator during World War II. In 1948, when the Senate created the Permanent Subcommittee on Investigations, Watt became its chief clerk. It was from this position that she managed the hearing rooms, prepared subpoenas, supervised committee records, and handled the committee's finances. From 1957 to 1960 she also served as the chief clerk of the Select Committee on Improper Activities in the Labor or Management Field, popularly known as the "Rackets Committee." In 1979, historian Donald Ritchie of the Senate

Historical Office asked Watt about her experiences with the Rackets Committee.

EXERPT FROM INTERVIEW WITH RUTH YOUNG WATT, CHIEF CLERK, PERMANENT SUBCOMMITTEE ON INVESTIGATIONS, 1948–79 OCTOBER 5, 1979

RITCHIE: Didn't you get started on the Teamster hearings while you were still in the Permanent Subcommittee?

WATT: I think it was those hearings on the Navy textile procurement. During the period that we were investigating that, this labor thing came up. That's where it got started and I believe it was Clark Mollenhoff that kept pounding away at Senator McClellan that they ought to have hearings on labor rackets. Then the Labor Committee decided they were going to do something about it. Then somebody put in a resolution for the Senate Labor Committee to have a special committee to review this thing. Then Senator McClellan got into it for the subcommittee and they compromised and put in to have a select committee with four members from the Labor Committee and four from the subcommittee.

RITCHIE: Was Mollenhoff around the office a lot in those days?

WATT: Yes.

RITCHIE: Basically trying to find out what you were doing, or was he providing information?

WATT: He was providing, too. He was close to the staff. He was from Iowa and LaVern Duffy was from Iowa, and they were good friends. And he and Bob were good friends, although I think Clark was always a strong Republican. He wrote for the *Des Moines Register.* He was there at every press conference, and he was around all the time, in fact he wrote one or two books on the committee. He was the one who started pushing to have this investigation into labor. . . .

RITCHIE: At one point you had 104 people working on the staff of the Rackets Committee, I read in one of the accounts.

WATT: That's right. We had forty-six on the payroll and we had more than that, we had GAO (General Accounting Office) people all over the country. They weren't on our payroll, they were being paid by GAO, but they were working for us. And we had offices all over the place. . . .

RITCHIE: Do you think that Kennedy handled that large staff effectively?

WATT: Yes. He had the knack. And then Kenny O'Donnell came after I don't know what period. Bob hadn't been there too long, maybe three or four months when Kenny O'Donnell came aboard, because I remember Kenny was up at Hyannis Port with us on that Fourth of July in '57.

RITCHIE: What was that occasion?

WATT: Bob had part of the staff up at his place at Hyannis Port working on the New York hearing. We went up for the Fourth of July, and Kenny was there.

RITCHIE: What was Kenny O'Donnell's role?

WATT: He was administrative assistant and he sat right outside of Bob's door and he was his memory, because he had a magnificent memory. Bob would say, "We did so-and-so at such-and-such a time, what was his name?" And Kenny could tell you; of course Bob was involved with so many things. But Kenny was really his right-hand man. They were a great team together. I had a great deal of admiration for both of them.

RITCHIE: Pierre Salinger also came on the committee staff.

WATT: He was the first on the payroll of the Rackets Committee. He had worked for Collier's and had some information on rackets so that he sold Bob on employing him. So they put him on the payroll on March 1st, I think it was.

RITCHIE: It was quite a colorful staff of people.

WATT: Yes, and we had James McShane who later became head of the United States Marshalls when President Kennedy came in (he died only a year after he was in). Of course, Pierre and Kenny. Larry O'Brien was never on our payroll, I don't know if he was on Senator Kennedy's payroll, but he was around so much I almost felt he must have been on Senator Jack Kennedy's payroll. He was a smart politician, smart campaigner. He was in and out of the office a lot, especially when we knew that Senator Kennedy was going to run for the presidency. They were running for President in our office after 5:00 in the evening. Kenny, and Larry, and Pierre and all those people were working on the campaign back in '59.

RITCHIE: They would all gather in Robert Kennedy's office?

WATT: Yes. You knew they were going to a campaign strategy meeting when you saw them come and go. But it would be after hours. . . .

RITCHIE: During the Rackets Committee hearings you had a lot of pretty tough characters testifying. You had Dave Beck, and Jimmy Hoffa, but you also had Vito Genovese. . . .

WATT: Oh, he was the scariest one. He was the only one that really frightened me.

RITCHIE: In what way?

WATT: I would stand in back of where the senators were when he was testifying, and he had the coldest eyes. He would look right through you and just make chills. He was about the coldest individual I think I've ever seen. We had the Gallo brothers, I think one of them was murdered.

RITCHIE: Joey Gallo.

WATT: Yes. He was testifying one day and sitting at the hearing table and he flicked his glass and it went right into an ashtray on the floor where the photographers sat facing him. It broke into a million pieces. So I had to sit down and clean it up. He said, "Oh, I wouldn't have done that if I'd known you had to clean it up'." So apparently he had done it on purpose, just to cause a diversion. Of course, that didn't stop Senator McClellan or Bobby Kennedy. The attendance was pretty good for those hearings. Jack—Senator Kennedy—came quite frequently. He would come when Bob would call and tell him it was going to be very interesting. I remember one day that he came into a hearing, it must have been when they knew he was going to run for the presidency because the press was flocking around him. He hadn't had any lunch and Evelyn Lincoln came in with a tray of lunch for him, and he took it and went into the telephone booth to try to eat it. The press was like this around him, so he never ate his lunch. I remember it very well, because he was in that little telephone booth with his lunch. No matter what he did it was news. When the Kennedys were around you felt it in the air. I don't know if I feel that way about Teddy Kennedy because I don't have much dealing with him, but for Senator John Kennedy and Robert Kennedy you just felt the excitement in the air when they were around. I don't know how to explain it. And when their father came to town everybody hopped! I remember one time he came during the hearings and he was going back to Boston. They had Eastern Airlines, Jack Kennedy's office, me, the SEC, and somebody else working on one reservation for him to get back to Boston! . . .

RITCHIE: Talking about some of those witnesses like Vito Genovese and Johnny Dio Dioguardi and all the others, did you ever fear for any physical violence?

WATT: No, never. I think it's true that they take care of their own when things don't go right, but not anybody else. I don't think that anybody had anything to fear. . . .

RITCHIE: Well, with the Rackets Committee alone you had some 1,500 witnesses.

WATT: Yes, and we paid every one of them. One time, when Dave Beck was testifying, we had some people in from Oregon. It had something to do with west coast labor unions. But we had two women that they subpoenaed, both were named Helen. One was "Big Helen" and the other was "Little Helen." They had been madams. They both were very respectable looking ladies, and one was a tall lady who lived in Oregon and was now happily married. The two of them were sitting there and Fred Othman, who was a newspaper man, said, "My God, Ruth, she looks just like my sister!" Anyway, she had come in from the west coast and one of the investigators had used his airline card to pay her way, and neglected to tell me, and I paid her again. I called her on the phone and wrote her a letter and told her that she'd been paid twice and I would be "out of pocket." I think I had a check back from her within a week. I was a little uneasy, you know, about having to pay a one-way fare to the west coast. . . .

RITCHIE: The Teamsters hearings seemed like a replay of the Army-McCarthy hearings in some ways: you had television cameras, you were in the Caucus Room.

WATT: I had the Caucus Room reserved the year around. Anybody who wanted it had to come to me. There wasn't the tension. The only time there was live television was during the Beck hearings, and that was Channel 5, I believe. Clark Mollenhoff was the one who was in charge of it, and was the voice. Other than that it was just the cameras for news.

RITCHIE: But you were in the papers quite frequently at that time. I've seen pictures of you handing subpoenas to Dave Beck and to Jimmy Hoffa. There seemed to be a little humor there as well, some of the characters went to great lengths not to answer the questions.

WATT: Oh, yes. Jimmy Hoffa was famous for that. He never claimed the Fifth Amendment, but would say, "I can't recall," and so on.

RITCHIE: What was your opinion of Hoffa? You must have seen a lot of him.

WATT: Oh, yes. It felt as though he lived with the staff in the daytime during the hearings. He was back and forth, even after the Rackets Committee was over he was back before the subcommittee in 1961. Of course, I was prejudiced, naturally, so I really didn't have the right focus on him as a person. I was prejudiced that he was a wheeler-dealer and was, we thought, part of the mob. And of course, we played right into his hands.

RITCHIE: What do you mean?

WATT: By having the hearings on Dave Beck who was president of the Teamsters Union. Following a prolonged investigation, Jimmy could step right in as president of Teamsters. So we always felt that we were responsible for him being president of the Teamsters Union. He was smart, but all these mobsters—you couldn't help but feel that he was tied in with them.

RITCHIE: Did Hoffa come to the offices before and after those hearings?

WATT: I can't remember that he was ever in that office. He might have been, but I can't remember.

RITCHIE: I wondered, because you see all the performances in the news and on television, I wondered if the relations between people changed at all when the cameras were turned off.

WATT: Oh, it was the same. It's not the same as on the floor of the Senate, but this was not politics. This was good over evil! It was a sincere thing. Everybody was trying to do a job. With the Teamsters Union I've heard it said that they don't care because they get their increases and they are interested only in a good living for their families. They don't know what's going on at the top. They're paying in their dues and getting their benefits and that's it—the welfare benefits, sickness, and their salary.

RITCHIE: I've heard that it was very hard to collect evidence on them because they destroyed so much of their paperwork.

WATT: Maybe they did, but we had an awful lot of files sitting in there. One time I think there was half a roomful of things that came in. I had to testify to that. Officially, I was responsible for them to be turned in, of course I never saw them, the investigators were the ones who did, but as chief clerk I was responsible officially. I can't remember which case it was that I testified, but I remember all those things in Room 160, files, great big bales of them. It might have been on the Sally Hucks case, that was a Hoffa case. She was a telephone operator at the Woodner, and she testified that she never got anything, but she had received a fur coat from him. The committee found out and it was turned over to Justice and I had to testify in that case. She went to jail. You see it was poor little people like that got it in the neck because the big ones were smart enough to get out of it. She had a good lawyer, but they had all the telephone tolls from the Woodner Hotel. And of course, Carmine Bellino was working on that, too. . . .

RITCHIE: It seemed like the whole mob was down there.

WATT: Yes, as time went on. I got used to all these strange names. And we had so many labor unions, the Teamsters was the biggest one, but we had the Bakers, and the Steamfitters, and all kinds of them. . . .

RITCHIE: The Rackets Committee had some interesting members, in fact it made a lot of reputations for John Kennedy and Barry Goldwater and others because of all the exposure they got from it. What were they like back then? Was there anybody in particular on the Rackets Committee that impressed you?

WATT: I thought they all were pretty outstanding. Senator McClellan, Senator Mundt—well, he had made his name as chairman of the Army-McCarthy hearings—Senator John Kennedy even before that.

RITCHIE: John Kennedy was on the Government Operations Committee but not on the Permanent Investigating Subcommittee.

WATT: That's right, but he was on the Rackets Committee because he was on Labor. I didn't have that much contact with Senator Jack Kennedy. I saw him in Hyannis Port once, and I saw him at the Rackets Committee, but he was not there every day. Bob made sure that when there was going to be publicity he came, and some days we didn't have that much. Bob was, after all, going to become chairman of the campaign for the presidency, and that helped him a lot. I told Senator McClellan one time, "Senator, Jack Kennedy would not be president if it hadn't been for you and this committee." He said, "Yes, people forget things so fast." And that's true, it's true of everybody; they want to know what have you done for me lately? . . .

RITCHIE: The person who seemed to be Robert Kennedy's chief antagonist on the committee was Barry Goldwater.

WATT: Well, he and Jack Kennedy were both presidential aspirants. He was conservative and Bob wasn't; their whole viewpoint was different; and one was a Republican and the other a Democrat.

RITCHIE: What did you think about Goldwater in those days?

WATT: I liked him. He was very nice. One time he called me up to his office to meet Bob Cummings and his wife, who had come to the hearings—that's in my photograph album. Edna Carver, his secretary, was my good friend. Then one time he came back from somewhere and brought a little bottle of perfume, I remember it had my name on the outside, I was quite impressed. Of course, he had that department store out in Arizona. I liked him very much.

RITCHIE: Homer Capehart was briefly on that committee, he succeeded someone.

WATT: When Senator Ives didn't run again in 1958.

RITCHIE: Capehart seems like an amusing character.

WATT: Wilma Miller, who was his secretary—we became very good friends afterwards—but she was very difficult when she was working for him at that point. When she was in his office I wasn't too happy going to that office. When I saw him in the hearing, why he didn't know me from Adam, he wasn't there that long and I didn't have that much contact with him. But I remember Wilma was very difficult. Later on, Senator McClellan gave her a job on the Patents Subcommittee after Senator Capehart was defeated, and I got to know her pretty well. But she was a difficult person when she was in authority.

RITCHIE: He was sort of a blustery little character.

WATT: More or less. He wasn't that little, he was kind of wide. But then he had a big tragedy in his life, some of his children were killed in an accident, about '58 or '59. Of course, we had all that tragedy in Senator McClellan's life, too, around that point, when Jimmy was killed in that private plane accident in '57 or '58. When the Rackets Committee started on the first day, Senator Goldwater and Senator Carl Hayden presented Senator McClellan with a gavel that was made out of Arizona ironwood. It had his initials on it, and I was custodian of it all those years up until he was no longer chairman of the subcommittee. But there was a little chip in it. When Senator McClellan's father died in 1958, Senator Ives took over for one day of hearings when he went out to the funeral, and we had a little board so the gavel wouldn't ruin that beautiful table in the Caucus Room. Well, Senator Ives on his first whack hit the corner of the board and took a chip out of that gavel. Senator McClellan couldn't figure out what happened, but of course we told him later. Arizona ironwood—you wouldn't think anything would damage it!

RITCHIE: Frank Church also was on that committee briefly.

WATT: He replaced Senator Pat McNamara. You see the first year Senator McNamara had defeated Senator Ferguson. McNamara was a big labor union man. After the first year he said, "We don't need this committee anymore, I'm getting off. We've served our purpose and I'm getting off." Well, probably the labor unions told him to do that. When he went, Senator Church came on to replace him. On the first day that Senator Church came to the committee he came over; they were voting and he was the first one there in the Caucus Room. I, of course, introduced myself to him and he said, "You know, I feel like what Harry Truman said when he first came to the Senate. He said, 'When I came to the Senate I wondered what I was doing here; and after I had been here six months I wondered what everybody else was doing here!'" That was the first time I had ever heard that when Senator Church told me. He's come a long way.

RITCHIE: He was very young at that point.

WATT: He had graduated from college and won an oratory contest or something. And when he made that keynote speech at the Democratic Convention he used college oratory. I was quite disappointed when I heard that in 1960. He's of course grown up since then, but it was definitely college oratory, the whole thing.

RITCHIE: Eventually when Robert Kennedy came back to the Senate, he was on the Government Operations Committee, but he never got on the Permanent Investigating Subcommittee, did he?

WATT: Yes, he was on the full committee, but he asked not to be put on the subcommittee.

RITCHIE: Why was that?

WATT: Well, after all he had been chief counsel and had all those people. He had other fish to fry anyway. . . .

RITCHIE: When you mentioned Kefauver, it reminded me: Did the Committee have access to the Kefauver Crime Committee papers?

WATT: I don't know. My biggest regret was that there were so many of the printed hearings around all the time that I never bothered to get a set for the committee. We never did have a set, we had to go to the library. All the papers went to the Commerce Committee, and I don't think that we had any of their files. Of course, we had access to the FBI files, and if we wanted a file we just wrote them. We wrote the Attorney General or J. Edgar Hoover.

RITCHIE: I've been through some of the Kefauver records at the Archives and I was struck by the mug shots and criminal records of some pretty frightening looking people.

WATT: That's right. We had many pictures and charts of the families. We had big charts on the walls, and then they were made smaller to fit into the printed hearings. They were put together by the staff. There were many of those families, and a lot of them have been killed in the meantime since then. The ones that were the most frightening were the narcotics hearings. Genovese was the head of that. Later on we had Joe Valachi, that was the first time we knew it was called "Cosa Nostra," he's the one that introduced that. . . .

Source: Watt, Ruth Young. "Ruth Young Watt, Chief Clerk, Permanent Subcommittee on Investigations, 1948–1979." Interview by Donald A. Ritchie. Oral History Project of the Senate Historical Office Available online at www.senate.gov/artandhistory/history/oral_history/Ruth_Young_Watt.htm.

Excerpt from Testimony of James B. Elkins, February 27, 1957

"Nail by nail, board by board," Time *magazine reported on March 18, 1957, "the special Senate committee headed by Arkansas Democrat John McClellan continued hammering together its case against U.S. labor racketeering." In the first week of its hearings, the committee focused on the activities of the International Brotherhood of Teamsters in Portland, Oregon. The star witness was James B. Elkins. A man who at various times in his life had been involved in bootlegging, narcotics, gambling, and other illegal ventures, Elkins was a member of a syndicate that included mobsters, Teamsters officials, and a Portland district attorney. When he believed his life was endangered, he became a witness before the McClellan committee. His mesmerizing testimony, replete with accounts of illegal tape recordings, threats of being thrown in a local lake "with a pair of concrete boots," and tales of bribery and packages of money hidden in manila envelopes, set the stage for other witnesses ready to reveal their own secrets about the ways and means of labor racketeering.*

EXCERPT FROM TESTIMONY OF JAMES B. ELKINS, FEBRUARY 27, 1957

MR. KENNEDY: Will you recount for the committee the conversation that you had with Mr. Frank Brewster?

MR. ELKINS: As near as I can remember it, I came into his room and I first sat down, in his little waiting room. Three men came in and looked me over for a couple of minutes and walked out. Then, he came in and I went in his place. I am looking around and he said, "You don't have to be so-and-so afraid of me. I don't wire up my place." I said, "I am not afraid of you wiring it up, Mr. Brewster." He said, "I am going to tell you to start with I don't like the people you represent." I said, "I don't represent any people, just Jim Elkins."

He said, "Well, I am going to tell you something else. I make mayors and I break mayors, and I make chiefs of police and I break chiefs of police. I have been in jail and I have been out of jail. There is nothing scares me."

I said, "I don't want to scare you. All I want to be is left alone." He talked a little more and he got red in the face and he said, "If you bother my 2 boys, if you embarrass my 2 boys, you will find yourself wading across Lake Washington with a pair of concrete boots." I believe that was the expression.

I said, "Let us name the boys."

THE CHAIRMAN: Who were the two boys?

MR. ELKINS: Clyde Crosby and Bill Langley.

THE CHAIRMAN: Crosby was what at that time?

MR. ELKINS: He had the job he has right now.

THE CHAIRMAN: Crosby was what?

MR. ELKINS: Whatever the position he holds, he is the big man for the Teamsters union in Portland and he is in charge of the Portland area, international representative or whatever he is.

THE CHAIRMAN: He was a big official or power in the Teamsters union at that time?

MR. ELKINS: That is correct.

THE CHAIRMAN: Who was Langley?

MR. ELKINS: He was the district attorney of Multnomah County, Portland, Oregon.

THE CHAIRMAN: And he was ordering you not to embarrass him?

MR. ELKINS: That is correct.

THE CHAIRMAN: If you did, you would find yourself walking through Lake Washington with a pair of concrete boots.

MR. ELKINS: That is correct.

THE CHAIRMAN: All right, go ahead.

MR. ELKINS: He also said, "Tom Maloney is a blubberheaded blabbermouthed so-and-so and I have known him 20 years, and I have put him in business 20 times and he messes up every time." Although he didn't say "mess up."

I told him I agreed with that, certainly, and he said Joe McLaughlin would be an asset to any man's organization.

THE CHAIRMAN: He said that or you said it?

MR. ELKINS: He said it. He said—"But I don't know what you're bellyaching about. You didn't let them make enough money. They could have done better in a popcorn stand."

THE CHAIRMAN: He was claiming you didn't let them make enough money?

MR. ELKINS: That is correct.

THE CHAIRMAN: Are those the two men who testified here yesterday?

MR. ELKINS: That is correct, yes, sir.

THE CHAIRMAN: They took the fifth amendment?

MR. ELKINS: That is correct; yes, sir.

THE CHAIRMAN: All right, proceed.

MR. KENNEDY: Will you go ahead?

MR. ELKINS: That is it. I just walked out, and I went on back home. Then I started catching more hell than I did before.

MR. KENNEDY: What happened to you then?

MR. ELKINS: They would call my wife and make threats, and then they would call at 2 o'clock in the morning and tie the phone up for a couple of hours.

MR. KENNEDY: How would they tie the phone up?

MR. ELKINS: They would call from some place and leave the receiver off. If they called from a roadside pay phone and left the receiver hanging, you can't use your phone.

They told me and my wife, "We are just a minute away and we are coming over to break both arms and both legs." I said, "Well we'll be waiting." My wife wanted to run next door to the neighbors, but I didn't want her out of the house, and I didn't want to leave her and the youngster there alone. So I just took a shotgun and sat by the door, but they didn't come.

THE CHAIRMAN: Did they ever come?

MR. ELKINS: Two fellows came when I wasn't home on two occasions and she called me and they would leave before I could get there.

MR. KENNEDY: How did you finally catch them there?

MR. ELKINS: Well, I left like I was going to leave and I doubled back in another car.

MR. KENNEDY: In another car?

MR. ELKINS: In another car, yes.

MR. KENNEDY: Then, what happened?

MR. ELKINS: Well, I pulled up to the curb, and I talked to them and they left and they didn't come back no more.

THE CHAIRMAN: You did what?

MR. ELKINS: I talked to them. Well, I pointed the shotgun at them and I talked to them, and they didn't come back any more.

MR. KENNEDY: Did you do anything else with them?

MR. ELKINS: Yes, I did. One of them, yes, I treated him a little rough.

MR. KENNEDY: What did you do with him?

MR. ELKINS: Well, I hit him on the head and knocked him around a little bit and put him back in the car and told his buddy that I was going to shoot the next person that came in my yard.

MR. KENNEDY: And they never came back?

MR. ELKINS: They never came back. Another time they called at 9 o'clock in the morning and they said, "Old man, we want to meet you right now," and my wife got excited when she heard the voice and she thought she knew them and so I took the phone and I said, "Well, I can't meet you right now, but when and where?" They said, "96th and Marine Drive." I said, "In the river or out of the river?" 96th and Marine Drive is on the banks of the Columbia River. And he said, "You just be there." But my wife raised such a fuss that I didn't go.

THE CHAIRMAN: You did not keep the appointment?

MR. ELKINS: No, I didn't keep the appointment.

MR. KENNEDY: How many telephone calls do you think that you received during this period of time?

MR. ELKINS: Maybe 20, and I don't believe over 20.

MR. KENNEDY: Were they at all times?

MR. ELKINS: Day and night, anytime, 2 or 3 o'clock in the morning sometimes. When they tied it up the longest was from about 1:30 until about 3:30.

MR. KENNEDY: The way they would tie it up was to put a call in to you and then leave their own phone off the hook.

MR. ELKINS: That is correct.

MR. KENNEDY: That ties your phone up?

MR. ELKINS: Your phone is tied up, that is correct. When I would listen on the receiver I could hear trucks go by occasionally. So first I thought they had cut my telephone line, and then I guess the telephone company or someone would come by to use this phone eventually and hung it up. The next day I called the telephone company and they explained to me what happened.

MR. KENNEDY: Did you ever take any measures to protect yourself?

MR. ELKINS: Yes, the Portland Police Department was trying to protect me but I live in the county and the Teamsters controlled the sheriff, so I didn't feel like I could get much protection there. So the city police attempted to try to cover me, but they were out of their jurisdiction. One of the boys was indicted for some simple thing, a Portland policeman.

MR. KENNEDY: What was that?

MR. ELKINS: He was eventually indicted.

MR. KENNEDY: For doing what?

MR. ELKINS: False swearing, they called it.

MR. KENNEDY: How long a period of time did this continue?

MR. ELKINS: About 7 months.

MR. KENNEDY: Did you put lights up in your house?

MR. ELKINS: Floodlights all of the way around, up in the trees and on the sides of the house.

MR. KENNEDY: When you were up visiting Frank Brewster he said to you that if you embarrassed his boys, you would be walking through Lake Washington with cement boots?

MR. ELKINS: That is correct.

MR. KENNEDY: You are sure that he said that?

MR. ELKINS: I am positive.

MR. KENNEDY: Was your other brother, Fred Elkins, ever threatened?

MR. ELKINS: No, not that I know of. He doesn't live in Oregon.

THE CHAIRMAN: Mr. Elkins, you have testified that you talked persuasively to two of those who came to visit you.

MR. ELKINS: Yes, sir.

THE CHAIRMAN: Did you identify the 2 men that you knew, those 2 that you had the encounter with?

MR. ELKINS: No, I did not. I didn't know them. They had a license that I had run down later and it was a stolen license plate and it wasn't a proper license plate.

THE CHAIRMAN: You tried to identify them later?

MR. ELKINS: That is right.

THE CHAIRMAN: And you ran into the difficulty of trying to trace a stolen license?

MR. ELKINS: That is right.

THE CHAIRMAN: Or someone using a stolen license?

MR. ELKINS: That is correct.

MR. KENNEDY: Now, Mr. Elkins, I would like to take you back to that meeting in early January of 1955 when you received the telephone call from Tom Maloney to come up to Seattle—

MR. ELKINS: That is right.

MR. KENNEDY: And meet with Tom Maloney and William Langley.

MR. ELKINS: That is correct.

MR. KENNEDY: Now, William Langley had just been elected district attorney; is that right?

MR. ELKINS: Yes, sir.

MR. KENNEDY: You came up and met Tom Maloney and William Langley at the Olympic Hotel.

MR. ELKINS: Yes.

MR. KENNEDY: In a room at the hotel and will you tell the committee what went on in that hotel room?

MR. ELKINS: Well, I asked what is the purpose of the meeting and they said it is just a discussion about what we are going to do.

MR. KENNEDY: Could you talk a little bit more into the microphone and also a little louder.

MR. ELKINS: They said they were going to have a discussion about what was going to take place when Langley went in, and I said, "In what way?" "Well," he said, "you are going to have a little gambling and a little this and a little that."

MR. KENNEDY: What is "a little of this and a little of that?"

MR. ELKINS: Card rooms, horse books, and I think he mentioned 3 or 4 houses of prostitution, bootlegging joints, punchboards.

MR. KENNEDY: Who said this to you?

MR. ELKINS: Bill said, "We are going to discuss what is going to go."

MR. KENNEDY: Bill is Bill Langley?

MR. ELKINS: Bill Langley.

MR. KENNEDY: He was the newly elected district attorney?

MR. ELKINS: Yes, that is correct.

MR. KENNEDY: And he was telling you what was to be allowed to go in the city?

MR. ELKINS: That is right. He said, "I want Tom in the picture. I am going to cut my take with him until he gets going."

MR. KENNEDY: What did he mean by that?

MR. ELKINS: Well, what the payoff was to him, he told me that he had to split it with Tom.

THE CHAIRMAN: That is Tom Maloney?

MR. ELKINS: That is correct.

MR. KENNEDY: Tom was to come down into Portland?

MR. ELKINS: That is right.

MR. KENNEDY: And you and Tom were to set up this town in this manner?

MR. ELKINS: That is right.

MR. KENNEDY: Having these horse books and having the card rooms and the gambling and after-hours places.

MR. ELKINS: I told him, "I won't be a party to the card rooms." They are operated under a license and they run their little poker game or pan game and it is gambling but it has been around there as many years as I have and I don't feel like trying to muscle in on them.

MR. KENNEDY: So what they were suggesting was to take a certain cut of the card rooms; is that right?

MR. ELKINS: That is right.

MR. KENNEDY: And the card rooms as they operated in Portland were independent and you felt that nobody could take a piece of them; is that right?

MR. ELKINS: That is right.

MR. KENNEDY: But the other things, the other operations, the gambling and the after-hour places, that was possible?

MR. ELKINS: Yes, sir.

MR. KENNEDY: Now, what did you say when Mr. Langley suggested opening the 3 or 4 houses of prostitution?

MR. ELKINS: Well, I passed it over, the first remark, because I knew we weren't going to do it.

MR. KENNEDY: Was that actually suggested by Maloney or was it suggested by Langley?

MR. ELKINS: It was suggested by Maloney.

MR. KENNEDY: Tom Maloney?

MR. ELKINS: Yes. He said: "It is okay with Bill for 3 or 4 houses and I am going to take you down and introduce you to Ann Thompson."

MR. KENNEDY: Who was Ann Thompson?

MR. ELKINS: Well, according to Tom, I didn't know her, she was a professional madam.

MR. KENNEDY: And what did he say about her?

MR. ELKINS: Well, he wanted to introduce me and he said he wanted her to supervise the houses.

MR. KENNEDY: What did you say to that?

MR. ELKINS: I got up to leave and he said: "There is no point in getting mad," Langley said. "You don't have to go and talk to her; it was just a suggestion."

MR. KENNEDY: He said it was just a suggestion and that you didn't have to get mad about it.

MR. ELKINS: That is right.

MR. KENNEDY: Have you run any houses of prostitution of your own?

MR. ELKINS: I [have] not.

MR. KENNEDY: You never have?

MR. ELKINS: No, sir.

MR. KENNEDY: You haven't gotten any income from any houses of prostitution?

MR. ELKINS: Not a nickel.

MR. KENNEDY: You are under indictment now for operating on prostitution?

MR. ELKINS: That is right.

MR. KENNEDY: Is the indictment against you a correct thing or not?

MR. ELKINS: No; it is as phony as it can be.

MR. KENNEDY: You never received any money from any madam?

MR. ELKINS: Not a nickel; no.

MR. KENNEDY: And this indictment against you now is not accurate or true?

MR. ELKINS: It is not.

MR. KENNEDY: But you have been indicted on it?

MR. ELKINS: I have; yes.

SENATOR MCCARTHY: Was this indictment obtained by the district attorney who was also indicted?

MR. KENNEDY: This was obtained by the State attorney who is not under indictment.

SENATOR MCCARTHY: The district attorney was not the same one?

MR. KENNEDY: That is Mr. Thornton, the State attorney, who is not under indictment. The district attorney is the one that is under indictment.

SENATOR MCCARTHY: Thank you.

MR. KENNEDY: But you say this is not true; you never received any monies from any madams.

MR. ELKINS: That is right. I was indicted jointly with two young fellows and one of them—I was asked by the grand jury if I had ever loaned this young fellow any money, and I told them that I had. But he didn't let me explain it was to operate bootlegging and afterhour spots, and gambling.

MR. KENNEDY: You had given this man, you had bankrolled this man, to operate a bootlegging place; is that right?

MR. ELKINS: That is correct.

MR. KENNEDY: And it developed that he also went into—

MR. ELKINS: It didn't develop. I still don't think that he ever did.

MR. KENNEDY: That he got into prostitution?

MR. ELKINS: He was supposed to have money with cabdrivers, which he admitted doing, when they would steer someone there for gambling, but that is the story the boys told me. One story I didn't know until after the indictment.

MR. KENNEDY: You hadn't even known one of the boys?

MR. ELKINS: That is correct.

MR. KENNEDY: But as far as you ever being concerned with prostitution, you never were.

MR. ELKINS: I have not.

MR. KENNEDY: So when it was suggested to you in the room, with Tom Maloney and the district attorney, you said you would not have anything to do with it; is that right?

MR. ELKINS: I said, "I don't want any part of any houses."

MR. KENNEDY: Did they also mention the position that Joe McLaughlin was to have? Was Joe McLaughlin's name mentioned?

MR. ELKINS: Well, Bill said that he met Joe, and he thought John Sweeney and Frank Brewster wanted Joe in the picture, but he didn't have too much to say about that at that trip because I left then.

MR. KENNEDY: And you went back to Portland?

MR. ELKINS: That is correct.

MR. KENNEDY: When was the next meeting?

MR. ELKINS: In 3 or 4 days John Sweeney called me and told me to come to Seattle in the next day or two and so I went up.

MR. KENNEDY: John Sweeney is now up in Seattle?

MR. ELKINS: John Sweeney is dead.

MR. KENNEDY: But I mean he was up at Seattle and Clyde Crosby replaced him in Portland.

MR. ELKINS: That is right. So I went to the Teamsters' hall in Seattle and Joe McLaughlin meets me in the hall and he takes me into a room and John Sweeney, Tom Maloney, and Joe McLaughlin and another man was in there, who they introduced me to, but I couldn't swear what his name is right now. Sweeney said: "He is one of the boys and you can talk freely in front of him." They talked about pinballs and punchboards and then he told me: "I want you to sit down with Tom."

MR. KENNEDY: Could you speak up a little bit?

MR. ELKINS: "I want you to sit down with Tom and Joe—," meaning Tom Maloney and Joe McLaughlin, and Frank Brewster has ordered me to send Joe McLaughlin down there to keep Tom out of trouble. So Joe is going to take care of the district attorney. You or Tom are not to tell the district attorney what to do. Let Joe handle that and

Joe can also give you some pointers on how to set up an operation of this type.

MR. KENNEDY: Did he say anything about Joe's experience?

MR. ELKINS: He said he had plenty of experience and he was a smart operator.

MR. KENNEDY: So what did you say to that?

MR. ELKINS: I didn't say anything and he didn't ask me anything. He was telling me and he didn't ask me.

MR. KENNEDY: So what happened then?

MR. ELKINS: Joe McLaughlin and Tom Maloney and I go together in the car and take a ride in it. We talked for about an hour and I told him I wouldn't try to cut in on any local people, but if he wanted to open a horse book or something of their own, I would help them. But I didn't feel like cutting them in on a couple of spots that I had of my own. I was talking about gambling and bootlegging.

MR. KENNEDY: This was while you were driving the car?

MR. ELKINS: No; we were parked alongside the curb and we were discussing that.

MR. KENNEDY: Was there any discussion about anything that you could do down there other than gambling and after-hour places?

MR. ELKINS: Yes; they were talking about anything, oh, Lord, that they could get their teeth in.

MR. KENNEDY: Was there any discussion about how the Teamsters or the Teamster union would help?

MR. ELKINS: That is correct. They said with the power of the Teamsters, and their weight behind it, Portland was not an open town and that the chief of police wouldn't go along with an open town, and they said either he will go along or the Teamsters will get him moved, meaning the chief of police.

MR. KENNEDY: They were going to get the chief of police moved?

MR. ELKINS: If he didn't go along. But they thought I was lying to them even at that time and they thought that I was operating under protection.

MR. KENNEDY: But they told you that they would have the help and assistance of the Teamster officials in Portland?

MR. ELKINS: That is correct.

MR. KENNEDY: And that Frank Brewster and John Sweeney were behind this operation?

MR. ELKINS: That is right.

Source: U.S. Senate. *Hearings Before the Senate Select Committee on Improper Activities in the Labor or Management Field,* 85th Congress, 1st Session, 86th Congress, Part 1, pp. 100–107.

Excerpt from Testimony of Dave Beck, March 27, 1957

As president of the Teamsters union, which comprised 1.4 million members, Dave Beck was a man of influence and wealth. The Select Committee on Improper Activities in the Labor or Management Field would soon prove that much of that wealth had come at the expense of the workers he represented. It is true that Beck's leadership had expanded the union's size and power. But it is also true that he had wantonly stolen Teamsters funds through simple graft. His palatial estate in Seattle, Washington, complete with a 45-seat movie house, had been financed by hundreds of thousands of Teamsters dollars that were not connected to his own salary. Because of the exposure of Beck's financial shenanigans by the Rackets Committee, the Teamsters would soon have to look for a new president. Beck would eventually be convicted on tax evasion and grand larceny charges. For a time, his home would not be the estate in Seattle but a jail cell in a Washington state prison on McNeil Island.

EXCERPT FROM TESTIMONY OF DAVE BECK MARCH 27, 1957

MR. KENNEDY: Tell me if this is true, that in March 1954 you came under income-tax investigation; that you found then that you were in difficulty because of the fact that you had taken some $320,000 from the union, so that you went to Fruehauf and asked them to give you some money so that you could stick it back into the treasury; that you arranged through Fruehauf to loan or borrow $200,000, and that you gave that money to the union in August of 1954?

Would you tell me if that is true?

MR. BECK: I must decline to answer the question because this committee lacks jurisdiction or authority under articles I, II, and III of the Constitution; further I decline to answer because I refuse to give testimony against myself, and invoke the 4th and 5th amendments; and further because the question is not relevant or pertinent to the investigation.

(At this point, Senator Goldwater withdrew from the hearing room.) . . .

SENATOR MCCARTHY: I had in mind, Mr. Chairman, that counsel would read at this time, here in public, a resume of the rest of the type of checks and financial transactions, and make them part of the record. We know what the answer will be.

THE CHAIRMAN: The check just presented will be made exhibit No. 131. . . . Mr. Counsel, if you can sum up a number of them, let us do so in order to expedite the hearings. I am convinced that we will continue to get the same resistance and lack of cooperation in the committee's efforts to discharge its duties and carry out its assignment. If we can in any way expedite it, let us try to do so.

MR. KENNEDY: Mr. Chairman, Mr. Dave Beck and the union, after this first accord was reached in December 1954, in which Mr. Beck paid the $200,000—he paid it in August 1954—this accord was reached, that he should pay more after they found out how much he owed, there was another accord reached and it was found he should pay another $50,000. Since that time he has repaid $20,000, making a total of $270,000 that he has restored. When he made the accord in December 1954, he stated that his accountants and attorneys had already spent over 700 hours on the books and records to try to determine how much money he had taken from the union.

THE CHAIRMAN: Who made that statement?

MR. KENNEDY: Dave Beck.

THE CHAIRMAN: Go ahead and recite the facts.

MR. CONDON: Mr. Chairman, I didn't follow that. Who said what to whom?

MR. KENNEDY: I will read you from the second paragraph. It is a letter signed "Yours very truly, Dave Beck," December 30, 1954. It is addressed to the Joint——

MR. CONDON: I just wanted to know to whom is the letter supposed to be written?

MR. KENNEDY: Joint Council 28, Building Association and Western Conference of Teamsters.

MR. CONDON: I understand.

THE CHAIRMAN: This purports to be Mr. Beck's statement over his signature.

(The witness consulted with his counsel.)

THE CHAIRMAN: We will give him a chance to see it.

MR. KENNEDY: It says:

> Today my attorneys and said accounting firm have advised me, after spending over 700 hours in examining my books and records and other sources of information, pertaining to my financial affairs, that to the best of their judgment and belief they have determined that the total amount due you as of December 31, 1953, amounts to $250,000.

Is there any question about that?
Mr. Beck——

THE CHAIRMAN: Ask Mr. Beck if he wrote the letter.

SENATOR MUNDT: Your client will be given a chance to deny that letter, Mr. Condon, if he wants to. I will ask him: Did you write that letter?. . . .

MR. BECK: I decline to answer on the grounds stated in my last answer.

MR. KENNEDY: Mr. Chairman, let me also ask Mr. Beck if it is not true that the Brown Equipment Co. was not being repaid as quickly as they expected to be, so that then Mr. Dave Beck had to go around to try to find a way to raise some new money. He then found the idea or had the idea of selling his house to the union, which, of course, the union had paid for originally, or at least a part of it, and also selling the furniture, which the union had paid for, through Mr. Nathan Shefferman. He came up with that idea of selling the house to the union, to raise the money and repay the loan to the Brown Equipment Co.

Is that a correct recitation of the facts?

MR. BECK: I must decline to answer the question, because this committee lacks jurisdiction or authority under articles I, II, and III of the Constitution ——

THE CHAIRMAN: All right. Consider the statement read, the objections read.

The Chair overrules the objections interposed by the witness, and his refusal to answer, and orders and directs him to answer the question, with the consent of the committee.

MR. BECK: I decline to answer on the grounds stated in my last answer.

THE CHAIRMAN: The Chair presents to you a check in the amount of $163,215, dated April 7, 1955, check No. 136, drawn on the American Security & Trust Co., signed by Dave Beck, as president, and John F. English, general secretary and treasurer, and drawn on the International Brotherhood of Teamsters, Chauffeurs, and so forth. The Chair asks you to examine the check and state whether or not you identify it, and if your signature appears thereon.

(Document handed witness.)
(The witness consulted with his counsel.)

MR. BECK: I must decline to answer the question, because this committee lacks jurisdiction or authority under articles I, II, and III of the Constitution ——

THE CHAIRMAN: All right. Consider your objections fully stated, the same as they have been before.

The Chair overrules your objections, and your refusal to answer, and, with the consent of the committee, orders and directs you to answer the question.

MR. BECK: I decline to answer on the grounds stated in my last answer.

SENATOR MCCARTHY: Mr. Chairman, could I make a suggestion? That is, that counsel give a resume of the balance of the questions he intends to ask. We know what the answer will be. It is getting late, and we all have a lot of work to do.

Source: U.S. Senate. *Hearings Before the Senate Select Committee on Improper Activities in the Labor or Management Field,* 85th Congress, 1st Session, Part 5, pp. 1676–1678.

Excerpt from Testimony of James R. Hoffa, August 23, 1957

Teamsters President Dave Beck had been a prime target of the Senate's Select Committee on Improper Activities in the Labor or Management Field, and its indefatigable counsel, Robert F. Kennedy, had secured the evidence to take him down. But the battle fought in the summer of 1957 that riveted the nation's attention on the committee was the confrontation between Kennedy and James R. Hoffa, the vice president of the Teamsters and now, with Beck's downfall, the man ready to take over the presidency. Kennedy and committee members were convinced that Hoffa had stolen union money and consorted with gangsters. But the wily and popular Hoffa was a difficult adversary. Confident that the committee could not touch him, he treated the racketeering investigation as more of a nuisance than a threat. He refused to answer questions. He mocked Kennedy. It would not be until the 1960s, after dogged and continuing investigation of the Teamsters by Kennedy as U.S. attorney general, that Hoffa would finally be brought to justice.

EXCERPT FROM TESTIMONY OF JAMES R. HOFFA, AUGUST 23, 1957

THE CHAIRMAN: Mr. Hoffa, you have been continuously asking us to refresh your memory.

MR. HOFFA: That is right, sir.

THE CHAIRMAN: Can you tell us how we can do it?

MR. HOFFA: Well, sir——

THE CHAIRMAN: How? After all, are you still taking the position that your memory has failed you?

MR. HOFFA: I don't say my memory has failed, but I say to the best of my recollection, I cannot recall the substance of this telephone call, nor place the facts together concerning what it pertains to.

THE CHAIRMAN: But, if these things do not refresh your memory, it would take the power of God to do it. The instrumentalities of mankind, obviously, are not adequate. Proceed.

MR. KENNEDY: It doesn't refresh your recollection—

"They are the best: they work for the U.N. and everywhere else?"

Listen to this carefully—

"And wherever you want to need 'em, any part of the country if you want to find out they're your people, you let me know."

What does that mean—

"If you want to find out they're your people you let me know?"

What does that mean? Who are these people?

MR. HOFFA: Well, Mr. Kennedy, I realize what the Chair just said, but I still must say to the best of my recollection, I cannot recall what that paragraph you read means at this time. I cannot recall it.

MR. KENNEDY: Mr. Hoffa, it is just beyond the powers of comprehension that you can't recall that. A reasonable man cannot believe you when you say that you can't recall that.

(The witness conferred with his counsel.)

MR. HOFFA: Well, I would say this to you. I just don't have a normal situation here in regards to the occupation I am in. I have strikes, I have people visiting me, meetings, telephone calls, and a hundred and one things. I cannot, to the best of my recollection, give you an answer to what this pertains to.

MR. KENNEDY: You have had the worst case of amnesia in the last 2 days I have ever heard of.

THE CHAIRMAN: Let us have order.

SENATOR MUNDT: Mr. Chairman, getting back to page two, I have a question.

You certainly can find a better answer than you have given, Mr. Hoffa, for a conversation where you, yourself, tell Dio that his man wanted $500 from you for supplies.

Let us get this picture. Here was a racketeer, who has a record in Sing Sing, who has a record of all kinds of violent activities in New York. He is sending you a man. His man comes out and he wants $500 for supplies. You certainly can tell us whether those supplies were dynamite for blowing up a building, if they were batteries or wires for this Minifon business, so that he can move in and record a secret conversation, or whether they were groceries for a starving family.

What were they?

I think this committee has a right to know, and I think that you certainly can recall an unusual circumstance like that. This isn't just an ordinary thing. Some of the times that you have said your memory has failed you, I have been inclined to think that there was a reason for it, that you could not remember an ordinary conversation, whether you walked into a hotel and rode up an elevator with a certain man or not. But when you tell the Committee that you cannot tell whether you ever used a Minifon yourself to walk in, sneak in, and under the cover of darkness take out of the meetings certain findings and facts and conversations, and tell us that you cannot remember whether you ever gave one of Dio's thugs $500 for supplies and, if so, you cannot remember what the supplies were for, you lose us. It is impossible.

I could not believe this if I were not sitting here listening to it. It would be easier for me to understand your saying "I take the fifth on it" because it is something to cover up.

But when you say you cannot remember, cannot remember whether you ever tried to pervert justice in grand jury, that is a terrible statement to make.

MR. HOFFA: Well, sir, I am sorry that is your position, but to the best of my recollection, I cannot recall, and this does not refresh my memory as to this conversation.

(At this point, Senator Kennedy entered the hearing room.)

SENATOR MUNDT: Do you remember giving them the $500?

MR. HOFFA: I say to the best of my recollection I do not recall the situation.

SENATOR MUNDT: Do you remember his asking for the $500?

MR. HOFFA: I can't recall, sir. I can't recall the conversation. I can't recall the situation, sir.

MR. KENNEDY: Now would you come over to page 5?

> Dio says:
>
> "A statement from Thomas L. Hickey, international vice president"
>
> —and he reads it to you—
>
> "The recent action of the executive council of the AFL in removing local 102 from the New York City taxi scene has cleared the way for New York City cab drivers to organize under the jurisdiction of the largest union in the A. F. of L."
>
> —That is your own union that is being referred to there—
>
> "and then the rest of the bull———. After I send them that telegram and everything."
>
> And Hoffa—
>
> "That stupid son of a ———."

(The witness conferred with his counsel.)

MR. KENNEDY: Why were you calling Mr. Tom Hickey a "stupid son of a ———" in connection with that statement?

MR. HOFFA: Well, I just don't have any independent recollection to this particular incident. To the best of my recollection, I cannot other than give the answers I am giving you.

MR. KENNEDY: Why was Tom Hickey a "stupid son of a ———" for making the statement that the Teamsters were going to organize the taxicabs? Why did you and Johnny Dio agree that Tom Hickey, a Teamster vice president in his own area, was a "stupid son of a ———" because he was trying to organize the taxicab drivers?

MR. HOFFA: Well, sir, I don't know. At that time the statement probably was made, but I don't recall it. I don't recall why. There may have been more to it than this conversation.

MR. KENNEDY: You cannot recall that?

MR. HOFFA: No, sir.

MR. KENNEDY: And Dio goes over on page 6 and says, *God alone is going to punish him*—He doesn't say evil old Tom Hickey—he is such a bad man—he is trying to organize the taxicab drivers for the Teamsters—that God alone is going to punish him, and you are joining in that conversation, Mr. Hoffa.

Can you explain that to us?

MR. HOFFA: Mr. Chairman, I cannot explain Dio's statement.

MR. KENNEDY: You did not oppose it. You said, "Right."

But we won't worry about that, Jim; you know, you said once 'don't rock the boat' and you said, "Right."

Is that the way you treat your fellow vice presidents in the Teamsters?

Jimmy Hoffa, ninth vice president of the Teamsters?

Or are you only interested in Jimmy Hoffa, not the Teamsters?

MR. HOFFA: I am interested in the International Brotherhood of Teamsters, and its members, and to the best of my recollection, I do not recall this conversation.

MR. KENNEDY: Well, then, from this conversation, you were interested in Johnny Dio and Jimmy Hoffa and not the Teamsters, Mr. Hoffa.

You call him *that old bas———will all be dead.*

Did you call Mr. Hickey that name, to Johnny Dio, a racketeer, a labor racketeer? Will you tell us about that?

MR. HOFFA: I have made the statement—

MR. KENNEDY: What is it?

MR. HOFFA: That I do not recall the conversation. To the best of my recollection, I am giving you my answers.

THE CHAIRMAN: Let us move to the next. Is there anything else on this one?

SENATOR CURTIS: Who is the "Bert" referred to on the top of page 7 in this conversation?

MR. HOFFA: Burke did you say?

SENATOR CURTIS: Yes.

MR. HOFFA: This particular one, I don't know what "Bert" I was talking about.

SENATOR CURTIS: It was Dio talking and it says:

> "Give my regards at home and to Bert and to everybody else."

MR. HOFFA: I don't recall, sir.

SENATOR CURTIS: Do you know whose home he was talking about?

MR. HOFFA: What home?

SENATOR CURTIS: It says:

Give my regards at home.

MR. HOFFA: Probably my home.

SENATOR CURTIS: You do not know who Bert was?

MR. HOFFA: I do not know this conversation. I cannot recall who Bert was.

SENATOR CURTIS: Do you know any "Bert"?

MR. HOFFA: Yes—

SENATOR CURTIS: And this Bert that you have in mind, does he know Dio?

(The witness conferred with his counsel.)

MR. HOFFA: I know Bert Brennan and he knows Dio and I don't know whether it was the conversation here or not.

SENATOR CURTIS: Bert who?

MR. HOFFA: Bert Brennan.

SENATOR CURTIS: And you do not know whether that was the Bert referred to?

MR. HOFFA: I cannot recall which Bert we were referring to.

SENATOR CURTIS: Well, what do you remember after having heard the transcription and having read the transcript of it?

(The witness conferred with his counsel.)

MR. HOFFA: Well, sir, I have no independent recollection at this time, as to what it referred to or who he referred to.

SENATOR CURTIS: I mean anywhere in the seven pages, do you remember anything?

MR. HOFFA: At this time I have no independent recollection of this conversation and if it would not have been played back and presented here, I would not have recalled or would not even remember that I made such a conversation.

SENATOR CURTIS: That is all.

THE CHAIRMAN: The audience may be at ease for a moment. We will take about a 2-minute recess.

(Brief recess.)

MR. FITZGERALD: May I address the Chair?

THE CHAIRMAN: You may.

MR. FITZGERALD: I have acted as counsel for Mr. Hoffa, and the counsel of record is Mr. Sol Gebb, of New York. I have worked with him on the case under which Mr. Hoffa is indicted with Mr. Brennan and Mr. Spindel in the southern district of New York, for conspiracy to violate section 605 of title 47 of the United States Code.

I am satisfied from the grand jury's investigations that this wiretapping recording that you read bears directly upon that, and is part of the Government's case, and will be so used in the southern district of New York.

Now, I am sure that the general counsel and the staff of this committee know that. I did not believe it possible that they would want to pursue a subject of this kind with a man under indictment.

MR. KENNEDY: Do you want to say this under oath, Mr. Fitzgerald?

MR. FITZGERALD: I am talking as counsel.

THE CHAIRMAN: Be brief. We agreed and the committee has held and I have held and I think you agreed that a Minifon could not be used for wiretapping, and the indictment is for wiretapping.

MR. FITZGERALD: This is not related to the Minifon. This partakes of every part of the indictment in New York. I say I don't think that the Chair or this committee realizing that, would want to pursue this inquiry further when Mr. Hoffa has to stand trial.

THE CHAIRMAN: All right, just a moment.

MR. FITZGERALD: I would like questioning deferred on it and I make it in good faith.

THE CHAIRMAN: Thank you very much. The Chair will not pursue the matter any further at this time.

Source: U.S. Senate. *Hearings Before the Senate Select Committee on Improper Activities in the Labor or Management Field*, 85th Congress, 1st Session, Part 13, pp. 5262–5266.

Excerpt from Testimony of Joseph Gallo and Lawrence Gallo, February 17, 1959

The Gallo brothers were gangland thugs, but colorful thugs. Joseph Gallo, dressed in black and wearing sunglasses, preened before the television cameras as Robert F. Kennedy, general counsel of the U.S. Senate committee, interrogated him. This was a long way from the rough Red Hook neighborhood on Brooklyn's industrial waterfront where he had grown up. Wisecracking, playing to the cameras, Gallo, known as "Crazy Joe" among his peers, relished the moment in the national spotlight, even dropping a glass for good effect. The committee was attempting to pin down Gallo and his brother, Larry, on the lucrative mob stronghold of jukebox vending. Neither Joseph nor Larry would offer up much information.

But the brothers were a spectacle to behold. Even Greenwich Village intellectuals and artists would later allow them access to their cliques. After Joe's gangland assassination in a Little Italy restaurant in 1972, Bob Dylan wrote a tribute called "Joey."

EXCERPT FROM TESTIMONY OF JOSEPH GALLO AND LAWRENCE GALLO FEBRUARY 17, 1959

THE CHAIRMAN: What is your principal business or occupation?

MR. JOSEPH GALLO: I respectfully decline to answer because I honestly believe my answer might tend to incriminate me.

THE CHAIRMAN: Are you what is known as a thug or a hoodlum? Is that the classification or category you would come in?

MR. JOSEPH GALLO: I respectfully decline to answer because I honestly believe my answer might tend to incriminate me.

THE CHAIRMAN: Are you also known as a racketeer and gangster?

MR. JOSEPH GALLO: I respectfully decline to answer because I honestly believe my answer might tend to incriminate me.

THE CHAIRMAN: What labor organization or union are you now associated with?

MR. JOSEPH GALLO: I respectfully decline to answer because I honestly believe my answer might tend to incriminate me.

THE CHAIRMAN: Proceed, Mr. Kennedy.

MR. KENNEDY: Mr. Chairman, going back to the Lombardozzi meeting in November of 1957, it is of some significance, because this was the very time, November of 1957, that the Gallos started or originated local 19, and it would indicate that Mr. Lombardozzi, at least, was initially informed and brought in on the setting up and establishment of local 19. Is that right, Mr. Gallo?

MR. JOSEPH GALLO: I respectfully decline to answer because I honestly believe my answer might tend to incriminate me.

MR. KENNEDY: Both of you, with some 40 arrests between you and some eight convictions, went into union work and established your own union, local 19, is that right?

MR. JOSEPH GALLO: I respectfully decline to answer because my answer may tend to incriminate me.

MR. KENNEDY: The fact is you were never interested in union work or you were never interested in the employees, were you, Mr. Gallo?

MR. JOSEPH GALLO: I respectfully decline to answer on the ground it may tend to incriminate me.

MR. KENNEDY: You had initially moved in on a man by the name of Clark, had you not, and taken over a part of his business?

MR. JOSEPH GALLO: I respectfully decline to answer on the ground it may tend to incriminate me.

MR. KENNEDY: And then you were operating these machines on a small scale and then along came local 1690. This was in the middle of 1957. Along came local 1690 and started placing picket lines in front of your various locations; is that right?

MR. JOSEPH GALLO: I respectfully decline to answer because the answer may tend to incriminate me.

MR. KENNEDY: You had no union at that time, so then the idea came to you that you would form local 19, and form your own union. Isn't that what you did—you formed your own union?

MR. JOSEPH GALLO: I respectfully decline to answer on the ground it may tend to incriminate me.

MR. KENNEDY: And then you started this period of harassment on the various jukebox owners in the New York area?

MR. JOSEPH GALLO: I respectfully decline to answer.

MR. KENNEDY: And at that time you had the backing of Carmine Lombardozzi, who had originally backed Al Cohen and his local union, but then he switched his backing to you. You also got some of the coin operators to join your union, the Jacob brothers, for instance. Isn't that right?

MR. JOSEPH GALLO: I respectfully decline to answer on the ground it may tend to incriminate me.

MR. KENNEDY: Then when the regular association would not join, the Jacob brothers and some of their followers walked out of the regular association and formed their own association, the United Coin Operators Association, isn't that right.

MR. JOSEPH GALLO: I respectfully decline to answer on the ground it may tend to incriminate me.

MR. KENNEDY: After this association was formed, they made a contract with you; is that right?

MR. JOSEPH GALLO: I respectfully decline to answer on the ground it may tend to incriminate me.

MR. KENNEDY: And your gangster-run union, at that time?

MR. JOSEPH GALLO: I respectfully decline to answer on the ground it may tend to incriminate me.

MR. KENNEDY: Then it was decided in order to get even more strength, you would switch your efforts from local 19, and this was after our investigation began, that you decided you would switch your efforts from local 19, which was an independent union, to a union which was well established, and that was the Teamsters Union, local 266?

MR. JOSEPH GALLO: I respectfully decline to answer on the ground it may tend to incriminate me.

MR. KENNEDY: So through the efforts of the underworld in New York City, the jurisdiction of the regular Teamster Union which would ordinarily have been in this field, local 202, was taken away by John O'Rourke in early 1958. The jurisdiction was taken away from them and switched to his gangster-run union of local 266 of the Teamsters Union; is that right?

MR. JOSEPH GALLO: I respectfully decline to answer on the ground it may incriminate me.

MR. KENNEDY: And this was the union that you, Lombardozzi, DeGrandis and the rest of the gangsters in New York were backing at that time?

MR. JOSEPH GALLO: I respectfully decline to answer on the ground it may tend to incriminate me.

MR. KENNEDY: Mr. DeGrandis in the meantime had had his difficulties because he had been kicked out of the Retail Clerks Union, where he had operated in the coin-machine business.

The Retail Clerks had come into his office to pick up his records and found only two things: a billy and a gun. Then he got out of there and was given a charter in the Teamsters Union. He formed that local in January 1958. Is that right?

MR. JOSEPH GALLO: I respectfully decline to answer on the ground it may tend to incriminate me.

MR. KENNEDY: That was local 266 of the Teamsters; is that right?

MR. JOSEPH GALLO: I respectfully recline—decline to answer on the ground it may tend to incriminate me.

MR. KENNEDY: Then what you did was you proceeded to work with the association. We have already had you identified as attending and being present at meetings of the association. You went around and started putting pressure on the various tavern owners that they should belong to this association, which would then automatically make them members of local 266 of the Teamsters; isn't that right?

MR. JOSEPH GALLO: I respectfully decline to answer on the ground it may tend to incriminate me.

MR. KENNEDY: Isn't it a fact that you have operated in that fashion in order to attempt to obtain control of all of the coin-machine businesses [in] the New York City area, and isn't that what your plan is?

MR. JOSEPH GALLO: I respectfully decline to answer because I honestly believe my answer may tend to incriminate me.

MR. KENNEDY: Isn't it a fact that, as an indication of the fact that you were switched from local 19 to 266, the records of the company that you have an interest in with your partner, Mr. Norman Clark, show that he began paying dues in local 266 in April of 1958? Is that right, that your own company started paying dues in local 266?

MR. JOSEPH GALLO: I respectfully decline to answer on the ground it may tend to incriminate me.

MR. KENNEDY: One of your chief associates has been the Jacob brothers, who are major operators in New York City. Isn't it a fact that you have gone down into West Virginia, into Pennsylvania, and into Ohio to help and assist them in their coin-machine route in those three States?

MR. JOSEPH GALLO: I respectfully decline to answer on the ground it may tend to incriminate me.

MR. KENNEDY: Isn't it a fact that you are going to attempt, through these underworld connections, to gain control over all of these operations in this area?

MR. JOSEPH GALLO: I respectfully decline to answer on the ground it might tend to incriminate me.

MR. KENNEDY: And if it was necessary, you would have somebody like Mr. Saul knocked on top of the head, or somebody like Mr. Green.

MR. JOSEPH GALLO: I respectfully decline to answer on the ground it may tend to incriminate me.

MR. KENNEDY: But you wouldn't do it yourself, would you, Mr. Gallo? You would have somebody go and do it for you, would you?

MR. JOSEPH GALLO: I respectfully decline to answer, Mr. Kennedy, on the ground it may tend to incriminate me.

MR. KENNEDY: Do you find it is much easier to have a big man go and do it rather than a little fellow like you?

MR. JOSEPH GALLO: I respectfully decline to answer on the ground it may tend to incriminate me.

THE CHAIRMAN: Are you a physical coward?

MR. JOSEPH GALLO: I respectfully decline to answer, Mr. Senator, on the ground it might tend to incriminate me.

THE CHAIRMAN: That might incriminate you to answer? Do you think it would? Do you think it would——

MR. JOSEPH GALLO: I respectfully decline to answer because I honestly believe my answer might tend to incriminate me.

THE CHAIRMAN: All right; proceed.

MR. KENNEDY: Have you anything else to tell us, Mr. Gallo?

MR. JOSEPH GALLO: I respectfully decline to answer on the ground it may tend to incriminate me, Mr. Kennedy.

THE CHAIRMAN: Senators, have you any questions of these talkative witnesses?

SENATOR ERVIN: Can you tell us of any honest day's work you ever did in your life?

MR. JOSEPH GALLO: I respectfully decline to answer that on the ground it may tend to incriminate me.

THE CHAIRMAN: You may stand aside.

Call the next witness.

Source: U.S. Senate. *Hearings Before the Senate Select Committee on Improper Activities in the Labor or Management Field*, 85th Congress, 2nd Session, Part 46, pp. 16842–16845.

Labor-Management Reporting and Disclosure Act of 1959, Bill of Rights of Members of Labor Organizations

In 1959, a coalition of Republicans and conservative southern Democrats worked to enact the passage of the Labor-Management Reporting and Disclosure Act, also known as the Landrum-Griffin Act for its sponsors, Democratic representative Phil Landrum of Georgia and Republican representative Robert Griffin of Michigan. The act was a direct response to the revelations by the Rackets Committee of corruption by officials of certain unions. The act required each union to provide regular, detailed accounts of its finances and membership. It provided for the protection of union funds and assets, the administration of trusteeships by labor organizations, and the election of officers of labor organizations. The act also guaranteed certain rights to all union members.

LABOR-MANAGEMENT REPORTING AND DISCLOSURE ACT OF 1959, BILL OF RIGHTS OF MEMBERS OF LABOR ORGANIZATIONS

SEC. 101. (a)

(1) EQUAL RIGHTS.—Every member of a labor organization shall have equal rights and privileges within such organization to nominate candidates, to vote in elections or referendums of the labor organization, to attend membership meetings and to participate in the deliberations and voting upon the business of such meetings, subject to reasonable rules and regulations in such organization's constitution and bylaws.

(2) FREEDOM OF SPEECH AND ASSEMBLY.—Every member of any labor organization shall have the right to meet and assemble freely with other members; and to express any views, arguments, or opinions; and to express at meetings of the labor organization his views, upon candidates in an election of the labor organization or upon any business properly before the meeting, subject to the organization's established and reasonable rules pertaining to the conduct of meetings: *Provided,* That nothing herein shall be construed to impair the right of a labor organization to adopt and enforce reasonable rules as to the responsibility of every member toward the organization as an institution and to his refraining from conduct that would interfere with its performance of its legal or contractual obligations.

(3) DUES, INITIATION FEES, AND ASSESSMENTS.—Except in the case of a federation of national or international labor organizations, the rates of dues and initiation fees payable by members of any labor organization in effect on the date of enactment of this Act shall not be increased, and no general or special assessment shall be levied upon such members, except—(A) in the case of a local organization, (i) by majority vote by secret ballot of the members in good standing voting at a general or special membership meeting, after reasonable notice of the intention to vote upon such question, or (ii) by majority vote of the members in good standing voting in a membership referendum conducted by secret ballot; or (B) in the case of a labor organization, other than a local labor organization or a federation of national or international labor organizations, (i) by majority vote of the delegates voting at a regular convention, or at a special convention of such labor organization held upon not less than thirty days' written notice to the principal office of each local or constituent labor organization entitled to such notice, or (ii) by majority vote of the members in good standing of such labor organization voting in a membership referendum conducted by secret ballot, or (iii) by majority vote of the members of the executive board or similar governing body of such labor organization, pursuant to express authority contained in the constitution and bylaws of such labor organization: *Provided,* That such action on the part of the executive board or similar governing body shall be effective only until the next regular convention of such labor organization.

(4) PROTECTION OF THE RIGHT TO SUE.—No labor organization shall limit the right of any member thereof to institute an action in any court, or in a proceeding before any administrative agency, irrespective of whether or not the labor organization or its officers are named as defendants or respondents in such action or proceeding, or the right of any member of a labor organization to appear as a witness in any judicial, administrative, or legislative proceeding, or to petition any legislature or to communicate with any legislator: *Provided,* That any such member may be required to exhaust reasonable hearing procedures (but not to exceed a four-month lapse of time) within such organization, before instituting legal or administrative proceedings against such organizations or any officer thereof: *And provided further,* That no interested employer or employer association shall directly or indirectly finance, encourage, or participate in, except as a party, any such action, proceeding, appearance, or petition.

(5) SAFEGUARDS AGAINST IMPROPER DISCIPLINARY ACTION.—No member of any labor organization may be fined, suspended, expelled, or otherwise disciplined except for nonpayment of dues by such organization or by any officer thereof unless such member has been (A) served with written specific charges; (B) given a reasonable time to prepare his defense; (C) afforded a full and fair hearing.

(b) Any provision of the constitution and bylaws of any labor organization which is inconsistent with the provisions of this section shall be of no force or effect.

Source: U.S. Department of Labor, "The Labor-Management Reporting and Disclosure Act of 1959"; www.dol.gov/compliance/laws/comp-lmrda.htm.

Bibliography

Baltakis, Anthony. "On the Defensive: Walter Reuther's Testimony Before the McClellan Labor Rackets Committee." *Michigan Historical Review* (1999).

Donnelly, Robert C. "Organizing Portland: Organized Crime, Municipal Corruption, and the Teamsters Union." *Oregon Historical Quarterly* (Fall 2003). Available at: http://www.historycooperative.org/journals/ohq/104.3/donnelly.html.

Goldfarb, Ronald. *Perfect Villains, Imperfect Heroes: Robert F. Kennedy's War Against Organized Crime.* New York: Random House, 1995.

Hamill, Pete. "The Lives They Lived: Victor Riesel and Walter Sheridan; In Defense of Honest Labor." *New York Times,* December 31, 1985.

Jacobs, Paul. "Extracurricular Activities of the McClellan Committee." *California Law Review* 51, no. 2 (May 1963).

Kennedy, Robert F. *The Enemy Within.* New York: Harper & Brothers, 1960.

McClellan, John L. *Crime Without Punishment.* New York: Duell, Sloan and Pearce, 1962.

Petro, Sylvester. "Power Unlimited: The Corruption of Union Leadership: A Report on the McClellan Committee Hearings." New York: Ronald Press, 1959.

Rovere, Richard. "Letter from Washington." *New Yorker,* May 25, 1957.

Salinger, Pierre. *P.S.: A Memoir.* New York: St. Martin's Griffin, 1995.

Schlesinger, Arthur M. Jr. *Robert Kennedy and His Times.* New York: Ballantine, 1978.

The Watergate Committee, 1973–74

By Keith W. Olson

Senate Resolution 60 establishing the Select Committee on Presidential Campaign Activities on February 7, 1973, identified three areas of investigation: the break-in and cover-up of the June 17, 1972, burglary of the Democratic National Committee headquarters in the Watergate office building in Washington, D.C.; illegal campaign financing; and the campaign of dirty tricks and other political espionage. The investigation soon revealed inseparable links between the break-in and cover-up and the unlawful finances, dirty tricks, and espionage. From the start the media and the public used the term *Watergate hearings* to encompass the variety of these activities.

The hearings proved devastating to the Nixon presidency and resulted in his resignation in August 1974. No other congressional investigation rivals Watergate in importance. All three branches of government became involved. The hearings' complexity and revelations engaged public attention to an unprecedented degree and helped forge a political consensus for President Richard Nixon to resign or face impeachment and conviction.

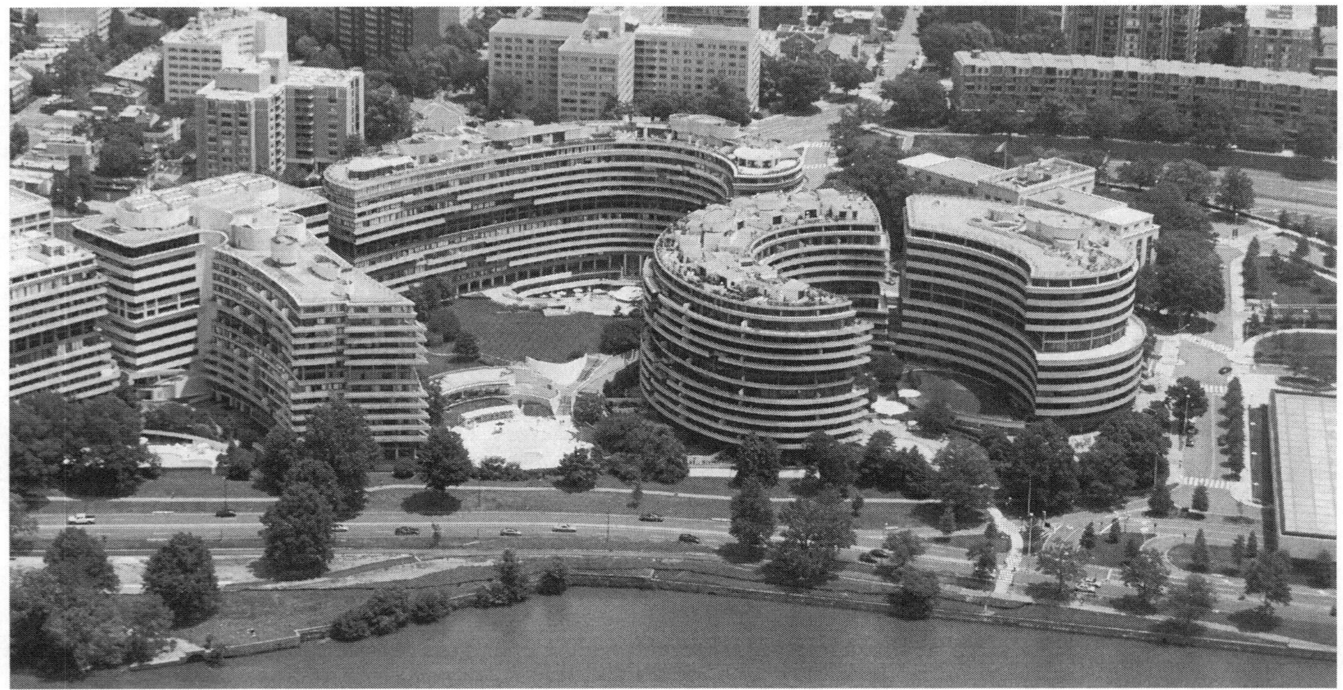

The Watergate complex, where the break-in occurred. (Frontpage/Shutterstock)

OVERVIEW

Background

Before June 17, 1972, *Watergate* was simply the name of a posh hotel and residence in Washington, D.C., near the Kennedy Center for the Performing Arts. On that date, however, a thwarted break-in of Democratic National Committee headquarters by a team of Republican operatives began to fix in the public mind and the national lexicon a much wider meaning of the word. *Watergate* would henceforth define a complex web of political scandals and excesses of executive power that would eventually bring down a president.

Congress Investigates

Unearthed by the investigative duo of Bob Woodward and Carl Bernstein of the *Washington Post,* revelations concerning the break-in at Democratic headquarters in the Watergate became an increasingly ominous political threat to President Richard Nixon and his Republican allies. In February 1973 the Senate established a committee to investigate the Watergate scandal. It was headed by Senator Sam Ervin of North Carolina. The committee's public hearings turned into a national sensation, especially the testimony of a number of White House officials including Chief of Staff H.R. Haldeman; Assistant to the President for Domestic Affairs John Ehrlichman; and counsel John Dean. When the committee learned of the existence of secret White House tape recordings, the hearings became the center of a major political and legal battle between Congress and the president over the release of the tapes. Gradually, federal judge John J. Sirica forced Nixon to make some of the recordings public. As evidence accumulated of the involvement of Nixon's close advisers in various crimes and the subsequent cover-up by those advisers and Nixon himself, the House of Representatives in 1974 authorized the Judiciary Committee to consider impeachment proceedings against the president.

Impact

With the release in July and August 1974 of many of the tape recordings from the Oval Office, the malfeasance of the president and his advisers became increasingly clear. The House Judiciary Committee voted to accept three of four proposed articles of impeachment. The final legal blow to the administration came with the decision of the U.S. Supreme Court that ordered the president to release additional tapes, one of which, known later as "the smoking gun," revealed that Nixon had participated in the Watergate cover-up as far back as June 23, 1972. On the evening of August 8, 1974, Nixon delivered a nationally televised speech announcing his resignation, effective the following day. The Watergate hearings had resulted in profound political upheaval: from President Nixon's resignation to the trials and convictions of a number of his close associates and to the declining fortunes of the Republican Party. Watergate also led to legislation seeking to tighten campaign financing laws, and it ushered in a period of more intensive journalistic investigations of political figures.

Origins of the Watergate Break-In and Cover-Up

The antecedents of the June 1972 burglary date back more than two years earlier. In February 1970, Tom C. Huston, a longtime Nixon aide, had proposed changes in the handling of internal security matters. One of Huston's proposals called for the establishment of an interagency group directed from the White House to coordinate intelligence gathering. In June 1970, the president met with the directors of the Central Intelligence Agency (CIA), the Federal Bureau of Investigation (FBI), the National Security Agency, and the Defense Intelligence Agency to establish the group, with FBI Director J. Edgar Hoover as chair and Huston as staff director.

Huston's plan called for a range of surveillance activities that included infiltration, burglaries, and mail openings. Three of the four directors of the intelligence agencies raised no objections. For several reasons, however, Hoover opposed the plan and told Attorney General John Mitchell that he would insist on Nixon's signature for all illegal operations. Nixon reluctantly retreated and abandoned the plan. One component of the plan, however, soon surfaced in another context. In June 1971, Nixon's reaction to the *New York Times*'s publication of the Pentagon Papers showed a deep distrust of the FBI, an inordinate desire for secrecy, and an excessive concern over unauthorized leaking of information from within his administration. To bypass the

CHRONOLOGY

1972

- *June 17:* Police arrest five men at 2:30 A.M. breaking into the offices of the Democratic National Committee at the Watergate hotel and office complex in Washington, D.C.
- *September 29:* In one of their many investigative reports on Watergate, Bob Woodward and Carl Bernstein of the *Washington Post* reveal that John Mitchell, while serving as attorney general, controlled a secret Republican fund used to finance widespread intelligence-gathering operations against the Democrats.
- *November 7:* President Nixon wins reelection in a landslide.

1973

- *January 30:* A federal jury finds former Nixon aides G. Gordon Liddy and James W. McCord Jr. guilty of conspiracy, burglary, and wiretapping in the Watergate incident.
- *April 30:* Nixon's top White House aides, H. R. Haldeman and John Ehrlichman, and Attorney General Richard Kleindienst resign over the scandal. Nixon fires White House counsel John Dean. Nixon addresses the nation.
- *May 17:* The Senate Watergate committee begins nationally televised hearings.
- *July 16:* Alexander Butterfield, former presidential appointments secretary, testifies that since 1971 Nixon had recorded all conversations and telephone calls in his offices.
- *July 23:* Nixon refuses to turn over the presidential tape recordings to the Senate Watergate committee or the special prosecutor.
- *October 20:* In the so-called Saturday Night Massacre, Nixon fires special prosecutor Archibald Cox. Attorney General Elliot Richardson and Deputy Attorney General William Ruckelshaus resign under protest. Pressure for impeachment mounts in Congress.
- *November 17:* Maintaining his innocence in all Watergate-related matters, Nixon declares, "I'm not a crook."

1974

- *April 30:* The White House releases more than 1,200 pages of edited transcripts of the Nixon tapes to the House Judiciary Committee, but the committee insists that the tapes themselves must be turned over.
- *July 24:* The Supreme Court rules unanimously that Nixon must turn over the tape recordings of 64 White House conversations.
- *July 27:* House Judiciary Committee passes the first of three articles of impeachment, charging obstruction of justice.
- *August 9:* Nixon becomes the first U.S. president to resign from office.

FBI, the president turned to his aide John Ehrlichman to stop the leaks. Ehrlichman organized the so-called Plumbers, a secret group with funding and jurisdiction solely at the discretion of the president.

In the summer of 1971, Nixon aides began working to monitor and shape the outcome of the Democratic primaries. With Democratic majorities in Congress and the closeness of the 1960 election, which Nixon lost, and the 1968 election, which he barely won, reelection was a constant priority within his administration. The president's drive for reelection exhibited characteristics that dovetailed with and mirrored other aspects of his administration: a predilection for secrecy, a desire for knowledge about opponents' plans, and a reliance on subordinates to conduct illegal activities such as telephone wiretapping, protective cover-ups of illegal operations, and "dirty tricks" to derail opponents' campaigns.

In June 1971, Nixon's concerns about internal intelligence shifted to the Pentagon Papers. Four years earlier President Lyndon B. Johnson's secretary of defense, Robert S. McNamara, had commissioned a detailed study of how the United States became involved in the Vietnam War. The resulting report was approximately 3,000 pages of narrative and 4,000 pages of documents that revealed, among other things, that four successive presidents—Harry Truman, Dwight Eisenhower, John F. Kennedy, and especially Johnson—had deceived and misled the public about Vietnam. Both Johnson and later Nixon vowed to keep the Pentagon Papers secret.

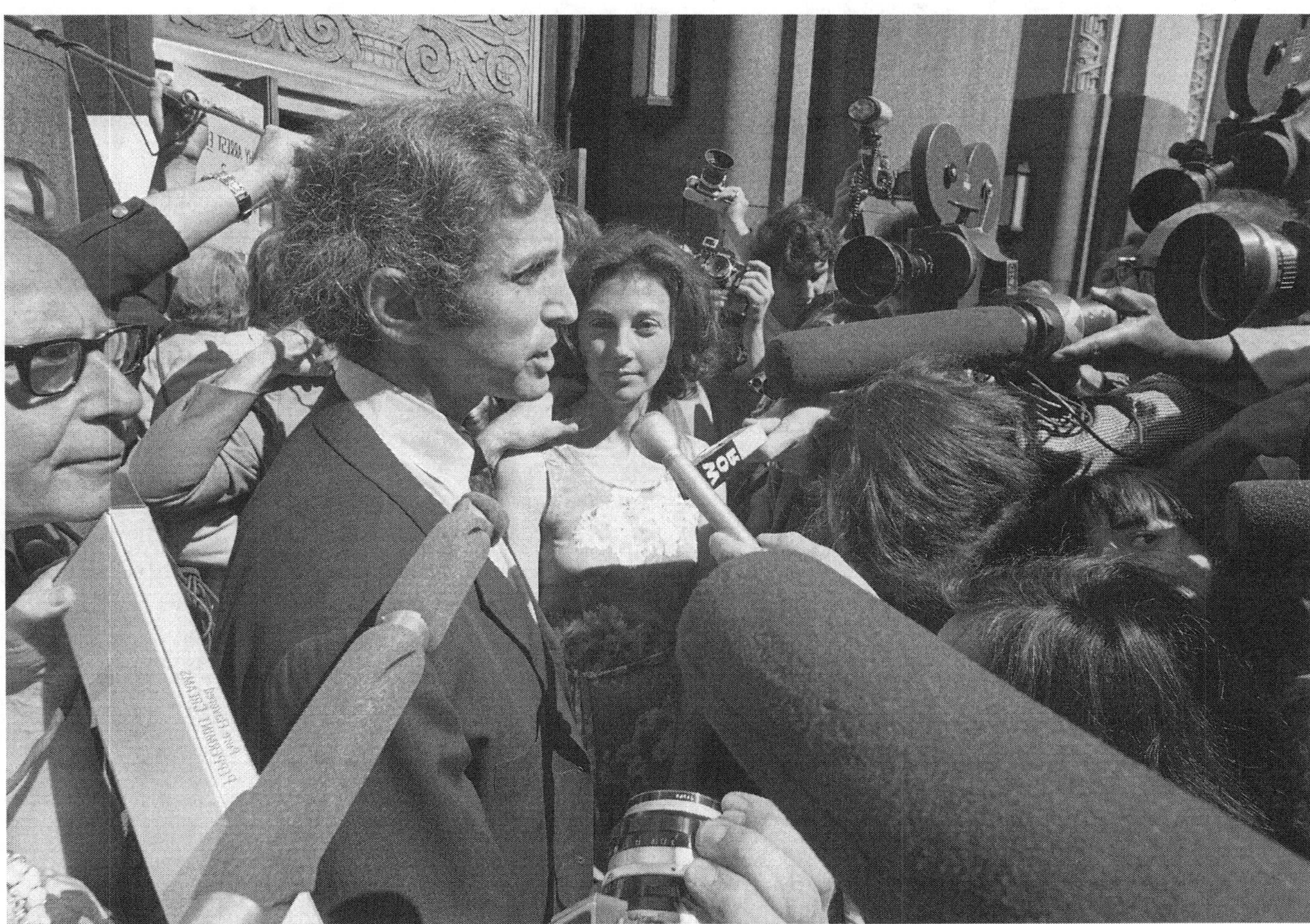

Daniel Ellsberg speaks to reporters at the Boston federal building on June 28, 1971. Ellsberg, charged in federal warrants with unauthorized possession of top secret documents—the Pentagon Papers—and failure to return them, arrived to surrender himself to the U.S. Attorney. (Associated Press)

Daniel Ellsberg, a Marine Corps veteran disillusioned with the Vietnam War, obtained a copy of the report and gave it to the *New York Times.* On June 13, 1971, the newspaper published the first of a planned series of articles based on the report. After three articles, the Justice Department obtained a temporary restraining order from a federal district court contending that their publication caused "immediate and irreparable harm" to national security. The case moved quickly to the Supreme Court, and on June 30 the court cited the First Amendment and overrode the federal district court. The Justice Department could not substantiate a charge of espionage against Ellsberg. Publication of the Pentagon Papers did not compromise national security, but it did tarnish the reputation of government officials.

A Los Angeles grand jury, however, indicted Ellsberg for violation of the criminal code, accusing him of releasing classified government documents to the public. Nixon wanted more than a conviction of Ellsberg; he wanted to discredit Ellsberg and the antiwar movement. To accomplish this, Nixon turned to Ehrlichman and his Plumbers. Ehrlichman assigned two of his aides, Egil Krogh Jr. and David Young Jr., to the task. The two shared an office in the Old Executive Office Building.

Soon the Plumbers gained two additional staff members: E. Howard Hunt, who was on the White House payroll, and G. Gordon Liddy, who was on the payroll of the Committee to Re-elect the President. Hunt had spent more than 20 years with the CIA and had participated in the 1954 overthrow of the elected government of Guatemala and the 1962 Bay of Pigs invasion of Cuba. Hunt also had published a steady stream of novels, many of them with a spy theme. Liddy was a lawyer who had five years' experience with the FBI and had served as an assistant district attorney in Dutchess County, New York. Before joining the Plumbers, Liddy was a special assistant to the assistant secretary of the treasury.

Young asked the CIA to prepare a psychological profile of Ellsberg, while Hunt requested false identification papers, disguises, and cameras. Nixon's assistant,

Charles Colson, raised the money. Liddy, Hunt, and three Cubans from Miami, whom Hunt had recruited, flew to Los Angeles. The team broke into the office of Lewis Fielding, Ellsberg's psychiatrist, and ransacked files, but they found nothing useful to discredit Ellsberg.

Late in 1971 the Plumbers attempted to identify the persons leaking government information to the newspaper columnist Jack Anderson. In his articles Anderson documented that Nixon secretly had supported Pakistan during the Indian-Pakistani War while he publicly declared the United States' neutrality. Nixon had Anderson followed, his telephoned tapped, his taxes audited, and his associates investigated. Hunt also devised plans to assassinate Anderson but stopped short of implementation.

The Plumbers never found Anderson's sources, but they did discover that a navy yeoman, Charles E. Radford, assigned to the Joint Chiefs of Staff, regularly stole "top secret 'eyes only'" documents from the National Security Council (NSC) and passed them to three admirals. In turn, the admirals gave the secret material to Admiral Thomas H. Moorer, chairman of the Joint Chiefs of Staff. The NSC had withheld the documents from the Joint Chiefs on the basis of national security. Denied access, the nation's top military officer had thus ordered espionage against his own government. National Security Adviser Henry Kissinger, his deputy, Alexander M. Haig, and Ehrlichman all supported Nixon's decision to cover up the espionage. Later the president reappointed Moorer to a second term as chairman of the Joint Chiefs of Staff.

Acceptance of a high-ranking military cover-up was not new for Nixon. On March 7, 1970, two years after the My Lai massacre in Vietnam, he explained to Kissinger: "It's a pretty cheap shot to allow the generals to be put on the rack for the My Lai business. It was covered up because it was in the interest of the country."

In May 1969, when the *New York Times* reported the previously secret bombing of Cambodia, Nixon, ardently supported by Kissinger, ordered illegal wiretaps on the telephones of 17 government officials and even members of Kissinger's staff.

During the cold war, presidents used national security to justify a wide range of illegal activity. Nixon accepted this exercise of presidential power and found support from high-ranking civilian and military officials. He ordered actions that exceeded those of his predecessors, but his actions fell within a recognizable broad pattern. The burglary of the Democratic Party national headquarters on June 17, 1972, therefore, seemed commonplace within the White House.

Reelection Campaign

Nixon's reelection campaign essentially paralleled, and at times intertwined with, the other activities of his administration. The mind-set remained the same, with an emphasis on secrecy and intelligence always central. A long list of subordinates was willing to violate the law on the president's behalf. The protective cover-up, the illegal telephone tapping, and the activities of the Plumbers all had their counterparts in the reelection campaign.

The early 1971 polls were unfavorable to Nixon. In January the Harris Poll found that if the presidential choices were Maine senator Edmund Muskie—considered the Democratic frontrunner—and Nixon, Muskie would win with 43 percent of the vote compared with 40 percent for Nixon. The next month the results were 44 percent to 39 percent in Muskie's favor. In January 1971 the Gallup Poll reported a 56 percent approval rating for the president, but that declined to 50 percent by March.

Late in March, Nixon adviser and speechwriter Patrick Buchanan sent Nixon an eight-page, single-spaced letter suggesting campaign strategy. Soon, with Nixon's approval, Buchanan started an evaluation of potential Democratic nominees. By May, the poll results favored Muskie 47 percent to 39 percent in a projected presidential election. To Buchanan, who was responsible for the preparation of the president's daily news summaries, the situation seemed clear. He subsequently wrote to Jeb Stuart Magruder, director of the Committee to Re-elect the President (CREEP), and Attorney General Mitchell, who had managed Nixon's 1968 campaign and planned to manage the 1972 campaign. "The first priority," Buchanan wrote, "is to trip up Muskie in the primaries."

"Dirty tricks" operations thus became a major theme of the primary and general election campaigns. H. R. Haldeman, Nixon's chief of staff, directed Dwight Chapin, the president's appointments secretary, and Gordon C. Strachan, an aide to Haldeman, to organize a covert program to disrupt the Democratic Party primaries. The operative who later became infamous was Donald Segretti, a lawyer who had served four years in the army, including one in Vietnam. At one point Segretti employed 28 people to undertake misdeeds.

The dirty-tricks campaign reached its most intense stage in the March 1972 Florida primary. One Segretti infiltrator stole Muskie stationery and sent out a fraudulent letter that discredited two of Muskie's opponents while at the same time discrediting him for supposedly sending the letter. The letter reported that police twice had arrested Minnesota senator Hubert H. Humphrey, the former vice president, for driving under the influence of alcohol while in the company of a prostitute. The letter also claimed that police twice had arrested

Washington senator Henry Jackson for homosexual activity and that Jackson had once fathered a child with an unmarried teenager. To further alienate voters, Segretti workers placed Muskie bumper stickers on top of Humphrey and Jackson stickers. Stink bombs twice exploded at Muskie picnics and also disrupted Muskie campaign headquarters. Telephone calls late at night asked voters to support Muskie. On primary day, Florida Democrats gave George Wallace a surprising victory with 42 percent of the vote while Muskie finished with an unexpectedly low 8.9 percent.

During the Wisconsin Democratic primary, which was held on April 4, 1972, Muskie suffered similar treatment from Segretti's operation. Fliers in black neighborhoods of Milwaukee invited voters to a free beer and free lunch picnic to meet Coretta Scott King, widow of Martin Luther King Jr., and the television star Lorne Greene. Those who came to the picnic found no food, no beer, and no celebrities. In the Wisconsin primary, Muskie finished in fourth place.

In January 1972 both Harris and Gallup Polls registered a virtual tie in voter preference for president in a Nixon-Muskie contest. Three months later Muskie's prospects had greatly dimmed. Nixon and his aides switched their strategy to support South Dakota senator George McGovern for the nomination on the belief that he would be the weakest Democratic candidate. According to Haldeman's diary, the president "made the point that the most effective way now for us to build up McGovern is to get out some fake polls showing him doing well in trial heats."

Independent of Segretti, both Magruder and Colson also ran dirty-tricks operations. The objective was the same—to deny Muskie the nomination and in doing so divide the Democratic Party. Smaller than the Segretti program, Magruder's team concentrated on four primaries, two of which, like Segretti's, were in Florida and Wisconsin. Colson, the president's special counsel, reported directly to Nixon. Once Colson proclaimed, "I would walk over my grandmother to help Richard Nixon."

Raising money is central to any political campaign. In this area Nixon relied on two men, Herbert W. Kalmbach and Maurice H. Stans. Starting early in 1969, Kalmbach maintained a secret fund to finance covert activities, and he and Stans raised millions of dollars from 19 well-known corporations that knowingly made illegal contributions.

In addition to illegal campaign contributions and three dirty-tricks programs, the Nixon reelection campaign placed great emphasis on intelligence gathering. This emphasis lay behind the Huston plan, the Plumbers, and the illegal telephone taps. Of all the intelligence activities, the one that produced the greatest impact came from Liddy.

For the reelection campaign, Mitchell wanted CREEP to have a lawyer serve as both general counsel and director of intelligence gathering. He assigned the search to White House counsel John Dean, who accepted Krogh's recommendation of Liddy. Mitchell interviewed Liddy and approved. Haldeman, Ehrlichman, and Magruder all found Liddy similarly suitable. Liddy, the experienced Plumber, FBI agent, and lawyer, started work on December 13, 1971.

On January 27, 1972, Liddy, Magruder, and Dean met in Mitchell's office and listened to Liddy's $1 million proposal, which included kidnapping, mugging, wiretapping, prostitutes, break-ins, and sabotage. Mitchell objected to the thrust of the report and to its cost. Eight days later the group again met in the attorney general's office and listened to Liddy's new plan, which had eliminated mugging, kidnapping, and prostitutes. Instead, Liddy offered a $500,000 budget that focused on electronic surveillance and surreptitious photography. The four men agreed on priorities. One was bugging the office of Lawrence O'Brien, the chairman of the Democratic National Committee (DNC), which had its headquarters in the Watergate complex in Washington, D.C.

On March 1, Mitchell resigned as attorney general and took charge of CREEP. At the end of the month, Mitchell approved a budget of $250,000 for the Liddy plan. Magruder told Mitchell that Colson had pressed for approval and that if Mitchell approved, Haldeman would concur. Mitchell and Magruder both wanted Liddy to tap the telephone of O'Brien's office as his first priority.

Hunt joined Liddy and arranged to recruit Miami-based Cubans as needed for the operation. James W. McCord Jr., a CREEP electronics expert, joined the group. The team consisted of seven individuals: Hunt, Liddy, McCord, and four Cuban operatives—Bernard L. Barker, Virgilio R. Gonzalez, Eugenio R. Martinez, and Frank A. Sturgis. On Memorial Day weekend, the team broke into O'Brien's DNC office at the Watergate and installed a tap on his telephone and on the telephone of the executive director of the Association of State Democratic Chairmen. Barker, the principal Cuban, photocopied some files. The mission, however, failed. One telephone tap and the copied documents provided no useful information, and the O'Brien tap proved insufficiently strong. Magruder told Liddy that Mitchell and Strachan shared his annoyance.

On June 17, 1972, McCord, Hunt, Liddy, and the four Cubans again broke into the DNC offices in the Watergate. A security officer spotted them and contacted the police. This time, they were apprehended. The June

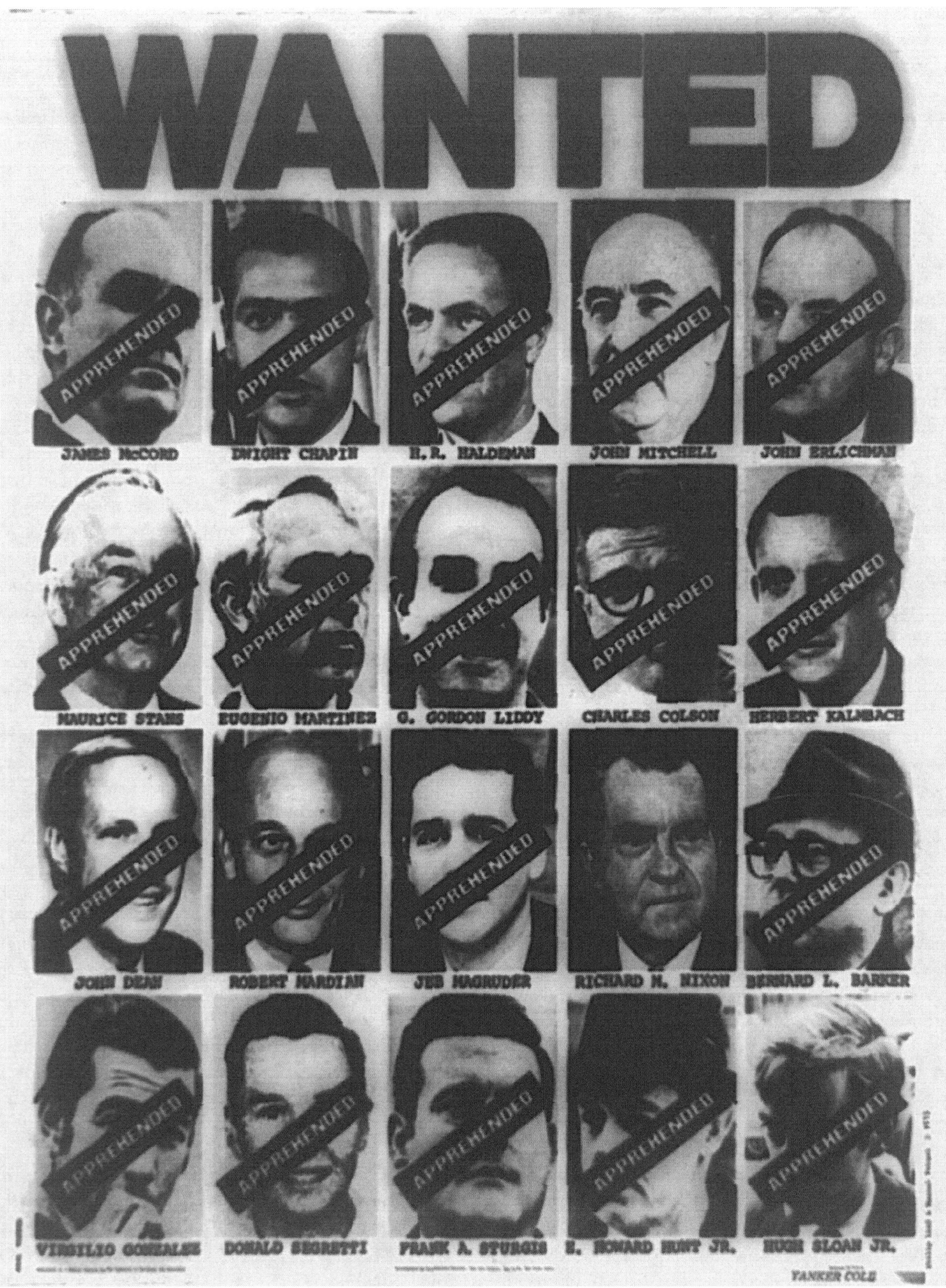

Political poster showing portraits of figures involved in the Watergate scandal, all labeled "apprehended"—except for Richard M. Nixon. (Library of Congress)

17 break-in and subsequent arrests led to the greatest constitutional crisis in the United States since the Civil War. Nevertheless, Haldeman later remembered the incident as unimportant "at the time it happened."

From the start, evidence surfaced that suggested the White House might be involved. Barker's address book and Martinez's telephone directory both had Hunt's name next to the term "W. House." A quick check revealed Hunt was on the White House payroll. Articles in the *Washington Post* by reporters Carl Bernstein and Bob Woodward in August and September traced the money that financed the break-in to a special CREEP account. The money originated with Nixon's Midwest finance-campaign chair, Kenneth Dahlberg, who had sent a check to Barker. Bernstein-Woodward articles in the *Post* kept the story alive during the fall but had little impact on the presidential campaign. Senator George McGovern gained the Democratic Party's nomination for president in July but lost to Nixon in a landslide in November.

All seven Watergate burglars pleaded not guilty. On January 10, 1973, they appeared before federal judge John J. Sirica. Hunt changed his plea to guilty, and the four Cubans immediately followed Hunt and changed their pleas. Liddy and McCord maintained their not-guilty pleas and stood trial. The jury found them guilty later in the month. Sirica, however, suspected a cover-up and delayed passing sentence.

On February 7, 1973, less than three weeks after Nixon's second inauguration, the Senate voted 77 to 0 to establish the Senate Select Committee on Presidential Campaign Activities. The impetus for forming the committee rested on widespread disapproval of the direct ties between the break-in and CREEP and the many dirty tricks that had taken place during the Democratic primary campaigns, including the fraudulent Muskie letter and the picnic invitation that provided none of the food or celebrities promised. Few Americans approved of one major party burglarizing the headquarters of the other major party and tapping telephones. The unanimous Senate vote reflected public opinion. A Senate investigation seemed appropriate.

Sam Ervin and the Committee

Senator Sam Ervin, the folksy Democrat from North Carolina, dominated the select committee from its origins to its final report. In retrospect, he proved the ideal senator to chair the investigation. In 1954 he had served as a member of the Senate committee that had investigated and then voted to "condemn" the conduct of Senator Joseph R. McCarthy (R-Wis.). Ervin enjoyed a reputation as a constitutional lawyer, quoted the Bible, and, despite his Harvard law degree with honors, came across as homespun. More than once, he called himself "just a country lawyer." He had a reputation as a conservative, having voted against Medicare in 1965, routinely supported the war in Vietnam, and displayed a paternalistic attitude toward blacks and women. Opponents of the committee had a difficult time stereotyping its chair as a liberal Nixon critic. At age 76, Ervin had no political ambition. He wanted, moreover, a wide investigative mandate to defuse possible charges of partisanship.

Ervin and Senate Majority Leader Mike Mansfield of Montana carefully selected the three colleagues who would serve as the other Democrats on the committee: Herman E. Tallmadge of Georgia, chairman of the Senate Committee on Agriculture who had ties to Republicans in the Midwest and Great Plains states; Joseph M. Montoya of New Mexico; and Daniel K. Inouye of Hawaii. All three were low-key with no apparent presidential ambitions. None of the Democratic members were from the Northeast or were ardent liberals.

The Republican Senate leadership named Howard Baker from Tennessee as vice chair of the committee. Politically ambitious within the Senate and the nation, Baker welcomed Ervin's desire for a wide mandate for the committee. In his statements and positions, Baker wanted to appear nonpartisan, but he quickly developed a back-channel connection to Nixon. Two other Republicans were appointed to the committee: Edward J. Gurney of Florida and Lowell P. Weicker Jr. of Connecticut. Senator Gurney had campaigned to get on the committee, enjoyed a favorable television image, and was totally loyal to the president. Senator Weicker viewed Nixon as an adversary. Unlike the Democrats, the Republicans on the committee lacked unity.

Ervin selected Professor Samuel Dash of Georgetown University Law School to serve as the committee's chief counsel. At Georgetown, Dash directed the Institute of Criminal Law and Procedure. His experience included district attorney of Philadelphia, trial lawyer for the Justice Department, and private practice. In addition, he had published an acclaimed study of electronic surveillance and had served as president of the National Association of Criminal Defense Lawyers. Like Ervin, he had graduated from Harvard Law School.

Baker selected Fred D. Thompson as minority counsel. A Nashville lawyer, Thompson had managed Baker's 1972 reelection campaign. Unlike Dash, Thompson had political ambitions—now 30, he already had lost an election for the House of Representatives.

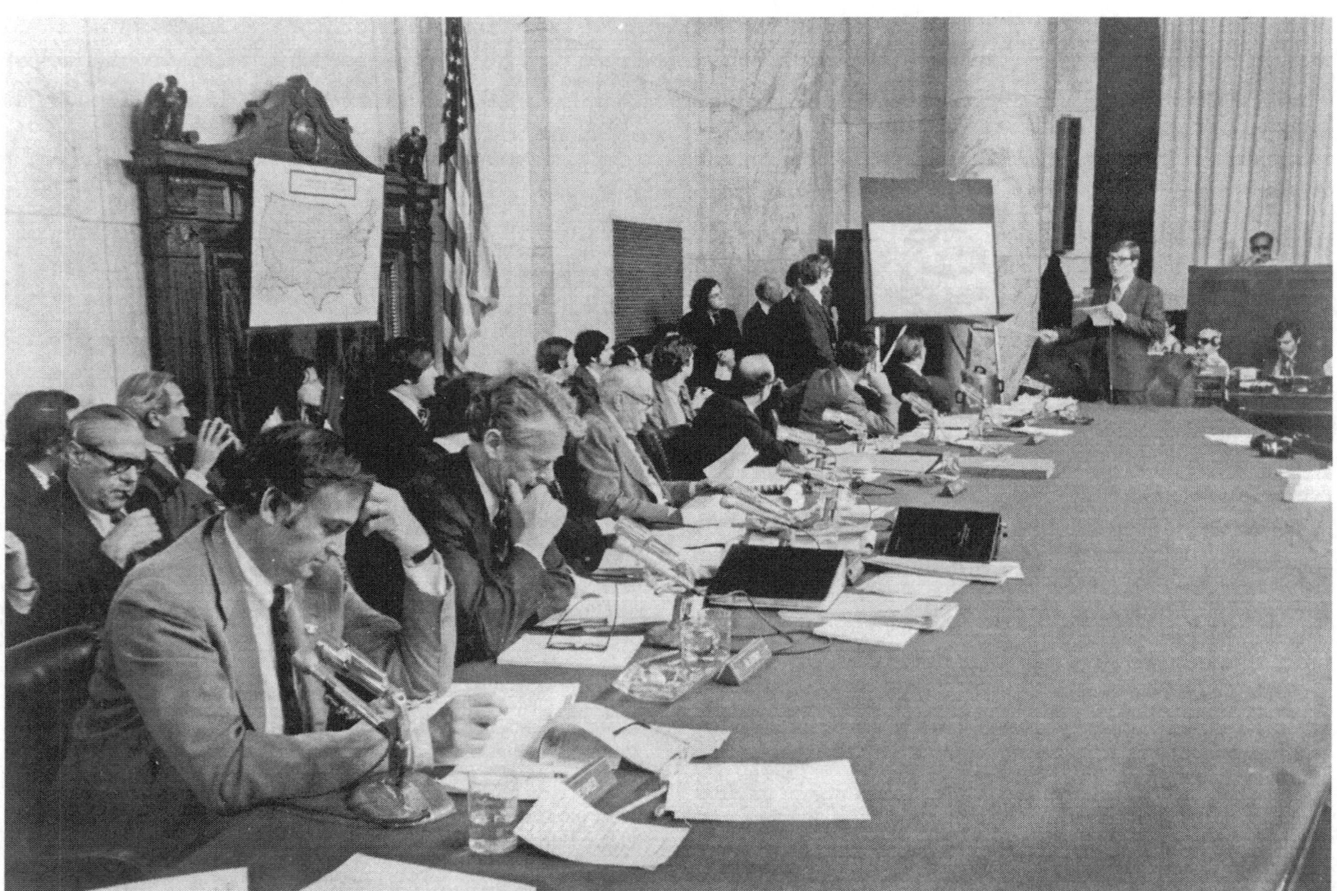

Watergate committee meeting in the Senate Caucus Room. From left to right at the table are senators Lowell Weicker Jr. (R-Conn.), Edward Gurney (R-Fla.), and committee chairman Sam Ervin (D-N.C.) (Library of Congress)

On February 21, 1973, the committee held its first meeting, at which it approved the appointments of Dash and Thompson. Dash expected the investigation to generate extensive records and consequently arranged for a computer system to maintain efficient record keeping. The computer staff eventually totaled 22 members. At peak operation, the committee employed more than 100 workers plus the computer group.

Between the end of February and the middle of May, a series of disclosures began to damage the image of the Nixon White House. On February 28 the Senate Judiciary Committee began its consideration of the confirmation of L. Patrick Gray as director of the FBI to replace J. Edgar Hoover, who had died the previous May. One document that Gray gave the committee stated that Dwight Chapin, Nixon's appointments secretary, had directed Herbert Kalmbach to pay Donald Segretti for his disruptive dirty-tricks campaign activities.

On March 23, Judge Sirica read in open court a letter from James McCord in which he described the pressure on the Watergate burglars to remain silent and to plead guilty. McCord also claimed that some people had committed perjury during the burglary trial. On April 3, in response to McCord's charges and Gray's testimony, Senator Weicker called for Haldeman to resign. Later Weicker told the press that Gray had burned two folders of documents that came from Hunt's White House office. Dean and Ehrlichman, moreover, had given Gray the folders soon after the June 1972 break-in. One folder contained documents doctored by Hunt that falsely implicated President John F. Kennedy in the November 1963 assassination of Ngo Dinh Diem, president of South Vietnam.

The next day, federal judge W. Matthew Byrne Jr. read aloud in his court a document about Hunt and Liddy, who, while on the White House and CREEP payrolls respectively, burglarized the office of Ellsberg's psychiatrist. Unknown to the public during these weeks, the FBI had been informing Nixon of the evidence implicating Haldeman, Ehrlichman,

From left to right: "plumber" G. Gordon Liddy, White House counsel John W. Dean, and Attorney General John Mitchell. All three played key roles in the Watergate scandal. (Associated Press)

and Attorney General Richard G. Kleindienst in the cover-up.

On April 30, buffeted by the disclosures, the president addressed the nation about Watergate. Maintaining his innocence in every aspect of the Watergate affair, he announced the resignations of Haldeman, Ehrlichman, and Kleindienst and the dismissal of White House counsel Dean.

The disclosures and Nixon's speech prompted Senator Charles H. Percy (R-Ill.) to introduce a "sense of the Senate" resolution requesting the president to appoint a special prosecutor to investigate Watergate. Ten other Republicans and seven Democrats cosponsored Percy's resolution. By voice vote, the Senate adopted the resolution on May 1, the day after the Nixon's address to the nation.

Public opinion polls reflected the impact of the damaging disclosures of late February to mid-May. At the end of January the president enjoyed his all-time high approval rating of 68 percent. By mid-May, only 44 percent of the public approved of his job performance. The mid-May poll results also reported that 96 percent of Americans had read or heard about Watergate and that 56 percent of the public believed the president had participated in the cover-up.

The Hearings Begin

On May 17, 1973, the committee met in the Caucus Room in the Old Senate Office Building, the site of several former Senate investigations. At 10 a.m., Chairman Sam Ervin called the meeting to order and in his prepared statement repeated the terms of the Senate authorizing resolution. The final report, he continued, "will reflect the considered judgment of the committee on whatever new legislation is needed to help safeguard the electoral process through which the President of the United States is chosen."

Ervin added that the hearings began "in an atmosphere of the utmost gravity," but he emphasized "that the purpose of these hearings is not prosecutorial or judicial but rather investigative and informative." The committee, he declared, would "provide full and open public testimony in order that the nation can proceed toward the healing of the wounds that now afflict the body politic."

Senator Howard Baker, the vice chair, spoke next and made several telling points. Repeating Ervin, Baker said, "We do not sit to pass judgment on the guilt or innocence of anyone." Rather, again echoing Ervin, Baker stated that the committee wanted "to develop the facts in full view of all the people of America." Most importantly, he pointed out that "virtually every action taken by this committee since its inception has been taken with complete unanimity of purpose and procedure. . . . This is not in any way a partisan undertaking, but rather it is a bipartisan search for the unvarnished truth."

The Watergate hearings were an enormous television spectacle. The Public Broadcasting Service (PBS) taped all 237 hours of testimony and replayed the hearings in the evenings on almost all of the 160 PBS stations nationwide. The three major networks—ABC, CBS, and NBC—carried the hearings for the first two weeks and then switched to a rotation whereby one channel covered the hearings while the other two channels aired their regular programs. Not since the Army-McCarthy hearings 20 years earlier had the nation been so riveted by a congressional investigation.

Samuel Dash planned the hearings carefully. For weeks prior to May 17, 1973, he and his staff interviewed participants in the break-in and the cover-up. The first witness, Robert Odle, the CREEP director of administration, discussed the transfer of personnel from the White House to CREEP. Odle also commented on the relationship and responsibilities of persons within CREEP, and on the constant liaison that H. R. Haldeman and Gordon C. Strachan maintained with CREEP.

The next day, May 18, James W. McCord Jr., the first of the burglars, testified. McCord began by characterizing the operation as "a very grave mistake, which I regret." Dash asked him why, after a long career as a law-enforcement officer without a blemish, he agreed to engage in two break-ins and illegal wiretapping. Citing the plan's support by higher-ups,

President Richard Nixon pounds his fist on the podium as he answers a question during his televised appearance before members of the National Broadcasters Association in Houston, Texas, on March 19, 1974. President Nixon declared that dragging out Watergate was dragging down America. (Associated Press)

McCord replied that Attorney General John Mitchell, in his own office, according to Liddy, had approved the plan, as had John Dean, "the top legal officer in the White House."

On the same day that McCord gave his testimony, Attorney General Elliot Richardson nominated Archibald Cox as special prosecutor to investigate Watergate. The Watergate investigation now spread its tentacles beyond the Congress and the news media. One of Cox's first requests, on June 3, was that the Senate suspend its hearings until after the completion of all trials.

Anthony T. Ulasewicz, Ehrlichman's assistant, appeared before the committee without an attorney. Ulasewicz had performed different types of jobs for Ehrlichman, including illegal telephone tapping, and in the summer of 1972 he had distributed "hush money" that Hunt had insisted be provided to cover the living expenses and legal fees of the Watergate defendants. Ulasewicz said he considered the investigative work he did for Ehrlichman to be "absolutely legal." But when Senator Daniel K. Inouye pressed the witness, he responded, "Yes, sir, I knew that it was wrong."

On May 24, Bernard L. Barker appeared. He was the first of the four burglars who had pleaded guilty back in January. During his testimony before the committee, Barker told of his participation in the September 1971 break-in of the office of Daniel Ellsberg's psychiatrist and of his participation in the two break-ins at the Democratic National Committee headquarters. A veteran of the 1961 Bay of Pigs operation, Barker said that he and the other three members of the group believed that their activities were a matter of national security.

At the start of proceedings on June 5, after observance of Memorial Day, Ervin read a statement on behalf of the committee. He reported that after careful consideration the committee unanimously declined to grant the request of Special Prosecutor Archibald Cox that the committee suspend hearings until after the completion of all trials. Ervin explained that under the

Senate resolution the committee had no authority to postpone or terminate its charge. The committee, furthermore, did not believe the hearings would impede a fair trial in a court.

Sally J. Harmony then took the witness oath. From March 13 to June 28, 1972, she had served as secretary to G. Gordon Liddy. She already had made four appearances before the grand jury. At the committee hearings, she told of typing a transcript of telephone logs and of photocopied documents from the Democratic National Committee. She also described how she created stationery with George McGovern letterhead.

Ervin concluded the morning session with the announcement that Liddy refused to testify privately to staff or in open hearings. He based his refusal on the rights granted under the Fifth and Sixth Amendments of the Constitution and on an immunity order under Title 18 of the United States Code.

Robert A. Reisner, former assistant to Jeb Stuart Magruder, appeared without counsel. Ervin commented that Reiner had met several times with the committee staff and had been "most cooperative." Reiner recounted that upon Magruder's orders he had helped shred politically sensitive office files.

Herbert L. Porter, the next witness, described working in the White House and then joining CREEP as director of the president's schedule. In his prepared statement Porter disassociated himself from knowledge of the break-in and cover-up. Under questioning he told how he, upon orders from Magruder, gave money to Liddy to pay for dirty tricks. Porter also admitted that Magruder had persuaded him to commit perjury before the grand jury and at the trial of the burglars.

Maurice H. Stans appeared next. He had served for three years as secretary of commerce before becoming chairman of CREEP's finance committee on February 15, 1972. In his prepared statement Stans insisted that he "had no knowledge of the Watergate break-in . . . or of the efforts to cover up after the event." He emphasized the complete separation in CREEP of the campaign committee and the finance committee. The finance committee raised money, he said, and the treasurer paid the bills. Stans, therefore, had not involved himself in payments to Liddy or those persons engaged in dirty tricks.

The first witnesses laid the foundation for the major testimony of Magruder. On June 14 the former director of CREEP began his appearances before the Watergate committee that would in the end fill 93 printed pages. He said that Attorney General Mitchell had approved Liddy's espionage plan to obtain intelligence that included burglary of the DNC headquarters. Charles Colson, he continued, had pressed for results. Magruder also reported that Gordon Strachan, Haldeman's assistant, had read summaries of the taped telephone conversations from the DNC. Strachan, according to Magruder, had prior knowledge of the break-in. Magruder also admitted that he had encouraged Porter to commit perjury. Finally Magruder confessed that he had perjured himself before the grand jury and at the trial of the burglars. Because of Magruder's position as director of CREEP until Mitchell took over on March 1, 1972, the charges and confessions he made carried credence. Nevertheless, the admissions, however revealing, did not portray a trail that led directly to the Oval Office.

John Dean Testifies

Dash had planned well in building the hearings to the most important witnesses. And now, on Monday, June 25, the committee prepared for the testimony that would shake the White House. Just 34 years old, White House counsel John Dean took the stand.

In response to a committee request, the chief judge of the federal district court had granted Dean an order of immunity for his testimony. Before reading his prepared statement, Dean commented: "It is a very difficult thing for me to testify about other people. It is far more easy for me to explain my own involvement in this matter, the fact that I was involved in obstructing justice, the fact that I assisted another in perjured testimony, the fact that I made personal use of funds that were in my custody." He added: "It is my honest belief that while the President was involved that he did not realize or appreciate at any time the implications of his involvement, and I think that when the facts come out I hope the President is forgiven." Finally, Dean stated that "Pursuant to the request of the committee I will commence with a general description of the atmosphere in the White House prior to June 1972."

For the next five hours Dean, in a steady, unemotional voice, read the 245 pages he had prepared. He opened with his conclusion, "The Watergate matter was an inevitable outgrowth of a climate of excessive concern over the political impact of demonstrators, excessive concern over leaks, an insatiable appetite for political intelligence, all coupled with a do-it-yourself White House staff, regardless of the law."

At length Dean explained the cover-up and told of the roles of John Ehrlichman, Haldeman, and Mitchell. Dean recalled that he left his first meeting with Nixon, on September 15, 1972, "with the impression that the

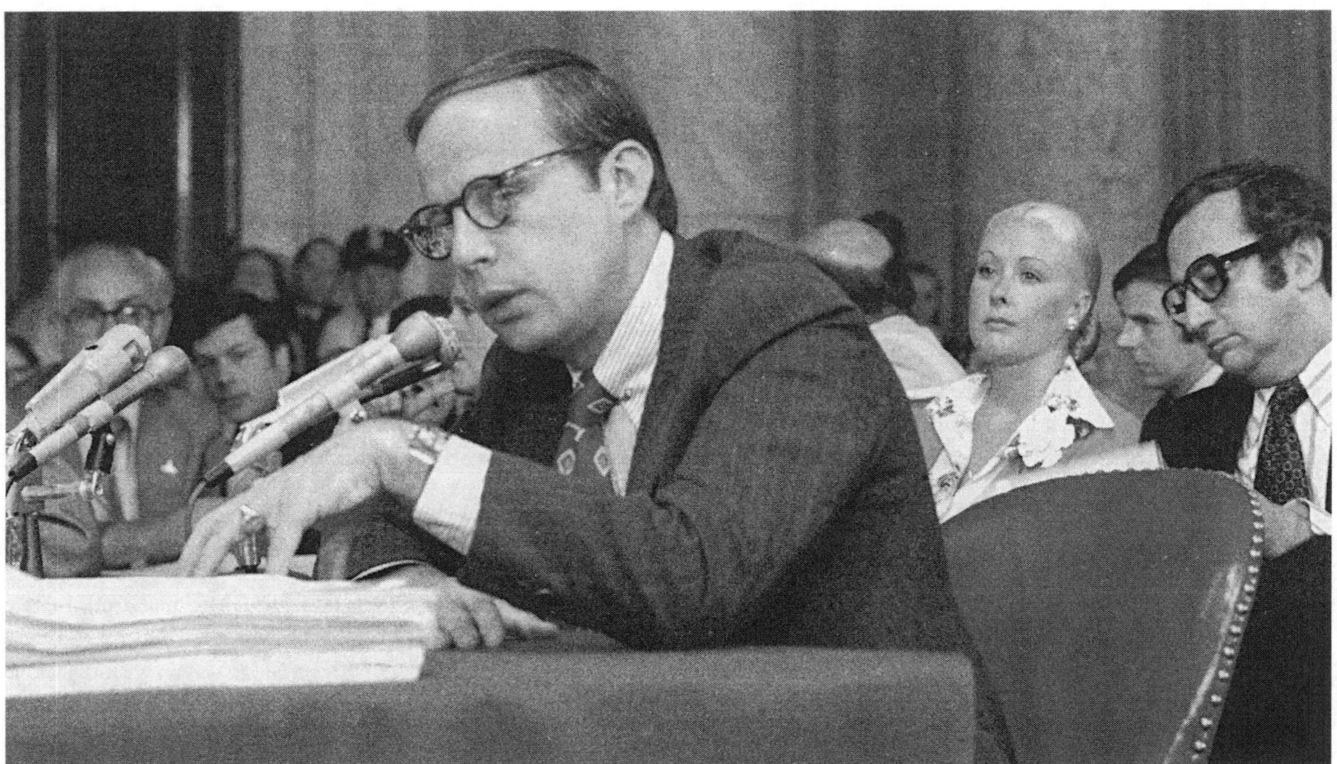

John W. Dean, former counsel to President Richard Nixon, testifies before the Senate committee investigating the Watergate break-in and other executive-branch misdeeds, June 27, 1973. His wife Maureen is seated behind him. (Associated Press)

President was well aware of what had been going on regarding the success of keeping the White House out of the Watergate scandal." Central to Dean's prepared statement was his discussion of the 15 meetings he had with the president from the end of February to late March 1973. At the meeting on March 21, 1973, Dean likened the cover-up to "a cancer growing on the Presidency and that if the cancer was not removed that the President himself would be killed by it." He told Nixon that offering E. Howard Hunt clemency and paying the expenses of the Watergate burglars in exchange for their silence constituted obstruction of justice. After he left the meeting Dean realized the president planned to continue the cover-up. Dean's description of events concurred with the testimonies of McCord, Magruder, and others.

Dean spent a week in the witness chair. For four days, majority and minority counsel and committee members bombarded him with questions. At one point, Dash addressed Dean, "I guess you are fully aware, Mr. Dean, of the gravity of the charges you have made under oath against the highest official in our land, the President of the United States." Dean replied, "Yes, I am." Baker framed the central question of Dean's testimony: "What did the President know and when did he know it?" Nixon supporters believed that in such a polarization the president would win because Dean had no evidence. Dean once stated that he was "quite willing to submit myself to a polygraph test on any issue of fact with any individual who says that what I am saying is less than truthful."

On June 28, the day before Dean finished, Hunt testified before the House Armed Services Subcommittee on Intelligence and admitted that the CIA had loaned him equipment. The next day, Colson said he had allowed a reporter to read classified State Department cables. On July 4, during the Senate's Independence Day recess. CBS-TV announced that Justice Department prosecutors recommended the indictment of Dean, Ehrlichman, Haldeman, and Mitchell. Two days later George A. Spater, chairman of American Airlines, admitted that his airline had illegally contributed $55,000 to Nixon's campaign. Three days after that the *New York Times* reported that Haldeman, Colson, Magruder, Strachan, and Dwight Chapin all had organized and directed the dirty tricks during the campaign and financed the operations with unreported campaign contributions.

John Mitchell Testifies

On July 10, the committee reconvened its investigation with John Mitchell as the first witness. Twice Mitchell's lawyers had requested that the committee withdraw its subpoena, and both times the committee refused. Upon advice of his lawyers, Mitchell offered no opening statement. Immediately he responded to questions about his position and actions concerning the Huston plan, the Committee to Re-elect the President, the Liddy plan, and the testimony of other witnesses. Committee members also questioned him about his relationship with Liddy, Magruder, Dean, Nixon, and others. Dash, for example, asked Mitchell, "Why didn't you at least recommend that Mr. Liddy be fired from his responsible position at the committee since obviously he was presenting to you an irresponsible plan?" Mitchell replied, "Well, in hindsight I probably should have done that, too."

Another time, Mitchell retorted, "I violently disagree with Mr. Magruder's testimony to the point that the Democratic National Committee was discussed as a target for electronic surveillance." Another time Dash explained to Mitchell that Hugh Sloan Jr., treasurer of CREEP, and Robert Reisner, deputy director of CREEP, swore under oath that Magruder told them that on March 30, 1972, Mitchell had approved of the Liddy plan.

Dash elicited from Mitchell his motive for concealing information from Nixon. Mitchell believed that the "White House horror stories," as he put it, would have damaged the president more than revelations about the break-in. On this important point Mitchell stated, "This was certainly my belief and rationale."

Mitchell defended the president, although he could not document Nixon's innocence. Rather, "I think I know the individual, I know his reactions to things. . . . I just do not believe that he had that information or had the knowledge." Mitchell asserted that if he had told Nixon about the Liddy plan, the break-in, and what Mitchell called the "White House horrors," he knew what Nixon would have done, "and it would be most detrimental to his political campaign."

At times Mitchell answered: "I don't know"; "I have no personal knowledge"; "I specifically deny"; "Well, I do not know"; "I don't recall"; and "I haven't any idea."

Minority counsel Fred D. Thompson inquired about Mitchell's role in paying the seven Watergate burglars for family support and legal fees. Thompson said that if the public learned of the payment it would be "embarrassing to say the least, if not illegal." Mitchell agreed but claimed he had no control over the money.

Senator Herman E. Talmadge asked Mitchell, "When you found out all these crimes and conspiracies and cover-ups were being committed, why on earth didn't you walk into the President's office and tell him the truth?" Mitchell answered that if he had done that, "it would affect him in his reelection." Talmadge continued, "You placed the expediency of the next election above your responsibilities as an intimate to advise the President of the peril that surrounded him? Here was the deputy campaign director involved, here were his two closest associates in his office involved, all around him were people involved in crime, perjury, accessory after the fact, and you deliberately refused to tell him." The former attorney general replied, "Senator, I think you have put it exactly correct." Senator Edward J. Gurney wanted to know if the president knew anything about the cover-up. Mitchell replied, "No, sir, I am thoroughly convinced that the President was unaware of it."

The next day Mitchell repeated some of his positions. "My reasons—my motives—had to do with an entirely different subject matter and that had to do with the White House horror stories, not the Watergate." Another time, regarding June 1972, Mitchell asserted, "I still believe that the most important thing to this country was the reelection of Richard Nixon. And I was not about to countenance anything that would stand in the way of that reelection."

Ervin asked Mitchell if he had been informed that Magruder planned to commit perjury before the grand jury in August 1972. The former attorney general replied, "That was correct, sir." In response to questioning by Senator Lowell P. Weicker, Mitchell admitted that despite being an attorney and former attorney general of the United States, he did not notify any officials in the Justice Department about what he knew about the break-in at the office of Ellsberg's psychiatrist.

During his questioning Dash made repeated references to Mitchell's logs to refresh his memory of dates, telephone calls, and conversations. Mitchell once commented that the examination of the committee was "much more intensive" than what he had experienced before the grand jury. At one point Dash asked: "Mr. Mitchell, you enjoy the distinction, and you have made it from time-to-time, that it was your purpose to not volunteer anything. Is there a distinction between your not volunteering anything and lying?" Dash soon followed with the question, "Since you may have given false testimony under oath on prior occasions, is there really any reason for this committee to believe your testimony now, especially to the issue of whether you did or did not give final approval . . . to the Liddy plan?"

At the conclusion of Mitchell's testimony on July 12, Ervin discussed a recent exchange of letters between him and the president. Ervin read the letter, dated July 12, to Nixon, "largely dictated by Senator Baker with suggestions from the other committee members." The responsibility of the committee and the position of the president as stated in his letter of June 6 "present the very grave possibility of a fundamental constitutional confrontation between the Congress and the Presidency," the committee's letter said. At 1 P.M. the committee unanimously adopted a resolution that stated that "the Committee is entitled to have access to every document in the possession of the White House or any Department or Agency of the Executive Branch of the Federal Government which is relevant." Second, the resolution repeated that "the Committee is anxious to avoid any confrontation with the White House in respect to this matter" and, therefore, authorized the committee chair to meet with the president to reconcile positions.

Alexander P. Butterfield's Revelation

The impact of the testimony of the next witness, Alexander P. Butterfield, the administrator of the Federal Aviation Administration, on July 16 is impossible to overestimate. Dash opened with a statement: "Mr. Chairman, at a staff interview with Mr. Butterfield on Friday, some significant information was elicited and was attended by the majority members of the staff and the minority members. The minority staff member elicited the information. Therefore, I would like to change the usual routine of the questioning and ask minority counsel Fred Thompson to begin the questioning of Mr. Butterfield."

From January 21, 1969, to March 14, 1973, Butterfield had served as a deputy assistant to the president. "My duties," he said, "were many and varied." These included "the collection of documents which will eventually go to the Nixon library." When Butterfield completed his job description, Thompson asked, "Are you aware of the installation of any listening devices in the Oval Office of the President?"

In his prepared statement Dean had commented that in one conversation with Nixon he thought the president's movements indicated he might be recording their conversation. After Butterfield's positive reply, Thompson asked the date of installation and whether the Old Executive Office Building had similar listening devices. Both rooms, Butterfield said, had voice-activated systems. Thompson next asked about the cabinet room and learned that a taping system operated there as well. In addition Thompson asked if there were devices on telephones in the Oval Office, the president's office in the Old Executive Office Building, and the Lincoln sitting room in the upstairs residence of the White House. Again the answer was yes. At Camp David, the president's retreat in Maryland, Butterfield continued, only the telephone on the president's desk, in his personal cabin, had a listening device. Butterfield added that the devices "were installed to record things of posterity, for the Nixon library. We had quite an elaborate setup at the White House for the collection and preservation of documents, and of things which transpired in the way of business of state."

Butterfield believed that neither Dean nor Ehrlichman knew of the taping systems and that no one had transcribed any of the tapes. Butterfield had given the director of the technical security division of the Secret Service the responsibility for storing the tapes. Near the end of Butterfield's appearance before the committee, Ervin read a letter he had received that day from J. Fred Buzhardt, counsel to the president. In the letter Buzhardt confirmed the facts of Butterfield's testimony and added that the system of recording conversations "is similar to that employed by the last Administration," a system that Nixon had "discontinued from 1969 until the spring of 1971."

Butterfield concluded his testimony with the opinion that the president planned to use the tapes "to present his defense. I believe, of course," Butterfield continued, "that the President is innocent of any crime or wrongdoing, that he is innocent, likewise, of any complicity."

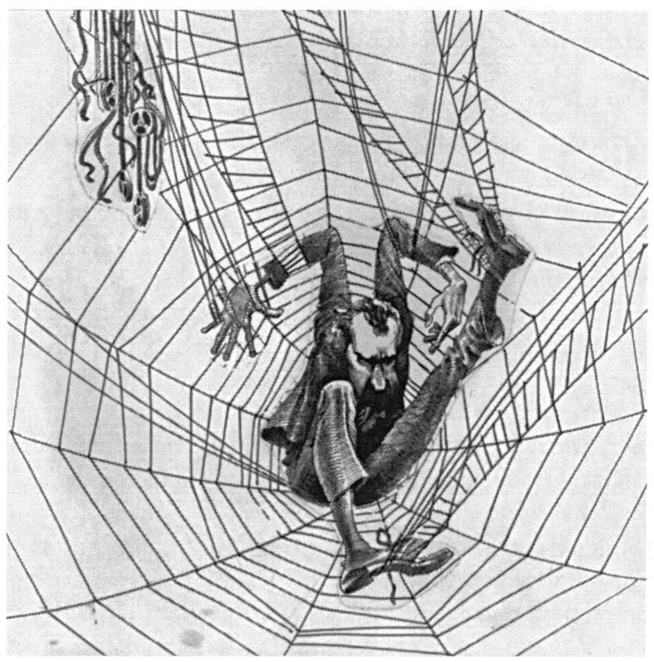

Political cartoon, drawn by Robert Pryor, of President Richard Nixon tangled in a spider's web of recording tapes that belied his assertions that he was not involved in Watergate-related crimes, 1974. (Library of Congress)

The tapes aroused intense, immediate curiosity. Logically they could answer questions that the testimony of witnesses had raised when their testimonies contradicted one another and when descriptions of conversations remained open to interpretation. The tapes could also reveal what the president knew and when he knew it. In addition to the committee, the special prosecutor and the grand jury both had reason to want access to the tapes.

Butterfield had offered straightforward testimony with no personal involvement in the conversations and events in question. The next witness, Herbert W. Kalmbach, the campaign fundraiser, contrasted markedly. With a desire "to clear my name," he opened with a prepared statement in which he denied "any prior knowledge of the Watergate break-in or participation in, the formulation of any planned conspiracy to cover up that incident or act of campaign sabotage or unethical activity." He told the committee that he had raised funds "to provide for the legal defense of the Watergate defendants and for the support of their families . . . in the belief that such was proper and necessary to discharge what I assumed to be a moral obligation." With common sense, he continued, "the fact that I had been directed to undertake these actions by the No. 2 and No. 3 men on the White House staff [Ehrlichman and Haldeman] made it absolutely incomprehensible to me that my actions in this regard could have been regarded in any way as improper or unethical."

After Kalmbach answered his last question, Ervin read into the record a letter that he had sent to President Nixon on July 17. The letter started, "Dear Mr. President: Today the Select Committee on Presidential Campaign Activities met and unanimously voted that I request that you provide the Committee with all relevant documents and tapes under control of the White House that related to the matters the Select Committee is authorized to investigate." The letter essentially repeated the July 12 request for documents and tapes.

The next four witnesses provided additional information and sometimes contradicted testimony of earlier witnesses. Fred C. LaRue, a special assistant to CREEP since 1972 and before that a consultant to the president, confessed to participation in the cover-up: "I am fully aware now that what I did then was wrong, both ethically and legally." As the questioning of LaRue neared its end, Ervin commented, "I can't resist the temptation to philosophize just a little bit about Watergate. The evidence thus far introduced or presented before this committee tends to show that men upon whom fortune had smiled benevolently and who possess great financial power, great political power, and great governmental power, undertook to nullify the laws of man and the laws of God for the purpose of gaining what history will call a very temporary political advantage. . . ." Ervin said that "those who participated in this effort to nullify the laws of man and the laws of God overlooked one of the laws of God which is set forth in the seventh verse of the sixth chapter of Galatians: 'Be not deceived. God is not mocked; for whatever a man soweth, that shall he also reap.'" Those present applauded.

Strachan, Haldeman's former staff assistant, testified next under a grant of immunity. He stated that he would tell the truth "even to the extent it might reflect adversely on me." He told of destroying documents, of payments to the Watergate defendants, and of Liddy's plan. In response to Senator Joseph M. Montoya, Strachan said, "To be 27 years old and walking into the White House and seeing the President on occasion . . . it's a pretty awesome-inspiring experience for a young man." Montoya told of young people writing to committee members expressing disillusionment with public service. He asked Strachan what advice "do you have for these young people?" Strachan replied, "My advice would be to stay away." His remark drew laughter from the audience.

Following a lunch recess, Ervin convened the afternoon session by reading a long letter from Nixon, dated July 23. In his letter Nixon wrote that he could not comply with the committee's request for tapes. The tapes, the president explained, "would not finally settle the central issues before your Committee. I personally listened to a number of them. The tapes are entirely consistent with what I know to be the truth and what I have stated to be the truth. However, as in any verbatim recording of informal conversations, they contain comments that persons with different perspectives and motivations would inevitably interpret in different ways." The president expanded on this point by adding, "On May 22 I described my knowledge of the Watergate matter and its aftermath in categorical and unambiguous terms that I know to be true." Nixon's May 22 statement was a response to the Senate Committee on Foreign Relations release of a CIA memorandum by Vernon Walters, deputy director of the CIA. That memorandum, dated several days after the break-in, recorded that the president wanted Walters to talk with the acting director of the FBI about its investigation.

After Senator Ervin read the president's letter, the committee voted unanimously to issue two subpoenas, one for the tapes and one for presidential papers. Ervin characterized Nixon's letter as remarkable: "If you will notice, the President says he has heard the tapes or some of them, and they sustain his position. But he says he's not going to let anyone else hear them for fear they might draw a different conclusion." The audience laughed. Ervin ended his comments by stating, "I deeply regret that the situation has arisen, because I think the Watergate tragedy is the greatest tragedy this country has ever suffered. I used to think that the Civil War was our country's greatest tragedy, but I do remember that there were some redeeming features in the Civil War in that there were some spirit of sacrifice and heroism displayed on both sides. I see no redeeming features in Watergate." Those present applauded. Senator Baker also noted his disappointment over the confrontation between Congress and the White House. News broadcasts and newsprint highlighted Ervin's statement about the "tragedy" of Watergate.

Returning to the questioning of Strachan, the committee learned the White House intended to have the Internal Revenue Service conduct a full-field audit of Clark Clifford, a prominent Democrat and former close adviser to President Harry Truman. Strachan reported further that Colson had prepared a list of 20 people who also would have their tax returns audited. In reply to Ervin's question if Haldeman knew of the intelligence operation, Strachan declared, "there is no doubt in my mind." He also said that Haldeman instructed him to destroy files that would be "politically embarrassing" if made public.

John Ehrlichman and H. R. Haldeman Testify

The next two witnesses were the president's closest aides. John Ehrlichman served as chief domestic adviser and H. R Haldeman as chief of staff. Ehrlichman, in the company of two attorneys, opened his appearance by reading a lengthy statement. Forcefully he declared, "I am here to refute every charge of illegal conduct on my part which has been made during the course of these hearings." He defended Nixon and accused John Dean of multiple falsehoods. The burglary of the office of Ellsberg's psychiatrist, Ehrlichman insisted, concerned national security.

For five days, Ehrlichman fended off questions. At times, Dash and Ehrlichman clashed. Ehrlichman: "Yes, in a literal sense, that is true." Dash: "Not in an actual sense." Ehrlichman: "Well, here I am dueling with a professor." To conclude, Ehrlichman repeated, "I did not cover up anything to do with Watergate."

Haldeman, the model of cooperation, presented a striking contrast to the pugnacious Ehrlichman. Like Ehrlichman, Haldeman insisted that neither he nor Nixon had any knowledge of the break-in or cover-up and identified Dean as the mastermind of the cover-up. At one point Haldeman exclaimed, "I don't know now whom to believe. I may add that until the recent period both John Mitchell and Jeb Magruder denied any Watergate involvement." Most startling to the committee was Haldeman's comment that to prepare for his appearance he had listened to the tapes of Nixon-Dean meetings of September 15, 1972, and March 21, 1973.

The Struggle over the Tapes

In many ways, the testimonies of Strachan, Ehrlichman, and Haldeman were anticlimactic. Butterfield's revelation on July 16 about the existence of the taping system shifted the focus of the hearings from unraveling the cover-up to a struggle over the release of the tapes. The committee, the special prosecutor, and federal judge John J. Sirica all asked the president to release the tapes, and Nixon, citing presidential confidentiality, refused.

Public opinion favored their release. Within three and a half weeks, three symbols of conservatism called for their release: the symbol of intellectual conservatism, William F. Buckley and the *National Review;* the symbol of corporate conservatism, the *Wall Street Journal;* and the symbol of political conservatism, Senator Barry Goldwater. Nixon's defenders believed the tapes would exonerate him, while Dean's supporters believed the opposite. Both sides wanted an answer to Baker's question: "What did the president know and when did he know it?"

The committee, meanwhile, continued its hearings, but the statements and answers they elicited only continued the pattern of confession, defiance, and, especially, contradictory testimonies. From August 7 until September 24 the committee recessed. On September 25 the committee closed Phase I, "Watergate Investigations." The next day it opened Phase II, "Campaign Practices." By November 12, the committee had conducted hearings on only 11 days. Beginning November 13, all hearings became executive sessions. Also in November the hearings entered Phase III, "Campaign Financing." The subjects the committee investigated during the autumn, winter, and spring of 1973–74 included campaign practices and finance, the Milk Fund issue regarding federal subsidies, and the finances of Charles G. "Bebe" Rebozo, a friend of Nixon's. In one way or another all these subjects had attracted national attention earlier. The center of political and public attention throughout these months was the struggle over control of the White House tapes.

Nixon's refusal to give up the tapes led to news conferences at which Watergate questions overwhelmingly dominated. Related issues also crowded into the news. On September 4, 1973, a Los Angeles grand jury had indicted Ehrlichman, Liddy, Egil Krogh Jr., and David Young Jr. for their roles in the burglary of the office of Ellsberg's psychiatrist. Four prominent corporations—American Airlines, Phillips Petroleum, Goodyear Tire and Rubber, and Minnesota Mining and Manufacturing—pleaded guilty to illegal campaign contributions. In mid-September, Donald Segretti pleaded guilty to four violations of campaign law and later before the committee stated, "my activities were wrong and have no place in the American political system." Late in September Vice President Spiro T. Agnew captured national attention over charges of bribery that led to his October 10 resignation following a plea bargain of federal income-tax evasion. On Friday evening, October 19, Nixon announced that rather than comply with a court order to transfer nine tapes to Sirica, he instead would submit summaries of the tapes authenticated by Mississippi senator John Stennis. Nixon ordered Attorney General Richardson to fire Special Prosecutor Archibald Cox and abolish his office. The terms of Cox's appointment, however, granted total independence. Richardson refused to fire Cox and resigned, as did his deputy, William Ruckelshaus. Solicitor General Robert H. Bork carried out Nixon's order. On Saturday evening the president's press secretary announced the series of events, and immediately the media dubbed the series of events the Saturday Night Massacre. Nixon had seriously misjudged the national mood, and he soon reestablished the office of the special prosecutor. He also turned over seven of the nine tapes and notified Sirica that two of the tapes did not exist.

On November 4, former attorney general Richard G. Kleindienst confessed to perjury during his confirmation hearing before the Senate. The next week *Time* published its first-ever editorial and called for Nixon's resignation. Throughout the autumn, public opinion polls recorded the steady erosion of confidence in the president. By November 1973, 83 percent of American disapproved of Nixon's handling of the tapes.

An angry crowd yells at President Nixon during the height of the Watergate scandal. (© Wally McNamee/CORBIS)

Out-of-the-Limelight Ending

The magnitude of the struggle over the tapes overshadowed all public issues from the summer of 1973 until President Nixon resigned in August 1974. His resignation ended the greatest constitutional crisis since the Civil War, a crisis that ultimately involved all three branches of the federal government and dominated public attention for more than a year.

To maintain custody of the tapes, Nixon attempted a series of stratagems. In November he released some tapes, but one contained an 18-and-a-half-minute erasure. The most dramatic stratagem came in May 1974, when he released transcripts of what he claimed were all the tapes. On July 24, the Supreme Court ruled the president had to release all tapes. One of the tapes recording a conversation on June 23, 1972, became known as the "smoking gun" tape because it revealed the president's involvement in the cover-up, obstruction of justice, and attempted misuse of a federal agency.

With impeachment in the House and conviction by the Senate all but a certainty, Nixon resigned the presidency on August 9, 1974. Six weeks earlier, on June 27, 1974, Senator Ervin had submitted the committee's 1,250-page final report to the Senate accompanied by a volume of exhibits and two volumes, totaling 2,157 pages, of appendixes to the hearings. Among the recommendations incorporated in the final report was the full disclosure of gifts, the establishment of a permanent Office of Public Attorney, individual and corporate campaign limits, and more congressional oversight.

THE WHITE HOUSE
WASHINGTON

August 9, 1974

Dear Mr. Secretary:

I hereby resign the Office of President of the United States.

Sincerely,

Richard Nixon

11.35 AM

The Honorable Henry A. Kissinger
The Secretary of State
Washington, D.C. 20520

HK

President Richard Nixon's resignation letter, August 9, 1974. (National Archives)

Ervin, whose service as chair earned him a favorable national reputation, accurately summarized the committee's work in his preface to the final report, calling it "one of the most comprehensive investigations in the history of Congress" and an assignment "successfully" completed. "It is my firm belief," he concluded, "that the bright light this committee has shed on the matter given it to study illuminated the American public's understanding and consciousness of the Watergate affair." That bright light drove President Nixon from office.

DOCUMENTS

Address by President Richard M. Nixon, April 30, 1973

By the end of April 1973, the web of Watergate, as one contemporary political cartoon suggested, was fast ensnaring the president of the United States. The Senate had established the Select Committee on Presidential Campaign Activities, chaired by Democratic senator Sam Ervin of North Carolina. Allegations of cover-ups and obstruction of justice by administration officials filled newspaper columns and television news. Although President Nixon claimed in an official statement from the White House that he had no prior knowledge of the Watergate break-in and other administration misdeeds, he decided to take forceful action on April 30. Appearing on national television, Nixon announced the dismissal of White House counsel John Dean and the resignations of trusted aides H.R. Haldeman and John Ehrlichman. He vowed to get the facts of Watergate out to the public and to get on with the work that the citizens of the United States expected from their president.

ADDRESS BY PRESIDENT RICHARD M. NIXON APRIL 30, 1973

Good evening:

I want to talk to you tonight from my heart on a subject of deep concern to every American.

In recent months, members of my Administration and officials of the Committee for the Re-election of the President—including some of my closest friends and most trusted aides—have been charged with involvement in what has come to be known as the Watergate affair. These include charges of illegal activity during and preceding the 1972 Presidential election and charges that responsible officials participated in efforts to cover up that illegal activity.

The inevitable result of these charges has been to raise serious questions about the integrity of the White House itself. Tonight I wish to address those questions.

Last June 17, while I was in Florida trying to get a few days rest after my visit to Moscow, I first learned from news reports of the Watergate break-in. I was appalled at this senseless, illegal action, and I was shocked to learn that employees of the Re-election Committee were apparently among those guilty. I immediately ordered an investigation by appropriate Government authorities. On September 15, as you will recall, indictments were brought against seven defendants in the case.

As the investigations went forward, I repeatedly asked those conducting the investigation whether there was any reason to believe that members of my Administration were in any way involved. I received repeated assurances that there were not. Because of these continuing reassurances, because I believed the reports I was getting, because I had faith in the persons from whom I was getting them, I discounted the stories in the press that appeared to implicate members of my Administration or other officials of the campaign committee.

Until March of this year, I remained convinced that the denials were true and that the charges of involvement by members of the White House Staff were false. The comments I made during this period, and the comments made by my Press Secretary in my behalf, were based on the information provided to us at the time we made those comments. However, new information then came to me which persuaded me that there was a real possibility that some of these charges were true, and suggesting further that there had been an effort to conceal the facts both from the public, from you, and from me.

As a result, on March 21, I personally assumed the responsibility for coordinating intensive new inquiries into the matter, and I personally ordered those conducting the investigations to get all the facts and to report them directly to me, right here in this office.

I again ordered that all persons in the Government or at the Re-election Committee should cooperate fully with the FBI, the prosecutors, and the grand jury. I also ordered that anyone who refused to cooperate in telling the truth would be asked to resign from government service. And, with ground rules adopted that would preserve the basic constitutional separation of powers between the Congress and the Presidency, I directed that members of the White House Staff should appear and testify voluntarily under oath before the Senate committee which was investigating Watergate.

I was determined that we should get to the bottom of the matter, and that the truth should be fully brought out—no matter who was involved.

At the same time, I was determined not to take precipitate action, and to avoid, if at all possible, any action that would appear to reflect on innocent people. I wanted to be fair. But I knew that in the final analysis, the integrity of this office—public faith in the integrity of this office—would have to take priority over all personal considerations.

Today, in one of the most difficult decisions of my Presidency, I accepted the resignations of two of my closest associates in the White House—Bob Haldeman, John Ehrlichman—two of the finest public servants it has been my privilege to know.

I want to stress that in accepting these resignations, I mean to leave no implication whatever of personal wrongdoing on their part, and I leave no implication tonight of implication on the part of others who have been charged in this matter. But in matters as sensitive as guarding the integrity of our democratic process, it is essential not only that rigorous legal and ethical standards be observed, but also that the public, you, have total confidence that they are both being observed and enforced by those in authority and particularly by the President of the United States. They agreed with me that this move was necessary in order to restore that confidence.

Because Attorney General Kleindienst—though a distinguished public servant, my personal friend for 20 years, with no personal involvement whatever in this matter—has been a close personal and professional associate of some of those who are involved in this case, he and I both felt that it was also necessary to name a new Attorney General.

The Counsel to the President, John Dean, has also resigned.

As the new Attorney General, I have today named Elliot Richardson, a man of unimpeachable integrity and rigorously high principle. I have directed him to do everything necessary to ensure that the Department of Justice has the confidence and the trust of every law abiding person in this country.

I have given him absolute authority to make all decisions bearing upon the prosecution of the Watergate case and related matters. I have instructed him that if he should consider it appropriate, he has the authority to name a special supervising prosecutor for matters arising out of the case.

Whatever may appear to have been the case before, whatever improper activities may yet be discovered in connection with this whole sordid affair, I want the American people, I want you to know beyond the shadow of a doubt that during my term as President, justice will be pursued fairly, fully, and impartially, no matter who is involved. This office is a sacred trust and I am determined to be worthy of that trust.

Looking back at the history of this case, two questions arise:

How could it have happened?

Who is to blame?

Political commentators have correctly observed that during my 27 years in politics I have always previously insisted on running my own campaigns for office.

But 1972 presented a very different situation. In both domestic and foreign policy, 1972 was a year of crucially important decisions, of intense negotiations, of vital new directions, particularly in working toward the goal which has been my overriding concern throughout my political career—the goal of bringing peace to America, peace to the world.

That is why I decided, as the 1972 campaign approached, that the Presidency should come first and politics second. To the maximum extent possible, therefore, I sought to delegate campaign operations, to remove the day-to-day campaign decisions from the President's office and from the White House. I also, as you recall, severely limited the number of my own campaign appearances.

Who, then, is to blame for what happened in this case?

For specific criminal actions by specific individuals, those who committed those actions must, of course, bear the liability and pay the penalty.

For the fact that alleged improper actions took place within the White House or within my campaign organization, the easiest course would be for me to blame those to whom I delegated the responsibility to run the campaign. But that would be a cowardly thing to do.

I will not place the blame on subordinates—on people whose zeal exceeded their judgment, and who may have done wrong in a cause they deeply believed to be right.

In any organization, the man at the top must bear the responsibility. That responsibility, therefore, belongs here, in this office. I accept it. And I pledge to you tonight, from this office, that I will do everything in my power to ensure that the guilty are brought to justice, and that such abuses are purged from our political processes in the years to come, long after I have left this office.

Some people, quite properly appalled at the abuses that occurred, will say that Watergate demonstrates the bankruptcy of the American political system. I believe precisely the opposite is true. Watergate represented a series of illegal acts and bad judgments by a number of individuals. It was the system that has brought the facts to light and that will bring those guilty to justice—a system that in this case has included a determined grand jury, honest prosecutors, a courageous judge, John Sirica, and a vigorous free press.

It is essential now that we place our faith in that system—and especially in the judicial system. It is essential that we let the judicial process go forward, respecting those safeguards that are established to protect the innocent as well as to convict the guilty. It is essential that in reacting to the excesses of others, we not fall into excesses ourselves.

It is also essential that we not be so distracted by events such as this that we neglect the vital work before us, before this Nation, before America, at a time of critical importance to America and the world.

Since March, when I first learned that the Watergate affair might, in fact, be far more serious than I had been led to believe, it has claimed far too much of my time and my attention.

Whatever may now transpire in the case, whatever the actions of the grand jury, whatever the outcome of any eventual trials, I must now turn my full attention—and I shall do so—once again to the larger duties of this office. I owe it to this great office that I hold, and I owe it to you—to my country.

I know that as Attorney General, Elliot Richardson will be both fair and he will be fearless in pursuing this case wherever it leads. I am confident that with him in charge, justice will be done.

There is vital work to be done toward our goal of a lasting structure of peace in the world—work that cannot wait, work that I must do.

Tomorrow, for example, Chancellor Brandt of West Germany will visit the White House for talks that are a vital element of "The Year of Europe," as 1973 has been called. We are already preparing for the next Soviet-American summit meeting later this year.

This is also a year in which we are seeking to negotiate a mutual and balanced reduction of armed forces in Europe, which will reduce our defense budget and allow us to have funds for other purposes at home so desperately needed. It is the year when the United States and Soviet negotiators will seek to work out the second and even more important round of our talks on limiting nuclear arms, and of reducing the danger of a nuclear war that would destroy civilization as we know it. It is a year in which we confront the difficult tasks of maintaining peace in Southeast Asia and in the potentially explosive Middle East.

There is also vital work to be done right here in America: to ensure prosperity, and that means a good job for everyone who wants to work; to control inflation, that I know worries every housewife, everyone who tries to balance a family budget in America; to set in motion new and better ways of ensuring progress toward a better life for all Americans.

When I think of this office—of what it means—I think of all the things that I want to accomplish for this Nation, of all the things I want to accomplish for you.

On Christmas Eve, during my terrible personal ordeal of the renewed bombing of North Vietnam, which after 12 years of war, finally helped to bring America peace with honor, I sat down just before midnight. I wrote out some of my goals for my second term as President.

Let me read them to you.

"To make it possible for our children, and for our children's children, to live in a world of peace.

"To make this country be more than ever a land of opportunity—of equal opportunity, full opportunity for every American.

"To provide jobs for all who can work, and generous help for those who cannot work.

"To establish a climate of decency, and civility, in which each person respects the feelings and the dignity and the God-given rights of his neighbor.

"To make this a land in which each person can dare to dream, can live his dreams—not in fear, but in hope—proud of his community, proud of his country, proud of what America has meant to himself and to the world."

These are great goals. I believe we can, we must work for them. We can achieve them. But we cannot achieve these goals unless we dedicate ourselves to another goal.

We must maintain the integrity of the White House, and that integrity must be real, not transparent. There can be no whitewash at the White House.

We must reform our political process—ridding it not only of the violations of the law, but also of the ugly mob violence, and other inexcusable campaign tactics that have been too often practiced and too readily accepted in the past, including those that may have been a response by one side to the excesses or expected excesses of the other side. Two wrongs do not make a right.

I have been in public life for more than a quarter of a century. Like any other calling, politics has good people, and bad people. And let me tell you, the great majority in politics—in the Congress, in the Federal Government, in the State Government—are good people. I know that it can be very easy, under the intensive pressures of a campaign, for even well-intentioned people to fall into shady tactics—to rationalize this on the grounds that what is at stake is of such importance to the Nation that the end justifies the means. And both of our great parties have been guilty of such tactics in the past.

In recent years, however, the campaign excesses that have occurred on all sides have provided a sobering demonstration of how far this false doctrine can take us. The lesson is clear: America, in its political campaigns, must not again fall into the trap of letting the end, however great that end is, justify the means.

I urge the leaders of both political parties, I urge citizens, all of you, everywhere, to join in working toward a new set of standards, new rules and procedures to ensure that future elections will be as nearly free of such abuses as they possibly can be made. This is my goal. I ask you to join in making it America's goal.

When I was inaugurated for a second term this past January 20, I gave each member of my Cabinet and each member of my senior White House Staff a special 4-year calendar, with each day marked to show the number of days remaining to the Administration. In the inscription on each calendar, I wrote these words: "The Presidential term which begins today consists of 1,461 days—no more, no less. Each can be a day of strengthening and renewal for America; each can add depth and dimension to the American experience. If we strive together, if we make the most of the challenge and the opportunity that these days offer us, they can stand out as great days for America, and great moments in the history of the world."

I looked at my own calendar this morning up at Camp David as I was working on this speech. It showed exactly 1,361 days remaining in my term. I want these to be the best days in America's history, because I love America. I deeply believe that America is the hope of the world. And I know that in the quality and wisdom of the leadership America gives lies the only hope for millions of people all over the world, that they can live their lives in peace and freedom. We must be worthy of that hope, in every sense of the word. Tonight, I ask for your prayers to help me in everything that I do throughout the days of my Presidency to be worthy of their hopes and of yours.

God bless America and God bless each and every one of you.

Source: Weekly Compilation of Presidential Documents, Richard Nixon, 1973, vol. 9, no. 18, 433–38.

Excerpt from Testimony of John Dean, June 25–29, 1973

In early June 1973, the* Washington Post *reported that White House counsel John Dean told Watergate investigators that he had discussed the cover-up with the president on many occasions. When he appeared before the Senate Select Committee on Presidential Campaign Activities for five days in late June 1973, Dean, in a dazzling display of recall, placed the president and several of his advisers in the middle of various Watergate-related activities. His opening statement detailed a program of political espionage activities unprecedented in its range and audacity.

EXCERPT FROM TESTIMONY OF JOHN DEAN JUNE 25–29, 1973

Mr. Dash. Mr. Dean, you have a statement you wish to present to the committee.

Mr. Dean. That is correct, Mr. Dash. But before I commence reading the rather lengthy statement I would just like to make a couple of comments. First of all, Mr. Chairman, and Mr. Vice Chairman and members of the committee, I sincerely wish I could say it is my pleasure to be here today but I think you can understand why it is not.

Mr. Dash. Mr. Dean, could you please take the microphone and put it closer so we can all hear.

Mr. Dean. Certainly. It is a very difficult thing for me to testify about other people. It is far more easy for me to explain my own involvement in this matter, the fact that I was involved in obstructing justice, the fact that I assisted another in perjured testimony, the fact that I made personal use of funds that were in my custody, it is far easier to talk about these things myself than to talk about what others did. Some of these people I will be referring to are friends, some are men I greatly admire and respect, and particularly with reference to the President of the United States, I would like to say this. It is my honest belief that while the President was involved that he did not realize or appreciate at any time the implications of his involvement, and I think that when the facts come out I hope the President is forgiven.

To one who was in the White House and became somewhat familiar with its interworkings, the Watergate matter was an inevitable outgrowth of a climate of excessive concern over the political impact of demonstrators, excessive concern over leaks, an insatiable appetite for political intelligence, all coupled with a do-it-yourself White House staff, regardless of the law. However, the fact that many of the elements of this climate culminated with the creation of a covert intelligence operation as a part of the President's reelection committee was not by conscious designs, rather an accident of fate.

These, of course, are my conclusions, but I believe they are well founded in fact. . . .

On September 15 the Justice Department announced the handing down of the seven indictments by the Federal grand jury investigating the Watergate. Late that afternoon I received a call requesting me to come to the President's Oval Office. When I arrived at the Oval Office I found Haldeman and the President. The President asked me to sit down. Both men appeared to be in very good spirits and my reception was very warm and cordial. The President then told me that Bob—referring to Haldeman—had kept him posted on my handling of the Watergate case. The President told me I had done a good job and he appreciated how difficult a task it had been and the President was pleased that the case had stopped with Liddy. I responded that I could not take credit because others had done much more difficult things than I had done. As the President discussed the present status of the situation I told him that all that I had been able to do was to contain the case and assist in keeping it out of the White House. I also told him that there was a long way to go before this matter would end and that I certainly could make no assurances that the day would not come when this matter would start to unravel.

Early in our conversation the President said to me that former FBI Director Hoover had told him shortly after he had assumed office in 1969 that his campaign had been bugged in 1968. The President said that at some point we should get the facts out on this and use this to counter the problems that we were encountering.

The President asked me when the criminal case would come to trial and would it start before the election. I told the President that I did not know. I said that the Justice Department had held off as long as possible the return of the indictments, but much would depend on which judge got the case. The President said that he certainly hoped that the case would not come to trial before the election.

The President then asked me about the civil cases that had been filed by the Democratic National Committee and the common cause case and about the counter suits that we had filed. I told him that the lawyers at the reelection committee were handling these cases and that they did not see the common cause suit as any real problem before the election because they thought they could keep it tied up in discovery proceedings. I then told the President that the lawyers at the reelection committee were very hopeful of slowing down the civil suit filed by the Democratic National Committee because they had been making ex parte contacts with the judge handling the case and the judge was very understanding and trying to accommodate their problems. The President was pleased to hear this and responded to the effect that, "Well, that's helpful." I also recall explaining to the President about the suits that the reelection committee lawyers had filed against the Democrats as part of their counteroffensive.

There was a brief discussion about the potential hearings before the Patman committee. The President asked me what we were doing to deal with the hearings and I reported that Dick Cook, who had once worked on Patman's committee staff, was working on the problem. The President indicated that Bill Timmons should stay on top of the hearings, that we did not need the hearings before the election.

The conversation then moved to the press coverage of the Watergate incident and how the press was really trying to make this into a major campaign issue. At one point in this conversation I recall the President telling me to keep a good list of the press people giving us trouble, because we will make life difficult for them after the election. The conversation then turned to the use of the Internal Revenue Service to attack our enemies. I recall telling the President that we had not made much use of this because the White House did not have the clout to have it done, that the Internal Revenue Service was a rather democratically oriented bureaucracy and it would be very dangerous to try any such activities. The President seemed somewhat annoyed and said that the Democratic administrations had used this tool well and after the election we would get people in these agencies who would be responsive to the White House requirements.

The conversation then turned to the President's post-election plans to replace people who were not on our team in all the agencies. It was at this point that Haldeman, I remember, started taking notes and he also told the President that he had been developing information on which people should stay and which should go after the election. I recall that several days after my meeting with the President, I was talking to Dan Kingsley, who was in charge of developing the list for Haldeman as to people who should be removed after the election. I told Kingsley that this matter had come up during my conversation with the President and he said he had wondered what had put new life into his project as he had received several calls from Higby about the status of his project within the last few days. The meeting ended with a conversation with the President about a book I was reading.

I left the meeting with the impression that the President was well aware of what had been going on regarding the success of keeping the White House out of the Watergate scandal and I also had expressed to him my concern that I was not confident that the cover up could be maintained indefinitely. . . .

Turning now to the handling of demands for White House money, I have previously discussed Mr. Kalmbach's raising the money for the first pressures for support money for silence. These pressures were continuous and following the election there were increasing pressures from Hunt for money for himself and the other indicted defendants as a means of assuring their silence. While this pressure had begun well before the election, it steadily grew after the election until the demands were being made directly to the White House for financial assistance. Before getting into the details of these pressures and how they were handled, I believe it might be helpful to explain the situation at the White House regarding the handling and availability of cash.

In early 1971, I was asked by Haldeman to assist in establishing the reelection committee in that they had no lawyer of their own. My activities resulted in my learning that there were large sums of cash that had been left over from the 1968 Nixon primaries and some funds had been left from the 1970 congressional fundraising efforts. These moneys, which were referred to as surplus moneys, were held by Kalmbach and controlled by Haldeman and Ehrlichman. I have submitted to the committee a memorandum prepared by Strachan of a meeting that was attended by Haldeman, Strachan, and myself on May 18, 1971, which reflects the tight controls Haldeman exercised over the surplus moneys held by Kalmbach. . . .

In this instance, I am referring to an expenditure of $813.

It was sometime prior to April 7, 1972, that I learned that cash was being sent to the White House. I was not told the amount, but I was asked by Strachan if I could suggest someone outside of the Government who might be willing to hold a large amount of cash in a safety deposit box. I told him I would have to think about it but later told him I couldn't think of anyone.

It was in late June or early July 1972, that I learned that $350,000 of the surplus money had been delivered to the White House prior to April 7, 1972. I was informed that the money came from the 1968 primaries and that the delivery was made before April 7 to insure that it not become a part of the 1972 campaign funds.

The $350,000 fund, as I have indicated, was held by Strachan but I do not know where he held it. It was shortly before Mr. Sloan was being called to testify in July that discussions commenced on how to make the $350,000 fund whole and get it out of the White House. There was no easy answer, because there was no place to send it out without reporting requirements. The concern was that Mr. Sloan would testify that he was aware of the disbursal of the $350,000 to the White House. This, in turn, would have created two problems: The White House would have been accused of having a secret slush fund if this became public, and second, a $6,800 expenditure out of a $22,000 authorization which had been made presented a potential campaign act violation for Haldeman, Colson, and Howard. I had numerous discussions about how to handle this problem with Mr. Stans and Mr. Parkinson but there was no easy answer.

I also discussed this matter with Mr. Haldeman, telling him that there was no easy answer. Finally, after the election, Stans indicated he had cash available and it was decided that Stans should provide $22,000 to Strachan to make the funds whole and then they could be removed from the White House and, if necessary, reported. This plan was approved by Haldeman, and Stans was so informed. On the morning of November 28, Stans called to request that Strachan come to his office to receive money that he had available. I do not know the source of the money or whether it was campaign money or any of the details about the $22,000 that Stans had made available. I could not locate Strachan, and Stans indicated that it should be picked up immediately but I cannot recall at this time the reason he called for the immediacy. Accordingly, I asked Mr. Fielding to pick up a package from Stans and give it to Strachan as soon as he could.

I informed Stans that Fielding would be over to pick up the package but he would not know what he was picking up and when I later learned that Stans had informed Fielding I was somewhat annoyed because I felt it was unfair to Fielding. The money was then given by Fielding to Strachan but no final decision had been made regarding how to dispose of the $350,000.

Having explained the status of the cash at the White House, I must now return to the pressure that was being placed on the White House for the use of these funds which I have just described for payments to the seven indicted individuals. This pressure began long before election day in that Paul O'Brien was receiving messages from William Bittman, Hunt's lawyer, that Hunt and others expected to have more support money and attorney's fees in exchange for continued silence. The initial payments by Kalmbach had not been sufficient. O'Brien reported this frequently to Mitchell, Mardian, LaRue, and myself. I, in turn, was reporting to Haldeman and Ehrlichman.

There were discussions in late July, August, and September of using these funds at the White House for these payments. I informed Haldeman of these discussions, but they were still in the discussion stage and no action was taken.

After the election, the pressure was greatly increased when Colson received a call from Mr. Hunt, which Colson recorded. Colson brought the recorded call to me and I, in turn, transcribed it onto a cassette tape. I have been informed by the committee counsel that the committee has in its possession a transcript of the conversation between Colson and Hunt in which Hunt makes demands for money. On November 15, I arranged a meeting with Haldeman and Ehrlichman so that they could hear the tape of the conversation Colson had had with Hunt and also to inform them of the increased and now threatening demands that were being transmitted through Hunt's lawyer to Mr. O'Brien and in turn on to the White House.

Haldeman and Ehrlichman were at Camp David at that time developing the plans for the reorganization of the executive branch for the second term of the Nixon administration. I departed on the morning of November 15 for Camp David with Mr. Walter Minnick, who was going to Camp David to discuss the reorganization plans with Ehrlichman. Mr. Minnick had been doing virtually all of the legal work at that time for Ehrlichman on the reorganization plan and was a member of Ehrlichman's staff. In fact, I was somewhat surprised that the counsel's office had not been more involved, or involved at all, prior to that time in the reorganization plans. After arriving at Camp David, Ehrlichman, Haldeman, and I went into the President's office in Laurel Lodge, which was empty. I have referred earlier to the fact that in this meeting the matter of Dwight Chapin's remaining at the White House was discussed.

It was after that discussion that I told them of the telephone conversation between Hunt and Colson and played the tape for them and also told them of the increasing demands being made for money. I told them I was going to New York that afternoon because Mitchell had requested that I come visit him regarding the demands being made and told them I would also play the tape for him. My instructions from this meeting were to tell Mitchell to take care of all these problems.

When we came out of this private meeting, Ehrlichman told Mr. Minnick, who had been waiting to meet with him, that we had been talking about reorganization matters. This position was taken because Minnick was at Camp David for that purpose and it would seem to be a very logical thing that I might be discussing with Haldeman and Ehrlichman. In fact, in our private meeting there was no discussion of the reorganization at all.

After a brief discussion about reorganization matters, I departed Camp David and returned to Washington and then flew to New York with Mrs. Stans. Stans had told me some days earlier that he was going to meet with Mr. Mitchell to discuss a number of matters about winding down the reelection committee and asked me to join him. . . .

Stans had arranged for the meeting with Mitchell to take place at the Metropolitan Club in New York City, because Stans was anxious to return to Washington as soon as the meeting was over and did not want to go down to Wall Street and get tied up in traffic. After the first part of the meeting where Stans and Mitchell discussed their problems, Stans departed and I played the tape for Mitchell. I recall that he had only one reaction to the tape and it was to the effect that it was certainly a self-serving tape for Colson and he wondered what the hell Hunt was talking about with regard to Mitchell's having perjured himself. I informed Mitchell that Ehrlichman and Haldeman had heard the tape and requested that he do what he could to solve the problem. I received no instruction or really any indication at all at that time from Mitchell regarding the matters that Hunt had raised in his conversation with Colson.

To the best of my recollection, it was the first week of December that Mitchell called me and said that we would have to use some of the $350,000 fund to take care of the demands that were being made by Hunt and the others for money. He indicated that the money that was taken out would be returned in order that the fund could be made whole again. He asked me to get Haldeman's approval.

Prior to Mitchell's call, I had been informed by Colson's secretary that Mrs. Hunt had called her at home on a number of occasions to discuss this problem with her in order that she might pass it on to Colson and get something done about the problem. Colson had sent his secretary, Miss Joan Hall, to me with these messages indicating that he did not want to talk to her about it but that she should pass the message on to me. I told Miss Hall not to talk to Mrs. Hunt and, if necessary, get an unlisted phone number.

After the phone call from Mitchell, I called Haldeman and described the situation in full to him and that I had told Mitchell that I was very reluctant to see White House money used but that he indicated that it would be returned as soon as they could raise some additional money. I told Haldeman that I did not think this was a good idea to further involve the White House in raising money for these men but I frankly had no answer. Haldeman said he did not like it either, but since we had the assurance that the money would be returned, I should inform Strachan that he could make the delivery of the money to the committee. Following my conversation with Haldeman I called Strachan and told him he should speak with LaRue and make a delivery to LaRue pursuant to LaRue's instruction. I also informed Strachan that he should anticipate the fact that we would get this money back in the near future. I do not recall how much money was delivered by Strachan but I believe it was either $40,000 or $70,000.

This delivery did not satisfy the demands and they continued to be relayed by Mr. Bittman to Mr. O'Brien, who, in turn, would relay them to Mr. Mitchell, Mr. LaRue, and myself. I, in turn, would tell Haldeman and Ehrlichman of the demands. I can recall LaRue and O'Brien coming to my office to discuss these demands and I told them that there could be no further use of the White House money and, in fact, to the contrary, Haldeman was expecting that that money which had been provided earlier was to be returned in full.

To the best of my recollection, it was some time shortly before the trial when the demands reached the crescendo point once again. O'Brien and LaRue came to my office and told me of the seriousness of the problem. Subsequently, Mitchell called me and told me that once again I should ask Haldeman to make available the necessary funds. I called Haldeman and told him of Mitchell's request and the situation and told him that I thought it was time to get the entire money out of the White House rather than continue as we were with, every few weeks, further bites being taken out of the apple. After we discussed the matter Haldeman said, send the entire damn bundle to them but make sure that we get a receipt for $350,000. After receiving my instructions from Haldeman I called Strachan and told him that he was to deliver the remainder of the money to LaRue but that he was to make certain that he got a receipt for $350,000. Strachan later told me that LaRue had refused to give him a receipt. . . .

Meeting of March 21

As I have indicated, my purpose in requesting this meeting particularly with the President was that I felt it necessary that I give him a full report of all the facts that I knew and explain to him what I believed to be the implication of those facts. It was my particular concern with the fact that the President did not seem to understand the implications of what was going on. For example, when I had earlier told him that I thought I was involved in an obstruction of justice situation he had argued with me to the contrary after I had explained it to him. Also, when the matter of money demands had come up previously he had very nonchalantly told me that that was no problem and I did not know if he realized that he himself could be getting involved in an obstruction of justice by having promised clemency to Hunt. What I had hoped to do in this conversation was to have the President tell me that we had to end the matter—now. Accordingly, I gave considerable thought to how I would present this situation to the President and try to make as dramatic a presentation as I could to tell him how serious I thought the situation was that the cover up continue.

I began by telling the President that there was a cancer growing on the Presidency and that if the cancer was not removed that the President himself would be killed by it. I also told him that it was important that this cancer be removed immediately because it was growing more deadly every day. I then gave him what I told him would be a broad overview of the situation and I would come back and fill in the details and answer any questions he might have about the matter.

I proceeded to tell him how the matter had commenced in late January and early February but that I did not know how the plans had finally been approved. I told him I had informed Haldeman what was occurring, and Haldeman told me I should have nothing to do with it. I told him that I had learned that there had been pressure from Colson on Magruder but I did not have all the facts as to the degree of pressure. I told him I did not know if Mitchell had approved the plans but I had been told that Mitchell had been a recipient of the wiretap information and that Haldeman had also received some information through Strachan.

I then proceeded to tell him some of the highlights that had occurred during the coverup. I told him that Kalmbach had been used to raise funds to pay these seven individuals for their silence at the instructions of Ehrlichman, Haldeman, and Mitchell and I had been the conveyor of this instruction to Kalmbach. I told him that after the decision had been made that Magruder was to remain at the reelection committee. I had assisted Magruder in preparing his false story for presentation to the grand jury. I told him that cash that had been at the White House had been funneled back to the reelection committee for the purpose of paying the seven individuals to remain silent.

I then proceeded to tell him that perjury had been committed, and for this cover up to continue it would require more perjury and more money. I told him that the demands of the convicted individuals were continually increasing and that with sentencing imminent, the demands had become specific.

I told him that on Monday the 19th, I had received a message from one of the reelection committee lawyers who had spoken directly with Hunt and that Hunt had sent a message to me demanding money. I then explained to him the message that Hunt had told Paul O'Brien the preceding Friday to be passed on to me. I told the President I'd asked O'Brien why to Dean, and O'Brien had asked Hunt the same question. But Hunt had merely said you just pass this message on to Dean. The message was that Hunt wanted $72,000 for living expenses and $50,000 for attorney's fees and if he did not get the money and get it quickly that he would have a lot of seamy things to say about what he had done for John Ehrlichman while he was at the White House. If he did not receive the money, he would have to reconsider his options.

I informed the President that I had passed this message on to both Haldeman and Ehrlichman. Ehrlichman asked me if I had discussed the matter with Mitchell. I had told Ehrlichman that I had not done so and Ehrlichman asked me to do so. I told the President I had called Mitchell pursuant to Ehrlichman's request but I had no idea of what was happening with regard to the request.

I then told the President that this was just typical of the type of blackmail that the White House would continue to be subjected to and that I didn't know how to deal with it. I also told the President that I thought that I would as a result of my name coming out during the Gray hearings be called before the grand jury and that if I was called to testify before the grand jury or the Senate committee I would have to tell the facts the way I know them. I said I did not know if executive privilege would be applicable to any appearance I might have before the grand jury. I concluded by saying that it is going to take continued perjury and continued support of these individuals to perpetuate the cover up and that I did not believe it was possible to continue it; rather I thought it was time for surgery on the cancer itself and that all those involved must stand up and account for themselves and that the President himself get out in front of this matter.

I told the President that I did not believe that all of the seven defendants would maintain their silence forever, in fact, I thought that one or more would very likely break rank.

After I finished, I realized that I had not really made the President understand because after he asked a few questions, he suggested that it would be an excellent idea if I gave some sort of briefing to the Cabinet and that he was very impressed with my knowledge of the circumstances but he did not seem particularly concerned with their implications.

It was after my presentation to the President and during our subsequent conversation the President called Haldeman into the office and the President suggested that we have a meeting with Mitchell, Haldeman, and Ehrlichman to discuss how to deal with this situation. What emerged from that discussion after Haldeman came into the office was that John Mitchell should account for himself for the pre-June 17 activities and the President did not seem concerned about the activities which had occurred after June 17.

After I departed the President's office I subsequently went to a meeting with Haldeman and Ehrlichman to discuss the matter further. The sum and substance of that discussion was that the way to handle this now was for Mitchell to step forward and if Mitchell were to step forward we might not be confronted with the activities of those involved in the White House in the cover up.

Accordingly, Haldeman, as I recall, called Mitchell and asked him to come down the next day for a meeting with the President on the Watergate matter.

In the late afternoon of March 21, Haldeman and Ehrlichman and I had a second meeting with the President. Before entering this meeting I had a brief discussion in the President's outer office of the Executive Office Building suite with Haldeman in which I told him that we had two options:

One is that this thing goes all the way and deals with both the preactivities and the postactivities, or the second alternative; if the cover up was to proceed we would have to draw the wagons in a circle around the White House and that the White House protect itself. I told Haldeman that it had been the White House's assistance to the reelection committee that had gotten us into much of this problem and now the only hope would be to protect ourselves from further involvement.

The meeting with the President that afternoon with Haldeman, Ehrlichman, and myself was a tremendous disappointment to me because it was quite clear that the cover up as far as the White House was concerned was going to continue. I recall that while Haldeman, Ehrlichman, and I were sitting at a small table in front of the President in his Executive Office Building office that I for the first time said in front of the President that I thought that Haldeman, Ehrlichman, and Dean were all indictable for obstruction of justice and that was the reason I disagreed with all that was being discussed at that point in time.

I could tell that both Haldeman, and particularly Ehrlichman, were very unhappy with my comments. I had let them very clearly know that I was not going to participate in the matter any further and that I thought it was time that everybody start thinking about telling the truth.

I again repeated to them I did not think it was possible to perpetuate the cover up and the important thing now was to get the President out in front. . . .

SENATOR GURNEY. Now, just in summary, Mr. Dean, I wonder if we can go over the salient points of the 5 days. Again as I understand it, to your own knowledge you have no knowledge that President Nixon was ever involved in the planning or the break-in at Watergate; is that correct?

MR. DEAN. I have no direct knowledge of that, that is correct.

SENATOR GURNEY. Then, in the year 1972 the only meeting you ever had with the President on Watergate was on September 15, is that correct?

MR. DEAN. Yes, and I believe we have been over that in detail.

SENATOR GURNEY. We have been over that in detail, and I don't think it would serve any purpose to go over it again.

In 1973 the two occasions that you did discuss Watergate with him prior to March 21, was that meeting on February 27, is that correct?

MR. DEAN. Well, as I, in answering Senator Baker's questions yesterday I don't know if you were present, Senator, we were going through all of the circumstantial situations leading up to the meetings that occurred in February and March, and the fact that there was a developing strategy that had occurred in California at the La Costa meetings and on the tail end of those and consistent with those I had a number of meetings with the President where subjects related to that particular California policy-setting meeting were being continually discussed.

SENATOR GURNEY. I understand that, but I mean the direct involvement of the possible criminal activities of Watergate, February 27 was the first meeting, was it not, when, as you testified, the question of obstruction of justice came up, isn't that correct?

MR. DEAN. That is correct.

SENATOR GURNEY. And you stated that you might be implicated in some way in that, and the President said no, he didn't think so. Isn't that the substance of that?

MR. DEAN. That is correct.

SENATOR GURNEY. Then, on March 13 you also—

MR. DEAN. That was, I believe, on the 28th that came up, Senator.

SENATOR GURNEY. Twenty-eighth, all right.

Then one other meeting on March 13 you had another conversation with him that involved this Executive clemency business, isn't that correct?

MR. DEAN. On March 13 we discussed both clemency and the fact that there was no money. The way the clemency discussion came up as you will recall is that at the end of another conversation I raised with him the fact that there were demands being made for money, for continued money there was no money around to pay it. He asked me how, you know, how much it was going to cost. I gave him my best estimate, which I said was $1 million or more. He, in turn, said to me, "Well, $1 million is certainly no problem to raise," and turned to Mr. Haldeman and made a similar comment and then he came back after, just a brief discussion on that, and I remember very clearly the way he pushed his chair away from his desk as he was looking back at Mr. Haldeman to get, you know, the same message through to Mr. Haldeman, you know, that $1 million is no problem.

Then he came back up, he rolled his chair back up toward the desk and said to me who is making the principal demands for this money at that point in time.

I said they were coming principally from Mr. Hunt through his attorney, and he turned to the discussion of the fact that he had talked with Mr. Ehrlichman and Mr. Colson about clemency for Mr. Hunt and he expressed annoyance at the fact that Mr. Colson had come to him contrary to an instruction that the President was aware of that Colson wasn't to raise this with him.

SENATOR GURNEY. So there were discussions—

MR. DEAN. Then we went on to discuss the delivery, you know, how this money was delivered and I told him that it was laundered and told him I was learning about things that I had never known about before, and I recall very vividly how Mr. Haldeman thought this was very funny and started laughing.

SENATOR GURNEY. So there were really two main discussions on Watergate, the money, the cover up money that you have just discussed and also the Executive clemency, and Mr. Haldeman was present during these discussions?

MR. DEAN. Well, Senator, not to take anything away from your interpretation but a lot of the discussion that occurred regarding the press conferences, the positions we were going to take on executive privilege, and the like, had direct implications on unraveling the Watergate.

SENATOR GURNEY. Well, I understand that. Indeed, I do, but I am talking about the criminal activities. Certainly press conferences, Executive clemency do not involve any criminal activity. I am just trying to pinpoint the criminal parts of it, and then, of course, there was the meeting on March 21.

MR. DEAN. I might add that in, as I told you in one point in time when I went to discuss this with counsel, who is an experienced prosecutor, he said that oftentimes intervening events show intention and purpose. That is why I have tried to report everything I know to the committee as fully as I know.

SENATOR GURNEY. I understand that, and I as a committee member am extremely glad you did, because I do think it sheds a lot of light and it will help the deliberations of the committee when other witnesses come before it. I am not in any way deprecating the importance of all of the events that surrounded these transactions in Watergate, but I am trying to pinpoint the criminal parts of it.

And that really is the sum and substance of your direct knowledge, direct conversations with the President on the criminal activity?

MR. DEAN. On the March 13 meeting.

SENATOR GURNEY. Well, I also said the March 21.

MR. DEAN. That is correct. We have gone over the March 21 meeting.

SENATOR GURNEY. Yes; we don't need to go over it again. I am just pinpointing that time and that date.

MR. DEAN. Then we jumped where the next in a series of meetings was in the April 15 period.

SENATOR GURNEY. Well, I realize that, but I am really not interested in that. I am not trying to cut you off here, but of course, the President himself later said that March 21 was the time when he first really realized the full implications. So I was just bringing us down to that date.

MR. DEAN. I would recall how that came up, that the President selected that date, was as the result of a discussion that had occurred on March 15—April 15, when he was searching his mind. I was being led through a series of rather leading questions by the President and at one point in the conversation, he said to me, do you recall what day it was that you gave me the report on some of the implications of the Watergate case? Then before I even got an answer out that I didn't remember the exact date in March, he said, I believe it was the 21st.

I said, I will have to check.

It was the next day that, when I was in his office again that afternoon, talking about a press statement that he was going to put out, he said, I have gotten the confirmation now and I believe it was the 21st. And he referred to it at that time as my cancer on the Presidency statement. That is the way I led that off and that is the way I had referred to it and that is the way he referred to it.

SENATOR GURNEY. Thank you, Mr. Dean.

Thank you, Mr. Chairman. I have no further questions.

SENATOR ERVIN. Senator Inouye, if you will yield for just a moment, Mr. Dash said he wanted to make a statement concerning his understanding of the rule of evidence.

MR. DASH. I think the question has come up from time to time and has been mentioned either by witnesses or by members of the committee as to admissibility of certain hearsay evidence. A memorandum of law has been submitted to all members of the committee. The leading case of the Supreme Court is *Krulewitch* v. *United States* and that case has been the position of the committee and the counsel working on the committee that even hearsay testimony, and most of the hearsay testimony admitted falls within this rule, is an exception to the hearsay rule.

The Supreme Court has ruled time and time again that where there is a conspiracy and there are overt acts—and I think at this stage of our hearings, there has been sufficient testimony which would go to a jury in a criminal case indicating that a conspiracy has occurred and that there have been overt acts—that therefore, the statements of a co-conspirator in the furtherance and in the course of the conspiracy, although hearsay, is an exception to the hearsay rule and is admitted in every court in this country.

Therefore, even Mr. McCord's testimony, which was initially hearsay, following up on the evidence of other witnesses which established the conspiracy and overt acts, that the Supreme Court has ruled in *Krulewitch* and other cases that that testimony is admissible and goes to a jury and is used against the defendants that may be charged as conspirators as any other testimony and is an exception to the hearsay rule.

Therefore, I think it should be made very clear and a memo has been given to every member of the committee that the hearsay evidence that has been admitted before this committee would be admissible in any court of law in this country under the *Krulewitch* decision, excepting conspiracy and co-conspirator's statements from the hearsay rule.

SENATOR GURNEY. What the chief counsel is saying, then, is that some people may be indicted on conspiracy, is that it, in addition to obstruction of justice and other things?

MR. DASH. Oh, quite certainly, Senator. The evidence before this committee, and I understand the evidence being considered by the prosecutors, includes the doctrine of conspiracy with two or more persons engaged in the commission of a crime that is a conspiracy. I understand that even Mr. LaRue, who just recently pleaded guilty, and this was made public knowledge, pleaded guilty to a conspiracy count rather than any other count, and that conspiracy is a major crime in this inquiry and in the inquiry made by a special prosecutor.

SENATOR GURNEY. Did you say Mr. LaRue pleaded guilty to conspiracy?

MR. DASH. Yes.

SENATOR GURNEY. I thought it was obstruction of justice?

MR. DASH. No; conspiracy to obstruct justice, Senator.

SENATOR BAKER. Mr. Chairman, could I say a word on this subject?

SENATOR ERVIN. Sure.

SENATOR BAKER. I do not mean to be facetious and I do not mean this to be critical of Mr. Dash, who is a fine lawyer, and Senator Gurney, who is a fine lawyer and a fine Senator, but this committee is too far gone to start worrying about hearsay and we are too deep into the business of finding the facts to try to second-guess what a court will admit or will not admit. I have spent a lifetime being surprised on what a court would admit or would not admit, depending on my point of view. I think it was Oliver Wendell Holmes who said lawyers spend their professional careers shoveling smoke and I have no desire to shovel smoke.

So I really recommend, Mr. Chairman, and once again, this is not a criticism of the committee or counsel, I recommend that we not think of ourselves as a court or a jury or a judge, and that we try to follow the facts, wherever they lead us, with the full foreknowledge that what we do will have little, if any, effect on how the rules of evidence are applied if there is in fact litigation, either civil or criminal, based on these same facts.

So I think that rules of this committee are important and the rule against hearsay and its exceptions—and the hearsay rule is virtually emasculated by the hundreds of exceptions to it—but I think the rules themselves are far less important than us getting along with the business at hand. So I very much hope that we do not fall into the business of extensive objections, the argument of objections, and the arguments about rules of law that may apply. If we get too far out of bounds, I think we ought to qualify the quality of the evidence so that we can take that into account. But I do not think, and I hope we do not start admitting and excluding evidence.

Thank you, Mr. Chairman.

SENATOR ERVIN. I would just like to make the observation that Felix Frankfurter wrote a very interesting article at the time about the Teapot Dome and he laid great stress on the wisdom of the fact that congressional committees should not be bound by technical rules of evidence. I do think, however, that it was well for Mr. Dash to make his statement, because I have read several articles by commentators who are not lawyers and who were criticizing the committee on the ground that it had received hearsay testimony. I am not concerned much about criticism, because I have been criticized very much over the years and I am sort of immune to it, but I think it is well for the general public to know that under the rules governing the admissibility of declarations of co-conspirators, the great bulk of the hearsay testimony that has been received in this case would have been admissible in a court of law for an indictment charging a conspiracy to obstruct justice.

I think the observations of my friend from Tennessee are correct, that we are not judges and we are not juries. We are members of a legislative body seeking to determine whether or not the facts before us indicate that new legislation may be necessary.

SENATOR BAKER. I might say, Mr. Chairman, that by explaining my point of view, I have fallen into the trap that the chairman just warned me against. He and I had a brief conversation a moment ago, and I am sure he will not think it a breach of confidence to repeat it. He said, "Howard," he said, "do not try to explain; your friends do not require it and your enemies will not believe it."

SENATOR ERVIN. I agree with you. I was not trying to explain, I was just trying to enlighten some of our commentators.

Source: U.S. Senate, Presidential Campaign Activities of 1972, Senate Resolution 60, Hearings Before the Select Committee on Presidential Campaign Activities of the United States Senate, 93rd Congress, 1st Session, Book 3, 914–15; 957–59; 967–71; 998–1000; 1521–25.

Excerpt from Testimony of Alexander P. Butterfield, July 16, 1973

The name of Alexander P. Butterfield on the witness list for the Senate Watergate committee did not stir excitement in the public mind. This was not John Mitchell or H. R. Haldeman or John Ehrlichman or John Dean, but an unknown former presidential appointments secretary in the Nixon White House. Nevertheless, it was the Butterfield testimony that profoundly changed the shape of the investigation and rattled an already shaken administration. Butterfield informed the Senate committee that the White House had a taping system and that since 1971 the president had recorded all conversations and telephone calls in his office. On those recordings, committee members immediately realized, were conversations that would likely reveal much of the truth about Watergate and its aftermath. Butterfield's revelations would set off a legal battle between the White House and the investigators about access to the tapes.

EXCERPT FROM TESTIMONY OF ALEXANDER P. BUTTERFIELD JULY 16, 1973

MR. BUTTERFIELD. My name is Alexander Porter Butterfield. I am the Administrator of the Federal Aviation Administration. My home address is 7416 Admiral Drive, Alexandria, Va.

SENATOR ERVIN. Thank you.

MR. DASH. Mr. Chairman, at a staff interview with Mr. Butterfield on Friday, some very significant information was elicited and was attended by the majority members of the staff and the minority members. The information was elicited by the minority staff member. Therefore, I would like to change the usual routine of the questioning and ask minority counsel to begin the questioning of Mr. Butterfield

MR. THOMPSON. Thank you, Mr. Dash. Mr. Butterfield, I understand you were previously an employee of the White House. Is that correct?

MR. BUTTERFIELD. That is correct.

MR. THOMPSON. Over what period of time were you employed by the White House?

MR. BUTTERFIELD. I would like to preface my remarks, if I may, Mr. Thompson, with one statement.

MR. THOMPSON. I am sorry, go right ahead.

MR. BUTTERFIELD. Although I do not have a statement as such, I would simply like to remind the committee membership that whereas I appear voluntarily this afternoon, I appear with only some 3 hours notice and without time to arrange for permanent counsel or for assistance by a temporary counsel.

That is all I have to say, Mr. Thompson.

MR. THOMPSON. During what period of time were you employed at the White House, Mr. Butterfield?

MR. BUTTERFIELD. I was at the White House as a deputy assistant to the President from the first day of the Nixon administration, January 21, 1969, until noon of March 14, 1973.

MR. THOMPSON. And what were your duties at the White House?

MR. BUTTERFIELD. My duties were many and varied, as a matter of fact, Mr. Thompson. I will try to state them briefly.

I was in charge of administration—that is to say that the staff secretary, who is the day-to-day administrator at the White House, reported directly to me. And, of course, I reported to Mr. Haldeman, as did everyone.

In addition to administration, I was responsible for the management and ultimate supervision of the Office of Presidential Papers and the Office of Special Files. Both of those offices pertained to the collection of documents which will eventually go to the Nixon library.

Third, I was in charge of security at the White House insofar as liaison with the Secret Service and the Executive Protective Service is concerned and insofar as FBI background investigations for prospective Presidential appointees is concerned.

A fourth duty was that I was the secretary to the Cabinet and had that duty not from January 21, 1969, but from November, I believe November 4, 1969, through until the day I departed, March 14 of this year.

I was additionally the liaison between the President and the Office of the President and all of the various support units. By that I mean the Office of the Military Assistant to the President and the Office of White House Visitors, again the Secret Service, the Executive Protective Service, the residence staff, Mrs. Nixon's staff—I served as sort of a conduit between all those elements and the Office of the President.

Finally, I was in charge of the smooth running of the President's official day, both in Washington, D.C., and at the western White House in San Clemente. I had nothing to do with the smooth running of his day in Florida or in Camp David, but I was responsible for the smooth implementation of the official events on his calendar in Washington and in the western White House.

That pretty well sums it up, sir.

MR. THOMPSON. You were employed on January 21, 1969, and continued to be employed until March 14 of this year, is that correct?

MR. BUTTERFIELD. That is correct.

MR. THOMPSON. Mr. Butterfield, are you aware of the installation of any listening devices in the Oval Office of the President?

MR. BUTTERFIELD. I was aware of listening devices; yes, sir.

MR. THOMPSON. When were those devices placed in the Oval Office?

MR. BUTTERFIELD. Approximately the summer of 1970. I cannot begin to recall the precise date. My guess, Mr. Thompson, is that the installation was made between—and this is a very rough guess—April or May of 1970 and perhaps the end of the summer or early fall 1970.

MR. THOMPSON. Are you aware of any devices that were installed in the Executive Office Building office of the President?

MR. BUTTERFIELD. Yes, sir, at that time.

MR. THOMPSON. Were they installed at the same time?

MR. BUTTERFIELD. They were installed at the same time.

MR. THOMPSON. Would you tell us a little bit about how those devices worked, how they were activated, for example?

MR. BUTTERFIELD. I don't have the technical knowledge, but I will tell you what I know about how those devices were triggered. They were installed, of course, for historical purposes, to record the President's business and they were installed in his two offices, the Oval Office and the EOB office. Within the west wing of the White House, there are several, at least three, perhaps four—the three that I know of—boxes called Presidential locator boxes. These are square boxes approximately 10 by 10 inches, and on them are several locations, about seven locations, which would tell where the President might be at any time, locations such as the residence—that is one of them; the south grounds is another; Oval Office is another; EOB office is still another; west wing, meaning west wing of the White House, is another; and out, I think, is the last one. When the President moves—east wing is still another and I think that covers all of the locations indicated on the box.

When the President moves from his Oval Office, for instance, to his Executive Office Building office and he departs the west wing and crosses the street, it is my understanding that the Secret Service agents, members of the Executive Protective Division who cover him—it is my understanding there are four, five, six of them—when he moves across the street, one of them covers the central location, which may be the switchboard under the east wing, or it may be the Secret Service Command Post, I don't know. If it is the Secret Service Command Post, it is in the Executive Office Building. It says the President is leaving the west wing and going to the EOB office. They would know this. And the little light moves from the Oval Office to EOB office. It doesn't actually move to the EOB office until the President actually enters the EOB office. As that light moves, there is a tie-in audio signal so that if one is preoccupied, as I might be, I realize that the locator box is indicating a change in the President's location and that kind of information was important to me. My office was located immediately adjacent to the President's Oval Office on the west side. My duties involved going in and out frequently and working directly with the President. Mr. Steve Bull, who at that time worked on the other side of the President, on the east side of the Oval Office, had one of these locator boxes, and Mr. Haldeman had a third. I believe there was a fourth in Mr. Chapin's office—in fact, I am sure there was a fourth in Mr. Chapin's office. We were probably the four who would be the most concerned, or at least most immediately concerned with the President's whereabouts and the fact that he was changing locations.

In that the Oval Office and the Executive Office Building office were indicated on this locator box, the installation was installed in such a way that when the light was on "Oval Office," the taping device was at least triggered. It was not operating, but it was triggered—it was spring-loaded, if you will, then it was voice-actuated. So when the light was on "Oval Office," in the Oval Office and in the Oval Office only, the taping device was spring-loaded to a voice-actuating situation. When the President went to the EOB office, the light was on. In the EOB office, there was the same arrangement. In those two offices, the arrangement was the same and the taping picked up all conversations or all noise in those two offices when the light was at those positions.

MR. THOMPSON. We discussed the Oval Office and the EOB office. What about the Cabinet room? Was there a taping device in the Cabinet room?

MR. BUTTERFIELD. Yes, sir, there was.

MR. THOMPSON. Was it activated in the same way?

MR. BUTTERFIELD. No, sir, it was not, and my guess is, and it is only my guess, is because there was no Cabinet room location per se on the locator box. There was only a west wing indication. When the light was on west wing that meant the President was in one of two places, the Cabinet room or the barbershop. When he went into the Cabinet room the light went to west wing. But he could have been someplace else in the west wing and so to insure the recording of business conversations in the Cabinet room a manual installation was made.

MR. THOMPSON. I do not want to hurry you, Mr. Butterfield, but I understand there is a vote in about 12 minutes so if we could go through it rather rapidly the first time, we might come back up and pick up some of the loose ends.

I understand the recording device in the Cabinet room was manually operated then, is that correct?

MR. BUTTERFIELD. That is correct.

MR. THOMPSON. There were buttons on the desk in the Cabinet room there that activated that device?

MR. BUTTERFIELD. There were two buttons.

MR. THOMPSON. Pardon me, was there also an activating device on your telephone?

MR. BUTTERFIELD. Yes, sir. There was an off-on button, one said "Haldeman" and one that said "Butterfield" that was on and off respectively, and one on my telephone.

MR. THOMPSON. How was the device usually activated, by the buttons or by your telephone activator?

MR. BUTTERFIELD. To my knowledge, the President never did pay any attention to the buttons at the Cabinet table. It was activated, the button on my telephone, by me.

MR. THOMPSON. So far as the Oval Office and the EOB office are concerned, would it be your testimony that the device would pick up any and all conversations no matter where the conversations took place in the room and no matter how soft the conversations might have been?

MR. BUTTERFIELD. With regard to the Oval and EOB offices?

MR. THOMPSON. Yes, sir.

MR. BUTTERFIELD. Yes, sir, it is my—

MR. THOMPSON. Was it a little more difficult to pick up in the Cabinet room?

MR. BUTTERFIELD. Yes, sir, it was a great deal more difficult to pick up in the Cabinet room.

MR. THOMPSON. All right. We have talked about the rooms, now if we could move on to telephones; are you aware of the installation of any devices on any of the telephones, first of all, the Oval Office?

MR. BUTTERFIELD. Yes, sir.

MR. THOMPSON. What about the Executive Office Building office of the President?

MR. BUTTERFIELD. Yes, sir. The President's business telephone at his desk in the Executive Office Building.

MR. THOMPSON. What about the Lincoln Room?

MR. BUTTERFIELD. Yes, sir, the telephone in the Lincoln sitting room in the residence.

MR. THOMPSON. What about Aspen cabin at Camp David?

MR. BUTTERFIELD. Only in, on the telephone at the President's desk in his study in the Aspen cabin, his personal cabin.

MR. THOMPSON. It is my understanding that this cabin was sometimes used by foreign dignitaries, was the device still present during those periods of time?

MR. BUTTERFIELD. No, sir, the device was removed prior to occupancy by chiefs of state, heads of government, and other foreign dignitaries.

MR. THOMPSON. All right. Would you state who installed these devices, all of these devices, so far as you know?

MR. BUTTERFIELD. I did not say, no, sir.

MR. THOMPSON. Well, who did?

MR. BUTTERFIELD. The Secret Service. The Technical Security Division of the Secret Service.

MR. THOMPSON. All right. You alluded to a reason for the installation of these devices. Would you state why, as far as your understanding is concerned, these devices were installed in these rooms?

MR. BUTTERFIELD. There was no doubt in my mind they were installed to record things for posterity, for the Nixon library. The President was very conscious of that kind of thing. We had quite an elaborate setup at the White House for the collection and preservation of documents, and of things which transpired in the way of business of state.

MR. THOMPSON. On whose authority were they installed, Mr. Butterfield?

MR. BUTTERFIELD. On the President's authority by way of Mr. Haldeman and Mr. Higby. . . .

MR. THOMPSON. . . Mr. Butterfield, as far as you know from your own personal knowledge, from 1970 until the present time all of the President's conversations in the offices mentioned and on the telephones mentioned, were recorded?

MR. BUTTERFIELD. That is correct, until I left. Someone could have taken the equipment out but until the day I left I am sure I would have been notified.

MR. THOMPSON. And as far as you know, those tapes are still available?

MR. BUTTERFIELD. As far as I know, but I have been away for 4 months, sir.

MR. THOMPSON. I have no further questions.

SENATOR ERVIN. Mr. Dash.

MR. DASH. Mr. Butterfield, just a few questions, because I think Mr. Thompson's questions have pretty much elicited most of the testimony. I think what you are saying was that at all times certainly in the White House itself, either in the Oval Office or in the Executive Office of the President where there was a locator light that whenever the President moved the locator light moved where the President was, it triggered the microphones and then whenever anybody started to speak in that office where the microphones were as the voice activated the device, the recording devices began to operate, is that not true?

MR. BUTTERFIELD. That is true, yes, sir.

MR. DASH. When someone finished speaking would it stop at that point or would there be some lag picked to pick up an answer?

MR. BUTTERFIELD. It was explained to me by those who installed the equipment that the equipment allowed for a lag so that no portion of a conversation would be omitted, so if I were talking to you and stopped talking just momentarily the tape would not stop, it would continue for a moment or two so that it would pick up your response if you should respond immediately.

Source: U.S. Senate, Presidential Campaign Activities of 1972, S. Res. 60, Hearings Before the Select Committee on Presidential Campaign Activities of the United States Senate, 93rd Congress, 1st Session, Book 5, 2073–79.

Excerpt from Testimony of John Ehrlichman, July 24–30, 1973

John Ehrlichman and his fellow UCLA alumnus, H. R. Haldeman, had been for many years among

Richard Nixon's most trusted advisers. For a time Ehrlichman was White House counsel, and he then assumed the office of chief domestic adviser. It was Ehrlichman who was most responsible for the creation of the so-called Plumbers, the group of ex-CIA agents and other veterans of clandestine work who were responsible for various undercover tasks, many of them illegal. It was a group of the Plumbers that police had caught at the Watergate complex. And now, in late July 1973, Ehrlichman, once a man who flaunted his power, sat before the Watergate committee shorn of his job, much of his dignity, and, soon, his freedom. In January 1975, he would be convicted of conspiracy, obstruction of justice, perjury, and other charges and would serve 18 months in a federal prison.

EXCERPT FROM TESTIMONY OF JOHN EHRLICHMAN JULY 24–30, 1973

SENATOR ERVIN. . . . Mr. Ehrlichman, do I understand that you are testifying that the Committee to Re-Elect the President and those associated with them constituted an eleemosynary institution that gave $450,000 to some burglars and their lawyers merely because they felt sorry for them?

[Applause and laughter.]

MR. EHRLICHMAN. I am afraid I am not your best witness on that, Mr. Chairman. I do not know what their motives were. I think those will appear in the course of the proceeding.

SENATOR ERVIN. You stated this was a defense fund just like that given to Angela Davis and to Daniel Ellsberg, did you not?

MR. EHRLICHMAN. I stated that was my understanding of it.

SENATOR ERVIN. Yes. Well, Daniel Ellsberg and the Angela Davis defense funds were raised in public meetings and the newspapers carried news items about it, did they not?

MR. EHRLICHMAN. I am not sure that we know who the donors to those funds were. I dare say there are many people in this country who contributed to those funds who would not want it known.

SENATOR ERVIN. Yes. But do you not think most of the people contributed their funds because they believed in the causes they stood for?

MR. EHRLICHMAN. I assume that.

SENATOR ERVIN. Well, certainly, the Committee To Re-Elect the President and the White House aides, like yourself, did not believe in the cause of burglars or wiretappers, did you?

MR. EHRLICHMAN. No.

SENATOR ERVIN. Can you—

MR. EHRLICHMAN. I didn't contribute a nickel, Mr. Chairman.

SENATOR ERVIN. Yes. [Laughter.]
You authorized somebody else to contribute?

MR. EHRLICHMAN. No, I would like to set that straight, if I might, Mr. Chairman.

The only reason that anybody ever came to me about Mr. Kalmbach raising money was because of this arrangement that we had entered into that we would protect Mr. Kalmbach if he wished to be protected from requests to raise money. Now that is—it was a situation where obviously he didn't wish to be protected. He made the judgment, he made it independent of me, and whether I conceded to it or not obviously didn't make any difference.

SENATOR ERVIN. Did he ever talk to you about that?

MR. EHRLICHMAN. Not until after the fact.

SENATOR ERVIN. I will ask you if he didn't come to you and not only talk about having known you a long time and you having known his family, but didn't he ask you whether it was a proper or legal operation?

MR. EHRLICHMAN. Mr. Chairman, the testimony is that that meeting, according to Mr. Kalmbach, was the 26th of July when he was long into this, and as I have already testified.

SENATOR ERVIN. He testified he had become dubious about the propriety of it and he went to you for reassurance?

MR. EHRLICHMAN. Well, as I—

SENATOR ERVIN. And he also testified when he got to you that you told him it was all right and to see that the money was delivered in secret because if he didn't deliver it in secret their heads would be in their laps. Didn't that occur?

MR. EHRLICHMAN. No. As a matter of fact, Mr. Chairman . . . I would be terribly slow to reassure Herb Kalmbach, whom I consider a good and close friend, of the propriety of any such undertaking, of any such undertaking without checking it first, if he had asked me, and I am testifying to you, Mr. Chairman, that he did not ask me.

SENATOR ERVIN. Well, you recall his testimony was to the effect that I have given you?

MR. EHRLICHMAN. You mean about the head in the lap business?

SENATOR ERVIN. Yes; that the heads would roll.

MR. EHRLICHMAN. I suspect that what was said there was that certainly Mr. Kalmbach's involvement—

SENATOR ERVIN. I am not asking about that. My question is, didn't he have a conversation in which you told him to do it in secret because otherwise "If it gets out, our heads will be in their laps"?

MR. EHRLICHMAN. I am trying to answer you, Mr. Chairman.

SENATOR ERVIN. Well, you can answer that yes or no. I have just 20 minutes at this time, and I want to ask my questions. [Laughter.]

I will put this question to you: Don't you consider that Herbert Kalmbach—

MR. EHRLICHMAN. I am perfectly willing to answer that, Mr. Chairman.

MR. WILSON. Let him answer that question, Mr. Chairman, please.

SENATOR ERVIN. He goes off and answers something I don't ask him.

MR. WILSON. Yes, but a "Yes" and "No" usually calls for explanation.

SENATOR ERVIN. Well, what is the answer, yes or no, that he had this conversation with Mr. Kalmbach?

MR. EHRLICHMAN. I had a conversation with Mr. Kalmbach, Mr. Chairman, and I have no doubt that we, if he says so, that we discussed the question of secrecy because I do recall his saying that Mr. Ulasewicz was carrying money back and forth.

Now, I had in my mind at that time the realization that this, what I considered to be a legitimate undertaking, could be terribly misconstrued if someone were to impute the efforts of the President's lawyer to this defense fund for Watergate burglars. I mean there is room for misunderstanding; I think you have stated the misunderstanding very eloquently in your opening question.

SENATOR ERVIN. So that was the reason that you made arrangements by which a gentleman in California, who resided in California, would deliver the money in cash and sometimes in laundry bags to an ex-policeman in New York, and allow the ex-policeman to come down and deliver the money under orders that he wasn't going to permit the people he delivered it to, to see him.

MR. EHRLICHMAN. Well, Mr. Chairman, as you know, I had nothing to do with those details at all. As a matter of fact, I was quite surprised to learn in the testimony here that there was what amounted to a laundering process where committee money or money held by people in the committee were passed through several hands and around to Mr. Kalmbach for eventual delivery, and this, of course, all predated any conversation that Mr. Kalmbach and I had.

SENATOR ERVIN. Well, I have always thought that if a political institution or committee enacted the role of an eleemosynary institution, it would, like the Pharisee, brag about it on all opportunities, and so you agreed with me that a Doubting Thomas might think that this money was routed in this clandestine way, not only to keep it secret but also to keep these people that were receiving the money secret? . . .

SENATOR ERVIN. Mr. Ehrlichman, you are a lawyer and you know that a psychiatrist is forbidden to divulge the information about his patient, don't you, without his patient's consent?

MR. EHRLICHMAN. Well, I think we are going to split hairs, it would be in circumstances—

SENATOR ERVIN. That is not splitting hairs. That is a Hippocratic oath which started back in ancient Greece and has been going ever since.

MR. EHRLICHMAN. I am not sure psychiatrists in every case are M.D.'s, but let's assume that for the sake of argument.

The fact is that as I have stated earlier, my assumption is that it is possible to get specific medical, and other kinds of confidential information, through a trained investigator if he knows what he is looking for without a violation of law.

SENATOR ERVIN. Mr. Ehrlichman, you are a lawyer and you know that a psychiatrist is forbidden by law to divulge the confidential information he gets from his patient, on examination of the patient, to make a diagnosis, without his client's consent. Now, don't you know that?

MR. EHRLICHMAN. I didn't know that was a matter of law. I know there is a privilege that exists as a matter of law, but I don't know that it's a criminal violation. It may well be. I just didn't know.

SENATOR ERVIN. Don't you know there's a statute to that effect in every State in this Union and the only statutes that make an exception to that is a judge in a court can require the physician or the psychiatrist to testify about his patient if he finds it's in the interests of justice?

MR. EHRLICHMAN. No, I didn't know that, Mr. Chairman.

SENATOR ERVIN. And yet you were adviser to the President of the United States?

MR. EHRLICHMAN. Well, I dare say there are a lot of things that I don't know, Mr. Chairman.

SENATOR ERVIN. Well, if you had known the law, I would submit that in all probability, you would also have known that the only way you could get the opinion of the psychiatrist, Ellsberg's psychiatrist, was by some surreptitious manner in some surreptitious fashion.

MR. EHRLICHMAN. I don't know what you mean by surreptitious, Mr. Chairman. I do know this from experience, that information of this kind is obtainable. Insurance adjusters obtain it, investigators obtain it, attorneys obtain it, and they obtain it through nurses, through nurses' aides, through all kinds of sources. And we would be kidding ourselves if we didn't admit that.

SENATOR ERVIN. You don't know what the word "surreptitious" means?

MR. EHRLICHMAN. Well, I don't know what you meant by it in that question, Mr. Chairman.

SENATOR ERVIN. Well, can't you answer? Don't you know, really?

MR. EHRLICHMAN. I did know the word. You were using it in a pejorative sense, Mr. Chairman, and I was not sure just how.

SENATOR ERVIN. Some people do things in illegal fashion, obtain information in illegal fashion. But I would assert as a lawyer that when you go to getting the record of a patient, of a doctor's recorded opinion of his patient, that you cannot get it legally without consent of the patient or without an order of a judge. The only other way you can get it is in an illegal or unethical way. . . .

MR. WILSON. . . . Now, my position is that if there is this reservoir of power, and your own committee, sir, in reporting out the Safe Streets Act bill in 1968 was willing to give an indication that there existed a reservoir of power for the purpose of, what I say, and this is my language, for the purpose of permitting the President to otherwise—to do what would otherwise be a crime, to protect the Nation against foreign intelligence and for the purpose of obtaining foreign intelligence.

Now, I know I am open to the attack, well, can he shoot somebody on the street, I am not going that far, and that is driving myself to a conclusion ad absurdum. As you know, as you all know, wiretapping is a form of invasion of the premises of the person who is overheard, and in the *Katz* and *Berger* cases, with which I am sure all of you are familiar, the Supreme Court has said now in this sophisticated age wiretapping is another kind of invasion of the privacy and premises of the man whose conversation is being bugged, so to speak.

So that we have squarely—we are not driving this problem any further today than saying that it is not a silly proposition. Mr. Chairman, you didn't call it silly, you maybe feel it was but you didn't say it—it is not a silly proposition for us to contend that an entry into the psychiatrist's office under grounds which would technically state burglary, because there is no Federal crime in that respect, is no different from an entry through his telephone system, and if your committee—and by your committee, I am not speaking of this august body, I am speaking of another august body, that is the Judiciary Committee, and I don't find that you, sir, or anyone else dissented from the philosophy of the report of the Senate which went out on the floor in support of that bill, that there is very likely a reservoir of constitutional power unlike the [1952] steel case, in the President in the matter of national security. That is the reason, sir, that I was so bold yesterday, and I want to apologize for what might have been a rude interruption, when I asked you to read the latter part of the first sentence or to protect national security information against foreign intelligence activities.

This is the kind of thing which I pick out of the symbol of 2511, lay it on top of the *Plamdon* case, and say that today there is no one living, indeed there is no one in this room, who can assert with categorical certainty that the President of the United States does not have the constitutional power to cause the entry under what would be otherwise illegal circumstances in pursuit of foreign intelligence, and I say again without fear of contradiction, that we are entitled to consider when we get to that point, that the fourth amendment may have vanished from the scene.

I think I must be running close to my 20 minutes, and I am like you are, Mr. Chairman, I don't want to trespass upon it. I do have some very excellent phrases from Justice Powell's decision. Let me just conclude by quoting one from a section in the opinion which has Roman numeral IV:

> We emphasize before concluding this opinion the scope of our decision as stated. At the outset this case involves only the domestic aspects of national security. We have not addressed and express no opinion as to the issues which may be involved with respect to activities of foreign powers or their agents.

There is a footnote that is interesting: "For the view that warrantless surveillance, though impermissible in domestic security cases, may be Constitutional where foreign powers are concerned." See *United States* v. *Smith* in a Fed. Sup. case decided in 1971, and a treatise, I am adding the word "treatise," by the American Bar Association Criminal Justice Project Standard relating to electronic surveillance in February 1971. See also *United States* v. *Clay* in 430 F. 2d 165.

Thank you, Mr. Chairman.

SENATOR ERVIN. Well, Mr. Wilson, I have enjoyed your argument. I have long known you to be one of the Nation's truly great lawyers, and I would like to say, I am sort of a country lawyer myself and sometimes I get sort of emphatic in the statement of my views, because I have never been able to straddle fences very well.

I agree with your interpretation of the case of *United States v. U.S. District Court.* In this case, the Government was taking a position which was long maintained by former Attorney General Mitchell, that the President had inherent power to exercise surveillance without a warrant from any court in respect to protecting against domestic subversion. And, of course, in the case you referred to, the Government took the position that section 2511.3 argued that except in national security surveillance, this warrant requirement, the Congress recognizes the President's authority to conduct such surveillances without prior judicial approval. Justice Powell said section 2511.3 can find no power as the language is wholly inappropriate for such a purpose. It merely provides that the act shall not be interpreted to limit or disturb such powers as the President may have under the Constitution.

Then his ultimate decision was and we therefore find the conclusion unacceptable that Congress intended to make clear that the act simply did not legislate with respect to domestic security surveillances.

I served on the Judiciary Committee when section 2511 of title 18 was drawn, and of course, if we had not put this in there, the same thing would have resulted, because Congress could not take away any constitutional powers of the President. So they put that in there because there was a controversy between some members of the committee having an opinion that the President almost has powers that would make an eastern potentate turn green with envy, and some people, like myself, on the committee felt that the Constitution limits and defines the powers of the President.

Some people believe in a doctrine of inherent powers. I do not believe the President has any power at all except such as the Constitution expressly gives him or such as are necessarily inferred from the expression of those powers. I think the Constitution was written that way to keep the President and, of course, the Congress, from exercising tyrannical power.

While I do not agree that this case has any application whatever to the situation—I agree with you that it has no application whatever to the situation. They discuss it. But where you and I part company is on the facts.

I think we have a rather anomalous situation here. Here was the Government—they were not prosecuting Ellsberg through the agents of the Department of Justice for giving papers to Russia. They were just merely charging him with stealing some papers that belonged to the Government, as I recall. And here were some employees of the White House that go out and for some strange reason, I guess they did not trust the Justice Department to do the prosecuting all by itself. So they decided they ought to go and try to steal some documents from the doctor of a man who was being prosecuted for stealing from the Government, which is quite a peculiar situation, really.

Now, I cannot see the slightest relationship between Dr. Fielding's, I believe his name was, notions of the mental state of Daniel Ellsberg and foreign intelligence activities. The only activity I think the doctor was engaged in was trying to determine what the mental state of his patient was. He was not engaged in any foreign intelligence activities and I think—this is my interpretation of the Constitution—I think that the emissaries that were sent out there for the plumbers to try to steal the doctor's notes were domestic subversion and not in defense of this country against foreign intelligence activities. . . .

SENATOR TALMADGE. Now, in matters involving national security, could the President authorize a forgery?

MR. EHRLICHMAN. Well, again, you are getting me into an area that obviously is a subject for the experts, and as Mr. Wilson pointed out this morning, the question of degree here can be carried to unreasonable lengths, and I am not prepared to answer where that line is. It is obviously a judicial question.

SENATOR TALMADGE. You do not think he could authorize murder, do you?

MR. EHRLICHMAN. I do not—as I say, I do not think I am the one to try to respond to that kind of question as to where the line is.

SENATOR TALMADGE. Well, you authorized the break-in, did you not? I was—I was trying to—

MR. EHRLICHMAN. No, sir, I did not.

SENATOR TALMADGE. You affirmed it yesterday in a memorandum that I saw; you said it was your signature provided it could not be traced.

MR. EHRLICHMAN. No, sir, I submit that that is not what that memorandum says.

SENATOR TALMADGE. Where is the document?

MR. EHRLICHMAN. What that memorandum says is that the investigation which had previously been authorized by me should also include an attempt to ascertain the contents of these files. There is nothing in there about the means to be pursued, and my testimony was, and continues to be, that my assumption was that that could be done by completely conventional investigatory means.

SENATOR TALMADGE. I will read the language "covert operation to be undertaken to examine all of the medical files still held by Ellsberg's psychiatrist."

How do you think you could examine all the medical files without a break-in?

MR. EHRLICHMAN. Well, it has occurred to me since, because I have been asked this question before, that one way that it could be done is through false pretenses, or through perfectly honest [laughter] means, one doctor to another, by recruiting the assistance of another psychiatrist or of a doctor or of a—someone who could get at them that way.

SENATOR TALMADGE. I do not think there is—

MR. EHRLICHMAN. I am not a trained investigator, Senator, and what I know from my own experience is that people who are investigators, as I mentioned yesterday, insurance adjusters, people of that kind have over the years brought to attorneys information of this kind which they have been given the assignment of gaining. It simply was not in contemplation that a break-in as such, would be engaged in. . . .

. . . The Justice Department had an investigation for prosecution purposes which was ongoing under Mr. Mardian. This was not intended to satisfy that need. This was intended to satisfy the President of the United States, who was saying how could a thing like this happen? What have we done to prevent it happening again? Is this Rand Corp., and all these other defense think tanks that are at fault in this or is our own Defense Department or is it the State Department or just where is the weakness in this?

SENATOR WEICKER. Mr. Ehrlichman, are you telling me that the break-in in Dr. Fielding's office was to satisfy the President of the United States?

MR. EHRLICHMAN. Well, now, you have [laughter] misunderstood me, Senator.

The President wanted very much to make sure that a thing like this could not happen again. How one learned whether Ellsberg acted alone, as a disgruntled employee of a think tank, whether he acted as a member of an international spy ring delivering secrets to a foreign embassy or just what his role was, where he fit, had to be determined in the opinion of the investigators by every available means.

Now, obviously, as we discussed yesterday, this business of the psychiatric profile—incidentally, Senator, I would like to refer to something that came in last night. As you all probably are very familiar on the committee, when you are a witness here you get all sorts of suggestions by telegram and telephone and so on, and someone overnight very kindly called in to suggest that the committee staff check the Warren Commission report and the Kerner Commission report for their references to the use of psychiatric profiles in domestic criminal acts, and that was something I did not know about but apparently, they felt that the use of the psychiatric profile is a very valid investigatory device and, of course, the CIA feels that, too. They have this section on it. Yes, we have the citations that were given us by a citizen who just wired in or called in. It is the Warren Commission report pages 26, 461, and 781; and the Kerner Commission report page 473. So this is apparently a technique of investigation which has considerable authenticity and dignity, and that, this business of trying to get additional information to permit the CIA psychiatric profile section to complete its work was the purpose of this additional task imposed upon these investigators. . . .

SENATOR TALMADGE. Mr. Ehrlichman, I judge you to be a highly intelligent, extremely articulate, faithful servant of the President of the United States; and I do not believe all this could take place in the White House without you knowing about it. Why did you not report it to the President of the United States?

MR. EHRLICHMAN. Well, now, you say, all this, Senator. We had on the one hand a very full scale investigation. On four separate occasions I was present when the Attorney General of the United States said, either to me or to the President directly, that the fruits of that very, very vigorous investigation satisfied him; that the only people indictable were the seven individuals who had been indicted. On repeated occasions, and this telephone call which we have just read little bits of, on March 28, 1973, was typical of the President's continual questing for additional information. Here he is on March 28 saying to the Attorney General, "Do you have anything more to give me over at the Department of Justice on this? What about this McCord letter? Do you have anything to tell me about John Mitchell? If you do, call me direct. Don't work through some staff person that is liable to keep it away from me."

SENATOR TALMADGE. Let me ask you this: Do you mean to tell me that you, as one of the highest officials in the land, sat there in the White House after authorizing the sum of $350,000 to pay for lawyers' fees, bail bond, and everything else on this cover up, supremely ignorant that you were obstructing justice?

MR. EHRLICHMAN. I had nothing whatever to do with the $350,000, Senator. I did not know the $350,000 existed.

SENATOR TALMADGE. I think the record authorizes you paid it, authorized the payment.

MR. EHRLICHMAN. If the record says that, the record is wrong because, Senator, it was not until well into the month of March of this year that I had even heard about the $350,000 fund. . . .

SENATOR WEICKER. . . . I would like to have your concept and I think this is very important; now we are questioning into the real events of the real business of this committee, what's your concept of political information. You see, unfortunately, thanks to the Committee to Re-Elect the President, and some of the witnesses who have appeared here, everybody thinks that the Senators at this table and others engaged in politics go running around hiring Ulasewicz' types "to dig up dirt on each other, and I just can't allow that to fly without contesting" it because really it's going to make elections rather interesting in the future if it does.

I wonder if you might, since you were the one who was responsible for hiring this man, and since we have had a description by this man of exactly what his job consisted of, which was dirt, I wonder if you might tell the committee what your concept is of politics here in the United States insofar as this type of activity is concerned?

MR. EHRLICHMAN. Well, I think that certainly there is room for improvement in the practice of politics in this country, there is no argument about that. But, at the same time, I think that each candidate who contests the candidacy of an incumbent has the obligation to come forward and contest the fitness of that incumbent for office both in terms of his voting record and in terms of his probity, and in terms of his morals, if you please, and any other facts that are important or germane to the voters of his district or State or the country, for that matter. I think a candidate for office assumes that burden of proof. He assumes the burden of proof of showing the unfitness of the incumbent and I don't think in our political system that is limited to his voting record or his absenteeism. If it were, we would countenance the perpetuation of scoundrels in office who were thieves or who were fraudulent or who were profligate or who were otherwise unfit for office, so I think it's perfectly competent for a challenger to meet head-on the issue of the fitness of an incumbent.

SENATOR WEICKER. Do you mean to tell me and this committee that you consider private investigators going into sexual habits, drinking habits, domestic problems, and personal social activities as a proper subject for investigation during the course of a political campaign?

MR. EHRLICHMAN. Senator, I know of my own knowledge of incumbents in office who are not discharging their obligation to their constituents because of their drinking habits, and it distresses me very much, and there is a kind of an unwritten law in the media that that is not discussed, and so the constituents at home have no way of knowing that you can go over here in the gallery and watch a Member totter onto the floor in a condition which, of at least partial inebriation which would preclude him from making any sort of a sober judgment on the issues that confront this country.

Now, I think that is important for the American people to know, and if the only way that it can be brought out is through his opponents in a political campaign, then I think that opponent has an affirmative obligation to bring that forward.

SENATOR WEICKER. Now, this is getting very interesting. [Laughter.]

Again we contrasted similar situations yesterday and again I am just not going to let these things get laid on the table without giving another side to the argument.

I have had eight election campaigns, 8 years, 6 against Democrats and 2 against Republicans. I suppose it would be considered self-serving to say that I have never done anything like that, so I won't. I will refer to my opponents. I know of no Democratic opponents out of the six and no Republican opponents out of the two that has ever done what Mr. Ulasewicz was doing or what you are, in effect, advocating here.

Now it seems to me it is up to the constituency, whatever that constituency happens to be, to make a determination of the fitness of the man or woman that they go ahead and elect, but do you really want to bring the political system of the United States, of our campaigns down to the level of what you are talking about right now?

MR. EHRLICHMAN. Well, I conceive of it this way, Senator. I know that in your situation your life style is undoubtedly impeccable and there wouldn't be anything at issue like that.

SENATOR WEICKER. I'm no angel.

MR. EHRLICHMAN. I thought you were.

SENATOR WEICKER. Believe me, I am not. I worry about you seeking people on the landscape here and I have a greater worry now before you here, and I will put it that way.

MR. EHRLICHMAN. I think you will agree with me, Senator, that someone with a serious drinking habit is of doubtful fitness for the kind of heavy duty that you bear, for instance, or that any Senator bears in the Senate of the United States. That is certainly a material question that has to be raised in a political campaign, at least so it seems to me.

Now, if that is not something that the incumbent's opponent should bring out, then you are leaving the constituency to the tender mercy of the journalists in the community as to whether or not that is reported to the constituency because they don't have any way of knowing really, especially the constituencies remote from here where people get here very seldom to make an observation. So, I would be very concerned about that and it seems to me that would be a very legitimate subject of inquiry. Maybe my standards are all haywire and everybody in the Congress ought to be immune from scrutiny on that subject, but that just seems to me to be an indefensible position on your part.

SENATOR WEICKER. You think we have no scrutiny around here?

MR. EHRLICHMAN. Sir?

SENATOR WEICKER. You think we have no scrutiny around here?

MR. EHRLICHMAN. Well, in all candor—

SENATOR WEICKER. I mean I have got news, let's count them, they are all over here at this stage of the game and they are all the time not just to hear you and I talk. If there is anything that is quite obvious in Washington, D.C., it is that every aspect of our lives, legislatively, personally, and in every way, is subject to the scrutiny of a free press and subject to the scrutiny, at least the Congress is subject to the scrutiny of a free press. [Laughter.]

And also, subject to the scrutiny of our constituency.

SENATOR BAKER. Our wives.

SENATOR WEICKER. And our wives, right. [Laughter.]

I want to state right now, and I, obviously you and I, are at loggerheads on a very basic issue here and one that I think not only relates to Mr. Ulasewicz' activities, and I am not so sure we don't come right back to the break-in in Daniel Ellsberg's office again, that I am quite satisfied that our systems, our institutions, are perfectly capable of passing decent judgments, fair judgments, hard judgments, on political figures, public officials, without the covert operations of men like Mr. Ulasewicz. . . .

MR. DASH. But you have testified and spent quite a bit of your time testifying, in answer to questions, that the break-in was actually a legal act in the interest of national security. Then taking your statement that you did not know in advance that is what they would do, nevertheless, you indicated that that was perfectly legal under the law in the interest of national security.

MR. EHRLICHMAN. I believe that is a sound position.

Source: U.S. Senate, Presidential Campaign Activities of 1972, S. Res. 60, Hearings Before the Select Committee on Presidential Campaign Activities of the United States Senate, 93rd Congress, 1st Session, Book 6, 2570–72; 2578–79; 2592–94; 2599–2600; Book 7, 2673–74; 2716–17; 2776–78; 2816.

Resignation Address of President Richard Nixon, August 8, 1974

For the first time in history, an American president resigned his office. Politically shredded by an inexorable process toward impeachment and embarrassed by the release of tape transcripts that demonstrated that he had lied about his role in the Watergate cover-up and other matters, a shaken Nixon gathered himself before television cameras on August 8, 1974, for the humbling task of resigning. The resignation became effective at noon the following day.

RESIGNATION ADDRESS OF PRESIDENT RICHARD NIXON AUGUST 8, 1974

Good evening.

This is the 37th time I have spoken to you from this office, where so many decisions have been made that shaped the history of this Nation. Each time I have done so to discuss with you some matter that I believe affected the national interest.

In all the decisions I have made in my public life, I have always tried to do what was best for the Nation. Throughout the long and difficult period of Watergate, I have felt it was my duty to persevere, to make every possible effort to complete the term of office to which you elected me.

In the past few days, however, it has become evident to me that I no longer have a strong enough political base in the Congress to justify continuing that effort. As long as there was such a base, I felt strongly that it was necessary to see the constitutional process through to its conclusion, that to do otherwise would be unfaithful to the spirit of that deliberately difficult process and a dangerously destabilizing precedent for the future.

But with the disappearance of that base, I now believe that the constitutional purpose has been served, and there is no longer a need for the process to be prolonged.

I would have preferred to carry through to the finish whatever the personal agony it would have involved, and my family unanimously urged me to do so. But the interest of the Nation must always come before any personal considerations.

From the discussions I have had with Congressional and other leaders, I have concluded that because of the Watergate matter I might not have the support of the Congress that I would consider necessary to back the very difficult decisions and carry out the duties of this office in the way the interests of the Nation would require.

I have never been a quitter. To leave my office before my term is completed is abhorrent to every instinct in my body. But as President, I must put the interest of America first. America needs a full-time President and a full-time Congress, particularly at this time with problems we face at home and abroad.

To continue to fight through the months ahead for my personal vindication would almost totally absorb the time and attention of both the President and the Congress in a period when our entire focus should be on the great issues of peace abroad and prosperity without inflation at home.

Therefore, I shall resign the Presidency effective at noon tomorrow. Vice President Ford will be sworn in as President at that hour in this office.

As I recall the high hopes for America with which we began this second term, I feel a great sadness that I will not be here in this office working on your behalf to achieve those hopes in the next 2½ years. But in turning over direction of the Government to Vice President Ford, I know, as I told the Nation when I nominated him for that office 10 months ago, that the leadership of America will be in good hands.

In passing this office to the Vice President, I also do so with the profound sense of the weight of responsibility that will fall on his shoulders tomorrow and, therefore, of the understanding, the patience, the cooperation he will need from all Americans.

As he assumes that responsibility, he will deserve the help and the support of all of us. As we look to the future, the first essential is to begin healing the wounds of this Nation, to put the bitterness and divisions of the recent past behind us, and to rediscover those shared ideals that lie at the heart of our strength and unity as a great and as a free people.

By taking this action, I hope that I will have hastened the start of that process of healing which is so desperately needed in America.

I regret deeply any injuries that may have been done in the course of the events that led to this decision. I would say only that if some of my judgments were wrong, and some were wrong, they were made in what I believed at the time to be the best interest of the Nation.

To those who have stood with me during these past difficult months, to my family, my friends, to many others who joined in supporting my cause because they believed it was right, I will be eternally grateful for your support.

And to those who have not felt able to give me your support, let me say I leave with no bitterness toward those who have opposed me, because all of us, in the final analysis, have been concerned with the good of the country, however our judgments might differ.

So, let us all now join together in affirming that common commitment and in helping our new President succeed for the benefit of all Americans.

I shall leave this office with regret at not completing my term, but with gratitude for the privilege of serving as your President for the past 5½ years. These years have been a momentous time in the history of our Nation and the world. They have been a time of achievement in which we can all be proud, achievements that represent the shared efforts of the Administration, the Congress, and the people.

But the challenges ahead are equally great, and they, too, will require the support and the efforts of the Congress and the people working in cooperation with the new Administration.

We have ended America's longest war, but in the work of securing a lasting peace in the world, the goals ahead are even more far-reaching and more difficult. We must complete a structure of peace so that it will be said of this generation, our generation of Americans, by the people of all nations, not only that we ended one war but that we prevented future wars.

We have unlocked the doors that for a quarter of a century stood between the United States and the People's Republic of China.

We must now ensure that the one quarter of the world's people who live in the People's Republic of China will be and remain not our enemies but our friends.

In the Middle East, 100 million people in the Arab countries, many of whom have considered us their enemy for nearly 20 years, now look on us as their friends. We must continue to build on that friendship so that peace can settle at last over the Middle East and so that the cradle of civilization will not become its grave.

Together with the Soviet Union we have made the crucial breakthroughs that have begun the process of limiting nuclear arms. But we must set as our goal not just limiting but reducing and finally destroying these terrible weapons so that they cannot destroy civilization and so that the threat of nuclear war will no longer hang over the world and the people.

We have opened the new relation with the Soviet Union. We must continue to develop and expand that new relationship so that the two strongest nations of the world will live together in cooperation rather than confrontation.

Around the world, in Asia, in Africa, in Latin America, in the Middle East, there are millions of people who live in terrible poverty, even starvation. We must keep as our goal turning away from production for war and expanding production for peace so that people everywhere on this earth can at last look forward in their children's time, if not in our own time, to having the necessities for a decent life.

Here in America, we are fortunate that most of our people have not only the blessings of liberty but also the means to live full and good and, by the world's standards, even abundant lives. We must press on, however, toward a goal of not only more and better jobs but of full opportunity for every American and of what we are striving so hard right now to achieve, prosperity without inflation.

For more than a quarter of a century in public life I have shared in the turbulent history of this era. I have fought for what I believed in. I have tried to the best of my ability to discharge those duties and meet those responsibilities that were entrusted to me.

Sometimes I have succeeded and sometimes I have failed, but always I have taken heart from what Theodore Roosevelt once said about the man in the arena, "whose face is marred by dust and sweat and blood, who strives valiantly, who errs and comes short again and again because there is not effort without error and shortcoming, but who does actually strive to do the deed, who knows the great enthusiasms, the great devotions, who spends himself in a worthy cause, who at the best knows in the end the triumphs of high achievements and who at the worst, if he fails, at least fails while daring greatly."

I pledge to you tonight that as long as I have a breath of life in my body, I shall continue in that spirit. I shall continue to work for the great causes to which I have been dedicated throughout my years as a Congressman, a Senator, a Vice President, and President, the cause of peace not just for America but among all nations, prosperity, justice, and opportunity for all of our people.

There is one cause above all to which I have been devoted and to which I shall always be devoted for as long as I live.

When I first took the oath of office as President 5½ years ago, I made this sacred commitment, to "consecrate my office, my energies, and all the wisdom I can summon to the cause of peace among nations."

I have done my very best in all the days since to be true to that pledge. As a result of these efforts, I am confident that the world is a safer place today, not only for the people of America but for the people of all nations, and that all of our children have a better chance than before of living in peace rather than dying in war.

This, more than anything, is what I hoped to achieve when I sought the Presidency. This, more than anything, is what I hope will be my legacy to you, to our country, as I leave the Presidency.

To have served in this office is to have felt a very personal sense of kinship with each and every American. In leaving it, I do so with this prayer: May God's grace be with you in all the days ahead.

Source: Weekly Compilation of Presidential Documents, Richard Nixon, 1974, vol. 10, no. 32, 1014–17.

Bibliography

Ben-Veniste, Richard, and George Frampton Jr. *Stonewall: The Real Story of the Watergate Prosecution.* New York: Simon & Schuster, 1977.

Bernstein, Carl, and Bob Woodward. *All the President's Men.* New York: Simon & Schuster, 1974.

Campbell, Karl. *Senator Sam Ervin, Last of the Founding Fathers.* Chapel Hill: University of North Carolina Press, 2007.

Committee on the Judiciary, House of Representatives, Ninety-third Congress, 2nd Session. *Impeachment of Richard M. Nixon, President of the United States: The Final Report of the Committee on the Judiciary, House of Representatives, Peter W. Rodino, Jr., Chairman.* New York: Viking Press, 1975.

Dash, Sam. *Chief Counsel: Inside the Ervin Committee—The Untold Story of Watergate.* New York: Random House, 1976.

Emery, Fred. *Watergate: The Corruption of American Politics and the Fall of Richard Nixon.* New York: Simon & Schuster, 1995.

Friedman, Leon, comp. and ed. *United States v. Nixon: The President Before the Supreme Court.* New York: Chelsea House, 1974.

Jaworski, Leon. *The Right and the Power: The Prosecution of Watergate.* New York: Reader's Digest Press, 1976.

Kurland, Philip. *Watergate and the Constitution.* Chicago: University of Chicago Press, 1978.

Kutler, Stanley, ed. *Abuse of Power: The New Nixon Tapes.* New York: Free Press, 1997.

Kutler, Stanley. *The Wars of Watergate: The Last Crisis of Richard Nixon.* New York: W. W. Norton, 1992.

Olson, Keith. *Watergate: The Presidential Scandal that Shook America.* Lawrence: University Press of Kansas, 2003.

Rozell, Mark J. "President Nixon's Conception of Executive Privilege: Defining the Scope and Limits of Executive Branch Secrecy." *Presidential Studies Quarterly* (1992), 323–35.

Sirica, John J. *To Set the Record Straight: The Break-In, the Tapes, the Conspirators, the Pardon.* New York: W.W. Norton, 1979.

U.S. Senate. Select Committee on Presidential Campaign Activities. *Final Report.* 93rd Congress, 2nd Session. Washington: Government Printing Office, 1974.

———. Select Committee on Presidential Campaign Activities of 1972. *Hearings.* 93rd Congress, 1st and 2nd Sessions. 26 vols. Washington Government Printing Office, 1974.

The Church Committee on Intelligence Activities Investigation, 1975–76

By David F. Rudgers

An Insular Intelligence Community

The passage of the National Security Act of 1947 heralded the emergence of the United States as the world's leading power and established the instrumentalities for managing the combination of diplomacy and military power that came to be called "national security affairs," which forever afterward defined the conduct of the U.S. government. Among those instrumentalities created was the unified National Military Establishment (which became the Department of Defense in 1949), a National Security Council (NSC) responsible to the president for coordinating policy across organizational lines, and, significantly, the country's first national intelligence organization—the Central Intelligence Agency (CIA).

While the CIA was never the largest of the entities composing what is commonly called the "intelligence community," it is the most multifaceted, long the most influential, and often the most controversial. In the post–World War II period, it engaged in all forms of intelligence collection (both secretly and overtly), produced independent intelligence analysis to inform U.S. leaders, pioneered the development of overhead reconnaissance technology, and carried out covert operations. As the cold war unfolded, covert operations increasingly came to define the nature of the CIA.

Although the CIA was initially intended to provide information to NSC policy makers, in the course of the cold war it became the secret, private enforcer for what has come to be called the "imperial presidency." All postwar presidents came to view covert operations as giving them a "third option" to traditional diplomacy and conventional military action in combating the menace perceived from the Soviet Union (and, after 1949, from the People's Republic of China).

The CIA is also unique because, unlike any other major intelligence organization, it was created by public legislation. Because of its clandestine nature and mission, however, it always operated largely outside the U.S. political process—its budgets secret, its administrative and personnel procedures separate from the regular executive-branch civil service, and its activities generally unexamined by the news media.

While Congress did take an early and active interest in the functioning of the CIA, such interest was never institutionalized into formal oversight committees but rather was based on the personal relationships that individual members of Congress, usually senior members of the armed services and appropriations committees of the House of Representatives and Senate, had with the directors of the CIA.

Nevertheless, efforts to establish formal oversight mechanisms were attempted over the years. Between 1947 and 1974, more than 200 resolutions were introduced in Congress calling for improved congressional oversight of the intelligence community. None of the resolutions were successful in gaining enough support to become law. It was not until the 1970s, when events triggered a massive sea change in both congressional and public attitudes about the cold war and the "imperial presidency," that serious challenges to the secrecy and insular operation of the CIA took form.

The 1970s–Challenging CIA Secrecy

The disastrous war in Vietnam in the 1960s and early 1970s, resulting in 56,000 American dead, deeply disturbed the American polity and caused a massive reaction against unchecked presidential authority. In the wake of the war, the Watergate scandal revealed a White House–centered criminal conspiracy that struck at the

OVERVIEW

Background

Alarmed by the Watergate scandal that exposed various illegal and nefarious government activities and also concerned about recent allegations of intelligence service misdeeds, the U.S. Senate on January 27, 1975, decided to establish an 11-member investigating committee. The U.S. Senate Select Committee to Study Governmental Operations with Respect to Intelligence Activities was chaired by Democratic senator Frank Church of Idaho. Texas senator John Tower served as vice chairman.

Congress Investigates

The committee was given nine months and 150 staffers to complete its work. Led by Democrats, the Church committee met resistance from the Republican administration of President Gerald R. Ford. Suspicious of Church's presidential ambitions and concerned over exposing American intelligence operations, the administration battled the committee over access to both documents and testimony from administration officials. Despite the resistance, the committee interviewed more than 800 individuals and conducted numerous public hearings, probing widespread intelligence abuses by the Central Intelligence Agency (CIA), the Federal Bureau of Investigation (FBI), and the National Security Agency (NSA). At the first televised hearing, staged in the Senate Caucus Room, Chairman Church dramatically displayed a CIA poison dart gun to highlight the committee's discovery that the CIA had directly violated a presidential order by maintaining stocks of shellfish toxin sufficient to kill thousands of people.

Impact

The panel issued its final report in May 1976 without the support of influential Republican members John Tower and Barry Goldwater. Despite its shortcomings, the inquiry demonstrated the need for perpetual surveillance of the intelligence community and resulted in the creation in 1976 of the Senate Select Committee on Intelligence. A similar committee in the House of Representatives was created in 1977. Also in reaction to the Church committee reports pushing for oversight, Congress passed the Foreign Intelligence Surveillance Act (FISA) of 1978, which established a court responsible for issuing warrants for domestic wiretapping activity.

very heart of constitutional government and led to the resignation of President Richard M. Nixon in August 1974 and his replacement by Vice President Gerald Ford. As historian John Robert Greene noted, the two events unleashed a "Power Earthquake" in Washington. By the end of 1974, "it was clear that Congress, not the Ford administration, controlled the national agenda."

The 1974 elections brought in a new group of Democratic senators and representatives who had gained office campaigning against Nixon's "imperial presidency" and the legacy of Watergate. Mired in the scandal were the revelations of the involvement of former CIA operatives such as E. Howard Hunt who had been deeply involved in the burglary of the Democratic National Committee headquarters at the Watergate hotel in Washington in 1972. As a result the CIA faced an unprecedented crisis of public confidence. For its part, Congress was now determined to assert increased authority over executive-branch intelligence activities.

The Senate in particular began to give serious consideration to the adequacy of senatorial oversight. On December 9–10, 1974, Senator Edmund Muskie (D-Maine) of the Committee on Government Operations chaired meetings on ways to strengthen such oversight. In the course of those meetings, senators began to promote resolutions to create congressional investigating committees to examine the intelligence agencies.

In the crosshairs of emerging congressional interest in U.S. intelligence policy was William Colby, director of the CIA since 1973. Polished and urbane, Colby was an Ivy-Leaguer trained as a lawyer. He had served in the CIA's World War II predecessor, the Office of Strategic Services (OSS), from 1942 to its dissolution in 1945. Specializing in covert operations and paramilitary actions, Colby rose steadily in the CIA and served in Vietnam prior to his appointment by President Nixon.

As an intelligence professional, Colby had been satisfied with the old order of things. Nevertheless, he

CHRONOLOGY

1974

- *Spring–Summer:* The Senate Watergate Committee makes public thousands of pages of documents relating to the Nixon administration's illegal activities, some which involve national intelligence agencies.
- *December 22:* Journalist Seymour Hersh publishes an article in the *New York Times* entitled "Huge C.I.A. Operation Reported in U.S. Against Anti-War Forces."

1975

- *January 4:* President Ford appoints a commission, headed by Vice President Nelson Rockefeller, to report on domestic spying.
- *January 27:* The Senate establishes the Select Committee to Study Governmental Operations with Respect to Intelligence Activities. Senator Frank Church (D-Idaho) is named chairman.
- *February 19:* The House of Representatives establishes a Select Committee on Intelligence to investigate allegations of "illegal or improper" activities of federal intelligence agencies. Its first chairman, Representative Lucien Nedzi (D-Mich.), was later replaced by Representative Otis G. Pike (D-N.Y.).
- *April 9:* Church committee holds its first official meeting.
- *May 15:* Church committee holds its first closed-door hearing, on the controversial issue of assassinations.
- *September 16:* Committee holds its first public hearings.
- *October:* Committee issues report entitled *Alleged Assassination Plots Involving Foreign Leaders.* The report is later published.
- *October 29:* Committee holds public hearings on National Security Agency (NSA), the first time in history that the NSA's actions were examined in a public forum.
- *November 2:* President Ford asks William Colby to resign as head of the CIA.

1976

- *January 29:* Two days before the Pike committee is scheduled to conclude its activities, the House votes to withhold public dissemination of the committee's final report.
- *April 26:* The Church committee issues the first volume of its final report.
- *May 19:* The Senate establishes the permanent Select Committee on Intelligence under the chairmanship of Senator Daniel K. Inouye (D-Hawaii) to carry out oversight of the nation's intelligence organizations.

1977

- *July 14:* The House of Representatives establishes the permanent Select Committee on Intelligence, first chaired by Representative Edward P. Boland (D-Mass.).

recognized that Vietnam and Watergate would change everything. He later reflected: "The lesson was clear. The old power structure of the Congress would no longer control their junior colleagues and hold off their curiosity about the secret world of intelligence. In this new era, CIA was going to have to fend for itself without that longtime special Congressional protection."

On December 22, 1974, the *New York Times* published a front-page article by investigative reporter Seymour Hersh headlined "Huge C.I.A. Operation Reported in U.S. Against Anti-War Forces." Hersh described how the CIA had conducted a "massive illegal domestic intelligence operation," initiated by President Lyndon Johnson, against critics of the Vietnam War, other domestic dissidents, and journalists considered unfriendly to U.S. policy. Hersh had been diligent in researching the story. On December 20, he had interviewed Colby, who confirmed the accuracy of what Hersh had uncovered but sought to convince him that the issue was a matter of little importance that should remain buried.

Daniel Schorr, a veteran investigative reporter for CBS News, later observed: "The disclosure that America's foreign intelligence agency had brought home its bag of espionage tricks to practice against American dissenters caused a public stir." On December 24, the chief of the CIA's Counterintelligence Staff, James Angleton, resigned. Noted Schorr: "The implication seemed obvious."

In the following weeks, other sensational stories about CIA activities poured out from newspapers and television. In addition to accounts of covert operations to overthrow foreign governments, the litany included plots to assassinate foreign leaders, secret drug experiments on unwilling subjects (in one case leading to the suicide of an Army scientist given LSD without his knowledge or consent), and the illegal opening of mail sent by U.S. citizens. So closely following Watergate, the revelations stimulated a flood of letters and telegrams to congressional offices demanding an investigation into charges of spying on U.S. citizens by the CIA and other government agencies.

Hersh's article caught President Ford by surprise. Ford read the article aboard Air Force One on his way to Vail, Colorado, for his annual Christmas skiing vacation. Jarred by the account and especially by the fact that he had not learned earlier of the scope of the matter, Ford turned for support to his secretary of state, Henry Kissinger. A Nixon hold-over, Kissinger dominated the making of U.S. foreign policy. As national security adviser since 1969, he had been Nixon's "sorcerer's apprentice," sandbagging the honorable but hapless secretary of state, William Rogers, whom he replaced in 1973. When Kissinger read the article, he quickly realized its possible ramifications. Soon, he fired off a memo to Ford that read: "We're concerned that we not act in such a way as to give credence to the allegations of the *New York Times* story and create the impression that a major problem actually exists and that the Ford Administration is confronted with a scandal of major proportions." At the same time, Kissinger also contacted White House Chief of Staff Donald Rumsfeld to plan strategy to combat the looming political crisis.

Shortly before Christmas, Colby presented Kissinger with a six-page report outlining other nefarious activities in which the CIA had been engaged. Later, Schorr wrote acerbically that "the burden of the CIA's red-faced defense was that [the violations] had not been 'massive.'"

On January 3, 1975, Ford met with Colby in the Oval Office. There, Colby dropped the other shoe. According to Ford, he learned that day for the first time of the existence of the CIA's "family jewels." This was the name given to a set of documents and reports detailing activities by the CIA over the span of over two decades that were considered likely illegal or inappropriate. The materials came to light during the stormy 17-week tenure of James Schlesinger as director of the Central Intelligence Agency from February to July 1973. At that time revelations had surfaced regarding the operational assistance given by the CIA for various criminal activities committed by Watergate conspirators. Clearly worried, on May 9, 1973, Schlesinger issued a memorandum to all CIA employees declaring, "I have ordered all senior operating officials of this Agency to report to me immediately on any activities now going on, or that have gone on in the past which might be construed to be outside the legislative charter of this Agency."

The result of Schlesinger's call for information was a cascade of material from entry-level clerks to staff officers, an outpouring of material on CIA misconduct totaling 693 pages. The activities included not only CIA connections with the Watergate conspiracy but also spying on anti–Vietnam War dissidents, wiretaps and surveillance of journalists, illegal break-ins and mail opening, the testing of psychotropic drugs without consent, and the exchange of information on U.S. citizens with other government agencies and local police departments.

On May 21, Colby, then head of the CIA's clandestine service, began reviewing the submissions and eventually boiled them down into a 70-page memorandum that a wag dubbed the "family jewels." Although Schlesinger left the CIA in July to become secretary of defense, he also left a time bomb ticking within the CIA and the Ford administration. Lamented Kissinger later: "Such a compilation was dynamite."

While Ford claimed that he only learned of the "family jewels" in his meeting with Colby on January 3, 1975, he had been forewarned. Kissinger had prepared a five-page note on December 25. He informed the president that the CIA had, indeed, engaged in activities that "clearly were illegal" and others that raised "profound moral objections."

The Rockefeller Commission

The dual impact of the Hersh article and the revelations of the "family jewels" launched a grand assault on the imperial presidency. President Ford's response to the revelations was a standard defensive tactic to head off a congressional investigation. On January 4, 1975, he signed an executive order establishing a "Commission on CIA Activities in the United States." The following day he announced that Vice President Nelson Rockefeller would serve as chairman of the commission. Six other members were selected from a list of more than two dozen prominent public figures.

The Rockefeller commission was given a mandate to investigate allegations of CIA domestic spying and other forms of misconduct and make recommendations for preventing future abuses. At a news conference, Ford said that he did not think that there was any conflict between the commission and the congressional investigation that seemed imminent. By early June 1975 the commission would complete its investigation and prepare a 299-page final report.

The Rockefeller commission report documented that over a 28-year period the CIA had engaged in numerous illegal activities that were often directly or indirectly authorized by presidents, particularly Johnson and Nixon. These included large-scale domestic surveillance of antiwar protesters and other dissidents as well as journalists and other U.S. citizens; a 21-year program of illegal mail interceptions and openings; illegal break-ins and wiretaps; and a program of testing LSD and other psychotropic drugs on unwitting subjects. The report did not find any direct CIA involvement in Watergate but described compliance with improper White House requests, subsequent destruction of possibly relevant files, and inadequate responses to FBI and Justice Department inquiries. A section on foreign, particularly Soviet, espionage in the United States was deleted at Kissinger's insistence in order to protect his friendly relations with the Soviet leadership. The report made 30 recommendations, including that a joint Senate-House intelligence committee be established, that the power of general counsels and inspectors general in intelligence agencies be strengthened, and that the president issue an executive order on intelligence operations and organization.

If Ford thought that the work of the Rockefeller commission would end the controversy, he was sadly mistaken. The report resulted in no important legislation and, except for providing a small amount of information, had no discernible impact on the work of the Church committee. When Senator Church saw the report, he declared that it was "just the tip of the iceberg," a comment that Daniel Schorr said reflected the "zeal on Capitol Hill for picking up where the Executive Branch had left off." Schorr added cynically: "The 'son of Watergate' . . . held promise of rich, political dividends."

The Creation of the Church Committee

"This was the post-Watergate Congress," William Colby wrote later in his memoirs, "with new and even some old members exultant in the muscle that they had used to bring down a President, willing and able to challenge the Executive as well as its own Congressional hierarchy, increasingly intense over morality in government, extremely sensitive to press and public pressures." The old congressional oligarchy of a few entrenched committee heads overseeing far-reaching intelligence activities was now under siege. Later, the CIA's official history of its legislative affairs declared that it was apparent "that the old way of doing oversight no longer sufficed."

On January 15, 1975, as the Rockefeller commission began its work in the executive branch, Colby testified in closed-door hearings conducted by the intelligence subcommittees of the Senate Armed Services and Appropriations Committees, co-chaired by Senators John Stennis (D-Miss.) and John McClellan (D-Ark.), respectively. It was, as Colby later commented, "a reasonably friendly panel" whose members "had been faithfully and patriotically protecting the CIA from public prying" for years. Although McClellan emerged from the hearings to declare himself "satisfied" with Colby's explanations regarding the Hersh article and other matters, the senators wished to release the testimony to the public.

Senator Frank Church (D-Idaho), left, talks with William E. Colby, director of the Central Intelligence Agency, during a meeting in Church's Washington office on February 27, 1975. Church, chairman of the Senate committee investigating intelligence agencies, met with Colby in an effort to ensure CIA cooperation in the investigation. (Associated Press)

Unfortunately for Colby, the CIA, and the administration, the testimony received extensive and detailed media coverage and scrutiny. Colby was chagrined to admit that his testimony "did not, as I had hoped, begin to quiet the storm whirling around the Agency. The years of total secrecy had made the CIA extremely vulnerable to suspicion and sensation. . . . So these improprieties I had conceded dominated the media, overriding my assertions that they were few and far between, and the storm continued unabated."

Meanwhile, on January 14 and 20, Democratic caucuses debated the issue of a Senate investigation of the CIA. Senator Church suggested setting up a special committee. Although opposed by Stennis and fellow Mississippi senator James Eastland, who chaired the Judiciary Committee, the caucus voted 45 to 7 to create a bipartisan select committee to investigate intelligence activities. As some senators left the meeting, they were overheard discussing "the end of an era."

On January 21, Senator John Pastore (D-R.I.), introduced Senate Resolution 21 to establish a "Select Committee to Study Government Operations with Respect to Intelligence Activities." Energetically debated over the next several days, the resolution was approved by an overwhelming 82–4 vote on January 27. The committee would have 11 members. It was given a nine-month tenure that was later lengthened. Senator Mike Mansfield (D-Ore.), president of the Senate and a strong supporter of congressional oversight of intelligence activities, wrote, "Neither witch hunt nor whitewash will be here conducted, and there will be no wholesale dismantling of our intelligence community. What we hope to attain is a full and objective analysis of the role of intelligence gathering in a free society today measured against current laws, practices, and policies in the intelligence community. It is a task that is long overdue."

Because it was a "select" committee, its members were chosen by the president of the Senate, with the recommendation of the majority and minority leaders of the upper house. The former, Mansfield, would choose six members and the chairman; the latter, Senator Hugh Scott (R-Pa.), would name five Republicans and the vice chairman. For his part, Mansfield sought a cross section of Senate Democrats, consciously breaking with the past by not choosing party oligarchs such as Stennis and McClellan, who had been major intelligence overseers in the past. Democrats on the committee included Church and Walter Huddleston of Kentucky, both of whom had shown a determination to increase oversight. Also included were Democrats Philip Hart of Michigan, Walter Mondale of Minnesota, Robert Morgan of North Carolina, and Gary Hart of Colorado. Scott selected Republicans John Tower of Texas, Charles Mathias of Maryland, Barry Goldwater of Arizona, and Howard Baker of Tennessee.

With the political stakes so high, the matter of selecting a chairman of the select committee became an issue of seminal importance. Mansfield's first choice was Philip Hart, a well-respected, 16-year veteran of the Senate. Hart, however, was seriously ill and unable to accept the post. Mansfield then turned to Frank Church, the third-ranking member of the Committee on Foreign Relations and chairman of its subcommittee on multinational corporations. Church lobbied hard for the position, and Mansfield responded with his appointment.

Scion of a politically minded family of Democrats in a heavily Republican state, where his father had served as governor, Church had been elected to the Senate in 1956 at the age of 32. In the Senate he developed a reputation as a loner. With a somewhat stuffy manner, he was sometimes chided for being "too earnest and moralistic" and was mockingly referred to as "Frank Sunday School" or "Frank Cathedral" (although few doubted his sincerity). He also developed a substantial reputation as an orator. His role model was Idaho's legendary Republican senator William Borah, who had become chairman of the Foreign Relations Committee, a position coveted by Church himself.

Although initially subscribing to the cold war consensus, Church was soured by the Vietnam War and the policy process leading up to the Bay of Pigs fiasco in 1961. Then, after participating in hearings on CIA activities in Laos in 1967 and 1969, he became an increasingly strong critic of the agency's influence on U.S. foreign policy. He concluded that Congress needed to reclaim the powers it had ceded to the presidency since World War II. His speeches and writings frequently condemned interventionism and called for a moral foreign policy. Unsurprisingly, he supported Senator Eugene McCarthy's attempts to strengthen congressional oversight bodies. In 1972, as chairman of the subcommittee on multinational corporations, he led an investigation into the role of such corporations in foreign policy, a probe that revealed routine bribery of foreign leaders.

Church was derided by "realists" such as Henry Kissinger as being hopelessly naïve about the state of the global order and the nature of the external threats the country faced, particularly from world communism. "Clearly," Kissinger grumbled, "Church came to the committee chair having already prejudged the Agency as a source of governmental misconduct."

A bigger problem for Church than his idealism was the general belief that he was using the committee's investigation to promote his presidential ambitions. Nowhere was this view more deeply entrenched than within the CIA. As intelligence writer Thomas Powers observed, "There wasn't a single CIA officer who doubted he was trying to launch himself toward the White House from the CIA's prostrate back." This view was also held within the select committee itself. In his memoirs, John Tower later wrote that Church "had his sights set on the White House" and that from "the beginning . . . thought that alleged improper and illegal intelligence-gathering activity began with Richard Nixon." A Republican staff member later said, "My whole vision of him is blurred by his drive for recognition, publicity, his obvious ambition for higher office."

While the charge of political ambition on Church's part is true, it is not entirely fair. Church did indeed see himself as a dark horse presidential contender, either in 1976 or 1980. He was a Democrat who won substantial election victories in a traditionally Republican state, and, as the fourth-youngest person ever elected to the U.S. Senate, seemed to have a long political career ahead of him. But despite the issue of Church's ambitions, he managed to keep the committee's activities on a predominately bipartisan plane. All members seemed determined to conduct a fair and thorough investigation and wished to protect the legitimate legislative interests and constitutional prerogatives of the Senate.

Once officially established, the select committee began to organize. It set up shop in a converted auditorium in the Dirksen Senate Office Building. Recruiting staff was not a major problem because of the potential impact of the committee. Many highly qualified applicants for staff positions appeared with backgrounds in academia, law, diplomacy, military service, and intelligence. Eventually the staff reached 135 people: 53 investigators, as well as press aides, researchers, secretaries, consultants, security officers, and other administrative support personnel.

It fell to Church to select the two key staff members: the staff director and the chief counsel. Named to the former post was William Miller, good-natured Foreign Service officer with considerable experience as a congressional staff member. Chosen as chief counsel was Frederick A.O. "Fritz" Schwarz Jr., a hard-charging and highly successful litigating lawyer from a major New York City law firm and a member of the family that founded the famous toy manufacturing company.

Thus organized, the select committee launched one of the most important congressional investigations in U.S. history. What became known as the "Year of Intelligence" was to many intelligence officers the "Year of the Firestorm" or the "Intelligence Wars." The CIA's official legislative history correctly called the investigation "the first probe of any consequence that Congress had ever conducted into Agency operations."

In the course of its 15-month existence, the select committee conducted 126 full committee meetings, 40 subcommittee meetings, 250 executive hearings, and 21 days of public hearings. In addition, it carried out 800 interviews of individuals and generated 110,000 pages of documentation. It published seven volumes of hearings, several detailed staff reports, and a six-volume "final report." The committee's investigation not only described the workings of the U.S. intelligence community and the making of U.S. intelligence policy in massive detail, but it also exposed the ugly underside of U.S. government conduct.

The Pike Committee

For its part the House of Representatives also sought to establish an investigative committee, but its efforts proved a farrago. On February 19, 1975, the chamber voted to establish the Select Committee on Intelligence, chaired by Representative Lucien Nedzi (D-Mich.) who had headed the intelligence subcommittee of the Committee on House Armed Services. Trouble began almost immediately, however. First, the committee was unable to agree on a staff director and became embroiled in other organizational disputes. Then, in June, the committee's Democratic members were outraged when the *New York Times* revealed that Colby had briefed Nedzi on the "family jewels" in 1973 and he had done nothing about it. Nedzi decided to resign as chairman of the new committee, but the House rejected his resignation. Nedzi then refused to serve. After more wrangling, the House abolished the committee on July 17 and replaced it with a new 13-member body chaired by Democratic representative Otis Pike of New York.

The Church Committee Congressional Investigation

As the investigation approached, Colby organized a strategy of engagement. Early on he believed that "you won't get away with stonewalling them." He also thought that if the committee could be persuaded to remain focused on domestic issues, the CIA might avoid damage to its overseas operations.

As soon as he learned of the establishment of the committee, Colby telephoned Church to offer his full cooperation. As the committee organized its staff and procedures, Colby devoted considerable time to developing ground rules by which the CIA would turn over material to investigators.

On February 27, 1975, Church and committee vice chairman John Tower met with Colby at the CIA's headquarters in Langley, Virginia. Colby's negotiations with Church and Tower were delicate, and the director applied all his lawyerly skills in the process. He pointed out to the senators that there were three categories of information: unclassified (which they could have freely); classified (which would require protection to prevent leaks); and certain highly sensitive material that should not face the risk of exposure (primarily the names of secret intelligence sources, foreign intelligence liaison arrangements, and the details of technical intelligence collection systems).

Colby requested that the committee staff sign secrecy agreements, that arrangements be made to protect committee records on a permanent basis, and that procedures be introduced to protect the identities of CIA employees from appearing in public documents. Within these parameters, Colby said, he would permit CIA officers to testify without regard to their secrecy oaths. The senators were agreeable, and Colby could later say that "I reached a fairly good, although not complete, understanding on these matters with Church and Tower, and thus I felt comfortable in instructing my subordinates to cooperate with the committee's investigators."

Colby also had to put his internal house in order, since his calculated stance was unsettling to those indoctrinated into a lifetime of secrecy. He did not agree with those who sought to resist the committee's inquiries. As a lawyer, he recognized that a defendant usually loses any attempt to suppress evidence, and, in 1975, the CIA was clearly the defendant. Rather, Colby felt disposed to releasing massive documentation and generally honoring the requests for documentation.

Colby told his colleagues that they could be sure "that any investigations would uncover all questionable conduct," so the CIA's only sensible recourse was to offer additional evidence "to try and put those in their true (and small) proportion." As a result, all employees were instructed to report all instances of past behavior that they considered improper.

Needless to say, many in the intelligence community objected to this approach, arguing that foreign intelligence was strictly an executive-branch function and that Congress could not be trusted to protect intelligence secrets. Colby's performance played to mixed reviews on the Church committee. Senator Goldwater, the body's conservative gadfly, was the most critical. He later said, "I never understand how a circumspect man like Colby could cave to so many big mouths in Congress." But Goldwater conceded: "In fairness to Colby, the times had targeted him and the agency."

Colby was not the only senior CIA officer influencing the Church committee. Hovering over its activities was the presence of former director Richard Helms. Director of the CIA from June 1966 to February 1973, Helms was, in the words of Schorr, "any casting director's model for a spymaster—tall, athletic, quick-witted and sardonic." Highly capable and a good administrator, Helms was also an amoral cold warrior with no sense of ethical constraints when it came to combating the Soviet adversary. However, with a strong sense of institutional loyalty, he refused to let the CIA be used by Nixon to cover up the unfolding Watergate scandal. An outraged Nixon forced him out, making him ambassador to Iran as a consolation. He held that position when the select committee began its work and became one of its primary targets, since his name appeared in documents relating to virtually every CIA activity in which the committee was interested: assassination plots and coup planning, clandestine mail openings, drug testing, spying on dissidents and journalists, and assistance to the Watergate burglars.

Helms also personified the antithesis to Colby's approach to the investigation. Helms and Colby were at loggerheads. Schorr observed: "The breach in the wall of secrecy that Congress now vowed to widen had already caused deep wounds inside the intelligence community. Many orthodox intelligence professionals were up in arms. Colby's belief that salvation lay in cooperation with investigations ran up against ingrained convictions that an intelligence secret was forever and its disclosure close to treason. The struggle had become personified in the Colby-Helms conflict."

At its first official meeting on April 9, the committee faced an issue that would be a constant source of tension—access to documents. Senator Huddleston asked: "What is the ultimate recourse if the agencies refuse to cooperate?" "The courts," Church answered, but pointed out that what the committee faced was essentially a political problem, not a legal one.

The documents issue would become the cutting edge of what became a congressional challenge to the "imperial presidency" unprecedented in postwar American politics. The man facing this challenge was "president-by-accident" Gerald Ford. In 1973 Nixon chose Ford, a longtime representative from Michigan, to replace his disgraced vice president, Spiro Agnew, who was forced to resign after investigations concerning his complicity in bribery. When Nixon himself resigned the following year, Ford's accession to the presidency was greeted with national relief.

Although the area of foreign affairs was never his strong point, Ford was not without experience in

Richard Helms, former CIA director, tells the Senate Intelligence Committee in Washington on September 17, 1975, that he intended to obey a presidential directive requiring the CIA to destroy its stockpiles of deadly poison, but that he never issued a written order to have it done. Helms said he "constantly" issued verbal instead of written orders. (Henry Griffin/Associated Press)

national intelligence matters. He had served as a member of the Intelligence Subcommittee of the House Committee on Appropriations. During his eight-year tenure on the subcommittee, he oversaw CIA covert operations in Algeria, Congo, Guatemala, and Turkey; paramilitary actions in Laos; the development of such technical intelligence collection systems as the U-2 aircraft and spy satellites; the organization of the Bay of Pigs disaster; and the CIA's rapidly expanding involvement in Vietnam. His press secretary Ronald Nessen later said of Ford's view of the Church investigation: "He was determined to deal with the CIA scandal in a way that would not damage America's necessary intelligence capacity. He believed he would be held accountable if he allowed the intelligence services to be crippled by excessive exposure and unwise restrictions."

As Ford organized his own executive branch team, he named as chief of staff Donald Rumsfeld. A GOP wheel horse, the hard-charging Rumsfeld had been a congressman, held several senior posts in the Nixon White House, and served as U.S. ambassador to NATO. His deputy (and protégé) was Richard Cheney, an ambitious young political scientist turned political activist.

Ford expressed much anxiety over the impending intelligence investigation. While he acknowledged that it was "entirely proper that this system be subject to congressional review," he insisted that "a sensationalized public debate over legitimate intelligence activities" was a "disservice to this Nation and a threat to our intelligence" because it "ties our hands while our potential enemies operate with secrecy, with skill, and with vast resources." Any investigation, he said, must be conducted with exceptional discretion and dispatch.

Ford was not reluctant to spell out his views on national security. In an interview for CBS News conducted by Walter Cronkite, Eric Sevareid, and Bob Schieffer on April 21, 1975, Ford strongly defended the practice of covert operations overseas. When Cronkite suggested that it might be antithetical in a democracy when the people had no awareness or input "into what government overseas they are going to knock off or what ones they are going to support," Ford bristled that the American people had to trust their elected officials.

The Church committee's greatest nemesis in the executive branch was not the president; it was his "national security czar," Henry Kissinger. A man of intellect and great cunning, Kissinger was a member of a Jewish refugee family from Nazi Germany who had settled in New York City in the 1930s. After World War II, through the critical influence of Fritz Kraemer, one of the nation's leading national security scholars, Kissinger rose in academia to become a senior professor at Harvard University. He attracted widespread attention in America's foreign policy establishment due to his ability to tell prominent men of affairs what they wanted to hear when they wanted to hear it—usually in a turgid prose style and a nearly incomprehensible German accent that gave many the mistaken impression that he possessed the wisdom and gravitas of "Old Europe."

Kissinger vaulted into a worldwide position of power with the admiring support of Nixon, who named him national security adviser in 1969 and secretary of state in 1973. Despite their vast differences in background and personality, they shared a crude *realpolitik* view of the world as well as a penchant for deceit, a loathing of a free press, and a relative disdain for elements of constitutional government.

Because Kissinger was an ardent cold warrior, he not only was a firm believer in waging the "secret war" against the Soviet Union overseas, but he also used the CIA to spy on Americans who opposed the Vietnam War. Observed journalist Tim Weiner: "From the start, Kissinger exerted ever-tightening control over the CIA's operations. . . . It became a one-man show. . . . The black operations of the United States were approved by Henry Kissinger."

By the beginning of Ford's presidency, Kissinger, aided by much self-promotion, was something of an American cultural icon. Through the scandals of the Nixon administration, he had managed to emerge with his reputation relatively unscathed. He was depicted in the media as "Super K," the indispensable man who kept U.S. foreign policy intact while Watergate raged. When Ford became president, Kissinger expected his dominant influence in the administration to continue.

Senator Frank Church, right, chairman of the Senate Intelligence Committee, speaks with Secretary of State Henry Kissinger on November 21, 1975, during one of the committee hearings on the activities of the CIA and other intelligence agencies. (Associated Press)

Although Ford had a high regard for his intellect and abilities, and he would remain as secretary of state until the end of Ford's presidency in 1977, Kissinger's stature in the new administration began to drop. Revelations began to appear publicly of Kissinger's major role in U.S. government plots to overthrow the democratically elected government of Chile in 1973. Kissinger's in-house critics began to bristle that Kissinger was a liability and a residue of Nixon that tainted the new administration. Rumsfeld emphasized that Kissinger's domination of foreign policy made Ford look increasingly less presidential. Increasingly, Ford became less dependent on Kissinger's advice.

As a result of the tortured political atmosphere, Colby's strategy of "managed cooperation" with the Church committee did not fare well with the White House. Colby himself later ruefully recalled, "It wasn't long before I felt very alone. Ford and his aides decided their best policy was to dissociate the White House from CIA's troubles and thus minimize their responsibility for the Agency's questionable practices in the past and the bad odor in the present. I agreed with them, and thought I should take the heat; the process added to my isolation. The wagons were drawn around—and I was left on the outside."

Throughout the committee's 15-month existence, its relationship with the executive branch was adversarial. The executive controlled the select committee's access to both information and witnesses. While the committee had subpoena power, Church did not use it, fearing that to do so would tie the committee up in court battles. For its part, the Ford White House periodically threatened to use claims of "executive privilege" with respect to material and testimony. Nevertheless, both sides backed off, willing to proceed through a series of accommodations.

But the committee proceeded amid contention from the beginning. On February 20, Colby complained to a House subcommittee that public criticism of past CIA activities undermined and endangered U.S. foreign intelligence operations. Church responded in a speech at the National Press Club in late February that the executive branch could not effectively investigate itself.

Ford remained concerned about sensitive information becoming public. In addition, the White House was particularly worried about public hearings that could bring Church considerable national exposure and easily could get out of control, exposing national security secrets. On February 21, Ford told Rumsfeld: "The question is how to plan to meet the investigation of the CIA." Rumsfeld promised to undertake "a damage-limiting operation for the President."

In February, Vice President Rockefeller met with Church and Tower and gave them a copy of the "family jewels," whose contents became the focus of the committee's investigation. On March 5, Church and Tower were invited to the White House to discuss procedures. Church brought with him a list of key documents (intelligence reports, policy directives, budget studies, legal authorities, and classified executive orders) that his committee wanted to see. Church thanked Ford for his initial cooperation and stated: "We will not be a wrecking crew. There will be no dismantling and no exposing of agents to danger. No sources will be compromised. We, however, do need information."

Church then asked Ford to facilitate the committee's work by permitting access to the various agency files. At this point Kissinger erupted: "Asking for information is one thing but going through the files is another." In an effort to calm the escalating tension, Ford said, "Senator Church is not asking for the right to go fishing in the files. I am certain all his requests would be relevant to the inquiry."

At a news conference on March 17, Ford was asked: "Will you be giving Congress all the material that is asked for as a part of its investigation of intelligence activities?" Ford responded: "I can assure you and others that we will do all we can to indicate maximum cooperation but until we have had an opportunity to review this request in detail, I am not in a position to give you a categorical answer."

The committee's request for documents hit the CIA hard. The list of requested materials included numerous CIA internal studies and histories as well as a wide variety of organizational and budgetary information. Although Colby proceeded to cooperate, many in the CIA, particularly partisans of Helms, favored stonewalling. Indeed, when it became clear that Colby would not do so, some acted on their own. David Atlee Phillips, a veteran clandestine service officer, resigned so he could speak out publicly. He and others established the Association of Retired Intelligence Officers and launched a project they called "Confound" in an effort to stymie the congressional investigation.

Despite Colby's efforts at cooperation, Ford's White House staff sought to keep close control over document release. On March 29, Robert McFarlane of the National Security Council staff submitted a detailed analysis of the various White House documents sought by the Church committee. The analysis conceded that most could be turned over, although other senior officials reviewing the list disagreed. By April 14, McFarlane asserted that no classified information should be provided to the committee until legal exchanges confirmed the president's exclusive right to make all final decisions about making secret information public.

Ford was not particularly happy with what was happening. There were no rules for orderly and uniform processing, which led to confusion and dispute. Nor were there clear guidelines for protecting sources and methods or strategies for focusing the investigation on important issues rather than on sensational ones.

To address the matter Ford created a special Intelligence Coordinating Group (ICG) to review requests for documents and other unfolding events of the congressional investigation. Despite the efforts at coordination and compromise, the positions of the major figures remained fixed: Colby favored maximum disclosure, and Kissinger urged maximum stonewalling.

Through April and May, the Church committee continued to press the document issue. After sending additional requests to the White House for documents, the committee received less than satisfactory cooperation. At the select committee's second formal session on April 16, Senator Philip Hart complained that the White House had "given us two go-to-hells. What is our response going to be?"

The CIA, meanwhile, announced that it and other intelligence organizations would assign "monitors" to accompany any present or former intelligence officers called to testify in order to "give advice if it became necessary." Senator Richard Schweiker (R-Pa.) spoke for all when he stated: "If the committee allowed this, we'd be the laughing stock of the Hill." Tower motioned the committee to repudiate the proposal, and it carried unanimously.

Eventually, through tough negotiation, the select committee largely succeeded in getting its way on access to documentary material. The committee agreed to accept two criteria: It would not ask for the names of agents and it would not ask for the methods by which the CIA obtained its information. Church recalled: "These were valid requests. They didn't interfere with the investigation of illegal activities infringing on the constitutional rights of Americans. We kept that agreement. In return we got a lot of information."

Assassinations

On May 15, 1975, the Church committee held its first closed-door hearing in a secret room in the Capitol once used by the Joint Atomic Energy Committee. The topic was the issue of assassinations. The assassination issue not only was an explosive one, it also cut across party lines. The issue became, in the words of one committee staff member, "the hottest item in town since Watergate."

For his part, Church was adamant about pursuing the topic and remained convinced afterward that exposing "CIA murder plots and murder attempts" overseas was one of the committee's major accomplishments. On May 15, Colby was the first witness at the committee's hearings on the subject. It did not go well. The CIA director did not shed much light on the subject. "It was like being a prisoner in the dock, there was a real interrogation," he later said. "I told them that our policy and our orders are very clear: We will have nothing to do with assassination." Church ended the hearing by saying that it is not enough to have orders. "We need to have a law which prohibits assassination in time of peace." Kissinger later said, "It is an act of insanity and national humiliation to have a law prohibiting the President from ordering assassination."

The hearings remained confrontational. By the time Colby left the witness table, it was clear that the CIA had planned murder. Emerging from the hearing, Church said on May 22 that Colby's testimony was "candid but

This Oliver W. Harrington cartoon shows Richard Nixon as an executioner, wearing nothing but a loincloth labeled "CIA" and standing beside a guillotine. The body of a beheaded woman labeled "Democracy" lies on the guillotine. (By Permission of Helma Harrington)

chilling" and later told the press: "It is simply intolerable that an agency of the United States government may engage in murder."

On July 23, after considerable argument, the committee voted, on a 6–5 party line, to issue an "interim report" on assassination plots. The question of its prior clearance by the full Senate was undecided.

Titled *Alleged Assassination Plots Involving Foreign Leaders,* the report chronicled one of the most sordid policies in the history of U.S. foreign relations. The committee reported that the CIA had planned, at President Dwight Eisenhower's direction, the assassination of Congolese leader Patrice Lumumba in 1960; planned numerous plots against Cuban leader Fidel Castro authorized by presidents John F. Kennedy and Lyndon Johnson between 1961 and 1965 (the CIA later admitted to eight—Castro claimed many more); cooperated with the assassins of General Rafael Trujillo, dictator of the Dominican Republic in 1961, and with the assassins of South Vietnam's authoritarian president Ngo Dinh Diem in 1961; colluded with the plotters against Chilean army chief of staff General Rene Schneider in 1970 (who was killed in a botched kidnapping attempt); and with the conspirators against Chilean president Salvador Allende, who died in the course of the military coup promoted by Nixon and Kissinger that overthrew him in 1973. Two other prospective targets, Presidents François "Papa Doc" Duvalier of Haiti and Sukarno of Indonesia, according to the report, died of natural causes.

The report also confirmed that, in no case, however, was the CIA or the U.S. government directly involved in any of the deaths. The CIA station chief in Congo refused to carry out the plot against Lumumba (who subsequently was overthrown and murdered by political enemies in 1961). The CIA also held back from final participation in the killings of Trujillo, Diem, and Schneider (whose killers acted on their own, and, according to the best evidence, said the report, Allende died by his own hand). Nevertheless, these revelations were disturbing. Far from being a "rogue elephant," as Church later observed, "the CIA operated as an arm of the presidency. This led presidents to conclude that they were 'super-godfathers' with enforcers. It made them feel above the law and unaccountable."

When President Ford ardently requested that the report not be made public, the committee, after contentious discussion during which Church threatened to resign his chairmanship if the panel bent to Ford's will, voted to submit the report to the full Senate, requesting that it meet in secret session to vote on its release to the public.

Whatever the Senate's wishes, the executive branch did not give in easily. After failing to get a court to enjoin publication of the report, Colby held a news conference in which he declared that its release would endanger lives. On November 20, the Senate gathered for one of its few closed sessions since World War II. A long and rancorous debate failed to reach a decision about making the report public. Seizing the moment, when the session ended, Church, acting on his own initiative, called a news conference to hand out copies of the report. A CIA official history of executive-legislative activities later observed: "It was the first time in history of executive-legislative relations that a committee of the Congress, with the putative support of its parent body, asserted the right to release a report a president contended was classified." Church declared: "We regard assassination plots as aberrations," and Mondale added that the United States "must not adopt the tactics of the enemy."

The release of the report was a bonanza for the media, and editorial comment ranged from condemnation of the CIA to equally strong criticism of the committee's action. Kissinger grumbled in a speech on November 24 that it was time to end "the self-flagellation that has done so much harm to this nation's capacity to conduct foreign policy." As if it were the aim of Congress, Kissinger added that "we cannot allow the intelligence service of this country to be dismantled."

Covert Action

Almost as controversial as the issue of assassination was that of covert action. Although the Church committee first requested CIA data on all covert activities, it later scaled back its request to information on five specific programs including U.S. participation in the 1973 overthrow of the government of Chile and the disastrous U.S. involvement in the post-independence civil war that ravaged Portugal's former West African colony of Angola in 1975.

For its review of covert operations, the committee received 14 CIA briefings and carried out more than 100 staff interviews, including 13 former ambassadors and a dozen CIA station chiefs. Sixty staff investigators were involved.

In responding to queries about covert operations, Colby was instructed by the White House to limit his response to specific time frames and topics. Only basic historical data would be given freely. More sensitive information would be "sanitized" before release. Other material could be reviewed only at CIA headquarters, and only notes could be taken and then reviewed by CIA offices before leaving the building. The most sensitive material could only be used indirectly in briefings and briefs. This category included everything about presidential authorizations and much about the operations themselves.

On October 23, Colby testified about covert operations in a closed hearing. When Church asked, "When does the CIA decide to resort to covert operations?" Colby recited a checklist: seriousness of the situation, level of cost in money and personnel, and chance of exposure and danger. Long skeptical of covert action, Church burst out, "The kind of intervention you are discussing has destroyed the moral leadership of our country throughout the world. Resistance, hostility, and hatred toward the United States—much of it stems from our covert actions. It has been 'counterproductive,' in that favorite Washington term."

On December 4, public hearings focusing on Chile began without the participation of either Colby or Kissinger, both of whom refused to appear. Church criticized the two; Tower and Goldwater, on the other hand, spoke out against public hearings on so sensitive a topic. Two former U.S. ambassadors to Chile, Ralph Duggan and Edward Korry, testified. Duggan called the secret intervention in Chile a "national disgrace." Korry, however, criticized the committee and the assassination report.

Ultimately, the Church committee produced six staff reports on CIA covert action programs. Only one (on Chile) was made public. Although detailing the CIA's vast intrigues against Allende, it could not prove direct CIA links to his 1973 overthrow and death.

Also in October 1975 the Church committee worked to reveal illegal CIA activities within the United States: clandestine mail openings and the monitoring of domestic dissent. Secret mail opening in the United States went back as far as the Civil War. The FBI became involved in the practice early in World War II, but Director J. Edgar Hoover abandoned it in 1966 because its questionable legality raised the threat of public criticism over privacy violations if exposed.

The CIA had no such concerns. Between 1953 and 1973, James Angleton's Counterintelligence Staff ran an extensive intercept program code-named HTLINGUAL, mainly out of the New York Post Office building. During the operation, more than 28 million letters (mostly to and from the Soviet Union) were checked against a mail-watch list; 215,820 were opened, and the contents photographed for distribution within the CIA. The watch list included Democratic senator Hubert Humphrey of Minnesota, scientist Linus Pauling, author John Steinbeck, the Ford and Rockefeller Foundations, and Harvard University.

The select committee held three days of public hearings on the program. The star witness in the lead-off hearing on September 24 was Angleton. Church and other members of the committee were outraged by such blatant lawlessness and when Angleton, Richard Helms, and other intelligence officials as well as two former postmasters general sought to defend the program, the hearings became particularly tense and contentious.

The CIA had become involved in monitoring domestic political dissent in the 1960s as a direct result of White House and Justice Department concern over urban riots, anti–Vietnam War protesters, campus takeovers by militant student radicals, and a perception of a general peril to domestic order. In the summer of 1967 President Johnson had ordered Helms to determine whether foreign agents, especially Communists, were fomenting the unrest. In response Helms created a special unit in the Counterintelligence staff to collect information about individuals and groups engaged in such activities. The unit, continued until 1974, found no credible evidence of foreign involvement. But during its course, the CIA accumulated files on more than 7,000 U.S. citizens and 6,000 groups.

Investigating the National Security Agency

The Church committee mainly concentrated on the CIA. Nevertheless, it did not ignore other components of the intelligence community, particularly the super-secret National Security Agency (NSA). Headquartered in a huge complex at Fort Meade, Maryland, the Defense Department component carried out the most sensitive form of intelligence performed by any nation—the collection of electronic communications and noncommunications signals, the breaking of foreign codes, and the creation of secure U.S. codes. Established in 1952 by a top-secret directive signed by President Harry Truman to unify military communication and signals intelligence activities, the NSA's existence was not acknowledged for many years and no reference to it appeared in the official *Government Organization Manual.*

In the course of the investigation, Church observed: "No statute establishes NSA or defines the permissible scope of its responsibilities." In addition, its technological capabilities made it, in the words of Mondale, "possibly the most single important intelligence source for this nation." This view also prompted Church to comment: "That capability at any time could be turned around on the American people and no American would have any privacy left, such is the capacity to monitor everything: telephone conversations, telegrams, it doesn't matter. There would be no place to hide."

As the Church committee took testimony in executive session from current and former NSA officers in the summer and fall of 1975, its mood became hostile as various NSA attorneys repeatedly argued over the committee's right to investigate the organization. The committee's attention was increasingly drawn to "G Group," which ran most of its domestic operations. Recognizing a serious problem, NSA director general Lew Allen contacted Frank Raven, a recently retired 33-year veteran of the organization who had headed G Group almost from its inception nearly 15 years earlier, to appear as the NSA's official representative.

A troubled Raven later recalled: "They were hanging NSA. NSA was getting deeper and deeper, and NSA didn't deserve it. They were on the defensive. Instead of trying to cooperate with the committee, and trying to find out what had happened, and who had done what, they had a chip on their shoulder and were fighting the committee every inch of the way." Raven did his part in the hearings by testifying with much candor.

The committee assigned the task of probing the NSA to a 30-year-old lawyer name L. Britt Snider. The entire question of holding public hearings on as secret a topic as the NSA and its activities was revolutionary, deeply divided the committee, and caused more contention with the executive branch. At a committee hearing on September 19, Goldwater opposed the idea of hearings on the NSA, saying, "We're in very, very ticklish waters."

At the beginning of October, Church announced that the committee would hold two days of public hearings on the NSA's past conduct. The Ford White House promptly panicked. On October 7, Ford telephoned Church personally in an attempt to convince him that public hearings on the NSA's electronic intelligence activities would endanger national security. He then sent Attorney General Edward Levi to argue against such hearings at a closed meeting with the committee.

Despite the intense White House pressure, Church pushed on. Two days of public hearings duly commenced on October 29, 1975. It was the first time in history that the NSA's activities were officially examined in a public forum. In his opening statement, Church emphasized how the committee had proceeded cautiously to protect technical secrets and that it was interested in examining activities of "questionable propriety and dubious legality." For his part, Tower called the open hearings a danger to national security.

At the hearings, Director Allen, accompanied by his deputy, Benson Buffam, and General Counsel Roy Banner, demonstrated a casual and largely indifferent attitude toward the legality of the NSA's activities. When asked by one of the committee members if the NSA's technical capabilities would allow it to monitor domestic conversations "if some person with malintent desired to do it," Allen offhandedly replied, "I suppose that such a thing is technically possible." As intelligence scholar Christopher Andrew later observed: "Though he gave no details of NSA's awesome technology his [Allen's] answers gave the American people their first glimpse of its phenomenal ability to pluck messages from the ether."

On October 29, Allen revealed an NSA program called "Operation Minaret." From 1966 to 1973, the NSA had intercepted messages of 1,680 citizens and groups targeted through lists supplied by the Defense Department, the FBI, and other agencies.

An even greater revelation, however, was "Operation Shamrock," described by Church as "probably the largest governmental interception program affecting Americans ever undertaken." It was initiated in August 1945, when offices of the Army's Signal Security Agency (later part of the NSA) approached officials of Western Union, RCA Global, and ITT World Communications in New York for purposes of securing access to foreign telecommunications traffic entering, leaving, or transiting the United States. After some initial reluctance on legal grounds, the companies eventually agreed to cooperate to varying degrees. In 1947 and 1949, the secretary of defense promised that this cooperation would never be disclosed.

Out of offices in New York, the NSA began sharing information with the FBI, the Secret Service, the CIA, and other agencies. The targets of the collection gathering were criminals, political dissidents, and activists. All were U.S. citizens, and no judicial warrants were sought for invading their privacy. By the 1970s the NSA had developed information on more than 600 citizens that could be shared with other government agencies. On May 12, 1974, the operation was terminated on the grounds that it was no longer useful.

The Church committee discovered Operation Shamrock through references in the "family jewels" and from a confidential source. Neither the White House nor the NSA wanted knowledge of Shamrock in the public domain. Nevertheless, as with the assassination report, the committee ignored presidential objectives. By a party-line vote, the committee decided to publish the report.

The Legacy of J. Edgar Hoover

One of the most conspicuous achievements of the Church committee was its official exposé of the infamous legacy of J. Edgar Hoover. During his long tenure as director (from 1924 until his death in 1972), Hoover ran the agency as a personal fiefdom, with scant supervision from attorneys general, virtually no oversight by Congress, and the indulgence of all presidents. With a genius for self-promotion and media manipulation, he established a fearsome reputation as a crime fighter, although he never personally arrested a single criminal and was highly selective about which crimes he chose to fight. In addition, as the country's leading counterespionage officer, his strident warnings against the "threat of Communist subversion" had great public resonance during the cold war. Because he equated such "subversion" with any form of political dissidence, his agents routinely spied on law-abiding people whose views or activities ran afoul of his malevolent prejudice, including Eleanor Roosevelt, Albert Einstein, scholar John Kenneth Galbraith, and humor journalist Art Buchwald. In addition, as a racist with strong ties to Southern law-enforcement agencies, Hoover focused much malice against African Americans involved in the civil rights movement.

Hoover died just as Watergate was breaking and the FBI was caught up in the wide-ranging scandal. His successor, Clarence Kelly, set out to reform the FBI. A former FBI agent, he had left the organization in 1961 to become police chief of Kansas City. He was an acknowledged professional law enforcement official. For the first time in the FBI's history, through the work of the Church committee, the public would now be given a detailed look into the FBI under Hoover.

Hoover was a consummate bureaucrat who never operated without some sort of official authorization. In June 1939, President Franklin D. Roosevelt issued a secret directive giving the FBI the sole responsibility for coordinating investigations under the espionage laws and for collecting domestic intelligence. In a somewhat ambiguous public directive, the president also directed the FBI to investigate groups that might violate certain federal laws and engage in "subversive activities." The FBI's cold war spying against "foreign" activities would easily shift to domestic dissenters during the turbulent 1960s.

After much haggling over the extent of documentation that the FBI should make available to the committee, some of it began to reach the members in August. What it unearthed, in the words of historian Frank Smist, was "dramatic evidence of the dangers an intelligence agency can present to those very freedoms it was originally created to protect."

The committee's most odious discovery was COINTELPRO (for "counterintelligence program"). COINTELPRO began in 1956 when Hoover requested authorization to conduct what would be domestic covert operations. When President Eisenhower asked what he had in mind, Hoover listed a range of activities: disinformation, mail interception, electronic surveillance, tax surveillance, forgeries, harassment, even clandestine trash inspection. Eisenhower made no objection. Hoover could get on with the work. His first target was the U.S. Communist Party (a personal obsession despite its lack of domestic political consequence). In 1961, he then went after the Socialist Workers Party, a Trotskyite group of equal inconsequence.

In April 1965 President Johnson told Hoover that he was certain that Communists were behind the anti–Vietnam War protests. Hoover knew he could not prove this but nevertheless fanned Johnson's paranoia by claiming that Communists could infiltrate leftist movements such as Students for a Democratic Society. Even though the CIA had already explored this ground, Hoover launched a COINTELPRO operation against the "New Left" in October 1968.

Even more shamefully, another such operation targeted African American groups, ranging from the Southern Christian Leadership Conference and the Congress of Racial Equality to the Nation of Islam and the Black Panthers. The operation, under Hoover's personal direction, also sought to destroy the career and reputation of civil rights leader Martin Luther King Jr.

While COINTELPRO dealt with misdeeds that went as far back as the Roosevelt administration, another one was unique to the Nixon administration, the Church committee revealed: the "Huston Plan." Thomas Huston was a former conservative Republican political activist who was hired by the Nixon White House and given internal security responsibilities. He began meeting with William Sullivan, the FBI deputy director responsible for domestic activities, including counterintelligence. In the summer of 1969 he brashly complained to Sullivan about the shortcomings of FBI intelligence concerning potential demonstrations. By 1970 President Nixon was so angered by attacks from the "New Left" that he directed Huston to devise a plan to strike at his radical critics. Relying on recommendations from counterintelligence specialists from various agencies, Huston prepared a massive internal spying plan. Under it, the intelligence agencies would receive authority to monitor the international communications of U.S. citizens, increase electronic surveillance of domestic critics and organizations, carry out secret (and illegal) break-ins of homes and establishments (one specific target was the highly respected Brookings Institution), and expand spying on college campuses. Nixon approved the plan.

Although some of Nixon's closest advisers supported the plan, Hoover was outraged when he saw it. Ever the crafty bureaucrat, he recognized that disaster would result if what he called the "jackals of the press" ever learned of the plan. Nixon reversed himself. Thus, in this one case, J. Edgar Hoover became the unlikeliest champion of American civil liberties.

The Church committee held public hearings on the Huston plan in late September. Huston admitted the plan had been wrongheaded but justified it in the context of the time and situation. Nixon flatly refused to cooperate with the committee on the matter.

Public Hearings and Poison Darts

The very idea of public hearings on hitherto secret intelligence activities was in itself revolutionary. In all, the Church committee held 21 days of public hearings that not only opened up the netherworld of U.S. government policy and external action but also, and to a considerable degree, displayed a great deal of political theater.

On September 16 public hearings began on the subject of biotoxic agents in U.S. government laboratories. Nixon had ordered all of them destroyed, but in violation of that order, a CIA scientist, it was discovered, decided to retain 11 grams of shellfish toxin (one gram could kill 5,000 people). What was this program and the mystery surrounding it?

Colby, Helms, and CIA scientists testified how, over a period of 18 years, the CIA had spent $3 million to develop poisons and biochemical weapons. Documents

Frank Church, Democratic senator from Idaho and chairman of the Senate Intelligence Committee, holds up a poison tranquilizer dart gun designed for use by the Central Intelligence Agency, September 17, 1975. Looking on is co-chairman of the committee, Republican senator John Tower of Texas. (Associated Press)

disclosed a capability to cause diseases and epidemics in people, livestock, and crops. Although Colby explained that the poisons had been kept through bureaucratic shortcomings rather than sinister intent, the revelations produced a media circus.

The hearings on poisons introduced to the world the "nondiscernible microbioinnoculator." This was a silent, electrically powered pistol designed to fire poison darts. The device, which was invented by the CIA, the device was a prototype of dubious effectiveness. It proved, however, to be a hit with committee members as well as Schorr and other television news correspondents. "Cameras moved in clucking and whining like an advancing army of mechanical insects," recalled Loch Johnson, special assistant to the committee. "Here was theater to give life to the hearings as Church had anticipated." Special CIA counsel Mitchell Rogovin later observed: "I myself brought the gun up and carried it like it was a dead fish. I wouldn't let Colby touch it. The press would have just loved to have gotten a picture of Colby carrying that gun."

Committee members had no such qualms. Church and Tower relished posturing with the device before news cameras. Photographs appeared in newspapers and magazines around the country.

Church Committee Impact on the Ford Administration

The public hearings ended Colby's career as CIA director and contributed to a massive internal shakeup of the Ford administration. Ever since the Hersh story in December 1974, the White House had become increasingly exasperated by Colby's cooperative approach with the committee, and he had few, if any, friends at court. Colby himself later remarked ruefully that "the impact of the toxin spectacular, and especially the fact that I had delivered the dart gun when Congress demanded it, blew the roof off."

The fall of Colby and the massive internal shakeup of which it was a major part had its genesis in the political travails facing Ford almost from the beginning of his accidental incumbency. Feuding among his staff and advisers had been constant. Rockefeller, Rumsfeld, Kissinger, Schlesinger—all frequently bickered and jockeyed for power.

Senator Frank Church, right, chairman of the Senate Intelligence Committee, chats with George H. W. Bush, President Ford's choice to be CIA director, prior to the start of hearings before the Senate Armed Services Committee December 16, 1975, on Capitol Hill. (Henry Griffin/Associated Press)

In late October 1975, Ford replaced Defense Secretary Schlesinger with Rumsfeld. Rumsfeld's deputy, Richard Cheney, replaced him as White House chief of staff. And in early November, the ax fell on Colby. He was replaced as CIA director by George H. W. Bush. Scion of a distinguished Connecticut family who had moved to Texas to prosper in the oil industry, he had served briefly as a congressman, Republican national chairman, and U.S. ambassador to the United Nations. At the time of his appointment as CIA director, he headed the U.S. diplomatic mission to the People's Republic of China.

For Senator Church the personnel changes of the Ford administration were ominous. As he left the committee room on November 3, he said: "There is no question in my mind that concealment is the new order of the day. Hiding evil is the trademark of a totalitarian government." Six days later he remarked on television that firing Colby was part of a pattern "to disrupt the investigation."

Nixon's View

The committee scored a victory early in 1976 when it finally got the views of former president Richard Nixon. Through his lawyer Nixon agreed to answer written questions under oath. The questions were carefully drafted and were classified. Nixon's lawyers cleared his answers with the White House and released them to the public on March 10.

Nixon argued that the presidency was "sovereign" and therefore was justified in breaking the law in certain circumstances, if deemed necessary in the "interests of national security." Surprised and outraged by the stance taken by the president on an issue central to the concept of the "imperial presidency," Church denounced the doctrine as pernicious and dangerous. Loch Johnson later observed: "Nixon's response did more to evoke the image of a CIA out of control than anything our committee had uncovered."

Weathering the Attacks

Church and the committee endured ferocious attack. In November, Church lamented: "We seemed to face increasing resistance on every front." From Republican *grande dame* Clare Booth Luce to former CIA director John McCone, the committee was lambasted for being overzealous and un-American. Angleton even saw its work as "a 'diabolical plot' by left-wingers to weaken the nation's defenses."

Conservative pundits shelled the committee with verbal assaults. William Safire, James K. Kilpatrick, Patrick Buchanan, and Paul Harvey charged that the committee's work was politically biased at best and dangerous to the nation's safety at worst. Such attacks took their toll. In December 1975 a Harris poll rated the committee at 38 percent positive, 40 percent negative, and 22 percent unsure. Quick to exploit this sentiment, President Ford asserted at a news conference that "we are going to have a strong intelligence community and we are not going to permit the Congress to dismantle America's intelligence community."

Unanticipated events overseas also militated against the committee. On December 23, 1975, Richard Welch, the CIA station chief in Greece, was shot to death by three masked gunmen outside his residence in Athens shortly after he was identified as a CIA officer in a Greek newspaper. Although his identity (as well as his residence) was long an open secret in the city, its impact in the United States was powerful. Colby, as well as CIA partisans in the media, were quick to blame his killing (at least in part) on the congressional investigation.

Two Republican senators even charged that the Church committee was responsible for exposing Welch's identify before his murder. Church angrily pointed out that the committee never published (or even possessed) Welch's name. Nevertheless, the damage was done. Letters calling him a "murderer" flooded Church's office, and a vigilante fringe group called "Veterans Against Communist Sympathizers" threatened to kill him. Public skepticism of the investigation, growing even before Welch's death, turned into a strong backlash.

The Ford administration was quick to exploit Welch's death to undermine the investigation. Colby himself went to Andrews Air Force Base to receive Welch's body. The funeral at Washington National Cemetery was nationally televised. All through the tributes to Welch and the ceremonies, the press and administration officials readily connected the event with the congressional investigation. Johnson summed up the issue accurately: "Nothing in the entire 16 months of the Church investigation was more unfair than this and similar pronouncements. In fact, the Committee had said nothing about Welch, or any other active CIA agent or officer, in any of its reports, press conferences or other public statements and we had never said a word about Greece."

Pike and Church Committee Acrimony

In the course of its investigations, a key factor for the Church committee was its relationship with its House counterpart led by Representative Otis Pike. There was only minimal contact between the two committees and no conferences or meetings. The main concern was the desire of both chairmen to avoid duplication of effort. Nevertheless, strong feelings of antipathy developed between the two bodies. The House committee greatly resented the media and public attention garnered by Church. Considerable ill will also developed over vastly different approaches to the investigations. Unlike the Church committee, the Pike committee was soon wracked with partisan and ideological discord, and, unlike the measured approach of the Church committee, it took a far more confrontational stand with the executive branch, particularly with Kissinger, that soon devolved into open conflict. In the end, when the acrimonious Pike committee hearings were completed, the full House repudiated its work by voting to suppress its final report. In February 1976, however, a copy was leaked to Schorr. Schorr, in turn, passed the copy to the New York City counterculture weekly, the *Village Voice,* which published it in two long, sensational installments.

Outraged, the House, on February 19, voted to investigate the matter. As a result, all 13 members of the Pike committee, as well as 32 staff members, had to testify under oath before the House Ethics Committee. The leaker was never identified. Schorr also was called to testify. He refused to reveal his source, however, and, while he was not prosecuted, he was eventually forced out of his position with CBS News.

Senator Frank Church holds a copy of the Rockefeller commission report on the CIA, which was later made public. Church pledged that his Senate select committee would probe beyond the Rockefeller commission's report. (© Bettmann/CORBIS)

Preparing the Final Church Committee Report

Under the cloud of the Welch assassination, the Church committee began the work of drafting its multivolume final report. The drafting was carried out between December 1975 and April 1976. In preparing the report, the committee divided into two subcommittees: a Foreign and Military Subcommittee, chaired by Walter Huddleston and including Gary Hart, Mathias, and Goldwater; and a Domestic Subcommittee, headed by Mondale and comprising Philip Hart, Morgan, Baker, and Schweiker.

The report comprised six volumes. For their part, Tower and Goldwater objected to the contents of three of the volumes and largely dissociated themselves from the committee's work altogether. The first volume appeared on April 26, 1976. It was entitled *Foreign and Military Intelligence.* It stated that between 1961 and 1975 the CIA had conducted more than 900 major projects and several thousand smaller ones, three-quarters of which had never been reviewed outside the organization itself. While the committee questioned whether the gains of covert actions outweighed the costs (particularly in the damage done to the nation's reputation globally), it did not recommend terminating them. Rather, it concluded that covert action should be employed only in exceptional cases where vital U.S. security interests were at stake.

The volume made 87 specific recommendations. Chief among them was that the Senate create a permanent oversight committee, which would be responsible for autho rizing the national intelligence budget. Its prior consent would also be required for launching any covert activity. It also proposed new legislation to replace the 1947 National Security Act in order to clarify the intelligence roles of the president, the National Security Council, and the CIA director, as well as to set forth the responsibilities of the various intelligence agencies. It also recommended that certain activities be prohibited altogether: political assassinations, the subversion of democratic governments, support for foreign police or security services that violated human rights, and the use of U.S. clergy or journalists for intelligence activities.

A few days later the committee released its second volume, entitled *Intelligence Activities and the Rights of Americans.* Soon the committee issued other staff reports and studies and further recommendations that composed the whole of the final report. The committee wanted vigorous Senate oversight to guarantee that the intelligence agencies obey the law. It recommended barring the CIA and other intelligence organizations, as well as the IRS and the Postal Service, from all domestic security. The report also recommended new legislation to protect the civil rights of Americans from violations due to new technologies.

In their informative account of the contemporary Justice Department, journalists Jim McGee and Brian Duffy correctly state: "The Church committee final report stands as one of the most important public documents in the history of American intelligence. Balanced in tone but firm in its judgments, the big volumes meticulously document how the nation's intelligence agencies have ignored and violated the Constitution." With the publication of its reports, the Church committee quietly went out of business.

The Impact

Evaluating the significance of the Church committee's work validates the axiom that "where you stand depends on where you sit." An "outsider" of liberal orientation like Daniel Schorr could write that, with the establishment of the Church committee, "a new era began in the monitoring of intelligence agencies long accustomed to reporting to uninquisitive armed services and appropriations committees." Conversely, a conservative national security affairs analyst like Angelo Codevilla observed: "The argument that underlay the Church committee hearings was that the U.S. had more to fear from a surfeit of intelligence than from external threats."

In his memoirs, Gerald Ford described the Church committee investigation as "sensational and irresponsible." Henry Kissinger described the committee's work as coalescing "into a powerful assault on American foreign policy" and said the "cumulative damage to the intelligence community lasted a long time" because of sensitive information revealed, secret identities and operations exposed, morale and initiative weakened, and careers damaged or ruined.

The spymasters also had their say. In his memoirs, Richard Helms later described the hearings as "a wanton breach of the secrecy understanding which existed between Congress and the [Central Intelligence] Agency until that time." William Colby was far less critical. He applauded congressional attempts to define more clearly the boundaries within which the CIA "should and should not operate." He concluded that the Church committee came "to fair conclusions about American intelligence reflecting proper differences and not merely the hysteria that I had feared might take over."

Scholars weighed in over the years. Loch Johnson, one of the participants in the Church committee's staff work, later became a noted scholar of intelligence issues. He also became one of the most articulate champions of the committee's work. In a scholarly study of the CIA, he observed that the "Year of Intelligence" had brought the "torch of democracy into the dark halls of the intelligence community. He noted: "Whatever one's views on this turn of events in 1975–77, one fact was clear to all—the nation had entered a new era in the conduct of its intelligence policy." Thomas Powers, in his outstanding account of Richard Helms and the CIA, wrote that the Church committee's work, after a year of immersion in the details of American intelligence, had "left the Senate with a feeling of shame. It was not the aims, or even the failures of American policy which generated this mood . . . but rather the melancholy discovery that American policy had been so often callous, reckless and offhand."

Whatever the views of the participants or the observers of the Church committee's work, there is no doubt that it generated pressure for reforming and revising national intelligence policy to tighten controls and correct past abuses. The first to act was Ford, who readily realized that the old ways of doing business were no longer valid, but who also understood the need to assert executive power at a time of unprecedented challenge to the "imperial presidency." At a news conference on February 17, 1976, Ford announced "plans for the first major reorganization of the intelligence community since 1947." A new executive order, he said, would centralize overall policy direction in the National Security Council and management under a committee headed by the incoming CIA director George H. W. Bush. In addition, a three-member oversight board of private citizens would be created. Further, he said, to "improve the performance of the intelligence agencies and to restore public confidence in them," he was issuing a "comprehensive set of public guidelines which will serve as legally binding charters for our intelligence activities." They would also, he said, "provide stringent protections for the rights of American citizens." Finally, he said, he would submit to Congress "special legislation to safeguard critical intelligence secrets." "We must not and will not," he said, "tolerate actions by our Government which will abridge the rights of our citizens," but, at the same time, "we much maintain a strong and effective intelligence capability." On February 13 Ford duly issued Executive Order 11905, "United States Foreign Intelligence Activities."

Although Church and most members of the committee thought that the executive order represented an improvement in intelligence oversight, neither they nor the staff were entirely satisfied. Mondale, in particular, stated that congressional legislation would be required for full reform. The Senate was first to act. On May 19, 1976, the Senate passed Resolution 400 to create the

Permanent Select Committee on Intelligence. Its first chairman was Daniel Inouye (D-Hawaii). For the first time in Senate history one committee had oversight for the entire intelligence community. The new body was the legitimate successor to the Church committee. Not only did it adopt its predecessor's legislative agenda but five former members of the Church committee were appointed to it.

It took the House of Representatives more than a year to pass House Resolution 658 in July 1977. The new permanent Select Committee on Intelligence was a unique legislative creation in that it was the only House select committee to have legislative authority and a standing committee staff. Its first chairman was Edward Boland (D-Mass.).

The creation of these committees was a seminal legislative event. The CIA's official history concluded that "both committees in their early years managed to carry out their responsibilities in a workmanlike fashion, putting through an intelligence authorization bill each year as well as other legislation. . . . Oversight inquiries took place behind closed doors, with few if any leaks of classified information."

The Department of Justice also took action as a result of the Church committee. As the committee's revelations concerning COINTELPRO became public, the Justice Department launched its own investigation of FBI activities. It was conducted by Henry Peterson, a trusted criminal lawyer who was the assistant attorney general in charge of the Criminal Division. He was vigorous in his efforts and concluded that the Internal Security Section of the Criminal Division had given the FBI free rein. He believed that was wrong, but also that the Justice Department was not entirely to blame since the nation's political leadership, both executive and legislative, had encouraged the FBI's zeal and had been unwilling to support the department's senior officials in dealing with J. Edgar Hoover. On March 10, 1976, Attorney General Edward H. Levi issued new regulations for FBI noncriminal investigations. Intrusive surveillance would be used only in cases involving violence or crime. Later, under Levi's direction, additional operational guidelines were issued that more clearly defined the FBI's role in intelligence gathering.

The Church committee's work also influenced congressional legislation. The Foreign Intelligence Surveillance Act (FISA) was introduced in mid-1978 by Senator Edward Kennedy (D-Mass.). It was his fourth effort in four years to secure such legislation. Although the Senate passed the legislation overwhelmingly, the bill met stiff resistance in the House. Nevertheless, on September 7, the House passed the bill, and President Jimmy Carter signed FISA into law on October 25, 1978.

FISA, for the first time, established procedures for conducting electronic surveillance within the United States. The attorney general was now required to approve all government applications and submit them, accompanied by appropriate justifications and certifications, to the newly established Foreign Intelligence Surveillance Court. This body, composed of seven district judges and three appellate judges appointed by the chief justice of the United States, meeting in secret, would issue warrants permitting the initiation of electronic surveillance actions that met predetermined standards. Among those standards were that the target be a foreign power or its agent; that no U.S. individual be targeted, unless there was probable cause that he or she was engaged in actions in violation of law for a foreign source that was likely to harm U.S. security; and that the use of the information uncovered be sharply restricted.

James Bamford, an unofficial chronicler of the NSA, called the Foreign Intelligence Surveillance Court "most certainly the strangest creation in the history of the federal judiciary. Its establishment was the product of a compromise between legislators who wanted the NSA and FBI . . . to follow the standard procedure of obtaining a court order required in criminal investigations and legislators who felt the agencies should have no regulation whatsoever in their foreign intelligence activities."

The court raised the fears of civil libertarians, but intelligence scholar John Oseth was correct in observing in 1985: "Indications are that the court created by the act has functioned substantially as originally intended—or, in the view of some, as originally feared. . . . In no case was a government request turned aside. . . . But the response on behalf of the new procedure is that it made operational planners more careful in selecting cases for which electronic surveillance was proposed."

A second significant piece of legislation followed in May 1980 when Congress approved a concise 750-word measure called the Intelligence Oversight Act of 1980. The legislation became law the following October as part of that year's Intelligence Authorization Act. The act established general reporting requirements to Congress by not only the CIA but also the other components of the intelligence community. The law, among other things, required that Congress be kept "fully and currently informed of all intelligence activities," including covert actions, and directed Congress to develop procedures to protect the information provided. Congress also was to be informed of "significant intelligence failures" as well as significant anticipated activities.

President Jimmy Carter, left, announces the Foreign Intelligence Surveillance Act of 1977 in the White House Rose Garden on May 17, 1977. The proposed plan is aimed at keeping the government from illegally spying on citizens. Standing behind Carter is Senator Edward Kennedy (D-Mass.), center, one of the sponsors of the bill, with Attorney General Griffin Bell at right. (Bob Daugherty/Associated Press)

Nevertheless, for the CIA, little changed as a result of the Church committee's work. Although the committee's findings led to restrictions and increased oversight, no real operational changes emerged. While the CIA's management was forced to accept the reality of institutionalized congressional oversight, its leadership generally continued to deny the legitimacy of the oversight and to believe that foreign intelligence remained exclusively a part of the executive branch. While the CIA did become more legalistic, its attorneys now acted in a fashion of corporate lawyers telling both CIA senior officials (as well as presidents) how to avoid doing what the law required. This mindset was highlighted later by a comment made by Richard Helms. In 1977 he was convicted of lying in his testimony before a congressional committee in 1973. After receiving a suspended sentence and paying a fine, Helms quipped that he considered his criminal conviction to be a "badge of honor."

After the work of the committee had finished, Senator Church commented, "Today, continuing congressional surveillance is built into the woodwork. We did the necessary job. Political will can't be guaranteed. The most we could do was to recommend that a permanent surveillance be established. We did that knowing that the Congress being a political animal will exercise its surveillance with whatever diligence the political climate of the time makes for."

In 1976 President Ford said, "Accountability is the real crux of how you can prevent abuses. . . . When you come right down to it, the person in this area who has the final responsibility is the President." Ford's view, a commonplace one in U.S. political thought, was borne out by events. His successor, Jimmy Carter, made intelligence reform a major part of his presidential platform and, on January 24, 1978, issued Executive Order 12036, which went beyond Ford's in tightening internal guidelines on intelligence activities that could infringe upon the rights and privacy of U.S. citizens at home and abroad. A reversal, however, began with the election of Ronald Reagan in 1980. Convinced of the expanding power of the Soviet Union as an "evil empire," President Reagan made "unleashing" the CIA not just a matter of policy but an article of faith. On December 4, 1981, Reagan signed Executive Order 1233, which undercut Carter's order by returning considerable discretion in surveillance operations to the CIA, authorizing it to conduct domestic covert operations, expanding its ability to gather intelligence on U.S. citizens, and weakening such executive oversight mechanisms as then existed. In March 1983 his administration also loosened the Levi guidelines for conducting FBI domestic security investigations.

Reagan's return to the "old order" of intelligence was highlighted and personified by his appointment of William J. Casey as CIA director in 1981. Like Reagan, Casey held a hard-line, almost messianic hostility toward the Soviet Union. A veteran of the wartime OSS, he saw himself as a true successor to its legendary chief, William Donovan, in combating the new "evil empire" as his venerated mentor had fought the old one. With such a crusader mentality, he naturally disdained legality and particularly the concept of congressional oversight. As the CIA's official history commented: "Casey knew he was obliged to deal with the oversight committees, not only because the law required it, but because there were things he wanted from the Congress, such as funding and legislation. But he never liked this part of his duties, seeing the committees as obstacles to the president's ability to carry out his responsibilities as commander-in-chief and leader of U.S. foreign policy."

As a result Casey had no qualms about lying to or otherwise misleading Congress, particularly concerning the clandestine and illegal (but soon very public) war launched by the Reagan administration to overthrow the leftist (but internationally recognized) government of Nicaragua. At one point his deceptions became so blatant that he received a severe public rebuke from Senator Goldwater, the former member of the Church committee who had had much disdain for its work. Ultimately Casey's duplicity would become criminal and lead to the major scandal known as "Iran-Contra."

Throughout the presidential administrations that followed the Church committee, the breakdown of congressional oversight would continue. In December 2007, *Washington Post* writer David Ignatius wrote: "It seems clear that the system of congressional oversight that was established in the mid-1970's to supervise isn't working."

The blame rests on the leaders in both the executive and legislative branches, of course. But in the last analysis, it is the American body politic that bears ultimate responsibility for the conduct of its leaders. The great Anglo-Irish playwright George Bernard Shaw once observed that in a democracy people always get the kind of government they deserve. Nevertheless, democracies can be self-correcting, for as another great resident of the British Isles, Winston Churchill, also noted, Americans always do the right thing after they have exhausted all other alternatives.

Former senator Gary Hart, a member of the Church committee, writing in his memoirs, summed up the matter aptly: "All the good intentions in the world cannot make up for the wrong circumstances. The people of America possess much more power than they think. They just do not use it often enough. Lethargy, lack of concern, personal preoccupation, defeatism, and cynicism sap the power of protest. . . . Thus, the last and most basic lesson for reform in a democracy: reform does not take place when the public is apathetic. . . . The corollary of this principle is that reform will continue, deepen, and take root in direct proportion to continued public demand."

DOCUMENTS

Executive Summary, Alleged Assassination Plots Involving Foreign Leaders: An Interim Report, November 20, 1975

One of the most sensational investigations conducted by the Church committee involved CIA plots to assassinate foreign leaders such as Fidel Castro of Cuba, Patrice Lumumba of Congo, Rafael Trujillo of the Dominican Republic, Ngo Dinh Diem of South Vietnam, and others. In November 1975, the committee issued an interim report, excerpts of which follow. According to Frederick Schwarz, chief counsel of the committee, "It was vital to make the politicians and the American people really believe that reform was necessary. You couldn't speak in abstractions; you had to have something real and concrete." This the assassination report provided in memorable, horrifying detail.

EXECUTIVE SUMMARY, ALLEGED ASSASSINATION PLOTS INVOLVING FOREIGN LEADERS: AN INTERIM REPORT NOVEMBER 20, 1975

The evidence establishes that the United States was implicated in several assassination plots. The Committee believes that, short of war, assassination is incompatible with American principles, international order, and morality. It should be rejected as a tool of foreign policy.

Our inquiry also reveals serious problems with respect to United States involvement in coups directed against foreign governments. Some of these problems are addressed here on the basis of our investigation to date; others we raise as questions to be answered after our investigation into covert action has been completed.

We stress the interim nature of this report. In the course of the Committee's continuing work, other alleged assassination plots may surface, and new evidence concerning the cases covered herein may come to light. However, it is the Committee's view that these cases have been developed in sufficient detail to clarify the issues which are at the heart of the Committee's mandate to recommend legislative and other reforms.

Thorough treatment of the assassination question has lengthened the Committee's schedule, but has greatly increased the Committee's awareness of the hard issues it must face in the months ahead. These issues include problems of domestic and foreign intelligence collection, counterintelligence, foreign covert operations, mechanisms of command and control, and assessment of the effectiveness of the total United States intelligence effort. The Committee intends, nevertheless, to complete, by February 1976, its main job of undertaking the first comprehensive review of the intelligence community.

A. Committee's Mandate

Senate Resolution 21 instructs the Committee to investigate the full range of governmental intelligence activities and the extent, if any, to which such activities were "illegal, improper, or unethical." In addition to that broad general mandate, the Committee is required to investigate, study, and make recommendations concerning various specific matters, several of which relate to the assassination issue.

Although the Rockefeller Commission initiated an inquiry into reported assassination plots, the Commission declared it was unable, for a variety of reasons, to complete the inquiry. At the direction of the President, the Executive Branch turned over to the Select Committee the work the Commission had done, along with certain other documents relating to assassination.

B. Committee Decision to Make Report Public

This report raises important questions of national policy. We believe that the public is entitled to know what instrumentalities of their Government have done. Further, our recommendations can only be judged in light of the factual record. Therefore, this interim report should be made public.

The Committee believes the truth about the assassination allegations should be told because democracy depends upon a well-informed electorate. We reject any contention that the facts disclosed in this report should be kept secret because they are embarrassing to the United States. Despite the temporary injury to our national reputation, the Committee believes that foreign peoples will, upon sober reflection, respect the United States more for keeping faith with its democratic ideal than they will condemn us for the misconduct revealed. We doubt that any other country would have the courage to make such disclosures.

The fact that portions of the story have already been made public only accentuates the need for full disclosure. Innuendo and misleading partial disclosures are not fair to the individuals involved. Nor are they a responsible way to lay the groundwork for informed public policy judgments.

C. Scope of Committee's Investigation

Investigating the assassination issue has been an unpleasant duty, but one that the Committee had to meet. The Committee has compiled a massive record in the months that the inquiry has been underway. The record comprises over 8,000 pages of sworn testimony taken from over 75 witnesses during 60 hearing days and numerous staff interviews. The documents which the Committee has obtained include raw files from agencies and departments, the White House, and the Presidential libraries of the Administrations of former Presidents Dwight Eisenhower, John Kennedy, and Lyndon Johnson.

We have obtained two types of evidence: *first,* evidence relating to the general setting in which the events occurred, the national policy of the time, and the normal operating procedures, including channels of command and control: and *second,* evidence relating to the specific events.

A Senate Committee is not a court. It looks to the past, not to determine guilt or innocence, but in order to make recommendations for the future. When we found the evidence to be ambiguous—as we did on some issues—we have set out both sides, in order that the evidence may speak for itself.

Despite the number of witnesses and documents examined by the Committee, the available evidence has certain shortcomings.

Many of the events considered occurred as long as fifteen years ago. With one exception, they occurred during the administrations of Presidents now dead. Other high officials whose testimony might have shed additional light on the thorny issues of authorization and control are also dead. Moreover, with the passage of time, the memories of those still alive have dimmed.

The Committee has often faced the difficult task of distinguishing refreshed recollection from speculation. In many instances, witnesses were unable to testify from independent recollection and had to rely on documents contemporaneous with the events to refresh their recollections. While informed speculation is of some assistance, it can only be assigned limited weight in judging specific events.

Although assassination is not a subject on which one would expect many records or documents to be made or retained, there were, in fact, more relevant contemporaneous documents than expected. In addition, in 1967 the Central Intelligence Agency had made an internal study of the Castro, Trujillo and Diem assassination allegations. That study was quite useful, particularly in suggesting leads for uncovering the story of the actual assassination activity. Unfortunately, the working papers relating to that investigation were destroyed upon the completion of the Report pursuant to instructions from CIA Director Richard Helms. . . . These notes were destroyed because of their sensitivity and because the information they contained had already been incorporated into the Report. In fairness to Director Helms, it should be added, however, that he was responsible for requesting the preparation of the Inspector General's Report and for preserving the Report.

Some ambiguities in the evidence result from the practice of concealing CIA covert operations from the world and performing them in such a way that if discovered, the role of the United States could be plausibly denied. An extension of the doctrine of "plausible deniability" has the result that communications between the Agency and high Administration officials were often convoluted and imprecise.

The evidence contains sharp conflicts, some of which relate to basic facts. But the most important conflicts relate not so much to basic facts as to differing perceptions and opinions based upon relatively undisputed facts. With respect to both kinds of conflicts, the Committee has attempted to set forth the evidence extensively to that it may speak for itself. . . . However, because the Committee's main task is to find lessons for the future, resolving conflicts in the evidence may be less important than making certain that the system which produced the ambiguities is corrected.

D. Summary of Findings and Conclusions

1. The Questions Presented

The Committee sought to answer four broad questions:

Assassination plots—Did the United States officials instigate, attempt, aid and abet, or acquiesce in plots to assassinate foreign leaders?

Involvement in other killings—Did United States officials assist foreign dissidents in a way which significantly contributed to the killing of foreign leaders?

Authorization—Where there was involvement by United States officials in assassination plots or other killings, were such activities authorized, and if so, at what levels of Government?

Communication and control—Even if not authorized in fact, were the assassination activities perceived by those involved to be within the scope of their lawful authority? If they were so perceived, was there inadequate control exercised by higher authorities over the agencies to prevent such misinterpretation?

2. Summary of Findings and Conclusions on the Plots

The Committee investigated alleged United States involvement in assassination plots in five foreign countries:

Country	Individual involved
Cuba	Fidel Castro
Congo (Zaire)	Patrice Lumumba
Dominican Republic	Rafael Trujillo
Chile	General Rene Schneider
South Vietnam	Ngo Dinh Diem

The evidence concerning each alleged assassination can be summarized as follows:

Patrice Lumumba (Congo/Zaire)—In the Fall of 1960, two CIA officials were asked by superiors to assassinate Lumumba. Poisons were sent to the Congo and some exploratory steps were taken toward gaining access to Lumumba. Subsequently, in early 1961, Lumumba was killed by Congolese rivals. It does not appear from the evidence that the United States was in any way involved in the killing.

Fidel Castro (Cuba)—United States Government personnel plotted to kill Castro from 1960 to 1965. American underworld figures and Cubans hostile to Castro were used in these plots and were provided encouragement and material support by the United States.

Rafael Trujillo (Dominican Republic)—Trujillo was shot by Dominican dissidents on May 31, 1961. From early in 1960 and continuing to the time of the assassination, the United States Government generally supported these dissidents. Some Government personnel were aware that the dissidents intended to kill Trujillo. Three pistols and three carbines were furnished by American officials, although a request for machine guns was later refused. There is conflicting evidence concerning whether the weapons were knowingly supplied for use in the assassination and whether any of them were present at the scene.

Ngo Dinh Diem (South Vietnam)—Diem and his brother, Nhu, were killed on November 2, 1963, in the course of a South Vietnamese General's coup. Although the United States Government supported the coup, there is no evidence that American officials favored the assassination. Indeed, it appears that the assassination of Diem was not part of the Generals' pre-coup planning but was instead a spontaneous act which occurred during the coup and was carried out without United States involvement or support.

General Rene Schneider (Chile)—On October 25, 1970, General Schneider died of gunshot wounds inflicted three days earlier while resisting a kidnap attempt. Schneider, as Commander-in-Chief of the Army and a constitutionalist opposed to military coups, was considered an obstacle in efforts to prevent Salvador Allende from assuming the office of President of Chile. The United States Government supported and sought to instigate a military coup to block Allende. U.S. officials supplied financial aid, machine guns and other equipment to various military figures who opposed Allende. Although the CIA continued to support coup plotters up to Schneider's shooting, the record indicates that the CIA had withdrawn active support of the group which carried out the actual kidnap attempt on October 22, which resulted in Schneider's death. Further, it does not appear that any of the equipment supplied by the CIA to coup plotters in Chile was used in the kidnapping. There is no evidence of a plan to kill Schneider or that United States officials specifically anticipated that Schneider would be shot during the abduction.

Assassination capability (Executive Action)—In addition to these five cases, the Committee has received evidence that ranking Government officials discussed, and may have authorized, the establishment within the CIA of a generalized assassination capability. During these discussions, the concept of assassination was not affirmatively disavowed.

Similarities and differences among the plots—The assassination plots all involved Third World countries, most of which were relatively small and none of which possessed great political or military strength. Apart from that similarity, there were significant differences among the plots:

(1) Whether United States officials initiated the plot, or were responding to requests of local dissidents for aid.

(2) Whether the plot was specifically intended to kill a foreign leader, or whether the leader's death was a reasonably foreseeable consequence of an attempt to overthrow the government.

The Castro and Lumumba cases are examples of plots conceived by United States officials to kill foreign leaders.

In the Trujillo case, although the United States Government certainly opposed his regime, it did not initiate the plot. Rather, United States officials responded to requests for aid from local dissidents whose aim clearly was to assassinate Trujillo. By aiding them, this country was implicated in the assassination, regardless of whether the weapons actually supplied were meant to kill Trujillo or were only intended as symbols of support for the dissidents.

The Schneider case differs from the Castro and Trujillo cases. The United States Government, with full knowledge that Chilean dissidents considered General Schneider an obstacle to their plans, sought a coup and provided support to the dissidents. However, even though the support included weapons, it appears that the intention of both the dissidents and the United States officials was to abduct General Schneider, not to kill him. Similarly, in the Diem case, some United States officials wanted Diem removed and supported a coup to accomplish his removal, but there is no evidence that any of those officials sought the death of Diem himself.

3. Summary of Findings and Conclusions on the Issues of Authority and Control

To put the inquiry into assassination allegations in context, two points must be made clear. First, there is no doubt that the United States Government opposed the various leaders in question. Officials at the highest levels objected to the Castro and Trujillo regimes, believed that the accession of Allende to power in Chile would be harmful to American interests, and thought of Lumumba as a dangerous force in the heart of Africa. Second, the evidence on assassination has to be viewed in the context of other, more massive activities against the regimes in question. For example, the plots against Fidel Castro personally cannot be understood without considering the fully authorized comprehensive assaults upon his regime, such as the Bay of Pigs invasion in 1961 and Operation MONGOOSE in 1962.

Once methods of coercion and violence are chosen, the probability of loss of life is always present. There is, however, a significant difference between a coldblooded, targeted, intentional killing of an individual foreign leader and other forms of intervening in the affairs of foreign nations. Therefore, the Committee has endeavored to explore as fully as possible the questions how and why the plots happened, whether they were authorized, and if so, at what level.

The picture that emerges from the evidence is not a clear one. This may be due to the system of deniability and the consequent state of the evidence which, even after our long investigation, remains conflicting and inconclusive. Or it may be that there were in fact serious shortcomings in the system of authorization so that an activity such as assassination could have been undertaken by an agency of the United States Government without express authority.

The Committee finds that the system of executive command and control was so ambiguous that it is difficult to be certain at what levels assassination activity was known and authorized. This situation creates the disturbing prospect that Government officials might have undertaken the assassination plots without it having been uncontrovertibly clear that there was explicit authorization from the President. It is also possible that there might have been a successful "plausible denial" in which Presidential authorization was issued but is now obscured. Whether or not the respective Presidents knew of or authorized the plots, as chief executive officer of the United States, each must bear the ultimate responsibility for the activities of his subordinates . . .

While we are critical of certain individual actions, the Committee is also mindful of the inherent problems in a system which relies on secrecy, compartmentalization, circumlocution, and the avoidance of clear responsibility. This system creates the risk of confusion and rashness in the very areas where clarity and sober judgment are most necessary.

Source: Washington, DC: USGPO, 1975. Available at http://www.maryferrell.org/mffweb/archive/viewer/showDoc.do?absPageId=147818.

Excerpt from Church Committee Report on Covert Action in Chile, 1963–73, December 18, 1975

In 1970 a physician named Salvador Allende, running as a socialist, was elected president of Chile. The CIA had deeply influenced Chilean politics in the past, but Allende's unlikely victory, achieved with 36 percent of the vote against a number of other candidates, provoked the Nixon administration to attempt to prevent his inauguration through a military coup. It failed, and Allende took office. Through the first years of Allende's presidency, the United States began, through covert action, to work toward destabilizing the Chilean economy by funding opposition political groups and encouraging a military coup. It trained opposition military leaders in guerrilla warfare and helped to fan street demonstrations against the government. In September 1973, the military launched an attack against civilian authority. Allende either was assassinated or committed suicide while defending (with an assault rifle) his socialist government against the coup. In late 1975, the Church committee released its report, "Covert Action in Chile, 1963–1973."

EXCERPT FROM CHURCH COMMITTEE REPORT ON COVERT ACTION IN CHILE, 1963–73 DECEMBER 18, 1975

CONGRESSIONAL OVERSIGHT

With regard to covert action in Chile between April 1964 and December 1974, CIA's consultation with its Congressional oversight committees—and thus Congress' exercise of its oversight function—was inadequate. The CIA did not volunteer detailed information; Congress most often did not seek it.

Beginning in 1973, numerous public allegations were made concerning activities undertaken by the CIA in Chile. In response, Congress began to assume greater control in the exercise of its oversight function—which it had badly neglected in the past—both in the number and depth of consultations with the Central Intelligence Agency. Prior to 1973 there were twenty meetings between Congressional committees and the CIA regarding Chile; these meetings were held with the House and Senate Armed Services and Appropriation Committees in their Intelligence Subcommittees. From March 1973 to December 1974 there were thirteen meetings held not only with these Committees, but also before the Senate Foreign Relations Subcommittee on Multinational Corporations and the House Foreign Affairs Subcommittee on Inter-American Affairs.

Based on CIA records, there was a total of fifty-three CIA Congressional briefings on Chile between 1964 and 1974. At thirty-one of these meetings, there was some discussion of covert action; special releases of funds for covert action were discussed at twenty-three of them. After January 1973 these briefings were concerned with past CIA covert activity. From information currently in the possession of the Committee and public sources, several tentative conclusions emerge: on several important occasions the CIA did not report on covert action until quite long after the fact; and in one case—Track II—it omitted discussion of an important, closely held operation, but one whose outcome reverberated on the foreign policy of the United States and carried implications for domestic affairs as well.

Of the thirty-three covert action projects undertaken in Chile with 40 Committee [executive branch review panel on covert operations] approval during the period 1963–1974, Congress was briefed in some fashion on eight. Presumably the twenty-five others were undertaken without Congressional consultation. These twenty-five projects included: the $1.2 million authorization in 1971, half of which was spent to purchase radio stations and newspapers while the other half went to support municipal candidates and anti-Allende political parties; and the additional expenditure of $815,000 in late 1971 to provide support to opposition parties.

Of the total of over thirteen million dollars actually spent by the CIA on covert action operations in Chile between 1963 and 1974, Congress received some kind of briefing (sometimes before, sometimes after the fact) on projects totaling about 7.1 million dollars. Further, Congressional oversight committees were not consulted about projects which were not reviewed by the full 40 Committee. One of these was the Track II attempt to foment a military coup in 1970. The other—a later CIA project involving contacts with Chilean military officers—was an intelligence collection project and thus did not come before the 40 Committee, even though in this instance the political importance of the project was clear.

Preliminary Conclusions

Underlying all discussion of American interference in the internal affairs of Chile is the basic question of why the United States initially mounted such an extensive covert action program in Chile—and why it continued, and even expanded, in the early 1970s.

Covert action has been a key element of U.S. foreign policy toward Chile. The link between covert action and foreign policy was obvious throughout the decade between 1964 and 1974. In 1964, the United States commitment to democratic reform via the Alliance for Progress and overt foreign aid was buttressed via covert support for the election of the candidate of the Christian Democratic party, a candidate and a party for which the Alliance seemed tailor made. During 1970 the U.S. Government tried, covertly, to prevent Allende from becoming President of Chile. When that failed, covert support to his opposition formed one of a triad of official actions: covert aid to opposition forces, "cool but correct" diplomatic posture, and economic pressure. From support of what the United States considered to be democratic and progressive forces in Chile we had moved finally to advocating and encouraging the overthrow of a democratically elected government.

Covert Action and U.S. Foreign Policy.

In 1964, the United States became massively involved in covert activity in Chile. This involvement was seen by U.S. policymakers as consistent with overall American foreign policy and the goals of the Alliance for Progress. The election of a moderate left candidate in Chile was a cornerstone of U.S. policy toward Latin America.

It is unclear from the record whether the 1964 election project was intended to be a one-time intervention in support of a good cause. It is clear that the scale of the involvement generated commitments and expectations on both sides. For the United States, it created assets and channels of funding which could be used again. For the Chilean groups receiving CIA funds, that funding became an expectation, counted upon. Thus, when opposition to Allende became the primary objective of covert action in 1970, the structure for covert action developed through covert assistance to political parties in 1964 was well established.

A fundamental question raised by the pattern of U.S. covert activities persists: *Did the threat to vital U.S. national security interests posed by the Presidency of Salvador Allende justify the several major covert attempts to prevent his accession to power?* Three American Presidents and their senior advisors evidently thought so.

One rationale for covert intervention in Chilean politics was spelled out by Henry Kissinger in his background briefing to the press on September 16, 1970, the day after Nixon's meeting with Helms. He argued that an Allende victory would be irreversible within Chile, might affect neighboring nations and would pose "massive problems" for the U.S. in Latin America.

> I have yet to meet somebody who firmly believes that if Allende wins, there is likely to be another free election in Chile. . . . Now it is fairly easy for one to predict that if Allende wins, there is a good chance that he will establish over a period of years some sort of communist government. In that case, we would have one not on an island off the coast (Cuba) which has not a traditional relationship and impact on Latin America, but in a major Latin American country you would have a communist government, joining, for example, Argentina . . . Peru . . . and Bolivia. . . . So I don't think we should delude ourselves on an Allende takeover and Chile would not present massive problems for us, and for democratic forces and for pro-U.S. forces in Latin America, and indeed to the whole Western Hemisphere.

Another rationale for U.S. involvement in the internal affairs of Chile was offered by a high-ranking official who testified before the Committee. He spoke of Chile's position in a worldwide strategic chess game in 1970. In this analogy, Portugal might be a bishop, Chile a couple of pawns, perhaps more. In the worldwide strategic chess game, once a position was lost, a series of consequences followed. U.S. enemies would proceed to exploit the new opportunity, and our ability to cope with the challenge would be limited by any American loss.

Executive Command and Control of Major Covert Action.

In pursuing the Chilean chess game, particularly the efforts to prevent Allende's accession to power or his maintaining power once elected, Executive command and control of major covert action was tight and well directed. Procedures within the CIA for controlling the programs were well defined and the procedures made Station officials accountable to their supervisors in Washington. Unilateral actions on the part of the Station were virtually impossible.

But the central issue of command and control is *Accountability:* procedures for insuring that covert actions are and remain accountable both to the senior political and foreign policy officials of the Executive Branch and to the Congress.

The record of covert activities in Chile suggests that, although established executive processes of authorization and control were generally adhered to, there were—and remain—genuine shortcomings to these processes:

Decisions about WHICH covert action projects are submitted to the 40 Committee were and are made within the CIA on the basis of the Agency's determination of the political sensitivity of a project.

The form in which covert action projects were cleared with Ambassadors and other State Department officials varied. It depended—and still depends—on how interested Ambassadors are and how forthcoming their Station Chiefs are.

Once major projects are approved by the 40 Committee, they often continue without searching re-examination by the Committee. The Agency conducts annual reviews of on-going projects, but the 40 Committee does not undertake a review unless a project is recommended for renewal, or there is some important change in content or amount.

There is also the problem of controlling clandestine projects not labeled "covert action." Clandestine collection of human intelligence is *not* the subject of 40 Committee review. But those projects may be just as politically sensitive as a "covert action"; witness U.S. contacts with the Chilean military during 1970–73. Similarly, for security reasons, ambassadors generally know CIA assets only by general description, not by name. That practice may be acceptable, provided the description is detailed enough to inform the ambassador of the risk posed by the development of a particular asset and to allow the ambassador to decide whether or not that asset should be used.

There remains the question of the dangers which arise when the very mechanisms established by the Executive Branch for insuring internal accountability are circumvented or frustrated.

By Presidential instruction, Track II was to be operated without informing the U.S. Ambassador in Santiago, the State Department, or any 40 Committee member save Henry Kissinger. The President and his senior advisors thus denied themselves the Government's major sources of counsel about Chilean politics. And the Ambassador in Santiago was left in the position of having to deal with any adverse political spillover from a project of which he was not informed.

The danger was greater still. Whatever the truth about communication between the CIA and the White House after October 15, 1970—an issue which is the subject of conflicting testimony—all participants agreed that Track II constituted a broad mandate to the CIA. The Agency was given to believe it had virtual *carte blanche* authority; moreover, it felt under extreme pressure to prevent Allende from coming to power, by military coup if necessary. It was given little guidance about what subsequent clearances it needed to obtain from the White House. Under these conditions, CIA consultation with the White House in advance of specific actions was less than meticulous.

The Role of the Congress.

In the hands of Congress rests the responsibility for insuring that the Executive Branch is held to full political accountability for covert activities. The record on Chile is mixed and muted by its incompleteness.

CIA records note a number of briefings of Congressional committees about covert action in Chile. Those records, however, do not reveal the timeliness or the level of detail of these briefings. Indeed, the record suggests that the briefings were often after the fact and incomplete. The situation improved after 1973, apparently as Congressional committees became more persistent in the exercise of their oversight function. Furthermore, Sec. 662 of the Foreign Assistance Act should make it impossible for major projects to be operated without the appropriate Congressional committees being informed.

The record leaves unanswered a number of questions. These pertain both to how forthcoming the Agency was and how interested and persistent the Congressional committees were. Were members of Congress, for instance, given the opportunity to object to specific projects before the projects were implemented? Did they want to? There is also an issue of jurisdiction. CIA and State Department officials have taken the position that they are authorized to reveal Agency operations only to the appropriate oversight committees.

Intelligence Judgements and Covert Operations.

A review of the intelligence judgements on Chile offered by U.S. analysts during the critical period from 1970–1973 has *not* established whether these judgements were taken into account when U.S. policy-makers formulated and approved U.S. covert operations. This examination of the relevant intelligence estimates and memoranda has established that the judgements of the analysts suggested caution and restraint while the political imperatives demanded action.

Even within the Central Intelligence Agency, processes for bringing considered judgements of intelligence analysts to bear on proposed covert actions were haphazard—and generally ineffective. This situation has improved; covert action proposals now regularly come before the Deputy Director for Intelligence and the appropriate National Intelligence Officer; but the operators still are separated from the intelligence analysts, those whose exclusive business it is to understand and predict foreign politics. For instance, the analysts who drafted the government's most prestigious intelligence analyses—NIEs—may not even have known of U.S. covert actions in Chile.

The Chilean experience does suggest that the Committee give serious consideration to the possibility that lodging the responsibility for national estimates AND conduct of operational activities with the same person—the Director of Central Intelligence—creates an inherent conflict of interest and judgement.

Effects of Major Covert Action Programs.

Covert Action programs as costly and as complex as several mounted by the United States in Chile are unlikely to remain covert. In Chile in 1964, there was simply too much unexplained money, too many leaflets, too many broadcasts. That the United States was involved in the election has been taken for granted in Latin America for many years.

The involvement in 1964 created a presumption in Chile and elsewhere in Latin America that the United States Government would again be involved in 1970. This made secrecy still harder to maintain, even though the CIA involvement was much smaller in 1970 than it had been in 1964.

When covert actions in Chile became public knowledge, the costs were obvious. The United States was seen, by its covert actions, to have contradicted not only its official declarations but its treaty commitments and principles of long standing. At the same time it was proclaiming a "low profile" in Latin American relations, the U.S. Government was seeking to foment a coup in Chile.

The costs of major covert ventures which are "blown" are clear enough. But there may be costs to pay even if the operations could remain secret for long periods of time. Some of these costs may accrue even within the calculus of covert operations: successes may turn to failures. Several officials from whom the Committee took testimony suggested that the poor showing of the Chilean Christian Democrats [PDC] in 1970 was, in some part, attributable to previous American covert support. Of course there were many causes of that poor showing, but in 1964 the PDC had been spared the need of developing some of its own grass roots organizations. The CIA did much of that for it. In 1970, with less CIA activity on behalf of the Christian Democratic Party, the PDC faltered.

Of course, the more important costs, even of covert actions which remain secret, are those to American ideals of relations among nations and of constitutional government. In the case of Chile, some of those costs were far from abstract: witness the involvement of United States military officers in the Track II attempt to overthrow a constitutionally-elected civilian government.

There are also long-term effects of covert actions. Many of those may be adverse. They touch American as well as foreign institutions. The Chilean institutions that the United States most favored may have been discredited within their own societies by the fact of their covert support. In Latin America particularly, even the suspicion of CIA support may be the kiss of death. It would be the final irony of a decade of covert action in Chile if that action destroyed the credibility of the Chilean Christian Democrats.

The effects on American institutions are less obvious but no less important. U.S. private and governmental institutions with overt, legitimate purposes of their own may have been discredited by the pervasiveness of covert action. Even if particular institutions were not involved in covert action, they may have been corrupted in the perception of Latin Americans because of the pervasiveness of clandestine U.S. activity.

In the end, the whole of U.S. policy making may be affected. The availability of an "extra" means may alter officials' assessment of the costs and rationales of overt policies. It may postpone the day when outmoded policies are abandoned and new ones adopted. Arguably, the 1964 election project was part of a "progressive" approach to Chile. The project was justified, if perhaps not actually sustained, by the desire to elect democratic reformers. By 1970, covert action had become completely defensive in character: to prevent the election of Allende. The United States professed a "low profile" but at the same time acted covertly to ensure that the Chilean elections came out right, "low profile" notwithstanding.

A special case for concern is the relationship between intelligence agencies and multinational corporations.

In 1970, U.S. Government policy prohibited covert CIA support to a single party or candidate. At the same time, the CIA provided advice to an American-based multinational corporation on how to furnish just such direct support. That raised all of the dangers of exposure, and eliminated many of the safeguards and controls normally present in exclusively CIA covert operations. There was the appearance of an improperly close relationship between the CIA and multinational companies when former Director John McCone used contacts and information gained while at the CIA to advise a corporation on whose Board of Directors he sat. This appearance was heightened because the contacts between the Agency and the corporation in 1970 extended to discussing and even planning corporate intervention in the Chilean electoral process.

The problem of cooperation is exacerbated when a cooperating company—such as ITT [International Telephone & Telegraph Co.]—is called to give testimony before an appropriate Congressional Committee. The Agency may then be confronted with the question of whether to come forward to set the record straight when it believes that testimony given on behalf of a cooperating company is untrue. The situation is difficult, for in coming forward the Agency may reveal sensitive sources and methods by which it learned the facts or may make public the existence of ongoing covert operations.

This report does not attempt to offer a final judgement on the political propriety, the morality, or even the effectiveness of American covert activity in Chile. Did the threat posed by an Allende presidency justify covert American involvement in Chile? Did it justify the specific and unusual attempt to foment a military coup to deny Allende the presidency? In 1970, the U.S. sought to foster a military coup in Chile to prevent Allende's accession to power; yet after 1970 the government—according to the testimony of its officials—did not engage in coup plotting. Was 1970 a mistake, an aberration? Or was the threat posed to the national security interests of the United States so grave that the government was remiss in not seeking his downfall directly during 1970–73? What responsibility does the United States bear for the cruelty and political suppression that have become the hallmark of the present regime in Chile?

On these questions Committee members may differ. So may American citizens. Yet the Committee's mandate is less to judge the past than to recommend for the future. Moving from past cases to future guidelines, what is important to note is that covert action has been perceived as middle ground between diplomatic representation and the overt use of military force. In the case of Chile, that middle ground may have been far too broad. Given the costs of covert action, it should be resorted to only to counter severe threats to the national security of the United States. It is far from clear that that was the case in Chile.

Source: http://foia.state.gov/Reports/ChurchReport.asp#C.TheRoleoftheCongress.

President Gerald R. Ford's Special Message to Congress Proposing Legislation to Reform the United States Foreign Intelligence Community, February 18, 1976

As the work of Church committee continued to reveal past misdeeds by U.S. intelligence agencies, President Gerald Ford, attempting to get in front of the political whirlwind, announced at a news conference on February 17, 1976, and in a message to the Congress on the following day that he was signing an executive order for the first major reorganization of the intelligence community since 1947. He said he was guided by two imperatives: that as Americans "we must not and will not tolerate actions by our Government which will abrogate the rights of our citizens," but at the same time "we must maintain an effective intelligence capability." In his message to Congress, he also proposed reform legislation. Although Ford's actions were positive steps, they did not slow down the work of the Church committee.

PRESIDENT GERALD R. FORD'S SPECIAL MESSAGE TO CONGRESS PROPOSING LEGISLATION TO REFORM THE UNITED STATES FOREIGN INTELLIGENCE COMMUNITY FEBRUARY 18, 1976

To the Congress of the United States:

By virtue of the authority vested in me by Article II, Section 2 and 3 of the Constitution, and other provisions of law, I have today issued an Executive Order [11905] pertaining to the organization and control of the United States foreign intelligence community. This order establishes clear lines of accountability for the Nation's foreign intelligence agencies. It sets forth strict guidelines to control the activities of these agencies and specifies as well those activities in which they shall not engage.

In carrying out my constitutional responsibilities to manage and conduct foreign policy and provide for the Nation's defense, I believe it essential to have the best possible intelligence about the capabilities, intentions and activities of governments and other entities and individuals abroad. To this end, the foreign intelligence agencies of the United States play a vital role in collecting and analyzing information related to the national defense and foreign policy.

It is equally as important that the methods these agencies employ to collect such information for the legitimate needs of the government conform to the standards set out in the Constitution to preserve and respect the privacy and civil liberties of American citizens.

The Executive Order I have issued today will insure a proper balancing of these interests. It establishes government-wide direction for the foreign intelligence agencies and places responsibility and accountability on individuals, not institutions.

I believe it will eliminate abuses and questionable activities on the part of the foreign intelligence agencies while at the same time permitting them to get on with their vital work of gathering and assessing information. It is also my hope that these steps will help to restore public confidence in these agencies and encourage our citizens to appreciate the valuable contribution they make to our national security.

Beyond the steps I have taken in the Executive Order, I also believe there is a clear need for some specific legislative actions. I am today submitting to the Congress of the United States proposals which will go far toward enhancing the protection of true intelligence secrets as well as regularizing procedures for intelligence collection in the United States.

My first proposal deals with the protection of intelligence sources and methods. The Director of Central Intelligence is charged, under the National Security Act of 1947, as amended, with protecting intelligence sources and methods. The Act, however, gives the Director no authorities commensurate with this responsibility.

Therefore, I am proposing legislation to impose criminal and civil sanctions on those who are authorized access to intelligence secrets and who willfully and wrongfully reveal this information. This legislation is not an "Official Secrets Act," since it would affect only those who improperly disclose secrets, not those to whom secrets are disclosed. Moreover, this legislation could not be used to cover up abuses and improprieties. It would in no way prevent people from reporting questionable activities to appropriate authorities in the Executive and Legislative Branches of the government.

It is essential, however, that the irresponsible and dangerous exposure of our Nation's intelligence secrets be stopped. The American people have long accepted the principles of confidentiality and secrecy in many dealings—such as with doctors, lawyers and the clergy. It makes absolutely no sense to deny this same protection to our intelligence secrets. Openness is a hallmark of our democratic society, but the American people have never believed that it was necessary to reveal the secret war plans of the Department of Defense, and I do not think they wish to have true intelligence secrets revealed either.

I urge the adoption of this legislation with all possible speed.

Second, I support proposals that would clarify and set statutory limits, where necessary, on the activities of the foreign intelligence agencies. In particular, I will support legislation making it a crime to assassinate or attempt or conspire to assassinate a foreign official in peacetime. Since it defines a crime, legislation is necessary.

Third, I will meet with the appropriate leaders of Congress to try to develop sound legislation to deal with a critical problem involving personal privacy—electronic surveillance. Working with Congressional leaders and the Justice Department and other Executive agencies, we will seek to develop a procedure for undertaking electronic surveillance for foreign intelligence purposes. It should create a special procedure for seeking a Judicial warrant authorizing the use of electronic surveillance in the United States for foreign intelligence purposes.

I will also seek Congressional support for sound legislation to expand judicial supervision of mail openings. The law now permits the opening of United States mail, under proper Judicial safeguards, in the conduct of criminal investigations. We need authority to open mail under the limitations and safeguards that now apply in order to obtain vitally needed foreign intelligence information.

This would require a showing that there is probably cause to believe that the sender or recipient is an agent of a foreign power who is engaged in spying, sabotage or terrorism. As is now the case the criminal investigations, those seeking authority to examine mail for foreign intelligence purposes[,] will have to convince a federal judge of the necessity to do so and accept the limitations upon their authorization to examine the mail provided in the order of the court.

Fourth, I would like to share my views regarding appropriate Congressional oversight of the foreign intelligence agencies. It is clearly the business of the Congress to organize itself to deal with these matters. Certain principles, however, should be recognized by both the Executive and Legislative Branches if this oversight is to be effective. I believe good Congressional oversight is essential so that the Congress and the American people whom you represent can be assured that the foreign intelligence agencies are adhering to the law in all of their activities.

Congress should seek to centralize the responsibility for oversight of the foreign intelligence community. The more committees and subcommittees dealing with highly sensitive secrets, the greater the risks of disclosure. I recommend that Congress establish a Joint Foreign Intelligence Oversight Committee. Consolidating Congressional oversight in one committee will facilitate the efforts of the Administration to keep the Congress fully informed of foreign intelligence activities.

It is essential that both the House and the Senate establish firm rules to insure that foreign intelligence secrets will not be improperly disclosed. There must be established a clear process to safeguard these secrets and effective measures deal with unauthorized disclosures.

Any foreign intelligence information transmitted by the Executive Branch to the Oversight Committee, under an injunction of secrecy, should not be unilaterally disclosed without my agreement. Respect for the integrity of the Constitution requires adherence to the principle that no individual member or committee, nor single House of Congress, can overrule an act of the Executive. Unilateral publication of classified information over the objection of the President, by one committee or one House of Congress, not only violates the doctrine of separation of powers, but also effectively overrules the actions of the other House of Congress, and perhaps even the majority of both Houses.

Finally, successful and effective Congressional oversight of the foreign intelligence agencies depends on mutual trust between the Congress and Executive. Each branch must recognize and respect the rights and prerogatives of the other if anything is to be achieved.

In this context, a Congressional requirement to keep the Oversight Committee "fully" informed is more desirable and workable as a practical matter than formal requirements for notification of specific activities to a large number of committees. Specifically, Section 662 of the Foreign Assistance Act, which has resulted in over six separate committee briefings, should be modified as recommended by the Commission on the Organization of the Government for the Conduct of Foreign Policy, and reporting should be limited to the new Oversight Committee.

Both the Congress and the Executive Branch recognize the importance to this Nation of a strong intelligence service. I believe it urgent that we take the steps I have outlined above to insure that America not only has the best foreign intelligence service in the world, but also the most unique—one which operates in a manner fully consistent with the Constitutional rights of our citizens.

Source: Gerald R. Ford. *Public Papers of the Presidents of the United States: Gerald R. Ford, 1976–77.* Vol. I. Washington, D.C.: Government Printing Office, 1979, pp. 362–66. Available at http://www.ford.utexas.edu/LIBRARY/speeches/760110.htm.

Excerpt from Final Report of the Select Committee to Study Governmental Operations With Respect to Intelligence Activities, April 1976

In April 1976, the Church committee released the second volume of its multi-volume final report. One of the committee staff members, Loch Johnson, later wrote that the report provided "a rich lode of information about the dark side of government heretofore concealed from the American people." In laying out the record, the report concluded that "the major premise of the programs was that a law enforcement agency has the duty to do whatever is necessary to combat perceived threats to the existing social and political order." Such a theory, wrote historian Richard Gid Powers in his authoritative work on the FBI, raised the record of abuses to "a level of epic evil" and "into a conscious campaign against civil liberties in America."

EXCERPT FROM FINAL REPORT OF THE SELECT COMMITTEE, APRIL 1976

I. INTRODUCTION AND SUMMARY

The resolution creating this Committee placed greatest emphasis on whether intelligence activities threaten the "rights of American citizens."

The critical question before the Committee was to determine how the fundamental liberties of the people can be maintained in the course of the Government's effort to protect their security. The delicate balance between these basic goals of our system of government is often difficult to strike, but it can, and must, be achieved. We reject the view that the traditional American principles of justice and fair play have no place in our struggle against the enemies of freedom. Moreover, our investigation has established that the targets of intelligence activity have ranged far beyond persons who could properly be characterized as enemies of freedom and have extended to a wide array of citizens engaging in lawful activity.

Americans have rightfully been concerned since before World War II about the dangers of hostile foreign agents likely to commit acts of espionage. Similarly, the violent acts of political terrorists can seriously endanger the rights of Americans. Carefully focused intelligence investigations can help prevent such acts. But too often intelligence has lost this focus and domestic intelligence activities have invaded individual privacy and violated the rights of lawful assembly and political expression. Unless new and tighter controls are established by legislation, domestic intelligence activities threaten to undermine our democratic society and fundamentally alter its nature.

We have examined three types of "intelligence" activities affecting the rights of American citizens. The first is intelligence collection—such as infiltrating groups with informants, wiretapping, or opening letters. The second is dissemination of material which has been collected. The third is covert action designed to disrupt and discredit the activities of groups and individuals deemed a threat to the social order. These three types of "intelligence" activity are closely related in the practical world. Information which is disseminated by the intelligence community or used in disruptive programs has usually been obtained through surveillance. Nevertheless, a division between collection, dissemination and covert action is analytically useful both in understanding why excesses have occurred in the past and in devising remedies to prevent those excesses from recurring.

A. Intelligence Activity: A New Form of Governmental Power to Impair Citizens' Rights

A tension between order and liberty is inevitable in any society. A Government must protect its citizens from those bent on engaging in violence and criminal behavior, or in espionage and other hostile foreign intelligence activity. Many of the intelligence programs reviewed in this report were established for those purposes. Intelligence work has, at times, successfully prevented dangerous and abhorrent acts, such as bombings and foreign spying, and aided in the prosecution of those responsible for such acts.

But, intelligence activity in the past decades has, all too often, exceeded the restraints on the exercise of governmental power which are imposed by our country's Constitution, laws, and traditions.

Excesses in the name of protecting security are not a recent development in our nation's history. In 1798, for example, shortly after the Bill of Rights was added to the Constitution, the Alien and Sedition Acts were passed. These Acts, passed in response to fear of pro French "subversion," made it a crime to criticize the Government. During the Civil War, President Abraham Lincoln suspended the writ of habeas corpus. Hundreds of American citizens were prosecuted for anti-war statements during World War I, and thousands of "radical" aliens were seized for deportation during the 1920 Palmer Raids. During the Second World War, over the opposition of J. Edgar Hoover and military intelligence, 120,000 Japanese-Americans were apprehended and incarcerated in detention camps.

Those actions, however, were fundamentally different from the intelligence activities examined by this Committee. They were generally executed overtly under the authority of a statute or a public executive order. The victims knew what was being done to them and could challenge the Government in the courts and other forums. Intelligence activity, on the other hand, is generally covert. It is concealed from its victims and is seldom described in statutes or explicit executive orders. The victim may never suspect that his misfortunes are the intended result of activities undertaken by his government, and accordingly may have no opportunity to challenge the actions taken against him.

It is, of course, proper in many circumstances—such as developing a criminal prosecution—for the Government to gather information about a citizen and use it to achieve legitimate ends, some of which might be detrimental to the citizen. But in criminal prosecutions, the courts have struck a balance between protecting the rights of the accused citizen and protecting the society which suffers the consequences of crime. Essential to the balancing process are the rules of criminal law which circumscribe the techniques for gathering evidence, the kinds of evidence that may be collected, and the uses to which that evidence may be put. In addition, the criminal defendant is given an opportunity to discover and then challenge the legality of how the Government collected information about him and the use which the Government intends to make of that information.

This Committee has examined a realm of governmental information collection which has not been governed by restraints comparable to those in criminal proceedings. We have examined the collection of intelligence about the political advocacy and actions and the private lives of American citizens. That information has been used covertly to discredit the ideas advocated and to "neutralize" the actions of their proponents. As Attorney General Harlan Fiske Stone warned in 1924, when he sought to keep federal agencies from investigating "political or other opinions" as opposed to "conduct . . . forbidden by the laws": "When a police system passes beyond these limits, it is dangerous to the proper administration of justice and to human liberty, which it should be our first concern to cherish. . . . There is always a possibility that a secret police may become a menace to free government and free institutions because it carries with it the possibility of abuses of power which are not always quickly apprehended or understood."

Our investigation has confirmed that warning. We have seen segments of our Government, in their attitudes and action, adopt tactics unworthy of a democracy, and occasionally reminiscent of the tactics of totalitarian regimes. We have seen a consistent pattern in which programs initiated with limited goals, such as preventing criminal violence or identifying foreign spies, were expanded to what witnesses characterized as "vacuum cleaners," sweeping in information about lawful activities of American citizens.

The tendency of intelligence activities to expand beyond their initial scope is a theme which runs through every aspect of our investigative findings. Intelligence collection programs naturally generate ever-increasing demands for new data. And once intelligence has been collected, there are strong pressures to use it against the target.

The pattern of intelligence agencies expanding the scope of their activities was well described by one witness, who in 1970 had coordinated an effort by most of the intelligence community to obtain authority to undertake more illegal domestic activity:

> The risk was that you would get people who would be susceptible to political considerations as opposed to national security considerations, or would construe political considerations to be national security considerations, to move from the kid with a bomb to the kid with a picket sign, and from the kid with the picket sign to the kid with the bumper sticker of the opposing candidate. And you just keep going down the line.

In 1940, Attorney General Robert Jackson saw the same risk. He recognized that using broad labels like "national security" or "subversion" to invoke the vast power of the government is dangerous because there are "no definite standards to determine what constitutes a 'subversive activity,' such as we have for murder or larceny." Jackson added:

> Activities which seem benevolent or helpful to wage earners, persons on relief, or those who are disadvantaged in the struggle for existence may be regarded as "subversive" by those whose property interests might be burdened thereby. Those who are in office are apt to regard as "subversive" the activities of any of those who would bring about a change of administration. Some of our soundest constitutional doctrines were once punished as subversive. We must not forget that it was not so long ago that both the term "Republican" and the term "Democrat" were epithets with sinister meaning to denote persons of radical tendencies that were "subversive" of the order of things then dominant.

This wise warning was not heeded in the conduct of intelligence activity, where the "eternal vigilance" which is the "price of liberty" has been forgotten. . . .

B. The Questions

We have directed our investigation toward answering the following questions:

Which governmental agencies have engaged in domestic spying?

How many citizens have been targets of Governmental intelligence activity?

What standards have governed the opening of intelligence investigations and when have intelligence investigations been terminated?

Where have the targets fit on the spectrum between those who commit violent criminal acts and those who seek only to dissent peacefully from Government policy?

To what extent has the information collected included intimate details of the targets' personal lives or their political views, and has such information been disseminated and used to injure individuals?

What actions beyond surveillance have intelligence agencies taken, such as attempting to disrupt, discredit, or destroy persons or groups who have been the targets of surveillance?

Have intelligence agencies been used to serve the political aims of Presidents, other high officials, or the agencies themselves?

How have the agencies responded either to proper orders or to excessive pressures from their superiors? To what extent have intelligence agencies disclosed, or concealed them from, outside bodies charged with overseeing them?

Have intelligence agencies acted outside the law? What has been the attitude of the intelligence community toward the rule of law?

To what extent has the Executive branch and the Congress controlled intelligence agencies and held them accountable?

Generally, how well has the Federal system of checks and balances between the branches worked to control intelligence activity?

C. Summary of the Main Problems

The answer to each of these questions is disturbing. Too many people have been spied upon by too many Government agencies and too much information has been collected. The Government has often undertaken the secret surveillance of citizens on the basis of their political beliefs, even when those beliefs posed no threat of violence or illegal acts on behalf of a hostile foreign power.

The Government, operating primarily through secret informants, but also using other intrusive techniques such as wiretaps, microphone "bugs," surreptitious mail opening, and break-ins, has swept in vast amounts of information about the personal lives, views, and associations of American citizens. Investigations of groups deemed potentially dangerous—and even of groups suspected of associating with potentially dangerous organizations—have continued for decades, despite the fact that those groups did not engage in unlawful activity. Groups and individuals have been harassed and disrupted because of their political views and their lifestyles. Investigations have been based upon vague standards whose breadth made excessive collection inevitable. Unsavory and vicious tactics have been employed—including anonymous attempts to break up marriages, disrupt meetings, ostracize persons from their professions, and provoke target groups into rivalries that might result in deaths. Intelligence agencies have served the political and personal objectives of presidents and other high officials. While the agencies often committed excesses in response to pressure from high officials in the Executive branch and Congress, they also occasionally initiated improper activities and then concealed them from officials whom they had a duty to inform.

Governmental officials—including those whose principal duty is to enforce the law—have violated or ignored the law over long periods of time and have advocated and defended their right to break the law.

The Constitutional system of checks and balances has not adequately controlled intelligence activities. Until recently the Executive branch has neither delineated the scope of permissible activities nor established procedures for supervising intelligence agencies. Congress has failed to exercise sufficient oversight, seldom questioning the use to which its appropriations were being put. Most domestic intelligence issues have not reached the courts, and in those cases when they have reached the courts, the judiciary has been reluctant to grapple with them.

Each of these points is briefly illustrated below, and covered in substantially greater detail in the following sections of the report.

1. The Number of People Affected by Domestic Intelligence Activity

United States intelligence agencies have investigated a vast number of American citizens and domestic organizations. FBI headquarters alone has developed over 500,000 domestic intelligence files, and these have been augmented by additional files at FBI Field Offices. The FBI opened 65,000 of these domestic intelligence files in 1972 alone. In fact, substantially more individuals and groups are subject to intelligence scrutiny than the number of files would appear to indicate, since typically, each domestic intelligence file contains information on more than one individual or group, and this information is readily retrievable through the FBI General Name Index.

The number of Americans and domestic groups caught in the domestic intelligence net is further illustrated by the following statistics:

- Nearly a quarter of a million first class letters were opened and photographed in the United States by the CIA between 1953–1973, producing a CIA computerized index of nearly one and one-half million names.
- At least 130,000 first class letters were opened and photographed by the FBI between 1940–1966 in eight U.S. cities.
- Some 300,000 individuals were indexed in a CIA computer system and separate files were created on approximately 7,200 Americans and over 100 domestic groups during the course of CIA's Operation CHAOS (1967–1973).
- Millions of private telegrams sent from, to, or through the United States were obtained by the National Security Agency from 1947 to 1975 under a secret arrangement with three United States telegraph companies.
- An estimated 100,000 Americans were the subjects of United States Army intelligence files created between the mid 1960's and 1971.
- Intelligence files on more than 11,000 individuals and groups were created by the Internal Revenue Service between 1969 and 1973 and tax investigations were started on the basis of political rather than tax criteria.
- At least 26,000 individuals were at one point catalogued on an FBI list of persons to be rounded up in the event of a "national emergency."

2. Too Much Information Is Collected for Too Long

Intelligence agencies have collected vast amounts of information about the intimate details of citizens' lives and about their participation in legal and peaceful political activities. The targets of intelligence activity have included political adherents of the right and the left, ranging from activists to casual supporters. Investigations have been directed against proponents of racial causes and women's rights; outspoken apostles of nonviolence and racial harmony; establishment politicians; religious groups; and advocates of new life styles. The widespread targeting of citizens and domestic groups, and the excessive scope of the collection of information, is illustrated by the following examples:

(a) The "Women's Liberation Movement" was infiltrated by informants who collected material about the movement's policies, leaders, and individual members. One report included the name of every woman who attended meetings, and another stated that each woman at a meeting had described "how she felt oppressed, sexually or otherwise."

Another report concluded that the movement's purpose was to "free women from the humdrum existence of being only a wife and mother," but still recommended that the intelligence investigation should be continued.

(b) A prominent civil rights leader and advisor to Dr. Martin Luther, Jr., was investigated on the suspicion that he might be a Communist "sympathizer." The FBI field office concluded he was not. Bureau headquarters directed that the investigation continue using a theory of "guilty until proven innocent":

> The Bureau does not agree with the expressed belief of the field office that - - - - - - - - - - - - - - - - - - is not sympathetic to the Party cause. While there may not be any evidence that - - - - - - - - - - - - - - - - - - is a Communist neither is there any substantial evidence that he is anti-Communist.

(c) FBI sources reported on the formation of the Conservative American Christian Action Council in 1971. In the 1950's, the Bureau collected information about the John Birch Society and passed it to the White House because of the Society's "scurillous attack" on President Eisenhower and other high Government officials.

(d) Some investigations of the lawful activities of peaceful groups have continued for decades. For example, the NAACP was investigated to determine whether it "had connections with" the Communist Party. The investigation lasted for over twenty-five years, although nothing was found to rebut a report during the first year of the investigation that the NAACP had a "strong tendency" to "steer clear of Communist activities." Similarly, the FBI has admitted that the Socialist Workers Party [SWP] has committed no criminal acts. Yet the Bureau has investigated the Socialist Workers Party for more than three decades on the basis of its revolutionary rhetoric—which the FBI concedes falls short of incitement to violence—and its claimed international links. The Bureau is currently using its informants to collect information about SWP members' political views, including those on "U.S. involvement in Angola," "food prices," "racial matters," the "Vietnam War," and about any of their efforts to support non-SWP candidates for political office.

(e) National political leaders fell within the broad reach of intelligence investigations. For example, Army Intelligence maintained files on Senator Adlai Stevenson and Congressman Abner Mikva because of their participation in peaceful political meetings under surveillance by Army agents. A letter to Richard Nixon, while he was a candidate for President in 1968, was intercepted under CIA's mail opening program. In the 1960's President Johnson asked the FBI to compare various Senators' statements on Vietnam with the Communist Party line and to conduct name checks on leading antiwar Senators.

(f) As part of their effort to collect information which "related even remotely" to people or groups "active" in communities which had "the potential" for civil disorder, Army intelligence agencies took such steps as: sending agents to a Halloween party for elementary school children in Washington, D.C., because they suspected a local "dissident" might be present; monitoring protests of welfare mothers' organizations in Milwaukee; infiltrating a coalition of church youth groups in Colorado; and sending agents to a priests' conference in Washington, D.C., held to discuss birth control measures.

(g) In the late 1960s and early 1970s, student groups were subjected to intense scrutiny. In 1970 the FBI ordered investigations of every member of the Students for a Democratic Society and of "every Black Student Union and similar group regardless of their past or present involvement in disorders." Files were opened on thousands of young men and women so that, as the former head of FBI intelligence explained, the information could be used if they ever applied for a government job.

In the 1960's Bureau agents were instructed to increase their efforts to discredit "New Left" student demonstrators by tactics including publishing photographs ("naturally the most obnoxious picture should be used"), using "misinformation" to falsely notify members events had been cancelled, and 18 writing "tell-tale" letters to students' parents.

(h) The FBI Intelligence Division commonly investigated any indication that "subversive" groups already under investigation were seeking to influence or control other groups. One example of the extreme breadth of this "infiltration" theory was an FBI instruction in the mid-1960's to all Field Offices to investigate every "free university" because some of them had come under "subversive influence."

(i) Each administration from Franklin D. Roosevelt's to Richard Nixon's permitted, and sometimes encouraged, government agencies to handle essentially political intelligence. For example:

- President Roosevelt asked the FBI to put in its files the names of citizens sending telegrams to the White House opposing his "national defense" policy and supporting Col. Charles Lindbergh.
- President Truman received inside information on a former Roosevelt aide's efforts to influence his appointments, labor union negotiating plans, and the publishing plans of journalists.
- President Eisenhower received reports on purely political and social contacts with foreign officials by Bernard Baruch, Mrs. Eleanor Roosevelt, and Supreme Court Justice William O. Douglas.
- The Kennedy Administration had the FBI wiretap a Congressional staff member, three executive officials, a lobbyist, and a Washington law firm. Attorney General Robert F. Kennedy received the fruits of an FBI "tap" on Martin Luther King, Jr. and a "bug" on a Congressman, both of which yielded information of a political nature.
- President Johnson asked the FBI to conduct "name checks" of his critics and of members of the staff of his 1964 opponent, Senator Barry Goldwater. He also requested purely political intelligence on his critics in

the Senate, and received extensive intelligence reports on political activity at the 1964 Democratic Convention from FBI electronic surveillance.

- President Nixon authorized a program of wiretaps which produced for the White House purely political or personal information unrelated to national security, including information about a Supreme Court justice.

3. Covert Action and the Use of Illegal or Improper Means

(a) Covert Action.—Apart from uncovering excesses in the collection of intelligence, our investigation has disclosed covert actions directed against Americans, and the use of illegal and improper surveillance techniques to gather information. For example:

(i) The FBI's COINTELPRO—counterintelligence program—was designed to "disrupt" groups and "neutralize" individuals deemed to be threats to domestic security. The FBI resorted to counterintelligence tactics in part because its chief officials believed that the existing law could not control the activities of certain dissident groups, and that court decisions had tied the hands of the intelligence community. Whatever opinion one holds about the policies of the targeted groups, many of the tactics employed by the FBI were indisputably degrading to a free society. COINTELPRO tactics included:

- Anonymously attacking the political beliefs of targets in order to induce their employers to fire them;
- Anonymously mailing letters to the spouses of intelligence targets for the purpose of destroying their marriages;
- Obtaining from IRS the tax returns of a target and then attempting to provoke an IRS investigation for the express purpose of deterring a protest leader from attending the Democratic National Convention;
- Falsely and anonymously labeling as Government informants members of groups known to be violent, thereby exposing the falsely labelled member to expulsion or physical attack;
- Pursuant to instructions to use "misinformation" to disrupt demonstrations, employing such means as broadcasting fake orders on the same citizens band radio frequency used by demonstration marshalls to attempt to control demonstrations, and duplicating and falsely filling out forms soliciting housing for persons coming to a demonstration, thereby causing "long and useless journeys to locate these addresses";
- Sending an anonymous letter to the leader of a Chicago street gang (described as "violence-prone") stating that the Black Panthers were supposed to have "a hit out for you." The letter was suggested because it "may intensify . . . animosity" and cause the street gang leader to "take retaliatory action."

(ii) From "late 1963" until his death in 1968, Martin Luther King, Jr., was the target of an intensive campaign by the Federal Bureau of Investigation to "neutralize" him as an effective civil rights leader. In the words of the man in charge of the FBI's "war" against Dr. King, "No holds were barred."

The FBI gathered information about Dr. King's plans and activities through an extensive surveillance program, employing nearly every intelligence-gathering technique at the Bureau's disposal in order to obtain information about the "private activities of Dr. King and his advisors" to use to "completely discredit" them.

The program to destroy Dr. King as the leader of the civil rights movement included efforts to discredit him with Executive branch officials, Congressional leaders, foreign heads of state, American ambassadors, churches, universities, and the press.

The FBI mailed Dr. King a tape recording made from microphones hidden in his hotel rooms which one agent testified was an attempt to destroy Dr. King's marriage. The tape recording was accompanied by a note which Dr. King and his advisors interpreted as threatening to release the tape recording unless Dr. King committed suicide.

The extraordinary nature of the campaign to discredit Dr. King is evident from two documents:

- At the August 1963 March on Washington, Dr. King told the country of his "dream" that:

  > all of God's children, black men and white men, Jews and Gentiles, Protestants and Catholics, will be able to join hands and sing in the words of the old Negro spiritual, "Free at last, free at last, thank God Almighty, I'm free at last."

  The Bureau's Domestic Intelligence Division concluded that this "demagogic speech" established Dr. King as the "most dangerous and effective Negro leader in the country." Shortly afterwards, and within days after Dr. King was named "Man of the Year" by Time magazine, the FBI decided to "take him off his pedestal," reduce him completely in influence," and select and promote its own candidate to "assume the role of the leadership of the Negro people."
- In early 1968, Bureau headquarters explained to the field that Dr. King must be destroyed because he was seen as a potential "messiah" who could "unify and electrify" the "black nationalist movement." Indeed, to the FBI he was a potential threat because he might "abandon his supposed 'obedience' to white liberal doctrines (non-violence)." In short, a non-violent man was to be secretly attacked and destroyed as insurance against his abandoning non-violence.

(b) Illegal or Improper Means.—The surveillance which we investigated was not only vastly excessive in breadth and a basis for degrading counterintelligence actions, but was also often conducted by illegal or improper means. For example:

(1) For approximately 20 years the CIA carried out a program of indiscriminately opening citizens' first class mail. The Bureau also had a mail opening program, but cancelled it in 1966. The Bureau continued, however, to receive the illegal fruits of CIA's program. In 1970, the heads of both agencies signed a document for President Nixon, which correctly stated that mail opening was illegal, falsely stated that it had been discontinued, and proposed that the illegal opening of mail should be resumed because it would provide useful results. The President approved the program, but withdrew his approval five days later. The illegal opening continued nonetheless. Throughout this period CIA officials knew that mail opening was illegal, but expressed concern about the "flap potential" of exposure, not about the illegality of their activity.

(2) From 1947 until May 1975, NSA received from international cable companies millions of cables which had been sent by American citizens in the reasonable expectation that they would be kept private.

(3) Since the early 1930's, intelligence agencies have frequently wiretapped and bugged American citizens without the benefit of judicial warrant. Recent court decisions have curtailed the use of these techniques against domestic targets. But past subjects of these surveillances have included a United States Congressman, a Congressional staff member, journalists and newsmen, and numerous individuals and groups who engaged in no criminal activity and who posed no genuine threat to the national security, such as two White House domestic affairs advisers and an anti–Vietnam War protest group. While the prior written approval of the Attorney General has been required for all warrantless wiretaps since 1940, the record is replete with instances where this requirement was ignored and the Attorney General gave only after-the-fact authorization.

Until 1965, microphone surveillance by intelligence agencies was wholly unregulated in certain classes of cases. Within weeks after a 1954 Supreme Court decision denouncing the FBI's installation of a microphone in a defendant's bedroom, the Attorney General informed the Bureau that he did not believe the decision applied to national security cases and permitted the FBI to continue to install microphones subject only to its own "intelligent restraint."

(4) In several cases, purely political information (such as the reaction of Congress to an Administration's legislative proposal) and purely personal information (such as coverage of the extra-marital social activities of a high-level Executive official under surveillance) was obtained from electronic surveillance and disseminated to the highest levels of the federal government.

(5) Warrantless break-ins have been conducted by intelligence agencies since World War II. During the 1960's alone, the FBI and CIA conducted hundreds of break-ins, many against American citizens and domestic organizations. In some cases, these break-ins were to install microphones; in other cases, they were to steal such items as membership lists from organizations considered "subversive" by the Bureau.

(6) The most pervasive surveillance technique has been the informant. In a random sample of domestic intelligence cases, 83% involved informants and 5% involved electronic surveillance. Informants have been used against peaceful, law-abiding groups; they have collected information about personal and political views and activities. To maintain their credentials in violence-prone groups, informants have involved themselves in violent activity. This phenomenon is well illustrated by an informant in the Klan. He was present at the murder of a civil rights worker in Mississippi and subsequently helped to solve the crime and convict the perpetrators. Earlier, however, while performing duties paid for by the Government, he had previously "beaten people severely, had boarded buses and kicked people, had [gone] into restaurants and beaten them [blacks] with blackjacks, chains, pistols." Although the FBI requires agents to instruct informants that they cannot be involved in violence, it was understood that in the Klan, "he couldn't be an angel and be a good informant."

4. Ignoring the Law

Officials of the intelligence agencies occasionally recognized that certain activities were illegal, but expressed concern only for "flap potential." Even more disturbing was the frequent testimony that the law and the Constitution were simply ignored. For example, the author of the so-called Huston plan testified:

QUESTION. Was there any person who stated that the activity recommended, which you have previously identified as being illegal opening of the mail and breaking and entry or burglary—was there any single person who stated that such activity should not be done because it was unconstitutional?

ANSWER. No.

QUESTION. Was there any single person who said such activity should not be done because it was illegal?

ANSWER. No.

Similarly, the man who for ten years headed FBI's Intelligence Division testified that:

> . . . never once did I hear anybody, including myself, raise the question: "Is this course of action which we have agreed upon lawful, is it legal, is it ethical or moral." We never gave any thought to this line of reasoning, because we were just naturally pragmatic.

Although the statutory law and the Constitution were often not "[given] a thought," there was a general attitude that intelligence needs were responsive to a higher law. Thus, as one witness testified in justifying the FBI's mail opening program:

> It was my assumption that what we were doing was justified by what we had to do . . . the greater good, the national security.

5. Deficiencies in Accountability and Control

The overwhelming number of excesses continuing over a prolonged period of time were due in large measure to the fact that the system of checks and balances—created in our Constitution to limit abuse of Governmental power—was seldom applied to the intelligence community. Guidance and regulation from outside the intelligence agencies—where it has been imposed at all—has been vague. Presidents and other senior Executive officials, particularly the Attorneys General, have virtually abdicated their Constitutional responsibility to oversee and set standards for intelligence activity. Senior government officials generally gave the agencies broad, general mandates or pressed for immediate results on pressing problems. In neither case did they provide guidance to prevent excesses and their broad mandates and pressures themselves often resulted in excessive or improper intelligence activity.

Congress has often declined to exercise meaningful oversight, and on occasion has passed laws or made statements which were taken by intelligence agencies as supporting overly-broad investigations.

On the other hand, the record reveals instances when intelligence agencies have concealed improper activities from their superiors in the Executive branch and from the Congress, or have elected to disclose only the less questionable aspects of their activities.

There has been, in short, a, clear and sustained failure by those responsible to control the intelligence community and to ensure its accountability. There has been an equally clear and sustained failure by intelligence agencies to fully inform the proper authorities of their activities and to comply with directives from those authorities. . . .

Source: Final Report of the Senate Select Committee to Study Governmental Operations with Respect to Intelligence Activities, Book II, April 26, 1976. Available at http://www.icdc.com/~paulwolf/cointelpro/churchfinalreportIIa.htm.

Excerpt from Senate Report of the Select Committee on Intelligence Regarding Legislation Authorizing the Use of Electronic Surveillance–The Foreign Intelligence Surveillance Act (FISA) of 1978

Passed in 1978, the Foreign Intelligence Surveillance Act (FISA) was a direct legislative result of the revelations of the Church committee. Although it took two years for Congress to complete its work, the passage of the law, in the words of historian James Bamford, "would at last bring under the rule of law an area of surveillance that had heretofore been considered far too sensitive even to discuss with another branch of government." The FISA legislation proved to be durable. Nevertheless, it would also on occasion be abused, challenged, and ignored.

EXCERPT FROM SENATE REPORT ON INTELLIGENCE, 1978

The Select Committee on Intelligence, to which was referred the bill (S. 1566) to amend title 18 United States Code, to authorize applications for a court order approving the use of electronic surveillance to obtain foreign intelligence information, having considered the same, reports favorably thereon with amendments and recommends that the bill, as amended, do pass. . . .

History of the Bill

The Foreign Intelligence Surveillance Act of 1977, S. 1566, was introduced by Senator Kennedy on May 18, 1977 to provide a statutory procedure to authorize applications for a court order approving the use of electronic surveillance within the United States to obtain foreign intelligence information. The bill, cosponsored by seven other Senators (Mr. Bayh, Mr. Eastland, Mr. Inouye, Mr. McClellan, Mr. Mathias, Mr. Nelson, and Mr. Thurmond), was referred to and considered by the Committee on the Judiciary. That committee reported the bill favorably on November 15, 1977; and it was referred to the Select Committee on Intelligence.

S. 1566 has its origin in S. 3197, The Foreign Intelligence Surveillance Act of 1976, 94th Congress, second session (1976). That legislation, also introduced by Senator Kennedy, had the same broad, bipartisan support, including that of the Ford administration, as S. 1566 and was the subject of Senate hearings by both the Subcommittee on Criminal Laws and Procedures of the Committee on the Judiciary and the Select Committee on Intelligence. S. 3197 was reported favorably by both Senate committees by a combined vote of 24 ayes and 2 nays, but the session ended before the full Senate could act on the legislation.

S. 1566 picks up where S. 3197 left off. Hearings were held by the Subcommittee on Criminal Laws and Procedures, chaired by Senator Kennedy at the request of Senator McClellan. Hearings were also held by the Subcommittee on Intelligence and the Rights of Americans, chaired by Senator Bayh, and included executive session hearings to consider classified information bearing upon the bill. Among those testifying before one or both of these subcommittees were Attorney General Griffin B. Bell; Director of the FBI Clarence M. Kelley; Director of Central Intelligence Stansfield Turner; Secretary of Defense Harold Brown; John Shattuck and Jerry Berman of the American Civil Liberties Union; Morton H. Halperin of the Center for National Security Studies; Steven Rosenfeld of the Committee on Federal Legislation of the Association of the Bar of the City of New York; and David Waiters of the American Privacy Foundation.

Broad-based support was voiced for S. 1566 throughout the hearings, with the administration indicating its support of the bill.

S. 1566 as reported has been amended in several respects to respond to the constructive criticisms and suggestions elicited in the hearings. As amended, the bill was approved by the Select Committee on Intelligence, 15–0, with a recommendation for favorable action.

Position of the Administration

The administration has supported the enactment of S. 1566 and supports its swift passage by the Senate. As Attorney General Bell stated in testifying in favor of the bill:

> I believe this bill is remarkable not only in the way it has been developed, but also in the fact that for the first time in our society the clandestine intelligence activities of our Government shall be subject to the regulation and receive the positive authority of a public law for all to inspect. President Carter stated it very well in announcing this bill when he said that "one of the most difficult tasks in a free society like our own is the correlation between adequate intelligence to guarantee our Nation's security on the one hand, and the preservation of basic human rights on the other." It is a very delicate balance to strike, but one which is necessary in our society, and a balance which cannot be achieved by sacrificing either our Nation's security or our civil liberties. In my view this bill strikes the balance, sacrifices neither our security nor our civil liberties, and assures that the abuses of the past will remain in the past and that the dedicated and patriotic men and women who serve this country in intelligence positions, often under substantial hardships and even danger, will have the affirmation of Congress that their activities are proper and necessary.

General Statement

I. Summary of the Legislation

S. 1566 amends title 18, United States Code, by adding after chapter 119 a new chapter 120 entitled "Electronic Surveillance Within the United States for Foreign Intelligence Purposes." The bill requires a court order for electronic surveillance as defined therein conducted for foreign intelligence purposes within the United States or targeted against the international communications of particular U.S. persons who are in the United States. The bill establishes the exclusive means by which such surveillance may be conducted. S. 1566 does not require a court order for electronic surveillance abroad, and the bill does not address the question whether the President has any constitutional power to conduct electronic surveillance of a U.S. person abroad without a court order to acquire foreign intelligence information, if such power exists.

Under S. 1566 the Attorney General, upon the general authorization of the President for the conduct of electronic surveillance within the United States for foreign intelligence purposes, may authorize applications to members of a special court for orders to conduct such surveillance. Applications are to be made to one of seven district judges publicly designated by the Chief Justice of the United States to serve staggered 7-year terms on a special court. Denials of such applications may be appealed to a special three-judge court of review and ultimately to the Supreme Court.

Approval of an application under the bill would require a finding by the court that the target of the surveillance is a "foreign power" or an "agent of a foreign power" and that the facilities or place at which the surveillance is to be directed are being used or are about to be used by a foreign power or an agent of a foreign power. A "foreign power" may include a foreign government, a faction of a foreign government, a foreign-based terrorist group, a foreign-based political organization, or an entity directed and controlled by a foreign government. An "agent of a foreign power" includes non-resident aliens who act as officers or employees of foreign powers or who act on behalf of foreign powers which engage in clandestine intelligence activities contrary to the interests of this country. U.S. persons meet the "agent of a foreign power" criteria if they engage in certain activities on behalf of a foreign power which involve or may involve criminal acts.

The court would also be required to find that procedures proposed in the application adequately minimize the acquisition and retention, and prohibit the dissemination, of information concerning U.S. persons which does not relate to national defense, foreign affairs, or the terrorist, sabotage, or clandestine intelligence activities of a foreign power. Additional limits are placed on the dissemination of information relating solely to national defense or foreign affairs.

Finally, a certification or certifications must be made by the Assistant to the President for National Security Affairs or an executive branch official or officials designated by the President from among those executive officers with responsibilities for national security or defense who are appointed by the President with the advice and consent of the Senate. Those officials would be required to certify that any information sought by the surveillance relates to, and if concerning a U.S. person is necessary to, the national defense or the successful conduct of foreign affairs of the United States or the ability of the United States to protect against grave hostile acts or the terrorist, sabotage, or clandestine intelligence activities of a foreign power. The court would be required to review each certification for surveillance of a U.S. person and to determine that the certification is not clearly erroneous.

The court could approve electronic surveillance for foreign intelligence purposes for a period of 90 days or, in the case of surveillance of a foreign government, faction, or entity openly controlled by a foreign government, for a period of up to 1 year. Any extension of the surveillance beyond that period would require a reapplication to the court and new findings as required for the original order.

Emergency surveillance without a court order would be permitted in limited circumstances, but a court order must be obtained within 24 hours of the initiation of the surveillance.

S. 1566 requires annual reports to the Administrative Office of the U.S. Courts and to the Congress of statistics regarding applications and orders for electronic surveillance. The Attorney General is also required, on a semiannual basis, to inform fully the House Permanent Select Committee on

Intelligence and the Senate Select Committee on Intelligence concerning all electronic surveillance under the bill; and nothing in the bill restricts the authority of those committees to obtain further information related to their congressional oversight responsibilities. The Senate committee is required to report annually to the Senate on the implementation of the bill.

II. Statement of Need

The purpose of the Foreign Intelligence Surveillance Act is to provide legislative authorization and regulation for all electronic surveillance conducted within the United States for foreign intelligence purposes. It has long been recognized that foreign intelligence electronic surveillance, exempted from the warrant provisions of the Omnibus Crime Control Act of 1968, could be subject to abuse. The report of the Senate Select Committee to Study Governmental Operations With Respect to Intelligence Activities, issued in 1976, provided firm evidence that foreign intelligence electronic surveillances involved abuses and that checks upon the exercise of these clandestine methods were clearly necessary.

The basic premise of the bill is that a court order for foreign intelligence electronic surveillances can be devised that is consistent with the "reasonable search" requirements of the Fourth Amendment. The Supreme Court has not ruled on the question of Fourth Amendment standards for electronic surveillance of foreign powers and their agents within the United States, although the Court in the *Keith* case required a judicial warrant for domestic security surveillances not involving foreign powers. Therefore, S. 1566 clarifies and advances the development of the law on a subject where uncertainty now exists.

The electronic surveillance authorized and regulated by this bill is designed to satisfy two broad types of intelligence requirements. First, it provides a means for the collection of "positive" foreign intelligence to enable the Government to understand and assess the capabilities, intentions, and activities of foreign powers. Second, it supplies a technique for use in foreign counterintelligence investigations to protect against clandestine intelligence activities, sabotage, and terrorism by or on behalf of foreign powers. The standards and procedures for electronic surveillance differ according to whether the primary purpose is collecting foreign intelligence or assisting foreign counterintelligence and counterterrorism investigations.

Source: U.S. Congress. Senate Report 95–701, 95th Congress, 2nd Session, 1978. Available at http://www.cnss.org/fisa.htm.

Bibliography

AARC Public Library, Church Committee Reports. http://www.aarclibrary.org/publib/contents/church/contents_church_reports.htm.

Ashby, LeRoy, and Rod Gramer. *Fighting the Odds: The Life of Senator Frank Church.* Pullman: Washington State University Press, 1994.

Bamford, James. *Body of Secrets: Anatomy of the Ultra-Secret National Security Agency.* New York: Doubleday, 2001.

Barrett, David. *The CIA and Congress: The Untold Story from Truman to Kennedy.* Lawrence: University Press of Kansas, 2005.

Breckinridge, Scott. *The CIA and the U.S. Intelligence System.* Boulder, Colo.: Westview Press, 1986.

Colby, William, and Peter Forbath. *Honorable Men: My Life in the CIA.* New York: Simon & Schuster, 1978.

Helms, Richard. *A Look Over My Shoulder: A Life in the Central Intelligence Agency.* New York: Random House, 2003.

Jeffreys-Jones, Rhodri. *Cloak and Dollar: A History of American Secret Intelligence.* New Haven, Conn.: Yale University Press, 2002.

Johnson, Loch K. *A Season of Inquiry: The Senate Intelligence Investigation.* Lexington: University Press of Kentucky, 1985.

McGee, Jim, and Brian Duffy. *Main Justice: The Men and Women Who Enforce the Nation's Criminal Laws and Guard Its Liberties.* New York: Simon & Schuster, 1997.

Oseth, John. *Regulating U.S. Intelligence Operations.* Lexington: University Press of Kentucky, 1985.

Powers, Richard Gid. *Secrecy and Power: The Life of J. Edgar Hoover.* New York: Free Press, 1987.

Powers, Thomas. *The Man Who Kept the Secrets: Richard Helms and the CIA.* New York: Knopf, 1979.

Prados, John. *Safe for Democracy: The Secret Wars of the CIA.* Chicago: Ivan R. Dee, 2006.

Ranelagh, John. *The Agency: The Rise and Decline of the CIA.* New York: Simon and Schuster, 1986.

Rudgers, David. *Creating the Secret State: The Origins of the Central Intelligence Agency, 1943–1947.* Lawrence: University Press of Kansas, 2000.

Schorr, Daniel. *Staying Tuned: A Life in Journalism.* New York: Pocket Books, 2001.

Smist, Frank. *Congress Oversees the Intelligence Community: 1947–1989.* Knoxville: University of Tennessee Press, 1990.

Snider, L. Britt. *The Agency and the Hill: The CIA's Relationship with Congress.* Washington: Center for the Study of Intelligence, Central Intelligence Agency, 2008

Stuart, Douglas. *Creating the National Security State: A History of the Law that Transformed America.* Princeton, N.J.: Princeton University Press, 2008.

Weiner, Tim. *Legacy of Ashes: The History of the CIA.* New York: Doubleday, 2007.

The Iran-Contra Hearings, 1987

By David L. Hostetter

The joint congressional hearings on the Iran-Contra Affair convened on May 5, 1987. They were the climactic act of the most dramatic political scandal of the Reagan administration. The hearings, which lasted until August 3, examined the clandestine operation in which Reagan administration officials arranged the sale of missiles to Iran in exchange for hostages held in Lebanon, with the proceeds from the missile sales going to the guerrillas, known as contras or counterrevolutionaries, then fighting against the Sandinista government of Nicaragua. The Sandinista National Liberation Front (FSLN) had won power by overthrowing the U.S.-backed Somoza regime in 1979. The joint committee of the Senate and the House of Representatives listened to more than 250 hours of testimony from 28 witnesses. At the conclusion of its investigation, the committee produced a 1,200-page report of its findings. At issue in the proceedings was the accountability under the Constitution of the executive branch to Congress. According to Senator Daniel Patrick Moynihan (D-N.Y.), "the very processes of American government were put in harm's way by a conspiracy of faithless or witless men: sometimes both."

The details of the Iran-Contra Affair became public knowledge in the autumn of 1986 because of a series of mistakes and mishaps. The ensuing scandal dominated the political news for most of the following year. Although it generally followed a tragic plot line, the Iran-Contra Affair included scenes of high suspense and

This 1987 cartoon by the Washington Post's *Herblock depicts President Ronald Reagan giving conflicting explanations for his role in the Iran-Contra Affair. Reagan's justification for trading arms for hostages and sending aid to the contra rebels in Nicaragua changed throughout the years of the scandal. Reagan, a movie actor prior to his entry into politics, is portrayed as unable to remmber his lines despite some 34 takes.* (A Herblock Cartoon, copyright by The Herb Block Foundation)

OVERVIEW

Background

The Iran-Contra Affair involved the clandestine operations in which Reagan administration officials arranged the sale of missiles to Iran in exchange for hostages held in Lebanon, with the proceeds from the missile sales going to the guerrillas, known as contras or counterrevolutionaries, fighting against the Sandinista government of Nicaragua. Provision of arms to the contras violated the Boland Amendment, which banned funding "for the purpose of overthrowing the government of Nicaragua." Because of a series of mistakes and mishaps in the autumn of 1986, details of the affair became public knowledge. Both the executive branch and Congress launched investigations into the affair. The Reagan administration initiated a commission chaired by former senator John Tower and appointed Lawrence Walsh as independent counsel. Meanwhile, the congressional leadership arranged for joint House-Senate hearings to examine the scandal.

Congress Investigates

The joint congressional hearings on the Iran-Contra Affair convened on May 5, 1987, and lasted until August 3. The joint committee listened to more than 250 hours of testimony from 28 witnesses. At the conclusion of its investigation, the committee produced a 1,200-page report of its findings. At issue in the proceedings was the accountability under the Constitution of the executive branch to Congress.

The intense debates about the powers of the president and Congress that took place in the House and Senate hearing rooms during the spring and summer of 1987 echoed arguments that had begun in the era of the Vietnam War and the Watergate scandal. Broadcast live on television, the hearings cast a harsh light on the wrongdoings of members of the Reagan administration while diffusing the question of whether President Ronald Reagan himself knew about the illegal aspects of the affair.

Impact

The hearings produced no "smoking gun" showing Reagan's direct consent for the illegal actions committed by his subordinates. But the congressional investigations revealed in vivid detail the lengths the Reagan administration was willing to go and the clandestine means it was willing to use to pursue foreign policy in violation of law that limited support to the contras. After the hearings ended and the committee's report was filed, the work of Walsh, the independent counsel, continued into the administration of Reagan's successor, George H. W. Bush.

On August 4, 1993, after six and a half years and $35.7 million, Walsh concluded the Iran-contra investigation and submitted his final report. By 1993 the statute of limitations on crimes that may have been committed prior to 1987 had expired. Walsh had brought indictments against 14 of the participants in the Iran-Contra Affair. The granting of limited immunity to key conspirators Oliver North and John Poindexter gave them grounds to have their convictions overturned on appeal. Six others convicted of crimes or facing trial were pardoned in 1992 as Bush completed his one term in office. The case of the Iran-Contra Affair was closed in legal terms, but it lived on in the politics of the nation.

moments of bizarre comedy. The intense debate that emanated from the House and Senate hearing rooms during the summer of 1987 echoed arguments over the powers of the president and Congress that began in the era of the Vietnam War and the Watergate scandal. Broadcast live on television, the hearings cast a harsh light on the wrongdoings of officials of the Reagan administration while obscuring the question of how much President Reagan knew about the illegal aspects of the affair.

The complex story of the series of clandestine operations that became known as the Iran-Contra Affair began on October 5, 1986, when an American, Eugene Hasenfus, parachuted out of a supply plane shot down by Sandinista soldiers over Nicaragua. Hasenfus served as the aircraft's kicker, responsible for dispensing the airdropped cargo by pushing it out of the plane's loading door to anti-Sandinista rebels in the jungle below. The 45-year-old Vietnam veteran had disobeyed orders by packing a parachute. After the Fairchild C-123K

CHRONOLOGY

1981

- *November 17:* President Ronald Reagan authorizes secret assistance to the Nicaraguan counterrevolutionaries known as contras.

1983

- *December 8:* First Boland Amendment, sponsored by Representative Edward Boland (D-Mass.), imposes limits on U.S. government aid to the contras.

1985

- *June 16:* Reagan says the United States will never deal with terrorists.
- *July 18:* National Security Adviser Robert McFarlane proposes trading arms for hostages to the president.
- *August 20–November 25:* United States delivers 522 anti-tank TOW missiles and surface-to-air Hawk missiles to Iran.
- *December 5:* Reagan signs finding retroactively authorizing the November missile shipment to Iran.

1986

- *January:* Reagan signs two findings authorizing arms deliveries to Iran. One thousand TOW missiles and spare parts for Hawk missiles are sent to Iran over the next seven months.
- *May 25:* McFarlane leads a delegation to Iran to deliver missile parts and negotiate for hostages.
- *October 5:* Nicaraguan soldiers shoot down a CIA contra-resupply plane. Eugene Hasenfus, an American, survives and is captured.
- *November 3:* The Lebanese newspaper *Al-Shiraa* reports arms-for-hostages deal with Iran.
- *November 6:* Reagan denies arms were sold to Iran. A week later he acknowledges weapons were sold to Iran but denies that arms were sold to win the release of American hostages.
- *November 19:* Reagan denies U.S. involvement in shipments prior to January 1986.
- *November 22:* A memo delineating diversion of funds to contras discovered in national security aide Oliver North's office.
- *November 25:* Attorney General Edwin Meese discloses diversion of Iran arms sales profits to contras.
- *December 1:* A special review board, known as the Tower Commission, is appointed by Reagan to investigate circumstances of the Iran-Contra Affair and the work of the National Security Council.
- *December 19:* Lawrence Walsh is appointed independent counsel on Iran-contra.

1987

- *January 6:* The Senate select committee on Iran-contra is created.
- *January 7:* The House select committee on Iran-contra is created.
- *February 26:* The Tower Commission issues its final report, which determines that Reagan did not know about the diversion of funds to the contras but should have provided better supervision of the National Security Council (NSC) staff. The report blames John Poindexter, the former national security adviser, for the illegal actions of NSC staff.
- *May 5:* Congress begins public hearings on the Iran-Contra Affair.

plane carrying him was hit by a shoulder-launched missile and began to plummet from the sky, Hasenfus jumped free, while the ensuing crash killed his crewmates. When Hasenfus pulled the ripcord on his parachute, he inadvertently unveiled the clandestine actions crafted by members of the Reagan administration to evade and subvert the will of Congress.

Discovered hiding in an abandoned house by Nicaraguan soldiers the day after being shot down, Hasenfus cooperated fully with his captors. At a news conference arranged by the Nicaraguan government, he admitted that he had willingly been part of what he believed to be a CIA initiative to supply the contra rebels. Records found at the crash site substantiated Hasenfus's confession and linked the operation to the White House. Hasenfus was tried and convicted, but Nicaragua's president, Daniel Ortega, pardoned him, releasing him in December as a Christmas peace offering to the American people.

- *July:* North and Poindexter testify publicly before Congress under grant of immunity.
- *August 3:* Congress concludes the hearings.
- *November 18:* Congress issues the Iran-contra report, which places responsibility for the crimes and misdeeds of administration officials on Reagan, but finds no evidence indicating the president's guilt or complicity.

1988

- *March 11:* McFarlane pleads guilty to withholding information from Congress.
- *March 16:* North, Poindexter, Richard Secord, and Albert Hakim are indicted on conspiracy to defraud the United States and other charges.
- *June 8:* Judge Gerhard Gesell orders separate trials for North, Poindexter, Secord, and Hakim due to problems caused by congressional grants of immunity.

1989

- *May 4:* North trial results in a three-count conviction.
- *November 8:* Secord pleads guilty to making false statements to Congress.
- *November 21:* Hakim pleads guilty to illegally supplementing the salary of a government official.

1990

- *February 16–17:* Former president Reagan gives videotaped deposition in Poindexter's trial. He admits that the Iran-Contra Affair was "a covert action that was taken at my behest."
- *April 7:* Poindexter is convicted on five counts.
- *July 20:* U.S. Court of Appeals for the District of Columbia Circuit vacates North's convictions and orders further hearings by trial court on the immunity issue.

1991

- *May 28:* The Supreme Court declines review of North case.
- *September 16:* The case against North is dismissed on motion of independent counsel after two days of hearings by the trial court.
- *October 7:* Elliott Abrams, former secretary of state for inter-American affairs, pleads guilty to withholding information from Congress.
- *November 15:* The U.S. Court of Appeals for the District of Columbia Circut reverses Poindexter's convictions.

1992

- *June 16:* Former secretary of defense Caspar W. Weinberger is indicted on five counts, including obstructing the congressional investigation and perjury.
- *December 24:* President George H. W. Bush pardons Weinberger, McFarlane, Abrams, and three others for all crimes they may have committed related to the Iran-Contra Affair. Walsh denounces the pardons.

1993

- *August 4:* Walsh concludes the Iran-contra investigation and submits the final report to the special court that had appointed him.

In the days following the Hasenfus revelations, Assistant Secretary of State for Inter-American Affairs Elliott Abrams and President Ronald Reagan publicly denied U.S. involvement with the contra supply operation. In the midterm elections held on November 4, the Democrats won a majority in the Senate, thus giving them control of both chambers of Congress. Meanwhile, the day before the elections, *Al-Shiraa,* a magazine based in Beirut, Lebanon, reported that the United States had sold anti-aircraft missiles to Iran. *Al-Shiraa* based its story on a leak from an Iranian dissident opposed to his government's dealings with the United States and Israel. The story broke in the American news media on November 5, the day after the elections. On November 6 President Reagan stated publicly that the *Al-Shiraa* allegations had "no foundation." By November 13 the president had modified his position, saying in a nationally televised speech that sale of the missiles had taken place, but that the transaction had been part of an elaborate policy intended to influence Iran and bring about the release of Americans being held hostage by Lebanese groups allied with Iran. Reagan emphasized that the administration "did not—repeat did not—trade weapons or anything else for hostages."

In the weeks between the elections and Thanksgiving, frenzied administration officials attempted to obscure the involvement of the White House in illegal activities. William J. Casey, director of the Central Intelligence Agency, Admiral John Poindexter, the national security adviser, and Lieutenant Colonel Oliver North, a member of the National Security Council (NSC) staff, worked together to coordinate the stories they would tell to Congress and the public. Testifying on Friday, November 21, in hearings of the House and Senate Select Committees on Intelligence, Casey and Poindexter both lied under oath, denying that the CIA knowingly conveyed missiles to Iran. Meanwhile, Attorney General Edwin Meese, on the president's authority, began collecting relevant information from the NSC in an effort to coordinate the administration's response.

Rather than deploy the Justice Department Criminal Division or the FBI in his inquiry, Meese relied instead on three members of his staff—Assistant Attorneys General Charles Cooper and William Bradford Reynolds along with Justice Department Chief of Staff John Richardson—to sift through the evidence. Poindexter and North, aware of Meese's probe, destroyed or changed thousands of pages of documents pertaining to the missile sales and the supplying of the contras. Retired Air Force General Richard V. Secord, who had worked with North on the contra supply operation, which they had dubbed "The Enterprise," also destroyed evidence in his possession. Despite the efforts of North, Poindexter, and Secord to cover up the illegal actions they had performed, Meese's investigators quickly came upon an April 4, 1986, memorandum that delineated the diversion of funds to the contras. Meese informed the president of the revealing memo on Monday, November 24. The president, claiming he had not known of the operation, worried that the diversion of funds would expose the arms sales to the Iranians.

Reagan appeared briefly in a televised midday news conference on Tuesday, November 25. After stating that his administration's approach to Iran was correct, he admitted that, "in one aspect implementation of that policy was seriously flawed." Reagan announced that he would appoint a special review board that would examine the workings of the NSC. The president also announced that Poindexter had resigned and that North had been "relieved of his duties." As the White House press corps burst into a cacophony of questions, Reagan turned the microphone over to Meese and exited the room. The attorney general then revealed the Iran-contra connection:

> In the course of the arms transfer, which involved the United States providing the arms to Israel and Israel, in turn, transferring the arms—in effect selling the arms—to representatives of Iran, certain monies which were received in the transaction between representatives of Israel and representatives of Iran were taken and made available to the forces in Central America who are opposing the Sandinista government there.

The reporters peppered Meese with questions about whether the president knew about the diversion of funds, who else in the White House had knowledge of the operations, and whether North had committed a crime. Meese said that only North knew the full extent of the programs and that the possibility of criminal wrongdoing was being explored. The NSC had never been the subject of a presidential commission inquiry.

On November 26, 1986, the president announced that the members of the special review board would be former senator John Tower, who would act as chair, former secretary of state Edmund Muskie, and former national security adviser Brent Scowcroft. Tower and Scowcroft were Republicans, Muskie was a Democrat. The Tower commission, as the group came to be known, interviewed 80 individuals, including the president. Reagan gave his testimony on December 2, 1986. During his discussion with the commission, he first said he had authorized the arms deal with Iran, but later he said he had not. On February 26, 1987, the commission submitted a 200-page report that criticized Reagan for not providing proper supervision to his staff and for not being aware of their actions. The commission placed most of the blame on Poindexter.

On December 19, 1986, Meese appointed Lawrence Walsh as independent counsel to investigate the Iran-Contra Affair. Walsh, a Republican who had served as a federal judge and in the Justice Department during the Eisenhower administration, went on to spend more than six years investigating the scandal. Walsh's efforts were often at cross-purposes with the congressional investigation.

The operations connected to the Iran-contra scandal joined two distinct goals of the Reagan administration's foreign policy: gaining release of hostages held in Lebanon by organizations allied with Iran and providing clandestine support for the counterrevolutionaries attacking the Nicaraguan government. The two issues, initially separate, were merged by administration officials willing to circumvent Congress by acting outside of the law and using funds obtained from one operation to support the other. Confrontations with Iran and allied groups in the Middle East, along with cold war tensions with nations aligned with the Soviet Union, motivated the Reagan administration to go beyond conventional operations and pursue illegal methods.

The Reagan Administration and Nicaragua

In the case of Nicaragua, the Reagan administration had escalated the United States' confrontation with the Sandinista regime almost immediately upon Reagan's taking office. Following a bloody struggle with the U.S.-backed dictatorship of Anastasio Somoza Debayle, which cost thousands of lives and brought havoc to the small Central American nation, the Sandinistas came to power in July 1979. Opposition to the initial coalition government, which was dominated by the Sandinista National Liberation Front (FSLN), arose almost immediately among supporters of the deposed dictator as well as others uneasy about Sandinista governance. In 1980 the two non-Sandinista members of the five-person ruling junta withdrew, leaving the FSLN in complete control. The Sandinistas pursued a program of land redistribution, public works, and education. The FSLN declared a policy of nonalignment in foreign affairs, but it developed warm relations with Cuba. Nicaragua's new position as an independent nation no longer under the control of a U.S.-supported dictator was not welcomed by the administration of President Jimmy Carter and became an immediate focus of attention for the more interventionist Reagan administration.

In February 1981 Reagan cut off economic aid to Nicaragua. By November of that year the administra-

Despite President Ronald Reagan's great popularity, the Iran-Contra Affair was an embarrassing and politically destructive episode that brought into question the president's grasp and knowledge of foreign-policy actions carried out under his leadership. (Library of Congress)

tion had authorized a clandestine program of aid to the opponents of the Sandinista regime. The contra forces were based in neighboring Honduras and Costa Rica. The CIA provided training to the Nicaraguan Democratic Force (FDN), the group in Honduras, throughout 1982. In November of that year *Newsweek* broke the news of the secret war, citing an interview with CIA Director William J. Casey. The *Boston Globe* ran an editorial criticizing the Reagan administration's attempt to impose its will on Nicaragua and its neighbors, especially through secret activities. The *Globe* editorial helped bring the issue to the attention of Congressman Edward P. Boland (D-Mass.).

As chair of the House Select Committee on Intelligence, Boland oversaw the approval of requests from the president for intelligence operations. The Reagan administration had forged ahead in aiding the contras without seeking congressional approval. When the 1983 Defense Authorization Act passed the House of Representatives in December, it included an amendment drafted by Boland that banned funding "for the purpose of overthrowing the government of Nicaragua." Although Reagan signed the bill and promised to abide by Boland's amendment, the administration and the CIA continued to solicit aid for the contras with the help of other countries. While the Democratic majority in the House generally opposed aiding the contras, the Republican-controlled Senate supported the administration's program. After the House and Senate versions of the Defense Authorization Act went through conference committee, the end result was a $24 million limit on contra aid for 1984.

Despite the limits imposed by Congress, the CIA and the NSC sought to aid the contras in a variety of ways. Robert McFarlane, Reagan's national security adviser, and Oliver North, the NSC's deputy director for political-military affairs, worked with the CIA to arrange for the mining of three key harbors in Nicaragua, justifying their actions by claiming that the American-made mines were meant to deter shipments of military supplies from Cuba and the Soviet Union. Reagan approved the plan in January 1984; subsequently the mines damaged several ships, killing two Nicaraguans and injuring sailors on a Soviet oil tanker.

The role of the U.S. government became known to the public through an article in the *Wall Street Journal.* Barry Goldwater (R-Ariz.), chairman of the Senate Select Committee on Intelligence, angered that the CIA had not informed him of or sought Senate approval for the mining, wrote a critical letter to Casey. Casey replied that he had informed Goldwater and the committee of the operation in March 1984, though he had said only that the harbors had been mined, not that the CIA had done it. The exchange between Goldwater and Casey led to greater scrutiny from the Senate Intelligence Committee, which from then on required that all secret operations be approved in advance and that all presidential findings on secret activities be shared with the committee. In October 1984 Congress took an additional step to rein in the administration by passing a second Boland Amendment, which prohibited any support from U.S. intelligence agencies for activities aimed at undermining the government of Nicaragua.

Determined to continue contra aid despite the intent of the Boland Amendments, the Reagan administration used the NSC, along with donations from private individuals and other countries, to keep the contras supplied. McFarlane, a former Marine, and North, then a Marine lieutenant colonel, worked to raise money for the contras at the behest of the National Security Planning Group (NSPG). Created by Reagan in 1981 to coordinate the execution of foreign policy among the many responsible departments, the NSPG included the president, the vice president, the secretaries of defense and state, and the national security adviser.

McFarlane embarked on his surreptitious diplomacy by seeking funds from the government of Saudi Arabia. In May 1984 the Saudis made an initial pledge of $1 million, which was deposited directly into the contras' account. When McFarlane reported to the president, "No one knows about this," Reagan replied, "Good. Let's make sure it stays that way." According to McFarlane, Reagan let it be known that he supported all efforts to solicit financial assistance for the contras. The president did his part for the cause by posing for photos with foreign donors and private American supporters alike. North and McFarlane garnered pledges of additional millions from the governments of Taiwan, Israel, and South Africa.

North, who worked with McFarlane to woo donors, also organized the transfer of weapons to the contras. Acting on the recommendation of Casey, North engaged Richard V. Secord, a retired Air Force major general experienced with the international arms trade as well as with covert operations. Secord, working with an Iranian-born businessman, Albert Hakim, obtained weapons with the money raised by North and McFarlane, then sold them to the contras at a profit. The first shipments of the illegally obtained weapons reached the contras in November 1984. In addition to weapons, North passed intelligence about Sandinista helicopter bases to the contras. North and Secord tried to use weapons transfers to unite the FDN contras in Honduras with a separate group attacking southern Nicaragua from Costa Rica. North and Secord's enterprise expanded to include airplanes, a ship, and paid staff. By the end of 1985 weapons were reaching the contras via airdrops from Southern Air Transport, a CIA-controlled airline. Thus the clandestine enterprise had become a substantial operation involving millions of dollars' worth of weapons and a sophisticated organizational structure.

McFarlane's and North's involvement with secret arms deals extended to the Middle East as well. Both the Carter and Reagan administrations perceived the regime in Iran, led by militant Shiite Muslim clerics who had overthrown the U.S.-backed shah in 1979 and established an Islamic republic, as a threat to American interests in the region. Radical students took the staff of the U.S. Embassy in Tehran hostage in November 1979 and held 53 Americans for 444 days, damaging the Carter administration and setting the stage for continued confrontation. Iran announced the freeing of the hostages six minutes after Ronald Reagan's swearing in as president on January 20, 1981.

Beginning in 1983, the Reagan administration enlisted other countries in "Operation Staunch," which was an effort to end arms sales to Iran. The United States also declared Iran a sponsor of international terrorism because of its ties to radical Islamic movements throughout the Middle East. American support for the 1983 Israeli invasion of Lebanon and the 1984 truck bombing of the Marine barracks in Beirut further heightened tensions between the United States and Iran's supporters. By 1985 Shiite Muslim radicals in Lebanon known as Hezbollah were holding seven Americans hostage.

Despite Reagan's public declarations that he would not negotiate with terrorists and hostage takers, the search for ways to influence the Iranian regime to gain release of the hostages was under way. Members of the administration disagreed over whether allowing arms sales to Iran, as recommended by a May intelligence report, was the proper course of action. While Secretary of Defense Caspar Weinberger and Secretary of State George Shultz opposed the idea of easing restriction on arms sales, National Security Adviser McFarlane and CIA Director Casey favored it. Discussions with the government of Israel produced a plan under which Israel would sell U.S.-made anti-tank TOW (tube-launched, optically-tracked, wire-guided) missiles to Iran and then the United States would sell more to Israel to replace them.

While hospitalized for removal of cancerous polyps in his intestine, Reagan met with McFarlane and gave him the approval to explore the arms-for-hostages deal. In August, McFarlane presented the plan to Reagan, Shultz, Weinberger, and Vice President George H. W. Bush. Despite the opposition of Weinberger and Shultz, Reagan gave verbal approval to McFarlane to move forward with the plan. On August 20, 1985, Israel delivered 96 TOW missiles to Iran. No hostages were released until another 408 TOWs were delivered on September 15. That day Lebanese kidnappers released Reverend Benjamin Weir, a Presbyterian minister who had been held for more than a year. McFarlane had asked for the release of William Buckley, CIA station chief in Beirut and a personal friend of Casey's, but Buckley had died of untreated pneumonia in June (Buckley's captors, Islamic Jihad, did not announce his death until October 4).

Although the delivery of missiles had prompted the release of only one hostage, McFarlane and his colleagues continued to pursue the arms-for-hostages arrangement. The next shipment, arranged by North and Secord, was intended to go through Portugal to obscure Israel's involvement. When the Portuguese government did not approve the passage of weapons through Lisbon, North and Secord procured a CIA-owned plane to pick up the missiles in Tel Aviv, Israel. The deal had been for delivery of 80 Hawk anti-aircraft missiles, but only 18 fit in the available plane. The Iranians were unhappy with the botched deal, which consisted of older-model Hawks that performed poorly when test-fired and which were emblazoned with the Israeli Star of David insignia.

By law the involvement of the CIA in providing a plane and negotiating with Portugal required presidential approval. In December 1985 Reagan signed a retroactive finding that granted approval to the CIA's dealings and justified it as part of an operation to trade arms for hostages. In January 1986 Reagan approved another finding that permitted the use of private contractors such as Secord to transport the weapons from Israel to Iran. By working with Secord, the administration sought to go around Congress while distancing itself from the operation. By the end of February 1986, 1,000 missiles had been delivered to Iran. Secord paid the CIA $3.7 million for the missiles and then sold them to the Iranian arms broker Manucher Ghorbanifar for $10 million. Ghorbanifar then marked up his shipments before delivering them to Iran. Despite the satisfaction of the Iranians with the arms provided by Secord and Ghorbanifar, no hostages were released.

The profits Secord made on the missile sales prompted North to propose using the money to help the contras. In the April 4 memorandum titled "Release of the Hostages in Beirut" that became known as the diversion memo, North outlined to Poindexter, who had taken over as national security adviser when McFarlane retired at the end of 1985, how monies gained from the arms sales could be applied to the contra cause. Part of the $6.3 million profit that Secord had brought in was diverted to the contras, while $800,000 was kept for the arms-for-hostages arrangement known as the Enterprise.

Frustrated with the failure of the arms deliveries to gain the hostages' freedom, North, Ghorbanifar, and McFarlane, serving as a special consultant, hatched a new plan in which spare parts for Hawk missiles would be exchanged for hostages. On May 25 a group that included North and McFarlane traveled secretly to Tehran aboard a disguised Israeli plane, accompanied by a cargo of spare parts. The group carried forged Irish passports and brought a bible signed by Reagan intended for the Ayatollah Ruhollah Khomeini, the leader of Iran, as well as a chocolate cake baked in the shape of a key purchased from a kosher bakery in Israel. The cake bearers traveled to Iran during the Muslim fast month of Ramadan. Upon arriving in Tehran, Iranian security agents confiscated the missile parts, the passports, and the gifts. After being taken to a hotel, the American delegates faced potential arrest by members of the Revolutionary Guard but were rescued by other Iranians who clashed with the guards in the hotel parking lot. The inept negotiators parlayed for three days without wresting any hostage release guarantees from the Iranians and left Tehran empty-handed. The efforts of Reagan administration officials to trade arms for hostages had put more than 1,500 weapons into the hands of the Iranians in exchange for the release of three hostages. Three more Americans were taken captive during the same period. Secretary of State Shultz characterized the transactions as "a hostage bazaar."

This Herblock cartoon lampoons the contradiction between President Reagan's resolute public denounciation of trading arms for hostages with the revelations that members of his administration did exactly that. Reagan's commanding image on the TV screen obscures his shady dealings with Iran, represented by a caricature of Ayatollah Khomeini. (A Herblock Cartoon, copyright by The Herb Block Foundation)

Three Investigations Launched

When the November 1986 revelations made the scope of the operations public, three investigations were launched: the Tower commission, the work of independent counsel Lawrence Walsh, and the Congressional Committees Investigating the Iran-Contra Affair. The Tower commission's conclusion shielded President Reagan from any sustained consideration of impeachment by Congress. Walsh's efforts were hampered by the congressional investigation, which granted immunity to many of the key players in order to get them to testify publicly.

With the Tower commission's efforts concluded and Walsh's investigation just beginning, attention turned to the congressional inquiry. In January 1987, the leadership of the House and the Senate had merged the efforts of the 11 members of the U.S. Senate Select Committee on Secret Military Assistance to Iran and the Nicaraguan Opposition and the 15 members of the parallel U.S. House of Representatives Select Committee to Investigate Covert Arms Transactions with Iran to form the Congressional Committees Investigating the Iran-Contra Affair. In March the committee chairs announced that joint hearings would be held. The committees bore responsibility for investigating four issues: sales of arms to Iran, diversion of funds to the contras, violations of federal law, and the National Security Council's role in foreign policy. The hearings went on to exceed the initial deadline of August 1, 1987; the final report would not appear until November.

By limiting the term and scope of the committee's investigation, the congressional leadership effectively defined the purpose of the hearings as a search for evidence that would serve as a so-called smoking gun, indicating that the president knew of and had approved the illegal activities. Because the Tower commission had already declared that Reagan was not party to the illegalities of the affair, Congress had set itself a task in which it could not live up to the precedent of the Watergate hearings, when the sworn testimony of administration witnesses led the House of Representatives to the brink of impeaching President Richard Nixon. The committee agreed not to subpoena either President Reagan or Vice President Bush, thus preventing any direct questioning of the leaders of the executive branch. Furthermore, the granting of immunity to key witnesses, intended to prompt honest and open testimony, served to hamper the later prosecution of those whom Special Prosecutor Walsh wanted to try because their congressional testimony could not be used against them in court. Another key player, CIA Director Casey, died May 7, 1987, of brain cancer.

Chairing the joint committee were Senator Daniel Inouye (D-Hawaii) and Representative Lee Hamilton (D-Ind.). Inouye had been a member of the Senate committee that investigated Watergate in 1973. Hamilton brought a wealth of experience from his years in the House. The Senate vice chairman of the committee was Senator Warren Rudman of New Hampshire, a conservative but independent Republican chosen by Inouye as a bow to bipartisanship. Dante Fascell (D-Fla.) served as Hamilton's vice chair on the House side. Both leaders wanted the investigation to focus on how the Iran-contra illegalities came about so that Congress could prevent such executive-branch subterfuge in the future. The sometimes unwieldy joint committee arrangement meant that the hearings alternated each week between the Senate Caucus Room in the Russell Senate Office Building and the House Foreign Affairs Committee Room in the Rayburn House Office Building.

The committee hired Arthur Liman as the chief counsel for the Senate and John Nields as chief counsel for the House. Both were eminently qualified for their duties, but they were not chosen with the prismatic effect of television in mind. In addition to Liman and Nields, the Republican minority of the House members, led by ranking member (and future vice president) Richard Cheney (R-Wyo.), oversaw its own minority counsel and committee staff.

From the outset of the hearings, the committee leadership and the majority of the witnesses worked from competing scripts. To accommodate the 26 members of the committee, a two-tiered riser had to be installed in the hearing room, which made them seem like grand inquisitors sitting in judgment of the beleaguered individuals who gave testimony. The hiring of Liman as the lawyer for the Senate and Nields as the counsel for the House was based on their professional qualifications, not their ability to project a likable persona to a television audience. Neither modified his appearance or his manner to improve the way in which he was perceived by the television audience when questioning witnesses. Liman, the gruff New Yorker whose unruly hair often draped into his eyes, and Nields, young-looking with a coif that brushed the collar of his suit jacket, often appeared as if they were imperious tribunes persecuting brave individuals who were only trying to do what they thought was right. The image they conveyed was at odds with the neat hair and military bearing of many of the witnesses. While the committee leadership strove for a balanced hearing to investigate the breadth and scope of the affair, the more media-savvy conspirators used the opportunity to win public sympathy for themselves and their efforts. Thus the committee ended up providing a platform for the administration's witnesses and their supporters among the Republican committee members.

The group of 28 witnesses questioned by the committee included contractors, contras, private funders, staffers from the NSC and the CIA, minor functionaries, and key cabinet secretaries. The first witness, Secord, set the confrontational pattern for the hearings. The former Air Force general, who testified for four days, contended that he had fully controlled the arms-for-hostages operation, replete with dummy corporations and Swiss bank accounts. Secord, with his close-cropped hair and military bearing, proved to be more appealing to the millions watching on television than Liman, whose hair often fell across his forehead as he questioned Secord. Liman's appearance and style prompted hateful letters from the public, many of them anti-Semitic.

Secord often replied to the committee in a dismissive and disdainful tone. Representative Henry Hyde (R-Ill.) chimed in to support Secord, questioning the line of inquiry that Liman pursued. Also damaging to the committee's efforts was the fact that the records of Secord's dealings with Hakim and Swiss banks were not yet available. Thus Secord set the combative tone for many of the witnesses that followed, which often kept members of the committee on the defensive.

The next witness was McFarlane. Alone among the witnesses, McFarlane expressed remorse for his actions. McFarlane had attempted suicide in February 1987 in response to the controversy over his role in the scandal. In the course of his testimony McFarlane affirmed that he had thought that North was working directly with Casey. Despite misgivings at the time, McFarlane detailed how he had falsified the chronology of events to help cover up the illegalities of the affair. McFarlane's reputation as a good soldier who always followed orders, gained during his service in Vietnam and in the Nixon administration, made him the tragic figure of the scandal: He went against his own better judgment and experience.

Following McFarlane were Robert Owen and Adolfo Calero. Owen had worked with contra leader Calero while working for the Nicaraguan Humanitarian

Former national security adviser Robert McFarlane testifies before the joint House Senate panel investigating the Iran-Contra Affair on Capitol Hill in Washington, July 15, 1987. McFarlane requested to return before the committee and called Lt. Col. Oliver North's testimony untrue in major areas. (Lana Harris/Associated Press)

Assistance Office of the State Department. He had collaborated with North to provide funding and assistance to the contras when such aid was proscribed by the Boland Amendments. Owen, who had been granted immunity, justified his illegal activities to aid the contras by claiming they had been noble and just. Calero, a Nicaraguan businessman educated at the University of Notre Dame who had opposed Somoza and the Sandinistas, also defended North and his efforts to aid the contras.

Hakim testified next. Hakim, a businessman of Iranian parentage who was raised in Beirut and educated in the United States, had worked with Secord on the Enterprise. Hakim's testimony undermined the credibility of both Secord and North. Members of the Enterprise had used money funneled into the Swiss bank accounts managed by Hakim for questionable expenditures. Hakim's willingness to engage in kickbacks to find a way to get American hostages released, while making profits from the associated arms deals, exemplified what came to be described as the privatizing of foreign policy. The proof of privatization was reinforced by the appearance of several wealthy donors who had been solicited by the White House to fund the contras.

The first major administration witness was Assistant Secretary of State Elliott Abrams. Abrams had been an important administration spokesperson for Reagan's confrontational interventionist policy in Central America. Abrams, a Harvard-trained lawyer, gave guarded answers about his involvement in the diversion to the contras of profits from the sale of arms to Iran. In the course of his testimony Abrams admitted that he had misled Congress about the funding of the contras. He had solicited the sultan of Brunei, a small Islamic monarchy on the island of Borneo in the south Pacific, which became another of the comedic episodes in the affair. When queried during congressional testimony as to whether he had sought funding from any Middle Eastern countries for the contras, Abrams had answered no. When confronted with this by the Iran-contra committee, Abrams claimed he had been honest because Brunei is not in the Middle East. The $2 million that Abrams garnered from the sultan ended up in the wrong Swiss bank account because of a clerical error by North's secretary, and thus was never received by the contras. Congressman Jack Brooks (D-Tex.), exasperated with Abrams's evasions, asked him, "Do you have to be authorized to tell the truth?"

The testimony of Glenn Robinette, a former CIA employee, added to the case for North's corruption. Secord had hired Robinette, who had worked in technical services creating false documents and James Bond–type gear for the CIA, to gather negative information on anti-contra activists who had brought suit against Secord and his allies. Robinette then aided North with the installation of a $13,800 security system for North's home in Northern Virginia. Secord and Hakim paid Robinette for the system, thus violating the prohibition against government employees receiving gratuities. Later, Robinette created backdated bills for the installation of the system to make it look like North had arranged for the installation himself. Republicans on the committee reacted especially negatively to Robinette's remarks, because now there was evidence that North had materially benefited from the Enterprise and then took steps to cover up his breaking of the law, tarnishing the claims of North and his collaborators that their misdeeds were inspired by noble motives.

Several witnesses gave testimony pertaining to legal reasoning during the period of the diversion of funds to the contras and the days after the Enterprise became known to the public. Bretton Sciaroni, a lawyer and the sole staff person of the president's Intelligence Oversight Board, explained his opinion that the Boland Amendments did not pertain to the NSC but only to the Department of Defense and the CIA. The goal of Sciaroni's work was to provide legal justification for North's operations. Assistant Attorney General Charles Cooper had worked with Attorney General Meese in November 1986 to investigate the revelations about the arms sales to Iran. Cooper had interviewed North at that time. The committee members were stunned by Cooper's tale of the casual pace of Meese's investigation, which had allowed North and others to destroy documents crucial to understanding the Enterprise. When asked whether he thought that North's testimony could be believed, Cooper stated that he did not think "an oath in any way enhances the obligation of truthfulness."

Despite the legal significance of the inquiry, public interest had waned in the weeks following Secord's testimony. The broadcast networks returned to their usual daytime schedules of soap operas, relegating the hearings to cable outlets CNN and C-SPAN. The viewing public was reawakened to the drama on Capitol Hill when Fawn Hall, who had been Oliver North's secretary, began her testimony. Having been granted immunity, Hall testified that she had helped North destroy phone logs and e-mail messages pertinent to his illegal actions. The young secretary, who wore her hair fashionably long and feathered, defended her actions and those of her superior. She stated that she understood her work for North to be part of the effort to recover American hostages and therefore legitimate. She justified the destruction of documentation that revealed North's clandestine actions by affirming her faith in North and claiming that, in pursuit of just ends, "sometimes you have to go above the written law."

Hall clearly articulated the "end justifies the means" logic that had driven the entire Enterprise. With her good looks and photogenic manner Hall won the popularity contest over the committee and gained a short-lived fame from what could have been her public humiliation. Hall's appearance contributed to the growing public sentiment that the committee members were persecuting well-meaning, loyal Americans who had been trying to do the right thing. The media furor over Hall's attractiveness, in contrast with the dour and serious all-male committee that had questioned her, underscored the victory of image over substance in the context of televised hearings and heightened the charged environment into which her former boss would enter.

The defining moments of the hearings came with the six days of testimony from North. The committee

The key figures of the Iran-Contra Affair as caricatures from Lewis Carroll's stories: National Security Council staffer Oliver North is the White Rabbit, holding a bag of payoff money; North's secretary Fawn Hall is Alice, busy shredding documents; the House and Senate are the timorous twins Tweedledum and Tweedledee; Retired Air Force Major General Richard Secord is the Walrus; Assistant Secretary Elliott Abrams is the Carpenter; William Casey, directory of the CIA, is the March Hare; and Attorney General Edwin Meese is the Dormouse. President Ronald Reagan reigns over the scene as the Mad Hatter while the Nicaraguan contras as Humpty Dumpty teeter precariously and the USSR as the Cheshire Cat looks on with a grin. (Library of Congress)

returned from its Independence Day recess to take part in what the historian Sean Wilentz has described as "a boiling hot piece of right wing performance art." North, who had generally worn civilian clothes while performing his NSC duties at the White House, appeared before the committee in his Marine uniform festooned with medals. Once granted partial immunity, ensuring that his congressional testimony could not be used against him in a criminal trial, North admitted that he had shredded documents, lied to Congress, misled the CIA, and engaged in subterfuge. In lengthy and combative responses, North and his counsel, Brendan Sullivan, used a variety of angles to put the committee back on its heels by making it seem that Congress opposed all covert action rather than actions about which it was not informed. What began as an investigation of North's misdeeds became a venue for a spirited defense of North's actions. North played the role of the lone combatant facing off against the tribunal, linking his past battles in Vietnam to the continuing battle of American light against Communist, terrorist darkness in Central America and the Middle East.

While Liman, Nields, and the committee members tried to pin North down on the details of his actions, North's performance in front of a television audience of millions spawned an effect unintended by his inquisitors. During North's six days of testimony, the "Olliemania" phenomenon led to an outpouring of public support for the colonel, which influenced the tone of the committee's questions. The Republican minority members were emboldened by the surge in support for North, using their question time to add to North's accolades. But the use of funds for private purposes such as the by-now infamous security fence at North's home created common ground between North's critics and supporters on the committee. The wispy garlands of noble sacrifice in defense of the nation frayed when exposed to the abrasive facts of the minor larceny represented by the receipts for fences and personal expenses for which North had used money diverted from the Enterprise.

Nonetheless, many on the committee and in the general public liked the idea of using the Iranian money to fund the contra "freedom fighters," which North described as a "neat idea." North's appearance served the administration's purposes by deflecting attention from the larger issue of its crimes and focusing it on the personality of North and his poignant personal story. North made it seem that Congress, not the administration, had damaged the national interest by blocking aid to the contras and interfering with sensitive operations related to the attempt to gain freedom for American hostages. The positive reaction to North's appearance at the hearing enabled him to go on to be an important conservative political figure and media personality in the years after the affair.

In contrast to North's passionate defense of the contras and the Enterprise in front of the committee, Poindexter's testimony returned the hearings to the tedious task of extracting information from a recalcitrant witness. The former national security adviser, first in his class at the Naval Academy and renowned for his encyclopedic recall of details, seemed to suffer from memory failure during his four days of testimony. In response to the committee's questioning, Poindexter gave variations of the reply of "I don't know" 184 times. Poindexter testified that he had never told the president about the diversion of funds from the sale of missiles to Iran to the Nicaraguan contras, but that he thought that Reagan would have approved of it. Poindexter's appearance sapped the hearings of dramatic tension because he laid to rest any hope of finding evidence that Reagan knew about the diversion of funds to the contras. According to Poindexter, there was no smoking gun because he had insulated the president from any knowledge of the diversion.

The witnesses who followed Poindexter included cabinet secretaries Shultz, Meese, and Weinberger. Secretary of State Shultz explained to Republican members of the committee why he had not resigned despite his opposition to the arm sales to Iran. Secretary of Defense Weinberger delivered a riposte to the Tower commission's contention that he had held himself aloof from the affair. Attorney General Meese defended his investigation of the affair. While these trusted advisers to the president revealed their disagreements and divisions, they did not directly implicate Reagan in the illegalities of the affair.

The final group of witnesses comprised men connected to the CIA. Joseph Fernandez, also known as Tomas Castillo, had served as CIA station chief in Costa Rica. Fernandez had worked with North to bolster the flagging southern front in the contra war against Nicaragua. Duane "Dewey" Clarridge had also worked for the CIA and helped to plan the clandestine mining of Nicaragua's harbors. Clair George, another CIA veteran, testified about the untrustworthiness of Manucher Ghorbanifar and his criticism of the evolution of the Enterprise. George indicated that the late William J. Casey had not heeded his warnings about the dangers of dealing with Ghorbanifar and forged ahead in league with North to create the clandestine network that had been revealed since October 1986.

The hearings concluded on August 3, 1987. The committee had heard 28 public witnesses and about 500 private testimonies. The committee staff had reviewed 300,000 documents. On November 18, 1987, the committee released its lengthy final report, which included a dissenting opinion from the Republican minority. While the minority dissent questioned the purpose and legitimacy of the investigation, the majority report concluded:

> The common ingredients of the Iran and Contra policies were secrecy, deception, and disdain for the law. A small group of senior officials believed that they alone know what was right. . . . They told neither the Secretary of State, the Congress, nor the American people of their actions. When exposure was threatened, they destroyed official documents and lied to

Cabinet officials, to the public and the elected representatives in Congress. They testified that they even withheld key facts from the President.

The Independent Counsel

The hearings had produced no smoking gun showing Reagan's direct consent for the illegal actions committed by his subordinates. The hearings had given wide exposure to the efforts of members of the Reagan administration to pursue foreign policy objectives in a clandestine manner. After the close of the hearings and the filing of the committee's report, the work of Lawrence Walsh, the independent counsel, continued past Reagan's term in office into the administration of his successor, George H. W. Bush.

As a result of Walsh's work, grand-jury indictments were brought against North, Poindexter, Secord, and Hakim in March 1988. The indictments comprised four charges: conspiring to obstruct the U.S. Congress, diverting public funds from arms sales to Iran to aid the contras in Nicaragua, stealing public funds for private ends, and lying to members of Congress and other government officials. In effect, the indictments charged the defendants with conducting a private foreign policy in violation of the Constitution.

Several obstacles blocked Walsh from initiating his prosecutions. The Reagan administration and a number of its former officials, also subject to independent-counsel investigations, argued that the independent-counsel law unconstitutionally denied the president important executive power. In June 1988, the U.S. Supreme Court rejected this argument and upheld the law's constitutionality. Then Iran-contra defendants Poindexter, North, Secord, and Hakim moved for dismissal of Walsh's charges. They argued that their compelled testimony before the joint congressional committees had violated their Fifth Amendment rights. U.S. District Judge Gerhard Gesell denied the motion, clearing the way for the trials to begin.

The refusal of the Justice Department and the White House to release classified information crucial to the case on the grounds that it was vital to national security hampered Walsh's prosecution. Without this information the prosecutor's case imploded, and thus Walsh had to drop the broader charges of conspiracy and diversion in favor of the less serious charges remaining in the indictments.

On May 4, 1989, Walsh won a conviction against North for obstructing Congress, destroying documents, and accepting an illegal gratuity. North's trial revealed evidence that suggested that both Reagan and Bush had larger roles in the Iran-Contra Affair than either the Tower commission or the congressional committees had determined. During the trial, North's attorneys attempted but failed to subpoena Reagan. In his 1992 memoir North contended that Reagan had known the arrangements of the Iran-Contra Affair. Judge Gesell sentenced North to two years' probation, 1,200 hours of community service, and a $150,000 fine.

North appealed. On July 20, 1990, the U.S. Court of Appeals for the District of Columbia suspended all three of North's felony convictions and overturned his conviction for destroying classified documents because of North's testimony before Congress. The appellate ruling affirmed the reasoning that North, Poindexter, Secord, and Hakim had presented before their trials: Congress's decision to grant immunity to North was in conflict with the Fifth Amendment protection of witnesses against self-incrimination. The appeals court directed the trial court to re-examine North's earlier testimony. The appellate judge, Laurence Silberman, had been the 1980 co-chair of the Reagan-Bush campaign's foreign-policy advisory group, and thus drew criticism for conflict of interest. On September 16, 1991, Judge Gesell dropped all charges against North.

Poindexter's trial followed a trajectory parallel to North's. After failing to win release of classified subpoenaed materials, Walsh narrowed his case to charges that Poindexter had provided false information and made false statements to Congress. Poindexter's counsel successfully subpoenaed former president Reagan, who became the first former president ordered to testify in a criminal trial regarding the conduct of affairs during his administration. Reagan provided an eight-hour videotaped deposition in which he stated frankly that the Iran-Contra Affair had been "a covert action taken at my behest." Under oath Reagan confirmed that he had played a leading part in initiating the actions investigated by Congress. But Poindexter failed to win access to the former president's diaries, which his attorneys argued were crucial to Poindexter's defense.

Walsh succeeded in convicting Poindexter. In testimony for the prosecution, North said that he had seen Poindexter destroy a high-level secret document, signed by the president, which detailed the Iran arms sales as an exchange-for-hostages deal. North also testified that Poindexter had instructed him to lie to Congress. Other testimony revealed that Poindexter had erased some 5,000 computer files after the Iran-contra story broke in the media in November 1986. On April 7, 1990, the jury convicted Poindexter on all five counts in the indictment. Sentenced on June 11, 1990, to six months in prison, he became the first Iran-contra defendant to receive a prison term. However, in November the Court of Appeals for the District of Columbia overturned Poindexter's conviction, ruling

Arrest photos of Lieutenant Colonel Oliver North. Involved in the sale of weapons to Iran to encourage the release of U.S. hostages and the subsequent diversion of funds to help the contra rebels of Nicaragua, North was convicted of three felony counts and sentenced to a three-year suspended prison term, two years' probation, $150,000 in fines, and 1,200 hours of community service. The convictions were vacated by an appeals court. North's sober countenance and nondescript business suit contrast with his aggressive performance during the hearings when he wore his Marine colonel's uniform bedecked with medals. (National Archives)

that Poindexter's congressional testimony had been unfairly used against him.

In March 1988, former national security adviser McFarlane pleaded guilty to four misdemeanor counts of withholding information from Congress and was fined a modest amount. Two private fund-raisers, Carl Channell and Richard Miller, pleaded guilty to using a tax-exempt organization to raise money to purchase arms for the contras. Channell was sentenced to probation, while Miller was ordered to perform public service. In November 1989, Secord, Hakim, and a corporation owned by Hakim all pleaded guilty to relatively minor counts. Abrams pleaded guilty to withholding information from Congress. He was placed on probation for two years, assigned 100 hours of community service, and made to pay a $50 fine. Republicans in Congress criticized the multimillion-dollar expenditures of Walsh's investigation as partisan politics.

In July 1991, Alan Fiers, who had served as chief of the CIA's Central American Task Force during the years of the Iran-Contra actions, plead guilty to two misdemeanor counts of withholding information from Congress. Fiers received a sentence in January 1992 of one year probation and 100 hours of community service.

In 1992, Walsh brought an indictment against the highest-ranking Reagan administration official to be charged in the Iran-Contra Affair: Caspar W. Weinberger, the former defense secretary. Weinberger was indicted on June 16, 1992, on five felony counts: one count of obstructing the congressional committees' investigations; two counts of making false statements to investigators working for Walsh and Congress; and two counts of perjury related to his congressional testimony. Penalties for each count were a maximum of five years in prison and up to $250,000 in fines.

Walsh based the case on evidence gathered from notes that Weinberger had written while serving for six years in the Reagan administration. These notes, many barely readable, were written on hundreds of small pieces of paper, which made up Weinberger's personal diary. Weinberger had given them to the Library of Congress, with the requirement that no one could read them without his personal consent. Throughout the Iran-contra investigations, Weinberger had repeatedly testified to Congress and the Tower commission that he had argued against the arms-for-hostages scheme when it was discussed by White House officials. Walsh did not make Weinberger's involvement an issue in the 1992 indictment. Instead, he focused on Weinberger's testimony under oath that he had not kept notes or a personal diary during the arms sale period. The discovery of the notes in the Library of Congress indicated that Weinberger had presented false testimony.

On June 19, 1992, Weinberger pleaded not guilty to all five felony charges. Judge Thomas F. Hogan set a tentative trial date of November 2, 1992, one day before the presidential election. This timing raised the question of whether Weinberger's trial would cause political embarrassment for President George H. W. Bush, who was campaigning against Bill Clinton. The Friday before the election, Walsh announced a new indictment against Weinberger, which centered on a note that had been written by Weinberger about a 1986 White House meeting. The note seemed to contradict Bush's claim that, as vice president, he had not been involved in the arms-for-hostages decision making. Senate Republicans asked the Justice Department to name an independent counsel to investigate whether the Clinton campaign had been behind the indictment, but the attorney general denied the request.

President Bush lost his race for reelection on November 3, 1992. In a Christmas Eve reprieve the following month, Bush pardoned Weinberger and five others implicated in the Iran-Contra Affair. The pardon cited Weinberger's record of public and military service, his recent ill health, and a desire to put Iran-contra to rest. Bush also pardoned former assistant secretary of state Abrams; former CIA officials Clair George, Duane Clarridge, and Alan Fiers; and former national security adviser McFarlane. Walsh accused Bush of furthering a cover-up and thwarting judicial process. He had long maintained that top Reagan administration officials had engaged in a cover-up to protect their president. Now, he promised, Bush would become the subject of his remaining investigation.

Bush's only testimony had taken place in a January 1988 videotaped deposition. An unsettled question was why Bush's personal diaries were withheld from prosecutors for six years; their existence was only disclosed to the independent counsel's office following the 1992 presidential election. Throughout 1993, Walsh sought to interview the former president but was blocked by Bush's attorneys. Bush consistently insisted on placing limits on any interview. Walsh refused those limits, complained that Bush was stalling the investigation, and ultimately abandoned the attempt to question Bush.

In 1993 Walsh chose not to indict former attorney general Meese. In 1986, Meese had claimed that Reagan had no knowledge of the arms sales to Iran. While Walsh contended that the statement was not true, he admitted that building a criminal case against Meese would have been difficult: Too much time had passed and could therefore have bolstered memory loss as a defense.

On August 4, 1993, after six-and-a-half years and $35.7 million, Walsh concluded the Iran-contra investigation and submitted his final report to the special court that had appointed him. By 1993 the statute of limitations on crimes that may have been committed prior to 1987 had expired. Walsh had brought indictments against 14 of the participants in the Iran-Contra Affair. The granting of limited immunity to North and Poindexter gave them grounds to have their convictions overturned on appeal. The case of the Iran-Contra Affair was closed in legal terms, but it lived on in the politics of the nation.

The Shadowlands

Senator Warren Rudman, co-chair during the Iran-contra hearings, succinctly summed up the stakes of the committee's work:

> Here was a case, the only one we know of, where the Congress's absolute power to fund the foreign policy of America was subverted by a White House that was determined to do something else, that converted American military hardware to money and that some of that money found its way into supporting a policy that the majority of the Congress opposed.

Rudman might have added that Congress also failed to bring the culprits to justice. Although the committee's majority recommended ways in which Congress could prevent such actions by the executive in the future, in practical terms the Iran-contra conspirators achieved much of what they had attempted and got away with it. By entering in the middle of the drama, as described by Maine senators and committee members George Mitchell and William Cohen, Congress was unable to determine the denouement of the story. The plot of the Watergate hearings was almost reversed, with Congress losing prestige and the administration successfully surviving its most serious scandal.

Several key players in the political drama that dominated the summer of 1987 went on to profit economically and politically from the attention they had gained from breaking the law. John Poindexter and Elliott Abrams worked in the administration of President George W. Bush. Dick Cheney, leader of the House Republicans on the Iran-contra committee, became Bush's vice president. Most prominently, North narrowly lost a bid to represent Virginia in the Senate in 1994 while successfully parlaying his fame into fortune. The unintended star of Congress's contribution to the

Iran-contra drama, who once pleaded that he was just a poor lieutenant colonel, went on to make a fortune as an author, entrepreneur, and media idol.

North and his family left the confines of their ill-gotten security fence for a mountain retreat in the Blue Ridge Mountains of Virginia they dubbed Narnia, a name borrowed from the children's fantasy stories of author C. S. Lewis. Thus Senator Moynihan's observation, that in the Iran-Contra Affair "the very processes of American government were put in harm's way by a conspiracy of faithless or witless men: sometimes both," may not be quite right. North and those he joined with shared a faith and used their wits, not in the furtherance of democracy but in the weaving of a myth that veiled their nefarious goals and illegal actions. And they won.

DOCUMENTS

Boland Amendment (Summary), 1983

Representative Edward P. Boland (D-Mass.), chair of the House Select Committee on Intelligence, oversaw the approval of requests from the president for intelligence operations. The Reagan administration had forged ahead in aiding the contras without seeking congressional approval. When the House of Representatives passed the 1983 Defense Authorization Act in December, it included an amendment drafted by Boland that banned such funding "for the purpose of overthrowing the Government of Nicaragua." Although President Ronald Reagan signed the bill and promised to abide by Boland's amendment, the administration and the CIA continued to solicit aid for the contras from private donors and other countries. While the Democratic majority in the House generally opposed aiding the contras, the Republican-controlled Senate supported the administration's program. After the House and Senate versions of the Defense Authorization Act went through conference committee, the end result was a $24 million limit on contra aid for 1984. This limitation prompted Reagan's advisers to seek illegal methods for funding the contras.

BOLAND AMENDMENT (SUMMARY), 1983

An amendment to prohibit covert assistance for military operations in Nicaragua and to authorize overt interdiction assistance. The overt interdiction assistance consists of assistance furnished by the President on terms he may dictate to any friendly country in Central America to enable that country to prevent the use of its territory for the transfer of military equipment from or through Cuba or Nicaragua or any other country. The assistance must be overt. For this overt aid $30,000,000 is provided for FY'83 and $50,000,000 is provided for FY'84.

Source: http://www.statemaster.com/encyclopedia/Boland-Amendment.

President Reagan's Address to the Nation on the Iran Arms and Contra Aid Controversy, November 13, 1986

On November 13, 1986, President Ronald Reagan, in a nationally televised speech, admitted that the sale of missiles to Iran had taken place. He explained the transaction as part of an elaborate policy intended to persuade Iran to pressure the Lebanese groups with which it was allied to release the Americans they held hostage.

PRESIDENT REAGAN'S SPEECH TO THE NATION, NOVEMBER 13, 1986

Good evening. I know you've been reading, seeing, and hearing a lot of stories the past several days attributed to Danish sailors, unnamed observers at Italian ports and Spanish harbors, and especially unnamed government officials of my administration. Well, now you're going to hear the facts from a White House source, and you know my name.

I wanted this time to talk with you about an extremely sensitive and profoundly important matter of foreign policy. For 18 months now we have had underway a secret diplomatic initiative to Iran. That initiative was undertaken for the simplest and best of reasons: to renew a relationship with the nation of Iran, to bring an honorable end to the bloody 6-year war between Iran and Iraq, to eliminate state-sponsored terrorism and subversion, and to effect the safe return of all hostages. Without Iran's cooperation, we cannot bring an end to the Persian Gulf war; without Iran's concurrence, there can be no enduring peace in the Middle East. For 10 days now, the American and world press have been full of reports and rumors about this initiative and these objectives. Now, my fellow Americans, there's an old saying that nothing spreads so quickly as a rumor. So, I thought it was time to speak with you directly, to tell you firsthand about our dealings with Iran. As Will Rogers once said, "Rumor travels faster, but it don't stay put as long as truth." So, let's get to the facts.

The charge has been made that the United States has shipped weapons to Iran as ransom payment for the release of American hostages in Lebanon, that the United States undercut its allies and secretly violated American policy against trafficking with terrorists. Those charges are utterly false. The United States has not made concessions to those who hold our people captive in Lebanon. And we will not. The United States has not swapped boatloads or planeloads of American weapons for the return of American hostages. And we will not. Other reports have surfaced alleging U.S. involvement: reports of a sealift to Iran using Danish ships to carry American arms; of vessels in Spanish ports being employed in secret U.S. arms shipments; of Italian ports being used; of the U.S. sending spare parts and weapons for combat aircraft. All these reports are quite exciting, but as far as we're concerned, not one of them is true.

During the course of our secret discussions, I authorized the transfer of small amounts of defensive weapons and spare parts for defensive systems to Iran. My purpose was to convince Tehran that our negotiators were acting with my authority, to send a signal that the United States was prepared to replace the animosity between us with a new relationship. These modest deliveries, taken together, could easily fit into a single cargo plane. They could not, taken together, affect the outcome of the 6-year war between Iran and Iraq nor could they affect in any way the military balance between the two countries. Those with whom we were in contact took considerable risks and needed a signal of our serious intent if they were to carry on and broaden the dialog. At the same time we undertook this initiative, we made clear that Iran must oppose all forms of international terrorism as a condition of progress in our relationship. The most significant step which Iran could take, we indicated, would be to use its influence in Lebanon to secure the release of all hostages held there.

Some progress has already been made. Since U.S. Government contact began with Iran, there's been no evidence of Iranian Government complicity in acts of terrorism against the United States. Hostages have come home, and we welcome the efforts that the Government of Iran has taken in the past and is currently undertaking.

But why, you might ask, is any relationship with Iran important to the United States? Iran encompasses some of the most critical geography in the world. It lies between the Soviet Union and access to the warm waters of the Indian Ocean. Geography explains why the Soviet Union has sent an army into Afghanistan to dominate that country and, if they could, Iran and Pakistan. Iran's geography gives it a critical position from which adversaries could interfere with oil flows from the Arab States that border the Persian Gulf. Apart from geography, Iran's oil deposits are important to the long-term health of the world economy.

For these reasons, it is in our national interest to watch for changes within Iran that might offer hope for an improved relationship. Until last year there was little to justify that hope. Indeed, we have bitter and enduring disagreements that persist today. At the heart of our quarrel has been Iran's past sponsorship of international terrorism. Iranian policy has been devoted to expelling all Western influence from the Middle East. We cannot abide that because our interests in the Middle East are vital. At the same time, we seek no territory or special position in Iran. The Iranian revolution is a fact of history, but between American and Iranian basic national interests there need be no permanent conflict.

Since 1983 various countries have made overtures to stimulate direct contact between the United States and Iran; European, Near East, and Far East countries have attempted to serve as intermediaries. Despite a U.S. willingness to proceed, none of these overtures bore fruit. With this history in mind, we were receptive last year when we were alerted to the possibility of establishing a direct dialog with Iranian officials. Now, let me repeat: America's longstanding goals in the region have been to help preserve Iran's independence from Soviet domination; to bring an honorable end to the bloody Iran-Iraq war; to halt the export of subversion and terrorism in the region. A major impediment to those goals has been an absence of dialog, a cutoff in communication between us. It's because of Iran's strategic importance and its influence in the Islamic world that we chose to probe for a better relationship between our countries.

Our discussions continued into the spring of this year. Based upon the progress we felt we had made, we sought to raise the diplomatic level of contacts. A meeting was arranged in Tehran. I then asked my former national security adviser, Robert McFarlane, to undertake a secret mission and gave him explicit instructions. I asked him to go to Iran to open a dialog, making stark and clear our basic objectives and disagreements. The 4 days of talks were conducted in a civil fashion, and American personnel were not mistreated. Since then, the dialog has continued and step-by-step progress continues to be made. Let me repeat: Our interests are clearly served by opening a dialog with Iran and thereby helping to end the Iran-Iraq war. That war has dragged on for more than 6 years, with no prospect of a negotiated settlement. The slaughter on both sides has been enormous, and the adverse economic and political consequences for that vital region of the world have been growing. We sought to establish communication with both sides in that senseless struggle, so that we could assist in bringing about a cease-fire and, eventually, a settlement. We have sought to be evenhanded by working with both sides and with other interested nations to prevent a widening of the war.

This sensitive undertaking has entailed great risk for those involved. There is no question but that we could never have begun or continued this dialog had the initiative been disclosed earlier. Due to the publicity of the past week, the entire initiative is very much at risk today. There is ample precedent in our history for this kind of secret diplomacy. In 1971 then-President Nixon sent his national security adviser on a secret mission to China. In that case, as today, there was a basic requirement for discretion and for a sensitivity to the situation in the nation we were attempting to engage.

Since the welcome return of former hostage David Jacobsen, there has been unprecedented speculation and countless reports that have not only been wrong but have been potentially dangerous to the hostages and destructive of the opportunity before us. The efforts of courageous people like Terry Waite have been jeopardized. So extensive have been the false rumors and erroneous reports that the risks of remaining silent now exceed the risks of speaking out. And that's why I decided to address you tonight. It's been widely reported, for example, that the Congress, as well as top executive branch officials, were circumvented. Although the efforts we undertook were highly sensitive and involvement of government officials was limited to those with a strict need to know, all appropriate Cabinet officers were fully consulted. The actions I authorized were, and continue to be, in full compliance with Federal law. And the relevant committees of Congress are being, and will be, fully informed.

Another charge is that we have tilted toward Iran in the Gulf war. This, too, is unfounded. We have consistently condemned the violence on both sides. We have consistently sought a negotiated settlement that preserves the territorial integrity of both nations. The overtures we've made to the Government of Iran have not been a shift to supporting one side over the other, rather, it has been a diplomatic initiative to gain some degree of access and influence within Iran—as well as Iraq—and to bring about an honorable end to that bloody conflict. It is in the interests of all parties in the Gulf region to end that war as soon as possible.

To summarize: Our government has a firm policy not to capitulate to terrorist demands. That no concessions policy remains in force, in spite of the wildly speculative and false stories about arms for hostages and alleged ransom payments. We did not—repeat—did not trade weapons or anything else for hostages, nor will we. Those who think that we have gone soft on terrorism should take up the question with Colonel Qadhafi. We have not, nor will we, capitulate to terrorists. We will, however, get on with advancing the vital interests of our great nation—in spite of terrorists and radicals who seek to sabotage our efforts and immobilize the United States. Our goals have been, and remain, to restore a relationship with Iran; to bring an honorable end to the war in the Gulf; to bring a halt to state-supported terror in the Middle East; and finally, to effect the safe return of all hostages from Lebanon.

As President, I've always operated on the belief that, given the facts, the American people will make the right decision. I believe that to be true now. I cannot guarantee the outcome. But as in the past, I ask for your support because I believe you share the hope for peace in the Middle East, for freedom for all hostages, and for a world free of terrorism. Certainly there are risks in this pursuit, but there are greater risks if we do not persevere. It will take patience and understanding; it will take continued resistance to those who commit terrorist acts; and it will take cooperation with all who seek to rid the world of this scourge.

Thank you, and God bless you.

Source: http://www.reagan.utexas.edu/archives/speeches/1986/111386c.htm.

President Reagan's News Conference, November 25, 1986

On November 25, 1986, President Ronald Reagan appeared briefly in a televised midday news conference to announce that he would appoint a special review board that would examine the workings of the National Security Council (NSC). The president also announced that Vice Admiral John Poindexter had resigned and that Lieutenant Colonel Oliver North had been "relieved of his duties." Reagan then turned the news conference over to Attorney General Edwin Meese. Meese stated that only North knew the full extent of the arms programs and that the possibility of criminal wrongdoing was being explored. The NSC had never before been the subject of a presidential commission inquiry.

PRESIDENT REAGAN'S NEWS CONFERENCE NOVEMBER 25, 1986

THE PRESIDENT: Last Friday, after becoming concerned whether my national security apparatus had provided me with a security—or a complete factual record with respect to the implementation of my policy toward Iran, I directed the Attorney General [Edwin Meese III] to undertake a review of this matter over the weekend and report to me on Monday. And yesterday Secretary Meese provided me and the White House Chief of Staff [Donald T. Regan] with a report on his preliminary findings. And this report led me to conclude that I was not fully informed on the nature of one of the activities undertaken in connection with this initiative. This action raises serious questions of propriety.

I've just met with my national security advisers and congressional leaders to inform them of the actions that I'm taking today. Determination of the full details of this action will require further review and investigation by the Department of Justice. Looking to the future, I will appoint a Special Review Board to conduct a comprehensive review of the role and procedures of the National Security Council staff in the conduct of foreign and national security policy. I anticipate receiving the reports from the Attorney General and the Special Review Board at the earliest possible date. Upon the completion of these reports, I will share their findings and conclusions with the Congress and the American people.

Although not directly involved, Vice Admiral John Poindexter has asked to be relieved of his assignment as Assistant to the President for National Security Affairs and to return to another assignment in the Navy. Lieutenant Colonel Oliver North [Deputy Director for

Political-Military Affairs] has been relieved of his duties on the National Security Council staff.

I am deeply troubled that the implementation of a policy aimed at resolving a truly tragic situation in the Middle East has resulted in such controversy. As I've stated previously, I believe our policy goals toward Iran were well founded. However, the information brought to my attention yesterday convinced me that in one aspect implementation of that policy was seriously flawed. While I cannot reverse what has happened, I'm initiating steps, including those I've announced today, to assure that the implementation of all future foreign and national security policy initiatives will proceed only in accordance with my authorization. Over the past 6 years we've realized many foreign policy goals. I believe we can yet achieve—and I intend to pursue—the objectives on which we all agree: a safer, more secure, and stable world.

And now, I'm going to ask Attorney General Meese to brief you.

REPORTER. What was the flaw?

Q[UESTION]. Do you still maintain you didn't make a mistake, Mr. President?

THE PRESIDENT. Hold it.

Q. Did you make a mistake in sending arms to Tehran, sir?

THE PRESIDENT. No, and I'm not taking any more questions. And in just a second, I'm going to ask Attorney General Meese to brief you on what we presently know of what he has found out.

Q. Is anyone else going to be let go, sir?

Q. Can you tell us—did Secretary Shultz—

Q. Is anyone else going to be let go? There have been calls for—

THE PRESIDENT. No one was let go. They chose to go.

Q. What about Secretary Shultz, Mr. President?

Q. Is Shultz going to stay, sir?

Q. How about Secretary Shultz and Mr. Regan, sir?

Q. What about Secretary Shultz, sir?

Q. Can you tell us if Secretary Shultz is going to stay?

Q. Can you give Secretary Shultz a vote of confidence if you feel that way?

THE PRESIDENT. May I give you Attorney General Meese?

Q. And who is going to run national security?

Q. What about Shultz, sir?

Q. Why won't you say what the flaw is?

Source: "Ronald Reagan Presidential Library, National Archives and Records Administration." Available at http://www.reagan.utexas.edu/archives/speeches/1986/112586a.htm.

Excerpt from Tower Commission Summary, February 26, 1987

On November 26, 1986, President Ronald Reagan announced that the members of the special review board would be former Texas senator John Tower, who would act as chair; former secretary of state Edmund Muskie; and former national security adviser Brent Scowcroft. Tower and Scowcroft were Republicans, Muskie was a Democrat. The Tower commission, as the group came to be known, interviewed 80 individuals, including the president. Reagan gave his testimony on December 2, 1986. During his discussion with the commission, he first said he had authorized the arms deal with Iran, but later he said he had not. On February 26, 1987, the commission submitted a 200-page report that criticized Reagan for not providing proper supervision to his staff and for not being aware of their actions. The commission placed most of the blame on Vice Admiral John Poindexter.

EXCERPT FROM TOWER COMMISSION SUMMARY, FEBRUARY 26, 1987

The arms transfers to Iran and the activities of the N.S.C. [National Security Council] staff in support of the contras are case studies in the perils of policy pursued outside the constraints of orderly process.

The Iran initiative ran directly counter to the Administration's own policies on terrorism, the Iran-Iraq war, and military support to Iran. This inconsistency was never resolved, nor were the consequences of this inconsistency fully considered and provided for. The result taken as a whole was a U.S. policy that worked against itself.

The Board believes that failure to deal adequately with these contradictions resulted in large part from the flaws in the manner in which decisions were made. Established procedures for making national security decisions were ignored. Reviews of the initiative by all the N.S.C. principals were too infrequent. The initiatives were not adequately vetted below the Cabinet level. Intelligence resources were underutilized. Applicable legal constraints were not adequately addressed. The whole matter was handled too informally, without adequate written records of what had been considered, discussed, and decided.

This pattern persisted in the implementation of the Iran initiative. The N.S.C. staff assumed direct operational control. The initiative fell within the traditional jurisdictions of the Departments of State, Defense, and C.I.A. Yet these agencies were largely ignored. Great reliance was placed on a network of private operators and intermediaries. How the initiative was to be carried out never received adequate attention from the N.S.C. principals or a tough working-level review. No periodic evaluation of the progress of the initiative was ever conducted. The result was an unprofessional and, in substantial part, unsatisfactory operation.

In all of this process, Congress was never notified. . . .

A FLAWED PROCESS

1. Contradictory Policies Were Pursued

The arms sales to Iran and the N.S.C. support for the contras demonstrate the risks involved when highly controversial initiatives are pursued covertly.

Arms Transfer to Iran

The initiative to Iran was a covert operation directly at odds with important and well-publicized policies of the Executive Branch. But the initiative itself embodied a fundamental contradiction. Two objectives were apparent from the outset: a strategic opening to Iran, and release of the U.S. citizens held hostage in Lebanon. The sale of arms to Iran appeared to provide a means to achieve both these objectives. It also played into the hands of those who had other interests—some of them personal financial gain—in engaging the United States in an arms deal with Iran.

In fact, the sale of arms was not equally appropriate for achieving both these objectives. Arms were what Iran wanted. If all the United States sought was to free the hostages, then an arms-for-hostages deal could achieve the immediate objectives of both sides. But if the U.S. objective was a broader strategic relationship, then the sale of arms should have been contingent upon first putting into place the elements of that relationship. An arms-for-hostages deal in this context could become counter-productive to achieving this broader strategic objective. In addition, release of the hostages would require exerting influence with Hezbollah, which could involve the most radical elements of the Iranian regime. The kind of strategic opening sought by the United States, however, involved what were regarded as more moderate elements. . . .

While the United States was seeking the release of the hostages in this way, it was vigorously pursuing policies that were dramatically opposed to such efforts. The Reagan Administration in particular had come into office declaring a firm stand against terrorism, which it continued to maintain. In December of 1985, the Administration completed a major study under the chairmanship of the Vice President. It resulted in a vigorous reaffirmation of U.S. opposition to terrorism in all its forms and a vow of total war on terrorism whatever its source. The Administration continued to pressure U.S. allies not to sell arms to Iran and not to make concessions to terrorists.

No serious effort was made to reconcile the inconsistency between these policies and the Iran initiative. No effort was made systematically to address the consequences of this inconsistency—the effect on U.S. policy when, as it inevitably would, the Iran initiative became known.

The Board believes that a strategic opening to Iran may have been in the national interest but that the United States never should have been a party to the arms transfers. As arms-for-hostages trades, they could not help but create an incentive for further hostage-taking. As a violation of the U.S. arms embargo, they could only remove inhibitions on other nations from selling arms to Iran. This threatened to upset the military balance between Iran and Iraq, with consequent jeopardy to the Gulf States and the interests of the West in that region. The arms-for-hostages trades rewarded a regime that clearly supported terrorism and hostage-taking. They increased the risks that the United States would be perceived, especially in the Arab world, as a creature of Israel. They suggested to other U.S. allies and friends in the region that the United States had shifted its policy in favor of Iran. They raised questions as to whether U.S. policy statements could be relied upon. . . .

N.S.C. Staff Support for the Contras

The activities of the N.S.C. staff in support of the contras sought to achieve an important objective of the Administration's foreign policy. The President had publicly and emphatically declared his support for the Nicaragua resistance. That brought his policy in direct conflict with that of the Congress, at least during the period that direct or indirect support of military operations in Nicaragua was barred.

Although the evidence before the Board is limited, no serious effort appears to have been made to come to grips with the risks to the President of direct N.S.C. support for the Contras in the face of these Congressional restrictions. . . .

2. The Decision-Making Process Was Flawed

Because the arms sales to Iran and the N.S.C. support for the contras occurred in settings of such controversy, one would expect that the decisions to undertake these activities would have been made only after intense and thorough consideration. In fact, a far different picture emerges.

Arms Transfers to Iran

The Iran initiative was handled almost casually and through informal channels, always apparently with an expectation that the process would end with the next arms-for-hostages exchange. It was subjected neither to the general procedures for interagency consideration and review of policy issues nor the more restrictive procedures set out in N.S.D.D. 159 for handling covert operations. This had a number of consequences:

(i) The Opportunity for a Full Hearing Before the President Was Inadequate. . . .
(ii) The Initiative Was Never Subjected to a Rigorous Review Below the Cabinet Level. . . .
(iii) The Process Was Too Informal.

The whole decision process was too informal. Even when meetings among N.S.C. principals did occur, often there was no prior notice of the agenda. No formal written minutes seem to have been kept. Decisions subsequently taken by the President were not formally recorded. An exception was the January 17 Finding, but even this was apparently not circulated or shown to key U.S. officials.

3. Implementation Was Unprofessional

The manner in which the Iran initiative was implemented and LtCol [Lieutenant-Colonel] North undertook to support the contras are very similar. This is in large part because the same cast of characters was involved. In both cases the operations were unprofessional, although the Board has much less evidence with respect to LtCol North's contra activities.

Arms Transfers to Iran

With the signing of the Jan. 17 Finding, the Iran initiative became a U.S. operation run by the N.S.C. staff. LtCol North made most of the significant operational decisions. He conducted the operation through Mr. Secord and his associates, a network of private individuals already involved in the contra resupply operation. To this was added a handful of selected individuals from the C.I.A.

But the C.I.A. support was limited. Two C.I.A. officials, though often at meetings, had a relatively limited role. One served as the point man for LtCol North in providing logistics and financial arrangements. The other (Mr. Allen) served as a contact between LtCol North and the intelligence community. By contrast, George Cave actually played a significant and expanding role. However, Clair George, Deputy Director for Operations, at C.I.A., told the Board: "George was paid by me and on the paper was working for me. But I think in the heat of the battle, . . . George was working for Oliver North."

Because so few people from the departments and agencies were told of the initiative, LtCol North cut himself off from resources and expertise from within the government. He relied instead on a number of private intermediaries, businessmen and other financial brokers, private operators, and Iranians hostile to the United States. Some of these were individuals with questionable credentials and potentially large personal financial interests in the transactions. This made the transactions unnecessarily complicated and invited kickbacks and payoffs. This arrangement also dramatically increased the risks that the initiative would leak. Yet no provision was made for such an eventuality. Further, the use of Mr. Secord's private network in the Iran initiative linked those operators with the resupply of the contras, threatening exposure of both operations if either became public.

The result was a very unprofessional operation. . . .

The implementation of the initiative was never subjected to a rigorous review. LtCol North appears to have kept VADM Poindexter fully informed of his activities. In addition, VADM Poindexter, LtCol North, and the C.I.A. officials involved apparently apprised Director Casey of many of the operational details. But LtCol North and his operation functioned largely outside the orbit of the U.S. Government. Their activities were not subject to critical reviews of any kind. . . .

N.S.C. Staff Support for the Contras

As already noted, the N.S.C. activities in support of the Contras and its role in the Iran initiative were of a piece. In the former, there was an added element of LtCol North's intervention in the customs investigation of the crash of the S.A.T. aircraft. Here too, selected C.I.A. officials reported directly to LtCol North. The limited evidence before the Board suggested that the activities in support of the Contras involved unprofessionalism much like that in the Iran operation.

4. Congress Was Never Notified

Congress was not apprised either of the Iran initiative or of the N.S.C. staff's activities in support of the Contras. . . .

The Board was unable to reach a conclusive judgment about whether the 1985 shipments of arms to Iran were approved in advance by the President. On balance the Board believes that it is plausible to conclude that he did approve them in advance. . . .

FAILURE OF RESPONSIBILITY

The N.S.C. system will not work unless the President makes it work. After all, this system was created to serve the President of the United States in ways of his choosing. By his actions, by his leadership, the President therefore determines the quality of its performance.

By his own account, as evidenced in his diary notes, and as conveyed to the Board by his principal advisors, President Reagan was deeply committed to securing the release of the hostages. It was this intense compassion for the hostages that appeared to motivate his steadfast support of the Iran initiative, even in the face of opposition from his Secretaries of State and Defense.

In his obvious commitment, the President appears to have proceeded with a concept of the initiative that was not accurately reflected in the reality of the operation. The President did not seem to be aware of the way in which the operation was implemented and the full consequences of U.S. participation.

The President's expressed concern for the safety of both the hostages and the Iranians who could have been at risk may have been conveyed in a manner so as to inhibit the full functioning of the system.

The President's management style is to put the principal responsibility for policy review and implementation on the shoulders of his advisors. Nevertheless, with such a complex, high-risk operation and so much at stake, the President should have insured that the N.S.C. system did not fail him. He did not force his policy to undergo the most critical review of which the N.S.C. participants and the process were capable. At no time did he insist upon accountability and performance review. Had the President chosen to drive the N.S.C. system, the outcome could well have been different. As it was, the most powerful features of the N.S.C. system—providing comprehensive analysis, alternatives and follow-up—were not utilized.

The Board found a strong consensus among N.S.C. participants that the President's priority in the Iran initiative was the release of U.S. hostages. But setting priorities is not enough when it comes to sensitive and risky initiatives that directly affect U.S. national security. He must ensure that the content and tactics of an initiative match his priorities and objectives. He must insist upon accountability. For it is the President who must take responsibility for the N.S.C. system and deal with the consequences.

Beyond the President, the other N.S.C. principals and the national security adviser must share in the responsibility for the N.S.C. system.

President Reagan's personal management style places an especially heavy responsibility on his key advisors. Knowing his style, they should have been particularly mindful of the need for special attention to the manner in which this arms-sale initiative developed and proceeded. On this score, neither the national security adviser nor the other N.S.C. principals deserve high marks.

It is their obligation as members and advisors to the council to ensure that the President is adequately served. The principal subordinates to the President must not be deterred from urging the President not to proceed on a highly questionable course of action even in the face of his strong conviction to the contrary.

In the case of the Iran initiative, the N.S.C. process did not fail, it simply was largely ignored. The national security adviser and the N.S.C. principals all had a duty to raise the issue and insist that orderly process be imposed. None of them did so.

All had the opportunity. While the national security adviser had the responsibility to see that an orderly process was observed, his failure to do so does not excuse the other N.S.C. principals. It does not appear that any of the N.S.C. principals called for more frequent consideration of the Iran initiative by the N.S.C. principals in the presence of the President. None of the principals called for a serious vetting of the initiative by even a restricted group of disinterested individuals. The intelligence questions do not appear to have been raised, and legal considerations, while raised, were not pressed. No one seemed to have complained about the informality of the process. No one called for a thorough re-examination once the initiative did not meet expectations or the manner of execution changed. While one or another of the N.S.C. principals suspected that something was amiss, none vigorously pursued the issue.

Mr. Regan also shares in this responsibility. More than almost any chief of staff of recent memory, he asserted personal control over the White House staff and sought to extend this control to the national security adviser. He was personally active in national security affairs and attended almost all the relevant meetings regarding the Iran initiative. He, as much as anyone, should have insisted that an orderly process be observed. In addition, he especially should have ensured that plans were made for handling any public disclosure of the initiative. He must bear primary responsibility for the chaos that descended upon the White House when such disclosure did occur.

Mr. McFarlane appeared caught between a President who supported the initiative and the Cabinet officers who strongly opposed it. While he made efforts to keep these Cabinet officers informed, the board heard complaints from some that he was not always successful. VADM Poindexter on several occasions apparently sought to exclude N.S.C. principals other than the President from knowledge of the initiative. Indeed, on one or more occasions Secretary Shultz may have been actively misled by VADM Poindexter.

VADM Poindexter also failed grievously on the matter of contra diversion. Evidence indicates that VADM Poindexter knew that a diversion occurred, yet he did not take the steps that were required given the gravity of that prospect. He apparently failed to appreciate or ignored the serious legal and political risks presented. His clear obligation was either to investigate the matter or take it to the President—or both. He did neither. Director Casey shared a similar responsibility. Evidence suggests that he received information about the possible diversion of funds to the contras almost a month before the story broke. He, too, did not move promptly to raise the matter with the President. Yet his responsibility to do so was clear.

The N.S.C. principals other than the President may be somewhat excused by the insufficient attention on the part of the national security adviser to the need to keep all the principals fully informed. Given the importance of the issue and the sharp policy divergences involved, however, Secretary Shultz and Secretary Weinberger in particular distanced themselves from the march of events. Secretary Shultz specifically requested to be informed only as necessary to perform his job. Secretary Weinberger had access through intelligence to details about the operation. Their obligation was to give the President their full support and continued advice with respect to the program or, if they could not in conscience do that, to so inform the President. Instead, they simply distanced themselves from the program. They protected the record as to their own positions on this issue. They were not energetic in attempting to protect the President from the consequences of his personal commitment to freeing the hostages.

Director Casey appears to have been informed in considerable detail about the specifics of the Iranian operation. He appears to have acquiesced in and to have encouraged North's exercise of direct operational control over the operation. Because of the N.S.C. staff's proximity to and close identification with the President, this increased the risks to the President if the initiative became public or the operation failed.

There is no evidence, however, that Director Casey explained this risk to the President or made clear to the President that LtCol North, rather than the C.I.A., was running the operation. The President does not recall ever being informed of this fact. Indeed, Director Casey should have gone further and pressed for operational responsibility to be transferred to the C.I.A.

Director Casey should have taken the lead in vetting the assumptions presented by the Israelis on which the program was based and in pressing for an early examination of the reliance upon Mr. Ghorbanifar and the second channel as intermediaries. He should also have assumed responsibility for checking out the other intermediaries involved in the operation. Finally, because Congressional restrictions on covert actions are both largely directed at and familiar to the C.I.A., Director Casey should have taken the lead in keeping the question of Congressional notification active.

Finally, Director Casey and, to a lesser extent, Secretary Weinberger should have taken it upon themselves to assess the effect of the transfer of arms and intelligence to Iran on the Iran-Iraq military balance, and to transmit that information to the President.

THE ROLE OF THE ISRAELIS

Conversations with emissaries from the Government of Israel took place prior to the commencement of the initiative. It remains unclear whether the initial proposal to open the Ghorbanifar channel was an Israeli initiative, was brought on by the avarice of arms dealers, or came as a result of an American request for assistance. There is no doubt, however, that it was Israel that pressed Mr. Ghorbanifar on the United States. U.S. officials accepted Israeli assurances that they had had for some time an extensive dialogue that involved high-level Iranians, as well as their assurances of Mr. Ghorbanifar's bona fides. Thereafter, at critical points in the initiative, when doubts were expressed by critical U.S. participants, an Israeli emissary would arrive with encouragement, often a specific proposal, and pressure to stay with the Ghorbanifar channel.

From the record available to the board, it is not possible to determine the role of key U.S. participants in prompting these Israeli interventions. There were active and ongoing consultations between LtCol North and officials of the Israeli Government, specifically David Kimche and Amiram Nir. In addition, Mr. Schwimmer, Mr. Nimrodi, and Mr. Ledeen, also in frequent contact with LtCol North, had close ties with the Government of Israel. It may be that the Israeli interventions were actively solicited by particular U.S. officials. Without the benefit of the views of the Israeli officials involved, it is hard to know the facts.

It is clear, however, that Israel had its own interests, some in direct conflict with those of the United States, in having the United States pursue the initiative. For this reason, it had an incentive to keep the initiative alive. It sought to do this by interventions with the N.S.C. staff, the national security adviser and the President. Although it may have received suggestions from LtCol North, Mr. Ledeen and others, it responded affirmatively to these suggestions by reason of its own interests.

Even if the Government of Israel actively worked to begin the initiative and to keep it going, the U.S. Government is responsible for its own decisions. Key participants in U.S. deliberations made the point that Israel's objectives and interests in this initiative were different from, and in some respects in conflict with, those of the United States. Although Israel dealt with those portions of the U.S. Government that it deemed were sympathetic to the initiative, there is nothing improper per se about this fact. U.S. decision-makers made their own decisions and must bear responsibility for the consequences.

AFTERMATH—THE EFFORTS TO TELL THE STORY

From the first hint in late October 1986 that the McFarlane trip would soon become public, information on the Iran initiative and contra activity cascaded into the press. The veiled hints of secret activities, random and indiscriminate disclosures of information from a variety of sources, both knowledgeable and otherwise, and conflicting statements by high-level officials presented a confusing picture to the American public. The board recognized that conflicts among contemporaneous documents and statements raised concern about the management of the public presentation of facts on the Iran initiative. Though the board reviewed some evidence on events after the exposure, our ability to comment on these events remains limited.

The board found evidence that immediately following the public disclosure, the President wanted to avoid providing too much specificity or detail out of concern for the hostages still held in Lebanon and those Iranians who had supported the initiative. In doing so, he did not, we believe, intend to mislead the American public or cover up unlawful conduct. By at least Nov. 20, the President took steps to insure that all the facts would come out. From the President's request to Mr. Meese to look into the history of the initiative, to his appointment of this board, to his request for an independent counsel, to his willingness to discuss this matter fully and to review his personal notes with us, the board is convinced that the President does indeed want the full story to be told.

Those who prepared the President's supporting documentation did not appear, at least initially, to share in the President's ultimate wishes. Mr. McFarlane described for the board the process used by the N.S.C. staff to create a chronology that obscured essential facts. Mr. McFarlane contributed to the creation of this chronology which did not, he said, present "a full and completely accurate account" of the events and left ambiguous the President's role. This was, according to Mr. McFarlane, done to distance the President from the timing and nature of the President's authorization. He told the board that he wrote a memorandum on Nov. 18, which tried to, in his own words, "gild the President's motives." This version was incorporated into the chronology. Mr. McFarlane told the board that he knew the account was "misleading, at least, and wrong, at worst." Mr. McFarlane told the board that he did provide the Attorney General an accurate account of the President's role.

The board found considerable reason to question the actions of LtCol North in the aftermath of the disclosure. The board has no evidence to either confirm or refute that LtCol North destroyed documents on the initiative in an effort to conceal facts from threatened investigations. The board found indications that LtCol North was involved in an effort, over time, to conceal or withhold important information. The files of LtCol North contained much of the historical documentation that the board used to construct its narrative. Moreover, LtCol North was the primary U.S. Government official involved in the details of the operation. The chronology he produced has many inaccuracies. These "histories" were to be the basis of the "full" story of the Iran initiative. These inaccuracies lend some evidence to the proposition that LtCol North, either on his own or at the behest of others, actively sought to conceal important information.

Out of concern for the protection of classified material, Director Casey and VADM Poindexter were to brief only the Congressional intelligence committees on the "full" story; the D.C.I. before the committees and VADM Poindexter in private sessions with the chairmen and vice chairmen. The D.C.I. and VADM Poindexter undertook to do this on November 21, 1986. It appears from the copy of the D.C.I.'s testimony and notes of VADM Poindexter's meetings that they did not fully relate the nature of events as they had occurred. The result is an understandable perception that they were not forthcoming.

The board is also concerned about various notes that appear to be missing. VADM Poindexter was the official note taker in some key meetings, yet no notes for the meetings can be found. The reason for the lack of such notes remains unknown to the board. If they were written, they may contain very important information. We have no way of knowing if they exist.

Source: Scowcroft, Brent. *Tower Commission Report.* New York: Bantam Books, 1987, pp. xiii–xxii.

Excerpt from Testimony of Oliver North to the Joint Hearings on the Iran-Contra Affair, July 8, 1987

At the end of the second day of testimony before the joint congressional committee by Lieutenant Colonel Oliver North on July 8, 1987, the House counsel, John Nields, confronted North and North's lawyer, Brendan Sullivan, with the established facts of North's lying to Congress so that he and others at the National Security Council could continue their illegal operations. North answered Nields's questions by justifying his actions, asserting that Congress could not be trusted with the facts because its members would leak vital secrets to the news media. Senate Chairman Daniel Inouye closed the day's testimony by refuting North's allegation, reminding North that the White House, not Congress, had leaked classified information. This excerpt is illustrative of the defiant and combative tone of North's testimony.

EXCERPT FROM TESTIMONY OF OLIVER NORTH, JULY 8, 1987

MR. NIELDS. There is a memorandum which was done by staff which is exhibit 126.

Do you have that in front of you?

MR. NORTH. I do.

MR. NIELDS. And it is dated August 6, 1986. Is that at or about the time when you had this interview?

MR. NORTH. Again I defer to the committee and Chairman Hamilton. I had such a meeting; if that is when it was—I don't remember the date.

MR. NIELDS. Then this was you personally talking to them?

MR. NORTH. It was on instructions of the National Security Adviser. I was instructed to meet with Chairman Hamilton and I believe many of the members of the committee.

MR. NIELDS. And they were interested in finding out the answers to the questions raised by the resolution of inquiry.

MR. NORTH. Exactly.

MR. NIELDS. Your fundraising activities?

MR. NORTH. Precisely.

MR. NIELDS. Military support for the Contras?

MR. NORTH. That's right.

MR. NIELDS. Questions about Mr. Owen, General Singlaub and John Hull?

[Witness confers with his attorney.]

MR. NORTH. Yes.

MR. NIELDS. The beginning of this memorandum that appears to be a description of what you said during that meeting. It says from Boland Amendment on, North explained strictures to Contras. Is that true, did you explain the strictures to the Contras?

MR. NORTH. I explained to them that there was no U.S. Government money until more was appropriated, yes.

MR. NIELDS. And it says never violated stricture, gave advice on human rights, civic action program.

MR. NORTH. I did do that.

MR. NIELDS. But I take it you did considerably more which you did not tell the committee about?

MR. NORTH. I have admitted that here before you today, knowing full well what I told the committee then. I think—and I think we can abbreviate this in hopes we can move on so that I can finish this week. I will tell you right now, counsel, and all the members here gathered, that I misled the Congress. I misled.

MR. NIELDS. At that meeting?

MR. NORTH. At that meeting.

MR. NIELDS. Face to face?

MR. NORTH. Face to face.

MR. NIELDS. You made false statements to them about your activities in support of the Contras?

MR. NORTH. I did. Furthermore, I did so with a purpose, and I did so with a purpose of hopefully avoiding the very kind of thing that we have before us now, and avoiding a shut-off of help for the Nicaraguan Resistance, and avoiding an elimination of the Resistance facilities in three Central American countries wherein we had promised those heads of state on my specific orders, on specific orders to me—I had gone down there and assured them of our absolute and total discretion.

MR. NIELDS. We do—

MR. NORTH. And I am admitting to you that I participated in preparation of documents for the Congress that were erroneous, misleading, evasive, and wrong, and I did it again here when I appeared before that committee convened in the White House Situation Room, and I make no excuses for what I did. I will tell you now that I am under oath and I was not then.

MR. NIELDS. We do live in a democracy, don't we?

MR. NORTH. We do, sir, thank God.

MR. NIELDS. In which it is the people, not one Marine lieutenant colonel, that get to decide the important policy decisions for the nation?

[Witness confers with his attorney.]

MR. NORTH. Yes.

MR. NIELDS. And part of the democratic process—

MR. NORTH. And I would point out that part of that answer is that this Marine lieutenant colonel was not making all of those decisions on his own. As I indicated yesterday in my testimony, Mr. Nields, I sought approval for everything that I did.

MR. NIELDS. But you denied Congress the facts.

MR. NORTH. I did.

MR. NIELDS. You denied the elected representatives of our people the facts upon which they needed to make a very important decision for this nation?

MR. NORTH. I did because of what I have just described to you as our concerns. And I did it because we have had incredible leaks from discussions with closed committees of the Congress. I was a part of, as people now know, the coordination for the mining of the harbors in Nicaragua. When that one leaked, there were American lives at stake and it leaked from a member of one of the committees, who eventually admitted it. When there was a leak on the sensitive intelligence methods that we used to help capture the Achille Lauro terrorists, it almost wiped out that whole channel of communications. Those kinds of things are devastating. They are devastating to the national security of the United States and I desperately hope that one of the things that can derive from all of this ordeal is that we can find a better way by which we can communicate those things properly with the Congress. I am not admitting that what happened in this is proper. I am not admitting—or claiming, rather—that what I did and my role in it in communicating was proper.

MR. NIELDS. Were you instructed to do it?

MR. NORTH. I was not specifically instructed, no.

MR. NIELDS. Were you generally instructed?

MR. NORTH. Yes.

MR. NIELDS. By whom?

MR. NORTH. My superiors. I prepared—

MR. NIELDS. Who?

MR. NORTH. I prepared draft answers that they signed and sent. I would also point out—

MR. NIELDS. What superior?

MR. NORTH. Well, look who signed—I didn't sign those letters to the—to this body.

MR. NIELDS. I am talking about the last—I'm talking about oral meeting in August of 1986.

MR. NORTH. I went down to that oral meeting with the same kind of understanding that I had prepared those memos in 1985 and other communications.

MR. NIELDS. Well you had a different boss, and in fairness, you ought to tell us whether he instructed you to do it, understood you did it, knew about it afterwards, or none of those.

MR. NORTH. He did not specifically go down and say, "Ollie, lie to the committee." I told him what I had said afterwards, and he sent me a note saying, "well done." Now, I would also like to point out one other thing. I deeply believe that the President of the United States is also an elected official of this land, and by the Constitution, as I understand it, he is the person charged with making and carrying out the foreign policy of this country. I believed from the moment I was engaged in this activity in 1984 that this was in furtherance of the foreign policy established by the President. I still believe that.

MR. NIELDS. Even—

MR. NORTH. I am not saying that what I did here was right. And I have just placed myself, as you know, counsel, in great jeopardy.

MR. NIELDS. Even the President—

[Witness confers with his attorney.]

MR. NIELDS. Even the President is elected by the people.

MR. NORTH. I just said that.

MR. NIELDS. And the people have the right to vote him out of office if they don't like his policies.

MR. NORTH. That is true.

MR. NIELDS. And they can't exercise that function if the policies of the President are hidden from them?

MR. NORTH. Wait a second. I mean, yesterday we talked about the need for this nation, which is a country at risk in a dangerous world, having the need to conduct covert operations and secret diplomacy and carry out secret programs. I mean, we talked at some length about that, and that can certainly be the subject of great debate, and this great institution can pass laws that say no such activities can ever be conducted again. But that would be wrong, and you and I know that. The fact is that this country does need to be able to conduct those kinds of activities, and the President ought not to be in a position, in my humble opinion, of having to go out and explain to the American people on a bi-weekly basis or any other kind that I, the President, am carrying out the following secret operations. It just can't be done. No nation in the world will ever help us again, and we desperately need that kind of help if we are to survive given our adversaries. And what I am saying to you, Mr. Nields, is the American people, I think, trust that the President will indeed be conducting these kinds of activities. They trust that he will do so with a good purpose and good intent. I will also admit to you that I believe there has to be a way of consulting with the Congress. There must be. I would also point out to you, Mr. Nields, that in June of 1986, not the Tower Commission, I gave a speech before the American Bar Association on very short notice, I stood on the podium with Senator Moynihan, and I advocated the formation of a small discreet joint intelligence committee with a very professional small staff in which the administration would feel comfortable confiding in planning and conducting and funding these kinds of activities. I still believe that to be a good and thoughtful thing to do. There has to be that kind of proposal that allows the administration to talk straightforward with the Congress.

MR. NIELDS. There came a time—

[Witness confers with his attorney.]

MR. NIELDS. There came a time when one of the resupply operation's planes went down in Nicaragua?

MR. NORTH. Yes.

MR. NIELDS. That was early October, 1986.

MR. NORTH. Yes.

MR. NIELDS. If you will turn to exhibit 133. Do you have that in front of you?

MR. NORTH. Yes.

MR. NIELDS. It is a PROF message from Mr. Cannistraro, it relates to the plane that went down, and in the middle of the page it discusses press guidance. Do you see that?

MR. NORTH. Yes.

MR. NIELDS. And the statement is, press guidance was prepared which states, no USG [U.S. government] involvement or connection but that we are generally aware of such support contracted by the Contras. Were you aware at the time that this was the press guidance for the Hasenfus plane?

MR. NORTH. I don't believe I was aware at that immediate moment, because, as I testified earlier, I believe I was overseas at that point. My recollection is that I was. But that is not inconsistent with what we had prepared as the press line if such a—if such an eventuality occurred.

MR. NIELDS. And then the next paragraph says, "UNO to be asked to assume responsibility for flight."

MR. NORTH. Right.

MR. NIELDS. And then it says, Elliott will follow up with Ollie to facilitate this.

MR. NORTH. Yes.

MR. NIELDS. Was Mr. Abrams aware that UNO was not responsible for the flight?

MR. NORTH. I think that the flight was certainly coordinated with people within UNO. UNO did indeed know about the flight. The flight happened to have been paid for by General Secord's operation, the airplane was paid for by his operation. The pilots were paid for by his operation. Those were not U.S. Government moneys, but those were certainly his activities, and I was the U.S. Government connection.

MR. NIELDS. And was Elliott Abrams aware of the fact that you were the U.S. Government connection?

MR. NORTH. You would have to ask Elliott Abrams exactly what he did know. But he called me to take care of getting the bodies home.

MR. NIELDS. Did he ask you whether you or the NSC had any connection with the airplane?

MR. NORTH. Counsel, he didn't have to ask me.

MR. NIELDS. Because he alr—

MR. NORTH. Any more than a congressman who called me up at one point and asked me to get an airdrop to the Indians had to ask me. He knew. I didn't have to tell him. I didn't have to write a memo to him. It was known. I would guess that that is probably why Chairman Hamilton convened his group in the situation room. I have no doubt about that. And what I want you to know is I still don't think that what we did was illegal.

MR. NIELDS. So you think—

MR. NORTH. Please. It was not right. It does not leave me with a good taste in my mouth. I want you to know lying does not come easy to me. I want you to know that it doesn't come easy to anybody, but I think we all had to weigh in the balance the difference between lives and lies. I had to do that on a number of occasions in both these operations, and it is not an easy thing to do.

MR. NIELDS. So you are telling us that you believe some Congressman knew of your connection, you have said that Izvestia knew of your connection, you said the Cubans knew of your connection, the Sandinistas—

MR. NORTH. I—

MR. NIELDS. I haven't finished the question yet—the Sandinistas knew of your connection, but exhibit 134 contains the administration's statement to the American people, it is a newspaper article about this flight; Washington Post, top left-hand column, "Top Reagan administration officials yesterday flatly denied any U.S. Government connection with the transport plane that the Sandinista

Government said it shot down in Nicaragua with three Americans and a man of Latin origin aboard." And the next exhibit, the committees have already heard, it is Elliott Abrams' statements on Evans and Novak absolutely guaranteeing that there was no U.S. Government connection, and particularly no NSC connection.

[Witness conferring with counsel.]

MR. NIELDS. Now the American people, I take it, in this country where we trust our government officials believed those statements.

MR. NORTH. Is that a question?

MR. NIELDS. Yes.

MR. NORTH. Well, I don't know. I cannot speak for the American people. I have never pretended to speak for the American people. But, I—

[Counsel conferring with witness.]

MR. NIELDS. Colonel North, I have only one more question.

MR. NORTH. Wait, wait—I am still trying to answer the last one. I am getting help here. I guess my problem is, counsel, that while I well recognize that there may well be a lot of American people who want to know, I was trying to weigh, and I am sure that others like Mr. McFarlane and Admiral Poindexter and Director Casey and Elliott Abrams and the Chief of the Central American Task Force and others were trying to weigh in their souls what would happen to those, for example, whom I had sent money to or enticed into this activity or published pamphlets in Managua, or ran radio broadcasts or blew things up or flew airplanes if the American Government stood up and announced it and that is, after all, the essence of deniability and I was that deniable link and I was supposed to be dropped like a hot rock when it all came down. And I was willing to serve in that capacity. I was not willing to become the victim of a criminal prosecution.

MR. NIELDS. I have only one more question, sir.

You have given this committee several speeches on the subject of covert operations.

MR. SULLIVAN. I object to that. Mr. Chairman, the witness has responded as frankly and as truthfully as he possibly can and I think that that is a pejorative term that mischaracterizes the extraordinary efforts of Colonel North to be frank with this committee. And I am tired, frankly, of going home at the end of the day and seeing members of this committee on the TV saying he is not being truthful, and that is another example of it. I request, Mr. Chairman, that that kind of tactic not be utilized. Thank you, sir.

CHAIRMAN INOUYE. I would like to advise the counsel that he may characterize this as something else, but as far as I am concerned, it was a very lengthy statement. Some people consider lengthy statements to be speeches. Counsel, proceed.

MR. NIELDS. I am perfectly happy to use the expression lengthy statements.

You have made several lengthy statements to the committee on the subject of covert operations.

MR. SULLIVAN. How about using lengthy answer, in order for him to get the truth before the committee?

CHAIRMAN INOUYE. Proceed.

MR. NIELDS. As a result of the fact that the operations you have been testifying about were conducted in the covert manner that you have been testifying about, as I understand your testimony, you and others put out a false version of facts relating to the 1985 HAWK shipment. You altered documents in official NSC files. You shredded documents shortly after you heard that representatives of the Attorney General of the United States were coming into your office to review them. You wrote false and misleading letters to the Congress of the United States. The Government lied to the American people about the connection to the Hasenfus plane. You received a personal financial benefit from operating funds of the covert organization without knowing where it came from.

MR. NORTH. Sir?

MR. NIELDS. I am referring to the security fence. Eight million dollars of operation funds was handled in a manner that you didn't know what had happened to it or whether it existed. My question to you is whether this is an inevitable—these things are inevitable consequences of conducting covert operations or whether these are things that happened because of this—these two particular covert actions? If you have an answer.

MR. NORTH. Well, I have tried over the course of the last 2 days, counsel, to answer every one of your questions accurately. I have tried to give you answers and explanations where needed for why I did what I did and the facts as they were known to me about what others did. I am not here to impugn the testimony of others or to make excuses for anything that I did. I have accepted the responsibility for those things that I did, and some of that has not come easily. I would also expect, as you keep raising the American people, that the tens of thousands of American people who have written to me and communicated with me since I was relieved of my duties at the NSC and in particular over the course of the last 2 days, some of them seem to believe and with very, very few exceptions, perhaps 50 out of 40,000 or 50,000, perhaps 50, the remaining 50,000 or so who have communicated seem to believe that they think it was right that somebody would do something under those circumstances and I tried to do it to the very best of my abilities. If they are found lacking, it is not for having tried not enough. I sincerely believe that I did everything within the law. I made serious judgment errors and I have admitted those, but I tried and I don't regret having done it.

MR. NIELDS. I have no further questions, Mr. Chairman.

CHAIRMAN INOUYE. Thank you very much. Colonel North, for the past 2 days, together with my colleagues on this panel, I have sat here very patiently listening to statements suggesting that Members of Congress cannot be trusted with the secrets of this land. Although I have not discussed this in public before, but I did serve on the Intelligence Committee for 8 years, serving as chairman for the first 2 years. In fact, it was my assignment to organize the Intelligence Committee. During that period, according to the Federal Bureau of Investigation, the Central Intelligence Agency and the National Security Agency, there wasn't a single leak from that Senate Select Committee on Intelligence. I am certain you are well aware that most of the leaks in this city come from the other side of Pennsylvania. Secondly, I am a recipient of the Distinguished Service Medal of Intelligence, the highest non-military decoration that can be given to a non-military person. And last year just before Mr. Casey went to the hospital, he presented me with a Central Intelligence Agency agency medal. Thirdly, a few days ago, General Odum, Director of the National Security Agency, communicated with me to advise me that since the creation of these two Select Committees, they have not seen any leaks emanating from these two committees. I don't know who you are talking about, but I can assure you that these committees, the House and the Senate Select Committees, can be trusted. The sessions of this day and yesterday have clearly demonstrated that if we had gone through the regular process that we have followed with all other witnesses, and that is going into executive session, taking depositions, we would not have had to have delays that we have experienced today over classified information. Like you, I do not wish to see secrets of this land inadvertently and accidentally made public. Accordingly, at the conclusion of tomorrow afternoon's session at five, the panel will enter into executive session to discuss matters of classification. The place will be announced tomorrow. We will stand in recess until 9:00 o'clock tomorrow morning, at which time Mr. Van Cleve will conduct the investigation.

Source: U.S. Congress. *Iran-Contra Investigation Joint Hearings Before the Senate Select Committee on Secret Military Assistance to Iran and the Nicaraguan Opposition and the House Select Committee to Investigate Covert Arms Transactions with Iran.* 100th Congress, 1st Session, 100–7, Part I, July 7, 8, 9, and 10, 1987, pp. 179–85. Testimony of Oliver L. North (Questioning by Counsels). Washington, D.C.: Government Printing Office, 1988.

Report of the Congressional Committees Investigating the Iran-Contra Affair, Executive Summary, November 18, 1987

The Iran-Contra hearings concluded on August 3, 1987. The congressional committee had heard 28 public witnesses and about 500 private testimonies. The committee staff had reviewed 300,000 documents. On November 18, 1987, the committee released its lengthy final report, which included a dissenting opinion from the Republican minority. While the minority dissent questioned the purpose and legitimacy of the investigation, the majority report concluded that the affair showed that members of the Reagan administration had conducted their actions with "secrecy, deception, and disdain for the law."

REPORT OF THE CONGRESSIONAL COMMITTEES, EXECUTIVE SUMMARY NOVEMBER 18, 1987

Dishonesty and Secrecy

The Iran-Contra affair was characterized by pervasive dishonesty and inordinate secrecy. North admitted that he and other officials lied repeatedly to Congress and to the American people about the contra covert action and Iran arms sales, and that he altered and destroyed official documents. North's testimony demonstrates that he also lied to members of the executive branch, including the Attorney General, and officials of the State Department, C.I.A. and N.S.C.

Secrecy became an obsession. Congress was never informed of the Iran or the contra covert actions, notwithstanding the requirement in the law that Congress be notified of all covert actions in a "timely fashion."

Poindexter said that Donald Regan, the President's chief of staff, was not told of the N.S.C. staff's fundraising activities because he might reveal it to the press. Secretary Shultz objected to third-country solicitation in 1984 shortly before the Boland Amendment was adopted; accordingly, he was not told that, in the same time period, the national security adviser had accepted an $8 million contribution from Country 2 even though the State Department had prime responsibility for dealings with that country. Nor was the Secretary of State told by the President in February 1985 that the same country had pledged another $24 million—even though the President briefed the Secretary of State on his meeting with the head of state at which the pledge was made. Poindexter asked North to keep secrets from Casey; Casey, North and Poindexter agreed to keep secrets from Shultz.

Poindexter and North cited fear of leaks as a justification for these practices. But the need to prevent public disclosure cannot justify the deception practiced upon members of Congress and executive branch officials by those who knew of the arms sales to Iran and of the contra support network. The State and Defense Departments deal each day with the most sensitive matters affecting millions of lives here and abroad. The Congressional Intelligence Committees receive the most highly classified information, including information on covert activities. Yet, according to North and Poindexter, even the senior officials of these bodies could not be entrusted with the N.S.C. staff's secrets because they might leak.

Poindexter told the Secretary of State in May 1986 that the Iran initiative was over, at the very time the McFarlane mission to Teheran was being launched. Poindexter also concealed from Cabinet officials the remarkable nine-point agreement negotiated by Hakim with the second channel. North assured the F.B.I. liaison to the N.S.C. as late as November 1986 that the United States was not bargaining for the release of hostages but seizing terrorists to exchange for hostages—a complete fabrication. The lies, omissions, shredding, attempts to rewrite history—all continued, even after the President authorized the Attorney General to find out the facts.

It was not operational security that motivated such conduct—not when our own Government was the victim. Rather, the N.S.C. staff feared, correctly, that any disclosure to Congress or the Cabinet of the arms-for-hostages and arms-for-profit activities would produce a storm of outrage.

As with Iran, Congress was misled about the N.S.C. staff's support for the contras during the period of the Boland Amendment, although the role of the N.S.C. staff was no secret to others. North testified that his operation was well-known to the press in the Soviet Union, Cuba and Nicaragua. It was not a secret from Nicaragua's neighbors, with whom the N.S.C. staff communicated throughout the period. It was not a secret from the third countries—including a totalitarian state—from whom the N.S.C. staff sought arms or funds. It was not a secret from the private resupply network which North recruited and supervised. According to North, even Ghorbanifar knew.

The Administration never sought to hide its desire to assist the contras so long as such aid was authorized by statute. On the contrary, it wanted the Sandinistas to know that the United States supported the contras. After enactment of the Boland Amendment, the Administration repeatedly and publicly called upon Congress to resume U.S. assistance. Only the N.S.C. staff's contra support activities were kept under wraps. The committees believe these actions were concealed in order to prevent Congress from learning that the Boland Amendment was being circumvented.

It was stated on several occasions that the confusion, secrecy and deception surrounding the aid program for the Nicaraguan freedom fighters was produced in part by Congress's shifting positions on contra aid.

But Congress's inconsistency mirrored the chameleon-like nature of the rationale offered for granting assistance in the first instance. Initially, Congress was told that our purpose was simply to interdict the flow of weapons from Nicaragua into El Salvador. Then Congress was told that our purpose was to harass the Sandinistas to prevent them from consolidating their power and exporting their revolution. Eventually, Congress was told that our purpose was to eliminate all foreign forces from Nicaragua, to reduce the size of the Sandinista armed forces, and to restore the democratic reforms pledged by the Sandinistas during the overthrow of the Somoza regime.

Congress had cast a skeptical eye upon each rationale proffered by the Administration. It suspected that the Administration's true purpose was identical to that of the Contras—the overthrow of the Sandinista regime itself. Ultimately Congress yielded to domestic political pressure to discontinue assistance to the contras, but Congress was unwilling to bear responsibility for the loss of Central America to communist military and political forces. So Congress compromised, providing in 1985 humanitarian aid to the contras; and the N.S.C. staff provided what Congress prohibited: lethal support for the contras.

Compromise is no excuse for violation of law and deceiving Congress. A law is no less a law because it is passed by a slender majority, or because Congress is open-minded about its reconsideration in the future.

Privatization

The N.S.C. staff turned to private parties and third countries to do the Government's business. Funds denied by Congress were obtained by the Administration from third countries and private citizens. Activities normally conducted by the professional intelligence services—which are accountable to Congress—were turned over to Secord and Hakim.

The solicitation of foreign funds by an Administration to pursue foreign policy goals rejected by Congress is dangerous and improper. Such solicitations, when done secretly and without Congressional authorization, create a risk that the foreign country will expect and demand something in return. McFarlane testified that "any responsible official has an obligation to acknowledge that every country in the world will see benefit to itself by ingratiating itself to the United States." North, in fact, proposed rewarding a Central American country with foreign assistance funds for facilitating arms shipments to the contras. And Secord, who had once been in charge of the U.S. Air Force's foreign military sales, said "where there is a quid, there is a quo."

Disdain for Law

In the Iran-contra affair, officials viewed the law not as setting boundaries for their actions, but raising impediments to their goals. When the goals and the law collided, the law gave way:

- The covert program of support for the contras evaded the Constitution's most significant check on executive power: The President can spend funds on a program only if he can convince Congress to appropriate the money.
- When Congress enacted the Boland Amendment, cutting off funds for the war in Nicaragua, Administration officials raised funds for the contras from other sources—foreign governments, the Iran arms sales and private individuals; and the N.S.C. staff controlled the expenditures of these funds through power over the Enterprise. Conducting the covert program in Nicaragua with funding from the sale of U.S. Government property and contributions raised by Government officials was a flagrant violation of the appropriations clause of the Constitution.
- In addition, the covert program of support for the contras was an evasion of the letter and spirit of the Boland Amendment. The President made it clear that while he opposed restrictions on military or paramilitary assistance to the contras, he recognized that compliance with the law was not optional. "[W]hat I might personally wish or what our Government might wish still would not justify us violating the law of the land," he said in 1983.

- A year later, members of the N.S.C. staff were devising ways to continue support and direction of contra activities during the period of the Boland Amendment. What was previously done by the C.I.A.—and now prohibited by the Boland Amendment—would be done instead by the N.S.C. staff.
- The President set the stage by welcoming a huge donation for the contras from a foreign government—a contribution clearly intended to keep the contras in the field while U.S. aid was barred. The N.S.C. staff thereafter solicited other foreign governments for military aid, facilitated the efforts of U.S. fund-raisers to provide lethal assistance to the contras and ultimately developed and directed a private network that conducted, in North's words, a "full-service covert operation" in support of the contras.
- This could not have been more contrary to the intent of the Boland legislation.

Numerous other laws were disregarded:

- North's full-service covert operation was a "significant anticipated intelligence activity" required to be disclosed to the intelligence committees of Congress under Section 501 of the National Security Act. No such disclosure was made.
- By executive order, a covert operation requires a personal determination by the President before it can be conducted by an agency other than the C.I.A. It requires a written finding before any agency can carry it out. In the case of North's full-service covert operation in support of the contras, there was no such personal determination and no such finding. In fact, the President disclaims any knowledge of this covert action.
- False statements to Congress are felonies if made with knowledge and intent. Several Administration officials gave statements denying N.S.C. staff activities in support of the contras which North later described in his testimony as "false" and "misleading, evasive and wrong."
- The application of proceeds from U.S. arms sales for the benefit of the contra war effort violated the Boland Amendment's ban on U.S. military aid to the contras, and constituted a misappropriation of Government funds derived from the transfer of U.S. property.
- The U.S. Government's approval of the pre-finding 1985 sales by Israel of arms to the Government of Iran was inconsistent with the Government's obligations under the Arms Export Control Act.
- The testimony to Congress in November 1986 that the U.S. Government had no contemporaneous knowledge of the Israeli shipments, and the shredding of documents relating to the shipments while a Congressional inquiry into those shipments was pending, obstructed Congressional investigations.
- The Administration did not make, and clearly intended never to make, disclosure to the intelligence committees of the finding—later destroyed—approving the November 1985 Hawk shipment, nor did it disclose the covert action to which the finding related.
- The committees make no determination as to whether any particular individual involved in the Iran-contra affair acted with criminal intent or was guilty of any crime. That is a matter for the independent counsel and the courts. But the committees reject any notion that worthy ends justify violations of law by Government officials; and the committees condemn without reservation the making of false statements to Congress and the withholding, shredding and alteration of documents relevant to a pending inquiry.
- Administration officials have, if anything, an even greater responsibility than private citizens to comply with the law. There is no place in Government for lawbreakers.

Who Was Responsible

Who was responsible for the Iran-contra affair? Part of our mandate was to answer that question, not in a legal sense (which is the responsibility of the independent counsel), but in order to reaffirm that those who serve the Government are accountable for their actions. Based on our investigation, we reach the following conclusions.

At the operational level, the central figure in the Iran-contra affair was Lieutenant Colonel North, who coordinated all of the activities and was involved in all aspects of the secret operations. North, however, did not act alone.

North's conduct had the express approval of Admiral John Poindexter, first as deputy national security adviser, and then as national security adviser. North also had at least the tacit support of Robert McFarlane, who served as national security adviser until December 1985.

In addition, for reasons cited earlier, we believe that the late Director of Central Intelligence, William Casey, encouraged North, gave him direction and promoted the concept of an extralegal covert organization. Casey, for the most part, insulated C.I.A. career employees from knowledge of what he and N.S.C. staff were doing. Casey's passion for covert operations—dating back to his World War II intelligence days—was well known. His close relationship with North was attested to by several witnesses. Further, it was Casey who brought Richard Secord into the secret operation, and it was Secord who, with Albert Hakim, organized the Enterprise. These facts provide strong reasons to believe that Casey was involved both with the diversion and with the plans for an "off-the-shelf" covert capacity.

The committees are mindful, however, of the fact that the evidence concerning Casey's role comes almost solely from North; that this evidence, albeit under oath, was used by North to exculpate himself; and that Casey could not respond. Although North told the committees that Casey knew of the diversion from the start, he told a different story to the Attorney General in November 1986, as did Casey himself. Only one other witness, Lieut. Col. Robert Earl, testified that he had been told by North during Casey's lifetime that Casey knew of the diversion.

The Attorney General recognized on November 21, 1986, the need for an inquiry. His staff was responsible for finding the diversion memorandum, which the Attorney General promptly made public. But as described earlier, his fact-finding inquiry departed from standard investigative techniques. The Attorney General saw Director Casey hours after the Attorney General learned of the diversion memorandum, yet he testified that he never asked Casey about the diversion. He waited two days to speak to Poindexter, North's superior, and then did not ask him what the President knew. He waited too long to seal North's offices. These lapses placed a cloud over the Attorney General's investigation.

There is no evidence that the Vice President was aware of the diversion. The Vice President attended several meetings on the Iran initiative, but none of the participants could recall his views.

The Vice President said he did not know of the contra resupply operation. His national security adviser, Donald Gregg, was told in early August 1987 by a former colleague that North was running the contra resupply operation, and that ex-associates of Edwin Wilson—a well-known ex-C.I.A. official convicted of selling arms to Libya and plotting the murder of his prosecutors—were involved in the operation. Gregg testified that he did not consider these facts worthy of the Vice President's attention and did not report them to him, even after the Hasenfus airplane was shot down and the Administration had denied any connection with it.

The central remaining question is the role of the President in the Iran-contra affair. On this critical point, the shredding of documents by Poindexter, North and others, and the death of Casey, leave the record incomplete.

As it stands, the President has publicly stated that he did not know of the diversion. Poindexter testified that he shielded the President from knowledge of the diversion. North said that he never told the President, but assumed that the President knew. Poindexter told North on November 21, 1986, that he had not informed the President of the diversion. Secord testified that North told him he had talked with the President about the diversion, but North testified that he had fabricated this story to bolster Secord's morale.

Nevertheless, the ultimate responsibility for the events in the Iran-contra affair must rest with the President. If the President did not know what his national security advisers were doing, he should have. It is his responsibility to communicate unambiguously to his subordinates that they must keep him advised of important actions they take for the Administration. The Constitution requires the President to "take care that the laws be faithfully executed." This charge encompasses a responsibility to leave the members of his Administration in no doubt that the rule of law governs.

Members of the N.S.C. staff appeared to believe that their actions were consistent with the President's desires. It was the President's policy—not an isolated decision by North or Poindexter—to sell arms secretly to Iran and to maintain the contras "body and soul," the Boland Amendment notwithstanding. To the N.S.C. staff, implementation of these policies became the overriding concern.

Several of the President's advisers pursued a covert action to support the contras in disregard of the Boland Amendment and of several statutes and executive orders requiring Congressional notification. Several of these same advisers lied, shredded documents and covered up their actions. These facts have been on the public record for months. The actions of those individuals do not comport with the notion of a country guided by the rule of law. But the President has yet to condemn their conduct.

The President himself told the public that the U.S. Government had no connection to the Hasenfus airplane. He told the public that early reports of arms sales for hostages had "no foundation." He told the public that the United States had not traded arms for hostages. He told the public that the United States had not condoned the arms sales by Israel to Iran, when in fact he had approved them and signed a finding, later destroyed by Poindexter, recording his approval. All of these statements by the President were wrong. Thus, the question whether the President knew of the diversion is not conclusive on the issue of his responsibility. The President created or at least tolerated an environment where those who did know of the diversion believed with certainty that they were carrying out the President's policies.

This same environment enabled a secretary who shredded, smuggled and altered documents to tell the committees that "sometimes you have to go above the written law"; and it enabled Admiral Poindexter to testify that "frankly, we were willing to take some risks with the law." It was in such an environment that former officials of the N.S.C. staff and their private agents could lecture the committees that a "rightful cause" justifies any means, that lying to Congress and other officials in the executive branch itself is acceptable when the ends are just, and that Congress is to blame for passing laws that run counter to Administration policy. What may aptly be called the "cabal of the zealots" was in charge.

In a constitutional democracy, it is not true, as one official maintained, that "When you take the king's shilling, you do the king's bidding." The idea of monarchy was rejected here 200 years ago and since then, the law—not any official or ideology—has been paramount. For not instilling this precept in his staff, for failing to take care that the law reigned supreme, the President bears the responsibility.

Fifty years ago Supreme Court Justice Louis Brandeis observed: "Our Government is the potent, the omnipresent teacher. For good or for ill, it teaches the whole people by its example. Crime is contagious. If the Government becomes a lawbreaker, it breeds contempt for law, it invites every man to become a law unto himself, it invites anarchy."

The Iran-contra affair resulted from a failure to heed this message.

Source: U.S. Congress. *Report of the Congressional Committees Investigating the Iran-Contra Affair: With Supplemental, Minority, and Additional Views,* pp. 3–24. 100th Congress, 1st session. Washington, D.C.: Government Printing Office, 1988.

Excerpt from Report of the Congressional Committees Investigating the Iran-Contra Affair, Minority View, November 18, 1987

The members of the Republican minority of the Congressional Committees Investigating the Iran-Contra Affair demanded the inclusion of their dissenting views in the committee's final report. The minority defended the intention of the Reagan administration's dealings with Iran and support for the contras. They questioned the intention of the committee's majority and supported the power of the executive in the realm of foreign policy.

EXCERPT FROM REPORT OF THE CONGRESSIONAL COMMITTEES, MINORITY VIEW NOVEMBER 18, 1987

Minority Report of
Representative Dick Cheney of Wyoming
Representative William S. Broomfield of Michigan
Representative Henry J. Hyde of Illinois
Representative Jim Courier of New Jersey
Representative Bill McCollum of Florida
Representative Michael DeWine of Ohio
Senator James McClure of Idaho
Senator Orrin Hatch of Utah

What the committees' report has done with the legal questions, however, is to issue a one-sided legal brief that pretends the Administration did not even have worthwhile arguments to make. As if that were not enough, the report tries to build upon these one-sided assertions to present a politicized picture of an Administration that behaved with contempt for the law. If nothing else would lead readers to view the report with extreme skepticism, the adversarial tone of the legal discussion should settle the matter.

Our View of the Iran-Contra Affair

The main issues raised by the Iran-contra affair are not legal ones, in our opinion. This opinion obviously does have to rest on some legal conclusions, however. We have summarized our legal conclusions at the end of this introductory chapter. The full arguments appear in subsequent chapters. In our view, the Administration did proceed legally in pursuing both its contra policy and the Iran arms initiative. We grant that the diversion does raise some legal questions, as do some technical and relatively insubstantial matters relating to the Arms Export Control Act. It is important to stress, however, that the Administration could have avoided every one of the legal problems it inadvertently encountered, while continuing to pursue the exact same policies as it did.

The fundamental issues, therefore, have to do with the policy decisions themselves, and with the political judgments underlying the way policies were implemented. When these matters are debated as if they were legal—and even criminal—concerns, it is a sign that interbranch intimidation is replacing and debasing deliberation. That is why we part company not only with the committees report's answers, but with the very questions it identifies as being the most significant. . . .

We do believe that virtually all of the N.S.C. staff's activities were legal, with the possible exception of the diversion of Iran arms sale proceeds to the resistance. We concede that reasonable people may take a contrary view of what Congress intended the Boland Amendments to mean. But we also agree with a letter from John Norton Moore, which appears as Appendix B to our report, that to the extent that the amendment was ambiguous, "well recognized principles of due process and separation of powers would require that it be interpreted to protect executive branch flexibility."

Notwithstanding our legal opinions, we think it was a fundamental mistake for the N.S.C. staff to have been secretive and deceptive about what it was doing. The requirement for building long-term political support means that the Administration would have been better off if it had conducted its activities in the open. Thus, the President should simply have vetoed the strict Boland Amendment in mid-October 1984, even though the Amendment was only a few paragraphs in an approximately 1,200 pages-long continuing appropriations resolution, and a veto therefore would have brought the Government to a standstill within three weeks of a national election. Once the President decided against a veto, it was self-defeating to think a program this important could be sustained by deceiving Congress. Whether technically illegal or not, it was politically foolish and counterproductive to mislead Congress, even if misleading took the form of artful evasion or silence instead of overt misstatement.

We do believe firmly that the N.S.C. staff's deceits were not meant to hide illegalities. Every witness we have heard told us his concern was not over legality, but with the fear that Congress would respond to complete disclosure with political reprisals, principally by tightening the Boland Amendments. That risk should have been taken.

We are convinced that the Constitution protects much of what the N.S.C. was doing—particularly those aspects that had to do with encouraging contributions and sharing information. The President's inherent constitutional powers are only as strong, however, as the President's willingness to defend them. As for the N.S.C. actions Congress could constitutionally have prohibited, it would have been better for the White House to have tackled that danger head on. Some day, Congress's decision to withhold resources may tragically require U.S. citizens to make an even heavier commitment to Central America, perhaps one measured in blood and not dollars. The commitment that might eliminate such an awful future will not be forthcoming unless the public is exposed to and persuaded by a clear, sustained and principled debate on the merits.

Source: U.S. Congress. *Report of the Congressional Committees Investigating the Iran-Contra Affair: With Supplemental, Minority, and Additional Views,* pp. 437–57. 100th Congress, 1st session. Washington, D.C.: Government Printing Office, 1988.

Walsh Report, Executive Summary, August 4, 1993

On August 4, 1993, after six and a half years and $35.7 million, Lawrence Walsh, the independent counsel, concluded the Iran-Contra investigation and submitted his final report to the special court *that had appointed him. By 1993 the statute of limitations on crimes that may have been committed before 1987 had expired. Walsh had brought indictments against 14 of the participants in the Iran-Contra Affair. The case of the Iran-Contra Affair was closed in legal terms, but it lived on in the nation's politics.*

WALSH REPORT, EXECUTIVE SUMMARY AUGUST 4, 1993

In October and November 1986, two secret U.S. Government operations were publicly exposed, potentially implicating Reagan Administration officials in illegal activities. These operations were the provision of assistance to the military activities of the Nicaraguan contra rebels during an October 1984 to October 1986 prohibition on such aid, and the sale of U.S. arms to Iran in contravention of stated U.S. policy and in possible violation of arms-export controls. In late November 1986, Reagan Administration officials announced that some of the proceeds from the sale of U.S. arms to Iran had been diverted to the contras.

As a result of the exposure of these operations, Attorney General Edwin Meese III sought the appointment of an independent counsel to investigate and, if necessary, prosecute possible crimes arising from them.

The Special Division of the United States Court of Appeals for the District of Columbia Circuit appointed Lawrence E. Walsh as Independent Counsel on December 19, 1986, and charged him with investigating:

(1) the direct or indirect sale, shipment, or transfer since in or about 1984 down to the present, of military arms, materiel, or funds to the government of Iran, officials of that government, persons, organizations or entities connected with or purporting to represent that government, or persons located in Iran;
(2) the direct or indirect sale, shipment, or transfer of military arms, materiel or funds to any government, entity, or person acting, or purporting to act as an intermediary in any transaction referred to above;
(3) the financing or funding of any direct or indirect sale, shipment or transfer referred to above;
(4) the diversion of proceeds from any transaction described above to or for any person, organization, foreign government, or any faction or body of insurgents in any foreign country, including, but not limited to Nicaragua;
(5) the provision or coordination of support for persons or entities engaged as military insurgents in armed conflict with the government of Nicaragua since 1984.

This is the final report of that investigation.

Overall Conclusions

The investigations and prosecutions have shown that high-ranking Administration officials violated laws and executive orders in the Iran/contra matter.

Independent Counsel concluded that:

- the sales of arms to Iran contravened United States Government policy and may have violated the Arms Export Control Act[1];
- the provision and coordination of support to the contras violated the Boland Amendment ban on aid to military activities in Nicaragua;
- the policies behind both the Iran and contra operations were fully reviewed and developed at the highest levels of the Reagan Administration;
- although there was little evidence of National Security Council [NSC] level knowledge of most of the actual contra-support operations, there was no evidence that any NSC member dissented from the underlying policy—keeping the contras alive despite congressional limitations on contra support;
- the Iran operations were carried out with the knowledge of, among others, President Ronald Reagan, Vice President George Bush, Secretary of State George P. Shultz, Secretary of Defense Caspar W. Weinberger, Director of Central Intelligence William J. Casey, and national security advisers Robert C. McFarlane and John M. Poindexter; of these officials, only Weinberger and Shultz dissented from the policy decision, and Weinberger eventually acquiesced by ordering the Department of Defense to provide the necessary arms; and
- large volumes of highly relevant, contemporaneously created documents were systematically and willfully withheld from investigators by several Reagan Administration officials;
- following the revelation of these operations in October and November 1986, Reagan Administration officials deliberately deceived the Congress and the public about the level and extent of official knowledge of and support for these operations.

In addition, Independent Counsel concluded that the off-the-books nature of the Iran and contra operations gave line-level personnel the opportunity to commit money crimes.

The Basic Facts of Iran/contra

The Iran/contra affair concerned two secret Reagan Administration policies whose operations were coordinated by National Security Council staff. The Iran operation involved efforts in 1985 and 1986 to obtain the release of

[1] Independent Counsel is aware that the Reagan Administration Justice Department took the position, after the November 1986 revelations, that the 1985 shipments of United States weapons to Iran did not violate the law. This post hoc position does not correspond with the contemporaneous advice given the President. As detailed within this report, Secretary of Defense Caspar W. Weinberger (a lawyer with an extensive record in private practice and the former general counsel of the Bechtel Corporation) advised President Reagan in 1985 that the shipments were illegal. Moreover, Weinberger's opinion was shared by attorneys within the Department of Defense and the White House counsel's office once they became aware of the 1985 shipments. Finally, when Attorney General Meese conducted his initial inquiry into the Iran arms sales, he expressed concern that the shipments may have been illegal.

Americans held hostage in the Middle East through the sale of U.S. weapons to Iran, despite an embargo on such sales. The contra operations from 1984 through most of 1986 involved the secret governmental support of contra military and paramilitary activities in Nicaragua, despite congressional prohibition of this support.

The Iran and contra operations were merged when funds generated from the sale of weapons to Iran were diverted to support the contra effort in Nicaragua. Although this "diversion" may be the most dramatic aspect of Iran/contra, it is important to emphasize that both the Iran and contra operations, separately, violated United States policy and law.[2] The ignorance of the "diversion" asserted by President Reagan and his Cabinet officers on the National Security Council in no way absolves them of responsibility for the underlying Iran and contra operations.

The secrecy concerning the Iran and contra activities was finally pierced by events that took place thousands of miles apart in the fall of 1986. The first occurred on October 5, 1986, when Nicaraguan government soldiers shot down an American cargo plane that was carrying military supplies to contra forces; the one surviving crew member, American Eugene Hasenfus, was taken into captivity and stated that he was employed by the CIA. A month after the Hasenfus shootdown, President Reagan's secret sale of U.S. arms to Iran was reported by a Lebanese publication on November 3. The joining of these two operations was made public on November 25, 1986, when Attorney General Meese announced that Justice Department officials had discovered that some of the proceeds from the Iran arms sales had been diverted to the contras.

When these operations ended, the exposure of the Iran/contra affair generated a new round of illegality. Beginning with the testimony of Elliott Abrams and others in October 1986 and continuing through the public testimony of Caspar W. Weinberger on the last day of the congressional hearings in the summer of 1987, senior Reagan Administration officials engaged in a concerted effort to deceive Congress and the public about their knowledge of and support for the operations.

Independent Counsel has concluded that the President's most senior advisers and the Cabinet members on the National Security Council participated in the strategy to make National Security staff members McFarlane, Poindexter and North the scapegoats whose sacrifice would protect the Reagan Administration in its final two years. In an important sense, this strategy succeeded. Independent Counsel discovered much of the best evidence of the cover-up in the final year of active investigation, too late for most prosecutions.

Scope of Report

This report provides an account of the Independent Counsel's investigation, the prosecutions, the basis for decisions not to prosecute, and overall observations and conclusions on the Iran/contra matters.

[2] See n. 1 above.

Part I of the report sets out the underlying facts of the Iran and contra operations. Part II describes the criminal investigation of those underlying facts. Part III provides an analysis of the central operational conspiracy. Parts IV through IX are agency-level reports of Independent Counsel's investigations and cases: the National Security staff, the private operatives who assisted the NSC staff, Central Intelligence Agency officials, Department of State officials, and White House officials and Attorney General Edwin Meese III.

Volume I of this report concludes with a chapter concerning political oversight and the rule of law, and a final chapter containing Independent Counsel's observations. Volume II of the report contains supporting documentation. Volume III is a classified appendix.

Because many will read only sections of the report, each has been written with completeness, even though this has resulted in repetition of factual statements about central activities.

The Operational Conspiracy

The operational conspiracy was the basis for Count One of the 23-count indictment returned by the Grand Jury March 16, 1988, against Poindexter, North, Secord, and Hakim. It charged the four with conspiracy to defraud the United States by deceitfully:

(1) supporting military operations in Nicaragua in defiance of congressional controls;
(2) using the Iran arms sales to raise funds to be spent at the direction of North, rather than the U.S. Government; and
(3) endangering the Administration's hostage-release effort by overcharging Iran for the arms to generate unauthorized profits to fund the contras and for other purposes.

The charge was upheld as a matter of law by U.S. District Judge Gerhard A. Gesell even though the Justice Department, in a move that Judge Gesell called "unprecedented," filed an amicus brief supporting North's contention that the charge should be dismissed. Although Count One was ultimately dismissed because the Reagan Administration refused to declassify information necessary to North's defense, Judge Gesell's decision established that high Government officials who engage in conspiracy to subvert civil laws and the Constitution have engaged in criminal acts. Trial on Count One would have disclosed the Government-wide activities that supported North's Iran and contra operations.

Within the NSC, McFarlane pleaded guilty in March 1988 to four counts of withholding information from Congress in connection with his denials that North was providing the contras with military advice and assistance. McFarlane, in his plea agreement, promised to cooperate with Independent Counsel by providing truthful testimony in subsequent trials.

Judge Gesell ordered severance of the trials of the four charged in the conspiracy indictment because of the immunized testimony given by Poindexter, North and Hakim to Congress. North was tried and convicted by a jury in May 1989 of altering and destroying documents, accepting an illegal gratuity and aiding and abetting in the obstruction of Congress. His conviction was reversed on appeal in July 1990 and charges against North were subsequently dismissed in September 1991 on the ground that trial witnesses were tainted by North's nationally televised, immunized testimony before Congress. Poindexter in April 1990 was convicted by a jury on five felony counts of conspiracy, false statements, destruction and removal of records and obstruction of Congress. The Court of Appeals reversed his conviction in November 1991 on the immunized testimony issue.

The Flow of Funds

The illegal activities of the private citizens involved with the North and Secord operations are discussed in detail in Part V. The off-the-books conduct of the two highly secret operations circumvented normal Administration accountability and congressional oversight associated with covert ventures and presented fertile ground for financial wrongdoing. There were several funding sources for the contras' weapons purchases from the covert-action Enterprise formed by North, Secord and Hakim:

(1) donations from foreign countries;
(2) contributions from wealthy Americans sympathetic to President Reagan's contra support policies; and
(3) the diversion of proceeds from the sale of arms to Iran.

Ultimately, all of these funds fell under the control of North, and through him, Secord and Hakim.

North used political fundraisers Carl R. Channell and Richard R. Miller to raise millions of dollars from wealthy Americans, illegally using a tax-exempt organization to do so. These funds, along with the private contributions, were run through a network of corporations and Swiss bank accounts put at North's disposal by Secord and Hakim, through which transactions were concealed and laundered. In late 1985 through 1986 the Enterprise became centrally involved in the arms sales to Iran. As a result of both the Iran and contra operations, more than $47 million flowed through Enterprise accounts.

Professional fundraisers Channell and Miller pleaded guilty in the spring of 1987 to conspiracy to defraud the Government by illegal use of a tax-exempt foundation to raise contributions for the purchase of lethal supplies for the contras. They named North as an unindicted co-conspirator.

Secord pleaded guilty in November 1989 to a felony, admitting that he falsely denied to Congress that North had personally benefited from the Enterprise. Hakim pleaded guilty to the misdemeanor count of supplementing the salary of North. Lake Resources Inc., the company controlled by Hakim to launder the Enterprise's money flow, pleaded guilty to the corporate felony of theft of Government property in diverting the proceeds from the arms sales to the contras and for other unauthorized purposes. Thomas G. Clines was convicted in September 1990 of four tax-related felonies for failing to report all of his income from the Enterprise.

Agency Support of the Operations

Following the convictions of those who were most central to the Iran/contra operations, Independent Counsel's investigation focused on the supporting roles played by Government officials in other agencies and the supervisory roles of the NSC principals. The investigation showed that Administration officials who claimed initially that they had little knowledge about the Iran arms sales or the illegal contra-resupply operation North directed were much better informed than they professed to be. The Office of Independent Counsel obtained evidence that Secretaries Weinberger and Shultz and White House Chief of Staff Donald T. Regan, among others, held back information that would have helped Congress obtain a much clearer view of the scope of the Iran/contra matter. Contemporaneous notes of Regan and Weinberger, and those dictated by Shultz, were withheld until they were obtained by Independent Counsel in 1991 and 1992.

The White House and Office of the Vice President

As the White House section of this report describes in detail, the investigation found no credible evidence that President Reagan violated any criminal statute. The OIC [Office of the Independent Counsel] could not prove that Reagan authorized or was aware of the diversion or that he had knowledge of the extent of North's control of the contra-resupply network. Nevertheless, he set the stage for the illegal activities of others by encouraging and, in general terms, ordering support of the contras during the October 1984 to October 1986 period when funds for the contras were cut off by the Boland Amendment, and in authorizing the sale of arms to Iran, in contravention of the U.S. embargo on such sales. The President's disregard for civil laws enacted to limit presidential actions abroad—specifically the Boland Amendment, the Arms Export Control Act and congressional-notification requirements in covert-action laws—created a climate in which some of the Government officers assigned to implement his policies felt emboldened to circumvent such laws.

President Reagan's directive to McFarlane to keep the contras alive "body and soul" during the Boland cut-off period was viewed by North, who was charged by McFarlane to carry out the directive, as an invitation to break the law. Similarly, President Reagan's decision in 1985 to authorize the sale of arms to Iran from Israeli stocks, despite warnings by Weinberger and Shultz that such transfers might violate the law, opened the way for Poindexter's subsequent decision to authorize the diversion. Poindexter told Congress that while he made the decision on his own and did not tell the President, he believed the President would have approved. North testified that he believed the President authorized it.

Independent Counsel's investigation did not develop evidence that proved that Vice President Bush violated any criminal statute. Contrary to his public pronouncements, however, he was fully aware of the Iran arms sales. Bush was regularly briefed, along with the President, on the Iran arms sales, and he participated in discussions to obtain third-country support for the contras. The OIC obtained no evidence that Bush was aware of the diversion. The OIC learned in December 1992 that Bush had failed to produce a diary containing contemporaneous notes relevant to Iran/contra, despite requests made in 1987 and again in early 1992 for the production of such material. Bush refused to be interviewed for a final time in light of evidence developed in the latter stages of OIC's investigation, leaving unresolved a clear picture of his Iran/contra involvement. Bush's pardon of Weinberger on December 24, 1992, pre-empted a trial in which defense counsel indicated that they intended to call Bush as a witness.

The chapters on White House Chief of Staff Regan and Attorney General Edwin Meese III focus on their actions during the November 1986 period, as the President and his advisers sought to control the damage caused by the disclosure of the Iran arms sales. Regan in 1992 provided Independent Counsel with copies of notes showing that Poindexter and Meese attempted to create a false account of the 1985 arms sales from Israeli stocks, which they believed were illegal, in order to protect the President. Regan and the other senior advisers did not speak up to correct the false version of events. No final legal determination on the matter had been made. Regan said he did not want to be the one who broke the silence among the President's senior advisers, virtually all of whom knew the account was false.

The evidence indicates that Meese's November 1986 inquiry was more of a damage-control exercise than an effort to find the facts. He had private conversations with the President, the Vice President, Poindexter, Weinberger, Casey and Regan without taking notes. Even after learning of the diversion, Meese failed to secure records in NSC staff offices or take other prudent steps to protect potential evidence. And finally, in reporting to the President and his senior advisers, Meese gave a false account of what he had been told by stating that the President did not know about the 1985 HAWK shipments, which Meese said might have been illegal. The statute of limitations had run out on November 1986 activities before OIC obtained its evidence. In 1992, Meese denied recollection of the statements attributed to him by the notes of Weinberger and Regan. He was unconvincing, but the passage of time would have been expected to raise a reasonable doubt of the intentional falsity of his denials if he had been prosecuted for his 1992 false statements.

The Role of CIA Officials

Director Casey's unswerving support of President Reagan's contra policies and of the Iran arms sales encouraged some CIA officials to go beyond legal restrictions in both operations. Casey was instrumental in pairing North with Secord as a contra-support team when the Boland Amendment in October 1984 forced the CIA to refrain from direct or indirect aid. He also supported the North-Secord combination in the Iran arms sales, despite deep reservations about Secord within the CIA hierarchy.

Casey's position on the contras prompted the chief of the CIA's Central American Task Force, Alan D. Fiers, Jr., to "dovetail" CIA activities with those of North's contra-resupply network, in violation of Boland restrictions. Casey's support for the NSC to direct the Iran arms sales and to use arms dealer Manucher Ghorbanifar and Secord in the operation, forced the CIA's Directorate of Operations to work with people it distrusted.

Following the Hasenfus shootdown in early October 1986, [Clair E.] George and Fiers lied to Congress about U.S. Government involvement in contra resupply, to, as Fiers put it, "keep the spotlight off the White House." When the Iran arms sales became public in November 1986, three of Casey's key officers—George, [Duane R.] Clarridge and Fiers—followed Casey's lead in misleading Congress.

Four CIA officials were charged with criminal offenses—George, the deputy director for operations and the third highest-ranking CIA official; Clarridge, chief of the European Division; Fiers; and [Joseph F.] Fernandez. George was convicted of two felony counts of false statements and perjury before Congress. Fiers pleaded guilty to two misdemeanor counts of withholding information from Congress. The four counts of obstruction and false statements against Fernandez were dismissed when the Bush Administration refused to declassify information needed for his defense. Clarridge was awaiting trial on seven counts of perjury and false statements when he, George and Fiers were pardoned by President Bush.

State Department Officials

In 1990 and 1991, Independent Counsel received new documentary evidence in the form of handwritten notes suggesting that Secretary Shultz's congressional testimony painted a misleading and incorrect picture of his knowledge of the Iran arms sales. The subsequent investigation focused on whether Shultz or other Department officials deliberately misled or withheld information from congressional or OIC investigators.

The key notes, taken by M. Charles Hill, Shultz's executive assistant, were nearly verbatim, contemporaneous accounts of Shultz's meetings within the department and Shultz's reports to Hill on meetings the secretary attended elsewhere. The Hill notes and similarly detailed notes by Nicholas Platt, the State Department's executive secretary, provided the OIC with a detailed account of Shultz's knowledge of the Iran arms sales. The most revealing of these notes were not provided to any Iran/contra investigation until 1990 and 1991. The notes show that—contrary to his early testimony that he was not aware of details of the 1985 arms transfers—Shultz knew that the shipments were planned and that they were delivered. Also in conflict with his congressional testimony was evidence that Shultz was aware of the 1986 shipments.

Independent Counsel concluded that Shultz's early testimony was incorrect, if not false, in significant respects, and misleading, if literally true, in others. When questioned about the discrepancies in 1992, Shultz did not dispute the accuracy of the Hill notes. He told OIC that he believed his testimony was accurate at the time and he insisted that if he had been provided with the notes earlier, he would have testified differently. Independent Counsel declined to prosecute because there was a reasonable doubt that Shultz's testimony was willfully false at the time it was delivered.

Independent Counsel concluded that Hill had willfully withheld relevant notes and prepared false testimony for Shultz in 1987. He declined to prosecute because Hill's claim of authorization to limit the production of his notes and the joint responsibility of Shultz for the resulting misleading testimony, would at trial have raised a reasonable doubt, after Independent Counsel had declined to prosecute Shultz.

Independent Counsel's initial focus on the State Department had centered on Assistant Secretary Elliott Abrams' insistence to Congress and to the OIC that he was not aware of North's direction of the extensive contra-resupply network in 1985 and 1986. As assistant secretary of state for inter-American affairs, Abrams chaired the Restricted Inter-Agency Group, or RIG, which coordinated U.S. policy in Central America. Although the OIC was skeptical about Abrams' testimony, there was insufficient evidence to proceed against him until additional documentary evidence inculpating him was discovered in 1990 and 1991, and until Fiers, who represented the CIA on the RIG, pleaded guilty in July 1991 to withholding information from Congress. Fiers provided evidence to support North's earlier testimony that Abrams was knowledgeable about North's contra-supply network. Abrams pleaded guilty in October 1991 to two counts of withholding information from Congress about secret Government efforts to support the contras, and about his solicitation of $10 million to aid the contras from the Sultan of Brunei.

Secretary Weinberger and Defense Department Officials

Contrary to their testimony to the presidentially appointed Tower Commission and the Select Iran/contra Committees of Congress, Independent Counsel determined that Secretary Weinberger and his closest aides were consistently informed of proposed and actual arms shipments to Iran during 1985 and 1986. The key evidence was handwritten notes of Weinberger, which he deliberately withheld from Congress and the OIC until they were discovered by Independent Counsel in late 1991. The Weinberger daily diary notes and notes of significant White House and other meetings contained highly relevant, contemporaneous information that resolved many questions left unanswered in early investigations.

The notes demonstrated that Weinberger's early testimony—that he had only vague and generalized information about Iran arms sales in 1985—was false, and that he in fact had detailed information on the proposed arms sales and the actual deliveries. The notes also revealed that Gen. Colin Powell, Weinberger's senior military aide, and Richard L. Armitage, assistant secretary of defense for international security affairs, also had detailed knowledge of the 1985 shipments from Israeli stocks. Armitage and Powell had testified that they did not learn of the November 1985 HAWK missile shipment until 1986.

Weinberger's notes provided detailed accounts of high-level Administration meetings in November 1986 in which the President's senior advisers were provided with false accounts of the Iran arms sales to protect the President and themselves from the consequences of the possibly illegal 1985 shipments from Israeli stocks.

Weinberger's notes provided key evidence supporting the charges against him, including perjury and false statements in connection with his testimony regarding the arms sales, his denial of the existence of notes and his denial of knowledge of Saudi Arabia's multi-million dollar contribution to the contras. He was pardoned less than two weeks before trial by President Bush on December 24, 1992.

There was little evidence that Powell's early testimony regarding the 1985 shipments and Weinberger's notes was willfully false. Powell cooperated with the various Iran/contra investigations and, when his recollection was refreshed by Weinberger's notes, he readily conceded their accuracy. Independent Counsel declined to prosecute Armitage because the OIC's limited resources were focused on the case against Weinberger and because the evidence against Armitage, while substantial, did not reach the threshold of proof beyond a reasonable doubt.

The Reagan, Bush and Casey Segments

The Independent Counsel Act requires a report as to persons not indicted as well as those indicted. Because of the large number of persons investigated, those discussed in individual sections of this report are limited to those as to whom there was a possibility of indictment. In addition there are separate sections on President Reagan and President Bush because, although criminal proceedings against them were always unlikely, they were important subjects of the investigation, and their activities were important to the action taken with respect to others.

CIA Director Casey is a special case. Because Casey was hospitalized with a fatal illness before Independent Counsel was appointed, no formal investigation of Casey was ever undertaken by the OIC. Casey was never able to give his account, and he was unable to respond to allegations of wrongdoing made about him by others, most prominently North, whose veracity is subject to serious question. Equally important, fundamental questions could not be answered regarding Casey's state of mind, the impact, if any, of his fatal illness on his conduct and his intent.

Under normal circumstances, a prosecutor would hesitate to comment on the conduct of an individual whose activities and actions were not subjected to rigorous investigation, which might exculpate that individual. Nevertheless, after serious deliberation, Independent Counsel concluded that it was in the public interest that this report expose as full and complete an account of the Iran/contra matter as possible. This simply could not be done without an account of the role of Director Casey.

Observations and Conclusions

This report concludes with Independent Counsel's observations and conclusions. He observes that the governmental problems presented by Iran/contra are not those of rogue operations, but rather those of Executive Branch efforts to evade congressional oversight. As this report documents, the competing roles of the attorney general—adviser to the President and top law-enforcement officer—come into irreconcilable conflict in the case of high-level Executive Branch wrongdoing. Independent Counsel concludes that congressional oversight alone cannot correct the deficiencies that result when an attorney general abandons the law-enforcement responsibilities of that office and undertakes, instead, to protect the President.

Independent Counsel asks the Congress to review the difficult and delicate problem posed to the investigations and prosecutions by congressional grants of immunity to principals. While recognizing the important responsibility of Congress for investigating such matters thoroughly, Congress must realize that grants of use immunity to principals in such highly exposed matters as the Iran/contra affair will virtually rule out successful prosecution.

Independent Counsel also addresses the problem of implementing the Classified Information Procedures Act (CIPA) in cases steeped in highly classified information, such as many of the Iran/contra prosecutions. Under the Act, the attorney general has unrestricted discretion to decide whether to declassify information necessary for trial, even in cases in which Independent Counsel has been appointed because of the attorney general's conflict of interest. This discretion is inconsistent with the perceived need for independent counsel, particularly in cases in which officers of the intelligence agencies that classify information are under investigation. This discretion gives the attorney general the power to block almost any potentially embarrassing prosecution that requires the declassification of information. Independent Counsel suggests that the attorney general implement standards that would permit independent review of a decision to block a prosecution of an officer within the Executive Branch and legitimate congressional oversight.

Classified Information

In addition to the unclassified Volumes I and II of this report, a brief classified report, Volume III, has been filed with the Special Division. The classified report contains references to material gathered in the investigation of Iran/contra that could not be declassified and could not be concealed by some substitute form of discussion.

Source: Walsh, Lawrence E. *Iran-Contra: The Final Report.* New York: Three Rivers Press, 1994, pp. xiii–xxii.

Bibliography

Abrams, Elliott. *Undue Process: A Story of How Political Differences Are Turned into Crimes.* New York: Easton Press, 1993.

Cannon, Lou. *President Reagan: The Role of a Lifetime.* New York: Touchstone, 1991.

Cohen, William S., and George J. Mitchell. *Men of Zeal: A Candid Inside Story of the Iran-Contra Hearings.* New York: Viking, 1988.

Draper, Theodore. *A Very Thin Line: The Iran-Contra Affairs.* New York: Hill & Wang, 1991.

Hamilton, Lee. *Report of the Congressional Committees Investigating the Iran-Contra Affair, with Supplemental, Minority, and Additional Views.* Washington, D.C.: U.S. Government Printing Office, 1987.

Kornbluh, Peter. *The Iran-Contra Scandal: The Declassified History.* New York: New Press, 1993.

Ledeen, Michael A. *Perilous Statecraft: An Insider's Account of the Iran-Contra Affair.* New York: Charles Scribner's Sons, 1988.

Leogrande, William M. *Our Own Backyard: The United States in Central America, 1977–1992.* Chapel Hill: University of North Carolina Press, 2000.

Lynch Michael E., and David Bogen, eds. *The Spectacle of History: Speech, Text, and Memory at the Iran-Contra Hearings.* Durham, N.C.: Duke University Press, 1996.

Mark, Clyde R. *Iran-Contra Affair: A Chronology.* Washington, D.C.: Congressional Research Service, 1987.

North, Oliver. *Under Fire: An American Story.* New York: Harper Collins, 1991.

Reagan, Ronald. *Ronald Reagan: An American Life.* New York: Simon & Schuster, 1990.

Report of the President's Special Review Board on the National Security Council and Iran (The Tower Commission Report). Washington, D.C.: U.S. Government Printing Office, 1987.

Shultz, George. *Turmoil and Triumph: Diplomacy, Power, and the Victory of the American Ideal.* New York: Charles Scribner's Sons, 1995.

Sklar, Holly. *Washington's War on Nicaragua.* Boston: South End Press, 1988.

Thelen, David. *Becoming Citizens in the Age of Television: How Americans Challenged the Media and Seized Political Initiative During the Iran-Contra Debate.* Chicago: University of Chicago Press, 1996.

Walsh, Lawrence E. *Final Report of the Independent Counsel for Iran Contra Matters.* Washington, D.C.: Government Reprints Press, 2001.

———. *Firewall: The Iran-Contra Conspiracy and Cover-Up.* New York: W. W. Norton & Company, 1997.

Wilentz, Sean. *The Age of Reagan: A History, 1974–2008.* New York: Harper Perennial, 2009.

Woodward, Bob. *Shadow: Five Presidents and the Legacy of Watergate.* New York: Simon & Schuster, 2000.

———. *Veil: The Secret Wars of the CIA, 1981–1987.* New York: Simon & Schuster, 2005.

The INSLAW Department of Justice Scandal, 1989–91

By Roger A. Bruns

When an individual of the stature of Elliot Richardson shouts "conspiracy," people tend to listen. In October 1991, Richardson alerted the public to a scandal that would become known as the INSLAW Affair. Members of the U.S. Department of Justice, Richardson charged, had likely committed a variety of crimes ranging from computer piracy to conspiracy. Richardson, a former U.S. attorney general, was the lawyer representing a computer company called INSLAW. Through machinations of the Justice Department, Richardson charged, INSLAW's software product had been stolen, the company had been systematically forced into bankruptcy, and INSLAW's good name had been destroyed in a sea of villainy and cover-up. Richardson considered the INSLAW Affair "a high-tech Watergate."

Richardson knew much about Watergate, the scandal that forced President Richard Nixon to resign in 1974. He was the attorney general under President Nixon who appointed the Watergate special prosecutor, Archibald Cox. When revelations about presidential misconduct emerged and as Cox was seeking the release of secret White House tape recordings of conversations in the Oval Office, Nixon summoned Richardson to the White House on October 20, 1973, and ordered the attorney general to fire Cox. Richardson resigned rather than execute the order.

Richardson's refusal to dismiss Cox became a crucial turning point in the Watergate imbroglio that brought down a president. Richardson's action stood as one of the era's great assertions of independence and the political sanctity of the separation of powers.

Now, 18 years after his role in the Watergate crisis, Elliot Richardson once again found himself in the middle of a constitutional confrontation, one that would pit the investigative power of Congress against the Justice Department and its claims of executive privilege. In the history of congressional investigations, the INSLAW Affair and the struggle it spawned would foreshadow future bitter collisions over Congress's authority to investigate.

The Beginnings of a Scandal

Long in need of adequate computer software to assist law enforcement officials across the country in their record keeping and tracking of criminal cases, the Justice Department in the 1970s turned to an organization called the Institute for Law and Social Research (INSLAW) to develop such a system. Founded by William Hamilton, a former analyst with the National Security Agency and onetime contract employee of the Central Intelligence Agency, INSLAW by the early 1980s

INSLAW president William Hamilton poses for a photograph, with a neon sign in the background saying Promis, one of the company's software products. (Photo by Cynthia Johnson/Time Life Pictures/Getty Images)

OVERVIEW

Background

In 1982, INSLAW Inc., a computer-software company based in Washington, D.C., that was owned by William and Nancy Hamilton, won a $10 million contract with the U.S. Department of Justice to install a sophisticated software program called PROMIS in U.S. attorneys' offices. Shortly after the installation of the software, the federal government reneged on the contract, refusing to pay most of the money specified in the agreement. INSLAW declared bankruptcy. Led by the famed attorney Elliot Richardson, INSLAW fought back, suing the department and winning a case in bankruptcy court in which the judge claimed that the department "took, converted, and stole" the computer program through "trickery, fraud, and deceit." Although the decision was eventually struck down on a technicality, investigative reporters and INSLAW attorneys began to find a series of bizarre connections between the INSLAW case and shadowy figures in the world of covert operations. The INSLAW matter had become scandalous, pointing to a government conspiracy that Richardson called "a high-tech Watergate."

Congress Investigates

In 1989, Representative Jack Brooks (D-Tex.), chairman of the House Committee on the Judiciary, launched an investigation into the INSLAW matter. The investigation ran into such a stone wall from the Justice Department that Brooks took the forceful step of issuing a subpoena to Attorney General Richard Thornburgh to release relevant documents. In 1992, the Judiciary Committee released a report accusing Justice Department officials of criminal misconduct and recommended the appointment of a special prosecutor.

Impact

Ultimately, a special prosecutor was never installed, the Justice Department was never held accountable, and INSLAW never received the money it was owed. The investigation itself illustrated a growing power struggle between the legislative and executive branches over congressional investigative authority. That battle would continue with increased tension and vehemence into the early years of the 21st century. The INSLAW story, packed with intrigue, remains as Representative Brooks characterized it after the investigation. "The legend of INSLAW as a government cover-up," he said in 1994, "has grown and grown."

had developed a software system it called PROMIS (Prosecutor's Management Information System). The PROMIS software proved to be a wildly successful invention.

At first, INSLAW was a nonprofit organization whose work was largely supported with grants from the Law Enforcement Assistance Administration (LEAA), part of the Justice Department. Later, when the LEAA was discontinued, INSLAW became a private company. Nevertheless, its relationship with the department continued. Edwin Meese, an adviser to President Ronald Reagan, was entranced by the potential of the PROMIS software, telling an April 1981 meeting of federal prosecutors that the software system was "one of the greatest opportunities for success in the future."

The PROMIS software was a case-management system for prosecutors. It had the ability to track people. "You can rotate the file by case, defendant, arresting officer, judge, defense lawyer," Hamilton said, "and it's tracking all the names of all the people in all the cases." For example, the system could provide a complete rundown of all federal cases in which a particular lawyer had been involved, all the cases in which the lawyer had represented a particular defendant, and at which stage in each of the cases there had been plea-bargain agreements. Thus, the system could help prosecutors determine strategies.

With a daunting network of nearly 600,000 lines of computer code, the PROMIS software also had the enormous potential of integrating many separate databases without extensive reprogramming. It could manipulate vast amounts of data from various sources of data. For the Justice Department, the software was a godsend. It enabled law enforcement agencies to keep up-to-the-minute tabs on cases as they wound their way through the courts. A U.S. attorney could sit before a computer

CHRONOLOGY

1982

- The Department of Justice signs a $10 million contract with INSLAW Inc. to install a computer program called PROMIS in the offices of 42 U.S. attorneys.

1985

- *February 7:* After the federal government withholds payments of nearly $2 million, INSLAW declares bankruptcy.

1988

- *January:* U.S. Bankruptcy Judge George Bason rules in favor of INSLAW and against the Justice Department in a civil trial and awards the company $6.8 million. Judge Bason finds that the department "took, converted, and stole" the PROMIS software from INSLAW through "trickery, fraud, and deceit."

1989

- Appellate court affirms Bason's decision.
- *August:* Representative Jack Brooks of Texas, chairman of the House Committee on the Judiciary, launches investigation into the INSLAW matter.

1991

- *May:* U.S. Court of Appeals in Washington reverses Bason's decision on grounds that bankruptcy courts lack jurisdiction over the case.
- *July 25:* Judiciary Committee subpoenas Attorney General Richard Thornburgh to turn over Justice Department documents related to investigation.
- *August 10:* Investigative journalist Danny Casolaro is found dead of an apparent suicide in a motel room in Martinsburg, West Virginia. Casolaro was working on a story that implicated various Republican officials connected to the INSLAW case in covert arms sales and clandestine covert operations.
- *September 10:* Judiciary Committee releases report accusing Justice Department officials of criminal misconduct and recommends the appointment of a special prosecutor.
- *October 21:* Elliot Richardson, attorney for INSLAW and former U.S. attorney general, publishes article in the *New York Times* characterizing the INSLAW scandal as "a high-tech Watergate."

1993

- *June:* Nicholas Bua, a former district judge appointed by Attorney General William Barr to investigate the case for the Justice Department, issues a report exonerating department officials of any wrongdoing.

1994

September 27: Attorney General Janet Reno issues a report stating that there was no need for an independent counsel or further investigation.

screen and quickly discover where any particular case stood, locate defendants and witnesses, follow the case motions, and find the histories of the case updated to the latest reports.

Before the advent of PROMIS, the federal government's law enforcement agencies all had separate databases that were not interconnected. The Justice Department, the CIA, the Internal Revenue Service, and a number of other agencies all had computer systems isolated from one another. The Justice Department itself in the late 1970s was composed of more than 30 semiautonomous regional U.S. Attorney offices. Each had a computer system to track case management for prosecutions, investigations, and civil litigations. Plaguing the system was the fact that the offices used as many as seven different programming languages, making the sharing of information among offices extraordinarily slow, if not nearly impossible. With the PROMIS software came the integration of the separate databases. It was a significant technological leap forward.

In 1982, INSLAW garnered a $10 million, three-year contract from the Justice Department to install the public domain PROMIS software system at the 20 largest U.S. Attorney's offices nationwide and in U.S. territories.

If successful, the company would install PROMIS software in the other 74 federal prosecutors' offices across the United States.

As INSLAW President William Hamilton eagerly looked forward to his company's future, he began to calculate the possible business that might follow that first contract with the Justice Department. He could imagine similar contracts from the Federal Bureau of Investigation, U.S. marshals' offices, the Immigration and Naturalization Service, U.S. Customs, and other federal agencies. He estimated the eventual market to automate the federal court system at as much as $3 billion. If INSLAW could continue its lucrative relationship with the federal government, a virtual fortune could be down the road.

Soon INSLAW upgraded the original PROMIS software. The company did not own the original version of PROMIS because it had been developed with LEAA funds. That version was in the public domain. But because it had funded a major upgrade with its own money, INSLAW did claim ownership of the upgraded product that came to be known as INSLAW's proprietary Enhanced PROMIS. It was over this new, modified version of PROMIS that INSLAW and the Justice Department soon became mired in an increasingly bitter dispute.

The conflict between the small company and the government agency centered on whether INSLAW had ownership of Enhanced PROMIS. At first, Justice Department officials seemed to recognize INSLAW's proprietary rights. Hamilton sent a letter to the department asking it to waive any proprietary rights it might claim to the enhanced version. In a reply dated August 11, 1982, a department lawyer wrote: "To the extent that any other enhancements (beyond the public domain PROMIS software) were privately funded by INSLAW and not specified to be delivered to the Department of Justice under any contract or other agreement, INSLAW may assert whatever proprietary rights it may have."

Soon after, however, the department's actions began to reverse the initial acknowledgment of those rights. In April 1983, the second year of the three-year contract, the government and INSLAW agreed to a modification. To obtain delivery of the Enhanced PROMIS version of the software, Justice agreed to pay license fees if it decided to substitute the new version for the original version in the various government facilities already using PROMIS. As part of the modified agreement, the department also agreed not to distribute the software to any other individuals or agencies in the United States and abroad.

But then the department began to back off its earlier recognition of INSLAW's proprietary rights and balked at paying fees for what it now claimed was public domain software. Justice Department officials also began to find fault with INSLAW's implementation services.

"I was so frustrated," Hamilton said. "INSLAW had always overfulfilled its quotas on those contracts. Even our enemies would say, 'Yeah, they're expensive, but they're awfully good.'" The department began withholding certain services payments in April 1983. Hamilton told Justice Department officials that their actions were jeopardizing the existence of the company.

What was behind the actions of the Justice Department? Speculation arose that the fracturing relations between INSLAW and the department had nothing to do with INSLAW's software product or the performance of the company but much to do with the interests of a longtime friend and powerful political ally to President Ronald Reagan—Edwin Meese.

Meese had joined Reagan's staff in California when the former movie actor became governor in 1967. As a legal affairs secretary and, finally, as chief of staff, Meese became one of Reagan's closest confidants. When Reagan won the White House in 1980, Meese followed him to Washington. He headed Reagan's transition team, then became counsel to the president, and in February 1985 he was named attorney general.

Meese's role in the INSLAW matter appeared to be centered on a longtime friend, Earl Brian. A former combat surgeon in Vietnam, Brian had also served in Reagan's administration in California as secretary of the state Department of Health and Welfare, the youngest person ever to occupy that position. Following Reagan's election to the presidency, Brian, like Meese, continued to serve Republican Party interests—most notably as a member of the White House Health Care Reduction Task Force, which reported to the attorney general.

But Brian's work in the 1980s was primarily not in government service but in major business dealings, most notably in information technology and software engineering. He headed a company called the Biotech Capital Corporation, the predecessor to Infotech, a parent company that extended over an empire that at various times had ties to United Press International, the Financial News Network, the Learning Channel, and the Hadron Corporation. Hadron was a new software company, a high-tech consulting firm that ventured into such areas as the development and design of aerospace systems, intelligence gathering, and developing treatments for toxic agents used in biological warfare.

In April 1983, Hamilton received a telephone call from Dominic Laiti, chairman of Hadron. Laiti told Hamilton that he wanted to buy INSLAW. When Hamilton clearly showed no interest in selling, Laiti pressed the issue. Hamilton later remembered him saying, "We have very good political contacts in the current administration. We can get this kind of business. . . . We have ways of making you sell."

When Hamilton continued to refuse, it became clear what Laiti had meant when he mentioned "ways of making you sell." It was within months of this telephone conversation, Hamilton said later, that the Justice Department completely stopped payment on its contract with INSLAW.

With the loss of its major source of revenue, INSLAW was soon reeling toward financial wreckage. On February 7, 1985, in the hope of gaining time to reorganize, William Hamilton, along with his wife, Nancy, filed for Chapter 11 bankruptcy protection. But, to the Hamiltons' complete astonishment, Justice Department attorneys began pressuring federal bankruptcy officials to force INSLAW out of reorganization and into liquidation. Why, the company and its lawyers wanted to know, were officials in the agency so determined to force INSLAW out of business?

The Hamiltons soon began to understand the situation. Anthony Pasciuto, the deputy director of the Executive Office for U.S. Trustees, which oversees bankruptcy estates on behalf of the court, said that the Justice Department was applying pressure on his office to convert INSLAW's Chapter 11 reorganization into a Chapter 7 liquidation, which would mean that all company assets, including the rights to the PROMIS software, would be sold at auction.

The Hamiltons learned of Brian's connection to Hadron and to Meese in the Justice Department. William and Nancy Hamilton came to believe that Justice was maneuvering to position Brian and Hadron to take advantage of the nearly $3 billion worth of data-

INSLAW owners Nancy and William Hamilton pose with a stack of computer tapes in their office; they sued the Justice Department for stealing their software. (Photo by Robert Sherbow/Time Life Pictures/Getty Images)

processing contracts that would likely be awarded in the years ahead.

To handle this matter, INSLAW hired several lawyers, the most celebrated of which, Elliot Richardson, advised the Hamiltons to sue the Justice Department in federal bankruptcy court. In June 1986, the Hamiltons filed a $30 million lawsuit against the department, charging that the disputes over the contract were a sham contrived by department officials who hoped to steer the contract to friends of the Reagan administration. The Justice Department, according to the suit, had committed "computer piracy."

The INSLAW case slowly made its way through the courts. In January 1988, George F. Bason Jr., a federal bankruptcy judge, ruled vigorously that the Justice Department had, as INSLAW charged, never paid for the enhanced version of the software it had distributed in U.S. attorneys' offices around the country. Bason's 216-page ruling cited numerous instances where testimony from Justice Department witnesses and others for the defense contradicted witnesses. Bason reached the conclusion that the department had indeed stolen the software by "trickery, fraud, and deceit" and that the department had unlawfully implemented the enhanced version of the PROMIS software. This decision, coming from a federal judge, was particularly damning.

Bason also found that Justice Department officials had made an overt effort to force INSLAW into liquidation bankruptcy, an action that would have placed the company's Enhanced PROMIS software up for public auction. Judge Bason pointed directly to a Justice Department official, C. Madison Brewer, who oversaw INSLAW's contract, as a principal figure in the scheming. Brewer was a former employee of INSLAW who had been dismissed. Top Justice Department officials, Bason said, purposely ignored repeated complaints that Brewer was extraordinarily biased and out to wage a war of revenge on his former employer.

Brewer, said Judge Bason, "was consumed by hatred for and an intense desire for revenge against Mr. Hamilton and against INSLAW." Bason said Brewer worked to scuttle INSLAW's other contracts with the department to "cut off INSLAW's financing and cash flow and try to drive them out of business."

Raising further charges against the entire Justice Department, the judge said officials there displayed "collective amnesia" when asked about INSLAW, about Brewer's former connections with the company, and about the validity of William Hamilton's accusations. The court awarded INSLAW $6.8 million in damages.

Shortly after the judge's decision, a Justice Department spokesman said, "As far as we're concerned, our conduct has been lawful and proper and we are quite confident that it will ultimately be vindicated."

Three months after the verdict, in a highly unusual and especially punitive move, Judge Bason was denied reappointment to the bench by the Justice Department that he had served for 14 years. His replacement, S. Martin Teel, was the chief Justice Department lawyer who had argued the department's case before Judge Bason.

In 1989 a federal appellate court affirmed Bason's decision, declaring that there was "convincing, perhaps compelling support for the findings set forth by the bankruptcy court." But later, in a stinging reversal for the Hamiltons and their attorneys, the District of Columbia Circuit Court of Appeals sided with the Justice Department on a technicality, finding that the bankruptcy court was not the proper court in which the INSLAW case should have originated. According to the ruling, the bankruptcy court had no rightful jurisdiction. INSLAW's case was thus lost, not on its merits, but on a technical point.

Elliot Richardson, the Hamiltons' lawyer, sent a letter to Attorney General Richard Thornburgh in 1989 regarding the litigation and the issues surrounding the INSLAW matter. He never received a reply. "I have never understood why," said Richardson. "I mean, I was attorney general when Thornburgh was a U.S. attorney. I appointed him chairman of a committee of U.S. attorneys, newly formed for the first time. I am a responsible former public official. I am not a wild-eyed nut." So why didn't Thornburgh respond to Richardson's letter? "You tell me," Richardson said. "I would have responded to a responsible lawyer whether I ever met him or not."

In October 1991, INSLAW filed an appeal for a writ of certiorari to the Supreme Court of the United States. The court denied the writ. Thus, if the Hamiltons wished to press their case further, they would have to start over in another lower court. But they lacked the financial resources for that kind of venture. Their legal crusade against the Justice Department had thus come to an end.

The INSLAW Affair, however, was just beginning. Indeed, the legal proceedings had only been a prelude to a congressional investigation that would soon begin to color the INSLAW Affair as a full-fledged conspiracy.

The Congressional Investigation Begins

By August 1989, the lawsuits and allegations surrounding INSLAW caught the attention of the new chairman of the House Judiciary Committee, Representative Jack Brooks (D-Tex.). That month, Brooks sent a letter to Attorney General Richard Thornburgh informing the Justice Department that Congress intended to launch a probe into the serious charges involving the contract with INSLAW. Brooks asked for the department's full cooperation with committee investigators. Thornburgh responded on August 21, 1989. Although he questioned the need for such an investigation, he offered to cooperate fully.

A former Marine colonel who served in the Pacific Theater in World War II, Jack Brooks had been elected in 1952 to the House of Representatives from the 2nd District of Texas. In 1989 he became chairman of the House Judiciary Committee. The brash, tough, cigar-smoking lawmaker was a relatively moderate Southern Democrat on such contentious issues as civil rights and labor. He was not one to back down from intimidation or gutter political infighting. When Brooks learned of the purported shenanigans taking place in the Justice Department, he pushed the Judiciary Committee ahead to attempt to learn the truth. With Brooks pressing the investigation, the INSLAW matter began to receive some mainstream media coverage, especially from *Washington Post* editorial writer Mary McGrory.

The committee's investigation, Brooks said, would focus on two principal questions. Did high-level department officials convert, steal, or otherwise misappropriate INSLAW's PROMIS software and attempt to put the company out of business? And did such officials, including Attorney General Edwin Meese and others, conspire to sell or in any way distribute INSLAW's Enhanced PROMIS to other federal agencies and foreign governments?

As the House investigation began in the fall of 1989, Brooks declared, "As incredible as this sounds, Federal Bankruptcy Judge George Bason, who will be testifying later, has already found much of the first part of the allegation to be true. In his decision on the INSLAW bankruptcy, Judge Bason ruled that the Department 'took, converted and stole' INSLAW's proprietary software using 'trickery, fraud and deceit.' The judge also severely criticized the decisions by high-level Department officials to 'ignore the ethical improprieties' on the part of the Justice Department officials involved in the case." The Justice Department, Brooks said, continued to deny any wrongdoing by its officials, maintaining that the matter was a simple case of a contract dispute. "It was all a little hard to swallow," said Brooks.

Brooks had Thornburgh's pledge to cooperate with the investigation. Perhaps Congress and the executive branch, he said, could work effectively together to probe the troubling questions of INSLAW.

But as the Judiciary Committee began its investigation and prepared to call witnesses, Brooks suddenly saw the specter of stonewalling instead of cooperation. Justice Department officials were soon resisting efforts

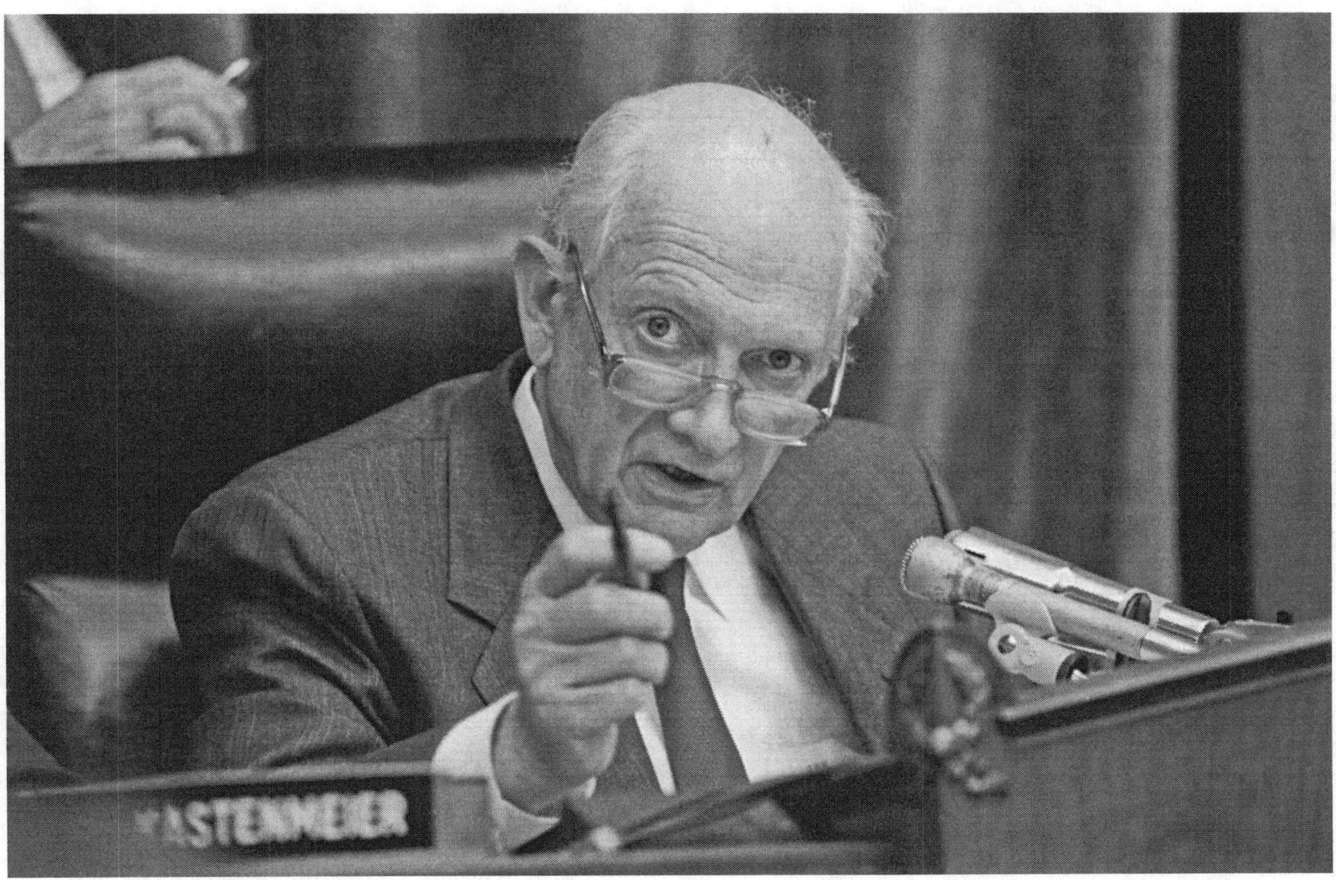

Representative Jack Brooks (D-Tex.), chairman of the House Committee on the Judiciary, was instrumental in pressing the investigation of the alleged computer software theft by the Department of Justice from the INSLAW Company. (Associated Press)

by committee staffers to see certain agency files. Some requests that department employees who had been involved with the INSLAW matter be available for questioning were now rebuffed.

The department's Office of Legislative Affairs then informed committee investigators that some of the requested information would be made available, but because of Privacy Act and trade-secret concerns, each request must be put in writing. Also, access to so-called Public Integrity Section files was not to be made available because its files were "highly sensitive, potentially hurtful, and . . . the information could be misused."

Both astonished and infuriated, Brooks fired off a letter to Thornburgh on January 9, 1990, arguing that the department's requirements were set up in such a way that would preclude Congress from obtaining objective information. He characterized the requirement that a department attorney accompany each witness as nothing short of intimidation.

It took a month of wrangling for the committee to persuade Thornburgh to abandon the demand that department counsel be present for employee depositions. But the dodges and weaves of the department continued. It was not until April 1990 that the attorney general and the chairman reached an agreement concerning access to information. The department agreed to provide free and unrestricted access to documents and employees.

Nevertheless, by midsummer of 1990, House Judiciary Committee investigators realized that all of the protestations of access were nothing more than a smoke screen. Justice Department officials began carefully scrutinizing each file relating to INSLAW, removing items that they deemed to be "privileged" or "attorney-client" materials. Some department officials privately admitted that there was concern at the highest levels of the agency that some of the "privileged" information would somehow end up in the hands of the INSLAW attorneys or the news media. By the end of the year, the department had withdrawn and tucked away nearly 200 files and individual documents. Obviously, as far as the committee investigators were concerned, the agreement was not working.

On December 5, 1990, the committee convened to address the department's refusal to provide access to "privileged" INSLAW documents. During this hearing,

Steven R. Ross, general counsel to the House Clerk, said, "The Attorney General's claimed basis for this withholding of documents is an attempt to create for himself and his functionaries within the Department an exemption from the constitutional principle that all executive officials, no matter how high or low, exercise their authority pursuant to law and that all such public officials are accountable to legislative oversight aimed at ferreting out waste, fraud, and abuse."

Ross also addressed a statement made by Assistant Attorney General Lee Rawls. Congressional investigations, Rawls had claimed, "are justifiable only as a means of facilitating the task of passing legislation." Such an interpretation by the Justice Department, Ross argued, was a total sham, a misunderstanding of congressional oversight responsibility. The Justice Department, Ross said, was in effect attempting to redefine the role of congressional investigations.

"What that proposed standard would do," Ross said, "would be to eradicate the time-honored role of Congress of providing oversight, which is a means that has been upheld by the Supreme Court on a number of occasions, by which the Congress can assure itself that previously passed laws are being properly implemented." Chairman Brooks again demanded full and unrestricted access to department employees and documents.

Meanwhile, as Brooks and others involved in the congressional investigation wrestled with officials at the Justice Department over impending testimony and access to documents, the strange tale of the INSLAW Affair was getting even stranger.

Bizarre Tales Unfold

As the stories about INSLAW's battles with the Justice Department began to receive national attention in the news media and as committee investigators began their research, the relatively simple tale of a contract dispute regarding computer software soon began to have layers of intrigue. Suddenly, a number of shadowy sources from the underground world of covert intelligence began making phone calls and sending memos about the INSLAW matter. A number of individuals contacted Hamilton and his attorney, Elliot Richardson, alleging that INSLAW Inc. had run into a strange mix of international plots and schemes. There was much more to the story, the sources insisted, than they had ever imagined.

Two main characters surfaced in the unfolding web of conspiracy tales. The first was Michael Riconosciuto, who contacted Hamilton in the spring of 1990. A figure who seemed straight out of a sinister spy thriller, Riconosciuto was an arms expert who also claimed advanced expertise in covert currency transfers, electronic surveillance, and computer-software design. He had served as the director of a federally funded research project to develop materials used in military and national security operations, including night-vision goggles, explosives, and biological and chemical weapons. Located on the reservation of the Cabazon Indians in Indio, California, the venture had been set up to assist the government in supporting various undercover enterprises in Central America and the Middle East. He was, Hamilton saw immediately, someone who was not reticent in hailing his own particular "advanced skills" in areas that aided intelligence operations.

Former U.S. attorney general Elliot Richardson served as attorney for INSLAW Inc. (Associated Press)

Riconosciuto also proved to be a figure whose background did not exactly inspire trust. He was, among other things, a suspected drug dealer. But Riconosciuto had something to tell Hamilton that would seem to make some weird but logical sense of his problems with the Justice Department. Riconosciuto claimed that individuals in the department had given the PROMIS software to American intelligence officers to resell in the international, underground intelligence market. Some of the money, he said, was made available to pay off various individuals who had engaged in backdoor military and diplomatic contacts outside the normal purview of congressional oversight.

One of the individuals who had been paid off, Riconosciuto recounted, was none other than Earl Brian. According to the story, Brian had been a member of Ronald Reagan's team in late 1980 that allegedly contacted Iranian leaders to orchestrate a deal that was later known as "the October Surprise"—the delaying of the release of 52 American hostages held by Iran until after the presidential election and until the Reagan administration took office.

Riconosciuto claimed that in payment for his part in the October Surprise, Brian was given the lucrative financial gold mine that resulted from the theft of the PROMIS software. Brian and others supposedly implicated in the October Surprise later adamantly denied that any such contacts with Iran about holding the hostages until Reagan took office ever occurred.

It was unclear why Riconosciuto had come to Hamilton with the story. But to Hamilton, the seemingly fanciful and fantastic assertion made sense. And Riconosciuto had more. He told Hamilton that the PROMIS software had been distributed to as many as 80 foreign and domestic intelligence agencies, including those of Iraq, Israel, Libya, and South Korea. Riconosciuto claimed that the Justice Department had altered PROMIS so that any agency using the software program could be subject to eavesdropping by the department itself. PROMIS, in other words, was being used as a kind of software Trojan horse. How did he know this? It was Riconosciuto himself, a master of computer hacking, who had been hired by the department to create the new "trapdoor" version of PROMIS. And who had given him the PROMIS software? Earl Brian.

The second primary source of the stories of the secret espionage use of PROMIS was a man named Ari Ben-Menashe. A former Israeli intelligence officer who had also served in the Israeli prime minister's office, Ben-Menashe claimed that he had been involved in numerous secret deals with foreign governments. Like Riconosciuto, Ben-Menashe was a man of dubious background and a growing reputation for making up false stories and accusations, a number of which he later published in a book titled *Profits of War: Inside the Secret U.S.-Israeli Arms Network* (1992).

At the time he came forward to make statements about the INSLAW Affair, Ben-Menashe had recently been acquitted in New York on arms-trading charges. The federal government had accused Ben-Menashe of conspiring to sell three transport planes to Iran. He had spent a year in prison awaiting trial. At the trial, he produced a diplomatic passport and other documents as evidence that his activities had been approved by the Israeli government.

Regardless of Ben-Menashe's shady background, his claims about his connection to the PROMIS software appeared to corroborate the growing pattern of charges pointing to the complicity of the Justice Department in the INSLAW Affair. Ben-Menashe claimed that in 1987, when he was a special consultant for intelligence affairs in the Israeli prime minister's office, he was at a meeting at the Israeli intelligence headquarters in Tel Aviv when Brian told the gathering that a number of U.S. agencies, such as the Central Intelligence Agency and the National Security Agency, were using versions of the PROMIS software. Later, Ben-Menashe said, he learned that Brian had given the software to Israel for use by its own intelligence agencies.

From the perspective of the Israelis, Ben-Menashe said, "PROMIS was a very big thing for us guys, a very, very big thing. . . . It was probably the most important issue of the '80s because it just changed the whole intelligence outlook. The whole form of intelligence collection changed. This whole thing changed it." PROMIS software, Ben-Menashe said, was the perfect tool for tracking Palestinian dissidents.

Ben-Menashe also appeared to give independent corroboration to Riconosciuto's claims that the INSLAW Affair centered on Earl Brian. Ben-Menashe said he learned that an Israeli master spy named Rafi Eitan, head of a secret unit in Israel's Defense Ministry, had claimed that he had acquired PROMIS software from Brian for the Israeli Defense Signals Intelligence Unit. He also said that the CIA had transferred $4 million into one of Brian's accounts in Phoenix as a payoff for the October Surprise.

In addition to Michael Riconosciuto and Ari Ben-Menashe, another figure from the shrouded underworld of espionage appeared on the scene to add yet more seasoning to the conspiracy stew that was suddenly the INSLAW Affair. Richard Babayan, described by the *St. Louis Post-Dispatch* as an Iranian arms trader, claimed that PROMIS had been sold to Iraq, Libya, and South Korea. Babayan also fingered Brian in the shadowy schemes, saying that a member of Iraqi intelligence had told him that it was Brian who had been the middleman in providing PROMIS to the Iraqis. Babayan also said he had been told that it was Brian who had sold PROMIS to the South Koreans as well.

The informants were certainly not what committee investigators would consider ideal witnesses. Nevertheless, the overall story that they independently presented seemed to Brooks and his committee to be compelling. Elliot Richardson said, "Why in the world would this one group of informers ever have come together and cooked up all this stuff? How did they keep it consistent from day to day among themselves as to who told what to whom? There is a hell of a load of stuff they've told to various people, including staffers, journalists, the Hamiltons, me. The picture they paint is relatively coherent and consistent

. . . and then you add the stonewalling by the Department of Justice. I have never understood why."

Brian denied all involvement in the INSLAW Affair. He rejected the statements of Ben-Menashe, Riconosciuto, and Babayan as fantasy. He had never met Riconosciuto, he said, and had no idea who Ben-Menashe was. In response to the claims that his friends in the White House and the Justice Department were attempting to force INSLAW into bankruptcy to pave the way for his own company to take over, Brian insisted he had never heard of INSLAW or the PROMIS software until much later, when he read reports of the case in newspapers and magazines. He denied any involvement in illegally transferring PROMIS to foreign intelligence services.

In addition, Brian adamantly rejected charges that he had been involved in the so-called October Surprise. In support of his claims, he provided investigators with evidence that he did not have a valid U.S. passport in 1980, when his activities with Iranian diplomats supposedly occurred. The investigators did not vigorously pursue other accusations that Brian had traveled on a passport under an assumed name.

In April 1991, Riconosciuto was arrested by federal agents in Washington State on the charge of manufacturing methamphetamines. He would face a jury several months later and claim at his trial that the Justice Department had set him up to discredit him as a witness in the INSLAW Affair. The jury convicted him on seven counts of distributing drugs. As Riconosciuto headed off to prison, U.S. Attorney Mark Bartlett commented to the news media, "He wants you to think he's a man of world intrigue. In fact he is a drug dealer, pure and simple."

The case for INSLAW and the Hamiltons was being seriously hurt by the credibility of its witnesses. But Representative Brooks and the House Judiciary Committee pressed on, determined to unearth the whole story. Unfortunately, he was facing at every turn an increasingly resistant attorney general.

The Committee Subpoenas the Attorney General

On July 8, 1991, Representative Brooks announced plans to hold regular authorization and oversight hearings to consider the Justice Department's 1992 fiscal-year budget request. Brooks indicated that as part of these hearings, he would be asking Thornburgh about his reneging on several previous commitments he had made to the committee to provide full and open access to the department's INSLAW files.

From the beginning of the authorization hearing, it was clear that Brooks intended to use this opportunity to hammer away at the manner in which Justice Department officials had treated requests for documents and testimony in the INSLAW matter. Brooks charged that the department seemed bent on using claims of executive privilege and playing politics at the expense of public scrutiny and agency accountability.

Chairman Brooks opened the hearing by lecturing the audience, including a number of department officials, about the legislative process in general and the constitutional process of checks and balances in particular. Oversight of the executive branch, Brooks explained, is at the heart of the constitutional mandate conferred by the founding fathers. It is an activity that anchors the architecture of constitutional government. Justice Department officials, he said, had continued throughout the INSLAW investigation to challenge the constitutional authority of the legislative branch. In their resistance, he said, they were undermining basic governmental processes.

On July 18, 1991, the committee was scheduled to hear testimony by Thornburgh. But as the panel gathered to begin the hearing, Chairman Brooks stared at an empty witness chair. Thornburgh had refused to show up. Brooks stated that Thornburgh "has turned his back on the very constitutional structure of government he has sworn to uphold. I am deeply saddened and amazed."

The chairman denounced Thornburgh in the strongest terms. "In light of the extreme importance of this proceeding," Brooks said, "it is particularly unfortunate and deeply disturbing."

The behavior of Thornburgh and his Justice Department colleagues toward the INSLAW matter, Brooks charged, had done great damage to relations between a duly authorized congressional investigation and the executive department. "I am shocked and saddened by the appearance of the empty chair before us and all the other chairs that he asked to be reserved for his people," Brooks continued. "The unanswered request and the delayed response are becoming the symbols of an increasingly remote and self-centered Justice Department that seems bent on expanding the accepted boundaries of executive branch power and prerogatives."

Finally, on July 25, 1991, the Judiciary Committee took an unusually forceful action. It subpoenaed the attorney general to turn over all the documents related to the INSLAW case that the department had withheld for one reason or another. Speculation raged around Capitol Hill and among reporters and pundits about how far this test of wills and struggle for power would go. If Thornburgh continued to withhold some of the materials, therefore defying the subpoena, would the committee find the attorney general in contempt of Congress? Would the showdown even lead to criminal proceedings? Brooks indicated to reporters that he had every intention of pushing as far as necessary to force the Justice Department to turn over the documents.

All standing committees have authority to compel witnesses to testify and produce evidentiary materials for investigations under their purview. Congressional power to compel testimony, known as inherent contempt, has been upheld in a number of Supreme Court decisions. Under the inherent contempt power, an individual can be brought before the House or Senate by the sergeant at arms, tried at the bar of the body, and even imprisoned in the U.S. Capitol. Although the inherent contempt power has been recognized by the Supreme Court as inextricably related to Congress's constitutionally based power to investigate, it rarely has been used. Brooks seemed on the verge of taking steps toward exercising this power against Thornburgh.

At that critical point in the confrontation, Thornburgh and the Justice Department backed down. Although Thornburgh continued to resist committee demands that he testify, he sent couriers up to Capitol Hill to deliver several hundred documents. The committee gained access to sensitive files of the Justice Department's Office of Professional Responsibility that had been withheld and received more than 400 additional documents that the department had described as related to "ongoing litigation and other highly sensitive matters and 'protected' under the claims of attorney-client and attorney work product privileges." But even as Brooks took some satisfaction in the delivery of the materials, he remained skeptical. Department officials announced that some of the material that they had intended to present to the committee had mysteriously disappeared.

The Suspicious Death of Danny Casolaro

In early August 1991, a 44-year-old freelance reporter named Danny Casolaro was found dead in a Martinsburg, West Virginia, motel room. His death immediately shook the INSLAW congressional investigation and added yet another layer of possible treachery to a story that seemed to grow more sordid at every turn. Casolaro was not a well-known writer, but he had published articles in a variety of periodicals and newspapers, including the *Providence Journal, Washington Star, National Enquirer,* and the Washington Crime News Service. He had written short stories, poetry, and a novel called *The Ice King*. Interested and skilled in computer science, he had cofounded a publication called *Computer Age,* which at the time was one of the few publications exploring a new but burgeoning field.

Friends of Casolaro said he was interested in conspiracy theories in history and became fascinated with the early published reports of the INSLAW matter, which came to his attention because of his ties to the computer field. By early 1990, even with some of the early work of the investigating committee now public, only a few reporters had shown much interest in the story. But Casolaro was fascinated. Why would the Justice Department take such a hard-line and aggressive stance against a small computer company? What was behind the rigid denials and stonewalling? Were there any other connections that would explain all of it?

Skilled in detective legwork around Washington, Casolaro had by the late 1980s already spent much time on the phone with Michael Riconosciuto. Shortly after Riconosciuto had been arrested by federal agents near Tacoma, Washington, on drug charges and claimed he had been "set up" because he had spoken out on INSLAW, Casolaro was on a plane headed west.

After extensive interviews with Riconosciuto and other informants who had come forward with claims about INSLAW, Casolaro concluded that the matter was linked to a variety of other government scandals involving a loose network of individuals engaged in profit-making clandestine intelligence operations.

Casolaro saw a connection running between individuals involved with INSLAW and the October Surprise, from arms trading to illegal covert operations. He also saw links with such scandals as the Iran-Contra Affair, in which the Reagan administration allegedly traded arms to Iran in an effort to bargain for the release of hostages. In addition Casolaro made connections between these events and a growing scandal involving the Bank of Credit and Commerce International, which he believed was a major financial conduit for these other enterprises.

They were tentacles of a huge conspiracy, he believed—what he called "the Octopus." His book, he promised, would blow out of the water this network of government camouflage, war profiteering, and fraud pulled off by a group of former intelligence officers—a profit-making cabal. Although Casolaro had not found a publisher for the book, family members and friends said he sounded upbeat about his research and excited about the revelations he had uncovered. But he told his brother and others that this was a high-risk venture in which he was involved, one which, if the wrong people found out, might place his life in jeopardy. If he turned up dead, he even told his brother, Anthony Casolaro, no one should believe that it was some mysterious accident.

Indeed, one of his close friends said that Casolaro told him he had received death threats for several months. One caller told Casolaro's housekeeper, "I will cut his body and throw it to the sharks." Anthony Casolaro said later that his brother had received a midnight call on August 5, shortly before a trip to Martinsburg, West Virginia. He did not say whom he was going to see in Martinsburg but said he was about to nail down the last details of the INSLAW matter.

On Saturday, August 10, a Sheraton Hotel maid found the body of Danny Casolaro in the bathtub of Room 517. His arms and wrists had been slashed. The previous evening he had called his mother to tell her he was heading home but would not be able to make it to his niece's birthday party. There was a suicide note in the room. It was not until the following Monday that Martinsburg police notified the family about Casolaro's death. The motel room had been sanitized by a cleaning company, and the body had been embalmed. His sister later said that the handwriting on the note looked like Danny's.

But Anthony Casolaro and other stunned family members insisted that this was not a suicide. What about the death threats? Where were many of Casolaro's notes and papers that he would have undoubtedly had with him? Where was the briefcase that he always carried with him? Where was his tape recorder?

Nevertheless, after reviewing the autopsy, the FBI agreed with Martinsburg police that this was a case of suicide. The family members, Elliot Richardson, and some members of the House INSLAW investigating committee had serious doubts. "It's hard to come up with any reason for [Casolaro's] death," concluded Richardson, "other than that he was deliberately murdered because he was so close to uncovering sinister elements in what he called 'the Octopus.'" During the three days preceding his death," Richardson said, "he told four friends in the course of four different telephone conversations that he was about to go to West Virginia to meet someone from whom he was confident of receiving definitive proof of what had happened to the PROMIS software and to INSLAW. . . . He was the only one who told people who have no reason to misrepresent what he said that he had hard evidence, and was on the point of getting conclusive evidence. No one else made that claim. . . . The idea that he committed suicide with a razor blade under these circumstances seems highly implausible."

As the House investigation of INSLAW continued, Chairman Brooks directed staff members to obtain sworn statements from FBI agents and other law-enforcement officials who had information about the Casolaro case. Although committee investigators found the case highly suspicious, they could reach no definitive conclusion about Casolaro's death. Also, as the investigation continued, the political divisions on the committee between Democrats and Republicans became increasingly glaring. Republicans began to see the investigation as a Democratic witch hunt designed solely to embarrass the Reagan administration. As Brooks added the Casolaro death to the investigation agenda, Republican members became even more resistant to calling additional witnesses.

Limited in resources and options in continuing the investigation, Brooks and his Democratic colleagues decided to conclude their work and call for the attorney general to appoint a special prosecutor to look into possible criminal actions involved in the INSLAW Affair.

In late summer, Richard Thornburgh resigned as attorney general to run for the U.S. Senate from Pennsylvania. *Washington Post* columnist Mary McGrory, one of the few mainstream journalists to give the INSLAW case serious attention, wrote, "The man who could have resolved the INSLAW case, Dick Thornburgh, resigned as attorney general on the day the West Virginia police came forward with their autopsy. Thornburgh calls INSLAW 'a little contract dispute' and refused to testify about it to the House Judiciary Committee. . . . Thornburgh's conduct is the most powerful reason for believing that Danny Casolaro really saw an octopus before he died."

Committee Issues Investigative Report, September 1992

On September 10, 1992, Brooks's committee issued a blistering, 230-page investigative report on the INSLAW Affair. The report asked that Attorney General William Barr, who had replaced Thornburgh, appoint an independent counsel to pursue allegations raised in the INSLAW Affair.

The report charged that high government officials had conspired to steal the PROMIS software and to distribute it internationally both for financial gain and for furthering intelligence and foreign-policy objectives: "The evidence . . . demonstrates that high-level Department officials deliberately ignored INSLAW proprietary rights and willfully drove the company into bankruptcy."

An independent counsel, the report said, could determine whether the attorney general had obstructed the congressional investigation, whether any Justice Department employees engaged in perjury or covered up their involvement in the matter, whether any relevant records were lost or destroyed by the department, and whether any private individuals were involved in the conspiracy.

The report attacked Meese's claims that he had no knowledge of bias against INSLAW by the Justice Department or its officials. Under oath, Meese said that he recalled no specific discussion with anyone about INSLAW's contract and the misuse of the PROMIS software. The congressional report revealed that Meese's testimony directly conflicted with that of a federal judge who said he had briefed Meese regularly on the whole issue and that Meese knew very well the details of the contract and the negotiations between the department and INSLAW.

The report pointed to a sworn statement made by Deputy Attorney General Arnold Burns to Office of Professional Responsibility investigators in 1988 as particularly revealing. Burns said that Justice Department attorneys had already advised him in 1986 that INSLAW's claim of proprietary rights was legitimate and that the department would probably lose the case in court on this issue. "Accepting this statement," the committee report said, "it is incredible that the Department, having made this determination, would continue to pursue its litigation of these matters. More than $1 million has been spent in litigation on this case by the Justice Department even though it knew in 1986 that it did not have a chance to win the case on merits. This clearly raises the specter that the Department actions taken against INSLAW in this matter represent an abuse of power of shameful proportions."

Aside from the facts of the INSLAW investigation itself, the report lambasted the Justice Department on the issues of stonewalling and cover-up. "One of the principal reasons the committee could not reach any definitive conclusion about INSLAW's allegations of a high criminal conspiracy at Justice was the lack of cooperation from the Department," the report stated. ". . . The Congress met with restrictions, delays and outright denials to requests for information and to unobstructed access to records and witnesses. . . . Attorney General Thornburgh repeatedly reneged on agreements made with this committee to provide full and open access to information and witnesses. . . . The Department failed to provide all the documents subpoenaed, claiming that some of the documents . . . had been misplaced or accidentally destroyed."

Chairman Brooks said that the report should be the starting point for a grand jury investigation. The owners of INSLAW, Brooks said, were "ravaged by the Justice Department . . . treated like dogs."

The committee also remained skeptical that the death of Danny Casolaro had been a suicide. "Based on the evidence collected by the committee," the report said, "it appears that the path followed by Danny Casolaro in pursuing his investigation into the INSLAW matter brought him in contact with a number of dangerous individuals associated with organized crime and the world of covert intelligence operations. The suspicious circumstances surrounding his death have led some law enforcement professionals and others to believe that his death may not have been a suicide. As long as the possibility exists that Danny Casolaro died as a result of his investigation into the INSLAW matter, it is imperative that further investigation be conducted."

On September 10, 1992, the entire Democratic membership of the committee wrote to Attorney General Barr reiterating the request for an independent counsel. One month later, the attorney general responded that he was unwilling to do so.

But with the political charges of conspiracy and cover-up surrounding the INSLAW Affair, Barr realized he had to do something. He decided to appoint Nicholas Bua, a retired judge in Chicago, to conduct an internal investigation for the Justice Department. In other words, the Justice Department would investigate itself.

Justice Department Bua Report Denies All

Nicholas Bua had been nominated to the federal bench in 1977 by President Jimmy Carter. When Attorney General Barr asked Bua to take on the Justice Department's own investigation of INSLAW in 1992, Bua had only recently retired.

In November 1992, Bill Clinton defeated President George H. W. Bush, who was bidding for a second term. Early in 1993, a new administration took over the reins of government in Washington. As Bua's investigation of INSLAW concluded, scores of Republican political appointees in the Justice Department turned their offices over to Democrats, led by new Attorney General Janet Reno, a state's attorney from Florida.

In June 1993, the new administration was handed a 267-page report from Bua and his staff of six federal prosecutors. The Bua report completely repudiated all of the various charges and allegations set forth by the Brooks report from the congressional investigation. "The allegations in this case seem to know no bounds," Bua and his team concluded, and "there is no credible evidence" of a conspiracy between department officials and "no connection between Earl Brian and anything related to INSLAW or PROMIS software."

"All of the actions" by department employees relating to the INSLAW computer firm were made in "good faith," the report asserted, and "there are no grounds for bringing criminal charges or disciplinary actions against those who dealt with the firm."

Bua attacked the credibility of the lineup of individuals upon which the Hamiltons' court case had rested and upon which Representative Brooks and his investigators had relied—from the convicted drug dealer Michael Riconosciuto to Ari Ben-Menashe, whose testimony, Bua insisted, was founded more on his hunger to publish a hot-selling book than in telling anything resembling the truth.

Finally, Bua rejected insinuations that the freelance journalist Danny Casolaro had been murdered in August 1991 because he was uncovering evidence of an "octopus" conspiracy linking INSLAW to other scandals. The physical evidence in Casolaro's hotel, Bua said, "strongly supports" police and FBI conclusions that it was a suicide.

William Hamilton and his attorney, Elliot Richardson, along with Brooks and the Democrats on the Judiciary Committee, had expected that Bua would attempt to exonerate the Justice Department. From the beginning, they questioned the decision by Barr to investigate the INSLAW Affair from within the department rather than to appoint a special prosecutor. They expected something of a whitewash from this report but had not expected the kind of total vindication of the department that it asserted.

Shortly after the release of the Bua report, Richardson issued a statement saying, "What I have seen of [the report] is remarkable both for its credulity in accepting at face value denials of complicity in wrongdoing against INSLAW and for its failure to pursue leads making those denials implausible."

On July 12, 1993, Hamilton submitted a 90-page rebuttal of the Bua report prepared by his lawyers to Associate Attorney General Webster Hubbell. He sent copies to each member of the House Judiciary Committee.

Representative Brooks and Representative Charlie Rose (D-NC) tried to enact a bill that would force a further investigation of the Justice Department and the death of Casolaro, and pay reparations to the owners of INSLAW. The bill died without any action by the Democratic leadership in the waning days of the 103rd Congress. More than a decade had passed since INSLAW had negotiated its now infamous contract with the Justice Department.

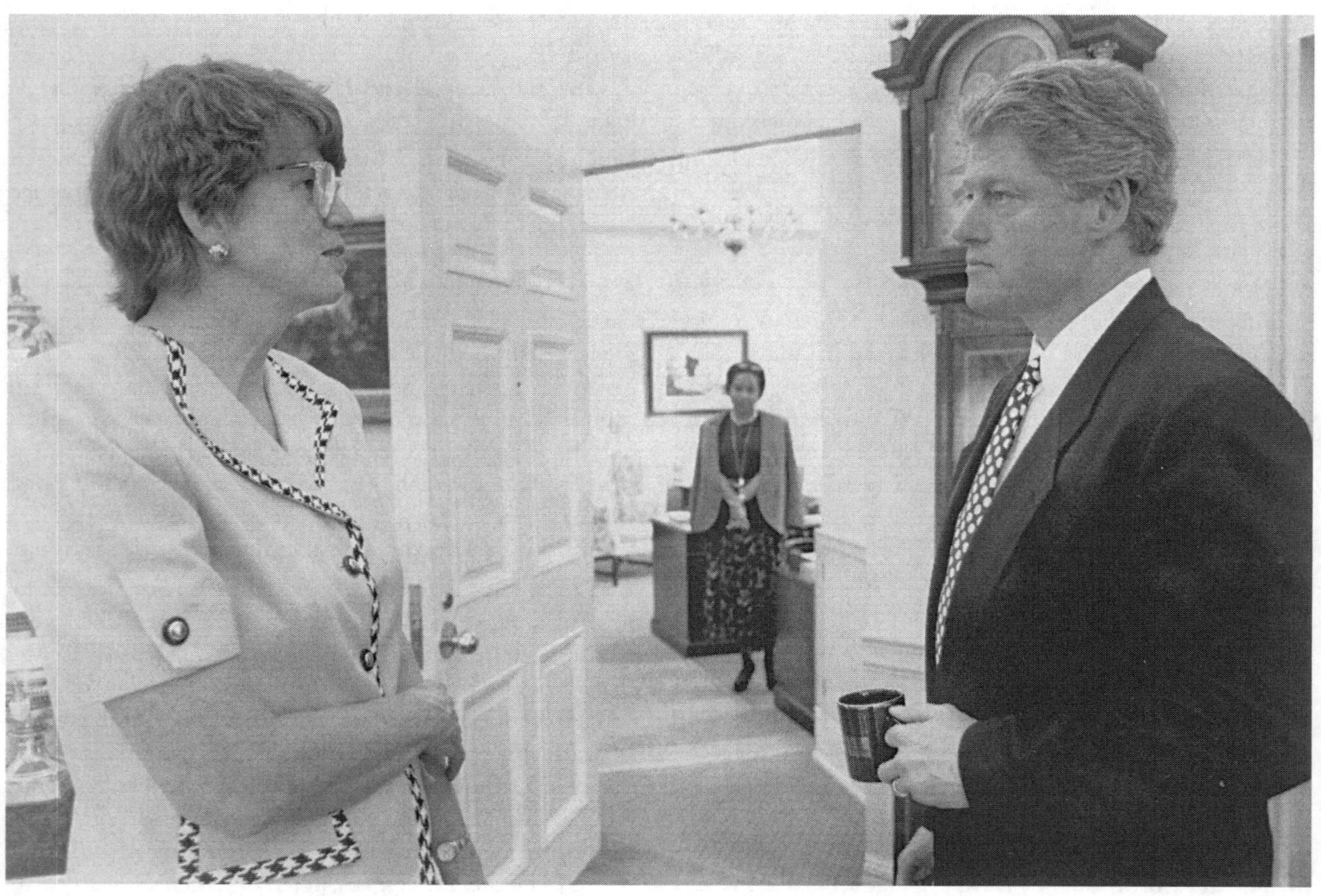

U.S. Attorney General Janet Reno speaks with President Bill Clinton. (Library of Congress)

Reno Rejects Independent Counsel

William Hamilton, accompanied by his attorney Elliot Richardson, met with Attorney General Janet Reno to plead their case shortly after the release of the Bua report. By this time, some former Justice Department officials had alleged that they had been told to shred documents relating to the INSLAW Affair that would be potentially damaging to a number of Reagan-era Justice Department officials. Hamilton and Richardson asked that the attorney general follow the recommendations of the House investigation and appoint a special prosecutor to conduct a nonpartisan investigation.

Instead, Reno did what her Republican counterpart had done—she ordered another internal investigation. Within a few weeks, on September 27, 1994, Reno sent both Congress and the news media another report that again asserted that there was no scandal and no need for an independent counsel or further investigation. "INSLAW was provided a full and fair opportunity to litigate its claims," said the report. "The ability of INSLAW and its counsel to keep this matter in the public spotlight by making a series of unsubstantiated allegations linking this affair to some of the major alleged conspiracies of the last 15 years should not be rewarded by acquiescing to their money demands." It was clear that the new administration had no interest in prolonging the INSLAW inquiry.

What about INSLAW's efforts to seek compensation for the huge financial losses it had incurred because of department actions? The Reno report rejected any notion that Hamilton and INSLAW should be paid one cent.

Chairman Brooks, along with Representative Richard Gephardt (D-Mo.), made abortive attempts to push legislation through Congress that would have provided financial relief to INSLAW. Their efforts were blocked by partisan votes.

Finally, in 1997, a U.S. federal claims court found that the enhancements to the PROMIS software were not under copyright protection to INSLAW. The court asserted that the Justice Department had acted properly in carrying out its obligations under the contract with the company. The legal and political actions in the INSLAW Affair had played themselves out.

The Octopus Swims On

After a decade and a half of controversy, of claims and counterclaims, of shady theories spun by shady and not-so-shady people, the INSLAW Affair finally had been buried by the Justice Department and federal courts. It had been relegated to the writings of a few individuals who continued to investigate the story and to insist that the whole matter had been, in fact, as Elliot Richardson claimed, bigger than Watergate. For all of its battles in Congress and the courts, William and Nancy Hamilton were unsuccessful in recovering any monies they claimed had been taken from their company by government fraud. No Justice Department officials were ever found culpable by a jury for their alleged misdeeds. The death of Danny Casolaro became a closed case, attributed to suicide.

But the echoes of the controversy persisted over the years. Earl Brian, whose name and career, he believed, had been besmirched by the INSLAW investigators, finally filed a lawsuit against Richardson for defamation of character. It was thrown out of court.

And things got worse for Brian. On October 17, 1996, after a four-month trial, a federal jury in Los Angeles convicted him on 10 counts of bank and securities fraud and conspiracy. He was sentenced to a four-and-a-half-year prison term. Federal investigators found that Brian and other executives used false interoffice billings and lease-back arrangements to collateralize loans totaling between $70 million and $100 million. Through the transactions, Brian had made off with $300,000 in stolen funds.

In 1999, British journalist Gordon Thomas published a history of the Israeli Mossad, the Institute for Intelligence and Special Operations. Titled *Gideon's Spies: The Secret History of the Mossad,* the book quoted admissions by a former longtime deputy director of the Mossad about the partnership between Israeli and U.S. intelligence in selling more than $500 million worth of licenses to a Trojan horse version of PROMIS to foreign intelligence agencies in order to spy on them.

In October 2001, a news report by Fox correspondent Carl Cameron indicated that the convicted spy and former FBI agent Robert Hanssen had provided a highly secret computer-software program to Russian organized crime figures. The software program was PROMIS.

Other investigative reports, some of which appeared on Fox News, indicated that a leader of a radical organization had bought the PROMIS software on the black market for $2 million to help the organization monitor U.S. intelligence agencies. His name was Osama bin Laden.

Congressman Brooks, William Hamilton, Elliot Richardson, and others pleading the case for INSLAW had been sorely disappointed that the congressional investigation had not led to a special prosecutor and possible indictments and that INSLAW never recovered large sums of money that the company and the congressional investigators charged had been stolen by the government. But Brooks did take some pride in the fact that the committee had not backed down in the face of executive intransigence.

Veteran FBI agent Robert Philip Hanssen, shown in this undated photo released by the FBI, was arrested for espionage on February 18, 2001. Agent Hanssen was charged with spying for the Soviet Union and Russia for more than 15 years. A Fox News report charged that Hanssen had provided PROMIS software to Russian organized crime figures. (FBI/Associated Press)

The Justice Department's unwillingness to allow congressional oversight into its affairs greatly hindered the committee's investigation, delaying inquires over several years. But the committee had persevered, resorting to the use of subpoena power and the threat of criminal contempt proceedings.

Brooks lauded the efforts of the committee in establishing several important precedents. Committee investigators were ultimately given unrestricted access to all contract, personnel, and administrative files of the Justice Department, including the sensitive files of the Office of Professional Responsibility. The committee had persuaded the FBI to permit one of its field agents to give a sworn statement to committee investigators. And, finally, under force of subpoenas, the Justice Department had provided documents that it had originally identified as related to ongoing litigation and "protected" under attorney-client and attorney work product privileges.

"The legend of INSLAW as a government cover-up has grown and grown," Chairman Brooks said later. Nevertheless, as with many historical events brimming with claims and counterclaims, all the intrigue may never be sorted out. The future revelation of historical documents may help piece together the web of machinations and secrecy surrounding the INSLAW Affair, but it is unlikely that the whole story will ever be explained to everyone's satisfaction.

One thing, nevertheless, is certain. The power struggle between the executive and legislative branches of government over congressional investigatory authority, exemplified so strongly in the INSLAW case, continued ever more aggressively early in the 21st century with the presidency of George W. Bush.

DOCUMENTS

News Release, U.S. House Committee on the Judiciary, August 11, 1992

In the summer of 1992, a few months before the presidential election, the House Committee on the Judiciary issued a news release anticipating a report that would outline the bizarre case of apparent computer software theft perpetrated by the U.S. Department of Justice and the extraordinary efforts to cover up illegal activities. Chaired by Representative Jack Brooks of Texas, the committee sided with the claims of INSLAW Inc. that its invention of so-called Enhanced PROMIS software had been essentially hijacked by the federal government at a considerable loss of money to the company. The committee called for the appointment of an independent counsel to sort out the claims and counterclaims and to determine whether purported illegalities should be prosecuted.

NEWS RELEASE, U.S. HOUSE COMMITTEE ON THE JUDICIARY, AUGUST 11, 1992

The ("INSLAW Affair") report concludes that there appears to be strong evidence, as indicated by the findings of two Federal court proceedings, as well as by the Committee investigation, that the Department of Justice "acted willfully and fraudulently," and "took, converted and stole," INSLAW's Enhanced PROMIS by "trickery, fraud and deceit." The report finds that these actions against INSLAW were implemented through the Project Manager from the beginning of the contract and under the direction of high-level Justice Department officials. The evidence presented in the report demonstrates that high-level Department officials deliberately ignored INSLAW's proprietary rights and misappropriated its PROMIS software for use at locations not covered under contract with the company. Justice then proceeded to challenge INSLAW's claims in court even though its own internal deliberations had concluded that these claims were valid and that the Department would most likely lose in court on this issue.

According to the report, the second phase of the Committee's investigation concentrated on the allegations that high-level officials at the Department of Justice conspired to drive INSLAW into insolvency and steal PROMIS. In this regard, the report states that several individuals testified under oath that INSLAW's PROMIS software was stolen and distributed internationally in order to provide financial gain to associates of Justice Department officials and to further intelligence and foreign policy objectives of the United States. Additional corroborating evidence was uncovered by the Committee which substantiated to varying degrees the information provided by these individuals.

(Chairman) Brooks stated, "Although (the Department of Justice was) faced with a growing body of evidence that serious wrongdoing had occurred which reached to the highest levels of the Department, both Attorney General Meese and Thornburgh ignored these findings of two Federal courts and refused to seek the appointment of an Independent Counsel."

Source: www.democraticunderground.com/discuss/duboard.php?az=view_all&address=1 25x196360.

House Judiciary Committee's Investigative Report: Extracts from Summary and Chapter 7, September 10, 1992

Ten years had passed since the U.S. Department of Justice awarded INSLAW Inc. a $10 million contract to set up its public-domain version of the software program known as PROMIS in 94 U.S. attorneys' offices across the country. In September 1992, after years of testimony, court filings, charges, and countercharges, the House Judiciary Committee released its report on the scandal. It was all here—the allegations of William Hamilton and his wife, Nancy, owners of INSLAW; the suspicions raised that U.S. Attorney General Edwin Meese, along with a number of friends, had engaged in fraud and cover-up; the various judicial decisions that settled nothing; the mysterious death of journalist Danny Casolaro, who many believed had been killed to prevent disclosures that would have implicated a number of people in positions of power; and the suggestion that the Justice Department may have destroyed incriminating evidence and obstructed justice.

HOUSE JUDICIARY COMMITTEE'S INVESTIGATIVE REPORT, SEPTEMBER 10, 1992

Summary

The Department of Justice has long recognized the need for a standardized management information system to assist law enforcement offices across the country in the recordkeeping and tracking of criminal cases. During the 1970s, the Law Enforcement Assistance Administration (LEAA) funded the development by INSLAW of a computer software system called the Prosecutor's Management Information System or PROMIS. This system was designed to meet the criminal prosecutor workloads of large urban jurisdictions; and by 1980, several large U.S. attorney's offices were using the PROMIS software. At this time, INSLAW (formerly called the Institute for Law and Social Research) was a nonprofit corporation funded almost entirely through Government grants and contracts. When President Carter terminated the LEAA, INSLAW converted the company to a for-profit corporation in 1981 to commercially market PROMIS.

The new corporation made several significant improvements to the original PROMIS software and the resulting product came to be known as INSLAW's proprietary Enhanced PROMIS. The original PROMIS was funded entirely with Government funds and was in the public domain.

In March 1982, the Justice Department awarded INSLAW, Inc., a $10 million, 3-year contract to implement the public domain version of PROMIS at 94 U.S. attorney's offices across the country and U.S. Territories. While the PROMIS software could have gone a long way toward correcting the Department's longstanding need for a standardized case management system, the contract between INSLAW and Justice quickly became embroiled in bitterness and controversy which has lasted for almost a decade. The conflict centers on the question of whether INSLAW has ownership of its privately funded "Enhanced PROMIS." This software was eventually installed at numerous U.S. attorney's offices after a 1983 modification to the contract. While Justice officials at the time recognized INSLAW's proprietary rights to any privately funded enhancements to the original public domain version of PROMIS, the Department later claimed that it had unlimited rights to all software supplied under the contract.

INSLAW attempted to resolve the matter several times but was largely met with indifference or hostility by Department officials. Eventually, the Department canceled part of the contract and, by February 1983, had withheld at least $1.6 million in payments. As a result, the company was driven to the brink of insolvency and was threatened with dissolution under chapter 7 of the bankruptcy laws. Department officials have steadfastly claimed the INSLAW controversy is merely a contract dispute which has been blown out of proportion by the media. INSLAW's owners, William and Nancy Hamilton, however, have persisted in their belief that the Department's actions were part of a high level conspiracy within Justice to steal the Enhanced PROMIS software.

A. INSLAW Allegations

Based on their knowledge and belief, the Hamiltons have alleged that high-level officials in the Department of Justice conspired to steal the Enhanced PROMIS software system. As an element of this theft, these officials, who included former Attorney General Edwin Meese and Deputy Attorney General Lowell Jensen, forced INSLAW into bankruptcy by intentionally creating a sham contract dispute over the terms and conditions of the contract which led to the withholding of payments due INSLAW by the Department. The Hamiltons maintain that, after driving the company into bankruptcy, Justice officials attempted to force the conversion of INSLAW's bankruptcy status from Chapter 11: Reorganization to Chapter 7: Liquidation. They assert that such a change in bankruptcy status would have resulted in the forced sale of INSLAW'S assets, including Enhanced PROMIS, to a rival computer company called Hadron, Inc., which, at the time, was attempting to conduct a hostile buyout of INSLAW. Hadron, Inc., was controlled by the Biotech Capital Corporation, under the control of Dr. Earl Brian, who was president and chairman of the corporation. The Hamiltons assert that even though the attempt to change the status of INSLAW's bankruptcy was unsuccessful, the Enhanced PROMIS software system was eventually provided to Dr. Brian by individuals from the Department with the knowledge and concurrence of then Attorney General Meese who had previously worked with Dr. Brian in the cabinet of California Governor Ronald Reagan and later at the Reagan White House. According to the Hamiltons, the ultimate goal of the conspiracy was to position Hadron and the other companies owned or controlled by Dr. Brian to take advantage of the nearly 3 billion dollars worth of automated data processing upgrade contracts planned to be awarded by the Department of Justice during the 1980s.

Information obtained by the Hamiltons through sworn affidavits of several individuals, including Ari Ben-Menashe, a former Israeli Mossad officer, and Michael Riconosciuto, an individual who claims to have ties to the intelligence community, indicated that an element of this ongoing criminal enterprise by Mr. Meese, Dr. Brian and others included the modification of the Enhanced PROMIS software by individuals associated with the world of covert intelligence operations. The Hamiltons claim the modification of Enhanced PROMIS was an essential element of the enterprise, because the software was subsequently distributed by Dr. Brian to intelligence agencies internationally with a "back door" software routine, so that U.S. intelligence agencies could covertly break into the system when needed. The Hamiltons also presented information indicating that PROMIS had been distributed to several Federal agencies, including the FBI, CIA, and DEA.

B. Committee Investigation

Due to the complexity and breadth of the INSLAW allegations against the Department of Justice, the committee's investigation focused on two principal questions: (1) Did high level Department officials convert, steal or otherwise misappropriate INSLAW'S PROMIS software and attempt to put the company out of business; and, (2) did high level Department of Justice officials, including Attorney General Edwin Meese and then Deputy Attorney General Lowell Jensen, and others conspire to sell, transfer, or in any way distribute INSLAW's Enhanced PROMIS to other Federal agencies and foreign governments?

1. Did the Department Convert, Steal or Misappropriate the PROMIS Software?

With regard to the first question, there appears to be strong evidence, as indicated by the findings in two Federal court proceedings as well as by the committee investigation, that the Department of Justice "acted willfully and fraudulently" and "took, converted and stole" INSLAW's Enhanced PROMIS by "trickery, fraud and deceit." It appears that these actions against INSLAW were implemented through the project manager from the beginning of the contract and under the direction of high-level Justice Department officials.

Just 1 month after the contract was signed, Mr. C. Madison "Brick" Brewer, the PROMIS project manager, raised the possibility of canceling the INSLAW contract. During an April 14, 1982, meeting of the PROMIS Project Team, Mr. Brewer and others discussed terminating the contract with INSLAW for [the] convenience of the government. Mr. Brewer did not recall the details of the meeting but said that if this recommendation was made, it was made "in jest." Based on notes taken at this meeting by Justice officials, Bankruptcy Court Judge George Bason found that Mr. Brewer's recommendation to terminate the INSLAW contract, "constituted a smoking gun that clearly evidences Brewer's intense bias against INSLAW, his single-minded intent to drive INSLAW out of business." By his own admission, Mr. Brewer became upset when INSLAW claimed that it had made enhancements to the public domain version of PROMIS using private funds. In his view, under the contract all versions of PROMIS were the government's property. It is clear from the record that Mr. Brewer and Mr. Videnieks (the PROMIS contracting officer), supported by high level Justice officials, continued to confront INSLAW at every turn. As Senior District Court Judge Bryant stated in his ruling on the case: "There was unending contention about payments under this contract and the rights of the respective parties."

Over the life of the contract, INSLAW made several attempts to reach an agreement with the Department over its proprietary rights to the Enhanced PROMIS software. The Department, however, steadfastly refused to conduct any meaningful negotiations and exhibited little inclination to resolve the controversy. In the meantime, INSLAW was pushed to the brink of financial ruin because the Department withheld at least $1.6 million in critical contract payments on questionable grounds, and in February 1985 was forced to file for protection under chapter 11 of the Bankruptcy Code in order to stay economically viable. INSLAW at this time had installed PROMIS at the 20 largest U.S. attorney's offices across the country as required by the contract. The Department had earlier canceled installation of PROMIS at the 74 smaller offices.

While refusing to engage in good faith negotiations with INSLAW, Mr. Brewer and Mr. Videnieks, with the approval of high level Justice Department officials, proceeded to take actions to misappropriate the Enhanced PROMIS software. These officials knew that INSLAW had installed Enhanced PROMIS at the 20 sites. Yet, without notice, and certainly without permission, the Department of Justice illegally copied INSLAW's Enhanced PROMIS software and installed it eventually at 25 additional U.S. attorney's offices. The Department reportedly also brought another 31 U.S. attorney's offices "on-line" to Enhanced PROMIS systems via telecommunications. INSLAW first learned of these unauthorized actions in September 1985, and notified the Department that it must remove the Enhanced PROMIS software or arrange for license agreements. When the Department refused, INSLAW subsequently filed a claim against Justice in the Federal Bankruptcy Court which eventually led to the Bankruptcy Court's finding that the Department's actions "were done in bad faith, vexatiously, in wanton disregard of the law and the facts, and for oppressive reasons to drive INSLAW out of business and to convert, by trickery, fraud and deceit, INSLAW's PROMIS software." When the case was appealed by the Department, Senior District Court Judge William Bryant concurred with the Bankruptcy Court and was very critical of the Department's handling of the case. In his ruling, at 49a, Judge Bryant stated:

> The Government accuses the bankruptcy court of looking beyond the bankruptcy proceeding to find culpability by the Government. What is strikingly apparent from the testimony and depositions of key witnesses and many documents is that INSLAW performed its contract in a hostile environment that extended from the higher echelons of the Justice Department to the officials who had the day-to-day responsibility for supervising its work.

Recently, the posture of some Department officials has been to attempt to exonerate the Department's handling of the INSLAW matter by citing the fact that the Court of Appeals has vacated the Bankruptcy and District Courts' judgment involving illegal misconduct of the Department including violations of the automatic stay provisions of the Bankruptcy Code. However, the D.C. Circuit's opinion was grounded primarily on jurisdictional questions and did not address the substantive merits of the findings of fact and conclusions of law of either the Bankruptcy Court or the ruling of the U.S. District Court.

Based on the facts presented in court and the committee's review of Department records, it does indeed appear that Justice officials, including Mr. Brewer and Mr. Videnieks, never intended to fully honor the proprietary rights of INSLAW or bargain in good faith with the company. The Bankruptcy Court found that:

> [The Department] engaged in an outrageous, deceitful, fraudulent game of cat and mouse, demonstrating contempt for both the law and any principle of fair dealing.

As the Bankruptcy and District Courts found on the merits, it is very unlikely that Mr. Brewer and Mr. Videnieks acted alone to violate the proprietary rights of INSLAW in this matter. In explaining his own actions, Mr. Brewer, the project manager, has repeatedly stated that he was not acting out any personal vendetta against INSLAW and that high level Department officials including Lowell Jensen were aware of every decision he made with regard to the contract. Mr. Brewer stated, under oath that "there was somebody in the Department at a higher level, looking over the shoulder of not just me but the people who worked for me."

The PROMIS Oversight Committee, headed by Deputy Attorney General Lowell Jensen, kept a close watch over the administration of the contract and was involved in every major decision. Mr. Jensen, who worked with former Attorney General Edwin Meese in the Alameda County district attorneys' offices, stated under oath that he kept the Attorney General regularly informed of all aspects of the INSLAW contract. The PROMIS Oversight Committee readily agreed with Mr. Brewer's recommendation to cancel part of INSLAW's contract for default because of the controversy regarding the installation of PROMIS in word processing systems at the 74 smaller U.S. attorneys' offices. Mr. Brewer's proposal was ultimately rejected only because a Justice contracts attorney advised the oversight committee that the Department did not have the legal authority to do so. Curiously, the recommendation to find INSLAW in default occurred shortly after INSLAW and the Department signed a modification to the contract (Mod. 12), which was supposed to end the conflict over proprietary rights.

Mr. Jensen, who is currently a Federal District Court judge in San Francisco, served at the Justice Department successively as Assistant Attorney General in charge of the Criminal Division, Associate Attorney General, and Deputy Attorney General between 1981 and 1986. The Bankruptcy court found that he "had a previously developed negative attitude about PROMIS and INSLAW" from the beginning (Findings No. 307–309) because he had been associated with the development of a rival case management system while he was a district attorney in California, and that this experience, at the very least, affected his judgment throughout his oversight of the contract. During a sworn statement, Judge Jensen denied being biased against INSLAW, but averred that he did not have complete recollection of the events surrounding his involvement in the contract. However, based on the committee's own investigation it is clear that Judge Jensen was not particularly interested or active in pursuing INSLAW's claims that Department officials were biased against the company and had taken action to harm the company. Perhaps most disturbing, he remembered very few details of the PROMIS Oversight Committee meetings even though he had served as its chairman and was certainly one of its most influential members. He stated that after a meeting with former Attorney General Elliot Richardson (representing INSLAW) regarding the alleged Brewer bias, he commissioned his deputy, Mr. Jay Stephens, to conduct an investigation of the bias charges. Based on this investigation, Judge Jensen said he concluded that there were no bias problems associated with the Department's handling of the INSLAW contract.

This assertion, however, contradicted Mr. Stephens, who testified during a sworn statement that he was never asked by Judge Jensen to conduct an investigation of the Brewer bias allegations raised by Mr. Richardson and others. Mr. Stephens' recollection of the events was sharp and complete in stark contrast to Judge Jensen's. As a result, many questions remain about the accuracy and completeness of Judge Jensen's recollections and statements. As for the PROMIS Oversight Committee, committee investigators were told that detailed minutes were not kept at any of the meetings, nor was there any record of specific discussions by its members affecting the INSLAW contract. The records that were available were inordinately sparse and often did not include any background of how and why decisions were made.

To date, former Attorney General Meese denies having knowledge of any bias against INSLAW by the Department or any of its officials. He stated, under oath, that he had little, if any, involvement with the INSLAW controversy and that he recalls no specific discussion with anyone, including Department officials about INSLAW's contract with Justice regarding the use or misuse of the PROMIS software. This statement is in direct conflict with Judge Jensen's testimony, that he briefed Mr. Meese regularly on this issue and that Mr. Meese was very interested in the details of the contract and negotiations.

One of the most damaging statements received by the committee is a sworn statement made by Deputy Attorney General Arnold Burns to Office of Professional Responsibility (OPR) investigators in 1988. In this statement, Mr. Burns stated that Department attorneys had already advised him (sometime in 1986) that INSLAW's claim of proprietary rights in the Enhanced PROMIS software was legitimate and that the Department had waived any rights in these enhancements. Mr. Burns was also told by Justice Attorneys that the Department would probably lose the case in court on this issue. Accepting this statement, it is incredible that the Department, having made this determination, would continue to pursue its litigation of these matters. More than $1 million has been spent in litigation on this case by the Justice Department even though it knew in 1986 that it did not have a chance to win the case on merits. This clearly raises the specter that the Department actions taken against INSLAW in this matter represent an abuse of power of shameful proportions.

2. *Was There a High Level Conspiracy?*

The second phase of the committee's investigation concentrated on the allegations that high level officials at the Department of Justice conspired to drive INSLAW into insolvency and steal the PROMIS software so it could be used by Dr. Earl Brian, a former associate and friend of then Attorney General Edwin Meese. Dr. Brian is a businessman and entrepreneur who owns or controls several businesses including Hadron, Inc., which has contracts with the Justice Department, CIA, and other agencies. The Hamiltons and others have asserted that Dr. Brian conspired with high level Justice officials to sell PROMIS to law enforcement and intelligence agencies worldwide. Former Attorney General Elliot Richardson, counsel to INSLAW, has alleged that the circumstances involving the theft of the PROMIS software system constitute a possible criminal conspiracy involving Mr. Meese, Judge Jensen, Dr. Brian, and several current and former officials at the Department of Justice. Mr. Richardson maintains that the individuals involved in the theft of the Enhanced PROMIS system have violated a plethora of Federal criminal statutes, including but not limited to: (1) 18 U.S.C. 654 (officer or employee of the United States converting the property of another); (2) 18 U.S.C. 1001 (false statements); (3) 18 U.S.C. 1621 (perjury); (4) 18 U.S.C 1503 (obstruction of justice); (5) 18 U.S.C. 1341 (mail fraud) and (6) 18 U.S.C. 371 (conspiracy to commit criminal offenses). Mr. Richardson further contends that the violations of Federal law associated in the theft of Enhanced PROMIS, the subsequent cover-up and the illegal distribution of PROMIS fulfill the requirements for prosecution under 18 U.S.C. 1961 et seq. (the Racketeer Influenced and Corrupt Organizations [RICO] statute).

As discussed earlier, the committee's investigation largely supports the findings of two Federal courts that the Department "took, converted, and stole INSLAW'S Enhanced PROMIS by trickery, fraud and deceit," and that this misappropriation involved officials at the highest levels of the Department of Justice. The recent ruling by the D.C. Circuit Court of Appeals does nothing to vitiate those conclusions, the product of an extensive record compiled under oath by two Federal jurists. While the Department continues to attempt to explain away the INSLAW matter as a simple contract dispute, the committee's investigation has uncovered other information which plausibly could suggest a different conclusion if full access to documents and other witnesses were permitted.

Several individuals have stated under oath that the Enhanced PROMIS software was stolen and distributed internationally in order to provide financial gain to Dr. Brian and to further intelligence and foreign policy objectives for the United States. While it should be acknowledged at the outset that some of the testimony comes from individuals whose past associations and enterprises are not commendable, corroborating evidence for a number of their claims made under oath has been found. It should be observed that these individuals provided testimony with the full knowledge that the Justice Department could—and would probably be strongly inclined to—prosecute them for perjury if they lied under oath. Moreover, we note that the Department is hardly in a position to negate summarily testimony offered by witnesses who have led less than an exemplary life in their choice of associations and activities. As indicated by the recent prosecution of Manuel Noriega, which involved the use of over 40 witnesses, the majority of whom were previously convicted drug traffickers, a witness's perceived credibility is not always indicative of the accuracy or usability in court of the information provided. Although the committee's investigation could not reach a definitive conclusion regarding a possible motive behind the misappropriation of the Enhanced PROMIS software, the disturbing questions raised, unexplained coincidences and peculiar events that have surfaced throughout the INSLAW case raise the need for further investigation.

One area which requires further investigation is the allegations made by Mr. Michael Riconosciuto. Mr. Riconosciuto, a shady character allegedly tied to U.S. intelligence agencies and recently convicted on drug charges, alleges that Dr. Brian and Mr. Peter Videnieks secretly delivered INSLAW's Enhanced PROMIS software to the Cabazon Indian Reservation, located in California, for "refitting" for use by intelligence agencies in the United States and abroad. When Dr. Brian was questioned about his alleged involvement in the INSLAW case, he denied under oath that he had ever met Mr. Riconosciuto and stated that he had never heard of the Cabazon Indian Reservation.

C. ADDITIONAL QUESTIONS

Suspicions of a Department of Justice conspiracy to steal INSLAW's PROMIS were fueled when Danny Casolaro—an investigative writer inquiring into those issues—was found dead in a hotel room in Martinsburg, WV, where he was to meet a source that he claimed was critical to his investigation. Mr. Casolaro's body was found on August 10, 1991, with his wrists slashed numerous times. Following a brief preliminary investigation by local authorities, Mr. Casolaro's death was ruled a suicide. The investigation was reopened later as a result of numerous inquiries from Mr. Casolaro's brother and others regarding the suspicious circumstances surrounding his death.

The Martinsburg Police investigation subsequently concluded in January 1992, that Mr. Casolaro's death was a suicide. Subsequently, Chairman Brooks directed committee investigators to obtain sworn statements from the FBI agent and two former Federal Organized Crime Strike Force prosecutors in Los Angeles who had information bearing on the Casolaro case. Sworn statements were obtained from former Federal prosecutors Richard Stavin and Marvin Rudnick on March 13 and 14, 1992. After initial resistance from the Bureau, a sworn statement was taken from FBI Special Agent Thomas Gates on March 25 and 26, 1992.

Special Agent Gates stated that Mr. Casolaro claimed he had found a link between the INSLAW matter, the activities taking place at the Cabazon Indian Reservation, and a Federal investigation in which Special Agent Gates had been involved regarding organized crime influence in the entertainment industry.

Special Agent Gates stated that Mr. Casolaro had several conversations with Mr. Robert Booth Nichols in the weeks preceding his death. Mr. Nichols, according to documents submitted to a Federal court by the FBI, has ties with organized crime and the world of covert intelligence operations. When he learned of Mr. Casolaro's death, Special Agent Gates contacted the Martinsburg, WV, Police Department to inform them of the information he had concerning Mr. Nichols and Mr. Casolaro. The Martinsburg Police have not commented on whether or not they eventually pursued the leads provided by Special Agent Gates.

Based on the evidence collected by the committee, it appears that the path followed by Danny Casolaro in pursuing his investigation into the INSLAW matter brought him in contact with a number of dangerous individuals associated with organized crime and the world of covert intelligence operations. The suspicious circumstances surrounding his death have led some law enforcement professionals and others to believe that his death may not have been a suicide. As long as the possibility exists that Danny Casolaro died as a result of his investigation into the INSLAW matter, it is imperative that further investigation be conducted.

D. EVIDENCE OF POSSIBLE COVER-UP AND OBSTRUCTION

One of the principal reasons the committee could not reach any definitive conclusion about INSLAW's allegations of a high criminal conspiracy at Justice was the lack of cooperation from the Department. . . . The Congress met with restrictions, delays and outright denials to requests for information and to unobstructed access to records and witnesses since 1988. The Department initially attempted to prevent the Senate Permanent Subcommittee on Investigations from conducting an investigation of the INSLAW affair. During this committee's investigation, Attorney General Thornburgh repeatedly reneged on agreements made with this committee to provide full and open access to information and witnesses. Although the day before a planned committee meeting to consider the issuance of a subpoena the Department promised full access to documents and witnesses, the committee was compelled to subpoena Attorney General Thornburgh to obtain documents needed to complete its investigation. Even then, the Department failed to provide all the documents subpoenaed, claiming that some of the documents held by the Department's chief attorney in charge of the INSLAW litigation had been misplaced or accidentally destroyed. The Department has not provided a complete accounting of the number of documents missing nor has it conducted an investigation to determine if the documents were stolen or illegally destroyed.

Questions regarding the Department's willingness and objectivity to investigate the charges of possible misconduct of Justice employees remain. That Justice officials may have too readily concluded that witnesses supporting the Department's position were credible while those who did not were ignored or retaliated against was, perhaps, most painfully demonstrated with the firing of Anthony Pasciuto, the former Deputy Director, Executive Office of the U.S. Trustees.

Mr. Pasciuto had informed the Hamiltons that soon after INSLAW filed for chapter 11 bankruptcy in 1985, the Justice Department had planned to petition the court to force INSLAW into chapter 7 bankruptcy and liquidate its assets including the PROMIS software. His source for this information was Judge Cornelius Blackshear who, at the time, was the U.S. Trustee for the Southern District of New York. Judge Blackshear subsequently provided INSLAW's attorneys with a sworn statement confirming what Mr. Pasciuto had told the Hamiltons. However, following a conversation with a Justice

Department attorney who was representing the Department in the INSLAW case, Judge Blackshear recanted his earlier sworn statement. Moreover, Judge Blackshear, under oath, could not or would not provide committee investigators with a plausible explanation of why he had recanted his earlier statements to INSLAW, Mr. Pasciuto and others regarding the Justice Department's efforts to force INSLAW out of business. He did confirm an earlier statement attributed to him that his recantation was a result of "his desire to hurt the least number of people." However, he would not elaborate on this enigmatic statement.

Similarly, Mr. Pasciuto, under strong pressure from senior Department officials, recanted his statement made to the Hamiltons regarding Judge Blackshear. It appears that Mr. Pasciuto may have been fired from his position with the Executive Office of U.S. Trustees because he had provided information to the Hamiltons and their attorneys which undercut the Department's litigating position before the Bankruptcy Court. This action was based on a recommendation made by the Office of Professional Responsibility (OPR). In a memorandum to Deputy Attorney General Burns, dated December 18, 1987, the OPR concluded that:

> In our view, but for Mr. Pasciuto's highly irresponsible actions, the department would be in a much better litigation posture than it presently finds itself. Mr. Pasciuto has wholly failed to comport himself in accordance with the standard of conduct expected of an official of his position.

Mr. Pasciuto now states he regrets having allowed himself to be coerced by the Department into recanting and has stated under oath to committee investigators that he stands by his earlier statements made to the Hamiltons that Judge Blackshear had informed him that the Department wanted to force INSLAW out of business. Certainly, Mr. Pasciuto's treatment by the Department during his participation in the INSLAW litigation raises serious questions of how far the Department will go to protect its interests while defending itself in litigation. Not unexpectedly, Mr. Pasciuto's firing had a chilling effect on other potential Department witnesses who might have otherwise cooperated with the committee in this matter. Judge Blackshear, on the other hand, was not accused of wrongdoing by the Department even though he originally provided essentially the same information as had Mr. Pasciuto.

Despite this series of obvious reversals, the Department, after limited investigation, has apparently satisfied itself that the sworn statements of its witnesses, including Judge Blackshear, have somehow been reconciled on key issues such that no false statements have been made by any of these individuals. This position is flatly in opposition to the Bankruptcy Court's finding that several Department officials may have perjured themselves which was never seriously investigated by the Department. In addition, there are serious conflicts and inconsistencies in sworn statements provided to the committee that have not been resolved. Equally important, the possibility that witnesses' testimony were manipulated by the Department in order to present a "united front" to the Congress and the public on the INSLAW case needs to be fully and honestly explored. The potential for a conflict of interest in the Department's carrying out such an inquiry is high, if not prudently manifest, and independent scrutiny is required. . . .

(EXCERPTS OF THE REPORT FROM CHAPTER VII)

VII. Top Department Officials Frustrated Committee's Investigation

The committee's investigation often encountered Department barriers to documents and agency personnel. While the committee could not prove that the Department deliberately conspired to conceal evidence of criminal wrongdoing, serious questions have been raised about the possible obstruction of a congressional investigation; destruction of Department documents; and, witness tampering by Department officials. . . .

The committee eventually overcame many of the obstacles put in its path by the Department and established several important precedents. First, committee investigators were ultimately given unrestricted access to all contract, personnel and administrative files of the agency, which consisted, in the INSLAW case, of several thousand documents. Second, access was given to the sensitive files of the Office of Professional Responsibility (OPR) which included not only the reports of that Office but individual interviews and sworn statements conducted during OPR investigation. Third, for the first time known to the committee, the FBI agreed to permit one of its field agents, Special Agent Thomas Gates, to give a sworn statement to committee investigators and to otherwise cooperate with the committee. Fourth, the Department agreed to allow Justice officials and employees to give sworn statements without a Department attorney present. Finally, under the force of a subpoena issued by the subcommittee, the Department provided more than 400 documents, which it had identified as related to ongoing litigation and other highly sensitive matters and "protected" under the claims of attorney-client and attorney work product privileges.

A. Department Attempts to Thwart Committee Inquiry

The committee's investigation began with an August 1989 letter from Chairman Brooks to Attorney General Thornburgh initiating an investigation into a number of serious allegations regarding the Department of Justice's (DOJ) handling of a contract with INSLAW, Inc. and asked for the Department's full cooperation with committee investigators.

Attorney General Thornburgh responded on August 21, 1989; and while seriously questioning the need for a comprehensive investigation, he stated:

> Nevertheless, I can pledge this Department's full cooperation with the committee in this matter, and I have so instructed all concerned agency employees, with the understanding that we will have to make arrangements to protect any information,

documents, or testimony that we may proffer to the committee from interested vendors and litigants, including INSLAW.

Armed with the Attorney General's pledge of cooperation, the committee nevertheless immediately encountered severe resistance by Justice officials when they were asked to provide access to agency files and personnel. On September 29, 1989, Department officials told committee investigators that they would not be given full and unrestricted access to agency files and individuals associated with the INSLAW contract. The Department insisted that committee investigators instead go through the cumbersome and lengthy process of putting all requests for documents, interviews and other materials in writing.

Initially, even INSLAW's contract files, which were readily accessible to the General Accounting Office (GAO), were denied to the committee. The Department also insisted that a Department attorney be present during any interviews of Department employees. During this time even individuals who had left the Department refused to be interviewed. This refusal possibly stems from pressure exerted by the Department which strongly believed that: "Justice has to speak through one voice," regarding the INSLAW matter.

As part of these negotiations the Department's Office of Legislative Affairs (OLA) informed committee investigators that some of the requested information would be made available, but because of Privacy Act and trade secret concerns the Department wanted the chairman to put each request in writing. The alternative was for the committee to obtain individual releases from as many as 50 individuals. The committee's request for access to the Public Integrity Section files was also denied. OLA also stated that the Office of Professional Responsibility was concerned with the Privacy Act and regarded its files "as highly sensitive, potentially hurtful, and is concerned that the information could be misused."

As a result of the Department's position, the chairman stated in a January 9, 1990, letter to the Attorney General that he could not devise any better way to preclude an Investigative body from obtaining objective and candid information, on any matter, than by intimidating employees who otherwise may cooperate with an investigation. He added that the presence of a Department attorney would undercut the committee's ability to interview persons in an open, candid, and timely manner, and he was deeply troubled by the continued lack of cooperation by Department employees. The chairman again personally informed the Attorney General of his concerns about the continued delays and resistance to providing needed information when they met on January 29, 1990.

The chairman requested immediate, full and unrestricted access to Department employees and documents. In a February 1990 response the Department agreed to allow its employees to be interviewed without Department counsel present. However, the Department delayed access to numerous files and negotiated for several months about the confidentiality of a variety of documents requested for the investigation. The Attorney General and the chairman reached another agreement in April 1990 on access to information. At this time, the Department agreed to provide free and unrestricted access to INSLAW files and Department employees. At the Department's fiscal year 1991 authorization hearings on May 16, 1990, Attorney General Thornburgh again indicated that the Department had decided to provide access to the committee for the INSLAW investigation:

> I have discussed with you and other members of this and other committees, our willingness to examine on a case-by-case basis any request that comes from the Congress. But rather than lay down a bunch of reasons why we can't release materials I prefer to discuss ways and means in which we can work with you and your staff. . . .

On June 15, 1990, the Department informed committee investigators that there were 64 boxes of INSLAW litigation files which they listed on a 422-page index. At this time, Department officials refused to give committee investigators the index because it included "privileged" information that the Department was concerned would be made available to INSLAW. Finally, on June 28, 1990, the Department's Acting Assistant Attorney General for Legislative Affairs agreed to provide the litigation file indices on the condition that they not be released to the public by the committee. However, Department officials refused to identify what documents were privileged or available. At the same time numerous interviews and sworn statements were being taken by committee investigators; however, these interviews were impaired by the lack of documentation from which to draw investigation-related questions. By letter dated September 6, 1990, the OLA Deputy Assistant Attorney General again refused to permit committee staff access to what he declared were "privileged" work-product and attorney/client documents. This judgment originated from Ms. Sandra Spooner, lead Department counsel on INSLAW's litigation, who reviewed each file and removed those she believed to be "privileged" attorney/client or work-product documents. Committee investigators finally gained access to the Department's "INSLAW Files" in late October 1990. However, soon thereafter the Department increased the number of documents and/or files withheld from an initial 175 to 190. On November 19, 1990, the Department again increased the number of documents and/or files withheld from the committee to 193.

The chairman protested the additional obstacles raised by the Department. The Attorney General responded that his pledge of free and unrestricted access did not include "privileged" attorney/client or work-product documents. This posture became the focus of a hearing on December 5, 1990.

The Judiciary Committee's Subcommittee on Economic and Commercial Law convened on December 5, 1990, to address the Department's refusal to provide access to "privileged" INSLAW documents. During this hearing Steven R. Ross, General Counsel to the House Clerk, stated that:

> the Attorney General's claimed basis for this withholding of documents is an attempt to create for himself and his functionaries within the Department an exemption from the constitutional principle that all executive officials, no matter how high or low, exercise their authority pursuant to law and that all such public officials are accountable to legislative oversight aimed at ferreting out waste, fraud, and abuse.

Mr. Ross added that the Department was attempting to redefine committee investigations to mean that congressional investigations are justifiable only as a means of facilitating the task of passing legislation. Mr. Ross stated:

> What that proposed standard would do would be to eradicate the time-honored role of Congress of providing oversight, which is a means that has been upheld by the Supreme Court on a number of occasions, by which the Congress can assure itself that previously passed laws are being properly implemented.

After providing several examples of Department attempts to withhold information by claiming attorney/client privilege, including Watergate, Ross concluded by stating:

> It is thus clear, in light of [the] history of claims by the Department that it may be excused from providing the Congress in general and this committee in particular with documents that it deems litigation sensitive, that Congress' broad power of investigation overcomes those litigious concerns.

B. Authorization and Oversight Hearings

On July 8, 1991, the committee chairman announced his plans to hold authorization and oversight hearings on July 11 and 18 to discuss the Department's fiscal year 1992 budget request. The chairman indicated that as part of these hearings, he would be asking, among other things, Attorney General Thornburgh about his failure to live up to the several previous commitments he had made to the committee to provide full and open access to the Department's INSLAW files.

Chairman Brooks opened the July 11, 1991, hearing by noting that oversight of executive branch policy and activity is at the heart of the congressional mandate as an integral component of the checks and balances architecture of constitutional government. He further noted that Department officials had continued to resist meaningful outside review of their activities by refusing to cooperate with GAO and congressional investigations.

Chairman Brooks expressed grave concern that the Department seemed increasingly bent on pursuing controversial theories of executive privilege and power at the expense of removing government from the sunshine of public scrutiny and accountability. This tendency appeared to be an increasing problem under the stewardship of Attorney General Thornburgh and had seriously hindered and delayed several congressional investigations, including the INSLAW case.

The chairman concluded the hearing by stating that the Judiciary Committee must carefully consider the actions needed to be taken to require production of documents requested from the Department and urged that all committee members attend the July 18, 1991, hearing, during which Attorney General Thornburgh would be asked to respond to these issues.

On July 18, 1991, the committee reconvened to review the Justice Department's fiscal year 1992 authorization request for appropriations and to hear the testimony of Attorney General Thornburgh. Unfortunately, the Attorney General decided at 7 P.M. the night before to refuse to appear.

Committee Chairman Brooks responded to the Attorney General's unprecedented nonappearance to a duly noticed hearing:

> In light of the extreme importance of this proceeding, it is particularly unfortunate and deeply disturbing that the Attorney General notified us last night, late last night that he would refuse to appear before us this morning. He refuses to attend for a myriad of reasons even though his appearance was duly scheduled for 1 full month.

The chairman noted the seriousness of the issues facing the Department and the need to resolve them as quickly as possible. He was particularly concerned with the Department's lack of cooperation with the committee on the INSLAW investigation. He concluded by expressing concern over the "great damage" that had been done to the relationship between the Judiciary Committee and the Justice Department stating:

> I am shocked and saddened by the appearance of the empty chair before us and all the other chairs that he asked to be reserved for his people. The unanswered request and the delayed response are becoming the symbols of an increasingly remote and self-centered Justice Department that seems bent on expanding the accepted boundaries of executive branch power and prerogatives.

C. The Department Reports Key Subpoenaed Documents Missing

On July 25, 1991, the Subcommittee on Economic and Commercial Law issued a subpoena to the Attorney General requiring that he provide all documents within the scope of the committee investigation listed in the subpoena.

On July 29, the Attorney General provided as many subpoenaed documents as possible, but stated that some documents were lost. . . .

Also, many documents that were provided were incomplete (i.e., missing pages or attachments), or were of such poor quality that they could not be read. . . .

During a July 31, 1991, subcommittee meeting convened to discuss the Attorney General's noncompliance with the subpoena, Chairman Brooks concluded:

My concern with the missing documents flows from the fact that our investigation is looking into allegations by those who claim that high level Department officials criminally conspired to force INSLAW into bankruptcy and steal its software. It is alleged this was done to benefit friends of then Attorney General Edwin Meese. Under these circumstances, I fully expected that the department would take great care in protecting all these documents. Unfortunately, the fact of missing documents will now leave lingering questions in the minds of some who have closely followed the investigation about whether documents may have been destroyed. . . .

Source: U.S. Congress. House. *The Inslaw Affair: Investigative Report by the Committee on the Judiciary* together with *Dissenting and Separate Views.* 102d Cong., 2d sess., September 10, 1992, H. Report 102-857, pages 1–10 and 92–101.

Excerpt from Comments by INSLAW Company on Judiciary Committee Investigative Report, 1992

Soon after the House Judiciary Committee issued its report on the INSLAW Affair, William Hamilton, founder and owner of INSLAW Inc., prepared his own comments to bolster the allegations made by the committee. Hamilton pointed particularly to the evidence that the U.S. Department of Justice had provided the PROMIS software to an Israeli official named Rafi Eitan, a member of the Israeli Ministry of Defense. The gift, in violation of INSLAW's propriety rights to the software, was part of an elaborate scheme, Hamilton charged, to distribute additional copies to other foreign intelligence agencies and law enforcement agencies so that the software could be monitored as a kind of "Trojan horse" spying device. Hamilton's comments went further. He accused the U.S. government of possibly arranging the murder of investigative reporter Danny Casolaro to prevent him from implicating the Justice Department in illegal activities relating to Inslaw and the PROMIS software. The INSLAW Affair, Hamilton charged, was no simple contractual dispute, as characterized by the government and some in the media, but a brutal, deadly exercise of government theft and perhaps worse.

EXCERPT FROM COMMENTS BY INSLAW COMPANY ON JUDICIARY COMMITTEE INVESTIGATIVE REPORT, 1992

Eleven years ago, the Justice Department's PROMIS Project Manager arranged for an Israeli Government official to visit INSLAW for a PROMIS briefing and demonstration. The Justice Department told INSLAW that the visitor was a prosecuting attorney from the Israeli Ministry of Justice who would be overseeing a project to computerize the public prosecution offices in Israel.

Three months after the visit, the Justice Department secretly turned over to a representative of the Israeli Government a copy of the PROMIS software, according to a contemporaneous internal Justice Department memorandum made public by the House Judiciary Committee in its September 1992 Investigative Report, *The INSLAW Affair.*

INSLAW followed up on this disclosure by the House Judiciary Committee by contacting the Israeli Ministry of Justice in Tel Aviv about the "prosecuting attorney" who had visited INSLAW ten years earlier in February 1983. After obtaining information from the Ministry about the current location of the prosecuting attorney, INSLAW consulted with two journalists in Tel Aviv. One journalist interviewed the now-retired prosecuting attorney at his home in Jerusalem. The prosecuting attorney bore no resemblance to the visitor to INSLAW and was unfamiliar with some important aspects of the visit to INSLAW, although he claimed to have been the February 1983 Israeli visitor to INSLAW. The other journalist told INSLAW that the prosecuting attorney's name has been used in the past as a pseudonym for Rafi Eitan, a legendary Israeli intelligence official.

INSLAW employees who had met with the Israeli visitor in February 1983 attempted to identify the visitor from a police-style photographic line-up. The process was videotaped in the studio of a national television network. The photographic line-up confirmed that the visitor to INSLAW was neither a prosecutor nor an attorney, but Rafi Eitan. At the time of the visit to INSLAW, Rafi Eitan was Director of LAKAM, a super-secret agency in the Israeli Ministry of Defense responsible for collecting scientific and technical intelligence information from other countries through espionage. Rafi Eitan became well known in the United States, several years after his visit to INSLAW, when Jonathan Pollard, a U.S. Navy civilian intelligence analyst, was arrested and charged with spying for Rafi Eitan and Israeli intelligence.

During the interim between Rafi Eitan's visit to INSLAW and the delivery of a copy of PROMIS to an Israeli official, the Government's PROMIS Project Manager and others in the Justice Department pressured INSLAW to deliver to the Justice Department, without any protection for INSLAW's property rights, the proprietary version of PROMIS that was not required to be delivered under INSLAW's PROMIS Implementation Contract.

The particular proprietary version of PROMIS that was the object of this Justice Department pressure was the version that INSLAW had demonstrated to the Israeli Government visitor and that operates on a VAX computer. INSLAW was operating this proprietary version of PROMIS on a computer at INSLAW's offices and using it to support each of the 10 largest U.S. Attorney's Offices, via telephone lines. Under its three-year contract, INSLAW was to provide this PROMIS computer time-sharing service on an interim basis until each of the U.S. Attorney's Offices acquired its own computer, and INSLAW thereafter was to install an earlier, public domain version of PROMIS on those computers.

The Justice Department explained this pressure to obtain immediate delivery of a copy of the proprietary VAX version of PROMIS by a suddenly-professed concern about INSLAW's financial viability.

In response to this professed concern, INSLAW offered to place a copy of the VAX version of PROMIS in escrow in a local bank; that would have been the accepted industry remedy for the professed problem. The Justice Department, however, rejected INSLAW's escrow offer and insisted on immediately obtaining physical custody of a copy of the proprietary VAX version of PROMIS.

The Justice Department eventually accomplished its objective of physical custody of a copy of the VAX version of PROMIS through a bilateral modification to the contract in which the Government committed itself, inter alia, not to disseminate the proprietary version of PROMIS outside the U.S. Attorney's Offices. This was the April 11, 1983 Modification #12 to the PROMIS Implementation Contract. None of the U.S. Attorney's Offices had a VAX computer, without which it is impossible to use a VAX version of PROMIS.

Two lower federal courts found that the Justice Department entered into Modification #12 in order to "steal" the proprietary version of PROMIS "through trickery, fraud and deceit." The House Judiciary Committee independently confirmed those findings in the course of a three-year-long investigation.

Rafi Eitan emerged again in the INSLAW affair in 1986 when INSLAW filed a lawsuit against the Justice Department over the theft of the PROMIS software. INSLAW's lead litigation counsel was fired by his law firm amid secret communications between the law firm and the two highest officials of the U.S. Justice Department. The Attorney General stated under oath and the Deputy Attorney General claimed to the Senate that the secret discussions were about the INSLAW case; the law firm claimed to the press that the secret discussions were about its concurrent representation in the Jonathan Pollard–Rafi Eitan espionage case.

In May 1986, three years to the month after the Justice Department secretly turned over a copy of PROMIS to an Israeli Government official, INSLAW and senior partners in the law firm that was then serving as INSLAW's litigation counsel reviewed a complaint, drafted by INSLAW's lead counsel, for the lawsuit against the Justice Department about the theft of the proprietary version of PROMIS. The complaint contained over 50 references to Jensen; included was a 23-paragraph section that described the "personal involvement" of then Deputy Attorney General D. Lowell Jensen in the INSLAW affair, beginning with Jensen's tenure as Assistant Attorney General for the Criminal Division during the first several years of the Reagan Administration. The law firm immediately rejected the complaint that had been drafted by the lead counsel and set about to redraft the complaint in its entirety, assigning two additional lawyers to the INSLAW case for that purpose. These lawyers soon produced a new complaint that omitted every reference to the role of D. Lowell Jensen. Prior to the filing of the revised complaint in U.S. Bankruptcy Court, the lead counsel inserted, at INSLAW's insistence, a single parenthetical reference to Jensen's role.

In October 1986, three months after INSLAW filed its lawsuit, the law firm fired INSLAW's lead counsel who had by then been a partner in the firm for 10 years. The lead counsel told INSLAW at the time that he had been fired for naming Jensen in the complaint. He also told INSLAW at the time that the Managing Partner had stated that Senior Partner Leonard Garment had instigated the firing.

On October 6, 1986, one week before Leonard Garment and the other members of the law firm's Senior Policy Committee met to vote on the decision to expel INSLAW's lead counsel from the firm, Garment had a social luncheon regarding INSLAW with Deputy Attorney General Arnold Burns. Garment never disclosed this fact either to INSLAW's lead counsel or to INSLAW. Burns had succeeded Jensen as Deputy Attorney General in the summer of 1986 when Jensen left the Justice Department to become a U.S. District Court Judge in San Francisco. During the luncheon, Burns complained to Garment about the litigation strategy that INSLAW's lead counsel was pursuing in its lawsuit against the Department and signalled to Garment his willingness to discuss a settlement, according to Burns' later disclosures to the Senate Permanent Investigations Subcommittee. Attorney General Meese also talked to Garment in October 1986 about INSLAW and about Garment's conversation with Burns relating to INSLAW, according to later sworn Justice Department responses to INSLAW interrogatories.

In early 1988, in statements to the press, Garment disclaimed any recollection of a discussion about INSLAW with Deputy Attorney General Burns and insisted that his October 1986 discussion with Attorney General Meese had been about Israel, not INSLAW. Moreover, Garment elaborated on this claim, reportedly telling at least one journalist that it was a discussion of a "back channel" communication that Garment had had with the Government of Israel about the Pollard case, which Garment described to the journalist as a national security problem affecting both Israel and the U.S. Justice Department.

The Israeli Government had retained Garment in an effort to prevent the indictment by the U.S. Justice Department of other Israeli officials involved in the Pollard espionage scandal. The central role of Rafi Eitan and Israeli intelligence in both the INSLAW affair and the Pollard espionage scandal may account for why Meese and Burns characterized the October 1986 discussions with Garment as having to do with INSLAW, while Garment insisted they were really about a national security problem of concern to both Israel and the U.S. Justice Department.

When Garment's law firm fired INSLAW's lead counsel, it agreed to make severance payments to him in excess of half-a-million dollars and contractually bound him to secrecy about the severance. Soon after firing INSLAW's lead counsel, the law firm, which had, by then, been representing INSLAW for almost a year, suddenly claimed to have discovered fatal deficiencies in the evidence available to prove the Justice Department's 1983 theft of PROMIS. The law firm presented INSLAW with a written ultimatum to concede to the Justice Department on that question or find new litigation counsel. INSLAW found new litigation counsel and proved in the U.S. Bankruptcy Court and the U.S. District Court that the Justice Department had stolen the PROMIS software in 1983.

A former Israeli intelligence official, Ari Ben-Menashe, published a book in the fall of 1992 entitled *Profits of War,* that contains specific claims about Rafi Eitan and the PROMIS software, many of which are plausible in view of the aforementioned facts. According to the author, a high-ranking member of the White House National Security Council staff was personally involved in the delivery of a copy of the proprietary version of PROMIS to Rafi Eitan during a visit by Rafi Eitan to Washington, D.C. in the early 1980's. Robert McFarlane, who during the relevant period was Deputy National Security Advisor to President Ronald Reagan, and Earl W. Brian, a private businessman who had been a member of the California cabinet of Governor Ronald Reagan, secretly presented INSLAW's proprietary software to Rafi Eitan, according to the author.

The objective of the alleged White House gift of INSLAW's software to Rafi Eitan and Israeli intelligence was for Israeli intelligence, through sales conducted by cutout companies, to disseminate PROMIS to foreign intelligence agencies, law enforcement agencies, and international commercial banks so that PROMIS could function in those target organizations as an electronic Trojan horse for Allied signal intelligence agencies, according to the author.

Among the individuals whose companies served as cutouts for the illegal dissemination of PROMIS by Israeli intelligence, according to the author, were Earl W. Brian and the late British publisher, Robert Maxwell. Earl W. Brian, for example, allegedly sold the proprietary version of PROMIS to Jordanian military intelligence, so that Israeli signal intelligence could surreptitiously access the computerized Jordanian dossiers on Palestinians.

When INSLAW sought redress in the federal courts in 1986 for the Justice Department's 1983 theft of PROMIS, Israeli intelligence intervened to obstruct justice, according to the author. While employed in Tel Aviv by Israeli military intelligence, Ben-Menashe claims to have seen a wire transfer of $600,000 to Earl W. Brian for use in financing a severance agreement between INSLAW's fired lead counsel and his law firm. Rafi Eitan drew the funds from a slush fund jointly administered by U.S. and Israeli intelligence, and Earl W. Brian was, in turn, to relay the money to Leonard Garment, according to the author. . . .

In piecing together the puzzle of the Government's theft of the proprietary version of PROMIS from INSLAW, we have noted the role of the Government's PROMIS Project Manager in sending Rafi Eitan to INSLAW under false pretenses and the alleged role of a senior White House National Security official in giving the proprietary version of PROMIS to Rafi Eitan. The missing piece to the puzzle appears to be the piece that links the actions of the Justice Department's PROMIS Project Manager with the alleged actions of the senior White House National Security official. Based on the available evidence, the missing piece appears to be D. Lowell Jensen, who was Assistant Attorney General for the Criminal Division at the time of the theft.

Jensen pre-approved virtually every decision taken by the Government's PROMIS Project Manager under INSLAW's contract, according to the latter's sworn testimony to the House Judiciary Committee. Jensen engineered INSLAW's problems with the Justice Department through specified top Criminal Division aides in order to give the PROMIS business to unidentified "friends," according to Justice Department officials whose statements and backgrounds INSLAW summarized in its July 11, 1993 rebuttal.

At the time of the 1983 theft, Jensen in the Criminal Division and Edwin Meese at the White House were planning to award a massive sweetheart contract to unidentified "friends" for the installation of PROMIS in every litigative office of the Justice Department, according to statements made in June 1983 by a Justice Department whistleblower to the staff of a Senator on the Judiciary Committee. The award was allegedly to take place once Meese left the White House to become Attorney General. Jensen and Meese had been close friends since the 1960's when they served together in the Alameda County, California, District Attorney's Office.

INSLAW has repeatedly given the Justice Department the names of senior Criminal Division officials under Jensen who either allegedly helped him implement the malfeasance against INSLAW or who allegedly witnessed it. On more than one occasion, INSLAW summarized for the Justice Department the circumstantial evidence that is at least partially corroborative of these allegations. Based on warnings from confidential informants in the Justice Department, INSLAW has repeatedly emphasized to the Justice Department the absolute necessity of placing these officials under oath before interrogating them, as well as the importance of a public statement by the Attorney General guaranteeing no reprisals. More than five years have elapsed since INSLAW began furnishing this information to the Justice Department. Not one of these Criminal Division officials has, it appears, ever been interrogated under oath regarding the INSLAW affair. And no Attorney General has seen fit to issue a public statement to Justice Department employees making it clear that the Attorney General wishes employees who have information about the INSLAW affair to come forward, and giving Justice Department employees the public assurance that reprisals will not be tolerated.

One of the senior Criminal Division officials who allegedly knows the whole story of Jensen's malfeasance against INSLAW is Mark Richard, the career Deputy Assistant Attorney General who has responsibility for intelligence and national security matters. In May 1988, the Chief Investigator of the Senate Judiciary Committee told INSLAW that a trusted source, who was in a position to observe Jensen's malfeasance, had identified Mark Richard as someone who not only knew the whole story but who was also "pretty upset" about it.

One of the organizational units that reports to Mark Richard is the Office of Special Investigations (OSI). OSI's publicly-declared mission is to locate and deport Nazi war criminals. The Nazi war criminal program is, however, a front for the Justice Department's own covert intelligence service, according to disclosures recently made to INSLAW by several senior Justice Department career officials.

One undeclared mission of this covert intelligence service has been the illegal dissemination of the proprietary version of PROMIS, according to information from reliable sources with ties to the U.S. intelligence community. INSLAW has, moreover, obtained a copy of a 27-page Justice Department computer printout, labeled "Criminal Division Vendor List." That list is actually a list of the commercial organizations and individuals who serve as "cutouts" for this secret Justice Department intelligence agency, according to intelligence community informants and a preliminary analysis of the computerized list. A significant proportion of the 100-plus companies on the list appear to be in the computer industry. The Justice Department's secret intelligence agency also has its own "proprietary" company that employs scores of agents of diverse nationalities, as well as individuals who appear to be regular employees of various departments and agencies of the U.S. Government or members of the U.S. Armed Forces, according to several sources.

According to written statements of which INSLAW has obtained copies, another undeclared mission of the Justice Department's covert agents was to insure that investigative journalist Danny Casolaro remained silent about the role of the Justice Department in the INSLAW scandal by murdering him in West Virginia in August 1991. INSLAW has acquired copies of two relevant written statements furnished to a veteran investigative journalist by a national security operative of the U.S. Government, several months after Casolaro's death. The individual who reportedly transmitted these written statements to the journalist by fax has testified under oath to being a national security operative for the FBI and the CIA. Partial corroboration for his claimed work for the FBI is reportedly available in the sworn testimony of several FBI agents during a recent criminal prosecution. One statement purportedly reflects the operative's personal knowledge and belief that Casolaro was killed by agents of the Justice Department and is allegedly written in the operative's own hand. The other statement is an excerpt from a typewritten set of questions and answers. The questions were posed to a senior CIA official by the investigative journalist; the answers, purportedly from the senior CIA official, were reportedly sent by fax to the journalist by the national security operative, who was acting as an intermediary. The following is the pertinent question and answer:

Q. Do you have any information for [San Francisco-based investigative journalist] George Williamson yet regarding the Danny Casolaro matter?

A. Yes. Casolaro appears to have been working as a free lance writer at the time of his death and was gathering material for a book. He was investigating the INSLAW case. He was on the trail of information that could have made the whole matter public and led to the exposure of the Justice Department and their involvement in the matter. Apparently he was very close to obtaining that information.

We do not agree with the consensus of opinion among the reporters who looked into the matter, that Casolaro committed suicide. Casolaro was murdered by agents of the Justice Department to insure his silence. The entire matter was handled internally by Justice, and our agency was not involved.

Although these allegations are profoundly disturbing, there is significant circumstantial evidence that bears on the plausibility of the allegations. As reported in INSLAW's July 11, 1993 rebuttal, Casolaro was scheduled to have his final, follow-up meeting with two sources on INSLAW in West Virginia the night before he died, and one of those sources was connected to the Justice Department's PROMIS Contracting Officer. As reported in this addendum, the meeting between Casolaro and those sources had allegedly been brokered by a covert intelligence operative for the U.S. Government, an Army Special Forces Major. This individual appeared in Casolaro's life during the final several weeks and introduced himself to Casolaro as one of the closest friends of the Government's PROMIS Contracting Officer. Finally, during the final week of his life, Casolaro told at least five confidants something that he had never told a single one of them at any other time during his year-long, full-time investigation: that he had just broken the INSLAW case. The preceding facts and the following information are noted in the July 11, 1993 rebuttal. Shortly after Casolaro was found dead, the aforementioned covert intelligence operative allegedly made the following statement, in words or substance, to a woman who had been present during several of his meetings with Casolaro:

> What Danny Casolaro was investigating is a business. If you don't want to end up like Danny or like the journalist who died a horrific death in Guatemala, you'll stay out of this. Anyone who asks too many questions will end up dead.

Not all of the secret Justice Department dissemination of PROMIS has gone through Rafi Eitan and Israeli intelligence. For example, in June 1983, the month after the Justice Department secretly conveyed a copy of PROMIS to a representative of the Government of Israel, it also, in partnership with the National Security Agency (NSA), secretly delivered a copy of PROMIS to the World Bank and the International Monetary Fund, according to a recent series of articles in the American Bankers International Banking Regulator. The Justice Department and its NSA partner conveyed a copy of the proprietary VAX version of PROMIS to the two international financial institutions so that the NSA could electronically monitor their operations. This is the same version of PROMIS that the Justice Department had asked INSLAW to demonstrate to Rafi Eitan in February 1983. As noted earlier, the Justice Department had committed itself not to disseminate the proprietary version of PROMIS outside the U.S. Attorney's Offices.

A second example is the alleged secret Justice Department conveyance of a copy of the proprietary IBM version of PROMIS to the CIA. In September 1993, CIA Director R. James Woolsey told INSLAW counsel Elliot L. Richardson that the CIA is using a PROMIS software system that it acquired from the NSA and that is identical to the PROMIS software that NSA uses internally and that is described on page 80 of the Bua Report. The application domain of the

NSA's PROMIS is the mission critical application of tracking the intelligence information it produces. The NSA's PROMIS operates on an IBM mainframe computer. This latest CIA disclosure underscores the difficulty the CIA has had in accounting for its PROMIS. The CIA initially told the House Judiciary Committee in writing that it had been unable to locate internally any PROMIS software. Approximately one year later, the CIA wrote again to the House Judiciary Committee, stating that components of the CIA were operating a software system called PROMIS but that it had purchased its PROMIS from a company in Massachusetts. That PROMIS operates on a personal computer with project management as the application domain. In both written reports, the CIA inexplicably failed to mention the PROMIS that operates on an IBM mainframe computer at the CIA and that is critical to the CIA's primary mission of producing intelligence information.

The third example is the alleged Justice Department secret dissemination of PROMIS to the NSA. Although the NSA is quoted in the Bua Report as claiming that it internally developed its PROMIS, the Toronto Globe and Mail reported in May 1986 that the NSA had purchased a PROMIS software system from a Toronto-based company. As shown in Exhibit A to INSLAW's July 11, 1993 rebuttal, Earl Brian's Hadron, Inc. sold INSLAW's PROMIS to the same Toronto company in 1983, in a transaction that also allegedly involved Edwin Meese, then Counsellor to the President.

The final example concerns the allegation that the Justice Department secretly distributed the proprietary VAX version of PROMIS to the U.S. Navy for an intelligence application on board nuclear submarines. The Navy confirmed to a reporter for Navy Times that it has a PROMIS software system and that it operates its PROMIS on a VAX computer in support of its nuclear submarines. The Navy's Undersea Systems Center in Portsmouth, Rhode Island, furthermore, notified the reporter in writing that its engineers had locally developed this VAX version of PROMIS; that its PROMIS is installed only at its land-based facility at Newport, Rhode Island; and that its PROMIS has never been installed on board any nuclear submarine. INSLAW has, however, obtained a document published by the same Undersea Systems Center in 1987 that reveals that its PROMIS is not only operating at the land-based "test facility" in Newport, but is also operational on board both attack class and "boomer" class submarines. The Navy, like the CIA and the NSA, clearly has difficulty in giving a credible accounting of its PROMIS software.

The Justice Department continues to try to convince INSLAW, Congress, the press and the American public that the INSLAW affair is, at best, a government contract dispute which could have been resolved long ago if INSLAW had submitted the dispute to the only forum deemed appropriate by the Justice Department: an Executive Branch Contract Appeals Board. What the evidence summarized in this addendum demonstrates, however, is that the essence of the INSLAW affair is radically different. The INSLAW affair was a premeditated, cynical and deceitful taking of INSLAW's software property by the chief law enforcement agency of the United States without due process of law and without compensation to INSLAW in violation of the Fourth Amendment to the Constitution.

Source: "The following information has been given to each member of the House Judiciary Committee and was placed on the Internet in electronic form by Bill Hamilton of Inslaw Corporation"; http://w2.eff.org/legal/cases/INSLAW/inslaw_hr.summary.

U.S. Justice Department News Release, September 27, 1994

With the release of the House Judiciary Committee's report on the INSLAW Affair and the circulation of further attacks by William Hamilton, INSLAW's president, on the U.S. Department of Justice, Attorney General William Barr faced intense pressure to appoint an independent counsel. In late 1991 Barr had launched his own internal Justice Department investigation. The agency, in effect, was investigating itself. To head the investigation he appointed retired judge Nicholas Bua of Illinois, who had been named to the federal bench in 1977 by Democratic President Jimmy Carter. As Bua worked on the investigation, the nation underwent a political transfer of power. In November 1992, Bill Clinton was elected president, and he was inaugurated in January 1993. Bua issued his report on the INSLAW matter shortly after the Clinton administration took power. But the Bua report, strongly exonerating the Justice Department, failed to stop a growing controversy. The new attorney general, Janet Reno, then asked members of the new administration now in the Justice Department to look into the scandal. In September 1994, the Justice Department upheld the findings of the Bua report. As the following news releases insisted, there was no scandal and no computer software theft, and there was no murder to cover it up.

U.S. JUSTICE DEPARTMENT NEWS RELEASE SEPTEMBER 27, 1994

NEW REPORT FINDS NO CREDIBLE BASIS FOR INSLAW CLAIMS, RECOMMENDS MATTER BE CLOSED

WASHINGTON, D.C.—Affirming findings of a special counsel appointed in the previous Administration, the Department of Justice today concluded that there is no credible evidence that Department officials conspired to steal computer software developed by INSLAW, Inc. or that the company is entitled to additional government payments.

The report also reaffirmed police findings that the death of J. Daniel Casolaro, a free-lance journalist investigating the INSLAW matter, was a suicide. It said there is no basis for asking for the appointment of an Independent Counsel, and recommended that the affair be closed.

The case began in 1982 when the Justice Department awarded a $10 million contract to INSLAW to install case management software called PROMIS in U.S. Attorneys' offices around the country. Since then, a series of disputes led to allegations by INSLAW that resulted in several lawsuits, two Congressional investigations, a number of internal Justice Department reviews including one by the Office of Professional Responsibility and another by the Public Integrity Section, the appointment of Nicholas Bua, a former federal judge, as special counsel whose six-member legal team issued a 267-page report in March 1993, and today's review of that report which runs another 187 pages.

Today's report states that the evidence compiled by Judge Bua fully supported the findings and conclusions he reached that there was no criminal wrongdoing in furtherance of the Department on the part of any past or present Justice Department employee. Says the report, "(T)here is no credible evidence that employees of the Department of Justice conspired with anyone to steal PROMIS or to injure INSLAW in any other way."

The report also concluded that the use of PROMIS by the Executive Office of United States Attorneys and in U.S. Attorneys' offices conforms with the contractual agreements that were made, and that INSLAW is not entitled as a matter of law to additional compensation for the use of its PROMIS software.

The report says INSLAW's contention that Justice Department officials conspired to destroy INSLAW and secretly profit from its work was based largely on alleged statements of anonymous sources, in and outside the Department. None came forward despite assurances from Attorney General Janet Reno that they would be protected from reprisals. Individuals who were identified as sources denied making the statements attributed to them by INSLAW. Two primary sources relied on by INSLAW were not credible: Michael Riconosciuto, currently serving a 30-year sentence on methamphetamine charges, and Ari Ben-Menashe, found by two Congressional investigations into the alleged "October Surprise" conspiracy to be totally untrustworthy.

Additional investigation was conducted into several relatively recent claims by INSLAW, and into matters which a House Judiciary Committee report recommended be subject to further review. For example, an MIT professor, Dr. Randall Davis, was hired to compare the computer code in INSLAW's PROMIS software with the code in the FBI's FOIMS software, which INSLAW contends is a pirated version of PROMIS. Dr. Davis concluded that there was no relation between FOIMS and PROMIS.

The report also concluded that there was no credible evidence that INSLAW's PROMIS was being used elsewhere in the government, or had been improperly distributed to a foreign government or entity, or that INSLAW related documents had been destroyed by the Justice Department Command Center, or that the Department had obstructed the reappointment of a bankruptcy judge who had ruled favorably to INSLAW and was later overturned.

The report rebuffed claims that PROMIS was stolen to raise money to reward individuals working for the release of American hostages in Iran, or to penetrate foreign intelligence agencies, or as part of a U.S.-Israeli slush fund connected with the late British publisher Robert Maxwell, or in aid of a secret U.S. intelligence agency concealed within the Office of Special Investigations Nazi-hunting unit which INSLAW asserts participated in illegal trafficking of PROMIS software and in the alleged murder of Mr. Casolaro.

The death of Mr. Casolaro was extensively investigated because of the allegations that he was murdered and because Judge Bua did not address the issue in significant detail. Today's report concurs in the conclusion of the Martinsburg, W. Va., Police Department that Mr. Casolaro committed suicide.

Extensive forensic evidence, including the autopsy, a blood spatter analysis and the toxicology report, strongly supports that conclusion. Many of Mr. Casolaro's friends described him as depressed. He also appeared to be greatly concerned about his professional failures, including his inability to generate income from his investigation into the INSLAW matter. He was suffering from multiple sclerosis.

Says the report, "There is no credible evidence that Mr. Casolaro was murdered."

In recommending that no additional compensation be paid to INSLAW, the report said the Department had adhered to the terms and conditions of its contract with INSLAW. Furthermore, it said, INSLAW had allowed some of its claims to languish for eight years before they were finally dismissed in late 1992. Currently, INSLAW is asking Congress to relieve it of the statutory time bar on the basis of an alleged conspiracy by the government, a conspiracy for which no credible evidence exists.

"INSLAW was provided a full and fair opportunity to litigate its claims," says the report. "The ability of INSLAW and its counsel to keep this matter in the public spotlight by making a series of unsubstantiated allegations linking this affair to some of the major alleged conspiracies of the last 15 years should not be rewarded by acquiescing to their money demands."

Source: www.fas.org/irp/news/1994/940927-555.htm.

New York Court of Appeals Finding, December 19, 1995

The INSLAW Affair involved a wide array of constitutional and legal challenges, ranging from the congressional investigation itself to a number of individual lawsuits. On October 21, 1991, Elliot Richardson, the former U.S. attorney general who was now a lawyer representing INSLAW Inc., published an article in the New York Times *titled "A High-Tech Watergate," which outlined the allegations surrounding the Inslaw Affair. In the article Richardson implicated*

Earl Brian, a former combat surgeon for the CIA, California's secretary of health and welfare under Governor Ronald Reagan, and a close friend of U.S. Attorney General Edwin Meese. Stung by the charges in the article, Brian sued Richardson for defamation of character. Unsuccessful in the first trial, Brian's lawyers moved for a decision by the New York Court of Appeals. Brian not only lost this case but was eventually convicted for fraud in later business dealings and served four years in prison.

NEW YORK COURT OF APPEALS FINDING DECEMBER 19, 1995

Earl W. Brian, M.D., Appellant v.
Elliot L. Richardson, Respondent

This defamation action concerns an article that was published on the Op Ed page of the *New York Times* on October 21, 1991. Although plaintiff alleged that the statement falsely accused him of participating in an illegal conspiracy, his complaint was dismissed on the theory that the publication was a non-actionable statement of the author's opinion. The correctness of this determination depends on the proper application of the principles established in *Immuno AG. v Moor-Jankowski* (77 NY2d 235, cert denied 497 US 1), in which this Court held that both the immediate context and the broader social context in which a published statement was made should be considered in determining whether the statement is one conveying opinion or fact.

The disputed article, entitled "A High-Tech Watergate," was written by defendant Elliot Richardson, a former United States Attorney General. In the article, defendant described his role as attorney for a software company, Inslaw, Inc., which had sold a computer-based case-tracking system to the United States Department of Justice. According to the article, the Department of Justice soon created a series of "sham" controversies regarding the software's cost and performance and eventually withheld payment, leading to Inslaw's bankruptcy. Meanwhile, defendant charged, the Department made illegal copies of the software.

The focus of the remainder of the article was a series of charges that came to defendant's attention regarding the use of this pirated software to further a subversive criminal conspiracy. According to the article, defendant had been told by former Justice Department employees that plaintiff Dr. Earl W. Brian, who had been "California health secretary under Gov. Ronald Reagan and a friend of Attorney General Edwin Meese 3d," was "linked to a scheme to take Inslaw's stolen software and use it to gain the inside track on a $250 million contract to automate Justice Department litigation divisions." Plaintiff was identified as the controlling shareholder of a corporation in which Attorney General Meese's wife also had an interest. Further, the article noted, this corporation controlled another computer company that had earlier launched an "aggressive" effort to acquire Inslaw.

The article also referred to claims made by a Michael Riconosciuto, "an out-of-fiction character believed by many knowledgeable sources to have C.I.A. connections," to the effect that Inslaw's software had been "stole[n]" "as part of a payoff to [plaintiff] for helping to get some Iranian leaders to collude in the so-called October surprise, the alleged plot by the Reagan campaign in 1980 to conspire with Iranian agents to hold up release of the American Embassy hostages until after election." According to the article, "other informants from the world of covert operations" not only "confirm[ed] and supplement[ed]" Riconosciuto's statements but also alleged that "scores of foreign governments now have [Inslaw's] software" and that plaintiff had been given the opportunity to sell this software as a reward. These sources identified the conspiracy's goals as follows: "to generate revenue for covert operations not authorized by Congress" and "to supply foreign intelligence agencies with a software system that would make it easier for U.S. eavesdroppers to read intercepted signals."

Defendant acknowledged that his informants "are not what a lawyer might consider ideal witnesses." However, defendant went on to argue that in his view their story was credible. According to defendant's theory, "the picture that emerges from the individual statements is remarkably detailed and consistent, all the more so because these people are not close associates of one another." Further, "[i]t seems unlikely that so complex a story could have been made up, memorized all at once and closely coordinated." Defendant noted that a skeptical free-lance journalist, one Danny Casolaro, had obtained "many leads" from the same informants and had been found dead in a hotel room after telling friends he was investigating evidence "linking Inslaw, the Iran-contra affair and the October surprise." Defendant opined that Casolaro had been murdered, although the authorities had concluded that his death was a suicide.

The remainder of the article discussed defendant's efforts to persuade Edwin Meese's successor, Attorney General Thornburgh, to investigate, as well as the Justice Department's purported resistance to a congressional investigation. The article ended with a review of defendant's own decision as former President Richard Nixon's Attorney General to utilize an independent prosecutor to investigate the Watergate affair. In the article's final paragraph, defendant argued that the question of the need for a special prosecutor to investigate the Inslaw affair was one that should be considered not only by the Justice Department, but also by Congress, other entities within the executive branch and, lastly, the public itself.

Following the article's publication, plaintiff commenced the present action for damages, alleging that it contained false and defamatory assertions about him and that defendant had published these assertions with reckless disregard for their accuracy. Specifically, plaintiff's complaint alleged that he had been defamed by the article's assertions that (1) he was part of a scheme to steal Inslaw's software to gain an unfair business advantage, (2) he was the beneficiary of politically motivated favoritism, (3) he had participated in a morally reprehensible scheme to delay the safe return of American hostages, (4) he had stolen software to foreign governments to advance illegal covert activities and (5) he had somehow been involved in the murder of an investigative journalist.

On February 26, 1993, the trial court dismissed the complaint, reasoning that "A High-Tech Watergate" would be understood by a reasonable reader "as a policy argument on a matter of public concern" and that its allegations were therefore not actionable under this Court's opinion in *Immuno AG. v Moor-Jankowski* (77 NY2d 235, supra). The dismissal was affirmed by the Appellate Division, which cited *Gross v New York Times* (82 NY2d 146) as well as *Immuno* and concluded that the article made clear to "the average reader or listener" that its accusations were "'merely a personal surmise'" built upon allegations and claims made by others (quoting, *Gross v New York Times,* supra, at 155). Both courts below stressed that the article in question was published on the Op Ed page of the newspaper, a space that is traditionally reserved for the expression of opinion and encouragement of public debate. Plaintiff then took a further appeal by permission of this Court.

The law governing defamation actions involving communications purporting to convey opinion has been explored in a quartet of recent Court of Appeals decisions (*Gross v New York Times Co.,* supra; 600 West 115th St. Corp. v. Von Gutfeld, 80 NY2d 130, cert denied __ US __, 113 S Ct 241; *Immuno AG. v Moor-Jankowski,* supra; *Steinhilber v Alphonse,* 68 NY2d 283). The essence of the tort of libel is the publication of a statement about an individual that is both false and defamatory. Since falsity is a sine qua non of a libel claim and since only assertions of fact are capable of being proven false, we have consistently held that a libel action cannot be maintained unless it is premised on published assertions of fact (*Gross v New York Times Co.,* supra, at 152-153; *Immuno AG. v Moor-Jankowski,* supra; see also, *Milkovich v Lorain Journal Co.,* 497 US 1, 17-21).

Distinguishing between assertions of fact and non-actionable expressions of opinion has often proved a difficult task. The factors to be considered are: "(1) whether the specific language in issue has a precise meaning which is readily understood; (2) whether the statements are capable of being proven true or false; and (3) whether either the full context of the communication in which the statement appears or the broader social context and surrounding circumstances are such as to 'signal'. . . readers or listeners that what is being read or heard is likely to be opinion, not fact'" (*Gross v New York Times Co.,* supra, at 153, quoting *Steinhilber v Alphonse,* supra, at 292; accord, *Immuno AG. v Moor-Jankowski,* supra). It is the last of these factors that lends both depth and difficulty to the analysis.

The significance of the context factor was explicated in *Immuno AG. v Moor-Jankowski* (supra). In that case, we rejected an analysis that would first search a publication for specific factual assertions and then hold those assertions actionable unless they were couched in figurative or hyperbolic language (id., at 254). Instead, we held that, in distinguishing between actionable factual assertions and non-actionable opinion, the courts must consider the content of the communication as a whole, as well as its tone and apparent purpose. Rather than sifting through a communication for the purpose of isolating and identifying assertions of fact, the court should look to the overall context in which the assertions were made and determine on that basis "whether the reasonable reader would have believed that the challenged statements were conveying facts about the libel plaintiff" (id., at 254, citing *Steinhilber v Alphonse,* supra, at 293).

In addition to considering the immediate context in which the disputed words appear, the courts are required to take into consideration the larger context in which the statements were published, including the nature of the particular forum. In *Immuno,* for instance, the challenged communication was a letter to the editor of a professional journal—a medium that is typically regarded by the public as a vehicle for the expression of individual opinion rather than "'the rigorous and comprehensive presentation of factual matter'" (77 NY2d, at 253, quoting 145 AD2d 114, 129). Similarly, in *600 W. 115th St. Corp. v Von Gutfeld* (supra, at 143–144), the alleged defamatory remarks were made at a public hearing, where the listeners presumably expect to hear vigorous expressions of personal opinion. In the same vein, the disputed statements in *Steinhilber v Alphonse* (supra, at 294) were made by the defendant union official as part of a recorded telephone message that was calculated to punish a "scab" in the aftermath of an acrimonious labor conflict. In that context, where the "'audience may anticipate [the use] of epithets, fiery rhetoric or hyperbole,'" we opined that statements which might otherwise be viewed as assertions of fact may take on an entirely different character (id., quoting *Information Control Corp. v Genesis One Computer Corp.,* 611 F2d 781, 784).

By way of contrast, in *Gross v New York Times* (supra, at 155–156), where the defendants' statements were held to be actionable assertions of fact, we stressed that the accusations had been made "in the course of a lengthy, copiously documented newspaper series that was written . . . after what purported to be a thorough investigation." Further, we noted that the articles appeared in the news section of the newspaper where, unlike the editorial section, the reader expects to find factual accounts (id., at 156). Finally, the identity, role and reputation of the author may be factors to the extent that they provide the reader with clues as to the article's import.

We emphasize that an article's appearance in the sections of a newspaper that are usually dedicated to opinion does not automatically insulate the author from liability for defamation. Despite our firm commitment to encouraging the robust exchange of ideas through these and similar media, we have never suggested that an editorial page or a newspaper column confers a license to make false factual accusations and thereby unjustly destroy individuals' reputations (see, e.g., *Immuno AG. v Moor-Jankowski,* supra, at 254). To the contrary, we have repeatedly emphasized that the forum in which a statement has been made, as well as the other surrounding circumstances comprising the "broader social setting," are only useful gauges for determining whether a reasonable reader or listener would understand the complained-of assertions as opinion or statements of fact.

In this case, the statements in dispute were made in an article that was published on the Op Ed page of a newspaper. Like the "letters to the editor" section in which the *Immuno* publication appeared, the Op Ed page is a forum traditionally reserved for the airing of ideas on matters of public concern.

Indeed, the common expectation is that the columns and articles published on a newspaper's Op Ed sections will represent the viewpoints of their authors and, as such, contain considerable hyperbole, speculation, diversified forms of expression and opinion. Thus, the "broader context" in which "A High-Tech Watergate" was published provided some signals to the reader that its contents were expressions of opinion.

The immediate context in which the challenged statements were made also supports the conclusion that the specific accusations of which plaintiff complains could not have been understood by a reasonable reader as assertions of fact that were proffered for their accuracy. At the outset of the article, defendant disclosed that he had been Inslaw's attorney, thereby signalling that he was not a disinterested observer (cf., *Immuno AG. v Moor-Jankowski,* supra, at 254). Further, the predominant tone of the article, which was rife with rumor, speculation and seemingly tenuous inferences, furnished clues to the reasonable reader that "A High-Tech Watergate" was something less than serious, objective reportage.

Finally, the purpose of defendant's article was to advocate an independent governmental investigation into the purported misuse of the software that Inslaw had sold to the Justice Department. To support this argument, defendant marshalled the relevant rumors and accusations that were floating around the Justice Department and strung them together with the few supporting "facts" that he had been able to glean from the public record and from private sources and personal knowledge. Indeed, without a recitation of the existing unresolved charges, defendant's call for a full-scale investigation would have made no sense. Given this contextual background, we conclude on this record that a reasonable reader would understand the statements defendant made about plaintiff as mere allegations to be investigated rather than as facts.

Significantly, most of the accusations about plaintiff that defendant recounted were identified in the article as mere "claims" that had been made by identified and unidentified sources. Further, although defendant unquestionably offered his own view that these sources were credible, he also set out the basis for that personal opinion, leaving it to the readers to evaluate it for themselves. Thus, there was no suggestion in the article that there were additional undisclosed facts on which its credibility assessment had been based (see, *Gross v New York Times Co.,* supra, at 153, citing *Hotchner v Castillo-Puche,* 551 F2d 910, 913, cert denied sub nom. *Hotchner v Doubleday & Co.,* 434 US 834).

To be sure, the fact that a particular accusation originated with a different source does not automatically furnish a license for others to repeat or publish it without regard to its accuracy or defamatory character. Here, however, the repeated charges were included in the article not necessarily to convince the reader of plaintiff's dishonesty but rather to demonstrate the need for an investigation that would establish the truth or falsity of the charges.

In sum, both the immediate context of the article itself and the broader context in which the article was published made it sufficiently apparent to the reasonable reader that its contents represented the opinion of the author and that its specific charges about plaintiff were allegations and not demonstrable fact. Under these circumstances, plaintiff failed to state a cognizable libel claim and his complaint was properly dismissed.

Accordingly, the order of the Appellate Division should be affirmed, with costs.

Source: www.law.cornell.edu/nyctap/I95_0246.htm.

U.S. Department of Justice News Release, August 4, 1997

In the summer of 1997, Inslaw Inc. and its owner, William Hamilton, suffered the last of the legal hammer blows that rendered futile their attempts to recover monies from the federal government. A Court of Federal Claims found INSLAW's charges of government theft and wrongdoing by the U.S. Department of Justice to be unfounded.

U.S. DEPARTMENT OF JUSTICE NEWS RELEASE AUGUST 4, 1997

Justice Department Successful Against INSLAW Claims in Federal Claims Court

WASHINGTON, D.C.—Ending a 10-year litigation dispute the Court of Federal Claims rejected claims by the software firm Inslaw that the Department of Justice illegally stole its software and distributed it world-wide, the Justice Department announced today.

According to a 186-page opinion, issued by Judge Christine Miller on July 31, 1997, there is "no merit to the claims" of a local software company that have fueled allegations of wrongdoing at the Department of Justice for a decade. The long-running dispute between Justice and Inslaw, Inc. centered around the company's claim that its PROMIS software, delivered to DOJ under a 1982 contract, had, in fact, been "stolen" by the government and was being disseminated world-wide.

The court's decision, issued after a three-week trial, rejected all of Inslaw's claims, finding that Inslaw had not shown it had any ownership rights to the software or that DOJ acted improperly in any way in connection with the software.

The Inslaw dispute received much press attention in 1988, when, in connection with Inslaw's bankruptcy filing, a District of Columbia bankruptcy judge used highly critical language in siding with Inslaw. That decision, which found that DOJ had taken software that was proprietary to Inslaw, was reversed on appeal, however. Judge Miller found that Inslaw's decision to take its case to the bankruptcy court rather than courts with certain jurisdiction to hear it, was a tactical one.

After the bankruptcy court's decision, the Department conducted several internal investigations, including inquiries by the Public Integrity Section of the Criminal Division and the Office of Professional Responsibility. In addition, former Attorney General William Barr appointed a special counsel, former District Judge Nicholas Bua, to conduct an independent investigation. Each inquiry found no merit to Inslaw's claims. Later, Attorney General Janet Reno initiated a new investigation, this one conducted by the Office of the Associate Attorney General. That investigation also concluded that Inslaw's claims were false.

The case was retried in the Court of Federal Claims in March of this year because Congress referred the case to the court for an advisory opinion as part of its consideration of whether to pass a private bill to compensate Inslaw. The court found that the claimed software enhancements are not proprietary to Inslaw, that DOJ acted justifiably regarding the software, that the government had unlimited rights in the PROMIS software it received, and the DOJ administered the 1982 contract in good faith. It also rejected Inslaw's copyright claim.

Assistant Attorney General Frank Hunger, head of the Civil Division said, "Both parties benefit from having a decision from a court with authority to resolve the matter—a court that has heard all the evidence," he said. "And the public benefits because all the evidence has been aired and they can be confident that the facts have finally been revealed. Certainly, the Department benefits from the lifting of the cloud that has hung over it for a decade."

Following the 1988 bankruptcy court decision, Inslaw's allegations of wrong-doing within DOJ expanded substantially to include alleged wide-spread dissemination of the software and its use by intelligence officials world-wide. Hunger said Judge Miller's decision "seems to put an end to that aspect of the Inslaw saga as well." The judge appointed a panel of independent experts to review the software Inslaw claimed were pirated versions of the PROMIS software. The experts found that Inslaw's allegations were false.

The decision of the Court of Federal Claims concludes not only that Inslaw has no legal claim against the United States, but also that it has no equitable claim. Courts generally consider only the parties' legal rights, but in congressional reference proceedings, the court is instructed to look to the equities as well as the law. Because the court concluded that the government, not Inslaw, owned the software at issue, and that DOJ officials acted properly in their dealings with Inslaw, Judge Miller concluded that there was no equitable basis for any of Inslaw's claims.

According to the court's opinion, the 1982 contract required Inslaw to install in U.S. Attorney's offices a non-proprietary, public-domain version of the PROMIS software. But, without notice to the government, Inslaw installed a different, allegedly proprietary version of the software and then asserted that the government could not use the software in other offices. The court found that only 12 of the more than 100 alleged enhancements actually existed and that Inslaw could not demonstrate that Inslaw, rather than the government, owned them.

Source: www.usdoj.gov/opa/pr/1997/August97/323civ.htm.

Bibliography

Barrett, Paul M. "Thornburgh, Brooks Clash Over Charge of Wrongdoing at Justice Department." *Wall Street Journal,* December 10, 1990, p. B7A.

Fisher, Louis. *The Politics of Executive Privilege.* Durham, N.C.: Carolina Academic Press, 2004.

Fricker, Mary, and Stephen Pizzo. "Outlaws at Justice: U.S. Department of Justice Stonewalls Inslaw Inc. Investigation." *Mother Jones,* May–June 1992, p. 30.

Fricker, Richard L. "Earl Brian: Reagan's 'Scandal Man' Off to Jail. *Consortium News,* 1997. http://www.consortiumnews.com/archive/xfile11.html.

Labaton, Stephen. "White House Gives Rationale for Balking at a Subpoena." *New York Times,* December 13, 1995.

Linsalata, Phil. "The Octopus File." *Columbia Journalism Review,* November/December 1991. Available at http://backissues.cjrarchives.org/year/91/6/octopus.asp.

Marcus, Ruth, and Susan Schmidt. "Legal Experts Uncertain on Prospects of Clinton Privilege Claim." *Washington Post,* December 14, 1995, p. A14.

McGrory, Mary. "Summer of the Octopus." *Washington Post,* August 18, 1991, p. C1.

Morganthau, Tom. "A Victim of Octopus." *Newsweek,* August 26, 1991, p. 21.

Richardson, Elliot. "A High-Tech Watergate." *New York Times,* October 21, 1991, A15.

U.S. Congress. House. *The Inslaw Affair: Investigative Report by the Committee on the Judiciary together with Dissenting and Separate Views.* 102d Cong., 2d sess., September 10, 1992. H. Report 102-857.

The Whitewater Investigation and Impeachment of President Bill Clinton, 1992–98

By Raymond W. Smock

Introduction: The Road from Whitewater to Impeachment

Never in American history has a president of the United States been the subject of investigations for criminal wrongdoing for so long and at such expense as was the case with President William Jefferson Clinton. The investigations, some major and some minor, including 11 by Congress and two by independent prosecutors, plus related investigations involving the FBI and other agencies of the federal government, were accompanied by massive media coverage, daily revelations, scandals both real and imagined, and a steady supply of rumors and innuendo fueled by Clinton's political enemies. Collectively the investigations and the speculations were known as Whitewater, named for an Arkansas real-estate firm, the Whitewater Development Corporation, which was established in 1978, the year Bill Clinton was first elected governor of Arkansas and 14 years before he ran successfully for president of the United States.

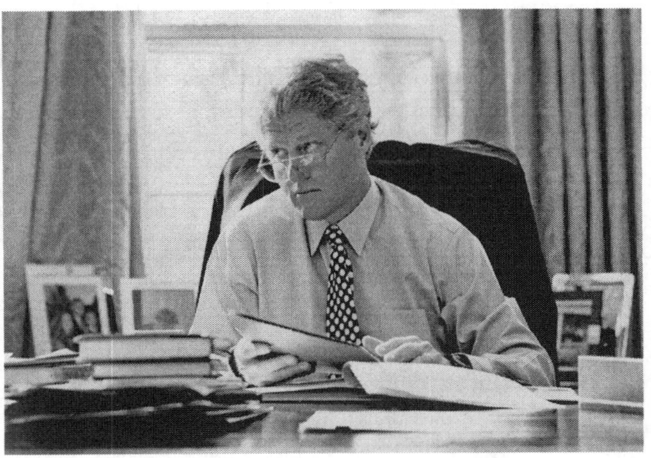

President Bill Clinton seated at his desk in the Oval Office, 1993. (Library of Congress)

In 1978, Bill Clinton and his wife, Hillary Rodham Clinton, became business partners with longtime Arkansas friends, businessman James B. McDougal and his wife, Susan, in a speculative real-estate venture to develop vacation homes in the Ozark Mountains along the White River. This investment and business partnership proved to be a colossal mistake that at the time none of the principals could possibly have foreseen. The Clintons eventually recovered most of their investment in the real-estate venture but lost $43,000 on the deal. Questions about the investment were raised by some of Clinton's political enemies in Arkansas before he ran for president. The matter got the attention of the nation during the presidential campaign of 1992. The Clintons' connection to the Whitewater Development Corporation, according to news accounts, had the appearance of a sweet deal designed to benefit and enrich the new governor. In hindsight, the sweetest thing about the real-estate deal was the way it was manipulated and purposely distorted by a wide range of the Clintons' political opponents and kept alive by journalists working on the assumption that where there was smoke there was fire. No president had come under such scrutiny since the Watergate investigations that nearly led to President Richard M. Nixon's impeachment almost two decades earlier. A new generation of journalists looked on Whitewater as their opportunity to be a part of history, and to further their careers in the process. The lure to investigate was strong.

There certainly was plenty of smoke, mostly in the financial and personal connections between the Clintons and the McDougals. Jim McDougal was a complex and talented Arkansas entrepreneur, a former congressional aide to Senator William Fulbright (D-Ark.), and a one-

OVERVIEW

Background

At the time Bill Clinton of Arkansas became the 42nd president of the United States in January 1993, the nation's politics was choked with bitterness and high levels of partisanship. Stung by defeat after holding the White House for three terms, Republicans assailed the new Democratic president as unfit for office, a usurper with a tainted past. Through right-wing radio talk programs and political-action groups, the opposition was bent on bringing down the president and crippling his agenda. The main attacks centered on Clinton's days as the governor of Arkansas and a so-called scandal dubbed Whitewater. The name came from the Whitewater Development Corporation, a business venture to build vacation homes in the Ozark Mountains along the banks of the White River, which Clinton and his wife, Hillary, had joined as business partners with their friends James and Susan McDougal in 1978. The term "Whitewater" came to encompass a number of charges of corruption leveled against the Clintons by their political opponents.

The Whitewater investigations included those run by the Senate and House of Representatives banking committees as well as another conducted by the House Committee on Government Reform and Oversight. But the national news media focused on the investigations of the special counsel, Robert B. Fiske Jr., and then, beginning in August 1994, the investigations conducted by the Office of Independent Counsel, headed by Kenneth W. Starr. It was the unrelenting Starr investigations that kept Whitewater alive. Much criminal wrongdoing and 15 major indictments and convictions came from the Starr investigations, but nothing criminal was attributed to either Bill or Hillary Clinton after one of the most expensive and lengthy investigations in U.S. history. Starr had not yet completed his own work when a bombshell news report rocked Washington and the nation—President Clinton, it was reported, had engaged in an illicit affair with a White House intern and employee, Monica S. Lewinsky. The Starr investigation veered dramatically away from Whitewater-related matters and toward a sex scandal and an inquiry into whether the president had committed perjury about his sexual relationship with Lewinsky. While the president lied to colleagues and the public about having sexual relations with Lewinsky, the illegal act of lying under oath occurred on January 17, 1998, when Clinton testified under oath in the Paula Corbin Jones sexual harassment lawsuit that he had not had a sexual relationship with Lewinsky. The Jones lawsuit, filed in 1994, was based on charges first made while Clinton was governor of Arkansas in 1991. When Clinton was deposed by Paula Jones's lawyers, it turned out to be the crucial link that triggered the investigation of the president's relationship with Lewinsky by the Office of Independent Counsel, headed by Starr. The charges of perjury, and additional charges of obstruction of justice in the president's attempts to cover up the affair, led the House of Representatives to impeach President Clinton in 1998. The Senate tried and acquitted him in 1999.

Congress Investigates

During the first two years of Clinton's term, the Whitewater charges were fueled by new developments. In May 1993, the administration fired seven employees in the White House Travel Office after serious accounting problems were discovered. The firings also made it possible to make room for Clinton friends to run the office. Then, in July 1993, the death of Vincent Foster, the deputy White House counsel, which had been ruled a suicide, generated speculation from Republican groups that he was tormented by Whitewater misdeeds and cover-ups or, worse, that he had been murdered.

time professor of political science. He turned to real-estate investments and eventually to the ownership of a small Arkansas savings and loan association, the Madison Guaranty Savings and Loan Association. McDougal eventually became caught up in the savings and loan industry fiasco of the 1980s that saw hundreds of savings and loans fail across the nation. By most accounts McDougal's mental health declined along with his business. His savings and loan was under investigation by the FBI when it failed in 1989. In 1992 and 1993 McDougal was investigated by the Resolution Trust Corporation (RTC), a federal entity created to investigate and resolve the savings and loan

In January 1994, Attorney General Janet Reno named Fiske, a New York lawyer and former U.S. attorney, as special counsel to investigate the Clintons' involvement in Whitewater. Fiske was later replaced by Starr, a former federal appeals court judge and U.S. solicitor. In the summer of 1994, the banking committees in the House and Senate began hearings on Whitewater. Although the committee investigations reported no malfeasance by the Clintons, Congress was not finished with the Whitewater matter.

In the 1994 congressional elections, Republicans swept into power in the House of Representatives for the first time in 40 years and also gained control of the Senate. In May 1995, the Senate formed a special Whitewater committee chaired by Senator Alfonse D'Amato (R-N.Y.). Following a year of intense investigation, the Special Whitewater Committee issued a 690-page majority report in June 1996 that charged the Clinton administration with abuse of power. The Democrats on the committee issued a blistering rebuttal, calling the committee's work a "legislative travesty."

Impact

The impact of the Whitewater investigations by Congress and the special prosecutors is still being felt in American politics. Millions of dollars were spent in investigating President Clinton (and often Hillary Clinton) throughout Clinton's two terms as president, causing a monumental distraction to the business of governance and crippling the American political process through excessive and relentless partisanship. That partisanship has not ended and seems to have become a standard mode of operation used by both parties. Much study remains to be done to analyze all the reasons that American national politics has evolved into the personal demonization of opponents and what this means to fundamental democratic institutions of American life and to the U.S. Constitution.

The impeachment of President Clinton only made the matter of defining the constitutional requirements of "high crimes and misdemeanors" more difficult. While perjury can be a serious crime, when the perjury involves lying about a sexual affair between consenting adults the question becomes is this what the Founders had in mind when they penned the Constitution, or has impeachment based on this charge had the effect of lowering the bar for future impeachments, while potentially trivializing the process. The public sentiment on private sexual affairs was mixed, as was how serious a crime it was to lie about the affairs. While some Americans considered it immoral, and many found it embarrassing and troublesome, most did not see this incident and lying about it under oath to be a significant enough offense to remove a president from office. The impeachment was almost entirely driven by partisan politics. Finally, Clinton's impeachment should be a warning to future political leaders in the federal government that previous standards of what constitutes news and the public's business, and what constitutes an impeachable crime, have been dramatically changed. Whatever standards of conduct that may have existed to protect the private lives of public officials are gone. While sex scandals and charges of sexual impropriety regarding prominent political leaders have surfaced from time to time throughout American history, the impeachment of the president, which the House managers insisted was not about sex but about perjury, was clearly about perjury related to a sexual relationship. It remains to be seen if fundamental American institutions, including the news media and the major political parties, can strike a better balance between the public and private actions of the nation's leaders.

industry failures, and he was indicted on and convicted of multiple felony counts based on that investigation and one conducted later by the federal Office of Independent Counsel (OIC), which was then investigating Bill Clinton. McDougal received a lighter sentence in return for his cooperation with the OIC in its investigation of Clinton.

Major newspapers like the *New York Times* and the *Washington Post* assigned investigative reporters to look into the Whitewater real-estate deal and related Arkansas matters as part of the vetting of Clinton when he ran for president in 1992. Mainstream news media acceptance of Whitewater as a topic of investigation

CHRONOLOGY

1978

- Bill Clinton, attorney general of Arkansas, and his wife, Hillary Clinton, partner with James and Susan McDougal to borrow $203,000 to form the Whitewater Development Corporation to build vacation homes in Arkansas's Ozark Mountains. Bill Clinton is elected governor of Arkansas.

1982

- James McDougal buys a small savings and loan and names it Madison Guaranty Savings and Loan Association, with assets of $3 million. After losing a reelection bid in 1980 after his first term, Clinton is again elected governor. Hillary Clinton, working with the Rose Law Firm, would later become one of the lawyers representing Madison Guaranty. Within two years, federal regulators begin to question the financial stability and lending practices of the bank.

1985

- McDougal holds a fund-raising event to help pay off a $50,000 Clinton campaign debt. Investigators determine some of the money was improperly withdrawn from depositor funds.

1986–1995

- During this time period, 747 savings-and-loan banks nationwide fail, causing scandals and criminal convictions for fraud and the loss of the life savings of many Americans, at a cost to taxpayers of $153 billion.

1989

- Madison Guaranty collapses and is bailed out by the federal government. McDougal is indicted on federal fraud charges.

1992

- While investigating the Madison collapse, the Federal Resolution Trust Corporation, an entity established by law in 1989 to resolve issues related to the failure of the savings-and-loan industry, names Bill and Hillary Clinton as "potential beneficiaries" of Madison's illegal activities. Bill Clinton is elected president of the United States.

1993

- *May:* White House fires seven employees in its travel office, possibly to make room for Clinton friends. An FBI investigation of the office begins. The news media call the incident Travelgate.
- *July 20:* Vincent Foster, the deputy White House counsel and a friend of President Clinton's since childhood, is found dead in a Northern Virginia park. Police rule the death a suicide. White House aides enter Foster's office shortly after his death, and speculation arises that files relating to Whitewater were removed from his office.

1994

- *January:* Attorney General Janet Reno names Robert B. Fiske Jr., a New York lawyer and former U.S. attorney, as special counsel to investigate the Clintons' involvement in Whitewater.
- *Summer:* Senate and House of Representatives banking committees begin hearings on Whitewater.
- *August 5:* Kenneth W. Starr succeeds Fiske as the independent counsel to investigate Whitewater-Madison matters.

1995

- *January 3:* Democratic majority on the Senate banking committee releases a report finding the Clintons broke no laws in Whitewater-related business.

had the unintended consequence of lending credence to less-careful journalists, pundits, and political enemies of the president, who gained cover for their partisan attacks by citing the *New York Times* and the *Washington Post* as their sources of information. As Arkansas journalist and media critic Gene Lyons said, "By the time House and Senate hearings on Whitewater began in late summer 1995, the Washington media had

- *January 4:* Republicans gain control of the U.S. House of Representatives for the first time in 40 years. Newt Gingrich of Georgia is elected speaker.
- *May 17:* Senate forms a special Whitewater committee chaired by Senator Alfonse D'Amato (R-N.Y.).
- *July 18:* Special committee begins hearings.
- *August 10:* House banking committee completes its investigation of Whitewater and finds no illegalities on the part of the Clintons.
- *November:* Monica S. Lewinsky accepts a paid job in the White House Office of Legislative Affairs and, two days later, begins an intimate affair with Clinton.
- *November 14–19:* Federal government is shut down due to an impasse over the federal budget between Republicans in Congress, led by Speaker Newt Gingrich, and the president. A month later, the government is shut down again over the budget, from December 16, 1995, to January 6, 1996.

1996

- *June 17:* Special Whitewater Committee issues a 690-page majority report charging that the Clinton administration misused its power. The Democratic minority labels the report a "legislative travesty."

1998

- *January 16:* Reno approves Starr's request for an expansion of the inquiry to include the Clinton-Lewinsky affair.
- *January 17:* President Clinton, testifying under oath to lawyers in a sexual-harassment case brought by Arkansas resident Paula Jones, denies having had an affair with Lewinsky.
- *August 17:* Clinton testifies at a grand-jury hearing that he had "inappropriate intimate contact" with Lewinsky but insists the evidence he gave in the Jones case was accurate.
- *September 9:* The Starr report is issued, outlining 11 possible grounds for impeachment. The House votes to make the 445-page report public. Whitewater is barely mentioned.
- *October 8:* House votes to begin impeachment proceedings against Clinton. House Committee on the Judiciary begins to draw up charges based on allegations made in the Starr Report.
- *December 11–12:* House Judiciary Committee approves four articles of impeachment.
- *December 15:* Representative Henry Hyde (R-Ill.) introduces impeachment resolution.
- *December 19:* Following more than 13 hours of debate over two days, the House approves, by narrow partisan majorities of 228–206 and 221–212, two of the four articles of impeachment against Clinton on the charges of perjury and obstruction of justice.

1999

- *January 7:* Senate formally begins Clinton's impeachment trial. Chief Justice William Rehnquist is sworn in as presiding officer.
- *January 25:* Senators deliberate in secret after hearing arguments to dismiss charges against the president.
- *January 27:* By identical votes of 56–44, the Senate does not dismiss charges against the president. Depositions are sought from Lewinsky and White House advisers Vernon Jordan and Sidney Blumenthal.
- *February 1:* Lewinsky is questioned by House managers and gives deposition in closed-door session at the Mayflower Hotel in Washington, D.C.
- *February 4:* Senate votes 70–30 not to have Lewinsky testify in person.
- *February 12:* Senate finds Clinton not guilty and acquits him of all charges. On Article 1, the charge of perjury, all 45 Democrats and 10 Republicans vote not guilty. On Article II, the charge of obstruction of justice, all 45 Democrats and 5 Republicans vote not guilty. It would have taken 67 votes to convict the president.

turned itself into a wholly owned subsidiary of the Republican Party."

The story that launched Whitewater on a national scale appeared on March 8, 1992, in the *New York Times*. The reporter, Jeff Gerth, did exhaustive research and spent considerable time in Arkansas. He would be one of the leading investigative journalists on the story as it unfolded over the next several years. Gerth's opening piece in the *New York Times* featured the headline "Clintons Joined S.&L. Operator in an Ozark Real Estate Venture." The headline, probably the work of editors rather than the author, actually was misleading and out of context. At the time the Clintons entered into their partnership in the Whitewater Development Corporation in 1978, Jim McDougal was not a savings and loan operator, and he would not become one until 1982.

The long, complex Whitewater investigations provide the essential context for explaining the impeachment of the president of the United States in 1998. After years of investigating Bill and Hillary Clinton, nothing had emerged from the official investigations of Whitewater and its related matters that led to criminal indictments of the Clintons. What the investigations did uncover, however, was a substantial web of corruption in Arkansas that would lead to indictments and jail sentences for Clinton associates. In addition to Jim and Susan McDougal, those indicted and convicted included Jim Guy Tucker, who succeeded Clinton as governor of Arkansas, and Webster L. Hubbell, a former law partner of Hillary Clinton in the Rose Law Firm in Little Rock. Hubbell followed Clinton to Washington and was the number-three man at the Justice Department when he was forced to step down following his conviction for mail fraud and tax evasion in connection with stealing $400,000 from Rose Law Firm clients and partners. Altogether there were 15 major indictments and convictions in the Arkansas investigations, with a number of those convicted receiving lighter sentences in exchange for their cooperation with the OIC in its investigation of the Clintons.

One seemingly minor aspect of the Whitewater investigations that ultimately had the most direct bearing on the impeachment of the president was a sexual-harassment accusation made against Bill Clinton by an Arkansas state employee, Paula Corbin Jones. Jones alleged that on May 8, 1991, she was escorted into a Little Rock hotel room by Arkansas state troopers, where she was sexually propositioned by the governor. This sex scandal, dubbed "Troopergate" in the news media, was first revealed in the pages of the conservative magazine *American Spectator* by the reporter David Brock. The *American Spectator* was funded by the billionaire conservative publisher Richard Mellon Scaife as part of his Arkansas Project, a $2.4 million enterprise designed to politically destroy Clinton and his aspirations for high office. This was not a secret conspiracy on the part of Scaife, but the open plan of a man who despised Clinton and his politics. When subsequent investigations of Troopergate revealed several Arkansas state troopers were paid for their stories, the scandal faded. Two years later, however, on May 6, 1994, Jones filed a sexual-harassment lawsuit against Clinton, now in his second year as president of the United States.

As the official Whitewater investigations of the OIC were winding down in early January 1998, a stunning new revelation that President Clinton had had an intimate relationship with a 21-year-old White House employee, Monica S. Lewinsky, suddenly and dramatically shifted the investigations away from Whitewater and became instead an all-out effort to determine if the president had lied about his sexual relationship with Lewinsky. The Jones lawsuit suddenly had resonance and relevance again. Clinton's sexual proclivities, with stories and rumors going far into his past, became front and center in American political life.

The Lewinsky affair was revealed publicly by Internet journalist Matt Drudge on January 19, 1998. Two days later the affair dominated all news media. The OIC had gotten wind of the affair only a few days earlier, on January 12, 1998, when a former White House employee then working at the Pentagon, Linda Tripp, a relatively minor witness in ongoing investigations conducted by the OIC, informed prosecutors that Lewinsky was about to perjure herself in the Jones case. Tripp had met Lewinsky in August 1996, when Lewinsky was transferred to a job at the Pentagon. Tripp became Lewinsky's friend and confidante, and a year later Tripp began taping her telephone conversations with Lewinsky as she systematically documented Lewinsky's earlier sexual encounters with President Clinton. Tripp had taken it upon herself to notify Jones's lawyers about the Lewinsky affair. To further their case, Jones's law-

Linda Tripp speaks to reporters outside the U.S. Courthouse in Washington. The U.S. government paid Tripp, a central figure in the Monica Lewinsky scandal, $595,000 as part of a settlement of lawsuits in which she accused U.S. officials of violating her privacy. Tripp's secret tapes of conversations with Lewinsky fueled the sex scandal that almost brought down President Bill Clinton. (Doug Mills/Associated Press)

yers were interested in getting statements from any women who may have been sexually involved with the president. When Jones's lawyers questioned Clinton on January 17, 1998, they already knew details of his relationship with Lewinsky.

The OIC prosecutors learned that Clinton's personal friend and adviser Vernon Jordan was trying to help Lewinsky find a job in New York City, and they made a connection and saw parallels between Jordan's relationship with Lewinsky and his earlier relationship with Hubbell, a pivotal Whitewater figure. Jordan had helped Hubbell find a lucrative consulting contract after he was forced to resign from the Justice Department in the wake of the Whitewater investigation, and later he helped Lewinsky find a job in New York. The OIC's presumption was that Jordan may have been acting on behalf of the president to silence witnesses against him.

The result of the new investigation into the Lewinsky affair focused on whether the president perjured himself in statements made under oath and whether he entered into an elaborate cover-up of the affair that amounted to obstruction of justice. On September 9, 1998, Kenneth W. Starr, the independent counsel, and his office issued a sensational referral to Congress, widely known as the Starr Report, outlining 11 reasons that the president of the United States should be impeached. Nothing in the Starr Report touched on charges against the president relating to Whitewater, after more than four years of investigation. The case against the president was based solely on his conduct in dealing with the Lewinsky sex scandal.

Travelgate and the Death of Vincent Foster

During President Clinton's first year in the White House, a series of White House missteps added to the scrutiny of the president under the widening umbrella of scandals and investigations known collectively as Whitewater. On May 19, 1993, White House chief of staff Thomas F. "Mack" McLarty directed David Watkins, the director of White House Administration, to fire seven employees in the White House Travel Office for corrupt practices, including the office's director, Billy Ray Dale, who had worked in the office since 1961 and served as director since 1982. The travel office was responsible for booking flights and other travel for members of the news media who accompanied the president when he traveled. The firings came after a brief FBI investigation found irregularities in the bookkeeping of the office, including an off-the-books ledger kept by Dale. White House deputy counsel Vincent Foster, a friend of Bill Clinton's since they were in kindergarten together, played a role in the internal investigations that led up to the dismissal of the seven employees.

The firing of the travel-office staff became known as "Travelgate," and it led to a number of investigations by the FBI, the Department of Justice, the General Accounting Office, the House of Representatives' Committee on Oversight and Government Reform, and eventually the OIC. What seemed like an embarrassing and bungled handling of a relatively minor incident blossomed into a full-fledged scandal with potentially illegal acts. While Travelgate eventually faded from public memory in light of subsequent events, especially the Lewinsky affair and the impeachment of the president, at the time Travelgate provided fuel to the Clinton's political enemies and made it possible for the president's critics to hone their story that the president was unethical and corrupt. Bumper stickers with the slogan "Impeach Clinton" had appeared almost immediately after his election.

The furor over the travel-office firings erupted when the new contractor selected for the travel business turned out to be World Wide Travel, a Little Rock, Arkansas, firm that was reputable but run by close friends of the Clintons'. The new head of the travel office was 25-year-old Catherine Cornelius, a distant cousin of President Clinton. Other Clinton friends, including Harry Thomason, the Hollywood television producer and chairman of the Clinton inauguration committee, were apparently interested in gaining business for their new air charter company. There were evident signs of cronyism that could not be wished away.

Critics charged that the White House used the FBI improperly to justify the firings. The FBI issued a report on May 28, 1993, stating that the White House had used no improper pressure and that agents acted responsibly. Under pressure to explain the firings, McLarty, with the help of Leon Panetta, director of the Office of Management and Budget, issued his own 80-page report on July 3, a candid assessment that blamed himself and other White House staff for handling the firings so badly and for giving the appearance that the FBI had been pressured into the investigation of the travel office. McLarty apologized for allowing some of the Clintons' personal friends to become involved in the travel-office contract. The report concluded, however, that nothing that had been done was a violation of any law. Another inquiry into the firings by the Justice Department's Office of Professional Responsibility concluded in a March 1994 report that the FBI had not been pressured and that no laws had been broken. Five of the White House Travel Office employees were reinstated to other positions in the executive branch, but Dale and his deputy chose to decline further government employment.

Dale was indicted by a federal grand jury on December 7, 1994, on embezzlement and criminal conversion charges, sparking a new round of news-media stories. Dale was acquitted on November 16, 1995, after a trial that included prominent journalists as character witnesses, including Sam Donaldson of ABC News. Dale may have kept sloppy books, which his lawyers admitted, but the jury determined that he had not stolen money. The following year, Congress passed relief bills to reimburse the fired travel-office workers for legal expenses they incurred in the amount of $150,000. A separate relief bill for Dale reimbursed him $500,000.

While none of the investigations implicated the president in the firings, Hillary Clinton would eventually become a subject of speculation about her role in the dismantling of the travel office. On January 5, 1996, a memo surfaced that was written two years earlier by Watkins. The memo stated that the First Lady was responsible for the firings and that "there would be hell to pay" from her if he and McLarty did not fire the travel-office staff. *New York Times* columnist William Safire wrote on January 8, 1996, that the nation was coming to the "sad realization that our First Lady—a woman of undoubted talents who was a role model for many in her generation—is a congenital liar." Two years later, the final report of the OIC exonerated Hillary Clinton of any criminal wrongdoing or direct involvement in the firing of the travel-office personnel, even though she had clearly expressed to White House staff that she wanted the workers replaced.

On July 20, 1993, in the early months of the Travelgate story, Foster, the deputy White House counsel, the president's longtime friend, and a former law partner of the First Lady in the Rose Law Firm, was found dead in a Northern Virginia park along the Potomac River. The cause of death was ruled a suicide, but extreme critics of the Clintons, including televangelist and onetime presidential candidate Pat Robertson and Reverend Jerry Falwell of Liberty University, asserted Foster may have been murdered to cover up White House wrongdoing in the Whitewater and Travelgate affairs.

The exploitation of Foster's death added a bizarre layer to the Whitewater and Travelgate stories. Within months several conservative foes of the president teamed up in a half-hour videotape, *Bill Clinton's Circle of Power,* produced by Patrick Matrisciana, founder of Citizens for Honest Government, and featuring Larry Nichols, a former Arkansas state employee fired by Clinton, who linked Bill Clinton to two dozen deaths caused by suicides, murders, and apparent accidents, suggesting that some of these individuals were silenced to cover up Clinton's involvement in a drug-smuggling operation in Mena, Arkansas, and other matters. Nichols called Clinton a "pathological liar." Falwell promoted *Bill Clinton's Circle of Power* on his *Old-Time Gospel Hour* television program.

Nichols had a history with Clinton and played a key role in the scandals that swirled around him during his years as governor. Clinton had fired Nichols from a state job as director of marketing for the Arkansas Development Finance Administration (ADFA) in 1988, when Associated Press stories linked Nichols to support for the contra rebels in Nicaragua. Nichols, while on the job as a state employee, had made hundreds of telephone calls to Nicaragua at the state's expense. Later he faced theft charges in Arkansas related to the sale of satellite television components that were never delivered. On October 19, 1990, Nichols filed a $3 million lawsuit against Clinton and held a news conference that included revelations of what he called the largest scandal ever perpetrated on the people of Arkansas. Nichols alleged that Clinton had misused ADFA funds and given the money to a string of mistresses, of whom he named five, including Gennifer Flowers, a nightclub singer, and two former beauty pageant winners who served as Miss Arkansas, including one who became Miss America.

When Clinton became a serious candidate for president in 1992, Nichols and Flowers sold their stories to the *Star* tabloid. Flowers claimed to have had a 12-year sexual relationship with Clinton. She was paid $150,000 for the story, and Nichols reportedly was paid $50,000 to describe in more detail the charges made in his lawsuit about Clinton using state funds on mistresses. Flowers had taped conversations with Clinton, which the *Star* billed as "love tapes." In early 1994, shortly after the appearance of the *Circle of Power* video, Matrisciana, with financial backing from Falwell's Liberty Alliance, produced *The Clinton Chronicles,* an 80-minute indictment of Clinton's alleged unethical and illegal activities, which included the *Circle of Power* theme of "suspicious" deaths tied to Clinton and expanded into other areas of alleged misconduct and moral lapses on the part of the president, including cocaine addiction, drug smuggling, womanizing, payoffs, the shredding of incriminating documents, and laundering of drug money through the ADFA. The Rose Law Firm figured in much of the nefarious schemes presented in the video. As in the earlier video, the main narration was supplied by Larry Nichols.

Copies of *The Clinton Chronicles* video were distributed to members of Congress. Approximately 300,000 copies were sold or given away. On June 30, 1994, Representative Philip M. Crane (R-Ill.) sent a cover letter with copies of the tape to his Republican colleagues in the House urging them to watch it. "If full documentary evidence of these allegations is ever

Shown here from left to right are Gennifer Flowers, who claimed in 1992 to be then-presidential candidate Bill Clinton's lover; Monica Lewinsky, who figured in the allegation of a cover-up by Bill Clinton; and Paula Jones, who accused Clinton of sexual harassment. (Associated Press)

allowed to be officially investigated and is ever confirmed," he wrote, "the Clinton Administration will be short-lived indeed." *The Clinton Chronicles* included the remarks of former representative William Dannemeyer (R-Calif.), who referred to the president as a pathological liar who should be impeached and urged Congress to investigate. Falwell produced a half-hour infomercial to promote *The Clinton Chronicles* that featured a blacked-out silhouette of a man described as an "investigative reporter." When Falwell asked the man why he wanted to conceal his identity, he said that two people he had planned to interview about Clinton's activities had been killed in separate plane crashes before they could be interviewed. The blackened silhouette concluded, "Jerry, are these coincidences? I don't think so." Later a reporter, Murray Waas, recognized the voice of the mystery man and identified him as none other than Matrisciana, the video's producer.

The mainstream news media had little trouble discounting and disproving virtually every aspect of the charges in *The Clinton Chronicles* and exposed Nichols's motives. Those promoting the video, especially Falwell, responded that the "liberal bias" of the media was protecting the president and was part of the cover-up. *The Clinton Chronicles,* however, despite its amazing tissue of lies and innuendo, did provide additional exposure of alleged extramarital affairs between Clinton and Flowers, Jones, and other named women. This part of the tape would come back to haunt the president.

The Special Prosecutors

In January 1994 as Whitewater matters and Foster's death dominated the news, Republicans, led by Senate minority leader Robert J. Dole (R-Kan.), called for the creation of an independent counsel to investigate. Congress began moving on a bill to reestablish the defunct Office of Independent Counsel, whose authorization had expired in 1992. Attorney General Janet Reno did not wait for the passage of the bill and appointed a special prosecutor, Robert B. Fiske Jr., under her own authority to provide an arm's-length independent investigation of Whitewater, Foster's death, and charges that the president had interfered with the investigation of the RTC as it examined the circumstances of Jim McDougal's defunct Madison Guaranty Savings and Loan. A 63-year-old New York Republican with impeccable nonpartisan credentials, Fiske had a distinguished career in government service and private practice. His appointment was highly praised by Republicans and Democrats alike. Fiske was given jurisdiction over the investigation of any federal crimes that Bill or Hillary Clinton may have committed in their relationships with Madison Guaranty Savings and Loan, the Whitewater Development Corporation, and Capital Management

Services, a small firm in Arkansas run by David Hale, a former municipal court judge, banker, and Little Rock businessman. Hale was the central witness in the trial of Jim and Susan McDougal. He pleaded guilty on March 22, 1994, to conspiring to defraud the Small Business Administration by stealing funds from a dummy business he had established. He was sentenced to jail but agreed to cooperate with Whitewater investigators.

Fiske would eventually become the forgotten man of the Whitewater investigations who was criticized by some Republicans for not finding the Clintons guilty of wrongdoing and for finding that Foster's death was a suicide. Fiske did not believe that the country would be well served by a lengthy investigation of a sitting president. He assembled his team and got to work quickly. On June 30, 1994, Fiske issued a preliminary report that cleared the Clintons of any wrongdoing or interference with the RTC and presented a thorough report on Foster's suicide. Fiske was quickly attacked by conservative Republicans as someone who was simply trying to protect the president. Many of Clinton's critics, despite the evidence, were not willing to believe that Foster had committed suicide.

On the same day Fiske issued his report, Clinton signed into law the Independent Counsel Reauthorization Act of 1994, which recreated the Office of Independent Counsel, first established in 1978. Clinton had earlier campaigned on the need for this law. The new law placed the selection of the independent counsel in the hands of a panel of judges in the Special Division of the United States Court of Appeals for the District of Columbia Circuit. Reno hoped that Fiske would be appointed to continue his investigations, but in what turned out to be a fateful and disastrous consequence for the Clintons, on August 5, 1994, Judge David Sentelle, a conservative Republican appointee, surprised everyone involved in the case when he replaced Fiske with Kenneth W. Starr, who would assume the head of the newly reestablished Office of Independent Counsel. Starr, a 48-year-old former

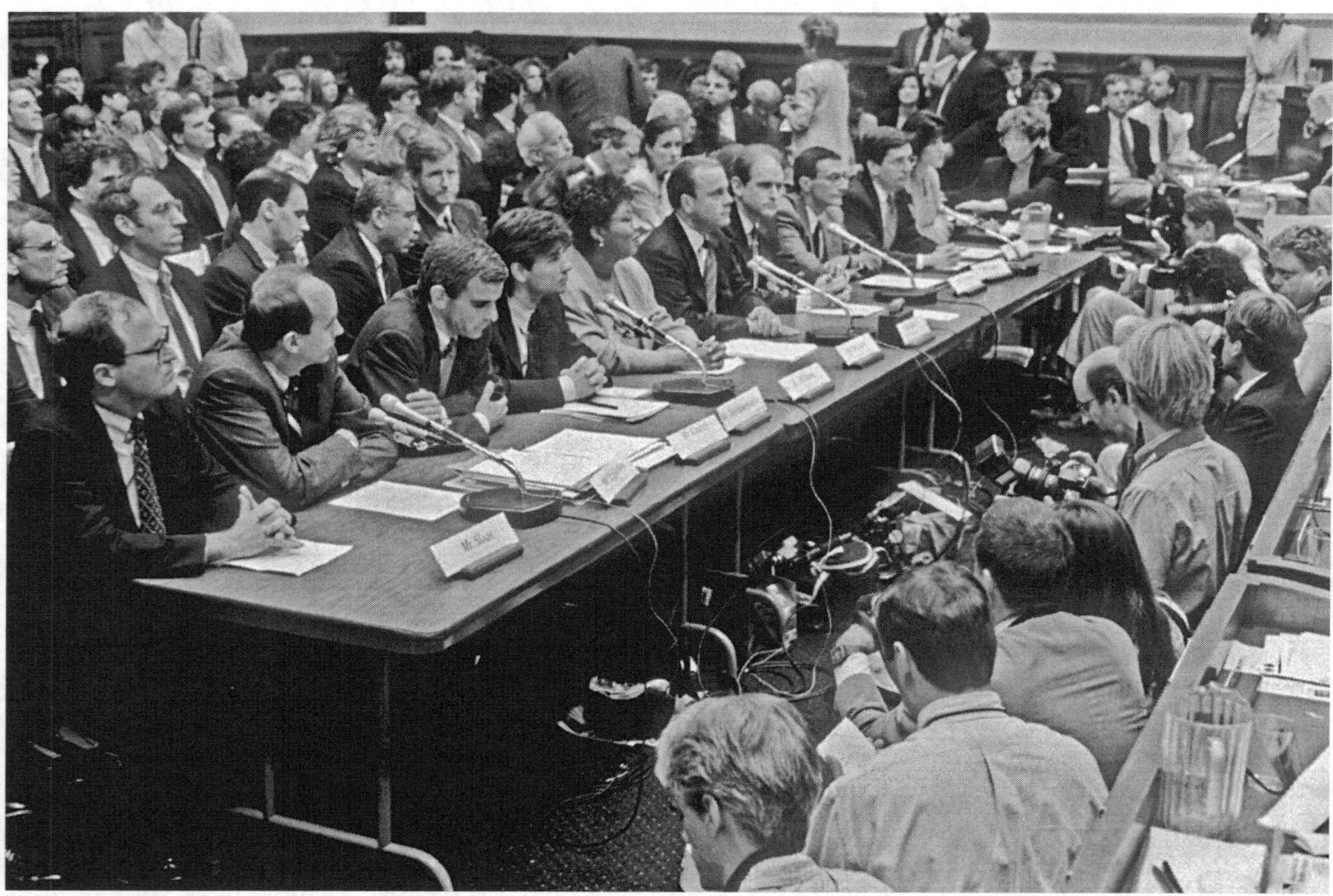

White House aides, from left, Clifford Sloan, Neil Eggleston, Bruce Lindsey, George Stephanopoulos, Margaret Ann Williams, Mack McLarty, Harold Ickes, John Podesta, Mark Gearan, and Lisa Caputo prepare to testify at a hearing on the Whitewater affair at the House Banking Committee on Capitol Hill, July 28, 1994. Hearings were opened to see if Treasury officials and the White House interfered with the Resolution Trust Corporation probe of the failed Madison Guaranty Savings and Loan in which the Clintons and James McDougal were partners. (Greg Gribson/Associated Press)

Court of Appeals judge appointed by President Ronald Reagan in 1983, had served as solicitor general from 1989 to 1993 in the George H. W. Bush administration.

Sentelle said he replaced Fiske because he was "compromised" by having been appointed by Reno, who was a member of the Clinton administration. The appointment of Starr was controversial from the beginning, despite his impeccable credentials. Just a week after his appointment, the *Washington Post* broke the story that Sentelle, a native North Carolinian, had gone to Capitol Hill to lunch with two old friends, the Republican senators from North Carolina, Jesse Helms and Lauch Faircloth, both of whom were critics of the Fiske investigation. What the *Post* could not report, however, was the actual conversation at that lunch. Sentelle later denied that they discussed Starr or Fiske. In an interview with author Ken Gormley years after he left office, Clinton described his feelings when Starr was appointed. "You know," Clinton said, "after Starr came in, there was no pretext about what he and all of his supporters were doing. I felt they were Wile E. Coyote in the pack and I was the Road Runner. And the chase was on."

Congressional Investigations

Various congressional committees in both the House and Senate did not wait for the completion of the Fiske and Starr investigations before launching inquiries of their own. An investigation into Foster's death by Representative William F. Clinger Jr. (R-Pa.), the ranking member of the House Committee on Government Operations, reported on August 12 that "all available facts lead to the undeniable conclusion that Vincent W. Foster, Jr. took his own life in Fort Marcy Park, Virginia on July 20, 1993." The Senate Committee on Banking, Housing, and Urban Affairs conducted its own investigation in late 1994 of Foster's death, basically reviewing the Park Police investigation that had originally determined Foster's death was a suicide. The Senate committee issued its report on January 3, 1995, just days before the opening of the 104th Congress, concluding once again that Foster died by his own hand.

The chairman of the House Banking, Finance, and Urban Affairs Committee, Henry Gonzalez (D-Tex.), resisted the idea of having his committee investigate Whitewater, but in the summer of 1994, he allowed the investigation to go forward. Republicans on the House banking committee wanted to continue the investigation of Foster's death, but Gonzalez refused to revisit the matter. The committee voted along party lines with Democrats opposed to another Foster probe while all Republicans on the committee voted in favor of further investigation. Gonzalez and the ranking member of the banking committee, Representative Jim Leach (R-Iowa), were a study in opposites, with Gonzalez seeking to limit the investigation and Leach demanding a full broad inquiry into the president's "arrogance of power." Leach had Republican staff members of the banking committee conduct their own investigation. Partisan tempers flared frequently on the topic of Whitewater. On July 29, 1994, Representative Peter King (R-N.Y.), a member of the banking committee, took to the floor of the House in a one-minute speech to complain about the tactics of the committee's Democratic majority. He accused Gonzalez of trying to "cover up the truth from the American people." He complained Representative Maxine Waters (D-Calif.), another committee member, had told him to "shut up" during the preceding day's hearing. King said "she is not going to tell me to shut up, she is not going to tell the American people to shut up, and I am not going to stop until we get to the root of Whitewater."

As Fiske was about to issue his preliminary report in June 1994, Gonzalez sought to have him testify before the House banking committee, but Fiske refused on the grounds that his investigation was ongoing. Playing down the Fiske report, Leach claimed that it only covered 5 percent of Whitewater matters. Holding congressional investigations simultaneously with the Fiske investigation presented problems for all involved. Fiske cautioned the House committee to avoid calling as witnesses Hubbell and several people connected to the RTC investigations because the congressional hearings might jeopardize the work of the special prosecutor.

With Republicans taking control of the House and Senate in 1995, the impediment of being in the minority was gone, and Republicans moved ahead with an active agenda of investigation into Whitewater. Leach became chairman of the House Banking, Finance and Urban Affairs Committee (which changed its name in 1995 to the House Banking and Financial Services Committee) and launched his own brief investigation beginning on August 5, 1995, focusing on matters of alleged White House interference with the RTC investigation of Jim McDougal's Madison Guaranty Savings and Loan. Nothing conclusive came from these hearings, but the following year Leach's committee looked into charges of guns-for-drugs deals with ties to the CIA and the contra rebels of Nicaragua at Mena Intermountain Regional Airport in Mena, Arkansas, some of which supposedly involved Clinton when he was governor.

The Senate took the lead with the most significant Whitewater investigation when Senator Alfonse D'Amato (R-N.Y.) became chairman of the Senate Banking, Housing and Urban Affairs Committee in 1995 and launched the Senate Special Committee to

Senate Whitewater Committee chairman Alfonse D'Amato, left, speaks with majority counsel Michael Chertoff during hearings, December 13, 1995. (Associated Press)

Investigate Whitewater Development Corporation and Related Matters. This special committee, commonly known as the Special Whitewater Committee, provided much ammunition for the news media as D'Amato became Clinton's chief adversary in the Senate, conducting his special committee as an anti-Clinton crusade. D'Amato's committee eventually issued a 690-page report that accused the president of abuse of power. Almost half of the report is written by the Democratic minority on the committee, led by ranking member Paul Sarbanes (D-Md.), which concluded that the president and the First Lady were not guilty of any wrongdoing in Whitewater or in relation to Foster's death. The report graphically demonstrated how partisan the investigation was, with completely different conclusions coming from the same set of facts.

The Whitewater committee was established by Senate Resolution 120 on May 17, 1995, with funding of $950,000. The Senate voted for the establishment of the committee by a vote of 96–3, showing broad bipartisan support for the investigation when the work first began. The committee lasted 347 days, held 60 days of public hearings, and deposed 274 witnesses, of which 139 testified before the committee. The committee examined a million pages of documents. In early 1996 the committee sought to extend its work and sought more funding. By this time many in the Senate, especially Democrats, had had enough of the committee. A compromise increased the funding for the investigation to a total of $1.4 million but fixed a termination date for the investigation of June 17, 1996.

The tenor of the Special Whitewater Committee was sensationalist from the beginning. At the opening hearing on July 18, 1995, Senator Frank Murkowski (R-Alaska) held up Foster's briefcase and tipped it upside down to show that nothing was inside, a reference to the fact that White House staff and possibly Hillary Clinton had gone through Foster's files after he was found dead. Murkowski was suspicious of the fact that a suicide note was not found until several days after Foster died. Other Republican members of the committee followed with a series of charges of wrongdoing, many connected to the disappearance of Foster's files. Eventually the committee returned to new conspiracy theories about Foster's death, even though the charges came mainly from a new video, *Unanswered: The Death of Vincent Foster,* involving Nichols, Clinton's Arkansas nemesis, and produced by Citizens for Honest Government, the same organization that had produced the earlier *Bill Clinton's Circle of Power* and *The Clinton Chronicles.* The overall investigation was held in phases, including the Foster phase, the Washington phase, and the Arkansas phase, as well as investigations into Rose Law Firm records and other matters.

In the majority report conclusion regarding Foster's death, the committee stated:

> After careful review of all the evidence, the Special Committee concludes that senior White House officials, particularly members of the Office of the White House Counsel, engaged in a pattern of highly improper conduct in their handling of the documents in Mr. Foster's office following his death. These senior White House officials deliberately prevented career law enforcement officers from the Department of Justice and Park Police from fully investigating the circumstances surrounding Mr. Foster's death, including whether he took his own life because of troubling matters involving the President and Mrs. Clinton. . . . This pattern of concealment and obstruction continues even to the present day.

The Democratic minority saw things differently and presented a detailed point-by-point rebuttal to the majority position on every aspect of the investigation.

> The Majority's pattern throughout these hearings has been to construct conclusions first and then to discard the facts as they become inconvenient. One after another, the partisan conspiracy theories about Whitewater—from the alleged shredding of documents at the Rose Law Firm, to the so-called "mystery phone call," to the "all-important" White House e-mails—have turned into dry holes. Lacking any cred-

ible case against the President, the Majority is now engaging in a blatantly political game of "tag" by tarring several witnesses with unsupportable suggestions of perjury in a bid to grab media attention.

The Process of Presidential Impeachment

The impeachment process described in several places in the U.S. Constitution had been used 13 times before 1998, when President Clinton was impeached. Most impeachment cases involved federal judges, as well as other officials, including one senator, William Blount, in 1797, and an associate justice of the Supreme Court, Samuel Chase, in 1804. Seven judges were convicted and removed from office, four were acquitted, and two resigned before their Senate trials. Only once before had a president of the United States been impeached: Andrew Johnson in 1868. Johnson was acquitted in the Senate, one vote shy of the two-thirds needed to convict. In the case of Nixon, the House Committee on the Judiciary voted on July 28, 1974, to send articles of impeachment to the floor of the House. Nixon resigned from office on August 9, 1974, before the House took action to impeach him.

Article 1, Section 2, of the Constitution gives the House of Representatives the "sole Power of Impeachment"; Section 3 gives the Senate the "sole Power to try all Impeachments" and states that if the president is impeached the chief justice presides over the trial. No conviction is possible without the "Concurrence of two thirds of the Members present." Article 2, Section 4, states that the president, the vice president, and all civil officers "shall be removed from office on Impeachment for, and conviction of, Treason, Bribery, and other High Crimes and Misdemeanors." While the Constitution is clear on the roles of each house of Congress in the impeachment process, the reasons for removing a president remained murky and subject to much legal debate, considerable public confusion, and the difficulty of appearing fair when the vote is along party lines.

The most important thing that can be said about an impeachment is that it does not resemble a conventional civil trial, especially those portrayed on television and in crime novels, where most Americans not trained in law get their impressions of the process. As the public watched the Clinton impeachment process unfold, many of the so-called experts appearing on television to explain the process based their understanding on the procedures used before petit juries, where charges are brought by a prosecutor, the defendant is indicted, the defendant has a lawyer, and the case goes before a judge and a jury of ordinary citizens picked from a pool of jurors. The jurors determine guilt or innocence based on their understanding of the case as it is presented to them and from any directives given by the judge before the jury begins deliberations. Once convicted, the judge passes sentence, often based on legal guidelines for the crime in question.

In the case of an impeachment, the charges against the president are brought by members of the House Judiciary Committee in a highly charged political atmosphere. The charges could come after a criminal investigation conducted outside of Congress, as was true with the Office of Independent Counsel investigation led by Starr, but that is not a requirement. It is the House that is the constitutional investigating body, with power to conduct its own investigation. The charges against the president must be shaped into articles of impeachment that describe the crime in constitutional terms as well as in the language of conventional law. The House then votes on the articles. Although it contains many individuals who have considerable legal experience as lawyers, prosecutors, and judges, the House must weigh politics as well as law, and the particular meaning of impeachable offenses as described in the Constitution. The House must decide if the charges seem fair, if they are justified, and if there is a good chance that the articles of impeachment can successfully be brought to trial in the Senate.

Once the president is impeached, the Senate trial does not represent anything known in a conventional court of law. The jury and the judges become one and the same in the Senate. The presiding officer is the chief justice of the United States, but he has little to do in the proceedings other than to keep order. The rules of the trial and how it is conducted, including who is called as a witness, the circumstances of the testimony, and allowable evidence, are all decided by the members of the Senate. The "prosecutors" in the Senate trial are a team of House members, known as House managers, consisting of members of the Judiciary Committee that originated the charges. While in conventional cases courts and juries determine guilt or innocence and then determine a range of potential punishments, in an impeachment there is only one result if convicted: removal from office.

Journalists covering the Clinton impeachment looked for analogies with the Watergate investigation of Nixon and generally ignored the only complete impeachment of a president in 1868, which seemed too long ago, too arcane, and not sufficiently relevant to the Clinton case. Likewise House members and staff tended to look at the Nixon example as their model. While this was helpful in determining the procedures followed by the Judiciary Committee, it was not a model for the actual impeachment or the Senate trial.

The Constitution describes the types of crimes for which a president or other government official can be impeached. In 1998, the meaning of "High Crimes and Misdemeanors" came under new scrutiny as members of Congress, the news media, and the public grappled with how the constitutional language fit with lying about a private sexual affair between consenting adults.

The Albatross of the Paula Jones Lawsuit

Had it not been for the Paula Jones sexual-harassment lawsuit, first filed on May 6, 1994, there may not have been sufficient grounds for an investigation of Clinton's sexual affair with Lewinsky. It was during the Jones case that the president first lied about having sexual relations with Lewinsky in testimony under oath, when questioned by lawyers representing Jones on January 17, 1998. The Jones case was an albatross for Clinton throughout his presidency. On August 10, 1994, the president filed a motion to dismiss the Jones lawsuit on grounds of presidential immunity, and in December that year U.S. District Judge Susan Webber Wright, in Little Rock, Arkansas, ruled that the trial could not take place until the president left office. Jones's lawyer appealed the decision to the U.S. Court of Appeals for the Eighth Circuit, in St. Louis, and on January 9, 1996, a three-judge panel ruled that the Jones case could go to trial. A week later, Clinton asked the Supreme Court to delay the trial until he was out of office. The Supreme Court heard the case on January 13, 1997. In a unanimous decision, handed down on May 27, 1997, the high court concluded that the Constitution did not protect the president from civil litigation relating to actions committed before he entered office (*Clinton v. Jones* 520 U.S. 681 [1997]). The long-delayed suit, with new lawyers for Jones, switched strategies in December 1997, reducing the amount of damages sought from $700,000 to $525,000, with Jones dropping charges against Clinton that he had defamed her.

When Starr got formal approval to expand his Whitewater investigation into possible charges of perjury and obstruction of justice in the Lewinsky affair, the Jones case was catapulted into a new realm. The connection was made between the two cases because Linda Tripp, who befriended Lewinsky and learned intimate details of the president's affair, had briefed Jones's lawyers on the affair between Lewinsky and the president. It was during the president's interview with Jones's lawyers on January 17, 1998, that the Lewinsky affair came up and the president denied the affair while under oath. Just 12 days after Clinton's deposition in the Jones case, Judge Wright ruled to exclude all evidence relating to Lewinsky from the Jones case because of the "inevitable effect of disrupting" the OIC investigation.

In February 1998, with the Starr investigation into the president's affair with Lewinsky under way, the president's lawyers asked Wright to dismiss the Jones case. In arguing against dismissal, Jones's attorneys filed 700 pages of documents alleging the president had made sexual advances toward other women and schemed to suppress the fact. Furthermore, without first-hand evidence, Jones's lawyers claimed Clinton had raped a woman in 1970. On April 1, 1998, Wright dismissed the Jones lawsuit, expressing exasperation with Jones and her team of lawyers: "Whether other women may have been subjected to workplace harassment, and whether such evidence has allegedly been suppressed, does not change the fact that plaintiff has failed to demonstrate that she has a case worthy of submitting to a jury." Wright's ruling did not take into account the truth or falsity of the charge that Clinton, when governor of Arkansas, had made sexual advances toward Jones in a hotel room in 1991. What she ruled on was the legal definition of sexual harassment. Jones failed to supply proof that she had been harmed in the workplace by the incident. The proof Jones cited was that her desk had been moved after the incident, that she was discouraged from applying for other state jobs, and that she did not receive flowers on Secretary's Day in 1992. Evidence showed that she kept her job and received satisfactory evaluations, cost-of-living increases, and one merit raise in the 19 months she remained at work following the 1991 incident.

Jones and her lawyers announced their plans to appeal Wright's dismissal of the case, and they did so on July 31, 1998. By October the U.S. Court of Appeals for the Eighth Circuit had heard the case and had taken it under advisement. While the court deliberated, Clinton reached an out-of-court settlement with Jones on November 13, 1998, paying her $850,000 while acknowledging no wrongdoing on his part. In early December the appeals court dismissed the case as a result of the settlement.

Opening the Impeachment Inquiry in the House Judiciary Committee

Once the Lewinsky affair became public in mid-January 1998, the OIC immediately began its investigation into the matter. Within weeks Starr announced that the inquiry was "moving very quickly and we've made very significant progress." Editorials in major newspapers raised the issue that perhaps the president should resign rather than face impeachment. On February 6, 1998, the president announced he would not resign.

The House Judiciary Committee, under the chairmanship of Representative Henry Hyde (R-Ill.), took preliminary steps to plan for an impeachment investigation in late January 1998, when the committee hired David Schippers, a Democrat, to be chief investigative counsel for the committee. Months before the Starr referral arrived on Capitol Hill, Judiciary Committee staff studied impeachment procedures and decided to follow the Watergate model if the referral from the OIC indicated impeachable offenses. The Judiciary Committee made plans to keep the material coming from the OIC in a special secure room in the Ford House Office Building several blocks from Capitol Hill, to limit access and avoid leaks of the information. House Republicans were divided over whether the material in the Starr referral should be made public. Speaker Newt Gingrich and Representative Bob Barr (R-Ga.) wanted the material made public, while Hyde and others thought public disclosure before an investigation by the Judiciary Committee would lead to chaos, with the news media poring over the details of the sex scandal.

On September 9, 1998, the OIC referral, soon to be known widely as the Starr Report, arrived in the House of Representatives. The 445-page document consisted of an introduction, a narrative of the events in the Lewinsky matter, and an analysis of the information that provided grounds to impeach the president. An appendix of six binders, totaling some 2,500 pages, provided detailed testimony and other supporting evidence. In addition, the House sergeant at arms received two identical sets of 17 boxes from the OIC that constituted all the material related to the investigation of the Lewinsky affair—one set for Republicans and the other set for Democrats.

Until the referral arrived, few people outside the OIC knew that it was entirely based on the Lewinsky affair, and that the only part of the referral that was originally part of the broader Whitewater investigation was the president's deposition in the Jones lawsuit. The OIC material was placed in the secure room, with a keypad combination lock on the door and armed Capitol Police officers guarding the door and keeping the hallway outside the room free of any unauthorized persons. Anyone going in or out of the room had to sign in. Nothing could be removed from the room, and no cameras, telephones, or recording devices could be taken in. Female members of the Judiciary Committee were even required to leave their purses outside. Republican and Democratic members of the Judiciary Committee had separate adjoining offices where they could listen to tape-recorded files.

On September 11, 1998, the House voted to receive the Starr referral and release to the public the first 445 pages, consisting of the introduction, narrative, and possible impeachable charges. The pressure to release more information to the public came from many members of Congress as well as from the news media. Gingrich and Richard Gephardt (D-Mo.), the House minority leader, decided to release parts of the OIC files. Additional staff members were allowed access to the files to help make the determination of what should become public information. But staff and members of the House found it difficult to decide what should be released and what should remain sealed. Schippers, chief investigative counsel of the Judiciary Committee, described the process as "just a mess." He wrote, "As it turned out, the staffers spent at least a full week, almost twenty-four hours a day, pulling material, taking words out, fighting over what they were going to leave in and take out."

The introduction to the Starr Report listed the charges against President Clinton and concluded that the president had

- lied under oath at a civil deposition while he was a defendant in a sexual-harassment lawsuit [Paula Jones suit deposition, Jan. 17, 1998];
- attempted to influence the testimony of a potential witness who had direct knowledge of facts that would reveal the falsity of his deposition testimony;
- attempted to obstruct justice by facilitating a witness's plan to refuse to comply with a subpoena;
- attempted to obstruct justice by encouraging a witness to file an affidavit that the President knew would be false, and then by making use of that false affidavit at his own deposition;
- lied to potential grand-jury witnesses, knowing that they would repeat those lies before a grand jury; and
- engaged in a pattern of conduct that was inconsistent with his constitutional duty to faithfully execute the laws.

> The evidence shows that these acts, and others, were part of a pattern that began as an effort to prevent the disclosure of information about the president's relationship with Lewinsky and continued as an ongoing effort to prevent the information from being disclosed in an ongoing criminal investigation.

The Starr Report shocked both friends and foes of the president with its graphic details about the president's 11 documented encounters with Lewinsky. Nothing in the tabloid press could match it for explicit details. Some Republicans and Democrats criticized the OIC and the House of Representatives for allowing such lurid details to become public knowledge. Just who benefited from the disclosures in the long run is still a subject of speculation. With this kind of information dominating news-media coverage, it became difficult for the OIC and the Judiciary Committee to keep the focus of the case on perjury, witness tampering, and obstruction of justice, and not just sex.

After a week of negotiations on what additional material in the Starr referral should go public, on September 18, 1998, Hyde and Representative John Conyers (D-Mich.), the ranking member of the Judiciary Committee, decided to release about 1½ boxes of the 17 boxes of material on the Lewinsky investigation. At the same time the committee released the four-hour tape of Clinton's August 17, 1998, testimony before the grand jury in the Jones lawsuit, and more than 3,000 pages of supporting documents, which included Lewinsky's testimony containing specific details of sexual encounters with the president. Three days later another batch of material, including Clinton's testimony before the grand jury in the Lewinsky case and a photograph of Lewinsky's semen-stained dress, became public. On September 24 the committee announced that it would soon bring a resolution to the floor of the House on the matter of impeachment. The committee released another 4,600 pages of documents on October 2, including tape recordings of conversations between Lewinsky and Tripp. The stage was set to move ahead with the impeachment.

On October 5, the Judiciary Committee voted 21 to 16, on a party-line vote, to recommend to the full House the adoption of a resolution calling for an impeachment investigation. It had been left to the committee to decide the grounds for impeachment. Other charges were still possible, including those related to the earlier Whitewater matters, Travelgate, and another matter dubbed "Filegate," in which the Clinton administration allegedly obtained raw FBI files on more than 900 political appointees in the Reagan and George H. W. Bush administrations. But the committee quickly decided that the case against the president would be based on his actions stemming from the Lewinsky affair and the president's aiding and abetting Lewinsky to give false testimony in the Jones case. In his statement before the committee on October 5, Schippers laid out the case for the charges against the president by citing 15 possible felonies. He distinguished these charges from the sensationalism of the sex scandal, which he said was not the important thing. It was the president's actions as a result of the affair: "Deplorable as the numerous sexual encounters related to the evidence may be, we chose to emphasize the consequences of those acts as they affect the administration of justice and the unique role the President occupies in carrying out his oath faithfully to execute the laws of the nation."

The full House voted on October 8 for House Resolution 581, which called for a broad investigation of the president by a vote of 258 to 176, with all Republicans and 31 Democrats voting in favor of the investigation. One Independent member, Bernard Sanders (I-Vt.), voted against the resolution. In his remarks during the debate, Hyde said:

> Today we will vote on an historic resolution to begin an inquiry into whether the president has committed impeachable offenses. All of us are pulled in many directions by our political parties, by philosophy and friendships. We're pulled by many competing forces, but mostly we're moved by our consciences. We must listen to that still small voice that whispers in our ear, "Duty, duty, duty."

Jerrold Nadler (D-N.Y.) did not think the proceedings would be fair:

> The president was not given the Starr report before it was made public, a violation of all the precedents. No debate on the committee occurred on the merits whatsoever. We spent the month on deciding what should be released and what should be kept in private. And then we heard the report of the two counsels, and then we discussed procedure, but not a minute of debate on the merits, on the evidence, on the standard of impeachment, on anything. And now, the supreme insult to the American people: an hour of debate on the House floor on whether to start for the third time in American history a formal impeachment proceeding. We debated two resolutions to name post offices yesterday for an hour and a half. An hour debate on this momentous decision: an insult to the American people, and another sign that this is not going to be fair.

Another Democrat, Robert Wexler of Florida, said:

> The global economy is crumbling, and we're talking about Monica Lewinsky! Saddam

> Hussein hides weapons, and we're talking about Monica Lewinsky! Genocide wracks Kosovo, and we're talking about Monica Lewinsky! Children cram into packed classrooms, and we're talking about Monica Lewinsky! Families can't pay their medical bills, and we're talking about Monica Lewinsky! . . . The president betrayed his wife. He did not betray the country. God help this nation if we fail to recognize the difference.

Ileana Ros-Lehtinen (R-Fla.) saw the case in terms of sexual-harassment laws applying equally to the president: "Our laws promise a remedy against sexual harassment. But if we say that lying about sex in court is acceptable or even expected, then we have made our sexual harassment laws nothing more than a false promise; a fraud upon our society, upon our legal system and upon women." The resolution gave the Judiciary Committee as a whole or any subcommittee the power to subpoena and interrogate witnesses. The language of the resolution made no specific reference to the Lewinsky affair or any potential charge that had come from the Starr referral. It said simply that the committee "is authorized and directed to investigate fully and completely whether sufficient grounds exist for the House of Representatives to exercise its constitutional power to impeach William Jefferson Clinton, President of the United States of America."

The vote to investigate the president came just a month before the midterm congressional elections on

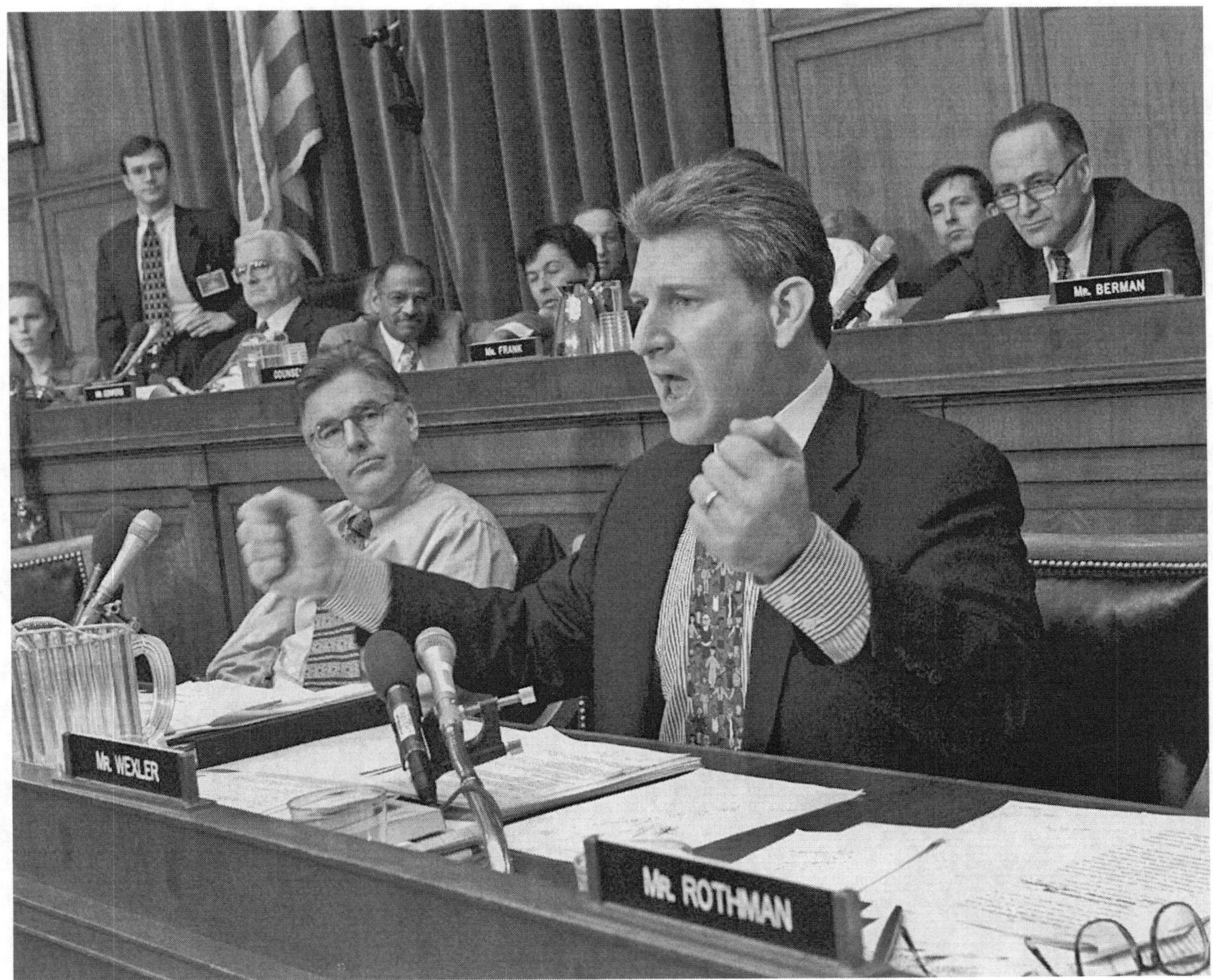

Representative Robert Wexler (D-Fla.) argues against President Clinton's impeachment, December 12, 1998. (© Susana Raab/CORBIS)

November 3, 1998. As the campaigns came down to the wire, Republican strategy shifted dramatically in a $10 million blitz of television ads directed against Democratic candidates over the president's affair with Lewinsky. In the House, Speaker Gingrich and Majority Leader Tom DeLay (R-Tex.) urged the Republican caucus to keep a united front on the impeachment question. But the strategy backfired: The Democrats picked up five seats in the House, and Republicans failed to achieve the 60-vote super-majority they had hoped to gain in the Senate. While a gain of five House seats seems like a small victory, the party controlling the White House historically has lost an average of 27 seats in midterm elections. Given the high expectations on the part of Republicans that the scandal would give them far greater control over Congress, it turned out to be a disaster. Before 1998, there was only one other midterm congressional election since the Civil War in which the party controlling the White House gained seats in Congress, and that was in 1934, during the presidency of Franklin D. Roosevelt. Some observers saw the election as a repudiation of the efforts to impeach the president. Polls showed that two-thirds of the American people were opposed to the impeachment. But neither popularity polls nor congressional elections were sufficient to deter the investigation, and members of both parties—through their votes and their remarks during the debate on House Resolution 581—demonstrated that the impeachment was going to continue.

The repercussions of the loss put a serious strain on congressional Republicans. Three days after the election, Gingrich announced he would not be a candidate for speaker when the new House convened in January 1999. Gingrich believed the sex scandal would destroy Clinton and help build a long period of Republican rule in Congress, similar to the 40 years that Democrats had controlled the House. But Gingrich's problems stemmed from more than his miscalculation about the Lewinsky scandal. He had fallen out of favor with members of his own party over missteps in his leadership going back to the 1995 shutdown of the government, ethics charges that plagued him throughout his tenure, and the passage of an omnibus appropriations bill in late 1998 that undercut the Republican agenda.

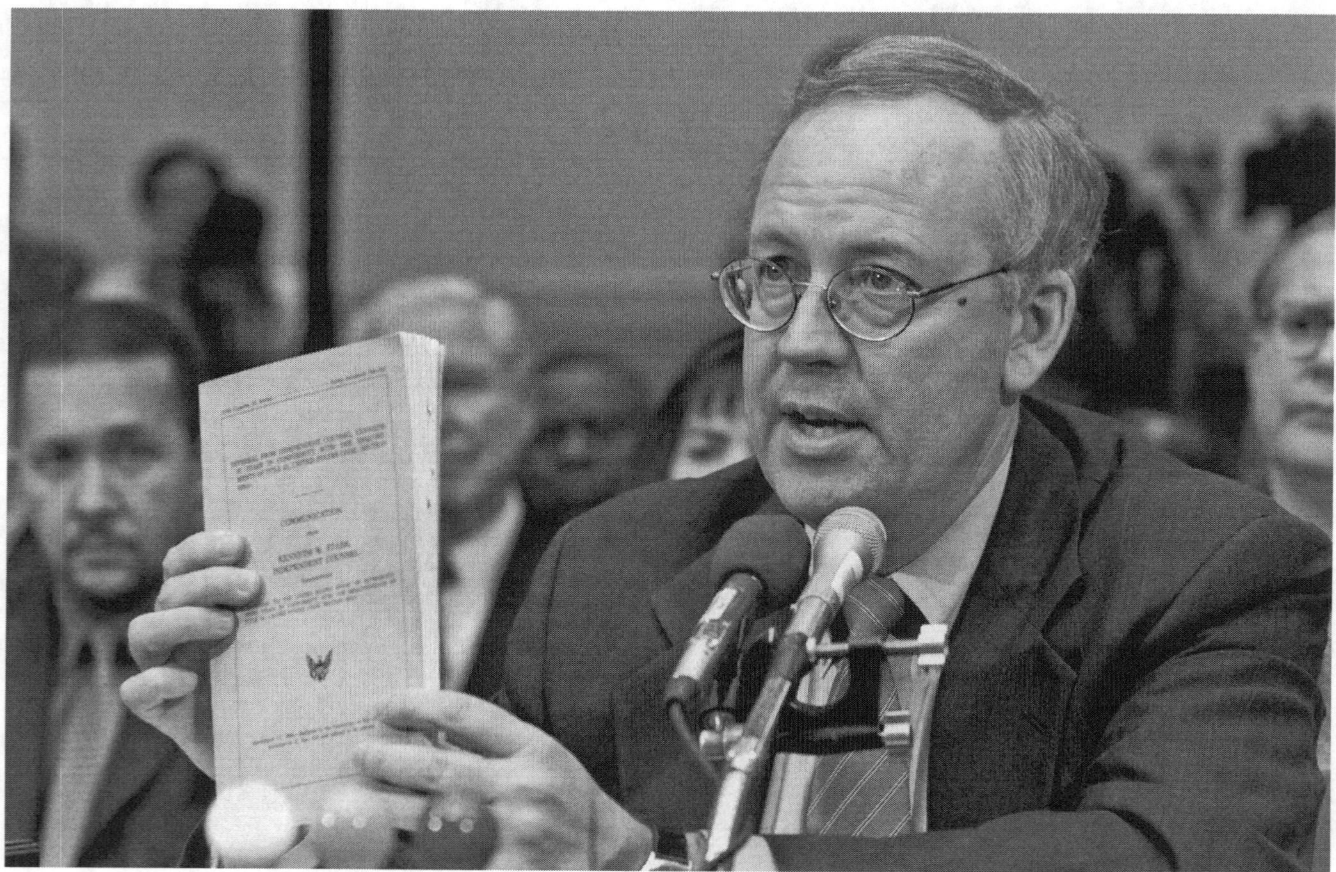

Independent Counsel Kenneth Starr refers to his report to Congress during a Capitol Hill hearing on Clinton's impeachment. (Doug Mills/Associated Press)

On November 5, 1998, Hyde, on behalf of the House Judiciary Committee, sent a list of 81 questions to Clinton asking him to admit or deny the facts laid out in the Starr Report. None of the questions asked the president directly if he had had sexual relations with Lewinsky. The committee lawyers purposely played down the details regarding the actual sex acts as the purpose of their inquiry and focused instead on potential perjury and obstruction-of-justice charges, with the heart of the matter being the president's attempts to influence Lewinsky's testimony in the Jones case. Questions 31 through 37 demonstrate the tone and character of the Hyde letter:

31. Do you admit or deny that on or about January 7, 1998, you had a discussion with Vernon Jordan in which he mentioned that he was assisting Monica Lewinsky in finding a job in New York?
32. Do you admit or deny that you viewed a copy of the affidavit executed by Monica Lewinsky on January 7, 1998, in the case of *Jones v. Clinton,* prior to your deposition in that case?
33. Do you admit or deny that you had knowledge that your counsel viewed a copy of the affidavit executed by Monica Lewinsky on January 7, 1998, in the case of *Jones v. Clinton,* prior to your deposition in that case?
34. Do you admit or deny that you had knowledge that any facts or assertions contained in the affidavit executed by Monica Lewinsky on January 7, 1998, in the case of *Jones v. Clinton* were not true?
35. Do you admit or deny that you viewed a copy of the affidavit executed by Monica Lewinsky on January 7, 1998, in the case of *Jones v. Clinton* at your deposition in that case on January 17, 1998?
36. Do you admit or deny that you had knowledge that your counsel viewed a copy of the affidavit executed by Monica Lewinsky on January 7, 1998, in the case of *Jones v. Clinton* at your deposition in that case on January 17, 1998?
37. Do you admit or deny that on or about January 9, 1998, you received a message from Vernon Jordan indicating that Monica Lewinsky had received a job offer in New York?

Clinton and his attorneys responded to the Hyde letter on November 27, answering all questions, though not all of them had definitive answers. The president's answers immediately met with objections from Republicans who found the president's response overly legalistic and evasive. In the case of the key questions cited above, the president answered them as follows:

Response to Request No. 31:

I told the grand jury that I was aware that Mr. Jordan was assisting Ms. Lewinsky in her job search in connection with her move to New York. App. at 526. I have no recollection as to whether Mr. Jordan discussed it with me on or about January 7, 1998.

Response to Request Nos. 32 and 33:

I do not believe I saw this affidavit before my deposition, although I cannot be absolutely sure. The record indicates that my counsel had seen the affidavit at some time prior to the deposition. *See* Dep. at 54.

Response to Request No. 34:

. . . . I was asked at my deposition in January about two paragraphs of Ms. Lewinsky's affidavit. With respect to Paragraph 6, I explained the extent to which I was able to attest to its accuracy. Dep at 202-03.

With respect to Paragraph 8, I stated in my deposition that it was true. Dep. at 204. In my August 17th grand jury testimony, I sought to explain the basis for that deposition answer. "I believe at the time that she filled out this affidavit, if she believed that the definition of sexual relationship was two people having intercourse, then this is accurate." App. at 473.

Response to Request Nos. 35 and 36:

I know that Mr. Bennett saw Ms. Lewinsky's affidavit during the deposition because he read portions of it aloud at the deposition. *See* Dep. at 202. I do not recall whether I saw a copy of Ms. Lewinsky's affidavit during the deposition.

Response to Request No. 37:

At some time, I learned that Ms. Lewinsky had received a job offer in New York. However, I do not recall whether I first learned of it in a message from Mr. Jordan or whether I learned it on that date.

On November 13, the president settled the long-standing Jones lawsuit, paying her $850,000 to drop the case with no apology for any wrongdoing on his part. The suit may have been settled, but the damage to the president's reputation continued.

Starr went before the Judiciary Committee on November 19 in a grueling 10-hour session where he came under fire from Democrats on the committee. Starr began with a 58-page prepared statement that outlined the charges against the president in the Jones case and the Lewinsky affair. "In short," he said, "the evidence suggests that the president repeatedly used the machinery of government and the powers of his office to conceal his relationship with Monica Lewinsky from the American people, from the judicial process in the Jones case, and from the grand jury." Starr gave a long recitation of the successes the OIC had had in prosecuting criminals in Whitewater matters related to the McDougals' Madison Guaranty Savings and Loan. Starr stopped short of connecting the president or the First Lady to any of the criminal charges in Whitewater, other than to suggest a pattern of deception. In the matter of both the White House Travel Office and Filegate, Starr said the president was not involved. Starr's statement made it clear that the only referrals he was making to the committee regarding possible impeachable offenses were strictly related to Lewinsky/Jones matters and that the four years of Whitewater investigations, despite their success in finding criminal activity in Arkansas, were not part of the case for impeachment.

The Starr testimony provided plenty of fodder for both the president's supporters and opponents. Democrats on the committee criticized Starr for not announcing sooner that his Whitewater investigations were all but abandoned months before. The OIC had kept silent through the midterm elections. During the questions that followed Starr's statement, the president's personal lawyer, David Kendall, got Starr to acknowledge that he never met Lewinsky during the whole eight months of the investigation and had never asked her a single question. In a blow to Starr, Sam Dash, the ethics adviser for the OIC, resigned in protest that Starr's statement had crossed the line into an advocacy position for impeachment.

On December 8 and 9, Clinton's lawyers who would lead the impeachment defense, Gregory Craig and White House counsel Charles Ruff, and three panels of witnesses made the case against impeachment before the Judiciary Committee. The first panel of experts addressed the topic "Historical Precedents and Constitutional Standards." The consensus of this panel, which included former U.S. attorney general Nicholas Katzenbach, Princeton history professor Sean Wilentz, Harvard professor Samuel Beer, and Yale Law professor Bruce Ackerman, was that the charges did not rise to impeachable offenses. The second panel dealt with the topic of "Abuse of Power." The panel consisted of three people who were members of the House Judiciary Committee during the impeachment debate regarding Nixon in 1974: former representatives Elizabeth Holtzman (D-N.Y.), Robert Drinan (D-Mass.), and Wayne Owens (D-Utah). All argued that Clinton's behavior did not rise to the level of impeachable offenses. The third panel discussed "How to Evaluate the Evidence," with testimony from James Hamilton, former assistant chief counsel to the Senate Watergate committee, and Richard Ben-Veniste, former assistant special prosecutor and chief of the Watergate task force. Hamilton argued that impeachment should be reserved for "great and dangerous offenses against the state," as the Founders envisioned it. He said Clinton's lying to the public and to his cabinet was wrong and disgraceful but not a danger to the state. Ben-Veniste said the impeachment was driven by partisanship that would damage the political process:

> I confess that I have spent more than one sleepless night considering whether anything that I can say will help extricate us all from the terrible mess that we're in. In my view, this process has suffered from too much partisanship, too much hypocrisy, too much sensationalism, and too little time for reflection. I ask whether impeachment will become still another arrow in the quiver of the warrior class of ever-more-truculent partisan politicians in Washington. If this is so, will we ever see an end to the gamesmanship of gotcha and payback that has already taken such a toll in the civility and comity within these hallowed halls?

On the second day of the hearing, the final panel on "Prosecutorial Standards" consisted of former U.S. attorney Thomas Sullivan, New York University Law School professor Ronald Noble, former Watergate taskforce leader Richard Davis, former acting deputy attorney general Edward Dennis, and former Massachusetts governor William Weld. Sullivan argued that in the "federal criminal justice system, indictments for obstruction of justice and perjury are relatively rare." In the matter of perjury, Sullivan said, "The law of perjury can be particularly arcane, including the requirements that the government prove beyond a reasonable doubt that the defendant knew his testimony to be false at the time he or she testified, that the alleged false testimony was material, and that any ambiguity or uncertainty about what the question or answer meant must be construed in favor of the defendant."

Noble argued that federal prosecutors and federal agents "ought to stay out of the private sexual lives of consenting adults." He gave 10 reasons why the charges against the president made a weak case:

> One, the alleged perjury occurred in a civil deposition and concerned private, lawful sexual conduct between consenting adults. Two, the alleged perjured testimony was deemed

inadmissible by the trial judge. Three, that evidence arguably was dismissed as immaterial by the trial judge. Four, in any event, the alleged perjured testimony was at most marginally relevant. Five, the alleged perjured testimony did not affect the outcome of the case. Six, the parties settled and the court dismissed the underlying civil suit. Seven, the settlement of the suit prevented the appellate court from ruling on the dismissal and on the materiality of the alleged perjured testimony. Eight, the theoretically harmed party knew of the alleged perjury prior to settlement. Nine, alleged—and I say, alleged—political enemies of the defendant funded the plaintiff's suit. Ten, a federal government informant conspired with one of the civil litigants to trap the alleged perjurer into perjuring himself.

President Bill Clinton gives video testimony before the grand jury empaneled by the U.S. District Court for the District of Columbia, August 17, 1998. (© Wally McNamee/CORBIS)

Dennis argued that moral outrage was insufficient grounds for an impeachment even if the moral outrage was justified. Weld, a former federal prosecutor during the Reagan administration, said, "I am pretty well convinced that adultery, fornication or even a false denial—false, I'm assuming perjury here—false denial of adultery or fornication—they do not constitute high crimes and misdemeanors within the meaning of the impeachment clause of the U.S. Constitution."

The final testimony on behalf of the president came from Ruff, the president's lawyer, who argued that the president's conduct—"morally reprehensible" as it was—did not constitute a high crime and misdemeanor: "Neither the president nor anyone speaking on his behalf will defend the morality of his personal conduct. The president had a wrongful relationship with Monica Lewinsky. He violated his sacred obligations to his wife and daughter. He misled his family, his friends, his colleagues and the public. And in doing so, he betrayed the trust placed in him not only by his loved ones but by the American people."

None of the panels during the two days of testimony had any particular evidence or facts related to the charges against the president, and this caused Hyde and other Republican committee members to question the value of the president's witnesses since they brought no facts to the case and did not argue the facts as presented in the Starr Report. Representative Bob Inglis (R-S.C.) complained that none of the witnesses offered anything new. Hyde asked Craig why there were no witnesses who had any firsthand knowledge of the facts in the case, and Craig replied that the president was presumed innocent until proven guilty and it was up to the committee to produce those who would testify about the facts.

As the Judiciary Committee began its deliberations on four articles of impeachment on December 11, Clinton issued another apology to the nation concerning his conduct, appearing in the White House Rose Garden to say, "Others are presenting my defense on the facts, the law and the Constitution. Nothing I can say now can add to that. What I want the American people to know, what I want the Congress to know is that I am profoundly sorry for all I have done wrong in words and deeds. I never should have misled the country, the Congress, my friends or my family. Quite simply, I gave in to my shame." On Capitol Hill many members of the Judiciary Committee left the hearing room to watch the president's remarks on television.

With the exception of Representative Lindsey Graham (R-S.C.), who voted against Article II, the 21 Republicans and 16 Democrats on the committee voted along party lines on each article of impeachment. Democrats argued that the articles were too vague and broad in language and did not refer to specific language the president used that could be considered perjury. As Representative Nadler noted:

> Article I . . . alleges that the president committed perjury. It is basic that we should be told before voting the specific words that are alleged to be perjurious. . . . What words specifically . . . are alleged to be perjurious? Could we have . . . those words, please, so that we can discuss them [and] . . . so that the Senate will know

what the allegation is, and the defense attorneys will know what they must defend against?

While the first three articles of impeachment dealt with perjury and obstruction of justice, the fourth article was a reflection of the outrage of many Republicans toward the insufficient, vague, and overly legalistic answers the president had given in his response to the 81 questions posed to him by Hyde. The fourth article accused the president of having failed "to respond to certain written requests for admission and willfully made perjurious, false and misleading sworn statements in response to certain written requests for admission propounded to him as part of the impeachment inquiry authorized by the House of Representatives of the Congress of the United States."

The Democrats on the committee tried to stop the articles of impeachment from going to the full House. On December 12, the committee took up an alternate measure to censure the president. The idea of a letter of rebuke to the president surfaced early in the debates over the Lewinsky scandal and was the preferred solution of those Democrats who wanted to express their strong disapproval of the president's actions without calling for his resignation or moving forward with impeachment. Polls indicated the public favored censure over impeachment, while other polls showed the president's popularity at an all-time high. The resolution of censure declared that the president had "egregiously failed" to uphold his oath of office and the implicit "high moral standards" of that oath. It recognized that the president "made false statements concerning his reprehensible conduct with a subordinate" and that he attempted to cover up his actions. The resolution stated that the president was not above the law and was still subject to "criminal and civil penalties." The committee rejected the censure resolution 22–14, with one Democrat, Bobby Scott of Virginia, voting no, and another Democrat, Maxine Waters of California, voting present. The last effort in the House to offer censure as an alternative came on December 19, the day the House voted to impeach the president. The Democrats offered a procedural motion to substitute a censure resolution and send the articles of impeachment back to the Judiciary Committee. This effort failed when acting speaker Ray LaHood (R-Ill.) ruled it not germane. House Democrats used this defeat to stage a temporary walkout, leaving the chamber and moving outside the Capitol, where they met with reporters to denounce the unfairness of the impeachment process.

When the full House of Representatives took up the Judiciary Committee's four articles of impeachment on December 19, only two articles survived. Article I, charging the president with perjury in his testimony to the grand jury in the Jones case and in his relationship with Lewinsky, passed the House 228–206. Article II, charging the president with perjury in his deposition in the Jones case, was defeated 229–205. Article III, charging the president with obstruction of justice and the cover-up of evidence in the Jones case, passed 221–212. Article IV, charging the president with making perjurious and misleading statements to Congress in his reply to the Judiciary Committee's 81 questions, was defeated 285–148, with many Republicans joining in opposition. The impeachment voting was largely a party-line vote, with a few exceptions. Four Republicans did not vote in favor of any of the articles of impeachment, five Democrats voted for three of the four articles, and one Democrat voted for all four. With four articles reduced to two, the House approved without objection House Resolution 611 calling for the impeachment of the president on two counts.

The political fallout from the impeachment drive had already claimed Gingrich, who announced after the midterm elections that he would not be a candidate for speaker in the 106th Congress. Gingrich resigned his seat in Congress on January 3, 1999, just days before the Senate impeachment trial began. In the meantime, Rep. Bob Livingston (R-La.), who earlier had said he would challenge Gingrich for the speakership and was the presumed heir apparent, surprised his colleagues and the nation by announcing his resignation from the House on the day the House voted to impeach the president. Livingston's own marital infidelity had become public information. In his speech Livingston urged the president to resign his office and then to the great surprise of everyone in the chamber said that he would follow his own advice to the president by resigning himself.

Representative Maxine Waters (D-Calif.) is seen at a hearing looking into the possible impeachment of President Clinton. (Photo by Karin Cooper/Getty Images)

The Senate Trial

On January 7, 1999, the 13 House managers, all members of the House Judiciary Committee, proceeded as a group from the House side of the Capitol to the Senate chamber for the opening exercise of the trial of President Clinton, the formal reading of the articles of impeachment. Thus would begin a clash of cultures between the two distinct chambers that make up the U.S. Congress. Some of the House managers had never set foot in the Senate chamber, and many of them knew little of the significant differences between the two bodies. The Republican members of the committee had been in charge of the impeachment process until this moment and had relentlessly led the effort to impeach the president. Things would be different in the Senate. The Senate had its own traditions and procedures, and it had the power to make the rules that would determine the way the trial unfolded. Even though the Republican Party controlled the Senate by a 55–45 margin, Senate tradition and procedure give each senator a stature and influence regardless of party identification.

One of the first acts on the part of Senate majority leader Trent Lott (R-Miss.) and the minority leader, Tom Daschle (D-S.D.), was to call a joint caucus of all 100 senators on the evening of January 7 to discuss the upcoming trial and to establish its rules and procedures. This was the first time in Senate history that such a caucus of both political parties was held. The choice of venue was no accident either. The senators met in the ornate Old Senate Chamber, a beautifully restored room that embodied so much of the Senate's "Golden Age" in the mid-19th century. Senator Robert C. Byrd (D-W.V.), age 81, an expert on the upper chamber's traditions, counseled his colleagues: "I try to take the long view of history that is yet before us. . . . our words and our deeds will be long remembered and long recorded. . . . The Nation will be watching us and I implore us all to conduct ourselves in a way that will bring honor to this body." But Senator Byrd minced no words in expressing his anger at the president and the House of Representatives. "The White House has sullied itself. The House has fallen into the black pit of partisan self-indulgence. The Senate is teetering on the brink of that same black pit."

This closed-door session gave senators the chance to speak their mind without the glare of television cameras or the press. Many were mad at Clinton or at the House for conducting such a partisan impeachment. During the meeting two political antagonists, Phil Gramm (R-Tex.) and Edward Kennedy (D-Mass.), agreed that the trial needed to be limited and of brief duration—not months, but weeks in length. This coming together of political rivals seemed to have a bracing effect on members of both parties. After more than two hours, the senators emerged with a plan to conduct the trial prudently to avoid further sensationalism, following rules of procedure established in the Senate trial of Andrew Johnson in 1868, and they agreed by a vote of 100 to 0. Lott and Daschle had agreed from the day the House voted for impeachment that the House had mishandled the process and that the Senate would have to find a way to cool the passions of the House managers and address the public perception that the impeachment was completely politicized. According to Ken Gormley's book *The Death of American Virtue: Clinton vs. Starr* (2010), Lott told Hyde before the Senate trial began, "I just did not want the United States Senate to become the scene of a loaded sex trial."

Barr, one of the House managers, later wrote a book on the impeachment, noting his disappointment when Lott agreed to hold the joint caucus. "That's right," he wrote, "there we were presenting a case supported by the majority of the membership of the U.S. House for removing the president from office, and all the Senate could think to do was get the guys together and hold hands and sing 'Kumbayah.'" Calling the caucus a "bipartisan love-fest," Barr saw the meeting as the first sign that the Senate "screwed the House impeachment managers big time" and that the Senate would only conduct a show trial. Schippers felt equally betrayed by the Senate's early decisions: "It was obvious from the onset that the Republican leadership was totally at the mercy of the polls. As long as the President's approval rating remained high, the Republican leaders were not about to rock the boat. They were more interested in preserving the self-proclaimed 'dignity' of the Senate than in performing the constitutional duty imposed upon them by the electorate."

The House managers, in their pretrial negotiations with the Senate, had asked if it was possible for Schippers to participate in presenting the case to the Senate. This important procedural question had no precedent in past impeachment trials. Never have House managers been allowed to be represented by counsel, even though the impeached official, in this case Clinton, was allowed to have counsel present his case. The Senate denied the House managers the right to be represented by counsel because it was the sole province of elected members to perform this constitutional duty. In terms of the general rules and procedures of the trial, from the issuance of special gallery passes for spectators to the duties of the presiding officer, the Senate followed the model of the 1868 impeachment trial of President Andrew Johnson. The Senate began a review of its own impeachment trial rules in 1974, with the impeachment

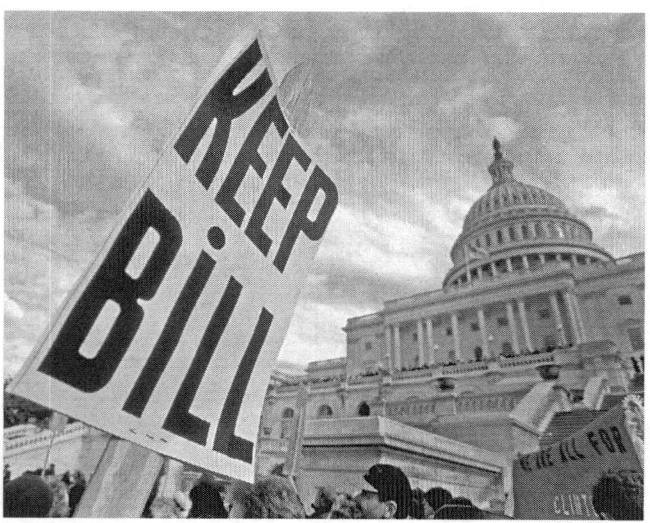

Demonstration in support of President Clinton in front of the Capitol, December 17, 1998. (© Brooks Kraft/Sygma/CORBIS)

of Nixon looming as a possibility, but any changes in the rules were dropped when the Nixon impeachment did not materialize. In 1986, as the Senate pondered the impeachment of Judge Harry E. Claiborne, its first impeachment trial of a judge in many years, the 1974 study of the impeachment rules was dusted off and a few minor modifications were made. But for all practical purposes the Clinton trial was conducted under rules that were 130 years old. The Senate precedent for most impeachments has been to close the deliberative phase of the trial to the public, while making the presentation of evidence open to public view. It would take a two-thirds vote of the Senate to change this rule, and none of the senators seemed to be willing to delay the trial to try to improve on rules long established for impeachment trials. The Senate had determined to limit the presentation of the House managers to the evidence gathered in the Starr investigation, which was the basis of the two articles of impeachment. Furthermore, the Senate limited the witnesses who would be called and, despite objections from the House managers, ruled out a personal appearance by Lewinsky.

The Senate trial began on January 14, 1999, with several days of opening statements by each of the 13 House managers. On January 22, Senator Byrd called for dismissal of the charges against the president in order to "end this sad and sorry time for our country." Under the trial rules any call for dismissal would only be in order after the senators had heard all the evidence. Byrd said he would introduce his motion to dismiss when the trial was completed. He said there was little likelihood that two-thirds of the Senate would convict the president and that number would not change by the time the trial ended. Byrd and many other Democrats and even some Republicans knew from the beginning of the trial that it was unlikely that two-thirds of the senators would vote for a conviction. Byrd's motion to dismiss was taken up on January 27 and defeated along party lines with only one Democratic senator, Russ Feingold of Wisconsin, voting with the majority. This vote was the first sign that the Senate was unlikely to muster a two-thirds vote necessary for a guilty verdict.

The impeachment trial, so rare an occurrence in the political life of the United States, took on monumental proportions, in ceremony, if not in substance. Chief Justice William Rehnquist, an expert on impeachments, wore a black robe with four gold stripes high on each sleeve. He was sworn in by 96-year-old Senator Strom Thurmond (R-S.C.), the president pro tempore of the Senate. The chief justice then administered the oath to all 100 senators, who came forward one by one to sign the Oath Book, taking souvenir pens back to their desks. The chief justice, as presiding officer, occasionally had to make rulings on procedure; otherwise, he was not a judge in the usual sense and he could not question the House managers or the president's defense team. The senators were the judges. This was made very clear in one of the early rulings from the chair. While the senators were not allowed to speak during the trial, they could submit written questions to the House managers. Senators were allowed to raise objections on procedural matters. At one point when Barr was speaking, Senator Tom Harkin (D-Iowa) rose to object to the use of the word "juror" to describe members of the Senate. Harkin cited *The Federalist Papers* to make the point that senators were not jurors in the usual sense of the word. Harkin explained that in regular juries the jurors are selected because they do not know the facts in the case, and regular jurors do not determine what constitutes evidence as senators do in determining the rules of a trial. The chief justice ruled that "the objection of the Senator from Iowa is well taken, that the Senate is not simply a jury; it is a court in this case. Therefore, counsel should refrain from referring to the Senators as jurors."

Each of the 13 House managers had a specific trial assignment in presenting the case to the Senate. The case against the president was summarized in a lengthy "Trial Memorandum of the U. S. House of Representatives," dated January 11, 1999, which served as the brief in the case. Each member of the Senate received a copy. Likewise, the president's defense team of lawyers presented a "Trial Memorandum of President William Jefferson Clinton," dated January 13, 1999. Chairman Hyde made opening and closing statements for the House managers. Representative James Sensenbrenner (R-Wis.)

delivered a one-hour introduction. Barr and fellow representatives Christopher Cannon (R-Utah), Steve Chabot (R-Ohio), and George Gekas (R-Pa.) each addressed how the president's conduct related to perjury and obstruction of justice. Representative Ed Bryant (R-Tenn.) outlined the facts in the case. Representatives Steve Buyer (R-Ind.), Charles Canady (R-Fla.), and Graham focused on how the president's conduct met the constitutional test for removal from office. Representative Asa Hutchinson (R-Ark.) discussed the facts as they related to obstruction of justice. Representative Bill McCollum (R-Fla.) summarized the factual aspects of the case, and Representative James Rogan (R-Calif.) discussed the issue of grand-jury perjury and also delivered closing remarks for the House managers' case.

Despite all the efforts of the House managers to keep the focus on the president's alleged acts of lying while under oath and his attempts to cover up his affair, it was almost impossible to separate the sensational private misconduct regarding the president's encounters with Lewinsky from the lies and cover-up about the affair. Hyde addressed this point in his summation following the presentations of the House managers:

> But I must say, despite massive and relentless efforts to change the subject, the case before you, Senators, is not about sexual misconduct, infidelity, adultery. Those are private acts and are none of our business.
>
> It's not even a question of lying about sex. The matter before this body is a question of lying under oath. This is a public act. The matter before you is a question of the willful, premeditated, deliberate corruption of the nation's system of justice through perjury and obstruction of justice.

The president's defense team consisted of private lawyers from the Washington firm of Williams & Connolly, led by Kendall, and staff of the Office of the White House Counsel—Ruff, Craig, Cheryl D. Mills, Bruce Lindsey, and Lanny Breuer. On January 19, 1999, Ruff made his opening statement in the president's defense. Ruff set the tone that would be followed throughout the defense, that the Jones lawsuit was nothing more than an effort to embarrass the president, that the case was eventually dismissed as not worthy of coming to trial, and that political enemies of the president were manipulating the Jones case. Ruff argued that the charges against the president did not rise to the level of impeachable crimes.

> And so what lesson can be learned from the process followed by the House? I suggest that what you have before you is not the product of the Judiciary Committee's well-considered, judicious assessment of their constitutional role. No, what you have before you is the product of nothing more than a rush to judgment.
>
> And so how should you respond to the managers' belated plea that more is needed to do justice? You should reject it. You have before you all that you need to reach this conclusion: There was no basis for the House to impeach, and there is no, and never will be any, basis for the Senate to convict.

On the evening of the day that Ruff began the defense, Clinton came to the House chamber to deliver his annual State of the Union address. The drama of that day could hardly be exaggerated. The president's impeachment trial was under way in the Senate, while the president was performing his constitutional duty to inform the nation on the state of the union. There was much speculation in the news media about how the president would act as he appeared before the very people who were trying him. Several people who would normally be at the State of the Union address stayed away, including the chief justice, Hyde, and a few other House managers; otherwise, the House and Senate assembled as usual to hear the address. The president delivered a remarkable hour-long speech that signaled he was still going about the task of conducting the nation's business despite his personal travails. By most accounts from Republicans and Democrats alike, it was one of the finest performances of his career. He did not mention the impeachment trial.

While the president had his team of lawyers refute the charges of the House managers, perhaps the most memorable speech of the trial came on January 21 from Dale Bumpers, the former Democratic senator from Arkansas. Bumpers had spent 24 years in the Senate and was well known to all its members. He was once a member of the most exclusive club, as the Senate is often called, unlike the House managers or the president's lawyers. He put the long investigation and the impeachment in human terms, including the personal cost that the president's transgressions had had on the First Family.

> But when I talk about the human element, I talk about what I thought was, on occasion, unnecessarily harsh and pejorative descriptions of the President. I thought that the language should have been tempered somewhat, to acknowledge that he is the President. To say constantly that

> the President lied about this and lied about that, as I say, I thought that was too much for a family that has already been about as decimated as a family can get.
>
> The relationship between husband and wife, father and child has been incredibly strained, if not destroyed. There's been nothing but sleepless nights, mental agony for this family for almost five years—day after day, from accusations of having assassinated, or had Vince Foster assassinated on down. It has been bizarre.

With occasional humor and a sweeping narrative, Bumpers's speech provided a refreshing counterpoint to the legalisms of the House managers and the president's defense team. Responding specifically to one of Hyde's charges that the president should be impeached to uphold the rule of law, Bumpers responded:

> Mr. Chairman, we've also learned that the rule of law includes presidential elections. That's a part of the rule of law in this country. We have an event, a quadrennial event in this country which we call "Presidential Elections." And that's the day when we reach across this aisle and hold hands, Democrats and Republicans. And we say, "Win or lose, we will abide by the decision." It is a solemn event, presidential elections, and it should not—they should not be undone lightly; or just because one side has the clout and the other one doesn't.

As the trial neared its end, the *New York Times* reported on January 31 that Starr was considering his own indictment of the president. The story, leaked by anonymous parties presumably associated with the OIC, said that Starr, after consultation with constitutional experts, had determined he had the authority to seek a grand-jury indictment of a sitting president. This raised anew an unresolved legal issue that had divided experts. Was impeachment the only remedy for a sitting president accused of a crime? Some experts believed that a president could only be prosecuted for a crime after he left office, or after he was removed from office by impeachment. Kendall, the president's private lawyer, thought the leak from the OIC was a blatant attempt to influence the outcome of the impeachment trial.

While Lewinsky did not testify before the Senate, the House managers hoped that a personal meeting with her for the purpose of questioning her further would lead to information that would convince the Senate that she needed to be questioned at the trial. Lewinsky was questioned for six hours by a select group of House managers on February 1 at the Mayflower Hotel in Washington, D.C., where she provided no new information and basically confirmed what the Clinton defense team said about her affidavit in the Jones case and related topics. Calling Lewinsky back to Washington turned out to be a disaster for the House managers. She was an impressive self-assured witness who, according to author Ken Gormley, "took command of the Republican congressmen and never lost the upper hand." Frustrated that the Senate limited the House managers to a few witnesses who appeared on video screens rather than in person, Hyde said, the Senate "did everything but put duct tape on our mouths."

"WHAT HAVE WE GOT THAT'S MORE LIKE A CLOSE SHAVE?"
IMPEACHMENT
CONGRESS
©1998 HERBLOCK

This Herblock cartoon, dated November 27, 1998, captures the idea that some members of Congress were willing to consider a reprimand or a censure of the president rather than the more extreme measure of removing him from office through the impeachment process. (A Herblock Cartoon, copyright by The Herb Block Foundation)

The final arguments and the conclusion of the presentations for both sides occurred on February 8, followed by three days of Senate deliberations in closed session. On February 12, the Senate convened for the vote on the two articles of impeachment. On the first article on perjury, the vote was 45 guilty and 55 not guilty. Ten Republicans voted not guilty, joining all the Democrats. Senator Arlen Specter (R-Pa.) voted according to Scottish law, that the charge was "not proved," but his vote was counted as not guilty. On the second article, dealing with obstruction of justice, the Senate split 50 guilty and 50 not guilty with five Republicans joining all the Democrats. In neither instance was the vote close to the 67 votes necessary for conviction. The president was acquitted by a comfortable margin.

The president's troubles were not over with his acquittal. On April 12, 1999, Judge Wright found Clinton in contempt of court for his false testimony in the Jones case. The president was fined $90,000 and ordered to pay court costs. Wright said, "There simply is no escaping the fact that the President deliberately violated this court's discovery orders and thereby undermined the integrity of the judicial system. Sanctions must be imposed, not only to redress the President's misconduct, but to deter others who might themselves consider emulating the President of the United States by engaging in misconduct that undermines the integrity of the judicial system."

Starr left the OIC in the fall of 1999. He wrote in the *Wall Street Journal* on Oct. 20, 1999, that, in retrospect, switching from the Whitewater investigation to the Lewinsky sex scandal had been a mistake. "Moving beyond Whitewater/Madison," Starr wrote, "slowed our progress, increased our costs, and fostered a damaging perception of empire building."

Starr's replacement as head of the OIC was Robert W. Ray, and the investigation into Clinton's conduct in the Jones case continued. News leaks suggested Ray was planning to convene a grand jury of his own to investigate the president. It was now in Ray's hands to finally put an end to the OIC investigation of the president and the First Lady. In the meantime, the Arkansas Supreme Court's Committee on Professional Conduct was planning disbarment proceedings against the president because he had "brought disrespect to the profession."

In the final deal between Ray and the president, made just days before Clinton left office in 2001, the president's law license was suspended for five years, he agreed to pay a $25,000 fine to the Committee on Professional Conduct, and he agreed to never seek reimbursement of legal fees from the OIC investigation. To finally close the books on all investigations against the president, Ray extracted an admission from the president that he "knowingly gave evasive and misleading testimony" in the Jones deposition. Clinton lied about his relationship with Lewinsky in the Jones deposition. The question remains, however, whether this perjury was an impeachable offense. A sufficient number of United States senators said it was not.

DOCUMENTS

Article from *New York Times*, March 8, 1992

Jeff Gerth was one of the leading investigative reporters for the New York Times *who helped launch the Whitewater story in the mainstream media with his extensive research and reporting. While aspects of the story had appeared in local Arkansas newspapers for several years without going anywhere, Gerth's articles took Whitewater to the national level. He continued to cover the story for the next several years, but none of his reporting had more influence than his first article, which appeared on the newspaper's front page on March 8, 1992. The timing was auspicious, coming just two days before Super Tuesday primaries in six states during the 1992 campaign. The article set the tone for most of the Whitewater charges and subsequent investigations. Journalist Gene Lyons subsequently attacked Gerth's reporting, stating, "It bears almost no relation to reality." Ken Gormley, author of* The Death of American Virtue: Clinton vs. Starr *(2010), quotes Bill Clinton from an interview given a decade after his presidency as saying, "I mean, you really got to hand it to the Republicans and the* New York Times *and the* Washington Post. *It's the first time in history we ever had a major investigation of a guy over an S&L [savings and loan] he didn't borrow money from and a land deal he lost money on." The headline—drafted by editors, not the reporter—starts the story out on the wrong foot since the Clintons entered into the partnership in the Whitewater Development Corporation four years before their business partner James McDougal purchased the Madison Guaranty Savings and Loan.*

ARTICLE FROM *NEW YORK TIMES* MARCH 8, 1992

Clintons Joined S.&L. Operator in an Ozark Real Estate Venture

Bill Clinton and his wife were business partners with the owner of a failing savings and loan association that was subject to state regulation early in his tenure as Governor of Arkansas, records show.

The partnership, a real estate joint venture that was developing land in the Ozarks, involved the Clintons and James B. McDougal, a former Clinton aide turned developer. It started in 1978, and at times money from Mr. McDougal's savings and loan was used to subsidize it. The corporation continues to this day, but does not appear to be active.

Mr. McDougal gave a detailed account of his relationship in several interviews in the last two weeks. This account, along with an examination of related local, state and Federal records and interviews with dozens of others in Arkansas, found the following:

- Available records covering the most active period of the real estate corporation, called Whitewater Development, appear to show that Mr. McDougal heavily subsidized it, insuring that the Clintons were under little financial risk in what turned out to be an unsuccessful enterprise. The corporation bought 200 acres of Ozark Mountain vacation property and planned to sell it in lots. During this period, the Clintons appear to have invested little money, so stood to lose little if the venture failed, but might have cashed in on their 50 percent interest if it had done well.
- The Clintons and Mr. McDougal disagree about what happened to Whitewater's records. Mr. McDougal says that at Mr. Clinton's request they were delivered to the Governor's mansion. The Clintons say many of them have disappeared. Many questions about the enterprise cannot be fully answered without the records.
- After Federal regulators found that Mr. McDougal's savings institution, Madison Guaranty, was insolvent, meaning it faced possible closure by the state, Mr. Clinton appointed a new state securities commissioner, who had been a lawyer in a firm that represented the savings and loan. Mr. Clinton and the commissioner deny giving any preferential treatment. The new commissioner approved two novel proposals to help the savings and loan that were offered by Hillary Clinton, Governor Clinton's wife and a lawyer. She and her firm had been retained to represent the association.
- The Clintons improperly deducted at least $5,000 on their personal tax returns in 1984 and 1985 for interest paid on a portion of at least $30,000 in bank loan payments that Whitewater made for them. The deductions saved them about $1,000 in taxes, but since the error was more than three years ago, Internal Revenue Service regulations do not require the Clintons to pay.

The complicated relationship between Mr. McDougal and the Clintons came to light in an investigation by The New York Times of the Clintons' tax records and business relationships. It raises questions of whether a governor should be involved in a business deal with the owner of a business regulated by the state and whether, having done so, the governor's wife through her law firm should be receiving legal fees for work done for the business.

Confusion Is Cited

Asked about these matters, the Clintons retained two lawyers to answer questions. The lawyers said the improper tax deductions were honest errors, made because there was confusion over who really owned a certain piece of Whitewater property and who was responsible for the loan taken out to buy it, Whitewater or the Clintons.

The deed for the land and the loan papers are all in the Clintons' names.

The lawyers said they were not in a position to answer questions about where the money that went into Whitewater came from. But generally, they said they thought neither the Clintons nor Mr. McDougal had profited from the venture. They also said the Clintons were once liable for about $100,000 in bank loans that financed Whitewater's original purchase of land. But the lawyers have only been able to find original documents showing $5,000 that the Clintons paid.

Some questions about the relationship and the Clintons' role in it may be difficult to resolve because of differing accounts and the missing records.

The two lawyers representing the Clintons are Susan P. Thomases, a longtime friend, and Loretta Lynch, a campaign aide, who participated in several hours of interviews at Ms. Thomases' Manhattan offices Thursday and Friday.

Payments on Debt

The records that are available, and Mrs. Thomases' account, show that Whitewater made payments between 1982 and 1985 on Mrs. Clinton's $30,000 real estate debt, reducing the debt by about $16,000 while also paying at least $14,000 in interest. At least one of those checks was signed by Mr. McDougal.

Mrs. Clinton originally borrowed the $30,000 from a bank also controlled by Mr. McDougal, Bank of Kingston, but "Hillary took the loan on behalf of the corporation," Ms. Thomases said. That, she explained, is why Whitewater made the payments.

The Clintons' 1984 and 1985 tax returns show that they took deductions for interest payments of $2,811 and $2,322 that Whitewater had made.

"It clearly is an error," Ms. Thomases said. She noted that the tax returns for those years were prepared by accountants in Arkansas.

The Clintons' gross income in 1984, as reported on their tax returns, was about $111,000 and they paid $22,280 in Federal taxes. In 1985, their reported income was about $102,000, and they paid $18,791 in Federal taxes.

Longtime Friendship

Mr. Clinton and Mr. McDougal had been friends since the 1960's. When Mr. Clinton became the nation's youngest

Governor at 32 years old, he took Mr. McDougal into his administration as an aide for economic development. It was at about this time that the men formed Whitewater.

A few years later Mr. McDougal, having left government in 1979, bought control of a small savings and loan association, Madison Guaranty, and built it into one of the largest state-chartered associations in Arkansas.

But over time, the savings and loan got in trouble, like many others around the country. Finally Federal regulators took the savings and loan away from Mr. McDougal, and a Federal grand jury charged him with fraud, though he was acquitted. The Clintons were not involved in those proceedings.

Mr. McDougal began having personal problems, too. He was found to be suffering from manic-depressive illness, though he was judged competent to stand trial. In the interviews, Mr. McDougal appeared stable, careful and calm.

A year after the Clintons and McDougals bought the Ozark Mountain property and founded Whitewater Development in 1979, the corporation bought a modular house for about $22,000 and placed it on one of its lots. That lot was then conveyed to Mrs. Clinton, and the deed indicates that she paid nothing for it. Ms. Thomases says this was an error by Whitewater. The deed, she said, should have shown the price and said that Mrs. Clinton paid.

But the house was carried on the books as a Whitewater corporate asset and used as a model house to attract other buyers, according to Whitewater records produced by Ms. Thomases. Because the records are incomplete, it is unclear exactly what happened. But about the same time, Mrs. Clinton personally borrowed $30,000 from Mr. McDougal's bank to pay for the house and the lot.

Ms. Thomases said Mrs. Clinton and the corporation regarded this as a corporate debt, though it was in Mrs. Clinton's name. The corporation included no one but the Clintons and the McDougals. It was this debt that Whitewater made payments on until the end of 1985.

One year after acquiring the property, Mrs. Clinton sold it for $27,500, with payments to be made over time, records show. It is not clear who received the buyer's down payment of $3,000. But Ms. Thomases said it was the corporation that took the loss on its books. A few years later, the buyer went bankrupt and stopped making payments, and then he died.

In 1988 Mrs. Clinton bought back the house from the estate of the buyer. Records show that she paid $8,000 and then resold the property a short time later for about $23,000, after closing costs. The Clintons reported a capital gain that year of $1,640.

Ms. Thomases explained that the capital gain was small because, as part of that transaction, Mrs. Clinton had to pay off Whitewater's remaining $13,000 debt on the property, originally incurred by Mrs. Clinton. The payments the previous owner had been making to Whitewater before he went bankrupt had been used to help pay off that debt.

Account Overdrawn

It was during the period when Whitewater was making the Clintons' loan payments that Madison Guaranty was putting money into Whitewater.

For example, Whitewater's check ledger shows that Whitewater's account at Madison was overdrawn in 1984, when the corporation was making payments on the Clintons' loan. Money was deposited to make up the shortage from Madison Marketing, an affiliate of the savings and loan that derived its revenues from the institution, records also show.

It was also in 1984 that Madison started getting into trouble. Federal examiners studied its books that year, found that it was violating Arkansas regulations and determined that correcting the books to adjust improperly inflated profits would "result in an insolvent position," records of the 1984 examination show.

Arkansas regulators received the Federal report later that year, and under state law the securities commissioner was supposed to close any insolvent institution.

As the Governor is free to do at any time, Mr. Clinton appointed a new securities commissioner in January 1985. He chose Beverly Bassett Schaffer, a lawyer in one of the firms that had been representing Madison.

Fund-Raising Ideas

Ms. Thomases, after talking to Mr. Clinton this week, said the Governor chose her because they were friends, and because he wanted to appoint a well qualified woman to an important post.

In interviews, Mrs. Schaffer, now a Fayetteville lawyer, said she did not remember the Federal examination of Madison but added that in her view, the findings were not "definitive proof of insolvency."

In 1985, Mrs. Clinton and her Little Rock law firm, the Rose firm, twice applied to the Securities Commission on behalf of Madison, asking that the savings and loan be allowed to try two novel plans to raise money.

Mrs. Schaffer wrote to Mrs. Clinton and another lawyer at the firm approving the ideas. "I never gave anybody special treatment," she said.

Madison was not able to raise additional capital. And by 1986 Federal regulators, who insured Madison's deposits, took control of the institution and ousted Mr. McDougal. Mrs. Schaffer supported the action.

Source: Jeff Gerth, "Clintons Joined S.&L. Operator in an Ozark Real-Estate Venture," *New York Times,* March 8, 1992, 1.

Excerpt from Senate Resolution Establishing a Special Whitewater Committee, May 17, 1995

Although the Office of the Special Prosecutor had been on the Whitewater trail since January 1994, Senate Republicans, fresh from successful congressional elections in November 1994 that gave them the majority, decided to push for a separate investigation. In May 1995, the Senate voted to create a special Whitewater committee with broad jurisdiction to investigate the political and personal finances of President Bill Clinton while he was governor of Arkansas as well as the charge that Whitewater papers may have been removed from the office of Vincent Foster, deputy White House counsel, after his death in July 1993. Chaired by Senator Alfonse D'Amato (R-N.Y.), the committee had the authority to examine a wide range of activities, including the actions of Madison Guaranty Savings and Loan, which was at the center of the Whitewater inquiry, and the Rose Law Firm in Arkansas, where Hillary Rodham Clinton and several former senior officials were partners. Only three Democrats voted to oppose the inquiry. The country would witness the phenomenon of two parallel, simultaneous inquiries on charges relating to Whitewater.

EXCERPT FROM SENATE RESOLUTION ESTABLISHING A SPECIAL WHITEWATER COMMITTEE, MAY 17, 1995

SECTION 1. ESTABLISHMENT OF SPECIAL COMMITTEE.

(a) ESTABLISHMENT—There is established a special committee administered by the Committee on Banking, Housing, and Urban Affairs to be known as the "Special Committee to Investigate Whitewater Development Corporation and Related Matters" (hereafter in this resolution referred to as the "special committee."

(b) PURPOSES—The purposes of the special committee are—

(1) to conduct an investigation and public hearings into, and study of, whether improper conduct occurred regarding the way in which White House officials handled documents in the office of White House Deputy Counsel Vincent Foster following his death;

(2) to conduct an investigation and public hearings into, and study of, the following matters developed during, or arising out of, the investigation and public hearings concluded by the Committee on Banking, Housing, and Urban Affairs prior to the adoption of this resolution—

(A) whether any person has improperly handled confidential Resolution Trust Corporation (hereafter in this resolution referred to as the "RTC") information relating to Madison Guaranty Savings and Loan Association or Whitewater Development Corporation, including whether any person has improperly communicated such information to individuals referenced therein;

(B) whether the White House has engaged in improper contacts with any other agency or department in the Government with regard to confidential RTC information relating to Madison Guaranty Savings and Loan Association or Whitewater Development Corporation;

(C) whether the Department of Justice has improperly handled RTC criminal referrals relating to Madison Guaranty Savings and Loan Association or Whitewater Development Corporation;

(D) whether RTC employees have been improperly importuned, prevented, restrained, or deterred in conducting investigations or making enforcement recommendations relating to Madison Guaranty Savings and Loan Association or Whitewater Development Corporation; and

(E) whether the report issued by the Office of Government Ethics on July 31, 1994, or related transcripts of deposition testimony—

(i) were improperly released to White House officials or others prior to their testimony before the Committee on Banking, Housing, and Urban Affairs pursuant to Senate Resolution 229 (103d Congress); or

(ii) were used to communicate to White House officials or to others confidential RTC information relating to Madison Guaranty Savings and Loan Association or Whitewater Development Corporation;

(3) to conduct an investigation and public hearings into, and study of, all matters that have any tendency to reveal the full facts about—

(A) the operations, solvency, and regulation of Madison Guaranty Savings and Loan Association, and any subsidiary, affiliate, or other entity owned or controlled by Madison Guaranty Savings and Loan Association;

(B) the activities, investments, and tax liability of Whitewater Development Corporation and, as related to Whitewater Development Corporation, of its officers, directors, and shareholders;

(C) the policies and practices of the RTC and the Federal banking agencies (as that term is defined in section 3 of the Federal Deposit Insurance Act) regarding the legal representation of such agencies with respect to Madison Guaranty Savings and Loan Association;

(D) the handling by the RTC, the Office of Thrift Supervision, the Federal Deposit Insurance Corporation, and the Federal Savings and Loan Insurance Corporation of civil or administrative actions against parties regarding Madison Guaranty Savings and Loan Association;

(E) the sources of funding and the lending practices of Capital Management Services, Inc., and its supervision and regulation by the Small Business Administration, including any alleged diversion of funds to Whitewater Development Corporation;

(F) the bond underwriting contracts between Arkansas Development Finance Authority and Lasater & Company; and

(G) the lending activities of Perry County Bank, Perryville, Arkansas, in connection with the 1990 Arkansas gubernatorial election;

(4) to make such findings of fact as are warranted and appropriate;

(5) to make such recommendations, including recommendations for legislative, administrative, or other actions, as the special committee may determine to be necessary or desirable; and

(6) to fulfill the constitutional oversight and informational functions of the Congress with respect to the matters described in this section.

SEC. 2. MEMBERSHIP AND ORGANIZATION OF THE SPECIAL COMMITTEE.

(a) MEMBERSHIP—

(1) IN GENERAL—The special committee shall consist of—

(A) the members of the Committee on Banking, Housing, and Urban Affairs; and

(B) the chairman and ranking member of the Committee on the Judiciary, or their designees from the Committee on the Judiciary.

(2) SENATE RULE XXV—For the purpose of paragraph 4 of rule XXV of the Standing Rules of the Senate, service of a Senator as the chairman or other member of the special committee shall not be taken into account.

(b) ORGANIZATION OF SPECIAL COMMITTEE—

(1) CHAIRMAN—The chairman of the Committee on Banking, Housing, and Urban Affairs shall serve as the chairman of the special committee (hereafter in this resolution referred to as the "chairman").

(2) RANKING MEMBER—The ranking member of the Committee on Banking, Housing, and Urban Affairs shall serve as the ranking member of the special committee (hereafter in this resolution referred to as the "ranking member").

(3) QUORUM—A majority of the members of the special committee shall constitute a quorum for the purpose of reporting a matter or recommendation to the Senate. A majority of the members of the special committee, or one-third of the members of the special committee if at least one member of the minority party is present, shall constitute a quorum for the conduct of other business. One member of the special committee shall constitute a quorum for the purpose of taking testimony.

(c) RULES AND PROCEDURES—Except as otherwise specifically provided in this resolution, the special committee's investigation, study, and hearings shall be governed by the Standing Rules of the Senate and the Rules of Procedure of the Committee on Banking, Housing, and Urban Affairs. The special committee may adopt additional rules or procedures not inconsistent with this resolution or the Standing Rules of the Senate if the chairman and ranking member agree that such additional rules or procedures are necessary to enable the special committee to conduct the investigation, study, and hearings authorized by this resolution. Any such additional rules and procedures shall become effective upon publication in the Congressional Record.

Source: U.S. Senate. S. Res. 120, 104th Cong. 1st. Sess., May 17, 1995. http://frwebgate.access.gpo.gov/cgi-bin/getdoc.cgi?dbname=104_cong_bills&docid=f:s r120ats.txt.pdf.

Senate Debate over Extending the Whitewater Committee Investigation, March 13, 1996

By early March 1996, the Senate Special Committee on Whitewater had held 10 months and 41 days of hearings. The Senate had voted almost unanimously to establish the committee. Now, with almost $1 million already spent by the investigation, Senator Alfonse D'Amato (R-N.Y.) and his Republican colleagues pressed for an extension of the inquiry and additional money. But the broad support that had existed when the committee was formed had deteriorated with the parade of witnesses and the contempt shown to those who defended President Bill Clinton. A number of Democratic senators, including Byron Dorgan of North Dakota, Daniel Inouye of Hawaii, and Paul Sarbanes of Maryland, assailed the request, labeling the inquiry a highly partisan assault on the president that had poisoned the nation's politics. The Democratic opposition ultimately forced a compromise on April 18, 1996. In return for an extension and an additional allotment of $450,000, Republicans agreed to end the public hearings by June 14.

SENATE DEBATE OVER EXTENDING THE WHITEWATER COMMITTEE INVESTIGATION MARCH 13, 1996

Mr. DORGAN. Mr. President, sometimes I walk into the Chamber of the Senate and I think that I have stumbled into the wrong Chamber. I hear the debate, and I think that is not what is being discussed. In the debate a few minutes ago it was said that the Democrats are stonewalling on Whitewater. I guess I do not understand. I must have missed something. We commissioned a Whitewater inquiry last May—May of last year. We provided nearly $1 million for a special investigative effort in the Congress last year.

Now we are saying we are willing to provide additional resources, and you ought to wrap this up in the next 5 weeks—5 weeks. And somehow we are stonewalling on Whitewater? I mean, it is plenty cold in Montana and North Dakota these days, and the heat bills are plenty high. I was thinking maybe if we took some of this hot air out there, it would heat the two States for the entire winter. Stonewalling on Whitewater? What on Earth are people talking about?

This is a manifestation of Parkinson's law. If you study Parkinson's law, one of his laws was that the amount of time needed to do a job always expands to the amount of time available to do the job. This is the manifestation of Parkinson's law. This inquiry, after spending $26 million on the independent counsel and still counting—this inquiry which is the political inquiry—now they want to extend to election 1996.

Some of us say maybe you ought to get up early in the morning now. Maybe you ought to go 5 days a week now. Maybe you ought to get the witnesses in now for the next 5 weeks and finish this investigation. As for me, it does not matter with respect to these records. Get a rental truck, back it up to the White House, get a vacuum cleaner, find a bunch of people that can read, and read all the records. As far as I am concerned, whatever the truth is let the truth come out. But do you need from last May until the election day of 1996 to demonstrate what this issue is? I think not. That is not what the issue is here. There is a right way to do things and a wrong way to do things.

We have said, in the next 5 weeks finish this investigation. Do your work. And what we are told by the other side is we are stonewalling. What a bunch of nonsense. While we are doing this, we are saying this is the most important thing for the Congress to do. Do you know what we are not doing? We are not having hearings on the issue of health care and Medicare and what we ought to do to solve that problem. Nobody is having hearings on the issue of jobs. Why are we losing jobs in this country? Why are jobs moving out of our country? Why does our Tax Code contain this insidious incentive that pays corporations to shut their plants in this country and move them overseas, and why does not somebody in this Congress do something about that? Nobody is holding hearings about what our monetary policy is doing to this country. Why cannot we have more than a 2.5-percent economic growth? What about the Fed and the Fed's policies? Nobody is talking about hearings on a whole range of issues dealing with the things that are central to people's lives.

This is the number of hearings. There were 41 days of hearings since last May on Whitewater, 12 days on crime, 3 days on education, no hearings on the economy and jobs, and no hearings on Medicare and health care. The question is, What is the priority?

I want to get to the bottom of Whitewater. We have had 100 FBI agents and independent counsel that spent $23 million, and we have had a special inquiry in Congress since last May. Now we have people telling us we want to go for another 4 or 5 months. You know that some of us serve here because we are interested in doing the people's business, part of which deals with the issue of jobs, health care, the economy, education, and a whole range of things. Get every record you want. Get every record you can. Study it forever. But I do not think we ought to have an unlimited amount of money given by the taxpayers for an unlimited inquiry to take us to election day 1996. Let us finish this in the next 5 weeks. Let us decide to do this and do it right; finish the testimony, finish the report, report back to the Senate, and then let us get on with the other business that confronts the American people.

We have enormous challenges. We have budget challenges. We have deficits. We have jobs, health care, and education. I have recited plenty of them to do. But the interesting thing is that no one seems very interested in focusing on those challenges. My constituents are interested. They are very interested in the question about what makes our education system work better. How do we advance the interest of our kids to have the best education system in the world? What do we do about jobs that are leaving the country? What kind of policies can we put in place to deal with that? That is what my constituents are interested in.

I am not suggesting that you have no business in the Whitewater inquiry. I voted for the funding last May for $1 million, and I will vote for additional funding. My objection is to what I think is kind of a thinly disguised approach by some to say we want unlimited time here; we want to work 2 or 3 days a week; we want to sort of move along leisurely. If you were hauling mail, you would go out and hire horses, I guess, and create some sort of "Pony Express" these days. That is the speed with which we see this inquiry moving.

All we are saying is let us get this job done. We have said we will provide appropriations for 5 weeks' additional inquiry, write a report, and let us finish it. There has been no other inquiry in the history of Congress that I am aware of that accepts this as a precedent. Nothing comes close to what you are suggesting and what has been done here. The Senator from Maryland has made that point over and over again. Yet we have people stand with indignation and say, "You all are stonewalling." What a bunch of nonsense.

I yield the floor.

Mr. SARBANES. I yield 6 minutes to the Senator from Hawaii.

The PRESIDING OFFICER. The Senator from Hawaii is recognized.

Mr. INOUYE. Mr. President, on May 17 of last year, this Senate voted 96 to 3 to create a special committee to investigate the so-called Whitewater affair. This bipartisan vote established the special committee with its primary purpose to get all the facts on Whitewater to the American people.

This bipartisan Senate vote imposed a February 29, 1996, deadline for the committee to complete its work to ensure that the facts were presented to the American people in a balanced and timely manner and before the country entered the politically charged atmosphere of a Presidential campaign.

Yet, as I listen intently to the ongoing debate, much of the bipartisan spirit which this body exhibited on May 17 no longer exists. Regretfully and sadly, it appears that the Republican majority has now chosen to forgo bipartisanship in an effort to indefinitely extend the special committee's mandate, at a cost of $600,000, and prolong the investigation into the 1996 Presidential campaign.

This Republican extension request is unprecedented, and it is unreasonable. The U.S. Senate has never before conducted an open-ended political investigation of a sitting American President during a Presidential election year.

During the course of this debate, reference has been made to the 1987 Iran-Contra hearings. The committee was able to complete its investigation in a 10-month period within the deadline set by the Congress. The Iran-Contra affair was an international event that had major consequences beyond our shores. It involved the constitutional relationship between the executive and legislative branches in the shaping of foreign policy. It involved the credibility of our foreign policy. It involved our relations with other countries and it involved the actions of our intelligence service and some of our Nation's most closely held secrets.

Because of the profound issues in question, we in Congress were compelled to investigate the episode, and for precisely the same reason we were compelled to ensure that the Iran-Contra investigation was conducted in an atmosphere free of partisanship and theatrics. I strongly believed then, as I do now, that the Nation would be ill-served by a congressional panel wantonly weakening a President for presumed political benefit.

The Iran-Contra Committee was obligated to investigate the conduct of the highest Government officers, and we were determined to let the facts lead us to where they willed. But we did not perform this task in a way that suggested to our adversaries that we were a nation divided. I believed we avoided this impression because of the lessons learned during the Watergate investigation.

The Senate committee that investigated Watergate, on which I served, had the same mandate as do today's select committees: to seek the facts about the event in question and propose legislation to prevent a repetition.

The structure of the Watergate Committee encouraged partisanship. There were majority and minority lawyers, majority and minority investigators, majority and minority secretaries and clerks. Even the committee's budget was divided into Democratic and Republican portions.

After the conclusion of the investigation, the committee's minority counsel and now our very distinguished colleague, Senator Fred Thompson, wrote that loyalty to the Republican minority was "one all-important criterion" for hiring his staff. "We are going to try our best to have a bipartisan investigation, but if it comes down to the question of us and them, I don't want to worry about who is us and who is them."

Mr. President, my one condition for assuming the role of chairman of the Senate Iran Committee was that there would be no majority and no minority staffs but a unified staff whose members reported to the committee as a whole and not to Democrats or Republicans. Our chief counsel, Mr. Arthur Liman, regarded all members of the committee as his clients, and, under his direction, our staff members worked side by side unconcerned whether their neighbor was one of us or one of them.

The structure of the staff would have been meaningless if the members of the committee were determined to make the Iran-Contra investigation a partisan matter. This did not happen.

Our colleague, former Senator Warren Rudman of New Hampshire and vice chair of this Senate Iran-Contra Committee, was empowered to make decisions in my absence. We collaborated on everything, and we divided the responsibility for witnesses among all members of the committee so the hearings became a collective matter. At no time during our closed committee meetings did any member raise political issues or hint at a Democratic attempt to smear the President or a Republican scheme to cover things up.

In comparison, nearly 17 months had elapsed from the date the Senate created the Watergate Committee until the committee report was published. The Watergate hearing itself dragged on for more than 8 months. The Iran-Contra Committee worked hard to accomplish its work within a 10-month period, hearings included. Yes, there were requests by Democrats and Republicans that we seek an indefinite time limit on the hearings, but the chairman of the House committee, Representative (Lee) Hamilton, and I, in conjunction with our vice chairs, strongly recommended against an open-ended investigation. We sought to ensure that our investigation was completed in a timely fashion to preserve the committee's bipartisanship and to avoid any exploitation of President Reagan during an election year.

The Special Committee on Whitewater has had 41 days of hearings, five public meetings, and now has made an unprecedented and unreasonable request to indefinitely extend the special committee's mandate. It will be a $600,000 tab, and I suppose it will prolong the investigation into the Presidential campaign with a possibility of politically damaging and embarrassing the incumbent President.

Mr. President, the Democrats are committed to ensuring that the American people know the facts on Whitewater but that it be done in the same bipartisan fashion as the Iran-Contra hearings, and not for the exploitation or for the embarrassment of the sitting President. . . .

MR. SARBANES. Mr. President, while the distinguished Senator from Hawaii is still in the Chamber, I commend him for his statement and underscore—underscore—the responsible manner in which he dealt with the Iran-Contra issue.

At the time, there were Members of the Congress, a Democratically-controlled Congress, who wanted to extend those hearings well into 1988, a Presidential election year, for political purposes. And that was obvious. The Republican leader of the Senate, Senator Dole, strongly urged there be a time limit on the work of the committee. He was fiercely opposed to the notion of an open-ended extension and was very clear in making that point in debate on the floor and off the floor in comments to the media.

Senator Inouye, who chaired the special committee in the Senate, and Congressman Hamilton rejected this proposal by some Democrats to prolong the hearing into the election year and therefore exploit, for political purposes, President Reagan's difficulties, and they settled on a reasonable time period. In fact, they moved it up in response to the representation made to them by Senator Dole.

It was Senator Dole at the time who pressed very hard that there should be a reasonable time limit, that it should stay out of the election year. In fact, Senator Dole, on the floor, said: "I am heartened by what I understand to be the strong commitment of both the chairman and vice chairman to avoid fishing expeditions. I am pleased to note that, as a result of a series of discussions which have involved myself, the majority leader, and the chairman and vice chairman designate of the committee, we have changed the date on which the committee's authorization will expire." And they moved it forward.

Senator Inouye took the lead in achieving that constructive and responsible result. I simply want to underscore it and contrast it with the situation we are now facing, where we have a proposal, now, for an unlimited time period, an additional $600,000.

I yield myself 1 more minute.

Furthermore, in order to complete its work, the Iran-Contra Committee, on which I was privileged to serve, under the very distinguished chairmanship of the Senator from Hawaii, held 21 days of hearings in the last 23 days, in late July and August, in order to complete its hearings. Contrast that with the work of this committee, which held 1 day of hearings in the last 2 weeks of its existence in the latter part of February; which held only 8 days of hearings in the entire month of February, whereas the Iran-Contra Committee held 21 days of hearings in order to wind the thing up.

The minority leader has made, I think, a very reasonable proposal in terms of providing some additional time to finish this matter up. The committee should intensify its schedule and complete it on time, and it ought to follow the example set by the distinguished Senator from Hawaii when he chaired the Iran-Contra Committee and worked assiduously to keep partisanship and politics out of the inquiry and to keep the inquiry out of the election year.

I yield the floor.

Source: Congressional Record, Senate, 104th Cong. 2nd Sess., Mar. 13, 1996, S1928-S1930.

Senate Special Committee's Whitewater Report: Conclusions on Arkansas Phase, June 17, 1996

The Senate Special Committee on Whitewater worked even longer than the Watergate investigating committee years earlier. There were 60 days of hearings, 10,729 pages of testimony, and 35,000 pages of depositions from 245 people. In the final committee report, the Republicans, as they had done throughout the hearings, accused Bill and Hillary Clinton of hiding criminal activity in their days in Arkansas. As the investigation progressed, it was First Lady Hillary Clinton, not President Clinton, who was at the center of the charges made in the report. In the eyes of the Republican investigators, she was leading a massive effort to conceal the truth, withhold documents, and mislead the committee. "Most roads lead from the First Lady and to the First Lady," said Senator Richard Shelby (R-Ala.) after the report was released. The Democrats, as they had done all along, accused the committee's chairman, Alfonse D'Amato (R-N.Y.), lawyer Michael Chertoff, who authored most of the report, and other Republicans on the committee of staging a political vendetta and witch hunt.

SENATE SPECIAL COMMITTEE'S WHITEWATER REPORT: CONCLUSIONS ON ARKANSAS PHASE, JUNE 17, 1996

The Special Committee's Arkansas Phase focused on the core allegations of improprieties and criminal misconduct concerning the activities of Madison Guaranty Savings and Loan Association ("Madison Guaranty"), Whitewater Development Corporation ("Whitewater"), Capital Management Services, Inc. ("CMS") and Lasater & Co. The Arkansas Phase was the last phase of the Committee's inquiry, and, in deference to the Independent Counsel's ongoing investigation, the Committee did not investigate thoroughly certain matters specified in Resolution 120, particularly the lending activities of the Perry County Bank in connection with the 1990 Arkansas gubernatorial election.

The convictions of three of the President and Mrs. Clinton's close Arkansas business and political associates in the recently concluded Tucker-McDougal trial in Little Rock marked a key turning point in the ongoing Whitewater affair. The jury's guilty findings against Governor Jim Guy Tucker and James and Susan McDougal, the Clintons' Whitewater business partners, demonstrate the seriousness of the matters under investigation in the Committee's Arkansas Phase. Simply put, Whitewater can longer be responsibly dismissed as "a cover-up without a crime."

The Arkansas jury unanimously concluded that James McDougal operated Madison Guaranty as, in effect, a criminal enterprise. The failure of Madison Guaranty cost American taxpayers more than $60 million. It is now clear that Madison and CMS, a small business investment company run by David Hale, were piggy banks for the Arkansas political elite.

Eight of the 24 counts of conviction relate directly to the Clintons' investment in Whitewater. The jury convicted on all of the counts concerning a loan from CMS to Susan McDougal's firm, Master Marketing. According to the testimony of an FBI agent at the Tucker-McDougal trial, approximately $50,000 of the loan was used to pay the expenses of Whitewater. Moreover, Mr. Hale testified at the trial that he discussed this fraudulent loan with then-Governor Clinton. Unfortunately, the Committee never heard the important testimony of Mr. Hale, who asserted his constitutional right not to testify. The Committee was unable to secure sufficient votes to grant Mr. Hale limited use immunity.

The recently-discovered Rose Law Firm billing records provide important new evidence relating to the Arkansas Phase. The records reveal Mrs. Clinton's previously undisclosed personal representation of Mr. McDougal's S&L before state regulators, seeking permission to raise additional money through the sale of stock. The records also show that Mrs. Clinton was repeatedly called on to do work related to the Madison land deal, known as Castle Grande, which federal S&L regulators found involved a series of fraudulent transactions. The Special Committee concludes that Mrs. Clinton's work on Castle Grande related to an effort to conceal the true nature of activities at Madison Guaranty.

The Special Committee also uncovered evidence that Mr. Clinton himself took an active role in obtaining one of the original Whitewater loans—one apparently approved as a favor after the bank's political lobbyist intervened. And Mr. Clinton's accountant testified that when he raised objections to early parts of Mr. McDougal's Whitewater proposal, Mr. Clinton pulled him aside and told him to "back off."

During the 1980s, Mr. McDougal and his allies obtained favorable results from their dealings with the Arkansas state government under Governor Clinton. At a time when Mr. McDougal was carrying the Clintons on their Whitewater loans, Mr. McDougal had a say in the making of state appointments, enjoyed personal access to the Governor and won valuable state leases for Madison. The Special Committee concludes that Governor Clinton's official and personal dealings with Mr. McDougal raised an apparent, if not an actual, improper conflict of interest.

Finally, the Clintons were not "passive" investors in the Whitewater real estate venture, as they have claimed. Indeed, the Clintons participated in important meetings concerning the Whitewater investment. The Special Committee concludes that the Clintons took an active role in obtaining and extending Whitewater-related loans.

Mrs. Clinton's legal work on Castle Grande related to an effort to conceal the true nature of the activities at Madison Guaranty.

The Castle Grande land development consisted of more than 1,000 acres of property near Little Rock purchased by Seth Ward, Webster Hubbell's father-in-law, and Madison Financial Corp. ("MFC")—Madison Guaranty's wholly-owned subsidiary. The land was sold in a series of transactions that caused nearly $4 million in losses to Madison Guaranty—losses ultimately borne by U.S. taxpayers.

Federal regulators have determined that Seth Ward acted as a "straw" man in the fraudulent Castle Grande transaction who simply held property in his name until MFC could find a buyer. In this way, Madison Guaranty was able to circumvent an Arkansas regulation that limited investment in real estate by a savings and loan. For his part in this sham deal, Mr. Ward earned over $300,000 in commissions on the sale of property.

Prior to the discovery of the Rose Law Firm billing records in the White House Residence, the nature and extent of Mrs. Clinton's work on Castle Grande was virtually unknown. The evidence obtained in the course of the Special Committee's investigation now establishes that Mrs. Clinton had direct and substantial involvement in Castle Grande.

The Rose billing records reflect that on April 7, 1986, Mrs. Clinton had a telephone conference with Madison Guaranty's chief loan officer, Don Denton. The records also reflect that on May 1, 1986, Mrs. Clinton prepared an option agreement under which MFC obtained the right to buy from Mr. Ward a small piece of property called Holman Acres for $400,000.

The background to the questionable transaction is as follows. In spring 1986, Mr. Ward approached John Latham, the President of Madison Guaranty, about collecting his commissions from the sham sales of real estate at Castle Grande. At the time, however, Madison Guaranty had come under scrutiny from federal banking regulators, who were examining the thrift and would have questioned the payment of such commissions.

Therefore, Seth Ward, Madison Guaranty, and Madison Financial executed a series of crossing loan transactions and promissory notes designed to pay Mr. Ward his commissions and fool the S&L's regulators. On March 31, 1986, Madison Guaranty loaned $400,000 to Mr. Ward. On April 7, 1986, MFC gave two promissory notes to Mr. Ward—one for $300,000 and the other for $70,943. Thus, Mr. Ward received his commissions from the $400,000 loan from Madison Guaranty, and MFC's notes effectively canceled his obligation to repay the loan and was the means by which he was able to keep his commissions.

The chief federal S&L examiner, James Clark, discovered the March 31 loan and April 7 notes during a 1986 examination and became concerned that there might be a connection between the crossing notes. Specifically, he suspected that the notes might represent a payment to Mr. Ward and thus a possibly improper investment by Madison Guaranty in MFC. Such investments by Madison Guaranty in its service corporation, MFC, were subject to a regulation limiting Madison's ability to invest in real estate.

When Mr. Clark inquired about the March 31 and April 7 notes, however, he was told that these notes were completely unrelated. He was told that the April 7 notes were related to MFC's plan to purchase Holman Acres from Mr. Ward. This transaction was to be accomplished through an as yet undrafted option agreement that would replace the notes, which existed simply to guarantee MFC's performance. In effect, the option agreement was a fictitious transaction designed to conceal the relationship between the March 31 loan and the April 7 notes.

According to Mr. Clark, the May 1, 1986, option prepared by Mrs. Clinton was used to disguise the fact that the crossing notes between Seth Ward, MFC, and Madison Guaranty were devised to pay commissions to Mr. Ward. In Mr. Clark's view, "the option was created 'in order to conceal the connection'" between the notes.

On April 7, 1986, Don Denton received a message that Mrs. Clinton had called. He returned the call and they discussed about the notes between Mr. Ward, MFC, and Madison Guaranty. Mr. Denton believed that Mrs. Clinton was preparing a $400,000 note between MFC and Mr. Ward, and he told her that such a note had already been prepared and executed. Mrs. Clinton asked him to send her whatever notes the S&L had executed with Mr. Ward. Mr. Denton did so, sending copies to Mrs. Clinton of the notes by courier.

Mr. Denton recalled that during this April 7 conversation he expressed concern to Mrs. Clinton with respect to the March 31 and April 1 notes because the note appeared to represent the payment by Madison Guaranty of an MFC obligation. Mrs. Clinton, however, "summarily dismissed" that Mr. Denton's concern in a manner that Mr. Denton took to mean that he ought to "take care of savings and loan matters, and she would take care of legal matters."

In sum, the Special Committee concludes that Mrs. Clinton's own work product—the May 1 option—was used to conceal the very transactions about which Mr. Denton expressed concern. This fact raises serious questions with respect to Mrs. Clinton's state of knowledge of the deceptive aspects of the transaction.

First, the billing records indicate that Mrs. Clinton was aware of the Arkansas regulation limiting the extent of Madison's investment in MFC. Indeed, the records reflect that on June 17, 1985, she reviewed a memorandum prepared by a Rose associate, Richard Massey, touching upon this regulation. More important, her conversation with Don Denton put her on notice—prior to the drafting of the critical May 1 option—that the notes exchanged by Mr. Ward, MFC, and Madison Guaranty were questionable. Thus, it appears that Mrs. Clinton was apprised of both the relevant law and facts that made the Castle Grande transaction irregular. Accordingly, an inference can be drawn that Mrs. Clinton might well have known that these documents were designed to conceal the true nature of the Madison-Ward transactions or that she consciously avoided the knowledge. At the very least, she was on notice to inquire further.

On June 13, 1996, the same day that the Special Committee received Mr. Denton's testimony, the Committee in a letter addressed to Mr. Kendall, Mrs. Clinton's counsel, requested that the First Lady attempt to refresh her recollection regarding the matters discussed by Mr. Denton and inform the Committee of what she recalls about them. The Special Committee's request was made in response to an earlier offer by Mrs. Clinton through a White House spokesman to answer in writing questions regarding the subject of the Special Committee's work.

On June 17, 1996, the Special Committee received an affidavit from Mrs. Clinton accompanied by a letter from Mr. Kendall. In the affidavit, Mrs. Clinton gave no indication as to her recollection regarding the subject matter of Mr. Denton's testimony. Instead, she simply requested that the Special Committee refer to Mr. Kendall's letter "addressing certain allegations recently made by Mr. Don Denton." In his letter, Mr. Kendall maintained that Mr. Denton's recollection is "wholly unreliable" but gave no indication as to the recollection of the First Lady. In sum, the First Lady has neither confirmed nor denied Mr. Denton's testimony.

Examination of Mrs. Clinton's involvement in Castle Grande cannot be viewed in isolation. The Special Committee also takes into account Mrs. Clinton's apparent failure to be more forthcoming about her role in Mr. McDougal's Castle Grande deal. When asked in 1995 about her knowledge of Castle Grande and some other land deals, Mrs. Clinton swore, under oath, "I do not believe I knew anything about any of these real estate parcels and projects." In light of the billing records, that statement appears incorrect on its face.

The Rose billing records reflect that Mrs. Clinton billed almost 30 hours to Castle Grande matters during the course of her representation of Madison Guaranty—more time than any other Rose attorney. And, in addition to the May 1 option and the phone call with Mr. Denton, Mrs. Clinton had 15 face-to-face or telephone conferences with Seth Ward, including one "regarding purchase from Brick Lile," the chairman of the company that sold the property to Mr. Ward and MFC.

In a sworn statement in 1996, Mrs. Clinton sought to explain her prior categorical denial of knowledge about Castle Grande by saying that she knew of the 1,000+ acre tract as "IDC"—the name of the company that sold the property and the matter to which she charged her billings. She further stated that she knew a small portion of the Castle Grande property, a trailer park, as Castle Grande Estates. The Committee finds it implausible that Mrs. Clinton would fail to recognize the name "Castle Grande" as referring to the larger development, given the testimony of Madison Guaranty insiders and federal regulators that the entire development was commonly known as Castle Grande.

The secreting of the Rose Law Firm billing records could have been motivated by a desire to conceal Mrs. Clinton's involvement in Castle Grande and, in particular, her involvement in work on the questionable April 7 notes and May 1 option could have motivated the secreting of the Rose Law Firm billing records. The jury in the recently concluded Tucker-McDougal trial convicted the defendants for crimes relating to the Castle Grande project. Prior to the discovery of the Rose billing records, Mrs. Clinton's role in Castle Grande was unknown. The desire to keep her role secret might have been the cause of the long absence of the billing records.

Webster Hubbell was significantly more involved in Castle Grande than he admitted in his Senate testimony.

Former Associate Attorney General and former Rose Law Firm partner Webster Hubbell has testified before the Special Committee and in other forums on several occasions. With respect to his testimony regarding his involvement in Castle Grande, Mr. Hubbell altered his story when he learned that Seth Ward was a nominee purchaser for MFC. In a December 1995 with the RTC, Mr. Hubbell stated that he understood as of September 1985, from Mr. Ward, that "Madison had limits on what it could own in its own name, and so Mr. Ward was going to own part of it until it could be sold."

And, in an interview with the RTC Office of Inspector General, Mr. Hubbell "said that Ward told him that he was negotiating on behalf of Madison to buy the IDC property, which would then be split up between Madison and Ward." In testimony before the Special Committee, however, Mr. Hubbell repeatedly testified that he was not aware of the deal between Madison and Ward until after the closing in early October 1985.

Mr. Hubbell was reluctant to answer questions regarding his own view of the legality of his father-in-law's role in the purchase of the IDC property. When asked if Mr. McDougal used Mr. Ward to evade a regulatory restriction, Mr. Hubbell answered, "I have never represented an S&L. I don't know whether it's illegal or not." When he was asked if he considered this transaction as a classic parking or warehousing transaction, Mr. Hubbell answered, "I think of parking and warehousing a little bit differently." When asked if he thought Mr. Ward could be considered a "straw man," Mr. Hubbell testified, "I didn't give it any consideration, you know. 'Straw man' means, to me, somebody who you clear title through."

Mr. Hubbell has denied advising Mr. Ward on the Castle Grande transaction. Specifically, he denied preparing a backdated September 24, 1985 letter or advising Mr. Ward on its preparation. There is evidence, however, that Mr. Hubbell may have prepared the backdated September 24, 1985, letter, which was found in his files at the Rose Law Firm. Martha Patton, Mr. Hubbell's secretary at Rose, has stated that although she does not recall typing the letter she believes that she did because the type is similar to that of the IBM typewriter that she used then, and the second page of the document is formatted in the style she used while a Rose secretary. She added that the letter appears to be "her style of typing . . ."

Former Madison chief loan officer Don Denton has indicated that Mr. Hubbell advised Mr. Ward on the Castle Grande matter. For example, Mr. Denton believed that the wording on the note, dated October 15, 1985, stating that Mr. Ward was not personally responsible for the note was prepared by Mr. Hubbell. Also, Mr. Denton believed that he had some conversations with Mr. Hubbell about the February 28, 1996, transaction.

Furthermore, Mr. Denton indicated in a recent interview that Mr. Hubbell was involved in the March 31 and April 7, 1986, notes between Mr. Ward, Madison Guaranty, and Madison Financial. He stated that he was "reasonably confident" that when Mrs. Clinton called him regarding these notes she was acting on Mr. Hubbell's behalf. Mr. Denton refused to say whether he ever dealt with Mr. Hubbell on the matter of the notes. He also declined to answer whether he had visited Mr. Hubbell's office at Rose regarding Mr. Ward or Madison Guaranty.

Mr. Hubbell may have provided inaccurate statements about his legal work on other occasions. In 1989 when the Rose Law Firm was retained to represent the FDIC in an action against Madison Guaranty's former accountants, Mr. Hubbell failed to disclose to regulators Rose's prior work for Madison. And in 1993 when he failed to disclose information he had learned the previous year from reading the Rose Law Firm billing records to FDIC investigators looking into the 1989 retention of Rose.

The Special Committee questions Mr. Hubbell's implausible claim that he did not advise Mr. Ward with respect to Castle Grande.

In 1985, Mr. McDougal retained Hillary Clinton to represent Madison Guaranty; the work was not brought in by a young associate.

The Special Committee concludes, based upon the substantial weight of the evidence, that Mr. McDougal hired Mrs. Clinton to represent Madison Guaranty Savings & Loan. Mrs. Clinton's statements that Richard Massey, then a young Rose Law Firm associate at the time, brought the client into the firm are not supported by the documentary or testimonial evidence received by the Committee.

Mr. McDougal made statements during the 1992 Clinton presidential campaign, as well as to the Los Angeles Times in 1993, that he put Mrs. Clinton on retainer as a favor to Bill Clinton. These McDougal statements are supported by others and by documentary evidence. Former Madison CEO John Latham confirmed that Mr. McDougal made the decision to retain the Rose Law Firm. Moreover, although President Clinton does not recall asking Mr. McDougal to place Mrs. Clinton on retainer, Mr. McDougal performed other favors for President Clinton when he was Governor by, among other things, substantial contributions, on behalf of the Clintons, on Whitewater loans.

Mrs. Clinton's markedly different account of how the business came to the Rose Law Firm is not confirmed by any attorney at the Rose Law Firm, including Mr. Massey. For example, Mrs. Clinton has repeatedly stated that Mr. Massey, then a first year associate at the Rose Law Firm, brought in Madison Guaranty as a client. She claims that Mr. Latham asked Mr. Massey whether he would be interested in representing Madison in connection with a proposed stock offering. Mrs. Clinton further explained that Mr. Massey was aware that she knew Mr. McDougal, so "he came to me and asked if I would talk with Jim to see whether or not Jim would let the lawyer and the officer go forward on this project. I did that, and I arranged that the firm would be paid $2,000 retainer."

Both Mr. Massey and Mr. Latham contradict Mrs. Clinton's version of events. Moreover, David Knight, a former partner of the Rose Law Firm, testified that he was involved in this meeting between Mr. Latham and Mr. Massey, and Mr. Latham did not hire Mr. Massey.

In a statement to the FDIC OIG in November 1994, Mrs. Clinton similarly told investigators that "she recalled Massey came to her and asked her to be the billing attorney which was a normal practice when an associate was handling the matter . . . Mrs. Clinton recalled that a Madison official (individual unknown) approached Rick Massey regarding a preferred stock offering in an effort to raise capital." In a sworn response to an RTC interrogatory in May 1995, Mrs. Clinton elaborated on her story. Mrs. Clinton stated that Mr. Massey approached her because "certain lawyers" in the Rose Law Firm were "opposed" to representing Mr. McDougal until Mr. McDougal paid an outstanding bill, and he was aware that Mrs. Clinton knew Mr. McDougal.

Mr. Massey, however, directly contradicted Mrs. Clinton's account stating that he was not responsible for bringing in Madison as a client. Specifically, Mr. Massey testified that Mr. Latham never offered him Madison's business and that he did not recall approaching Mrs. Clinton with a proposal to represent Madison. Contrary to Mrs. Clinton's unsworn statement of November 1994 to the RTC, Mr. Massey also testified that he did not ask Mrs. Clinton to be the billing attorney. Mr. Knight agrees that Mr. Massey did not secure an offer of business, and he—Mr. Knight—further testified that he would have expected to know about such an offer if it had happened.

Mrs. Clinton claimed that she became involved in discussions about the Madison retainer because of an outstanding debt Mr. McDougal, through his Madison Bank & Trust, owed to the Rose Law Firm in 1985.

Documentary evidence and testimony provided to the Special Committee, however, indicated that the outstanding balance of Rose's bill to Madison Bank & Trust was paid in November 1984, months prior to Rose's retainer in April 1985. Furthermore, Gary Bunch, President of Madison Bank & Trust, provided the Special Committee with documents showing that the legal fees owed to the Rose Law Firm were paid in late October 1984. Mr. Bunch further testified that Mr. McDougal directed him in October 1984 to pay the outstanding Rose Law Firm bill for the Madison Bank & Trust matter in full.

Following the discovery of the Rose billing records and the testimony of Mr. Massey before the Special Committee, Mrs. Clinton's story changed in a February 1996 interview with RTC investigators. She claimed, for the first time, that the late Vincent Foster initially informed her that Mr. Massey wanted to do legal work for Madison.

Mrs. Clinton's statements conflict internally and with the testimony of others involved in the events surrounding Rose's Madison retainer. Over the next several months, it was Mrs. Clinton—not Mr. Massey—that officials at Madison Guaranty, including Seth Ward and Jim McDougal, sought out for representation. Finally, Mr. Massey, Mr. Knight, Mr. Latham and Mr. Bunch, all unrelated and with no apparent reason to mislead the Special Committee, contradict Mrs. Clinton's assertion that she did not bring Madison Guaranty to the Rose Law Firm as a client.

Mrs. Clinton had a substantive contact with Beverly Bassett Schaffer about Madison Guaranty's proposal to issue preferred stock.

The Rose billing records and Beverly Bassett Schaffer contradict Mrs. Clinton's statements that she did not speak directly to Beverly Bassett Schaffer, the Arkansas Securities Commissioner in charge of state regulation of Madison Guaranty, about Madison Guaranty's proposed preferred stock transaction.

Prior to the discovery of the billing records, Mrs. Clinton claimed in her sworn responses to RTC interrogatories in May 1995 that she called the Arkansas Securities Department to find out "to whom Mr. Massey should direct any inquiries" on the proposed stock deal, but she did not recall to whom she spoke.

The Rose billing records reflect that Mrs. Clinton called Ms. Schaffer the day before the Rose Law Firm submitted Madison's proposal to do preferred stock offering to the Arkansas Securities Department. In testimony before the Special Committee, Ms. Schaffer directly contradicted Mrs. Clinton and stated that the substance of the proposal was discussed during the phone call, and that Ms. Schaffer told Mrs. Clinton that her agency would approve the proposal.

Mr. Massey likewise contradicted Mrs. Clinton's account of this important telephone call. Mr. Massey testified that he drafted the proposal and knew exactly to whom the proposal should be sent. Mr. Massey also testified that Mrs. Clinton never gave any instructions to him about whom he should address the transmission letter.

This conversation has at least the appearance of an attempt by the then-Governor's wife to lobby to influence the activities of state regulators on behalf of private clients. Thus, both Ms. Schaffer and Mrs. Clinton may have motive to hide this event from public scrutiny. The fact that Ms. Schaffer recalls that the phone call included a discussion of the substance of Madison Guaranty's stock proposal, which she approved two weeks later, supports the Special Committee's conclusion that a substantive call occurred.

Governor Clinton's official and personal dealings with James McDougal raised an apparent, if not an actual, improper conflict of interest.

Governor Clinton's official and personal dealings with Jim McDougal, beyond appearances, raised an apparent, if not actual, conflict of interest. Although Mr. McDougal was carrying the Clintons on the Whitewater loans, then Governor Clinton—using the power of his high political office—consistently acted favorably on Mr. McDougal's other business ventures and accepted many of the recommendations Mr. McDougal made regarding proposed state action. These favors took the form of influence in appointments, the awarding of lucrative state leases, and beneficial decisions relating to state regulators. This favoritism was critical to Mr. McDougal, whose savings & loan was experiencing serious financial trouble.

Of course, from the standpoint of Governor Clinton, if Madison Guaranty failed or Mr. McDougal experienced financial troubles, the Clintons could be liable for the full Whitewater debt. Thus, Governor Clinton had reason to act in a way to ensure the viability of Mr. McDougal's savings & loan, even if such action was adverse to the interests of the state. For example, documents indicate that Governor Clinton played a role in the award of contracts for state leases to Madison.

Perhaps the most blatant example of the problems created by this conflict of interest related to certain legislation. In 1987, Governor Clinton vetoed a water bill that favored a utility, Castle Sewer & Water, owned by R. D. Randolph and Jim Guy Tucker, two business associates of Mr. McDougal. Mr. Randolph and Mr. Tucker threatened Governor Clinton by reminding him of a questionable 1985 Madison fundraiser, and the possibility of litigation related to Rose's representation of Madison on the utility issue. Shortly thereafter, Governor Clinton called the legislature into a special session and then signed the bill, as Mr. McDougal's associates desired.

The Clintons took an active role in obtaining and extending Whitewater-related loans; they were not "passive" investors in Whitewater.

The Clintons were not "passive investors" in the Whitewater real estate venture. Indeed, they actively sought and obtained Whitewater loans and extensions. Based largely on Mr. Clinton's official position, state bankers routinely gave the Clintons beneficial treatment on Whitewater-related loans, often disregarding banking regulations and sound lending practices.

Whitewater was a "no cash" deal. Mr. Clinton actively participated in obtaining the initial down payment loan [for] the Whitewater investment. He enlisted bank lobbyist Paul Berry to grant him and James McDougal an unsecured loan for the down payment. This loan was just one of the Whitewater loans that would not have been made under what the lending officer characterized as "ordinary circumstances."

Moreover, the Clintons actively participated in key meetings concerning the Whitewater real estate investment. At the outset of the investment, Mr. Clinton met with Mr. McDougal about the structure of the financing. When Mr. Clinton's personal accountant, Gaines Norton, raised serious questions about the lawfulness of Mr. McDougal's plans, Mr. Clinton told him to "back off." This indicates a conscious avoidance of learning the facts about the Whitewater transactions.

Also early in the investment, Mrs. Clinton had at least two meetings with bank officials to renew Whitewater loans. Although few payments of principal were being made, and the Clintons often refused to provide the required loan documents and financial statements, Mrs. Clinton's continued meetings and conversations with reluctant bank officials helped to secure the extension of Whitewater loans. Again and again, bankers looked the other way when the Clintons failed to make principal payments on the Whitewater loan or failed to submit the required financial statements, many times due to Governor Clinton's public office. Finally, after 1986, Mrs. Clinton essentially took control of the Whitewater investment. Mrs. Clinton sought power of attorney over the investment, paid back taxes and attempted to collect all the Whitewater documents.

In fact, it appears that in many instances where the Clintons got involved with the Whitewater loans, the banking regulations were either "bent" or broken. For example, federal and state regulators cited Mrs. Clinton's irregular out of territory and often past due loan in connection with Whitewater Lot 13 and prohibited the bank from renewing the loan. Governor Clinton's Bank Commissioner Marlin Jackson may have assisted the Clintons in obtaining a new loan at a bank he then regulated. Later, Mr. Jackson improperly used government stationery in connection with securing loan renewals for the Clintons. Mr. Jackson used his government position to act as a go-between for the Clintons in their dealings with a state-regulated bank was clearly inappropriate. This action raises serious questions of whether Mr. Jackson misused his official position to influence improperly bank action to benefit the wholly private interests of the Clintons.

Governor Clinton's office steered state bond work to Dan Lasater.

The Special Committee was very concerned about Governor Clinton's troubling relationship with Arkansas businessman Dan Lasater. In 1980, Mr. Lasater entered the securities business with the firm of Collins, Locke & Lasater. In January 1985, a Little Rock paper reported that a federal bankruptcy judge found, in open court, that Mr. Lasater lied under oath during the bankruptcy trial of his former business partner, George Locke, and also found that Mr. Lasater was involved in a conspiracy to defraud Mr. Locke's creditors. In February 1985, widely-reported accounts of sworn testimony in federal court put Governor Clinton on notice that Mr. Lasater was a cocaine user and the subject of a drug investigation. On October 23, 1986, Mr. Lasater was indicted on drug charges for possession and distribution of cocaine.

Mr. Lasater contributed substantial sums of money to Governor Clinton, "loaned" $8,000 to the Governor's brother, Roger, to pay a drug debt, and, at the Governor's request, gave Roger a job.

The Special Committee identified three instances in which Governor Clinton or his aides inappropriately sought to take actions intended to benefit Mr. Lasater. First, in February 1983, Senior Economic Adviser to the Governor, Bob Nash, while acting in his official capacity, improperly directed Charles Stout, the Chairman of the Arkansas Housing Development Board ("AHDA"), to grant lucrative state bond underwriting contracts to Mr. Lasater's firm, Collins, Locke & Lasater. Mr. Nash directed AHDA Chairman Stout to award 15% of AHDA's bond-business to Mr. Lasater's firm. This order represented an unprecedented interference by the Governor's office into the otherwise independent and competitive underwriting selection process of the agency. Mr. Nash did not suggest that the AHDA should include other Arkansas firms. Rather, Mr. Nash's order specifically directed that Mr. Lasater's firm be included. Mr. Nash's directive had the weight and influence of the Governor's office behind it, and, as a result, the AHDA Board bowed to the Governor's order awarded a substantial amount of state bond business to Mr. Lasater's firm. Prior to Mr. Stout's order, Mr. Lasater's firm had not received AHDA bond business. In addition, the Stephens firm, the largest bond firm in Little Rock, questioned whether Mr. Lasater's firm was qualified to participate in these offerings.

Second, in late 1983, Governor Clinton sought to use the power of his office to benefit Mr. Lasater when the Governor personally called and asked Linda Garner, the State Insurance Commissioner, to include Collins, Locke and Lasater as a manager for the multi-billion dollar securities portfolio for which she was acting as receiver in connection with her responsibilities as Insurance Commissioner. Governor Clinton did not attempt to intervene on behalf of any other financial firms. The Committee has concluded that this contact represents another instance where Governor Clinton inappropriately tried to influence an appointed state official to direct business opportunities to Mr. Lasater.

Third, the Governor's office extended itself to monitor and to facilitate Mr. Lasater's company's efforts to secure the underwriting contract for a $29 million dollar bond financing for a police radio system in 1985.

In each of these three instances, the Special Committee concludes that Mr. Lasater received inappropriate assistance from the Governor and his office. Given Mr. Lasater's past problems, it is far from clear why Mr. Lasater would be entitled to preferential treatment.

The Clintons took a series of erroneous tax deductions related to Whitewater.

The Special Committee concludes that the Clintons took a series of erroneous Whitewater deductions, often in error, on their personal federal income tax returns. From 1978 to the early 1990s, the Clintons invested a total of $42,192 in Whitewater. During this same period, the Clintons deducted $42,656 of their Whitewater related expenses on their federal income tax returns—almost $500 more than their total investment in the corporation. From 1992 to this date, the Clintons have admitted taking improper deductions of $7,928 and omitting income of $8,171 on their federal income tax returns during the period of their Whitewater investment. Based on its analysis of the available evidence, the Special Committee concludes that the Clintons could have understated their income on Whitewater-related items by as much as an additional $33,771, for a total increase in taxable income of $49,870.

Source: U.S. Congress. Senate. *Final Report of the Special Committee to Investigate Whitewater Development Corporation and Related Matters Together with Additional and Minority Views.* (S. Rpt. 104–280). Washington, D.C.: Government Printing Office, 1996.

Excerpt from Starr Report Outlining Grounds for Impeachment of President Clinton, September 9, 1998

Kenneth W. Starr, a federal judge on the U.S. Court of Appeals for the District of Columbia for six years under President Ronald Reagan, served as U.S. solicitor general from 1989 to 1993 under President George H. W. Bush. At one time he was a leading candidate to become a justice of the U.S. Supreme Court. In 1994, Starr replaced Robert B. Fiske Jr. as the independent counsel investigating the Whitewater scandal. Although the charges and denials surrounding the Whitewater investigation appeared to be limping to an ambiguous conclusion, with no hard evidence indicating criminal malfeasance by President Bill Clinton, the president's affair with Monica S. Lewinsky breathed new life into Starr's work. Starr laid out his case against Clinton in a 445-page report to Congress released in September 1998. It became a bestseller, filled with details about the intimate relationship between Clinton and Lewinsky. The report laid the foundation for Clinton's impeachment, charging that the president had lied under oath about his relationship with Lewinsky, as well as in his deposition in the Paula Jones case, and had obstructed justice.

EXCERPT FROM STARR REPORT SEPTEMBER 9, 1998

Pursuant to Section 595(c) of Title 28, the Office of Independent Counsel (OIC) hereby submits substantial and credible information that President Clinton obstructed justice during the *Jones v. Clinton* sexual harassment lawsuit by lying under oath and concealing evidence of his relationship with a young White House intern and federal employee, Monica Lewinsky. After a federal criminal investigation of the President's actions began in January 1998, the President lied under oath to the grand jury and obstructed justice during the grand jury investigation. There also is substantial and credible information that the President's actions with respect to Monica Lewinsky constitute an abuse of authority inconsistent with the President's constitutional duty to faithfully execute the laws.

There is substantial and credible information supporting the following eleven possible grounds for impeachment:

1. President Clinton lied under oath in his civil case when he denied a sexual affair, a sexual relationship, or sexual relations with Monica Lewinsky.
2. President Clinton lied under oath to the grand jury about his sexual relationship with Ms. Lewinsky.
3. In his civil deposition, to support his false statement about the sexual relationship, President Clinton also lied under oath about being alone with Ms. Lewinsky and about the many gifts exchanged between Ms. Lewinsky and him.
4. President Clinton lied under oath in his civil deposition about his discussions with Ms. Lewinsky concerning her involvement in the *Jones* case.
5. During the *Jones* case, the President obstructed justice and had an understanding with Ms. Lewinsky to jointly conceal the truth about their relationship by concealing gifts subpoenaed by Ms. Jones's attorneys.
6. During the *Jones* case, the President obstructed justice and had an understanding with Ms. Lewinsky to jointly conceal the truth of their relationship from the judicial process by a scheme that included the following means: (i) Both the President and Ms. Lewinsky understood that they would lie under oath in the *Jones* case about their sexual relationship; (ii) the President suggested to Ms. Lewinsky that she prepare an affidavit that, for the President's purposes, would memorialize her testimony under oath and could be used to prevent questioning of both of them about their relationship; (iii) Ms. Lewinsky signed and filed the false affidavit; (iv) the President used Ms. Lewinsky's false affidavit at his deposition in an attempt to head off questions about Ms. Lewinsky; and (v) when that failed, the President lied under oath at his civil deposition about the relationship with Ms. Lewinsky.
7. President Clinton endeavored to obstruct justice by helping Ms. Lewinsky obtain a job in New York at a time when she would have been a witness harmful to him were she to tell the truth in the *Jones* case.
8. President Clinton lied under oath in his civil deposition about his discussions with Vernon Jordan concerning Ms. Lewinsky's involvement in the *Jones* case.
9. The President improperly tampered with a potential witness by attempting to corruptly influence the testimony of his personal secretary, Betty Currie, in the days after his civil deposition.
10. President Clinton endeavored to obstruct justice during the grand jury investigation by refusing to testify for seven months and lying to senior White House aides with knowledge that they would relay the President's false statements to the grand jury—and did thereby deceive, obstruct, and impede the grand jury.
11. President Clinton abused his constitutional authority by (i) lying to the public and the Congress in January 1998 about his relationship with Ms. Lewinsky; (ii) promising at that time to cooperate fully with the grand jury investigation; (iii) later refusing six invitations to testify voluntarily to the grand jury; (iv) invoking Executive Privilege; (v) lying to the grand jury in August 1998; and (vi) lying again to the public and Congress on August 17, 1998—all as part of an effort to hinder, impede, and deflect possible inquiry by the Congress of the United States.

Source: U.S. Congress. House Document 105-310: *Communication from Kenneth W. Starr, Independent Counsel, Transmitting a Referral to the United States House of Representatives Filed in Conformity with the Requirements of Title 28, United States Code, Section 595(c).* Washington: Government Printing Office, 1998. [The best-known printing is *The Starr Report: The Findings of Independent Counsel Kenneth W. Starr on President Clinton and the Lewinsky Affair.* New York: Public Affairs, 1998.]

Executive Summary of President Clinton's Memorandum Concerning the Starr Report, September 11, 1998

The White House was quick to respond to the Starr Report. On September 11, 1998, President Bill Clinton's personal lawyer, David Kendall, accompanied by White House counsel Charles Ruff and other White House lawyers, held a news conference to release a preliminary memorandum on the report. In his opening statement Kendall charged that independent counsel Kenneth W. Starr and his fellow investigators had engaged in an unrestrained, politically motivated personal assault on the president. "This is not a news story," Kendall said. "A man tried to keep an inappropriate relationship private. The President has acknowledged his personal wrongdoing and sought forgiveness from his family, Ms. Lewinsky, the Cabinet, the Congress, and the country. In light of that acknowledgment, the salacious allegations in this referral are simply intended to humiliate, embarrass, and politically damage the President. In short, this is personal and not impeachable."

EXECUTIVE SUMMARY OF PRESIDENT CLINTON'S MEMORANDUM CONCERNING THE STARR REPORT SEPTEMBER 11, 1998

Summary of Key Points of the President's Case in Anticipation of the Starr Report

1. The President has acknowledged a serious mistake—an inappropriate relationship with Monica Lewinsky. He has taken responsibility for his actions, and he has apologized to the country, to his friends, leaders of his party, the cabinet and most importantly, his family.
2. This private mistake does not amount to an impeachable action. A relationship outside one's marriage is wrong—and the President admits that. It is not a high crime or misdemeanor. The Constitution specifically states that Congress shall impeach *only* for "treason, bribery or other high crimes and misdemeanors." These words in the Constitution were chosen with great care, and after extensive deliberations.
3. "High crimes and misdemeanors" had a fixed meaning to the Framers of our Constitution—it meant wrongs committed against our system of government. The impeachment clause was designed to protect our country against a President who was using his official powers against the nation, against the American people, against our society. It was never designed to allow a political body to force a President from office for a very personal mistake.
4. Remember—this report is based entirely on allegations obtained by a grand jury—reams and reams of allegations and purported "evidence" that would never be admitted in court, that has never been seen by the President or his lawyers, and that was not subject to cross-examination or any other traditional safeguards to ensure its credibility.
5. Grand juries are not designed to search for truth. They do not and are not intended to ensure credibility, reliability, or simple fairness. They only exist to accuse. Yet this is the process that the Independent Counsel has chosen to provide the "evidence" to write his report.
6. The law defines perjury very clearly. Perjury requires proof that an individual knowingly made a false statement while under oath. Answers to questions that are literally true are *not* perjury. Even if an answer doesn't directly answer the question asked, it is not perjury if it is true—no accused has an obligation to help his accuser. Answers to fundamentally ambiguous questions also can never be perjury. And nobody can be convicted of perjury based on only one other person's testimony.
7. The President did not commit perjury. Most of the illegal leaks suggesting his testimony was perjurious falsely describe his testimony. First of all, the President never testified in the Jones deposition that he was not alone with Ms. Lewinsky. The President never testified that his relationship with Ms. Lewinsky was the same as with any other intern. To the contrary, he admitted exchanging gifts with her, knowing about her job search, receiving cards and notes from her, and knowing other details of her personal life that made it plain he had a special relationship with her.
8. The President has admitted he had an improper sexual relationship with Ms. Lewinsky. In a civil deposition, he gave narrow answers to ambiguous questions. As a matter of law, those answers could not give rise to a criminal charge of perjury. In the face of the President's admission of his relationship, the disclosure of lurid and salacious allegations can only be intended to humiliate the President and force him from office.
9. There was no obstruction of justice. We believe Betty Currie testified that Ms. Lewinsky asked her to hold the gifts and that the President never talked to her about the gifts. The President admitted giving and receiving gifts from Ms. Lewinsky when he was asked about it. The President never asked Ms. Lewinsky to get rid of the gifts and he never asked Ms. Currie to get them. We believe that Ms. Currie's testimony supports the President's.
10. The President never tried to get Ms. Lewinsky a job after she left the White House in order to influence her testimony in the Paula Jones case. The President knew Ms. Lewinsky was unhappy in her Pentagon job after she left the White House and did ask the White House personnel office to treat her fairly in her job search. He never instructed anyone to hire her, or even indicated that he very much wanted it to happen. Ms. Lewinsky was never offered a job at the White House after she left—and it's pretty apparent that if the President had ordered it, she would have been.
11. The President did not facilitate Ms. Lewinsky's interview with Bill Richardson, or her discussions with Vernon Jordan. Betty Currie asked John Podesta if he could help her with her New York job search which led to an interview with Bill Richardson, and Ms. Currie also put her in touch with her longtime friend, Mr. Jordan. Mr. Jordan has made it clear that this is the case, and, as a private individual, he is free to offer job advice wherever he sees fit.
12. There was no witness tampering. Betty Currie was not supposed to be a witness in the Paula Jones case. If she was not called or going to be called, it was impossible for any conversations the President had with her to be witness tampering. The President testified that he did not in any way attempt to influence her recollection.
13. There is no "talking points" smoking gun. Numerous illegal leaks painted the mysterious talking points as the proof that the President or his staff attempted to suborn the perjury of Monica Lewinsky or Linda Tripp. The OIC's spokesman said that the "talking points" were the "key" to Starr even being granted authority to investigate the President's private life. Yet in the end, Ms. Lewinsky has apparently admitted the talking points were written by her alone [or with Ms. Tripp's assistance], and the President was not asked one single question about them in his grand jury appearance.

14. Invocation of privileges was not an abuse of power. The President's lawful assertion of privileges in a court of law was only made on the advice of his Counsel, and was in significant measure validated by the courts. The legal claims were advanced sparingly and as a last resort after all attempts at compromise by the White House Counsel's office were rejected to protect the core constitutional and institutional interests of this and future presidencies.
15. Neither the President nor the White House played a role in the Secret Service's lawful efforts to prevent agents from testifying to preserve its protective function. The President never asked, directed or participated in any decision regarding the protective function privilege. Neither did any White House official. The Treasury and Justice Departments independently decided to respond to the historically unprecedented subpoenas of Secret Service personnel and to pursue the privilege to ensure the protection of this and future presidents.
16. The President did not abuse his power by permitting White House staff to comment on the investigation. The President has acknowledged misleading his family, staff and the country about the nature of his relationship with Ms. Lewinsky, and he has apologized and asked for forgiveness. However, this personal failing does not constitute a criminal abuse of power. If allowing aides to repeat misleading statements is a crime, then any number of public officials are guilty of misusing their office for as long as they fail to admit wrong doing in response to any allegation about their activities.
17. The actions of White House attorneys were completely lawful. The White House Counsel attorneys provided the President and White House officials with informed, candid advice on issues raised during this investigation that affected the President's official duties. This was especially necessary given the fact that impeachment proceedings against the President were a possible result of the OIC's investigation from Day One. In fact, throughout the investigation, the OIC relied on the White House Counsel's office for assistance in gathering information and arranging interviews and grand jury appearances. The Counsel's office's actions were well known to the OIC throughout the investigation and no objection was ever voiced.

Source: http://icreport.access.gpo.gov/report/rebuttal1.htm. See also, *The Starr Report: The Findings of Independent Counsel Kenneth W. Starr on President Clinton and the Lewinsky Affair.* New York: Public Affairs, 1998, 359–62.

Resolution of Impeachment of President Clinton, December 15, 1998

A month after independent counsel Kenneth W. Starr issued his report, the House of Representatives voted on October 8, 1998, for impeachment proceedings to begin against President Bill Clinton. The task of drawing up the charges against the president was now in the hands of the House Judiciary Committee, chaired by Representative Henry Hyde (R-Ill.). For two months the committee labored to define the impeachment charges. In the second week of December, the members approved four articles charging Clinton with lying under oath and obstruction of justice. On December 15, Chairman Hyde introduced the impeachment resolution in the House.

RESOLUTION OF IMPEACHMENT OF PRESIDENT CLINTON DECEMBER 15, 1998

Resolved, That William Jefferson Clinton, President of the United States, is impeached for high crimes and misdemeanors, and that the following articles of impeachment be exhibited to the United States Senate:

Articles of impeachment exhibited by the House of Representatives of the United States of America in the name of itself and of the people of the United States of America, against William Jefferson Clinton, President of the United States of America, in maintenance and support of its impeachment against him for high crimes and misdemeanors.

Article I

In his conduct while President of the United States, William Jefferson Clinton, in violation of his constitutional oath faithfully to execute the office of President of the United States and, to the best of his ability, preserve, protect, and defend the Constitution of the United States, and in violation of his constitutional duty to take care that the laws be faithfully executed, has willfully corrupted and manipulated the judicial process of the United States for his personal gain and exoneration, impeding the administration of justice, in that: On August 17, 1998, William Jefferson Clinton swore to tell the truth, the whole truth, and nothing but the truth before a Federal grand jury of the United States. Contrary to that oath, William Jefferson Clinton willfully provided perjurious, false and misleading testimony to the grand jury concerning one or more of the following:

(1) the nature and details of his relationship with a subordinate Government employee;
(2) prior perjurious, false and misleading testimony he gave in a Federal civil rights action brought against him;
(3) prior false and misleading statements he allowed his attorney to make to a Federal judge in that civil rights action; and

(4) his corrupt efforts to influence the testimony of witnesses and to impede the discovery of evidence in that civil rights action.

In doing this, William Jefferson Clinton has undermined the integrity of his office, has brought disrepute on the Presidency, has betrayed his trust as President, and has acted in a manner subversive of the rule of law and justice, to the manifest injury of the people of the United States.

Wherefore, William Jefferson Clinton, by such conduct, warrants impeachment and trial, and removal from office and disqualification to hold and enjoy any office of honor, trust, or profit under the United States.

Article II

In his conduct while President of the United States, William Jefferson Clinton, in violation of his constitutional oath faithfully to execute the office of President of the United States and, to the best of his ability, preserve, protect, and defend the Constitution of the United States, and in violation of his constitutional duty to take care that the laws be faithfully executed, has willfully corrupted and manipulated the judicial process of the United States for his personal gain and exoneration, impeding the administration of justice, in that:

(1) On December 23, 1997, William Jefferson Clinton, in sworn answers to written questions asked as part of a Federal civil rights action brought against him, willfully provided perjurious, false and misleading testimony in response to questions deemed relevant by a Federal judge concerning conduct and proposed conduct with subordinate employees.

(2) On January 17, 1998, William Jefferson Clinton swore under oath to tell the truth, the whole truth, and nothing but the truth in a deposition given as part of a Federal civil rights action brought against him. Contrary to that oath, William Jefferson Clinton willfully provided perjurious, false and misleading testimony in response to questions deemed relevant by a Federal judge concerning the nature and details of his relationship with a subordinate Government employee, his knowledge of that employee's involvement and participation in the civil rights action brought against him, and his corrupt efforts to influence the testimony of that employee.

In all of this, William Jefferson Clinton has undermined the integrity of his office, has brought disrepute on the Presidency, has betrayed his trust as President, and has acted in a manner subversive of the rule of law and justice, to the manifest injury of the people of the United States.

Wherefore, William Jefferson Clinton, by such conduct, warrants impeachment and trial, and removal from office and disqualification to hold and enjoy any office of honor, trust, or profit under the United States.

Article III

In his conduct while President of the United States, William Jefferson Clinton, in violation of his constitutional oath faithfully to execute the office of President of the United States and, to the best of his ability, preserve, protect, and defend the Constitution of the United States, and in violation of his constitutional duty to take care that the laws be faithfully executed, has prevented, obstructed, and impeded the administration of justice, and has to that end engaged personally, and through his subordinates and agents, in a course of conduct or scheme designed to delay, impede, cover up, and conceal the existence of evidence and testimony related to a Federal civil rights action brought against him in a duly instituted judicial proceeding.

The means used to implement this course of conduct or scheme included one or more of the following acts:

(1) On or about December 17, 1997, William Jefferson Clinton corruptly encouraged a witness in a Federal civil rights action brought against him to execute a sworn affidavit in that proceeding that he knew to be perjurious, false and misleading.

(2) On or about December 17, 1997, William Jefferson Clinton corruptly encouraged a witness in a Federal civil rights action brought against him to give perjurious, false and misleading testimony if and when called to testify personally in that proceeding.

(3) On or about December 28, 1997, William Jefferson Clinton corruptly engaged in, encouraged, or supported a scheme to conceal evidence that had been subpoenaed in a Federal civil rights action brought against him.

(4) Beginning on or about December 7, 1997, and continuing through and including January 14, 1998, William Jefferson Clinton intensified and succeeded in an effort to secure job assistance to a witness in a Federal civil rights action brought against him in order to corruptly prevent the truthful testimony of that witness in that proceeding at a time when the truthful testimony of that witness would have been harmful to him.

(5) On January 17, 1998, at his deposition in a Federal civil rights action brought against him, William Jefferson Clinton corruptly allowed his attorney to make false and misleading statements to a Federal judge characterizing an affidavit, in order to prevent questioning deemed relevant by the judge. Such false and misleading statements were subsequently acknowledged by his attorney in a communication to that judge.

(6) On or about January 18 and January 20–21, 1998, William Jefferson Clinton related a false and misleading account of events relevant to a Federal civil rights action brought against him to a potential witness in that proceeding, in order to corruptly influence the testimony of that witness.

(7) On or about January 21, 23 and 26, 1998, William Jefferson Clinton made false and misleading statements

to potential witnesses in a Federal grand jury proceeding in order to corruptly influence the testimony of those witnesses. The false and misleading statements made by William Jefferson Clinton were repeated by the witnesses to the grand jury, causing the grand jury to receive false and misleading information.

In all of this, William Jefferson Clinton has undermined the integrity of his office, has brought disrepute on the Presidency, has betrayed his trust as President, and has acted in a manner subversive of the rule of law and justice, to the manifest injury of the people of the United States.

Wherefore, William Jefferson Clinton, by such conduct, warrants impeachment and trial, and removal from office and disqualification to hold and enjoy any office of honor, trust, or profit under the United States.

Article IV

Using the powers and influence of the office of President of the United States, William Jefferson Clinton, in violation of his constitutional oath faithfully to execute the office of President of the United States and, to the best of his ability, preserve, protect, and defend the Constitution of the United States, and in disregard of his constitutional duty to take care that the laws be faithfully executed, has engaged in conduct that resulted in misuse and abuse of his high office, impaired the due and proper administration of justice and the conduct of lawful inquiries, and contravened the authority of the legislative branch and the truth seeking purpose of a coordinate investigative proceeding, in that, as President, William Jefferson Clinton refused and failed to respond to certain written requests for admission and willfully made perjurious, false and misleading sworn statements in response to certain written requests for admission propounded to him as part of the impeachment inquiry authorized by the House of Representatives of the Congress of the United States. William Jefferson Clinton, in refusing and failing to respond and in making perjurious, false and misleading statements, assumed to himself functions and judgments necessary to the exercise of the sole power of impeachment vested by the Constitution in the House of Representatives and exhibited contempt for the inquiry.

In doing this, William Jefferson Clinton has undermined the integrity of his office, has brought disrepute on the Presidency, has betrayed his trust as President, and has acted in a manner subversive of the rule of law and justice, to the manifest injury of the people of the United States.

Wherefore, William Jefferson Clinton, by such conduct, warrants impeachment and trial, and removal from office and disqualification to hold and enjoy any office of honor, trust, or profit under the United States.

Source: U.S. House of Representatives. Resolution of Impeachment of President Clinton, H. Res. 611, 105th Cong., 2d sess. Report No. 105–830, Dec. 15, 1998, http://icreport.access.gpo.gov/hr611rh.txt.

Closing Defense Argument at the Impeachment Trial of President Clinton: Dale Bumpers, January 21, 1999

On January 21, 1999, Dale Bumpers, the longtime senator from Bill Clinton's home state of Arkansas who had recently retired after four terms, returned to the Senate for one of the most important missions of his career—to persuade his former colleagues to spare the president of the United States the ultimate humiliation of removal from office. A recurring theme running throughout his speech was that the prosecution had been overzealous, willing to go to extraordinary lengths to bring down the president—$50 million, teams of FBI agents, and an overwhelming desire to win that trumped all notions of fairness and reason. When he finished, a group of senators from both parties rushed to his side to congratulate Bumpers for an exquisite piece of oratory. "Very impressive!" Senator Strom Thurmond (R-S.C.) shouted, not that Bumpers had persuaded his old friend to change his vote. But the speech, a mixture of constitutional exegesis and good old-fashioned humor, solidified Clinton's tenuous hold on his support. He would survive the Senate vote and finish out his term.

CLOSING DEFENSE ARGUMENT BY DALE BUMPERS, JANUARY 21, 1999

THE CHIEF JUSTICE. The Chair recognizes Mr. Counsel Bumpers to continue the presentation in the case of the President.

MR. COUNSEL BUMPERS. Mr. Chief Justice, my distinguished House managers from the House of Representatives, colleagues, I have seen the look of disappointment on many faces, because I know a lot of people really thought they would be rid of me once and for all. (Laughter.)

I have taken a lot of ribbing this afternoon. But I have seriously negotiated with some people, particularly on this side, about an offer to walk out and not deliver this speech in exchange for a few votes. (Laughter.)

I understand three have it under active consideration. (Laughter.)

It is a great joy to see you, and it is especially pleasant to see an audience which represents about the size of the cumulative audience I had over a period of 24 years. (Laughter.)

I came here today for a lot of reasons. One was that I was promised a 40-foot cord. I have been shorted 28 feet. Chris Dodd said he didn't want me in his lap. I assume he arranged for the cord to be shortened.

I want to especially thank some of you for your kind comments in the press when it received some publicity that I would be here to close the debate on behalf of the White House counsel and the President.

I was a little dismayed by Senator Bennett's remark. He said, "Yes, Senator Bumpers is a great speaker, but he was never persuasive with me because I never agreed with him." (Laughter.)

I thought he could have done better than that. (Laughter.)

You can take some comfort, colleagues, in the fact that I am not being paid, and when I finish, you will probably think the White House got their money's worth. (Laughter.)

I have told audiences that over 24 years, I went home almost every weekend and returned usually about dusk on Sunday evening. And you know the plane ride into National Airport, when you can see the magnificent Washington Monument and this building from the window of the airplane—I have told these students at the university, a small liberal arts school at home, Hendrix—after 24 years of that, literally hundreds of times, I never failed to get goose bumps.

The same thing is true about this Chamber. I can still remember as though it was yesterday the awe I felt when I first stepped into this magnificent Chamber so full of history, so beautiful. And last Tuesday, as I returned, after only a short 3-week absence, I still felt that same sense of awe that I did the first time I walked in this Chamber.

Colleagues, I come here with some sense of reluctance. The President and I have been close friends for 25 years. We fought so many battles back home together in our beloved Arkansas. We tried mightily all of my years as Governor and his, and all of my years in the Senate when he was Governor, to raise the living standard in the delta area of Mississippi, Arkansas and Louisiana, where poverty is unspeakable, with some measure of success; not nearly enough.

We tried to provide health care for the lesser among us, for those who are well off enough they can't get on welfare, but not making enough to buy health insurance. We have fought about everything else to improve the educational standards for a State that for so many years was at the bottom of the list, or near the bottom of the list, of income, and we have stood side by side to save beautiful pristine areas in our State from environmental degradation.

We even crashed a twin engine Beech Bonanza trying to get to the Gillett coon supper, a political event that one misses at his own risk. We crashed this plane on a snowy evening at a rural airport off the runway sailing out across the snow, jumped out—jumped out—and ran away unscathed, to the dismay of every politician in Arkansas. (Laughter.)

The President and I have been together hundreds of times at parades, dedications, political events, social events, and in all of those years and all of those hundreds of times we have been together, both in public and in private, I have never one time seen the President conduct himself in a way that did not reflect the highest credit on him, his family, his State and his beloved Nation.

The reason I came here today with some reluctance—please don't misconstrue that, it has nothing to do with my feelings about the President, as I have already said—but it is because we are from the same State, and we are long friends. I know that necessarily diminishes to some extent the effectiveness of my words. So if Bill Clinton, the man, Bill Clinton, the friend, were the issue here, I am quite sure I would not be doing this. But it is the weight of history on all of us, and it is my reverence for that great document—you have heard me rail about it for 24 years—that we call our Constitution, the most sacred document to me next to the Holy Bible.

These proceedings go right to the heart of our Constitution where it deals with impeachment, the part that provides the gravest punishment for just about anybody—the President—even though the framers said we are putting this in to protect the public, not to punish the President. Ah, colleagues, you have such an awesome responsibility. My good friend, the senior Senator from New York, has said it well. He says a decision to convict holds the potential for destabilizing the Office of the Presidency. And those 400 historians—and I know some have made light about those historians, are they just friends of Bill?

Last evening, I went over that list of historians, many of whom I know, among them C. Vann Woodward. In the South we love him. He is the preeminent southern historian in the Nation. I promise you—he may be a Democrat, he may even be a friend of the President, but when you talk about integrity, he is the walking personification, exemplification of integrity.

Well, colleagues, I have heard so many adjectives to describe this gallery and these proceedings—historic, memorable, unprecedented, awesome. All of those words, all of those descriptions are apt. And to those, I would add the word "dangerous," dangerous not only for the reasons I just stated, but because it is dangerous to the political process. And it is dangerous to the unique mix of pure democracy and republican government Madison and his colleagues so brilliantly crafted and which has sustained us for 210 years.

Mr. Chief Justice, this is what we lawyers call "dicta"—this costs you nothing. It is extra. But the more I study that document, and those 4 months at Philadelphia in 1787, the more awed I am. And you know what Madison did—the brilliance was in its simplicity—he simply said: Man's nature is to get other people to dance to their tune. Man's nature is to abuse his fellow man sometimes. And he said:

The way to make sure that the majorities don't abuse the minorities, and the way to make sure that the bullies don't run over the weaklings, is to provide the same rights for everybody. And I had to think about that a long time before I delivered my first lecture at the University of Arkansas last week. And it made so much sense to me.

But the danger, as I say, is to the political process, and dangerous for reasons feared by the framers about legislative control of the Executive. That single issue and how to deal with impeachment was debated off and on for the entire 4 months of the Constitutional Convention. But the word "dangerous" is not mine. It is Alexander Hamilton's—brilliant, good-looking guy—Mr. Ruff quoted extensively on Tuesday afternoon in his brilliant statement here. He quoted Alexander Hamilton precisely, and it is a little arcane. It isn't easy to understand.

So if I may, at the expense of being slightly repetitious, let me paraphrase what Hamilton said. He said: The Senate had a unique role in participating with the executive branch in appointments; and, two, it had a role—it had a role—in participating with the executive in the character of a court for the trial of impeachments. But he said—and I must say this; and you all know it—he said it would be difficult to get a, what he called, well-constituted court from wholly elected Members. He said: Passions would agitate the whole community and divide it between those who were friendly and those who had inimical interests to the accused; namely, the President. Then he said—and these are his words: The greatest danger was that the decision would be based on the comparative strength of the parties rather than the innocence or guilt of the President.

You have a solemn oath, you have taken a solemn oath, to be fair and impartial. I know you all. I know you as friends, and I know you as honorable men. And I am perfectly satisfied to put that in your hands, under your oath.

This is the only caustic thing I will say in these remarks this afternoon, but the question is, How do we come to be here? We are here because of a 5-year, relentless, unending investigation of the President, $50 million, hundreds of FBI agents fanning across the Nation, examining in detail the microscopic lives of people—maybe the most intense investigation not only of a President, but of anybody ever.

I feel strongly about this because of my State and what we have endured. So you will have to excuse me, but that investigation has also shown that the judicial system in this country can and does get out of kilter unless it is controlled. Because there are innocent people—innocent people—who have been financially and mentally bankrupt.

One woman told me 2 years ago that her legal fees were $95,000. She said, "I don't have $95,000. And the only asset I have is the equity in my home, which just happens to correspond to my legal fees of $95,000." And she said, "The only thing I can think of to do is to deed my home." This woman was innocent, never charged, testified before a grand jury a number of times. And since that time she has accumulated an additional $200,000 in attorney fees.

Javert's pursuit of Jean Valjean in Les Miserables pales by comparison. I doubt there are few people—maybe nobody in this body—who could withstand such scrutiny. And in this case those summoned were terrified, not because of their guilt, but because they felt guilt or innocence was not really relevant. But after all of those years, and $50 million of Whitewater, Travelgate, Filegate—you name it—nothing, nothing. The President was found guilty of nothing—official or personal.

We are here today because the President suffered a terrible moral lapse of marital infidelity—not a breach of the public trust, not a crime against society, the two things Hamilton talked about in Federalist Paper No. 65—I recommend it to you before you vote—but it was a breach of his marriage vows. It was a breach of his family trust. It is a sex scandal. H.L. Mencken one time said, "When you hear somebody say, 'This is not about money,' it's about money." (Laughter)

And when you hear somebody say, "This is not about sex," it's about sex.

You pick your own adjective to describe the President's conduct. Here are some that I would use: indefensible, outrageous, unforgivable, shameless. I promise you the President would not contest any of those or any others.

But there is a human element in this case that has not even been mentioned. That is, the President and Hillary and Chelsea are human beings. This is intended only as a mild criticism of our distinguished friends from the House. But as I listened to the presenters, to the managers, make their opening statements, they were remarkably well prepared and they spoke eloquently—more eloquently than I really had hoped.

But when I talk about the human element, I talk about what I thought was, on occasion, an unnecessarily harsh, pejorative description of the President. I thought that the language should have been tempered somewhat to acknowledge that he is the President. To say constantly that the President lied about this and lied about that—as I say, I thought that was too much for a family that has already been about as decimated as a family can get. The relationship between husband and wife, father and child, has been incredibly strained, if not destroyed. There has been nothing but sleepless nights, mental agony, for this family, for almost 5 years, day after day, from accusations of having Vince Foster assassinated, on down. It has been bizarre.

I didn't sense any compassion. And perhaps none is deserved. The President has said for all to hear that he misled, he deceived, he did not want to be helpful to the prosecution, and he did all of those things to his family, to his friends, to his staff, to his Cabinet, and to the American people. Why would he do that? Well, he knew this whole affair was about to bring unspeakable embarrassment and humiliation on himself, his wife whom he adored, and a child that he worshipped with every fiber of his body and for whom he would happily have died to spare her or to ameliorate her shame and her grief.

The House managers have said shame, an embarrassment is no excuse for lying. The question about lying—that is your decision. But I can tell you, put yourself in his position—and you have already had this big moral lapse—as to what you would do. We are, none of us, perfect. Sure, you say, he should have thought of all that beforehand. And indeed he should, just as Adam and Eve should have, just as you and you and you and you and millions of other people who have been caught in similar circumstances should have thought of it before. As I say, none of us is perfect.

I remember, Chaplain—the Chaplain is not here; too bad, he ought to hear this story. This evangelist was holding this great revival meeting and in the close of one of his meetings he said, "Is there anybody in this audience who has ever known anybody who even comes close to the perfection of our Lord and Savior, Jesus Christ?" Nothing. He repeated the challenge and, finally, a little-bitty guy in the back held up his hand. "Are you saying you have known such a person? Stand up." He stood up and said, "Tell us, who was it?" He said, "My wife's first husband."

Make no mistake about it: Removal from office is punishment. It is unbelievable punishment, even though the framers didn't quite see it that way. Again, they said—and it bears repeating over and over again—they said they wanted to protect the people. But I can tell you this: The punishment of removing Bill Clinton from office would pale compared to the punishment he has already inflicted on himself. There is a feeling in this country that somehow or another Bill Clinton has gotten away with something. Mr. Leader, I can tell you, he hasn't gotten away with anything. And the people are saying: "Please don't protect us from this man." Seventy-six percent of us think he is doing a fine job; 65 to 70 percent of us don't want him removed from office.

Some have said we are not respected on the world scene. The truth of the matter is, this Nation has never enjoyed greater prestige in the world than we do right now. I saw Carlos Menem, President of Argentina, a guest here recently, who said to the President, "Mr. President, the world needs you." The war in Bosnia is under control; the President has been as tenacious as anybody could be about Middle East peace; and in Ireland, actual peace; and maybe the Middle East will make it; and he has the Indians and the Pakistanis talking to each other as they have never talked to each other in recent times.

Vaclav Havel said, "Mr. President, for the enlargement of the North Atlantic Treaty Organization, there is no doubt in my mind that it was your personal leadership that made this historic development possible." King Hussein: "Mr. President, I've had the privilege of being a friend of the United States and Presidents since the late President Eisenhower, and throughout all the years in the past I have kept in touch, but on the subject of peace, the peace we are seeking, I have never, with all due respect and all the affection I held for your predecessors, known someone with your dedication, clear-headedness, focus, and determination to help resolve this issue in the best way possible."

I have Nelson Mandela and other world leaders who have said similar things in the last 6 months. Our prestige, I promise you, in the world, is as high as it has ever been.

When it comes to the question of perjury, you know, there is perjury and then there is perjury. Let me ask you if you think this is perjury: On November 23, 1997, President Clinton went to Vancouver, BC. And when he returned, Monica Lewinsky was at the White House at some point, and he gave her a carved marble bear. I don't know how big it was. The question before the grand jury, August 6, 1998:

> What was the Christmas present or presents that he got for you?

ANSWER: Everything was packaged in the Big Black Dog or big canvas bag from the Black Dog store in Martha's Vineyard and he got me a marble bear's head carving. Sort of, you know, a little sculpture, I guess you would call, maybe.

QUESTION: Was that the item from Vancouver?

ANSWER: Yes.

QUESTION (on the same day of the same grand jury): When the President gave you the Vancouver bear on the 28th, did he say anything about what it means?

ANSWER: Hmm.

QUESTION: Well, what did he say?

ANSWER: I think he—I believe he said that the bear is the—maybe an Indian symbol for strength—you know, to be strong like a bear.

QUESTION: And did you interpret that to be strong in your decision to continue to conceal the relationship?

ANSWER: No.

The House Judiciary Committee report to the full House, on the other hand, knowing the subpoena requested gifts, is giving Ms. Lewinsky more gifts on December 28 seems odd. But Ms. Lewinsky's testimony reveals why he did so. She said that she "never questioned that we would not ever do anything but keep this private, and that meant to take whatever appropriate steps needed to be taken to keep it quiet."

They say:

> The only logical inference is that the gifts, including the bear symbolizing strength, were a tacit reminder to Ms. Lewinsky that they would deny the relationship, even in the face of a Federal subpoena.

She just got through saying "no." Yet, this report says that is the only logical inference. And then the brief that came over here accompanying the articles of impeachment said, "On the other hand, more gifts on December 28 . . ." Ms. Lewinsky's testimony reveals her answer. She said that she "never questioned that we were ever going to do anything but keep this private, and that meant to take whatever appropriate steps needed to be taken to keep it quiet."

Again, they say in their brief:

> The only logical inference is that the gifts, including the bear symbolizing strength, were a tacit reminder to Ms. Lewinsky that they would deny the relationship even in the face of a Federal subpoena.

Is it perjury to say the only logical inference is something when the only shred of testimony in the record is, "No, that was not my interpretation. I didn't infer that." Yet, here you have it in the committee report and you have it in the brief. Of course, that is not perjury.

First of all, it is not under oath. But I am a trial lawyer and I will tell you what it is; it is wanting to win too badly. I have tried 300, 400, maybe 500 divorce cases. Incidentally, you are being addressed by the entire South Franklin County, Arkansas, Bar Association. I can't believe there were that many cases in that little town, but I had a practice in surrounding communities, too. In all those divorce cases, I would guess that in 80 percent of the contested cases perjury was committed. Do you know what it was about? Sex. Extramarital affairs. But there is a very big difference in perjury about a marital infidelity in a divorce case and perjury about whether I bought the murder weapon, or whether I concealed the murder weapon or not. And to charge somebody with the first and punish them as though it were the second stands our sense of justice on its head.

There is a total lack of proportionality, a total lack of balance in this thing. The charge and the punishment are totally out of sync. All of you have heard or read the testimony of the five prosecutors who testified before the House Judiciary Committee—five seasoned prosecutors. Each one of them, veterans, said that under the identical circumstances of this case, they would never charge anybody because they would know they couldn't get a conviction. In this case, the charges brought and the punishment sought are totally out of sync. There is no balance; there is no proportionality.

But even stranger—you think about it—even if this case had originated in the courthouse rather than the Capitol, you would never have heard of it. How do you reconcile what the prosecutors said with what we are doing here? Impeachment was debated off and on in Philadelphia for the entire 4 months, as I said. The key players were Gouverneur Morris, a brilliant Pennsylvanian; George Mason, the only man reputed to be so brilliant that Thomas Jefferson actually deferred to him; he refused to sign the Constitution, incidentally, even though he was a delegate because they didn't deal with slavery and he was a strict abolitionist. Then there was Charles Pinckney from South Carolina, a youngster at 29 years old; Edmund Randolph from Virginia, who had a big role in the Constitution in the beginning; and then, of course, James Madison, the craftsman. They were all key players in drafting this impeachment provision.

Uppermost in their minds during the entire time they were composing it was that they did not want any kings. They had lived under despots, under kings, and under autocrats, and they didn't want any more of that. And they succeeded very admirably. We have had 46 Presidents and no kings. But they kept talking about corruption. Maybe that ought to be the reason for impeachment, because they feared some President would corrupt the political process. That is what the debate was about—corrupting the political process and ensconcing one's self through a phony election; maybe that is something close to a king.

They followed the British rule on impeachment, because the British said the House of Commons may impeach and the House of Lords must convict. And every one of the colonies had the same procedure—the House and the Senate. In all fairness, Alexander Hamilton was not very keen on the House participating. But here were the sequence of events in Philadelphia that brought us here today. They started out with maladministration and Madison said, "That is too vague; what does that mean?" So they dropped that. They went from that to corruption, and they dropped that. Then they went to malpractice, and they decided that was not definitive enough. And they went to treason, bribery, and corruption. They decided that still didn't suit them.

Bear in mind one thing: During this entire process, they are narrowing the things you can impeach a President for. They were making it tougher. Madison said, "If we aren't careful, the President will serve at the pleasure of the Senate." And then they went to treason and bribery. Somebody said that still is not quite enough, so they went to treason and bribery. And George Mason added, "or other high crimes and misdemeanors against the United States." They voted on it, and on September 10 they sent the entire Constitution to a committee they called the Committee on Style and Arrangement, which was the committee that would draft the language in a way that everybody would understand—that is, well crafted from a grammatical standpoint. But that committee, which was dominated by Madison and Hamilton, dropped "against the United States." And the stories will tell you that the reason they did that was because they were redundant, because that committee had no right to change the substance of anything, and they would not have dropped it if they had not felt that it was redundant. Then they put it in for good measure. And we can always be grateful for the two-thirds majority.

This is one of the most important points of this entire presentation. First of all, the term "treason and bribery"—nobody quarrels with that. We are not debating treason and bribery here in this Chamber. We are talking about other high crimes and misdemeanors. And where did "high crimes and misdemeanors" come from? It came from the English law. And they found it in English law under a category which said distinctly "political" offenses against the state.

Let me repeat that. They said "high crimes and misdemeanors" was to be because they took it from English law where they found it in the category that said offenses distinctly "political" against the state.

So, colleagues, please, for just one moment, forget the complexities of the facts and the tortured legalisms—and we have heard them all brilliantly presented on both sides. And I am not getting into that.

But ponder this: If high crimes and misdemeanors was taken from English law by George Mason, which listed high crimes and misdemeanors as "political" offenses against the state, what are we doing here? If, as Hamilton said, it had to be a crime against society or a breach of the public trust, what are we doing here? Even perjury, concealing, or deceiving an unfaithful relationship does not even come close to being an impeachable offense. Nobody has suggested that Bill Clinton committed a political crime against the state.

So, colleagues, if you are to honor the Constitution, you must look at the history of the Constitution and how we got to the impeachment clause. And, if you do that, and you do that honestly, according to the oath you took, you cannot—you can censor Bill Clinton, you can hand him over to the prosecutor for him to be prosecuted, but you cannot convict him. You cannot indulge yourselves the luxury or the right to ignore this history.

There has been a suggestion that a vote to acquit would be something of a breach of faith with those who lie in Flanders field, Anzio, Bunker Hill, Gettysburg, and wherever. I did not hear that. I read about it. But I want to say, and, incidentally, I think it was Chairman Hyde who alluded to this and said those men fought and died for the rule of law.

I can remember a cold November 3 morning in my little hometown of Charleston, Arkansas. I was 18 years old. I had just gotten one semester in at the university when I went into the Marine Corps. So I was to report to Little Rock to be inducted. My, it was cold. The drugstore was the bus stop. I had to be there by 8 o'clock to be sworn in. And I had to catch the bus down at the drugstore at 3 o'clock in the morning. So my mother and father and I got up at 2 o'clock, got dressed, and went down there. I am not sure I can tell you this story. And the bus came over the hill. I was rather frightened anyway about going. I was quite sure I was going to be killed, only slightly less frightened that Betty would find somebody else when I was gone.

The bus came over the schoolhouse hill and my parents started crying. I had never seen my father cry. I knew I was in some difficulty. Now, as a parent, at my age, I know he thought he was giving not his only begotten son, but one of his begotten sons. Can you imagine? You know that scene. It was repeated across this Nation millions of times. Then, happily, I survived that war, saw no combat, was on my way to Japan when it all ended. I had never had a terrible problem with dropping the bomb, though that has been a terrible moral dilemma for me because the estimates were that we would lose as many as a million men in that invasion.

But I came home to a generous government which provided me under the GI bill an education in a fairly prestigious law school, which my father could never have afforded. I practiced law in this little town for 18 years, loved every minute of it. But I didn't practice constitutional law. And I knew very little about the Constitution. But when I went into law school, I did study constitutional law, Mr. Chief Justice. It was very arcane to me. And trying to read the Federalist Papers, de Tocqueville, all of those things that law students are expected to do, that was tough for me. I confess.

So after 18 years of law practice, I jumped up and ran for Governor. I served as Governor for 4 years. I guess I knew what the rule of law was, but I still didn't really have much reverence for the Constitution. I just did not understand any of the things I am discussing and telling you. No. My love for that document came day after day and debate after debate right here in this Chamber.

Some of you read an op-ed piece I did a couple of weeks ago when I said I was perfectly happy for my legacy, that during my 24 years here I never voted for a constitutional amendment. And it isn't that I wouldn't. I think they were mistaken not giving you fellows 4 years. (Laughter.)

You are about to cause me to rethink that one. (Laughter.)

The reason I developed this love of it is because I saw Madison's magic working time and time again, keeping bullies from running over weak people, keeping majorities from running over minorities, and I thought about all of the unfettered freedoms we had. The oldest organic law in existence made us the envy of the world.

Mr. Chairman, we have also learned that the rule of law includes Presidential elections. That is a part of the rule of law in this country. We have an event, a quadrennial event, in this country which we call a Presidential election, and that is the day when we reach across this aisle and hold hands, Democrats and Republicans, and we say, win or lose, we will abide by the decision. It is a solemn event, a Presidential election, and it should not be undone lightly or just because one side has the clout and the other one doesn't.

And if you want to know what men fought for in World War II, for example, in Vietnam, ask Senator Inouye. He left an arm in Italy. He and I were with the Presidents at Normandy, on the 50th anniversary, but we started off in Anzio. Senator Domenici, were you with us? It was one of the most awesome experiences I have ever had in my life. Certified war hero. I think his relatives were in an internment camp. So ask him, what was he fighting for? Or ask Bob Kerrey, certified Medal of Honor winner, what was he fighting for? Probably get a quite different answer. Or Senator Chafee, one of the finest men ever to grace this body and certified Marine hero of Guadalcanal, ask him. And Senator McCain, a genuine hero, ask him. You don't have to guess; they are with us, and they are living, and they can tell you. And one who is not with us in the Senate anymore, Robert Dole, ask Senator Dole what he was fighting for. Senator Dole had what I thought was a very reasonable solution to this whole thing that would handle it fairly and expeditiously.

The American people are now and for some time have been asking to be allowed a good night's sleep. They are asking for an end to this nightmare. It is a legitimate request. I am not suggesting that you vote for or against the polls. I understand that. Nobody should vote against the polls just to show their mettle and their courage. I have cast plenty of votes against the polls, and it has cost me politically a lot of times. This has been going on for a year, though.

In that same op-ed piece, I talked about meeting Harry Truman my first year as Governor of Arkansas. I spent an hour with him—an indelible experience. People at home kid me about this because I very seldom make a speech that I don't mention this meeting. But I will never forget what he said: "Put your faith in the people. Trust the people. They can handle it." They have shown conclusively time and time again that they can handle it.

Colleagues, this is easily the most important vote you will ever cast. If you have difficulty because of an intense dislike of the President—and that is understandable—rise above it. He is not the issue. He will be gone. You won't. So don't leave a precedent from which we may never recover and almost surely will regret.

If you vote to acquit, Mr. Leader, you know exactly what is going to happen. You are going to go back to your committees. You are going to get on with this legislative agenda. You are going to start dealing with Medicare, Social Security, tax cuts, and all those things which the people of this country have a nonnegotiable demand that you do. If you vote to acquit, you go immediately to the people's agenda. But if you vote to convict, you can't be sure what is going to happen.

James G. Blaine was a Member of the Senate when Andrew Johnson was tried in 1868, and 20 years later he recanted. He said, "I made a bad mistake." And he said, "As I reflect back on it, all I can think about is that having convicted Andrew Johnson would have caused much more chaos and confusion in this country than Andrew Johnson could ever conceivably have created."

And so it is with William Jefferson Clinton. If you vote to convict, in my opinion, you are going to be creating more havoc than he could ever possibly create. After all, he has only got 2 years left. So don't, for God sakes, heighten the people's alienation, which is at an all-time high, toward their Government. The people have a right, and they are calling on you to rise above politics, rise above partisanship. They are calling on you to do your solemn duty, and I pray you will.

Thank you, Mr. Chief Justice.

Source: Congressional Record, U.S. Senate, 106th Cong., 1st sess., 1217–1221.

Bibliography

Baker, Peter. *The Breach: The Inside Impeachment and Trial of William Jefferson Clinton.* New York: Scribner, 2000.

Barr, Bob. *The Meaning of Is: The Squandered Impeachment and Wasted Legacy of William Jefferson Clinton.* Atlanta: Stroud & Hall, 2004.

Ben-Veniste, Richard. *The Emperor's New Clothes: Exposing the Truth from Watergate to 9/11.* New York: Simon & Schuster, 2009.

Branch, Taylor. *The Clinton Tapes: Wrestling History with the President.* New York: Simon & Schuster, 2009.

Brown, Lowell H. *High Crimes and Misdemeanors in Presidential Impeachment.* New York: Palgrave Macmillan, 2010.

Brownstein, Ronald. *The Second Civil War: How Extreme Partisanship Has Paralyzed Washington and Polarized America.* New York: Penguin, 2007.

Busby, Robert. *Defending the American Presidency: Clinton and the Lewinsky Scandal.* New York: Palgrave Macmillan, 2001.

Blumenthal, Sidney. *The Clinton Wars.* New York: Farrar, Straus and Giroux, 2003.

Conason, Joe, and Gene Lyons. *The Hunting of the President: The Ten-Year Campaign to Destroy Bill and Hillary Clinton.* New York: Thomas Dunne, 2000.

Denton, Jr., Robert E., and Rachel L. Holloway. *Images, Scandal, and Communication Strategies of the Clinton Presidency.* Westport, Conn.: Praeger, 2003.

Dershowitz, Alan. *Sexual McCarthyism, Clinton, Starr, and the Emerging Constitutional Crisis.* New York: Basic Books, 1998.

Duffy, Brian. "Whitewater on the Rise: The President and His Campaign Must Contend with a Newly Invigorated Investigation." *U.S. News & World Report,* June 10, 1996.

Gartner, John D. *In Search of Bill Clinton: A Psychological Biography.* New York: St. Martin's Press, 2008.

Gerth, Jeff, and Don Van Natta Jr. *Her Way: The Hopes and Ambitions of Hillary Rodham Clinton.* New York: Little Brown, 2007.

Gormley, Ken. *The Death of American Virtue: Clinton vs. Starr.* New York: Crown, 2010.

Hamilton, Nigel. *Bill Clinton: Mastering the Presidency.* New York: Public Affairs Press, 2007.

Harris, John. *The Survivor: Bill Clinton in the White House.* New York: Random House Trade Paperbacks, 2006.

Klaidman, Daniel, and Michael Isikoff. "The Most Dangerous Man in Washington." *Newsweek,* December 2, 1996.

Klein, Joe. *The Natural: The Misunderstood Presidency of Bill Clinton.* New York: Broadway, 2003.

Kyvig, David E. *The Age of Impeachment: American Constitutional Culture Since 1960.* Lawrence: University Press of Kansas, 2008.

Lyons, Gene. *Fools for Scandal: How the Media Invented Whitewater.* New York: Franklin Square Press, 1996.

McDougal, Jim, and Curtis Wilkie. *Arkansas Mischief: The Birth of a National Scandal.* New York: Henry Holt, 1998.

McDougal, Susan, with Pat Harris. *The Woman Who Wouldn't Talk: Why I Refused to Testify Against the Clintons & What I Learned in Jail.* New York: Carroll & Graf, 2003.

Malti-Douglas, Fedwa. *Partisan Sex: Bodies, Politics and the Law in the Clinton Era.* New York: Peter Lang, 2009.

Marion, Nancy. *The Politics of Disgrace: The Role of Political Scandal in American Politics.* Durham, N.C.: Carolina Academic Press, 2010.

Matrisciana, Patrick, ed. *The Clinton Chronicles Book.* Hemet, Calif.: Jeremiah Books, 1994.

Posner, Richard. *An Affair of State: The Investigation, Impeachment, and Trial of President Clinton.* Cambridge, Mass.: Harvard University Press, 2000.

Rosell, Mark, and Clyde Wilcox, eds. *The Clinton Scandal and the Future of American Government.* Washington, D.C.: Georgetown University Press, 2000.

Schippers, David P. (with Alan P. Henry). *Sell Out: The Inside Story of President Clinton's Impeachment.* Washington, D.C.: Regnery, 2000.

Snyder, K. Alan. *Mission Impeachable: The House Managers and the Historic Impeachment of President Clinton.* Vienna, Va.: Allegiance Press, 2001.

The Starr Report: The Findings of Independent Counsel Kenneth W. Starr on President Clinton and the Lewinsky Affair. New York: Public Affairs, 1998.

Stewart, James. *Blood Sport: The President and His Adversaries.* New York: Simon & Schuster, 1996.

U.S. Congress. Senate. *Final Report of the Special Committee to Investigate Whitewater Development Corporation and Related Matters. 104th Cong., 2nd sess., June 17, 1996.* Washington, D.C.: U.S. Government Printing Office, 1996. http://frwebgate.access.gpo.gov/cgi-bin/getdoc.cgi?dbname=104_cong_reports&docid =f:sr280.104.pdf.

U.S. Congress. House Document 105–310: *Communication from Kenneth W. Starr, Independent Counsel, Transmitting a Referral to the United States House of Representatives Filed in Conformity with the Requirements of Title 28, United States Code, Section 595(c).* Washington: Government Printing Office, 1998.

Waldman, Amy. "The Real Blood Sport: The Whitewater Scandal Machine." *Washington Monthly,* May 1996.

Woodward, Bob. *Shadow: Five Presidents and the Legacy of Watergate.* New York: Simon & Schuster, 1999. [Paperback edition, 2005].

The 9/11 Commission, 2002–04

By Gail Russell Chaddock

For Americans waking to clear, ice-blue skies on September 11, 2001, the terrorist attacks on the United States marked a new world. Nineteen terrorists commandeered four airplanes and crashed two of them into the World Trade Center in New York City and one into the Pentagon near Washington, D.C., and the fourth crashed into a field in Pennsylvania. Nearly 3,000 people died in the horrific events of September 11, what President George W. Bush called "the first war of the 21st century."

Until the September 11 attacks, which soon became known as 9/11, few Americans had heard of Saudi exile Osama bin Laden, who three years earlier had called on Muslims to kill Americans and their allies anywhere in the world. U.S. bases in the Middle East and its "occupation" of Islam's holiest places, bin Laden said, showed that Americans had declared war against God, his messenger, and Muslims. A financier of the anti-Soviet resistance in Afghanistan, bin Laden had launched al-Qaeda—"the foundation" or base—in the late 1980s. Afghanistan had been a training ground and rallying point for young Muslim fighters, backed at the time by U.S. arms and covert funding. But for bin Laden the fight with the Soviets was only the beginning.

Bin Laden and other Islamist terrorist leaders held a worldview of extreme intolerance. By the early 1990s, they had shifted their view of the immediate enemy from the Soviet Union to the United States, which bin Laden described as "the head of the snake." The bombings of U.S. embassies in Nairobi, Kenya, and Dar es Salaam, Tanzania, on August 7, 1998, and the attack on the U.S.S. *Cole* in a Yemeni harbor on October 12, 2000, marked the seriousness of that threat.

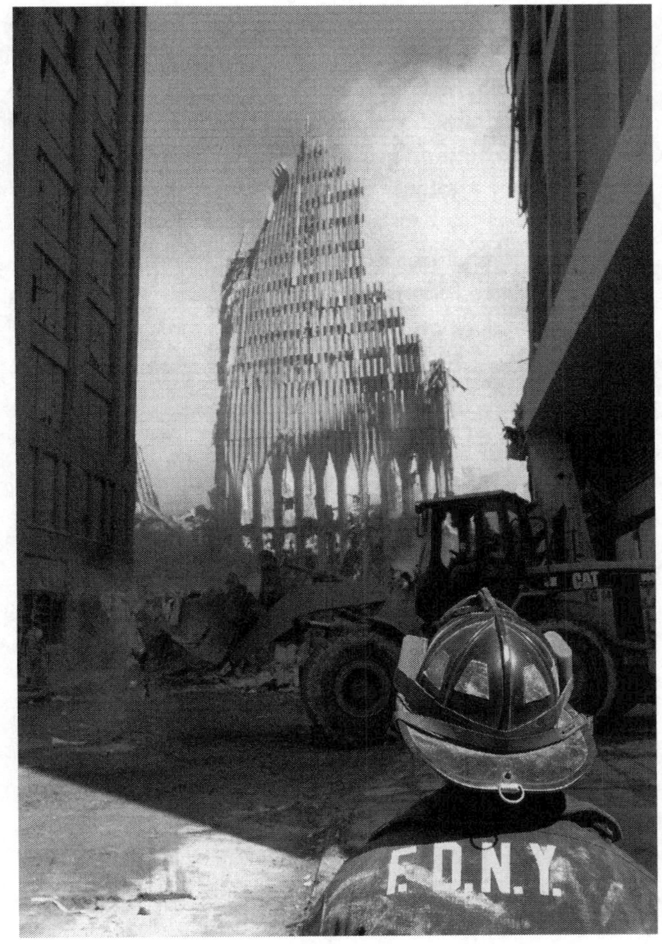

The nation was shocked and horrified by the destruction of the tallest buildings in New York City, when terrorists flew two hijacked commercial airliners filled with passengers into the Twin Towers of the World Trade Center on the morning of September 11, 2001. Here a New York City firefighter looks up at the remains of the South Tower. (U.S. Navy Photo by Photographer's Mate 2nd Class Jim Watson)

OVERVIEW

Background

On September 11, 2001, Islamist terrorists, piloting hijacked airliners, crashed two planes into the Twin Towers of the World Trade Center in New York City. A third plane veered into the side of the Pentagon near Washington, D.C. A fourth airliner, believed to be headed toward the White House or the U.S. Capitol, crashed in a field in Pennsylvania after passengers battled to take back the plane. Nearly 3,000 people, including citizens of some 90 nations, were killed in the attacks. In an instant, countering terrorism became the top national security priority for the United States. On September 14, FBI officials released the names of the 19 terrorists on the four flights. Government sources began to link the attacks to Osama bin Laden and his al-Qaeda network of terrorists. Congress set aside, for a season, bitter partisan fights to respond to the crisis, including establishing disaster relief, aid to the families of attack victims, and new powers of surveillance and detention for law enforcement. President George W. Bush said that in a new, global "war on terror," the United States would be targeting not only terrorists but also those who financed or sheltered them.

Congress Investigates

The intelligence community had been investigating al-Qaeda prior to the 9/11 attacks. In February 1998, bin Laden publicly called for a jihad, or holy war, against American civilians and military personnel anywhere in the world. With some exceptions, Congress outsourced much of the investigation of the terrorist threat to independent commissions. No fewer than a dozen blue-ribbon panels from 1989 to the 2001 attacks had investigated the nation's intelligence and counterterrorism capabilities and found the system wanting. Congress largely ignored the recommendations. But the events of September 11—and mounting pressure from the families of victims of that day's attacks—moved Congress to pursue its own investigation of what went wrong and how to prevent it from happening again.

President Bush and Vice President Richard Cheney urged lawmakers to hold off on a probe that they said would distract intelligence officials from the ongoing war on al-Qaeda in Afghanistan. But on February 14, 2002, House and Senate intelligence committees announced the first-ever joint, bicameral investigation by two standing committees. The investigation focused narrowly on what the intelligence community knew—or should have known—about the terrorist threat, what was done with the information, and why it failed to prevent the attacks. Meanwhile, the 9/11 families stepped up lobbying for an independent investigation with a broader mandate to probe all aspects of the 9/11 attacks, including the response on the ground. The families also questioned whether Congress could fairly investigate its own role in the failures leading up to the 9/11 attacks, especially underfunding of intelligence and counterterrorism capacity, they said. In November

By early summer 2000, the first of the 19 al-Qaeda terrorists arrived in the United States to begin flight training. During the summer, bin Laden and senior al-Qaeda leaders in Afghanistan started recruiting the rest of the operatives for the attack. Fifteen of the 19 hijackers came from Saudi Arabia, where it was easier to acquire a U.S. visa. Until the September 11 attacks, concerns about terrorism had barely registered on American public opinion polls or in Congress. The events of September 11, 2001, unfolded like a slow nightmare from which no one could awake in time.

At 8:46 A.M., hijacked American Airlines Flight 11 crashed into the North Tower of the World Trade Center in New York City.

At 9:03 A.M., United Airlines Flight 175 banked left into the South Tower of the World Trade Center, where the public-address system minutes earlier had directed tenants to stay on their floors. No one who heeded that advice survived.

At 9:38 A.M., American Airlines Flight 77 gunned its engines and slammed into the west wall of the Pentagon, once dubbed the world's safest building.

At 10:06 A.M., United Airlines Flight 93 plowed into a field in Shanksville, Pennsylvania, as unarmed passengers battled to regain the cockpit. At the time of the crash, the airliner was just 20 minutes from its likely target, the U.S. Capitol or the White House.

2002, Congress created an independent National Commission on Terrorist Attacks Upon the United States. Popularly known as the 9/11 Commission, the 10-member panel was headed by former New Jersey governor Thomas Kean, a Republican appointed by President Bush, and Lee Hamilton, a former congressman from Indiana, appointed by Democratic congressional leaders. Republican and Democratic congressional leaders each appointed four of the other eight commissioners. Like the Joint Inquiry, the 9/11 Commission spent much of its time negotiating with the Bush administration over access to documents. During 11 months, the Joint Inquiry reviewed 500,000 pages of documents and held 22 hearings. It released nonclassified portions of its report on December 20, 2002. The Joint Inquiry's final report was released on July 24, 2003, heavily redacted. By contrast, the 9/11 Commission fought to get as much as possible onto the public record in a bid to defuse the conspiracy theories that quickly formed around the events of 9/11. In all, 9/11 Commission staff reviewed more than 2.5 million pages of documents and interviewed some 1,200 individuals in 10 countries on national security, law enforcement, intelligence, diplomacy, border control, commercial aviation, terrorist financing, and congressional oversight. The 9/11 Commission issued its final report on July 22, 2004, endorsed unanimously by the 10 commissioners.

Impact

The Joint Inquiry produced the first public timeline of events leading up to the 9/11 attacks and identified critical points where U.S. intelligence and law-enforcement officials had failed to "connect the dots." It was limited in its work by a short mandate—the investigation had to be completed by the end of the 107th Congress—and difficulties gaining access to documents and declassifying its findings. The 9/11 Commission had a much wider mandate to study facts and circumstances related to the attack. Its final report read like a spy thriller and sat on the *New York Times* best-seller list for 26 weeks. It was nominated for a National Book Award, a first for a government publication. Most of its 41 recommendations, including the creation of a director of national intelligence and a National Counterterrorism Center, were voted into law. With strong support from families of victims of the 9/11 attacks, the commissioners won access to many documents denied to the congressional Joint Inquiry, including some access to the presidential Daily Briefs. But Congress did not act on the recommendation that the 9/11 commissioners said would be among the most difficult and the most important: creating a single, principal point of oversight and review for homeland security. Nor did Congress give the new national intelligence director the budget authority that the 9/11 Commission also deemed essential. In the end, Congress overhauled the executive branch but declined to reform itself.

By midmorning, nearly 3,000 people had perished, including 343 firefighters and 60 police officers in New York City. Sixteen acres of New York's financial district were reduced to a smoldering ditch. The searches for those who didn't make it home and the funerals and memorial services went on for months.

In Washington, members of Congress rallied on the east steps of the Capitol at 7 P.M. to show unity and resolve. "When America suffers, we as a Congress stand united and we stand together," said House Speaker Dennis Hastert (R-Ill.). "We stand strongly united behind the president," said Senate majority leader Tom Daschle (D-S.D.). Addressing the nation from the Oval Office, President Bush said: "These acts of mass murder were intended to frighten our nation into chaos and retreat. But they have failed. Our nation is strong."

For a time, there was little talk on Capitol Hill of fixing blame, beyond the terrorists, for the most lethal attack on the U.S. territory since Pearl Harbor in 1941. There would be an investigation of the lapses and failures that enabled the attacks, but not yet, members said. "It's impossible to overstate the sense of unity and common purpose we felt," said Senator Bob Graham

(continues on page 1098)

CHRONOLOGY

1993

- *February 26:* Fifteen-hundred-pound truck bomb detonates in the underground garage of the World Trade Center in New York City, killing six and injuring more than 1,000. The FBI arrests conspirator Mohammed Salameh after he returns to the rental office to get back his $400 deposit for a truck linked to the bombing. Mastermind Ramzi Yousef, convicted in November 1997, said that he had hoped to kill 250,000 people.

1994

- *December 24:* Armed Islamic Group hijacks Air France Flight 8969 in Algiers to fly the plane into the Eiffel Tower. Flight is diverted to Marseilles, where an elite French counterterrorism squad stages a rescue on the tarmac, killing all four terrorists. Videos of the rescue are broadcast worldwide.

1996

- *June 25:* A truck bomb explodes outside U.S. military housing in Khobar Towers, Saudi Arabia, killing 19 and wounding 515.
- *August 23:* Osama bin Laden issues a public *fatwa,* or religious decree, authorizing attacks on Western military targets in Saudi Arabia.

1998

- *February 23:* Bin Laden publicly calls for *jihad,* or holy war, against U.S. civilians and military personnel anywhere in the world.
- *August 7:* Near-simultaneous bombing of U.S. embassies in Nairobi, Kenya, and Dar es Salaam, Tanzania, kill 301, injure more than 5,000. President Bill Clinton orders cruise missile strikes on suspected al-Qaeda sites in Afghanistan and Sudan.

1999

- *December 14:* Algerian jihadist Ahmed Ressam arrested attempting to cross from Vancouver to Washington State. He is arrested after running away. Inspectors find explosives in his rental car. He is later linked to a plot to blow up Los Angeles Airport.

2000

- *January 5–8:* Meeting of al-Qaeda operatives in Malaysia. Two individuals from the Malaysia meeting—Khalid al-Mihdhar and Nawaf al-Hazmi—enter the United States.
- *October 12:* Bombing of U.S.S. *Cole* in a Yemeni harbor kills 17 sailors and injures 39 others. U.S. intelligence links attacks to bin Laden. *Cole* investigation renews CIA interest in the Malaysia meeting.

2001

- *May–August:* Intelligence Community receives numerous reports indicating an impending terrorist attack.
- *July 10:* FBI Phoenix field office sends electronic communication to FBI headquarters warning of terrorists training in flight schools for attacks.
- *August 6:* President George W. Bush receives an intelligence briefing warning that bin Laden might be planning to attack. The briefing was entitled "Bin Ladin Determined To Strike in US."
- *August 23:* CIA requests that al-Mihdhar and al-Hazmi be added to watchlists. Both are already in the United States. FBI begins search.
- *September 11:* American Airlines Flight 11 with 92 people aboard crashes into the North Tower of the World Trade Center in New York City; United Airlines Flight 175, with 65 people aboard, crashes into the South Tower; American Airlines Flight 77 crashes into the Pentagon, killing the 64 people on board and 125 people in the nation's military headquarters. The Capitol and White House are evacuated; South Tower of World Trade Center collapses into the streets, sending hundreds of onlookers running for their lives; United Airlines Flight 93 crashes into a Pennsylvania field, killing all 44 on board after passengers struggled with hijackers believed to be intent on crashing the aircraft into the Capitol or the White House; the World Trade Center's North Tower collapses, releasing a massive

cloud of debris and smoke; government sources begin to link the attacks to bin Laden.

- *September 14:* The Justice Department releases the names of 19 hijackers who commandeered the planes.
- *October 7:* The United States launches attack on al-Qaeda camps in Afghanistan.

2002

- *February 14:* The Senate and House intelligence committees launch investigation of intelligence failures leading up to the 9/11 attacks. Congress authorizes $3.2 million for the Joint Inquiry to expire at the end of the 107th Congress, or by Jan. 3, 2003.
- *November 27:* President Bush signs law creating the National Commission on Terrorist Attacks Upon the United States. Popularly known as the 9/11 Commission, the independent, bipartisan commission is chartered to prepare a full and complete account of the circumstances surrounding the September 11, 2001, terrorist attacks, including preparedness for and the immediate response to the attacks. President appoints former secretary of state Henry Kissinger to chair the commission. Democratic congressional leadership appoints former Senate majority leader George Mitchell (D) of Maine as vice chair.
- *December 11:* Mitchell resigns as vice chair; former representative Lee Hamilton (D-Ind.) appointed to replace him.
- *December 13:* Kissinger resigns as chair.
- *December 16:* Former governor Thomas Kean (R) of New Jersey is appointed to replace him.
- *December 20:* Joint Inquiry releases nonclassified portions of its final report, after nine public hearings.

2003

- *January 27:* First meeting of the commission held in Washington; Philip Zelikow announced as executive director.
- *March 28:* Congress approves commission budget increase, to $14 million.
- *March 20:* The United States, acting without the approval it sought from the United Nations, attacks Iraq.
- *July 24:* Joint Inquiry releases declassified version of its 832-page final report, with strikeouts and redactions in the text.
- *October 15:* 9/11 Commission issues its first subpoena to the Federal Aviation Administration.
- *November 6:* 9/11 Commission issues subpoena to Department of Defense.
- *December 9:* Former senator Bob Kerrey (D-Neb.) replaces resigning senator Max Cleland (D-Ga.) on commission.

2004

- *July 22:* 9/11 Commission issues its 567-page final report. Commissioners announce that they will continue working together to encourage implementation of commission recommendations as the nonprofit 9/11 Public Discourse Project.
- *August 2:* President Bush announces executive orders based on commission recommendations.
- *August 20:* Commission votes to encourage National Archives and Records Administration to review 9/11 Commission records not currently available to the public with the goal of releasing to the public as much information as possible by January 2, 2009.
- *August 21:* 9/11 Commission disbands. Commission records are transferred to the National Archives for preservation and public access.
- *October 6:* The Senate passes Collins-Lieberman bill implementing 9/11 Commission recommendations by a vote of 96 to 2.
- *October 8:* The House passes 9/11 Recommendations Implementation Act by a vote of 282 to 134. Negotiations stall over a compromise agreement between the House and Senate.
- *December 3:* President Bush writes to congressional leaders in support of the bill.
- *December 6:* Conference committee announces agreement on bill implementing the 9/11 Commission recommendations, including new language

(continues)

(continued)

that the new director of national intelligence would not "abrogate the responsibilities" of the Department of Defense.

- *December 7:* The House passes the Intelligence Reform and Terrorism Prevention Act by a vote of 336 to 75.
- *December 8:* The Senate passes the Intelligence Reform and Terrorism Prevention Act by a vote of 89 to 2.
- *December 17:* President Bush signs the Intelligence Reform and Terrorism Prevention Act before the 9/11 commissioners and staff and 9/11 families.

2005

- *August 29:* Hurricane Katrina batters Gulf Coast, topping levees in New Orleans and flooding 80 percent of New Orleans. Delays in getting help to the area signal ongoing problems in emergency response and raise new doubts that the lessons of 9/11 have been assimilated.
- *December 5:* 9/11 Public Discourse Project releases its fifth and final report on the implementation of the 9/11 Commission recommendation. The average grade on 41 recommendations was C-.

2009

- *January 14:* The National Archives and Records Administration (NARA) opens more than 150 cubic feet of records of the 9/11 Commission, representing some 35 percent of the commission's archived textual records. Before it closed in 2004, the commission voted to encourage the release of its records to the fullest extent possible in January 2009. NARA staff was unable to process the entire collection by January 2009, citing the collection's volume and the large percentage of national security classified files. Because the commission was part of the legislative branch, its records are not subject to the Freedom of Information Act.

(continued from page 1095)

(D-Fla.), who chaired the Senate Select Committee on Intelligence. "Every issue that had divided us as a people and as parties seemed trivial in comparison with what we were now facing." Even the most strident partisans didn't want to be seen as engaging in a "blame game" when the nation was still in peril. "It's not over," said Senator Ted Stevens (R-Alaska). "It's not going to be over for a long time."

Congress Defers to the White House

As in past national crises, the devastation of the 9/11 attacks—and the fear that new attacks could be imminent—shifted initiative to the White House. A president widely dismissed as irrelevant in the summer of 2001 soared to approval ratings greater than 90 percent. Congressional leaders, some barely on speaking terms, vowed to work across party lines to respond to the crisis. "We are in complete agreement, and we will act together as one," said House minority leader Richard Gephardt (D-Mo.) at a news briefing on September 13. "There is no division between the parties, between the Congress and the president." It was, for a time, the honeymoon Bush never got after the long, bitter recount in the 2000 presidential election. Bush was on the phone with congressional leaders several times a day. He had 7 A.M. breakfasts with congressional leaders—no staff, no notes. For a time, the White House drove the congressional agenda.

From partisan gridlock, Congress shifted into overdrive to help the victims of the 9/11 attacks, rebuild the economy, and tighten the nation's defenses to fight a faceless and apparently stateless enemy. Major new laws passed rapidly and often with no dissent. On September 13, Congress voted unanimously to pass a bill (HR 2884) easing the federal tax burden on families of 9/11 victims. On September 14, lawmakers also unanimously backed the president's request for $40 billion for disaster relief and counterterrorism (HR 2888). A resolution to use "all necessary and appropriate force" against those who planned or aided the 9/11

New York City firefighters work in the rubble of the World Trade Center towers, September 11, 2001. (Library of Congress)

attacks (S.J. Res. 23) passed the same day with only one dissenting vote. Ten days after the attacks, Congress passed a $15 billion airline bailout bill. In addition to aid and loan guarantees, it created a victim-compensation fund for 9/11 families, while limiting the damages they could win if they opted instead to sue the airlines.

But even in the new era of good feeling, lawmakers complained that the White House wasn't treating Congress like a partner in what Bush called the "war on terror." Members of Congress on both sides of the aisle said that the official briefings on terrorism didn't add to what they had already read in the morning papers. Moreover, Democrats said that the Bush administration was using fear of further terrorist attacks to drive its legislative priorities. Attorney General John Ashcroft told lawmakers that if they did not grant the government significant new powers of surveillance and detention by September 21, they could be held accountable for future attacks. On the eve of a key House vote on the USA Patriot Act (HR 3162), the Federal Bureau of Investigation (FBI) issued a warning that new terrorist attacks on American soil could take place within days. "I think it is important for the American people to know their government is on full alert," Bush said in a news conference on October 11. The USA Patriot Act passed the Senate on October 24 with just one dissenting vote and later cleared the House by a vote of 357 to 66.

Pollsters and strategists signaled that national security could be the key issue in the 2002 midterm elections, and the president's party had a lock on it. Some Democrats called for a full congressional investigation of circumstances leading up to the 9/11 attacks. After visits with families of attack victims, Senator Robert Torricelli (D-N.J.) called for a board of inquiry along the lines of the panel that had investigated the 1941 Japanese attack on Pearl Harbor six decades earlier. "Congress shouldn't be shielding itself," he said. Senator Joseph Lieberman (D-Conn.) called on the president to set up an independent commission. But an ongoing sense of siege, especially in the U.S. Capitol, held in check the calls for investigations into what went wrong on 9/11.

Another terrorist attack, this time biological in nature, struck the Capitol on October 15, when an intern in Daschle's office opened a letter containing deadly anthrax powder. The anthrax attacks marked a high-water mark in public fears of terrorism, with 6 in 10 Americans reporting that they were worried about being a victim of terrorism. In such a climate of vulnerability, calls for an all-out probe of the intelligence and law-enforcement agencies charged with keeping the nation and the Capitol safe got little traction. The Hart Senate Office Building closed for decontamination for three months. Bush said the attacks might be linked to Osama bin Laden, the mastermind of the 9/11 attacks. (On August 8, 2008, the Justice Department announced that a civilian biological researcher at Fort Detrick, Maryland, who had committed suicide a week before, was the sole person responsible for the attacks. Several members of Congress disputed that account.)

Lapses, Gaps, and Conspiracy Theories

As Congress focused on the immediate fallout of the attacks, the news media and citizen investigators using the Internet conducted their own probes into the events of 9/11. None had Congress's authority to subpoena witnesses, access classified documents, or fund the agencies they were investigating. But the questions they raised—especially regarding discrepancies in official accounts of the government's preparation for and response to the attacks—helped mobilize families of victims to press Congress and the White House for answers. These unanswered questions fueled demands for an independent investigation.

Bloggers competed to produce the most complete, minute-by-minute timeline of the events: Why was Flight 11 in the air for 24 minutes, off course, without transponder or radio contact, before fighters were ordered to intercept it? Why was Flight 77 in the air for 35 minutes after Flight 11 hit the North Tower of the World Trade Center, without a single plane able to intercept it? In March 2002, Malcontentx, an anonymous Toronto blogger, posted a 140-page document, "Unanswered Questions," that became a key resource for 9/11 families. "At the moment, (since our governments seem uninterested in carrying out an open review of the events surrounding Sept. 11) it is up to us citizens to carry on the search for the truth ourselves," he wrote. Lawyers, doctors, pilots, and engineers set up their own collaborative investigations over the Internet, raising questions of their own: Was the collapse of World Trade Center Building 7 the result of controlled demolition, rather than fires in the neighboring Twin Towers? Did spikes in stock trading on companies hurt by the 9/11 attacks signal foreknowledge?

Such questions fueled a wide range of conspiracy theories and added to pressure from the public, especially from the 9/11 families, for an official investigation. In the end, there were two official probes of the attacks. House and Senate intelligence panels launched a Joint Inquiry into Intelligence Community Activities Before and After the Terrorist Attacks of September 11, 2001, on February 14, 2002. Its scope was limited to intelligence failures. At the urging of 9/11 families, Congress authorized and Bush approved the National Commission on Terrorist Attacks Upon the United States, known as the 9/11 Commission, on November 27, 2002. The two probes overlapped by about eight months.

Congress Probes Intelligence Failures

There was no shortage of issues for Congress to investigate after the attacks—the response of air traffic controllers and the Federal Aviation Administration, law enforcement, border security, foreign policy. But Congress's first move was to examine failures of the U.S. intelligence community. "As with previous national shocks and setbacks that involved anything foreign, Americans wanting to find explanations for 9/11 and to assign blame turned immediately and reflexively toward intelligence," said Paul Pillar, a retired analyst for the Central Intelligence Agency (CIA) who testified before both the Joint Inquiry and the 9/11 Commission.

No fewer than a dozen blue-ribbon panels from 1989 to the 2001 attacks had investigated the nation's intelligence and counterterrorism capabilities and found the system wanting. These included the Commission on the Roles and Capabilities of the United States Intelligence Community (1996), known as the Aspin-Brown Commission; the National Commission on Terrorism (2000), or Bremer Commission; and the U.S. Commission on National Security in the 21st Century, or the Hart-Rudman Commission, which reported to the secretary of defense on February 15, 2001.

Many of these reports signaled the need for a comprehensive strategy to protect the United States, including improving coordination and information sharing on terrorist threats among the 14 government intelligence agencies and organizations. The director of the CIA, for example, had the responsibility but not the authority to coordinate activities across the intelligence community. The Pentagon controlled 80 percent of the intelligence community's budget and the hiring and firing decisions that went with it. Of the 340 recommendations to reform the intelligence community, only 35 were fully implemented, according to a study by Amy Zegart. The vast majority of recommendations resulted in no action at all, she said.

Before 9/11, both the Senate Select Committee on Intelligence and the House Permanent Select Committee on Intelligence had identified weaknesses in how the intelligence community was functioning, including the need to boost funding for human intelligence and to upgrade technology. By late summer 2001, the Senate intelligence panel had drafted legislation based on the recommendations of the Hart-Rudman and Bremer commissions, with plans to take it up in the fall. After the 9/11 attacks, however, demands for reform shot up the agenda. In October, Senator Richard Shelby (R-Ala.), the ranking Republican on the Senate intelligence panel, called on CIA director George Tenet to resign over the intelligence failures on his watch. Critics said it was a bid to deflect attention from the Bush White House. Tenet, who had served under both Presidents Clinton and Bush, told Congress that the CIA needed more people, better communications, and better information-technology support. "We were doing the best we could," he said.

Plans for a joint congressional investigation were set in motion just days after the attacks in private talks between Senator Graham and Republican Representative Porter Goss, fellow Floridians who chaired the Senate and House intelligence committees. The key to the 9/11 attacks was a failure of intelligence, so it made sense for their panels to take the lead in the investigation, Graham said. He and Goss agreed that the investigation should be a joint effort and must be clearly bipartisan, backed by congressional leadership and the White House. With the support of their ranking members, they took the proposal to congressional leaders on September 25. Graham and Goss made the case that a joint investigation would be less taxing to federal agencies than separate, competing probes. At the White House that evening, President Bush and Vice President Richard Cheney promised to cooperate.

The prospect of a congressional investigation did not derail proposals for an independent probe. Democrats on the House intelligence panel, led by Representative Nancy Pelosi (D-Calif.) pushed for a strong, independent commission with subpoena power as part of the House Intelligence Authorization Act for Fiscal Year 2002 (HR 2883). In response, Goss proposed an amendment on the House floor limiting the commission's scope and stripping it of subpoena power. On October 5, 2001, the House voted to establish an independent commission to investigate the 9/11 attacks as part of the Intelligence Authorization Act for Fiscal Year 2002 (HR 2883), a move the White House strongly opposed. President Bush urged Congress to confine its investigation to the two intelligence committees and to focus on how to prevent future attacks. A backward-looking investigation, the president said, would distract the FBI and the CIA from the work they needed to do to keep the nation safe. In his memoir, *Like No Other Time,* Daschle wrote that Cheney told him that the leaders of the war on terror—especially the FBI and CIA—were too busy to go back through their records or to "waste time" preparing testimony. "In his message there was an implied threat: If you keep pushing for this [independent investigation], we're going to say that you're interfering with the war effort," Daschle added. At the urging of the president and with Daschle's support, conferees dropped the independent investigation from the conference report. (Daschle still lost his reelection bid in 2004 after a Republican campaign that charged him with being obstructionist.)

The Congressional Joint Inquiry

On February 14, 2002, the Senate and House intelligence committees announced the launch of the first joint, bicameral investigation by two standing committees in congressional history. Congress authorized $3.2 million for the Joint Inquiry to expire at the end of the 107th Congress, or by January 3, 2003. The investigation focused narrowly on what the intelligence community knew—or should have known—about the international terrorist threat to the United States before September 11, 2001. A factual review was to include what was done with that information and why it failed to prevent the attacks. The mandate also included identifying and fixing any system problems that contributed to such a failure.

"When the Intelligence Community fails to provide timely and accurate threat information, it is a grave matter," said co-chair Graham, at the start of the Joint Inquiry. Graham, a former two-term governor of Florida and a Senate centrist, developed into one of the Bush administration's strongest critics after 9/11, especially over what

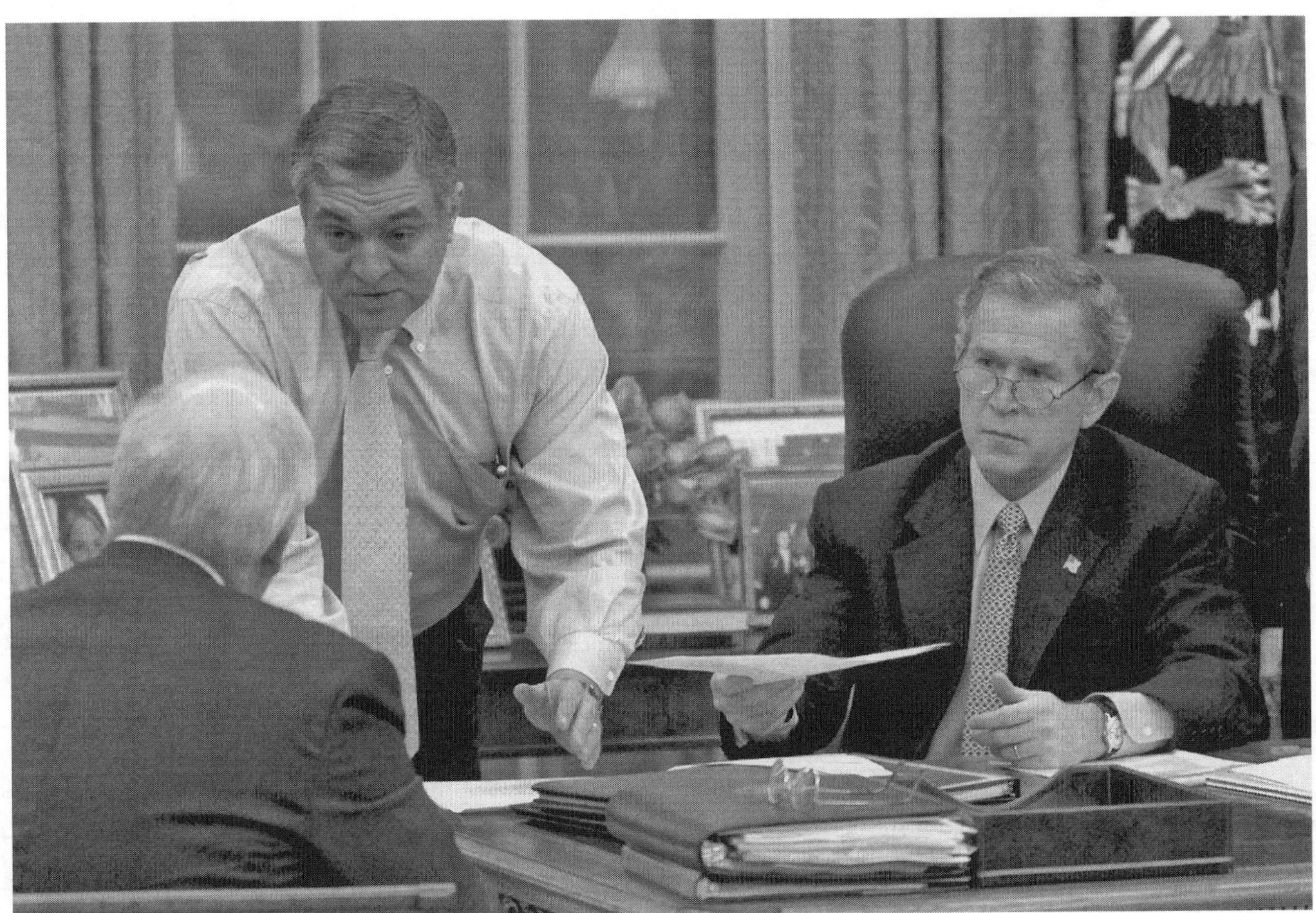

CIA Director George Tenet, left, meets with President George W. Bush, right, and Vice President Dick Cheney, foreground, in the Oval Office. (©Eric Draper/The White House/Reuters/CORBIS)

he saw as a cover-up of the role of the Kingdom of Saudi Arabia in financing terrorist activity.

The three other Joint Inquiry leaders cut sharply different political profiles. Shelby, a former Democrat, remained a strong critic of the CIA—especially of its director—throughout the Joint Inquiry. Some have claimed there was no intelligence failure on September 11th," Shelby said, "but the fact that nearly 3,000 Americans perished on that day strongly suggests otherwise."

On the House side, Goss, a former Army intelligence officer and CIA clandestine agent, was CIA director Tenet's strongest defender on Capitol Hill after the 9/11 attacks. He said Congress should look to itself for failing to recognize the threat and adequately fund antiterrorism efforts. Goss had met regularly with Bush and Cheney before September 11 and was among those House and Senate leaders evacuated to a secure location after the attacks. While he denied rumors in the fall of 2001 that he was in line for Tenet's job, Goss replaced Tenet as CIA director in September 2004. As a leader of the Joint Inquiry, he called for a fact-driven review. "We will not be driven by outside pressures," he said on June 4.

Representative Nancy Pelosi, the top Democrat on the House intelligence panel and party whip, was focused on regaining control of the House. She and Goss maintained a strong working relationship on the Joint Inquiry and both backed the investigation's conclusions. In 2006, she would lead Democrats back to power on a campaign that included a call to fully implement the recommendations of the 9/11 Commission. Pelosi often spoke of the need to honor those who lost their lives on September 11 and their families, "who are looking to us for answers."

As a mark of trust, Graham, Goss, Shelby, and Pelosi set a ground rule that no decisions would be made unless all four agreed. At Graham's urging, the leaders also agreed to hire a separate joint staff to conduct the 9/11 investigation. The permanent staff was needed to continue oversight responsibilities, Graham said, a decision that the permanent staff came to resent.

With the clock running down on the 107th Congress, the Joint Inquiry had less than 11 months to complete its investigation. A first step was to bring on new staff members and set up five investigative teams, assigned mainly to the CIA, the FBI, and the National Security Agency (NSA). They also gathered material from the Treasury, Defense, State, Transportation, and Energy departments, as well as private-sector individuals and organizations. The 24 new specialists brought experience in law enforcement, investigations, oversight, and, especially, intelligence. With 37 lawmakers on the Joint Inquiry, members of Congress outnumbered the new joint staff. After the Joint Inquiry's first business meeting on June 4, 2002, Goss predicted "heavy membership participation." But over time, some panel members complained that the new staff had evolved into a largely independent operation. Members missed being briefed by personal staff. "Many members of our joint committee have found it exceedingly difficult to get information about the inquiry," said Shelby at the first public hearing on September 18, 2002. "They're frustrated by what a lot of them perceive to be efforts to limit their ability to participate in this inquiry fully."

The investigation hit an early glitch with the resignation on May 1 of L. Britt Snider, the Joint Inquiry's staff director. The first public hearings, initially set to begin in May, were put off until September. A former inspector general for the CIA and special adviser to Tenet, Snider stepped down after reports that he had proposed hiring a CIA employee who had failed an agency polygraph test. But Snider's departure also reflected views within the congressional leadership, most notably Shelby, on whether an executive director with close ties to Tenet could lead a hard-hitting investigation of the CIA. He was replaced by Eleanor Hill, a former federal prosecutor who also served as staff director of the Senate Permanent Subcommittee on Investigation and inspector general of the Department of Defense. Both Hill and Snider had worked on the 1986 Iran-contra investigation, Hill as a staff liaison for Senator Sam Nunn (D-Ga.) and Snider for Senator William Cohen (R-Maine).

"When we started this," Hill said, "it was a catastrophic, traumatic moment for this country. People were panicked, people felt unsafe. The country needed reassurances, and the country also needed to move beyond this and to feel that whatever had been missed was fixed and we could go on into the future." Lawmakers of both parties credited Hill with getting the investigation back on track and tightening the focus on investigation. A veteran of congressional investigations, Hill said she accepted the job only after assurances that the staff would be free to conduct a thorough investigation: "I really felt that 9/11 was such a cataclysmic event for the country that at least the leadership realized that we had to put politics aside here, get to the bottom of what happened, move the country forward, and fix what was wrong," she said. "I think to the extent we were able to be successful, a lot of it came from the fact that the leadership did that." A first step was to develop a timeline of events. Over 11 months, staff reviewed 500,000 pages of documents and conducted some 300 interviews, as well as briefings and panels involving nearly 600 individuals from intelligence-community agencies, state and local entities, the private sector, and foreign governments. The Joint Inquiry also held 22 hearings, including nine public hearings in September and October 2002. "It was a huge amount of investigative work in a limited time frame," Hill said.

In the nine months before the Joint Inquiry held its first public meeting, intelligence agencies and other congressional panels had begun releasing their own versions of events. "If you look at the hearings and statements being issued by committees and agencies, what you see is the assumption and the position of a lot of the agencies was: We did everything that we could possibly have done," Hill said. Over time, that's an assumption the Joint Inquiry—along with the news media, whistleblowers, and families of 9/11 victims—would begin to take apart.

Connecting the Dots

The congressional probe produced a timeline of events and an analysis of missed opportunities that went beyond what agencies had pieced together on their own. It became the main narrative on intelligence failures regarding the 9/11 attacks. "The Intelligence Community failed to fully capitalize on available and potentially important information," the Joint Inquiry concluded in its final report. But it did not find what 9/11 families called the smoking gun: tactical intelligence about where, when, or how an attack would be carried out—and evidence that politicians deliberately ignored it.

To build a timeline—who knew what, when, and what they did with what they knew—the Joint Inquiry staff asked agencies for access to all of the analysis produced on terrorism and al-Qaeda from 1994 until the 2001 attacks. That included any intelligence that an attack was imminent or the nature of the attack, information about the 19 hijackers—their backgrounds, how they entered the United States, their support networks and activities leading up to the attacks—and how they avoided detection. Despite assurances from the White House, the CIA director, and the heads of the intelligence-community agencies that access to highly classified information would be complete and unprecedented, access was a challenge throughout the investigation. In an appendix to their final report, the Joint Inquiry noted that there were areas where no access was allowed and others where access was achieved "only after extensive discussions and delays or under conditions that limited the scope of the Inquiry's work." Battles with agencies to get secret documents declassified for public hearings or the final report were more bruising still.

Most notably, the White House denied the Joint Inquiry access to the President's Daily Brief (PDB) and barred CIA officials from answering questions on how the presidential briefs were prepared. Intelligence officials advised the Joint Inquiry about the content of an August 6, 2001, PDB titled "Bin Ladin Determined To Strike in US." This and other leaks led staff to conclude that the PDBs were critical to an understanding of what Presidents Clinton and Bush knew about the terrorist threat and what they did about it. Even the statement on why access to PDBs was important was redacted in the Joint Inquiry's final report. Staff members were also denied access to intelligence-community budget requests, NSA planning documents and contractual information, and Pentagon documents on 13 military options reportedly prepared for operations against bin Laden. Intelligence-community agencies insisted that agency representatives be present to monitor all interviews of their personnel, and the Joint Inquiry accepted those terms.

Even with these limitations, the Joint Inquiry staff assembled a body of evidence of missed opportunities and a narrative to explain them that challenged and later supplanted the official government accounts of the events leading up to 9/11. One of the most dramatic examples of the power of congressional investigation involved the closed testimony of Coleen Rowley, a Minneapolis FBI agent. In late October 2001, FBI headquarters summoned agents from the Phoenix and Minneapolis offices to Washington to establish a timeline of FBI actions before 9/11. The timeline seemed to be making the case that "nobody could have foreseen this or stopped this," said Rowley. She disagreed. In August 2001, a month before the attacks, FBI field agents in Minneapolis had identified Zacarias Moussaoui—a student pilot who wanted to learn to fly planes but not land them—as a threat, but FBI headquarters refused to pursue a warrant allowing agents to search the hard drive of his computer. The bureau also failed to connect the Moussaoui investigation, the heightened threat environment in the summer of 2001, and the July 10 warning from an FBI agent in Phoenix that bin Laden might be sending terrorists to the United States for flight training to use planes to conduct terrorist activity. Rowley recommended including these items in the official timeline but was overruled. On May 16, 2002, she was called in for a debriefing by the Joint Inquiry staff—at FBI headquarters, with an FBI official present—on a legal issue involving the "wall" between intelligence and law enforcement. When asked if she had anything she wanted to add, she handed them a memo outlining these concerns, then hand-delivered copies to the director of the FBI and two Joint Inquiry members, Senators Dianne Feinstein (D-Calif.) and Shelby. "I think that if that [congressional] Inquiry had not been going on and

FBI Agent Coleen Rowley from the Minneapolis FBI field office testifies before the Senate Judiciary Committee on June 6, 2002. The committee investigated intelligence failures leading up to the 9/11 attacks. In a 13-page memo, Rowley accused FBI headquarters of putting roadblocks in the way of Minneapolis field agents trying to investigate Zacarias Moussaoui, who was later convicted of conspiring with the hijackers in the September 11 attacks. (Joe Marquette/ Associated Press)

if I had not been called as a witness, I definitely would not have written it on my own," Rowley said.

In closed hearings, the Joint Inquiry questioned witnesses on issues ranging from the evolution of the terrorist threat to airplanes as weapons, covert action, the Moussaoui and Phoenix memo, information sharing, and reorganization of the intelligence community. Tenet, National Security Agency director Michael Hayden, FBI director Robert Mueller, Deputy Secretary of State Richard Armitage, former National Security advisers Samuel Berger and Brent Scowcroft, and Deputy Secretary of Defense Paul Wolfowitz testified in open hearings. Richard Clarke, special adviser to the president for cyberspace security, testified in a closed hearing, but National Security Adviser Condoleezza Rice did not, as the White House claimed executive privilege.

The Public Hearings

As a veteran of the Iran-contra investigation, Eleanor Hill recalled the disappointment of seeing the findings of that congressional investigation ignored. For the most part, the public does not have time to follow nine months of narrow, courtroom-style interrogation, she concluded. In a bid to make the public hearings more accessible, she organized them around staff statements to frame witness testimony. "They need to have hearings that underscore the big issues, the most critical testimony, and do it in a way that the public can hear enough of it to understand what the issue is," she said.

The first public hearing opened in Room 216 of the Hart Senate Office Building on September 18, 2002. "These public hearings are part of our search for truth," Senator Graham said, "not to point fingers [or] to pin blame, but with the goal of identifying and correcting whatever systemic problems might have prevented our government from detecting and disrupting al-Qaeda's plot." Chairman Goss cautioned the audience, packed with family members of 9/11 victims, not to expect that all secrets would be shared. "So today, we begin the process of open hearings," he said, "with the understanding not everything can be discussed in this forum, as much as we would like to share it with America, but that much can and should be explained to our nation, which is our goal. And we will go as far as we can." But for Shelby and many of the 9/11 families, assigning blame was the point. "I think it's important that the American people know where we stand as we begin to discuss publicly why their multi-million-dollar intelligence community was unable to detect and prevent the worst single attack on American soil in our history," said Shelby. "I will continue," he said, "to support this effort and support our chairmen, but there may come a day very soon when it will become apparent that ours must be only a prelude to further inquiries." Prominent 9/11 family groups also demanded an investigation that included accountability for the lapses that enabled the attacks. "We need people to be held accountable for their failures," testified Kristen Breitweiser, co-chairperson of September 11th Advocates and a witness at the first Joint Inquiry public hearing.

Public hearings wound down in October with top intelligence officials responding to recommendations for change. In a much anticipated hearing on October 17, Tenet said that he and other executive-branch officials were well aware of the danger of an al-Qaeda attack, especially in midsummer 2001, but saw the attack coming most likely in the Middle East. He also told lawmakers that he had requested increases of more than $2 billion annually for fiscal years 2000 through 2005, but that Congress had approved "only small portions of these requests."

The Long Fight Over Declassification

Each Joint Inquiry staff report had to be cleared for public presentation. Those negotiations with intelligence agencies were arduous and often went on right up until the night before a public hearing. For the first hearing, Tenet refused to declassify any reference to the intelligence community providing information to the president or White House—a position that only further convinced 9/11 families that the congressional inquiry was headed for a whitewash. But these mini-battles before each public hearing were only a prelude to the ordeal of declassifying the final report, which went on for six months after the Joint Inquiry formally shut down.

The Joint Inquiry released the unclassified elements of its final report on December 10, 2002. That included the cover page, a table of general contents, a list of findings and conclusions, without accompanying narrative, and the recommendations. The rest of the report was held in the secure facilities of the House and Senate intelligence panels, pending declassification. Seven months later, the 900-page report was released, but with redactions and strikeouts throughout. Twenty-seven pages covering foreign support for the hijackers while they were in the United States were stricken almost entirely, fueling speculation of a cover-up over a possible Saudi role in financing terrorism. "In the view of the Joint Inquiry," the report concluded, "this gap in U.S. intelligence coverage is unacceptable, given the magnitude and immediacy of the potential risk to U.S. national security. The intelligence community needs to address this area of concern as aggressively and as quickly as possible." Even that statement, which was in brackets, signaled that language was changed during declassification.

The intelligence community pushed hard for a final report that was scrubbed and entirely declassified. But Hill and the joint staff, with the support of congressional leaders, insisted that it be presented to the public with the redactions clearly presented in context. The 900-page declassified version of the report was released on July 24, 2003.

While nine members submitted additional or supplementary views, no member of the Joint Inquiry voted against it. In his 135-page statement of additional views, Shelby named six leaders of the intelligence community that he said had failed in significant ways. "Too much has happened for us to be able to conclude that the American people and our national security interests can be protected simply by throwing more resources at agencies still fundamentally wedded to the pre-September 11 status quo," he wrote.

Even with those limitations, the Joint Inquiry's framing of the issue around "missed opportunities" and the evidence developed to support that claim became the main narrative of the events surrounding September 11, 2001—and a critical assist to the independent commission that followed it.

The 9/11 Families Push for an Independent Commission

Meanwhile, the families of the victims of 9/11 were gaining confidence as players on Capitol Hill. For many activists, trust that Washington would do right by the families took a hit when Congress passed a $15 billion bailout that shielded the airlines from liability just 10 days after the attacks. "When we figured that they had taken away our rights, that was very upsetting, because they limited the liability of the airlines and anyone else who would be held responsible for 9/11," said Carie Lemack, a founder of Families of September 11th. Her mother, Judy Larocque, had been a passenger on American Airlines Flight 11.

Early on, the families questioned whether Congress could fairly investigate its own failures, including lapses in oversight and funding that could have contributed to vulnerabilities on September 11. They scanned press reports and Internet sites for new questions and information, wrote letters, held vigils, organized conference calls, convened strategy sessions—and refused to go away. They met with White House officials and members of Congress, focusing on those from the areas hardest hit by the attacks. The families were not all of one mind. Their groups included Voices of September 11th, Families of September 11th, the Skyscraper Safety Campaign, September 11th Advocates, Coalition of 9/11 Families, and 9/11 Families for a Secure America. Leaders of these groups formed the 12-member Family Steering Committee, which lobbied hard to create the 9/11 Commission and then closely followed its work.

Mary Fetchet, a member of the Family Steering Committee and founding director of Voices of September 11th, lost her son Brad in the attack on the World Trade Center. "We had different goals," she said of the various groups. "Some wanted accountability. I was concerned about just understanding what the failures were and to build a framework so that our government would be more prepared to respond in the event of terrorist attacks." Many 9/11 family activists saw Congress as part of the problem. Working closely with the families, Representative Timothy Roemer (D-Ind.) called for an independent bipartisan commission. He was the only Joint Inquiry member to also serve on the 9/11 Commission. "The families were the driving force, the gravitas," he said. "They had this overwhelming moral authority, and they usually got what they wanted."

What the families of victims wanted was answers. They doubted whether the Joint Inquiry, with a mandate limited to intelligence, could fairly answer them. The Joint Inquiry's clashes with the Bush White House over the release of documents or testimony by top admin-

September 11 family members Mary Fetchet, left, of New Canaan, Connecticut, holding a photograph of her son Brad, killed in Tower 2, and Carie Lemack of Boston, right, holding a photograph of her mother, Judy Larocque, who died on American Airlines flight 11, attend a vigil outside the White House on December 6, 2004, for passage of legislation that would revamp the nation's intelligence agencies. (Susan Walsh/Associated Press)

istration officials only reinforced those concerns. More than a year before the release of the Joint Inquiry report, the families began lobbying Congress and the White House for an independent investigation.

Congress Punts to an Independent Commission

It was more than 14 months after the 9/11 attacks before Congress approved the creation of an independent investigative commission. From September 2001 through May 2002, four measures to create an independent panel with subpoena power failed. Sponsors included Senator Torricelli, Representative Pelosi, Senator Charles Grassley (R-Iowa), Senator John McCain (R-Ariz.), Senator Lieberman, and Representative Roemer. Meanwhile, disclosures from the Joint Inquiry, as well as ongoing investigations in the news media, fueled calls for a broader, independent investigation. On May 15, CBS News broadcast the first reports that Bush had received the secret intelligence briefing on August 6, 2001 titled "Bin Ladin Determined To Strike in US." The report renewed pressure on Congress to find out what the president knew and when he knew it.

On June 11, 2002, the 9/11 families rallied outside the Capitol to demand the creation of an independent commission. On July 25, Roemer tried again to form a 10-member independent commission through an amendment to the Intelligence Authorization Act for 2003. After intense debate, the measure passed 219 to 188. Twenty-five Republicans broke with the White House to vote for the amendment. The Senate passed a similar measure in September. The families kept up pressure on the White House to agree to an independent investigation. On September 20, White House spokesman Ari Fleischer reported that the families "have made compelling arguments." Still, negotiations with Congress over the powers and makeup of the 9/11 Commission went on until November 15. The White House drew a line on two issues: (1) that 6 of 10 commissioners would be required to invoke the commission's subpoena powers, and (2) that the chairman, appointed by the White House, would not share power with a co-chair, appointed by congressional Democrats. Congress agreed, and on November 27, 2002, Bush signed Public Law 107–306 creating the National Commission on Terrorist Attacks Upon the United States, with the revisions the White House had requested.

While the Joint Inquiry was limited to investigating intelligence failures, the 9/11 Commission, as the new panel became known, was tasked with probing intelligence, the response on the ground, and everything else—facts and circumstances relating to law-enforcement agencies, diplomacy, immigration, nonimmigrant visas, border control, the flow of financial assets to terrorist organizations, commercial aviation, the role of congressional oversight and resource allocation, and "other facts and circumstances deemed relevant." Initially funded at a mere $3 million, the commission was required to release its final report within 18 months. (By contrast, the Clinton-era Whitewater investigation of a botched real-estate deal took six years at a cost to taxpayers of $50 million, and the commission investigating the *Challenger* space shuttle disaster in 1986 had a $75 million budget.) The White House worried that a report released any later than May 27 could affect the 2004 presidential election.

The commission got off to a slow start. Bush's pick for chairman, former secretary of state Henry Kissinger, was short-lived. Kissinger withdrew on December 13, 2002, citing concerns over requirements to disclose clients of his international consulting firm. His decision came a day after meeting with a delegation of 9/11 family members, who grilled him on whether his client list included Saudis or members of the bin Laden family. "He wouldn't share that information with us," said Fetchet, of the Family Steering Committee. The panel's vice chairman, George Mitchell, a former senator and former Senate majority leader, resigned on December 11, citing time constraints with his consulting business. Kissinger and Mitchell were replaced by former

New Jersey governor Tom Kean (pronounced cane), a Republican, as chairman and former Indiana representative Lee Hamilton, a Democrat, as vice chair. When the call from the White House came to chair the 9/11 Commission, Kean was president of Drew University in Madison, N.J., 30 miles west of Manhattan. He knew many families and victims of the attacks. "In towns around me, we had funerals for six months," he said. The son of a U.S. representative and grandson of a U.S. senator, Kean served consecutive terms as speaker of the state assembly, then as governor from 1982 to 1990. President Clinton appointed him to serve on the 1997 President's Initiative on Race. Known for a capacity to work across party lines, Kean knew Trenton and Newark better than he knew the corridors of power in Washington.

Hamilton knew Washington. During his 34 years in the U.S. House of Representatives, he chaired the International Relations Committee and the Permanent Select Committee on Intelligence. In 1987, he chaired the House Select Committee to Investigate Covert Arms Transactions With Iran. (His Republican counterpart on that panel was Wyoming representative Richard Cheney.) After retiring from the House in 1999, Hamilton moved a few blocks down Pennsylvania Avenue to direct the Woodrow Wilson Center for International Scholars. He served on the Hart-Rudman Commission, which famously warned in 1999 that "America will become increasingly vulnerable to hostile attack on our homeland, and our military superiority will not entirely protect us. . . . Americans will likely die on American soil, possibly in large numbers."

The other eight commissioners were appointed by congressional leaders. On the House side, Democrats appointed former representative Tim Roemer, who had not run for reelection in 2002, and Jamie Gorelick, vice chair of Fannie Mae and a former deputy attorney general in the Clinton administration. As a member of the Joint Inquiry, Roemer had developed strong ties with 9/11 families. Senate Democrats appointed former senator Max Cleland of Georgia and Washington lawyer Richard Ben-Veniste. Cleland had just lost a bitter reelection bid, amid Republican charges that he was "soft" on national security. He resigned from the commission after a year and was replaced by former Nebraska senator Bob Kerrey, president of the New School in New York City. A tough interrogator, Ben-Veniste had served on both the Watergate and Whitewater investigations. House Republican leaders tapped Washington lawyer Fred Fielding, who had served as legal counsel in the Nixon and Reagan White Houses—and would later serve as legal counsel in the Bush White House—and former Illinois governor Jim Thompson. Senate Republican leader Trent Lott of Mississippi named former Washington senator Slade Gorton. At the urging of the 9/11 families, McCain, an early supporter of an independent commission, had a say on the other Republican appointment, former secretary of the navy John Lehman.

"We were set up to fail," Kean and Hamilton wrote in their joint account of the 9/11 Commission, *Without Precedent: The Inside Story of the 9/11 Commission* (2006). At their first meeting on December 18, 2002, the new chair and vice chair talked through challenges: A month into its 18-month mandate, the commission had no offices, no staff, no security clearances, a massive mandate, inadequate funding, and a toxic campaign season fast approaching. If the commission was to have a chance at success, the commissioners had to avoid splintering on party lines, prevent leaks that could damage credibility, and win the support of the 9/11 families for the final report.

Kean and Hamilton wrote, "The breadth of the mandate was exceeded by the emotional weight of 9/11: a singularly shocking, painful, and transformative event in American history that was, in many ways, ongoing. We stepped into moving streams: a congressional inquiry into the attacks was winding down; family members of victims were demanding answers to tough questions; the wounds of regions such as the New York and Washington areas were still fresh; and the nation was fighting a war against terrorism around the world, preparing to go to war in Iraq, and receiving periodic terror alerts at home."

At Kean's suggestion, the two leaders agreed to function as cochairs. That meant no decisions on key issues, including staff hires, unless both agreed. They accepted news-media invitations on the condition that they appeared together. They agreed to set up an integrated staff, to signal that the commission was nonpartisan. They assigned staff to the commission, not to individual commissioners, in part to limit prospects for minority reports. Most importantly, they agreed to keep the process open: to hold public hearings to the extent possible and to draft a report with a narrative compelling enough to be read. "In general, secrecy is a precursor to cynicism and conspiracy theories," they wrote. "We wanted to give an authoritative account of 9/11; we did not want to give fodder to conspiracy theorists who could question why we were undertaking our investigation in secret."

At Gorton's urging, Kean and Hamilton hired University of Virginia professor Philip Zelikow as executive director. At the Kennedy School of Government

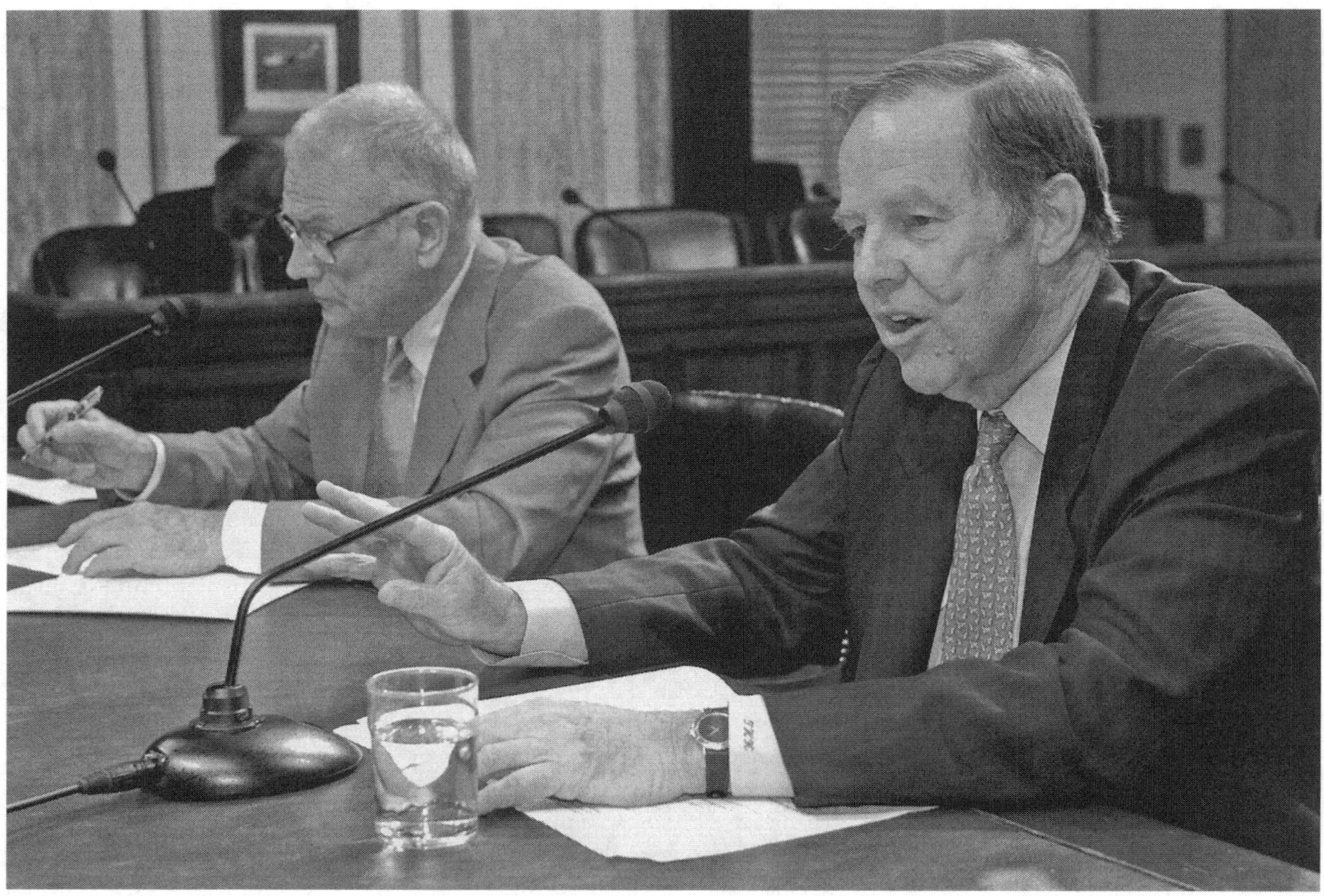

9/11 Commission Chairman Tom Kean, right, and Vice Chairman Lee Hamilton, left. (Associated Press)

at Harvard University, he had led the Catastrophic Terrorism Study Group in 1998. Other commissioners questioned whether an academic had the temperament to lead a tough investigation. Tireless, brilliant, and combative, Zelikow become a lightning rod for critics over his ties to the Bush administration: He had served on Bush's national-security transition team in 2000–01 and, in 1995, coauthored a book on German unification with Rice. He recruited a staff of more than 60, including 5 of the 26 staff who had served on the congressional Joint Inquiry. "We benefited from and built on their work, but they also had other problems, too," Zelikow said. "The Joint Inquiry was too narrowly focused, given the scope of the committee responsibilities. I had more freedom in composing a staff, which included some of the best folks from the Joint Inquiry." Even staff who complained about Zelikow's people skills credited his capacity to move the investigation along and help shape a compelling narrative. Until White House Counsel Alberto Gonzales refused to talk to him, Zelikow also led efforts to negotiate access to documents and witnesses at the White House.

Most of the staff recruited to work with the 9/11 Commission already had security clearances and extensive experience in intelligence, law enforcement, or congressional investigation. Deputy Director Christopher Kojm worked with Hamilton on the Iran-Contra Investigation and the House International Relations Committee, before moving to the State Department as deputy assistant secretary for intelligence policy. General Counsel Daniel Marcus served as associate attorney general in the second Clinton administration. A broad and diverse staff included accountants, systems engineers, federal and state prosecutors, money laundering experts, an ex-air marshal, senior intelligence analysts (including an agent who ran CIA operations in Afghanistan), police officers, law professors, historians, and a novelist. Team leaders included John Farmer Jr., a former attorney general of New Jersey; Douglas MacEachin, a former deputy director of intelligence at the CIA; Michael Hurley, a career CIA operations officer; Dietrich Snell, deputy attorney general of New York; and John Roth, a former chief of the asset forfeiture and money laundering division of the

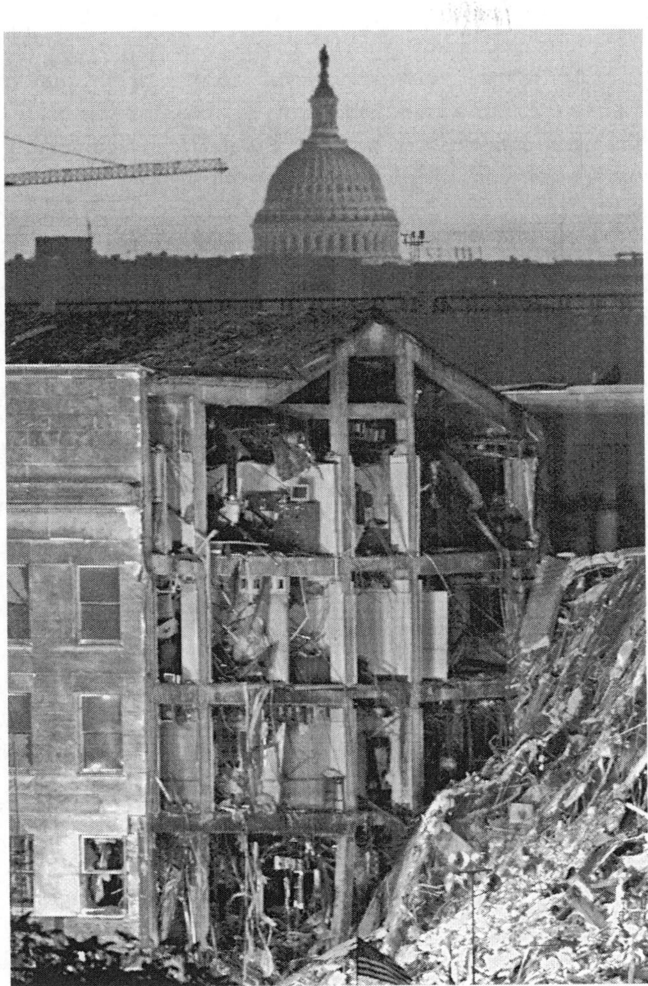

The dome of the Capitol building in Washington is visible behind the crash site at the Pentagon at sunrise on September 16, 2001. Eighty-five remains were recovered from the Pentagon, the Defense Department said. According to the department, 188 people—military and civilian employees at the Pentagon and the passengers and crew in the hijacked airplane—were believed killed when the plane crashed into the military complex on September 11. (Stephen J. Boitano/Associated Press)

Justice Department. Kevin Shaeffer, a staff member who retired from the navy after injuries in the 9/11 attack on the Pentagon, was assigned to review the emergency response in New York and Northern Virginia.

At their first meeting on January 17, 2003, commissioners seated themselves by party affiliation. Kean asked them to alternate seats by party. "We got to know each other as people," Kean said. "That's how we developed into a bipartisan effort. Democrats caucused together for the first two months. Republicans wanted to caucus, but I never allowed it. . . . Eventually, it was a different world." How a commission appointed by highly partisan people managed to work across party lines is a point of pride for many who served on the commission. Others, including critics among 9/11 families, blame the commission for not being partisan enough—that is, not being willing to assign blame for failures of 9/11 to specific individuals or administrations. "If there had been any attempt to cast blame, there would have been a divided report and it would have been useless. We would have wasted our time and the taxpayers' money," said Commissioner Gorton. Instead, he said, the commission came to understand its work as finding facts, period: "We listed all of the facts and all of the incidents that we think led to 9/11. If you think that means Bush screwed up, that's fine. If you think that means Clinton screwed up, fine. It became implicit in the minds of all of us that we had to write a history without adjectives. It wasn't up to us to express opinions or to cast blame."

The Fight for Access to Key Information

As the 9/11 Commission began meeting in the spring of 2003, the Joint Inquiry was still battling with the Bush administration to declassify the final version of its report, which was not released until July 2003, riddled with redactions. The 9/11 commissioners had expected to build on the work of the Joint Inquiry, but early on it was a struggle even to gain access to the Joint Inquiry's closed hearings or final report. As of April 2003, only commissioners and six designated staff members had clearance to read even a redacted version of the Joint Inquiry report. Moreover, Goss, the Joint Inquiry's cochair, declined to share documents obtained from U.S. intelligence agencies. He said that they were intermixed with congressionally privileged material and the congressional staff did not have the resources to sort them out.

Even Commissioner Roemer, who had served on the Joint Inquiry, was not allowed to review the Joint Inquiry report in its unredacted form. At a March 20 meeting, Roemer noted his "sense of urgency and his strong sense that the commission is off to a disturbingly slow start with respect to clearances, access to the Joint Inquiry report, and access to executive branch documents." He also expressed concern that the White House was not yet backing the commission's request for $11 million in supplemental funding. Congressional backers cried foul. "Frankly, I am amazed and disappointed that questions regarding the funding of the commission persist given its bipartisan leadership and the heavy-lifting it is being asked to perform by the end of May 2004," said Senator Charles Schumer (D-N.Y.).

Shelby and Senator Lindsey Graham (R-S.C.) criticized the Bush administration for resisting the committee's requests for information related to the attacks. In a March 21, 2003, letter, Senator McCain urged the commission to use subpoena power to obtain needed documents or testimony. He also urged the commission to fully investigate and make public the role of Saudi policy and money in the rise of a global terrorist network deeply hostile to the United States. "The U.S. government's reluctance to address this issue directly must not extend to your work," he added. Senator Lieberman called on the commission to answer why more aggressive intelligence tactics and military options against bin Laden were not used and whether "specific international partnerships" would have rooted him out sooner. By April, prospects were brightening. On April 3, the White House made good on its commitment to allocate $9 million to the commission from the Emergency Response Fund that Congress had created after the attacks. The Senate approved $11 million for the commission in its supplemental appropriations bill. The House bill added none.

Negotiations over the terms of access to executive-branch documents and officials occupied much of 2003. At a May 1, 2003, meeting, Roemer said he felt strongly that no individual in the administration should block the Commission's statutorily mandated access to Joint Inquiry documents. Kean and Hamilton agreed that Roemer was "exactly right on the underlying merits," but Kean added that "where the Commission decides to make a stand on access to information is a very important question." "Subpoenas take a lot of time in court," he said in an interview. "We could have gone out of existence. I didn't know whether we would win in courts. Presidential privilege is something often protected in the courts." Instead, the commission took the issue to the American public. In their first interim report on July 8, 2003, Kean and Hamilton told a news briefing that "the coming weeks will determine whether we can do our job within the time allotted. . . . Extensive and prompt cooperation from the U.S. government, the Congress, state and local agencies, and private firms is essential."

As the commissioners negotiated with the Bush administration over access, the working groups used what information they had to develop the first comprehensive account of the facts and circumstances surrounding the attacks. The commission organized nine teams to work on al-Qaeda and the organization of the 9/11 attack, intelligence, counterterrorism policy, terrorist financing, border security, law enforcement, aviation and transportation security, the response to the attacks at the national level, and the emergency response in New York and northern Virginia and at local levels. Zelikow directed the teams to start preparing timelines and monographs for their subjects and to develop a list of essential questions: "Be sure you have considered some of the questions suggested by family groups or interested members of Congress or suggested at our initial hearings," he wrote in an April 3, 2003, memo to staff. "Test sample questions against this criterion: if this question is not answered, or at least reasonably addressed, can the Commission's work be considered successful?" The commission hired two staff members to keep in touch with the families.

In all, staff reviewed more than 2.5 million pages of documents and interviewed some 1,200 individuals in 10 countries. Staff members say that the direction they heard most often from commission leaders was "What are the facts?" Kean and Hamilton often cited the commission's congressional mandate: Tell what happened and make recommendations so it doesn't happen again. "It's amazing how many disputes can be resolved by just getting facts straight," said Hamilton, in an interview.

Probing U.S. Air Defense

One of the most difficult elements of the 9/11 narrative was sorting out why the military's air defenders failed to shoot down the hijacked planes. Even coming to terms on a timeline—when did the Federal Aviation Administration (FAA) notify the North American Aerospace Defense Command (NORAD) about the hijacked planes, and how did NORAD respond?—was complicated by official misstatements and delays in producing requested documents. When and how civilian leaders weighed in on events of the day was even more obscure. These lapses in the official account in turn fueled the persistent conspiracy theories on the events of September 11, including the view that U.S. officials deliberately allowed the attacks to happen The questions especially concerned 9/11 families, who pressed the commission to find out what could have been done to thwart the hijacked planes—and who was accountable for not doing it.

The fact-finding team ran into stiff resistance from the start. On May 7 and July 2, 2003, the commission requested logs, tapes, radar transmissions, after-action reviews, and any records of contacts with NORAD or with hijacked flights. After the FAA confirmed that all requested materials had been sent, the commission found out otherwise. During on-site interviews in FAA command centers in Boston, New York, Cleveland, and Indianapolis, staff learned that key primary documents had not been shared with the commission. These included tapes of FAA responses to calls on September 11 and records of contacts with NORAD. After renewed pressure from the commission, the FAA delivered some 20 boxes of additional material on October 10. During a break in a public hearing on October 14, team leader John Farmer briefed commissioners on how gaps in access had set back his investigation, jeopardizing the commission's May 27, 2004, deadline.

The briefing reignited the debate within the 9/11 Commission over the need for subpoenas. Commissioner Gorelick said the FAA's delayed response confirmed the need to issue subpoenas across the board. If the Commission had to wait for evidence of failure, it would be too late for a subpoena to work and too late for the commission to do its job, she said, according to meeting minutes released by the National Archives in January 2009. Given this provocation, the commission needs to use all the tools it has, said Commissioner Ben-Veniste, a Democrat. Commissioner Thompson, a Republican, said that a subpoena in that context would be viewed as a political act. In the interest of unity, the commission struck a compromise: It would issue its first subpoena to the FAA, but with a warning to the rest of the executive branch that additional subpoenas would be issued, if necessary. The commission also added six staff members to work through the evidence. "We were demonstrating—to the White House, the executive branch agencies, the 9/11 families, and the public—that if we were pushed sufficiently, we would push back," wrote Kean and Hamilton in *Without Precedent*.

Meanwhile, the Pentagon side of the investigation raised similar issues. An official Air Force account of the response on September 11 credited a "remarkable job" by the air defenders. "We were able to respond quickly Sept. 11 because we had a robust command and control structure in place and some fighter aircraft on rapid reaction alert," wrote Maj. Gen. Larry K. Arnold, now retired, who commanded the Continental U.S. Region for NORAD in 2001, in the foreword to *Air War Over America* (2003). NORAD officials told the 9/11 Commission at a public hearing on May 23, 2003, that NORAD was aware of the hijacking of United Airlines Flight 93 at 9:16 A.M. They assured commissioners that fighters from Langley Air Force Base in Virginia had been scrambled—that is, ordered to take off in haste—to meet the threat to Washington. Officials said that these orders included authority to shoot down the civilian aircraft, which crashed in a field in Pennsylvania before the fighters could intercept it. But elements of the official account didn't hold up. On a visit to the NEADS (Northeast Air Defense Sector) facility in Rome, New York, staff found tapes and transcripts from more than 20 phone banks that had not been shared with the commission. To date, NORAD had provided only one garbled transcript of the 9/11 events in response to commission requests for documents. Trust in NORAD had been shattered, Executive Director Zelikow told commissioners at a November 6 meeting. The incident prompted commissioners to issue their second subpoena, this time for NORAD documents.

With subpoenaed logs, notes, and recordings, 9/11 Commission staff constructed a minute-by-minute account of events of the day that showed that much of the official account was false: It understated the confusion of the day and the disconnect between top government officials and the response on the ground. NORAD told the commission in May 2003 that it had been notified about the hijacking of American Airlines Flight 77 at 9:24 A.M., or some 14 minutes before the flight crashed into the Pentagon, and that it had scrambled jets to go after United 93 and American 77. But commission staff later found that there had been no notification that Flight 77 was a hijacking before it crashed and that the Langley jets had been directed to fly east over the Atlantic Ocean. At 9:36 A.M., NORAD received notice that an unidentified plane was six miles from the White House. Only then did the scrambled fighters head toward Washington, but it was too late. NORAD's account of the response to United 93 was also misleading. The official timeline presented to the commission at a hearing on May 23, 2003, set the hijacking of Flight 93 at 9:16 A.M., or 47 minutes before the crash. But FAA tapes and the United 93 flight data recorder show that the plane was not hijacked until after the pilot's last transmission at 9:28 A.M. What NORAD and FAA officials failed to tell the commission was that the reason Langley fighters had been scrambled was to respond to reports of a threat from American Airlines Flight 11—the plane that had crashed into the North Tower of the World Trade Center. Commission staff found that the mistaken report that American 11 was heading toward Washington appeared in more logs and tapes than any other single event on the morning of September 11.

The commission also had difficulty confirming official accounts of the shoot-down order. Vice President Cheney told the commission that he had issued a shoot-down order just after 10 A.M., after discussing it in a phone conversation with Bush. The president confirmed that conversation. But the commission found nothing in logs or notes on either end of the call to document that such a call took place. The order that eventually reached NORAD pilots was to identify the planes, not shoot them down, and it did not reach NORAD until after all the planes had crashed. In drafting the final report, the commission noted that recordkeeping that morning was incomplete.

At its last public hearing on June 17, 2004, the 9/11 Commission laid out staff analysis of the air war, including a timeline, recordings of key conversations, and graphics depicting the movements of hijacked

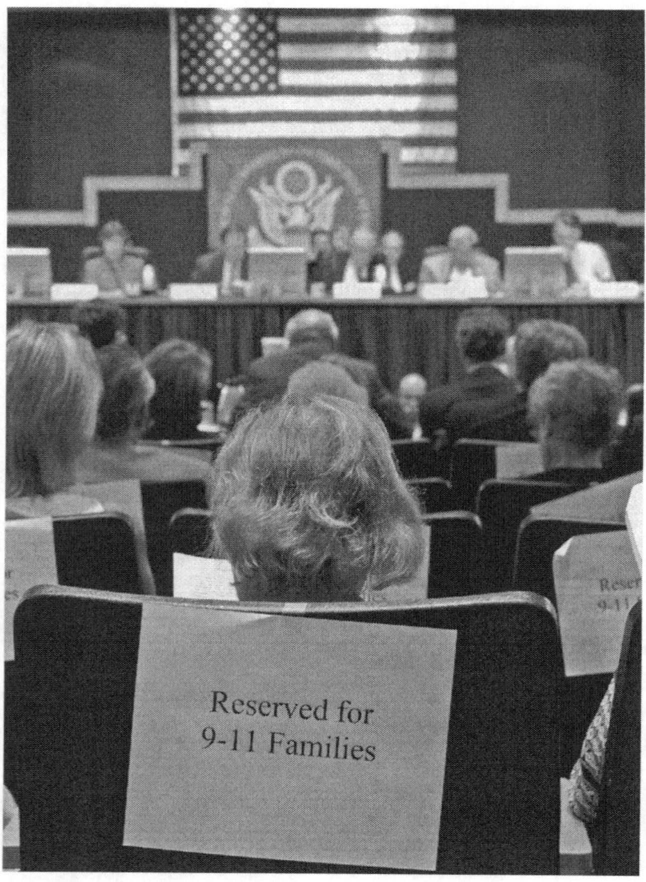

Family members of the victims of the September 11 terrorist attacks sit in the 9/11 Commission public hearing on June 16, 2004, in Washington. (Evan Vucci/Associated Press)

planes and military aircraft on September 11. "We do not believe that an accurate understanding of the events of this morning reflects discredit on the operational personnel from NEADS or FAA facilities," said Zelikow in presenting the staff report. In their final report, commissioners played down the frustrations of the investigation, concluding simply: "NORAD and the FAA were unprepared for the type of attacks launched against the United States on September 11, 2001. They struggled, under difficult circumstances, to improvise a homeland defense against an unprecedented challenge they had never before encountered and never trained to meet." In private, commissioners debated at length whether to investigate why the FAA and NORAD had given false accounts. They decided that the issue was outside their mandate and referred it to the inspectors general of the Departments of Transportation and Defense. Sixteen months later, the inspectors general reported that there was no proof of deliberate falsification, but rather "a lack of attention to details" and inadequate recordkeeping. Citing recently declassified tapes and transcripts, chief investigator Farmer challenged that view. "The events of the day as entered in the records were both unmistakable and unmistakably different from what officials had claimed," wrote Farmer in his book, *The Ground Truth: The Untold Story of America Under Attack on 9/11* (2009). "History should record that whether through unprecedented administrative incompetence or orchestrated mendacity, the American people were misled about the nation's response to the 9/11 attacks. . . . The story they were told gave a false assurance that by the time the last hijacked plane was heading for Washington, some ninety minutes after the attacks began, the military, from the commander in chief on down, had reasserted control over American airspace and was prepared to respond to the final attack. . . . That wasn't true."

What the President Knew and When He Knew It

For many 9/11 families, no issue was as important as fixing accountability for what went wrong—and the buck stopped at the White House. No single document captured the public imagination as powerfully as the Presidential Daily Brief of August 6, 2001, titled "Bin Ladin Determined To Strike in US." The rumored title alone convinced critics, including the 9/11 families, that the White House had been too passive in the face of an urgent terrorist threat. Bush was on vacation in Crawford, Texas, during the month of August 2001. The day after receiving the August 6 PDB, the president played golf at a private club on Lake Waco, jogged at the ranch, read a little, and went bass fishing. Later in the week, he gave a speech on stem-cell research, an issue he often discussed with visitors that summer. Looking back, the president chose the wrong issue to worry about, critics said. For Bush, who was running for reelection in 2004 on his record on national security, the prospect of giving a commission created by Congress access to secret White House briefings was unacceptable. Administration negotiators said that presidents need advisers who give candid advice, and that is less likely if presidents are forced to disclose that advice.

The congressional Joint Inquiry tried, without success, to gain access to the August 6 PDB. National Security Adviser Rice publicly confirmed the existence of that PDB in May 2002, but she refused to release its contents or appear before the Joint Inquiry to answer questions about it. The commission spent months negotiating terms of access with the White House to see all PDBs relevant to its mission. The White House opposed the request, citing executive privilege. In the end, a review team of four—Kean, Hamilton, Gorelick, and Zelikow—was allowed to read some 20 PDBs that

that the White House deemed relevant. Gorelick and Zelikow alone were given access to some 300-plus other PDBs, which they summarized in a document prepared for the full commission. The 9/11 families following the negotiations opposed the deal. "As it now stands a limited number of commissioners will have restricted access to a limited number of PDB documents. This will prevent a full uncovering of the truth and is unacceptable," said the Family Steering Committee in a statement.

Showdowns at the Public Hearings

Once the documents started flowing, the nine work teams prepared lines of questioning for interviews. With the May deadline fast approaching, commissioners debated whether to hold public hearings. Many prominent commissions had not. But the 9/11 Commission was committed to an open process. From March 31, 2002, through December 8, the commission held six public policy hearings on issues ranging from civil-aviation security to the nature of al-Qaeda, state sponsorship of terrorism, challenges within the Islamic world, whether to create a director of national intelligence, best practices for emergency preparedness, and the tradeoff between liberty and security at home. The purpose was to educate the public on the terrorist threat, but the public barely noticed. The hearings also brought relations between the commission and the 9/11 families to a low point. The families wanted to see top officials, under oath, answer tough questions, not an academic seminar. But those critical months also gave the staff more time to analyze documents and prepare questions. At a news briefing to present the commission's second interim report, Hamilton acknowledged the impatience of many to see results. "We are engaged in what may be the largest investigation of the United States government actions and policies in American history," he said on September 23, 2002. "Waiting for the right answers is better than rushing to judgment with the wrong ones."

What these six policy hearings in 2002 lacked in drama was amply made up in the last six, which convened top officials in both the Clinton and Bush administrations to answer questions on national security in the spring of 2003. Cribbing from a strategy used by the Joint Inquiry, the 9/11 Commission organized these "factual hearings" around introductory staff statements that laid out findings. The statements were tightly edited for brevity and maximum impact. It was a good way to present a complex investigation in a very short period of time to the American people. For the 9/11 Commission, staff statements also served the critical secondary purpose of facilitating the process of declassification. Since staff findings were based at least in part on classified material, the commission submitted the text to the administration for prepublication review. Once in the public domain, the evidence could also be used in the commission's final report, thus avoiding the pages of redactions that broke up the Joint Inquiry report.

The factual phase of the hearings began on January 26, 2004, with a staff statement on how the 19 hijackers entered the United States. The opening statement challenged the official account that all the hijackers had been in the United States legally. New data showed that at least six of the 19 hijackers had violated immigration laws while in the United States, three had made false statements on visa applications that could have been detected, eight carried passports that showed evidence of fraudulent manipulation, and five had aroused enough suspicion at customs or immigration checkpoints to require additional screening. Staff called them all missed opportunities, then turned to officials from key agencies to account for why these chances were missed. That first hearing also included dramatic testimony from Jose Melendez-Perez, the immigration inspector at Orlando International Airport who blocked the alleged 20th hijacker, likely to have meant to be on Flight 93, from entering the country. "Your actions in doing your job efficiently and competently may well have contributed to saving the Capitol or the White House," said Ben-Veniste, prompting a sustained ovation from the audience.

On January 27, 2004, Hamilton and Kean held a news conference to formally request Congress to extend the deadline for completing the report by at least 60 days. That would be 60 days closer to the 2004 presidential election, which already was turning on national security issues, and close to the Democratic National Convention, which was set to convene at the end of July. "We are aware of the political arguments back and forth about whether an extension is a good thing. We have decided that the right course is simply this: Put aside the politics and just ask for the time we really need," they said. With the public support of the 9/11 families, the White House and Congress agreed to give the commission until July 26 to complete its final report, and another month to close down.

The commission then turned to its highest-profile public hearings, which Kean and Hamilton later described as "a perfect storm of outsize personalities, disputed facts, global events, and partisan politics." The next few hearings put the 9/11 Commission on the map of public consciousness, but also raised partisan tensions within the commission to a boil. The commission had invited top national security officials in both the Clinton and Bush administrations to appear over a two-day period, March 23 and 24, 2004: Secretary of State Colin Powell and his predecessor, Madeleine Albright; Secretary of Defense Donald Rumsfeld and his predecessor, William Cohen; and Berger and Rice, as well as Tenet and Clarke, who both had served in both the Clinton and Bush administrations. All would testify publicly and under oath. On February 23, the Bush administration declined to allow Rice to appear in public, citing executive privilege. The refusal was a blow, but not unexpected. Rice had already responded to questions in private over several hours. The White House said that no presidential adviser had ever testified before Congress. Since the 9/11 Commission was voted on and established by Congress, White House spokesmen said, a request from the commission was in effect a request by Congress. "I argued that precedent had nothing to do with us," said Kean. "We argued very publicly that we needed documents that Congress had never seen, such as the President's Daily Briefing, and that we needed access to the president himself, because if we couldn't answer the question 'What did the president know and when did he know it?,' our report would have no credibility. Many of the families absolutely believed that the president had advance knowledge of the attacks." The commission made the case that Rice's presence was needed to reassure the public, and she must testify, along with the others, under oath.

In the end, what forced the Rice testimony weren't arguments of the commission, but the controversy raised by the public testimony of Clarke—and the book that he rushed to press just two days before his public testimony, *Against All Enemies: Inside America's War on Terror*. The book reinforced the view that Bush was inattentive to calls for urgent action on al-Qaeda. Appearing before the commission on March 24, Clarke addressed the 9/11 families in his opening statement: "Your government failed you, those entrusted with protecting you failed you, and I failed you. We tried hard, but that doesn't matter, because we failed. And for that failure, I would ask, once all the facts are out, for your understanding and your forgiveness."

National Security Adviser Condoleezza Rice testifies before the 9/11 Commission in Washington, April 8, 2004. (©David Coleman/Alamy)

Family members seated behind him in the cavernous Room 216 in the Hart Senate Office Building described the moment as breathtaking—the first government apology for what happened to those lost on that day. But to the 9/11 Commission, whose effectiveness depended on banking the fires of partisanship and presenting a united front, Clarke's critique of the Bush administration was also a moment of maximum danger. Commissioners Thompson and Lehman, both nominated by Republicans, grilled Clarke on the motives for his statements. "Mr. Clarke, as we sit here this afternoon, we have your book and we have your press briefing [a background briefing to a handful of reporters that made no reference to the charges in his book] of August 2002. Which is true?" asked Thompson. "I was a special assistant to the president, and I made the case I was asked to make," said Clarke. "You've got a real credibility problem," said Lehman. The apology to the families made news around the world. So did his criticism of the president. In the next few days, Rice and Clarke traded swipes on television news shows. Commissioners kept up the pressure for the White House to relent. Rice told reporters: "I would like nothing better in a sense than to be able to go up and do this, but I have a responsibility to maintain what is a long-standing constitutional separation between the executive and the legislative branch."

The controversy moved from a commission hearing to the floor of the Senate and House. "It is one thing for Mr. Clarke to dissemble in front of the media, in front of the press, but if he lied under oath to the United States Congress, it's a far, far more serious matter," said Senate Majority Leader Lott, charging that Clarke had told one story to the congressional Joint Inquiry in closed testimony in July 2002, and a harsher version to the 9/11 Commission. Without consulting with Democrats on his panel, Goss, the House Intelligence Committee chair, sent a copy of Clarke's Joint Inquiry testimony to the executive branch for declassification. "This is a stunning violation that can only feed the impression that sensitive materials are being selectively declassified for political reasons, rather than national security or the public interest," argued Representative Jane Harman (D-Calif.), the ranking Democrat on the panel.

For many family members, the appearance of Rice before the commission, under oath, would be the high point of the investigation. In preparation for Rice's appearance before the panel, the staff drafted a memo with competing statements by Rice and Clarke on 30 issues. Clarke said that Bush failed to act prior to September 11 on the threat from al-Qaeda despite repeated warnings. Rice said that terrorism was an urgent priority, but not the only priority of the new administration. "When viewed side by side," Kean and Hamilton wrote, "it was striking how much the disagreement was one of interpretation, and not of facts." In the end, the public pressure on the White House the week after Clarke's testimony was too much, especially in a campaign season focused on national security. On March 30, the White House agreed to allow Rice to testify in public under oath and—a surprise—also dropped its objections to the president and vice president meeting with the full commission to respond to questions.

The announcement of Rice's April 8 appearance prompted a flood of questions that the 9/11 families and the public wanted answered. Many family members were convinced that Bush knew of the attacks in advance, and they wanted the commissioners to ask tough enough questions to get Rice to admit it. Each commissioner had 15 minutes to ask questions, with no follow-up. Moreover, unlike other witnesses, Rice read her entire statement. The Bush administration, she stated, had kept Clarke and the Clinton administration counterterrorism team on the National Security Council staff "to ensure continuity of operations while we developed new policies." The new strategy to defeat al-Qaeda, released on September 4, 2001, she said, "was the very first major national security policy directive of the Bush administration—not Russia, not missile defense, not Iraq, but the elimination of al-Qaeda." The threats reported in the spring and summer of 2001 were "not specific as to time, nor place, nor manner of attack. . . . There was no silver bullet that could have prevented the 9/11 attacks." Kean asked the first question on behalf of several 9/11 family members: "Did you ever see or hear from the FBI, from the CIA, from any other intelligence agency, any memos or discussions or anything else between the time you got into office and 9/11 that talked about using planes as bombs?" "To the best of my knowledge," Rice replied, "that possibility of using planes as bombs was never briefed to us. . . . You have to depend to a certain degree on the intelligence agencies to sort, to tell you what is actually relevant, what is actually based on sound sources, what is speculative."

In a reversal from the Clarke questioning, the volleys came mainly from Democrats. Citing the August 6 PDB, Ben-Veniste took a chance by asking Rice if she could recall the title of the then-classified document. Rice could have simply refused to answer, but she didn't. "I believe the title was 'Bin Laden Determined to Attack Inside the United States.'" (The title is "Bin Ladin Determined To Strike in US.") "It was historical information based on old reporting," she said. "There was no new threat information. And it did not, in fact, warn of any coming attacks inside the United States."

But what caught fire in news reports and on the Internet was the official confirmation, for the first time, of the title of the August 6 memorandum. Ben-Veniste pressed to have the PDB declassified, and, two weeks later, the White House did so. In his memoir, Ben-Veniste reports getting several death threats in his office after questioning Rice—and a gentle caution from commission leaders. "Tom [Kean] and Lee [Hamilton] noted at our next meeting that the Clarke and Rice hearings had tested the commission's bipartisanship and that we needed to be sensitive to perceptions," he said. "I could live with that." Had the venue been a courtroom, instead of a hearing room where a witness could run out the clock with "long, convoluted answers," Ben-Veniste says, he would have pushed the significance of the August PDB "and what it meant to the question of her perception of what her responsibilities were—or what the president perceived that his responsibilities were."

By contrast, the commission's interview with former president Clinton on April 8 was subdued. A key point was whether Clinton had authorized the CIA to kill bin Laden. Clinton followed the line laid out by Berger, his former national security adviser. (Berger later pleaded guilty to a misdemeanor charge of removing highly classified documents from the National Archives related to the 9/11 investigation. The commission confirmed that they had already reviewed the documents at issue.) Clinton told commissioners that there should have been no doubt as to his intentions to kill or capture bin Laden: After the bombings of U.S. embassies in Kenya and Tanzania in 1998, Clinton had ordered air strikes against suspected al-Qaeda sites in Afghanistan and Sudan. But he said that those down the chain of command in the CIA took a more cautious interpretation of the directive to focus on capturing, rather than killing, bin Laden. Commenting on this interview in their final report, commissioners wrote, "It showed the complexity of how a president's orders and intentions move through the government, particularly in the secret world of national security."

Commission Under Fire

There was one last dramatic moment in the final public hearings that the commission had not anticipated—an attack on one of its own. The issue in the April 13–14 hearings was how and why American intelligence and law-enforcement agencies had failed to connect the dots—an image developed during the Joint Inquiry investigations—to detect the terrorist plot and stop it. The key recommendations of the 9/11 Commission grow out of this critical narrative. The congressional Joint Inquiry had released the main elements of this account of missed opportunities: The CIA had highly significant information regarding two of the 9/11 hijackers, Khalid al-Mihdhar and Nawaf al-Hazmi, but waited 18 months, until August 2001, to inform the FBI and add their names to watch lists.

A Phoenix FBI field-office agent had drafted a memo in July 2001 that warned of the possibility of "a coordinated effort" by bin Laden to send students to U.S. flight schools to train for terrorist activity. The agent proposed seeking authority to obtain visa information concerning individuals trying to attend flight schools, but FBI headquarters took no action until after 9/11. The FBI's Minneapolis field office detained Moussaoui, a French national, on suspicion that he was training for a terrorist act. Even with the surge of threat reports in the summer of 2001, no one connected these elements. In one of the commission's rare leaks, Attorney General Ashcroft woke up to headlines the morning of his hearing on April 13, 2004, reporting that he had been uninterested in counterterrorism and would be treated harshly by the commission. Instead, Ashcroft went on the offensive. "The single greatest structural cause for the September 11th problem was the wall that segregated or separated criminal investigators and intelligence agents," he said. "Government erected this wall, government buttressed this wall, and before September 11 government was blinded by this wall." Someone built this wall, he added, citing a March 1995 Justice Department memo written by then-deputy attorney general Gorelick. "I have declassified it for you and the public to review. Full disclosure compels me to inform you that the author . . . is a member of the commission," he said.

Outraged at what they saw as an unfair attack—including selective declassification of documents—the commissioners rallied around their colleague. "Don't you ask those questions. That's for me," Gorton told Gorelick, before grilling Ashcroft on why, if the "wall" was so disabling, the Justice Department had reaffirmed the policy in a memo on August 6, 2001. (The commission staff raced to get copies of this memo to the hearing room.) Gorelick did not respond to Ashcroft's version of events, a decision she now says she regrets. "As valiant and thoughtful as my fellow commissioners were in trying to set the record straight, I actually regret agreeing with them that I would not speak out myself, because there remains so much out there that is false," she said in an e-mail message. The "wall" predated the Clinton administration.

The history of tensions between intelligence and criminal investigations dates from the 1930s, when President Franklin D. Roosevelt granted the FBI dual intelligence and law-enforcement responsibilities. Congressional investigations of unlawful FBI spying against

This cartoon shows Attorney General John Ashcroft describing how questions on the appropriateness of his actions threaten security, during a Senate Judiciary Committee hearing on the U.S. government's policies in the war against terrorism, following the September 11 terrorist attacks. (Kevin Kallaugher/Baltimore Sun, www.kaltoons.com)

domestic dissidents between 1956 and 1971 and CIA abuses disclosed by the Senate Church committee and the House Pike committee resulted in legislation that ended the FBI's domestic intelligence role and set up a wall between federal law enforcement and intelligence. In 1978 Congress passed the Foreign Intelligence Surveillance Act (FISA) to ensure that foreign intelligence-gathering did not undermine constitutional protections. In a March 1995 memo, signed by Gorelick, the Justice Department set up procedures to help investigate death threats against the judge, prosecutor, and witnesses in the trial of plotters of the 1993 World Trade Center bombing, including limits on coordination between intelligence and criminal investigators and sharing requirements if intelligence investigators developed information that "reasonably indicated" the commission of a "significant federal crime." But over time, misunderstandings and cultural barriers distorted the application of these reforms. A 1999 investigation by the Department of Justice found that the 1995 procedures were "largely misunderstood and often misapplied, resulting in undue reluctance among FBI agents to provide information to criminal investigators and prosecutors." A 9/11 staff monograph on the "wall" between intelligence and law-enforcement investigations, declassified in May 2009, concluded that "the information sharing failures in the summer of 2001 were not the result of legal barriers but of the failure of individuals to understand that the barriers did not apply to the facts at hand. Simply put, there was no legal reason why the information could not have been shared."

Still, the bid to make Gorelick the issue was a flashpoint in the 9/11 investigation: In the two weeks after the Ashcroft hearing, Gorelick faced calls for her resignation from conservative newspapers and from Republicans in Congress. She also received hate mail and a death threat. Seventy-five Republican House members signed a letter questioning her role in the Clinton Justice Department on the issue. The bid to target Gorelick shifted attention from issues in the Bush/Ashcroft Justice Department to the Clinton team. An attack on one of its members could also discredit the findings of the 9/11 Commission at a critical point in the investigation. After the hearing, the Justice Department declassified more Gorelick memos on its Web site, with her handwriting in the margins.

No Precedent: Access to the Oval Office

On April 29, the 9/11 Commission met with Bush and Cheney in the Oval Office. No investigative commission had ever questioned a sitting president. Initially, the White House had agreed to meet only with the 9/11 Commission's chair and vice chair, only for an hour and on the condition that Cheney be present. In response, the 9/11 families pressed for public hearings before all 10 commissioners. On March 30, the White House agreed to a meeting with the full commission. The night before the meeting, Kean called Andrew Card, the White House chief of staff, to complain that the attorney general had acted unfairly and in bad faith in using selectively declassified information on Gorelick in such a political way. He said it would be the first issue the commission would raise with the president. In fact, it was the first issue the president raised with the commission.

As commissioners gathered in the Oval Office, Bush said that he disapproved of what the attorney general had done and that the Gorelick memos would be removed from the Web site. Instead of an hour, the meeting went on for more than three, as the president agreed to answer all questions. The answers were no surprise: The spike of threats before the 9/11 attacks were not actionable and appeared mainly directed overseas, the president said. Commissioners asked about how the administration was organized to fight terrorism and what intelligence was most useful to him. Cheney spoke only when asked a question. As with the commission's meeting with Clinton, there was no recording or transcript of the meeting, and the president did not testify under oath. "I'm glad I took the time," said Bush after the meeting. "This is an important commission, and it's important that they asked the questions they asked so that they can help make recommendations necessary to protect our homeland." The commissioners issued a joint statement that they found the president and vice president "forthcoming and candid."

The Final Report: Just the Facts

By the time the commission members settled into debating and drafting their final report, the terms set at the outset by Kean and Hamilton had settled into habit: Tell what happened and make recommendations so it doesn't happen again. Both chairs were veterans of commissions that had disappeared without a trace. Avoiding that outcome, they said, required maintaining consensus among commissioners, both on the facts of the investigation and the recommendations derived from them. That meant no 200-page minority report, such as the one then-Representative Cheney had added to the 1987 Iran-contra report or the 135-page statement that Shelby had appended to the Joint Inquiry. Several chapters went through 20 hands-on revisions by commissioners before approval. "The point we made time and time again was that if the report was going to have any impact, it had to be unanimous," wrote Kean and Hamilton. "All ten commissioners had been in and around politics for decades, and nearly all of us commented that the atmosphere in Washington was currently as partisan as we had ever seen it. . . . When it became apparent that we could reach agreement on the facts of 9/11 and on our recommendations, we saw that we had a chance to make a point about how politics could still work in a bipartisan manner."

The final report was to have a different tone than staff reports. It was to draw all the evidence into a single narrative, written for a broad audience. Toward the end of 2003, Zelikow and the front office began early drafts of the final report, drawing on evolving team monographs. In addition, the commission was reviewing and finalizing staff monographs, to be published in classified form. Rolling drafts of the report and monographs were revised by commissioners and staff through the spring of 2004.

Commissioners had little difficulty describing the character of the new enemy the nation faced. "We learned about an enemy who is sophisticated, patient, disciplined, and lethal," the report concluded. But some commissioners balked at an early draft on the role of U.S. policy toward Israel in promoting terrorism. At a March 2 meeting, Gorton told colleagues, "If this is the way the report goes, I'm not going to sign it." He wrote out a few pages of alternative language on the Muslim sense of grievance that described centuries of losing cultural, military, and political battles with the West. Several commissioners endorsed this approach. "The report does not say they attacked us because we support Israel, and that was my doing," said Gorton, in an interview. Hamilton recalls extensive negotiations over the language on this issue that was resolved only when commissioners could agree that Osama bin Laden used American policy toward Israel as a means of inciting and recruiting terrorists. The final language in the report on this issue reads: "Right or wrong, it is simply a fact that American policy regarding the Israeli-Palestinian conflict and American actions in Iraq are dominant staples of popular commentary across the Arab and Muslim world. That does not mean U.S.

U.S. forces killed Osama bin Laden in May 2011. (Associated Press)

choices have been wrong. It means those choices must be integrated with America's message of opportunity to the Arab and Muslim world."

The 9/11 Commission report offered 41 recommendations. The ones that attracted the most attention concerned how to protect against and prepare for terrorist attacks. Drawing on recommendations from the Joint Inquiry, the commission proposed an overhaul of national intelligence to promote unity of effort in the intelligence community. That included creating a national intelligence director to oversee the intelligence community and a new counterterrorism center to help break down barriers to sharing information among agencies. Since more than 80 percent of spending by the U.S. intelligence community falls under the Pentagon's budget, the commission stated, the new national intelligence director would also need budgetary authority over all intelligence agencies, including those within the Defense Department. The events of 9/11 showed that stronger leadership was needed: The fact that CIA Director Tenet could issue a directive in 1998 stating, "We are at war" with al-Qaeda, to no effect on the intelligence community, was unacceptable, the commission concluded.

But the recommendation the commission described as "among the most difficult and important" was reforming congressional oversight of intelligence and homeland security. Leaders of the Department of Homeland Security now appear before at least 88 committees and subcommittees of Congress. The commission proposed creating a single, principal committee to oversee the Intelligence Community.

From the start, the commissioners wanted to write a report to be read. An early draft of the report led with an extended historical section. That was rejected in favor of a gripping narrative on the four flights. The writing was a team product. The novelist John Updike, writing in the *New Yorker* (November 24, 2004), described the King James Version of the Bible as "our language's lone masterpiece produced by committee, at least until this year's 9/11 Commission Report." Staff describing the drafting process often referred to Hamilton's style points: Be descriptive, dispassionate, simple, concise, and frankly understated. This is not to be a document reflecting judgments of passion. Tell the story, lay out the facts in as much detail as you can, and let the judgments be those of the readers as they evaluate the evidence. Sentences were to be noun, verb. No adjectives. ("Adjectives are where you get the bias," Hamilton said.) If a sentence has dependent clauses, rewrite the sentence. In the final tense weeks of drafting, staff members also recall an editor saying, often: "I've got a box of periods on my desk, and I'm going to use them."

Legacy

The 9/11 Commission released its 567-page report on July 22, 2004, but, unlike most government reports, it was not just a government publication with a bland cover. Kean and Zelikow also negotiated a deal with W. W. Norton to publish a commercial version of the report with 600,000 copies available in bookstores the day of the release. Just a week after its publication, the report was selling out in bookstores, and the commission's Web site, www.9-11commission.gov, was flooded with traffic. John Kerry, the Democratic presidential candidate, dubbed the report a "blueprint for action" and urged extending the commission's mandate for another 18 months. Kerry said that if he were elected president he would create a powerful national intelligence director. On August 2, President Bush announced support for a director of national intelligence and a counterterrorism center. One by one, politicians up for reelection were pressed by voters to take a position on the 9/11 Commission report. Some candidates even ran on a platform to carry out all 41 recommendations.

Despite criticism over the course of the investigation, the 9/11 families overall embraced the report and pushed Congress to implement it.

In a rare move, Congress convened some two dozen hearings on commission recommendations through the August recess. Kean and Hamilton testified together before seven congressional committees. Over all, commissioners made more than 20 appearances before congressional panels. The Senate passed its version of legislation implementing the 9/11 recommendations on October 5 by a vote of 96 to 2. At the urging of the chairman of the House Committee on Armed Services, Representative Duncan Hunter (R-Calif.), the House bill reduced the proposed budgetary powers of the director of national intelligence. The bill, which passed 282 to 134 on October 7, also cracked down on illegal immigration, including outlawing the issuance of driver's licenses to those in the country illegally. After Bush's reelection in November, Congress got back to negotiations over the final form of a bill. On December 7, the anniversary of the attacks on Pearl Harbor, the House passed the Intelligence Reform and Terrorism Prevention Act by a vote of 336 to 75. The Senate passed the bill on December 8 by a vote of 89 to 2. "We are rebuilding a structure that was designed for a different enemy in a different time, a structure that was designed for the Cold War and has not proved agile enough to deal with the threats of the 21st century," said Senator Susan Collins (R-Maine), who led the drive to pass the bill as chair of the Governmental Affairs Committee. When Tenet issued his "We are at war" memorandum on December 4, 1998—"I want no resources or people spared in this effort, either inside CIA or the [Intelligence] Community"—it had little impact. With a new, empowered director of national intelligence, that would never happen again, Collins said. "This legislation will ensure that in the future, when such a clear, concise order is issued, it will mobilize and galvanize the resources we can bring to bear." The creation of a National Counterterrorism Center, as also recommended by the 9/11 Commission, she added, would demolish the barriers, or "information stovepipes," that block essential sharing of intelligence.

While the commission formally disbanded on August 21, 2004, commissioners continued to travel around the country promoting the implementation of their recommendations. Their work was supported by foundation grants for a lobbying effort called the 9/11 Public Discourse Project, which disbanded on December 31, 2005.

In the years after the 9/11 Commission made its recommendations for improving homeland security, Congress overhauled national intelligence and spent billions to upgrade security for air traffic, ports, and other critical infrastructure. Congress created a new director of national intelligence and the National Counterterrorism Center to promote priorities and sharing of information across agency lines, but at the urging of the Pentagon, lawmakers left budgetary and personnel control ambiguous. Turf battles over personnel between the national intelligence director and the CIA made headlines for much of the first year of the Obama administration. The FBI launched ambitious reform, including upgrading antiquated systems. Moreover, the intelligence director developed into a significant bureaucracy in its own right. But the reform deemed essential to all others—streamlining congressional oversight—never occurred. Some 108 congressional committees and subcommittees now claim oversight of the U.S. Department of Homeland Security. That is up 20 from the 9/11 Commission's count of 88 in 2004—a system it then dubbed "dysfunctional."

"The 9/11 Commission was necessary because the families of the victims didn't trust the Joint Inquiry, didn't trust Congress," said Commissioner Kerrey in an interview. "That's why the recommendations for Congress to reform itself were so important, and they haven't done it, and it's a problem." Mary Fetchet, the 9/11 family member, said: "I thought that if it was legislated, it would be implemented. I certainly didn't want another person to perish in the way that my son did. But what I've found is that we had to continue to be involved, because legislation is just the first step."

One of the most enduring legacies of the 9/11 Commission is that people continued to talk about it long after it ended. On Capitol Hill, it is viewed as the gold standard of nonpartisan, independent investigation—so much so that lawmakers now typically punt difficult issues, such as explaining the near-collapse of the U.S. financial system in 2008, to an independent commission "like the 9/11 Commission." In a sharp break with the fate of most congressional commissions, the 9/11 Commission's report was widely read. More than 6 million people downloaded copies from the commission's official Web site, in addition to those who made its commercial versions best-sellers.

The commissioners did not succeed in their aim of defusing conspiracy theories. The official report attributes the events of 9/11 to a conspiracy by the Islamist terrorist group al-Qaeda. There's a lively and growing cottage industry in alternative conspiracy theories, conducted mainly over the Internet and foreign mainstream news media. But much of the speculation focuses on issues that the 9/11 Commission did not take up. For critics of the 9/11 Commission's account, most notably the 9/11 "truth

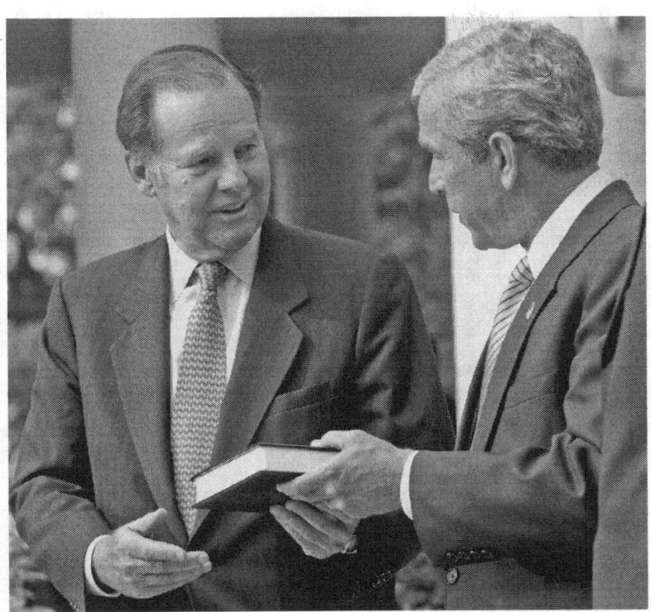

President Bush, right, receives a copy of the September 11 Commission's report from Thomas H. Kean, chairman of the commission, during a ceremony in the Rose Garden of the White House on July 22, 2004. Bush praised the recommendations in the report as "very constructive," though his administration reacted coolly toward a central proposal to establish a national intelligence director. (Pablo Martinez Monsivais/Associated Press)

movement," the collapse of Building 7 in the World Trade Center complex is a smoking gun. The 47-story building was not hit by planes and collapsed nearly seven hours after the Twin Towers. The 2008 report by the National Institute of Standards and Technology attributes the collapse of Building 7 to the effects of fire. Critics say the investigation missed evidence that the building was brought down by explosives in a controlled demolition. For the 9/11 truth movement, wrote David Ray Griffin, the leading critic of the 9/11 Commission's work, the collapse of Building 7 was "the part of the official story that, by being most vulnerable to critique, could be used to bring down the whole body of lies."

Mainstream criticism focuses on two issues: Did the Commission get the facts right? And were its recommendations effective in derailing future terrorist plots? Much of the documentation developed by the 9/11 Commission is still classified and exempt from the Freedom of Information Act, including the CIA interviews with detainees that provided much of the detail in the commission's account of the plot. The CIA never permitted direct access to detainees, but did put to detainees some questions proposed by 9/11 Commission staff. Looking back, several commissioners question whether they should have pushed harder for direct access to detainees—or more robust assurances that torture was not used in the answers they received.

Another line of criticism focuses on whether the 9/11 Commission recommendations for institution change are helpful. Critics such as Judge Richard Posner argue that centralizing control over intelligence is a formula for group think and will not make the nation safer. "The tighter organization proposed by the 9/11 Commission and endorsed by the Intelligence Reform Act," he wrote, "is likely to impede the flow of intelligence data and reduce the diversity of methods and agency cultures that promotes innovative intelligence."

But the main legacy of the 9/11 Commission will be whether its recommendations in fact provide a stronger defense against terrorism.

DOCUMENTS

Phoenix Memo, FBI, July 10, 2001

On July 10, 2001, an agent in the FBI's Phoenix field office e-mailed a memo to FBI headquarters and the New York field office warning of suspicious activity at Arizona flight schools. The memo, marked "routine," notes an "inordinate number of individuals of investigative interest"—Sunni Muslims from Kenya, Pakistan, Algeria, the United Arab Emirates, India, and Saudi Arabia—learning to fly commercial airplanes and studying aviation security and other aviation subjects. The agent suggested that this could be part of a plan to prepare terrorists to attack civil aviation targets. He recommended that FBI headquarters develop ties with civil aviation programs around the country, seek visa information on students seeking to attend flight schools, and circulate the ideas in the memo to the intelligence community. "Basically what I wanted was an analytic product. I wanted this discussed with the Intelligence Community. I wanted to see if my hunches were correct," the agent told the Joint Inquiry. The memo was sent to six people in the Usama Bin Ladin and Radical Fundamentalist Units at FBI headquarters and to two agents on the international terrorism squad in New York. (Note the FBI's variant spelling of Osama bin Laden.) On August 7, 2001, specialists in the two units opted to close the matter. The

9/11 Commission concluded that even if the memo had been broadly shared and its recommendations acted on promptly, "we do not believe it would have uncovered the plot. It might well, however, have sensitized the FBI so that it might have taken the Moussaoui matter more seriously the next month." Portions of the document were redacted before it was released, as shown by the black bars in the text.

PHOENIX MEMO, FBI, JULY 10, 2001

Precedence: ROUTINE *Date: 07/10/2001*

To: Counterterrorism *Attn: RFU*

SSA ▇▇▇▇▇

IRS ▇▇▇▇▇

New York ▇▇▇▇▇

From: Phoenix

Contact: SA ▇▇▇▇▇

Approved By: ▇▇▇▇▇

Drafted By: ▇▇▇▇▇

Case Id #: ~~(S)~~ ▇▇▇▇▇ *(Pending)*

Title: ~~(S)~~ [ZAKARIA MUSTAPHA SOUBRA;

[IT-OTHER ▇▇▇▇▇*]*

Synopsis: ~~(S)~~ UBL ▇▇▇▇▇ *supporters attending civil aviation universities/colleges in the State of Arizona.*

~~(S)Derived From~~ : G-3

~~Declassify On~~ : X1

~~(s)~~

~~(U)~~ Full Field Investigation Instituted: 04/17/2000 (NONUSPER)

Details: (S) [The purpose of this communication is to advise the Bureau and New York of the possibility of a coordinated effort by USAMA BIN LADEN (UBL) to send students to the United States to attend civil aviation universities and colleges. Phoenix has observed an inordinate number of individuals of investigative interest who are attending or who have attended civil aviation universities and colleges in the State of Arizona. The inordinate number of these individuals attending these types of schools and fatwas ▇▇▇▇▇ gives reason to believe that a coordinated effort is underway to establish a cadre of individuals who will one day be working in the civil aviation community around the world. These individuals will be in a position in the future to conduct terror activity against civil aviation targets.

~~(S)~~ Phoenix believes that the FBI should accumulate a listing of civil aviation universities/colleges around the country. FBI field offices with these types of schools in their area should establish appropriate liaison: FBIHQ should discuss this matter with other elements of the U.S. intelligence community and task the community for any information that supports Phoenix's suspicions. FBIHQ should consider seeking the necessary authority to obtain visa information from the USDOS on individuals obtaining visas to attend these types of schools and notify the appropriate FBI field office when these individuals are scheduled to arrive in their area of responsibility.

~~(S)~~ Phoenix has drawn the above conclusion from several Phoenix investigations to include captioned investigation and the following investigations: ▇▇▇▇▇, a Saudi Arabian national and two Algerian Islamic extremists ▇▇▇▇▇

~~(S)~~ Investigation of ZAKARIA MUSTAPHA SOUBRA was initiated as the result of information provided by ▇▇▇▇▇ a source who has provided reliable information in the past. The source reported during April 2000 that SOUBRA was a supporter of UBL and ▇▇▇▇▇ SOUBRA arrived in Arizona from London, England on 08/27/1999 on an F-1 student visa to attend EMBRY RIDDLE UNIVERSITY (ERU), Prescott, Arizona. ERU only teaches courses related to the field of aviation. SOUBRA is an Aeronautical Engineering student at ERU and has been taking courses in "international security" relating to aviation. SOUBRA, within weeks of his arrival at Prescott, Arizona, ▇▇▇▇▇ supporting UBL, at Mosques located throughout Arizona. SOUBRA has also organized anti United States and Israeli demonstrations in the area of ARIZONA STATE UNIVERSITY (ASU), Tempe, Arizona. He has also established and organized an Islamic student association on the ERU campus organizing the Muslim student population on the ERU campus.

~~(S)~~ Phoenix has identified several associates of SOUBRA at ERU who arrived at the university around the same time that he did. These individuals are Sunni Muslims who have the same radical fundamentalists views as SOUBRA. They come from Kenya, Pakistan, United Arab Emirates, India, Saudi Arabia and Jordan. SOUBRA's associates are (s)

(S) ▇▇▇▇▇

▇▇▇▇▇

~~(S)~~ ▇▇▇▇▇

▇▇▇▇▇

~~(S)~~ ▇▇▇▇▇

▇▇▇▇▇

~~(S)~~

~~(S)~~

~~(S)~~

~~(S)~~

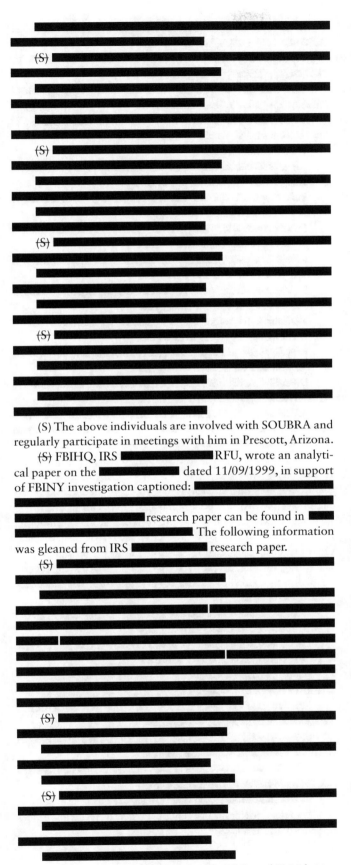

(S) The above individuals are involved with SOUBRA and regularly participate in meetings with him in Prescott, Arizona.

~~(S)~~ FBIHQ, IRS [redacted] RFU, wrote an analytical paper on the [redacted] dated 11/09/1999, in support of FBINY investigation captioned: [redacted] research paper can be found in [redacted] The following information was gleaned from IRS [redacted] research paper.

~~(S)~~

~~(S)~~

~~(S)~~

~~(S)~~ "The Fatwa is jihad against the U.S. and British government, armies, interests, **airports** (emphasis added by FBI Phoenix), and instructions and it has been given because of the U.S. and British aggression against Muslims and the Muslim land of Iraq . . .we . . . confirm that the only Islamic Fatwa against this explicit aggression is Jihad. Therefore the message for the British governments or any other government of non-Muslim countries is to stay away from Iraq, Palestine, Pakistan, Arabia, etc . . . or face full scale war of Jihad which it is the responsibility and the duty of every Muslim around the world to participate in . . .We . . .call upon . . . Muslims around the world including Muslims in the USA and in Britain to confront by all means whether verbally, financially, politically or militarily the U.S. and British aggression and do their Islamic duty in relieving the Iraqi people from the unjust sanctions."

~~(S)~~ SOUBRA was interviewed by FBI Phoenix on 04/07/2000 and 05/11/2000 at his residence. On 04/07/2000, interviewing Agents observed photocopied photographs of UBL, IBN HATTAB and wounded Chechnyan Mujahadin tacked to his livingroom wall. SOUBRA admitted to [redacted] in the State of Arizona. SOUBRA stated that he considers the United States Government and U.S. Military forces in the Gulf as "legitimate military targets of Islam." He also stated that the targeting of the U.S. Embassies in Africa was "legitimate." OUBRA denied having received any military training. However, Phoenix believes that SOUBRA was being less than truthful in this regard. SOUBRA was defiant towards interviewing Agents and it was clear that he was not intimidated by the FBI presence. It is obvious that he is a hard-core Islamic extremist who views the U.S. as an enemy of Islam. Investigation of SOUBRA is continuing.

~~(S)~~

~~(S)~~

~~(S)~~

~~(S)~~

~~(S)~~

~~(S)~~

~~(S)~~

~~(S)~~ Phoenix believes that it is more than a coincidence that subjects who are supporters of UBL are attending civil aviation universities/colleges in the State of Arizona. As receiving offices are aware, Phoenix has had significant UBL associates/operatives living in the State of Arizona and conducting activity in support of UBL. [WADIH EL-HAGE, a UBL lieutenant recently convicted for his role in the 1998 bombings of U.S. Embassies in Africa, lived in Tucson, Arizona for several years during the 1980s.

[

~~(S)~~ This information is being provided to receiving offices for information, analysis and comments.

LEAD (s) :

Set Lead 1:

COUNTERTERRORISM

AT WASHINGTON, DC

(S) The RFU/UBLU is requested to consider implementing the suggested actions put forth by Phoenix at the beginning of this communication.

Set Lead 2:

NEW YORK
AT NEW YORK, NEW YORK
(S) Read and Clear

Source: www.gpoaccess.gov/serialset/creports/911.html.

President's Daily Brief, August 6, 2001

No document prompted as much speculation on what the president knew and when he knew it as an item in the August 6, 2001, President's Daily Brief (PDB) titled "Bin Ladin Determined To Strike in US" The first news reports of the existence of the August 6, 2001, PDB appeared in May 2002. Reports that President George W. Bush knew of impending attacks from al-Qaeda and did not respond outraged 9/11 families and fueled momentum for an independent investigation. Responding to the controversy, National Security Adviser Condoleezza Rice described the August 6 PDB as a historical document with no actionable intelligence. "I want to reiterate, it was not a warning. There was no specific time, place, or method mentioned," she said in a statement on May 16, 2002. The congressional Joint Inquiry attempted to gain access to the August 6 PDB, without success. The 9/11 Commission requested unprecedented access to all PDBs related to Osama bin Laden, al-Qaeda, the Taliban, and key countries such as Afghanistan, Pakistan, and Saudi Arabia. A four-member 9/11 Commission review team was given access to some 300 PDBs, which were shared with the full commission in a summary report. In its final report, the commission describes the president as saying that the August 6 item told him that al-Qaeda was dangerous, which he had known since he had become president. If his advisers had told him there was an al-Qaeda cell in the United States, they would have moved to take care of it. But that never happened, he said. On April 10, 2004, the item related to al-Qaeda in the August 6 PDB was declassified and reprinted in newspapers and over the Internet. The White House also declassified the text of an item from the PDB received by President Bill Clinton on December 4, 1998, titled "Bin Ladin Preparing to Hijack U.S. Aircraft and Other Attacks." On December 8, 1998, the Federal Aviation Administration had issued a security directive requiring more intensive screening of passengers at all three New York airports.

PRESIDENT'S DAILY BRIEF, AUGUST 6, 2001

Bin Ladin Determined To Strike in US

Clandestine, foreign government, and media reports indicate Bin Ladin since 1997 has wanted to conduct terrorist attacks in the US. Bin Ladin implied in US television interviews in 1997 and 1998 that his followers would follow the example of World Trade Center bomber Ramzi Yousef and "bring the fighting to America."

After US missile strikes on his base in Afghanistan in 1998, Bin Ladin told followers he wanted to retaliate in Washington, according to a [redacted] service.

An Egyptian Islamic Jihad (EIJ) operative told an [redacted] service at the same time that Bin Ladin was planning to exploit the operative's access to the US to mount a terrorist strike.

The millennium plotting in Canada in 1999 may have been part of Bin Ladin's first serious attempt to implement a terrorist strike in the US. Convicted plotter Ahmed Ressam has told the FBI that he conceived the idea to attack Los Angeles International Airport himself, but that Bin Ladin lieutenant Abu Zubaydah encouraged him and helped facilitate the operation. Ressam also said that in 1998 Abu Zubaydah was planning his own US attack.

Ressam says Bin Ladin was aware of the Los Angeles operation.

Although Bin Ladin has not succeeded, his attacks against the US Embassies in Kenya and Tanzania in 1998 demonstrate that he prepares operations years in advance and is not deterred by setbacks. Bin Ladin associates surveilled our Embassies in Nairobi and Dar es Salaam as early as 1993, and some members of the Nairobi cell planning the bombings were arrested and deported in 1997.

Al-Qa'ida members—including some who are US citizens—have resided in or traveled to the US for years, and the group apparently maintains a support structure that could aid attacks. Two al-Qa'ida members found guilty in the conspiracy to bomb our Embassies in East Africa were US citizens, and a senior EIJ member lived in California in the mid-1990s.

A clandestine source said in 1998 that a Bin Ladin cell in New York was recruiting Muslim-American youth for attacks.

We have not been able to corroborate some of the more sensational threat reporting, such as that from a [redacted] *service in 1998 saying that Bin Ladin wanted to hijack a US aircraft to gain the release of "Blind Shaykh" 'Umar 'Abd al-Rahman and other US-held extremists.*

Nevertheless, FBI information since that time indicates patterns of suspicious activity in this country consistent with preparations for hijackings or other types of attacks, including recent surveillance of federal buildings in New York.

The FBI is conducting approximately 70 full field investigations throughout the US that it considers Bin Ladin-related. CIA and the FBI are investigating a call to our Embassy in the UAE in May saying that a group of Bin Ladin supporters was in the US planning attacks with explosives.

Declassified and Approved for Release, 10 April 2004

Sources: http://govinfo.library.unt.edu/911/report/index.htm; http://news.findlaw.com/hdocs/docs/terrorism/80601pdb.html; www.gwu.edu/~nsarchiv/NSAEBB/NSAEBB116/pdb8-6-2001.pdf.

President Bush's Address to the Nation, September 11, 2001

On the morning of September 11, 2001, President George W. Bush arrived for a scheduled appearance at Emma E. Booker Elementary School in Sarasota, Florida, to promote an education bill. Moments before he arrived, he learned about an airplane crash at the World Trade Center in New York City. The president continued with his planned activities at the school, including reading to second-grade children in one of the classrooms. At 9:06 A.M., White House Chief of Staff Andrew Card told the president: "A second plane hit the other tower, and America's under attack." Bush stayed in the classroom another 10 minutes. At 9:29 A.M. he made his first statement on the day's events. "Today we've had a national tragedy. Two airplanes have crashed into the World Trade Center in an apparent terrorist attack on our country," he told students and reporters. The president boarded Air Force One at 9:55 A.M. to return to Washington, but the Secret Service, Vice President Richard Cheney, and advisers strongly argued against it. At 10:10 A.M., Air Force One headed to Offutt Air Force Base in Nebraska. At 3:15 P.M., the president opened a videoconference with advisers with the words, "We're at war." George Tenet, the director of national intelligence, told the president that the CIA was still assessing who was responsible but that early signs pointed to al-Qaeda. Against the advice of advisers, the president returned to Washington in the late afternoon. At 8:30 P.M., he addressed the nation from the Oval Office.

PRESIDENT BUSH'S ADDRESS TO THE NATION SEPTEMBER 11, 2001

Today, our fellow citizens, our way of life, our very freedom came under attack in a series of deliberate and deadly terrorist acts. The victims were in airplanes or in their offices: secretaries, business men and women, military and federal workers, moms and dads, friends and neighbors. Thousands of lives were suddenly ended by evil, despicable acts of terror. The pictures of airplanes flying into buildings, fires burning, huge—huge structures collapsing have filled us with disbelief, terrible sadness, and a quiet, unyielding anger. These acts of mass murder were intended to frighten our nation into chaos and retreat. But they have failed. Our country is strong.

A great people has been moved to defend a great nation. Terrorist attacks can shake the foundations of our biggest buildings, but they cannot touch the foundation of America. These acts shatter steel, but they cannot dent the steel of American resolve. America was targeted for attack because we're the brightest beacon for freedom and opportunity in the world. And no one will keep that light from shining. Today, our nation saw evil—the very worst of human nature—and we responded with the best of America. With the daring of our rescue workers, with the caring for strangers and neighbors who came to give blood and help in any way they could.

Immediately following the first attack, I implemented our government's emergency response plans. Our military is powerful, and it's prepared. Our emergency teams are working in New York City and Washington D.C. to help with local rescue efforts. Our first priority is to get help to those who have been injured, and to take every precaution to protect our citizens at home and around the world from further attacks. The functions of our government continue without interruption. Federal agencies in Washington which had to be evacuated today are reopening for essential personnel tonight and will be open for business tomorrow. Our financial institutions remain strong, and the American economy will be open for business as well.

The search is underway for those who were behind these evil acts. I have directed the full resources of our intelligence and law enforcement communities to find those responsible and to bring them to justice. We will make no distinction between the terrorists who committed these acts and those who harbor them.

I appreciate so very much the members of Congress who have joined me in strongly condemning these attacks. And on behalf of the American people, I thank the many world leaders who have called to offer their condolences and assistance. America and our friends and allies join with all those who want peace and security in the world, and we stand together to win the war against terrorism.

Tonight, I ask for your prayers for all those who grieve, for the children whose worlds have been shattered, for all whose sense of safety and security has been threatened. And I pray they will be comforted by a Power greater than any of us, spoken through the ages in Psalm 23:

Even though I walk through the valley of the shadow of death, I fear no evil for you are with me.

This is a day when all Americans from every walk of life unite in our resolve for justice and peace. America has stood down enemies before, and we will do so this time. None of us will ever forget this day, yet we go forward to defend freedom and all that is good and just in our world.

Thank you. Good night. And God bless America.

Source: www.americanrhetoric.com/speeches/gwbush911addresstothenation.htm.

Excerpt from Coleen Rowley's Memorandum to FBI Director Robert Mueller, May 21, 2002

After the 9/11 attacks, FBI director Robert Mueller told Congress that the FBI had received no warning of a terrorist plot by Arab extremists to hijack airplanes to use as weapons. On May 21, 2002, Coleen Rowley, the chief legal adviser to the FBI's Minneapolis field office, produced a 13-page memorandum to the contrary. She was called to Washington on five days' notice to brief the Joint Inquiry on the investigation of the suspected terrorist Zacarias Moussaoui, who had been arrested on August 15, 2001, on a visa violation. Local agents wanted to push for a warrant to search the hard drive of his computer, but efforts were stymied at FBI headquarters, and the search did not take place. In December 2001, Moussaoui was charged with conspiring in the September 11 attacks. Rowley had been expected to give information to support the FBI's legal position on the case, and she did. But at the end of the briefing, Joint Inquiry staff asked Rowley if she had anything to add. She handed them a memorandum, drafted the night before, that described how facts in the investigation had been omitted or distorted to avoid "institutional embarrassment." She also hand-delivered copies of the memorandum to Mueller and to Senators Richard Shelby (R-Ala.) and Dianne Feinstein (D-Calif.), and to members of the Senate Select Committee on Intelligence and of the Joint Inquiry. The memorandum was leaked to Time *magazine, which later named Rowley and two other whistle-blowers "Person of the Year." The memorandum seized public attention as Exhibit A of the case for institutional failure to connect the dots leading up to the 9/11 disaster. This key document appears here as an excerpt of the edited version that was seen by the public for the first time in the June 3, 2002, issue of* Time, *which was available on May 26, just five days after the date of the memorandum.*

EXCERPT FROM ROWLEY MEMORANDUM MAY 21, 2002

FBI Director Robert Mueller
FBI Headquarters, Washington, D.C.

Dear Director Mueller:

I feel at this point that I have to put my concerns in writing concerning the important topic of the FBI's response to evidence of terrorist activity in the United States prior to September 11th. The issues are fundamentally ones of INTEGRITY and go to the heart of the FBI's law enforcement mission and mandate. Moreover, at this critical juncture in fashioning future policy to promote the most effective handling of ongoing and future threats to United States citizens' security, it is of absolute importance that an unbiased, completely accurate picture emerges of the FBI's current investigative and management strengths and failures.

To get to the point, I have deep concerns that a delicate and subtle shading/skewing of facts by you and others at the highest levels of FBI management has occurred and is occurring. The term "cover up" would be too strong a characterization, which is why I am attempting to carefully (and perhaps over laboriously) choose my words here. I base my concerns on my relatively small, peripheral but unique role in the Moussaoui investigation in the Minneapolis Division prior to, during and after September 11th and my analysis of the comments I have heard both inside the FBI (originating, I believe, from you and other high levels of management) as well as your Congressional testimony and public comments.

I feel that certain facts, including the following, have, up to now, been omitted, downplayed, glossed over and/or mischaracterized in an effort to avoid or minimize personal and/or institutional embarrassment on the part of the FBI and/or perhaps even for improper political reasons:

1) The Minneapolis agents who responded to the call about Moussaoui's flight training identified him as a terrorist threat from a very early point. The decision to take him into custody on August 15, 2001, on the INS "overstay" charge was a deliberate one to counter that threat and was based on the agents' reasonable suspicions. While it can be said that Moussaoui's overstay status was fortuitous, because it allowed for him to be taken into immediate custody and prevented him receiving any more flight training, it was certainly not something the INS coincidentally undertook of their own volition. I base this on the conversation I had when the agents called me at home late on the evening Moussaoui was taken into custody to confer and ask for legal advice about their next course of action. The INS agent was assigned to the FBI's Joint Terrorism Task Force and was therefore working in tandem with FBI agents.

2) As the Minneapolis agents' reasonable suspicions quickly ripened into probable cause, which, at the latest, occurred within days of Moussaoui's arrest when the French Intelligence Service confirmed his affiliations with radical fundamentalist Islamic groups and activities connected to Osama Bin Laden, they became desperate to search the computer lap top that had been taken from Moussaoui as well as conduct a more thorough search of his personal effects. The agents in particular believed that Moussaoui signaled he had something to hide in the way he refused to allow them to search his computer.

3) The Minneapolis agents' initial thought was to obtain a criminal search warrant, but in order to do so, they needed to get FBI Headquarters' (FBIHQ's) approval in order to ask for DOJ OIPR's approval to contact the United States Attorney's Office in Minnesota. Prior to and even after receipt of information provided by the French, FBIHQ personnel disputed with the Minneapolis agents the existence of probable cause to believe that a criminal violation had occurred/was occurring. As such, FBIHQ personnel refused to contact OIPR to attempt to get the authority. While reasonable minds may differ as to whether probable cause existed prior to receipt of the French intelligence information, it was certainly established after that point and became even greater with successive, more detailed information from the French and other intelligence sources. The two possible criminal violations initially identified by Minneapolis Agents were violations of Title 18 United States Code Section 2332b (Acts of terrorism transcending national boundaries, which, notably, includes "creating a substantial risk of serious bodily injury to any other person by destroying or damaging any structure, conveyance, or other real or personal property within the United States or by attempting or conspiring to destroy or damage any structure, conveyance, or other real or personal property within the United States") and Section 32 (Destruction of aircraft or aircraft facilities). It is important to note that the actual search warrant obtained on September 11th was based on probable cause of a violation of Section 32.[1] Notably also, the actual search warrant obtained on September 11th did not include the French intelligence information. Therefore, the only main difference between the information being submitted to FBIHQ from an early date which HQ personnel continued to deem insufficient and the actual criminal search warrant which a federal district judge signed and approved on September 11th, was the fact that, by the time the actual warrant was obtained, suspected terrorists were known to have highjacked planes which they then deliberately crashed into the World Trade Center and the Pentagon. To say then, as has been iterated numerous times, that probable cause did not exist until after the disastrous event occurred, is really to acknowledge that the missing piece of probable cause was only the FBI's (FBIHQ's) failure to appreciate that such an event could occur. The probable cause did not otherwise improve or change. When we went to the United States Attorney's Office that morning of September 11th, in the first hour after the attack, we used a disk containing the same information that had already been provided to FBIHQ; then we quickly added Paragraph 19 which was the little we knew from news reports of the actual attacks that morning. The problem with chalking this all up to the "20–20 hindsight is perfect" problem (which I, as all attorneys who have been involved in deadly force training or the defense of various lawsuits are fully appreciative of) is that this is not a case of everyone in the FBI failing to appreciate the potential consequences. It is obvious, from my firsthand knowledge of the events and the detailed documentation that exists, that the agents in Minneapolis who were closest to the action and in the best position to gauge the situation locally, did fully appreciate the terrorist risk/danger posed by Moussaoui and his possible co-conspirators even prior to September 11th. Even without knowledge of the Phoenix communication (and any number of other additional intelligence communications that FBIHQ personnel were privy to in their central coordination roles), the Minneapolis agents appreciated the risk. So I think it's very hard for the FBI to offer the "20–20 hindsight" justification for its failure to act! Also intertwined with my reluctance in this case to accept the "20–20 hindsight" rationale is first-hand knowledge that I have of statements made on September 11th, after the first attacks on the World Trade Center had already occurred, made telephonically by the FBI Supervisory Special Agent (SSA) who was the one most involved in the Moussaoui matter and who, up to that point, seemed to have been consistently, almost deliberately thwarting the Minneapolis FBI agents' efforts (see number 5). Even after the attacks had begun, the SSA in question was still attempting to block the search of Moussaoui's computer, characterizing the World Trade Center attacks as a mere coincidence with Minneapolis' prior suspicions about Moussaoui. . . .

5) The fact is that key FBIHQ personnel whose job it was to assist and coordinate with field division agents on terrorism investigations and the obtaining and use of FISA searches (and who theoretically were privy to many more sources of intelligence information than field division agents), continued to, almost inexplicably, throw up roadblocks and undermine Minneapolis' by-now desperate efforts to obtain a FISA search warrant, long after the French intelligence service provided its information and probable cause became clear. HQ personnel brought up almost ridiculous questions in their apparent efforts to undermine the probable cause. In all of their conversations and correspondence, HQ personnel never disclosed to the Minneapolis agents that the Phoenix Division had, only approximately three weeks earlier, warned of Al Qaeda operatives in flight schools seeking flight training for terrorist purposes!

Nor did FBIHQ personnel do much to disseminate the information about Moussaoui to other appropriate intelligence/law enforcement authorities. When, in a desperate 11th hour measure to bypass the FBIHQ roadblock, the Minneapolis Division undertook to directly notify the CIA's Counter Terrorist Center (CTC), FBIHQ personnel actually chastised the Minneapolis agents for making the direct notification without their approval! . . .

7) Although the last thing the FBI or the country needs now is a witch hunt, I do find it odd that (to my knowledge) no inquiry whatsoever was launched of the relevant FBIHQ personnel's actions a long time ago. Despite FBI leaders' full

knowledge of all the items mentioned herein (and probably more that I'm unaware of), the SSA, his unit chief, and other involved HQ personnel were allowed to stay in their positions and, what's worse, occupy critical positions in the FBI's SIOC Command Center post September 11th. (The SSA in question actually received a promotion some months afterward!) It's true we all make mistakes and I'm not suggesting that HQ personnel in question ought to be burned at the stake, but, we all need to be held accountable for serious mistakes. I'm relatively certain that if it appeared that a lowly field office agent had committed such errors of judgment, the FBI's OPR would have been notified to investigate and the agent would have, at the least, been quickly reassigned. I'm afraid the FBI's failure to submit this matter to OPR (and to the IOB) gives further impetus to the notion (raised previously by many in the FBI) of a double standard which results in those of lower rank being investigated more aggressively and dealt with more harshly for misconduct while the misconduct of those at the top is often overlooked or results in minor disciplinary action. From all appearances, this double standard may also apply between those at FBIHQ and those in the field.

8) The last official "fact" that I take issue with is not really a fact, but an opinion, and a completely unsupported opinion at that. In the day or two following September 11th, you, Director Mueller, made the statement to the effect that if the FBI had only had any advance warning of the attacks, we (meaning the FBI) may have been able to take some action to prevent the tragedy. Fearing that this statement could easily come back to haunt the FBI upon revelation of the information that had been developed pre-September 11th about Moussaoui, I and others in the Minneapolis Office immediately sought to reach your office through an assortment of higher level FBIHQ contacts, in order to quickly make you aware of the background of the Moussaoui investigation and forewarn you so that your public statements could be accordingly modified. When such statements from you and other FBI officials continued, we thought that somehow you had not received the message and we made further efforts. Finally when similar comments were made weeks later, in Assistant Director Caruso's congressional testimony in response to the first public leaks about Moussaoui we faced the sad realization that the remarks indicated someone, possibly with your approval, had decided to circle the wagons at FBIHQ in an apparent effort to protect the FBI from embarrassment and the relevant FBI officials from scrutiny. Everything I have seen and heard about the FBI's official stance and the FBI's internal preparations in anticipation of further congressional inquiry, had, unfortunately, confirmed my worst suspicions in this regard. After the details began to emerge concerning the pre-September 11th investigation of Moussaoui, and subsequently with the recent release of the information about the Phoenix EC, your statement has changed. The official statement is now to the effect that even if the FBI had followed up on the Phoenix lead to conduct checks of flight schools and the Minneapolis request to search Moussaoui's personal effects and laptop, nothing would have changed and such actions certainly could not have prevented the terrorist attacks and resulting loss of life. With all due respect, this statement is as bad as the first! It is also quite at odds with the earlier statement (which I'm surprised has not already been pointed out by those in the media!). I don't know how you or anyone at FBI Headquarters, no matter how much genius or prescience you may possess, could so blithely make this affirmation without anything to back the opinion up than your stature as FBI Director. The truth is, as with most predictions into the future, no one will ever know what impact, if any, the FBI's following up on those requests would have had. Although I agree that it's very doubtful that the full scope of the tragedy could have been prevented, it's at least possible we could have gotten lucky and uncovered one or two more of the terrorists in flight training prior to September 11th, just as Moussaoui was discovered, after making contact with his flight instructors. It is certainly not beyond the realm of imagination to hypothesize that Moussaoui's fortuitous arrest alone, even if he merely was the 20th hijacker, allowed the hero passengers of Flight 93 to overcome their terrorist hijackers and thus spare more lives on the ground. And even greater casualties, possibly of our Nation's highest government officials, may have been prevented if Al Qaeda intended for Moussaoui to pilot an entirely different aircraft. There is, therefore at least some chance that discovery of other terrorist pilots prior to September 11th may have limited the September 11th attacks and resulting loss of life. Although your conclusion otherwise has to be very reassuring for some in the FBI to hear being repeated so often (as if saying it's so may make it so), I think your statements demonstrate a rush to judgment to protect the FBI at all costs. I think the only fair response to this type of question would be that no one can pretend to know one way or another.

Mr. Director, I hope my observations can be taken in a constructive vein. They are from the heart and intended to be completely apolitical. Hopefully, with our nation's security on the line, you and our nation's other elected and appointed officials can rise above the petty politics that often plague other discussions and do the right thing. You do have some good ideas for change in the FBI but I think you have also not been completely honest about some of the true reasons for the FBI's pre-September 11th failures. Until we come clean and deal with the root causes, the Department of Justice will continue to experience problems fighting terrorism and fighting crime in general.

I have used the "we" term repeatedly herein to indicate facts about others in the Minneapolis Office at critical times, but none of the opinions expressed herein can be attributed to anyone but myself. I know that those who know me would probably describe me as, by nature, overly opinionated and sometimes not as discreet as I should be. Certainly some of the above remarks may be interpreted as falling into that category, but I really do not intend anything as a personal criticism of you or anyone else in the FBI, to include the FBIHQ personnel who I believe were remiss and mishandled their duties with regard to the Moussaoui investigation. Truly my only purpose is to try to provide the facts within my purview so that an accurate assessment can be obtained and we can learn from our mistakes. I have pointed out a few of the things that I think should be looked at but there are many, many more.

An honest acknowledgment of the FBI's mistakes in this and other cases should not lead to increasing the Headquarters bureaucracy and approval levels of investigative actions as the answer. Most often, field office agents and field office management on the scene will be better suited to the timely and effective solution of crimes and, in some lucky instances, to the effective prevention of crimes, including terrorism incidents. The relatively quick solving of the recent mailbox pipe-bombing incidents which resulted in no serious injuries to anyone are a good example of effective field office work (actually several field offices working together) and there are hundreds of other examples. Although FBIHQ personnel have, no doubt, been of immeasurable assistance to the field over the years, I'm hard pressed to think of any case which has been solved by FBIHQ personnel and I can name several that have been screwed up! Decision-making is inherently more effective and timely when decentralized instead of concentrated.

Your plans for an FBI Headquarters' "Super Squad" simply fly in the face of an honest appraisal of the FBI's pre-September 11th failures. The Phoenix, Minneapolis and Paris Legal Attache Offices reacted remarkably exhibiting keen perception and prioritization skills regarding the terrorist threats they uncovered or were made aware of pre-September 11th. The same cannot be said for the FBI Headquarters' bureaucracy and you want to expand that?! Should we put the counterterrorism unit chief and SSA who previously handled the Moussaoui matter in charge of the new "Super Squad"?! You are also apparently disregarding the fact the Joint Terrorism Task Forces (JTTFs), operating out of field divisions for years, (the first and chief one being New York City's JTTF), have successfully handled numerous terrorism investigations and, in some instances, successfully prevented acts of terrorism. There's no denying the need for more and better intelligence and intelligence management, but you should think carefully about how much gate keeping power should be entrusted with any HQ entity. If we are indeed in a "war," shouldn't the Generals be on the battlefield instead of sitting in a spot removed from the action while still attempting to call the shots?

I have been an FBI agent for over 21 years and, for what it's worth, have never received any form of disciplinary action throughout my career. From the 5th grade, when I first wrote the FBI and received the "100 Facts about the FBI" pamphlet, this job has been my dream. I feel that my career in the FBI has been somewhat exemplary, having entered on duty at a time when there was only a small percentage of female Special Agents. I have also been lucky to have had four children during my time in the FBI and am the sole breadwinner of a family of six. Due to the frankness with which I have expressed myself and my deep feelings on these issues, (which is only because I feel I have a somewhat unique, inside perspective of the Moussaoui matter, the gravity of the events of September 11th and the current seriousness of the FBI's and United States' ongoing efforts in the "war against terrorism"), I hope my continued employment with the FBI is not somehow placed in jeopardy. I have never written to an FBI Director in my life before on any topic. Although I would hope it is not necessary, I would therefore wish to take advantage of the federal "Whistleblower Protection" provisions by so characterizing my remarks.

Sincerely

Coleen M. Rowley
Special Agent and Minneapolis Chief Division Counsel

Source: www.time.com/time/covers/1101020603/memo.html.

Excerpt from Testimony of Richard A. Clarke Before the Joint Inquiry, June 11, 2002

As chief counterterrorism adviser on the National Security Council under presidents Bill Clinton and George W. Bush, Richard A. Clarke was in a position to comment on the priority and attention both presidents gave to the threat posed by al-Qaeda. In closed testimony before the Joint Inquiry in 2002, Clarke was sparing in his criticism of either man. By contrast, in public testimony two years later before the 9/11 Commission on March 24, 2004 (see below), Clarke criticized President Bush for failing to focus urgently on the terrorist threats prior to 9/11. Due to Clarke's critical testimony of Bush in 2004, Republican leaders pushed to have this 2002 document declassified ahead of schedule to allow the public to see his less critical assessment of the president. In this testimony Clarke revealed that by October 2000 the United States had conducted 11 Predator unmanned reconnaissance flights over Afghanistan that located Osama bin Laden "either twice or three times" but with no subsequent success in capturing or killing him. This document was declassified in November 2004, after the presidential election.

EXCERPT FROM TESTIMONY OF RICHARD A. CLARKE JUNE 11, 2002

MR. CLARKE: Thank you, Mr. Chairman, Mr. Chairman, and members. Thank you for this opportunity to brief you today, and thank you for honoring the White House's request that it be in a briefing format.

My understanding is that you would like me to walk through the last 10 years, during which I have chaired the Interagency Counterterrorism Coordinating Committee, and I will be glad to do that. We have a PowerPoint briefing to do that for you. I will try to move through that rapidly, though, because I recognize your desire to get to the questions.

Let me first say, again, who I am and what I did. My name is Richard Clarke, and I was the chairman of the NSC [National Security Council] Counterterrorism Committee from 1992—late in 1992, through October of 2002. Prior to that, in the Reagan administration, I was a Deputy Assistant Secretary of State for Intelligence in the Bureau of Intelligence at the State Department, in charge of analysis.

In the first Bush administration, I was the Assistant Secretary of State for Political-Military Affairs. . . .

That after-action report concluded that we needed significantly to step up FBI and other Federal law enforcement activities in the United States in order to find, to root out and to *prevent* al-Qa'ida sleeper cells in the United States. The Senate Intelligence Committee asked me to brief on the results of that after-action review, and I briefed Senator Shelby and others in February of 2000. A copy of that briefing has been provided today for you.

At about the same time, we contemplated additional military strikes against Afghanistan on three occasions. We had missiles ready to launch against facilities in which we believed bin Laden to be at the time. The decision was made by the CIA Director—on the recommendation of the CIA Director not to launch those attacks, because the intelligence was not of sufficient quality to ensure that bin Laden would have been there.

In retrospect, we now know that on only one of those three occasions was the intelligence correct. On the other two occasions, we would have been attacking facilities that were al-Qa'ida, but bin Laden would not have been present.

That caused us to look for another way of finding bin Laden, and we asked the community management staff and the JCS [Joint Chiefs of Staff] J-3 to look at finding a second source of information about where bin Laden was, so that when we had intelligence information from HUMINT sources that he was at a particular location, we could confirm it.

And by October of 2000, we had the Predator flying over Afghanistan. We flew 11 missions before the weather prevented further operations for the winter, and on those 11 missions we found bin Laden either twice or three times, definitively twice, potentially a third time.

In October of 2000, the USS Cole was attacked in Yemen. The CIA and FBI did not conclude in the remaining months of the Clinton administration that bin Laden and al-Qa'ida was culpable for that attack. However, it seemed clear to us at the time that he was.

In 2001, the Bush administration, immediately upon coming into office, asked for a review of how we were organized on terrorism, on homeland security and on cybersecurity. The recommendation of that review was that we split the counterterrorism portfolio from the cyberterrorism portfolio. That was agreed by May in the principals committee, and I asked to be assigned to the cybersecurity portfolio, since I had done counterterrorism for 10 years.

The Bush administration also tasked in February a policy review of al-Qa'ida. That was developed over the course of the spring and resulted in a draft Presidential directive to eliminate al-Qa'ida. That Presidential directive was finalized by the principals in the first week in September.

Source: http://intelligence.senate.gov/107351.pdf.

Conclusions of the Joint Inquiry into Intelligence-Community Activities Before and After the Terrorist Attacks of September 11, 2001, July 23, 2003

On February 14, 2002, the House and Senate intelligence committees launched an investigation into the terrorist attacks of September 11, 2001—the first joint, bicameral inquiry by two standing committees in congressional history. The Bush administration opposed a congressional probe, citing concerns that it would distract senior officials from the ongoing "war on terror." But public pressure for an investigation, especially from families of the victims of 9/11, trumped those reservations. The Joint Inquiry hoped to discover what the intelligence community knew or should have known prior to 9/11, and what could be done to prevent such attacks in the future. A professional staff, led by Washington attorney Eleanor Hill, spent months negotiating access to documents and witnesses with the Bush administration and intelligence agencies—and another seven months working to declassify the final report. The Joint Inquiry reviewed some 500,000 pages of documents and conducted more than 600 interviews and briefings. In an unusual move for intelligence committees, much of the review was conducted in open public hearings. Even with limitations on access, the Joint Inquiry produced the most detailed timelines to date of al-Qaeda plans to attack the United States and of missed opportunities to thwart them. Its work provided the basis for one of the most dramatic chapters in the 9/11 Commission's final report, "The System Was Blinking Red." On December 20, 2002, the Joint Inquiry released nonclassified portions of its final report, including the title page, the table of contents, a list of findings and conclusions, and recommendations. The declassified final report, still heavily redacted, was released on July 23, 2003.

CONCLUSIONS OF THE JOINT INQUIRY JULY 23, 2003

In short, for a variety of reasons, the Intelligence Community failed to capitalize on both the individual and collective significance of available information that appears relevant to the events of September 11. As a result, the Community missed opportunities to disrupt the September 11th plot by denying entry to or detaining would-be hijackers; to at least try to unravel the plot through surveillance and other investigative work within the United States; and, finally, to generate a heightened state of alert and thus harden the homeland against attack.

No one will ever know what might have happened had more connections been drawn between these disparate pieces of information. We will never definitively know to what extent the Community would have been able and willing to exploit fully all the opportunities that may have emerged. The important point is that the Intelligence Community, for a variety of reasons, did not bring together and fully appreciate a range of information that could have greatly enhanced its chances of uncovering and preventing Usama Bin Ladin's plan to attack these United States on September 11, 2001.

SYSTEMIC FINDINGS

Our review of the events surrounding September 11 has revealed a number of systemic weaknesses that hindered the Intelligence Community's counterterrorism efforts before September 11. If not addressed, these weaknesses will continue to undercut U.S. counterterrorist efforts. In order to minimize the possibility of attacks like September 11 in the future, effective solutions to those problems need to be developed and fully implemented as soon as possible.

1. Finding: Prior to September 11, the Intelligence Community was neither well organized nor equipped, and did not adequately adapt, to meet the challenge posed by global terrorists focused on targets within the domestic United States. Serious gaps existed between the collection coverage provided by U.S. foreign and U.S. domestic intelligence capabilities. The U.S. foreign intelligence agencies paid inadequate attention to the potential for a domestic attack. The CIA's failure to watchlist suspected terrorists aggressively reflected a lack of emphasis on a process designed to protect the homeland from the terrorist threat. As a result, CIA employees failed to watchlist al-Mihdhar and al-Hazmi. At home, the counterterrorism effort suffered from the lack of an effective domestic intelligence capability. The FBI was unable to identify and monitor effectively the extent of activity by al-Qa'ida and other international terrorist groups operating in the United States. Taken together, these problems greatly exacerbated the nation's vulnerability to an increasingly dangerous and immediate international terrorist threat inside the United States.

2. Finding: Prior to September 11, 2001, neither the U.S. Government as a whole nor the Intelligence Community had a comprehensive counterterrorist strategy for combating the threat posed by Usama Bin Ladin. Furthermore, the Director of Central Intelligence (DCI) was either unwilling or unable to marshal the full range of Intelligence Community resources necessary to combat the growing threat to the United States.

3. Finding: Between the end of the Cold War and September 11, 2001, overall Intelligence Community funding fell or remained even in constant dollars, while funding for the Community's counterterrorism efforts increased considerably. Despite those increases, the accumulation of intelligence priorities, a burdensome requirements process, the overall decline in Intelligence Community funding, and reliance on supplemental appropriations made it difficult to allocate Community resources effectively against an evolving terrorist threat. Inefficiencies in the resource and requirements process were compounded by problems in Intelligence Community budgeting practices and procedures.

4. Finding: While technology remains one of this nation's greatest advantages, it has not been fully and most effectively applied in support of U.S. counterterrorism efforts. Persistent problems in this area included a lack of collaboration between Intelligence Community agencies, a reluctance to develop and implement new technical capabilities aggressively, the FBI's reliance on outdated and insufficient technical systems, and the absence of a central counterterrorism database.

5. Finding: Prior to September 11, the Intelligence Community's understanding of al-Qa'ida was hampered by insufficient analytic focus and quality, particularly in terms of strategic analysis. Analysis and analysts were not always used effectively because of the perception in some quarters of the Intelligence Community that they were less important to agency counterterrorism missions than were operations personnel. The quality of counterterrorism analysis was inconsistent, and many analysts were inexperienced, unqualified, under-trained, and without access to critical information. As a result, there was a dearth of creative, aggressive analysis targeting Bin Ladin and a persistent inability to comprehend the collective significance of individual pieces of intelligence. These analytic deficiencies seriously undercut the ability of U.S. policymakers to understand the full nature of the threat, and to make fully informed decisions.

6. Finding: Prior to September 11, the Intelligence Community was not prepared to handle the challenge it faced in translating the volumes of foreign language counterterrorism intelligence it collected. Agencies within the Intelligence Community experienced backlogs in material awaiting translation, a shortage of language specialists and language-qualified field officers, and a readiness level of only 30% in the most critical terrorism-related languages used by terrorists.

7. Finding: [Prior to September 11, the Intelligence Community's ability to produce significant and timely signals intelligence on counterterrorism was limited by NSA's failure to address modern communications technology aggressively, continuing conflict between Intelligence Community agencies, NSA's cautious approach to any collection of intelligence relating to activities in the United States, and insufficient collaboration between NSA and the FBI regarding the potential for terrorist attacks within the United States].

8. Finding: The continuing erosion of NSA's program management expertise and experience has hindered its contribution to the fight against terrorism. NSA continues to have mixed results in providing timely technical solutions to modern intelligence collection, analysis, and information sharing problems.

9. Finding: The U.S. Government does not presently bring together in one place all terrorism-related information from all sources. While the CIA's Counterterrorist Center does manage overseas operations and has access to most Intelligence Community information, it does not collect terrorism-related information from all sources, domestic and foreign. Within the Intelligence Community, agencies did not adequately share relevant counterterrorism information, prior to September 11. This breakdown in communications was the result of a number of factors, including differences in the agencies' missions, legal authorities and cultures. Information was not sufficiently shared, not only between different Intelligence Community agencies, but also within individual agencies, and between the intelligence and the law enforcement agencies.

10. Finding: Serious problems in information sharing also persisted, prior to September 11, between the Intelligence Community and relevant non-Intelligence Community agencies. This included other federal agencies as well as state and local authorities. This lack of communication and collaboration deprived those other entities, as well as the Intelligence Community, of access to potentially valuable information in the "war" against Bin Ladin. The Inquiry's focus on the Intelligence Community limited the extent to which it explored these issues, and this is an area that should be reviewed further.

11. Finding: Prior to September 11, 2001, the Intelligence Community did not effectively develop and use human sources to penetrate the al-Qa'ida inner circle. This lack of reliable and knowledgeable human sources significantly limited the Community's ability to acquire intelligence that could be acted upon before the September 11 attacks. In part, at least, the lack of unilateral (i.e., U.S.-recruited) counterterrorism sources was a product of an excessive reliance on foreign liaison services.

12. Finding: During the summer of 2001, when the Intelligence Community was bracing for an imminent al-Qa'ida attack, difficulties with FBI applications for Foreign Intelligence Surveillance Act (FISA) surveillance and the FISA process led to a diminished level of coverage of suspected al-Qa'ida operatives in the United States. The effect of these difficulties was compounded by the perception that spread among FBI personnel at Headquarters and the field offices that the FISA process was lengthy and fraught with peril.

13. Finding: [*redacted*]

14. Finding: [Senior U.S. military officials were reluctant to use U.S. military assets to conduct offensive counterterrorism efforts in Afghanistan, or to support or participate in CIA operations directed against al-Qa'ida prior to September 11. At least part of this reluctance was driven by the military's view that the Intelligence Community was unable to provide the intelligence needed to support military operations. Although the U.S. military did participate in [*redacted*] counterterrorism efforts to counter Usama Bin Ladin's terrorist network prior to September 11, 2001, most of the military's focus was on force protection].

15. Finding: The Intelligence Community depended heavily on foreign intelligence and law enforcement services for the collection of counterterrorism intelligence and the conduct of other counterterrorism activities. The results were mixed in terms of productive intelligence, reflecting vast differences in the ability and willingness of the various foreign services to target the Bin Ladin and al-Qa'ida network. Intelligence Community agencies sometimes failed to coordinate their relationships with foreign services adequately, either within the Intelligence Community or with broader U.S. Government liaison and foreign policy efforts. This reliance on foreign liaison services also resulted in a lack of focus on the development of unilateral human sources.

16. Finding: [The activities of the September 11 hijackers in the United States appear to have been financed, in large part, from monies sent to them from abroad and also brought in on their persons. Prior to September 11, there was no coordinated U.S. Government-wide strategy to track terrorist funding and close down their financial support networks. There was also a reluctance in some parts of the U.S. Government to track terrorist funding and close down their financial support networks. As a result, the U.S. Government was unable to disrupt financial support for Usama Bin Ladin's terrorist activities effectively].

RELATED FINDINGS

17. Finding: Despite intelligence reporting from 1998 through the summer of 2001 indicating that Usama Bin Ladin's terrorist network intended to strike inside the United States, the United States Government did not undertake a comprehensive effort to implement defensive measures in the United States.

18. Finding: Between 1996 and September 2001, the counterterrorism strategy adopted by the U.S. Government did not succeed in eliminating Afghanistan as a sanctuary and training ground for Usama Bin Ladin's terrorist network. A range of instruments was used to counter al-Qa'ida, with law enforcement often emerging as a leading tool because other means were deemed not to be feasible or failed to produce results. While generating numerous successful prosecutions, law enforcement efforts were not adequate by themselves to target or eliminate Bin Ladin's sanctuary. The United States persisted in observing the rule of law and accepted norms of international behavior, but Bin Ladin and al-Qa'ida recognized no rules and thrived in the safe haven provided by Afghanistan.

19. Finding: Prior to September 11, the Intelligence Community and the U.S. Government labored to prevent attacks by Usama Bin Ladin and his terrorist network against the United States, but largely without the benefit of an alert, mobilized and committed American public. Despite intelligence information on the immediacy of the threat level in the spring and summer of 2001, the assumption prevailed in the U.S. Government that attacks of the magnitude of September 11 could not happen here. As a result, there was insufficient effort to alert the American public to the reality and gravity of the threat.

20. Finding: Located in Part Four Entitled "Finding, Discussion and Narrative Regarding Certain Sensitive National Security Matters."

Source: www.gpoaccess.gov/serialset/creports/911.html.

Excerpt from Testimony of Richard A. Clarke Before the 9/11 Commission, March 24, 2004

Two days after publishing his memoir, Against All Enemies: Inside America's War on Terror *(2004) and after his appearance on the television news program* 60 Minutes, *former Clinton and Bush counterterrorism adviser Richard A. Clarke gave public testimony before the 9/11 Commission. In his book and in his public testimony, Clarke was highly critical of President George W. Bush for his failure to act forcefully against the danger signs that were evident before the 9/11 attacks. In his book, Clarke called President Bush "inattentive," while praising President Clinton for recognizing "terrorism as the major post–Cold War threat" and who "acted to improve our counterterrorism capabilities." Clarke's testimony in 2004 contrasted significantly from his testimony before the Joint Inquiry on June 11, 2002 (see above). Clarke began with an apology to the victims of the 9/11 attacks and laid the blame directly on the government when he said, "your government failed you, those entrusted with protecting you failed you and I failed you." Clarke was critical of National Security Adviser Condoleezza Rice for not alerting the president earlier to an antiterrorism strategy that had been developed before Bush was inaugurated. Clarke portrayed the road to 9/11 as one that had featured many danger signs that the Bush administration should not have ignored.*

EXCERPT FROM TESTIMONY OF RICHARD A. CLARKE, MARCH 24, 2004

CLARK: I welcome these hearings because of the opportunity that they provide to the American people to better understand why the tragedy of 9/11 happened and what we must do to prevent a re-occurrence.

I also welcome the hearings because it is finally a forum where I can apologize to the loved ones of the victims of 9/11.

To them who are here in the room, to those who are watching on television, your government failed you, those entrusted with protecting you failed you and I failed you. We tried hard, but that doesn't matter because we failed.

And for that failure, I would ask—once all the facts are out—for your understanding and for your forgiveness.

With that, Mr. Chairman, I'll be glad to take your questions. . . .

ROEMER: Well, let's say, Mr. Clarke—I think this is a fair question—let's say that you asked to brief the president of the United States on counterterrorism.

CLARK: Yes.

ROEMER: Did you ask that?

CLARK: I asked for a series of briefings on the issues in my portfolio, including counterterrorism and cybersecurity.

ROEMER: Did you get that request?

CLARK: I did. I was given an opportunity to brief on cybersecurity in June. I was told I could brief the president on terrorism after this policy development process was complete and we had the principals meeting and the draft national security policy decision that had been approved by the deputies committee.

ROEMER: Let's say, Mr. Clarke, as gifted as you might be in eloquence, and silver-tongued as anyone could be, and let's say—let's imagine—that instead of saying no, you asked for this briefing to the president—you said you didn't get it after 8 months of talking—let's say you get this briefing in February, after your memo to Dr. Rice on September the 25th, and you meet with the president of the United States in February and you brief him on terrorism, tell me how you convinced the president to move forward on this and get this principals meeting that doesn't take place until September the 4th moved up so that you can do something about this problem?

CLARK: Well, I think the best thing to have done, if there had been a meeting with the president in February, was to show him the accumulated intelligence that al Qaeda was strong and was planning attacks against the United States, against friendly governments. It was possible to make a very persuasive case that this was a major threat and this was an urgent problem.

ROEMER: And you think this would have sped up the deputies' process and the principals' process?

CLARK: No.

ROEMER: Do you think the president would have reached down then and said something to the national security team to . . .

CLARK: I don't know . . .

ROEMER: . . . to expedite this? What . . .

CLARK: Don't know.

ROEMER: . . . You worked for President Clinton. You saw what meetings with presidents could do there. Is this a magical solution? Or is it something that president might say right back to you, "Listen, Dick, I've got many other things I've got to do here, in the Middle East peace process, Bosnia, Kosovo, the Korean peninsula"? How likely is it that we are able to see some kind of result from a meeting like that?

CLARK: I think it depends, in part, on the president.

President Bush was regularly told by the director of Central Intelligence that there was an urgent threat. On one occasion—he was told this dozens of times in the morning briefings that George Tenet gave him. On one of those occasions, he asked for a strategy to deal with the threat.

Condi Rice came back from that meeting, called me, and relayed what the president had requested. And I said, "Well, you know, we've had this strategy ready since before you were inaugurated. I showed it [to] you. You have the paperwork. We can have a meeting on the strategy any time you want."

She said she would look into it. Her looking into it and the president asking for it did not change the pace at which it was considered. And as far as I know, the president never asked again; at least I was never informed that he asked again.

Sources: http://transcripts.cnn.com/TRANSCRIPTS/0403/24/bn.00.html; http://govinfo.library.unt.edu/911/archive/hearing8/index.htm.

Excerpt from Testimony of Condoleezza Rice Before the 9/11 Commission, April 8, 2004

Citing executive privilege, the White House at first declined to allow National Security Adviser Condoleezza Rice to appear before either the Joint Inquiry or the 9/11 Commission. But public testimony by former counterterrorism chief Richard A. Clarke challenged whether Rice and others in the Bush administration had given the terrorist threat adequate attention. On the eve of the 9/11 attacks, Rice had been preparing a paper on missile defense, an early priority of the Bush White House. After the 9/11 attacks, Rice said that no one had anticipated that terrorists would use airplanes as weapons to fly into buildings, a statement that angered families of the victims of 9/11 and that Rice later revised. After Clarke's testimony, the Family Steering Committee called on Rice to testify under oath before the 9/11 Commission. "We believe that testifying before the Commission in a public forum is Ms. Rice's moral obligation given her responsibility as National Security Advisor to protect our nation," the Family Steering Committee said in a March 27, 2004, statement. "The death of nearly 3,000 innocent people warrants such a moral precedent." Meanwhile, Rice was defending the Bush administration's strategy in frequent interviews. No one, including Clarke, had yet presented the president with a comprehensive plan to eliminate al-Qaeda, she said. The president, she added, was tired of "swatting flies." The 9/11 Commission staff prepared an 11-page document contrasting Clarke's and Rice's views on some 30 topics. "When viewed side-by-side, it was striking how much the disagreement was one of interpretation, and not of facts," commission chair Tom Keane and vice chair Lee Hamilton wrote.

EXCERPT FROM TESTIMONY OF CONDOLEEZZA RICE, APRIL 8, 2004

MR. KEAN: Thank you very much, Dr. Rice. We appreciate your statement, your attendance and your service.

I have a couple of questions. As we understand it, when you first came into office, you'd just been through a very difficult campaign. In that campaign neither the President nor his opponent, to the best of my knowledge, ever mentioned al Qaeda. There had been almost no congressional action or hearings about al Qaeda; very little bit in the newspapers. And yet you walk in and Dick Clarke is talking about al Qaeda should be our number one priority, Sandy Berger tells you you'll be spending more time on that than anything else. What did you think, and what did you tell the President as you hit that kind of, I suppose, new information for you.

MS. RICE: Well, in fact, Mr. Chairman, it was not new information. I think we all knew about the 1998 bombings. We knew that there was speculation that the 2000 Cole attack was al Qaeda. There had been, I think, documentaries about Osama bin Laden. I myself had written for an introduction to a volume on bioterrorism done at Stanford that I thought that we wanted not to wake up one day and find that Osama bin Laden had succeeded on our soil. It was on the radar screen of any person who studied or worked in the international security field.

But there's no doubt that I think the briefing by Dick Clarke, the earlier briefing during the transition by Director Tenet and, of course, what we talked with about (sic) Sandy Berger gave you a heightened sense of the problem and a sense that this was something that the United States had to deal with.

I have to say that of course there were other priorities, and indeed, in the briefings with the Clinton administration they emphasized other priorities—North Korea, the Middle East, the Balkans.

One doesn't have the luxury of dealing only with one issue if you are the United States of America. There are many urgent and important issues. . . .

I do think early on in these discussions we asked a lot of questions about whether Osama bin Laden himself ought to be so much the target of interest or whether—what was that going to do to the organization if, in fact, he was put out of commission. And I remember very well the director saying to President Bush, well, it would help but it would not stop attacks by al Qaeda nor destroy the network.

MR. KEAN: I've got a question now I'd like to ask you. It was given me by a number of members of the families. Did you ever see or hear from the FBI, from the CIA, from any other intelligence agency any memos or discussions or anything else between the time you got into office and 9/11 that talked about using planes as bombs?

MS. RICE: Let me address this question because it has been on the table. I think that concern about what I might have known or we might have known was provoked by some statements that I made in a press conference.

I was in a press conference to try and describe the August 6th memo, which I've talked about here in my opening remarks and which I talked about with you in the private session. And I said at one point that this was a historical memo, that it was not based on new threat information, and I said no one could have imagined them taking a plane, slamming it into the Pentagon—I'm paraphrasing now—into the World Trade Center, using planes as a missile.

As I said to you in the private session, I probably should have said "I" could not have imagined, because within two days, people started to come to me and say, "Oh, but there were these reports in 1998 and 1999, the intelligence community did look at information about this."

To the best of my knowledge, Mr. Chairman, this kind of analysis about the use of airplanes as weapons actually was never briefed to us. I cannot tell you that there might not have been a report here or a report there that reached somebody in our midst. . . .

All that I can tell you is that it was not in the August 6th memo, using planes as a weapon, and I do not remember any reports to us, a kind of strategic warning that planes might be used as a weapon. In fact, there were some reports done in '98 and '99. I think I was—I was certainly not aware of them at the time that I spoke. . . .

MR. BEN-VENISTE: . . . The extraordinary high terrorist attack threat level in the summer of 2001 is well documented. And Richard Clarke's testimony about the possibility of an attack against the United States homeland was repeatedly discussed from May to August within the intelligence community, and that is well documented. You acknowledged to us in your interview of February 7, 2004 that Richard Clarke told you that al Qaeda cells were in the United States. Did you tell the President at any time prior to August 6 of the existence of al Qaeda cells in the United States?

MS. RICE: First, let me just make certain—

MR. BEN-VENISTE: If you could just answer that question—

MS. RICE: Well, first—

MR. BEN-VENISTE: —because I only have a very limited—

MS. RICE: I understand, Commissioner, but it's important—

MR. BEN-VENISTE: Did you tell the President? (Applause.)

MS. RICE: It's important that I also address—it's also important, Commissioner, that I address the other issues that you have raised. So I will do it quickly, but if you'll just give me a moment.

MR. BEN-VENISTE: Well, my only question to you is whether you told the President.

MS. RICE: I understand, Commissioner, but I will—if you will just give me a moment, I will address fully the questions that you've asked.

First of all, yes, the August 6th PDB was in response to questions of the President.

In that sense he asked that this be done. It was not a particular threat report. And there was historical information in there about various aspects of al Qaeda's operations. Dick Clarke had told me, I think in a memorandum—I remember it as being only a line or two—that there were al Qaeda cells in the United States.

Now, the question is, what did we need to do about that? And I also understood that that was what the FBI was doing, that the FBI was pursuing these al Qaeda cells. I believe in the August 6th memorandum it says that there were 70 full-field investigations under way of these cells. And so there was no recommendation that we do something about this, but the FBI was pursuing it.

I really don't remember, Commissioner, whether I discussed this with the President.

MR. BEN-VENISTE: Thank you.

MS. RICE: I remember very well that the President was aware that there were issues inside the United States. He talked to people about this. But I don't remember the al Qaeda cells as being something that we were told we needed to do something about.

MR. BEN-VENISTE: Isn't it a fact, Dr. Rice, that the August 6th PDB warned against possible attacks in this country? And I ask you whether you recall the title of that PDB.

MS. RICE: I believe the title was "Bin Laden Determined to Attack Inside the United States." Now, the PDB—

MR. BEN-VENISTE: Thank you. . . .

MR. BEN-VENISTE: Well, if you are willing—if you were willing to declassify that document, then others can make up their minds about it.

Let me ask you a general matter. Beyond the fact that this memorandum provided information—not speculative, but based on intelligence information—that bin Laden had threatened to attack the United States and specifically Washington, D.C., there was nothing reassuring, was there, in that PDB?

MS. RICE: Certainly not. There was nothing reassuring. But I can also tell you that there was nothing in this memo that suggested that an attack was coming on New York or Washington, D.C. There was nothing in this memo as to time, place, how or where. This was not a threat report to the President or a threat report to me. It's a matter—

MR. BEN-VENISTE: We agree that there were no specifics. . . .

Source: http://govinfo.library.unt.edu/911/archive/hearing9/9-11Commission_Hearing_2004-04-08.htm.

Excerpt from Executive Summary of the 9/11 Commission Final Report, July 22, 2004

From the start, the 9/11 commissioners and staff aimed to produce a final report that would be not only accurate but a compelling narrative history, accessible even to school children. Chairman Tom Kean and vice chair Lee Hamilton had both served on commissions whose final reports were ignored by both the public and Congress. This report, they told staff, would be more than a doorstop. Commission teams produced timelines, monographs, and staff statements that, over time, helped produce a common voice. Kean and Hamilton enforced an editorial style that was concise, dispassionate, and understated. They told staff to let the facts tell the story and let the recommendations grow out of the facts. Chapter outlines of the final narrative were in draft form by spring 2003. Over time, some 30 staffers had a hand in drafting the final report. In the final months, 10 commissioners worked through up to 20 drafts of individual chapters, line by line. High-profile public hearings from January to June 2004 helped prime public interest in the final report. Public interest kept up pressure on the Bush administration to declassify material for the final report. On July 22, the 9/11 Commission released its 567-page final report as both a government report and a commercial release, which sold out in a week. Within days, candidates on both sides of the aisle were competing to endorse its recommendations. President Bush signed the Intelligence Reform and Terrorism Prevention Act on December 17, 2004.

EXCERPT FROM THE EXECUTIVE SUMMARY OF THE 9/11 COMMISSION FINAL REPORT JULY 22, 2004

WE PRESENT THE NARRATIVE of this report and the recommendations that flow from it to the President of the United States, the United States Congress, and the American people for their consideration. Ten Commissioners—five Republicans and five Democrats chosen by elected leaders from our nation's capital at a time of great partisan division—have come together to present this report without dissent.

We have come together with a unity of purpose because our nation demands it. September 11, 2001, was a day of unprecedented shock and suffering in the history of the United States. The nation was unprepared. . . .

Who Is the Enemy?

Who is this enemy that created an organization capable of inflicting such horrific damage on the United States? We now know that these attacks were carried out by various groups of Islamist extremists. The 9/11 attack was driven by Usama Bin Ladin.

In the 1980s, young Muslims from around the world went to Afghanistan to join as volunteers in a jihad (or holy struggle) against the Soviet Union. A wealthy Saudi, Usama Bin Ladin, was one of them. Following the defeat of the Soviets in the late 1980s, Bin Ladin and others formed al Qaeda to mobilize jihads elsewhere.

The history, culture, and body of beliefs from which Bin Ladin shapes and spreads his message are largely unknown to many Americans. Seizing on symbols of Islam's past greatness, he promises to restore pride to people who consider themselves the victims of successive foreign masters. He uses cultural and religious allusions to the holy Qur'an and some of its interpreters. He appeals to people disoriented by cyclonic change as they confront modernity and globalization. His rhetoric selectively draws from multiple sources-Islam, history, and the region's political and economic malaise.

Bin Ladin also stresses grievances against the United States widely shared in the Muslim world. He inveighed against the presence of U.S. troops in Saudi Arabia, which is the home of Islam's holiest sites, and against other U.S. policies in the Middle East....

1998 to September 11, 2001

The August 1998 bombings of U.S. embassies in Kenya and Tanzania established al Qaeda as a potent adversary of the United States.

After launching cruise missile strikes against al Qaeda targets in Afghanistan and Sudan in retaliation for the embassy bombings, the Clinton administration applied diplomatic pressure to try to persuade the Taliban regime in Afghanistan to expel Bin Ladin. The administration also devised covert operations to use CIA-paid foreign agents to capture or kill Bin Ladin and his chief lieutenants. These actions did not stop Bin Ladin or dislodge al Qaeda from its sanctuary.

By late 1998 or early 1999, Bin Ladin and his advisers had agreed on an idea brought to them by Khalid Sheikh Mohammed (KSM) called the "planes operation." It would eventually culminate in the 9/11 attacks. Bin Ladin and his chief of operations, Mohammed Atef, occupied undisputed leadership positions atop al Qaeda. Within al Qaeda, they relied heavily on the ideas and enterprise of strong-willed field commanders, such as KSM, to carry out worldwide terrorist operations. KSM claims that his original plot was even grander than those carried out on 9/11-ten planes would attack targets on both the East and West coasts of the United States. This plan was modified by Bin Ladin, KSM said, owing to its scale and complexity. Bin Ladin provided KSM with four initial operatives for suicide plane attacks within the United States, and in the fall of 1999 training for the attacks began. New recruits included four from a cell of expatriate Muslim extremists who had clustered together in Hamburg, Germany. One became the tactical commander of the operation in the United States: Mohamed Atta.

U.S. intelligence frequently picked up reports of attacks planned by al Qaeda. Working with foreign security services, the CIA broke up some al Qaeda cells. The core of Bin Ladin's organization nevertheless remained intact. In December 1999, news about the arrests of the terrorist cell in Jordan and the arrest of a terrorist at the U.S.-Canadian border became part of a "millennium alert." The government was galvanized, and the public was on alert for any possible attack.

In January 2000, the intense intelligence effort glimpsed and then lost sight of two operatives destined for the "planes operation." Spotted in Kuala Lumpur, the pair were lost passing through Bangkok. On January 15, 2000, they arrived in Los Angeles.

Because these two al Qaeda operatives had spent little time in the West and spoke little, if any, English, it is plausible that they or KSM would have tried to identify, in advance, a friendly contact in the United States. We explored suspicions about whether these two operatives had a support network of accomplices in the United States. The evidence is thin simply not there for some cases, more worrisome in others.

We do know that soon after arriving in California, the two al Qaeda operatives sought out and found a group of ideologically like-minded Muslims with roots in Yemen and Saudi Arabia, individuals mainly associated with a young Yemeni and others who attended a mosque in San Diego. After a brief stay in Los Angeles about which we know little, the al Qaeda operatives lived openly in San Diego under their true names. They managed to avoid attracting much attention.

By the summer of 2000, three of the four Hamburg cell members had arrived on the East Coast of the United States and had begun pilot training. In early 2001, a fourth future hijacker pilot, Ham Hanjour, journeyed to Arizona with another operative, Nawaf al Hazmi, and conducted his refresher pilot training there. A number of al Qaeda operatives had spent time in Arizona during the 1980s and early 1990s.

During 2000, President Bill Clinton and his advisers renewed diplomatic efforts to get Bin Ladin expelled from Afghanistan. They also renewed secret *efforts* with some of the Taliban's opponents—the Northern Alliance—to get enough intelligence to attack Bin Ladin directly. Diplomatic efforts centered on the new military government in Pakistan, and they did not succeed. The efforts with the Northern Alliance revived an inconclusive and secret debate about whether the United States should take sides in Afghanistan' civil war and support the Taliban's enemies. The CIA also produced a plan to improve intelligence collection on al Qaeda, including the use of a small, unmanned airplane with a video camera, known as the Predator.

After the October 2000 attack on the *USS Cole,* evidence accumulated that it had been launched by al Qaeda operatives, but without confirmation that Bin Ladin had given the order. The Taliban had earlier been warned that it would be held responsible for another Bin Ladin attack on the United States. The CIA described its findings as a "preliminary judgment"; President Clinton and his chief advisers told us they were waiting for a conclusion before deciding whether to take military action. The military alternatives remained unappealing to them.

The transition to the new Bush administration in late 2000 and early 2001 took place with the *Cole* issue still pending. President George W Bush and his chief advisers accepted that al Qaeda was responsible for the attack on the *Cole,* but did not like the options available for a response.

Bin Ladin's inference may well have been that attacks, at least at the level of the *Cole,* were risk free.

The Bush administration began developing a new strategy with the stated goal of eliminating the al Qaeda threat within three to five years.

During the spring and summer of 2001, U.S. intelligence agencies received a stream of warnings that al Qaeda planned, as one report put it, "something very, very, very big." Director of Central Intelligence [DCI] George Tenet told us, "The system was blinking red."

Although Bin Ladin was determined to strike in the United States, as President Clinton had been told and President Bush was reminded in a Presidential Daily Brief article briefed to him in August 2001, the specific threat information pointed overseas. Numerous precautions were taken overseas. Domestic agencies were not effectively mobilized. The threat did not receive national media attention comparable to the millennium alert.

While the United States continued disruption efforts around the world, its emerging strategy to eliminate the al Qaeda threat was to include an enlarged covert action program in Afghanistan, as well as diplomatic strategies for Afghanistan and Pakistan. The process culminated during the summer of 2001 in a draft presidential directive and arguments about the Predator aircraft, which was soon to be deployed with a missile of its own, so that it might be used to attempt to kill Bin Ladin or his chief lieutenants. At a September 4 meeting, President Bush's chief advisers approved the draft directive of the strategy and endorsed the concept of arming the Predator. This directive on the al Qaeda strategy was awaiting President Bush's signature on September 11, 2001.

Though the "planes operation" was progressing, the plotters had problems of their own in 2001. Several possible participants dropped out; others could not gain entry into the United States (including one denial at a port of entry and visa denials not related to terrorism). One of the eventual pilots may have considered abandoning the planes operation. Zacarias Moussaoui, who showed up at a flight training school in Minnesota, may have been a candidate to replace him.

Some of the vulnerabilities of the plotters become clear in retrospect. Moussaoui aroused suspicion for seeking fast-track training on how to pilot large jet airliners. He was arrested on August 16, 2001, for violations of immigration regulations. In late August, officials in the intelligence community realized that the terrorists spotted in Southeast Asia in January 2000 had arrived in the United States.

These cases did not prompt urgent action. No one working on these late leads in the summer of 2001 connected them to the high level of threat reporting. In the words of one official, no analytic work foresaw the lightning that could connect the thundercloud to the ground.

As final preparations were under way during the summer of 2001, dissent emerged among al Qaeda leaders in Afghanistan over whether to proceed. The Taliban's chief, Mullah Omar, opposed attacking the United States. Although facing opposition from many of his senior lieutenants, Bin Ladin effectively overruled their objections, and the attacks went forward.

September 11, 2001

The day began with the 19 hijackers getting through a security checkpoint system that they had evidently analyzed and knew how to defeat. Their success rate in penetrating the system was 19 for 19. They took over the four flights, taking advantage of air crews and cockpits that were not prepared for the contingency of a suicide hijacking.

On 9/11, the defense of U.S. air space depended on close interaction between two federal agencies: the Federal Aviation Administration (FAA) and North American Aerospace Defense Command (NORAD). Existing protocols on 9/11 were unsuited in every respect for an attack in which hijacked planes were used as weapons.

What ensued was a hurried attempt to improvise a defense by civilians who had never handled a hijacked aircraft that attempted to disappear, and by a military unprepared for the transformation of commercial aircraft into weapons of mass destruction.

A shootdown authorization was not communicated to the NORAD air defense sector until 28 minutes after United 93 had crashed in Pennsylvania. Planes were scrambled, but ineffectively, as they did not know where to go or what targets they were to intercept. And once the shootdown order was given, it was not communicated to the pilots. In short, while leaders in Washington believed that the fighters circling above them had been instructed to "take out" hostile aircraft, the only orders actually conveyed to the pilots were to "ID type and tail."

Like the national defense, the emergency response on 9/11 was necessarily improvised.

In New York City, the Fire Department of New York, the New York Police Department, the Port Authority of New York and New Jersey, the building employees, and the occupants of the buildings did their best to cope with the effects of almost unimaginable events unfolding furiously over 102 minutes. Casualties were nearly 100 percent at and above the impact zones and were very high among first responders who stayed in danger as they tried to save lives. Despite weaknesses in preparations for disaster, failure to achieve unified incident command, and inadequate communications among responding agencies, all but approximately one hundred of the thousands of civilians who worked below the impact zone escaped, often with help from the emergency responders.

At the Pentagon, while there were also problems of command and control, the emergency response was generally effective. The Incident Command System, a formalized management structure for emergency response in place in the National Capital Region, overcame the inherent complications of a response across local, state, and federal jurisdictions....

GENERAL FINDINGS

Since the plotters were flexible and resourceful, we cannot know whether any single step or series of steps would have defeated them. What we can say with confidence is that none of the measures adopted by the U.S. government from 1998 to 2001 disturbed or even delayed the progress of the al Qaeda plot. Across the government, there were failures of imagination, policy, capabilities, and management.

Imagination

The most important failure was one of imagination. We do not believe leaders understood the gravity of the threat. The terrorist danger from Bin Ladin and al Qaeda was not a major topic for policy debate among the public, the media, or in the Congress. Indeed, it barely came up during the 2000 presidential campaign.

Al Qaeda's new brand of terrorism presented challenges to U.S. governmental institutions that they were not well-designed to meet. Though top officials all told us that they understood the danger, we believe there was uncertainty among them as to whether this was just a new and especially venomous version of the ordinary terrorist threat the United States had lived with for decades, or it was indeed radically new, posing a threat beyond any yet experienced.

As late as September 4, 2001, Richard Clarke, the White House staffer long responsible for counterterrorism policy coordination, asserted that the government had not yet made up its mind how to answer the question: "Is al Qida a big deal?"

A week later came the answer.

Policy

Terrorism was not the overriding national security concern for the U.S. government under either the Clinton or the pre-9/11 Bush administration.

The policy challenges were linked to this failure of imagination. Officials in both the Clinton and Bush administrations regarded a full U.S. invasion of Afghanistan as practically inconceivable before 9/11.

Capabilities

Before 9/11, the United States tried to solve the al Qaeda problem with the capabilities it had used in the last stages of the Cold War and its immediate aftermath. These capabilities were insufficient. Little was done to expand or reform them.

The CIA had minimal capacity to conduct paramilitary operations with its own personnel, and it did not seek a large-scale expansion of these capabilities before 9/11. The CIA also needed to improve its capability to collect intelligence from human agents.

At no point before 9/11 was the Department of Defense fully engaged in the mission of countering al Qaeda, even though this was perhaps the most dangerous foreign enemy threatening the United States.

America's homeland defenders faced outward. NORAD itself was barely able to retain any alert bases at all. Its planning scenarios occasionally considered the danger of hijacked aircraft being guided to American targets, but only aircraft that were coming from overseas.

The most serious weaknesses in agency capabilities were in the domestic arena. The FBI did not have the capability to link the collective knowledge of agents in the field to national priorities. Other domestic agencies deferred to the FBI.

FAA capabilities were weak. Any serious examination of the possibility of a suicide hijacking could have suggested changes to fix glaring vulnerabilities-expanding no-fly lists, searching passengers identified by the CAPPS *screening* system, deploying federal air marshals domestically, hardening cockpit doors, alerting air crews to a different kind of hijacking possibility than they had been trained to expect. Yet the FAA did not adjust either its own training or training with NORAD to take account of threats other than those experienced in the past.

Management

The missed opportunities to thwart the 9/11 plot were also symptoms of a broader inability to adapt the way government manages problems to the new challenges of the twenty-first century. Action officers should have been able to draw on all available knowledge about al Qaeda in the government. Management should have ensured that information was shared and duties were clearly assigned across agencies, and across the foreign-domestic divide.

There were also broader management issues with respect to how top leaders set priorities and allocated resources. For instance, on December 4, 1998, DCI Tenet issued a directive to several CIA officials and the DDCI [Deputy Director of Central Intelligence] for Community Management, stating: "We are at war. I want no resources or people spared in this effort, either inside CIA or the Community." The memorandum had little overall effect on mobilizing the CIA or the intelligence community. This episode indicates the limitations of the DCI's authority over the direction of the intelligence community, including agencies within the Department of Defense.

The U.S. government did not find a way of pooling intelligence and using it to guide the planning and assignment of responsibilities for joint operations involving entities as disparate as the CIA, the FBI, the State Department, the military, and the agencies involved in homeland security....

RECOMMENDATIONS

Three years after 9/11, the national debate continues about how to protect our nation in this new era. We divide our recommendations into two basic parts: What to do and how to do it.

WHAT TO DO? A GLOBAL STRATEGY

The enemy is not just "terrorism." It is the threat posed specifically by Islamist terrorism, by Bin Ladin and others who draw on a long tradition of extreme intolerance within a minority strain of Islam that does not distinguish politics from religion, and distorts both.

The enemy is not Islam, the great world faith, but a perversion of Islam. The enemy goes beyond al Qaeda to include the radical ideological movement, inspired in part by al Qaeda, that has spawned other terrorist groups and violence. Thus our strategy must match our means to two ends: dismantling the al Qaeda network and, in the long term, prevailing over the ideology that contributes to Islamist terrorism.

The first phase of our post-9/11 efforts rightly included military action to topple the Taliban and pursue al Qaeda. This work continues. But long-term success demands the use of all elements of national power: diplomacy, intelligence, covert action, law enforcement, economic policy, foreign aid, public diplomacy, and homeland defense. If we favor one tool while neglecting others, we leave ourselves vulnerable and weaken our national effort.

What should Americans expect from their government? The goal seems unlimited: Defeat terrorism anywhere in the world. But Americans have also been told to expect the worst: An attack is probably coming; it may be more devastating still.

Vague goals match an amorphous picture of the enemy. Al Qaeda and other groups are popularly described as being all over the world, adaptable, resilient, needing little higher-level organization, and capable of anything. It is an image of an omnipotent hydra of destruction. That image lowers expectations of government effectiveness.

It lowers them too far. Our report shows a determined and capable group of plotters. Yet the group was fragile and occasionally left vulnerable by the marginal, unstable people often attracted to such causes. The enemy made mistakes. The U.S. government was not able to capitalize on them.

No president can promise that a catastrophic attack like that of 9/11 will not happen again. But the American people are entitled to expect that officials will have realistic objectives, clear guidance, and effective organization. They are entitled to see standards for performance so they can judge, with the help of their elected representatives, whether the objectives are being met.

We propose a strategy with three dimensions: (1) attack terrorists and their organizations, (2) prevent the continued growth of Islamist terrorism, and (3) protect against and prepare for terrorist attacks.

Attack Terrorists and Their Organizations

- Root out sanctuaries. The U.S. government should identify and priortize actual or potential terrorist sanctuaries and have realistic country or regional strategies for each, utilizing every element of national power and reaching out to countries that can help us.
- Strengthen long-term U.S. and international commitments to the future of Pakistan and Afghanistan.
- Confront problems with Saudi Arabia in the open and build a relationship beyond oil, a relationship that both sides can defend to their citizens and includes a shared commitment to reform.

Prevent the Continued Growth of Islamist Terrorism

In October 2003, Secretary of Defense Donald Rumsfeld asked if enough was being done "to fashion a broad integrated plan to stop the next generation of terrorists." As part of such a plan, the U.S. government should

- Define the message and stand as an example of moral leadership in the world. To Muslim parents, terrorists like Bin Ladin have nothing to offer their children but visions of violence and death. America and its friends have the advantage-our vision can offer a better future.
- Where Muslim governments, even those who are friends, do not offer opportunity, respect the rule of law, or tolerate differences, then the United States needs to stand for a better future.
- Communicate and defend American ideals in the Islamic world, through much stronger public diplomacy to reach more people, including students and leaders outside of government. Our efforts here should be as strong as they were in combating closed societies during the Cold War.
- Offer an agenda of opportunity that includes support for public education and economic openness.
- Develop a comprehensive coalition strategy against Islamist terrorism, using a flexible contact group of leading coalition governments and fashioning a common coalition approach on issues like the treatment of captured terrorists.
- Devote a maximum effort to the parallel task of countering the proliferation of weapons of mass destruction.
- Expect less from trying to dry up terrorist money and more from following the money for intelligence, as a tool to hunt terrorists, understand their networks, and disrupt their operations.

Protect against and Prepare for Terrorist Attacks

- Target terrorist travel, an intelligence and security strategy that the 9/11 story showed could be at least as powerful as the effort devoted to terrorist finance.
- Address problems of screening people with biometric identifiers across agencies and governments, including our border and transportation systems, by designing a comprehensive screening system that addresses common problems and sets common standards. As standards spread, this necessary and ambitious effort could dramatically strengthen the world's ability to intercept individuals who could pose catastrophic threats.
- Quickly complete a biometric entry-exit screening system, one that also speeds qualified travelers.
- Set standards for the issuance of birth certificates and sources of identification, such as driver's licenses.
- Develop strategies for neglected parts of our transportation security system. Since 9/11, about 90 percent of the nation's $5 billion annual investment in transportation security has gone to aviation, to fight the last war.
- In aviation, prevent arguments about a new computerized profiling system from delaying vital improvements in the "no-fly" and "automatic selectee" lists. Also, give priority to the improvement of checkpoint screening.
- Determine, with leadership from the President, guidelines for gathering and sharing information in the new security systems that are needed, guidelines that integrate safeguards for privacy and other essential liberties.
- Underscore that as government power necessarily expands in certain ways, the burden of retaining such powers remains on the executive to demonstrate the value of such powers and ensure adequate supervision of how they are used, including a new board to oversee the implementation of the guidelines needed for gathering and sharing information in these new security systems.
- Base federal funding for emergency preparedness solely on risks and vulnerabilities, putting New York City and Washington, D.C., at the top of the current list. Such

assistance should not remain a program for general revenue sharing or pork-barrel spending.

- Make homeland security funding contingent on the adoption of an incident command system to strengthen teamwork in a crisis, including a regional approach. Allocate more radio spectrum and improve connectivity for public safety communications, and encourage widespread adoption of newly developed standards for private-sector emergency preparedness-since the private sector controls 85 percent of the nation's critical infrastructure.

HOW TO DO IT? A DIFFERENT WAY OF ORGANIZING GOVERNMENT

The strategy we have recommended is elaborate, even as presented here very briefly. To implement it will require a government better organized than the one that exists today, with its national security institutions designed half a century ago to win the Cold War. Americans should not settle for incremental, ad hoc adjustments to a system created a generation ago for a world that no longer exists.

Our detailed recommendations are designed to fit together. Their purpose is clear: to build unity of effort across the U.S. government. As one official now serving on the front lines overseas put it to us: "One fight, one team."

We call for unity of effort in five areas, beginning with unity of effort on the challenge of counterterrorism itself

- unifying strategic intelligence and operational planning against Islamist terrorists across the foreign-domestic divide with a National Counterterrorism Center;
- unifying the intelligence community with a new National Intelligence Director;
- unifying the many participants in the counterterrorism effort and their knowledge in a network-based information sharing system that transcends traditional governmental boundaries;
- unifying and strengthening congressional oversight to improve quality and accountability; and strengthening the FBI and homeland defenders.

Unity of Effort: A National Counterterrorism Center

The 9/11 story teaches the value of integrating strategic intelligence from all sources into joint operational planning-with both dimensions spanning the foreign-domestic divide.

- In some ways, since 9/11, joint work has gotten better. The effort of fighting terrorism has flooded over many of the usual agency boundaries because of its sheer quantity and energy. Attitudes have changed. But the problems of coordination have multiplied. The Defense Department alone has three unified commands (SOCOM, CENTCOM, and NORTHCOM) that deal with terrorism as one of their principal concerns.
- Much of the public commentary about the 9/11 attacks has focused on "lost opportunities." Though characterized as problems of "watchlisting," "information sharing," or "connecting the dots," each of these labels is too narrow They describe the symptoms, not the disease.
- Breaking the older mold of organization stovepiped purely in executive agencies, we propose a National Counterterrorism Center (NCTC) that would borrow the joint, unified command concept adopted in the 1980s by the American military in a civilian agency, combining the joint intelligence function alongside the operations work.
- The NCTC would build on the existing Terrorist Threat Integration Center and would replace it and other terrorism "fusion centers" within the government. The NCTC would become the authoritative knowledge bank, bringing information to bear on common plans. It should task collection requirements both inside and outside the United States.
- The NCTC should perform joint operational planning, assigning lead responsibilities to existing agencies and letting them direct the actual execution of the plans.
- Placed in the Executive Office of the President, headed by a Senate confirmed official (with rank equal to the deputy head of a cabinet department) who reports to the National Intelligence Director, the NCTC would track implementation of plans. It would be able to influence the leadership and the budgets of the counterterrorism operating arms of the CIA, the FBI, and the departments of Defense and Homeland Security.
- The NCTC should not be a policymaking body. Its operations and planning should follow the policy direction of the president and the National Security Council.

Unity of Effort: A National Intelligence Director

Since long before 9/11—and continuing to this day—the intelligence community is not organized well for joint intelligence work. It does not employ common standards and practices in reporting intelligence or in training experts overseas and at home. The expensive national capabilities for collecting intelligence have divided management. The structures are too complex and too secret.

- The community's head—the Director of Central Intelligence—has at least three jobs: running the CIA, coordinating a 15-agency confederation, and being the intelligence analyst-in-chief to the president. No one person can do all these things.
- A new National Intelligence Director should be established with two main jobs: (1) to oversee national intelligence centers that combine experts from all the collection disciplines against common targets like counterterrorism or nuclear proliferation; and (2) to oversee the agencies that contribute to the national intelligence program, a task that includes setting common standards for personnel and information technology.
- The national intelligence centers would be the unified commands of the intelligence world—a long-overdue reform for intelligence comparable to the 1986 Goldwater-Nichols law that reformed the organization of national defense. The home services—such as the CIA, DIA (Defense Information Agency], NSA [National Security Agency], and FBI—would organize, train, and equip the best intel-

ligence professionals in the world, and would handle the execution of intelligence operations in the field.

- This National Intelligence Director (NID) should be located in the Executive Office of the President and report directly to the president, yet be confirmed by the Senate. In addition to overseeing the National Counterterrorism Center described above (which will include both the national intelligence center for terrorism and the joint operations planning effort), the NID should have three deputies:
- For foreign intelligence (a deputy who also would be the head of the CIA)
- For defense intelligence (also the under secretary of defense for intelligence)
- For homeland intelligence (also the executive assistant director for intelligence at the FBI or the under secretary of homeland security for information analysis and infrastructure protection)
- The NID should receive a public appropriation for national intelligence, should have authority to hire and fire his or her intelligence deputies, and should be able to set common personnel and information technology policies across the intelligence community.
- The CIA should concentrate on strengthening the collection capabilities of its clandestine service and the talents of its analysts, building pride in its core expertise.
- Secrecy stifles oversight, accountability, and information sharing. Unfortunately, all the current organizational incentives encourage over classification. This balance should change; and as a start, open information should be provided about the overall size of agency intelligence budgets.

Unity of *Effort:* Sharing Information

The U.S. government has access to a vast amount of information. But it has a weak system for processing and using what it has. The system of "need to know" should be replaced by a system of "need to share."

The President should lead a government-wide effort to bring the major national security institutions into the information revolution, turning a mainframe system into a decentralized network. The obstacles are not technological. Official after official has urged us to call attention to problems with the unglamorous "back office" side of government operations.

- But no agency can solve the problems on its own to build the network requires an effort that transcends old divides, solving common legal and policy issues in ways that can help officials know what they can and cannot do. Again, in tackling information issues, America needs unity of effort.

Unity of *Effort:* Congress

Congress took too little action to adjust itself or to restructure the executive branch to address the emerging terrorist threat. Congressional oversight for intelligence—and counterterrorism—is dysfunctional. Both Congress and the executive need to do more to minimize national security risks during transitions between administrations.

- For intelligence oversight, we propose two options: either a joint committee on the old model of the joint Committee on Atomic Energy or a single committee in each house combining authorizing and appropriating committees. Our central message is the same: the intelligence committees cannot carry out their oversight function unless they are made stronger, and thereby have both clear responsibility and accountability for that oversight.
- Congress should create a single, principal point of oversight and review for homeland security. There should be one permanent standing committee for homeland security in each chamber.
- We propose reforms to speed up the nomination, financial reporting, security clearance, and confirmation process for national security officials at the start of an administration, and suggest steps to make sure that incoming administrations have the information they need.

Unity of *Effort:* Organizing America's Defenses in the United States

We have considered several proposals relating to the future of the domestic intelligence and counterterrorism mission. Adding a new domestic intelligence agency will not solve America's problems in collecting and analyzing intelligence within the United States. We do not recommend creating one.

- We propose the establishment of a specialized and integrated national security workforce at the FBI, consisting of agents, analysts, linguists, and surveillance specialists who are recruited, trained, rewarded, and retained to ensure the development of an institutional culture imbued with a deep expertise in intelligence and national security.
- At several points we asked: Who has the responsibility for defending us at home? Responsibility for America's national defense is shared by the Department of Defense, with its new Northern Command, and by the Department of Homeland Security. They must have a clear delineation of roles, missions, and authority.
- The Department of Defense and its oversight committees should regularly assess the adequacy of Northern Command's strategies and planning to defend against military threats to the homeland.

* * *

- The Department of Homeland Security and its oversight committees should regularly assess the types of threats the country faces, in order to determine the adequacy of the government's plans and the readiness of the government to respond to those threats.

We call on the American people to remember how we all felt on 9/11, to remember not. only the unspeakable horror but how we came together as a nation-one nation. Unity of purpose and unity of effort are the way we will defeat this enemy and make America safer for our children and grandchildren.

We look forward to a national debate on the merits of what we have recommended, and we will participate vigorously in that debate.

Excerpt from 9/11 Commission Staff Report on the "Wall Between Intelligence and Law Enforcement Investigations," August 20, 2004

Congress's investigation of the abuses in domestic intelligence gathering in the mid-1970s led to a shake-up of the intelligence establishment, including the creation of permanent oversight committees in the House and Senate. It also created a "wall" between federal law enforcement and the intelligence community. The 1978 Foreign Intelligence Surveillance Act (FISA) set up a new court to review requests for domestic surveillance whose primary purpose was to obtain foreign intelligence information. Over time, the new procedures were widely misunderstood and misapplied and muted the ability of both law enforcement and intelligence efforts to deal with the growing threat from Islamic terrorists. The commission staff drafted this monograph to explain the origins and culture of the wall. The report makes the case for new legal procedures and changes in the existing cultures within the intelligence community, law-enforcement agencies, and the court when facing the challenges of international terrorism. This report was declassified on May 20, 2009.

EXCERPT FROM 9/11 COMMISSION STAFF REPORT, AUGUST 20, 2004

Legal Barriers to Information Sharing: The Erection of a Wall Between Intelligence and Law Enforcement Investigations

Commission on Terrorist Attacks Upon the United States

Staff Monograph

Barbara A. Grewe

Senior Counsel for Special Projects

August 20, 2004

As the threat of terrorism from radical Islamic groups developed, the FBI had both law enforcement and intelligence responsibilities in response to the threat. And it had different tools to use depending on whether its investigation was designated as an intelligence matter or a criminal matter. For criminal matters it could apply for and use traditional criminal warrants. For intelligence matters it could apply to a special court, known as the Foreign Intelligence Surveillance Court (FISC), for warrants pursuant to the Foreign Intelligence Surveillance Act (FISA) of 1978. This law governs electronic surveillance and physical searches of foreign powers and their agents within the United States. This divergence in purposes for the respective types of investigations and concerns about using intelligence techniques to advance law enforcement interests led to information sharing barriers being erected between the investigations. This paper will describe the history and development of the various barriers and their impact on the 9/11 story.

The History of Tensions Between Intelligence and Criminal Investigations

. . . In 1978 Congress passed the Foreign Intelligence Surveillance Act (FISA). This law regulated intelligence collection directed at foreign powers and agents of foreign powers in the United States. It was a compromise. FISA did not require traditional court approval of a warrant, but established a special new court, the Foreign Intelligence Surveillance Court (FISC), to review requests for surveillance pursuant to this law. The Department of Justice created an Office of Intelligence Policy and Review (OIPR). OIPR would be responsible, *inter alia,* for presenting surveillance applications to the FISA court.

Because of longstanding concerns regarding the use of non-criminal warrants to obtain evidence for criminal matters the 1978 act was interpreted by the courts, the Congress, and the Justice Department, to require that a search be approved only if its "primary purpose" was to obtain foreign intelligence information. The FISA application process required a certification from a high-ranking Executive Branch official, such as the Director of the FBI, that the purpose of the desired surveillance was to obtain foreign intelligence information. In other words, the FISA process could not be used to circumvent traditional criminal warrants to build a criminal case or to spy upon domestic targets unrelated to foreign powers. If a prosecution became or was perceived to have become the primary purpose of FISA coverage, the FISA court could terminate the surveillance and the criminal court could suppress any of the information obtained or derived from the FISA coverage. The Justice Department interpreted these rulings to mean that criminal prosecutors could be briefed on FISA-related information but could not direct or control its collection.

There was, however, some recognition that evidence collected via a FISA warrant could be used in subsequent criminal proceedings. How and when it could be used was the subject of significant debate. Through the 1980s and early 1990s informal information sharing procedures allowed FBI agents to brief criminal prosecutors on what was being collected during FISA surveillances. There were no written guidelines governing such contacts. The prosecutors understood that they could not manipulate the process to direct the FISA collection to advance their criminal matters. Whether and when the FBI shared information pertinent to possible criminal investigations was left solely to the judgment of the FBI. There were no requirements that OIPR be apprised of such information sharing.

The Creation of the July 1995 Procedures

The prosecution of Aldrich Ames for espionage in early 1994 raised concerns about the prosecutors' role in intelligence investigations. Over the course of the Ames investigation FBI Director Freeh and Attorney General Reno signed nine certifications that the information being sought was for the purpose of collecting foreign intelligence information. Some of these certifications were made after a decision had been made to criminally prosecute Ames and he was talking to the prosecutors.

Richard Scruggs, the acting head of OIPR, became worried that because of the numerous prior consultations between FBI agents and criminal prosecutors, the judge handling the criminal case might rule that the FISA warrants had been misused. If that happened, Ames might escape conviction. Scruggs complained to Attorney General Reno about the absence of any information sharing controls. Almost immediately Scruggs began imposing information sharing procedures for FISA material. As a result, OIPR became the gatekeeper for the flow of FISA information to criminal prosecutors. The FBI was not permitted to brief criminal prosecutors on information gathered from FISA surveillance without OIPR's approval. . . .

On July 19, 1995, the "Procedures for Contacts Between the FBI and the Criminal Division Concerning Foreign Intelligence and Foreign Counterintelligence Investigations" were issued by the Attorney General. The procedures required that the Criminal Division be notified when a foreign counterintelligence (FCI) or foreign intelligence (FI) investigation developed facts or circumstances that "reasonably indicate that a significant federal crime has been, is being, or may be committed." The FISA court officially incorporated these procedures in future FISA orders as accepted procedures to govern information sharing.

It is important to understand what these procedures did and did not do. First, these procedures only applied to information gathered by the FBI as part of an intelligence investigation. They did not control information gathered by the CIA or the NSA. [Redacted] Thus, information from the CIA and NSA could be shared with criminal investigators and/or prosecutors without complying with these procedures and any notice to or involvement by OIPR.

Second, despite OIPR's proposals to the contrary, these procedures said nothing about information sharing within the FBI. FBI agents working intelligence matters could freely share information with agents working on parallel criminal matters. The only controls were on information sharing between the FBI and criminal prosecutors.

Third, the procedures compelled information sharing when there was evidence of a significant criminal offense. Both the FBI and OIPR had an independent obligation to notify the Criminal Division when this threshold was met. The procedures clearly rejected OIPR's view that it should have the gatekeeper role in deciding what intelligence information should or could be shared with criminal prosecutors. They did not ban information sharing under any circumstances.

Finally, the limits on information sharing were solely on the advice-giving role of prosecutors, not the sharing itself. The procedures specifically endeavored to prevent even the appearance of direction and control. They limited the type of advice that the criminal prosecutors could give to agents working on the intelligence matters. Such advice could preserve the possibility of a criminal prosecution but could not direct activities so as to enhance such a prosecution. . . .

The March 1995 Gorelick Memorandum

Mary Jo White became the United States Attorney for the Southern District of New York (SDNY) in the spring of 1993, shortly after the first World Trade Center bombing and the discovery of the so-called Landmarks Plot to simultaneously bomb New York City tunnels and landmarks. Her attorneys and the FBI agents in the New York Field Office worked tirelessly to bring to prosecution the perpetrators of the attack and the plot.

By the early spring of 1995 the trial of the plotters was underway. During the trial the FBI learned of death threats against the judge, the prosecutors, and witnesses at the trial. Criminal pen registers on relevant telephones were already in place to try to learn who was behind the threats. It was decided, however, that these techniques were not providing adequate information, and there was continuing concern for the safety of government officials and witnesses. White and her staff suggested that an intelligence investigation be opened to aggressively address the ongoing threats.

Because any intelligence surveillance or physical searches within the United States required a FISA warrant, the FBI would need to convince OIPR to present a warrant application to the Foreign Intelligence Surveillance Court. The FBI believed, however, that because there was already an open criminal matter on these individuals and the threats, OIPR would reject such an application because it would appear that the primary purpose of such surveillance was the criminal case, not an intelligence investigation. [redacted]

This request was very troubling to OIPR. There is ample evidence that some individuals in OIPR believed that once it was decided that a case would become a criminal matter, the intelligence investigation had to be terminated. This view was not without some basis in the law. The seminal case on the primary purpose standard, *United States v. Truong Dinh Hung*, supported such a view. The court in *Truong*, which involved a pre-FISA search but was decided after the passage of FISA, upheld the admission of evidence gathered in the intelligence investigation prior to the matter becoming a criminal investigation. Once the Criminal Division wrote a memorandum indicating that it was going to open a criminal matter, the court held the primary purpose was no longer intelligence and all information gathered after that point was suppressed. The Truong case became the foundation for subsequent cases holding that the primary purpose standard also applied to surveillance authorized under FISA. . . .

Reports of Problems with the July 1995 Procedures and Efforts at Reform

The July 1995 procedures were intended to permit a reasonable degree of information sharing between FBI agents conducting intelligence investigations and Criminal Division prosecutors.

They were also intended, however, to ensure that the FBI would be able to obtain continuing FISA coverage and later be able to use the fruits of such coverage in criminal cases. If the FISA court or a subsequent criminal court held that the primary purpose was something other than intelligence collection, renewal of coverage could be denied or evidence could be suppressed. As all parties to the procedures agreed, this could be a very delicate balance with substantial risks to national security if the process was not adequately managed. All agreed that some management was required. They disagreed as to how this management should be exercised. As a result the procedures were widely misunderstood and misapplied. This resulted in far less information sharing and coordination between the FBI and the Criminal Division in practice than was allowed in theory under the July 1995 procedures.

OIPR's leadership was very risk averse and thus took a very conservative approach as to how much information sharing could take place and when. It believed that the earlier and the more frequent the contact between the FBI and the Criminal Division, the more likely that the court would find that the primary purpose standard was not met. During the debate over the procedures OIPR argued that information sharing should be minimized and worried that the FBI and the Criminal Division wanted to meet more often than OIPR deemed wise. Over time OIPR, and eventually the FISC itself, began to see mere contacts between the FBI and the Criminal Division as a proxy for improper direction and control. Significantly, OIPR viewed its role primarily as an officer of the FISA court and therefore responsible for stewardship of the court's responsibilities. It viewed its role as an advocate for its institutional clients as secondary. This would materially affect how OIPR handled the subsequent problems that arose regarding FISA applications. . . .

Broader Complaints Regarding Application of the Procedures

General concerns about the application of the procedures persisted, however, so that in October 1997 the Attorney General announced that she wanted to improve information sharing between the FBI and the Criminal Division in foreign intelligence matters. She established a working group consisting of OIPR, the FBI, and the Criminal Division to recommend changes. It was chaired by Daniel Seikaly, Deputy Director of EONS. During the working group meetings the FBI conceded that its agents were going to OIPR to ask permission to approach the Criminal Division rather than contacting the Criminal Division directly as mandated by the 1995 procedures. The Criminal Division complained that the FBI Office of General Counsel and OIPR had opined that mere contacts between investigators and the Criminal Division created an appearance of improper direction and control. It also complained that it had heard that if too much contact occurred that OIPR would refuse to present any further FISA applications in the particular case. Seikaly concluded that the Attorney General's memorandum was being "ignored" by both the FBI and OIPR. . . .

While the Department of Justice was considering reforms to the 1995 procedures to increase information sharing, the FISA court—with OIPR's concurrence—imposed additional restrictions. Over the course of 2000 OIPR had informed the FISA court of numerous errors in prior FISA applications, particularly as to the existence and nature of any parallel criminal investigations. The court reacted by imposing additional restrictions on information sharing. For all Bin Ladin-related FISAs the court ordered that no information obtained from such FISAs could be shared with criminal prosecutors (including the United States Attorney's Office in New York or anyone in the Criminal Division) or FBI agents working on any related criminal matter without the court's permission.

In November 2000 the court added a requirement that no one in the FBI or the Department of Justice, including persons working solely on intelligence investigations, could see any FISA material before signing a form acknowledging that they understood the restrictions on sharing any of the information they obtained. One attorney in the FBI's National Security Law Unit reported at the time that, based on his discussions with OIPR, he believed the FISA court would no longer permit criminal prosecutors to give any advice to the FBI agents working on intelligence matters. The attorney also believed that the court's wall was about to be applied to more FISA applications and thus supersede the 1995 procedures entirely.

The parties returned in December that year with slight modifications but still no unanimity on reform. OIPR continued to insist that Criminal Division advice had to be restricted. The Attorney General again rejected the proposal on the grounds that it was not unanimous.

The December reform attempt also suffered from the court's unhappiness with the numerous factual errors in the applications it had received, including erroneous descriptions of the walls between intelligence and criminal investigations. Reform proponents recognized that even if the Attorney General had approved the reforms, the FISA court would also have had to approve the new procedures. The reform proponents recognized that the court would be unlikely to approve any changes that sought to increase information sharing, let alone expand the type of advice the prosecutors could provide to intelligence agents. Thus, achieving reform would likely require an appeal to the FISC court of review. This was considered particularly risky because the court of review had never before convened. Moreover, one of its judges had previously indicated doubts about the constitutionality of the FISA statute. Thus an appeal could risk the ability to obtain future FISA warrants.

The problems with errors in FISA applications continued. On March 9, 2001, Chief Judge Lamberth of the FISA court wrote to Attorney General John Ashcroft that because of the continued errors on a series of FISA applications, the FISA court was banning a supervisory FBI agent who had been involved in preparing the particular applications. . . .

The Erection of Internal FBI Walls

By the Summer of 2001, internal walls between FBI agents working on intelligence matters and FBI agents working on criminal matters were in place, at least in matters relating to Bin Ladin. These walls did not preclude information sharing between the agents but governed the circumstances and means by which the information could be shared. We sought to determine when and why such procedures were implemented.

The July 1995 procedures were silent on the issue of information sharing within the FBI. We found no witnesses who recalled when internal FBI information sharing procedures were first instituted. Jim Baker, head of OIPR since 2001, said he was not aware of any documents establishing internal FBI walls. He believed the concept was already in place when he arrived in 1996. Former FBI General Counsel Larry Parkinson believed that the absence of such procedures was an oversight. Given the fact that Scruggs had originally proposed such walls prior to the creation of the July 1995 procedures and the March 1995 memorandum included them, it appears more likely that the parties to the July 1995 procedures intentionally rejected internal FBI walls. We found no documents reporting any discussion of such walls during the development of the July 1995 procedures.

The absence of discussion may also be a reflection that there was no perceived need for internal FBI walls to satisfy the primary purpose standard. Although the FBI had different designations for investigations depending on whether they were an intelligence or criminal matter—terrorism intelligence investigations were designated as 199 cases and criminal terrorism investigations were designated as 265 cases—the FBI did not distinguish between agents. All agents attended the same academy and received most of their training in how to conduct criminal cases. Any agent on a counterterrorism squad could work both 199 and 265 cases. These separate designations for different types of investigations were an internal administrative matter for the FBI and had no impact on whether criminal charges could be instituted.

More significantly perhaps, FBI agents had no authority to actually institute criminal proceedings. Only Department of Justice prosecutors could open a case in a grand jury, present witnesses, and obtain an indictment. Applications for criminal warrants and the filing of criminal charges in the district court required approval of a prosecutor. The series of cases applying the primary purpose standard routinely found that cases became criminal when prosecutors became involved. They did not consider what internal designation the FBI used to file its cases and did not look to see whether an agent wore an intelligence or criminal hat. It was solely the presence of prosecutors that changed the nature of the cases in the courts' eyes. Thus, while prosecutors could not direct or control the FISA process, any FBI agent could do so. . . .

This linear approach—first intelligence case and then criminal case—worked fairly well in traditional FCI matters. An investigation of a potential spy was first an intelligence investigation to determine who and what were involved. When this information was gathered criminal charges could be instituted, the individual would be arrested, his access to sensitive materials would end, and the criminal case could proceed.

As the respective parties would come to realize, terrorism cases were not so neat. There could be multiple plots and overlapping participants, and bringing criminal charges against one set of individuals did not end the need for ongoing intelligence. This was clearly demonstrated with regard to Bin Ladin. He was first indicted in June 1998 but he was not apprehended and he continued to plan and execute more terrorist acts. In August 1998 he directed the East Africa embassy bombings and a superseding indictment was brought. Concerns about additional plots around the Millennium required extensive intelligence gathering about possible future acts while Bin Ladin remained criminally charged for prior acts. These scenarios altered the traditional view of sequential investigations.

Thus, it is clear why an internal FBI wall was in place in the March 1995 memorandum but not the July 1995 procedures. In the cases covered by the March memorandum the sequence of cases had been reversed—the criminal case preceded the intelligence case. Thus, OIPR was concerned that agents who were working on an active criminal case—and thus working closely with and often at the direction of criminal prosecutors—could be perceived to be directing FISA coverage for the ongoing criminal case. The July procedures, however, implicitly presumed sequential cases. . . .

In December 1999 there was overwhelming concern about possible terrorist attacks scheduled to coincide with the Millennium. Record numbers of FISA applications were being filed with the court. Many of these applications provided for coverage of individuals and facilities believed to be related to Bin Ladin. The problem was that there was already a criminal indictment returned against Bin Ladin. This posed a dilemma for OIPR. Normally once a criminal case was opened OIPR would no longer present applications for FISA coverage. Here, however, Bin Ladin was not in custody and there was fear that he was planning further attacks. Thus, there was an acute need for additional intelligence collection and it needed to be approved quickly. OIPR and the FISA court resolved this dilemma by making the court the wall and specifying that information gathered pursuant to these particular FISA warrants could not be shared with criminal prosecutors or FBI agents working on the Bin Ladin-related criminal cases without first obtaining the court's permission. Thus, a distinction was made between agents collecting new intelligence and those assigned to particular criminal investigations. . . .

Because of the court's dissatisfaction with the lax manner in which information had been shared, it began requiring that all persons within the FBI and the Department of Justice who received information from this FISA coverage sign a certification that they understood the court's limits on how and when such information could be shared. Although the additional restrictions applied only to specific FISA warrants, it is apparent that the FBI began applying these additional restrictions to its handling of other unrelated FISA coverage. Thus, by late November 2000 the incentive to share information with fellow agents all but disappeared.

The NSA Caveats

The National Security Agency (NSA) also placed restrictions on the sharing and use of information it collected. Initially these restrictions merely governed the use of its reporting in criminal matters. In December 1999, however, the NSA began placing new, more restrictive caveats on its Bin Ladin-related reporting. These caveats precluded sharing the information contained in these NSA reports with criminal prosecutors or investigators without obtaining OIPR's permission.

These new caveats were the result of NSA's and the Department of Justice's overabundance of caution. During the Millennium crisis the Attorney General authorized electronic surveillance of three individuals overseas. Because these searches were not within the United States, no FISA warrant was required. The Attorney General could authorize these searches pursuant to Executive Order 12333. The information that led to these targets, however, had initially been obtained from FISA-authorized surveillances. Thus, in an abundance of caution, the Attorney General conditioned these surveillances on a requirement that any reporting from these surveillances bear caveats preventing the sharing of any of the reporting with criminal investigators or prosecutors without first obtaining OIPR's permission.

Because of the complexity of determining which Bin Ladin-related reporting was derived from these particular authorizations, NSA decided to place identical caveats on all Bin Ladin-related reporting, not just that authorized by the Attorney General. These caveats were added to NSA's Bin Ladin-related reporting on December 30, 1999. . . .

The Wall in the Summer of 2001

Attorney General John Ashcroft testified to the Commission that specific information sharing failures in the summer of 2001 arose from Attorney General Reno's July 1995 procedures and specifically from the March 1995 memorandum signed by Deputy Attorney General Gorelick. A review of the facts surrounding the information sharing failures, however, demonstrate that the Attorney General's testimony did not fairly and accurately reflect the significance of the 1995 documents and their relevance to the 2001 discussions.

There were three occasions in the summer of 2001 when questions were raised regarding what information could be shared and with whom. One occasion involved decisions whether to seek a criminal warrant or a FISA warrant for Zacarias Moussaoui's laptop computer and other possessions. The other two of these occasions related to information gathered by the NSA in December 1999 regarding Khalid al Mihdhar and Nawaf al Hazmi. We examined these incidents to determine what, if any, role the July 1995 procedures had on the failure to share relevant information.

The Moussaoui Investigation

On August 15, 2001, the Minneapolis FBI Field Office received information that an individual named Zacarias Moussaoui was taking flight lessons at the Pan Am International Flight Academy in Eagan, Minnesota. Moussaoui had attracted the attention of the academy's flight instructors because, among other factors, despite having little knowledge of flying he wanted to learn how to "take off and land" a Boeing 747. The Minneapolis FBI agent assigned to investigate further was extremely suspicious of Moussaoui's intentions and believed he might be intending to hijack a plane.

Because it was not clear that there was sufficient information of a criminal plot, the agent opened an intelligence investigation. The agent went promptly to work on gathering information regarding Moussaoui's intentions. Minneapolis and FBI Headquarters debated whether Moussaoui should be arrested immediately or surveilled to obtain further information. Because it was not clear that Moussaoui could be imprisoned for criminal charges, the FBI case agent decided the most important thing to do was to prevent Moussaoui from obtaining any further training he could later use to carry out a potential attack. As a French national who had overstayed his visa, Moussaoui could be detained immediately by the Immigration and Naturalization Service (INS). The INS arrested Moussaoui on the immigration violation on August 16. A deportation order was signed on August 17, 2001.

Upon arresting Moussaoui it was determined that he had a laptop computer and a bag containing numerous papers and other materials. The FBI case agent believed that whatever Moussaoui had planned might be described in either the laptop or the other papers. The agent could not examine these materials, however, without obtaining a search warrant. The agent contacted the Minneapolis USAO and gave some hypothetical information similar to the Moussaoui facts to determine whether there was sufficient information to obtain a criminal search warrant. The Assistant United States Attorney told the agent they were close to having sufficient information. The agent did not ask for a final opinion on a criminal warrant and did not present an application for such a warrant to the USAO. . . .

At one point the Minneapolis Field Office indicated that it wanted to open a parallel criminal investigation of Moussaoui on the belief that he was planning to conduct a hijacking. FBI Headquarters ordered Minneapolis not to open a criminal case because it believed that the existence of a parallel criminal case might have a negative impact of the FISA court's willingness to authorize a FISA warrant. There was nothing in the law or the July 1995 procedures that precluded opening a parallel criminal case. Headquarters's decision was based solely on its and OIPR's beliefs about possible reactions of the FISA court, not on actual rules governing the circumstances. . . .

Eventually FBI Headquarters determined that there was insufficient information linking Moussaoui to a foreign power to obtain a FISA warrant and decided not to send an application to OIPR for its consideration. FBI Headquarters decided to deport Moussaoui without obtaining a FISA warrant to search his belongings.

Once the decision was made not to seek a FISA warrant, there was no barrier preventing the Field Office from returning to the USAO in Minneapolis to seek a possible criminal warrant. The concern of Part B about retaining the possibility of a future FISA warrant was no longer relevant once any idea of obtaining a FISA warrant had been abandoned. The witnesses all said, however, that they just did not think about that option at the time. Once the idea of obtaining a criminal warrant had been abandoned in favor of trying to obtain a FISA warrant, no one gave a criminal warrant another thought.

In sum, the central question of whether a FISA warrant should have been applied for or could have been obtained was not governed by the July 1995 procedures. The sole issue in the Moussaoui matter that the procedures governed was the circumstances under which the Field Office could have contacted the local USAO to discuss a possible criminal case once an intelligence case had already been opened. As FBI Headquarters never pursued obtaining the required permission, we cannot say whether it would have been granted. . . .

Conclusion

As the review of the facts demonstrates, whatever the merits of the March 1995 Gorelick memorandum and the Attorney General's July 1995 procedures on information sharing, they did not control the decisions that were made in the summer of 2001. The Gorelick memorandum applied to only two specific cases, neither of which was involved (or even still existed) in the summer of 2001. The July 1995 procedures did not govern the sharing of information gathered by NSA, CIA, the State Department, or INS and thus did not apply to the information regarding Hazmi and Mihdhar that the analyst had to share with the criminal agent. Moreover, the July 1995 procedures did not govern whether information could be shared among FBI agents. . . .

What had happened was a growing battle within the Department of Justice during the 1990s, and between parts of Justice and the FISA court, over the scope of OIPR's screening function and the propriety of using FISA-derived information in criminal matters. The FISA court's concern with FBI sloppiness also began to take a toll, resulting in [redacted] the FBI being required to separately designate criminal and intelligence agents; and the court banning one FBI supervisor from appearing before it. By late 2000, these factors had culminated in a set of complex rules and a widening set of beliefs—a bureaucratic culture—that discouraged FBI agents from even seeking to share intelligence information. Neither Attorney General Reno nor Attorney General Ashcroft acted to resolve the conflicting views within the Department of Justice or challenged the strict interpretation of the FISA statute espoused by the FISA court and OIPR.

It is clear, therefore, that the information sharing failures in the summer of 2001 were not the result of legal barriers but of the failure of individuals to understand that the barriers did not apply to the facts at hand. Simply put, there was no legal reason why the information could not have been shared.

Source: http://fas.org/irp/eprint/wall.pdf.

Statement on the Need to Reform Congress by Chairman Thomas Kean and Vice Chair Lee Hamilton, Final Report of the 9/11 Public Discourse Project, December 5, 2005

After the 9/11 Commission formally disbanded on August 24, 2004, the 10 commissioners continued to work together to educate the public, promote the 41 commission recommendations, and keep an eye on how Congress implemented reform. Deputy Executive Director Christopher Kojm headed the 9/11 Public Discourse Project, which began its work immediately after the 9/11 Commission ended its work, and the 9/11 Commission's spokesman, Alvin Felzenberg, continued as lead press contact. Cribbing from the experience responding to Hurricane Katrina, Kean and Hamilton called for faster implementation of key reforms. We are safer, but not as safe as we need to be, they said: "Many obvious steps that Americans assume have been completed have not been." Kean and Hamilton believed progress had been made in strengthening U.S. defenses against terrorism and noted the creation of a National Counterterrorism Center and a director of national intelligence. But much work remained, including the need to improve the sharing of intelligence information and the need for reforms within the FBI. One area, however, where improvement was needed that had not been addressed was that of congressional oversight. In all the reforms instituted since 9/11, Congress had yet to reform itself.

STATEMENT ON THE NEED TO REFORM CONGRESS, DECEMBER 5, 2005

. . . Now more than ever Congress needs powerful Intelligence and Homeland Security oversight Committees.

Why?—Because the Congress has provided powerful authorities to the Executive branch in order to protect us. It has created a Director of National Intelligence, a National Counterterrorism Center, and given the Executive branch powers to investigate citizens and inspect their documents.

Congress now needs to be an effective check and balance on the Executive branch in carrying out the counterterrorism policies of the United States.

Because so much information is classified, Congress is the only source of independent oversight on the full breadth of intelligence and homeland security issues before our country.

Last year, the word we heard most often on Capitol Hill describing this oversight was "dysfunctional."

The oversight Committees need stronger powers over the budget, and exclusive jurisdiction. When too many Committees are responsible, nobody is responsible.

The Congress cannot play its proper role under the Constitution to provide a check and balance on the actions of the Executive if its oversight committees are weak.

Strong oversight by the Congress protects our liberties and makes our policies better. Our freedom and safety depend on robust oversight by the Congress. . . .

Finally, we call upon our elected leaders. The first purpose of government, in the preamble of our Constitution, is to "provide for the common defense." We have made clear, time and again, what we believe needs to be done to make our country safer and more secure: The responsibility for action, and leadership, rests with Congress and the President.

We ask each of you to recall that day, September 11th, 2001. It was a day of unbearable suffering. It was also a day when we were united as Americans. We came together as citizens with a sense of urgency, and with a sense of purpose.

We call upon our elected leaders to come together with that same sense of urgency and purpose.

The terrorists do not target Republicans or Democrats—they target Americans. We will not defeat them as Republicans or Democrats—we will defeat them by working together.

We call upon our political leaders to act as one again, on a bipartisan basis, to take all necessary steps to make our country safer and more secure. The American people deserve no less.

Sources: http://govinfo.library.unt.edu/911/report/911Report_Exec.htm; www.9-11pdp.org/press/2005-12-05_statement.pdf.

Bibliography

Bergen, Peter L. *Holy War, Inc.: Inside the Secret World of Osama bin Laden.* New York: Touchstone/Simon & Schuster, 2002.

Ben-Veniste, Richard. *The Emperor's New Clothes: Exposing the Truth from Watergate to 9/11.* New York: Thomas Dunne Books, 2009. Chapter 5.

Clarke, Richard A. *Against All Enemies: Inside America's War on Terror.* New York: Free Press, 2004.

Cleland, Max. *Heart of a Patriot: How I Found the Courage to Survive Vietnam, Walter Reed and Karl Rove.* New York: Simon & Schuster, 2010.

Coll, Steve. *Ghost Wars: The Secret History of the CIA, Afghanistan, and Bin Laden, from the Soviet Invasion to September 10, 2001.* New York: Penguin Press, 2004.

Dale Scott, Peter. *The Road to 9/11: Wealth, Empire, and the Future of America.* Berkeley and Los Angeles: University of California Press, 2007.

Diamond, John. *The CIA and the Culture of Failure: U.S. Intelligence from the End of the Cold War to the Invasion of Iraq.* Palo Alto, Calif.: Stanford University Press, 2008.

Farmer, John. *The Ground Truth: The Untold Story of America Under Attack on 9/11.* New York: Riverhead Books, 2009.

Felzenberg, Alvin S. *Governor Tom Kean: From the New Jersey Statehouse to the 9-11 Commission.* New Brunswick, N.J.: Rivergate Books, 2006.

Filson, Leslie. *Air War Over America: Sept. 11 Alters Face of Air Defense Mission.* Tyndall Air Force Base, Fla.: Headquarters 1st Airforce, 2003.

Graham, Bob. *Intelligence Matters: The CIA, the FBI, Saudi Arabia, and the Failure of America's War on Terror.* Lawrence: University Press of Kansas, 2008.

Hersh, Seymour. *Chain of Command: The Road from 9/11 to Abu Ghraib.* New York: Harper Perennial, 2005.

Johnson, Loch K. *A Season of Inquiry: Congress and Intelligence.* Chicago: Dorsey Press, 1988.

Kean, Thomas, and Lee Hamilton. *Without Precedent: The Inside Story of the 9/11 Commission.* New York: Vintage, 2007.

Kitts, Kenneth. *Presidential Commissions & National Security: The Politics of Damage Control.* Boulder, Colo.: Lynne Rienner, 2006.

National Commission on Terrorist Attacks. *The 9/11 Commission Report: Final Report of the National Commission on Terrorist Attacks upon the United States.* New York: W. W. Norton & Company, 2004.

Pillar, Paul R. *Good Literature and Bad History: The 9/11 Commission's Tale of Strategic Intelligence.* London: Intelligence and National Security, 2006.

Posner, Gerald. *Why America Slept: The Failure to Prevent 9/11.* New York: Random House, 2003.

Posner, Richard. *Preventing Surprise Attacks: Intelligence Reform in the Wake of 9/11.* Stanford, Calif.: Hoover Institution, 2005.

Ray Griffin, David. *The Mysterious Collapse of World Trade Center 7: Why the Final Official Report about 9/11 Is Unscientific and False.* Northampton, Mass.: Olive Branch Press, 2010.

Senate Committee on Intelligence and House Permanent Select Committee on Intelligence. *Joint Inquiry into Intelligence Community Activities Before and After the Terrorist Attacks of September 11, 2001.* Washington, D.C.: Government Printing Office, 2002.

Shenon, Philip. *The Commission: The Uncensored History of the 9/11 Investigation.* New York: Twelve, 2008.

Smith, Dennis. *Report from Ground Zero: The Story of the Rescue Efforts at the World Trade Center.* New York: Viking Penguin, 2003.

Tenet, George. *At the Center of the Storm: My Years at the CIA.* New York: Harper Collins, 2007.

Thompson, Paul. *The Terror Timeline: A Comprehensive Chronicle of the Road to 9/11—and America's Response.* New York: Harper Collins, 2004.

Wright, Lawrence. *The Looming Tower: Al-Qaeda and the Road to 9/11.* New York: Alfred A. Knopf, 2006.

Zegart, Amy B. *Spying Blind: The CIA, the FBI and the Origins of 9/11.* Princeton, N.J.: Princeton University Press, 2007.

Official Internet Resources

The National Commission on Terrorist Acts Upon the United States: www.9-11commission.gov/. The 9/11 Commission's Web site includes the final report, hearings, staff monographs and statements, lists of witnesses, news releases, and audio, video, and transcripts of public events. The site was frozen on September 20, 2004. Noting can be added, deleted, or altered. The official government edition was released on July 22, 2004. It is available on the Internet at www.gpoaccess.gov/911/Index.html.

The 9/11 Public Discourse Project: www.9-11pdp.org/. After the 9/11 Commission disbanded, the 10 commissioners set up a nonprofit entity to track and assess implementation of commission recommendations. The Web site includes transcripts of hearings, reports, and public statements.

9/11 Commission papers at the National Archives: www.archives.gov/research/9-11-commission/. The National Archives and Records Administration has opened more than 150 cubic feet of records of the 9/11 Commission—just over one-third of the collection. Documents include summaries of more than 1,200 interviews, or Memorandums for the Record (MFR); the front-office files, including agendas and minutes of commission meetings; work plans, notes on interviews, requests for documents, and other records of eight work teams; and news clippings and files of the 9/11 Commission's New York Office. Nearly two-thirds of the collection has yet to be processed or is still classified.

Other Internet Resources

Ahmed, Nafeez. The Cutting Edge. http://nafeez.blogspot.com/.

Architects and Engineers for 9/11 Truth. www.ae911truth.org/.

Hence, Kyle F., and Ray Nowosielski. 9/11 Citizens Watch. http://911citizenswatch.org.

MalcontentX. "Unanswered Questions." www.communitycurrency.org/MainIndexMX.html

9/11Blogger.com. www.911blogger.com.

9/11Truth.org. www.911Truth.org.

Pilots for 9/11 Truth. http://pilotsfor911truth.org/.

Ryan, Kevin, Frank Legge, and Steven Jones. Journal of 9/11 Studies. www.journalof911studies.com/.

Thompson, Paul, et al. "Complete 9/11 Timeline," History Commons. www.historycommons.org/project.jsp?project=911_

Interviews (all by the author):

Ben-Veniste, Richard (member, National Commission on Terrorist Attacks Upon the United States), October 5, 2009. Phone interview.

Byman, Daniel (staff member, House/Senate Joint Inquiry and staff member National Commission on Terrorist Attacks Upon the United States). September 28, 2009. Phone interview.

Casazza, Patty (member, 9-11 Family Steering Committee). January 9, 2010. Phone interview.

Cinquegrana, Rick (deputy director, House/Senate Joint Inquiry). September 30, 2009. Phone interview.

Dunkee, William (minority staff director, Senate Select Committee on Intelligence). March 30, 2009. Phone interview.

Farmer, John (former attorney general, New Jersey; staff member, National Commission on Terrorist Attacks Upon the United States). September 14, 2009. Phone interview.

Felzenburg, Alvin (principal spokesman, National Commission on Terrorist Attacks Upon the United States and the 9/11 Public Discourse Project). December 11, 2009. Washington, D.C.

Fetchett, Mary (founding director, Voices of September 11). July 10, 2009. Phone Interview.

Fielding, Fred (member, National Commission on Terrorist Attacks Upon the United States). January 29, 2010. Law office, Washington D.C.

Gorelick, Jamie (member, National Commission on Terrorist Attacks Upon the United States). October 28, 2009. Phone interview, e-mails.

Gorton, Slade (former Republican senator from Oregon; member, National Commission on Terrorist Attacks Upon the United States). June 8, 2009. Law office, Washington, D.C.

Hamilton, Lee (former Democratic representative from Indiana; vice chair, National Commission on Terrorist Attacks Upon the United States). April 21, 2009, and January 7, 2010. Washington D.C.

Hence, Kyle (cofounder, 9/11 Citizens Watch). January 6, 2010. Phone interview.

Hill, Eleanor (director, House/Senate Joint Inquiry). March 25 and April 29, 2009. Law office, Washington D.C.

Jacobson, Michael (staff member, House/Senate Joint Inquiry). September 30, 2009. Phone interview.

Johnson, Loch (professor of political science, University of Georgia). April 17, 2009. Phone interview.

Kean, Thomas (former Republican governor, New Jersey; chair, National Commission on Terrorist Attacks Upon the United States). April 2, 2009, and January 29, 2010. Phone interviews.

Kerrey, Bob (former Democratic senator from Nebraska; member, National Commission on Terrorist Attacks Upon the United States). January 12, 2010. Phone interviews.

Kojm, Christopher (deputy director, National Commission on Terrorist Attacks Upon the United States). May 29, 2009. Washington D.C.

Latas, Jeff (cofounder, Pilots for 9/11Truth; former president, U.S. Air Force Investigative Board; commercial pilot). February 10, 2010. Phone interview.

Lemack, Carie (co-founder Families of September 11). May 5, 2009. The Christian Science Monitor Bureau, Washington D.C.

MalcontentX (anonymous author, "Unanswered Questions"). February 10, 2010. Phone interview.

Pillar, Paul (former senior analyst, Central Intelligence Agency; director of studies, security studies program, Georgetown University). May 27, 2009. Georgetown University office.

Roemer, Timothy (former Democratic representative from Indiana; member, House/Senate Joint Inquiry and the National Commission on Terrorist Attacks Upon the United States). April 20, 2009. Center for National Policy, Washington D.C.

Rowley, Coleen (former Minneapolis FBI agent). August 24, 2009, and January 29, 2010. Phone interviews.

Schiavo, Mary (attorney, Motley Rice). August 25, 2009. Phone interview.

Snider, L. Britt (first staff director, House/Senate Joint Inquiry). September 29, 2009. Phone interview.

Webster, William (former director, Federal Bureau of Investigation; former director, Central Intelligence Agency). May 21, 2009. Law office, Washington D.C.

Zegart, Amy (associate professor of public policy, University of California at Los Angeles). July 10, 2009. Phone interview.

Zelikow, Philip (executive director, 9/11 Commission). E-mail message to author, May 14, 2009.

Zogby, John (pollster and president, Zogby International). January 9, 2010. Phone interview.

The Hurricane Katrina Inquiry, 2005–06

By Roger A. Bruns

> We were abandoned. City officials did nothing to protect us. We were told to go to the Superdome, the Convention Center, the interstate bridge for safety. We did this more than once. In fact, we tried them all for every day over a week. We saw buses, helicopters and FEMA [Federal Emergency Management Agency] trucks, but no one stopped to help us. We never felt so cut off in all our lives. When you feel like this you do one of two things, you either give up or go into survival mode. We chose the latter. This is how we made it. We slept next to dead bodies, we slept on streets at least four times next to human feces and urine. There was garbage everywhere in the city. Panic and fear had taken over.
>
> —*Patricia Thompson, New Orleans citizen and evacuee (House Select Bipartisan Committee to Investigate the Preparation for and Response to Hurricane Katrina, December 6, 2005)*

It was the greatest natural disaster in the United States in more than a century. On August 29, 2005, Hurricane Katrina blasted into the historic Louisiana city of New Orleans. The storm became a tragedy of grievous proportions in lives and damage. More than 1,800 people perished. Katrina, unlike the horrendous storm a hundred years earlier, was not a mysterious occurrence, the news of which trickled through the pages of the nation's newspapers days after the event. Here, in New Orleans, with a worldwide television-viewing audience watching the unfolding events, the horror was palpable: the surging waters; the desperate families, most of them African Americans, trying to find shelter; the frightened calls for help; the growing hopelessness as ancient levees fractured; and the increasing awareness that assistance was disorganized.

Apathy and Neglect

They had known it was coming. For many years, weather experts, geologists, and others in the scientific community warned of the potential horrific consequences if an especially strong hurricane rocked New Orleans and the surrounding Gulf region. The existence of the city, surrounded by the waters of Lake Pontchartrain and the Mississippi River, depended on an aging system of levees. A break in the levees would mean a city engulfed in water.

In a number of reports, experts warned that in the event of a major hurricane the levees would likely crack, and thousands of residents in the lower sections of New Orleans would face a massive wall of water that could

Water from a levee along the Inner Harbor Navigational Canal pours into the city after the structure broke under the force of Hurricane Katrina. An estimated 80 percent of New Orleans was under floodwaters after levees broke around Lake Ponchartrain. The water level in New Orleans continued to rise, forcing the evacuation of thousands of residents, many of whom took refuge in the Superdome. (©Vincent Laforet/EPA/CORBIS)

OVERVIEW

Background

One of the most devastating natural disasters in the history of the United States, the hurricane called Katrina that struck the Gulf Coast in 2005, tested the effectiveness and determination of the country's governmental first responders to protect lives, especially in the city of New Orleans, Louisiana. Those government agencies and officials, for the most part, performed with abysmal coordination and lack of speed. More than 1,800 Americans lost their lives; thousands of others were injured and rendered homeless. Why had federal, state, and local officials not taken decisive action in evacuating New Orleans when evidence of the potential catastrophe had become known days before the hurricane hit the coast? What failures in planning and execution led to such loss and suffering?

Congress Investigates

Although Democratic members of Congress called for the appointment of a national commission to investigate the Katrina disaster, Republicans, who controlled both houses of Congress, decided to limit the investigation. Congress conducted narrow inquiries in both the Senate and the House of Representatives.

Impact

The George W. Bush administration initially pledged to cooperate with congressional investigators. When the investigative work in committees of both houses got under way, however, the White House began to stonewall, citing issues of separation of powers and executive privilege. Even though the investigations were led by Republican members of Congress, the administration refused repeated requests for testimony and documents.

The reports from both the Senate and House committees attacked the performance of the president, the Department of Homeland Security, the Federal Emergency Management Agency, and others involved in the Katrina disaster. Nevertheless, because of the resistance of the Bush administration in cooperating with the inquiries, the efforts by Congress to investigate Katrina were compromised. Three years after the disaster, a number of investigations relating to Katrina continued in several congressional committees. The reports from House and Senate investigations addressed many important questions about the lack of preparedness and the breakdown of emergency relief at the federal, state, and local levels. New Orleans and most of the Gulf Coast, however, remain as vulnerable to major hurricanes as these areas were before Katrina.

result in thousands of deaths. Scientists worked up computer models that plotted the likely paths of destruction through the city, in which a ravaging force of wind and water would require rooftop rescues of those who had not evacuated. They told of the likelihood of a water supply suddenly turned toxic, a disease-carrying gumbo of waste and pollution.

On June 24, 2002, more than three years before Katrina struck, the New Orleans *Times-Picayune,* in a story titled "The Big One," warned that "a major hurricane could decimate the region, but flooding from an even moderate storm could kill thousands. It's just a matter of time."

Three years before Katrina, journalist Daniel Zwerdling of National Public Radio produced several reports on the dangers of a hurricane hitting New Orleans. His reports were eerily prescient. After Katrina hit, Zwerdling contacted a number of scientists who had provided the information in the stories. Later he said sadly, "A couple of them started crying when I asked them after Katrina what it was like to see some of their predictions come alive."

In July 2004, the Federal Emergency Management Agency (FEMA) conducted a disaster exercise to assess the needs and readiness of the agency and others to respond to a severe hurricane. The exercise concluded that a fleet of buses would be needed to evacuate 100,000 people from New Orleans because they would have no other way out. The exercise also predicted widespread flooding in hospitals and nursing homes, desperate conditions at an undersupplied Louisiana Superdome, and a lack of responders and resources to mount search-and-rescue missions.

Thus, city, state, and national leaders knew of the dangers of the weakening infrastructure of New Orleans. They knew of the critical necessity for proper

CHRONOLOGY

2005

- *August 26:* The National Hurricane Center warns that Hurricane Katrina is expected to reach Category 4 intensity before making landfall in Mississippi or Louisiana. In anticipation of the possible devastation, Governor Haley Barbour of Mississippi and Governor Kathleen Blanco of Louisiana declare states of emergency.
- *August 27:* President George W. Bush declares a state of emergency in Louisiana. Highways leading out of New Orleans fill up with traffic.
- *August 28:* The National Hurricane Center issues a dire warning that a catastrophic hurricane is about to hit. As Katrina winds reach 175 mph, Mayor Ray Nagin of New Orleans orders a mandatory evacuation of the city.
- *August 29:* Katrina hits the Gulf Coast. In New Orleans, two major flood-control levees are breached, and the National Weather Service reports "total structural failure" in parts of the city. Ten thousand people take refuge in the Louisiana Superdome. Many die in flooded neighborhoods ravaged by as much as 20 feet of water.
- *August 30:* New Orleans is left with no power, no drinking water, dwindling food supplies, and fires. Thousands seek refuge in city shelters.
- *August 31:* President Bush flies over the Gulf Coast in Air Force One to survey the damage. Evacuations from the Louisiana Superdome to the Houston Astrodome begin.
- *September 1:* In New Orleans, stranded people remain in buildings, on roofs, or gathered in large groups on higher ground. Violence disrupts relief efforts as authorities rescue trapped residents and try to evacuate thousands of others. More than 1,800 would perish as a result of Katrina.
- *September 2:* The U.S. Senate Committee on Homeland Security and Governmental Affairs announces the beginning of an investigation into the response to Katrina.
- *September 3:* Officials clear tens of thousands of evacuees from the Louisiana Superdome and the Convention Center, where they were living in squalid conditions with little food or water.
- *September 12:* Amid charges of incompetence, Michael Brown, director of the Federal Emergency Management Agency, resigns.
- *September 15:* The U.S. House of Representatives creates the Select Bipartisan Committee to Investigate the Preparation for and Response to Hurricane Katrina.
- *September 27:* Former FEMA director Michael Brown testifies before the House select committee.

2006

- *February 15:* The House select committee issues a report on Katrina.
- *May:* The Senate Committee on Homeland Security and Governmental Affairs issues a Katrina report.
- *October 4:* President Bush signs the Post-Katrina Emergency Reform Act.

disaster and evacuation plans. They knew all of this, and they did little.

New Orleans, with its diverse heritage, rich history and tradition, unique architecture, and cultural mix, was also a city with much poverty. Although a mecca for tourists, New Orleans at the time of Katrina had a large population of individuals living in poverty—nearly 30 percent. African Americans made up more than 65 percent of the city.

Many people living in the low-lying areas of the city did not have automobiles or television sets—the usual trappings necessary for transportation and information. Hidden from the upper enclaves of New Orleans society, many of these individuals were living on welfare, often in woefully substandard conditions. They had no credit cards. Many were illiterate. Even if an evacuation notice reached them, many did not have the means to leave the area. It was well known that any successful attempt to evacuate such a population would have to find sufficient means to spread the word about an impending disaster and provide ways for the people to leave, presumably by a fleet of buses or other vehicles.

Although a group of city officials had begun steps to contract with a variety of transportation companies to help move residents who could not evacuate on their own in case of a hurricane, the officials had not yet signed the contracts. The New Orleans Fire Department, the official lead agency for urban search and rescue in a city surrounded by water, owned no boats. The police had only seven. Not only were New Orleans officials unprepared for the disaster, but Louisiana and the federal government also were not ready. With budget dilemmas facing governments at all levels, money for infrastructure and disaster planning was woefully lacking. The emergency-response capability of the United States, once the envy of countries across the world, had slipped dangerously because of budget cuts and neglect. The city of New Orleans was ill-prepared to face what was coming.

The Storm Approaches

At 11 A.M. on Friday, August 26, 2005, with both local and national weather forecasters warning of a major catastrophic storm headed toward New Orleans, Kathleen Blanco, governor of Louisiana, declared a state of emergency for the state. Nevertheless, she did not notify President George W. Bush until Saturday about the kinds of federal relief that were needed. Her request was in a form letter used by governors to communicate with federal officials.

On Saturday, August 27, at noon, New Orleans mayor Ray Nagin said at a news briefing in City Hall that "although the track could change, forecasters believe Hurricane Katrina will affect New Orleans. We may call for a voluntary evacuation later this afternoon or tomorrow afternoon." Nagin's reluctance to call an immediate and mandatory evacuation appeared to some observers as a breathtakingly tepid response to a budding catastrophe. Reports from the National Hurricane Center indicated that the storm was gaining intensity by the minute and its track was straight toward New Orleans. These were precious minutes, and they were wasting away.

Neither Governor Blanco nor Mayor Nagin saw the need to activate emergency plans to deploy buses or rescue boats. Nagin was concerned that a hasty mandatory evacuation might subject his office to future lawsuits from hotels and other businesses if the hurricane passed harmlessly by New Orleans.

In facing such a crisis as Katrina, federal officials in Washington were supposed to follow the so-called National Response Plan, which had been formed to establish clear lines of communication in case of a disaster. The plan was designed to create a formal chain of command and a flow of orders and directions to the mobilization teams. Under the plan, the president was supposed to trigger the response to a threat by declaring an emergency. In the case of a crisis as critical as Katrina, the secretary of the Department of Homeland Security (DHS), a new agency created after the September 11, 2001, terrorist attacks to protect American lives in the event of a national disaster, was then supposed to declare that the particular emergency was an "Incident of National Significance." That declaration would have mobilized all federal agencies, all state and local officials, and all major relief agencies that had prepared to follow the plan.

The problem with any bureaucratic set of directions that rarely needs to be used is that success depends on communication. If one link is weak, the entire chain of command can snap. In the case of Katrina, when Michael Chertoff, secretary of homeland security, was informed of the possible severity of the coming hurricane, he did not quickly respond to the outlines prescribed in the National Response Plan. He did not declare Katrina an "Incident of National Significance," as called for in the plan, he did not officially appoint a principal federal official to take charge of mobilization efforts, and he did not communicate that choice to the appropriate government agencies.

Michael Brown was head of FEMA, the DHS agency logically suited to take command of the emergency. But Brown had little background in taking on a situation such as this. Before joining FEMA, he was the judges and stewards commissioner for the International Arabian Horse Association. Brown received a briefing on August 27 from the National Hurricane Center. Nevertheless, having received no orders from Chertoff, his boss, Brown issued no orders. He waited. Meanwhile, the Weather Channel and local and national weather forecasters continued to plot the storm's seemingly inexorable path toward the city.

Without the designation as the principal official in charge, FEMA's Brown only haltingly began to line up the National Guard, other U.S. military personnel, and his own FEMA organizational team. Flustered, Brown telephoned Chertoff, saying, "I am having a horrible time. I can't get a unified command established."

Historian Douglas Brinkley, who lived in New Orleans and helped in rescue efforts, later interviewed survivors and published a stirring book on the disaster, *The Great Deluge* (2006). Brinkley wrote that a stronger personality than Brown might have overcome this obstacle. "But even Brown's GOP allies knew he was weak-kneed," Brinkley said. "The question that still haunts the events of Monday, August 29, was not, however, why Michael Brown needed post-Katrina direction and so much instruction from his boss. The important question was why Chertoff was so callous, both to Brown's specific relief needs and to the apocalyptic needs of the entire Gulf Coast region. Brown tried to maneuver around Chertoff, to appeal directly to President Bush, but it was hard to get through to the White House."

And so the tragedy unfolded under a nearly paralyzed bureaucracy. Throughout the government agencies, frantic officials wondered who was in charge. By late afternoon on Saturday, August 27, Blanco had ordered the Louisiana State Police to open all lanes of the interstate highways to outbound traffic. The roads soon filled with streams of cars and other vehicles. But in the lower areas of the city, among those most at risk for severe flooding, the sense of urgency had not taken hold. Somehow, city and state officials had not prepared the most vulnerable for what was progressively being seen as a possible tragedy of immense proportions. These people did not have cars in which to join the mass exodus on the freeways. Even though the signs were ominous, many of the residents decided to ride out the storm. Most had ridden out others.

But Katrina was not like the others. Nick Felton, president of the New Orleans Firefighters Union, told other civic leaders that he immediately needed emergency food and supplies. When one official suggested that Felton might be acting a bit alarmist, he said, "Aren't you guys watching the Weather Channel?" Felton had been through both Hurricane Betsy (1965) and Hurricane Camille (1969), and, he said, "This damn thing, at least on the Weather Channel, looked far worse."

On Sunday, August 28, at 10:11 A.M., no one had any doubts about the severity of the storm that was about to hit shore. The National Hurricane Center issued a bulletin to government officials and the media that, in full detail, predicted the catastrophic effects of the monster called Katrina. A hurricane of "unprecedented strength" would render the area around New Orleans "Uninhabitable For Weeks," the bulletin declared. It talked about destruction of homes, possible collapse of office buildings, airborne debris, uprooted trees, a vicious surge of water, and sustained hurricane winds: "PERSONS . . . PETS . . . AND LIVESTOCK EXPOSED TO THE WINDS WILL FACE CERTAIN DEATH IF STRUCK."

This was no longer some fanciful nightmare scenario; this was a nightmare come to life. So alarming was the warning that Brian Williams of *NBC Nightly News* at first thought the warning might be a hoax. As he soon learned, "it was real, every word of it."

About the same time as the terrifying alert from the National Hurricane Center, Mayor Nagin shook off the cloud of doubt and indecision. He finally decided to order a mandatory evacuation. "I wish I had better news," he said at a news conference, "but we're facing the storm most of us have feared. This is going to be an unprecedented event." He told those citizens who had no means of transportation out of the city to make their way to the Louisiana Superdome.

But where were the buses? Where were the trains that could have been used to get citizens out of the lower areas of the city? Amtrak officials later said they had offered the use of the trains to evacuate people but the city had declined. On Sunday, several trains left the New Orleans station with only a few passengers on board. At 8:30 P.M., the last train departed with many empty cars.

In the early evening of Sunday, August 28, an eerie calm pervaded the New Orleans riverbanks; birds flew skittishly about. As Mayor Nagin left the city's command center for a suite at the Hyatt hotel, light rain began to fall.

The Horror

On August 28, the evening before Katrina made landfall, the Department of Homeland Security issued a report stating that the hurricane had been upgraded to Category 5 and that "any storm rated Category 4 or greater . . . will likely lead to severe flooding and/or levee breaching. This could leave the New Orleans metro area submerged for weeks or months." The White House received the report at 1:47 A.M. on Monday, August 29. President Bush later stated that levee breaches were unanticipated.

In those early Monday-morning hours, the wind and sea blasted the Gulf Coast. By 6 A.M. Katrina was a Category 4 storm, with winds raging at over 150 miles an hour. Within two hours, a giant storm surge blasted water into the low-lying areas of the city, soon flooding most streets with 10 to 15 feet of water. At St. Rita's Nursing Home in St. Bernard Parish, southeast of New Orleans, water rushed in and killed 35 bedridden patients.

Through the next hours and days, as the storm passed through the city and levees were breached by the rampaging waters, the images defied any semblance of normalcy. Amid the surging waters, a motorboat sat atop a house. In the debris piling up in an area of the Ninth Ward, a Mack truck lay on its side. A mattress tottered on a telephone pole. The façade of a church stood erect; the rest of the church had been totally washed away.

Seven residents on top of a building chalked a message on the roof that read "Help. The water is rising." A man holding a baby uncovered the body of a dead elderly man slumped outside the Convention Center. Prisoners from New Orleans Parish Prison sat on a freeway overpass after their jail was evacuated by authorities. The owner of A. J. Produce Co. painted these words on the side of his business establishment: "Looters will be shot."

A New Orleans *Times-Picayune* reporter named Doug MacCash discovered floating balls of ants. "In addition to all of the other horrors befalling New Orleanians during the flood," he wrote, "was the creepy discovery that red ants form themselves into floating clusters to avoid drowning. As I paddled along Carrollton Avenue on Wednesday, I saw two glittering, golf ball-sized masses of ants floating beside our canoe."

Species of all kinds, including humans, tried desperately to survive. In the attics of hundreds of houses in New Orleans, family members, along with their pet dogs and cats, breathed their last gasps, pounding on the roofs above as the waters rushed over them.

Legendary pianist, singer, and songwriter Dr. John, a native of New Orleans whose blues and boogie-woogie sounds had taken root many years before in his hometown, said after the hurricane: "People told these epic stories: being in the attic with the water rising, seeing their grandfather's body in the tree outside." The musician likened the destruction of much of his beloved city to that of a hydrogen bomb. "I remember seeing dead rats," he said. "A rat is a hard critter to kill."

Thousands of people were trapped. The darkness and despair gripping the city spawned unconfirmed, alarming reports of marauders, looters, and rapists running rampant. Many of the reports turned out to be pure fiction; some did not. One report that gained surprising currency was that someone spotted a shark lurking in the fetid waters flooding the city streets.

The main destination for those wading through the waters became the Louisiana Superdome. In 1975, the Superdome had hosted its first National Football League game. One of the most celebrated marvels of American architecture, the magnificent domed stadium could hold more than 75,000 spectators for football games. On one occasion, the Rolling Stones played before a crowd of more than 80,000, with many of the crowd using the stadium field. The Superdome stood on relatively high ground. Although it was built to withstand winds of more than 200 miles an hour, some experts feared that floodwaters could possibly reach the second floor in a severe storm. Nevertheless, in late August 2005, the Superdome became the city's major shelter. It had not been so equipped.

Even as Katrina approached, city officials had not stockpiled sufficient food and supplies for people seeking refuge. No one seemed to grasp early on the possibility that, should the floodwaters break through the levees, thousands of people might be forced to use the Superdome as a shelter of last resort.

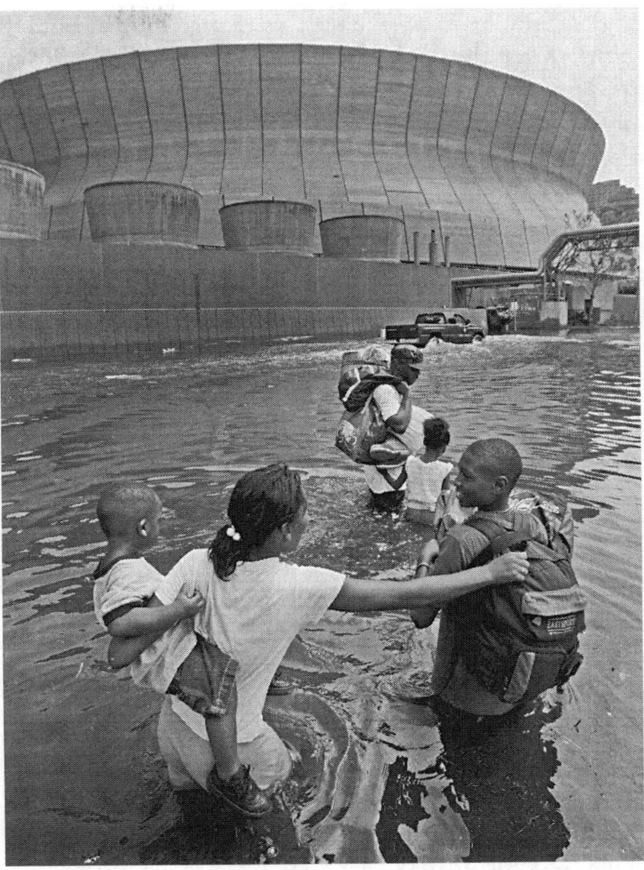

New Orleans residents make their way to the Superdome through rising floodwater from Hurricane Katrina in New Orleans on August 30, 2005. (© Michael Ainsworth/Dallas Morning News/CORBIS)

The Louisiana National Guard did deliver three truckloads of water and seven truckloads of food to supply 15,000 people for three days. But the Superdome had no water purification system, no designated medical staff, no chemical toilets, and no antibiotics.

Approximately 9,000 residents and 550 National Guardsmen rode out the first night in the Superdome as Katrina came ashore. Colonel Thomas Beron of the Louisiana National Guard later described conditions in the building as increasingly grim. The power went out, and the dome was mostly dark. Inside, with no air-conditioning, the sweltering August heat of New Orleans stifled the storm's refugees. Toilets began to overflow.

"And the other part," said Beron, "is that we had about 10,000 to 12,000 people who took shelter. . . . We think about 18,000 or 15,000 people came in the next few days afterward, where they were up on their roofs and waded to the Superdome. So, we really had overcrowding. And then, to top that off, the Superdome roof started leaking. Initially, we had people in the studio—

in the stadium seats, like they were watching a football game. When the roof started leaking, we got afraid that the Superdome roof might collapse. So, we had to move people out of those seats and into the hallways. And that just made it more tough for those people inside, no question about it."

David Duplantier, a 16-year veteran of the New Orleans Police Department, was on patrol at the Superdome on Sunday, August 28. He was in the building for more than a week. "The roof literally looked like an eggshell," he recalled. "It started to peel. And you could hear the wind." Even with the floodwaters rising around the Superdome, he said, the people never stopped coming in.

One woman attempting to help the few rescue workers was startled to see the scene taking shape on part of Interstate 10 after the winds and rains had left. "I've never seen so many people," she said later. "They were all on the elevated portion of the interstate and many were sitting in the sun in wheelchairs waiting for buses. They were all obviously sunburned, obviously dehydrated, very listless. . . . It was horrible. People literally crying for water."

Communications systems were woefully inadequate. In the early hours of the crisis, mobile communications units developed by FEMA were at Barksdale Air Force Base in Shreveport, Louisiana, and did not make it to the state's emergency operations center in Baton Rouge until the day after the storm hit. Also, most of the U.S. Forest Service's 5,000 radios—the largest civilian cache in the United States—remained unused.

In St. Bernard Parish, Larry Ingargiola, director of the local Office of Emergency Preparedness, lost all landline and cell-phone communications after the storm made landfall. As his building flooded, he climbed to the roof with his family. From his rooftop perch, he got word of the breached levees from Louisiana Department of Wildlife and Fisheries officials who rode by in boats. Ingargiola, the local official in charge of emergency preparedness, was without communications for two days.

Mayor Nagin's command center at the Hyatt hotel also lost all communications. The mayor managed to transmit some information to his emergency managers by walking back to City Hall. It was not until five days after landfall that Mayor Nagin had a cell phone. He spent much time leaning out of windows in hopes of getting a signal.

In the two years before Katrina struck, New Orleans law-enforcement officials had asked Congress for $105 million to upgrade its communications network. When those attempts failed, they approached the Department of Homeland Security, which also turned them down. Now, with the ravages of the storm laying waste to much of the communications network, the police, along with other first responders, were nearly helpless in transferring information. The raging winds and water destroyed more than 3,000 phone lines. Most callers who dialed 911 got a busy signal.

Homeland Security Secretary Michael Chertoff said later that he understood shortly after Katrina hit that the levees had not broken and that New Orleans "had dodged a bullet." He said he saw the information in a headline. Later, President Bush said the same thing. "There was a sense of relaxation," said Bush. "I myself thought we had dodged a bullet. You know why? Because I was listening to people, probably over the airways, say, the bullet has been dodged."

Thus, Bush and Chertoff, the major figures responsible for responding to a national disaster, said their information had come from the news media. With the vast array of government communications systems and bureaucracy at their disposal, such statements were no less than shocking.

It was not until the morning of August 31, two days after the waters began pouring through the neighborhoods of the city, that administration officials gave any public indication that a full-scale catastrophe was occurring on their watch, despite the fact that for many hours television reporters such as Anderson Cooper on CNN were providing graphic on-site evidence to an international audience. How did television commentators reach trapped residents before emergency responders? It was a question that would sorely embarrass government officials at all levels.

As thousands of people crammed into the stagnating confines of the Superdome, others made their way about 10 blocks to the Convention Center, a sprawling building nearly a mile long near the Mississippi River. The center was never intended to be used as a shelter. Captain M. A. Pfeiffer, an operations officer for the New Orleans Police Department, explained that the center "was supposed to be a bus stop where they dropped people off for transportation. The problem was, the transportation never came."

Along with about 2,000 other survivors inside the center, a man named Tony Cash waited for help. "It was as if all of us were already pronounced dead," he said. "It was as if somebody already had the body bags. Wasn't nobody coming to get us." By Tuesday, August 30, the numbers inside the center had expanded to nearly 20,000. "The lights never came on, for some reason, all the way," said Cash.

At the Convention Center, the atmosphere was surreal. As the hours slowly dragged by, more than 250

Hurricane Katrina's devastation of New Orleans, August 30, 2005. (Caitlin Mirra/Shutterstock)

troops from the Louisiana National Guard were camped out within the building's confines, separated from the rest of the crowd by a wall and their own trucks, fearful that the crowd would break in. The guardsmen waited for orders that did not come for three days.

At the Tulane Medical Center, officials in charge of evacuating patients had been told informally by the state emergency operations center that they could use National Guard buses to move patients. But the National Guard insisted on proof of authorization before they provided the buses. In desperation, medical-center personnel began to load patients into the backs of pickup trucks.

And so, as federal relief slogged along in the first critical hours and days of the disaster, bodies began floating in the waters. Even with the mandatory evacuation notice, no government agency was prepared to provide the necessary transportation to rescue those with no means to escape.

After the first day of flooding, several news sources reported that Fats Domino, a founding father of rock 'n roll and rhythm and blues, was missing. Domino was a true son and soul of New Orleans—born on Jourdan Avenue in the Ninth Ward in 1928. The legendary singer and pianist sold more than 65 million records in the 1950s and 1960s. For many years after the height of his career, Domino lived only a few blocks from his birthplace.

On the morning after Katrina hit, the drummer Ernest "Box" Fontenant managed to reach Domino's house on Caffin Avenue and found the famous entertainer stranded on the first floor with waters rising. Fontenant carried Domino on his back to the second floor. There, along with Domino's wife, Rosemary, and a few others, they huddled, waiting for help. After a few hours, a boat arrived, rescued the group from a balcony, and left them on a bridge.

Later, Domino and his family were taken to the Baton Rouge apartment of the local college-football hero JaMarcus Russell. For three days, with telephones and other communications cut off, the public did not know of Domino's fate. Indeed, after some of the water subsided, someone scrawled the following words on the outside of Domino's house: "RIP Fats. You will be missed."

Unlike many in his neighborhood, Fats Domino survived, although he lost much of the memorabilia of his career. Later, he said, "You can replace pianos, you see. You can't replace life, and we got out alive."

For the most part, many of the medical facilities in the lower areas of New Orleans had been left to struggle on their own. The patients, those least able to evacuate the city, often faced unimaginable horror and, on many occasions, death. Wilda Sim-McManus, a patient at Memorial Medical Center, later described the deteriorating conditions: "The sewer lines had all backed up, and we were down there in all that stifling heat and this odor was horrendous. People were trying to get into the hospital just to get to higher ground, and they weren't allowing that. . . . They boarded the doors up and we were just in there smothering. . . ."

At midday on Wednesday, August 31, Marty Bahamonde, one of the few FEMA employees who had managed to reach New Orleans, sent a message to Brown. "Sir, I know that you know the situation is past critical," said Bahamonde. "Here are some things you might not know. Hotels are kicking people out, thousands gathering in the streets with no food or water. Hundreds still being rescued from homes. The dying patients at the DMAT [Disaster Medical Assistance Team] tent being medivacd. Estimates are many will die within hours. Evacuation in process. Plans developing for dome evacuation but hotel situation adding to problem. We are out of food and running out of water at the dome, plans in works to address the critical need. FEMA staff is OK and holding own. DMAT staff working in deplorable conditions. The sooner we can get the medical patients out, the sooner we can get them out. Phone connectivity impossible."

To this desperate plea for help, Brown responded with these 12 words: "Thanks for the update. Anything specific I need to do or tweak?"

On September 2, President Bush arrived for a meeting in Alabama to meet with governors and federal officials involved in the Katrina disaster response. He said, "And the federal government's job is big, and it's massive, and we're going to do it. Where it's not working right, we're going to make it right. Where it is working right, we're going to duplicate it elsewhere. We have a responsibility, at the federal level, to help save life, and that's the primary focus right now. Every life is precious, and so we're going to spend a lot of time saving lives, whether it be in New Orleans or on the coast of Mississippi." To FEMA Director Michael Brown, Bush said, "Brownie, you're doing a heck of a job." From that moment on, many in the news media would call him "Heckava Job Brownie." Amid the uproar over his incompetence, Brown resigned on September 12.

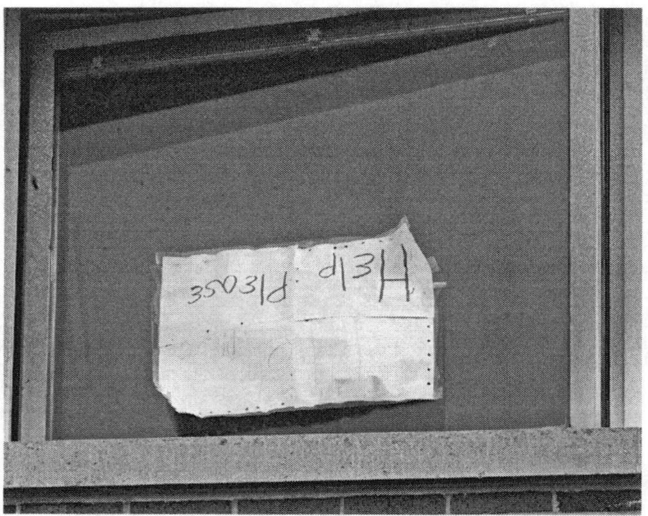

A sign placed upside-down on a window at Memorial Medical Center in New Orleans on Monday, September 12, 2005. More than 40 bodies were recovered on Sunday from the 317-bed hospital. (Rick Bowmer/Associated Press)

Not only did FEMA slog through bureaucratic red tape and misinformation, but it also blocked outside assistance from coming to the immediate rescue of people trapped in the flooded streets and homes of the city. Robert Dummett, state coordinator of the Florida Airboat Association, which had 500 airboat pilots at the ready to help pick up victims trapped in floodwaters, said, "We cannot get deployed to save our behinds." The pilots, he said, spent thousands of dollars of their own money stocking their boats and swamp buggies with food, water, medical supplies, and fuel, and they "are physically sick, watching the New Orleans coverage and knowing that the resources to help these poor people is sitting right in our driveways."

When a Florida congressman reported to FEMA officials that the airboaters from his state were ready to go to New Orleans, a FEMA representative told him that citizen volunteers were not being allowed into the ravaged city because of safety issues.

A survivor of Katrina later said, "The people of New Orleans were stranded in a flood and were allowed to die. The military had personnel stationed just 40 miles outside the city, and they could have moved in and gotten people out sooner. People were allowed to die."

Congress Investigates

Senator Hillary Rodham Clinton (D-N.Y.) pushed to establish a congressional commission on Katrina much like the one that had been formed to investigate the tragedies of September 11, 2001. Clinton's idea was to "examine the Federal, State, and local response to the devastation wrought by Hurricane Katrina in the Gulf Region of the United States especially in the States of Louisiana, Mississippi, Alabama, and other areas impacted in the aftermath and make immediate corrective measures to improve such responses in the future." Although opinion polls following Katrina indicated strongly that the public favored the idea of such a panel, Republicans in Congress were not eager to let an outside body pass judgment on the performance of the federal government in the storm disaster. Senator Clinton's motion failed.

Senator Pete Domenici (R-N.M.) said, "We don't need an outside committee every time there is a problem in this country. As a longtime senator, I cannot believe what I'm hearing. . . . Implicit is that we will play politics. I don't believe it."

Instead, the Republican leadership in Congress decided to proceed with its own investigations. On September 2, 2005, Senator Susan Collins (R-Maine), chairman of the Senate Committee on Homeland Security and Governmental Affairs, together with its ranking member, Senator Joseph Lieberman (D-Conn.), announced that the committee would conduct an investigation into the preparation for and response to Hurricane Katrina. On September 14, the Senate Committee held its first hearing. By April 2006, the Senate committee would hold a total of 23 hearings and conduct formal interviews with more than 325 witnesses.

On September 15, 2005, the House of Representatives approved HR 437, which created its own Select Bipartisan Committee to Investigate the Preparation for and Response to Hurricane Katrina. The committee was to investigate the development, coordination, and execution by local, state, and federal authorities of emergency response plans and other activities in preparation for Hurricane Katrina, and the local, state, and federal government response to the disaster.

Dennis Hastert (R-Ill.), Speaker of the House, appointed Representative Tom Davis (R-Va.) as committee chairman. One of the few politically moderate members of the Republican Party in Congress, Davis, whose Northern Virginia district was minutes from Washington, called the first meeting of the committee for September 22.

But Democrats, chafing as the minority in both houses of Congress and taking continuing partisan shots from the Republican Bush White House, brushed aside the assurances of Davis and others that the Republicans would take a fair look at the Katrina tragedy. Led by Minority Leader Nancy Pelosi (D-Calif.), Democrats continued calling for an independent commission and refused to be a part of the Republican-led investigation. Pelosi declared, "I am not going to, as leader, validate what I consider to be a whitewash."

The House select committee was thus made up entirely of Republicans, though a number of Democratic representatives began participating in some of the sessions, especially Representatives Charles Melancon (D-La.) and Gene Taylor (D-Miss.), whose states were so directly affected by Katrina. However, both Melancon and Taylor supported their Democratic colleagues. The two sent a letter to President Bush saying, "We applauded your decision after September 11 [2001] to create an independent commission to honor the families of the victims. We believe that the victims of Katrina deserve no less than the victims of September 11."

Governor Blanco also suggested an independent panel. "Only an independent, nonpartisan commission investigation that commands full support from the executive and legislative branches will accomplish what we need," said Blanco.

But Committee Chairman Tom Davis pressed on, urging members to put aside partisan bickering. "The task before us is considerable," he said. "The American people want the facts. It's about getting the facts, not getting even."

Taking a pointed shot at Pelosi, Davis declared, "While Nancy Pelosi was hunkered down this morning issuing more partisan, divisive press releases, serious-minded Members of Congress were preparing to question former FEMA director Mike Brown as part of our investigation to get to the bottom of what went wrong in the response to Hurricane Katrina. This is the job of Congress. It is our responsibility to investigate what went wrong, what should have been done differently, and how to do it better in the future. In our system of checks and balances, the Congress has both the duty and the obligation to ask the tough questions the actions [sic] of government officials—local, state, and federal."

Operating on a tight timeline, the House Committee would hold nine hearings and review more than 500,000 pages of documents. Shortly after both the Senate and House committees began their work, President Bush promised to cooperate fully with the congressional inquiries. "The United States Congress also has an important oversight function to perform," said Bush during a televised address from Jackson Square in New Orleans. "Congress is preparing an investigation, and I will work with members of both parties to make sure this effort is thorough."

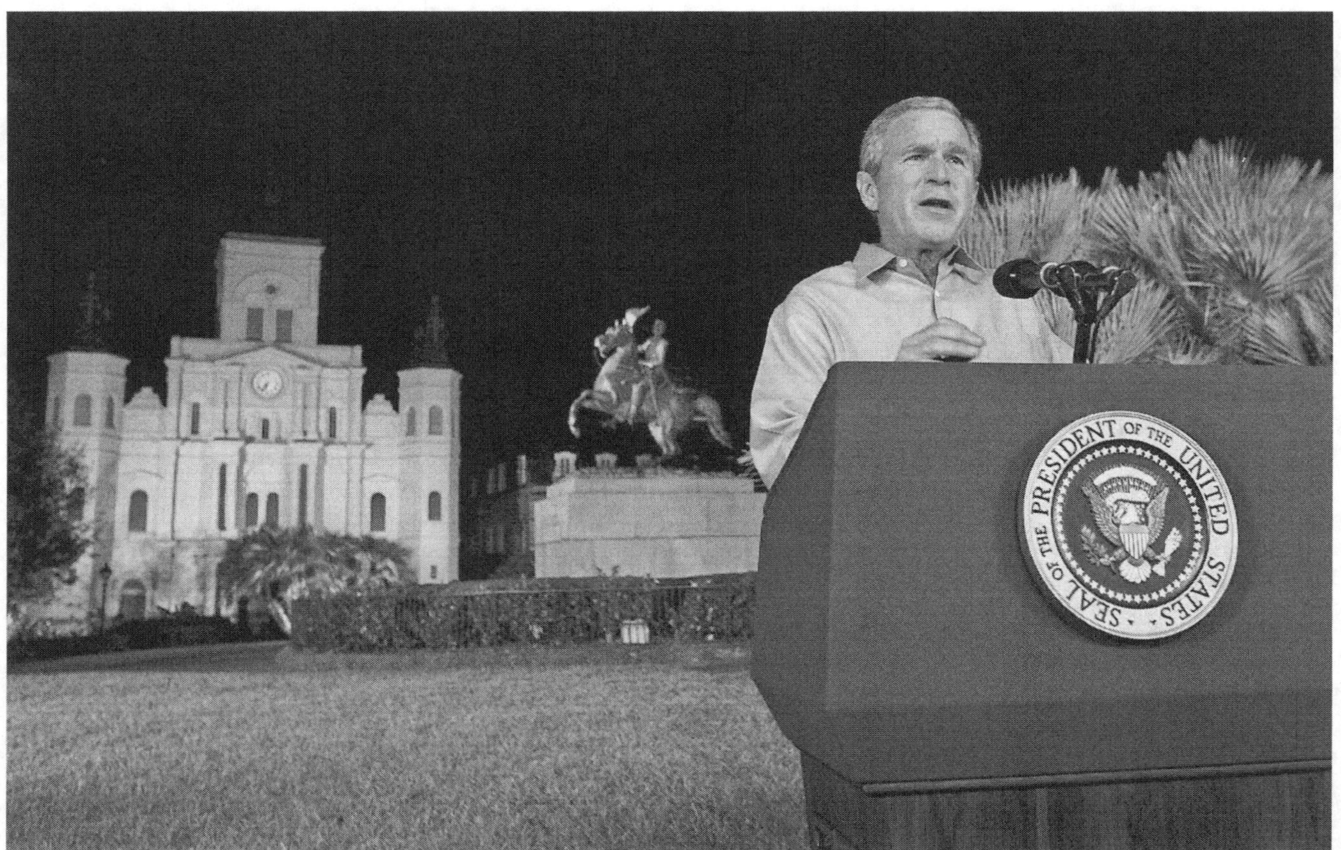

President Bush concludes his remarks following his nationally televised address from Jackson Square in New Orleans, September 15, 2005. (Susan Walsh/Associated Press)

Nevertheless, by January 2006, the Bush administration began to turn hostile toward the congressional inquiries, even though they were being run by Republicans in both chambers of Congress. Citing confidentiality of executive-branch communications, administration spokesmen announced that White House officials had decided not to turn over certain White House documents and e-mail correspondence about Hurricane Katrina or make senior White House officials available for sworn testimony.

Democrats reacted with fury. "A lot of federal government employees who we've interviewed, they've been told by the White House that they can't answer any questions about communications they had with people at the White House," Senator Lieberman told ABC News. "Now, that's stonewalling. For the administration to simply tell people in the federal government they can't talk to our investigators about any of the conversations they had with people at the White House is unacceptable." Lieberman threatened to request subpoenas for documents and testimony if the administration continued to stonewall.

"Now, the issue you bring up goes to separation-of-powers issues," said Scott McClellan, Bush's press secretary, during a White House briefing. All presidents, he said, have believed that they had the right to confidential conversations with their advisers. President Bush was merely asserting the same right. "That's what this is about. That's the bottom line here. "

Senate Committee Chairman Susan Collins was especially annoyed when certain administration officials who were not even part of the president's staff announced that they, too, would not testify because of executive-confidentiality and executive-privilege issues. "I completely disagree with that practice," Collins said. Nevertheless, she backed away from the White House challenge, deciding against any strong-arm confrontation with the president over basic governmental powers between the executive and legislative branches.

Chairman Davis of the House committee also threatened to subpoena the White House when it rejected his requests for documents. Davis also backed off, however, deciding instead to accept a deal for restricted access involving two briefings from Kenneth Rapuano, a second-level Bush official who had been one of those in command as the hurricane struck.

Representative Davis later defended his meek challenge of the White House, saying that a subpoena fight would have prevented the committee from obtaining enough information to meet its February 15, 2006, deadline for a report and to produce recommendations in time for congressional and administration action before the next hurricane season. But Davis was never comfortable with his decision, later admitting that the final report did not capture much about Bush's actions and those of other administration officials during the crisis. "It is a mystery to many of us what he knew and when he knew it," Davis said, "and the White House went out of their way in their briefings not to reveal that."

In the midst of the battle over documents and witnesses, Senator Clinton once again called for the creation of an independent commission that would have been made up of non-federal-government employees, appointed by the president and Democratic and Republican leaders in Congress. Charging that the Bush administration had been withholding documents and testimony from both the House and Senate committees, Clinton said, "Just as with 9/11, we did not get to the point where we believed we understood what happened until an independent investigation was conducted." Clinton's motion for an independent commission again failed along party lines, just as it had failed a few months earlier.

The White House's entrenched position on the rights of the executive branch to defy congressional investigative power did not waver, either. The Bush administration continued to deny access to whatever documents or testimony it wished.

As the investigation proceeded, Senator Lieberman again pointedly attacked Bush for his cavalier position. "Almost every question our staff has asked federal agency witnesses regarding conversations with or involvement of the White House has been met with a response that they could not answer on direction of the White House," a frustrated Lieberman declared.

Other Democrats charged the White House with stonewalling. "Until those officials who are responsible appear before this committee, anything else is part of the administration's cover-up," said Senator Mark Dayton (D-Minn.). Senator Mark Pryor (D-Ark.) added, "If this committee is not allowed to do its job, the families affected by Hurricane Katrina deserve to get a full accounting in a setting where politics does not play a role."

Representative Christopher Shays (R-Conn.) not only attacked the president for failing to cooperate fully with the investigations, but he also hammered Bush for his dilatory leadership in Katrina. The slow, uncommunicative response during the Katrina crisis amounted to a paralysis of leadership that enhanced the tragedy, Shays said. "When you have a natural disaster, the president needs to be hands-on," he said, "and if anyone in his staff gets in the way, he needs to push them away. . . . The response was pathetic."

The White House continued to stonewall throughout the Senate and House investigations. Chertoff, the secretary of homeland security, did appear briefly before both committees in February 2006, but the main focus of the testimony centered on the one individual upon whom President Bush had lavished praise in the immediate aftermath of the storm—the former head of FEMA, Michael Brown.

The Grilling of Michael Brown

On September 27, 2005, four weeks after Katrina struck, Michael Brown testified before the House select committee. It was as if an assault team awaited him in the hearing room.

By this time, Brown had become the public face of the government's incompetent response to Katrina. More than President Bush, more than Secretary of Homeland Security Michael Chertoff, more than Mayor Ray Nagin, more than any other single individual, Brown took the fusillade of criticism. Although he had quickly resigned his position as head of FEMA after the tragedy, he remained on the government payroll as a consultant. "Heckava Job Brownie" was still being paid to offer advice on emergency preparedness. No one, it seemed, was held accountable by the Bush administration for the Katrina debacle.

Now, anxiously sitting before the committee, he became a symbol of everything that had gone wrong in the days after August 29, 2005. Through hours of grueling testimony, Brown fought off his attackers. One of the most persistent was Representative Gene Taylor (D-Miss.). "I do wish you had taken the time to visit the folks who were devastated by this storm for more than a photo op," Taylor said. "Maybe you would realize that things happened that were beyond the comprehension of the local elected officials." Taylor reacted with special anger at Brown's attempts to place primary responsibility for the failed response at the state and local level. In Taylor's own congressional district, several individuals attempting to rescue neighbors had to loot a Wal-Mart store to get the necessary food and supplies and had to wait several days before any help from FEMA arrived. Taylor shouted at Brown that FEMA "fell on [its] face" during Katrina. It rated "an F-minus in my book."

Brown fired back at his critics, those who lampooned not only his overall credentials to handle the job at FEMA but also his credibility on the Katrina disaster. Brown blamed the failures largely on others, especially Governor Blanco and Mayor Nagin and other Louisiana state and local officials. The man who used to oversee Arabian horse shows dodged and weaved through his congressional testimony, finally declaring that his biggest mistake was that he failed to realize how ill-equipped the state and local machinery was to handle the crisis and how incompetent its management. "My biggest mistake was not recognizing by Saturday [August 27] that Louisiana was dysfunctional," Brown said during his House testimony.

Shortly after Brown left the hearing room, an insulted Governor Blanco leveled her own shot. In a statement issued by her office, she said, "It clearly demonstrates the appalling degree to which Mr. Brown is either out of touch with the truth or reality."

Michael Brown, former director of the Federal Emergency Management Agency, testifies before a House select committee investigating the preparation and response to Hurricane Katrina, September 27, 2005. (Associated Press)

Following Brown's testimony, CNN news analyst Jack Cafferty lampooned the former FEMA head for admitting "that he is not—quote—'a superhero,' which is something that I had already figured out all by myself. What I didn't know was, according to Brown, the whole Katrina fiasco was the fault of local lawmakers. I also didn't know Brown is still on the payroll. Brown said yesterday that he's being paid for about a month as a consultant to FEMA. So, help me out here. The guy who resigned in disgrace after bungling the response to Katrina is being paid taxpayer money by the government to be a consultant. Yes, that makes sense, right? You can't make this stuff up."

On February 10, 2006, Brown was back in front of Congress, this time before the Senate Homeland Security and Governmental Affairs Committee. Like its counterpart in the House of Representatives had done a few months earlier, the committee relentlessly pummeled the man who had been widely condemned as perhaps the most derelict in responding to Hurricane Katrina.

Senator Norm Coleman (R-Minn.) said to the beleaguered Brown, "You're not prepared to, kind of, put a mirror in front of your face and recognize your own inadequacies and say, 'You know something? I made some big mistakes. I wasn't focused. I didn't get things done.'" Coleman charged that Brown "didn't provide the leadership," and added, "I'm not sure you got it."

Brown angrily responded, "I absolutely resent you sitting here saying that I lacked the leadership to do that, because I was down there pushing everything that I could."

Some Senate committee members suggested that Brown was being used by the Bush administration as a scapegoat to hide all of their other various failings. Senator Patrick Leahy (D-Vt.) expressed sympathy for the position in which the beleaguered Brown found himself.

Committee Chairman Susan Collins said, "By almost any measure, FEMA's response to Katrina has to be judged a failure. The response was riddled with missed opportunities and poor decision-making, and failed leadership." But Collins leveled criticism at others, especially Chertoff and the Department of Homeland Security: "The responsibility for FEMA's failed response must be shared by DHS. The Department's lack of preparedness for the Katrina catastrophe manifested itself in a variety of ways. Instead of springing into action or, better yet, acting before the storm made landfall, the Department appears to have moved haltingly, and, as a result, key decisions were either delayed or made based on questionable assumptions."

And so, as Michael Brown walked away from his congressional questioners, he knew at least that others realized that the blame for Katrina was not his alone.

The Reports of the House and Senate Committees

Despite Democrats' suspicions that the House committee report would be a whitewash, Representative Davis and his colleagues did focus on the administration's dilatory and unresponsive actions in the wake of the disaster. The report declared, "It remains difficult to understand how government could respond so ineffectively to a disaster that was anticipated for years, and for which specific dire warnings had been issued for days," the report declared. "This crisis was not only predictable, it was predicted."

Released on February 15, 2006, the 749-page report of the House committee was titled "A Failure of Initiative: The Final Report of the Select Bipartisan Committee to Investigate the Preparation for and Response to Hurricane Katrina." The report concluded that Katrina tested all levels of government involved in disaster relief and that all levels of government failed. The report confirmed the news accounts about the shocking inability of all three levels of government to meet their obligations to the public, characterizing the response to Katrina as "a litany of mistakes, misjudgments, lapses, and absurdities all cascading together, blinding us to what was coming and hobbling any collective effort to respond."

The House report castigated the actions of Chertoff, who, the report charged, had ignored or forgotten the protocols of the National Response Plan, and had delayed before handing off the catastrophe to FEMA's Brown. Although 100,000 residents remained in New Orleans, Chertoff had made no effort to ensure that buses had been secured to evacuate them, the report concluded.

Interviewed shortly after the release of the House report, Chairman Davis was especially critical of both DHS and FEMA. "They could have pre-positioned a lot more ice, food, that kind of thing, water on the ground for emergency use. We could have had different evacuation centers than they had. . . . The whole infrastructure was completely overwhelmed. . . . At the end of the day with a storm of this size the federal government has got to take the lion's share of the credit or blame for what happens."

Although limited by an uncooperative administration that withheld information and witnesses, the House report did take aim at the incompetent and ill-prepared response that contributed to the deaths of more than 1,800 people and the virtual destruction of a major American city. If Democrats had feared that the House committee would be a thinly veiled whitewash of the administration, those fears proved unfounded.

The House committee concluded that the failures of Katrina resulted from a lack of performance, not a lack of plans. The Republican committee attacked not only Nagin, Blanco, Brown—the usual suspects—but it also attacked the party's leader. Inexplicably, the president and other White House officials acted with little sense of urgency, failing to recognize the enormity of the crisis and then acting almost perfunctorily as it went on. The report declared that Bush had responded too passively, and it noted that "earlier presidential involvement might have resulted in a more effective response." Davis went even further, asking why Bush and White House chief of staff Andrew H. Card Jr. remained on vacation during the storm, leaving only the deputy homeland-security adviser in command at the White House. "What does that tell you?" Davis asked.

Unfortunately, the House committee lacked much of the background information that could have provided greater insight into the disaster. But Davis and his colleagues did not have the stomach for a showdown with the Bush administration over claims of executive privilege. The committee settled for what it was able to uncover without administration cooperation. Nevertheless, it concluded, "If this is what happens when we have advance warning, we shudder to imagine the consequences when we do not. Four and a half years after 9/11, America is not ready for prime time."

In May 2006, the Senate Homeland Security and Governmental Affairs Committee issued a 750-page report titled "Hurricane Katrina: A Nation Still Unprepared." Also hampered by the lack of cooperation from the White House, the Senate panel asserted in its own report that a catastrophe in the Gulf region and especially New Orleans had been predicted for many years, and that a lack of leadership and resources at all levels of government prevented proper training and response. The panel's main recommendation was for the dismantling and restructuring of FEMA.

Under the leadership of James Lee Witt during the 1990s, FEMA had performed well in responding to a number of weather-related disasters. But Katrina was something different. This was a sledgehammer smashing into a major American city, the kind of disaster that many Americans began to think might occur through a terrorist attack. This was on the scale of tragedy for which DHS had been created in the first place. Now, in the wake of Katrina, many began to wonder whether

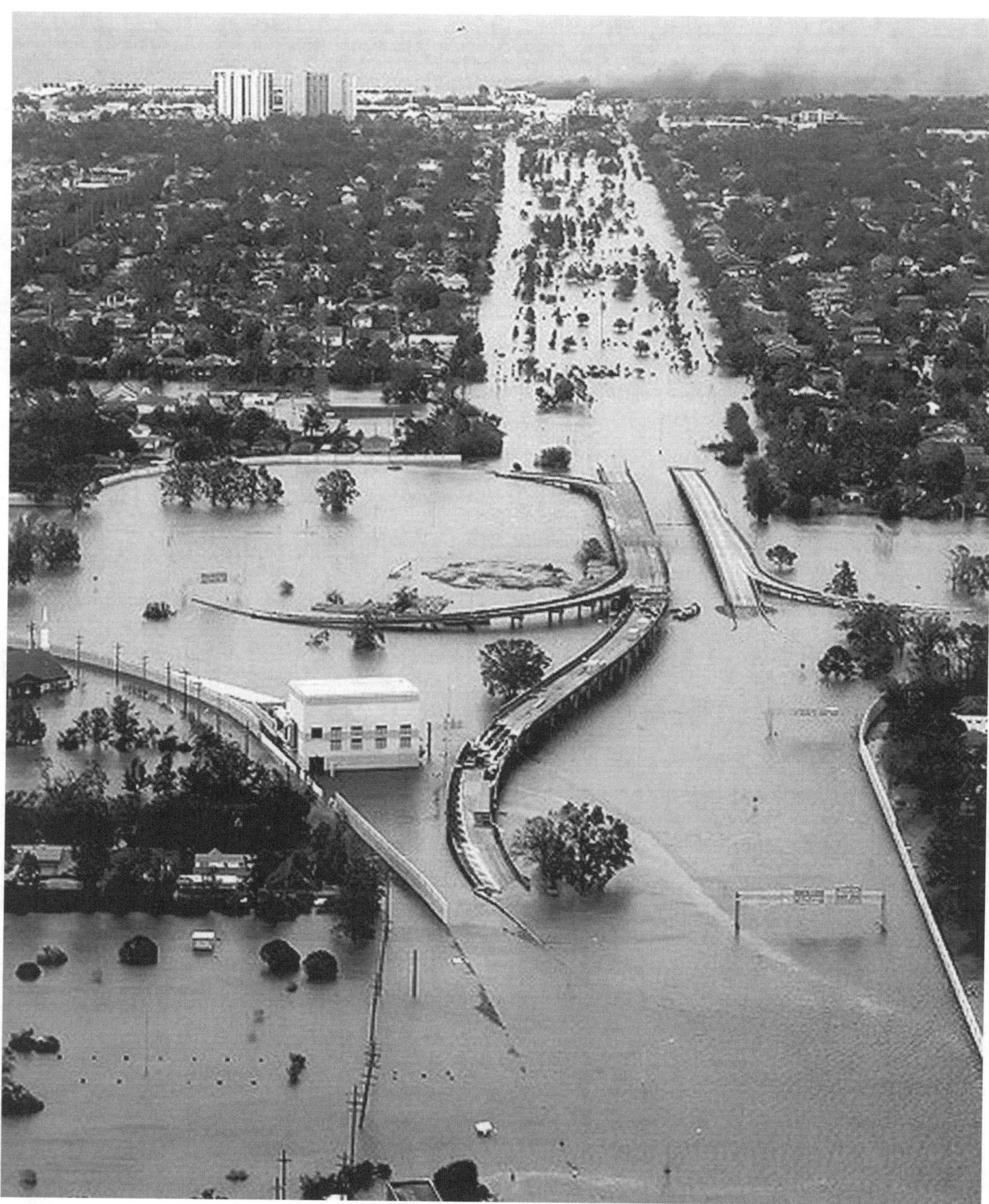

New Orleans, Louisiana, in the aftermath of Hurricane Katrina. Shown here is flooded Interstate 10 at West End Boulevard and the surrounding area, with Lake Pontchartrain in the background. A breach in the levee of the 17th Street Canal, located just beyond the left edge of this photograph, was responsible for much of the flooding of the city in the hours after the hurricane. (U.S. Coast Guard, Petty Officer 2nd Class Kyle Niemi)

FEMA was still the organizational mechanism through which disaster response should be coordinated.

Indeed, Witt himself had warned that the bureaucracy created after the September 11 attacks could hamper rescue efforts by FEMA in future crises. In March 2004, Witt had told Congress, "I assure you that we could not have been as responsive and effective during disasters as we were during my tenure as FEMA director, had there been layers of federal bureaucracy between myself and the White House."

Both congressional reports were critical of government officials at all levels. Mayor Nagin, Governor Blanco, DHS Secretary Chertoff, and FEMA Director Brown all came under withering fire. Both Nagin and Blanco had responded too slowly, the reports said, and had failed to prepare the state and the city for a disaster that had been predicted for years.

Chertoff also had failed to anticipate the likely consequences of the storm, the reports charged, and had done relatively little to procure the buses, boats, and aircraft that could have saved countless additional lives in rescue operations. The criticism of Brown took on an air of mockery and ridicule, especially regarding his lack of training for the job and his feckless response in the unfolding early days of the hurricane.

And yet, the reports utterly failed to ask for accountability. There were no calls for firings of administration personnel, no suggestions of criminal responsibility. None of the individuals in the chain of command who should have saved lives lost their jobs, except for Brown, who resigned after unrelenting pressures from the media, only to be rehired by the Bush administration as a disaster-planning consultant, a move that took cynicism to new levels.

The Question of Race

African Americans constituted 67.3 percent of the population of New Orleans at the time of the Katrina disaster. Many were poor. Approximately 28 percent of the citizens of the city lived below the poverty line on an income of $15,000 or less. Most of the poor resided in the lower-lying areas of the city most vulnerable to flooding. As Brinkley, the historian, has written of the separate enclaves of New Orleans: "The core of the city, built geographically in concentric circles around the mansion residents, the tourism world, and the shipping industry, rarely took the poverty-stricken neighborhoods into account. Poor neighborhoods occupied the majority of New Orleans's 181 square miles, stretching mile after mile with dilapidated houses and people on porches, people with nowhere to go. Bifurcated, if not officially segregated, New Orleans gave the impression of a city that didn't even know itself."

Most statistical analyses indicate that more than 1,800 people lost their lives from the effects of Katrina. In some areas, such as the Lower Ninth Ward and New Orleans East in Orleans Parish and areas in St. Bernard Parish, many hundreds, although surviving the first onslaught of flooding, perished in the weeks after Katrina from the effects of dislocation and the lack of medical facilities and proper housing.

Various statistical analyses in the years following the tragedy did not indicate that African Americans died at any greater rate than their population in the city. A study by the Louisiana Department of Health and Hospitals, for example, asserted that white residents, who made up less than 30 percent of the population, represented 36 percent of the storm's fatalities. Nevertheless, because the residents of New Orleans were overwhelmingly African American, the issue of race became a central focus in the discussion of Katrina.

At a benefit produced by NBC called "A Concert for America," on September 2, 2005, singer Kanye West startled some observers by charging that the reason so many people in New Orleans had been left virtually to fend for themselves for so long was the element of racism. "You know," West said, "it's been five days because most of the people are black. . . . George Bush doesn't care about black people." West went on: "I hate the way they portray us in the media. If you see a black family, it [the media] says they're looting. See a white family, it says they're looking for food."

Following Katrina, many New Orleans residents were evacuated to Houston, Texas. Then-senator Barack Obama (D-Ill.), touring shelter facilities in the Houston Astrodome, said: "There seemed to be a sense that this other America was somehow not on people's radar screen . . . and that . . . does have to do with historic indifference on the part of government to the plight of those who are disproportionately African American."

In both congressional investigations, a few of the witnesses echoed West's charges and the observations of Senator Obama. "No one is going to tell me it wasn't a race issue," said Patricia Thompson, a New Orleans evacuee. "Yes, it was an issue of race. Because of one thing: When the city had pretty much been evacuated, the people that were left there mostly was black."

"They died from abject neglect," Leah Hodges, a community activist, told the Senate investigating committee. "We left body bags behind. . . . The people of New Orleans were stranded in a flood and were allowed to die." One resident said she was "one sunrise from being consumed by maggots and flies."

Victims of Hurricane Katrina stay at the Astrodome stadium in Houston, Texas, where 16,000 evacuees received food and shelter, September 4, 2005. (©Carlos Barria/Reuters/CORBIS)

According to a Gallup poll, 6 out of every 10 black New Orleans residents said if most of Katrina's victims were white, relief would have arrived sooner.

What if the city had been composed mostly of white Americans? Would the response by government officials have been as dilatory and haphazard? Many people from New Orleans certainly believed that was the case. The issue was delicately ignored in the final reports of the congressional committees. It remains a haunting question.

Seeking Reform

Soon after the two committees completed their work in early 2006, legislators pushed for reform that would guarantee that the response to another Katrina would never again stain the country's history. Senators Susan Collins and Joseph Lieberman, who led the Senate investigation, called for FEMA to be removed from the Department of Homeland Security. Lieberman proposed that Congress rebuild the agency within the Department of Health and Human Services. Collins, calling FEMA a "shambles and beyond repair," agreed with the Senate committee report that called for a new agency. Their efforts were not successful.

Congress did pass the Post-Katrina Emergency Reform Act, which President Bush signed into law on October 4, 2006. Stemming from the congressional investigations and the suggestions made by the committees to strengthen emergency preparedness, the act made a number of organizational and administrative changes for FEMA that attempted to prepare and protect against future threats like Katrina. Many critics claimed that these changes lacked muscle and money and amounted to nothing more than political gamesmanship and bureaucratic tinkering.

The White House also warded off attempts in Congress to pass legislation that would have created a federally financed reconstruction program for Louisiana to bail out home owners and mortgage lenders. The state would have to use community-development money already appropriated by Congress, the administration declared, fearing that such legislation would exacerbate the budget deficit. For many Louisiana residents, who saw the federal government pouring billions of dollars into the Iraq War week after week, the declaration of concern for budget deficits seemed hollow, baseless, and cruel.

By late 2008, more than three years after the storm, Congress had not stopped investigating Katrina. Both houses of Congress in several committees continued to press on with inquiries relating to a number of issues, ranging from suspect contract arrangements to fraudulent relief payments. Representative Henry Waxman (D-Calif.), chairman of the House Committee on Oversight and Government Reform, for example, held a series of hearings examining the reasons that thousands of trailers provided by FEMA after Katrina for temporary housing for the homeless and displaced were found to contain toxic levels of formaldehyde gas.

Congress thus continued to search for answers to the abject failure of governments to respond to the crisis. How could a major city in the United States endure such destruction and human misery when so many resources to relieve such suffering existed but had not been deployed? The issue was one of competence and determination. Too many people in positions of power and too many government agencies charged with safeguarding the American people had failed abysmally. For these reasons, Katrina remains a shameful event in American history.

DOCUMENTS

Excerpt from Testimony of Michael Brown, September 27, 2005

By the time he testified before the House select committee to investigate the Katrina disaster in September 2005, Michael Brown, former head of the Federal Emergency Management Agency (FEMA), had become something of a Bush administration fall guy. In the wake of the hurricane's destruction, the president had uttered his sincere but soon infamous greeting of "Brownie, you're doing a heck of a job" when the two met days after the storm. By the time of Bush's remark, it was evident to almost everyone who had paid any attention to the horrors that befell the victims of Katrina and the ineptitude of the federal emergency response, especially by FEMA, that Brown's work had been anything but praiseworthy. He resigned as director on September 12. On September 27, Representative Gene Taylor (D-Miss.) was one of several members of Congress who grilled the hapless Brown unmercifully.

EXCERPT FROM TESTIMONY OF MICHAEL BROWN, SEPTEMBER 27, 2005

REPRESENTATIVE GENE TAYLOR (D-MISS.): Mr. Brown, how much are the citizens of this country paying you now?

BROWN: Well, that's public record. I think it's $148,000 a year.

TAYLOR: OK. Mr. Brown, looking at page three of your testimony, you say: It's inherently impractical to expect the federal government to respond to every disaster, whatever size, in every community across the nation, the federal government is simply not a first responder, never has been, should never be.

I do wish you had taken the time to visit the folks who were devastated by this storm for more than a photo op. Maybe you would realize that things happened that were beyond the comprehension of the local elected officials.

They parked their vehicles in places that had never flooded. And yet they flooded. So they had no vehicles. Their uniforms were in buildings that had never flooded. They had no uniforms. The meals they were counting on eating, even the canned food that you make reference to, was lost under a wall of salt water.

See, things happen that sometimes folks can't comprehend. And that's why they're counting on their nation to come bail them out. Their nation let them down.

As I said before, looting the Wal-Mart should not be the first response of the local entity. Looking to their nation to help them should be. And the nation should be able to come forward with exact times and quantities when things are going to be delivered and not the lame excuse that I must have heard a hundred times: Help is on the way.

What assurances can you give me that, based on what has happened and the mistakes that were made—and I hope you'll admit your mistakes; that's the best way to learn from them—that you as a consultant are going to work to see to it that this doesn't happen again, or are we going to see this happen the next time there's a major hurricane or natural disaster or act of terror?

BROWN: Mr. Taylor, let me assure you that I have been to plenty of disasters. I have had friends die by terrorist incidents. I lost my Sunday school teacher in the bombing of the Alfred P. Murrow [Murrah] Building [in Oklahoma City in 1995]. I know what death and destruction is.

So I don't expect you to lecture me about not knowing how people suffer. I know how they suffer. I saw the death and the destruction in the tsunami in South Asia. I smelled the rotten bodies. I know what that is like. I don't need you to lecture me about what death and destruction is.

TAYLOR: I thought I'd ask a consultant on the federal payroll . . .

BROWN: Congressman, you let me finish. I know what death and destruction is and I know how much people suffer.

And it breaks my heart. I pray for these people every night. So don't lecture me about knowing what disaster is like.

TAYLOR: So we should never . . .

BROWN: Let me explain to you, also, that I am committed—I am absolutely committed to making certain that these deficiencies that we've identified, that FEMA, that I've put my heart and soul in, that my family has sacrificed for the past four and a half years, that it gets the need and attention that it gets.

I'm not up here for a photo op. I'm not up here because this is fun. I'm up here because I want to see our government work properly.

I want to see that it takes care of our citizens in a way that is proper and that we fix some of these things.

So I would kindly appreciate it if you wouldn't lecture me about those things.

TAYLOR: If I may, going back to your statement, it should never be the first responder, what if the first responders are killed, like they were in the twin towers? What if the first responders don't have fuel? What if they don't have food?

What do we do then? Do we sit back and say, Well, you guys screwed up. And we do nothing—as you did.

Or are we going to change that for next time?

BROWN: On September 11th, we had firefighters respond from all over this country. We have the Emergency Management Assistance Compact fully utilized.

TAYLOR: (off-mike)

BROWN: So the federal government was still—please let me finish.

The federal government, even on September 11th, was not the first responder. It was the firefighters of this country who put their lives on the line every single day to protect those communities that came and responded to the attacks in New York and at the Pentagon.

TAYLOR: I think . . .

BROWN: It was not the federal government that came in and did that.

TAYLOR: The first responders in the case of September 11th were local. So what you're saying is if something happens to them, there's no place for us to immediately . . .

BROWN: You're not listening to me, Congressman.

TAYLOR: (off-mike)

BROWN: Firefighters came from all over this country. That's why we have—are you aware of the mutual aid compacts that exist between states, so that if one state is overwhelmed and needs additional firefighters or medical workers or police officers, that other states under this compact of mutual aid can send those to the states, that help?

That's why the federal government should not be the first responders. State and locals do that. And a system is in place to make that work.

TAYLOR: Who's the chief of the National Guard Bureau?

BROWN: I don't know.

TAYLOR: In your capacity as the director of FEMA, knowing that the states are responsible for responding and that the greatest asset they have is the National Guard, you don't know the name of the chief of the National Guard Bureau?

BROWN: Do you know the name of the emergency manager in Colorado?

TAYLOR: I don't hold that job. You did. So let's back up.

BROWN: I do.

TAYLOR: At what point did you ever contact the chief of the National Guard Bureau in the wake of Hurricane Katrina and ask for his help?

BROWN: Actually, I think I did talk to the chief. I think he was in Baton Rouge, and I did talk to him.

But I talked to the person . . .

TAYLOR: If I may—I'm asking the questions. You're the witness.

BROWN: . . . responsible . . .

TAYLOR: I'm asking the questions.

BROWN: Let me answer your first question.

I spoke to the person at the National Guard who's responsible, General Landreneau, the governor's adjutant general.

TAYLOR: I'm talking about the chief of the National Guard Bureau for the whole nation.

BROWN: You can play this game all day, sir.

TAYLOR: I'm not playing a game. I'm asking you a question.

BROWN: I don't know his name.

TAYLOR: OK. Did you ever speak to him in the wake of Hurricane Katrina, at all?

BROWN: Yes, I think he came to my office and I did speak to him.

TAYLOR: When?

BROWN: I don't recall. I'd have to go back. . . .

TAYLOR: As someone whose testimony says you are a facilitator of information and resources, that's obviously a resource, so at what time did you ask for his resource? What day?

BROWN: I didn't ask him. I asked General Landreneau, who was in charge of the National Guard.

TAYLOR: Of one state.

BROWN: Yes. And I also spoke to—and if he is listening, I apologize, I don't remember his name, but I also spoke to the adjutant general in Mississippi.

TAYLOR: What's the name of the chief of naval operations?

Did you at any time in all this, as someone who prides himself on . . .

BROWN: No, because I spoke . . .

TAYLOR: . . . being the facilitator of information and help, since you only have 2,000 employees, and since they had a sizable contingent in south Mississippi, did you speak to him? And when did you speak to him?

BROWN: No. Instead, I spoke to the commander at NORTHCOM, and I spoke to Deputy Secretary England. I didn't need to speak to the naval commander.

TAYLOR: So when did you speak to Deputy Secretary England?

(crosstalk)

TAYLOR: After the storm, that you spoke to him . . .

(crosstalk)

BROWN: I had an e-mail from Secretary England, I believe on Monday, as a matter of fact.

TAYLOR: OK. And it was in regard to what?

BROWN: What they were doing and what they were providing.

TAYLOR: And what were you asking of him as someone who is a facilitator of other people's . . .

BROWN: He had already offered. He was already offering.

TAYLOR: I know he's offering, so what did you ask for?

BROWN: We asked for the *Bataan,* that was already moving up the Gulf Coast. I think at that time, or maybe the next day, we asked for the USS *Comfort.* And there was a third ship, whose name I don't recall right now.

TAYLOR: In the coordination of other people's assets that you make reference to, how well was the *Comfort* used?

BROWN: I think it was misused.

TAYLOR: Why?

BROWN: The state of Mississippi put a request in for the USS *Comfort* for medical purposes.

For those in the public who don't understand, the *Comfort* is basically a hospital ship, provides medical care.

The state of Mississippi made a request for the USS *Comfort* for medical purposes. That request was then withdrawn, because they no longer needed it. Mississippi had a need for housing. So I made the rational decision that if we could put a cruise ship that was not being utilized, in the Port of Houston, in Mississippi, which is obviously better used for housing, could even move the *Comfort* to New Orleans.

TAYLOR: Are you aware in your capacity of a facilitator of other people's assets that the state of Mississippi would not certify the *Comfort,* which is good enough to patch up Marines and soldiers who suffer the most horrible of wounds?

The state of Mississippi had never certified the *Comfort* as a state-recognized hospital. And therefore people who were picked up by the ambulance—remember, the bridges between the coastal counties are gone, so if you are hurt in Jackson County, the assets in Gulfport or Biloxi are no longer available to you.

Were you aware that those people could not be delivered to the *Comfort*? I would think as the coordinator of all these events that maybe you would have been aware of that, maybe you would have picked up the phone to Governor Barbour or someone and said, We've got this great asset here, why aren't you using it? Why didn't that happen?

BROWN: Because they no longer needed it. I was informed that the state of Mississippi no longer needed the USS *Comfort* because they had the hospitals open and they would rather take people to the hospitals than to the ship.

TAYLOR: I was informed last Friday . . .

BROWN: You and I have a difference of opinion.

TAYLOR: . . . by the head of American Medical Response that they were told they could not deliver the patients there and that in frustration the doctors of the *Comfort* went into town and started practicing medicine literally on street corners or anyplace they could just to feel that they were doing something.

I would think, in your capacity as the federal emergency management association, you could have done a little bit better than that.

BROWN: Well, first, I would think that you would know it's the Federal Emergency Management Agency and not an association, that we're an agency of the federal government.

And second of all, that decision about what to do with the USS *Comfort* was made by me on the day that I was sent back to Washington, D.C. So what occurred after that, I have no knowledge of, Congressman.

TAYLOR: Don't you think it would have made sense to follow up and see that that asset that you asked for was being used properly?

BROWN: Congressman, I just told you that I did that. And I made a rational decision, because based on the information that was given to me, the state of Mississippi—the state of Mississippi, who is the one who is the responder in this incident, said they no longer needed the USS *Comfort.* So I made a rational decision to move the *Comfort* to New Orleans and to move a cruise ship into Pascagoula.

After I left, that decision was apparently overruled or changed.

TAYLOR: All right.

In the lessons learned department, you said earlier that we should not be in the business of providing gasoline. If you saw the paper last week, you saw people pushing their vehicles down the highway in Texas in the stalled traffic for fear of running out of fuel. That made you aware of a heck of a lot of people who could have and would have left south Mississippi, gone and stayed with relatives, if fuel had only been available for them.

Since you kind of came and visited but left quickly you may not be aware that when the electricity goes down, so do the fuel pumps. So even if it's in the tank at the station, it's not being available to the public.

In the wake of all this, do you think it would be prudent for FEMA to rethink its position on delivering fuel to people, to help them evacuate, to help them run the generators, so that they don't have to become a burden on the citizens of this country?

BROWN: No, I do not, because I don't think that it's a wise policy decision to supply every man, woman and child or family with five gallons of gasoline, which is a dangerous commodity to begin with. And if we do it beforehand, we preposition it, it's going to wash away in floodwaters or it's going to be taken to a shelter. I just think that's a bad idea.

TAYLOR: So we got you to where you think every individual, even if they're 80 years old and incapacitated, ought to be responsible for having two or three days' worth of food, or heck with them.

You said we can't put one—referring to communications gear—in every county, and now we shouldn't even try to expedite people leaving a disaster area.

Mr. Brown, I'm certainly glad you came before this committee today. I think the public needed to know how you felt on these subjects.

Source: http://www.uncommonthought.com/mtblog/linked_files/BrownCongressionalTestimony.html.

Staff Report for Representative Charles Melancon, November 2, 2005

The Third Congressional District of Louisiana, a predominantly rural region encompassing most of southeastern Louisiana and surrounding the city of New Orleans and Orleans Parish, has a rich history flavored with a unique Cajun and Creole culture. With bayous, rivers, and streams that run into marshes and wetlands on their way to the Gulf of Mexico, the area is below sea level. The Third District took a devastating hit by Hurricane Katrina, ravaging Jefferson, St. Bernard, and Plaquemines parishes, including many suburban New Orleans communities. Hurricane Katrina and the subsequent failure of the New Orleans levee system caused massive flooding that displaced hundreds of thousands of people. At the time of Katrina, the Third District of Louisiana was represented in Congress by Charles Melancon, a Democrat. Soon after the testimony of Michael Brown, who had served as director of the Federal Emergency Management Agency during the disaster, Representative Melancon asked his staff to review the record of e-mail messages and other materials of Brown in the aftermath of Katrina.

STAFF REPORT FOR REPRESENTATIVE CHARLES MELANCON, NOVEMBER 2, 2005

To date, the Department of Homeland Security has provided few of the documents requested by Reps. Melancon and Davis. One exception, however, involves the e-mails of Michael Brown, the former director of the Federal Emergency Management Agency. Although it does not appear that the Department has provided a complete set of e-mails involving Mr. Brown, the Department has produced more than 1,000 pages of e-mail correspondence from Mr. Brown's office. About 100 pages of these e-mails were produced on October 14, 2005. The remainder, about 900 pages of e-mails, were produced on October 18, 2005.

At the request of Rep. Melancon, this staff analysis summarizes some of the key e-mails involving Mr. Brown. These e-mails paint a portrait of Mr. Brown that differs significantly from Mr. Brown's testimony before Congress about his actions. In his appearance before the House select committee, Mr. Brown described himself as an effective leader. He said, "I get it when it comes to emergency management. I know what it's all about."

The e-mails, however, reveal that Mr. Brown made few decisions and seemed out of touch. In the midst of the crisis, Mr. Brown found the time to exchange e-mails about his appearance, his reputation, and other nonessential matters. But few of his e-mails demonstrated leadership or a command of the challenges facing his agency.

Although the Brown e-mails provide a unique window into FEMA's decision-making process, they do not appear to be a complete set of Mr. Brown's e-mails. Mr. Brown testified before the select committee that he "exchanged e-mails" with White House officials, including White House chief of staff Andrew Card, yet none of these e-mails are included. There are also no e-mails between Mr. Brown and Secretary

Chertoff. Moreover, despite the requests of Reps. Melancon and Davis, the select committee has not received any of the relevant e-mails and communications involving Homeland Security Secretary Michael Chertoff, Defense Secretary Donald Rumsfeld, Army Corps of Engineers Commander Carl Strock, Health and Human Services Secretary Michael Leavitt, and White House chief of staff Andrew Card. The continued failure of Administration officials to comply with these document requests will impede congressional oversight of the federal response to Hurricane Katrina.

Mr. Brown's Testimony

On September 27, 2005, Michael Brown appeared before the House select committee to defend his response to Hurricane Katrina. At the hearing, Mr. Brown testified that "FEMA pushed forward with everything that it had, every team, every asset that we had, in order to help what we saw as being a potentially catastrophic disaster." He testified that he had made only two mistakes:

> First, I failed initially to set up a series of regular briefings to the media about what FEMA was doing throughout the Gulf Coast region. . . . Second, I very strongly personally regret that I was unable to persuade Governor Blanco and Mayor Nagin to sit down, get over their differences and work together. I just couldn't pull that off.

Mr. Brown also testified to his own leadership skills. Asked what credentials he brought to his job as FEMA Director, he said, "Management skills. . . . Organizational skills. . . . You need to be able to lead people, put the right people in place, put good people around you . . . not yes people but people who are going to argue and give you the pros and cons of the decisions that you have to make, and then be willing to make those decisions and carry forward with it."

Mr. Brown's E-Mails

The e-mails from Mr. Brown paint a different picture of Mr. Brown than Mr. Brown conveyed during the hearing. They reveal that Mr. Brown made few decisions and seemed out of touch. A number of the e-mails address nonessential matters such as what Mr. Brown should wear, how he could defend his reputation, and even who would care for his dog. Other e-mails are devoted to banter with Mr. Brown's staff. There are few e-mails that show Mr. Brown taking charge or issuing tasking orders. . . .

There are almost no e-mails from Mr. Brown in which he makes decisions and communicates them to his subordinates. In the e-mails, Mr. Brown receives incoming messages about specific problems, but rarely reacts.

On Wednesday, August 31, 2005, at 12:20 p.m., Marty Bahamonde, one of the only FEMA employees on the ground in New Orleans, sent a desperate message to Mr. Brown: "Sir, I know that you know the situation is past critical. Here are some things you might not know. Hotels are kicking people out, thousands gathering in the streets with no food or water. Hundreds still being rescued from homes. The dying patients at the DMAT tent being medivac. Estimates are many will die within hours. Evacuation in process. Plans developing for dome evacuation but hotel situation adding to problem. We are out of food and running out of water at the dome, plans in works to address the critical need. FEMA staff is OK and holding own. DMAT staff working in deplorable conditions. The sooner we can get the medical patients out, the sooner we can get them out. Phone connectivity impossible."

Mr. Brown responded to Mr. Bahamonde at 12:24 p.m. This is Mr. Brown's full response: "Thanks for the update. Anything specific I need to do or tweak?"

This indecisive response is not uncommon. Two days later, on Friday, September 2, 2005, Mr. Brown received a message with the subject "Medical help." At the time, thousands of patients were being transported to the New Orleans airport, which had been converted to a makeshift hospital.

Because of a lack of ventilators, medical personnel had to ventilate patients by hand for as long as 35 hours.

The text of the e-mail read: "Mike, Mickey and other medical equipment people have a 42 ft trailer full of beds, wheelchairs, oxygen concentrators, etc. They are wanting to take them where they can be used but need direction. Mickey specializes in ventilator patients so can be very helpful with acute care patients. If you could have someone contact him and let him know if he can be of service, he would appreciate it. Know you are busy but they really want to help."

Mr. Brown, however, did not respond to this message until four days later, when he finally forwarded it to FEMA Deputy chief of staff Brooks Altshuler and Deputy Director of Response Michael Lowder. The text of Mr. Brown's e-mail read: "Can we use these people?" . . .

The e-mails of former FEMA Director Michael Brown provide telling insights into the federal response to Hurricane Katrina. They depict a leader who seemed overwhelmed and rarely made key decisions. Many of the e-mails address superficial subjects—such as Mr. Brown's appearance or reputation—rather than the pressing response needs of Louisiana and Mississippi. Few of the e-mails show Mr. Brown taking command or directing the response. The credibility and thoroughness of the congressional investigation into the response to Hurricane Katrina will hinge on access to key documents and communications. To date, there are significant gaps in the e-mails involving Mr. Brown that have been provided to Congress. Other key officials—including Secretary Chertoff, Secretary Rumsfeld, Secretary Leavitt, and White House chief of staff Andrew Card—have not provided any of their communications. The select committee will not be able to fulfill its objectives if these documents are not produced in a timely manner.

Source: http://i.a.cnn.net/cnn/2005/images/11/03/brown.emails.analysis.pdf.

Testimony of Leah Hodges, December 6, 2005

The devastation wrought by Hurricane Katrina in loss of life, property, physical and mental injury, family displacement, and overall human tragedy was enormous. For the members of the investigating committees, it was not enough simply to calculate the numbers. They, and the nation, needed to see beyond the statistics and to hear from some of those who faced the awful days following Katrina. One of those individuals was a college student named Leah Hodges, who testified before the House committee on December 6, 2005.

TESTIMONY OF LEAH HODGES DECEMBER 6, 2005

I wish to thank everyone who is listening today for the chance to communicate my story. I come to Congress today representing not just myself, but hundreds, even thousands of other New Orleans residents who experienced the same or similar traumatic experiences and witnessed the same or similar events.

I come from a family of musicians. Before Hurricane Katrina, we were planning a musical family reunion. I had taken time off from pursuing my law degree to care for my sick granddad. I was also in the process of working with community leaders on setting up music and art workshops for youths. The manual I was writing for the workshops was severely damaged in the flood. I intend to finish it.

But I have also started a new project, which is all about my experience as a detainee at the Highway 10 causeway.

Let me begin with a few general points.

1. I don't need to point out the failures of the President, the Governor of Louisiana and the Mayor of New Orleans, as these individuals have already claimed responsibility for everything that happened to us as the result of the hurricane and its aftermath.
2. The people of New Orleans were stranded in a flood and were allowed to die. The military had personnel stationed just 40 miles outside the city, and they could have moved in and gotten people out sooner. People were allowed to die.
3. Animals from the animal shelter and fish from the fish aquarium were evacuated before the people.
4. The President and local officials issued "shoot to kill orders" and people were shot. People who asked for help were threatened with being shot. My niece and her fiancé, they needed gas. Her fiancé asked military for help and they told him "if you don't get back inside we will shoot you."
5. Bodies are still being found every day in New Orleans. Most people in New Orleans do not believe the official body counts.
6. The devastation that hit New Orleans was foreseeable and avoidable, and because it was not avoided, New Orleans was turned into a mass grave.
7. As a hurricane survivor, I and my family were detained, not rescued.

My family was ordered to evacuate our home. We were directed to evacuation points. Beforehand, I, my mother, my brother and two sisters visited a nursing home where the elderly clients had been abandoned by the owners and staff. There were five elderly persons there; the others had been evacuated earlier, perhaps by family. The day before the flood, the manager had come and told everyone they had to get out. Taking the keys to the bus that the home used to transport the senior citizens, the manager left them stranded. We rescued them. We shared all our food and provisions. When we approached the police and asked for help, they refused to help us. Instead, they threatened to shoot my baby brother.

We were then lured to the so-called evacuation points. This was several days after the hurricane had struck. The city was flooded. Soldiers had showed up with M16s and military weapons. They had declared New Orleans and Jefferson Parish a war zone. They loaded us onto military trucks after they told us they would take us to shelters where our basic needs would be met.

We were dropped off at a site where we were fenced in, and penned in with military vehicles. The armed military personnel brought in dogs. There we were subjected to conditions only comparable to a concentration camp.

We were in a wide open space along the interstate and under the Highway 10 causeway. The overpass provided little shade, however. During the days, we were exposed to the hot sun. August is the hottest month in New Orleans. It was early September and still extremely hot. Our skin blistered. My mother's skin is still not fully healed.

We were just three miles from an airport, but we were detained there for several days. Many of those who were there when we arrived had already been there several days. On any given day there were at least ten thousand people in the camp. On my last day there, I would estimate there were still three thousand detainees. By that time, nearly all the white people had been selected to evacuate first. They were put on buses and shipped out, leaving the remaining population 95 percent black.

There was muck and trash all over the causeway. Nothing was done to clean it up. At night, we were subject to sleep deprivation as low-flying helicopters were deliberately flown right over us. They would throw up the muck and trash, so that it would get all over us, even the pregnant women, the elderly, the infirm.

The military did not bring anything to help keep any of us alive. Not even a first aid kit. But they had body bags. They were doing nothing for the pregnant women. Some women miscarried. I know that conditions at the Convention Center were much the same. My niece was there. She was pregnant and she was terrified that her unborn baby had died. When she asked the military for help, they told her to wait until she was sure the baby was dead and then talk to them.

When I later spoke of my experience to a state trooper, he told me: "I would have rebelled." They set us up so that we would rebel, so that they could shoot us. At one point they brought in two truckloads of dogs and let the dogs out.

We would circulate through the camp to assist the sick and elderly and pregnant. One day, when I was on my way to get some water, I met a friend. He was a fellow musician. He told me that he wanted to try to get word out to the news media. But he was afraid to leave his family. I told him I would look after his family. But while he was gone I also had to circle back and check on my own family. I found that my brother had come up with an idea. He had persuaded a woman who was pregnant and due for labor to fake as if she were in labor. They told those in charge that she needed medical attention or she could have a miscarriage, and that got her out.

There was an old man from the senior center, he was an amputee. We had to carry him to the bathroom. They would not assist in caring for our people. The heat was unbearable. We got to the point we were so afraid of losing him to a heat stroke. We told them he was in a diabetic coma, that's how we got him out.

Mother is a cardiac patient, born with an enlarged heart. She suffers extreme hypertension. For three days I pleaded with them for care, and they would not do anything. Finally, on the third day, someone came out to check her blood pressure. The sphygmomanometer did not appear to be in working condition. I told the man, who was from the Coast Guard, to take my blood pressure first. The thing fell to pieces in his hands. It never worked.

The camp was so big, and people were scattered. People were deliberately kept apart. One woman was not allowed to see her two children.

At the camp, they lied and told us all the buses were going to the same place. They wouldn't tell us when the buses were coming. Meanwhile, my mother sat in the blazing hot sun. . . .

On the last day they refused to give food and water to the ill for 24 hours.

People died in the camp. We saw the bodies lying there.

They were all about detention, as if it were Iraq, like we were foreigners and they were fighting a war. They implemented war-like conditions. They treated us worse than prisoners of war. Even prisoners of war have rights under the Geneva Convention.

Source: Select Bipartisan Committee to Investigate the Preparation for and Response to Hurricane Katrina, http://i.a.cnn.net/cnn/2005/images/11/03/brown.emails.analysis.pdf.

Executive Summary of Report of House Select Bipartisan Committee to Investigate the Preparation for and Response to Hurricane Katrina, February 15, 2006

Headed by the moderate Republican Tom Davis of Virginia, the House select committee on Katrina was not the partisan whitewash that most of the Democrats in the House had predicted. Although hampered by the refusal of President Bush and other administration officials to turn over much of the documentation that would have been valuable in assessing the lack of preparedness of the Katrina disaster, Davis and his colleagues on the committee were not hesitant in their final report issued on February 15, 2006, to attack the administration for its lack of urgency and bumbling communication and coordination. They called the report "A Failure of Initiative." "It remains difficult to understand how government could respond so ineffectively to a disaster that was anticipated for years and for which specific dire warnings had been issued for days," said Davis.

EXECUTIVE SUMMARY OF REPORT OF HOUSE COMMITTEE ON HURRICANE KATRINA FEBRUARY 15, 2006

The Select Committee identified failures at all levels of government that significantly undermined and detracted from the heroic efforts of first responders, private individuals and organizations, faith-based groups, and others.

The institutional and individual failures we have identified became all the more clear when compared to the heroic efforts of those who acted decisively. Those who didn't flinch, who took matters into their own hands when bureaucratic inertia was causing death, injury, and suffering. Those whose exceptional initiative saved time and money and lives.

We salute the exceptions to the rule, or, more accurately, the exceptions that proved the rule. People like Mike Ford, the owner of three nursing homes who wisely chose to evacuate his patients in Plaquemines Parish before Katrina hit, due in large part to his close and long-standing working relationship with Jesse St. Amant, Director of the Plaquemines Office of Emergency Preparedness.

People like Dr. Gregory Henderson, a pathologist who showed that not all looting represented lawlessness when, with the aid of New Orleans police officers, he raided pharmacies for needed medication and supplies and set up ad hoc clinics in downtown hotels before moving on to the Convention Center.

But these acts of leadership were too few and far between. And no one heard about or learned from them until it was too late. The preparation for and response to Hurricane Katrina show we are still an analog government in a digital age. We must recognize that we are woefully incapable of storing, moving, and accessing information—especially in times of crisis. Many of the problems we have identified can be categorized as "information gaps"—or at least problems with information-related implications, or failures to act decisively because information was sketchy at best. Better information would have been an optimal weapon against Katrina. Information sent to the right people at the right place at the right time.

Information moved within agencies, across departments, and between jurisdictions of government as well.

Seamlessly. Securely. Efficiently. Unfortunately, no government does these things well, especially big governments. The federal government is the largest purchaser of information technology in the world, by far. One would think we could share information by now. But Katrina again proved we cannot.

We reflect on the 9/11 Commission's finding that "the most important failure was one of imagination." The Select Committee believes Katrina was primarily a failure of initiative. But there is, of course, a nexus between the two. Both imagination and initiative—in other words, *leadership*—require good information. And a coordinated process for sharing it. And a willingness to use information—however imperfect or incomplete—to fuel action.

With Katrina, the reasons reliable information did not reach more people more quickly are many, and these reasons provide the foundation for our findings. In essence, we found that while a national emergency management system that relies on state and local governments to identify needs and request resources is adequate for most disasters, a catastrophic disaster like Katrina can and did overwhelm most aspects of the system for an initial period of time. No one anticipated the degree and scope of the destruction the storm would cause, even though many could and should have.

The failure of local, state, and federal governments to respond more effectively to Katrina—which had been predicted in theory for many years, and forecast with startling accuracy for five days—demonstrates that whatever improvements have been made to our capacity to respond to natural or man-made disasters, four and a half years after 9/11, we are still not fully prepared. Local first responders were largely overwhelmed and unable to perform their duties, and the National Response Plan did not adequately provide a way for federal assets to quickly supplement or, if necessary, supplant first responders.

The failure of initiative was also a failure of agility. Response plans at all levels of government lacked flexibility and adaptability. Inflexible procedures often delayed the response. Officials at all levels seemed to be waiting for the disaster that fit their plans, rather than planning and building scalable capacities to meet whatever Mother Nature threw at them. We again encountered the risk-averse culture that pervades big government, and again recognized the need for organizations as agile and responsive as the 21st century world in which we live.

One-size-fits-all plans proved impervious to clear warnings of extraordinary peril. Category 5 needs elicited a Category 1 response. Ours was a response that could not adequately accept civilian and international generosity, and one for which the Congress, through inadequate oversight and accounting of state and local use of federal funds, must accept some blame.

In crafting our findings, we did not guide the facts. We let the facts guide us. The Select Committee's report elaborates on the following findings, which are summarized in part here, in the order in which they appear:

- The accuracy and timeliness of National Weather Service and National Hurricane Center forecasts prevented further loss of life. The Hurricane Pam exercise reflected recognition by all levels of government of the dangers of a catastrophic hurricane striking New Orleans.
- Implementation of lessons learned from Hurricane Pam was incomplete. Levees protecting New Orleans were not built for the most severe hurricanes.
- Responsibilities for levee operations and maintenance were diffuse.
- The lack of a warning system for breaches and other factors delayed repairs to the levees.
- The ultimate cause of the levee failures is under investigation, and results to be determined.

The failure of complete evacuations led to preventable deaths, great suffering, and further delays in relief.

- Evacuations of general populations went relatively well in all three states.
- Despite adequate warning 56 hours before landfall, Governor Blanco and Mayor Nagin delayed ordering a mandatory evacuation in New Orleans until 19 hours before landfall.
- The failure to order timely mandatory evacuations, Mayor Nagin's decision to shelter but not evacuate the remaining population, and decisions of individuals led to an incomplete evacuation.
- The incomplete pre-landfall evacuation led to deaths, thousands of dangerous rescues, and horrible conditions for those who remained.
- Federal, state, and local officials' failure to anticipate the post-landfall conditions delayed post-landfall evacuation and support.

Critical elements of the National Response Plan were executed late, ineffectively, or not at all.

- It does not appear the President received adequate advice and counsel from a senior disaster professional.
- Given the well-known consequences of a major hurricane striking New Orleans, the Secretary should have designated an Incident of National Significance no later than Saturday, two days prior to landfall, when the National Weather Service predicted New Orleans would be struck by a Category 4 or 5 hurricane and President Bush declared a federal emergency.
- The Secretary should have convened the [National] Interagency Incident Management Group [a group comprised of local, state, and federal entities with fire protection responsibilities to improve the ability of fire protection forces in emergencies] on Saturday, two days prior to landfall, or earlier to analyze Katrina's potential consequences and anticipate what the federal response would need to accomplish.

- The Secretary should have designated the Principal Federal Official [PFO] on Saturday, two days prior to landfall, from the roster of PFOs who had successfully completed the required training, unlike then-FEMA Director Michael Brown. Considerable confusion was caused by the Secretary's PFO decisions.
- A proactive federal response, or push system, is not a new concept, but it is rarely utilized.
- The Secretary should have invoked the Catastrophic Incident Annex [an established set of strategies for coordinating responses in case of mass casualties] to direct the federal response posture to fully switch from a reactive to proactive mode of operations.
- Absent the Secretary's invocation of the Catastrophic Incident Annex, the federal response evolved into a push system over several days.
- The Homeland Security Operations Center failed to provide valuable situational information to the White House and key operational officials during the disaster.
- The White House failed to de-conflict varying damage assessments and discounted information that ultimately proved accurate.
- Federal agencies, including DHS, had varying degrees of unfamiliarity with their roles and responsibilities under the National Response Plan and National Incident Management System [which establishes standardized incident management processes, protocols, and procedures that all responders—federal, state, tribal, and local—use to coordinate and conduct response actions].
- Once activated, the Emergency Management Assistance Compact enabled an unprecedented level of mutual aid assistance to reach the disaster area in a timely and effective manner.
- Earlier presidential involvement might have resulted in a more effective response.

DHS and the states were not prepared for this catastrophic event.

- While a majority of state and local preparedness grants are required to have a terrorism purpose, this does not preclude a dual use application.
- Despite extensive preparedness initiatives, DHS was not prepared to respond to the catastrophic effects of Hurricane Katrina.
- DHS and FEMA lacked adequate trained and experienced staff for the Katrina response.
- The readiness of FEMA's national emergency response teams was inadequate and reduced the effectiveness of the federal response.

Massive communications damage and a failure to adequately plan for alternatives impaired response.

- Massive inoperability had the biggest effect on communications, limiting command and control, situational awareness, and federal, state, and local officials' ability to address unsubstantiated media reports.
- Some local and state responders prepared for communications losses but still experienced problems, while others were caught unprepared.
- The National Communication System met many of the challenges posed by Hurricane Katrina, enabling critical communication during the response, but gaps in the system did result in delayed response and inadequate delivery of relief supplies.

Command and control was impaired at all levels, delaying relief.

- Lack of communications and situational awareness paralyzed command and control.
- A lack of personnel, training, and funding also weakened command and control.
- Ineffective command and control delayed many relief efforts.

The military played an invaluable role, but coordination was lacking.

- DOD [Department of Defense]/DHS coordination was not effective during Hurricane Katrina.
- DOD, FEMA, and the state of Louisiana had difficulty coordinating with each other, which slowed the response.
- National Guard and DOD response operations were comprehensive, but perceived as slow. Coordination with other responders could improve.
- The Army Corps of Engineers provided critical resources to Katrina victims, but pre-landfall contacts were not adequate.
- DOD has not yet incorporated or implemented lessons learned from joint exercises in military assistance to civil authorities that would have allowed for a more effective response to Katrina.
- The lack of integration of National Guard and active duty forces hampered the military response.
- Northern Command does not have adequate insight into state response capabilities or adequate interface with governors, which contributed to a lack of mutual understanding and trust during the Katrina response.
- Even DOD lacked situational awareness of post-landfall conditions, which contributed to a slower response.
- DOD lacked an information sharing protocol that would have enhanced joint situational awareness and communications between all military components.
- Joint Task Force Katrina command staff lacked joint training, which contributed to the lack of coordination between active duty components.
- Joint Task Force Katrina, the National Guard, Louisiana, and Mississippi lacked needed communications equipment and the interoperability required for seamless on-the-ground coordination.
- EMAC [The Emergency Management Assistance Compact, a congressionally ratified organization that provides form and structure to interstate mutual aid] processing, pre-arranged state compacts, and Guard equipment packages need improvement.

- Equipment, personnel, and training shortfalls affected the National Guard response.
- Search and rescue operations were a tremendous success, but coordination and integration between the military services, the National Guard, the Coast Guard, and other rescue organizations was lacking.

The collapse of local law enforcement and lack of effective public communications led to civil unrest and further delayed relief.

- A variety of conditions led to lawlessness and violence in hurricane stricken areas.
- The New Orleans Police Department was ill-prepared for continuity of operations and lost almost all effectiveness.
- The lack of a government public communications strategy and media hype of violence exacerbated public concerns and further delayed relief.
- EMAC and military assistance were critical for restoring law and order.
- Federal law enforcement agencies were also critical to restoring law and order and coordinating activities.

Medical care and evacuations suffered from a lack of advance preparations, inadequate communications, and difficulties coordinating efforts.

- Deployment of medical personnel was reactive, not proactive.
- Poor planning and pre-positioning of medical supplies and equipment led to delays and shortages.
- New Orleans was unprepared to provide evacuations and medical care for its special needs population and dialysis patients, and Louisiana officials lacked a common definition of "special needs."
- Most hospital and Veterans Affairs Medical Center emergency plans did not offer concrete guidance about if or when evacuations should take place.
- New Orleans hospitals, Veterans Affairs Medical Center, and medical first responders were not adequately prepared for a full evacuation of medical facilities.
- The government did not effectively coordinate private air transport capabilities for the evacuation of medical patients.
- Hospital and Veterans Affairs Medical Center emergency plans did not adequately prepare for communication needs.
- Following Hurricane Katrina, New Orleans Veterans Affairs Medical Center and hospitals' inability to communicate impeded their ability to ask for help.
- Medical responders did not have adequate communications equipment or operability.
- Evacuation decisions for New Orleans nursing homes were subjective and, in one case, led to preventable deaths.
- Lack of electronic patient medical records contributed to difficulties and delays in medical treatment of evacuees.
- Top officials at the Department of Health and Human Services and the National Disaster Medical System do not share a common understanding of who controls the National Disaster Medical System under Emergency Support Function.
- Lack of coordination led to delays in recovering dead bodies.
- Deployment confusion, uncertainty about mission assignments, and government red tape delayed medical care.

Long-standing weaknesses and the magnitude of the disaster overwhelmed FEMA's ability to provide emergency shelter and temporary housing.

- Relocation plans did not adequately provide for shelter. Housing plans were haphazard and inadequate.
- State and local governments made inappropriate selections of shelters of last resort. The lack of a regional database of shelters contributed to an inefficient and ineffective evacuation and sheltering process.
- There was inappropriate delay in getting people out of shelters and into temporary housing—delays that officials should have foreseen due to manufacturing limitations.
- FEMA failed to take advantage of the Department of Housing and Urban Development's expertise in largescale housing challenges.

FEMA logistics and contracting systems did not support a targeted, massive, and sustained provision of commodities.

- FEMA management lacked situational awareness of existing requirements and of resources in the supply chain. An overwhelmed logistics system made it challenging to get supplies, equipment, and personnel where and when needed.
- Procedures for requesting federal assistance raised numerous concerns.
- The failure at all levels to enter into advance contracts led to chaos and the potential for waste and fraud as acquisitions were made in haste.
- Before Katrina, FEMA suffered from a lack of sufficiently trained procurement professionals. DHS procurement continues to be decentralized and lacking a uniform approach, and its procurement office was understaffed given the volume and dollar value of work.
- Ambiguous statutory guidance regarding local contractor participation led to ongoing disputes over procuring debris removal and other services.
- Attracting emergency contractors and corporate support could prove challenging given the scrutiny that companies have endured.

Contributions by charitable organizations assisted many in need, but the American Red Cross and others faced challenges due to the size of the mission, inadequate logistics capacity, and a disorganized shelter process.

Source: U. S. Congress. House. "A Failure of Initiative: The Final Report of the Select Bipartisan Committee to Investigate the Preparation for and Response to Hurricane Katrina." 109th Cong., 2nd sess., 2006, H. Rep. 109-377. Available at http://katrina.house.gov/.

Excerpt Regarding Michael Chertoff from Senate Committee Report on Department of Homeland Security, 2006

Michael Chertoff was no stranger to congressional investigations. The influential lawyer had been special counsel for the Senate Whitewater Committee, which delved into various accusations against President Bill Clinton and Hillary Rodham Clinton in the 1990s. When Chertoff was approved by the Senate in 2003 for a federal judgeship, the only dissenting vote was that of Senator Hillary Rodham Clinton of New York. And now, in February 2006, Chertoff was the figure at the witness table answering questions about his role as secretary of the Department of Homeland Security during the Katrina disaster. Although Chertoff took responsibility for his department's inadequate response to Katrina, he refused to admit that the Bush administration did not take the hurricane seriously. Instead, Chertoff lamented that he had trusted Michael Brown, director of the Federal Emergency Management Agency, to lead the federal response effort. "If I knew then what I know now about Mr. Brown's agenda," Chertoff declared, "I would have done something different." Like the report of the House committee on Katrina, the Senate report took Chertoff to task for many more lapses than trusting Michael Brown.

EXCERPT REGARDING MICHAEL CHERTOFF FROM SENATE COMMITTEE REPORT ON DEPARTMENT OF HOMELAND SECURITY, 2006

Federal Preparations

The National Response Plan (NRP) was intended to form the basis of the federal government's response to disasters and for its interaction with state and local governments during such events. The response to the Hurricane Katrina disaster varied across the federal government.

The Department of Homeland Security (DHS), which is charged with preparing for and responding to domestic incidents, whether terrorist attacks or natural disasters, failed to lead an effective federal response to Hurricane Katrina. DHS did not fully adapt or adequately train to meet its obligations under the NRP before Hurricane Katrina. Nor did the Department address the known deficiencies of the Federal Emergency Management Agency (FEMA), such as staffing shortages, inadequate training, poor commodities tracking, and insufficient plans for post-disaster communications. In the critical days before landfall, DHS leadership mostly watched from the sidelines, allowed FEMA to take the lead, and missed critical opportunities to help prepare the entire federal government for the response. . . .

Department of Homeland Security

DHS and its leaders failed to prepare the nation adequately for the unprecedented devastation of Hurricane Katrina. . . . DHS failed to fully adapt and appropriately train to meet the requirements of the NRP in the nine months between its promulgation and Hurricane Katrina. Nor did the Department address FEMA's deficiencies such as staffing shortage, weaknesses in commodities tracking, and insufficient plans for post-disaster communications. . . .

As Katrina was bearing down on the Gulf Coast, they failed to take reasonable steps during that period to create a full awareness and a sense of urgency across the federal government about the impending catastrophe. DHS's actions and inactions during the days immediately prior to landfall had consequences in the days that followed.

Besides DHS's failure to organize, train, and equip its personnel under the NRP, poor preparation, and missed opportunities led to responders' improvising actions because they had no clear plan to guide them. The failures of the response flowed logically from these mistakes made before landfall.

DHS Leadership in the Days Before Landfall

The job of leading the federal response to a catastrophe rests with the Secretary of DHS. In the days before Katrina made landfall, DHS Secretary Michael Chertoff's efforts in this regard fell short of what was reasonably expected of him. Secretary Chertoff testified that he saw his role as "lead[ing] the entire Department, imparting strategic guidance and direction based upon the plan developed, priorities established, and information provided. I also work with the President and other Department heads and deal with governors, members of Congress and other officials."

Secretary Chertoff testified that over the course of the weekend before landfall, he "followed planning activities closely" and "stayed in continual contact with senior DHS and FEMA officials and my experienced advisors."

On the Saturday before landfall, Secretary Chertoff was at home working on unrelated matters, and his only apparent Katrina-related activity was to receive a briefing about that day's FEMA video teleconference [VTC]. These video teleconferences are a means by which key federal and state personnel involved in emergency management share information about their disaster preparations, including the latest weather forecasts, the progress of evacuations, and the pre-positioning of commodities.

On Sunday, Secretary Chertoff participated in the FEMA VTC. He heard assurances from then-FEMA Director Michael Brown and others that preparations were well in hand. For instance, Brown told attendees on the conference call "I want that supply chain jammed up as much as possible. . . . Just keep jamming those lines full as much as you can with commodities" and "get to the edge of the envelope. . . . If you feel like you are missing go ahead and do it. I'll figure out some way to justify it."

Secretary Chertoff offered to assist Brown in enlisting aid from other DHS components: "If there's anything that you need from Coast Guard or any other components that you're not getting, please let us know."

Brown told Secretary Chertoff, "I appreciate it. . . . The Coast Guard and ICE [Immigration and Customs Enforcement] and all of the others have been incredibly good to us." Secretary Chertoff also asked, "Are there any DOD [Department of Defense] assets that might be available? Have we reached out to them [DOD], and have we I guess made any kind of arrangement in case we need some additional help from them?" Brown responded that there were DOD assets at the State Emergency Operations Center [EOC] in Baton Rouge that were "fully engaged."

Secretary Chertoff testified that he did not second-guess statements he heard on the Sunday VTC—including those by state emergency managers and state National Guard officials who, as he termed it, "express[ed] very clearly their satisfaction with the state of affairs."

During the August 28 conference call, Brown asked the Acting Deputy Director of the Louisiana Office of Homeland Security and Emergency Preparedness, Colonel Jeff Smith, if there were "any unmet needs, anything that we're not getting to you that you need" to which Colonel Smith responded, "Mike, no . . . it looks like those resources that are en route are going to—to be a good first shot." Colonel Smith also cautioned that, "Naturally, once we get into this thing . . . I'm sure that things are going to come up that maybe some of even our best planners hadn't even thought about. So I think flexibility is going to be the key." He also stated that it would be important to "cut through any potential red tape when those things do arise."

The Mississippi representative on the call said, "FEMA has been great. You're leaning forward, and we appreciate that." He later said, "We've got everything that we need from the federal government." Secretary Chertoff thought the emergency management officials on that call had hundreds of years of combined professional experience managing hurricanes.

Secretary Chertoff also spoke with Governors [Haley] Barbour of Mississippi, [Kathleen] Blanco of Louisiana, and [Bob] Riley of Alabama that day. The Secretary and other senior leaders did not take affirmative steps prior to landfall, beyond his statements on the Sunday VTC, to ensure that DHS components with operational responsibilities under the NRP [National Response Plan] were prepared to respond. Instead, the evidence suggests that Secretary Chertoff and DHS responded to Katrina as if DHS headquarters had no special responsibilities outside the normal course of operations.

Despite assurances and lack of affirmative requests from the governors of the Gulf states, the Secretary still should have taken additional steps to better prepare his Department for the coming storm. From all corners, the message throughout the weekend, especially at the Saturday and Sunday VTCs, was that a catastrophe was about to strike the Gulf Coast, and the greater New Orleans area in particular. The head of the National Hurricane Service [Center], Max Mayfield, had been making calls to leaders in parishes, cities, states, and the federal government. The Hurricane Pam exercise in 2004 had predicted that flooding from a catastrophic storm—what had been known for years among meteorologists and government officials as the "New Orleans scenario"—might kill as many as 60,000. In the weekend conference call, Brown referred to the approaching storm as the "big one." As Mayfield said, "I think the wisest thing to do here is plan on a Category 5 hurricane . . . no matter where it hits it's going to have an impact over a very, very large area. . . . I don't think any model can tell you with any confidence right now whether the levees will be topped or not, but that's obviously a very, very grave concern."

During the weekend, as Katrina neared New Orleans, there was a need for initiative, for recognition of the unprecedented threat and the equally unprecedented response it required. Leadership—direction, encouragement, a sense of purpose and urgency—was needed. Secretary Chertoff did not provide it.

For example, he did not ask specifically what preparations were under way, how much material was being prepositioned, and whether it would be enough. And though the DHS Inspector General had issued a draft report in June 2005 stating that FEMA's logistics systems had performed poorly during the four Florida hurricanes in 2004, Secretary Chertoff did not inquire whether the system could handle the expected impact of Katrina. The Committee has found no evidence to suggest that anyone, including Secretary Chertoff, attempted to determine if the system could handle the expected impact of Katrina. Similarly, a DHS study had concluded that FEMA's procurement office was understaffed. Yet the Secretary did not ask whether this important office was up to the coming task. Although he has stated repeatedly that he relied on Brown as his "battlefield commander," aside from on the Sunday VTC, according to Brown, Secretary Chertoff did not talk to his "commander" directly over the weekend, either while Brown was in Washington or after he left for the Gulf on Sunday afternoon.

In view of Secretary Chertoff's testimony that he stayed in contact with "senior DHS and FEMA officials and [his] experienced advisors," this omission is particularly inexplicable. Because Secretary Chertoff was placing so much faith in Brown to lead the preparations and response, it was incumbent on the Secretary to do more than just have a brief management conversation with him in front of dozens of state, local, and federal officials—including the President of the United States—on a VTC. Secretary Chertoff should have called Brown privately to discuss in more detail the status of preparations and the level of cooperation Brown was getting from DHS and other government departments.

Conversely, Brown failed to inform the Secretary of the FEMA deficiencies that he has since claimed in testimony and media interviews to have known about at the time. These two key players' failure to communicate is evidence of the profound dysfunction then existing between DHS and FEMA leadership.

Additionally:

- There should have been a plan to maintain situational awareness at the Homeland Security Operations Center (HSOC). The Director of DHS' Operations Center,

Matthew Broderick, testified "there was no plan." The HSOC plans months in advance for events such as the Super Bowl, yet no effort was being made to identify sources of information specific to New Orleans and the Gulf Coast, such as local National Weather Service stations or local media outlets. Rather, the intention was to rely exclusively on FEMA officials and the very state and local entities that would be bearing the brunt of the storm's fury to provide situational awareness. Secretary Chertoff bears ultimate responsibility for ensuring that there is such a plan.

The National Communications System (NCS) never developed a plan to restore communications to emergency responders, such as the police and fire departments, after a catastrophic disaster. Instead, the NCS intended to rely solely on the private sector to restore communications capabilities. Additionally, Peter Fonash, the Director of NCS, was not familiar with the "New Orleans scenario," until the day before landfall. The Secretary bears ultimate responsibility for this lack of preparation.

- The investigation uncovered no evidence that anyone coordinated with the Department of Justice (DOJ) to determine which agency was going to take the lead under Emergency Support Function 13, Public Safety and Security. . . . There was no DOJ representative at the Public Safety and Security desk at the FEMA National Response Coordination Center (NRCC), FEMA's national operations center in charge of overall coordination of the response at the national level. Each of the Emergency Support Functions is represented there to coordinate activities in their area of expertise. Additionally DOJ did not have a response plan (either for itself or to coordinate with DHS) to execute Public Safety and Security responsibilities following a natural disaster.
- The investigation uncovered no evidence that senior DHS leadership contacted the leadership of Immigration and Custom Enforcement (ICE), Customs and Border Patrol (CBP), Federal Protective Service (FPS) or the Secret Service to assess their planning and preparation—or even to determine if they *were* planning and preparing. There was confusion over staffing the Public Safety and Security desk at the NRCC—FPS had attempted to send a representative to the desk, only to be rebuffed by FEMA. Moreover, ICE was going forward with a previously scheduled conference in Baltimore for its Special Agents in Charge (SACs), and the New Orleans SAC was still planning to fly out Sunday morning to attend the conference rather than remain in the area to lead his office's response efforts after the storm had passed.

In addition, the Secretary has broader responsibilities that reach across the federal government. Yet, there is no evidence, nor any testimony by the Secretary, that he reached out to other Cabinet secretaries to assess their level of preparedness, to determine if they were coordinating efforts with DHS, or to ensure that they responded quickly and fully to any requests that might come from DHS or FEMA.

Finally, it is reasonable to expect that the Secretary would be engaged with the President during critical times in a catastrophe. The Committee was unable to develop any record as to whether the Secretary was in fact keeping the President informed in the pre-storm period. The lack of plans to maintain situational awareness, the lack of coordination in the deployment of federal law enforcement assets, and the communications problems at all levels of government all resulted in part from some of the pre-landfall inaction described above. Much was expected of Secretary Chertoff, and there were things that only he, as a Cabinet secretary, could do. In his testimony before the Committee, U.S. Comptroller General David Walker (the head of the non-partisan Government Accountability Office, which is commonly referred to as the investigative arm of Congress) described the unique leverage of such a position: "No matter how capable the person [leading the response effort] might be, level matters in this town, unfortunately, especially with regard to certain departments and agencies like the Department of Defense. *Hierarchy is real.*"

Source: U.S. Congress. Senate. Committee on Homeland Security and Governmental Affairs. *Hurricane Katrina: A Nation Still Unprepared.* 109th Cong., 2d sess., 2006. S. Rep. 163-168.

Excerpt from Executive Summary of the Report of the Senate Committee on Homeland Security and Governmental Affairs, May 2006

The Senate committee probing the Katrina disaster, headed by Susan Collins, Republican from Maine, and Joseph Lieberman, Democrat from Connecticut, issued its own report in May 2006, three months after the House report had been made public. It echoed many of the criticisms leveled by the House committee. Throughout the investigation, Senator Lieberman had been outspoken about the refusal of the White House to cooperate. At one point he said that his staff had been almost totally stonewalled. "There's been no assertion of executive privilege, just a refusal to answer," Lieberman said. "I have been told by my staff that almost every question our staff has asked federal agency witnesses regarding conversations with or involvement of the White House has been met with a response that they could not answer on direction of the White House." Despite Lieberman's dismay over White House intransigence, the committee did not take aggressive action to challenge the White House. Although the report was stinging in its criticism, it lacked documented authority. Thus, the work of neither the House nor the Senate committee resulted in any formal actions against those responsible for neglect. The Senate committee made a number of recommendations, most notably calling for the creation of a "New National Emergency Management System for the 21st Century." That proposal, containing a number of useful suggestions, would be blown away by the strong winds of politics.

EXCERPT FROM EXECUTIVE SUMMARY OF SENATE REPORT, MAY 2006

Hurricane Katrina was an extraordinary act of nature that spawned a human tragedy. It was the most destructive natural disaster in American history, laying waste to 90,000 square miles of land, an area the size of the United Kingdom. In Mississippi, the storm surge obliterated coastal communities and left thousands destitute. New Orleans was overwhelmed by flooding. All told, more than 1,500 people died. Along the Gulf Coast, tens of thousands suffered without basic essentials for almost a week.

But the suffering that continued in the days and weeks after the storm passed did not happen in a vacuum; instead, it continued longer than it should have because of—and was in some cases exacerbated by—the failure of government at all levels to plan, prepare for and respond aggressively to the storm. These failures were not just conspicuous; they were pervasive. Among the many factors that contributed to these failures, the Committee found that there were four overarching ones: 1) long-term warnings went unheeded and government officials neglected their duties to prepare for a forewarned catastrophe; 2) government officials took insufficient actions or made poor decisions in the days immediately before and after landfall; 3) systems which officials relied on to support their response efforts failed; and 4) government officials at all levels failed to provide effective leadership.

These individual failures, moreover, occurred against a backdrop of failure, over time, to develop the capacity for a coordinated, national response to a truly catastrophic event, whether caused by nature or man-made. The results were tragic loss of life and human suffering on a massive scale, and an undermining of confidence in our governments' ability to plan, prepare for, and respond to national catastrophes.

Effective response to mass emergencies is a critical role of every level of government. It is a role that requires an unusual level of planning, coordination and dispatch among governments' diverse units. Following the terrorist attacks of 9/11, this country went through one of the most sweeping reorganizations of federal government in history. While driven primarily by concerns of terrorism, the reorganization was designed to strengthen our nation's ability to address the consequences of both natural and man-made disasters. In its first major test, this reorganized system failed. Katrina revealed that much remains to be done.

The Committee began this investigation of the preparations for and response to Hurricane Katrina within two weeks of the hurricane's landfall on the Gulf Coast. The tragic loss of life and human suffering in Katrina's wake would have been sufficient in themselves to compel the Committee's attention. But the conspicuous failures in governments' emergency preparedness and response added a sense of urgency to the investigation—not only because of our heightened national awareness of the dangers of both terrorist acts and natural disasters, but because so much effort had been directed towards improvement.

Our investigation has been bipartisan, and has examined in detail the actions of officials of local, state and federal government departments and agencies. Though suffering was pervasive across the Gulf Coast, the Committee focused most of its efforts on the response in New Orleans, where massive flooding presented extraordinary challenges to responders and victims alike. In addition, the investigation centered largely on the initial response to the hurricane in the critical week or so after the storm hit. We have conducted formal interviews of more than 325 witnesses, reviewed over 838,000 pages of documentation, and conducted 22 public hearings with 85 witnesses in the course of our information gathering efforts. Our report, more than 700 pages long, includes 86 findings and 185 recommendations.

Most of our hearings focused on what went wrong in Katrina. Two of our hearings, however, examined the successes: the effective and heroic search and rescue efforts by the U.S. Coast Guard; and the outstanding performance of certain members of the private sector in restoring essential services to the devastated communities and providing relief to the victims. These successes shared some important traits. The Coast Guard and certain private sector businesses both conducted extensive planning and training for disasters, and they put that preparation into use when disaster struck. Both moved material assets and personnel out of harm's way as the storm approached, but kept them close enough to the front lines for quick response after it passed. Perhaps most important, both had empowered front-line leaders who were able to make decisions when they needed to be made. . . .

The Roles of the Different Levels of Government in Disaster Response

Assessing the government's response to Katrina requires at the outset an understanding of the roles of government entities and their leaders and the framework within which they operate. Every level of government, and many components within each level, play important roles. At every level of government, the chief executive has the ultimate responsibility to manage an emergency response.

It has long been standard practice that emergency response begins at the lowest possible jurisdictional level—typically the local government, with state government becoming involved at the local government's request when the resources of local government are (or are expected to be) overwhelmed. Similarly, while the federal government provides ongoing financial support to state and local governments for emergency preparedness, ordinarily it becomes involved in responding to a disaster at a state's request when resources of state and local governments are (or are expected to be) overwhelmed. Louisiana's Emergency Operations Plan explicitly lays out this hierarchy of response.

During a catastrophe, which by definition almost immediately exceeds state and local resources and significantly disrupts governmental operations and emergency services, the role of the federal government is particularly vital, and it would reasonably be expected to play a more substantial role in response than in an "ordinary" disaster.

Long-Term and Short-Term Warnings Went Unheeded

The Committee has worked to identify and understand the sources of government's inadequate response and recovery efforts. And while this report does not purport to have identified every such source, it is clear that there was no lack of information about the devastating potential of Katrina, or the uncertain strength of the levees and floodwalls protecting New Orleans, or the likely needs of survivors. Nonetheless, top officials at every level of government—despite strongly worded advisories from the National Hurricane Center (NHC) and personal warnings from NHC Director Max Mayfield—did not appear to truly grasp the magnitude of the storm's potential for destruction before it made landfall.

The potentially devastating threat of a catastrophic hurricane to the Gulf region has been known for forty years: New Orleans experienced flooding in some areas of remarkably similar proportions from Hurricane Betsy in 1965, and Hurricane Camille devastated the Gulf Coast in 1969. More recently, numerous experts and governmental officials had been anticipating an increase in violent hurricanes, and New Orleans' special and growing vulnerability to catastrophic flooding due to changing geological and other conditions was widely described in both technical and popular media.

Hurricane Georges hit the Gulf in 1998, spurring the state of Louisiana to ask FEMA for assistance with catastrophic hurricane planning. Little was accomplished for the next six years. Between 2000 and 2003, state authorities, an emergency-preparedness contractor, and FEMA's own regional staff repeatedly advised FEMA headquarters in Washington that planning for evacuation and shelter for the "New Orleans scenario" was incomplete and inadequate, but FEMA failed to approach other federal agencies for help with transportation and shelter or to ensure that the City and State had the matters in hand.

Then, in 2004, a White House aide received a briefing on the catastrophe on a scenario whose characteristics foreshadowed most of Katrina's impacts. While this hypothetical "Hurricane Pam" exercise resulted in draft plans beginning in early 2005, they were incomplete when Katrina hit. Nonetheless, some officials took the initiative to use concepts developed in the drafts, with mixed success in the critical aspects of the Katrina response. However, many of its admonitory lessons were either ignored or inadequately applied. . . .

The specific danger that Katrina posed to the Gulf Coast became clear on the afternoon of Friday, August 26, when forecasters at the National Hurricane Center and the National Weather Service saw that the storm was turning west. First in phone calls to Louisiana emergency management officials and then in their 5 p.m. EDT Katrina forecast and accompanying briefings, they alerted both Louisiana and Mississippi that the track of the storm was now expected to shift significantly to the west of its original track to the Florida panhandle. The National Hurricane Center warned that Katrina could be a Category 4 or even a 5 by landfall. By the next morning, Weather Service officials directly confirmed to the Governor of Louisiana and other state and local officials that New Orleans was squarely at risk. . . .

Preparation Proved Insufficient

Some coastal towns in Mississippi went to extraordinary lengths to get citizens to evacuate, including sending people door-to-door to convince and cajole people to move out of harm's way. The State of Louisiana activated more than twice the number of National Guard troops called to duty in any prior hurricane, and achieved the largest evacuation of a threatened population ever to occur. The City of New Orleans issued its first ever mandatory evacuation order. The Coast Guard readied its personnel, pre-positioned its equipment, and stood by to begin search and rescue operations as quickly as humanly possible. Departing from usual practice, the Governors of the three affected states requested, and President Bush issued, emergency declarations before the storm made landfall.

But however vigorous these preparations, ineffective leadership, poor advance planning and an unwillingness to devote sufficient resources to emergency management over the long term doomed them to fail when Katrina struck. Despite the understanding of the Gulf Coast's particular vulnerability to hurricane devastation, officials braced for Katrina with full awareness of critical deficiencies in their plans and gaping holes in their resources. While Katrina's destructive force could not be denied, state and local officials did not marshal enough of the resources at their disposal.

In addition, years of short-changing federal, state and local emergency functions left them incapable of fully carrying out their missions to protect the public and care for victims. For example, the lack of survivable, interoperable communications, which Governor Haley Barbour said was the most critical problem in his state, occurred because of an accumulation of decisions by federal, state, and local officials that left this long standing problem unsolved.

The Committee believes that leadership failures needlessly compounded these losses. Mayor Nagin and Governor Blanco—who knew the limitations of their resources to address a catastrophe—did not specify those needs adequately to the federal government before landfall. For example, while Governor Blanco stated in a letter to President Bush two days before landfall that she anticipated the resources of the state would be overwhelmed, she made no specific request for assistance in evacuating the known tens of thousands of people without means of transportation, and a senior state official identified no unmet needs in response to a federal offer of assistance the following day.

The state's transportation secretary also ignored his responsibilities under the state's emergency operations plan, leaving no arm of the state government prepared to obtain and deliver additional transportation to those in New Orleans who lacked it, when Katrina struck. In view of the long-standing role of requests as a trigger for action by higher levels of government, the state bears responsibility for not signaling its needs to the federal government more clearly.

Compounded by leadership failures of its own, the federal government bears responsibility for not preparing effectively for its role in the post storm response. FEMA was unprepared for a catastrophic event of the scale of Katrina. Well before Katrina, FEMA's relationships with state and local officials, once a strength, had been eroded in part because certain preparedness grant programs were transferred elsewhere in the Department of Homeland Security; not as important to state and local preparedness activities, FEMA's effectiveness was diminished. In addition, at no time in its history, including in the years before it became part of DHS, had FEMA developed—nor had it been designed to develop—response capabilities sufficient for a catastrophe nor had it developed the capacity to mobilize sufficient resources from other federal agencies, and the private and nonprofit sectors.

Moreover, FEMA's Director, Michael Brown, lacked the leadership skills that were needed. Before landfall, Brown did not direct the adequate pre-positioning of critical personnel and equipment, and willfully failed to communicate with Secretary Chertoff, to whom he was supposed to report. Earlier in the hurricane season, FEMA had pre-positioned an unprecedented amount of relief supplies in the region. But the supplies were not enough. Similarly, while both FEMA and the Department of Health and Human Services made efforts to activate the federal emergency health capabilities of the National Disaster Medical System (NDMS) and the U.S. Public Health Service, only a limited number of federal medical teams were actually in position prior to landfall to deploy into the affected area. Only one such team was in a position to provide immediate medical care in the aftermath of the storm.

More broadly, DHS—as the department charged with preparing for and responding to domestic incidents, whether terrorist attacks or natural disasters—failed to effectively lead the federal response to Hurricane Katrina. DHS leadership failed to bring a sense of urgency to the federal government's preparation for Hurricane Katrina, and Secretary Chertoff himself should have been more engaged in preparations over the weekend before landfall. Secretary Chertoff made only top-level inquiries into the state of preparations, and accepted uncritically the reassurances he received. He did not appear to reach out to the other Cabinet Secretaries to make sure that they were readying their departments to provide whatever assistance DHS—and the people of the Gulf—might need.

Similarly, had he invoked the Catastrophic Incident Annex (CIA) of the NRP, Secretary Chertoff could have helped remove uncertainty about the federal government's need and authority to take initiative before landfall and signaled that all federal government agencies were expected to think—and act—proactively in preparing for and responding to Katrina. The Secretary's activation of the NRP CIA could have increased the urgency of the federal response and led the federal government to respond more proactively rather than waiting for formal requests from overwhelmed state and local officials. Understanding that delay may preclude meaningful assistance and that state and local resources could be quickly overwhelmed and incapacitated, the NRP CIA directs federal agencies to pre-position resources without awaiting requests from the state and local governments. Even then, the NRP CIA holds these resources at mobilization sites until requested by state and local officials, except in certain prescribed circumstances.

The military also had a role to play, and ultimately, the National Guard and active duty military troops and assets deployed during Katrina constituted the largest domestic deployment of military forces since the Civil War. And while the Department of Defense (DOD) took additional steps to prepare for Katrina beyond those it had taken for prior civil support missions, its preparations were not sufficient for a storm of Katrina's magnitude. Individual commanders took actions that later helped improve the response, but these actions were not coordinated by the Department. The Department's preparations were consistent with how DOD interpreted its role under the National Response Plan, which was to provide support in response to requests for assistance from FEMA.

However, additional preparations in advance of specific requests for support could have enabled a more rapid response. In addition, the White House shares responsibility for the inadequate pre-landfall preparations. To be sure, President Bush, at the request of FEMA Director Michael Brown, did take the initiative to personally call Governor Blanco to urge a mandatory evacuation. As noted earlier, he also took the unusual step of declaring an emergency in the Gulf States prior to Katrina making landfall. On the other hand, the President did not leave his Texas ranch to return to Washington until two days after landfall, and only then convened his Cabinet as well as a White House task force to oversee federal response efforts.

Response at All Levels of Government Was Unacceptable

The effect of the long-term failures at every level of government to plan and prepare adequately for a catastrophic hurricane in the Gulf was evident in the inadequate preparations before Katrina's landfall and then again in the initial response to the storm.

Search and Rescue

Flooding in New Orleans drove thousands of survivors to attics and rooftops to await rescue. Some people were trapped in attics and nursing homes and drowned as the dirty waters rose around them. Others escaped only by chopping their way through roofs. Infrastructure damage complicated the organization and conduct of search-and-rescue missions in New Orleans and elsewhere. Destruction of communications towers and equipment in particular limited the ability of crews to communicate with one another, undermining coordination and efficiency. Rescuers also had to contend with weapons fire, debris, and polluted water.

The skill and dedication of Louisiana Department of Wildlife and Fisheries officials and others working in these adverse conditions stand out as a singular success story of the hurricane response. Applying a model developed in the Hurricane Pam exercise, rescue teams in Louisiana brought hurricane victims to high ground, where they were supposed to receive food, water, medical attention, and transport to shelters. Here, too, there were problems. Poor communications delayed state and federal officials learning about where rescuees had been dropped, in turn slowing shipments of food and water to those areas. The City of New Orleans was unprepared to help people evacuate, as many buses from the city's own fleet were submerged, while at the same time officials had not arranged in advance for drivers for those buses that were available.

The storm also laid waste to much of the city's police, whose headquarters and several district offices, along with hundreds of vehicles, rounds of ammunition, and uniforms were all destroyed within the first two days of landfall. Planning for search and rescue was also insufficient. FEMA, for instance, failed to provide boats for its search and rescue teams even though flooding had been confirmed by Tuesday. Moreover, interagency coordination was inadequate at both the state and federal levels. While the Louisiana Department of Fisheries and Wildlife and FEMA are responsible for interagency search and rescue coordination at the state and federal levels respectively, neither developed adequate plans for this mission. Staggeringly, the City of New Orleans Fire Department owned no boats, and the New Orleans Police Department owned five. Meanwhile, widespread communications failures in Louisiana and Mississippi were so bad that many officers reverted to either physically running messages from one person to another, or passing messages along a daisy chain of officers using radios with limited range.

Situational Awareness

While authorities recognized the need to begin search-and-rescue missions even before the hurricane winds fully subsided, other aspects of the response were hindered by a failure to quickly recognize the dimensions of the disaster. These problems were particularly acute at the federal level. The Homeland Security Operations Center (HSOC)—charged with providing reliable information to decision-makers including the Secretary and the President—failed to create a system to identify and acquire all available, relevant information, and as a result situational awareness was deeply flawed. With local and state resources immediately overwhelmed, rapid federal mobilization of resources was critical.

Yet reliable information on such vital developments as the levee failures, the extent of flooding, and the presence of thousands of people in need of life-sustaining assistance at the New Orleans Convention Center did not reach the White House, Secretary Chertoff or other key officials for hours, and in some cases more than a day. FEMA Director Michael Brown, then in Louisiana, contributed to the problem by refusing to communicate with Secretary Chertoff opting instead to pass information directly to White House staff. Moreover, even though senior DHS officials did receive on the day of landfall numerous reports that should have led to an understanding of the increasingly dire situation in New Orleans, many indicated they were not aware of the crisis until sometime Tuesday morning.

DHS was slow to recognize the scope of the disaster or that FEMA had become overwhelmed. On the day after landfall, DHS officials were still struggling to determine the "ground truth" about the extent of the flooding despite the many reports it had received about the catastrophe; key officials did not grasp the need to act on the less-than-complete information that is to be expected in a disaster. DHS leaders did not become fully engaged in recovery efforts until Thursday, when in Deputy Secretary Michael Jackson's words, they "tried to kick it up a notch"; after that, they did provide significant leadership within DHS (and FEMA) as well as coordination across the federal government. But this effort should have begun sooner.

The Department of Defense also was slow to acquire information regarding the extent of the storm's devastation. DOD officials relied primarily on media reports for their information. Many senior DOD officials did not learn that the levees had breached until Tuesday; some did not learn until Wednesday. As DOD waited for DHS to provide information about the scope of the damage, it also waited for the lead federal agency, FEMA, to identify the support needed from DOD. The lack of situational awareness during this phase appears to have been a major reason for DOD's belated adoption of the forward-looking posture necessary in a catastrophic incident.

Post-Storm Evacuation

Overwhelmed by Katrina, the city and state turned to FEMA for help. On Monday, Governor Blanco asked FEMA Director Michael Brown for buses, and Brown assured the state the same day that 500 buses were en route to assist in the evacuation of New Orleans and would arrive within hours. In spite of Brown's assurances and the state's continued requests over the course of the next two days, FEMA did not direct the U.S. Department of Transportation to send buses until very early on Wednesday, two days after landfall, and the buses did not begin to arrive at all until Wednesday evening and not in significant numbers until Thursday. Concerned over FEMA's delay in providing buses—and handicapped by the Louisiana Department of Transportation and Development's utter failure to make any preparation to carry out its lead role for evacuation under the state's emergency plan—Governor Blanco directed members of her office to begin locating buses on Tuesday and approved an effort to commandeer school buses for evacuation on Wednesday. But these efforts were too little, too late. Tens of thousands of people were forced to wait in unspeakably horrible conditions until as late as Saturday to be evacuated.

Logistics and Military Support

Problems with obtaining, communicating and managing information plagued many other aspects of the response as well. FEMA lacked the tools to track the status of shipments, interfering with the management of supplying food, water, ice and other vital commodities to those in need across the Gulf Coast. So too did the incompatibility of the electronic systems used by federal and state authorities to manage requests for assistance, which made it necessary to transfer requests from the state system to the federal system manually.

Supplies of commodities were especially problematic. Federal shipments to Mississippi did not reach adequate levels until 10 days after landfall. The reasons for this are unclear, but FEMA's inadequate "surge capacity"—the ability to quickly ramp up the volume of shipments—is a likely cause. In both Mississippi and Louisiana, there were additional problems in getting the supplies the "last mile" to individuals in need. Both states planned to make supplies available for pickup at designated distribution points, but neither anticipated the problems people would face in reaching those points, due to impassable roads or other issues.

And in Louisiana, the National Guard was not equipped to assume this task. One of Louisiana's greatest shortages was portable toilets, which were requested for the Superdome but never arrived there, as more than 20,000 people were forced to reside inside the Dome without working plumbing for nearly a week.

For their part, Louisiana and Mississippi relied heavily on support from other states to supplement their own emergency resources. Both states were parties to an interstate agreement known as the Emergency Management Assistance Compact (EMAC), which provides a system for sharing National Guard troops and other resources in natural disasters. As in many other areas of Katrina response, however, the magnitude of the demands strained the EMAC process and revealed limitations in the system.

Paperwork burdens proved overwhelming. Louisiana experienced difficulties processing the volume of incoming resources. On Wednesday, August 31, the federal National Guard Bureau, which ordinarily serves a coordinating function within the Department of Defense, relieved Louisiana and Mississippi of many of the bureaucratic responsibilities by making direct requests for available troops to state Adjutants General. This process quickly resulted in the largest National Guard deployment in U.S. history, with 50,000 troops and supporting equipment arriving from 49 states and four territories within two weeks. These forces participated in every aspect of emergency response, from medical care to law enforcement and debris removal, and were considered invaluable by Louisiana and Mississippi officials.

Although this process successfully deployed a large number of National Guard troops, it did not proceed efficiently, or according to any pre-existing plan or process. There is, in fact, no established process for the large-scale, nation-wide deployment of National Guard troops for civil support. In addition, the deployments of National Guard troops were not coordinated with the federal Northern Command, which was overseeing the large-scale deployments and operations of the active-duty military.

While the National Response Plan has specific procedures for active-duty involvement in natural disasters, their deployment raised unforeseen issues and was initially a source of frustration to Governor Blanco. The Governor directed her Adjutant General to secure additional troops on the day after landfall, but federal and state officials did not coordinate her requests well, and ground troops didn't arrive in significant numbers for several days. The Defense Department chose to rely primarily on the deployment of National Guard troops (versus federal active duty troops) pursuant to its declared strategy and because it believed they were best suited to the required tasks, including performing law enforcement. In addition, the need to resolve command issues between National Guard and active duty forces—an issue taken up (but not resolved) in a face-to-face meeting between President Bush and the Governor on Air Force One on the Friday after landfall, may have played a role in the timing of active duty troop deployments. The issue became moot as the two forces stayed under their separate commands, an arrangement that turned out to work well in this case thanks to the cooperation of the respective commanders.

While the large numbers of active-duty troops did not arrive until the end of the first week following landfall, National Guard troops did, and the Department of Defense contributed in other important ways during that period. Early in the week, DOD ordered its military commanders to push available assets to the Gulf Coast. They also streamlined their ordinarily bureaucratic processes for handling FEMA requests for assistance and emphasized movement based on vocal commands with the paperwork to follow, though some FEMA officials believe that DOD's approval process continued to take too long. They provided significant support to search-and-rescue missions, evacuee airlifts, logistics management of buses arriving in the State for evacuation, and other matters.

Toward the end of the week, with its own resources stretched thin, FEMA turned to DOD to take over logistics for all commodity movements. The Department of Defense acceded to the request, and provided some logistics assistance to FEMA. However, it did not undertake the complete logistical take-over initially requested by FEMA because that was not needed.

By Tuesday afternoon, the New Orleans Superdome had become overcrowded, leading officials to turn additional refugees away. Mayor Nagin then decided to open the Morial Convention Center as a second refuge of last resort inside the city, but did not supply it with food or water. Moreover, he communicated his decision to open the Convention Center to state and federal officials poorly, if at all. That failure, in addition to the delay of shipments due to security concerns and DHS's own independent lack of awareness of the situation, contributed to the paucity of food, water, security or medical care at the Convention Center, as a population of approximately 19,000 gathered there.

Those vital commodities and services did not arrive until Friday, when the Louisiana National Guard, assisted by Guard units from five other states, brought in relief supplies provided by FEMA, established law and order, and then evacuated the Convention Center on Saturday within eight hours.

Law Enforcement

Law enforcement outside the Superdome and the Convention Center was a problem, and was fueled by several contributing factors, including erroneous statements by top city officials inflaming the public's perception of the lawlessness in New Orleans. Without effective law enforcement, real or imagined safety threats interrupted virtually every aspect of the response. Fearing for their personal safety, medical and search and rescue teams withdrew from their missions. FEMA and commercial vendors of critical supplies often refused to make deliveries until military escorts could be arranged. In fact, there was some lawlessness, yet for every actual act there were rumors of dozens more, leading to widespread and inaccurate reporting that severely complicated a desperate situation. Unfortunately, local, state, and federal officials did little to stanch this rumor flow. Police presence on the streets was inadequate, in part because in a matter of hours Katrina turned the New Orleans police department [NOPD] from protectors of the public to victims of the storm. Nonetheless, most New Orleans police officers appear to have reported for duty, many setting aside fears about the safety of their families or the status of their homes.

Even so, the ability of the officers who remained to perform their duties was significantly hampered by the lack of basic supplies. While supplies such as weapons and ammunition were lost to flooding, the NOPD leadership did not provide its officers with basic necessities such as food; nor did the department have logistics in place to handle supplies. Members of the NOPD also identified the lack of a unified command for this incident as a major problem; eight members of the Command Staff were extremely critical of the lack of leadership from the city's Office of Emergency Preparedness (OEP). The department's rank and file were unfamiliar with both the department's and the city's emergency-operations manuals and other hurricane emergency procedures. Deficiencies in the NOPD's manual, lack of training on this manual, lack of familiarity with it, or a combination of the three resulted in inadequate protection of department resources.

Federal law-enforcement assistance was too slow in coming, in large part because the two federal departments charged under the NRP with providing such assistance—DHS and the Department of Justice (DOJ)—had done almost no pre-storm planning. In fact, they failed to determine even well into the post-landfall period which of the two departments would assume the lead for federal law enforcement under the NRP. As a result, later in the week, as federal law-enforcement officers did arrive, some were distracted by a pointless "turf war" between DHS and DOJ over which agency was in the lead. In the end, federal assistance was crucial, but should have arrived much sooner.

Health Care

Safety concerns were only one of numerous challenges faced by health-care providers. There were numerous other challenges, including the following.

- Medical teams had to triage more than 70,000 rescuees and evacuees and provide acute care to the sick and wounded. While officials used plans developed in Hurricane Pam as a helpful framework for managing this process, existing emergency-room facilities were overwhelmed by the volume of patients. Local and state officials quickly set up temporary field hospitals at a sports arena and a K-mart in Baton Rouge to supplement hospital capacity.
- New Orleans had a large population of "special needs patients," individuals living at home who required ongoing medical assistance. Before Katrina struck, the City Health Department activated a plan to establish a care facility for this population within the Superdome and provided transportation to evacuate several hundred patients and their caregivers to Baton Rouge. While Superdome facilities proved useful in treating special needs patients who remained behind, they had to contend with shortages of supplies, physical damage to the facility necessitating a post-landfall relocation of patients and equipment to an area adjacent to the Dome, and a population of more than 20,000 people using the Superdome as a refuge of last resort.

  Also, FEMA's Disaster Medical Assistance Teams which provide the invaluable resources of pharmacies and hospital equipment, arrived at the Superdome on the night following landfall, but left temporarily on Thursday, before the evacuation of the Superdome's special needs population was completed, because of security concerns.
- In Louisiana, hospitals had to evacuate after landfall on short notice principally due to loss of electrical power. While hospitals had evacuated some of their patients before landfall, they had retained others thought to be too frail for transport, and believed by staying open they would be available to serve hurricane victims. Their strategy became untenable after landfall when power was lost, and their backup generators were rendered inoperable by flooding and fuel shortages. The Louisiana Department of Health and Hospitals stepped in to arrange for their evacuation; while successful, it had to compete with search and rescue teams for helicopters and other needed resources.
- Many nursing homes in and around New Orleans lacked adequate evacuation plans. While they were required to have plans on file with local government, there was no process to ensure that there were sufficient resources to evacuate all the nursing homes at once, and dozens of patients who were not evacuated died. When evacuation became necessary, some sent their patients to the

Superdome, where officials struggling to handle the volume of patients already there were obliged to accept still more.

Long-Term Factors Contributed to the Poor Response

Actions taken—and failures to act—well before Katrina struck compounded the problems resulting from the ineffective leadership that characterized the immediate preparations for the hurricane and the post-landfall response. A common theme of these earlier actions is underfunding emergency preparedness. While the Committee did not examine the conflicting political or budget priorities that may have played a role, in many cases the shortsightedness associated with the underfunding is glaring. Among notable examples are the following:

- The Louisiana Office of Homeland Security and Emergency Preparedness [LOHSEP], the state counterpart to FEMA, suffered chronic staffing problems and employee turnover due to underfunding. LOHSEP's Planning Chief also testified that lack of resources prevented the agency from meeting its schedule for periodic review and updates of state emergency plans.
- The Office of Emergency Preparedness for New Orleans, long known to be among the nation's cities most vulnerable to a catastrophic hurricane, had a staff of only three. Its police and fire departments, responsible for search and rescue activities, had five and no boats, respectively. In 2004, the city turned down a request by the New Orleans Fire Department to fund the purchase of six additional boats.
- The Hurricane Pam exercise faced repeated delays due to funding constraints. It took nearly five years for the federal government to approve the state's initial funding request, and the limited funding finally granted necessitated last-minute cutbacks in the scope of the exercise. Follow-up workshops were delayed by funding shortfalls—some as small as the $15,000 needed for participants' travel expenses—shortfalls that either the state or federal government should have remedied.
- Numerous witnesses testified that FEMA's budget was far short of what was needed to accomplish its mission, and that this contributed to FEMA's failure to be prepared for a catastrophe. FEMA witnesses also universally pointed out that the agency has suffered for the last few years from a vacancy rate of 15 to 20 percent (i.e., between 375 to 500 vacant positions in a 2,500-person agency), including several at key supervisory levels. FEMA sought additional funding but did not receive it. The Committee found that FEMA's budget shortages hindered its preparedness.

  We also found inadequate training in the details of the recently promulgated National Response Plan was a contributing factor in shortcomings in government's performance. Louisiana emergency management officials and National Guardsmen were receiving basic NRP and incident command system (ICS) training two days after the storm hit. Certain FEMA officials, also, were inadequately trained on the NRP and ICS. Only one large-scale federal exercise of the NRP took place before Katrina, the DHS Top Officials 3 exercise in April 2005, approximately three months after the NRP was issued. . . .

  The Committee also identified significant planning failures that predated Katrina. One of the most remarkable stories from this investigation is the history of planning for the 100,000 people in New Orleans believed to lack the means to evacuate themselves. Dating back to at least 1994, local and state officials have known about the need to address this problem. For its part, the federal government, which knew about this problem for some time, neither monitored their planning nor offered assistance. This evacuation problem was not included in the Pam exercise and, during follow up meetings in the summer of 2005, New Orleans officials informed counterparts from FEMA, other federal agencies, and the state preparedness agency that the City was not able to provide for the necessary pre-storm evacuation, but nothing was done to resolve the issue.
- The City of New Orleans, with primary responsibility for evacuation of its citizens, had language in its plan stating the city's intent to assist those who needed transportation for pre-storm evacuation, but had no actual plan provisions to implement that intent. In late 2004 and 2005, city officials negotiated contracts with Amtrak, riverboat owners and others to pre-arrange transportation alternatives, but received inadequate support from the city's Director of Homeland Security and Emergency Preparedness, and contracts were not in place when Katrina struck. As Katrina approached, notwithstanding the city's evacuation plans on paper, the best solution New Orleans had for people without transportation was a private-citizen volunteer carpool initiative called Operation Brothers' Keepers and transit buses taking people—not out of the city, but to the Superdome. While the Superdome provided shelter from the devastating winds and water, conditions there deteriorated quickly. Katrina's "near miss" ripped the covering off the roof, caused leaking, and knocked out the power, rendering the plumbing, air conditioning, and public announcement system totally useless.
- The Louisiana Department of Transportation and Development, whose Secretary had personally accepted departmental responsibility under the state's emergency operations plan to arrange for transportation for evacuation in emergencies, had done nothing to prepare for that responsibility prior to Katrina. While the Secretary attempted to defend his inaction in a personal appearance before the Committee, the Committee found his explanations rang hollow, and his account of uncommunicated doubts and objections to state policy disturbing. Had his department identified available buses or other means of transport for evacuation within the state in the months before the hurricane, at a minimum the State would have been prepared to evacuate people stranded in New Orleans after landfall more quickly than it did.
- FEMA and the U.S. Department of Transportation, charged under the National Response Plan with sup-

porting state and local government transportation needs (including evacuation) in emergencies, did little to plan for the possibility that they would be called on to assist with post-landfall evacuation needs, despite being on notice for over a month before Katrina hit that the state and local governments needed more buses and drivers—and being on notice for years that tens of thousands of people would have no means to evacuate.

- Though much attention had been paid to addressing communications shortfalls, efforts to address interoperability—as well as simply operability—were inadequate. There was little advance preparation regarding how responders would operate in an area with no power and where virtually all forms of pre-existing communications were destroyed. And while satellite phones were available to some, they either did not function properly or officials were not trained on how to use these relatively complex devices. Moreover, the National Communications System, the agency within DHS that is primarily responsible under the National Response Plan for providing communications support to first responders during disasters, had no plans to do so.

These planning failures would have been of far less consequence had the system of levees built to protect New Orleans from flooding stayed intact, as they had in most prior hurricanes. But they did not, and the resulting inundation was catastrophic. The levee failures themselves turned out to have roots long pre-dating Katrina as well. While several engineering analyses continue, the Committee found deeply disturbing evidence of flaws in the design and construction of the levees. For instance, two major drainage canals—the 17th Street and London Avenue Canals—failed at their foundations, prior to their flood walls being met with the water heights for which they were designed to protect central New Orleans. Moreover, the greater metropolitan New Orleans area was literally riddled with levee breaches caused by massive overtopping and scouring of levees that were not "armored," or properly designed, to guard against the inevitable cascading waters that were sure to accompany a storm of the magnitude of Hurricane Katrina.

The Committee also discovered that the inspection and maintenance regime in place to ensure that the levees, flood walls and other structures existing to protect the residents of the greater New Orleans area was in no way commensurate with the risk posed to these persons and their property.

Equally troubling was the revelation of serious disagreement—still unresolved months after Katrina—among officials of several government entities over who had responsibility, and when, for key levee issues including emergency response and levee repair. Such conflicts prevented any meaningful emergency plans from being put in place and, at the time of Katrina, none of the relevant government agencies had a plan for responding to a levee breach. While the deadly waters continued to pour into the heart of the city after the hurricane had passed, the very government agencies that were supposed to work together to protect the city from such a catastrophe not only initially disagreed about whose responsibility it was to repair the levee breaches, but disagreed as to how the repairs should be conducted. Sadly, due to the lack of foresight and overall coordination prior to the storm, such conflicts existed as the waters of Lake Pontchartrain continued to fill central New Orleans.

Waste, Fraud and Abuse

Besides overwhelming many government emergency-response capabilities, Katrina severely affected the government's ability to properly track and verify its costs when it contracted for disaster relief goods and services. While the Committee did not specifically include this issue in its investigation, the Committee was aware of wasteful, and sometimes fraudulent and abusive spending practices, and held two hearings on the subject.

It takes money to prepare, respond and recover from a disaster, and typically the bigger the disaster, the more money it takes. As of March 8, 2006, the federal government had committed $88 billion to the response, recovery and rebuilding efforts. Unfortunately, not all of this money has been wisely spent. Precious taxpayer dollars have been lost due to waste, fraud and abuse. Among the problems that have come to the Committee's attention are FEMA's lack of financial controls, failures to ensure eligibility of individuals receiving disaster-related assistance, and poor contracting practices, including use of no bid contracts.

A notable example of the resulting wastefulness was FEMA's purchase of 25,000 manufactured homes that are virtually useless because FEMA's own regulations prohibit them being installed in a flood plain. In a similar vein, FEMA's lack of controls in dealing with hotels providing temporary housing for evacuees resulted in instances where hotels charged for empty rooms; individuals held multiple rooms; hotel rooms were used as storage units for personal goods; individuals stayed at resorts; and hotels charged rates as high as $400 per night.

Recommendations: A New National Emergency Management System for the 21st Century

Our report sets out seven foundational recommendations together with a series of supporting "building blocks," or tactical recommendations, all designed to make the nation's emergency preparedness and response system strong, agile, effective, and robust. Hurricane Katrina exposed flaws in the structure of FEMA and DHS that are too substantial to mend.

Our first foundational recommendation is to abolish FEMA and replace it with a stronger, more capable structure, to be known as the National Preparedness and Response Authority (NPRA). To take full advantage of the substantial range of resources DHS has at its disposal, NPRA will remain within DHS. Its Director would be assured of having sufficient access and clout by having the rank of Deputy Secretary, and having a direct line of communication to the President during catastrophes. The Director would also serve as the Advisor to the President for national emergency management, in a manner akin to the Chairman of the Joint Chiefs of Staff.

To ensure capable and qualified leadership, senior NPRA officials would be selected from the ranks of professionals with experience in crisis management, in addition to substantial management and leadership experience, whether in the public, private or nonprofit sector.

Our second foundational recommendation is to endow the new organization with the full range of responsibilities that are core to preparing for and responding to disasters. These include the four central functions of comprehensive emergency management—mitigation, preparedness, response and recovery—which need to be integrated. In addition, NPRA would adopt an "all-hazards plus" strategy for preparedness. In preparing our nation to respond to terrorist attacks and natural disasters, NPRA must focus on building those common capabilities—for example survivable, interoperable communications and evacuation plans—that are necessary regardless of the incident. At the same time, it must not neglect to build those unique capabilities—like mass decontamination in the case of a radiological attack or water search and rescue in the case of flooding—that will be needed for particular types of incidents. NPRA's mandate should also include overseeing protection of critical infrastructure, such as energy facilities and telecommunications systems, both to protect such infrastructure from harm and to ensure that such infrastructure is restored as quickly as possible after a natural disaster or terrorist attack.

Our third foundational recommendation is to enhance regional operations to provide better coordination between federal agencies and the states and establish regional strike teams. Regional offices should be adequately staffed, with representation from federal agencies outside DHS that are likely to be called on to respond to a significant disaster in the region. They should provide coordination and assist in planning, training, and exercising of emergency preparedness and response activities; work with states to ensure that grant funds are spent most effectively; coordinate and develop inter-state agreements; enhance coordination with NGOs and the private sector; and provide personnel and assets, in the form of Strike Teams, to be the federal government's first line of response to a disaster. The Strike Teams would consist of, at a minimum, a designated FCO; personnel trained in incident management, public affairs, relief and recovery, and communications support; a Defense Coordinating Officer (DCO); and liaisons to other federal agencies. These regional Strike Teams should coordinate their training and exercises with the state and local officials and the private sector entities they will support when disasters occur.

Our fourth foundational recommendation is to build a true, government-wide operations center to provide enhanced situational awareness and manage interagency coordination in a disaster. Currently, there is a multiplicity of interagency coordinating structures, with overlapping missions, that attempt to facilitate an integrated federal response. Three of these structures—the Homeland Security Operations Center (HSOC), the National Response Coordination Center (NRCC), and the Interagency Incident Management Group (IIMG)—should be consolidated into a single, integrated entity—a new National Operations Center (NOC). The NOC would include representatives of all relevant federal agencies, and should provide for one clearly defined emergency management line of communication from the states to the federal government. The NOC would include representatives of all relevant federal agencies, and should provide for one clearly defined emergency management line of communication from the states to the federal government and from the federal government to the states. It would also include a strong analytic team capable of sorting through and assessing information and determining which pieces would become part of the common operating picture.

To improve its performance in future disasters, the NOC should establish clear protocols and procedures to ensure that reports are received and reviewed, at appropriate levels, in a timely manner. When there is notice of a potential major disaster, the NOC should implement plans, including one for securing information from the Department of Defense, for obtaining post-disaster situational awareness, including identifying sources of information and data particular to the region in which the disaster may occur and, where appropriate, bringing in individuals with particular knowledge or expertise about that region.

Our fifth foundational recommendation is to renew and sustain commitments at all levels of government to the nation's emergency management system. FEMA emergency response teams have been reduced substantially in size, are inadequately equipped, and training for these teams has been all but eliminated. If the federal government is to improve its performance and be prepared to respond effectively to the next disaster, we must give NPRA—and the other federal agencies with central responsibilities under the National Response Plan—the necessary resources to accomplish this. We must fund NPRA commensurate with the significance of its mission and ensure that those funds are well-spent. To be full partners in the national preparedness effort, states and localities will need additional resources as well.

The Administration and DHS must also ensure that federal leaders of all agencies with an emergency support role understand their key responsibilities under the National Response Plan and the resources they need to effectively carry out the comprehensive planning required, while also training and exercising on NIMS, NRP and other operational plans. To fully integrate state and local officials into the system, there should be established an advisory council to NPRA made up of state and local officials and first responders. The advisory council should play an integral role in ensuring that the full range of activities of the new organization—including developing response plans, conducting training and exercises, formulating preparedness goals, effectively managing grants and other resources—are done in full consultation and coordination with, and take into account the needs and priorities of, states and localities. DHS and the NPRA should more fully integrate the private and nonprofit sectors into their planning and preparedness initiatives. Among other things, they should designate specific individuals at the national and regional levels to work directly with private sector organizations. Where appropriate, private sector representatives should also be included in planning, training and exercises.

Our sixth foundational recommendation is to strengthen the underpinning of the nation's response to disasters and catastrophes. Despite their shortcomings and imperfections, the National Response Plan (NRP) and National Incident Management System (NIMS), including the ESF structure currently represent the best approach available to respond to multi-agency, multi-jurisdictional emergencies. Federal, state and local officials and other responders must commit to supporting the NRP and NIMS and working together to improve the performance of the national emergency management system. We must undertake further refinements of the NRP and NIMS, develop operational plans, and engage in training and exercises to ensure that everyone involved in disaster response understands them and is prepared to carry them out.

In particular, the NRP should be strengthened to make the unity of effort concept very clear, so that everyone understands the concept and their roles in establishing unity, and there should be clarification of the importance of integrating agencies with ESF responsibilities into the ICS, rather than their operating in "stovepipes." The roles and responsibilities of the Principal Federal Official and the Federal Coordinating Officer are overlapping and were a source of confusion during Hurricane Katrina. The Stafford Act should be amended to clarify the roles and responsibilities of the Federal Coordinating Officer, and the NRP should be revised to eliminate the PFO position for Stafford Act-declared emergencies and disasters. It should also be amended to ensure that the Act addresses response to all disasters and catastrophes, whether natural or man-made.

Our seventh foundational recommendation is to improve the nation's capacity to respond to catastrophic events. DHS should ensure that the Catastrophic Incident Annex is fully understood by the federal departments and agencies with responsibilities associated with it. The Catastrophic Incident Supplement should be completed and published, and the supporting operational plans for departments and agencies with responsibilities under the CIA should be completed. These plans should be reviewed and coordinated with the states, and on a regional basis, to ensure they are understood, trained and exercised prior to an emergency.

DHS must also develop the national capabilities—especially surge capacity—it needs to respond to catastrophic disasters, ensuring it has sufficient full time staff, response teams, contracting personnel, and adequately trained and sufficiently staffed reserve corps to ramp up capabilities, as needed. These capabilities must be scalable so that NPRA can draw on the appropriate resources from supporting ESF agencies to respond to a disaster irrespective of cause, size, or complexity.

Conclusion

Our Report can do justice neither to the human suffering endured during and after Katrina nor to the dimensions of the response. As to the latter, we have identified many successes and many failures; no doubt there are others in both categories we have missed. The Committee shares the view expressed by President Bush shortly after Katrina that our nation can do better.

Avoiding past mistakes will not suffice. Our leadership and systems must be prepared for catastrophes we know will be unlike Katrina, whether due to natural causes or terrorism. The Committee hopes to help meet that goal through the recommendations in this Report, because almost exactly four years after 9/11, Katrina showed that the nation is still unprepared.

Source: U.S. Congress. Senate Committee on Homeland Security and Governmental Affairs. *Hurricane Katrina: A Nation Still Unprepared.* 109th Cong., 2d sess., 2006. S. Rep. 109-322.

Bibliography

American's Intelligence Wire. "Congress Investigates Katrina Response; President Bush Visits Disaster Zone; Katrina Chaos Exaggerated by Local Officials?" (Parts 1 and 2) September 27, 2005. Available at http://find.galegroup.com/itx/start.do?prodId=GRGM.

Brinkley, Douglas. *The Great Deluge: Hurricane Katrina, New Orleans, and the Mississippi Gulf Coast.* New York: William Morrow, 2006.

Brownstein, Ronald. "Partisan Snub of Republican Katrina Inquiry Now Looks Petty." *Los Angeles Times,* February 19, 2006, A20.

Gunderson, Edna. "A Musical Icon Rebuilds His Life, Home, and Music." *USA Today*, September 23, 2007. Available at www.usatoday.com/life/music/news/2007-09-20-fats domino-cover-main_N.htm.

Ink, Dwight. "An Analysis of the House Select Committee and White House Reports on Hurricane Katrina." *Public Administration Review* (November/December 2006), 800.

"Katrina Panel Close to Conclusion: Plenty of Warning, Paucity of Planning." *Emergency Preparedness News* (February 7, 2006), 17.

Lipton, Eric. "White House Declines to Turn Over Storm Papers." *New York Times*, January 25, 2006. Available at www.nytimes.com/2006/01/25/politics/25katrina.html.

Neuman, Johanna. "The Nation: Report Details Katrina Communications Fiasco." *Los Angeles Times,* May 3, 2006, A4.

Staff Report for Representative Charles Melancon, U.S. House of Representatives. "Hurricane Katrina Document Analysis: The E-Mails of Michael Brown," November 2, 2005. Available at http://i.a.cnn.net/cnn/2005/images/11/03/brown.emails.analysis.pdf.

U.S. Congress. House. "A Failure of Initiative: The Final Report of the Select Bipartisan Committee to Investigate the Preparation for and Response to Hurricane Katrina." 109th Cong., 2d sess., 2006. H. Rep. 109-377. Available at www.gpoaccess.gov/Katrinareport/mainreport.pdf.

U.S. Congress. Senate Committee on Homeland Security and Governmental Affairs. *Hurricane Katrina: A Nation Still Unprepared.* 109th Cong., 2d sess., 2006. S. Rep. 109-322. Available at www.gpoaccess.gov/serialset/creports/katrinanation.html.

White House Office of the Press Secretary. "President Arrives in Alabama, Briefed on Hurricane Katrina." News release, September 2, 2005. Available at http://georgewbush-whitehouse.archives.gov/news/releases/2005/09/20050902-2.html.

INDEX

Bold page numbers indicate a main discussion of a topic. *Italic* page numbers indicate a photograph or illustration. Page numbers followed by *c* indicate chronology entries.

A

B

C

D

G

H

J

L

N

O

S

T

X

Y

Z